University Casebook Series

December, 1979

ACCOUNTING AND THE LAW, Fourth Edition (1978), with Problems Pamphlet (Successor to Dohr, Phillips, Thompson & Warren)

> George C. Thompson, Professor, Columbia University Graduate School of Business.
> Robert Whitman, Professor of Law, University of Connecticut.
> Ellis L. Phillips, Jr., Member of the New York Bar.
> William C. Warren, Professor of Law Emeritus, Columbia University.

ACCOUNTING FOR LAWYERS, MATERIALS ON, (1978) (Temporary Edition)

> David R. Herwitz, Professor of Law, Harvard University.

ADMINISTRATIVE LAW, Seventh Edition (1979), with 1979 Problems Supplement (edited in association with Paul R. Verkuil, Dean and Professor of Law, Tulane University)

> Walter Gellhorn, University Professor, Columbia University.
> Clark Byse, Professor of Law, Harvard University.
> Peter L. Strauss, Professor of Law, Columbia University.

ADMIRALTY, Second Edition (1978), with Documentary Supplement

> Jo Desha Lucas, Professor of Law, University of Chicago.

ADVOCACY, INTRODUCTION TO, Second Edition (1976)

> Board of Student Advisers, Harvard Law School.

ADVOCACY, see also Lawyering Process

AGENCY-ASSOCIATIONS-EMPLOYMENT-PARTNERSHIPS, Second Edition (1977)

> Reprinted from Conard, Knauss & Siegel's Enterprise Organization.

AGENCY, see also Enterprise Organization

ANTITRUST AND REGULATORY ALTERNATIVES (1977)

> Louis B. Schwartz, Professor of Law, University of Pennsylvania.
> John J. Flynn, Professor of Law, University of Utah.

ANTITRUST SUPPLEMENT—SELECTED STATUTES AND RELATED MATERIALS (1977)

> John J. Flynn, Professor of Law, University of Utah.

BIOGRAPHY OF A LEGAL DISPUTE, THE: An Introduction to American Civil Procedure (1968)

> Marc A. Franklin, Professor of Law, Stanford University.

BUSINESS ORGANIZATION, see also Enterprise Organization

BUSINESS PLANNING (1966), with 1979 Problem Supplement

> David R. Herwitz, Professor of Law, Harvard University.

i

BUSINESS TORTS (1972)

Milton Handler, Professor of Law Emeritus, Columbia University.

CIVIL PROCEDURE, see Procedure

CLINIC, see also Lawyering Process

COMMERCIAL AND CONSUMER TRANSACTIONS, Second Edition (1978)

William D. Warren, Dean of the School of Law, University of California, Los Angeles.
William E. Hogan, Professor of Law, Cornell University.
Robert L. Jordan, Professor of Law, University of California, Los Angeles.

COMMERCIAL LAW, CASES & MATERIALS ON, Third Edition (1976)

E. Allan Farnsworth, Professor of Law, Cornell University.
John Honnold, Professor of Law, University of Pennsylvania.

COMMERCIAL PAPER, Second Edition (1976)

E. Allan Farnsworth, Professor of Law, Columbia University.

COMMERCIAL PAPER AND BANK DEPOSITS AND COLLECTIONS (1967), with Statutory Supplement.

William D. Hawkland, Professor of Law, University of Illinois.

COMMERCIAL TRANSACTIONS—Text, Cases and Problems, Fourth Edition (1968)

Robert Braucher, Professor of Law Emeritus, Harvard University, and
The late Arthur E. Sutherland, Jr., Professor of Law, Harvard University.

COMPARATIVE LAW, Third Edition (1970)

Rudolf B. Schlesinger, Professor of Law, Hastings College of the Law.

COMPETITIVE PROCESS, LEGAL REGULATION OF THE, Second Edition (1979), with Statutory Supplement

Edmund W. Kitch, Professor of Law, University of Chicago.
Harvey S. Perlman, Professor of Law, University of Virginia.

CONFLICT OF LAWS, Seventh Edition (1978)

Willis L. M. Reese, Professor of Law, Columbia University, and
Maurice Rosenberg, Professor of Law, Columbia University.

CONSTITUTIONAL LAW, Fifth Edition (1977), with 1979 Supplement

Edward L. Barrett, Jr., Professor of Law, University of California, Davis.

CONSTITUTIONAL LAW, Ninth Edition (1975), with 1979 Supplement

Gerald Gunther, Professor of Law, Stanford University.

CONSTITUTIONAL LAW, INDIVIDUAL RIGHTS IN, Second Edition (1976), with 1979 Supplement

Gerald Gunther, Professor of Law, Stanford University.

CONTRACT LAW AND ITS APPLICATION, Second Edition (1977)

Addison Mueller, Professor of Law Emeritus, University of California, Los Angeles.
Arthur I. Rosett, Professor of Law, University of California, Los Angeles.

CONTRACT LAW, STUDIES IN, Second Edition (1977)

Edward J. Murphy, Professor of Law, University of Notre Dame.
Richard E. Speidel, Professor of Law, University of Virginia.

CONTRACTS, Third Edition (1977)

John P. Dawson, Professor of Law Emeritus, Harvard University, and
William Burnett Harvey, Professor of Law and Political Science, Boston
University.

CONTRACTS, Second Edition (1972), with Statutory Supplement

E. Allan Farnsworth, Professor of Law, Columbia University.
William F. Young, Jr., Professor of Law, Columbia University.
Harry W. Jones, Professor of Law, Columbia University.

**CONTRACTS, Second Edition (1978), with Statutory and Administrative Law
Supplement (1978)**

Ian R. Macneil, Professor of Law, Cornell University.

**COPYRIGHT, Unfair Competition, and Other Topics Bearing on the Protection
of Literary, Musical, and Artistic Works, Third Edition (1978)**

Benjamin Kaplan, Professor of Law Emeritus, Harvard University, and
Ralph S. Brown, Jr., Professor of Law, Yale University.

CORPORATE FINANCE, Second Edition (1979)

Victor Brudney, Professor of Law, Harvard University.
Marvin A. Chirelstein, Professor of Law, Yale University.

CORPORATE READJUSTMENTS AND REORGANIZATIONS (1976)

Walter J. Blum, Professor of Law, University of Chicago.
Stanley A. Kaplan, Professor of Law, University of Chicago.

**CORPORATION LAW, BASIC, Second Edition (1979), with Documentary
Supplement**

Detlev F. Vagts, Professor of Law, Harvard University.

**CORPORATIONS, Fourth Edition—Unabridged (1969), with 1977 Supplement
and 1978 Special Supplement**

William L. Cary, Professor of Law, Columbia University.

**CORPORATIONS, Fourth Edition—Abridged (1970), with 1977 Supplement and
1978 Special Supplement**

William L. Cary, Professor of Law, Columbia University.

CORPORATIONS, THE LAW OF: WHAT CORPORATE LAWYERS DO (1976)

Jan G. Deutsch, Professor of Law, Yale University.
Joseph J. Bianco, Professor of Law, Yeshiva University.

CORPORATIONS COURSE GAME PLAN (1975)

David R. Herwitz, Professor of Law, Harvard University.

CORPORATIONS, see also Enterprise Organization

CREDIT TRANSACTIONS AND CONSUMER PROTECTION (1976)

John Honnold, Professor of Law, University of Pennsylvania.

CREDITORS' RIGHTS, see also Debtor-Creditor Law

iii

CRIMINAL LAW, Second Edition (1979)

Fred E. Inbau, Professor of Law Emeritus, Northwestern University.
James R. Thompson, Professor of Law Emeritus, Northwestern University.
Andre A. Moenssens, Professor of Law, University of Richmond.

CRIMINAL PROCEDURE, CONSTITUTIONAL (1977), with 1980 Supplement

James E. Scarboro, Professor of Law, University of Colorado.
James B. White, Professor of Law, University of Chicago.

CRIMINAL PROCEDURE (1974), with 1977 Supplement

Fred E. Inbau, Professor of Law Emeritus, Northwestern University.
James R. Thompson, Professor of Law Emeritus, Northwestern University.
James B. Haddad, Professor of Law, Northwestern University.
James B. Zagel, Chief, Criminal Justice Division, Office of Attorney General of Illinois.
Gary L. Starkman, Assistant U. S. Attorney, Northern District of Illinois.

CRIMINAL JUSTICE, THE ADMINISTRATION OF, Second Edition (1969)

Francis C. Sullivan, Professor of Law, Louisiana State University.
Paul Hardin III, Professor of Law, Duke University.
John Huston, Professor of Law, University of Washington.
Frank R. Lacy, Professor of Law, University of Oregon.
Daniel E. Murray, Professor of Law, University of Miami.
George W. Pugh, Professor of Law, Louisiana State University.

CRIMINAL JUSTICE ADMINISTRATION AND RELATED PROCESSES, Successor Edition (1976), with 1979 Supplement

Frank W. Miller, Professor of Law, Washington University.
Robert O. Dawson, Professor of Law, University of Texas.
George E. Dix, Professor of Law, University of Texas.
Raymond I. Parnas, Professor of Law, University of California, Davis.

CRIMINAL JUSTICE, LEADING CONSTITUTIONAL CASES ON (1979)

Lloyd L. Weinreb, Professor of Law, Harvard University.

CRIMINAL LAW, Second Edition (1975)

Lloyd L. Weinreb, Professor of Law, Harvard University.

CRIMINAL LAW AND ITS ADMINISTRATION (1940), with 1956 Supplement

The late Jerome Michael, Professor of Law, Columbia University, and
Herbert Wechsler, Professor of Law, Columbia University.

CRIMINAL LAW AND PROCEDURE, Fifth Edition (1977)

Rollin M. Perkins, Professor of Law Emeritus, University of California, Hastings College of the Law.
Ronald N. Boyce, Professor of Law, University of Utah.

CRIMINAL PROCESS, Third Edition (1978), with 1979 Supplement

Lloyd L. Weinreb, Professor of Law, Harvard University.

DAMAGES, Second Edition (1952)

The late Charles T. McCormick, Professor of Law, University of Texas, and
The late William F. Fritz, Professor of Law, University of Texas.

DEBTOR-CREDITOR LAW (1974), with 1978 Case-Statutory Supplement

William D. Warren, Dean of the School of Law, University of California, Los Angeles.
William E. Hogan, Professor of Law, Cornell University.

UNIVERSITY CASEBOOK SERIES—Continued

DECEDENTS' ESTATES (1971)

The late Max Rheinstein, Professor of Law Emeritus, University of Chicago.
Mary Ann Glendon, Professor of Law, Boston College Law School.

DECEDENTS' ESTATES AND TRUSTS, Fifth Edition (1977)

John Ritchie III, Professor of Law Emeritus, University of Virginia.
Neill H. Alford, Jr., Professor of Law, University of Virginia.
Richard W. Effland, Professor of Law, Arizona State University.

DECEDENTS' ESTATES AND TRUSTS (1968)

Howard R. Williams, Professor of Law, Stanford University.

DOMESTIC RELATIONS, Third Edition (1978)

Walter Wadlington, Professor of Law, University of Virginia.
Monrad G. Paulsen, Dean of the Law School, Yeshiva University.

DOMESTIC RELATIONS, see also Family Law

DYNAMICS OF AMERICAN LAW, THE: Courts, the Legal Process and Freedom of Expression (1968)

Marc A. Franklin, Professor of Law, Stanford University.

ELECTRONIC MASS MEDIA, Second Edition (1979)

William K. Jones, Professor of Law, Columbia University.

ENTERPRISE ORGANIZATION, Second Edition (1977), with Statutory and Formulary Supplement (1979)

Alfred F. Conard, Professor of Law, University of Michigan.
Robert L. Knauss, Dean of the School of Law, Vanderbilt University.
Stanley Siegel, Professor of Law, University of California, Los Angeles.

ENVIRONMENTAL PROTECTION, SELECTED LEGAL AND ECONOMIC ASPECTS OF (1971)

Charles J. Meyers, Dean of the Law School, Stanford University.
A. Dan Tarlock, Professor of Law, Indiana University.

EQUITY AND EQUITABLE REMEDIES (1975)

Edward D. Re, Adjunct Professor of Law, St. John's University.

EQUITY, RESTITUTION AND DAMAGES, Second Edition (1974)

The late Robert Childres, Professor of Law, Northwestern University.
William F. Johnson, Jr., Adjunct Professor of Law, New York University.

ESTATE PLANNING PROBLEMS (1973), with 1977 Supplement

David Westfall, Professor of Law, Harvard University.

ETHICS, see Legal Profession, also Professional Responsibility

EVIDENCE, Third Edition (1976)

The late David W. Louisell, Professor of Law, University of California, Berkeley.
John Kaplan, Professor of Law, Stanford University.
Jon R. Waltz, Professor of Law, Northwestern University.

v

UNIVERSITY CASEBOOK SERIES—Continued

EVIDENCE, Sixth Edition (1973), with 1980 Supplement

The late John M. Maguire, Professor of Law Emeritus, Harvard University.
Jack B. Weinstein, Professor of Law, Columbia University.
James H. Chadbourn, Professor of Law, Harvard University.
John H. Mansfield, Professor of Law, Harvard University.

EVIDENCE (1968)

Francis C. Sullivan, Professor of Law, Louisiana State University.
Paul Hardin, III, Professor of Law, Duke University.

FAMILY LAW, see also Domestic Relations

FAMILY LAW (1978)

Judith C. Areen, Professor of Law, Georgetown University.

FAMILY LAW: STATUTORY MATERIALS, Second Edition (1974)

Monrad G. Paulsen, Dean of the Law School, Yeshiva University.
Walter Wadlington, Professor of Law, University of Virginia.

FEDERAL COURTS, Sixth Edition (1976), with 1979 Supplement

The late Charles T. McCormick, Professor of Law, University of Texas.
James H. Chadbourn, Professor of Law, Harvard University, and
Charles Alan Wright, Professor of Law, University of Texas.

FEDERAL COURTS AND THE FEDERAL SYSTEM, Second Edition (1973), with 1977 Supplement

The late Henry M. Hart, Jr., Professor of Law, Harvard University.
Herbert Wechsler, Professor of Law, Columbia University.
Paul M. Bator, Professor of Law, Harvard University.
Paul J. Mishkin, Professor of Law, University of California, Berkeley.
David L. Shapiro, Professor of Law, Harvard University.

FEDERAL RULES OF CIVIL PROCEDURE, 1978 Edition

FEDERAL TAXATION, see Taxation

FUTURE INTERESTS AND ESTATE PLANNING (1961), with 1962 Supplement

The late W. Barton Leach, Professor of Law, Harvard University, and
James K. Logan, formerly Dean of the Law School, University of Kansas.

FUTURE INTERESTS (1958)

The late Philip Mechem, Professor of Law Emeritus, University of Pennsylvania.

FUTURE INTERESTS (1970)

Howard R. Williams, Professor of Law, Stanford University.

GOVERNMENT CONTRACTS, FEDERAL (1975), with 1980 Supplement

John W. Whelan, Professor of Law, Hastings College of the Law.
Robert S. Pasley, Professor of Law Emeritus, Cornell University.

HOUSING (THE ILL-HOUSED) (1971)

Peter W. Martin, Professor of Law, Cornell University.

INJUNCTIONS (1972)

Owen M. Fiss, Professor of Law, Yale University.

V7204—6f

UNIVERSITY CASEBOOK SERIES—Continued

INSTITUTIONAL INVESTORS, 1978

David L. Ratner, Professor of Law, Cornell University.

INSURANCE (1971)

William F. Young, Professor of Law, Columbia University.

INTERNATIONAL LAW, see also Transnational Legal Problems and United Nations Law

INTERNATIONAL LEGAL SYSTEM (1973), with Documentary Supplement

Noyes E. Leech, Professor of Law, University of Pennsylvania.
Covey T. Oliver, Professor of Law, University of Pennsylvania.
Joseph Modeste Sweeney, Professor of Law, Tulane University.

INTERNATIONAL TRADE AND INVESTMENT, REGULATION OF (1970)

The late Carl H. Fulda, Professor of Law, University of Texas.
Warren F. Schwartz, Professor of Law, University of Virginia.

INTERNATIONAL TRANSACTIONS AND RELATIONS (1960)

Milton Katz, Professor of Law, Harvard University, and
Kingman Brewster, Jr., formerly President, Yale University.

INTRODUCTION TO THE STUDY OF LAW (1970)

E. Wayne Thode, Professor of Law, University of Utah.
J. Leon Lebowitz, Professor of Law, University of Texas.
Lester J. Mazor, Professor of Law, Hampshire College.

INTRODUCTION TO LAW, see also Legal Method, also On Law in Courts, also Dynamics of American Law

JUDICIAL CODE: Rules of Procedure in the Federal Courts with Excerpts from the Criminal Code, 1978 Edition

The late Henry M. Hart, Jr., Professor of Law, Harvard University, and
Herbert Wechsler, Professor of Law, Columbia University.

JURISPRUDENCE (Temporary Edition Hard Bound) (1949)

Lon L. Fuller, Professor of Law Emeritus, Harvard University.

JUVENILE COURTS (1967)

Hon. Orman W. Ketcham, Juvenile Court of the District of Columbia.
Monrad G. Paulsen, Dean of the Law School, Yeshiva University.

JUVENILE JUSTICE PROCESS, Second Edition (1976), with 1980 Supplement

Frank W. Miller, Professor of Law, Washington University.
Robert O. Dawson, Professor of Law, University of Texas.
George E. Dix, Professor of Law, University of Texas.
Raymond I. Parnas, Professor of Law, University of California, Davis.

LABOR LAW, Eighth Edition (1977), with Statutory Supplement, and 1979 Case Supplement

Archibald Cox, Professor of Law, Harvard University, and
Derek C. Bok, President, Harvard University.
Robert A. Gorman, Professor of Law, University of Pennsylvania.

LABOR LAW (1968), with Statutory Supplement and 1974 Case Supplement

Clyde W. Summers, Professor of Law, University of Pennsylvania.
Harry H. Wellington, Dean of the Law School, Yale University.

LAND FINANCING, Second Edition (1977)

Norman Penney, Professor of Law, Cornell University.
Richard F. Broude, of the California Bar.

LAW, LANGUAGE AND ETHICS (1972)

William R. Bishin, Professor of Law, University of Southern California.
Christopher D. Stone, Professor of Law, University of Southern California.

LAWYERING PROCESS (1978), with Civil Problem Supplement and Criminal Problem Supplement

Gary Bellow, Professor of Law, Harvard University.
Bea Moulton, Professor of Law, Arizona State University.

LEGAL METHOD, Second Edition (1952)

Noel T. Dowling, late Professor of Law, Columbia University,
The late Edwin W. Patterson, Professor of Law, Columbia University, and
Richard R. B. Powell, Professor of Law, University of California, Hastings College of the Law.
Second Edition by Harry W. Jones, Professor of Law, Columbia University.

LEGAL METHODS (1969)

Robert N. Covington, Professor of Law, Vanderbilt University.
The late E. Blythe Stason, Professor of Law, Vanderbilt University.
John W. Wade, Professor of Law, Vanderbilt University.
The late Elliott E. Cheatham, Professor of Law, Vanderbilt University.
Theodore A. Smedley, Professor of Law, Vanderbilt University.

LEGAL PROFESSION (1970)

Samuel D. Thurman, Dean of the College of Law, University of Utah.
Ellis L. Phillips, Jr., Member of the New York Bar.
The late Elliott E. Cheatham, Professor of Law, Vanderbilt University.

LEGISLATIVE AND ADMINISTRATIVE PROCESSES (1976)

Hans A. Linde, Professor of Law, University of Oregon.
George Bunn, Professor of Law, University of Wisconsin.

LEGISLATION, Third Edition (1973)

The late Horace E. Read, Vice President, Dalhousie University.
John W. MacDonald, Professor of Law Emeritus, Cornell Law School.
Jefferson B. Fordham, Professor of Law, University of Utah, and
William J. Pierce, Professor of Law, University of Michigan.

LOCAL GOVERNMENT LAW, Revised Edition (1975)

Jefferson B. Fordham, Professor of Law, University of Utah.

MASS MEDIA LAW (1976), with 1979 Supplement

Marc A. Franklin, Professor of Law, Stanford University.

MENTAL HEALTH PROCESS, Second Edition (1976)

Frank W. Miller, Professor of Law, Washington University.
Robert O. Dawson, Professor of Law, University of Texas.
George E. Dix, Professor of Law, University of Texas.
Raymond I. Parnas, Professor of Law, University of California, Davis.

MUNICIPAL CORPORATIONS, see Local Government Law

NEGOTIABLE INSTRUMENTS, see Commercial Paper

NEW YORK PRACTICE, Fourth Edition (1978)

Herbert Peterfreund, Professor of Law, New York University.
Joseph M. McLaughlin, Dean of the Law School, Fordham University.

OIL AND GAS, Fourth Edition (1979)

Howard R. Williams, Professor of Law, Stanford University,
Richard C. Maxwell, Professor of Law, University of California, Los Angeles, and
Charles J. Meyers, Dean of the Law School, Stanford University.

ON LAW IN COURTS (1965)

Paul J. Mishkin, Professor of Law, University of California, Berkeley.
Clarence Morris, Professor of Law Emeritus, University of Pennsylvania.

OWNERSHIP AND DEVELOPMENT OF LAND (1965)

Jan Krasnowiecki, Professor of Law, University of Pennsylvania.

PARTNERSHIP PLANNING (1970) (Pamphlet)

William L. Cary, Professor of Law, Columbia University.

PERSPECTIVES ON THE LAWYER AS PLANNER (Reprint of Chapters One through Five of Planning by Lawyers) (1978)

Louis M. Brown, Professor of Law, University of Southern California.
Edward A. Dauer, Professor of Law, Yale University.

PLANNING BY LAWYERS, MATERIALS ON A NONADVERSARIAL LEGAL PROCESS (1978)

Louis M. Brown, Professor of Law, University of Southern California.
Edward A. Dauer, Professor of Law, Yale University.

PLEADING AND PROCEDURE, see Procedure, Civil

POLICE FUNCTION (1976) (Pamphlet)

Chapters 1-11 of Miller, Dawson, Dix & Parnas' Criminal Justice Administration, Second Edition.

PREVENTIVE LAW, see also Planning by Lawyers

PROCEDURE—Biography of a Legal Dispute (1968)

Marc A. Franklin, Professor of Law, Stanford University.

PROCEDURE—CIVIL PROCEDURE, Second Edition (1974)

James H. Chadbourn, Professor of Law, Harvard University.
A. Leo Levin, Professor of Law, University of Pennsylvania.
Philip Shuchman, Professor of Law, University of Connecticut.

PROCEDURE—CIVIL PROCEDURE, Fourth Edition (1978), with 1979 Supplement

The late Richard H. Field, Professor of Law, Harvard University.
Benjamin Kaplan, Professor of Law Emeritus, Harvard University.
Kevin M. Clermont, Professor of Law, Cornell University.

PROCEDURE—CIVIL PROCEDURE, Third Edition (1976), with 1978 Supplement

Maurice Rosenberg, Professor of Law, Columbia University.
Jack B. Weinstein, Professor, of Law, Columbia University.
Hans Smit, Professor of Law, Columbia University.
Harold L. Korn, Professor of Law, Columbia University.

UNIVERSITY CASEBOOK SERIES—Continued

PROCEDURE—PLEADING AND PROCEDURE: State and Federal, Fourth Edition (1979)

The late David W. Louisell, Professor of Law, University of California, Berkeley.
Geoffrey C. Hazard, Jr., Professor of Law, Yale University.

PROCEDURE—FEDERAL RULES OF CIVIL PROCEDURE, 1978 Edition

PROCEDURE PORTFOLIO (1962)

James H. Chadbourn, Professor of Law, Harvard University, and
A. Leo Levin, Professor of Law, University of Pennsylvania.

PRODUCTS AND THE CONSUMER: DECEPTIVE PRACTICES (1972)

W. Page Keeton, Professor of Law, University of Texas.
Marshall S. Shapo, Professor of Law, University of Virginia.

PRODUCTS AND THE CONSUMER: DEFECTIVE AND DANGEROUS PRODUCTS (1970)

W. Page Keeton, Professor of Law, University of Texas.
Marshall S. Shapo, Professor of Law, University of Virginia.

PRODUCTS LIABILITY AND SAFETY (1980)

W. Page Keeton, Professor of Law, University of Texas.
David G. Owen, Professor of Law, University of South Carolina.
John E. Montgomery, Professor of Law, University of South Carolina.

PROFESSIONAL RESPONSIBILITY (1976), with 1979 Problems, Cases and Readings, Supplement, 1979 Statutory (National) Supplement, and 1979 Statutory (California) Supplement

Thomas D. Morgan, Professor of Law, University of Illinois.
Ronald D. Rotunda, Professor of Law, University of Illinois.

PROPERTY, Fourth Edition (1978)

John E. Cribbet, Dean of the Law School, University of Illinois.
Corwin W. Johnson, Professor of Law, University of Texas.

PROPERTY—PERSONAL (1953)

The late S. Kenneth Skolfield, Professor of Law Emeritus, Boston University.

PROPERTY—PERSONAL, Third Edition (1954)

The late Everett Fraser, Dean of the Law School Emeritus, University of Minnesota—Third Edition by
Charles W. Taintor II, late Professor of Law, University of Pittsburgh.

PROPERTY—REAL—INTRODUCTION, Third Edition (1954)

The late Everett Fraser, Dean of the Law School Emeritus, University of Minnesota.

PROPERTY—REAL PROPERTY AND CONVEYANCING (1954)

Edward E. Bade, late Professor of Law, University of Minnesota.

PROPERTY, MODERN REAL, FUNDAMENTALS OF (1974), with 1979 Supplement

Edward H. Rabin, Professor of Law, University of California, Davis. •

PROPERTY, REAL, PROBLEMS IN (Pamphlet) (1969)

Edward H. Rabin, Professor of Law, University of California, Davis.

PROSECUTION AND ADJUDICATION (1976) (Pamphlet)

Chapters 12–16 of Miller, Dawson, Dix & Parnas' Criminal Justice Administration, Second Edition.

UNIVERSITY CASEBOOK SERIES—Continued

PUBLIC UTILITY LAW, see Free Enterprise, also Regulated Industries

REAL ESTATE PLANNING (1974), with 1978 Supplement

Norton L. Steuben, Professor of Law, University of Colorado.

RECEIVERSHIP AND CORPORATE REORGANIZATION, see Creditors' Rights

REGULATED INDUSTRIES, Second Edition, 1976

William K. Jones, Professor of Law, Columbia University.

RESTITUTION, Second Edition (1966)

John W. Wade, Professor of Law, Vanderbilt University.

SALES (1980)

Marion W. Benfield, Jr., Professor of Law, University of Illinois.
William D. Hawkland, Chancellor, Louisiana State University Law Center.

SALES AND SALES FINANCING, Fourth Edition (1976)

John Honnold, Professor of Law, University of Pennsylvania.

SECURITY, Third Edition (1959)

The late John Hanna, Professor of Law Emeritus, Columbia University.

SECURITIES REGULATION, Fourth Edition (1977), with 1979 Selected Statutes
Supplement and 1979 Cases and Releases Supplement

Richard W. Jennings, Professor of Law, University of California, Berkeley.
Harold Marsh, Jr., Member of the California Bar.

SENTENCING AND THE CORRECTIONAL PROCESS, Second Edition (1976)

Frank W. Miller, Professor of Law, Washington University.
Robert O. Dawson, Professor of Law, University of Texas.
George E. Dix, Professor of Law, University of Texas.
Raymond I. Parnas, Professor of Law, University of California, Davis.

SOCIAL WELFARE AND THE INDIVIDUAL (1971)

Robert J. Levy, Professor of Law, University of Minnesota.
Thomas P. Lewis, Dean of the College of Law, University of Kentucky.
Peter W. Martin, Professor of Law, Cornell University.

TAX, POLICY ANALYSIS OF THE FEDERAL INCOME (1976)

William A. Klein, Professor of Law, University of California, Los Angeles.

TAXATION, FEDERAL INCOME (1976), with 1979 Supplement

Erwin N. Griswold, Dean Emeritus, Harvard Law School.
Michael J. Graetz, Professor of Law, University of Virginia.

TAXATION, FEDERAL INCOME, Second Edition (1977), with 1979 Supplement

James J. Freeland, Professor of Law, University of Florida.
Stephen A. Lind, Professor of Law, University of Florida.
Richard B. Stephens, Professor of Law Emeritus, University of Florida.

TAXATION, FEDERAL INCOME, Volume I, Personal Tax (1972), with 1979
Supplement; Volume II, Corporate and Partnership Taxation, Second
Edition (1980)

Stanley S. Surrey, Professor of Law, Harvard University.
William C. Warren, Professor of Law Emeritus, Columbia University.
Paul R. McDaniel, Professor of Law, Boston College Law School.
Hugh J. Ault, Professor of Law, Boston College Law School.

V7204—11f

UNIVERSITY CASEBOOK SERIES—Continued

TAXATION, FEDERAL WEALTH TRANSFER (1977)

Stanley S. Surrey, Professor of Law, Harvard University.
William C. Warren, Professor of Law Emeritus, Columbia University, and
Paul R. McDaniel, Professor of Law, Boston College Law School.
Harry L. Gutman, Instructor, Harvard Law School and Boston College Law School.

TAXES AND FINANCE—STATE AND LOCAL (1974)

Oliver Oldman, Professor of Law, Harvard University.
Ferdinand P. Schoettle, Professor of Law, University of Minnesota.

TAXATION OF INDIVIDUALS, PARTNERSHIPS AND CORPORATIONS, PROBLEMS in the (1978)

Norton L. Steuben, Professor of Law, University of Colorado.
William J. Turnier, Professor of Law, University of North Carolina.

TORT LAW AND ALTERNATIVES: INJURIES AND REMEDIES, Second Edition (1979)

Marc A. Franklin, Professor of Law, Stanford University.

TORTS, Third Edition (1976)

The late Harry Shulman, Dean of the Law School, Yale University.
Fleming James, Jr., Professor of Law Emeritus, Yale University.
Oscar S. Gray, Professor of Law, University of Maryland.

TORTS, Sixth Edition (1976)

The late William L. Prosser, Professor of Law, University of California, Hastings College of the Law.
John W. Wade, Professor of Law, Vanderbilt University.
Victor E. Schwartz, Professor of Law, University of Cincinnati.

TRADE REGULATION (1975), with 1979 Supplement

Milton Handler, Professor of Law Emeritus, Columbia University.
Harlan M. Blake, Professor of Law, Columbia University.
Robert Pitofsky, Professor of Law, Georgetown University.
Harvey J. Goldschmid, Professor of Law, Columbia University.

TRADE REGULATION, see Antitrust

TRANSNATIONAL LEGAL PROBLEMS, Second Edition (1976), with Documentary Supplement

Henry J. Steiner, Professor of Law, Harvard University.
Detlev F. Vagts, Professor of Law, Harvard University.

TRIAL, see also Lawyering Process

TRIAL ADVOCACY (1968)

A. Leo Levin, Professor of Law, University of Pennsylvania.
Harold Cramer, Esq., Member of the Philadelphia Bar, (Maurice Rosenberg, Professor of Law, Columbia University, as consultant).

TRUSTS, Fifth Edition (1978)

The late George G. Bogert, James Parker Hall, Professor of Law Emeritus, University of Chicago.
Dallin H. Oaks, President, Brigham Young University.

TRUSTS AND SUCCESSION (Palmer's), Third Edition (1978)

Richard V. Wellman, Professor of Law, University of Georgia.
Lawrence W. Waggoner, Professor of Law, University of Michigan.
Olin L. Browder, Jr., Professor of Law, University of Michigan.

UNIVERSITY CASEBOOK SERIES—Continued

UNFAIR COMPETITION, see Competitive Process and Business Torts

UNITED NATIONS IN ACTION (1968)

Louis B. Sohn, Professor of Law, Harvard University.

UNITED NATIONS LAW, Second Edition (1967), with Documentary Supplement (1968)

Louis B. Sohn, Professor of Law, Harvard University.

WATER RESOURCE MANAGEMENT, Second Edition (1980)

Charles J. Meyers, Dean of the Law School, Stanford University.
A. Dan Tarlock, Professor of Law, Indiana University.

WILLS AND ADMINISTRATION, 5th Edition (1961)

The late Philip Mechem, Professor of Law, University of Pennsylvania, and
The late Thomas E. Atkinson, Professor of Law, New York University.

WORLD LAW, see United Nations Law

University Casebook Series

V7204—14f

CASES AND MATERIALS

ON

FUNDAMENTALS

OF

FEDERAL INCOME TAXATION

By

JAMES J. FREELAND

STEPHEN A. LIND

RICHARD B. STEPHENS
Professors of Law, University of Florida

SECOND EDITION

Mineola, New York
THE FOUNDATION PRESS, INC.
1977

F., L. & S. Fed.Income Tax. 2d Ed. UCB
4th Reprint—1980

To our students
and to students elsewhere who feel
they have benefited from use of
the first edition of this book.

*

PREFACE

Tax books are perishable—not much affected by freeze but fragile when it comes to political heat. Early in 1976 the authors of this book agreed that an accretion of comparatively minor developments—legislative, administrative, and judicial actions which, although not cataclysmic, were important—prompted a revision. Legislative tax thunder always rumbles in the background, and so a second edition of this book was undertaken by the authors (and brought almost to completion in September) with the idea that the usually minor Congressional product could be incorporated before the manuscript went to the publishers. Then came the Tax Reform Act of 1976. Three months of intensive work were required to take account of its extensive changes. This may be the first book to be twice revised in moving from its first to its second edition. But it is up to date essentially through 1976.

As its title indicates, the purpose of this book is to aid in the teaching of the fundamentals of the federal income tax. The accomplishment of such a purpose involves, first, a selective determination of basic principles and concepts and, second, a decision of the manner and depth of treatment of the matters that are deemed fundamental. There is wide room for disagreement on both points. Nevertheless the authors are confident that a thoughtful study of the materials presented in this book will afford the student a good income tax foundation. Those who do not proceed beyond the fundamentals may be inadequately informed, but at least they will have a useful awareness of how the federal income tax impinges on practically everything that goes on in our society and economy. Others will have a good basis for enlarging their tax knowledge through advanced law school courses, or graduate study, or practice, or some combination of all three.

Although the major tax legislation of 1976 is captioned "Reform," it moves us further away from the dream of simplicity or even of some simplification. The demands made of the tax lawyer are heavy; but legal educators need to keep in mind that a practitioner must be a lawyer first and a *tax* lawyer only second. The tax lawyer should receive the bulk of his specialized training either through graduate study or, in the time-honored tradition of the legal profession, through his own scholarly efforts in practice. In law school some tax study may be essential for all, but not to the point that law school becomes trade school at the expense of the study of jurisprudence, comparative law and other courses needed to develop perspective.

Beyond basic income tax instruction graduate tax programs, including that at the University of Florida College of Law, offer graduate instruction, which may lead to an LL.M. in Taxation, in subjects such as the following:

Income Tax Accounting	Income Taxation of Trusts and Estates
State and Local Taxation	Estate Planning
Corporate Taxation	Partnership Taxation
Advanced Corporate Tax Problems	Tax Procedure
Corporate Reorganization	Investigation and Prosecution of Tax Fraud
United States Taxation of Foreign Income	Deferred Compensation
Estate and Gift Taxation	Federal Tax Research
Apportionment of Death Taxes	Tax Exempt Organizations

Other areas not identified are sometimes studied by way of supervised research and independent study courses.

The approach taken in this book to various aspects of the income tax varies from one of great attention to detail to one of very general descriptive notes. These differences are not haphazard. For one thing, the authors, aware of time limitations, are certain that to present a uniformly general survey approach to income taxation would be a meaningless exercise, a serious disservice to students and a waste of faculty energy and time. A substantial amount of detailed study and analysis, selectively presented, is the only way to achieve a basic understanding of what federal taxation is all about.

What we have done is attempt to make the detailed study portions of the book serve a second purpose of giving the student a tight grasp of tax concepts and principles that are of wide application and importance. For example, the "gotcha" (I.R.C. § 1245, the first broad recapture provision which makes its appearance in Chapter 22) is examined closely both as to purpose and effect, because both it and other related recapture provisions crop up repeatedly, and they frequently affect all types of taxpayers, individuals, trusts, partnerships, corporations, and so forth. On the other hand, with regard to restrictions on deductions (considered in Chapter 15) the effect of illegality or impropriety on the deductibility of an expenditure, although it has been the subject of several interesting and highly "teachable" Supreme Court decisions, is relegated to an explanatory note, that discusses the cases, because the problem is of far less frequent occurrence. Similarly, we are content to present the constitutional status of the income tax by way of a note. When the modern income tax was first enacted in 1913, almost every conceivable constitutional objection was raised against it; and various objections dealt with in the note should be known to the student, even though they do not have much current importance. Students should also have some understanding of tax procedure, which they can get from Chapters 28, 29 and 30, presented largely as text, even if busy instructors find no class time for this material.

There are some matters that must be classified as important which are not dealt with in detail. For example, deferred compensation arrangements, touched on in Chapter 20, affect the lives of millions of taxpaying employers and employees. And the tax rules applicable to trusts, partnerships, and corporations, accorded only sparing recognition in Chapter 14 with regard to problems of assignment of income, also must be classified as important on the basis of any similar numerical test. Nevertheless, it simply cannot all be done in a basic course. And so, of necessity, some important matters are alluded to in notes but not considered in detail and are left for development in additional income tax courses. The first edition of this book anticipated this trend which continues. A study of the taxation of individuals is the beginning, and it will serve as the cornerstone on which additional income tax courses can rest.

Brief note treatment of some matters not presented in detail reflects an effort to resist the academic compulsion to appear erudite. The purpose of such notes is only to create a general awareness and we have tried to keep in mind the boy who received a Christmas book telling him "more than he wanted to know about penguins." We *do* know more about some of these "penguins," but it is more than we choose to tell. In this spirit we have resisted the inclination to let the second edition "grow." Nevertheless, references are included to more nourishing books and articles that may be of assistance if, at another time, the student would undertake his own detailed exploration of the area.

The authors have attempted to take account of the fact that students arrive at their first law school tax course with a wide variety of educational and other experiences. Those who have little accounting background are apprehensive and likely to feel they "will not like tax." This attitude, as we know, is not fully justified, and experience has shown that many of these people have found a new dimension in tax law. Nevertheless, in many instances in which instruction is bound to encroach on the domain of the accountant, an effort is made, sometimes through informative comment such as the note on depreciation in Chapter 22 and on inventories in Chapter 19, to render the material manageable regardless of the student's background knowledge. Sometimes we are sneaky, too, for example by using the innocuous caption "Timing," rather than the intimidating term "Accounting." Moreover if, partly due to past lack of experience, the present study seems to get off to a slow beginning, the student may anticipate a quickening pace as later chapters unfold. In fact, most students will discern a mounting crescendo with something in the nature of fireworks at the end of the show. If an instructor deems procedure (Chapters 28 through 30) too unlike fireworks, he can select his own high note on which to end.

Many of the judicial opinions and other documents quoted in this work have fallen prey to our editorial license. Deletions are indicated conventionally by the use of ellipses and asterisks, and editorial additions are bracketed. Where necessary, footnotes are renumbered to take account of omissions. In general, the materials included are based on the status of the law toward the end of 1976.

The authors acknowledge an indebtedness to the hundreds of law students who have passed through their classes over a combined teaching period of about sixty years. Not only have these young men and women served as guinea pigs for various experiments; their perception and insight have been a part of the continuing education of their instructors, making former students substantial contributors to the form and substance of this book. Some graduate students who have worked directly with the authors should be recognized by name. They are: Bernie Barton, Nat Doliner, Jack Levine, Sharon Selk and Chuck Tallant.

Colleagues have also been most helpful. In pre-publication mimeographed form the first edition of this book was used by Professors Arthur Andrews of the University of Arizona, Bruce Peterson of the University of Tulsa, and Joel Rabinovitz, of the University of California at Los Angeles. With the advent of graduate tax study at Florida and the increase in the number of full-time tax instructors to seven, the authors have had the benefit of helpful comments from lawyers closer to home, namely, Professors Dennis Calfee, David Hudson, Larry Lokken and Doug Miller. Paul Lipton of Milwaukee, who teaches the investigation and prosecution of tax fraud as an adjunct professor at Florida, was kind enough to offer comments on Part B of Chapter 28. Each has made suggestions that are reflected in this volume for which the authors are grateful. A word of thanks is also due to the graduate tax faculty of the New York University School of Law, with whom the authors have had close professional association.

PREFACE

Credit for the preparation of the index goes to Betty Taylor, University of Florida Law Librarian, who in keeping with previously demonstrated skills has admirably accomplished this task.

The essential procedure of mind to machine to publisher was accomplished by Merry James, Linda Powell and Lee Ann Williams under the gentle guidance of Beth Kaster and despite the impatient directions of the authors.

JAMES J. FREELAND
STEPHEN A. LIND
RICHARD B. STEPHENS

May, 1977

*

SUMMARY OF CONTENTS

	Page
PREFACE	XVII
TABLE OF INTERNAL REVENUE CODE SECTIONS	XXXI
TABLE OF TREASURY REGULATIONS	XLIX
TABLE OF INTERNAL REVENUE RULINGS	LIII
TABLE OF MISCELLANEOUS RULINGS	LV
TABLE OF CASES	LVII

PART ONE: INTRODUCTION

Chapter

1. Orientation	1
2. The Tax Practitioner's Tools	25

PART TWO: IDENTIFICATION OF INCOME SUBJECT TO TAXATION

3. Gross Income: The Scope of Section 61	36
4. The Exclusion of Gifts and Inheritances	64
5. Limitations in Employment Relationships	99
6. Awards	124
7. Gain from Dealings in Property	141
8. Annuities and Life Insurance Proceeds	188
9. Discharge of Indebtedness	199
10. Damages and Related Receipts	204
11. Separation and Divorce	219
12. Other Exclusions from Gross Income	253

PART THREE: IDENTIFICATION OF THE PROPER TAXPAYER

13. Assignment of Income	262
14. Income Producing Entities	300

PART FOUR: DEDUCTIONS IN COMPUTING TAXABLE INCOME

15. Business Deductions	342
16. Deductions for Profit-Making, Nonbusiness Activities	428
17. Deductions Not Limited to Business or Profit-Seeking Activities	465
18. Deductions for Individuals Only	496

PART FIVE: THE YEAR OF INCLUSION OR DEDUCTION

Chapter   Page
19. Fundamental Timing Principles _____ 537
20. How Ineluctable is the Integrity of the Taxable Year? _____ 598

PART SIX: THE CHARACTERIZATION OF INCOME AND DEDUCTIONS

21. Capital Gains and Losses _____ 635
22. Characterization of Gain on the Sale of Depreciable Property 721
23. Deductions Affected by Characterization _____ 808

PART SEVEN: DEFERRAL AND NONRECOGNITION OF INCOME AND DEDUCTIONS

24. Deferred Reporting of Gains _____ 847
25. Disallowance of Losses _____ 886
26. Nonrecognition Provisions _____ 895

PART EIGHT: CONVERTING TAXABLE INCOME INTO TAX LIABILITY

27. Computations _____ 947

PART NINE: FEDERAL TAX PROCEDURE

28. Introduction _____ 970
29. Refund Procedures _____ 994
30. Deficiency Procedures _____1000

Index _____1023

TABLE OF CONTENTS

		Page
PREFACE		XVII
TABLE OF INTERNAL REVENUE CODE SECTIONS		XXXI
TABLE OF TREASURY REGULATIONS		XLIX
TABLE OF INTERNAL REVENUE RULINGS		LIII
TABLE OF MISCELLANEOUS RULINGS		LV
TABLE OF CASES		LVII

PART ONE: INTRODUCTION

CHAPTER 1. ORIENTATION		1
A.	A Look Forward	1
B.	A Glimpse Backward	6
C.	The Income Tax and the United States Constitution	14
D.	The Road Ahead	21
CHAPTER 2. THE TAX PRACTITIONER'S TOOLS		25
1.	Legislative Materials	25
2.	Administrative Materials	29
3.	Judicial Materials	31
4.	Unofficial Tax Materials	34

PART TWO: IDENTIFICATION OF INCOME SUBJECT TO TAXATION

CHAPTER 3. GROSS INCOME: THE SCOPE OF SECTION 61		36
A.	Introduction to Income	36
B.	Equivocal Receipt of Financial Benefit	37
C.	Income Without Receipt of Cash or Property	53
CHAPTER 4. THE EXCLUSION OF GIFTS AND INHERITANCES		64
A.	Rules of Inclusion and Exclusion	64
B.	The Income Tax Meaning of Gift	66
C.	The Income Tax Meaning of Inheritance	89
CHAPTER 5. LIMITATIONS IN EMPLOYMENT RELATIONSHIPS		99
A.	Fringe Benefits	99
B.	Exclusions for Meals and Lodging	116
CHAPTER 6. AWARDS		124
A.	Prizes	124
B.	Scholarships and Fellowships	133

Page

CHAPTER 7.   GAIN FROM DEALINGS IN PROPERTY 141
  A.   Factors in the Determination of Gain 141
  B.   Determination of Basis 142
    1.   Cost as Basis 142
    2.   Property Acquired by Gift 146
    3.   Property Acquired from a Decedent 154
  C.   The Amount Realized 159
  D.   Determination of Gain 178

CHAPTER 8.   ANNUITIES AND LIFE INSURANCE PROCEEDS 188

CHAPTER 9.   DISCHARGE OF INDEBTEDNESS 199

CHAPTER 10.   DAMAGES AND RELATED RECEIPTS 204
  A.   Compensation for Injuries or Sickness: Statutory
    Exclusions 205
  B.   Personal Injuries not Subject to Statutory Rules 214
  C.   Recoveries for Injuries to Business or to Property 215

CHAPTER 11.   SEPARATION AND DIVORCE 219
  A.   Support vs. Property Settlements 219
  B.   Periodic Alimony Payments 231
  C.   Other Aspects of Alimony Payments 236
    1.   Child Support 236
    2.   Indirect Benefits 241
    3.   Divorce 247
  D.   Nondeductible Alimony 248

CHAPTER 12.   OTHER EXCLUSIONS FROM GROSS INCOME 253
  A.   Miscellaneous Statutory Exclusions 253
  B.   Federal Taxes and State Activities 256

PART THREE: IDENTIFICATION OF THE
PROPER TAXPAYER

CHAPTER 13.   ASSIGNMENT OF INCOME 262
  A.   Introduction 262
  B.   Income from Services 264
  C.   Income from Property 275
  D.   Anticipatory Assignment for Value 292

CHAPTER 14.   INCOME PRODUCING ENTITIES 300
  A.   Introduction 300
  B.   Trusts and Estates 304
  C.   Partnerships 322
  D.   Corporations 331

PART FOUR: DEDUCTIONS IN COMPUTING
TAXABLE INCOME

Page

CHAPTER 15. BUSINESS DEDUCTIONS 342
A. Introduction 342
B. The Anatomy of the Business Deduction Workhorse:
   Section 162 344
   1. "Ordinary and Necessary" 344
   2. "Expenses" 348
   3. "Carrying On" Business 356
C. Specific Business Deductions 363
   1. "Reasonable" Salaries 363
   2. Travel "Away from Home" 369
   3. Necessary Rental and Similar Payments 383
   4. Expenses for Education 396
D. Miscellaneous Business Deductions 405
   1. Introduction 405
   2. Business Losses 410
E. Restrictions on Deductions 413
   1. Artificial Losses 413
   2. Other Statutory Restrictions on Deductions 418
   3. Illegality or Impropriety 420
   4. Depreciation, Depletion, and Amortization 427

CHAPTER 16. DEDUCTIONS FOR PROFIT-MAKING, NONBUSINESS
   ACTIVITIES 428
A. Section 212 Expenses 428
B. Charges Arising Out of Transactions Entered into for
   Profit 455

CHAPTER 17. DEDUCTIONS NOT LIMITED TO BUSINESS OR
   PROFIT-SEEKING ACTIVITIES 465
A. Interest 465
B. Taxes 472
C. Casualty and Theft Losses 475
   1. Nature of Losses Allowed 475
   2. Timing Casualty Losses 487
   3. Measuring the Loss 488
D. Bad Debts and Charitable Contributions 495

CHAPTER 18. DEDUCTIONS FOR INDIVIDUALS ONLY 496
A. Personal and Dependency Exemptions 496
B. The Concept of Adjusted Gross Income 504
C. The Standard Deduction 507
D. Extraordinary Medical Expenses 511
E. Moving Expenses 525
F. Political Contributions 536

PART FIVE: THE YEAR OF INCLUSION OR DEDUCTION

Page

CHAPTER 19. FUNDAMENTAL TIMING PRINCIPLES _____ 537
  A. Introduction _____ 537
  B. The Cash Receipts and Disbursements Method _____ 541
     1. Receipts _____ 541
     2. Disbursements _____ 551
  C. The Accrual Method _____ 559
     1. Income Items _____ 559
     2. Deduction Items _____ 584

CHAPTER 20. HOW INELUCTABLE IS THE INTEGRITY OF THE
            TAXABLE YEAR? _____ 598
  A. Taxpayer's Restoration of Previously Taxed Income ___ 598
  B. The Tax Benefit Doctrine _____ 608
  C. Income Averaging _____ 613
     1. Statutory Averaging _____ 613
     2. Do-it-Yourself Averaging _____ 620
     3. Statutory Do-it-Yourself Averaging _____ 628
  D. The Carryover and Carryback Devices _____ 631

PART SIX: THE CHARACTERIZATION OF INCOME AND DEDUCTIONS

CHAPTER 21. CAPITAL GAINS AND LOSSES _____ 635
  A. Introduction _____ 635
  B. The Mechanics of Capital Gains _____ 640
  C. The Mechanics of Capital Losses _____ 650
  D. The Meaning of "Capital Asset" _____ 660
     1. The Statutory Definition _____ 660
     2. "Income" Property _____ 670
     3. The Corn Products Doctrine _____ 680
  E. The Sale or Exchange Requirement _____ 689
     1. Introduction _____ 689
     2. Correlation with Prior Transactions _____ 703
  F. The Holding Period _____ 713

CHAPTER 22. CHARACTERIZATION OF GAIN ON THE SALE OF
            DEPRECIABLE PROPERTY _____ 721
  A. Depreciation _____ 721
     1. Introduction _____ 721
     2. Special Rules on Personalty _____ 758
     3. Special Rules on Realty _____ 759

TABLE OF CONTENTS

Page

CHAPTER 22. CHARACTERIZATION OF GAIN ON THE SALE OF DEPRECIABLE PROPERTY—Continued

B. Sales and Exchanges of Depreciable Property _____ 762
    1. The Section 1231 Hotchpot _____ 762
    2. Characterization Under Section 1239 _____ 779
    3. Recapture Under Section 1245 _____ 786
    4. Recapture Under Section 1250 _____ 795
    5. Other Recapture Concepts _____ 801

CHAPTER 23. DEDUCTIONS AFFECTED BY CHARACTERIZATION PRINCIPLES _____ 808

A. Bad Debts and Worthless Securities _____ 808
B. The Charitable Deduction _____ 823

PART SEVEN: DEFERRAL AND NONRECOGNITION OF INCOME AND DEDUCTIONS

CHAPTER 24. DEFERRED REPORTING OF GAINS _____ 847
A. Timing and Character of Gain in an Open Transaction __ 847
B. Timing and Character of Gain in a Closed Transaction __ 855
    1. Transactions Not Involving a § 453 Installment Election _____ 855
        a. Cash Method Taxpayers _____ 855
        b. Accrual Method Taxpayers _____ 872
    2. Transactions Under a § 453 Election _____ 874

CHAPTER 25. DISALLOWANCE OF LOSSES _____ 886
A. Losses Between Related Taxpayers _____ 886
B. Wash Sales _____ 894

CHAPTER 26. NONRECOGNITION PROVISIONS _____ 895
A. Introduction _____ 895
B. Like Kind Exchanges _____ 897
C. Involuntary Conversions _____ 914
D. Sale of a Principal Residence _____ 929
E. Other Nonrecognition Provisions _____ 942

PART EIGHT: CONVERTING TAXABLE INCOME INTO TAX LIABILITY

CHAPTER 27. COMPUTATIONS _____ 947
A. Classification of Taxpayers _____ 947
B. Minimum Tax _____ 953
C. Maximum Tax on Personal Service Income _____ 960
D. Credits Against Tax _____ 962

TABLE OF CONTENTS

PART NINE: FEDERAL TAX PROCEDURE

Page

CHAPTER 28. INTRODUCTION 970
   A. Civil Liability for Tax 970
   B. The Profile of a Tax Fraud Case 981

CHAPTER 29. REFUND PROCEDURES 994

CHAPTER 30. DEFICIENCY PROCEDURES 1000

Index 1023

TABLE OF INTERNAL REVENUE CODE SECTIONS

Section	Page	Section	Page
1	263	2(b)(1)(A)(ii)	950
	342	2(b)(1)(B)	950
	640	2(b)(2)(B)	950
	641	2(b)(2)(C)	950
	648	2(c)	950
	947		952
	952	3	342
	961		947
	1003		952
1(a)	23		953
	220	3(a)	952
	262	11	23
	263		301
	342		619
	508		648
	947		649
	948		947
	949	11(a)	331
	951	23(k)(4)	817
	952	24(b)	891
1(a)(2)	949	31	962
1(b)	23		963
	947	31(b)	964
	950	33	320
1(c)	23		969
	262	34	254
	263		969
	508	35	969
	619	35(a)	969
	641	37	962
	642		964
	644	37(c)(1)	968
	646	38	801
	846		804
	947		962
	950		966
	951	40	966
	952	40–43	962
	960	41	409
	961		419
1(d)	23		536
	263		967
	508	41(c)	536
	947	42	968
	951	43	968
2	420	43(c)(2)	968
	421	44	969
	947	44A	497
2(a)	263		505
	947		511
	949		536
2(b)	947		962
	950		968
2(b)(1)(A)	950	44A(c)(2)	968

Section	Page	Section	Page
44A(d)	968	62(4)	642
46	966		653
46–48	804		655
	962	62(5)	721
46–50	801		732
46(a)(1)(A)	806		769
46(a)(1)(B)	806	62(10)	630
46(d)	806	62(13)	220
47	807		504
	966	63	262
47(a)	807		342
47(b)	807		507
48	966		808
48(c)(2)(A)	806	63(a)	342
49	804	63(b)	221
50	804		343
50A	966		506
50B	966	64	786
51	952		795
56	648	66–97	715
	960	71	204
56–58	259		219
	953		220
56(a)	648		229
56(c)	954		248
57(a)(1)	469		249
57(a)(9)(A)	648		252
57(b)	469	71–84	64
61	18	71(a)	219
	36		229
	37		230
	49		231
	53		232
	64		234
	114		248
	204		249
	314		250
	405		251
	498		252
61(a)	29		496
61(a)(1)	106		498
	254		540
61(a)(7)	64	71(a)(1)	231
	301		234
61(a)(12)	199	71(a)(2)	220
62	343		232
	504		234
	505		504
	506	71(a)(3)	220
	507		232
	509		235
	808	71(b)	236
	953		251
	962		496
62(1)	721		498
	732	71(c)	231
	769		232
	817		252
62(2)	817	71(c)(1)	230
62(3)	641		252
	642		

TABLE OF INTERNAL REVENUE CODE SECTIONS

Section	Page	Section	Page
71(c)(2)	230	101(b)(2)(B)(i)–(iii)	86
	232	101(c)	188
	249		190
71(d)	248	101(d)	188
	249		189
	250		190
72	191	101(d)(1)(B)	190
	192	101(e)	241
	194	102	65
	249		87
	470		98
72(a)	188		189
	193		204
72(b)	188		251
72(c)	188		303
72(c)(1)	192		491
72(c)(2)	193		677
72(c)(3)	192	102(a)	64
72(d)	191		65
72(e)	188		66
	193		75
72(e)(1)(B)	194		76
72(h)	188		86
	194		89
72(k)	219		199
72(m)(3)	110		396
73	263	102(b)	64
	947		65
74	52		66
	124		89
	133		396
	134		670
74(a)	134		677
79	99		678
	110	102(b)(1)	65
79(a)	110	102(b)(2)	65
79(a)(2)	110	103	18
79(b)(1)	110		253
79(b)(2)	110		259
79(b)(3)	110		303
80	204		470
82	525	103(a)	256
83	631	103(b)	256
84	17	103(c)	256
101	194	103(d)	256
	209	103(g)(24)	470
	470	104	205
101–124	64		206
101(a)	188		207
	189		208
	193		209
101(a)(1)	188		212
101(a)(2)	188		213
101(a)(2)(A)	188		214
101(a)(2)(B)	188		215
101(b)	85	104–106	204
	86		205
101(b)(1)	86	104(a)	209
101(b)(1)–101(b)(2)(B)	66		210
101(b)(2)	86	104(a)(1)	206
101(b)(2)(B)	86		212

TABLE OF INTERNAL REVENUE CODE SECTIONS

Section	Page	Section	Page
104(a)(2)	206	117	133
	207		134
	208		135
	214		136
	215		137
	216		138
	217		139
104(a)(3)	209	117(a)	134
	210	117(a)(1)(A)	134
	211	117(a)(2)	134
	212	117(b)	134
104(a)(4)	210	117(b)(1)	135
	211	117(b)(2)	135
104(a)(5)	210	117(b)(2)(A)	135
	211	119	116
104(b)	210		122
105	206	121(a)–(c)	929
	209	121(b)(1)	941
	210	121(d)(7)	929
105(a)	211	122	253
105(b)	205	123	216
	211		488
	212	141	221
105(c)	211		343
	212		507
	213		642
105(d)	211		649
	213	141–144	505
105(e)	209		506
	212	141(a)	509
105(f)	212	141(c)	509
105(g)	211	142	507
106	209	142(a)	947
	210	143	496
107	116		507
	122	143(b)	510
108(a)	199		947
109	253		950
	254		952
110	253	144(a)	507
111	204		947
	206		952
	612	151	496
111(a)	608		633
	808		642
111(b)	608		649
	808		652
112	253		950
	254	151(a)–(d)	496
112(d)	254	151(b)	496
113	253		968
	254	151(e)	496
114	253		497
115	256		498
115(a)	260		968
116	64	151(e)(1)(A)	498
	65	151(e)(1)(B)	498
	253	151(e)(2)	498
	254	151(e)(3)	498
	320	151(e)(4)	498
	969		

TABLE OF INTERNAL REVENUE CODE SECTIONS

Section	Page	Section	Page
152	211	162(b)	405
	212		823
	496	162(c)	421
152(a)	497	162(c)(2)	425
152(a)(9)	497	162(c)(3)	476
152(a)(10)	497	162(e)	410
152(b)	497		418
152(b)(2)	497		419
152(b)(5)	420		423
	421	162(f)	422
	497		426
152(c)	497	162(g)	422
	511	163	254
152(d)	497		320
152(e)	498		418
152(e)(2)(A)	498		419
152(e)(2)(B)	498		468
162	207		469
	320		1001
	343	163(a)	465
	344		540
	347	163(b)	465
	352		468
	353	163(c)	468
	354	163(d)	465
	358		469
	359	164	320
	361		474
	394	164(a)	472
	407		474
	408		540
	409	164(a)(3)	969
	410	164(b)	472
	418	164(c)	472
	420	164(c)(2)	669
	424	164(d)(1)	472
	431	165	410
	432		413
	474		476
	523	165(a)	410
	524		455
	559		475
	605		490
	629	165(b)	411
162(a)	343		412
	344		455
	348		488
	356	165(c)	410
	358		475
	396		476
	405		650
	406		915
	411	165(c)(1)	343
	540		410
162(a)(1)	363		411
162(a)(1–3)	405		475
162(a)(2)	358		476
	369		490
162(a)(3)	383		892
	393		
	395		

Section	Page	Section	Page
165(c)(2)	343	167(b)	721
	359		758
	411	167(b)(2)–(4)	751
	432	167(b)(4)	732
	435	167(c)	721
	455		732
	464		751
	475	167(d)	1015
	476	167(f)	726
	490		758
	892		759
165(c)(3)	411		761
	476		786
	487		794
	488	167(g)	721
	490		726
	612	167(h)	320
165(d)	421		393
165(e)	487	167(j)	759
165(f)	650	167(k)	734
	808		759
165(g)	475		801
	667		802
	698	167(m)	355
165(g)(1)	635		725
	808	167(m)(2)	725
165(g)(2)	808	167(n)	759
165(h)	487	167(o)	759
166	814		762
166(a)–(e)	808	168	802
166(a)(2)	815	168(i)	802
166(c)	588	169	721
	815		734
166(d)	667		802
	698	170	410
	814		808
166(d)(1)(B)	635		844
166(d)(2)(A)	814	170(a)	540
	815	170(a)(1)	823
166(d)(2)(B)	814	170(b)	505
	815	170(b)(1)(A)	823
166(g)	588		846
167	158	170(b)(1)(A)(ii)	134
	159		844
	408		846
	409	170(b)(1)(B)	823
	722	170(b)(1)(C)	823
	727	170(b)(1)(C)(iii)	845
	730	170(b)(1)(E)	823
	758	170(b)(1)(F)	505
	786		633
	795	170(b)(2)	823
167(a)	393	170(c)	823
	721	170(c)(2)	844
	752		846
167(a)(1)	343	170(d)(1)	633
	411	170(d)(1)(A)	823
167(a)(2)	343		844
	432	170(e)	18
	455		666

TABLE OF INTERNAL REVENUE CODE SECTIONS

Section	Page	Section	Page
170(e)(1)	823	212	431
170(e)(1)(A)	288		432
170(e)(2)	823		453
170(f)(2)(B)	845		455
170(f)(3)(A)	845		464
170(f)(3)(B)(iii)	845		474
170(f)(3)(B)(iv)	845		540
172	612		605
	631		629
	633	212(1)	343
	634		352
172(a)	632		431
172(b)(1)(A)	632	212(2)	343
172(b)(1)(A)(ii)	632		431
172(b)(1)(B)	632		453
172(b)(1)(C–G)	632		454
172(b)(2)	632	212(3)	431
172(b)(2)(A)	633		454
172(b)(3)(E)	632	213	205
172(c)	633		206
172(d)	633		208
172(d)(2)(B)	633		210
172(d)(3)	633		521
172(d)(5)	633		522
172(d)(6)	633		523
175	803		524
	804		633
179	758	213(a)	205
	759		218
	761		511
	786		540
	794	213(a)(1)	505
179(a)	758	213(b)	205
179(b)	758		505
179(c)	758		511
179(d)(1)	758	213(e)	211
179(d)(9)	758		511
182	145		521
	803	213(e)(1)(B)	521
	804	213(f)	511
183	343	214	505
	413		968
	475	215	219
	803		220
184	734		231
186	216		232
187	734		248
188	734		249
	966		250
189	465		251
	472		496
	721		504
	758		540
190	355	217	26
191	759		525
208(a)	557		534
212	320		535
	407		536
	418	217(c)(2)(B)	535
	424	217(g)	26
	428		

Section	Page	Section	Page
218	409	271(a)	808
	419	271(c)	419
	536	273	670
	967		677
218(c)	536		678
	967	274	407
219(a)	630		408
219(b)	630		409
242	969	274(a)	405
261–281	343	274(a)(1)	407
262	219		762
	356	274(a)(1)(A)	407
	396	274(a)(1)(B)	407
	406		410
	407		757
	476	274(b)	405
262–279	808		407
263	354	274(b)(1)	66
263(a)	348		87
	354	274(c)	369
	721		383
	757		405
263(a)(1)	354		407
263(c)	804	274(d)	405
263(f)	355		408
	726	274(e)	405
264(a)(2)	469		407
264(a)(3)	469	274(h)	383
	470		408
264(b)	469	275	472
264(c)	470	275(a)(4)	969
265(2)	259	276	405
	465		418
	470	276(a)(1)	410
265(4)	470	276(c)	410
266	471	278	418
267	891		419
	892	279	419
	893	280A	418
	894		420
	895		
267(a)(1)	886	Subchapter C	300
267(a)(2)	392	301	301
	418	301–395	300
	471	316	301
	584	318	785
	597	331	762
267(b)	418	332	942
	886	333	942
267(c)	886	334	942
267(c)(4)	88	341(e)	3
267(d)	886	351	942
	894	358	942
	895	362	942
269	301	362(b)	942
	420	368	942
270	415	385	469
271	410	401	629
	418	401(a)	628
	419		
	808		

TABLE OF INTERNAL REVENUE CODE SECTIONS

Section	Page	Section	Page
401(a)(4)	628	453(a)	874
402(a)	629		882
402(a)(1)	191		943
402(a)(2)	191		944
402(b)	628		945
402(e)(4)(A)	86	453(b)	874
403(a)	629	453(b)(2)(A)	873
403(b)	630	453(d)	320
404(a)	210		882
	629		883
404(a)(2)	629		943
404(a)(4)	316	453(d)(1)	882
404(a)(5)	629	453(d)(1)–(3)	874
404(a)(8)	630	453(d)(2)	882
404(a)(9)	630		944
404(e)	630		945
408(d)	631		946
408(e)	631	453(d)(3)	882
408(f)	631		883
409(b)	631	453(d)(4)	883
409(c)	631	455	559
421–425	631		579
441	537	456	559
441(a)–(e)	537		579
441(b)(2)	537	461(a)	537
441(g)	537		551
442	537		584
443(a)(2)	537	461(f)	584
443(b)	537	461(g)	465
446	537		468
	541		551
	578		557
446(b)	539		558
	579		579
446(c)	538	462	578
446(c)(4)	539		587
446(e)	540		589
451	319	465	413
451(a)	319	482	301
	537		331
	541		468
	559	483	465
451(b)	319		468
452	578		874
	589	483(f)(2)	468
453	538	501(a)	629
	637	501(c)	260
	678	501(c)(3)	135
	855	501(c)(17)	629
	873	501(d)	260
	874	511(a)(2)(B)	260
	882	512	703
	883	514	703
	884	534	1014
	885	611	735
	895	612	735
	896	613	735
	941	613(b)	735
	943	613(d)	736
	945	613A(b)	736
		613A(c)(3)	736

TABLE OF INTERNAL REVENUE CODE SECTIONS

Section	Page	Section	Page
613A(c)(5)	736	675	304
641	301		315
	302	676	304
641–692	301		313
642(h)	653		314
643(a)	302	677	252
644	304		304
651	251		314
	302		315
	393	677(a)	251
651(b)	302		315
652	251	677(b)	251
	302		315
	316		316
	393	678	304
652(a)	302		314
652(b)	303		315
	678		316
661	251	678(b)	315
	302	678(c)	316
	319	679	304
	320		314
	393		316
661(a)	302	682	220
661(b)	303		248
662	251		251
	302	682(a)	251
	316	682(b)	251
	319	691	317
	320		318
	393		319
662(a)	302		320
662(b)	303		321
	678		882
663	320	691(a)	319
665–668	291	691(a)(1)(A)	319
	302	691(a)(1)(C)	320
671	304	691(a)(2)	320
	314	691(a)(3)	320
	396	691(a)(4)	882
671–675	314		883
671–678	251	691(b)	320
	392	691(b)(1)(A)	320
	393	691(b)(1)(B)	320
	394	691(b)(2)	320
672(a)	304	691(c)	321
	315	691(c)(1)(A)	321
672(b)	304	691(c)(1)(B)	321
	315	691(c)(2)	321
672(c)	304	701	300
672(d)	304		322
673	304	Subchapter K	300
	314	701–771	300
	393	703	300
673(c)	314	704(a)	300
674	304	704(e)	322
674(a)	315		331
674(b)	315		392
674(c)	315		393
674(d)	315		394
			395

xl

Section	Page	Section	Page
704(e)(1)	330	1014(b)(6)	154
707(c)	322		156
721	942	1014(c)	319
722	942	1014(d)	154
723	942	1015	155
731	942		156
732	942		168
741	762		677
801(g)(1)(A)	191		678
852(b)(5)(B)	470		726
901(a)	969		795
911	253	1015(a)	146
	255		178
	256		713
	534	1015(d)	186
911(a)	255	1015(d)(1)(A)	146
	536		178
911(a)(1)	255	1015(d)(4)	146
911(a)(2)	255		178
911(b)	255	1015(d)(6)	146
911(c)	255		178
1001	696		187
1001(a)	141	1016	786
	178	1016(a)(1)	142
	850	1016(a)(2)	721
	896		733
1001(a)–(c)	847		786
1001(b)	141	1016(a)(2)(B)	733
	159	1016(a)(23)	157
	852	1017	30
	872		199
	873	1019	146
1001(b)(2)	472		253
1001(c)	141		254
	165	1023	17
	896		154
	897		156
	914		157
1001(e)	670		189
	678		254
1001(e)(1)	678		318
1001(e)(3)	678		321
1002	165		658
1011(a)	178		677
	847		678
1011(b)	154		713
	823		795
1012	141		915
	142	1023(a)(2)	156
	178		158
1014	155	1023(b)(1)	677
	156	1023(b)(2)(A)	319
	189	1023(b)(2)(B)	189
	677	1023(b)(3)(A)	156
	896	1023(c)	157
1014(a)	154		321
	155	1023(d)	156
	713		157
1014(b)	677		158
1014(b)(1)	154	1023(d)(2)	157
1014(b)(2)–(9)	155	1023(e)	157

TABLE OF INTERNAL REVENUE CODE SECTIONS

Section	Page	Section	Page
1023(f)(1)	156	1038(a)	943
1023(g)(3)	158	1038(b)	944
1023(g)(4)	187		946
1023(h)	157	1038(b)(1)	943
	159		945
	896	1038(b)(2)	944
1023(h)(1)	157		945
	158	1038(b)(2)(B)	946
1023(h)(2)(B)	158	1038(c)	944
	159		946
1031	637	1038(c)(1)	944
	896	1038(c)(2)	944
	897	1039	942
	904		943
	905	1039(a)	943
	912	1039(b)(2)	943
	913	1039(b)(3)	943
	928	1039(d)	943
	929	1040	689
1031(a)	897		942
1031(d)	942	1055	468
1032	942	1056(a)	758
1033	215	1056(d)	726
	637		758
	914	1091	894
	915		895
	928	1091(a)	894
	929	1091(d)	894
	943		895
1033(a)	915	1201	648
	928		649
1033(a)(1)	914	1201–1223	215
1033(a)(2)	914	1201(a)	640
1033(a)(2)(E)	915		648
1033(a)(3)	914		649
1033(b)	914	1201(a)(1)(B)	649
	915	1201(a)(2)	649
1033(f)	914	1201(b)	640
	928		641
	929		642
1033(f)(1)	914		643
1033(f)(2)	914		647
1033(f)(4)	914		649
1033(g)	914	1201(b)(1)	643
	928		645
1034	215		646
	932	1201(b)(2)	643
1034(a)	931		644
1034(a)–(e)	929		645
1034(c)(5)	931		646
1034(j)	929	1201(b)(3)	643
1035	943		645
1036	942		646
1037	943	1201(c)	640
1038	874		643
	883		645
	942		646
	943		
	945		
	946		

TABLE OF INTERNAL REVENUE CODE SECTIONS

Section	Page	Section	Page
1202	633	1212(b)(1)(B)	654
	640		656
	641		657
	642		658
	643	1212(b)(2)	653
	645		654
	646		656
	647		657
	648	1212(b)(2)(A)	655
	649		657
	960	1212(b)(2)(B)	654
1211	475		655
	639		656
	656	1212(b)(2)(B)(i)	656
	808		657
1211(a)	650	1212(b)(2)(B)(ii)	657
	658	1212(b)(3)	653
1211(b)	640	1221	640
	650		650
	651		660
	653		666
	654		667
	655		678
	658		699
1211(b)(1)	652		762
	653		777
	655		778
1211(b)(1)(A)	652	1221(1)	665
	659		778
1211(b)(1)(B)	652	1221(2)	667
	653	1221(3)	699
	655		845
	659	1221(6)	666
1211(b)(1)(C)	651	1222	640
	652		650
	653		689
	659		713
1211(b)(1)(C)(i)	651		762
	653		786
1211(b)(1)(C)(ii)	655		795
1211(b)(3)	652		808
	653		896
1212	475	1222(2)	650
	639	1222(3)	641
	654	1222(4)	641
	1000		650
1212(a)	650	1222(6)	641
	658	1222(7)	641
1212(a)(1)	658		642
1212(a)(1)(A)(ii)	658	1222(10)	650
1212(b)	650		653
	653		656
	656	1222(11)	640
	659		641
1212(b)(1)	653	1223	667
	654	1223(1)	713
	656		897
	657	1223(2)	713
1212(b)(1)(A)	655		719
		1223(4)	894
		1223(7)	929

xliii

Section	Page	Section	Page
1223(11)	713	1242–1244	667
1231	215	1245	215
	476		667
	495		777
	637		778
	667		786
	698		787
	762		789
	777		791
	778		792
	786		793
	795		795
	911		796
	914		801
	915		802
1231(a)	777		804
	896		874
1231(b)(1)(B)	778		966
1232	667	1245(a)	786
	689		795
	698	1245(a)(2)	795
	699	1245(a)(2)(B)	791
1232(a)(2)(E)	699	1245(a)(2)(C)	791
1232(a)(3)(E)	699	1245(a)(2)(D)	791
1233	689	1245(a)(3)	789
	713	1245(a)(3)(C)	791
	717	1245(a)(3)(D)	791
	718	1245(a)(4)	791
1233(b)	717	1245(b)	787
1234	660		792
	667	1245(b)(1)	786
1234(b)	717	1245(b)(2)	786
1235	667	1245(b)(4)	897
	689		905
	698		914
	699	1245(c)	786
	700	1245(d)	786
	850	1250	215
1235(b)	699		778
1236	660		786
	668		789
1237	660		794
	668		795
	669		796
1237(a)	668		799
	669		800
1237(a)(1)	669		801
1237(a)(2)(C)	669		802
1237(b)(1)	669		804
1237(b)(2)	669		845
1238	801		846
	802		874
1239	667		885
	779		914
	785	1250–1252	667
1239(b)(3)	785	1250(a)	795
1239(c)	785	1250(a)(1)	800
1241	667	1250(a)(1)(B)	795
	670		800
	689	1250(a)(1)(B)(iii)	801
	698	1250(a)(2)(B)	795

Section	Page	Section	Page
1250(a)(2)(B)(iv)	801	1312(1)	999
1250(a)(3)(B)	795	1314	998
1250(b)(1)	795	1341	599
1250(b)(3)	795		600
1250(b)(4)	795		604
	801		605
1250(c)	789		606
	795		607
1250(d)	787		608
1250(d)(1)	795		612
1250(d)(2)	795	1341(a)	598
1250(d)(4)	897	1341(a)(1)	605
	914	1341(a)(1)–(3)	604
1250(d)(4)(A)	905	1341(a)(2)	605
1250(h)	795		606
1250(i)	786	1341(a)(3)	605
	795	1341(a)(4)	600
1251	801	1341(a)(5)	600
	802	1341(b)(1)	598
	803	1341(b)(2)	598
	804		604
1251(b)(2)(B)	803	1342	204
1251(b)(2)(E)	803	1346	204
1251(e)(1)(A)	802	1347	204
1252	801	1348	960
	803		961
	804		962
1252(a)	804		968
1253	689	1348(a)	960
	698	1351	204
	700	1371–1379	301
1253(d)	723	1372(a)	1005
1254	667	1372(e)(5)	1005
	801	1396	980
	804	1551	301
1301	613	2001	158
	618	2031	154
	620	2032	154
	628	2033	319
	633	2035	155
	637	2035(b)	1015
	640	2039(c)	630
	678	2053	321
1301–1305	318	2056	156
1302	618		948
1302(a)	628	2201	979
1302(a)(1)	613	2501(a)(5)	19
1302(b)(1)	613	2504(c)	1015
1302(b)(2)	613	2513	948
1302(c)	613	2516	249
1303	613	2517	630
1303(c)(2)(C)	620	2523	948
1304(a)	613	3401(a)	963
1304(c)(2)	613	3401(c)(6)	963
1305	613	3401(f)	963
1311	1015	3402	963
1311–1315	999		995
1311 et seq.	998	3402(a)	963
	1018	3402(m)	963
1311(a)	998	3402(n)	963
1311(b)	998	3403	963

Section	Page	Section	Page
6001	994	6401(b)	963
6012(a)	970		995
6013	220	6402	994
	248		996
	263	6402(a)	996
	420	6411	632
	421	6501	1000
	1020	6501(a)	1000
6013(a)	262		1015
	496	6501(b)	1000
	947	6501(b)(1)	1000
	949	6501(c)	1000
6013(d)	496	6501(c)(1)	1000
	947		1002
6013(d)(3)	949		1015
	1002	6501(c)(2)	1000
6013(e)	949		1015
	1000	6501(c)(3)	1000
	1003	6501(c)(4)	976
6013(e)(2)	1003		1000
6015	963		1021
	995	6501(e)	642
6020	983		1014
6042	972		1015
6072	418	6501(e)(1)(A)	1000
	535	6502	979
6072(a)	970	6502(a)	980
6151(a)	970	6503(a)	975
6153	963	6503(a)(1)	1000
	995	6511	994
6201(a)(3)	971	6511(a)	535
6201(c)	263		994
6211(a)	1000		997
6212	1007		1015
6212(a)	1000	6511(b)	994
6212(b)(1)	1000	6511(c)	994
	1020	6511(d)(1)	808
6212(c)(1)	1000		994
6213	1000	6511(d)(2)(A)	632
	1007	6512(a)	976
6213(a)	975		994
	979		996
	1000		1006
	1007	6512(b)	976
6213(b)	1000	6513	995
6213(b)(1)	971	6513(a)	994
	1000	6513(b)	994
6213(b)(3)	995	6532(a)	994
	1000	6532(a)(1)	996
6213(c)	1000	6532(a)(3)	999
6213(d)	975	6601(a)	1000
	1000		1001
	1021	6611(a)	994
6214(a)	1000	6611(f)(1)	632
6301	980	6621	994
6302	980		1000
6315	962		1001
	995		
6321	980	6651	1001
6323(f)	980	6651(a)	1000
6331	980	6653	1000

TABLE OF INTERNAL REVENUE CODE SECTIONS

Section	Page
6653(a)	1000
	1002
6653(b)	949
	1000
	1002
	1003
	1019
6654	963
6851	1007
6851(a)	1007
6861	975
	1000
	1007
6861(a)	1000
6861(b)	1000
	1007
6901	980
6901(a)	980
6901(c)	980
6902(a)	980
	1013
7121	1000
	1015
	1017
7121(b)(1)	1015
7121(b)(2)	1015
7122	1000
	1016
7201	51
	1019
	1020
7201–7203	986
7206	51
7206(1)	985
	1020
7207	987
7210	984
7421	1000
7421(a)	979
	1007
7422	994
	996
	1000
7422(a)	994
	996
	1000
7422(b)	994
	1000
7422(c)	1018

Section	Page
7422(e)	976
	994
	996
	1000
	1006
7422(f)	994
7441	1018
7454(a)	1013
7454(b)	1014
7463	1008
7481	1018
7482	976
	1000
7482(a)	978
	1004
7482(b)	1004
7482(b)(2)	1005
7502	1007
7502(a)	994
7502(c)	1008
7602	983
	984
	985
7602–7604	972
7605(b)	984
7608(b)	983
7621	972
7701	666
7701(a)(3)	630
7701(a)(17)	219
7701(a)(26)	362
7701(b)	405
7805	29
7805(b)	1017
8001–8023	27

1939 Code

Section	Page
12(d)	948
22(a)	29
22(b)(2)	191
22(b)(5)	215
22(k)	219
	231
23(a)(1)	358
23(a)(1)(A)	358
23(m)	735
23(t)	802
23(u)	219
51(b)	948
124	802
124A	802
3760	1015

*

xlvii

TABLE OF TREASURY REGULATIONS

Proposed Regulations

Section	Page
1.82–1(a)	525
1.217–1	525
1.217–2(b)	525
1.217–2(c)	525
1.217–2(d)(1)	525
1.1253–2(d)(7)	700
1.1253–2(d)(9)	700

Regulations

Section	Page
1.48–1(o)(2)	806
1.61–1	37
1.61–2(a)(1)	37
	53
	99
1.61–2(d)(1)	37
	106
1.61–2(d)(2)(i)	53
	142
1.61–2(d)(2)(ii)(a)	99
1.61–4(a)	290
1.61–6(a)	178
1.61–11(b)	253
1.61–12(a)	199
1.61–14	50
1.61–14(a)	37
1.62–1(a)	504
1.62–1(b)	504
1.62–1(c)	504
1.62–1(d)	504
1.71–1(a)	219
	231
1.71–1(b)	231
1.71–1(b)(4)	219
	229
1.71–1(c)	248
1.71–1(d)	231
1.71–1(d)(3)	232
1.71–1(e)	236
1.72–2(b)(1)	194
1.72–2(b)(3)	191
1.72–4(a)	188
1.72–4(a)(4)	194
1.72–4(d)(3) Ex.	191
1.72–7(a)	188
	193
1.72–7(b)	188
	193
1.72–7(b) Ex.	193
1.72–9 (tables)	188
1.72–9 (table 1)	193
	198

Section	Page
1.72–9 (table 2)	193
1.72–9 (table 3)	193
1.72–11(c)(2)	194
1.72–11(d)(1)	188
1.72–15(g)	210
1.74–1	124
1.74–1(a)(1)	133
1.79–3(d)	110
1.86–23(e)(1)	490
1.86–23(h)(1)	490
1.86–113(b)(1)	490
1.101–1(a)(1)	188
1.101–1(b)(1)	188
1.101–1(c)	188
1.101–2(d)(2) Ex. 1	86
1.101–3(a)	190
1.101–4(a)(1)	188
1.101–4(c)	190
1.101–4(h)	190
1.102–1(a)	66
	89
1.102–1(b)	66
	89
1.104–1(a)	204
1.104–1(b)	206
	213
1.104–1(c)	204
	207
1.104–1(d)	204
1.105–1(a)	204
1.105–2	204
1.105–3	204
	212
1.105–4(g)	214
1.106–1	204
1.107–1(a)	122
1.111–1(a)(1)	608
1.111–1(a)(2)	608
1.111–1(b)(1)	608
1.111–1(b)(2)(i)	608
1.111–1(b)(2)(ii)	608
1.116–1(b)	254
1.116–1(c)	255
1.117–1	133
1.117–1(a)	134
1.117–1(b)(1)	134
1.117–2(a)	133
1.117–2(b)(1)	133
1.117–2(b)(2)	133
1.117–2(b)(2)(i)	140

Section	Page	Section	Page
1.117-2(b)(2)(ii)	135	1.165-1(d)(2)(i)	612
	140	1.165-1(d)(2)(iii)	612
1.117-2(b)(3) Ex. 2	140	1.165-1(d)(3)	487
1.117-3	133	1.165-1(e)	475
1.117-3(a)	135	1.165-3(a)(1)	412
1.117-3(c)	135	1.165-3(a)(2)	412
1.117-3(d)	134	1.165-3(c)	413
1.117-3(e)	135	1.165-5(a)-(c)	808
1.117-4(c)	133	1.165-7(a)(1)	475
	136		487
1.117-4(c)(1)	136	1.165-7(a)(2)	488
1.117-4(c)(2)	136	1.165-7(a)(3)	475
1.119-1	116	1.165-7(b)	488
1.121-2(a)	929		490
1.141-1(a)	507	1.165-7(b)(1)	411
1.141-1(e)	509	1.165-7(b)(4)	490
1.141-1(f)	507	1.165-7(b)(5)	475
1.142	507	1.165-8(a)(1)	475
1.143	507	1.165-8(a)(2)	487
1.144-1(a)	507	1.165-8(c)	488
1.151-1(b)	496	1.165-8(d)	475
1.151-2(a)	498	1.165-9(b)	455
1.152-1(a)	497	1.165-11(a)-(d)	487
1.152-4(a)	498	1.166-1	808
1.162-1(a)	344	1.166-2	808
1.162-2	369		814
1.162-2(a)	382	1.166-4	588
1.162-2(b)	382	1.166-5	808
1.162-2(c)	382	1.166-5(b)	817
1.162-2(e)	381	1.167(a)-1	721
1.162-4	348	1.167(a)-2	722
	353	1.167(a)-3	721
	721		723
1.162-5	396	1.167(a)-5	412
1.162-5(a)	397	1.167(a)-6	721
1.162-5(b)(2)(i)	359	1.167(a)-9	721
1.162-5(b)(3)(i)	359	1.167(a)-10	721
1.162-6	356	1.167(a)-11	725
1.162-7	363	1.167(a)-11(c)(1)(i)	726
1.162-8	363	1.167(a)-11(c)(2)(ii)	725
1.162-9	363	1.167(a)-11(c)(2)(iii)	725
1.162-11	383	1.167(a)-11(d)(2)	355
1.162-12	418		726
1.162-14	405	1.167(b)-0	721
1.162-17	506	1.167(b)-1(a)	721
1.162-17(b)(1)	348	1.167(b)-2(a)	721
1.162-17(b)(2)	348	1.167(b)-3(a)(1)	721
1.162-17(b)(3)	348	1.167(c)-1(a)(1)	721
1.162-20	405	1.167(f)-1(a)	758
	410	1.167(f)-1(b)(1)	758
	418	1.167(g)-1	455
1.162-20(c)(2)(ii)(b)	419	1.170A-1(g)	845
1.162-20(c)(3)	410	1.170A-8(e)	633
1.163-1	465	1.172-5(a)(3)(ii)	633
1.163-4(a)(1)	467	1.179-1(a)-(d)	758
1.164-1(a)	472	1.179-2(a)	758
1.164-2	472	1.179-3(a)	758
1.164-3	472	1.179-3(b)	758
1.164-5	472	1.179-3(f)	758
1.165-1(b)	411	1.212-1(g)	428
1.165-1(d)(2)	487	1.212-1(h)	455

1

Section	Page	Section	Page
1.212–1(k)	428	1.455–1	559
1.212–1(*l*)	428	1.461–1(a)(1)	551
1.212–1(m)	428	1.461–1(a)(2)	584
1.213–1(a)(1)	511	1.471–1	581
1.213–1(b)(1)(i)	511	1.471–2	583
1.213–1(e)	511	1.471–2(b)	583
1.213–1(e)(1)(v)	521	1.471–4	583
1.213–1(g)(1)–1(g)(3)(iii)	206	1.643(c)–1	252
1.213–1(g)(2)	218	1.651(b)–1	303
1.215–1	248	1.652(b)–2	303
1.262–1(b)(5)	369	1.662(a)–4	316
1.262–1(b)(7)	428	1.662(b)–1	303
1.262–1(b)(8)	409	1.671–1	304
1.263(a)–1(b)	354	1.673(a)–1	304
1.263(a)–2	348	1.676(a)–1	304
1.263(a)–3	355	1.676(b)–1	304
1.263(f)–(1)	726	1.678(c)–1(b)	316
1.266–1(b)(1)	471	1.691(a)–2	319
1.266–1(b)(2)	471	1.704–1(e)(1)	322
1.267(d)–1(a)	886	1.704–1(e)(2)(i)	322
1.267(d)–1(c)(3)	886	1.704–1(e)(2)(i)–(iii)	394
1.274–2(a)	405	1.704–1(e)(2)(viii)	322
1.274–2(c)	405	1.704–1(e)(3)(i)	322
	407	1.704–1(e)(3)(i)(6)	331
1.274–2(d)	405	1.753–1(b)	319
	407	1.871–2(b)	255
1.274–2(d)(4)	407	1.911–1(a)(2)	255
1.274–2(e)(4)	408	1.911–1(b)(8–11)	255
1.274–4(d)(2)(v)	383	1.911–2(c)	255
1.274–5	408	1.1001–1(a)	141
1.446–1(a)–1(c)(1)	537		159
1.446–1(a)(2)	538		178
1.446–1(c)(1)(i)	541		847
1.446–1(c)(1)(iii)	538		853
1.446–1(c)(1)(iv)(b)	539	1.1001–1(e)	146
1.446–1(c)(2)	581		154
1.446–1(d)	539	1.1011–1	178
1.446–1(e)	540	1.1012–1(a)	142
1.451–1(a)	541	1.1012–2	178
	559	1.1014–1(a)	154
1.451–2	541	1.1014–2(a)(5)	156
1.451–3(b)(1)	539	1.1014–3(a)	154
1.451–3(b)(2)	539	1.1014–4	670
1.451–5	580	1.1014–5	670
1.451–5(a)(1)	580		677
1.451–5(a)(2)	580	1.1015–1(a)	146
1.451–5(a)(3)	580	1.1015–1(b)	670
1.451–5(b)(2)	580		677
1.451–5(c)	580	1.1015–1(c)	670
1.451–5(c)(4)	580	1.1015–4	146
1.453–1(a)–(c)	874		154
1.453–4	874		186
1.453–4(c)	885	1.1017–1	30
1.453–5(b)(2)	883	1.1017–1(a)	199
	945	1.1031(a)–1	897
1.453–5(b)(6)	945	1.1031(a)–1(c)	904
1.453–6(a)	872	1.1031(b)–1(b)	897
	873	1.1031(b)–1(b) Ex. 1	897
1.453–6(a)(2)	853	1.1031(d)–(1)	897
1.453–9(a)	874	1.1031(d)–1(e)	914
1.453–9(b)	874	1.1033(c)–1(b)	914

Section	Page	Section	Page
1.1034-1(a)	929	1.1250-2(a)(1)	795
1.1034-1(b)	929	1.1250-2(b)(1)	795
1.1034-1(c)(3)	929	1.1303-1(a)	613
	932	1.1303-1(c)	613
1.1034-1(c)(4)	929	1.1341-1(a)	598
1.1038-1(h) Ex. 1	945	1.1341-1(a)(2)	605
1.1091-1(g)	894	1.1341-1(b)(1)(i)	598
1.1091-2	894	1.1341-1(b)(1)(ii)	598
1.1223-1(i)	716	20.2031-1(b)	945
	718	31.3401(c)-1	963
1.1231-1	762	39.22(b)(2)-2	191
1.1233-1(a)(3)	716	301.6203-1	970
1.1235-2(b)	699	301.6213-1(b)(1)	971
1.1235-2(c)	700	301.6402-2(a)(2)	974
1.1236-1(d)(1)(ii)	668	301.6402-3	974
1.1237-1(a)(4)	669		995
1.1245-1(a)(1)-(3)	786	301.6402-3(a)(6)	996
1.1245-1(b)(1)	786	601.104(c)	980
1.1245-1(c)	786	601.105(b)(2)	972
1.1245-1(d)	786	601.105(b)(2)(ii)	972
1.1245-2(a)(1)-2(a)(3)(i)	786	601.105(b)(3)	972
1.1245-2(a)(7)	786	601.105(c)(5)	973
1.1245-2(c)(4)	905	601.105(d)	972
1.1245-6(d)	874		973
1.1250-1(a)(1)-(a)(3)(ii)	795	601.105(e)	974
1.1250-1(c)(1)	795	601.105(e)(2)	975
1.1250-1(c)(4)	795	601.106(a)(1)	973
1.1250-1(c)(6)	874	601.106(a)(2)	978
	885	601.106(b)	973
1.1250-1(e)(1)	795	601.106(d)(2)	1017
1.1250-1(e)(2)	795	601.107(b)(2)	982
		601.107(c)	983

TABLE OF INTERNAL REVENUE RULINGS

Rulings with accompanying text are indicated by italic type.

Revenue Ruling	Page	Revenue Ruling	Page
53–162	845	66–34	253
54–9	396	*66–97*	*714*
54–19	208	66–110	111
54–457	523	66–111	725
54–465	*551*	*66–167*	*270*, 883
54–607	718	67–221	167
55–58	700	*67–246*	*827*
55–157	883	*67–254*	*921*
55–159	883	*67–255*	*922*
55–422	80	67–380	791
55–608	418	*67–437*	*606*
55–713	111	*67–442*	*247*
56–19	522	68–37	216
56–399	497	68–153	605
57–54	209	68–246	883
57–234	931	68–419	883
57–315	396	*68–531*	*491*
57–352	758	68–643	557
57–463	*584*	69–62	412
57–560	136, 138	*69–102*	*288*, *296*
58–40	688	69–154	212
58–89	133	*69–188*	*465*, *467*, 558
58–353	700	*69–462*	*877*
58–418	205, 214	*69–487*	*794*
60–31	*620*, *627*, 628	70–101	341
60–43	904	70–151	561
60–223	359	70–217	253
60–226	699	70–341	253
60–326	86	70–344	716
60–351	260	70–399	928
61–95	382	70–435	627
61–119	904	70–474	409
62–102	*85*, 86	70–475	409
62–189	522	70–476	409
62–210	522	70–477	845
63–66	291	*71–41*	*924*
63–136	76	*71–112*	*826*
63–144	407, 408	71–132	260, 261
63–232	*476*	71–158	503
63–273	522	71–159	503
64–224	422	71–195	653
64–236	*444*	71–425	76
64–237	*920*	71–470	362
64–267	522	71–536	253
64–328	111	72–45	206
65–13	354	72–164	190
65–34	503	72–191	206
65–185	883	72–208	580
65–254	605	72–226	522
66–7	*713*	72–381	716

TABLE OF INTERNAL REVENUE RULINGS

Revenue Ruling	Page	Revenue Ruling	Page
72–400	206	75–169	408
72–462	122	75–187	523
72–545	454	75–230	208
72–583	19	75–280	138
72–592	494	75–291	897, 912
73–113	823	75–292	897, 912
73–155	209	75–302	525
73–175	498, 499	75–316	523, 524
73–200	522	75–319	523
73–201	522	75–358	843
73–256	139	75–380	381
74–72	214	75–432	377
74–178	698	75–438	931
74–265	722	75–457	883
74–294	471	75–460	617, 619
74–411	931	75–499	206
74–540	139	75–538	777
74–581	272	76–2	26
74–603	212	76–83	166
74–613	883	76–96	52
75–11	291	76–110	878
75–12	468	76–121	253
75–45	205, 207, 209, 214	76–177	656
75–85	530	76–216	931
75–120	359, 360, 361	76–255	508, 951
75–126	208	76–301	904, 913
75–127	208	76–319	926
75–150	758		

TABLE OF MISCELLANEOUS RULINGS

	Page		Page
Commissioner's Delegation		Rev.Proc. 64–44	1016
Order No. 11 (Rev, 6)	1016	Rev.Proc. 65–13	724
Commissioner's Delegation		Rev.Proc. 66–53	1016
Order No. 97 (Rev. 10)	1015	Rev.Proc. 67–1	1017
G.C.M. 13745	270	Rev.Proc. 68–16	1016
G.C.M. 14407	260	Rev.Proc. 70–21	580
G.C.M. 20021	577	Rev.Proc. 71–21	579
G.C.M. 21503	716	Rev.Proc. 72–1	30
I.T. 3369	578	Rev.Proc. 72–3	30
I.T. 3452	719	Rev.Proc. 72–9	30
I.T. 4026	86	Rev.Proc. 72–10	355
Mim. 6463	409		725
Mim. 6490	700	Rev.Proc. 72–18	471
Rev.Proc. 62–21	724	Rev.Proc. 72–52	540
	725	Rev.Proc. 76–29	30
	726	T.D. 4422	724
Rev.Proc. 64–13	995		

*

TABLE OF CASES

The principal cases are in italic type. A selection of other cases cited is listed; they are in roman type. References are to Pages.

Adler v. Comm'r, 522
Agar v. Comm'r, 214
Agnellino v. Comm'r, 986
Akers v. Scofield, 51
Alabama Coca-Cola Bottling Co., 409
Alabama-Georgia Syrup Co., 354
Alderson v. Comm'r, 912
Allen v. Comm'r, 1003
Allen, Mary Frances, 479
Alter, Robert H., 408
American Automobile Ass'n v. United States, 578
Amidon v. Kane, 20
Ander, Katherine, 487
Anderson v. Comm'r, 712
Andresen v. Maryland, 988, 989
Andress, Jr., Wm., 409
Andrews, Curtis R., 578
Appleby, Comm'r v., 412
Application of (see name of party)
Armston Co. v. Comm'r, 394
Arrowsmith v. Comm'r, 703
Artnell Co. v. Comm'r, 572
Artstein, Maurice, 817
Asmar, Robert, 1003
Austin v. Comm'r, 288
Automobile Club of Michigan v. Comm'r, 578
Ayer, United States, v., 979

Backus v. United States, 1017
Bagley & Sewall Co., Comm'r v., 684
Baier, Estate of v. Comm'r, 435
Baker v. Comm'r, 232
Bank of Commerce, United States v., 984
Bardwell v. Comm'r, 229
Barker v. United States, 669
Barrett, United States v., 123
Bassett, Robert S., 525
Beacon Publishing Co. v. Comm'r, 578, 587
Beckley, John L., 757
Beckwith v. United States, 987
Bell Electric Co., 588
Bellis v. United States, 987
Bell's Estate v. Comm'r, 676

Bennett, Clayburn M. v. U. S., 932
Berenson v. Comm'r, 703
Bernatschke v. United States, 221, 229
Bess, United States v., 980
Beth W. Corp. v. United States, 166
Bhalla, Chander P., 137
Bieberdorf, Fredrick A., 138
Bilder, Comm'r v., 513, 521
Billingsley, United States v., 984
Bingler v. Johnson, 29, 136
Blair v. Comm'r, 250, 279, 676, 678
Blanton, George L., 605
Blewitt, Jr., Roy E., 361
Bloomington Coca-Cola Bottling Co. v. Comm'r, 897
Blum, Nathan, 852
Bodzin, Stephen, A., 420
Boland, J. L., 355
Bon v. United States, 669
Borge v. Comm'r, 337
Borrelli, Donald, 717
Bosch & Second Nat. Bank of New Haven, Estate of, Comm'r v., 284
Botany Worsted Mills v. United States, 1017
Bounds v. United States, 87
Bowers v. Lumpkin, 432, 769
Boykin v. Comm'r, 717
Boylston Market Ass'n, Comm'r v., 555
Bradley, James Parks, 241
Bresler, David, 712
British Transp. Comm'n v. Gourly, 208
Brooke v. United States, 394
Brooks v. United States, 208
Brown v. Allen, 1014
Brown v. Comm'r, 395, 712
Brown v. Helvering, 578
Brown, Clay, Commissioner v., 703
Brown, United States v., 989
Brunn, Helvering v., 17, 18
Brushaber v. Union Pacific Railroad Co., 16
Budlong, Culver M., 1020
Bugbee, Howard S., 808
Burck v. Comm'r, 557
Burnet v. Logan, 628, 847, 850, 852, 853, 871
Burnet v. Sanford & Brooks Co., 540

Burns, Stix, Friedman & Co., 32

Butler, Frank L., 395

Byrum, Paul J., 1014

Cammarano v. United States, 419, 423

Campbell v. Prothro, 17, 288–290

Carasso, Max, 521

Carey v. Comm'r, 361

Carrieres, Jean C., 165

Castner Co., George L., 873, 874

Century Electric Co. v. Comm'r, 29, 899

Cesarini v. United States, 37

Chandler v. Comm'r, 53

Chesapeake Corp. of Virginia, 354

Christensen, Harold A., 406

Clapham, Robert G., 932

Clifford, Helvering v., 309

Clifton Investment Co. v. Comm'r, 917

Coerver, Robert A., 382

Cohan v. Comm'r, 406

Cole, U. S. ex rel. v. Helvering, 996

Collector v. Day, 257, 258

Collins v. Comm'r, 166

Colorado Springs Nat. Bank v. United States, 358

Commissioner v. —— (see opposing party)

Computing & Software, Inc., 723

Conti, Elmer W., 347

Corbett v. Comm'r, 360

Corliss v. Bowers, 304, 313, 314

Corn Products Refining Co. v. Comm'r, 666, 680

Correll, United States v., 29

Couch v. United States, 985, 988

Coughlin v. Comm'r, 402

Cowan, Virginia Luty v. United States, 86

Cowden v. Comm'r, 857

Crane v. Comm'r, 29, 168

Cremona, Leonard, 361

Crichton, Comm'r v., 898

Cromer, United States v., 984

Cromwell v. County of Sac., 1018

Culbertson, Comm'r v., 322

Cummings, Nathan, 713

Cummings v. Comm'r, 712

Cunningham v. Bay Drilling Co., 207

Curcio v. United States, 988

Daniel, Jr., Richard T., 252

Daniels, F. H., 522

Davis, United States v., 159, 250, 698

Dean, J. Simpson, 57, 468

Decision, Inc., 578

Deltide Fishing & Rental Tools v. United States, 778

Deming, Jr., Robert O., 209

Denny, Reginald, 523

Deputy v. duPont, 467

Dilks, Lorenzo C., 49

Disney, United States v., 382

Dixon v. United States, 1017

Doehring, Kenneth W., 1005

Domenie, Johan, 359, 464

Donaldson v. United States, 984

Donaldson, United States v., 985

Donovan v. Campbell, Jr., 523

Dorl, Emma R., 976

Dorsey, Stephen H., 851, 853, 872

Dougherty Co., P. v. Comm'r, 353

Dowell v. United States, 408

Duberstein, Comm'r v., 66, 76, 88, 136, 491

Dunn Construction Co. v. United States, 885

Dysart v. United States, 998

Ebner, G. G., 409

Edwards, Jessie Lee, 167

Ehrhart v. Comm'r, 137

Eichbauer, Leonard J., 497

Eickmeyer, Allen G., 700

Eisner v. Macomber, 17, 636

Elliot, Jane U., 487

Ellis v. United States, 251

Elmer v. Comm'r, 883

Empey, United States v., 630

Enochs v. Williams Packing & Navagation Co., 979

Estate of —— (see name of party)

Executor v. United States, 284

Fackler, John D., 557

Fairid-Es-Sultaneh v. Comm'r, 149

Faloona Gerald R., 139

Fanelli, J. A., 215

Farina v. McMahon, 51

Farmer's & Merchant's Bank v. Comm'r, 216

Farnsworth & Chambers Co. v. Phinney, 995

Farrara, Chester, 578

Faucher, B. A., 817

Fausner v. Comm'r, 381

Felix, Albert T., 395

Felt & Tarrant Mfg. Co., United States v., 997

Fetzer Refrigerator Co. v. United States, 597

Fielding, Leonard T., 137
Fifth & York Co. v. United States, 578
First Nat. Bank & Trust Co. of Chickasha v. United States, 342, 412
First Savings & Loan Ass'n, 873
Fischer, C. Fink, 523
Fisher v. Comm'r, 77
Fisher v. United States, 985
Fitch, David C., 668
Fleischman, Meyer J., 445
Flora v. United States, 995
Flowers v. United States, 497
Forbes v. Hassett, 1014
Ford v. United States, 997
Forman Co. v. Comm'r, 468
Frazell, United States v., 1016
Frankel, Genevieve E. v. United States, 86
Frank, Morton, 356, 464, 769
Fribourg Navigation Co. v. Comm'r, 29, 793
Fryer, Robert C., 409
Furner v. Comm'r, 360
Furumizo v. United States, 208

Garber, Inc., S., 578, 588
Gardin, Ronald L., 382
Garner v. United States, 20
Generes, United States v., 359, 818
Gerard, Raymon, 511
Gerhardt, Helvering v., 257, 258
Gerstacker v. Comm'r, 522
Ghastin, Burl J., 123
Giannini, Comm'r v., 263, 265
Giblin v. Comm'r, 816
Glenshaw Glass Co., Comm'r v., 45, 216
Goldman, Alvin L., 382, 536
Goldstein, United States v., 982
Goldwater, Estate of Leo J., 248
Golsen, Jack E., 19, 469, 713, 1005
Gooding Amusement Co. v. Comm'r, 469
Gordy, R. E., 669
Gould v. Gould, 219
Graphic Press, Inc. v. Comm'r, 915
Graves v. People of State of New York ex rel. O'Keefe, 16, 257, 258, 260
Gray v. Darlington, 636
Green, William H., 408
Gregory v. Helvering, 508, 913
Greisdorf, L. D., 523
Grier v. United States, 768
Grossman, Jacob, 814
Grunwald, Arnold P., 523
Gulftex Drug Co., 688

Haden Co., W. D. v. Comm'r, 912
Haft, Harold, 360
Hagen Advertising Displays, Inc. v. Comm'r, 578, 588
Hamilton Memorial Gardens, Inc. v. Comm'r, 588
Handy Button Machine Co., 471
Harolds Club v. Comm'r, 363
Harrold v. Comm'r, 588
Harsh Investment Corp. v. United States, 725
Hartung v. Comm'r, 534
Harvey v. Comm'r, 382
Haslam, Charles J., 818
Hawkins, C. A., 214
Heffner, United States v., 987
Heidel, James B., 619
Heidt v. Comm'r, 348
Heim v. Fitzpatrick, 299
Heiner v. Donnan, 20
Heininger, Comm'r v., 423
Heisler v. United States, 735
Helvering v. ——— (see opposing party)
Helvering, U. S. ex rel. Cole v., 996
Hembree v. United States, 138
Hertz Corp. v. United States, 751
Hess v. Comm'r, 86
Higgins v. Comm'r, 428, 668
Hill v. Comm'r, 397
Hill, Nora Payne, 32, 1008
Hitchcock Co., E. R. v. United States, 915
Hochschild v. Comm'r, 352
Hoffman, Abbott, 1008, 1020
Holding v. Comm'r, 913
Hollywood Baseball Ass'n v. Comm'r, 777, 778
Holt, Harold, 19
Hoover Motor Express Co., v. United States, 426
Hope, Karl, 605
Hornung, Paul V., 547
Horrmann, William C., 455, 769
Horst, Helvering v., 17, 18, 250, *275,* 313
Hort v. Comm'r, 216, 670
Houlette, Richard T., 932
House v. Comm'r, 1005
Hoven, Vernon, 717
Hudock, Frank, 487
Hudson, Galvin, 694, 872
Hughes, William, 534
Hundley, Jr., C. R., 359
Huntington, Wassace, 882
Hunt Foods, Inc., 699
Hunt, Winoma Bell, 521

Hurlburt, Estate of Coid, 855
Hylton v. United States, 15

Idaho Power Co., Comm'r v., 758
Illinois Merchants Trust Co., Executor, 353
Imbesi v. Comm'r, 415, 765
Imel v. United States, 166
Inaja Land Co., 851
Independent Life Ins. Co., Helvering v., 53
Indian Trail Trading Post, Inc. v. Comm'r, 471
In re ——— (see name of party)
International Flavors & Fragrances v. Comm'r, 689
International Shoe Machine Corp. v. United States, 666, 769
Irwin v. Gavit, 65
Israelson v. United States, 471

Jackson, Jr., Lewis B., 230
Jacobs, J. H., 522
James v. United States, 50, 564, 588
Johnson, Estate of Leslie E., 260, 630
Jordan Marsh Co. v. Comm'r, 904

Kahler, Charles F., 542
Kaiser, United States v., 76
Keener, Seth E., 535
Keeton, United States v., 123
Kelly v. Comm'r, 521, 523
Kenan v. Comm'r, 689
Kenfield, Kenneth R., 361
Kentucky Utilities Co. v. Glenn, 492
Kern v. Granquist, 942
Key Homes, Inc., 873
KFOX, Inc. v. United States, 723
Kimbell v. United States, 712
King v. United States, 979
Kintner, United States, v., 630
Kirby Lumber Co., United States v., 139, 199
Kirschenmann v. Westover, 394
Klein, Estate of v. Comm'r, 699
Knetsch v. United States, 469
Knowland, J. R., 216
Knowlton v. Moore, 18, 19
Knoxville v. Knoxville Water Co., 722
Knuckles v. Comm'r, 214
Kowalski, Robert J., 123
Kralstein, Max, 87
Kraut, Aaron, 703
Kroon v. United States, 491
Kub, Shirley E., 1002
Kunsman, Donald H., 487

Kurkjian, John, 424
Kurzner v. United States, 630

Lafko, United States v., 985
Laing v. United States, 1007
Laird v. United States, 726
Landa v. Comm'r, 230
Land, Ben C., 230
Lane, Blanche E., 51
Lanning, George R., 382
Laster, Anna E., 248
Laughlin, Estate of Hazel S., 684
Lavery v. Comm'r, 541
Lawrence, Arthur, 19, 1004
Leahey, United States v., 987
Leathers v. United States, 139
Lee, Harold K., 248
Lentin v. Comm'r, 426
Leonardo, Application of, 988
Leslie Co. v. Comm'r, 259, 471, 905
Lester, Comm'r v., 236
Levitt v. United States, 259, 471
Levy v. United States, 361
Lewis v. Reynolds, 997, 1014
Lewis, United States v., 598, 600
Licht, Rose, 487
Liebes & Co. v. Comm'r, 216
Liftin, Comm'r v., 872
Lilly v. Comm'r, 424
Loose v. United States, 559
Lowe, Alvin G., 217
Lowry v. United States, 458
Lucas v. Earl, 263, 264
Ludey, United States v., 723
Lyeth v. Hoey, 89
Lykes v. United States, 431
Lyon Co. v. United States, 396

McAllister v. Comm'r, 676
McBride, Jr., A. F., 412
McCauley, P., 497
McCulloch v. Maryland, 256
McDonald v. Comm'r, 361
McDonald v. United States, 361
MacDonald, Jr., John E., 137
McDonell, Allen J., 125
McGarry's Inc. v. Rose, 984
McGuire v. United States, 333
McGuire, United States v., 301
McKinney, Worthy W., 168
McMahon, Inc., W. O., 578
McNeill v. Comm'r, 894
McShain, John, 915
McWeeney v. New York, New Haven & Hartford Railroad Co., 207
McWilliams v. Comm'r, 886

Mahana v. United States, 219
Malat v. Riddell, 664, 666
Malone v. United States, 178
Maness v. United States, 361
Manhattan Co. of Va., 355
Mansfield Journal Co. v. Comm'r, 688
Manton, Martin T., 51
Manton, United States v., 51
Mariorenzi v. Comm'r, 471
Markey v. Comm'r, 381
Markus v. Comm'r, 534
Marlett, Carolyn C., 814
Marquis, Sarah, 835
Marshall v. United States, 883
Martino, Joseph, 361
Martinon v. Fitzgerald, 980
Masline, John R., 382
Masser, Harry G., 916, 927
Massey Motors, Inc. v. United States, 747
Mathews v. Comm'r, 392, 394
Mauldin v. Comm'r, 660
Maxwell, United States v., 1003
Mazzei, Raymond, 422, 481
Meadows, Della M., 535
Melnik v. United States, 397
Mercantile Trust Co. of Baltimore, 912
Merchants' Loan & Trust Co. v. Smietanka, 636
Merians, Sidney, 454
Merrill, Ted F., 717
Merritt v. Comm'r, 894
Metropolitan Building Co. v. Comm'r, 673
Meyer, Estate of, 897
Meyer v. United States, 215
M. H. S. Co., 915
Midland Empire Packing Co., 348
Midland Ross Corp., United States v., 699
Miller v. Standard Nut Margarine Co., 979
Miller, Estate of Minnie v. Comm'r, 893
Miller, Jr., Andrew O., 255
Mills, Ernest H., 229
Minzer, Comm'r v., 111
Miranda v. Arizona, 982
Mitchell v. Comm'r, 712, 785
Mitchell, Helvering v., 1002, 1019
Mittleman, Meyer, 217
Modernaire Interiors, Inc., 578
Moloney v. United States, 988
Montgomery v. Comm'r, 517, 521
Montgomery, John E., 488, 612
Morelan, United States v., 123

Morrill v. United States, 305, 314, 315
Mt. Morris Drive-In Theatre Co. v. Comm'r, 351
Musselman Hub-Brake Co. v. Comm'r, 418
Musso, Sr. v. Comm'r, 1007

Nachman v. Comm'r, 723
Nathan, Julia, 230
National Alfalfa Dehydrating & Milling Co., Comm'r v., 467
Newburger, Andrew M., 248
Newbury, Blanche C., 230
New Capital Hotel, Inc., 569
Newhouse, George R., 468
Newton, Ellery W., 408
New York v. United States, 257, 260
New York ex rel. Cohn v. Graves, 16
Nichols v. Comm'r, 361
Nichols v. Coolidge, 20
Nichols, Horace E., 474
Nogle v. United States, 995
North American Oil Consolidated v. Burnet, 561

Oaks, Alden B., 395
Oaks, United States v., 985
Ochs v. Comm'r, 523
Old Colony Trust Co. v. Comm'r, 43, 249
Olk v. United States, 88
124 Front Street, Inc., 897
O'Neill, United States v., 630
Osceola Heard Davenport, 165
Overton v. Comm'r, 331, 394
Owens v. United States, 1002
Owens, Helvering v., 488

Pacific Grape Products Co. v. Comm'r, 580, 588
Pacific Ins. Co. v. Soule, 15
Paduano, Gerald F., 468
Paine v. Comm'r, 698
Panhandle Oil Co. v. Mississippi ex rel. Knox, 257
Parker, United States v., 779, 785
Parmer v. Comm'r, 291
Parr v. United States, 138
Paul v. Comm'r, 720
Perry v. United States, 394
Philadelphia Park Amusement Co. v. United States, 142
Phinney v. Mauk, 229
Phipps Estate, Henry, 412
Pike, Joseph P., 601
Pnipps v. United States, 259

Poe v. Seaborn, 947
Pollock v. Farmers' Loan & Trust Co., 14, 15, 257, 258, 979
Popular Library, Inc., 578
Porter, Hazel, 230
Portland General Electric Co. v. United States, 758
Powell, United States v., 984
Poyner v. Comm'r, 80
Prichard Funeral Home, 578
Primuth, David J., 361
Primuth, David J. v. Comm'r, 359
Proskey, Aloysius J., 138
Protiva, James D., 360
Puckett, Paul E., 1005
Pulliam, David R., 892
Pulvers v. Comm'r, 478
Putnam v. Comm'r, 815

Rainbow Gasoline Corp., 468
Ramsey Scarlett Co., 487
Raytheon Products Corp. v. Comm'r, 216
Reed, Grace P. v. United States, 86
Reese, Elmer L., 137
Regenstein v. Edwards, 354
Reis, C. A., 1014
Reisine, Barry, 361
Reisman, George F., 248
Reisman v. Caplin, 983, 984
Resorts International, Inc. v. Comm'r, 700
Rice, Florence G. v. United States, 86
Rider, J. A., 412
Rife v. Comm'r, 988
Robertson, William E., 168
Robinson, John, 408
Robinson, Ray S., 627
Robinson v. Comm'r, 880
Rochelle, United States v., 49
Rodeway Inns of America, 723
Rogers, John M., 912
Romm v. Comm'r, 1002
Rose v. Comm'r, 521
Rosenberg, Thelma, 976
Rosenspan v. United States, 369
Rossman Corp. v. Comm'r, 426
Ruehmann, Albert III, 360
Rundell, Jr., William K., 138
Runyon v. United States, 215
Rutkin v. United States, 50, 421
Ryker, Ann Hairston, 229

Salvatore, Susie, 284
Sanders v. United States, 1003

Sanford v. Comm'r, 408
Saperstein, Estate of A. M., 817
Schall v. Comm'r, 78
Schlude v. Comm'r, 578
Schuessler v. Comm'r, 584
Schulz, James, 406
Schwab v. Comm'r, 230
Scudder, Louise M., 1002
Seay, Dudley G., 206, 214
Seed, Harris W., 359
Shafpa Realty Corp., 871
Shainberg, Herbert, 725
Shanahan, James A., 490
Shapiro, Comm'r v., 979
Sharon, Joel A., 736
Sharp v. United States, 752
Sheahan, United States v., 932
Sheldon v. Comm'r, 291
Silverman v. Comm'r, 122
Simon, United States v., 605
Simplified Tax Records, Inc., 589
Skelly Oil Co., United States v., 707
Skemp v. Comm'r, 395
Smith v. Comm'r, 913
Smith, Comm'r v., 106, 815
Smith, Estate of v. Comm'r, 291, 490
Smith, Harold S., 217
South Dade Farms v. Comm'r, 578
South Tacoma Motor Co., 578
Spreckles v. Helvering, 453
Spring City Foundry Co. v. Comm'r, 559, 872, 873
Springer v. United States, 15, 883
Stair v. United States, 1017
Stanton v. United States, 75
Starr, Estate of v. Comm'r, 383, 395, 697
State Fish Corp., 216
Stayton, Jr., William H., 49
Steele v. Suwalski, 503
Steen, In re v. United States, 884
Steffke, Estate of Wesley A., 248
Steinberg v. United States, 51
Stern, Comm'r v., 980
Stern, Julius Long, 891
Stern, United States v., 988
Stewart, Anita Quinby, 251
Stewart, J. B., 382
Stockdale v. Insurance Companies, 20
Stolk, William Co., 932
Stone, Nathaniel M., 1019
Stranahan, Estate of v. Comm'r, 292
Stratton's Independence, Ltd. v. Howbert, 734
Strickland v. Comm'r, 253
Strother v. Comm'r, 852

Suarez, Efrain T., 1014
Sullivan Corp., Alice Phelan v. Comm'r, 608
Sullivan, United States v., 20, 50, 51, 421
Sunnen, Comm'r v., 1018, 1019
Sun Oil Co., 394
Surasky v. United States, 439
Susskind v. United States, 997
Sutter, Richard A., 406
Sweeney v. United States, 979
Swenson Land & Cattle Co., 471
Sylvan, Fred, 1008

Taft v. Bowers, 146
Tait v. Western Maryland Railway Co., 1018
Tanenbaum, Marc H., 122
Tank Truck Rentals, Inc. v. Comm'r, 425, 426
Tatum v. Comm'r, 290
Taylor v. Campbell, 229
Taylor, Helvering v., 1014
Taylor-Winfield Corp., 699
Tellier, Comm'r v., 424
Textile Mills Securities Corp. v. Comm'r, 422
Thoene, J. J., 522
Toledo TV Cable Co., 723
Town & Country Food Co., 883
Travis v. Comm'r, 578
Traxler, Duane, M., 1008, 1020
Trent v. Comm'r, 817
Turnbull, Inc., Transferee, 980
Turner, Reginald, 108
Turnipseed, Leon, 497

United Draperies v. Comm'r, 425
United Railways & Electrical Co. of Baltimore v. West, 727
United States v. ——— (see opposing party)
United States Junior Chamber of Commerce v. United States, 116

Valley Title Co., 897
Vander Poel, Francis & Co., 554
Van Orman v. Comm'r, 231
VanZandt v. Comm'r, 393
Varian, Estate of v. Comm'r, 33
Veenstra & De Haan Coal Co., 578
Villafranca, Frederick, J., 588
Virginian Hotel Corp. v. Helvering, 733

Wallace v. United States, 166
Wall Corp., United States v., 985
Waller, William, 194
Walz Frances R., 164
Warden v. Hayden, 988
Waring v. Comm'r, 851, 872
Warren Jones Co. v. Comm'r, 862
Wasnok, Stephen P., 765, 768
Welch v. Helvering, 344, 396
Western Oaks Building Corp., 873
Western Wine & Liquor Co., 688
Westinghouse Broadcasting Co. v. Comm'r, 723
Whipple v. Comm'r, 815
Whipple, A. J., 815
White v. Fitzpatrick, 386, 392
White, J. P., 494
Whitfield Jr., L. B., 354
Wide Acres Rest Home, Inc., 578
Wilcox, Comm'r v., 49, 50, 388
Wiles v. Comm'r, 166
Williams v. McGowan, 32, 726, 773, 801
Williams, Jay A., 544
Wills v. Comm'r, 128
Willis, Inc., C. G., 928
Wilner, Ellis H., et al. v. United States, 86
Wilson v. United States, 123
Windle Co., W. W., 688
Winmill, Helvering v., 29
Wisconsin Cheeseman v. United States, 471
Wiseley v. Comm'r, 1002
Wissing v. Comm'r, 1003
Wolder v. Comm'r, 94
Woodsam Associates, Inc. v. Comm'r, 178
Woolrich Woolen Mills v. United States, 355
World Airways, Inc., 588
Worthy, Jr., Ford S., 410
Wren, Clifford H., 165
Wright Motor Co., United States v., 985
Wrobleski v. Bingler, 139

Yeomans, Betsy Lusk, 409
Young, United States v., 988
Your Health Club, Inc., 578

Zimmerman & Sons, Inc. v. United States, 355
Zimmern v. Comm'r, 353

†

CASES AND MATERIALS

ON

FUNDAMENTALS OF
FEDERAL INCOME TAXATION

PART ONE: INTRODUCTION

CHAPTER 1. ORIENTATION

A. A LOOK FORWARD

The question is: What can you tell a law student that will help to make him a good tax student? We have no universal *vade mecum* and no hope to emulate the wisdom of Polonius in his advice to Laertes. Nevertheless, having watched hundreds of law students in the beginning, middle, and never-ending process of learning about the federal income tax, the authors offer a few remarks that may be helpful.

A student may find unexpected excitement in the study of the income tax. The uninitiated are likely to think of taxes as a kind of sterile game of questions and answers, largely involving only arithmetic and little philosophy. Forget it! Nice reasoning and a careful consideration of underlying (often non-tax) policy considerations lurk behind every legislative tax effort, every administrative determination of the Treasury Department, every judicial decision in cases of tax controversy, and all but routine struggles of taxpayers, their counsel, and students to arrive at proper tax conclusions.

Every tax has an inescapable regulatory effect. To impose a tax on a transaction is to some extent to discourage it. To relieve from tax a transaction otherwise subject to the exaction tends on the other hand to encourage it. The present income tax statute has many special provisions in the form of exceptions and preferences that, according to some, defeat the laudable objective of a "comprehensive tax base" and an even-handed tax treatment of all financial incre-

ments that can properly be called income. To those who do not
benefit from a particular special provision it is usually a "loophole." See Blum, "The Effects of Special Provisions in the Income
Tax on Taxpayer Morale," Joint Committee on the Economic Report, Federal Tax Policy for Economic Growth and Stability 251
(1955), reprinted in Sander and Westfall, Readings in Federal Taxation 41 (Foundation Press 1970). Yet there may be no complete
escape from this, and the elusive comprehensive tax base may not
be realistically attainable. See Bittker, "A 'Comprehensive Tax Base'
as a Goal of Income Tax Reform," 80 Harv.L.Rev. 925 (1967), reprinted in Sander and Westfall, Readings in Federal Taxation 91
(Foundation Press 1970). In any event, the point is the federal income tax is far from a neutral, revenue-raising device; it has a profound impact on what people do. Whether its regulatory aspects are
deliberate or incidental, when is Congress using the carrot and when
the stick to bring about a certain result through the use of the taxing power? This is a question the student should consider as he
works his way through this book. See Surrey, "Tax Incentives as a
Device for Implementing Government Policy: A Comparison with
Direct Government Expenditures," 83 Harv.L.Rev. 705 (1970), reprinted in Sander and Westfall, Readings in Federal Taxation 153
(Foundation Press 1970). See also Bittker, "Accounting for Federal 'Tax Subsidies' in the National Budget," 22 Nat.Tax Journal
244 (1969), and Surrey and Hellmuth, "The Tax Expenditure Budget
—Response to Professor Bittker," 22 Nat.Tax Journal 528 (1969)
and, generally, Klein, *Policy Analysis of the Federal Income Tax*, c. 4
(Foundation Press 1976).

You are undertaking a study in communication. English majors
take heart; the use of the language is as important here as it is in any
area of the law. But of course other prior training and experience
are likewise helpful. There is no such thing as pure tax law. Instead, tax principles relate to events and transactions that would
go on even if there were no federal income tax, although many
events and transactions are shaped by an awareness of relevant tax
principles. There is a clue here to the nature of your study. You
must be sure you understand what it is that is happening which
gives rise to the tax question. You may have to learn a little (or
a little more) about the respective rights and obligations of a mortgagor and mortgagee before you can properly appraise the tax consequences of their transactions; you may have to ponder the nature
of interspousal payments in cases of divorce or separation before you
can attempt to say how the tax laws will treat either spouse; and
you must learn about annuity and endowment contracts if you would
like to discover how Congress taxes (or relieves from tax) amounts
that are received under such agreements. In the pages that follow,
a case or a note will often be of assistance in this subordinate but
important endeavor. As you know, taxes are so pervasive that the

above examples could be extended indefinitely. But, while these remarks are intended as a word of caution to the neophyte, an encouraging note should also be detected. It is the very diversity of circumstances giving rise to tax questions that makes tax study appealing to many. It is difficult to imagine any more broadening endeavor, for tax questions lead one into all segments of law and society often raising, at least indirectly, broad social, economic, and political considerations. For example, in this book you will encounter the so-called low income allowance for taxpayers at or near the poverty level, see Dodyk, "The Tax Reform Act of 1969 and the Poor," 71 Colum.L.Rev. 758 (1971), and the maximum tax on earned income which benefits taxpayers at the other end of the economic scale, see Ostarch, "The Maximum Tax on Earned Income: How It Operates and the Planning Possibilities Available," 11 Taxation for Accountants 304 (1973). Every substantive course in any law school's curriculum has an outer ripple of tax ramifications.

The communications study being undertaken is learning to decipher the messages of the Internal Revenue Code. This is not quite akin to foreign language study for, after all, the Code is written in English; and it is quite correct in matters of grammar and syntax. If it falters occasionally rhetorically (see, e. g., I.R.C. (26 U.S.C.A.) § 341(e)), this is not the usual rule. The messages are there, in general written with about as much clarity as is possible, allowing for the complexity of the thoughts expressed. The origin of the present statute, indicated briefly in the next part of this chapter, may increase your respect for the document with which you are dealing. Our suggestion here, then, is not to throw down the statute in exasperation when an initial look at a provision does not provide much nourishment. Struggle with the language, rejecting the notion that it is not understandable and with confidence that persistence will pay off. This is an essential part of your training. The cryptic language of the Code has a key, a style which you, as have others before you, can learn to decipher.

Just reading the Internal Revenue Code in cold blood is neither very much fun nor very productive. It must be read with an eye toward the circumstances to which its messages are directed. As you move into this course you will quickly see how hopeless it would be to try to teach the fundamentals of federal income taxation with the Code as the only material to be studied by students. Among other things, this explains repeated references in the pages that follow to selected provisions in the Regulations. For there, sometimes by way of narrative and often by way of illustration, you will gain an understanding of what the cryptic statutory rules are all about. We venture this prediction concerning the progress of a student who goes about his study in the right way: (1) He will read the assigned provision in the statute without very much comprehension. (2) He will study the assigned material in the Regulations with growing awareness. (3) He will return to what seems almost new statutory language, even discovering words in the statute which initially he did not realize were there. This third phase involves what German psychologists call a "gestalt." A student once more quaintly characterized the third stage as "hitting the Ah hah! button."

The process just described suggests growth but not maturity and, admittedly, the "gestalt" does not always arrive on schedule. Moreover, even as general awareness grows, different people will derive somewhat different meanings from the same language, much as two cooks following the same recipe will bake rather different cakes. And so there is need for further effort toward understanding. The materials that appear in the following pages of this book, cases, rulings, committee reports, notes, problems, etc., are presented as an aid to that effort.

Tax practice is of two main types: (1) An application of tax principles to past events or transactions, and (2) Advice as to how tax principles will apply to proposed events or transactions. The more interesting and rewarding activity is of the latter, planning type. But in either case, a prediction is called for. The tax practitioner must attempt to say how the administration and the courts will deal with the circumstances with which he is presented; indeed he must often, also, attempt to foresee possible *legislative* change. We now begin to see the need for a kind of two-phase approach to tax study—what may be called a Why? Why? approach.[1]

Why do we postulate a particular answer to a tax problem? The bible tells us so. That is, the Code provides, or seems to provide, this answer. But then *why* did Congress write this provision into the Code? Here we are in the realm of policy; why are we concerned with this second "why?" To be sure, a great many tax questions can be answered routinely without major struggle. But by his second year a law student is aware of the frailties of the language, of the necessarily short-hand nature of statutory language, of substantial uncertainties as to meaning in varying circumstances. The second "why?" calls for knowledge that may bear heavily on meaning in cases of obscurity; and it also has a direct bearing on the matter of predicting possible legislative change. For example: Why did Congress provide the investment tax credit in 1962? Why did Congress terminate it in 1969? Was its restoration in 1971 predictable? What about further tinkering with the credit in 1975, a gloomy economic year? Why did the Tax Reform Act of 1976 extend the 10 percent credit for four years and make other minor changes? When will it likely be curtailed or again terminated?[2]

1. Since the first edition of this book was published, the authors have learned that, while the normal owl says "Who? Who?", the psychotic owl says "Why? Why?" but we persist.

2. A helpful introductory guide to tax policy thought and analysis is found in Klein, *Policy Analysis of the Federal Income Tax: Text and Readings* (Foundation Press 1976).

There are several by-products to seeking an understanding of the reasons behind tax legislation. For one thing, it makes the study far more interesting; a comparison might be the appeal of Euclidian geometry over elementary arithmetic. Secondly, the knowledge acquired has much longer life and usefulness. Finally, this is the *only* way to develop any comfortable feel for prediction in areas that cannot properly be regarded as settled. Of course, the policy reasons behind a statutory provision are not always discernible; one recalls the tradesman's classic reply: "There's no reason for it; it's just our policy!" But if there really is no reason (or perhaps no longer is any reason) for a legislative rule, is this in itself a basis for predicting legislative change, or at least narrow judicial interpretation?

It is also a truism that "the life of the law is not logic but experience." Judicial notions of what is sound policy often affect the way in which statutory language is read and not infrequently present the student with surprise interpretations quite at variance with his own possibly reasonable, literal reading of the statute. Thus, experience is essential to tax practice but, on any given matter, some experience can be gained quite quickly vicariously. As a student you begin the process of gaining experience by reliving the tax controversies of others, which are presented in numerous cases and rulings that appear in the pages that follow. The controversies of others serve as a catalyst to your analysis of the Code.

In most parts of this book problems appear, which the student is expected to work out. Usually, he can arrive at supportable answers on the basis of the related, assigned materials. Proper effort in this regard teaches the required close reading of the statute and, gradually, yields a more comfortable feeling about wading into fresh thickets of Code verbiage. But enough difficult questions and questions to which authoritative answers seem surprising are included to create also a healthy skepticism. In many instances in which answers are elusive or unexpected a case or ruling is cited, which may be considered when the student has attempted his own analysis. The discovery, appraisal and persuasive use of precedent are as important in tax cases as in others.

Now it must be admitted that tax study presents the student with a mass of material, statutory and otherwise. Practice is of course no different in this respect. It is equally obvious that not everything can be learned at the same time, and the authors feel that initial study must be episodic rather than comprehensive. As in other law school courses, you must constantly ask yourself where you are. And you may not always be quite sure, just as the blind man's initial impression of an elephant depends upon whether he first grasps the trunk or the tail. We venture three suggestions here. After examining the brief historical and constitutional discussions that follow in the next two segments of this chapter, study the last portion entitled "The

Road Ahead". An effort is made there to give you an overview of
the areas covered by this book. It would then be wise to take a careful look at the table of contents. While it will not now be perfectly
meaningful, it will give you a start toward orientation. And, as you
proceed with your study, pay attention to chapter headings and sub-
headings. This is obviously good practice in any course as an aid to
directing pre-class efforts. Finally, as you go along consciously prepare your own notes for subsequent review. Again this is not a
novel thought. But it can well be said that in the course of tax study
knowledge grows with geometric rather than arithmetic progression;
and the more you learn the greater your learning capacity. That
which is obscure and difficult at the beginning of the course will
become relatively clear and easy toward the end, as broader comprehension aids perception. Hours spent in review at the end may
provide a greater yield than hours spent at the beginning, but only
if the requisite hours *were* spent at the beginning.

B. A GLIMPSE BACKWARD

Historians often give too little recognition to the federal income
tax despite its profound impact on political, economic, and social
developments in the United States.[1] We do not attempt in any comprehensive way to fill that gap. An excellent brief "Historical Review" appears in Surrey, Warren, McDaniel, and Ault, Federal Income Taxation: Cases and Materials, vol. 1, pp. 1–36 (Foundation
Press 1972), which includes references to principal historical source
materials; and a useful "Brief History" of early developments may
be found in Griswold and Graetz, *Federal Income Taxation: Principles and Policies*, pp. 2–10 (Foundation Press 1976). Among other
works looking back more comprehensively at income taxation in the
United States are Paul, Taxation in the United States (1954), and
Blakey, The Federal Income Tax (1940). Probing the legislative history of specific statutory provisions is facilitated by Seidman, Legislative History of Federal Income Tax Laws, 1953–1939 (1954);
Seidman, Legislative History of Federal Income Tax Laws, 1938–1861
(1938); Goldstein, Barton's Federal Tax Laws Correlated (1968).
There are numerous historical references in subsequent chapters of
this book, which are an aid to understanding specific provisions
in the income tax laws. Some further comments are in order here
regarding the origin of the present income tax statute.

1. See, e. g., Samuel Eliot Morison's
   otherwise excellent History of the
   American People (1965).

The Congressional Joint Committee on Internal Revenue Taxation has summarized the first one hundred and fifty years of internal revenue taxation as follows: [2]

LAWS PRIOR TO 1939

"The first internal-revenue tax law was enacted on March 3, 1791, and imposed a tax on distilled spirits and stills. This was followed by legislation imposing taxes upon carriages, retail dealers in wines and foreign spirituous liquors, snuff, refined sugar, property sold at auction, legal instruments, real estate, and slaves. All of these taxes and the offices created for their enforcement were abolished in 1802. During this first era of taxation the internal-revenue receipts amounted to only $6,758,764.26. Comparing this with the receipts for the fiscal year 1938, amounting to $5,658,765,314, it will be noted that the Internal Revenue Service collects at the present time more than twice as much from internal-revenue taxes in one day as the original organization collected in 10 years. [The "present time" was 1939. Collections now approach three hundred billion dollars annually. Ed.]

"Due to the necessities occasioned by the War of 1812, internal-revenue taxes were again imposed in 1813. These taxes were levied on refined sugar, carriages, distillers, sales at auction, distilled spirits, manufactured articles, household furniture, watches, gold, silver, plated ware, jewelry, real estate, and slaves. An officer known as the Commissioner of Revenues was in charge of the administration of such taxes. All these taxes were repealed by the act of December 23, 1817, and the office of Commissioner of Revenues was discontinued, effective upon the completion of the collection of the outstanding taxes. The collections during the 5-year period from 1813 to 1818 amounted to $25,833,449.43.

"For a period of 43 years, namely, 1818 to 1861, no internal-revenue taxes were imposed. On July 6, 1861, an act was passed imposing a tax on incomes and real property. No income tax was ever collected under this act, and all of the tax collected on real property was returned to the States under authority of the act of March 2, 1891.

"The act of July 1, 1862, is largely the basis of our present system of taxation. It contained the first law under which any income tax was collected, and it created the office of Commissioner of Internal Revenue. It taxed practically everything which Congress thought was susceptible of yielding revenue. The three sources of revenue which remained for a long time the backbone of the internal

----

2. "Codification of Internal Revenue Law," p. IX (1939), reproduced at 26 U.S.C.A. XIX–XX.

revenue system, namely, spirits, tobacco, and beer, received particular attention from the lawmakers.

"The internal-revenue laws were first codified in the Revised Statutes of 1873, Title XXXV, which was made absolute law. A perfected edition of the Revised Statutes was prepared in 1878, but was only prima facie, not absolute, law. The internal-revenue laws were again codified in Title 26 of the United States Code, which was enacted as prima facie law in 1924. Scrutiny of the Code was invited in its preface for the purpose of correcting errors, eliminating obsolete matter, and restatement.

"In 1930, the Joint Committee on Internal Revenue Taxation published a complete substitute for Title 26 of the United States Code, containing all the law of a permanent character, relating exclusively to internal revenue, in force on December 1, 1930. This was not a mere duplication of the old Title, for in addition to correcting errors and eliminating obsolete matter, certain omitted provisions were added and the Title completely rearranged in a manner considered logical and useful.

"In 1933, a new edition was published containing the internal-revenue laws in force on July 16, 1932. This edition was substituted for Title 26 of the United States Code, and was prima facie law. A third edition was published in 1938, containing the internal-revenue laws in force at the beginning of that year."

Prior to 1939, the mere ascertainment of statutory provisions that might affect the determination of a tax question threw the tax practitioner into the hodge-podge of the Statutes at Large. Happily, a 1939 development relieved the practitioner (but not necessarily the scholar) from this awkwardness, except as regards transitional problems that reached back to earlier years. The Report of the Ways and Means Committee on the Bill that became the Internal Revenue Code of 1939 [3] included the following statement:

THE NEED OF AN INTERNAL REVENUE CODE

"The need for enactment into absolute law of a codification of internal revenue laws has long been recognized. The last such enactment was in 1874, when the Revised Statutes were adopted. If the need for enactment into law of a codification was recognized in 1874, when only 17 volumes of the Statutes at Large had been published and our internal revenue was derived almost entirely from taxes on liquor and tobacco, that need must be much greater today, when 34 additional volumes have been published and our internal revenue is derived from more than a hundred separate sources.

3. H.Rep. No. 6, 76th Cong. 1st Sess.
(1939), 1939–2 C.B. 532–533.

"The United States Code is itself the culmination of more than 30 years' effort. Due to the mass of legislation contained in that Code, it was thought best by the Congress to put it through a testing period before its enactment into law. It was, therefore, made only prima facie evidence of the law, and scrutiny of it was invited for the purpose of correcting errors, eliminating obsolete matter, and restatement.

"The review and correction of the internal revenue title was begun by the staff of the Joint Committee on Internal Revenue Taxation after the enactment of the Revenue Act of 1928. The first edition of the work was published in 1930 and the second, in 1933. The second edition was substituted for title 26 of the United States Code and became, therefore, prima facie evidence of the law.

"It has now been nearly 13 years since the United States Code was enacted as prima facie law and more than 8 years since the first edition of the Internal Revenue Code was published by the staff of the joint committee. However, because the internal revenue title is not the law, but only prima facie evidence thereof, it can not be relied upon and it is still necessary to go to the many volumes of the Statutes at Large to determine what the law actually is. The great mass of internal revenue legislation since 1873, scattered through 34 volumes of the Statutes at Large, makes such a recourse an exceedingly difficult undertaking, even for the most experienced lawyer. Statutes are repeated in subsequent Acts in almost identical language, with no reference to prior Acts or any expressed intention to amend or repeal. Provisions of a permanent character are included in riders and provisos and are hidden in various Acts. Amendments are often involved and obscure. Inconsistencies and duplications abound.

"The only practical way to determine with certainty that the Internal Revenue Code is actually the law is to enact it, as was done with the Revised Statutes of 1873. It is believed that it has had a sufficient testing period to make it acceptable as free from error.

* * *

"This Code contains all the law of a general and permanent character relating exclusively to internal revenue in force on January 2, 1939. In addition, it contains the internal revenue law relating to temporary taxes, the occasion for which arises after the enactment of the Code. The following should be noted in connection with the general character of the Code:

"First. It makes no changes in existing law.

"Second. It makes liberal use of catchwords, headlines, different types, indentations, and other typographical improvements.

"Third. By a system of cross-references, it correlates not only its own provisions but also provisions of the United States Code not relating exclusively to internal revenue.

"Fourth. To obviate confusion with the law itself, the cross-references are in type different from that containing the law.

"Fifth. It is arranged with a view of giving prominence to matters which concern the ordinary transactions of the ordinary classes of taxpayers.

"The preparation of this Code began with the collection and examination of all original statutes relating to internal revenue, without reference to the United States Code. This procedure allowed an independent check to be made subsequently against that Code. The next step was the elimination of obsolete matter and those temporary provisions relating to taxes the occasion for which arose prior to the effective date of the Code. The most striking examples of the temporary laws which are omitted are the income tax provisions of the Revenue Act of 1936 and prior Revenue Acts. While these provisions remain in force for the purpose of administering the taxes for the earlier years, they do not affect the current tax situation.

"After the elimination of the obsolete and temporary provisions from the whole body of internal revenue law, the remaining provisions were checked against the United States Code. The care in the preparation of the United States Code and in the present codification gives assurance of the accuracy of the final product. Moreover, every provision has been carefully reviewed and checked by the Treasury Department and conferences have been held and agreements reached on all issues.

"There are many laws of a general character which, though relating to internal revenue, apply also to other objects. To codify such laws under internal revenue, however, would disrupt the entire title structure of the United States Code and render complete codification of Federal law impossible. In only a few instances has any provision been taken from any title of the United States Code other than the internal revenue title, and then only for the reason that such provision relates exclusively to internal revenue. The great value of the United States Code is thus preserved. Moreover, detailed cross-references compensate for any deficiency due to such a procedure by acquainting the reader both with the general subject of the provision referred to and its location in the United States Code."

The 1939 effort was largely a matter of sorting and putting together currently operative internal revenue statutes—*codification.* Even so, the result was the tax practitioner's "bible," the Internal Revenue Code of 1939. Wholesale *revision* of the internal revenue laws was first accomplished in 1954, yielding a new (King James Version?) "bible" for the practitioner. When the 1954 legislation was presented to the Senate, Senator Millikin, Chairman of the Senate Finance Committee said: [4]

---

4. 100 Cong.Rec. 8536 (1954), reproduced at 26 U.S.C.A. XXI.

INTERNAL REVENUE CODE OF 1954

"Mr. President, the Senate has before it H.R. 8300, a bill to revise the internal revenue laws of the United States. The bill contains over 820 pages.

"The need for revenue revision is evident from the fact that many of our revenue statutes are antiquated and ill-adapted to present-day conditions. Some have not been changed since the days of the Civil War. We have not had a complete revision of the internal revenue laws since 1875, more than 79 years ago.

"In 1939, Congress enacted a codification of existing internal revenue laws. The 1939 code collected all the internal revenue laws in one document, eliminated obsolete matter and made typographical improvements in titles and cross-references. That code did not change the existing law, so that many of the complications and inequities of existing law were continued. It has been over 15 years since the 1939 code was enacted.

"Since 1939, over 200 internal revenue statutes have been enacted, including 14 major revenue acts. I cannot too strongly emphasize the value of the 1939 code, which was enacted with the unanimous support of both parties. Without the basic work undertaken in the 1939 code, it would not have been possible to have H.R. 8300 ready for enactment at this time.

"H.R. 8300 is the culmination of studies on tax revision extending over a period of nearly 2½ years. The Joint Committee on Taxation instructed its staff to make a study of tax revision in the spring of 1952. In July of that year, the staff prepared a questionnaire seeking suggestions from farm, labor and business groups, and from individual taxpayers, on how to improve the internal revenue laws. Over 17,000 replies were received from this questionnaire, coming from every State in the country.

"The answers to this questionnaire were digested, and the staff of the Joint Committee on Internal Revenue Taxation and the Treasury Department began a study of this digest and other suggestions early in 1953. Groups in various sections of the country became revision conscious, and were encouraged to submit plans and make suggestions to improve the internal revenue laws.

"The Ways and Means Committee began hearings on revenue revision on June 16, 1953. A total of 504 witnesses were heard; and, in addition, 1,000 statements were submitted for the record. All this data was assembled and analyzed by the staffs of the Joint Committee on Internal Revenue Taxation and the Treasury.

"The Committee on Ways and Means began its executive sessions on the revenue revision bill on January 13, 1954; and those sessions continued until March 9, 1954. On January 20, 1954, the President in his budget message made 25 recommendations for tax revision, 23 of which were incorporated in the House version of the bill.

"The bill passed the House on March 18, 1954, by a majority of [sic] 259 votes—309 yeas, 80 nays. The bill was referred to the Senate Finance Committee on March 23, 1954. The Senate Finance Committee held public hearings from April 7 to April 23. A total of 130 witnesses were heard and approximately 420 statements were submitted for the record. The executive sessions by the committee lasted 5 weeks. In our deliberations, care was given toward meeting the objections of the witnesses to the House version of the bill. Suggestions not submitted to the Ways and Means Committee were also considered, and the Senate Finance Committee amendments contain many of these suggestions.

"I believe this bill has had the most thorough study and analysis of any tax bill ever presented to the Congress. Testimony had not been taken in the Ways and Means Committee on the text of the House version of the bill. Before our committee, witnesses were given an opportunity to raise objections to the final text of the House version.

"Constructive criticisms were received from business, agricultural, labor, law, accounting, and engineering groups. Our committee gave particular attention to the criticisms of the technical provisions of the bill; for example, the provisions relating to corporate distributions and reorganizations have been completely revised, to meet constructive objections. I believe that the committee amendments considerably improve the provisions of the House version of the bill, and remove meritorious objections developed in the testimony. In cases where it was not possible to find an adequate solution to meet the criticism of a House provision, your committee has restored existing law. * * *"

As in the case of its predecessor, the 1954 Code has been amended many times. Nevertheless, as amended, it is *the* statutory law on federal internal revenue taxation. A major revision occurred in 1969. The Staff of the Joint Committee on Internal Revenue Taxation has said of the 1969 revision:[5]

"The Tax Reform Act of 1969 (H.R. 13270) is a substantive and comprehensive reform of the income tax laws. As the House and Senate Committee Reports suggest, there was no prior tax reform bill of equal substantive scope.

"The congressional consideration of this Act lasted eleven months and one day. . . .

"From time to time, since the enactment of the present income tax over 50 years ago, various tax incentives or preferences have been added to the internal revenue laws. Increasingly in recent years, taxpayers with substantial incomes have found ways of gaining tax ad-

5. "General Explanation of the Tax Reform Act of 1969," p. 1 (1970).

vantages from the provisions that were placed in the code primarily to aid limited segments of the economy. In fact, in many cases these taxpayers have found ways to pile one advantage on top of another. The House and Senate agreed that this was an intolerable situation. It should not have been possible for 154 individuals with adjusted gross incomes of $200,000 or more to pay no Federal income tax on 1966 income. Ours is primarily a self-assessment system. If taxpayers are generally to pay their taxes on a voluntary basis, they must feel that these taxes are fair. Moreover, only by sharing the tax burden on an equitable basis is it possible to keep the tax burden at a level which is tolerable for all taxpayers. It is for these reasons that the amendments in this Act contain some 41 categories of tax reform provisions described in summary fashion at the end of this section.

"Despite the comprehensive scope of the Tax Reform Act of 1969, the committees recognized that much remains to be done. In some cases, income tax problems had to be postponed for further analysis and study. Moreover, the entire area of estate and gift tax reform lies outside the scope of this Act and remains an area for future consideration. * * * "

Despite the enactment of the Tax Reform Act of 1976 and rather extensive changes in the estate and gift taxes, general tax reform of the kind contemplated by the Committee is still undone. Since the publication of the first edition of this book there have been four significant revisions of the 1954 code. Three were undertaken in an effort to stimulate the economy. The Revenue Act of 1971 provided tax reductions for individuals and tax incentives for business to give a shot in the arm to a then sagging economy.[6] The Tax Reduction Act of 1975 provided further reductions for individuals and corporations in an attempt to check the sharpest economic decline since the 1930s,[7] and the Revenue Adjustment Act of 1975 extended the Reduction Act's relief into 1976.[8] Despite the broader scope of the 1976 legislation, it also included tax cuts designed to stimulate business.

As these remarks indicate, "What's past is prologue," and our income tax provisions should be expected to undergo further and perhaps constant and very likely extensive change. Nevertheless, students should not feel that their learning in this area is evanescent. The fundamentals of federal income taxation remain remarkably constant. And that is what this book is about. Certainly many of the details presented will be altered and some soon. But the student should join the authors in a search for basic concepts and policy considerations

6. Pub.Law 92–178. See H.Rep.No.92–533, 92d Cong. 1st Sess. (1971), 1972–1 C.B. 498.

7. Pub.Law 94–12. See H.Rep.No.94–19, 94th Cong. 1st Sess. (1975), 1975–19 I.R.B. 47.

8. Pub.Law 94–164. See Sen.Rep.No. 94–548, 94th Cong. 1st Sess. (1975), 1976–6 I.R.B. 20.

supporting basic principles. Such an approach is not only an aid in predicting change but also in understanding changes as they occur.

C. THE INCOME TAX AND THE UNITED STATES CONSTITUTION

The very limited purpose of this note is to present what every good Boy Scout should know about the constitutional aspects of the federal income tax. The treatment of the subject is neither comprehensive nor detailed and, indeed, may reasonably be termed superficial. Nevertheless, these matters are relatively quiescent these days and for most purposes the elementary thoughts presented may be sufficient. The investigation and prosecution of tax fraud are not given detailed consideration in this book; but of course they are areas in which constitutional issues are constantly at the forefront.[1]

THE POWER TO TAX

The federal government's power to tax is derived from Article 1, Section 8, clause 1 of the Constitution of the United States, which confers on Congress the "power to lay and collect taxes, duties, imposts and excises * * *." If no other constitutional provision affected the taxing power, this would clearly be enough to authorize the imposition of an income tax. However, Section 2, clause 3 and Section 9, clause 4 of Article 1 require that "direct" taxes be apportioned among the several states in accordance with their respective populations. Further, Article 1, Section 8, clause 1 reads: "all duties, imposts, and excises shall be uniform throughout the United States." These provisions provide the substance for Mr. Justice Chase's famous quote: "[T]he power of Congress to tax is a very extensive power. It is given in the Constitution, with only * * * two qualifications. Congress * * * must impose direct taxes by the rule of apportionment, and indirect taxes by the rule of uniformity." [2]

What is the difference between a "direct" tax and an "indirect" tax? A direct tax is a tax demanded from the very person who is intended to pay it. An indirect tax is a tax paid primarily by a person who can shift the burden of the tax to someone else, or who at least is under no legal compulsion to pay the tax.[3] By way of example, a tax at a flat rate on all persons is a direct tax. In contrast,

---

1. See Crowley and Manning, *Criminal Tax Fraud—Representing the Taxpayer before Trial* (P.L.I.1976); Balter, *Tax Fraud and Evasion*, (Warren, Gorham and Lamont 4th Ed.1976); Lipton, "Constitutional Protection for Books and Records in Tax Fraud Investigations," *Tax Fraud*, p. 75 (I.C. L.E.1973). A brief note on procedure in tax fraud cases appears in Chapter 28, infra, at page 981.

2. License Tax Cases, 5 Wall. (U.S.) 462, 471 (1866).

3. Pollock v. Farmers' Loan & Trust Co., 157 U.S. 429, 558 (1895).

a sales tax is an indirect tax, because it is imposed on the seller who may shift it to the purchaser. A person may avoid an indirect tax by not buying the article subject to the tax.

APPORTIONMENT AMONG THE STATES

The rule of apportionment to which direct taxes must conform requires that, after Congress has established a sum to be raised by direct taxation, the sum must be divided among the states in proportion to their respective populations. This determines the share that must be collected within each particular state. There would be no inequality (but query as to unfairness) *among the states* in a tax at a flat rate on all persons, because a capitation tax is self-apportioning. But inequality of a sort would result if an unapportioned direct tax were levied on all carriages within the United States and a particular state had only 5% of the population but 10% of the carriages. Of course one might wonder today whether it was bad for a small state with many carriages to bear more of the federal tax burden than a more populous state with few.

Congress once did enact an unapportioned tax on carriages which appeared to be a direct tax. However, it was held not to be direct but rather an excise tax on the *use* of carriages and therefore valid.[4] The court was influenced by dicta in prior opinions indicating direct taxes are only capitation taxes or taxes on land.

As one ponders the possible use of direct taxes as federal revenue raising measures, he is likely to come to the conclusion that (1) a failure to provide an apportionment rule might make it possible for a central taxing authority improperly to burden some states to the great advantage of others, but (2) application of an apportionment rule might create inter-personal inequities at least as bad as the interstate inequities sought to be avoided. Perhaps it is for these reasons that Congress does not enact direct taxes, unless the income tax is still properly so classified.

What is the proper classification of the income tax? Prior to the enactment of the Income Tax Act of 1894 the United States Supreme Court had found that a tax on the premiums received by an insurance company[5] and a tax on income which an individual derived in part from professional earnings and in part from the interest on bonds[6] were not direct taxes. In the landmark case of Pollock v. Farmers' Loan & Trust Co.,[7] the Court was asked to decide the constitutionality of an income tax statute that included as income rents from real estate. On the principle that substance must prevail over form, the Court held that a tax on the income from property so bur-

4. Hylton v. United States, 3 Dall. (U. S.) 171 (1796).

5. Pacific Insurance Co. v. Soule, 7 Wall (U.S.) 433 (1868).

6. Springer v. United States, 102 U.S. 586 (1880).

7. Supra note 3.

dened the property as to be the equivalent of a tax on the property. The Court held the intention of the drafters of the Constitution was to prevent the imposition of tax burdens on accumulations of property, except in accordance with the rule of apportionment,[8] and for this reason invalidated the tax. This decision was met with great criticism. At the time individual incomes varied sharply from state to state and it was observed that the effect of the decision, if income taxes had to be subject to the rule of apportionment, might be to cause a citizen in Massachusetts to pay only 2.8% of his income while a citizen in Minnesota had to pay 32.9% of his income.[9] There is also language in later Supreme Court opinions criticizing the *Pollock* case as an erroneous application of a principle of constitutional law.[10]

THE 16TH AMENDMENT

The foregoing capsule tax history may help in understanding the 16th Amendment. In the Amendment, emphasis is to be placed on the phrase "from whatever source derived," not on the "power" language. The power was already reposed in Congress by Article I. What the 16th Amendment provides is that income taxes shall not be subject to the rule of apportionment regardless of the *sources* from which the taxed income is derived.[11] With appropriate emphasis the Amendment reads:

AMENDMENT XVI

The Congress shall have power to lay and collect taxes on incomes, *from whatever source derived*, without apportionment among the several States, and without regard to any census or enumeration.

It matters not that a tax on salary income may be an excise and a tax on rental income a direct tax; Congress may enact a statute that taxes both without concern for the apportionment requirement.

Another reason it is important not to look at the 16th Amendment as an isolated power-granting provision is that, if it were so read, it might appear to authorize an unapportioned tax on incomes only if Congress taxed *all* incomes regardless of source. This would invalidate a provision granting an exemption of some income, such as municipal bond interest, or perhaps invalidate an entire taxing act making such an exemption, an argument which the Supreme Court has rejected.[12] The primary message of the 16th Amendment is that, for future income taxes, the principle (apportionment) upon

8. Supra note 3 at 583.

9. Seligman, *The Income Tax*, p. 587 (MacMillan Company 1914).

10. E. g., Graves v. N.Y. ex rel. O'Keefe, 306 U.S. 466, 480 (1939),

citing New York ex rel. Cohn v. Graves, 300 U.S. 308, 313 (1937).

11. Brushaber v. Union Pacific Railroad Co., 240 U.S. 1 (1916).

12. Id. at 21.

which the *Pollock* case invalidated the 1894 income tax statute shall be laid aside.

Despite the relatively minor role that constitutional issues such as apportionment now play in federal tax practice, reference may be made here to one interesting issue that seems to loom on the horizon. In 1974 Congress added I.R.C. § 84 to the Internal Revenue Code, which treats as income subject to tax appreciation inherent in property, if a taxpayer gives the property to a political organization. A possible related future development has been the repeated proposal to tax pre-death appreciation in a decedent's property upon its transmission at the time of his death.[13] It can be argued that provisions of this type attempt to tax property rather than income, because under traditional notions the gain, which could become income, has not been "realized" by the taxpayer. The conclusion could be that the attempted tax is direct and therefore invalid because not apportioned.

At an early date the concept of realization entered the federal tax picture when the Supreme Court stressed that the 16th Amendment applied to gains *derived* from capital or labor and that, with respect to gains on property, income included profit gained through a sale or conversion of the property.[14] A later opinion added: [15]

> While it is true that economic gain is not always taxable as income, * * * [g]ain may occur as a result of exchange of property, payment of taxpayer's indebtedness, relief from a liability, or other profit realized from the completion of a transaction.

It has never been determined, however, that mere appreciation in property that continues to be held by the taxpayer is within the "incomes" concept of the 16th Amendment and, indeed, to this time it has been generally supposed that appreciation or gain is not "realized" and thus not brought within the "incomes" concept by a mere gift of appreciated property.[16] If I.R.C. § 84 is to be sustained, it will be under judicial tax doctrine newly announced, because § 84 pretty much requires that we treat any *disposition* of appreciated

---

13. E. g., S.Bill 2345, 94th Cong. 1st Sess. (1975). The Revenue Act of 1976 by the enactment of I.R.C. § 1023 takes a carryover basis approach to the problem of how to deal with appreciation in a decedent's property. This important development is dealt with in chapter 7, infra.

14. Eisner v. Macomber, 252 U.S. 189, 207 (1920).

15. Helvering v. Bruun, 309 U.S. 461, 469 (1940).

16. Compare Helvering v. Horst, 311 U. S. 112 (1940), with Campbell v. Prothro, 209 F.2d 331 (5th Cir. 1954). Dicta in *Horst* seems to imply that the concept of "realization" may be a matter of administrative convenience only supporting a postponement of tax to the final event of enjoyment of the income by the taxpayer. Helvering v. Horst, supra at 116. One commentator, embracing the *Horst* dicta, suggested some years ago that therefore the doctrine of realization is not a constitutional mandate at all, but only one of expedience, inviting administrative discretion. Surrey, "The Supreme Court and the Federal Income Tax: Some Implications of the Recent Decisions", 35 Ill.L.Rev. 779, 791 (1941).

property,[17] not just its "sale or conversion", as giving rise to realized gain within the "incomes" concept of the 16th Amendment.[18]

Perhaps we have waded in a little too deep here for this introductory discussion; a briefer look now at the uniformity requirement.

UNIFORMITY AMONG THE STATES

The other qualification imposed by the Constitution on the federal taxing power is the rule of uniformity. Article 1, Section 8, clause 1 states:

> * * * but all duties, imposts, and excises shall be uniform throughout the United States.

This provision does not expressly mention "taxes"; can it successfully be argued that a direct "tax" is to be differentiated from "Duties, Imposts, and Excises" and is therefore free from the uniformity requirement? No. An income tax is in the nature of an excise, the government literally "excising" and taking for its use a portion of the taxpayer's gain. If as when it taxes rental income from property the present income tax may be termed direct, it does not escape the uniformity requirement. Of course, a direct tax that had to be apportioned could not be imposed uniformly, a temporary effect of *Pollock*, criticized at the time. But when the 16th Amendment removed the income tax from the apportionment requirement, it clearly left it fully subject to the constitutional requirement of uniformity.[19]

If it follows that all federal income taxation must be uniform throughout the United States, what then is the meaning of the constitutional term "uniform?" It might appear that if both A and B have $10,000 of income but A is taxed on her *salary* income and B is not taxed on his municipal bond *interest*,[20] the income tax is not being imposed in a uniform manner. However, it is well settled that the Constitution requires only geographic uniformity.[21] Although under principles dating back at least to *Brushaber*[22] certain exemptions may be constitutional, this does not mean that Congress can exempt the state bond interest of New Yorkers while taxing that kind of

---

17. The question here must not be confused with the assignment of income issue principally involved in Helvering v. Horst, supra note 16. Mere appreciation in property is certainly not ripe "fruit" which when later plucked by another to whom it has been given may be attributed to the transferor. See Helvering v. Horst and other materials at page 275, infra. When the transferee disposes of the property the gain may indeed have vanished. Helvering v. Bruun, supra note 15, may be similarly differentiated.

18. The somewhat parallel treatment under I.R.C. § 170(e), reducing the deduction allowed for charitable contributions of appreciated property, avoids the realization issue.

19. See Seligman, supra note 9 at 622.

20. Compare I.R.C. § 61 with § 103.

21. Knowlton v. Moore, 178 U.S. 41 (1900).

22. Supra note 11.

income of California residents. Similarly, the incomes of A and B may be subjected to different rates of tax; if A is taxed on part of her income at a higher rate than B pays, the constitutional uniformity requirement is not offended if it is because of different income levels and a graduated rate table and not because A and B are merely in different places.[23] Whenever some manner or mode of taxation is used somewhere in the United States, the same manner or mode must be used everywhere throughout the United States.[24]

Notwithstanding the constitutional fiat of uniformity, in the practical application of the income tax laws some lack of uniformity creeps in, even in the geographical sense. There are always uncertainties in the interpretation of statutes, tax or otherwise, but perhaps more in the tax area than in others. Crystallized differences in meaning develop in various parts of the country. A New York district judge may hold a person taxable on an alleged item of income which is held *not* taxable by a district judge in California. On appeal, the 2nd and 9th Circuits may similarly differ. A Court of Claims decision which is not appealable to a Court of Appeals may reach even a third view. Unless the matter goes to the Supreme Court, in a practical sense the law is different on the east and west coasts and possibly in one trial forum without regard to geography.

Prior to 1970, the Tax Court said it was never bound to follow decisions of the Courts of Appeal as to issues of law when the same issue appeared before the Tax Court for later decision.[25] This was the Court's settled view even when the appeal in the later case would be to an appellate court that had previously expressly overruled the Tax Court.[26] The Tax Court advanced an important argument that a part of its mission as a court not subject to geographic division was to work towards a uniform interpretation of the tax laws throughout the nation, a mission best accomplished by adhering to its own views until the Supreme Court took a hand in the matter. However, the Tax Court has changed its position and now decides cases on the basis of the law in the circuit to which an appeal will lie.[27]

In recent years even the Treasury has indicated it will sometimes apply different tax principles in different circuits depending on the law as determined by the controlling court of appeals.[28] These disparities are hardly more palatable than direct geographic discrimination by Congress, which the Constitution expressly condemns. Can it be said that, even if a taxing *statute* is seemingly untainted, an

23. Cf. Knowlton v. Moore, supra note 21 at 84.

24. Ibid.

25. Arthur Lawrence, 27 T.C. 713 (1957).

26. Harold Holt, 23 T.C. 469, 473 (1954).

27. Jack E. Golsen, 54 T.C. 742 (1970).

28. E. g., Rev.Rul. 72–583, 1972–2 C.B. 534, no longer of substantive significance because of the addition of I.R.C. § 2501(a)(5).

unconstitutional lack of uniformity may arise by virtue of inconsistent *judicial* and *administrative* action?

DUE PROCESS

Congress sometimes makes use of its taxing power in a retrospective manner, but this generally does not offend any constitutional proscription. It has long been settled that Congress may impose an income tax measured by the income of a prior year or by income of the year of the enactment earned before the enactment date.[29] In fact, the 16th Amendment became operative March 1, 1913, and the imposition of a tax on income earned after that date was upheld even though the taxing statute was not enacted until October 3, 1913.[30] If question can be raised about retrospective taxation, the Fifth Amendment seems the likely weapon. But in *Brushaber* [31] the Court expressly held that the due process clause of the Fifth Amendment "is not a limitation upon the taxing power conferred upon Congress by the Constitution * * *,". Although the Fifth Amendment may not limit the taxing power, it can vitiate a statute which, while masquerading as a tax, in reality amounts to a confiscation. If a supposed taxing statute is so arbitrary or capricious as to amount to spoliation or confiscation it will be invalid as a denial of due process. Dicta in *Brushaber* [32] supports this proposition.[33]

The principal message here is that most taxing statutes are not vulnerable to constitutional attack. The Supreme Court will clearly not attempt to determine in the countless circumstances that arise whether Congress has nicely balanced the tax burden or is instead depriving some taxpayers of property in a discriminatory manner that might be considered denial of due process. But there is always the chance that Congress may go too far.[34]

SELF–INCRIMINATION

One of the vexatious problems in current tax litigation arises out of the Fifth Amendment provision that "[n]o person * * * shall be compelled in any criminal case to be a witness against himself." It is of course well-settled that requiring a taxpayer to file an income tax return does not violate that Fifth Amendment privilege; rather, the proper place to raise the objection is in the return itself.[35] But to what extent, if at all, does the Fifth Amendment privilege apply in tax investigations? A summary analysis of this question appears in Part B of Chapter 28 infra, beginning at page 981.

29. Stockdale v. The Insurance Companies, 20 Wall. (U.S.) 323, 331 (1874).

30. Supra note 11.

31. Id. at 24.

32. Ibid.

33. Ibid.; and see Heiner v. Donnan, 285 U.S. 312 (1932); Nichols v. Coolidge, 274 U.S. 531, 542 (1926).

34. A Pennsylvania income tax statute was surprisingly held to offend the state constitution and therefore to be invalid in Amidon v. Kane, 444 Pa. 38, 279 A.2d 53 (1973).

35. United States v. Sullivan, 274 U.S. 259 (1927); Garner v. United States, 424 U.S. 648, 1976–1 U.S.T.C. para. 9301 (1976).

D. THE ROAD AHEAD

Although Wordsworth's ambling dreamer happily happened up-on a host of golden daffodils, one better embarks on a journey or project with a destination or goal clearly in mind. The goal in this course is to expose the fundamentals of income taxation by exploring the manner in which many basic transactions and events bear upon an individual's liability for income tax. This note summarizes the steps by which this book works toward that goal; a course has been set for which this note is a skeletal road map to the destination.

You have survived the scattered but important introductory ma-terial in most of Part One, although there may be some things to re-turn to there. Part Two of this book seeks to corral all items re-quired to be included in a taxpayer's gross income. Listing of course is impossible. Instead, an examination is made of judicial and ad-ministrative interpretation of the broad congressional language "in-come from whatever source derived" and its constitutional counter-part. This is followed by a detailed study of the Code sections by which Congress specifically excludes from or includes in gross income all or parts of specified items. The purpose here is not to memorize a laundry list, but much more to learn to manage the language of the Code, really a new language or at least *patois*.

After learning to identify gross income, a question may be: Who is to pay tax on it? Part Three of the book examines the so-called assignment-of-income doctrine which is aimed at preventing the arti-ficial shifting of tax liability among individuals and other taxable entities. All right! Macy's won't pay Gimbel's tax. But there are challenging problems here which will unfold in due time.

Once one has gathered all items of income and assigned them to the proper taxpayer (in tax parlance, has determined his gross in-come for the year), various deductions are allowed to reach the net figure "taxable income", the base to which the tax rates are applied. Congress might have imposed a tax on gross income but, after all, fair is fair and almost as a required matter of legislative grace it determined instead to allow numerous statutory deductions. Part Four of this book considers these deductions.

Individuals are not the only taxpayers under our federal taxing system. Corporations, trusts, and estates pay income taxes as well and, while not actually taxed as an entity, a partnership also must determine its "taxable income". While this book emphasizes indi-vidual income tax liability, nevertheless, principles and concepts in-volved in determining tax liability (gross income, taxpayer identifi-cation, taxable income, rates, credits, etc.) are often similar or the same for all affected entities. Some of this spill-over is especially apparent in Part Four which treats deductions in four chapters dealing respectively with: business deductions; deductions for profit-making, non-business activities; deductions not limited to business or profit-making activities; and deductions for individuals only. The material includes cases and rulings relevant to but not specifically directed to individual taxpayers.

In determining taxable income for the year, three additional questions must be considered with respect to each item of income or deduction. They are: (1) For what taxable year is an item income or deductible? This will soon be seen to be quite important when *graduated* rate tables and statutes limiting the period of liability or of refund recovery are considered. (2) What is the character (capital gain or loss, or ordinary income or loss) of various items? Tax advantages and limitations too attend such determinations. (3) Is gain or loss immediately to be recognized? Some items seemingly taxable or deductible get a deferment, sometimes essential or at least helpful, at others disadvantageous or even disastrous.

The timing matters identified in number (1), above, are considered in Part Five of the book. Conventional usage might cause the first chapter there to be entitled Tax Accounting, which normally puts the fear of God into Political Science majors who conjure up thoughts of balance sheets, debits and credits, and electronic calculators. The concepts involved will prove much less frightening when actually encountered. Our income taxing system is based on annual reporting (tax liability is determined and paid on a twelve month basis), and principles of tax accounting seek to say into what annual period an income or deduction item is properly included. These matters can be wonderfully complex; but the fundamental rules, the things with which we are concerned here, are really pretty simple.

The second question mentioned above is known as characterization of income and deductions. Congress has determined that income from some sources is to be given preferential treatment (taxed at lower rates) and, concurrently, deductions of losses from such preferential sources are to be subject to limitations. Part Six of the book illustrates that one must characterize each item of income or deduction and see whether the items when combined are to be given preferential treatment or subjected to limitations. Some deductions are not considered until Part Six because they cannot be intelligently considered separately from the characterization concept. Also, beware! Part Six is the den of the "Gotcha!" Enter with care, at your own risk. The "Gotcha!" is a sneaky kind of character assassin.

In some situations, even though one has income or loss, even *realized* income or loss, nevertheless Congress has seen fit not immediately to accord it tax consequences. Part Seven examines the non-recognition or deferral of some gains and the non-recognition or sometimes outright disallowance of some losses.

Consideration of all of the above leads to the determination of taxable income, next to be converted into tax liability. Part Eight of the book explains that conversion. Different rates of tax are applied to various classifications of taxpayers. Corporations are taxed at essentially stepped rates found in § 11, while estates and trusts are taxed at the graduated rates in § 1(d). Individuals are further classified into various categories: married taxpayers filing joint returns and surviving spouses § 1(a), heads of households § 1(b), unmarried individuals § 1(c), and married individuals filing separately § 1(d), for which separate graduated rate tables are provided. Part Eight studies the development of these individual classifications. Under the graduated rate tables, as the amount of one's taxable income increases, the applicable tax rate increases too, applicable that is to each additional increment of income. All individuals, regardless of their total income, pay at the same rate (14%) on the first few dollars of their taxable income (within classifications), and the progression continues in this parallel fashion up through the higher reaches of the rate tables.

The fact that taxes are imposed at graduated rates often explains taxpayer efforts to reduce taxable income for the year by shifting income to another (low bracket) year, or by assigning it to a related (low bracket) taxpayer. A close examination of the rate tables listed above will help explain some technical terms used throughout the course. A taxpayer's marginal tax rate is the highest rate applicable to any portion of one's income. Sometimes the term "effective tax rate" is used to describe the percentage of a taxpayer's total taxable income which must be paid as tax liability. For example, under § 1(a), married taxpayers filing a joint return with a taxable income of $50,000 have tax liability of $17,060. While they pay tax at a marginal rate of 50% (or may be said to be in the 50% rate bracket), some would say they are paying at an effective rate of only 34%, that percentage of their taxable income. The term "effective tax rate" should be used with care, however, because there is far from universal agreement on its meaning.

Part Eight also illustrates some additional special taxes and tax rates; and it introduces tax credits. Tax credits are subtracted from the amount of tax otherwise actually to be paid. They are therefore preferable to deductions used to determine taxable income. Credits reduce tax dollar for dollar, while deductions are effective in reducing tax only to the extent of one's marginal tax rates.

We have reached the Moon but not the Millenium. Nobody is perfect, and mistakes are made in federal taxes as much or more as anywhere. Tax procedures are available for correcting mistakes and by administrative and judicial proceedings for settling inevitable controversies. Still in a fundamental way Part Nine, the last three chapters of this book, deals with these phenomena.

Chapter 2 which follows here is still introductory, dealing as it does with the tax practitioner's tools. From there, in the words of your favorite Baedeker, as the sun settles softly behind the blue mountains that reach down to the shimmering sea, it's off to Part Two and Gross Income!

Bon voyage!

CHAPTER 2. THE TAX PRACTITIONER'S TOOLS

In any matter governed by statutory law, as are all federal tax questions, the approach to an answer is two-fold. (1) The statutory law, all such law that bears on the problem must first be found. (2) The proper meaning must be ascribed to such law.[1] The first step *can* always be accomplished and very well better be. The second step involves opinion, judgment, and often controversy, but there are guides, sometimes controlling, that must be discovered and appraised.

To some extent this course emphasizes well-settled tax principles of wide application, basic statutory concepts that have a well-burnished gloss. But an effort is made as well to help the student develop a technique for proceeding with some assurance when, as is so often the case, answers are elusive or obscure. A feel for a tax solution is not an innate gift so much as it is a result of a broad understanding of the phenomena of our federal taxing system. A beginning toward such understanding can be made by attaining an awareness of legislative, administrative, and judicial procedures that affect federal taxes, identifying the products of such procedures, and pondering the effect such products have on the solution of a tax problem. When we speak of such "products" we are referring to the *primary* materials of federal taxation, which are discussed immediately below. Secondary (unofficial) materials, often indispensible in the proper use of the primary materials, are discussed more briefly at the end of this chapter.

1. LEGISLATIVE MATERIALS

a. **The Code.** The taxing power of the federal government is vested in Congress. Congress exercises its power by enacting legislation. Therefore, the exercise of the federal taxing power is by *statute* and, as far as internal taxes are concerned, the current statutory document is the Internal Revenue Code of 1954. It is fair to say in this area that the Code is *the* law; other materials to which the researcher resorts are only aids to establishing the meaning of the Code, sometimes challenging, at times persuasive, and occasionally controlling. All tax decisions and controversies center around the meaning of provisions of the Code.[2]

---

1. There is a third facet to which most students receive a jolting introduction when they enter practice; all the relevant facts must be *ascertained*.

2. The improvement in tax teaching in the law schools has been dramatic in the past thirty years. Much credit for this goes to Erwin Griswold, one time professor and long time dean of the Harvard Law School, and more recently Solicitor General of the United States. And one of the world's few possessors of a solid gold golf putter. In broadest outline, the organization of this book is similar to his innovative casebook, Cases on Federal Taxation, first published by Foundation Press in 1940. Moreover, present day stress on THE STATUTE (and the regulations) also largely originated with him. Whether known or acknowledged, many tax practitioners trained in the past three dec-

Of course the plenary taxing power of Congress is subject to some restraints; federal taxing statutes must square with the requirements of the Constitution much the same as any other federal statute. However, beyond the brief comments in Chapter 1, discussion of the point will not be extended here because only infrequently in recent years has a civil tax case turned on a constitutional issue.

Not all the statutory law of federal income taxation can be found in the Internal Revenue Code. Some provisions affecting tax liability appear in other federal statutes.[3] But this is highly unusual, and the Code is the basic, and often the only relevant statutory document. By-products of the legislative process should now be briefly noted.

b. **Bills.** The formal beginning of the tax legislative process is the introduction of a bill in the House of Representatives where, under the Constitution, bills for raising revenue are supposed to originate.[4] As a matter of fact, most bills involving comprehensive tax legislation have had their origin in the Treasury Department, but they enter the legislative branch when they are introduced by a member of the House. The introduction of a tax bill, which is given publicity by the press and tax informational services, alerts the public to proposed changes in the law. But post-enactment examination of the bills introduced and the changes made in them as they passed through Congress rarely sheds much light on the final statutory product.

c. **Hearings.** Upon submission, in both the Senate and the House tax bills are usually referred to committees. In the House the Ways and Means Committee to which a tax bill is referred may hold quite extensive hearings on the proposed legislation. Important officials of the Treasury Department appear with a prepared statement and are questioned by committee members. But many others may also appear, some merely representing themselves and others representing various trade associations, industry groups, professional societies, etc. Similar proceedings may take place in the Finance Committee in the Senate. Transcripts of these hearings are published and can be the source of much interesting material reflecting both private and governmental policy views on tax matters. But the hear-

---

ades, and most tax instructors who have come along in that period, all are to some extent indebted to Erwin Griswold.

3. Pub.L. 93–490, 1974–2 C.B. 451, without amending the Code fixed some special rules for the deductibility of moving expenses of armed forces personnel at variance with I.R.C. § 217. Rev.Rul. 76–2, 1976–1 I.R.B. 9. Section 506(c) of the Tax Reform Act of 1976 added new subsection 217(g) which deals with moving expenses

of the armed forces. Section 2117 of the same act, however, limits tax liability potentially arising out of cancellation of certain student loans, without amending the Code.

4. A sophisticated analysis of the tax legislative process appears in Surrey, "The Congress and the Tax Lobbyist—How Special Tax Provisions Get Enacted," 70 Harv.L.Rev. 1145 (1957), reprinted in Sander and Westfall, Readings in Federal Taxation, 3 (1970).

ings are only rarely useful in attempting to give meaning to the statutes ultimately enacted.

d. **Committee Reports.** When the Ways and Means Committee brings a bill back to the floor of the House, a report accompanies the bill. Basically, the report seeks to explain to the other House members just what the bill is designed to do, usually with illustrations. Later, when the Finance Committee reports its bill to the Senate another committee report emerges. These reports are the most important part of the so-called "legislative history" of a statute and, in this country, practitioners, the Treasury, and the courts often resort to them as guides to the meaning of the legislation. As a matter of fact, a good bit of approved literary piracy goes on here. The House committee report may borrow heavily from statements before the committee by Treasury officials. When the Senate committee prepares its report with respect to parts of the bill that have not been altered, the Senate report comments are likely to be identical to the comments in the House report. This custom-sanctioned plagiarism is usually carried one step further when the Treasury issues new regulations under the statute as enacted, echoing the language of the committee reports.

Usually a tax bill emerges from the Senate in a form somewhat different from the form in which it was passed by the House. Before such a bill can go to the president, the disagreeing votes of the two houses must be reconciled. This task is undertaken by a conference committee, made up of Senate and House members. When agreement is reached in the committee, the managers report the bill back to their respective houses, generally resulting in passage in the newly agreed form. The conference committee report is often a rather brief and cryptic document, mainly identifying the areas of disagreement on which each house receded. But it may be accompanied by a statement on the part of the managers of the bill which is informative as to the reasons for action taken in conference. And the conference committee may also issue an explanation of the bill as it has been developed by the committee members. There is always the possibility that such reports and explanations will afford some insight into the meaning of new legislation, which would be missed upon a reading of the bare words of the statute.

Distinct from *ad hoc* conference committees is the permanent Joint Committee on Internal Revenue Taxation, made up of five members of the Finance Committee and five members of the Ways and Means Committee. Its role in Congress is collateral to the formal legislative process.[5] Nevertheless, it has a staff of experts and authority, among other things, to investigate the tax laws and their administration, and some of its publications are enlightening as to the likelihood of changes in the law or as to the meaning of recent statutory changes.

5. See I.R.C. (26 U.S.C.A.) §§ 8001–8023.

e. **Debates.** Our legislative process contemplates parliamentary debate of proposed legislation. A tax bill is no exception. Congressional proceedings, including such debates, are published in the Congressional Record. This product of the legislative process may also have a bearing on the meaning ultimately accorded a new statute. But, of all the subordinate legislative materials mentioned, the committee reports are clearly the most significant.

f. **Prior Laws.** The modern income tax dates from 1913, the year in which the Sixteenth Amendment was ratified. From then until 1939, Congress enacted numerous internal revenue acts among which the controlling statutory law was scattered. In 1939, the internal revenue laws were codified, first as the Internal Revenue Code of 1939. Thereafter, for fifteen years, internal revenue legislation took the form of additions to or other changes in that Code. Wholesale revision in 1954 produced the current Internal Revenue Code of 1954, which has now been the subject of many additions, deletions, and other changes. This suggests two problems for the student and practitioner. (1) If we are not talking about tax liability for the current year (questions controlled by the Code as most recently amended), what was the status of the statutory law as of the year with which we are concerned? (2) If we find a case bearing on a tax problem, a current problem, did the decision in that case rest on provisions of statutory law that are the same as or at least similar to the current provisions? If not, the case is obviously irrelevant. Generally, the opinion will set out the pertinent statute, either in the text or in the margin, so that it can be compared with the current provisions. Where the problem arises otherwise, the so-called "Cumulative Changes Service," published by Prentice-Hall may save time that otherwise would have to be spent searching for the effective date provisions of numerous amendatory acts.

g. **Treaties.** In the hierarchy of laws in the United States, a federal statute and a treaty enjoy equal status. Treaties made under the authority of the United States are the supreme law of the land, along with laws made in pursuance of the Constitution, and the Constitution itself. Consequently, a tax treaty, of which we now have many, can supersede a provision of the Internal Revenue Code. The point is made as a precautionary gesture but will not be further explored here.

Generally it is the practice in this casebook to delete from a judicial opinion or its footnotes the quotation of statutory language that is essentially the same as that appearing in the Code in its present form. When that is done a reference to the current Code provision replaces the footnote, as it is assumed that students will have the Code available. Opinions quoting language no longer in the Code or substantially different from the Code's present language are not changed in this respect. A comparative analysis may have to be undertaken by the student to see what current relevance the case may have despite the statutory changes, an effort that has educational value in and of itself. Statutory assignments throughout the book will usually quickly bring the student to the current provisions with which the old should be compared. The matter discussed here is illustrated in *Glenshaw Glass* set out in Chapter 3, where the Court quotes I.R.C. (1939) § 22(a) in the text and then in footnote 11 discusses a minor change of language in the parallel I.R.C. (1954) § 61(a).

2. ADMINISTRATIVE MATERIALS

a. **Regulations.** The Secretary of the Treasury is given general authority to "prescribe all needful rules and regulations for the enforcement" of the Internal Revenue Code.[6] This is a lawful congressional delegation of subordinate legislative authority. Under it the regulations promulgated become a kind of proliferation of the statute. But all three branches of government may play a part here. In the final analysis, the *judiciary* has the right to say whether the regulations promulgated by the *executive* conform to the statute enacted by the *legislature*. Interpretative regulations may be dismissed as not the law if they are at variance with the statute. However, the student should not lightly assume that a regulation is invalid. Even where a provision in the "Regs." seems to stretch the statute pretty far, it will likely be sustained if it reflects a consistent, long-standing interpretation by the Treasury or, as a practical matter, if it happens to coincide with notions of sound policy and is reasonable.[7] Not infrequently courts have accorded interpretative regulations "force of law" status.[8]

In this course, principal emphasis is placed on the Code and the Regulations. And students should learn at once to think of the initial approach to a tax question as follows: (1) What Code provisions bear on the problem? (2) Do the Regs. shed any light on their meaning in the setting at hand? This is not the end, but it is the right beginning for the solution of a tax problem.

---

6. I.R.C. (26 U.S.C.A.) § 7805.

7. See e. g., Bingler v. Johnson, 394 U.S. 741, 89 S.Ct. 1439 (1969).

8. See e. g., Helvering v. Winmill, 305 U.S. 79, 59 S.Ct. 45 (1938); Crane v. Comm'r, 331 U.S. 1, 67 S.Ct. 1047 (1947), upholding a provision of the Regulations, stating: "As the * * * provision of the Regulations has been in effect since 1918, and as the relevant statutory provision has been repeatedly re-enacted since then in substantially the same form, the * * * [Regulation] may itself be considered to have the force of law." 331 U.S. at

7 and 8, 67 S.Ct. at 1051; Fribourg Navigation Co. v. Comm'r, 383 U.S. 272, 283, 86 S.Ct. 862, 868, 869 (1966); Century Electric Co. v. Comm'r, 192 F.2d 155 (8th Cir. 1951), cert. den., 342 U.S. 954, 72 S.Ct. 625 (1952). Perhaps the high-water mark appears in U. S. v. Correll, 389 U.S. 299, 88 S.Ct. 445 (1967), in which the Supreme Court said: "The role of the judiciary in cases of this sort begins and ends with assuring that the Commissioner's regulations fall within his authority to implement the congressional mandate in some reasonable manner." 389 U.S. at 307, 88 S.Ct. at 450.

Some Treasury Regulations are more than mere interpretations of the statute. Congress sometimes carves out areas in which the Treasury can actually make, not merely interpret, the rules.[9] Such qualified or restricted delegations of legislative power seem no longer to be subject at all to attack on constitutional grounds (the separation of powers doctrine), and consequently regulations of this sort are even less vulnerable in the courts than are interpretative regulations.

The Regulations are especially valuable to the student, often enabling him to move from the general and abstract language of the statute to a specific, concrete example of its application. The practitioner, as a student, is of course accorded the same opportunity. Nevertheless, in using the Regulations it is well to remember that they are generally subordinate to the statute and, in any instance in which an exact answer must be achieved, it is entirely improper to rely on the Regulations (or on instructions on a tax form, which generally have about the same status) as a substitute for the statute. Indeed, it may well be necessary to go beyond both, as further comments below will indicate.

b. **Rulings.** The Regulations are not the only income tax documents emanating from the Treasury Department. However, at this point we discuss only one other, the Revenue Ruling (others are Revenue Procedures and Technical Information Releases). Revenue Rulings are issued under the same statutory authority as the Regulations. They are generally the Treasury's answer to a specific question raised by a taxpayer concerning his tax liability. In the interest of a uniform application of the tax laws, they are published to provide precedents for use in the disposition of like cases. While they do not have the force and effect of regulations, they do at least reflect the current policies of the Internal Revenue Service. The Service will not invariably respond to a request for a ruling. See Rev. Proc. 72–3, 1972–1 C.B. 698 (procedure for rulings, determination letters and closing agreements), and Rev.Proc. 72–9, 1972–1 C.B. 719 ("no ruling" areas); see also Rev.Proc. 76–29, 1976–1 C.B. 85, reflecting an accelerated response to ruling requests. Published Revenue Rulings appear first in the weekly Internal Revenue Bulletin and then, in more permanent form, in the semi-annual Cumulative Bulletin. See Rev.Proc. 72–1, 1972–1 C.B. 693. Since 1939, the Cumulative Bulletin has also been a source for the tax legislation committee reports, otherwise rather elusive documents. A student should not delay in making the acquaintance of "C.B.".

c. **Acquiescences.** The Internal Revenue Service publishes its acquiescence or nonacquiescence in the Tax Court's determination of issues adverse to the government. Such actions do not of course

---

9. See I.R.C. (26 U.S.C.A.) § 1017; Reg. § 1.1017–1.

affect the taxpayer who has just won his case but, in essence, the Service is saying either we will or we will not continue to contest the point as it arises in *other* cases. Less methodically, notice is given from time to time whether the Treasury will follow a decision of the Court of Claims, a district court, or court of appeals; obviously, Supreme Court decisions are controlling. These indications of adherence to or shifts in Treasury views, first published in the Internal Revenue Bulletin and eventually appearing in the Cumulative Bulletin, are of course of great importance in tax planning.

In addition to its essentially legislative and administrative activities, the Treasury performs a quasi-judicial function as well. If a deficiency in tax is asserted by the Treasury, or if the taxpayer claims a refund on the ground he has overpaid his tax, the initial decision of any ensuing controversy must be made by the Treasury. But such determinations give rise to no published opinions or reports, and procedures for judicial review always take the form of trials *de novo*. It will be important at another time to consider intra-agency procedures [10] but, as we are here mainly concerned with the *materials* of federal taxation and no such *materials* are generated by such procedures, we turn now to the judicial process.

3. JUDICIAL MATERIALS

The decisional process serves to put the meat on the skeletal law of the statute. In broad perspective the Code lays down bare legal norms and cursory fact norms, sometimes clearly and separately identifiable and sometimes coalescing and indistinguishable. When a tax controversy gets into court, the court's function, at least at the trial level, is to identify the problem, determine the relevant facts (findings of fact) and interpret and apply the Code provisions. In essence the tribunal must draw a line in each case; that is the primary job of the courts. The growing body of decisions in many areas of the tax law takes on a meaningful profile which can have significant value as an aid in predicting the outcome of future controversies involving similar issues. Thus lines drawn by the courts in prior decisions can be plotted and are useful tools to the tax practitioner planning prospective transactions and are essential to the practitioner in deciding whether to litigate an issue that is the subject of current administrative controversy.

An appellate tribunal can of course review the findings of fact as determined by the trial court, but in general it cannot reject such findings unless they are virtually entirely unsupported by evidence. Hence the function of the appellate process is not so much fact line drawing as it is interpretation. You will discover that appellate courts are rather adept at enunciating legal norms or rules or tests,

10. See Part Nine, Federal Tax Procedures, Chapters 28–30, infra.

which are then applied by trial courts in specific factual settings. Generally speaking, the appellate tribunal is at its best when the issue before it is a question of law. Thus, for example in Williams v. McGowan [11] the only issue the Court of Appeals had to decide was whether the sale of a proprietorship business was a sale of an entity or whether such a sale was a sale of each constituent asset separately. The facts were clear and undisputed. The Code did not provide a ready answer. The Court held as a matter of law that a proprietorship is simply an aggregate of many things, not an entity.

The cases presented in this casebook are representative, not only of the substantive areas of tax law, but also of what courts do. In your study of other law school courses you have become generally aware of the federal court structure—district courts, courts of appeals and the Supreme Court. You now meet two new federal courts, perhaps for the first time: The United States Tax Court and the United States Court of Claims.

a. Trial Courts

(1) *Tax Court Decisions.* If the Commissioner of Internal Revenue asserts a deficiency in income tax (charges in effect that the taxpayer has paid less than he owed) for any year, one thing the taxpayer can do is petition the Tax Court for a redetermination of the deficiency (or hopefully, a decision that no additional tax is due). As such suits are always between the taxpayer and the Commissioner (who is represented by attorneys in the office of the Chief Counsel of the Treasury Department), such cases are usually cited using only the taxpayer's name, e. g., Nora Payne Hill, 13 T.C. 291 (1949). The Tax Court, created as the Board of Tax Appeals in 1924 and changed in name only in 1942 was, until 1970, an *independent* administrative agency in the executive branch of the government. The Tax Reform Act of 1969 established the Tax Court as an Article I Court to be known as the United States Tax Court. Though not an Article III Court (the judiciary article of the Constitution) the United States Tax Court is now a de jure court albeit under the Legislative Article of the Constitution.[12]

It may be well to recognize three categories of Tax Court decisions. (1) The Court sits in divisions so that only one of the sixteen regular judges hears and decides a case. A Tax Court case is always tried without a jury before one of the judges. Such cases *may* be officially reported in the Tax Court (formerly B.T.A.) Reports, after required review by the Chief Judge. (2) The decision may not be officially reported if it involves primarily factual determinations and

11. 152 F.2d 570 (2d Cir. 1945), set out infra at page 773.

12. This action was held constitutional in Burns, Stix, Friedman and Co., Inc., 57 T.C. 392 (1971); and it is fairly clear the Tax Court now has power to punish for contempt and to enforce its orders. See Dubroff, "The United States Tax Court: An Historical Analysis," 40 Albany L.R. 7 (1975).

the application only of settled legal principles. Commerce Clearing House and Prentice-Hall, however, do publish such so-called "Memorandum Decisions." (3) Some officially reported decisions are, upon determination of the Chief Judge prior to publication, reviewed by the entire court. In such instances, the Court can reject the decision of the judge who heard the case. Constitutional challenge to this procedure has been rejected.[13] In any event, a decision that has the concurrence of all the judges of the Tax Court (or which has at least been considered by all) may have somewhat greater weight than the decision of a single judge. Still in the final analysis, it will usually be the judge's insight and the persuasiveness of his opinion, whether the case is reported, reviewed by the Court or merely a memorandum decision, which will determine whether it will be followed administratively and by other courts.

(2) *District Court Decisions.* When a tax deficiency is asserted the taxpayer's judicial remedy is not limited to suit in the Tax Court. He can pay the deficiency, file an administrative claim for refund and, upon its denial or prolonged administrative inaction, file suit in the district court for a refund. Fact issues may be determined by a jury if the plaintiff demands a jury trial. The same procedure is open to him even if he merely asserts that initially he overpaid his tax.[14] The tax decisions in the district courts emerge in the Federal Supplement.

(3) *Court of Claims Decisions.* An alternate forum for refund suits is the Court of Claims.[15] A Court of Claims case is heard by a Trial Judge, prior to July, 1973, called a Commissioner, who renders a report. Usually after further pleadings and oral argument, the Court of Claims makes its decision largely upon the Trial Judge's report, often adopting the report as its own. Court of Claims decisions appear in the Federal Reporter, Second Series. The Trial Judges' reports are published by Commerce Clearing House and Prentice Hall. Although the reports are not final decisions of the Court, they may indicate how the Court of Claims will rule and in any event are replete with reasoning and documentation. Court of Claims decisions are final unless, upon petition, the Supreme Court grants certiorari. However, such potential finality, important as it may be to the litigant, does not elevate Court of Claims decisions above those of the Tax Court or the district courts as valuable precedent in other cases.

b. **Appellate Courts.**

(1) *Court of Appeals Decisions.* Tax decisions of the district courts and of the Tax Court can be appealed (as of right) by either

---

13. Estate of Varian v. Comm'r, 396 F. 2d 753 (9th Cir. 1968).

14. See Chapter 29, infra.

15. See Brown, "Tax Refund Cases in the Court of Claims," 32 N.Y.U. Inst. on Fed.Tax. 1305 (1974).

party to the courts of appeals. Decisions on such appeals are of course reported in the Federal Reporter. It is not uncommon, as such appeals fan out to the eleven circuits, to find divergent views expressed on like questions in the several courts of appeal. This is often unsettling in matters of tax planning and often a factor taken into account in the forum-shopping stage of tax litigation.[16]

(2) *Supreme Court Decisions.* Many tax decisions in the Supreme Court represent that Court's determination (upon petition for certiorari) to settle a point on which the courts of appeals have taken divergent positions. Even so, the activities of the Tax Court, although its decisions are sometimes upset on judicial review, are so much more extensive that they clearly have more positive effect on the development of the tax law and on a uniform administration of the tax laws than the occasional forays of the Supreme Court.

Judicial decisions in federal tax cases (*except* those of the Tax Court) are collected in two important series of reports: (1) *United States Tax Cases* (cited, e. g., 67–2 U.S.T.C. para. ——) published by Commerce Clearing House, Inc., and (2) *American Federal Tax Reports* (cited —— A.F.T.R. ——) published by Prentice-Hall, Inc. Thus, in contrast to the space now occupied by complete sets of the Federal Supplement, the Federal Reporter and the United States Reports, a complete set of federal tax (other than Tax Court) cases is compressed into about 15 feet of bookshelf space.

4. UNOFFICIAL TAX MATERIALS

Federal tax practice would be almost impossible without the help of the major tax services. This is partly because of the bulk of material and partly because in detail tax principles are constantly changing. The Standard Federal Tax Reporter of Commerce Clearing House, Inc., and Federal Taxes published by Prentice-Hall, Inc., both do an elaborate job of indexing and digesting tax materials and keep their subscribers current by way of weekly advance sheet reports. Prentice-Hall publishes separately a Federal Tax Citator, which is the most comprehensive tool for "Shepardizing" tax cases. A more modest, selective citator volume is included in the C.C.H. service. Somewhat similar research assistance may be found in the *Federal Tax Coordinator,* published by the Research Institute of America, and Rabkin and Johnson, *Federal Income, Gift and Estate Tax* published by Matthew Bender & Co.

The most important income tax encyclopedia is Mertens, Law of Federal Income Taxation, now published in loose-leaf form and kept current by fairly frequent supplements. The Bureau of National Affairs, Inc. publishes an extensive series of Tax Management portfolios, which are constantly revised. West Publishing Company

---

16. Consider again the Constitutional requirement that federal taxes be uniform throughout the United States discussed in Chapter 1 at page 14, supra.

includes within its Hornbook Series, Chommie, *Federal Income Taxation* (2d edition 1973).

There is a great deal of excellent literature available on federal income tax problems. As would be expected, all the major law reviews publish tax articles from time to time. The Tax Law Review (a New York University Law School publication) is made up exclusively of tax writing, generally of a detailed and scholarly nature, and the University of Florida Law Review publishes a similar annual tax issue. Two other tax periodicals more practitioner oriented are The Journal of Taxation and Taxes. Commerce Clearing House publishes, and keeps up to date, a loose-leaf volume entitled Federal Tax Articles. The indexing—by subject, Code section and author—is good, and a brief description of the subject matter of each listed article is presented. For tax articles, all that the volume purports to cover, this service is somewhat superior to the better-known Index to Legal Periodicals.

Annual Institutes, such as the New York University Institute on Federal Taxation, the Southern Federal Tax Institute, and the Tax Institute of the University of Southern California yield volumes of papers usually addressed to current tax problems. And there are numerous useful treatises on special areas of tax law.

Further specific reference is made in the chapters that follow to helpful unofficial materials. The literature cited is of varying quality and depth and, as to some that may be classified as superficial, the editors' objective is to identify materials that may be helpful to the beginning student.

PART TWO: IDENTIFICATION OF INCOME SUBJECT TO TAXATION

CHAPTER 3: GROSS INCOME: THE SCOPE OF SECTION 61

A. INTRODUCTION TO INCOME

Internal Revenue Code: Section 61.

The federal income tax is imposed annually, at graduated rates, on a net figure known as "taxable income." Taxable income is "gross income" less certain authorized deductions. The scope of the gross income concept is taken as the starting point for this course, just as gross income is the starting point in the computation of tax liability.

Code section 61 defines gross income as "all *income* from whatever source derived." It may appear that Congress has violated a cardinal principle against defining a word in terms of the very word being defined—"water" means "water". But this of course is not the case. "Gross income" is a distinct statutory concept which could as well have been called "gross take" or something of the sort. If it wished to, which of course it does not, Congress could define gross income to include only amounts received as salary or wages or as dividends or in some other very restricted manner. Under the statutory definition, the meaning of the term "gross income" depends initially upon the meaning accorded "income." According to the legislative history of section 61, S.Rep.No. 1622, 83rd Cong. 2d Sess., page 168 (1954), "the word income is used as in section 22(a) [§ 61 of the 1954 Code] in its constitutional sense. It [was] not intended [in § 61 of the 1954 Code] to change the concept of income that obtains under section 22(a) [of the 1939 Code]." A long standing question has therefore been: What is "income"?

The term "income" in the Code, "incomes" in the Sixteenth Amendment, has a tax meaning that may vary from the meaning accorded the term in other contexts. A finder's treasure trove may not be "income" to the economist because it is not a recurring kind of receipt; but is it "income" in the tax sense? It may be that for some purposes one has income if his wealth increases by way of an appreciation in his investments; but does such appreciation constitute income for tax purposes? Still it should not be understood that the question is always broad and elusive. The statute itself offers some illustrations in section 61; and there are two important series of statutory rules of inclusion and exclusion which are taken up beginning with Chapter 4. Moreover, in recent years important court decisions have greatly narrowed the area of uncertainty, and long-standing administrative practice has added some clarification.

There is a comprehensive analysis of the concept of gross income in Magill, "Taxable Income" (1945); see also Sneed, "The Configurations of Gross Income" (1967) and Lowndes, "Current Conceptions of Taxable Income," 25 Ohio St.L.J. 151 (1964).

B. EQUIVOCAL RECEIPT OF FINANCIAL BENEFIT

Internal Revenue Code: Section 61.
Regulations: Sections 1.61–1, –2(a)(1), –2(d)(1), –14(a).

CESARINI v. UNITED STATES

District Court of the United States, Northern District of Ohio, 1969.
296 F.Supp. 3.
Aff'd per curiam, 428 F.2d 812, 6th Cir. 1970.

YOUNG, DISTRICT JUDGE. This is an action by the plaintiffs as taxpayers for the recovery of income tax payments made in the calendar year 1964. Plaintiffs contend that the amount of $836.51 was erroneously overpaid by them in 1964, and that they are entitled to a refund in that amount, together with the statutory interest from October 13, 1965, the date which they made their claim upon the Internal Revenue Service for the refund.

Plaintiffs and the United States have stipulated to the material facts in the case, and the matter is before the Court for final decision. The facts necessary for a resolution of the issues raised should perhaps be briefly stated before the Court proceeds to a determination of the matter. Plaintiffs are husband and wife, and live within the jurisdiction of the United States District Court for the Northern District of Ohio. In 1957, the plaintiffs purchased a used piano at an auction sale for approximately $15.00, and the piano was used by their daughter for piano lessons. In 1964, while cleaning the piano, plaintiffs discovered the sum of $4,467.00 in old currency, and since have retained the piano instead of discarding it as previously planned. Being unable to ascertain who put the money there, plaintiffs exchanged the old currency for new at a bank, and reported the sum of $4,467.00 on their 1964 joint income tax return as ordinary income from other sources. On October 18, 1965, plaintiffs filed an amended return with the District Director of Internal Revenue in Cleveland, Ohio, this second return eliminating the sum of $4,467.00 from the gross income computation, and requesting a refund in the amount of $836.51, the amount allegedly overpaid as a result of the former inclusion of $4,467.00 in the original return for the calendar year of 1964. On January 18, 1966, the Commissioner of Internal Revenue rejected taxpayers' refund claim in its entirety, and plaintiffs filed the instant action in March of 1967.

Plaintiffs make three alternative contentions in support of their claim that the sum of $836.51 should be refunded to them. First, that the $4,467.00 found in the piano is not includable in gross income under Section 61 of the Internal Revenue Code. (26 U.S.C. § 61) Secondly, even if the retention of the cash constitutes a realization of ordinary income under Section 61, it was due and owing in the year the piano was purchased, 1957, and by 1964, the statute of limitations provided by 26 U.S.C. § 6501 had elapsed. And thirdly, that if the treasure trove money is gross income for the year 1964, it was entitled to capital gains treatment under Section 1221 of Title 26. The Government, by its answer and its trial brief, asserts that the amount found in the piano is includable in gross income under Section 61(a) of Title 26, U.S.C., that the money is taxable in the year it was actually found, 1964, and that the sum is properly taxable at ordinary income rates, not being entitled to capital gains treatment under 26 U.S.C. §§ 1201 *et seq.*

After a consideration of the pertinent provisions of the Internal Revenue Code, Treasury Regulations, Revenue Rulings, and decisional law in the area, this Court has concluded that the taxpayers are not entitled to a refund of the amount requested, nor are they entitled to capital gains treatment on the income item at issue.

The starting point in determining whether an item is to be included in gross income is, of course, Section 61(a) of Title 26 U.S.C., and that section provides in part:

"Except as otherwise provided in this subtitle, *gross income means all income from whatever source derived*, including (but not limited to) the following items: * * *" (Emphasis added.)

Subsections (1) through (15) of Section 61(a) then go on to list fifteen items specifically included in the computation of the taxpayer's gross income, and Part II of Subchapter B of the 1954 Code (Sections 71 *et seq.*) deals with other items expressly included in gross income. While neither of these listings expressly includes the type of income which is at issue in the case at bar, Part III of Subchapter B (Sections 101 *et seq.*) deals with items specifically *excluded* from gross income, and found money is not listed in those sections either. This absence of express mention in any of the code sections necessitates a return to the "all income from whatever source" language of Section 61(a) of the code, and the express statement there that gross income is "not limited to" the following fifteen examples. Section 1.61–1(a) of the Treasury Regulations, the corresponding section to Section 61 (a) in the 1954 Code, reiterates this broad construction of gross income, providing in part:

"Gross income means all income from whatever source derived, unless excluded by law. *Gross income includes income realized in any form*, whether in money, property, or services. * * * " (Emphasis added.)

The decisions of the United States Supreme Court have frequently stated that this broad all-inclusive language was used by Congress to exert the full measure of its taxing power under the Sixteenth Amendment to the United States Constitution. Commissioner of Internal Revenue v. Glenshaw Glass Co., 348 U.S. 426, 429, 75 S.Ct. 473, 99 L. Ed. 483 (1955); Helvering v. Clifford, 309 U.S. 331, 334, 60 S.Ct. 554, 84 L.Ed. 788 (1940); Helvering v. Midland Mutual Life Ins. Co., 300 U.S. 216, 223, 57 S.Ct. 423, 81 L.Ed. 612 (1937); Douglas v. Willcuts, 296 U.S. 1, 9, 56 S.Ct. 59, 80 L.Ed. 3 (1935); Irwin v. Gavit, 268 U.S. 161, 166, 45 S.Ct. 475, 69 L.Ed. 897 (1925).

In addition, the Government in the instant case cites and relies upon an I.R.S. Revenue Ruling which is undeniably on point:

"The finder of treasure-trove is in receipt of taxable income, for Federal income tax purposes, to the extent of its value in United States currency, for the taxable year in which it is reduced to undisputed possession." Rev.Rul. 61, 1953–1, Cum.Bull. 17.

The plaintiffs argue that the above ruling does not control this case for two reasons. The first is that subsequent to the Ruling's pronouncement in 1953, Congress enacted Sections 74 and 102 of the 1954 Code, § 74, expressly *including* the value of prizes and awards in gross income in most cases, and § 102 specifically *exempting* the value of gifts received from gross income. From this, it is argued that Section 74 was added because prizes might otherwise be construed as non-taxable gifts, and since no such section was passed expressly taxing treasure-trove, it is therefore a gift which is non-taxable under Section 102. This line of reasoning overlooks the statutory scheme previously alluded to, whereby income from all sources is taxed unless the taxpayer can point to an express exemption. Not only have the taxpayers failed to list a specific exclusion in the instant case, but also the Government *has* pointed to express language covering the found money, even though it would not be required to do so under the broad language of Section 61(a) and the foregoing Supreme Court decisions interpreting it.

The second argument of the taxpayers in support of their contention that Rev.Rul. 61, 1953–1 should not be applied in this case is based upon the decision of Dougherty v. Commissioner, 10 T.C.M. 320, P–H Memo. T.C., ¶51,093 (1951). In that case the petitioner was an individual who had never filed an income tax return, and the Commissioner was attempting to determine his gross income by the so-called "net worth" method. Dougherty had a substantial increase in his net worth, and attempted to partially explain away his lack of reporting it by claiming that he had found $31,000.00 in cash inside a used chair he had purchased in 1947. The Tax Court's opinion deals primarily with the factual question of whether or not Dougherty actually *did* find this money in a chair, finally concluding that he did not, and from this petitioners in the instant case argue that if such found money is clearly gross income, the Tax Court would not have reached the fact question, but merely included the $31,000.00 as a matter of law. Petitioners argue that since the Tax Court did not include the sum in Dougherty's gross income until they had found as a fact that it *was not* treasure trove, then by implication such discovered money is not taxable. This argument must fail for two reasons. First, the *Dougherty* decision precedes Rev.Rul. 61, 1953–1 by two years, and thus was dealing with what then was an uncharted area of the gross income provisions of the Code. Secondly, the case cannot be read as authority for the proposition that treasure trove is not includable in gross income, even if the revenue ruling had not been issued two years later.[1]

In partial summary, then, the arguments of the taxpayers which attempt to avoid the application of Rev.Rul. 61, 1953–1 are not well taken. The *Dougherty* case simply does not hold one way or another on the problem before this Court, and therefore petitioners' reliance upon it is misplaced. The other branch of their argument, that found money must be construed to be a gift under Section 102 of the 1954 Code since it is not expressly included as are prizes in Section 74 of the Code, would not even be effective were it being urged at a time prior to 1953, when the ruling had not yet been promulgated. In addition to the numerous cases in the Supreme Court which uphold the broad sweeping construction of Section 61(a) found in Treas.Reg. § 1.61–1(a), other courts and commentators writing at a point in time before the ruling came down took the position that windfalls, including found monies, were properly includable in gross income under Section 22(a) of the 1939 Code, the predecessor of Section 61(a) in the 1954 Code. See, for example, the decision in Park & Tilford Distillers Corp. v. United States, 107 F.Supp. 941, 123 Ct.Cl. 509 (1952);[2] and Com-

---

1. The Dougherty Court, after carefully considering the evidence before it on the factual question of whether or not the taxpayer actually found the $31,000.00 as claimed, stated:
"In short, we do not believe the money was in the chair when the chair was acquired by the petitioner.
"Where the petitioner got the money which he later took from the chair and in what manner it was obtained by him, we do not know. It is accordingly impossible for us to conclude and hold the $31,000 here in question was not acquired by him in a manner such as would make it income to him within the meaning of the statute. Such being the case, *we do not reach the question whether money, if acquired in the manner claimed by the petitioner, is income under the statute.*" (Emphasis added.) 10 T.C.M. 320 at 323 (1951).

2. In this taxpayer's suit for a refund of corporation taxes, Judge Madden of the Court of Claims stated at pages 943–944: " * * * It is not, and we

ment, "Taxation of Found Property and Other Windfalls," 20 U.Chi.L. Rev. 748, 752 (1953).[3] While it is generally true that revenue rulings may be disregarded by the courts if in conflict with the code and the regulations, or with other judicial decisions, plaintiffs in the instant case have been unable to point to any inconsistency between the gross income sections of the code, the interpretation of them by the regulations and the courts, and the revenue ruling which they herein attack as inapplicable. On the other hand, the United States *has* shown a consistency in letter and spirit between the ruling and the code, regulations, and court decisions.

Although not cited by either party, and noticeably absent from the Government's brief, the following Treasury Regulation appears in the 1964 Regulations, the year of the return in dispute :

"§ 1.61–14   Miscellaneous items of gross income.

"(a) In general.   In addition to the items enumerated in section 61(a), there are many other kinds of gross income   *   *   *.   *Treasure trove, to the extent of its value in United States currency, constitutes gross income for the taxable year in which it is reduced to undisputed possession.*" (Emphasis added.)

Identical language appears in the 1968 Treasury Regulations, and is found in all previous years back to 1958. This language is the same in all material respects as that found in Rev.Rul. 61–53–1, Cum.Bull. 17, and is undoubtedly an attempt to codify that ruling into the Regulations which apply to the 1954 Code. This Court is of the opinion that Treas.Reg. § 1.61–14(a) is dispositive of the major issue in this case if the $4,467.00 found in the piano was "reduced to undisputed possession" in the year petitioners reported it, for this Regulation was applicable to returns filed in the calendar year of 1964.

This brings the Court to the second contention of the plaintiffs: that if any tax was due, it was in 1957 when the piano was purchased, and by 1964 the Government was blocked from collecting it by reason of the statute of limitations. Without reaching the question of whether the voluntary payment in 1964 constituted a *waiver* on the part of

think could not rationally be, suggested that Congress lacks the power to tax windfalls as income. * * * A windfall may, of course, be a gift, and thus expressly exempt from income tax. But if, as in the instant case, the windfall is clearly not a gift, but a payment required by a statute * * * we do not see how its exemption could be reconciled with the reiterated statements that Congress intended, by Section 22(a), to tax income to the extent of its constitutional power." 107 F.Supp. at 943, 944.

3. This article, after stating arguments both ways on the question, and thus

suggesting by implication that the area was not clearly defined at that time, went on to state at page 752: "Perhaps a more appropriate interpretation of Section 22(a) would be to hold that all windfalls * * * are taxable income under its sweeping language. * * * Insofar as the policy of Section 22(a) is to impose similar tax burdens on persons in similar circumstances, there is no basis for distinguishing value received as windfall and * * * value received as salary." Footnote 50 of the Comment indicates that the article was in printing when Rev.Rul. 61–53–1 came out.

the taxpayers, this Court finds that the $4,467.00 sum was properly included in gross income for the calendar year of 1964. Problems of when title vests, or when possession is complete in the field of federal taxation, in the absence of definitive federal legislation on the subject, are ordinarily determined by reference to the law of the state in which the taxpayer resides, or where the property around which the dispute centers is located. Since both the taxpayers and the property in question are found within the State of Ohio, Ohio law must govern as to when the found money was "reduced to undisputed possession" within the meaning of Treas.Reg. § 1.61–14 and Rev.Rul. 61–53–1, Cum.Bull. 17.

In Ohio, there is no statute specifically dealing with the rights of owners and finders of treasure trove, and in the absence of such a statute the common-law rule of England applies, so that "title belongs to the finder as against all the world except the true owner." Nieder-lehner v. Weatherly, 78 Ohio App. 263, 69 N.E.2d 787 (1946), appeal dismissed, 146 Ohio St. 697, 67 N.E.2d 713 (1946). The *Niederlehner* case held, *inter alia,* that the owner of real estate upon which money is found does not have title as against the finder. Therefore, in the instant case if plaintiffs had resold the piano in 1958, not knowing of the money within it, they later would not be able to succeed in an action against the purchaser who *did* discover it. Under Ohio law, the plaintiffs must have actually *found* the money to have superior title over all but the true owner, and they did not discover the old currency until 1964. Unless there is present a specific state statute to the contrary,[4] the majority of jurisdictions are in accord with the Ohio rule.[5] Therefore, this Court finds that the $4,467.00 in old currency was not "reduced to undisputed possession" until its actual discovery in 1964, and thus the United States was not barred by the statute of limitations from collecting the $836.51 in tax during that year.

Finally, plaintiffs' contention that they are entitled to capital gains treatment upon the discovered money must be rejected. * * *

[This portion of the opinion is omitted. The characterization of income and its tax significance are considered in Chapter 21, infra. Ed.]

---

4. See, for example, United States v. Peter, 178 F.Supp. 854 (E.D.La.1959) where it is held that under the Louisiana Civil Code and the Code D'Napolean the finder of treasure does not own it, and can only become the owner if no one else can prove that the treasure is his property.

5. See Weeks v. Hackett, 104 Me. 264, 71 A. 858, 860 (1908) for a review of the authorities in jurisdictions where the finder is the owner as against all but the true owner. Also, see Finding Lost Goods 36A C.J.S. § 5, p. 422 (1961).

OLD COLONY TRUST CO. v. COMMMISSIONER

Supreme Court of the United States, 1929.
279 U.S. 716, 49 S.Ct. 499.

MR. CHIEF JUSTICE TAFT delivered the opinion of the Court.

*   *   *

William M. Wood was president of the American Woolen Company during the years 1918, 1919 and 1920. In 1918 he received as salary and commissions from the company $978,725, which he included in his federal income tax return for 1918. In 1919 he received as salary and commissions from the company $548,132.27, which he included in his return for 1919.

August 3, 1916, the American Woolen Company had adopted the following resolution, which was in effect in 1919 and 1920:

"Voted: That this company pay any and all income taxes, State and Federal, that may hereafter become due and payable upon the salaries of all the officers of the company, including the president, William M. Wood; the comptroller, Parry C. Wiggin; the auditor, George R. Lawton; and the following members of the staff, to wit: Frank H. Carpenter, Edwin L. Heath, Samuel R. Haines, and William M. Lasbury, to the end that said persons and officers shall receive their salaries or other compensation in full without deduction on account of income taxes, State or Federal, which taxes are to be paid out of the treasury of this corporation."

This resolution was amended on March 25, 1918, as follows:

"Voted: That, in referring to the vote passed by this board on August 3, 1916, in reference to income taxes, State and Federal, payable upon the salaries or compensation of the officers and certain employees of this company, the method of computing said taxes shall be as follows, viz:

" 'The difference between what the total amount of his tax would be, including his income from all sources, and the amount of his tax when computed upon his income excluding such compensation or salaries paid by this company.' "

Pursuant to these resolutions, the American Woolen Company paid to the collector of internal revenue Mr. Wood's federal income and surtaxes due to salary and commissions paid him by the company, as follows:

Taxes for 1918 paid in 1919 . . . . $681,169.88
Taxes for 1919 paid in 1920 . . . .   351,179.27

The decision of the Board of Tax Appeals here sought to be reviewed was that the income taxes of $681,169.88 and $351,179.27 paid by the American Woolen Company for Mr. Wood were additional income to him for the years 1919 and 1920.

The question certified by the Circuit Court of Appeals for answer by this Court is:

"Did the payment by the employer of the income taxes assessable against the employee constitute additional taxable income to such employee?"

* * *

Coming now to the merits of this case, we think the question presented is whether a taxpayer, having induced a third person to pay his income tax or having acquiesced in such payment as made in discharge of an obligation to him, may avoid the making of a return thereof and the payment of a corresponding tax. We think he may not do so. The payment of the tax by the employers was in consideration of the services rendered by the employee and was a gain derived by the employee from his labor. The form of the payment is expressly declared to make no difference. Section 213, Revenue Act of 1918, c. 18, 40 Stat. 1065.* It is therefore immaterial that the taxes were directly paid over to the Government. The discharge by a third person of an obligation to him is equivalent to receipt by the person taxed. The certificate shows that the taxes were imposed upon the employee, that the taxes were actually paid by the employer and that the employee entered upon his duties in the years in question under the express agreement that his income taxes would be paid by his employer. This is evidenced by the terms of the resolution passed August 3, 1916, more than one year prior to the year in which the taxes were imposed. The taxes were paid upon a valuable consideration, namely, the services rendered by the employee and as part of the compensation therefor. We think therefore that the payment constituted income to the employee.

This result is sustained by many decisions.   * * *

Nor can it be argued that the payment of the tax * * * was a gift. The payment for services, even though entirely voluntary, was nevertheless compensation within the statute. This is shown by the case of Noel v. Parrott, 15 F.2d 669. There it was resolved that a gratuitous appropriation equal in amount to $3 per share on the outstanding stock of the company be set aside out of the assets for distribution to certain officers and employees of the company and that the executive committee be authorized to make such distribution as they deemed wise and proper. The executive committee gave $35,000 to be paid to the plaintiff taxpayer. The court said, p. 672:

"In no view of the evidence, therefore, can the $35,000 be regarded as a gift. It was either compensation for services rendered, or a gain or profit derived from the sale of the stock of the corporation, or both; and, in any view, it was taxable as income."

---

* The legislative history of the 1954 Code makes it clear that, while § 61 omits the phrase "in whatever form paid," the definition of gross income still includes "income realized in any form." Sen.Rep.No.1622, 83d Cong. 2d Sess. 168 (1954). Ed.

It is next argued against the payment of this tax that if these payments by the employer constitute income to the employee, the employer will be called upon to pay the tax imposed upon this additional income, and that the payment of the additional tax will create further income which will in turn be subject to tax, with the result that there would be a tax upon a tax. This it is urged is the result of the Government's theory, when carried to its logical conclusion, and results in an absurdity which Congress could not have contemplated.

In the first place, no attempt has been made by the Treasury to collect further taxes, upon the theory that the payment of the additional taxes creates further income, and the question of a tax upon a tax was not before the Circuit Court of Appeals and has not been certified to this Court. We can settle questions of that sort when an attempt to impose a tax upon a tax is undertaken, but not now. United States v. Sullivan, 274 U.S. 259, 264; Yazoo & Mississippi Valley R. R. v. Jackson Vinegar Co., 226 U.S. 217, 219. It is not, therefore, necessary to answer the argument based upon an algebraic formula to reach the amount of taxes due. The question in this case is, "Did the payment by the employer of the income taxes assessable against the employee constitute additional taxable income to such employee?" The answer must be "Yes."

[The separate opinion of MR. JUSTICE MCREYNOLDS has been omitted. Ed.]

COMMISSIONER v. GLENSHAW GLASS CO.*

Supreme Court of the United States, 1955.
348 U.S. 426, 75 S.Ct. 473.
Rehearing den., 349 U.S. 925, 75 S.Ct. 657.

MR. CHIEF JUSTICE WARREN delivered the opinion of the Court.

This litigation involves two cases with independent factual backgrounds yet presenting the identical issue. The two cases were consolidated for argument before the Court of Appeals for the Third Circuit and were heard *en banc*. The common question is whether money received as exemplary damages for fraud or as the punitive two-thirds portion of a treble-damage antitrust recovery must be reported by a taxpayer as gross income under § 22(a) of the Internal Revenue Code of 1939.[1] In a single opinion, 211 F.2d 928, the Court of Appeals affirmed the Tax Court's separate rulings in favor of the taxpayers. 18 T.C. 860; 19 T.C. 637. Because of the frequent recurrence of the question and differing interpretations by the lower courts of this

---

* See Wright, "The Effect of the Source of Realized Benefits upon the Supreme Court's Concept of Taxable Receipts," 8 Stan.L.Rev. 164 (1956). Ed.

1. 53 Stat. 9, 53 Stat. 574, 26 U.S.C.A. § 22(a). [See note 11, infra. Ed.]

Court's decisions bearing upon the problem, we granted the Commissioner of Internal Revenue's ensuing petition for certiorari.   348 U.S. 813.

The facts of the cases were largely stipulated and are not in dispute.   So far as pertinent they are as follows:

Commissioner v. Glenshaw Glass Co.—The Glenshaw Glass Company, a Pennsylvania corporation, manufactures glass bottles and containers.   It was engaged in protracted litigation with the Hartford-Empire Company, which manufactures machinery of a character used by Glenshaw.   Among the claims advanced by Glenshaw were demands for exemplary damages for fraud [2] and treble damages for injury to its business by reason of Hartford's violation of the federal antitrust laws.[3]   In December, 1947, the parties concluded a settlement of all pending litigation, by which Hartford paid Glenshaw approximately $800,000.   Through a method of allocation which was approved by the Tax Court, 18 T.C. 860, 870–872, and which is no longer in issue, it was ultimately determined that, of the total settlement, $324,529.94 represented payment of punitive damages for fraud and antitrust violations.   Glenshaw did not report this portion of the settlement as income for the tax year involved.   The Commissioner determined a deficiency claiming as taxable the entire sum less only deductible legal fees.   As previously noted, the Tax Court and the Court of Appeals upheld the taxpayer.

Commissioner v. William Goldman Theatres, Inc.—William Goldman Theatres, Inc., a Delaware corporation operating motion picture houses in Pennsylvania, sued Loew's, Inc., alleging a violation of the federal antitrust laws and seeking treble damages.   After a holding that a violation had occurred, William Goldman Theatres, Inc. v. Loew's, Inc., 150 F.2d 738, the case was remanded to the trial court for a determination of damages.   It was found that Goldman had suffered a loss of profits equal to $125,000 and was entitled to treble damages in the sum of $375,000.   William Goldman Theatres, Inc. v. Loew's, Inc., 69 F.Supp. 103, aff'd, 164 F.2d 1021, cert. denied, 334 U.S. 811.   Goldman reported only $125,000 of the recovery as gross income and claimed that the $250,000 balance constituted punitive damages and as such was not taxable.   The Tax Court agreed, 19 T.C. 637, and the Court of Appeals, hearing this with the *Glenshaw* case, affirmed.   211 F.2d 928.

It is conceded by the respondents that there is no constitutional barrier to the imposition of a tax on punitive damages.   Our question

---

2. For the bases of Glenshaw's claim for damages from fraud, see Shawkee Manufacturing Co. v. Hartford-Empire Co., 322 U.S. 271; Hazel-Atlas Glass Co. v. Hartford-Empire Co., 322 U.S. 238.

3. See Hartford-Empire Co. v. United States, 323 U.S. 386, 324 U.S. 570.

is one of statutory construction: are these payments comprehended by § 22(a)?

The sweeping scope of the controverted statute is readily apparent:

"SEC. 22.   GROSS INCOME.

"(a) GENERAL DEFINITION.—'Gross income' includes gains, profits, and income derived from salaries, wages, or compensation for personal service . . . of whatever kind and in whatever form paid, or from professions, vocations, trades, businesses, commerce, or sales, or dealings in property, whether real or personal, growing out of the ownership or use of or interest in such property; also from interest, rent, dividends, securities, or the transaction of any business carried on for gain or profit, *or gains or profits and income derived from any source whatever.* * * *" (Emphasis added.)[4]

This Court has frequently stated that this language was used by Congress to exert in this field "the full measure of its taxing power." Helvering v. Clifford, 309 U.S. 331, 334; Helvering v. Midland Mutual Life Ins. Co., 300 U.S. 216, 223; Douglas v. Willcuts, 296 U.S. 1, 9; Irwin v. Gavit, 268 U.S. 161, 166. Respondents contend that punitive damages, characterized as "windfalls" flowing from the culpable conduct of third parties, are not within the scope of the section. But Congress applied no limitations as to the source of taxable receipts, nor restrictive labels as to their nature. And the Court has given a liberal construction to this broad phraseology in recognition of the intention of Congress to tax all gains except those specifically exempted. Commissioner v. Jacobson, 336 U.S. 28, 49; Helvering v. Stockholms Enskilda Bank, 293 U.S. 84, 87–91. Thus, the fortuitous gain accruing to a lessor by reason of the forfeiture of a lessee's improvements on the rented property was taxed in Helvering v. Bruun, 309 U.S. 461. Cf. Robertson v. United States, 343 U.S. 711; Rutkin v. United States, 343 U.S. 130; United States v. Kirby Lumber Co., 284 U.S. 1. Such decisions demonstrate that we cannot but ascribe content to the catchall provision of § 22(a), "gains or profits and income derived from any source whatever." The importance of that phrase has been too frequently recognized since its first appearance in the Revenue Act of 1913[5] to say now that it adds nothing to the meaning of "gross income."

Nor can we accept respondents' contention that a narrower reading of § 22(a) is required by the Court's characterization of income in Eisner v. Macomber, 252 U.S. 189, 207, as "the gain derived from capital, from labor, or from both combined."[6] The Court was there

4. See note 1, supra.

5. 38 Stat. 114, 167.

6. The phrase was derived from Stratton's Independence, Ltd. v. Howbert, 231 U.S. 399, 415, and Doyle v. Mitch-

endeavoring to determine whether the distribution of a corporate stock dividend constituted a realized gain to the shareholder, or changed "only the form, not the essence," of his capital investment. Id., at 210. It was held that the taxpayer had "received nothing out of the company's assets for his separate use and benefit." Id., at 211. The distribution, therefore, was held not a taxable event. In that context—distinguishing gain from capital—the definition served a useful purpose. But it was not meant to provide a touchstone to all future gross income questions. Helvering v. Bruun, supra, at 468–469; United States v. Kirby Lumber Co., supra, at 3.

Here we have instances of undeniable accessions to wealth, clearly realized, and over which the taxpayers have complete dominion. The mere fact that the payments were extracted from the wrongdoers as punishment for unlawful conduct cannot detract from their character as taxable income to the recipients. Respondents concede, as they must, that the recoveries are taxable to the extent that they compensate for damages actually incurred. It would be an anomaly that could not be justified in the absence of clear congressional intent to say that a recovery for actual damages is taxable but not the additional amount extracted as punishment for the same conduct which caused the injury. And we find no such evidence of intent to exempt these payments.

It is urged that re-enactment of § 22(a) without change since the Board of Tax Appeals held punitive damages nontaxable in Highland Farms Corp., 42 B.T.A. 1314, indicates congressional satisfaction with that holding. Re-enactment—particularly without the slightest affirmative indication that Congress ever had the Highland Farms decision before it—is an unreliable indicium at best. Helvering v. Wilshire Oil Co., 308 U.S. 90, 100–101; Koshland v. Helvering, 298 U.S. 441, 447. Moreover, the Commissioner promptly published his nonacquiescence in this portion of the Highland Farms holding [7] and has, before and since, consistently maintained the position that these receipts are taxable.[8] It therefore cannot be said with certitude that

---

ell Bros. Co., 247 U.S. 179, 185, two cases construing the Revenue Act of 1909, 36 Stat. 11, 112. Both taxpayers were "wasting asset" corporations, one being engaged in mining, the other in lumbering operations. The definition was applied by the Court to demonstrate a distinction between a return on capital and "a mere conversion of capital assets." Doyle v. Mitchell Bros. Co., supra, at 184. The question raised by the instant case is clearly distinguishable.

8. The long history of departmental rulings holding personal injury recoveries nontaxable on the theory that they roughly correspond to a return of capital cannot support exemption of punitive damages following injury to property. See 2 Cum.Bull. 71; I–1 Cum.Bull. 92, 93; VII–2 Cum.Bull. 123; 1954–1 Cum.Bull. 179, 180. Damages for personal injury are by definition compensatory only. Punitive damages, on the other hand, cannot be considered a restoration of capital for taxation purposes.

7. 1941–1 Cum.Bull. 16.

Congress intended to carve an exception out of § 22(a)'s pervasive coverage. Nor does the 1954 Code's [9] legislative history, with its reiteration of the proposition that statutory gross income is "all-inclusive," [10] give support to respondents' position. The definition of gross income has been simplified, but no effect upon its present broad scope was intended.[11] Certainly punitive damages cannot reasonably be classified as gifts, cf. Commissioner v. Jacobson, 336 U.S. 28, 47–52, nor do they come under any other exemption provision in the Code. We would do violence to the plain meaning of the statute and restrict a clear legislative attempt to bring the taxing power to bear upon all receipts constitutionally taxable were we to say that the payments in question here are not gross income. See Helvering v. Midland Mutual Life Ins. Co., supra, at 223.

Reversed.

Mr. Justice Douglas dissents.

Mr. Justice Harlan took no part in the consideration or decision of this case.

NOTE

The Supreme Court in *Glenshaw Glass* attempts to define gross income or at least to indicate some requirements of gross income [1] when it refers to "undeniable accessions to wealth, clearly realized, and over which the taxpayers have complete dominion." Within these requirements, do borrowers have income on the receipt of loans? Clearly not; loans are based on concurrently acknowledged obligations to repay which, offsetting the receipt, negate any accession to wealth.[2] Of course if the borrower has no intent to repay a "loan" and the lender is unaware of that fact, the "loan" is not a loan but an illegal appropriation of the would-be creditor's property, which is income to the so-called borrower under I.R.C. § 61.[3]

9. 68A Stat. 3 et seq. Section 61(a) of the Internal Revenue Code of 1954, 68A Stat. 17, is the successor to § 22 (a) of the 1939 Code.

10. H.R.Rep. No. 1337, 83d Cong., 2d Sess. A18; S.Rep. No. 1622, 83d Cong., 2d Sess. 168.

11. In discussing § 61(a) of the 1954 Code, the House Report states:
"This section corresponds to section 22 (a) of the 1939 Code. While the language in existing section 22(a) has been simplified, the all-inclusive nature of statutory gross income has not been affected thereby. Section 61(a) is as broad in scope as section 22(a).
"Section 61(a) provides that gross income includes 'all income from whatever source derived.' This definition

is based upon the 16th Amendment and the word 'income' is used in its constitutional sense." H.R.Rep. No. 1337, supra, note 10, at A18.

A virtually identical statement appears in S.Rep. No. 1622, supra, note 10, at 168.

1. In other opinions the Supreme Court has not attempted an all encompassing definition of gross income. See, for example, Comm'r v. Wilcox, 327 U.S. 404, 407 (1946).

2. Lorenzo C. Dilks, 15 B.T.A. 1294 (1929); William H. Stayton, Jr., 32 B.T.A. 940 (1935).

3. United States v. Rochelle, 384 F.2d 748 (5th Cir. 1967).

At one time the line between loans and illegal income was difficult to draw. Initially, in Commissioner v. Wilcox [4] the Supreme Court did not tax embezzlers, because they could be compelled by victims to return the property involved. It analogized embezzlers to borrowers who, as suggested above, achieved no accession to wealth. Would a burglar's status be the same? Later in Rutkin v. United States,[5] the Court distinguished the receipts of an extortionist from those of an embezzler on the ground that an extortionist is less likely to be asked for repayment, taxing that kind of illegal loot. Still later, however, in James v. United States [6] the Court overruled *Wilcox* outright, deciding that illegal gain is income despite a legal obligation to make restitution.[7]

Beginning students in income taxation or anyone else for that matter may reasonably question whether gross income includes wealth acquired by illegal means, but the Supreme Court has left little doubt. Supplying an affirmative answer in *James*, the Court provided the following convenient summary of the area: [8]

It had been a well-established principle * * * that unlawful, as well as lawful gains are comprehended within the term "gross income". Section 11B of the Income Tax Act of 1913 provided that "the net income of a taxable person shall include gains, profits, and income * * * from * * * the transaction of any *lawful* business carried on for gain or profit, or gains or profits and income derived from any source whatever. * * *" (Emphasis supplied.) 38 Stat. 167. When the statute was amended in 1916, the one word "lawful" was omitted. This revealed, we think, the obvious intent of that Congress to tax income derived from both legal and illegal sources, to remove the incongruity of having the gains of the honest laborer taxed and the gains of the dishonest immune. Rutkin v. United States, supra, at p. 138; United States v. Sullivan, 274 U.S. 259, 263. Thereafter, the Court held that gains from illicit traffic in liquor are includible within "gross income". Ibid. * * * And, the Court has pointed out, with approval, that there "has been a widespread and settled administrative and judicial recognition of the taxability of unlawful gains of many kinds," Rutkin v. United States, supra, at p. 137. These include protection payments made to racketeers, ran-

4. Supra, note 1.

5. 343 U.S. 130 (1952).

6. 366 U.S. 213 (1961).

7. The *James* case which is involved with timing is included in the text in Chapter 19, infra page 564. The series of cases is discussed in Libin and

Haydon, "Embezzled Funds as Taxable Income: A Study in Judicial Footwork," 61 Mich.L.Rev. 425 (1963) and Bittker, "Taxing Income from Unlawful Activities," 25 Case West.L. Rev. 130 (1974).

8. Supra note 6 at 218. See also Reg. § 1.61–14.

som payments paid to kidnappers, bribes, money derived from the sale of unlawful insurance policies, graft, black market gains, funds obtained from the operation of lotteries, income from race track bookmaking and illegal prize fight pictures. Ibid.[9]

The taxation of illegal gains has caused some interesting results. It was the evasion of income tax laws and not a conviction of murder, robbery, or some similar crime that led to the conviction and imprisonment of gangster Al Capone in 1931.[10] A taxpayer's attempt to create some black letter law (bathed perhaps in red light) failed when the Tax Court said, in effect: Madame, the wages of sin are not exempt from taxation! [11] One judge who disagreed with treating illegal pilfering the same as legal profiting was Judge Martin Manton of the Second Circuit Court of Appeals who felt such action was degrading to the government.[12] Ironically, the same Judge Manton was later held liable for tax on bribes accepted to influence his decisions,[13] after having been convicted,[14] imprisoned and disbarred for accepting the bribes. The Commissioner has been successful in taxing some scurrilous swindlers. In Akers v. Scofield [15] an ingenious scheme involving maps, hidden "gold" bars, and an intrigued and probably greedy widow was successful up to a point but hit the fiscal fan when the Commissioner successfully taxed the swindler's proceeds. In a more timely vein, the Commissioner has been successful in taxing gains on the illegal sale of narcotics.[16]

Although the judicial opinions speak in terms of the question whether an illegal receipt is gross income and, if so, when, a third dimension of this problem is less often expressed. If a pickpocket's daily take is gross income, his failure to report it ultimately on his Form 1040 is itself a crime.[17] And it is of course a federal crime. One wonders therefore how much a desire to add a federal sanction to existing state sanctions for various offenses may affect the seeming effort to define and time the receipt of gross income.

9. Reporting of such gains can raise important 5th Amendment self-incrimination questions. See United States v. Sullivan, 274 U.S. 259 (1927), and Chapter 28, Part B of the text, infra page 981.

10. See Bittker, supra note 7.

11. Blanche E. Lane, 15 T.C.M. 1088 (1956).

12. The argument was offered in his concurring opinion in Steinberg v. United States, 14 F.2d 564, 569 (2d Cir. 1926).

13. Martin T. Manton, 7 T.C.M. 937 (1948). Judge Manton's philosophy is considered in greater detail in the Bittker article cited supra note 7.

14. United States v. Manton, 107 F.2d 834 (2d Cir. 1938), cert. den. 309 U.S. 664 (1940).

15. 167 F.2d 718 (5th Cir. 1948), cert. den. 335 U.S. 823 (1948).

16. Farina v. McMahon, 1958–2 U.S. T.C. para. 9938 (D.N.Y.1958).

17. See, e. g., I.R.C. §§ 7201 and 7206.

PROBLEMS

1. Winner attends the opening of a new department store. All persons attending are given free raffle tickets for a digital watch worth $200. Disregarding any possible application of I.R.C. § 74, must Winner include anything within gross income when she wins the watch in the raffle?

2. Would the results to the taxpayer in the *Cesarini* case be different if instead of discovering $4467 in old currency in the piano, he discovered that the piano, a Steinway, was the first Steinway piano ever built and it is worth $5000?

3. Employee has worked for Employer's incorporated business for several years at a salary of $40,000 per year. Another company is attempting to hire Employee but Employer persuades him to agree to stay for at least two more years by giving him 2% of the company's stock, which is worth $20,000, and by buying Employee's spouse a new car worth $5000. How much income does Employee realize from these transactions?

4. Insurance Adjuster refers his clients to an auto repair firm that gives him a kickback of 10% of billings on all referrals.

   (a) Does Adjuster have gross income?

   (b) Even if the arrangement violates local law?

5. Owner agrees to rent Tenant his lake house for the summer for $4000.

   (a) How much income does Owner realize if he agrees to charge only $1000 if Tenant makes certain improvements to the house at a cost to Tenant of $3000?

   (b) Is there a difference in result to Owner in (a), above, if Tenant effects exactly the same improvements but does all the labor himself and incurs a total cost of only $500? *[handwritten: fmv of Value received]*

   (c) Are there any tax consequences to Tenant in part (b), above? *[handwritten: Satisfaction of 2,500 Debt]*

6. Under a nationally advertised plan, Consumer purchases a new automobile from Dealer at a cost of $5500 and subsequently receives a $500 cash rebate from the manufacturer. Must Consumer include the $500 rebate in income? See Rev.Rul. 76–96, 1976–1 C.B. 23. *[handwritten: Reduction of Purchase Price]*

C. INCOME WITHOUT RECEIPT OF CASH OR PROPERTY

Internal Revenue Code: Section 61.
Regulations: Sections 1.61–2(a)(1), –2(d)(2)(i).

HELVERING v. INDEPENDENT LIFE INSURANCE CO.*

Supreme Court of the United States, 1934.
292 U.S. 371, 54 S.Ct. 758.

[This case raised the question whether a taxpayer must include in gross income the rental value of a building owned and occupied by the taxpayer. Whether or not the statute purported to subject that value to the income tax, it was the taxpayer's position that such a tax was foreclosed by Article I, § 9, cl. 4 of the Constitution, which requires the apportionment of direct taxes. See the discussion of basic constitutional principles in Chapter 1 at page 14.   The Court sustained this position, saying in part:]

If the statute lays taxes on the part of the building occupied by the owner or upon the rental value of that space, it cannot be sustained, for that would be to lay a direct tax requiring apportionment. * * * The rental value of the building used by the owner does not constitute income within the meaning of the Sixteenth Amendment.

CHANDLER v. COMMISSIONER

United States Court of Appeals, Third Circuit, 1941.
119 F.2d 623.

Before ALLEN, HAMILTON, and MARTIN, CIRCUIT JUDGES.

* * *

Rental Value of Brandywine Lodge. Brandywine Farms Corporation was organized in 1926. Chandler owned all its capital stock from 1926 until February 8, 1930, when he transferred all the shares to the trust herein involved. The main business of the corporation consisted in the purchase and sale of stocks. It also owned approximately 450 acres of farm land at Pocopson, Chester County, Pennsylvania. During the taxable years 1934 and 1935 Chandler and his family occupied Brandywine Lodge, a dwelling house located upon this property, rent free. Its reasonable rental value was stipulated to be $4,000 per annum. Chandler performed substantial services for the corporation

---

* See Goode, The Individual Income Tax, pp. 120–129 (1964), reprinted in Sander and Westfall, Readings in Federal Taxation, 290 (Foundation Press 1970); Marsh, "The Taxation of Imputed Income," 58 Pol.Sci.Q. 514 (1943). Ed.

and was its president during the taxable years in question. The Commissioner included the rental value of the residence in Chandler's gross income. The Board found that the privilege of using the Lodge rent free was given to Chandler by the corporation not as a gratuity but as compensation for the services which he rendered and that the value of that privilege was therefore properly included as income.

Somewhat similar situations existed in Hillman v. Commissioner, 3 Cir., 71 F.2d 688 and Richards v. Commissioner, 5 Cir., 111 F.2d 376, which are cited to us by Chandler. In the Hillman case the taxpayer conveyed property to a family corporation whose entire stock was owned by the taxpayer, his wife and children. The taxpayer and his family occupied rent free a house owned by the corporation which paid the taxes out of corporate income. The Commissioner included the estimated rental value of the family residence in the taxpayer's gross income; the Board sustained the Commissioner except that it reduced the amount of the rental value. This court reversed on the ground that in the absence of an express agreement to pay rent none may be implied, since the parties involved were all members of the family. In the Richards case the taxpayers, husband and wife, owned all the stock of a corporation which held title to two residences occupied by the taxpayers and their children rent free. The purpose of having title in the corporation was to create interests which were readily transferable in the event of the death of either or both taxpayers. The Commissioner included the rental value in the taxpayers' income, and was sustained by the Board. The Circuit Court of Appeals reversed, the majority holding that the rent free use of the residence was a gift.

Chandler relies upon the Hillman and Richards cases as authority for his position that the rental value of a house occupied by the taxpayer as a family residence rent free, where title is held by a family corporation controlled by the taxpayer, is not income to him. It is possible to distinguish these cases, for in neither was there a finding by the Board such as was made in the present case that the right to occupy the house rent free was granted by the corporation as compensation for services rendered by the taxpayer. Of greater significance, we think, is the fact that this court in the Hillman case and the Circuit Court of Appeals for the Fifth Circuit in the Richards case failed to give any effect to the separate existence of the corporation holding title to the property. As indicated in the dissenting opinion in the Richards case corporations are separate taxpayers whose existence as entities separate from their stockholders is seldom ignored in tax matters. See White's Will v. Commissioner, 3 Cir., 119 F.2d 619. A corporate officer or stockholder may receive the right to use corporate property rent free in lieu of a money compensation for services rendered or as a dividend, but it may not be presumed that the corporate directors have given away as a gratuity a valuable right to use the corporate property. Ordinarily such action would be beyond their power. Noel v. Parrott, 4 Cir., 15 F.2d 669, certiorari denied, 273 U.S. 754, 47 S.Ct. 457, 71 L.Ed. 875; Wolter v. Johnston, 3 Cir., 34 F.2d 598, 68 A.L.R. 1211, certiorari denied, 280 U.S. 606, 50 S.Ct. 153, 74 L.Ed. 650; Fletcher, Cyc.Corp., Perm.Ed., § 2939. Reasoning such as that advanced in the Hillman case that a gift is presumed because of the family relationship between the parties overlooks, we think, the fact that a corporation is not "related" to its stockholders, directors and officers. That purely artificial modern concept, the stock company, does not form a segment in the oldest of all human relationships, the family circle. The corporate "person" may be deemed by a fiction of the law to have abilities normally ascribed to man but that fiction cannot be indulged to the extent of endowing the corporation with feelings of love and affection for its stockholders, officers and directors. It is only because of the love and affection which a normal human donor feels for members of his family that it is presumed by the law that a transfer of property by him to them is a gift. The basis for such a presumption is entirely absent when the donor is a corporation. We are not persuaded by the rationale of either opinion and insofar as Hillman v. Commissioner, supra, is in conflict with our decision it is overruled.

Chandler argues that the Board erred in finding that the right to occupy Brandywine Lodge rent free was compensation and claims that this right arose by reason of the express terms of the trust agreement, but in this contention he again ignores the fact that the corporation which provided the Lodge is a separate entity which is not a party to the trust agreement. We conclude that the rental value of Brandywine Lodge was properly included in Chandler's income.

Maintenance Expenses of Brandywine Lodge. Brandywine Farms Corporation paid the following maintenance and operating expenses during 1934 and 1935:

	1934	1935
General expense	$ 288.22	$ 366.54
Oil and gas	1241.79	1257.08
Stable supplies	222.70	158.05
Coal	89.76	75.68
Auto expense	206.78	175.68
Garden supplies	952.91	376.17
Telephone	421.34	363.16
Electricity	722.01	605.13
Fertilizer and feed	75.95	96.30
Poultry expense	254.10	337.18
Stable food	313.39	225.95
Household salaries	6045.75	4650.00
Total	10,834.70	8,686.92

The Board allocated to the corporation as ordinary and necessary expenses in carrying on its business the following:

	1934	1935
General expense	$144.11	$183.27
Fertilizer and feed	75.95	96.30
Household salaries	432.00	432.00
Total	$652.06	$711.57

Everything in excess of these operating expenses of the corporation was treated by the Commissioner as maintenance expenses for Chandler's residence, and consequently as his income. The Commissioner was sustained by the Board, which deemed these expenditures "personal, living, or family expenses" of Chandler within the meaning of Section 24(a) (1) of the Revenue Act of 1934, 26 U.S.C.A. Int.Rev. Acts page 675,* which had the effect of discharging his family obligations.

Chandler contends that the burden was upon the Commissioner to establish the relative sums expended for the Lodge property and the farm property as a whole, that the Commissioner did not meet this burden and that the Board had no basis for the allocation which was made. The Board based its allocation upon the testimony of Harry D. Brown, Jr., the treasurer of Brandywine Farms Corporation for 1934 and 1935. It accepted his estimate that 50% of the item designated general expenses, 40% of the salary of one of the farm employees and all of the costs for fertilizer and seed were expended on behalf of the farms. He also testified that all of the expenditures for stable food, and the bulk of the oil and gas expenditures were for the Lodge and the home of the overseer. There is no direct testimony that the remaining expenditures were for the Lodge but the very nature of some of the expenditures makes this a reasonable conclusion. As to them the Board had to speculate to a certain extent in order to make its allocation. It is significant that Chandler, who is in the best position to know if any of the expenditures allocated to the Lodge were in fact for the farm, has not attacked the Board's action save in very general terms. We conclude that the Board was justified in the allocation which it made.

Chandler argues that no part of these expenditures was income to him. He relies upon Commissioner v. Plant, 2 Cir., 76 F.2d 8, as well as upon Hillman v. Commissioner, supra, and Richards v. Commissioner, supra, previously discussed. Commissioner v. Plant is clearly distinguishable. In that case the taxpayer as beneficiary of a trust was permitted to use as a summer residence a house owned by the trustees. The expenditures made were for the preservation of the trust res. In the present case Chandler was under a legal obligation to provide and maintain a home for his family suitable to their station in life. The payment by the corporation of the ex-

* See I.R.C. § 262. Ed.

penses of maintaining the home selected by Chandler as his family residence did in legal effect discharge this obligation. Hill v. Commissioner, 8 Cir., 88 F.2d 941. That the substantial discharge of a legal obligation of the taxpayer represents for tax purposes a distribution to him is now well settled. Helvering v. Fitch, 309 U.S. 149, 60 S.Ct. 427, 84 L.Ed. 665. There was no error in including in Chandler's income the costs of maintaining his home at Brandywine Lodge.

Rent and Assessments of Park Avenue Apartment. The trustee paid $6,190.06 in 1934 and $5,658.48 in 1935 for rent and assessments on the Park Avenue apartment in New York City, occupied by Chandler and his family as a family residence for at least four months of each year. For the reasons already stated we are of the opinion that these payments were properly treated as income to Chandler under the terms of Section 24(a) (1) of the Revenue Act of 1934.

The decision of the Board of Tax Appeals is affirmed.

J. SIMPSON DEAN *

Tax Court of the United States, 1961.
35 T.C. 1083. (NA).   *Non Acquiescence*

Opinion   *Commissioner disagrees & will try again*

RAUM, JUDGE: The Commissioner determined deficiencies in income tax against petitioners for 1955 and 1956 in the amounts of $13,875.61 and $16,383.86, respectively. Petitioners are husband and wife; they filed joint returns for 1955 and 1956 with the director of internal revenue at Wilmington, Delaware. To the extent that the deficiencies still remain in controversy they raise the question whether petitioners were entitled to deduct as interest the amounts of $9,243.38 in 1955 and $26,912.02 in 1956 representing interest on loans on life insurance policies which had accrued and which was paid by them after they had made irrevocable assignments of such policies to their children. An amended answer filed by the Commissioner claims increases in the deficiencies already determined by adding thereto the amounts of $105,181.50 and $119,796.78 for 1955 and 1956, respectively. Such increases raise a single issue, unrelated to the original deficiencies, namely, whether petitioners realized taxable income to the extent of the alleged economic benefit derived from the interest-free use of funds which they had borrowed from a family corporation controlled by them. The facts have been stipulated.

* * *

[Only the portion of the opinion dealing with the interest-free loans is presented.]

* See O'Hare, "The Taxation of Interest-Free Loans," 27 Vand.L.Rev. 1085 (1974), and Schlifke, "Taxing as Income the Receipt of Interest-Free Loans," 33 U.Chi.L.Rev. 346 (1966). Ed.

The Commissioner's amended answer charged petitioners with income equal to interest at the alleged legal rate in Delaware (6 percent) with respect to loans which they had obtained upon non-interest-bearing notes from their controlled corporation, Nemours Corporation, and which were outstanding during 1955 and 1956. The theory of the amended answer was that the petitioners realized income to the extent of the economic benefit derived from the free use of borrowed funds from Nemours, and that such economic benefit was equal to interest at the legal rate in Delaware, alleged to be 6 percent per annum. However, the Commissioner's brief has reduced the amount of his additional claim so that the income thus attributed to petitioners is measured, not by the legal rate of interest, but by the prime rate, since it is stipulated that petitioners could have borrowed the funds at the prime rate. As thus reduced, the additional income which the Commissioner seeks to charge to petitioners is $65,648.79 for 1955 and $97,931.71 for 1956. The facts in relation to this issue have been stipulated as follows:

9. Prior to December 17, 1954 the entire issued and outstanding capital stock of Nemours Corporation, hereinafter referred to as Nemours, organized under the laws of the State of Delaware with principal office in Wilmington, Delaware, consisting of 36,172 shares of no par common, was owned by the petitioners, as follows:

J. Simpson Dean _____ 7,249 shares
Paulina duPont Dean _____ 28,923 shares

10. On December 17, 1954 each of the petitioners made a gift of 2,000 shares of the stock of Nemours to the above-mentioned trusts created by them in 1937 for the benefit of their children. In the years 1955 and 1956 the petitioners owned 32,172 shares of no par common of Nemours.

11. For the taxable year 1955 Nemours was a personal holding company under section 542 of the Internal Revenue Code of 1954 and filed its Federal income tax returns as such.

12. For the taxable year 1956 Nemours filed its Federal income tax return as a regular business corporation. By notice of deficiency dated March 2, 1960, respondent determined that Nemours was a personal holding company for the year 1956. An appeal from such determination was taken by Nemours and the matter is now pending before this Court in Docket No. 86863, entitled Nemours Corporation v. Commissioner of Internal Revenue.

13. Petitioner J. Simpson Dean owed Nemours on non-interest bearing notes the following amounts:

Period	Amount
January 1, 1955 to January 10, 1955	$302,185.73
January 11, 1955 to December 31, 1955	223,861.56
January 1, 1956 to December 31, 1956	357,293.41

14. Petitioner Paulina duPont Dean owed Nemours on non-interest bearing notes the following amounts:

Period	Amount
January 1, 1955 to December 31, 1955	$1,832,764.71
January 1, 1956 to December 31, 1956	2,205,804.66

15. The following are the prime rates of interest and the dates on which changes were made in such rates at which the petitioners could have borrowed money during the years 1955 and 1956:

January 1, 1955	3%
August 15, 1955	3¼%
October 20, 1955	3½%
April 20, 1956	3¾%
September 1, 1956	4%
December 31, 1956	4%

16. Interest computed at the prime rates shown in the preceding paragraph on the non-interest bearing notes of the petitioners for the taxable years 1955 and 1956 would be as follows:

Year 1955:	Amount
J. Simpson Dean	$7,203.98
Paulina duPont Dean	58,444.81
Total	$65,648.79

Year 1956:	Amount
J. Simpson Dean	$13,651.59
Paulina duPont Dean	84,280.12
Total	$97,931.71

[Paragraph 17 of the stipulation, objected to by respondent as to relevancy,[1] states that if petitioners had paid interest to Nemours, the corporation would have made dividend distributions to petitioners equal to the amount of such interest, and further sets forth the effect, taxwise and otherwise, upon petitioners, Nemours, and the trusts, based upon that hypothesis as well as certain other assumptions.]

The theory of the Commissioner's amended answer, as modified in his brief, undoubtedly had its origin in a statement by this Court in a Memorandum Opinion involving certain gift taxes of these taxpayers, Paulina duPont Dean, T.C. Memo. 1960–54, on appeal (C.A. 3), where it was said:

Viewed realistically, the lending of over two million dollars to petitioners without interest might be looked upon as a means of passing on earnings (certainly potential earnings) of Nemours in lieu of dividends, to the extent of a reasonable interest on such loans. * * *

1. We find it unnecessary to rule upon that objection, since we reach the result herein without reliance upon paragraph 17.

The amended answer herein was filed within several months after the foregoing Memorandum Opinion had been promulgated. The statement quoted above was mere dictum and we have not been directed to any case holding or even suggesting that an interest-free loan may result in the realization of taxable income by the debtor, or to any administrative ruling or regulation taking that position. Although the question may not be completely free from doubt we think that no taxable income is realized in such circumstances.

In support of its present position, the Government relies primarily upon a series of cases holding that rent-free use of corporate property by a stockholder or officer may result in the realization of income. Charles A. Frueauff, 30 B.T.A. 449 (rent-free use of corporation's apartment); Reynard Corporation, 30 B.T.A. 451 (rent-free use of corporation's house); Percy M. Chandler, 41 B.T.A. 165, affirmed 119 F.2d 623 (C.A.3) (rent-free use of corporation's apartment and lodge); Paulina duPont Dean, 9 T.C. 256 (rent-free use of corporation's house); Dean v. Commissioner, 187 F.2d 1019 (C.A.3), affirming a Memorandum Opinion of this Court (rent-free use of corporation's house); Rodgers Dairy Co., 14 T.C. 66 (personal use of corporation's automobile). Cf. Louis Greenspon, 23 T.C. 138, affirmed on this point but reversed on other grounds 229 F.2d 947 (C.A.8) (farm expenses paid by corporation); Alex Silverman, 28 T.C. 1061, affirmed 253 F.2d 849 (C.A.8) (wife's travel expenses paid by corporation); Chester Distributing Co. v. Commissioner, 184 F.2d 514 (C.A.3), affirming per curiam a Memorandum Opinion of this Court (personal entertainment expenses paid by corporation). These cases bear a superficial resemblance to the present case, but reflection convinces us that they are not in point. In each of them a benefit was conferred upon the stockholder or officer in circumstances such that had the stockholder or officer undertaken to procure the same benefit by an expenditure of money such expenditure would not have been deductible by him. Here, on the other hand, had petitioners borrowed the funds in question on interest-bearing notes, their payment of interest would have been fully deductible by them under section 163, I.R.C.1954. Not only would they not be charged with the additional income in controversy herein, but they would have a deduction equal to that very amount. We think this circumstance differentiates the various cases relied upon by the Commissioner, and perhaps explains why he has apparently never taken this position in any prior case.

We have heretofore given full force to interest-free loans for tax purposes, holding that they result in no interest deduction for the borrower, A. Backus, Jr. & Sons, 6 B.T.A. 590; Rainbow Gasoline Corporation, 31 B.T.A. 1050; Howell Turpentine Co., 6 T.C. 364, reversed on another issue 162 F.2d 316 (C.A.5); D. Loveman & Son Export Corporation, 34 T.C. 776, nor interest income to the lender, Combs Lumber Co., 41 B.T.A. 339; Society Brand Clothes, Inc., 18 T.C. 304; Brandtjen & Kluge, Inc., 34 T.C. 416. We think it to be equally true that an interest-free loan results in no taxable gain to the borrower,[2] and we hold that the Commissioner is not entitled to any increased deficiency based upon this issue.

Reviewed by the Court.

Decision will be entered under Rule 50.

FISHER, J., concurs in the result.

[handwritten marginalia: entire court looked at case]

[handwritten marginalia: Today Rule 155]

[handwritten marginalia: Decision on point, need to go back + calculate dollar value of loan, list]

OPPER, J., concurring: The necessity is not apparent to me of deciding more on the second issue than that there can be no deficiency. If petitioners were in receipt of some kind of gross income, possibly comparable to that dealt with in such cases as Charles A. Frueauff, 30 B.T.A. 449 (1934), the corresponding interest deduction would perhaps exactly offset and nullify it. But because that would mean that there is no deficiency, it would not necessarily follow that there was no gross income, as the present opinion, in my view, gratuitously holds. Certainly the statement that "an interest-free loan results in no taxable gain to the borrower" is much too broad a generalization to make here.

Suppose, for example, that in such a case as Charles A. Frueauff, supra, the property made available without charge to the shareholder-officer was rented by him to another, instead of being occupied for personal use. Would the fact that he could presumably deduct as a business or nonbusiness expense the hypothetical rental value theoretically paid by him to the corporation, section 212, I.R.C.1954, and thereby completely offset any gross income, lead us to conclude, as here, contrary to that whole line of cases, that there could be no gross income in the first place?

Or suppose the facts showed that the indebtedness was "incurred * * * to purchase or carry obligations * * * the interest on which is wholly exempt from * * * taxes." Sec. 265(2), I.R.C. 1954.

This being apparently a case of first impression, the present result seems peculiarly unfortunate in deciding a point that need not be passed on. To make matters worse, the burden here is on respondent, since the issue was first raised by his answer;[1] and thus in this lead-

---

2. As recently as 1955, this was also the view of the Commissioner. In Rev.Rul. 55–713, 1955–2 C.B. 23, in sanctioning the so-called split-dollar insurance scheme, it is said at page 24: "In the instant case, the substance of the insurance arrangement between the parties is in all essential respects the same as if Y corporation makes annual loans without interest, of a sum of money equal to the annual increases in the cash surrender value of the policies of insurance taken out on the life of B. The mere making available of money does not result in realized income to the payee or a deduction to the payor."

1. See, e. g., Rainbow Gasoline Corporation, 31 B.T.A. 1050 (1935), decided partly for petitioner and partly for respondent entirely on the question of burden of proof.

ing case all factual conclusions and inferences must be favorable to petitioners. Cf., e. g., Spheeris v. Commissioner, 284 F.2d 928 (C.A.7, 1960), affirming a Memorandum Opinion of this Court. Disposition of the issue as one of generally applicable law is hence doubly unnecessary.

TIETJENS, WITHEY, and DRENNEN, JJ., agree with this concurring opinion.

———

BRUCE, J., dissenting: I respectfully dissent from the opinion of the majority with respect to the second issue. In my opinion the present case is not distinguishable in principle from such cases as Paulina duPont Dean, 9 T.C. 256; Chandler v. Commissioner, 119 F.2d 623 (C.A.3), affirming 41 B.T.A. 165, and other cases cited by the majority, wherein it was held that the rent-free use of corporate property by a stockholder or officer resulted in the realization of income. "Interest" in the sense that it represents compensation paid for the use, forbearance, or detention of money, may be likened to "rent" which is paid for the use of property.

I agree with Judge Opper in his concurring opinion that "the statement that 'an interest-free loan results in no taxable gain to the borrower' is much too broad a generalization to make here." I do not wish to infer that the interest-free loan of money should be construed as resulting in taxable income to the borrower in every instance. However, it is difficult to believe that the interest-free loan of in excess of $2 million ($2,563,098.07 throughout 1956) by a personal holding company to its majority stockholders (its only stockholders prior to December 17, 1954) did not result in any economic benefit to the borrower.

In my opinion, the statement that "had petitioners borrowed the funds in question on interest-bearing notes, their payment of interest would have been fully deductible by them under section 163, I.R.C. 1954," is likewise too broad a generalization to make here.

Section 163(a) states the "General Rule" to be that "There shall be allowed as a deduction all interest paid or accrued within the taxable year on indebtedness." Section 265(2) provides, however, that—

No deduction shall be allowed for—

* * * * * * *, * * *

(2) INTEREST.—Interest on indebtedness incurred or continued to purchase or carry obligations * * * the interest on which is wholly exempt from the taxes imposed by this subtitle.

Section 265(2) is specifically included in the cross references contained in subsection (c) of section 163 and is therefore clearly intended as an exception to, or limitation upon, section 163(a). For obligations, the interest on which is wholly exempt from taxes, see section 103 of the Internal Revenue Code of 1954.

It is recognized that the burden with respect to the issue here presented by his amended answer is upon the respondent. This burden, however, was, in my opinion, discharged by the stipulated facts presented. It was incumbent upon the petitioners, if such were the facts, to plead and establish that had they been required to pay interest on the loans in question they would have been entitled to deduct such interest from their gross income. They have done neither. It is well established that deductions are matters of legislative grace and must be clearly established.

On the record presented herein, I do not agree that "had petitioners borrowed the funds in question on interest-bearing notes, their payment of interest would have been fully deductible by them under section 163," and that the inclusion in the gross income of the petitioners of an amount representing a reasonable rate of interest on the loans in question would therefore result in no deficiency.

PROBLEMS

1. Vegy grows vegetables in his garden. Does Vegy have gross income when: *Not suff*

1.61-4b (a) Vegy harvests his crop? *No   No realized income*

(b) Vegy and his family consume $100 worth of vegetables? *No*

(c) Vegy sells vegetables for $100? *Yes - realized income*

(d) Vegy exchanges $100 worth of vegetables with Charlie for $100 worth of tuna which Charlie caught? *Yes 100 of income*

(e) Vegy agrees with Grocer to sell his vegetables in Grocer's market which previously did not have a vegetable section. Grocer pays $50 per month to landlord for the portion of the market used by Vegy but Grocer does not charge Vegy any rent. Vegy keeps all proceeds from his sales. *No taxable income*

2. Doctor needs to have his income tax return prepared. Lawyer would like a general physical check up. Doctor would normally charge $100 for the physical and Lawyer would normally charge $100 for the income tax return preparation.

(a) What tax consequences to each if they simply swap services without any money changing hands?

(b) Does Lawyer realize any income when he fills out his own tax return?

CHAPTER 4. THE EXCLUSION OF GIFTS AND INHERITANCES

A. RULES OF INCLUSION AND EXCLUSION

Internal Revenue Code: Section 102(a) and (b) first sentence.

As Chapter 3 illustrates, gross income is a very broad concept. Over the years, numerous administrative and judicial decisions have gone a long way toward delineating its scope. Nevertheless, partly because of past uncertainties and partly because of a desire to accord special treatment for some types of receipts or benefits, Congress has been unwilling to rely on gross income, unexplained or only generally defined, as the starting point in the computation of federal income tax liability. Instead, two series of sections have undertaken to say that certain items are specifically includible in gross income, or partially includible, I.R.C. (26 U.S.C.A.) §§ 71–84, and other items are specifically excludible from gross income, or partially excludible, §§ 101–124. As cases such as *Cesarini* and *Glenshaw Glass* set out in Chapter 3 indicate, these special statutory rules do not purport to be exhaustive; some questions remain to be answered without special statutory help under the general definition of gross income in I.R.C. (26 U.S.C.A.) § 61. But of course when an explicit statutory provision is applicable it takes precedence over the general definition. Thus, although dividends are given as an illustration of an item of gross income in § 61 (a) (7), up to $100 of dividend income may be excluded from gross income by reason of the special rules of § 116. In the materials that follow, be sure to differentiate exclusions from gross income from deductions available in determining taxable income which have a similar but not identical effect.

It is not possible to present a definition of gross income that will answer all questions which may arise. But here is a kind of check-list that may be helpful and which will be more meaningful as the study of gross income progresses:

Gross income includes the receipt of any financial benefit which is:

1. Not a mere return of capital, and

2. Not accompanied by a contemporaneously acknowledged obligation to repay, and

3. Not excluded by a specific statutory provision, and (as will be seen)

4. Not within the concept of a tax-free fringe benefit.

A comparatively simple, long-standing exclusionary rule is found in § 102. We begin with it. It often comes as a surprise to a taxpayer who has grown accustomed to the income tax bite to learn that when Uncle Harry died and left him securities worth $10,000 the amount will not appear at all on his Form 1040. The section may safely be read fairly literally and is as generous as it sounds. Could Congress tax such receipts as income?

Of course if the securities received produce dividends for the taxpayer, the dividends must be treated as income, except for the $100 exclusion under § 116. Perhaps redundantly, the statute makes this clear in § 102(b) (1).

Somewhat less certain at an earlier time was the taxpayer's status if Uncle Harry left him the right only to the income from securities, perhaps by way of a trust under which the securities themselves were to be retained for a remainderman who would get them upon the taxpayer's death. In the famous case of Irwin v. Gavit, 268 U.S. 161, 45 S.Ct. 475 (1924), the Supreme Court held, in effect, that language such as now appears in § 102(a), excluding from gross income property acquired by bequest, did not exclude a gift *of the income* from property. A codification of that principle now appears in § 102(b) (2).

We are steering you away from the last two sentences of § 102 (b). A gift, perhaps in trust, may assure the taxpayer of a steady flow of money over a period of years or for his life. A question then arises whether this is an excluded gift of property or an included gift of the income from property, or partly each. These last two sentences are a partial answer to the question; but the final answer is left to Subchapter J, §§ 641–692. The broad outline of Subchapter J is suggested in Chapter 14, infra at page 301; but its provisions must be studied in detail before the full significance of the last two sentences of § 102(b) can be grasped. Such study is generally undertaken in a separate course on the income taxation of trusts and estates.

Some other questions that arise in the application of § 102 are manageable here and are suggested in the materials that follow in this chapter.

B. THE INCOME TAX MEANING OF GIFT

Internal Revenue Code: Sections 101(b)(1) through (2)(B), first sentence; 102(a), (b) first sentence; 274(b)(1).
Regulations: Section 1.102–1(a), (b).

COMMISSIONER v. DUBERSTEIN *

Supreme Court of the United States, 1960.
363 U.S. 278, 80 S.Ct. 1190.

MR. JUSTICE BRENNAN delivered the opinion of the Court.

These two cases concern the provision of the Internal Revenue Code which excludes from the gross income of an income taxpayer "the value of property acquired by gift." [1] They pose the frequently recurrent question whether a specific transfer to a taxpayer in fact amounted to a "gift" to him within the meaning of the statute. The importance to decision of the facts of the cases requires that we state them in some detail.

No. 376, Commissioner v. Duberstein. The taxpayer, Duberstein,[2] was president of the Duberstein Iron & Metal Company, a corporation with headquarters in Dayton, Ohio. For some years the taxpayer's company had done business with Mohawk Metal Corporation, whose headquarters were in New York City. The president of Mohawk was one Berman. The taxpayer and Berman had generally used the telephone to transact their companies' business with each other, which consisted of buying and selling metals. The taxpayer testified, without elaboration, that he knew Berman "personally" and had known him for about seven years. From time to time in their telephone conversations, Berman would ask Duberstein whether the latter knew of potential customers for some of Mohawk's products in which Duberstein's company itself was not interested. Duberstein provided the names of potential customers for these items.

One day in 1951 Berman telephoned Duberstein and said that the information Duberstein had given him had proved so helpful that he wanted to give the latter a present. Duberstein stated that Berman owed him nothing. Berman said that he had a Cadillac as a gift for Duberstein, and that the latter should send to New York for it; Berman insisted that Duberstein accept the car, and the latter finally did so, protesting however that he had not intended to be compensated for

---

* See Klein, "An Enigma in the Federal Income Tax: The Meaning of the Word 'Gift'," 48 Minn.L.Rev. 215 (1963). Ed.

1. The operative provision in the cases at bar is § 22(b)(3) of the 1939 Internal Revenue Code. The correspond-

ing provision of the present Code is § 102(a).

2. In both cases the husband will be referred to as the taxpayer, although his wife joined with him in joint tax returns.

the information. At the time Duberstein already had a Cadillac and an Oldsmobile, and felt that he did not need another car. Duberstein testified that he did not think Berman would have sent him the Cadillac if he had not furnished him with information about the customers. It appeared that Mohawk later deducted the value of the Cadillac as a business expense on its corporate income tax return.

Duberstein did not include the value of the Cadillac in gross income for 1951, deeming it a gift. The Commissioner asserted a deficiency for the car's value against him, and in proceedings to review the deficiency the Tax Court affirmed the Commissioner's determination. It said that "The record is significantly barren of evidence revealing any intention on the part of the payor to make a gift. * * * The only justifiable inference is that the automobile was intended by the payor to be remuneration for services rendered to it by Duberstein." The Court of Appeals for the Sixth Circuit reversed. 265 F. 2d 28.

No. 546, Stanton v. United States. The taxpayer, Stanton, had been for approximately 10 years in the employ of Trinity Church in New York City. He was comptroller of the Church corporation, and president of a corporation, Trinity Operating Company, the church set up as a fully owned subsidiary to manage its real estate holdings, which were more extensive than simply the church property. His salary by the end of his employment there in 1942 amounted to $22,500 a year. Effective November 30, 1942, he resigned from both positions to go into business for himself. The Operating Company's directors, who seem to have included the rector and vestrymen of the church, passed the following resolution upon his resignation: "Be it Resolved that in appreciation of the services rendered by Mr. Stanton * * * a gratuity is hereby awarded to him of Twenty Thousand Dollars, payable to him in equal instalments of Two Thousand Dollars at the end of each and every month commencing with the month of December, 1942; provided that, with the discontinuance of his services, the Corporation of Trinity Church is released from all rights and claims to pension and retirement benefits not already accrued up to November 30, 1942."

The Operating Company's action was later explained by one of its directors as based on the fact that, "Mr. Stanton was liked by all of the Vestry personally. He had a pleasing personality. He had come in when Trinity's affairs were in a difficult situation. He did a splendid piece of work, we felt. Besides that .   .   . he was liked by all of the members of the Vestry personally." And by another: "[W]e were all unanimous in wishing to make Mr. Stanton a gift. Mr. Stanton had loyally and faithfully served Trinity in a very difficult time. We thought of him in the highest regard. We understood that he was going in business for himself. We felt that he was entitled to that evidence of good will."

On the other hand, there was a suggestion of some ill-feeling between Stanton and the directors, arising out of the recent termination of the services of one Watkins, the Operating Company's treasurer, whose departure was evidently attended by some acrimony. At a special board meeting on October 28, 1942, Stanton had intervened on Watkins' side and asked reconsideration of the matter. The minutes reflect that "resentment was expressed as to the 'presumptuous' suggestion that the action of the Board, taken after long deliberation, should be changed." The Board adhered to its determination that Watkins be separated from employment, giving him an opportunity to resign rather than be discharged. At another special meeting two days later it was revealed that Watkins had not resigned; the previous resolution terminating his services was then viewed as effective; and the Board voted the payment of six months' salary to Watkins in a resolution similar to that quoted in regard to Stanton, but which did not use the term "gratuity." At the meeting, Stanton announced that in order to avoid any such embarrassment or question at any time as to his willingness to resign if the Board desired, he was tendering his resignation. It was tabled, though not without dissent. The next week, on November 5, at another special meeting, Stanton again tendered his resignation which this time was accepted.

The "gratuity" was duly paid. So was a smaller one to Stanton's (and the Operating Company's) secretary, under a similar resolution, upon her resignation at the same time. The two corporations shared the expense of the payments. There was undisputed testimony that there were in fact no enforceable rights or claims to pension and retirement benefits which had not accrued at the time of the taxpayer's resignation, and that the last proviso of the resolution was inserted simply out of an abundance of caution. The taxpayer received in cash a refund of his contributions to the retirement plans, and there is no suggestion that he was entitled to more. He was required to perform no further services for Trinity after his resignation.

The Commissioner asserted a deficiency against the taxpayer after the latter had failed to include the payments in question in gross income. After payment of the deficiency and administrative rejection of a refund claim, the taxpayer sued the United States for a refund in the District Court for the Eastern District of New York. The trial judge, sitting without a jury, made the simple finding that the payments were a "gift,"[3] and judgment was entered for the taxpayer. The Court of Appeals for the Second Circuit reversed. 268 F.2d 727.

The Government, urging that clarification of the problem typified by these two cases was necessary, and that the approaches taken by the Courts of Appeals for the Second and the Sixth Circuits were in conflict, petitioned for certiorari in No. 376, and acquiesced in the taxpayer's petition in No. 546. On this basis, and because of the im-

---

3. See note 14, infra.

To be made a

portance of the question in the administration of the income tax laws, we granted certiorari in both cases. 361 U.S. 923.

The exclusion of property acquired by gift from gross income under the federal income tax laws was made in the first income tax statute [4] passed under the authority of the Sixteenth Amendment, and has been a feature of the income tax statutes ever since. The meaning of the term "gift" as applied to particular transfers has always been a matter of contention.[5] Specific and illuminating legislative history on the point does not appear to exist. Analogies and inferences drawn from other revenue provisions, such as the estate and gift taxes, are dubious. See Lockard v. Commissioner, 166 F.2d 409. The meaning of the statutory term has been shaped largely by the decisional law. With this, we turn to the contentions made by the Government in these cases.

First. The Government suggests that we promulgate a new "test" in this area to serve as a standard to be applied by the lower courts and by the Tax Court in dealing with the numerous cases that arise.[6] We reject this invitation. We are of opinion that the governing principles are necessarily general and have already been spelled out in the opinions of this Court, and that the problem is one which, under the present statutory framework, does not lend itself to any more definitive statement that would produce a talisman for the solution of concrete cases. The cases at bar are fair examples of the settings in which the problem usually arises. They present situations in which payments have been made in a context with business overtones —an employer making a payment to a retiring employee; a businessman giving something of value to another businessman who has been of advantage to him in his business. In this context, we review the law as established by the prior cases here.

The course of decision here makes it plain that the statute does not use the term "gift" in the common-law sense, but in a more colloquial sense. This Court has indicated that a voluntary executed transfer of his property by one to another, without any consideration or compensation therefor, though a common-law gift, is not necessarily a "gift" within the meaning of the statute. For the Court has shown that the mere absence of a legal or moral obligation to make such a payment does not establish that it is a gift. Old Colony Trust Co. v. Commissioner, 279 U.S. 716, 730. And, importantly, if the payment proceeds primarily from "the constraining force of any moral or legal duty," or from "the incentive of anticipated benefit" of an economic nature, Bogardus v. Commissioner, 302 U.S. 34, 41, it is not a gift.

4. § II.B., c. 16, 38 Stat. 167.

5. The first case of the Board of Tax Appeals officially reported in fact deals with the problem. Parrott v. Commissioner, 1 B.T.A. 1.

6. The Government's proposed test is stated: "Gifts should be defined as transfers of property made for personal as distinguished from business reasons."

And, conversely, "[w]here the payment is in return for services rendered, it is irrelevant that the donor derives no economic benefit from it." Robertson v. United States, 343 U.S. 711, 714.[7] A gift in the statutory sense, on the other hand, proceeds from a "detached and disinterested generosity," Commissioner v. LoBue, 351 U.S. 243, 246; "out of affection, respect, admiration, charity or like impulses." Robertson v. United States, supra, at 714. And in this regard, the most critical consideration, as the Court was agreed in the leading case here, is the transferor's "intention." Bogardus v. Commissioner, 302 U.S. 34, 43. "What controls is the intention with which payment, however voluntary, has been made." Id., at 45 (dissenting opinion).[8]

The Government says that this "intention" of the transferor cannot mean what the cases on the common-law concept of gift call "donative intent." With that we are in agreement, for our decisions fully support this. Moreover, the *Bogardus* case itself makes it plain that the donor's characterization of his action is not determinative—that there must be an objective inquiry as to whether what is called a gift amounts to it in reality. 302 U.S., at 40. It scarcely needs adding that the parties' expectations or hopes as to the tax treatment of their conduct in themselves have nothing to do with the matter.

It is suggested that the *Bogardus* criterion would be more apt if rephrased in terms of "motive" rather than "intention." We must confess to some skepticism as to whether such a verbal mutation would be of any practical consequence. We take it that the proper criterion, established by decision here, is one that inquires what the basic reason for his conduct was in fact—the dominant reason that explains his action in making the transfer. Further than that we do not think it profitable to go.

Second. The Government's proposed "test," while apparently simple and precise in its formulation, depends frankly on a set of "principles" or "presumptions" derived from the decided cases, and concededly subject to various exceptions; and it involves various corollaries, which add to its detail. Were we to promulgate this test as a matter of law, and accept with it its various presuppositions and stated consequences, we would be passing far beyond the require-

---

7. The cases including "tips" in gross income are classic examples of this. See, e. g., Roberts v. Commissioner, 176 F.2d 221.

8. The parts of the *Bogardus* opinion which we touch on here are the ones we take to be basic to its holding, and the ones that we read as stating those governing principles which it establishes. As to them we see little distinction between the views of the Court and those taken in dissent in *Bogardus*. The fear expressed by the dissent at 302 U.S., at 44, that the prevailing opinion "seems" to hold "that every payment which in any aspect is a gift * * * relieved of any tax" strikes us now as going beyond what the opinion of the Court held in fact. In any event, the Court's opinion in *Bogardus* does not seem to have been so interpreted afterwards. The principal difference, as we see it, between the Court's opinion and the dissent lies in the weight to be given the findings of the trier of fact.

ments of the cases before us, and would be painting on a large canvas with indeed a broad brush. The Government derives its test from such propositions as the following: That payments by an employer to an employee, even though voluntary, ought, by and large, to be taxable; that the concept of a gift is inconsistent with a payment's being a deductible business expense; that a gift involves "personal" elements; that a business corporation cannot properly make a gift of its assets. The Government admits that there are exceptions and qualifications to these propositions. We think, to the extent they are correct, that these propositions are not principles of law but rather maxims of experience that the tribunals which have tried the facts of cases in this area have enunciated in explaining their factual determinations. Some of them simply represent truisms: it doubtless is, statistically speaking, the exceptional payment by an employer to an employee that amounts to a gift. Others are over-statements of possible evidentiary inferences relevant to a factual determination on the totality of circumstances in the case: it is doubtless relevant to the over-all inference that the transferor treats a payment as a business deduction, or that the transferor is a corporate entity. But these inferences cannot be stated in absolute terms. Neither factor is a shibboleth. The taxing statute does not make nondeductibility by the transferor a condition on the "gift" exclusion; nor does it draw any distinction, in terms, between transfers by corporations and individuals, as to the availability of the "gift" exclusion to the transferee. The conclusion whether a transfer amounts to a "gift" is one that must be reached on consideration of all the factors.

Specifically, the trier of fact must be careful not to allow trial of the issue whether the receipt of a specific payment is a gift to turn into a trial of the tax liability, or of the propriety, as a matter of fiduciary or corporate law, attaching to the conduct of someone else. The major corollary to the Government's suggested "test" is that, as an ordinary matter, a payment by a corporation cannot be a gift, and, more specifically, there can be no such thing as a "gift" made by a corporation which would allow it to take a deduction for an ordinary and necessary business expense. As we have said, we find no basis for such a conclusion in the statute; and if it were applied as a determinative rule of "law," it would force the tribunals trying tax cases involving the donee's liability into elaborate inquiries into the local law of corporations or into the peripheral deductibility of payments as business expenses. The former issue might make the tax tribunals the most frequent investigators of an important and difficult issue of the laws of the several States, and the latter inquiry would summon one difficult and delicate problem of federal tax law as an aid to the solution of another.[9] Or perhaps there would

9. Justice Cardozo once described in memorable language the inquiry into whether an expense was an "ordinary and necessary" one of a business:

be required a trial of the vexed issue whether there was a "constructive" distribution of corporate property, for income tax purposes, to the corporate agents who had sponsored the transfer.[10] These considerations, also, reinforce us in our conclusion that while the principles urged by the Government may, in nonabsolute form as crystallizations of experience, prove persuasive to the trier of facts in a particular case, neither they, nor any more detailed statement than has been made, can be laid down as a matter of law.

Third. Decision of the issue presented in these cases must be based ultimately on the application of the fact-finding tribunal's experience with the mainsprings of human conduct to the totality of the facts of each case. The nontechnical nature of the statutory standard, the close relationship of it to the data of practical human experience, and the multiplicity of relevant factual elements, with their various combinations, creating the necessity of ascribing the proper force to each, confirm us in our conclusion that primary weight in this area must be given to the conclusions of the trier of fact. Baker v. Texas & Pacific R. Co., 359 U.S. 227; Commissioner v. Heininger, 320 U.S. 467, 475; United States v. Yellow Cab Co., 338 U.S. 338, 341; Bogardus v. Commissioner, supra, at 45 (dissenting opinion).[11]

This conclusion may not satisfy an academic desire for tidiness, symmetry and precision in this area, any more than a system based on the determinations of various fact-finders ordinarily does. But we see it as implicit in the present statutory treatment of the exclusion for gifts, and in the variety of forums in which federal income tax cases can be tried. If there is fear of undue uncertainty or overmuch

"One struggles in vain for any verbal formula that will supply a ready touchstone. The standard set up by the statute is not a rule of law; it is rather a way of life. Life in all its fullness must supply the answer to the riddle." Welch v. Helvering, 290 U.S. 111, 115. The same comment well fits the issue in the cases at bar.

10. Cf., e. g., Nelson v. Commissioner, 203 F.2d 1.

11. In *Bogardus*, the Court was divided 5 to 4 as to the scope of review to be extended the fact-finder's determination as to a specific receipt, in a context like that of the instant cases. The majority held that such a determination was "a conclusion of law or at least a determination of a mixed question of law and fact." 302 U.S., at 39. This formulation it took as justifying it in assuming a fairly broad standard of review. The dissent took a contrary view. The approach of this part of the Court's ruling in *Bogardus*, which we think was the only part on which there was real division among the Court, see note 8, supra, has not been afforded subsequent respect here. In *Heininger*, a question presenting at the most elements no more factual and untechnical than those here—that of the "ordinary and necessary" nature of a business expense—was treated as one of fact. Cf. note 9, supra. And in Dobson v. Commissioner, 320 U.S. 489, 498, n. 22, *Bogardus* was adversely criticized, insofar as it treated the matter as reviewable as one of law. While *Dobson* is, of course, no longer the law insofar as it ordains a greater weight to be attached to the findings of the Tax Court than to those of any other fact-finder in a tax litigation, see note 13, infra, we think its criticism of this point in the *Bogardus* opinion is sound in view of the dominant importance of factual inquiry to decision of these cases.

litigation, Congress may make more precise its treatment of the matter by singling out certain factors and making them determinative of the matter, as it has done in one field of the "gift" exclusion's former application, that of prizes and awards.[12] Doubtless diversity of result will tend to be lessened somewhat since federal income tax decisions, even those in tribunals of first instance turning on issues of fact, tend to be reported, and since there may be a natural tendency of professional triers of fact to follow one another's determinations, even as to factual matters. But the question here remains basically one of fact, for determination on a case-by-case basis.

One consequence of this is that appellate review of determinations in this field must be quite restricted. Where a jury has tried the matter upon correct instructions, the only inquiry is whether it cannot be said that reasonable men could reach differing conclusions on the issue. Baker v. Texas & Pacific R. Co., supra, at 228. Where the trial has been by a judge without a jury, the judge's findings must stand unless "clearly erroneous." Fed.Rules Civ.Proc., 52(a). "A finding is 'clearly erroneous' when although there is evidence to support it, the reviewing court on the entire evidence is left with the definite and firm conviction that a mistake has been committed." United States v. United States Gypsum Co., 333 U.S. 364, 395. The rule itself applies also to factual inferences from undisputed basic facts, id., at 394, as will on many occasions be presented in this area. Cf. Graver Tank & Mfg. Co. v. Linde Air Products Co., 339 U.S. 605, 609–610. And Congress has in the most explicit terms attached the identical weight to the findings of the Tax Court. I.R.C., § 7482 (a).[13]

Fourth. A majority of the Court is in accord with the principles just outlined. And, applying them to the *Duberstein* case, we are in agreement, on the evidence we have set forth, that it cannot be said that the conclusion of the Tax Court was "clearly erroneous." It seems to us plain that as trier of the facts it was warranted in con-

---

12. I.R.C., § 74, which is a provision new with the 1954 Code. Previously, there had been holdings that such receipts as the "Pot O' Gold" radio giveaway, Washburn v. Commissioner, 5 T.C. 1333, and the Ross Essay Prize, McDermott v. Commissioner, 80 U.S. App.D.C. 176, 150 F.2d 585, were "gifts." Congress intended to obviate such rulings. S.Rep. No. 1622, 83d Cong., 2d Sess., p. 178. We imply no approval of those holdings under the general standard of the "gift" exclusion. Cf. Robertson v. United States, supra.

13. "The United States Courts of Appeals shall have exclusive jurisdiction to review the decisions of the Tax Court . . . in the same manner and to the same extent as decisions of the district courts in civil actions tried without a jury. * * * The last words first came into the statute through an amendment to § 1141(a) of the 1939 Code in 1948 (§ 36 of the Judicial Code Act, 62 Stat. 991). The purpose of the 1948 legislation was to remove from the law the favored position (in comparison with District Court and Court of Claims rulings in tax matters) enjoyed by the Tax Court under this Court's ruling in Dobson v. Commissioner, 320 U.S. 489. Cf. note 11, supra. See Grace Bros., Inc. v. Commissioner, 173 F.2d 170, 173.

cluding that despite the characterization of the transfer of the Cadillac by the parties and the absence of any obligation, even of a moral nature, to make it, it was at bottom a recompense for Duberstein's past services, or an inducement for him to be of further service in the future. We cannot say with the Court of Appeals that such a conclusion was "mere suspicion" on the Tax Court's part. To us it appears based in the sort of informed experience with human affairs that fact-finding tribunals should bring to this task.

As to *Stanton*, we are in disagreement. To four of us, it is critical here that the District Court as trier of fact made only the simple and unelaborated finding that the transfer in question was a "gift." [14] To be sure, conciseness is to be strived for, and prolixity avoided, in findings; but, to the four of us, there comes a point where findings become so sparse and conclusory as to give no revelation of what the District Court's concept of the determining facts and legal standard may be. See Matton Oil Transfer Corp. v. The Dynamic, 123 F.2d 999, 1000–1001. Such conclusory, general findings do not constitute compliance with Rule 52's direction to "find the facts specially and state separately * * * conclusions of law thereon." While the standard of law in this area is not a complex one, we four think the unelaborated finding of ultimate fact here cannot stand as a fulfillment of these requirements. It affords the reviewing court not the semblance of an indication of the legal standard with which the trier of fact has approached his task. For all that appears, the District Court may have viewed the form of the resolution or the simple absence of legal consideration as conclusive. While the judgment of the Court of Appeals cannot stand, the four of us think there must be further proceedings in the District Court looking toward new and adequate findings of fact. In this, we are joined by MR. JUSTICE WHITTAKER, who agrees that the findings were inadequate, although he does not concur generally in this opinion.

Accordingly, in No. 376, the judgment of this Court is that the judgment of the Court of Appeals is reversed, and in No. 546, that the judgment of the Court of Appeals is vacated, and the case is remanded to the District Court for further proceedings not inconsistent with this opinion.

It is so ordered.

---

14. The "Findings of Fact and Conclusions of Law" were made orally, and were simply: "The resolution of the Board of Directors of the Trinity Operating Company, Incorporated, held November 19, 1942, after the resignations had been accepted of the plaintiff from his positions as controller of the corporation of the Trinity Church, and the president of the Trinity Operating Company, Incorporated, whereby a gratuity was voted to the plaintiff, Allen [*sic*] D. Stanton, in the amount of $20,000 payable to him in monthly installments of $2,000 each, commencing with the month of December, 1942, constituted a gift to the taxpayer, and therefore need not have been reported by him as income for the taxable years 1942, or 1943."

[Concurring and dissenting opinions of Messrs. JUSTICE HARLAN, WHITTAKER, DOUGLAS and BLACK have been omitted. Ed.]

MR. JUSTICE FRANKFURTER, concurring in the judgment in No. 376 and dissenting in No. 546, [said in part:]

*   *   *

The Court has made only one authoritative addition to the previous course of our decisions. Recognizing Bogardus v. Commissioner, 302 U.S. 34, as "the leading case here" and finding essential accord between the Court's opinion and the dissent in that case, the Court has drawn from the dissent in *Bogardus* for infusion into what will now be a controlling qualification, recognition that it is "for the triers of the facts to seek among competing aims or motives the ones that dominated conduct." 302 U.S. 34, 45 (dissenting opinion). All this being so in view of the Court, it seems to me desirable not to try to improve what has "already been spelled out" in the opinions of this Court but to leave to the lower courts the application of old phrases rather than to float new ones and thereby inevitably produce a new volume of exegesis on the new phrases.

Especially do I believe this when fact-finding tribunals are directed by the Court to rely upon their "experience with the mainsprings of human conduct" and on their "informed experience with human affairs" in appraising the totality of the facts of each case. Varying conceptions regarding the "mainsprings of human conduct" are derived from a variety of experiences or assumptions about the nature of man, and "experience with human affairs," is not only diverse but also often drastically conflicting. What the Court now does sets fact-finding bodies to sail on an illimitable ocean of individual beliefs and experiences. This can hardly fail to invite, if indeed not encourage, too individualized diversities in the administration of the income tax law. I am afraid that by these new phrasings the practicalities of tax administration, which should be as uniform as is possible in so vast a country as ours, will be embarrassed. By applying what has already been spelled out in the opinions of this Court, I agree with the Court in reversing the judgment in Commissioner v. Duberstein.

But I would affirm the decision of the Court of Appeals for the Second Circuit in Stanton v. United States.

*   *   *

NOTE

The Supreme Court in *Duberstein*, agreeing with the Tax Court decision, held that the question whether a transfer of money or property constitutes a gift within the exclusion of I.R.C. (26 U.S.C.A.) § 102(a) is an issue of fact to be determined by the trial court. In Stanton v. United States, the Supreme Court considered the findings of fact, as determined by the district court sitting without a jury, to be inadequate. The case was therefore remanded. The district court, on remand with more detailed findings of facts, held that Stanton had received a gift;[1] and the court of appeals affirmed.[2]

There are two interesting side effects of the *Duberstein* case. First, the Supreme Court in United States v. Kaiser,[3] decided on the same day as *Duberstein*, upheld a jury verdict of gift largely on the basis of its *Duberstein* rationale. In this case Kaiser, a non-union member, received strike benefits (subsistence payments) from the union which was striking the Kohler Company in Wisconsin. The district court entered judgment N.O.V. for the United States.[4] The court of appeals reversed, upholding the verdict for the taxpayer.[5] The Supreme Court, affirming the court of appeals, again emphasized the factual nature of the issue. On the other hand, in Madonna J. Colwell[6] the Tax Court differentiated *Kaiser* in a similar setting. Strike benefits received by a non-union member who honored a picket line but did not participate in strike activities were included in his income. Based primarily on the factor that the payments were made without union awareness of taxpayer's financial status, the Tax Court concluded that the union's interest was not charitable but to further the effectiveness of the strike. The final message should be clear. In this area, the law (I.R.C. (26 U.S.C.A.) § 102(a)) is simple and concise. The facts give rise to the complexity, and cases such as these are generally won or lost at the trial level. This is the result in the trilogy of *Duberstein, Stanton* and *Kaiser*.

The second point is now relevant. Recall that in the *Duberstein* opinion, the Supreme Court expressly refused to lay down a test for determining whether a payment or transfer of property constitutes a gift, aware that its "conclusion may not satisfy an academic desire for tidiness, symmetry and precision in this area * * *".[7] However, earlier in its opinion, the Court, quoting language from some of its own decisions handed down many years ago involving this same issue, gratuitously said: "A gift in the statutory sense * * * proceeds from a 'detached and disinterested generosity,' * * * 'out of affection, respect, admiration, charity or like impulses' * * *, the most critical consideration * * * is the transferor's 'intention'."[8] Perhaps the message was not intended as the formu-

[handwritten margin note: Not withstanding the verdict — judgment entered by court for the plaintiff even though there has been a verdict for the defendant]

1.   186 F.Supp. 393 (E.D.N.Y.1960).

2.   287 F.2d 876 (2d Cir. 1961).

3.   363 U.S. 299, 80 S.Ct. 1204 (1960).

4.   158 F.Supp. 865 (E.D.Wis.1958).

5.   262 F.2d 367 (7th Cir. 1958).

6.   64 T.C. 584 (1975). Compare also Rev.Rul. 63–136, 1963–2 C.B. 19, welfare payments not for services and those made under work training programs are not income, with Rev.Rul. 71–425, 1971–2 C.B. 76, which while generally excluding amounts received under work training programs, taxes the entire amount if it exceeds the welfare payment that would be made absent the program, except such part as exceeds the value of the services performed.

7.   Comm'r v. Duberstein, 363 U.S. 278, 290, 80 S.Ct. 1190, 1199 (1960); see p. 72 supra.

8.   Id. at 285; see p. 70 supra.

lation of criteria. But even so, it is á test of sorts, and the lower courts use those criteria in resolving the factual controversy of gift or no gift in cases decided subsequent to *Duberstein*.[9]

FISHER v. COMMISSIONER

United States Court of Appeals, Second Circuit, 1932.
59 F.2d 192.

SWAN, CIRCUIT JUDGE. The single issue presented by this appeal is whether an amount of $6,000 received by the taxpayer in 1924 from his employer was a gift, as he contends, or additional compensation for services, as the Commissioner contends. The facts were stipulated, and, without opinion, the Board found that the amount in question was compensation for services, with the result that a tax deficiency of $528.97 was adjudged.

After twenty-four years of service in the employ of Holmes Electric Protective Company, the petitioner voluntarily handed in his resignation, in December, 1924, to take effect at the end of the year. Starting as an office boy in 1900, he had risen to the position of general traffic manager, with a salary of $10,000 per year. This salary was paid him for the year 1924, and in addition he received from the company on December 23d the $6,000 herein involved. During the preceding October he had been told by his superior officer, Mr. Allen, that when he should actually leave the employ of the company "it would do something for him," but he had no intimation of what that would be until the sum in question was received. Never before had his employer paid him any bonus or other addition to his regular salary, nor had there ever been any agreement that he should receive anything more than the salary which from time to time he had agreed to accept. It was not the practice of the company to pay a bonus to any of its officers or employees, nor had it ever done so. Neither in the year 1924 nor in any previous year had the petitioner performed services outside the scope of the duties of his position. The making of the $6,000 payment was not formally authorized or ratified by any vote of the executive committee or of the board of directors of the company, but it was informally approved by a majority of the members of the executive committee, one of whom was the president of the corporation which held all the stock of the Holmes Company. On the books of the latter it was charged to salary account, and was so reported on its informational tax return (form 1099), and the total sum of $16,000 was included as a deduction in the consolidated income tax return filed on behalf of the Holmes Company and the parent corporation with which it was affiliated.

Upon these facts it is urged that the $6,000 payment must necessarily have been a gift, since it was not paid pursuant to any

9. E. g. Max Kralstein, 38 T.C. 810
     (1962); acq., 1963–2 C.B. 4.

contract obligation of the employer, nor as compensation for extra services rendered by the employee beyond the terms of his employment, nor, his resignation being voluntary, as compensation for the loss of his employment. But the mere fact that the employer was under no legal duty to pay is not conclusive that the payment was a nontaxable gift. Section 213(a) of the Revenue Act of 1924 (43 Stat. 267, 26 USCA § 954(a)), defines gross income to include "gains, profits, and income derived from salaries, wages, or compensation for personal service * * * of whatever kind and in whatever form paid." In Old Colony Trust Co. v. Commissioner, 279 U.S. 716, 730, 49 S.Ct. 499, 504, 73 L.Ed. 918, the Supreme Court said that "the payment for services, even though entirely voluntary" may nevertheless be "compensation within the statute," citing with approval Noel v. Parrott, 15 F.2d 669 (C.C.A. 4); and in Lucas v. Ox Fibre Brush Co., 281 U.S. 115, 50 S.Ct. 273, 74 L.Ed. 733, it was held that an employer might deduct reasonable compensation voluntarily paid to employees for services rendered in prior years. The doctrine that bonus payments and gratuitous "additional compensation" for past services may constitute taxable income has been frequently recognized in decisions of the lower federal courts and of the Board of Tax Appeals. See Noel v. Parrott, supra. * * * Whether a payment in a given case shall be deemed taxable compensation or a gift exempt from tax depends upon the intention of the parties, and particularly that of the employer, to be determined from the facts and circumstances surrounding the transaction. In the case at bar, the Holmes Company clearly indicated its intention by charging the payment upon its books to salary account and so reporting it in its tax returns. It is urged that these were the acts of subordinate officials not shown to have been authorized to so treat the payment, but surely the burden of proving their lack of authority, if such was the fact, was upon the taxpayer. Nor is there merit in the petitioner's contention that the sole stockholder approved the payment and hence presumptively intended to make a gift rather than to pay additional compensation. There was no action by the corporate stockholder; its president would have no authority by virtue of his office to give away its property. On the record presented, the Board's finding that the payment was additional compensation was amply justified.

Order affirmed.

SCHALL v. COMMISSIONER *

United States Court of Appeals, Fifth Circuit, 1949.
174 F.2d 893.

McCORD, CIRCUIT JUDGE. This appeal involves the income tax liability of petitioners, Charles Schall and Daisy B. Schall, for the

* See Zipperstein, "Taxation of Clergymen," 41 Taxes 219 (1963). Ed.

year 1943. The Tax Court found a deficiency in income and victory taxes for the year in question of $17.75.

The question presented is whether the Tax Court correctly held that the sum of $2,000 received by petitioner during the tax year involved, from a church of which he had formerly been Pastor constitutes taxable income within the meaning of Section 22(a) of the Internal Revenue Code, 26 U.S.C.A. § 22(a).

The material facts, as found by the Tax Court and revealed by the record, are without dispute, and may be summarized as follows:

Petitioner, Dr. Charles Schall, became pastor of the Wayne Presbyterian Church of Wayne, Pennsylvania, in October, 1921, at a salary of $6,000 per year. He served continuously in that capacity for eighteen years, when he was stricken with a heart attack which necessitated his resignation. After a severe and protracted illness, during which he remained in a hospital for eight months, he was advised by his physician to move to Florida in order to escape the rigorous climate and winters of Pennsylvania.

The congregation of the Wayne Presbyterian Church knew of Dr. Schall's condition, of the advice of his physician, and of his financial inability to move to Florida. Accordingly, at a meeting held on June 28, 1939, it recommended that his resignation be accepted, and unanimously adopted the following resolution:

"Whereas the pastor of this Church, Rev. Dr. Charles Schall, has become incapacitated for the further service as pastor and has requested the Congregation to join in a petition to Chester Presbytery to dissolve the pastoral relation; and

"Whereas the Congregation *moved by affectionate regard for him and gratitude* for his long and valued ministry among them, desire that he should continue to be associated with them in an honorary relation;

"Now, Therefore, Be It Resolved that, effective upon formal dissolution by Presbytery, Rev. Charles Schall be constituted Pastor Emeritus of this church with salary or honorarium amounting to Two Thousand Dollars ($2000.) annually, payable in monthly installments, with no pastoral authority or duty, and that the Session of this Church be requested to report this action to Presbytery. * * * "

Dr. Schall had made no request of the congregation that the above or any other amount be paid to him after his resignation, and had no knowledge that this resolution would be adopted. He did not agree to render any services in consideration for same, and since his resignation has performed no pastoral services for the Church whatever. Moreover, his testimony is forthright, and clear to the effect that he regarded the proposed payments "as an outright gift". It is without dispute that since his illness and resignation, Dr. Schall has resided continuously in the state of Florida.

We are of opinion the Tax Court clearly erred in holding that the payments to petitioner were taxable income. Bogardus v. Commissioner, 302 U.S. 34, 58 S.Ct. 61, 82 L.Ed. 32; Bass v. Hawley, 5 Cir., 62 F.2d 721. Where, as here, all the facts and circumstances surrounding the adoption of the resolution clearly prove an intent to make a gift, the mere use of the terms "salary" and "honorarium" do not convert the gift into a payment for services. Bogardus v. Commissioner, 302 U.S. 34, 44, 58 S.Ct. 61, 82 L.Ed. 32. Moreover, " * * * a gift is none the less a gift because inspired by gratitude for past faithful service of the recipient * * *". Frank T. Knowles, 5 T.C. 525; Bogardus v. Commissioner, 302 U.S. 34, 58 S.Ct. 61, 82 L.Ed. 32. Manifestly, these payments to petitioner were non-taxable gifts, within the orbit of the rule defining same, as enunciated by this court in the case of Bass v. Hawley, 5 Cir., 62 F.2d 721, at page 723:

" * * * That only is a gift which is purely such, not intended as a return of value or made because of any intent to repay another what is his due, but bestowed only because of *personal affection* or *regard* or *pity*, or from general motives of philanthropy or charity. * * *"

It follows that the decision of the Tax Court should be, and the same is hereby,

Reversed.

NOTE

In Revenue Ruling 55–422 [1] the Service accepted the philosophy of the *Schall* decision and stated that it would not continue to litigate the issue. The Ruling recognized that "there was a far closer personal relationship between the recipient and the congregation than is found in lay employment relationships * * *." The distinction was further pointed up in Alvin T. Perkins [2] taxing a minister on pension payments received not directly from his congregation, but from a more remote church organization which normally provided pensions to retired ministers.

POYNER v. COMMISSIONER *

United States Court of Appeals, Fourth Circuit, 1962.
301 F.2d 287.

SOBELOFF, CHIEF JUDGE. Not the least of the difficulties often faced by a recently widowed woman is the loss of her husband's finan-

---

1. 1955–1 C.B. 14.

2. 34 T.C. 117 (1960).

* See Rothman, "Voluntary Payments to Widows of Corporate Executives:

Gifts or Income?," 62 Mich.L.Rev. 1216 (1964). Ed. and Burke, "Corporate Payments to Widows: What Genre under the Internal Revenue Code?" 34 Pitt.L.R. 91 (1972).

cial support. However, for many widows of ranking employees in companies, this cause for worry has been alleviated by the practice of the employer making payments to the widow for limited periods following the husband's death, frequently by continuing to pay her the salary her husband would have received had he lived. The Commissioner of Internal Revenue has since 1950 [1] sought to treat such payments as ordinary income to the widow under the general provisions of section 61 of the Internal Revenue Code, 26 U.S.C.A. § 61.[2] The widows, on the other hand, have contended with considerable success in the courts that the payments were gifts, hence not includible in gross income under section 102.[3] The issue in the present case is of this character. We are asked by a widow to reverse a decision of the Tax Court which treats as ordinary income the payments made to her by a corporation of which for 38 years her husband had been president and majority stockholder.[4]

The statutory definition of a "gift" which is excluded from a person's gross income by section 102 and the function of an appellate court in reviewing the findings of the trier of fact in these cases have recently received extensive attention by the Supreme Court. Commissioner v. Duberstein, 363 U.S. 278, 80 S.Ct. 1190, 4 L.Ed.2d 1218 (1960). A study of this decision indicates that in any given case there are three steps which must be followed in reaching a conclusion. First, the trier of fact must make findings as to the basic facts, the actual happenings. These findings may not be upset if found by a jury unless the reviewing court is convinced that reasonable men could make only contrary findings, or, if found by a judge without a jury, unless clearly erroneous.

Second, the trier of fact must draw from these basic findings his inferences as to the "dominant reason" for the payments—the answer to the question why the payments were made. This determination too is one of fact as to which appellate review is restricted to the clearly erroneous standard where, as in the present case, a judge sat without a jury. The scope of review is therefore limited to ascertaining whether the trier of fact considered the correct criteria in making the factual inferences and whether the finding as to dominant motive is sufficiently supported in the evidence.[5]

1. I.T. 4027, 1950–2 Cum.Bull. 9.

2. [I.R.C. § 61(a) (1) is omitted. Ed.]

3. [I.R.C. § 102(a) is omitted. Ed.]

4. 35 T.C. 65 (1960). For general discussions of the issues involved in this case, and summaries of the course of Treasury rulings and judicial decisions concerning corporate payments to widows under section 102 and its predecessors, see Crown, Payments to Corporate Executives' Widows, N.Y.

U. 19th Inst. on Fed.Tax. 815 (1961); Pelisek, Tax Treatment of Payments to the Widows of Corporate Officers and Employees, 44 Marq.L.Rev. 16 (1960).

5. This restricted scope of review was applied in Kaiser v. United States, 363 U.S. 299, 80 S.Ct. 1204, 4 L.Ed.2d 1233 (1960), and by the courts of appeals in United States v. Stanton, 287 F.2d 876 (2d Cir. 1961), and United States v. Kasynski, 284 F.2d 143 (10th Cir. 1960). In defining the proper scope

Third, the lower court must decide whether the dominant reason, as found, for the payments is such as to require gift treatment and an escape from taxation under section 102, or income treatment and taxation under section 61. This question, involving the proper meaning of the statutory term "gift," is one of law as to which an appellate court may make an independent judgment. To give guidance in the decision of future cases, the majority opinion in Duberstein summarized earlier cases, citing specific examples of motives which require as a matter of law either the conclusion that the payments are a gift or that they are income, as those terms are used in the Internal Revenue Code.[6]

Now we shall see how this three-stage approach was followed in the case before us. The basic facts are undisputed since the parties submitted the case to the Tax Court upon stipulation. Over a span of 38 years before his death on January 31, 1956, Mervin G. Pierpont, the taxpayer's husband, served as the president of the Loewy Drug Company, a wholesale drug distributor in Baltimore. Throughout the entire period, he owned two-thirds of the outstanding stock, the rest being owned by Morton L. Lazarus. The company had paid him all amounts owed for his services. On March 22, 1956, the Board of Directors of the company passed a resolution whereby a 1954 Cadillac, valued at $3,245.14, was transferred to his widow. The resolution stated that "in recognition of the services rendered by the late Mervin G. Pierpont, this Corporation pay to his widow as a continuance of his salary the sum of Three Thousand, Two Hundred Forty-Five Dollars and Fourteen Cents * * *." By a similar resolution passed the following month, the company undertook to pay his widow $600 per month either until the payments aggregated $20,000 or until further action by the Board. She received under the two resolutions a total of $9,910.05 in 1956 and $7,800.00 in 1957 when the payments were terminated upon the liquidation of the company. It was stipulated in the Tax Court that the payments were "not made pursuant to any

---

of appellate review, the Supreme Court in *Duberstein* specifically adopted the view of the dissenters in Bogardus v. Commissioner, 302 U.S. 34, 39, 44, 58 S.Ct. 61, 64, 82 L.Ed. 32 (1937). The majority had there held that drawing factual inferences from the basic facts as to the reasons for the payments was "a conclusion of law or at least a determination of a mixed question of law and fact," a question to which the clearly erroneous standard of review did not apply so that an appellate court could more independently exercise its own judgment. The courts of appeals, however, did not consistently use this approach. Compare Simpson v. United States, 261 F.2d 497, 500 (7th Cir.

1958) (broad review), with United States v. Allinger, 275 F.2d 421, 423 (6th Cir. 1960) (narrow review). In Bounds v. United States, 262 F.2d 876, 880 (4th Cir. 1958), relying on the majority's opinion in *Bogardus*, we felt at liberty to apply the broad scope of review in reversing the findings of the District Court as to motive. Consequently, we would be guilty of no inconsistency were we to reach a different result here, having proceeded in Bounds according to a now unacceptable standard for review.

6.   363 U.S. at 285, 80 S.Ct. 1190, 4 L. Ed.2d 1218.

contract, plan, policy, practice, or understanding made or in effect prior to the Decedent's death." However, there is no mention in the stipulation as to who were the directors who authorized the payments and what were their relationships to the widow; neither are we told to whom Pierpont devised his controlling interest in the company, or what the widow's personal financial status may have been.

In her 1956 tax return the widow reported as a gift the $9,910.05 received in that year. The Commissioner, however, determined that it was income to her, applied the $5000 exclusion provided for employee death benefits by section 101(b),[7] and asserted a tax deficiency of $1,-376.22 on the remaining $4,910.05. The sums paid the widow had been fully deducted by the company as an expense of doing business.

From the stipulated facts, the Tax Court proceeded to draw factual inferences as to motive. Referring to the two corporate resolutions which authorized the payments, the Tax Court said that they "suggest that the dominant intention of the donor was to pay additional compensation in respect of the decedent's services." In addition, the court found that there was "nothing in the record that would lead us to conclude that the alleged gifts 'proceed[ed] from a detached and disinterested generosity * * * out of affection, respect, admiration, charity or like impulses,'" motives which the Supreme Court recognized in Duberstein as indicating gift treatment. The Tax Court then summarized its findings and conclusions by saying that "the payments in controversy were not intended as a 'gift,'" and treated them as income.

We think that the findings of the Tax Court regarding the dominant reason for the payments, based as they are upon the stipulated facts, cannot be sustained. The decisions in the Tax Court prior to the Duberstein case[8] established a set of factors to be evaluated in discovering the dominant motive for such payments to widows, and our decision in Bounds v. United States, 262 F.2d 876 (4th Cir. 1958), recog-

---

7. [I.R.C. § 101(b) is omitted. Ed.]

Before us the Government expressly declined to advance the argument that section 101(b) now requires all payments from an employer, made by reason of the death of an employee, to be included in the recipient's gross income, subject only to the $5,000 exclusion. This position finds support in our dictum in Bounds v. United States, 262 F.2d 876, 878 n. 2 (4th Cir. 1958), and in the dictum of Judge Dimock in Rodner v. United States, 149 F.Supp. 233, 236–38 (S.D.N.Y. 1957). It has been specifically rejected in Reed v. United States, 177 F. Supp. 205, 209 (W.D.Ky.1959), aff'd per curiam, 277 F.2d 456 (6th Cir. 1960); Cowan v. United States, 191 F.Supp. 703, 705 (N.D.Ga.1960); Frankel v. United States, 192 F.Supp. 776 (D.Minn.1961); and by Judge Weinfeld in Wilner v. United States, 195 F.Supp. 786, 787–90 (S.D.N.Y. 1961). In view of the Government's position, we are not called upon to reconsider this issue.

[This issue became moot with the issuance of Rev.Rul. 62–102, which is set out immediately after this case. Ed.]

8. E. g., Florence S. Luntz, 29 T.C. 647 (1958); Estate of John A. Maycann, 29 T.C. 81 (1957); Estate of Arthur W. Hellstrom, 24 T.C. 916 (1955); Louise K. Aprill, 13 T.C. 707 (1949); see Pelisek, supra note 4, at 20 n. 20.

nized and followed these criteria. The clearest formulation appears in Florence S. Luntz, 29 T.C. 647, 650 (1958), where the Tax Court listed the following as the five factors to be considered:

"(1) the payments had been made to the wife of the deceased employee and not to his estate; (2) there was no obligation on the part of the corporation to pay any additional compensation to the deceased employee; (3) the corporation derived no benefit from the payment; (4) the wife of the deceased employee performed no services for the corporation; and (5) the services of her husband had been fully compensated."

The stipulated facts directly respond to every one of the five factors, and in each instance the response is favorable to the widow. This being so, we see no justification for the Tax Court's finding that "there is no solid evidence that they [the directors authorizing the payments] were motivated in any part by the widow's needs or by a sense of generosity or the like." In every prior Tax Court case, essentially identical facts were held sufficient to support the conclusion that the dominant motive was sympathy for the taxpayer's widowed position. The only evidence on which the Tax Court specifically relies for its contrary finding is the wording of the authorizing corporate resolutions. While the language of the resolutions certainly merits consideration, never before has such language been deemed sufficient by itself, and in the face of the other above specified factors, to support a finding that the payments were compensation for services rendered.[9] As the facts stipulated in this case do not differ from those deemed conclusive in past cases, a contrary finding seems to us without warrant.

The Supreme Court in Duberstein did not destroy the authority of the earlier Tax Court cases and the guides enunciated in them for discovering motivation. The plea addressed by the Government to the Supreme Court in Duberstein to establish a new test defining "gift" was expressly rejected. The Court limited itself to summarizing earlier decisions as to which particular dominant motivations, when adequately supported by the evidence, result in income treatment, and which result in gift treatment. An enumeration of the criteria, by which the trier of fact shall determine in every type of case what that dominant reason is, was deemed inadvisable, if not futile. The Court preferred to leave the development of such criteria to a case-by-case approach in the lower courts.

---

9. See Bounds v. United States, 262 F. 2d 876, 881–82 (4th Cir. 1958). The language of the corporate resolution here is no doubt modeled after the sample resolution in I.T. 3329, 1939–2 Cum.Bull. 153. See Pelisek, *supra* note 4, at 22–23. I.T. 3329 was in this respect revoked in 1950 by I.T. 4027, 1950–2 Cum.Bull. 9, but without any appreciable effect on the course of decision in the Tax Court. See Estate of Arthur W. Hellstrom, 24 T.C. 916, 919 (1955).

On the other hand, Duberstein cannot be read as limiting inquiry by the trier of fact solely to the factors recognized by the earlier decisions. The objective is to discover which motive is dominant in a field of co-existing motives. In the task of sorting out the varying motives, the development of more reliable criteria by the triers of fact should not be curtailed. Indeed, the Tax Court since Duberstein has considered it necessary to inquire into the widow's stock holdings in the company [10] and the knowledge or lack of it on the part of the Board of her financial status following the death of her husband.[11] The Tax Court in the present case also seems to have thought that the directors' knowledge of "the widow's needs" was an important factor. These subjects are certainly relevant, and inquiry may properly be directed to them, and whatever other factors the trier of fact might think helpful.

Nevertheless, none of the facts stipulated in the present case touches upon those additional factors which since Duberstein have been important. The stipulations were made before Duberstein and covered only the criteria which had up to that time been formulated and treated by the Tax Court and this circuit as decisive. It would be unfair now to allow findings to stand, which are adverse to the taxpayer because of her silence on matters never deemed pertinent in earlier litigation. While, as we have indicated, it is perfectly proper for the court to broaden the field of inquiry beyond that previously established, this should not be done without affording an opportunity to the taxpayer, and to the Government as well, to amplify the record. Of course, we do not undertake to dictate the result to be reached upon the broadened inquiry. Additional data which the parties will be free to produce may have the effect of confirming or overcoming the result which the five Luntz factors, standing alone, were held to require in the earlier cases.

Decision vacated and case remanded for proceedings not inconsistent with this opinion.

REVENUE RULING 62–102 [1]

1962–2 Cum.Bull. 37.

The Internal Service will no longer contend that section 101(b) of the Internal Revenue Code of 1954 applies to limit to $5,000 the exclusion from gross income of an amount paid to the widow of a de-

---

10. Estate of Rose A. Russek, 20 CCH Tax Ct.Rep. 123 (January 31, 1961); see Ivan Y. Nickerson, 19 CCH Tax Ct.Mem. 1508 (1960) (payment, to children of deceased employee).

1961); Ray I. Martin, 36 T.C. No. 56 (June 21, 1961); Mildred W. Smith, 20 CCH Tax Ct.Rep. 775 (May 29, 1961); Estate of Rose A. Russek, 20 CCH Tax Ct.Rep. 123 (January 31, 1961).

11. Estate of Julius B. Cronheim, 20 CCH Tax Ct.Rep. 1144 (August 17,

1. Based on Technical Information Release 371, dated March 19, 1962.

ceased employee, where the payment otherwise qualifies as a gift excludable under section 102(a) of the Code.

The Service has abandoned its former contention in view of adverse decisions in the cases of Grace P. Reed et al. v. United States, 177 F.Supp. 205 (1959), affirmed without opinion, 277 F.2d 456 (1960); Virginia Luty Cowan v. United States, 191 F.Supp. 703 (1960); Genevieve E. Frankel et al. v. United States, 192 F.Supp. 776 (1961); and Ellis H. Wilner et al. v. United States, 195 F.Supp. 786 (1961). The Government withdrew this argument in its defense of the case of Florence G. Rice v. United States, 197 F.Supp. 223 (1961).

Revenue Ruling 60–326, C.B. 1960–2, 32, is modified accordingly.

The Service will continue to argue that, in extending section 101 (b) of the Code to noncontractual payments, Congress assumed that such payments did not qualify as gifts, thereby endorsing the Service's ruling in I.T. 4027, C.B. 1950–2, 9, that widows' payments generally are not gifts.

NOTE

It should be recognized that the exclusion under I.R.C. (26 U.S. C.A.) § 101(b) (1) applies only to amounts that "are paid by reason of the death of the employee." Since the purpose of § 101(b) is to place a limited portion of employee death benefits on an equal footing with regular life insurance benefits, § 101(b) (2) (B) requires that in order to receive the exemption the right to the amount received must be created by the employee's death and not represent benefits that he could have enjoyed if living.[1] Thus, if payments made at death represent a mere liquidation of nonforfeitable retirement benefits that the decedent would have received personally had he survived, the § 101 (b) exclusion has no application. For example, assume a taxpayer had a vested right to receive $1200 a year for 10 years under an arrangement calling for continuation of the payments to his estate if he died prematurely. If he died after six years, the remaining $4800 paid to his estate would not be excluded under § 101(b).[2] However, the exclusion is allowed, even if the decedent had a nonforfeitable right to payment, if the payments are made under certain qualified pensions plans and are made within one taxable year of the recipient.[3]

As Revenue Ruling 62–102 reproduced above points out, even though I.R.C. (26 U.S.C.A.) § 101(b) allows a $5000 exclusion without the need to classify the item as a "gift", the section is not exclusive, and any excess amount properly identified as a "gift" is excluded

1. Regulations imposing the same requirement under I.R.C. (26 U.S.C.A.) § 101(b) (1) prior to the 1954 addition of § 101(b) (2) were upheld in Hess v. Comm'r, 271 F.2d 104 (3d Cir. 1959).

2. Reg. § 1.101–2(d) (2) Example 1.

3. I.R.C. (26 U.S.C.A.) §§ 101(b)(2)(B) (i)–(iii), 402(e)(4)(A). For the tax treatment of amounts not excluded, see Ferguson, Freeland and Stephens, Federal Income Taxation of Estates and Beneficiaries, 171–175 (Little, Brown 1970).

by § 102. A damper on classifying such items as gifts may have been created in 1962 when Congress enacted I.R.C. (26 U.S.C.A.) § 274(b) (1), which limits the deduction for business "gifts", with minor exceptions, to $25 per donee per year. The paying employer's tax considerations are now hostile to those of the payee in this respect.

Labelling and treating the payment as compensation does not necessarily require a finding that it is not a gift and is income to the employee.[4] Nevertheless, under *Duberstein* it is certainly a factor in the determination.

PROBLEMS

1. As the Note at page 75 of the text makes clear, the application of the § 102 exclusion usually raises a factual question, the transferor's intent. It is, therefore, unrealistic to expect a pat answer to the question whether employer-employee transfers are gifts. Nevertheless, what seem to be the possibilities in the somewhat comparable situations below?   *Items of Nominal value are not included in gross income*

Rev Ruling 59-58

    a. (1) Employer gives employee a ham at Christmas. *Not taxable*

       (2) Employee gives employer a ham at Christmas. *Not taxable*

$25 value is for deduction. Not for consideration of inclusion in gross income.

    b. (1) Employer gives all employees $100 black and white T.V.s at Christmas. *Amount Not Nominal*

       (2) Same, except that Employer's son Employee S gets a $500 color T.V. *Son has $100. gross income.*

    c. (1) Employer gives Employee a $40 battery-run Timex watch on retirement. *Non Taxable —*

       (2) Employer gives Employee a $2000 gold-plated Rolex watch on retirement.

    d. Same as c, above, except that:

       (1) The $40 watch is purchased with funds collected by soliciting employee's fellow employees.

       (2) The $2000 Rolex is purchased with $1000 solicited from employee's fellow employees and $1000 contributed by employer. See Max Kralstein, 38 T.C. 810 (1962).

    e. Employer gives retiring employee a check for $5000. Employer is:

       (1) The congregation for whom employee has served as minister of the gospel.

       (2) The central fiscal organization of the church for which employee has served as bookkeeper.

    f. At the Heads Eye Casino in Vegas, Lucky Louie:

       (1) gives the maitre d' a $50 tip to assure a good table. *Taxable*

    4. Bounds v. U. S., 262 F.2d 876 (4th Cir. 1958).

Compensation for services rendered

(2) gives the croupier a $50 "toke" after a good night with the cubes. See Olk v. United States, 536 F.2d 876 (9th Cir. 1976). *Taxable for services rendered.*

2.

a. If a gratuitous transfer of property or money is between fairly closely-related members of a family (Let's use the I.R.C. § 267(c)(4) "family" definition, for example.), is it reasonable to think that it might "generate" income which the government can properly tax?

b. As a practical matter, however, is there any real need to carve out a specific gift exclusion for such transfers?

c. Should it be considered significant that the parties also have some other relationships such as employer-employee or as business partners?

d. "Gifts should be defined as transfers of property made for personal as distinguished from business reasons." Comm'r v. Duberstein, footnote 6, supra page 69. Would this Treasury-proposed test rejected by the Court be useful?

3. Our system of self-assessment requires the taxpayer to make the initial determination of gift or income, and tax administration procedures give the Commissioner the power to challenge that decision. If judicial controversy develops, why is the decision of the trial court so important, and what role may an appellate court play?

4. Employee was employed by Corporation for a good many years. When he died the corporate board took note of his death and agreed with the suggestion of one board member that although the corporation had paid him his full salary under his contract nevertheless Employee had been sadly undercompensated. The board voted $15,000 to his widow, Mary, which was promptly paid to her. What tax treatment should Mary accord the $15,000?

C. THE INCOME TAX MEANING OF INHERITANCE

Internal Revenue Code: Section 102(a), (b), first sentence.
Regulations: Section 1.102–1(a), (b).

LYETH v. HOEY

Supreme Court of the United States, 1938.
305 U.S. 188, 59 S.Ct. 155.

MR. CHIEF JUSTICE HUGHES delivered the opinion of the Court.

The question presented is whether property received by petitioner from the estate of a decedent in compromise of his claim as an heir is taxable as income under the Revenue Act of 1932.

Petitioner is a grandson of Mary B. Longyear who died in 1931, a resident of Massachusetts, leaving as her heirs four surviving children and the petitioner and his brother, who were sons of a deceased daughter. By her will, the decedent gave to her heirs certain small legacies and the entire residuary estate, amounting to more than $3,000,000, was bequeathed to trustees of a so-called Endowment Trust, created April 5, 1926, the income from which was payable to another set of trustees under another trust described as the Longyear Foundation. The main purpose of the latter trust was to preserve "the records of the earthly life of Mary Baker Eddy," the founder of the Christian Science religion.

When the will was offered for probate in Massachusetts there was objection by the heirs upon the grounds, among others, of lack of testamentary capacity and undue influence. After hearing, at which a statement was made by the respective parties of their proposed evidence, the probate court granted a motion for the framing of issues for trial before a jury. In that situation a compromise agreement was entered into between the heirs, the legatees, the devisees and the executors under the will, and the Attorney General of Massachusetts. This agreement provided that the will should be admitted to probate and letters testamentary issued; that the specific and pecuniary bequests to individuals should be enforced; that the bequest of the residuary estate to the Endowment Trust should be disregarded; that $200,000 should be paid to the heirs and a like amount to the Endowment Trust, and that the net residue of the estate, as defined, should be equally divided between the trustees of the Endowment Trust and the heirs. The net residue to which the heirs were thus entitled was to be payable in units of stock owned by the decedent in certain corporations, Longyear Estate, Inc., Longyear Corporation and Longyear Realty Corporation, and for that purpose a unit was to consist of three shares, one share of each corporation.

The compromise was approved by the probate court pursuant to a statute of Massachusetts (Mass.Gen.Laws 1932, c. 204, §§ 15–17) and a decree was entered on April 26, 1932, admitting the will to probate, issuing letters testamentary to the executors and directing them "to administer the estate of said deceased in accordance with the terms of said will and said agreement of compromise." Owing to the Depression and the necessity of discharging pecuniary legacies amounting to about $300,000, which were entitled to priority in payment before distribution of the residue, the heirs undertook to finance one-half of these legacies and the residuary legatees the other one-half. For this purpose the heirs formed a corporation known as Longyear Heirs, Inc., to which they assigned their interests in the estate in exchange for common stock. Preferred stock was issued to the pecuniary legatees.

In July, 1933, the executors distributed to Longyear Heirs, Inc., as assignee of the petitioner, his distributable share of the estate consisting of $80.17 in cash and a certificate of deposit for 358 units, each unit representing one share of each of the three corporations mentioned in the compromise agreement. The Commissioner of Internal Revenue valued this distributable share at $141,484.03 and treated the whole amount as income for the year 1933 in which it was received. An additional tax of $56,389.65 was assessed, which petitioner paid in October, 1936, with interest. Claim for refund was then filed and on its rejection this suit was brought against the collector.

On motion of petitioner the District Court entered a summary judgment in his favor, 20 F.Supp. 619, which the Circuit Court of Appeals reversed. 96 F.2d 141. Because of a conflict with the decision of the Circuit Court of Appeals of the Fourth Circuit in Magruder v. Segebade, 94 F.2d 177, certiorari was granted.

The Court of Appeals overruled the contentions of petitioner that the property he received was within the statutory exemption (§ 22(b) (3) of the Revenue Act of 1932) and, further, that the property was not income either under the statute or under the Sixteenth Amendment of the Federal Constitution. As the view of the Court of Appeals upon these questions determined the rights of the parties, it was found unnecessary to discuss certain affirmative defenses set up by the answer of the respondent and these defenses are not pressed in this court.

First. By § 22(b) (3) of the Revenue Act of 1932, there is exempted from the income tax—

"The value of property acquired by gift, bequest, devise, or inheritance. * * *"

Whether property received by an heir from the estate of his ancestor is acquired by inheritance, when it is distributed under an agreement settling a contest by the heir of the validity of the decedent's will, is a question upon which state courts have differed. The question has arisen in the application of state laws of taxation. In Massachusetts, the rule is that when a will is admitted to probate under a compromise agreement, the state succession tax is applied to the property "that passes by the terms of the will as written and not as changed by any agreement for compromise." Baxter v. Treasurer, 209 Mass. 459, 463; 95 N.E. 854, 856. Although under the Massachusetts statute relating to compromise [1] it is the practice to insert a clause in the court's decree that the estate is to be administered in accordance with the agreement, "yet the rights of the parties so far as they rest upon the agreement are contractual and not testamentary." Ellis v. Hunt, 228 Mass. 39, 43; 116 N.E. 956. See, also, Brandeis v. Atkins, 204 Mass. 471, 474; 90 N.E. 861; Copeland v. Wheelwright, 230 Mass. 131, 136; 119 N.E. 667. Thus, when a contest was withdrawn under a compromise and the residuary estate was divided equally between the legatee and the heirs, it was held that the tax was properly levied upon the entire residuary legacy and that the administrators with the will annexed had no right to pay out of the share transferred to the heirs one-half of the tax thus collectible from the legatee unless the compromise agreement expressly or impliedly so provided. Brown v. McLoughlin, 287 Mass. 15, 17; 190 N.E. 795. Several States have a similar rule.[2] In other States the amount received by an heir under an agreement compromising a contest of his ancestor's will is considered to be received by virtue of his heirship and is subject to an inheritance tax unless the statute exempts him.[3]

In the instant case, the Court of Appeals applied the Massachusetts rule, holding that whether the property was received by way of inheritance depended "upon the law of the jurisdiction under which this taxpayer received it." We think that this ruling was erroneous. The question as to the construction of the exemption in the federal statute is not determined by local law. We are not concerned with the peculiarities and special incidences of state taxes or with the policies they reflect. Undoubtedly the state law determines what persons are qualified to inherit property within the jurisdiction. Mager v. Grima, 8 How. 490, 493; Maxwell v. Bugbee, 250 U.S. 525, 536, 537. The local law determines the right to make a testamentary disposition of such property and the conditions essential to the validity of wills, and the state courts settle their construction. Uterhart v. United States, 240 U.S. 598, 603. The State establishes the procedure governing the probate of wills and the processes of administration. Petitioner's status as heir was thus determined by the law of Massachusetts. That law also regulated the procedure by which his rights as an heir could

1. Massachusetts General Laws 1932,   3. [Citations omitted. Ed.]
   Chap. 204, §§ 13–18.

2. [Citations omitted. Ed.]

be vindicated. The state law authorized its courts to supervise the making of agreements compromising contests by heirs of the validity of an alleged will of their ancestor, in order that such compromises shall be just and reasonable with respect to all persons in interest.[4] But when the contestant is an heir and a valid compromise agreement has been made and there is a distribution to the heir from the decedent's estate accordingly, the question whether what the heir has thus received has been "acquired by inheritance" within the meaning of the federal statute necessarily is a federal question. It is not determined by local characterization.

In dealing with the meaning and application of an act of Congress enacted in the exercise of its plenary power under the Constitution to tax income and to grant exemptions from that tax, it is the will of Congress which controls, and the expression of its will, in the absence of language evidencing a different purpose, should be interpreted "so as to give a uniform application to a nationwide scheme of taxation." Burnet v. Harmel, 287 U.S. 103, 110. Congress establishes its own criteria and the state law may control only when the federal taxing act by express language or necessary implication makes its operation dependent upon state law. Burnet v. Harmel, supra. See Burk-Waggoner Oil Assn. v. Hopkins, 269 U.S. 110, 111, 114; Weiss v. Wiener, 279 U.S. 333, 337; Morrissey v. Commissioner, 296 U.S. 344, 356. Compare Crooks v. Harrelson, 282 U.S. 55, 59; Poe v. Seaborn, 282 U.S. 101, 109, 110; Blair v. Commissioner, 300 U.S. 5, 9, 10. There is no such expression or necessary implication in this instance. Whether what an heir receives from the estate of his ancestor through the compromise of his contest of his ancestor's will should be regarded as within the exemption from the federal tax should not be decided in one way in the case of an heir in Pennsylvania or Minnesota and in another way in the case of an heir in Massachusetts or New York,[5] according to the differing views of the state courts. We think that it was the intention of Congress in establishing this exemption to provide a uniform rule.

Second. In exempting from the income tax the value of property acquired by "bequest, devise, or inheritance," Congress used comprehensive terms embracing all acquisitions in the devolution of a decedent's estate. For the word "descent," as used in the earlier acts,[6] Congress substituted the word "inheritance" in the 1926 Act and the subsequent revenue acts as "more appropriately including both real and personal property." [7] Thus the acquisition by succession to a de-

---

4. See Note 1. Such agreements are "entirely valid outside of the statute." Ellis v. Hunt, 228 Mass. 39, 44, 116 N.E. 956.

5. See Notes 2 and 3.

6. See Act of October 3, 1913, c. 16, § II, 38 Stat. 167; Revenue Acts of 1918, 1921 and 1924, § 213(b) (3).

7. Revenue Act of 1926, § 213(b) (3); Acts of 1928 and 1932, § 22(b) (3). Sen.Rep. No. 52, 69th Cong., 1st Sess., p. 20.

cedent's estate whether real or personal was embraced in the exemption. Further, by the "estate tax," Congress has imposed a tax upon the transfer of the entire net estate of every person dying after September 8, 1916,[8] allowing such exemptions as it sees fit in arriving at the net estate. Congress has not indicated any intention to tax again the value of the property which legatees, devisees or heirs receive from the decedent's estate.

Petitioner was concededly an heir of his grandmother under the Massachusetts statute. It was by virtue of that heirship that he opposed probate of her alleged will which constituted an obstacle to the enforcement of his right. Save as heir he had no standing. Seeking to remove that obstacle, he asserted that the will was invalid because of want of testamentary capacity and undue influence. In accordance with local practice, he asked the probate court to frame these issues for a jury trial. It then became necessary for him to satisfy the court that the issues were substantial. Issues are not to be framed unless it appears from statements by counsel of expected evidence or otherwise that there is a "genuine question of fact supported by evidence of such a substantial nature as to afford ground for reasonable expectation of a result favorable to the party requesting the framing of issues." Briggs v. Weston, 294 Mass. 452, 2 N.E.2d 466; Smith v. Patterson, 286 Mass. 356, 190 N.E. 536. Petitioner satisfied that condition and the probate court directed the framing of jury issues. It was in that situation, facing a trial of the issue of the validity of the will, that the compromise was made by which the heirs, including the petitioner, were to receive certain portions of the decedent's estate.

There is no question that petitioner obtained that portion, upon the value of which he is sought to be taxed, because of his standing as an heir and of his claim in that capacity. It does not seem to be questioned that if the contest had been fought to a finish and petitioner had succeeded, the property which he would have received would have been exempt under the federal act. Nor is it questioned that if in any appropriate proceeding, instituted by him as heir, he had recovered judgment for a part of the estate, that part would have been acquired by inheritance within the meaning of the act. We think that the distinction sought to be made between acquisition through such a judgment and acquisition by a compromise agreement in lieu of such a judgment is too formal to be sound, as it disregards the substance of the statutory exemption. It does so, because it disregards the heirship which underlay the compromise, the status which commanded that agreement and was recognized by it. While the will was admitted to probate, the decree also required the distribution of the estate in accordance with the compromise and, so far as the latter provided for distribution to the heirs, it overrode the will. So far as the will became effective under the agreement it was because of the heirs'

---

8. Act of September 8, 1916, c. 463, Title II, 39 Stat. 777.

consent and release and in consideration of the distribution they received by reason of their being heirs. Respondent agrees that the word "inheritance" as used in the federal statute is not solely applicable to cases of complete intestacy. The portion of the decedent's property which petitioner obtained under the compromise did not come to him through the testator's will. That portion he obtained because of his heirship and to that extent he took in spite of the will and as in case of intestacy. The fact that petitioner received less than the amount of his claim did not alter its nature or the quality of its recognition through the distribution which he did receive.

We are not convinced by the argument that petitioner had but "the expectations" of an heir and realized on a "bargaining position." He was heir in fact. Whether he would receive any property in that capacity depended upon the validity of his ancestor's will and the extent to which it would dispose of his ancestor's estate. When, by compromise and the decree enforcing it, that disposition was limited, what he got from the estate came to him because he was heir, the compromise serving to remove *pro tanto* the impediment to his inheritance. We are of the opinion that the exemption applies.

In this view we find it unnecessary to consider the other questions that have been discussed at the bar.

The judgment of the Circuit Court of Appeals is reversed and that of the District Court is affirmed.

Reversed.

WOLDER v. COMMISSIONER *

United States Court of Appeals, Second Circuit, 1974.
493 F.2d 608.

OAKES, CIRCUIT JUDGE: These two cases, involving an appeal and cross-appeal in the individual taxpayers' case and an appeal by the Commissioner in the estate taxpayer's case, essentially turn on one question: whether an attorney contracting to and performing lifetime legal services for a client receives income when the client, pursuant to the contract, bequeaths a substantial sum to the attorney in lieu of the payment of fees during the client's lifetime. In the individual taxpayers' case, the Tax Court held that the fair market value of the stock and cash received under the client's will constituted taxable income under § 61, Int.Rev.Code of 1954, and was not exempt from taxation as a bequest under § 102 of the Code. From this ruling the individual taxpayers, Victor R. Wolder, the attorney, and his wife, who signed joint returns, appeal.

* * *

---

* See Kemp, "Federal Tax Aspects of Will Contests," 23 U.Miami L.Rev. 72 (1968); Schenk, "Tax Effects of Will Contests and Compromises," 10 Tulane Tax Inst. 214 (1961). Ed.

There is no basic disagreement as to the facts. On or about October 3, 1947, Victor R. Wolder, as attorney, and Marguerite K. Boyce, as client, entered into a written agreement which, after reciting Mr. Wolder's past services on her behalf in an action against her ex-husband for which he had made no charge, consisted of mutual promises, first on the part of Wolder to render to Mrs. Boyce "such legal services as she shall in her opinion personally require from time to time as long as both . . . shall live and not to bill her for such services," and second on the part of Mrs. Boyce to make a codicil to her last will and testament giving and bequeathing to Mr. Wolder or to his estate "my 500 shares of Class B common stock of White Laboratories, Inc." or "such other . . . securities" as might go to her in the event of a merger or consolidation of White Laboratories. Subsequently, in 1957, White Laboratories did merge into Schering Corp. and Mrs. Boyce received 750 shares of Schering common and 500 shares of Schering convertible preferred. In 1964 the convertible preferred was redeemed for $15,845. In a revised will dated April 23, 1965, Mrs. Boyce, true to the agreement with Mr. Wolder, bequeathed to him or his estate the sum of $15,845 and the 750 shares of common stock of Schering Corp. There is no dispute but that Victor R. Wolder had rendered legal services to Mrs. Boyce over her lifetime (though apparently these consisted largely of revising her will) and had not billed her therefor so that he was entitled to performance by her under the agreement, on which she had had a measure of independent legal advice. At least the New York Surrogate's Court (DiFalco, J.) ultimately so found in contested proceedings in which Mrs. Boyce's residuary legatees contended that the will merely provided for payment of a debt and took the position that Wolder was not entitled to payment until he proved the debt in accordance with § 212, New York Surrogate's Court Act.[1]

* * *

Wolder argues that the legacy he received under Mrs. Boyce's will is specifically excluded from income by virtue of § 102(a), Int. Rev.Code of 1954, which provides that "Gross Income does not include the value of property acquired by gift, bequest, devise or inheritance * * *" See also Treas.Reg. 1.102–1(a). The individual taxpayer, as did dissenting Judge Quealy below, relies upon United States v. Merriam, 263 U.S. 179, 44 S.Ct. 69, 68 L.Ed. 240 (1923), and its progeny for the proposition that the term "bequest" in § 102 (a) has not been restricted so as to exclude bequests made on account of some consideration flowing from the beneficiary to the decedent. In *Merriam* the testator made cash bequests to certain persons who were named executors of the estate, and these bequests were " 'in

1. Subsequently another surrogate held that the estate would not be obligated under the so-called tax clause in Mrs. Boyce's will to reimburse Mr. Wolder for any income tax payable by him by reason of the bequest made to him in accordance with the 1947 contract.

lieu of all compensation or commissions to which they would otherwise be entitled as executors or trustees.'" 263 U.S. at 184, 44 S.Ct. at 70. The Court held nevertheless that the legacies were exempt from taxation, drawing a distinction—which in a day and age when we look to substance and not to form strikes us as of doubtful utility—between cases where "compensation [is] fixed by will for services to be rendered by the executor and [where] a legacy [is paid] to one upon the implied condition that he shall clothe himself with the character of executor." 263 U.S. at 187, 44 S.Ct. at 71. In the former case, Mr. Justice Sutherland said, the executor "must perform the services to earn the compensation" while in the latter case "he need do no more than in good faith comply with the condition [that he be executor] in order to receive the bequest." The Court went on to take the view that the provision in the will that the bequest was in lieu of commissions was simply "an expression of the testator's will that the executor shall not receive statutory allowances for the services he may render." While the distinction drawn in the *Merriam* case hardly stands economic analysis, Bank of New York v. Helvering, 132 F.2d 773 (2d Cir. 1943), follows it on the basis that it is controlling law.[2]

But we think that *Merriam* is inapplicable to the facts of this case, for here there is no dispute but that the parties did contract for services and—while the services were limited in nature—there was also no question but that they were actually rendered. Thus the provisions of Mrs. Boyce's will, at least for federal tax purposes, went to satisfy her obligation under the contract. The contract in effect was one for the postponed payment of legal services, i. e., by a legacy under the will for services rendered during the decedent's life.

Moreover, the Supreme Court itself has taken an entirely different viewpoint from *Merriam* when it comes to interpreting § 102(a), or its predecessor, § 22(b)(3), Int.Rev.Code of 1939, in reference to what are gifts. In Commissioner v. Duberstein, 363 U.S. 278, 80 S.Ct. 1190, 4 L.Ed.2d 1218 (1960), the Court held that the true test is whether in actuality the gift is a bona fide gift or simply a method for paying compensation. This question is resolved by an examination of the intent of the parties, the reasons for the transfer, and the parties' performance in accordance with their intentions—"what the basic reason for [the donor's] conduct was in fact—the dominant

2. One also doubts the present day validity of the underlying philosophical premise of Merriam, that "If the words are doubtful, the doubt must be resolved against the government and in favor of the taxpayer." 263 U.S. at 188, 44 S.Ct. at 71. In White v. United States, 305 U.S. 281, 292, 59 S.Ct. 179, 184, 83 L.Ed. 172 (1938), after noting for the majority that it was not "impressed" by this very argument, Mr. Justice Stone said, "It is the function and duty of courts to resolve doubts. We know of no reason why that function should be abdicated in a tax case more than in any other where the rights of suitors turn on the construction of a statute and it is our duty to decide what that construction fairly should be."

reason that explains his action in making the transfer." 363 U.S. at 286, 80 S.Ct. at 1197. See also Carrigan v. Commissioner, 197 F.2d 246 (2d Cir. 1952); Fisher v. Commissioner, 59 F.2d 192 (2d Cir. 1932). There are other cases holding testamentary transfers to be taxable compensation for services as opposed to tax-free bequests. Cotnam v. Commissioner, 263 F.2d 119 (5th Cir. 1959); Mariani v. Commissioner, 54 T.C. 135 (1970); Cohen v. United States, 241 F.Supp. 740 (E.D.Mich.1965); Davies v. Commissioner, 23 T.C. 524 (1954). True, in each of these cases the testator did not fulfill his contractual obligation to provide in his will for payment of services rendered by the taxpayer, forcing the taxpayers to litigate the merits of their claims against the estates, whereas in the case at bar the terms of the contract were carried out. This is a distinction without a difference, and while we could decline to follow them in the case at bar, we see no reason to do so.

Indeed, it is to be recollected that § 102 is, after all, an exception to the basic provision in § 61(a) that "Except as otherwise provided in this subtitle, gross income means all income from whatever source derived, including . . . (1) Compensation for services, including fees, commissions and similar items . . . . ." The congressional purpose is to tax income comprehensively. Commissioner v. Jacobson, 336 U.S. 28, 49, 69 S.Ct. 358, 93 L.Ed. 477 (1949). A transfer in the form of a bequest was the method that the parties chose to compensate Mr. Wolder for his legal services, and that transfer is therefore subject to taxation, whatever its label whether by federal or by local law may be. See also Hort v. Commissioner, 313 U.S. 28, 31, 61 S.Ct. 757, 85 L.Ed. 1168 (1941).

Taxpayer's argument that he received the stock and cash as a "bequest" under New York law and the decisions of the surrogates is thus beside the point. New York law does, of course, control as to the extent of the taxpayer's legal rights to the property in question, but it does not control as to the characterization of the property for federal income tax purposes. United States v. Mitchell, 403 U.S. 190, 197, 91 S.Ct. 1763, 29 L.Ed.2d 406 (1971); Commissioner v. Duberstein, 363 U.S. at 285, 44 S.Ct. at 69; Morgan v. Commissioner, 309 U.S. 78, 80–81, 60 S.Ct. 424, 84 L.Ed. 585 (1940); Higt v. United States, 256 F.2d 795, 800 (2d Cir. 1958). New York law cannot be decisive on the question whether any given transfer is income under § 61(a) or is exempt under § 102(a) of the Code. We repeat, we see no difference between the transfer here made in the form of a bequest and the transfer under Commissioner v. Duberstein, supra, which was made without consideration, with no legal or moral obligation, and which was indeed a "common-law gift," but which was nevertheless held not to be a gift excludable under § 102(a).

* * *

PROBLEMS

1. Consider whether it is likely that § 102 applies in the following circumstances:

(a) Father leaves Daughter $20,000 in his will.

(b) Father dies intestate and Daughter receives $20,000 worth of real estate as his heir.

(c) Father leaves several family members out of his will and Daughter and others attack the will. As a result of a settlement of the controversy Daughter receives $20,000.

(d) Father leaves Daughter $20,000 in his will stating that the amount is in appreciation of Daughter's long and devoted service to him.

(e) Father leaves Daughter $20,000 pursuant to a written agreement under which Daughter agreed to care for Father in his declining years.

(f) Same agreement as in (e), above, except that Father died intestate and Daughter successfully enforced her $20,000 claim under the agreement against the estate.

(g) Same as (f), above, except that Daughter settles her $20,000 claim for a $10,000 payment.

(h) Father appointed Daughter executrix of his estate and Father's will provided Daughter was to receive $20,000 for services as executrix.

(i) Father appointed Daughter executrix of his estate and made a $20,000 bequest to her in lieu of all compensation or commissions to which she would otherwise be entitled as executrix.

CHAPTER 5. LIMITATIONS IN EMPLOYMENT RELATIONSHIPS

A. FRINGE BENEFITS

Internal Revenue Code: See Section 79.
Regulations: Section 1.61–2(a)(1), –2(d)(2)(ii)(a).

SUMMARY AND EXPLANATION OF DISCUSSION DRAFT OF PROPOSED REGULATIONS ON FRINGE BENEFITS

Issued by the Office of the Assistant Secretary of the Treasury for Tax Policy September 2, 1975, and published in the Federal Register on September 5, 1975.

The following document contains a discussion draft of proposed regulations dealing with the subject of fringe benefits. In general, the proposed regulations codify practices that have grown up over more than 60 years. Those practices and precedents constitute a practical interpretation of statutory language which is so elastic that it provides only general guidance. With the definition of "income" —as in the case of other broad concepts such as "due process" or "equal protection"—most of the law must be discovered in a study of the ways in which the language has been interpreted. Thus, for example, official interpretations outstanding for decades hold that such things as travel passes for railroad employees or supper money for employees who work overtime are not to be included in income. These conclusions are carried forward into the proposed regulations, although a logical argument to the contrary could be made if we were writing on a clean slate.

It is not anticipated that any regulations dealing with such a question will be definitive. It is hoped only that they will provide guidelines which give a better and more uniform sense of direction. That, in turn, should provide results which are more equitable.

Public and Congressional Comment and Criticism Invited.

Ordinarily, regulations are published first in proposed form and then, after comment and revision, in final form. In this case they are being published as a discussion draft prior to publication in proposed form because of the nature of the subject and the desirability of obtaining the broadest possible public comment. The taxability of fringe benefits is not solely a question for tax technicians, as the following discussion explains. The administrative and procedural results which have grown up over many years have come to affect in some degree nearly everyone who works, and have evolved perhaps as much from what laymen view as "income" as from any abstract economic theory or legislative guidance. The proposed rules are an effort, in the common law tradition, to restate and rationalize those results and it seems desirable to have comment from laymen and technicians alike before announcing semifinal positions in proposed form.

As we publish these proposed regulations, the tax writing committees of Congress are embarking on a reconsideration of a substantial segment of the tax law. In that effort, Congress, too, may wish to focus on certain aspects of the proposals and, perhaps, to modify the results proposed. While we believe Treasury has authority to deal with these issues through the adoption of regulations, Treasury would not object to workable legislative changes or expansion. The lines drawn in the proposals fall in gray areas and could well be different in a number of respects and still be sound.

The following summary and discussion are published in the hope that an explanation of the considerations underlying the precedents and the proposed rules will better focus public discussion.

I. Summary

General rules.

(1) Employees do not have taxable compensation where the benefit is on hand anyway, it costs nothing additional to provide it, and it is not limited to top executives.

(2) If a benefit does not qualify under (1), then its tax status is determined by looking at all of the facts and circumstances. Among the factors indicating whether or not a benefit is not taxable are:

- Whether the employer incurs a substantial and identifiable cost.

- Whether the expense is clearly related to the employer's business.

- Whether the benefit is exact reimbursement of an unusually large personal expense incurred by the employee on account of the employer's business.

- Whether the benefit is limited to top executives.

(3) Small amounts are not taxed.

Some examples illustrating the general rules.

(1) Airline employees and travel agents are not taxed on travel passes.

(2) Store employees are not taxed on merchandise discounts.

(3) An interior decorator is not taxed on the purchase of furniture for personal use at wholesale prices.

(4) Use of a business jet is not taxed where employees and their guests use otherwise empty seats. But a flight made only for personal entertainment purposes of an executive and spouse is taxed.

(5) Benefits to insure safety are not taxed. Examples are taxi fare home at night from a plant in an unsafe area and bodyguards after a threat by terrorists.

(6) Cars are not taxed to the extent required for the job. A specific example deals with and exempts transportation provided the President, and those cabinet officers, ambassadors, and consuls, for whom Congress has impliedly recognized that transportation to and from home is "official." Officials not covered by Congressional authorization are taxable on the personal use of government cars, including commuting between their homes and offices. Another example covers officials such as fire chiefs, who must be on duty at all hours.

Also not taxed are cars for outside salesmen who pay for gas for personal use.

Cars are not taxed where they are provided to take an executive from his office to business appointments, but there is tax to the extent the car is used for commuting. The use of "demonstrators" by employees of an auto agency who do not primarily use the car for business is taxed.

(7) Free parking spaces in a company garage are not taxed under most circumstances.

(8) Having one's secretary type a personal letter is not taxed.

(9) Payment of bar association dues by a law firm is not taxed.

(10) Periodic social functions of a firm are not taxed to employees.

(11) Tuition-free American-style schools operated for overseas employees are not taxed to the employee.

(12) The use of a free company day care center results in income that may be offset by a deduction expressly allowed by statute.

II. *Discussion.*

The taxation of economic benefits which individuals receive in kind has been troublesome since our income tax system began in 1913. Fringe benefits have proliferated as our industries and working conditions have grown ever more complex. Generalized principles have been slow to develop, and there has inevitably been non-uniformity of treatment of different taxpayers in similar situations.

The statutory definition of "gross income"—like most broad and sweeping definitions—fails to provide certainty in a multitude of individual situations. As a result, interpreting and applying the definition have become major tasks for the courts and administrative officials. As in the case of such other broad phrases as "due process" and "equal protection," a substantial gloss on the statutory language has evolved and become a part of the law.

Our Anglo-American system of law rests firmly on precedent, but as precedents amass, it has been the role of jurists and scholars to rationalize the accumulation and to seek the threads of underlying principle. In the process, some precedents are discarded as defective; others are recognized as correct conclusions, but for reasons different from those advanced at the time; and the entire process is subject to constant revision for, as Cardozo said, "If we were to state the law today as well as human minds can state it, new problems, arising almost overnight, would encumber the ground again." [1] This constant and dynamic search for organizing principles is the genius of our legal system. The proposed regulations represent a limited effort to apply that process to a narrow but vexing area of the tax law, in which more than half a century of judicial and administrative precedent have produced considerable confusion and uncertainty.

There are no general principles which will accommodate every judicial decision and administrative action that has occurred in the last 62 years, for a number of those decisions and actions are inconsistent with each other and with the general lines of precedent that have developed. The attempt has been to discover those organizing principles which best conform to the body of precedent and which themselves represent sound and equitable policies.

The proposals are presented with the awareness that the principles expressed are not all-encompassing and that the principles will themselves require modification in time, for it is no doubt necessary to a sound and practical income tax that the content of "income" should remain somewhat fluid, so that the application of the tax can keep pace with changing conditions. [2]

It is intended that the proposed regulations be viewed as broad principles suggesting a rationale and path to a reasonable solution in particular cases. They are essentially different from those highly technical provisions of the Code and regulations intended to deal definitively with all aspects of a narrow problem. They are not to be construed or applied in a narrow and literal fashion to exclude every situation which fails to be described by the precise language employed. "As in other sciences, so in politics, it is impossible that all things should be precisely set down in writing; for enactments must be universal, but actions are concerned with particulars." [3]

1. Cardozo, "The Growth of the Law" (1924), p. 19. These lectures, addressed in part to the then current effort of the American Law Institute to "restate" the law in a number of areas, contain a discussion of this process.

2. Cf. Surrey and Warren, *Federal Income Taxation*, 1972, vol. 1, p. 115.

3. Aristotle, *Politics*, Book II, quoted by Cardozo, op. cit.

The Definition of "Income."

The Internal Revenue Code states simply that

> Gross income means all income from whatever source derived. . . .

As a definition, that language has an obvious defect, for to say that gross income includes income still fails to tell us what income is. The statutory language should be viewed rather as broad authorization to reach such items as may be appropriate, in the context of our overall system. It is clearly broad enough to encompass almost any economic benefit, but it is equally clear that it has not been construed to do so. To the uninitiated layman the language may appear sufficient. For perhaps the great majority of taxpayers, no ambiguities exist. Income from wages and salaries, dividends, interest from savings deposits, and the like are universally regarded as income under any definition, and for the majority that appears to take care of all of the problems. But students of the tax law know better, and most of the hundreds of pages of the Internal Revenue Code were written to help draw the lines between what will and what will not be treated as income.

Even for theoretical economists, there has been great confusion as to exactly what constitutes income. The classic work on the subject is Professor Simons', *Personal Income Taxation* (1938), which comments on the task of defining "income":

> Many writers have undertaken to formulate definitions, and with the most curious results. Whereas the word is widely used in discussions of justice in taxation and without evident confusion, the greatest variety and dissimilarity appear, as to both content and phraseology, in the actual definitions proposed by particular writers. The consistent recourse to definition in terms which are themselves undefinable (or undefined or equally ambiguous) testifies eloquently to the underlying confusion.[4]

Professor Simons' own theoretical definition of income (generally known as the Haig-Simons definition) has become the definition perhaps most widely accepted among economists.

However, the theoretical definitions of income have not been used for the practical purpose of assessing taxes, except as a frame of reference against which to judge the existing system. Thus, Professor Simons, himself, says:

> If one accepts our definition of income, one may be surprised that it has ever been proposed seriously as a basis for taxation . . . One may remark at the outset that no government has ever undertaken to graduate taxes really on

4. Simons, op. cit., pp. 41–42.

the basis of personal income. The actual tax base is merely something calculated according to more or less carefully defined methods; and these methods may be regarded as designed to give results which are in most instances something like true personal income. Indeed, every income tax is, and probably must be, based largely on presumptions. . . . Tax laws do not really define income but merely set up rules as to what must be included and what may be deducted; and such rules by no means define income because they are neither exhaustive nor logically coherent. . . . Indeed, if there be any excuse for a treatise like this, it must lie in the importance of maintaining some broad—and perhaps quite "impractical"—conception in terms of which existing and proposed practices in income taxation may be examined, tested, and criticized.[5]

It is sometimes asserted simply that income includes any "economic benefit" received, and "economic benefit" is the germ of the more elegant theoretical definition which Professor Simons developed. But the concept of "economic benefit" does not explain 60 years of actual experience. Nor does it conform to public understanding and custom. The fact that economic logic and theory are separated by a substantial gap from the legal rules that have actually developed is neither unique nor undesirable, for as Justice Holmes said:

The life of the law has not been logic; it has been experience. The felt necessities of the time, the prevalent moral and political theories, intuitions of public policy, avowed or unconscious, even the prejudices which judges share with their fellow-men, have had a good deal more to do than the syllogism in determining the rules by which men should be governed.[6]

A few examples will suffice to show that the concept of "economic benefit" does not explain the law:

(1) Social security, welfare, and unemployment compensation payments are not taxable as income under our system. There is no section of the Code which so provides. The exclusion grew up as a result of administrative action, undoubtedly in response to what Justice Holmes called "the felt necessities of the times."

(2) Persons who purchase life insurance pay premiums which are in effect invested on their behalf. Income from those investments is not taxed to the purchaser, notwithstanding that they clearly represent economic benefits.

(3) Taxpayers who invest money in the purchase of a house realize income in kind consisting of the right to live in the house.

5. Pp. 103–106.   6. Holmes, *The Common Law*, p. 1.

That income is not taxed under our tax system although there is nothing in the Code which expressly excludes it.   (Such income has been taxed at various times under other systems.)   A taxpayer who invests the same money in stocks or bonds with the intention of using the income to rent a house, on the other hand, must pay tax on the income from the stocks and bonds, which reduces the amount available to pay rent.

(4) Meals and lodging provided to taxpayers by their employers clearly constitute an economic benefit but are not taxable to the extent they are provided "for the convenience of the employer."   This exclusion was initiated early by administrative ruling and existed for 40 years on that basis.   In 1954, it was written into the Internal Revenue Code in somewhat modified fashion.

(5) Entertainment, meals, travel, and lodging received in a business context are in large part untaxed under current statutory provisions.   At the higher levels of today's business communities, individuals' personal and business lives tend to meld into an indistinguishable whole, and many persons spend much of their lives in such activities.   It is a legitimate conjecture whether the restaurant and resort industries would be decimated without these provisions.

(6) Large elaborate offices for executives, attended with employees and accompanied by working conditions designed to provide every creature comfort and convenience are commonplace and obviously constitute an economic benefit which has both personal and business aspects.   Those benefits are not taxed.

(7) A great variety of miscellaneous benefits provided by employers have been held administratively not to constitute income. Examples include group-term life insurance and compensation for tornado damage.

None of the economic benefits in the foregoing examples was originally excluded from income because of a clear and specific statutory exclusion.   Nor were they excluded because of insurmountable administrative considerations.   For the billions of dollars of additional revenues which could be obtained from these sources, it would obviously be possible to devise workable administrative rules.

The results are better explained by what Justice Holmes called "the prevalent moral and political theories," than by strict theory. The attitude of labor unions on some of these items is interesting as an expression of one view as to "prevalent theories."   Justice Goldberg speaking in his earlier role as General Counsel, CIO, took the following position:

> The line between [compensation and conditions of employment] is, perhaps, not susceptible of precise definition. The reason it is not is because the line is really an institutional and sociological one.   It depends very much on what

our current conception of the relative responsibilities of employer and employee happen to be. The question is whether the benefit in question is one which we regard as a proper responsibility which employers should supply for employees as a condition of employment wholly apart from the compensation for their work. And the answers to that question vary from time to time.

> To the extent that benefits are usually or normally provided by employers, even though they may involve a saving to an employee over alternative methods of providing this facility by himself, then, to that extent the provision of such benefits should not be considered as compensation to the employee but as the provision of improved conditions of work.

Applying these views to employer-provided insurance, he concluded the benefit to be nontaxable, stating:

> How about insurance? With this principle in mind, are the insurance programs negotiated by unions just a disguised way of paying compensation, or are they offered on a service basis as a condition of employment? Clearly the latter.[7]

The Internal Revenue Code as presently interpreted by the regulations and the better reasoned case law requires more than a finding that an employee enjoyed an economic benefit. Section 61(a)(1) of the Code speaks of "compensation *for* services." The regulations condition taxability upon finding a situation where "services are *paid for* other than in money." Treas.Reg. Sec. 1.61–2(d)(1). And, in the Supreme Court's words, section 61 "is broad enough to include in taxable income any economic or financial benefit conferred on the employee *as compensation*." Comm'r v. Smith, 324 U.S. 177, 181 (1945) (emphasis added). The notion of a bargain between employer and employee—that there must be a payment *in exchange for* services—has been added as an essential element for the taxation of compensation, including fringe benefits.

Policy Considerations.

> In sum, there is no easy or entirely satisfactory answer as to how all economic benefits should be taxed or not taxed. Professor Simons says with respect to income in kind:

> There is here an essential and insuperable difficulty, even in principle. The problem . . . certainly is not amenable to reasonable solution on the basis of simple rules which could be administered by revenue agents. . . . At all events, let it be recognized that one faces here one of the real imponderables of income definition.[8]

7. Quoted in Surrey and Warren, op.   8. Simons, op. cit., pp. 123–24.
cit., p. 139.

The principles governing the taxation of fringe benefits inescapably involve a large degree of judgment not reducible to a single formulistic test or tests. Simple mechanical formulas are not possible. In reaching the judgments embodied in the proposed regulations, the following policy considerations were taken into account.

(1) *Present practices in general are codified.* Sixty-two years of experience must be given great weight. The practices which have developed provide a reasonable and pragmatic guide to which economic benefits are appropriate for taxation. The general rules of the proposed regulations excluding benefits inherent in the employer's business under certain circumstances deal with a category of clear economic benefits that have not been generally taxed and which, we believe, generally should not be taxed. The first eight factors set out in the proposed regulations are distillations of principles from experience and are applications of the ninth factor, which states that an item is not taxed if it is not thought of as constituting compensation paid for services. While these factors necessarily lack particularity in many respects, they are much more specific than the statutory language and far preferable to some simplistic theory (such as "economic benefit") that is at odds with our national conception of what realistically constitutes taxable compensation for services. In some instances, where precedent was slim, or unconvincing, questions have been resolved in favor of taxpayers. In other cases, rules were resolved against taxpayers even though good arguments would be made for a contrary result. For example, in the case of executive transportation furnished by employers, it might arguably have been reasonable to hold that private transportation was not taxable to the extent it was furnished to permit the executive to perform work while commuting. However, the line of precedent with respect to commuting expense is so extensive and so firmly established that such a rule did not appear to be an administrative option.

(2) *Statutory authority is broad but not mandatorily all-encompassing.* The statutory definition of income is very broad. That broad scope provides the residual authority to deal with new forms of compensation and other income generally as they develop without having to amend the statute each time. Inherent in that authority is the flexibility and, indeed, the necessity to distinguish between economic benefits which should be taxed and those which should not. The draft regulations do not extend the reach of the income tax to fringe benefits so far as they could legally, but only so far as they may practically.

(3) *Equity among taxpayers.* As indicated earlier, many high-income persons, particularly those whose business and personal lives are in effect melded, enjoy major economic benefits in the form of meals, lodging, travel, and entertainment, much of which goes untaxed under rules that are statutory. When this is occurring in so

widespread a fashion, it seems particularly unfair, for example, to tax ordinary airline employees for traveling in otherwise empty seats or to tax retail clerks for discounts received on goods purchased from their employers.

If all taxpayers had fringe benefits or other benefits in kind and those benefits were roughly in proportion to their other income, then the uniform exclusion of all such benefits from tax would be as equitable as tax matters are likely ever to be and would probably contribute to a more efficient and effective tax system, as it would avoid the valuation and withholding problems discussed below. But the non-uniform exclusion of such benefits—exclusions for some but not others—would be clearly inequitable. Thus, in drafting the proposed regulations a special effort was made to be sure that ordinary taxpayers in the lower and middle income classes were treated in a fashion as generous as that which very high income taxpayers already enjoy, subject to the overriding principle that the integrity of the system must be protected.

(4) *Valuation problems.* Valuation of benefits in kind is extremely difficult in many, if not most cases, and the necessity for valuation vastly complicates the tax law. What is the value to a stewardess of riding in an otherwise empty seat? In most cases the privilege would not be worth to her the retail price of a ticket, i. e., she would not make the trip if she had to pay for it. Thus, in Reginald Turner, 13 T.C.M. 462 (1954), the court dealt with taxpayers who had won a free trip to South America and stated:

> The winning of the tickets did not provide them with something which they needed in the ordinary course of their lives and for which they would have made an expenditure in any event, but merely gave them an opportunity to enjoy a luxury otherwise beyond their means. Their value to the petitioners was not equal to their retail cost.

Similarly, how would one tax free or subsidized medical and recreational services and facilities for employees? Or company cafeteria meals provided at prices less than the prices prevailing in comparable restaurants? Valuation of such items comes very close to valuing working conditions as such, an undertaking that would encounter almost insurmountable difficulties.[9] In general, it is desirable to avoid the complications of taxing such items, unless their omission constitutes a serious threat to the tax base or creates inequities that are significant in the context of the system as a whole.

(5) *Withholding considerations.* Our system relies on wage withholding to collect most of the personal income tax. In 1972, $91 billion of $110 billion personal income tax collected was withheld

---

9. See Vickrey, *Agenda for Progressive Taxation* (1947), p. 123.

from wages. The system works well only because almost all of the tax is collected automatically on cash payments. Withholding involves only easy arithmetic applied to unambiguous dollar amounts. Audit of withheld amounts is easy. If we should attempt to include in the withholding base every economic benefit enjoyed by great numbers of employees, the operation of the system would be seriously jeopardized. Taxpayers would have many ingenious theories to justify exclusion from gross income and, when taxed, there would be an infinity of valuation problems, of the kind referred to above.

This reliance on a simple self-executing system to collect most income tax leads to the policy judgment that, as a general rule, only those fringe benefit cases which threaten the integrity of the basic system should be taxed. Thus, the proposed regulations reach private junkets on corporate aircraft, personal use of company cars (and drivers) by executives, and discriminatory use of company facilities generally. While the proposed regulations reach these obvious cases, they do not involve the esoteric problems of taxing, and thus valuing, for example, the right to occupy an otherwise empty seat on a commerical flight. Employee discounts and free travel for airline flight attendants do not threaten the integrity of our income tax system. There is a great risk that trying to tax these and similar items would threaten the continued success of our self-assessment system.

(6) *Retroactivity.* In some cases, notwithstanding that existing precedent might have supported an assertion of taxability, it is in fact the case that tax has not been generally collected. This is true, for example, in the case of automobiles and automobile transportation provided in a variety of situations. In such cases, it seems unfair to impose heavy tax liabilities retroactively on unsuspecting laymen. Thus, in a few instances, the proposed regulations would exercise the statutory discretion given by the Code to the Secretary to apply administrative rules on a nonretroactive basis.

Conclusion.

The proposed regulations are published for discussion as an attempt to provide guidelines that will afford greater degrees of certainty, uniformity, and fairness in an area which has become steadily more significant. They will not provide simple formulas which can be mechanically applied by revenue agents. That is not a defect, as present law provides no such formula either, except insofar as the broad sweep of the existing statutory language may in practicality give a revenue agent the personal discretion to include anything and everything that appears to result in economic benefit to the employee —an obviously unsatisfactory state of affairs. There is no way to avoid judgments in this difficult area, and we can only work to insure that those judgments are as sound and uniform as possible.

The draft regulations are published in the hope that they will provide the basis for prescribing better guidelines to that end.

Office of the
Assistant Secretary for Tax Policy
September 2, 1975

NOTE

When an area of fringe benefits threatens to get out of hand, Congress sometimes steps in with express legislation. In 1964 Congress added I.R.C. (26 U.S.C.A.) § 79 which imposes a limit on the amount of group term life insurance which an employer can provide tax-free for an employee.[1] Prior to that time group term life insurance premiums paid for an employee were not included in his income at all and, while Congress recognized the desirability of employers providing employee protection, the amounts of coverage on some employees was so great that Congress determined its compensatory nature should not be entirely ignored. A maximum of $50,000 was imposed on the amount of employer-paid coverage that could be provided tax free.[2] For purposes of determining the taxable portion of premium payments, the cost of group insurance is determined under uniform tables provided in the regulations.[3] The ceiling limitation does not apply: (1) if the premiums are paid for individuals whose employment has been terminated and who have either reached retirement age or are disabled,[4] or (2) if the employer or a charity is the beneficiary of the proceeds of the policy.[5]

Restrictions on the scope of allowable fringe benefits have also been imposed administratively. An example is the treatment of so-called "split-dollar" life insurance arrangements between employers and employees. Under such arrangements, which are outside the group insurance rules of § 79, an insurance contract is purchased on the life of the employee. The employer provides the funds to pay the annual premium to the extent of the increase in cash surrender value each year and the employee pays the balance of the premium. At the employee's death the amount of the cash surrender value of the policy is paid to the employer and any excess benefits go to the employee's designated beneficiary. While the initial cost of the policy falls primarily on the employee, subsequent premiums are paid principally by the employer. Initially the Service regarded such trans-

1. See Walker, "Group Life Insurance," 23 N.Y.U. Inst. on Fed.Tax. 153 (1965).

2. I.R.C. (26 U.S.C.A.) § 79(a). In effect, the ceiling is raised to the extent that the employee contributes to the cost of the insurance. I.R.C. (26 U.S.C.A.) § 79(a)(2).

3. Reg. § 1.79–3(d).

4. I.R.C. (26 U.S.C.A.) § 79(b)(1).

5. I.R.C. (26 U.S.C.A.) § 79(b)(2). See also § 79(b)(3), providing a further exception in the case of insurance purchased under a qualified employer's benefit plan described in I.R.C. (26 U.S.C.A.) § 72(m)(3).

actions as merely interest-free loans to the employee which did not constitute income to him.[6] In a change of administrative policy, the Service now regards the transaction as one in which the earnings on the employer's investment in the contract are "applied to provide current life insurance protection to the employee from year to year, without cost to the employee."[7] The Service has ruled that, since the effect of the "split-dollar" arrangement is "to provide an economic benefit to the employee represented by the amount of the annual premium cost that he should bear and of which he is relieved,"[8] the employee has income to that extent.

COMMISSIONER v. MINZER

United States Court of Appeals, Fifth Circuit, 1960.
279 F.2d 338.

JONES, CIRCUIT JUDGE. We are here concerned with the liability of Sol Minzer and Adele Minzer, his wife, for a federal income tax deficiency for the year 1954. The transactions from which the controversy stems were those of Sol Minzer and he will be referred to as the taxpayer. No issues of fact are presented.

In 1954 the taxpayer was an insurance agent or broker. During that year he procured or kept in force policies of insurance upon his life. As a representative of the insurance companies which had issued the policies he became entitled to commissions on the policies to the same extent as though the insurance had been on the life of someone else. He received the commissions, or the benefit of them, upon these policies on his own life either by remitting the premiums, less commissions, to the companies, or by remitting the premiums in their entirety and receiving back from the companies their checks to him for the amounts of the commissions. The taxpayer did not include these commissions as taxable income in his return for 1954. The Commissioner of Internal Revenue recomputed the tax by the inclusion of the commissions as income and made a deficiency determination. The Tax Court held for the taxpayer. 31 T.C. 1130. Seven judges dissented. The Commissioner brings the case to us for review.

The Tax Court, or those of the Court who subscribed to the prevailing opinion, placed their decision upon the narrow ground that

---

6. Rev.Rul. 55–713, 1955–2 C.B. 23.

7. Rev.Rul. 64–328, 1964–2 C.B. 11, 13.

8. Id. at 13 and 15. Rev.Rul. 64–328 is modified by Rev.Rul. 66–110, 1966–1 C.B. 12. For a discussion of "split-dollar" life insurance including the possibility that the government's analysis of it is improper and that it is nothing more than an interest-free loan under the *J. Simpson Dean* case, Chapter 3, supra at page 57, see Chommie, Federal Income Taxation, pp. 59–60 (2d Edit. 1973); an earlier discussion of the problem appears in Redeker, "Split-Dollar Insurance," 15 N.Y.U. Inst. on Fed.Tax. 249 (1957).

the taxpayer was a broker and not an employee and hence the transactions were outside the terms of Income Tax Regulations Section 61–2(d)(2).[1] In the prevailing opinion of the Tax Court an unwillingness is expressed to apply the prior administrative rulings [2] holding that commissions received or retained by a life insurance agent on policies upon his own life are income to the agent. This ruling would have been followed by the Tax Court if it had found an employer-employee relationship between the insurance companies and the taxpayer.

The contract between one of the insurance companies, Western States Life Insurance Company, is designated as an agency contract and the taxpayer is therein referred to as "the agent." The contract with the other company, Occidental Life Insurance Company, is called a brokerage agreement. In both contracts the taxpayer was authorized to solicit and submit applications for life insurance and in each

1. [Reg. § 1.61–2(d)(2) is omitted. See also I.R.C. § 83, added long after the decision in this case. Ed.]

2. "Information is requested relative to the basis on which a ruling relating to insurance commissions was made.
"The particular ruling, which is one of several rulings contained in Treasury Decision 2137, reads as follows:
"Commission retained by agent on his own life insurance policy.—A commission retained by a life insurance agent on his own life insurance policy is held to be income accruing to the agent, and should be included in his return of income for the assessment of the income tax.
"If a life insurance company reduces the standard charge of an insurance policy to a purchaser and the relationship of employer and employee does not exist, the amount by which the policy is reduced can not be considered income at the time of purchase for the reason that it is not 'gain derived from capital, from labor, or from both combined,' nor 'profit gained through a sale or conversion of capital assets' within the meaning of the definition of income as stated in Eisner v. Macomber, 252 U.S. 189, 40 S.Ct. 189, 64 L.Ed. 521; T.D. 3010, C.B. 3, 25. The Board of Tax Appeals has held that the purchase of property at a bargain price does not result in taxable income where the sale is consummated by two persons dealing at arms' length. (See Appeal of Manomet Cranberry Co., 1 B.T.A. 706, C.B. IV–1, 3.)

"The reason that the commission allowed an insurance agent on a policy taken out on his own life is considered income is that the relationship of employer and employee exists between the insurance company and the agent, and inasmuch as the insurance company is under contract to pay the agent commissions on all policies of insurance secured by him, no distinction can logically be made between a commission paid to the agent on account of a policy written on his own life and a commission paid to the agent on account of a policy written on the life of some one else. The commission is paid to the agent as compensation for services rendered as an employee, i. e., on account of business obtained, regardless of whose life is insured, and is 'gain derived from labor,' and therefore taxable income. Furthermore, it is immaterial whether the agent remits to the company the standard charge for such insurance (namely, the amount that would be charged any other person under like conditions) and receives a check for his commission, or whether he remits to the company the standard charge minus his commission. The net result is the same. The agent receives taxable income to the extent of the commission, either actually or constructively. It follows that the amount of commission paid by the insurance company should be reported as income by the insurance agent." G.C.M. 10486, XI–1 C.B. 14.

contract the percentage of premiums which the taxpayer should receive as commissions was specified. The relationships created by the contracts were substantially the same. It does not seem to us that the tax incidence is dependent upon the tag with which the parties label the connection between them. The agent or broker, or by whatever name he be called, is to receive or retain a percentage of the premiums on policies procured by him, called commissions, as compensation for his service to the company in obtaining the particular business for it. The service rendered to the company, for which it was required to compensate him, was no different in kind or degree where the taxpayer submitted his own application than where he submitted the application of another. In each situation there was the same obligation of the company, the obligation to pay a commission for the production of business measured by a percentage of the premiums. In each situation the result was the same to the taxpayer. The taxpayer obtained insurance, which the companies were prohibited by law from selling to him at any discount. 14 Vernon's Tex. Civ.Stat. Insurance Code, Art. 21.21. It cannot be said that the insurance had a value less than the amount of the premiums. It must then be said that a benefit inured to the taxpayer to the extent of his commissions. The benefit is neither diminished nor eliminated by referring, as does the Tax Court, to the word "commission" as a verbal trap. The commissions were, we conclude, compensation for services and as such were income within the meaning of 26 U.S.C.A. (I.R.C.1954) § 61(a)(1).

While, as we have tried to indicate, the Commissioner's contention is sound in principle, it is also to be supported by the long-standing administrative rulings which are to be given great weight. Lykes v. United States, 343 U.S. 118, 72 S.Ct. 585, 96 L.Ed. 791; Helvering v. R. J. Reynolds Tobacco Co., 306 U.S. 110, 59 S.Ct. 423, 83 L.Ed. 536; Massachusetts Mutual Life Insurance Co. v. United States, 288 U.S. 269, 53 S.Ct. 337, 77 L.Ed. 739. The weight so given is not, in our opinion, lightened by the conclusion in the General Counsel's Memorandum, G.C.M. 10486, that there was an employer-employee relationship existing, and the stress there placed upon such relationship, although we think the ruling is applicable as well to independent contractors and others as to those in a technical common law master and servant category.

The Commissioner's position is sustained by precedent as well as upon principle and by administrative ruling. A case such as that before us has recently been decided by the Third Circuit with the result that commissions on insurance paid with respect to policies of the agent were held to be income taxable to him. Ostheimer v. United States, 3 Cir., 1959, 264 F.2d 789. We are in accord with that court's conclusions that the agent did not receive a bargain purchase and that the commissions were neither discounts nor rebates.

It is argued that the doctrine urged by the Commissioner represents an unprecedented extension of the concept of income as is found in Eisner v. Macomber, 252 U.S. 189, 40 S.Ct. 189, 190, 64 L.Ed. 521. There taxable income was characterized as "the gain derived from capital, from labor, or from both combined." We cannot see that our decision in any way expands the Eisner v. Macomber principle. On the contrary we think our determination is within it. But if the Eisner v. Macomber statement is regarded as a deterrent to the decision we have reached, we are taken from under its interdict by a later case from the Supreme Court where it is said that the phrase in Eisner v. Macomber "was not meant to provide a touchstone to all future gross income questions". Commissioner of Internal Revenue v. Glenshaw Glass Co., 348 U.S. 426, 75 S.Ct. 473, 477, 99 L.Ed. 483. See Commissioner of Internal Revenue v. LeBue, 351 U.S. 243, 76 S.Ct. 800, 100 L.Ed. 1142.

It follows that the decision of the Tax Court must be and it is hereby

Reversed.

CAMERON, CIRCUIT JUDGE.

I dissent.

PROBLEMS

1. Did the Treasury give adequate recognition to the *Glenshaw Glass* case when issuing its fringe benefit discussion? (Note that this and questions 2–4 all relate to the Treasury's fringe benefit discussion, supra page 99.)

    (a) After *Glenshaw Glass* is the word "income" in § 61 as elastic as is suggested in the first paragraph of the Treasury's discussion?

    (b) Could *Glenshaw Glass* be said to wipe the slate clean justifying a change in result with respect to travel passes and supper money if the Treasury so desired?

    (c) If "economic benefit" does not "explain 60 years of actual experience", is it not at least the root stock of the income concept since *Glenshaw Glass*?

2. An equitable result for the taxation of fringes is sought to assure that "lower and middle income classes [are] treated in a fashion as generous as * * * very high income taxpayers * * *."

    (a) Is this a proper objective? What about the self-employed, the retired, and others who have no fringe benefits?

    (b) If an airline stewardess had to pay tax on the regular cost of an airline ticket for the seat "given" her, she would be faced with about the same tax circumstance as a self-employed person with similar income who uses *after-tax* income to buy a vacation airline ticket. Is that bad?

(c) Why does it seem "unfair" to tax "unsuspecting laymen" on the value of the use of company cars beyond fringe or business activities when most taxpayers never have received these benefits, taxable or otherwise?

3. Is a finding that something is not "compensation *for* services," or that "services" are not being "paid for other than in money," or that an employee received a benefit other than "as compensation" relevant to the question whether an employee has gross income? That which is not a gift or otherwise expressly excluded may be income even if not "compensation" or paid for services. But return to this question after studying *McDonell,* infra page 125. For something received by an employee from an employer to be income must it at least be conferred *as a benefit*? If conferred as a benefit, must the benefit be *"in exchange for services?"*

4. To what extent is the question whether something is income dependent on the ease with which it may be valued? What if we tried to tax as income the fair club value of the company's tennis courts? It would seem sound at least to tax it only if the employee used the courts. And should the inclusion be at a cut rate, e. g. half of the charge of a membership at municipal courts?

5. If the *conclusions* in the proposed regulations seem desirable, is there a better way to reach them? Is the Treasury really on a quest for an "income" definition? In England "Inland Revenue", the I.R.S. counterpart, has authority to make concessions. Is that what goes on here? Should Congress legislate expressly on the items that appear in the examples? Give the I.R.S. the power to grant concessions with guidelines like the "Summary?"

6. A is employed by Sears and salaried. Sears, let us say, gives A a 10% courtesy discount, standard for most employee purchases. A works in garden tools and sells himself a $500 ride-on mower for $450. B is employed by Montgomery Ward, but all else is much the same. However, he is a commission salesman. He sells himself a $500 ride-on mower and his employer, let us say, pays him a 10% commission on the sale. The net cost to each is $450. What tax result to A and B? Is there any difference in their situations that would support a different tax result?

B. EXCLUSIONS FOR MEALS AND LODGING

Internal Revenue Code: Sections 107; 119.
Regulations: Section 1.119–1.

THE UNITED STATES JUNIOR CHAMBER OF COMMERCE v. THE UNITED STATES

Court of Claims of the United States, 1964.
167 Ct.Cl. 392, 334 F.2d 660.

JONES, SENIOR JUDGE. This is a suit by The United States Junior Chamber of Commerce to recover $747.89 as alleged erroneously assessed withholding and F.I.C.A. taxes,[1] together with interest thereon, for the years 1959 and 1960. The principal issue for our determination is the applicability, under the facts of this case, of the exclusionary rule contained in § 119 of the Internal Revenue Code of 1954.

Plaintiff is a nonprofit corporation, incorporated under the laws of the State of Missouri. It was organized for "such educational and charitable purposes as will promote and foster the growth and development of young men's civic organizations in the United States." Among its activities are such programs as the promotion of interest in youth athletic programs, safe driving programs, and community and school development programs. The headquarters and principal offices of plaintiff are located in Tulsa, Oklahoma. Plaintiff owns and maintains a residential building in Tulsa, known as the "U.S. Jaycee White House" (hereinafter referred to as the House), which is the official residence and home of the president of plaintiff during his term of office.

The president of plaintiff is its chief executive officer and is elected at the annual meeting by a majority vote of plaintiff's membership. He is elected for a term of one year only, and may not succeed himself in office. During the years involved in this suit, plaintiff had three presidents who, prior to their election, lived and worked in North Carolina, Iowa, and Pennsylvania, respectively. At the expiration of their terms of office, each president returned to his respective residence and employment.

The by-laws of plaintiff provide, in pertinent part, that:

"Because of the benefits and convenience accruing to the Corporation by having the President and his family, if any,

---

1. F.I.C.A. are the initials of the Federal Insurance Contributions Act, the tax under which is commonly known as the social security tax.

reside in Tulsa in the home built by the Corporation for the President, the President and his family shall reside at the U.S. Jaycee White House in Tulsa, during his tenure of office."

In accordance with the by-laws, each of the above-mentioned three presidents lived in the House during his term of office. None of the presidents paid plaintiff any rent while so residing there, and all expenses of operating and maintaining the House were paid by plaintiff. It was plaintiff's policy to recognize the building as the private residence of its president and his family during his term of office, and visits to the House by members were not approved unless a specific invitation had been extended by the president in residence. The present controversy is concerned with the question whether or not the fair rental value of the House is excludable from the gross income of plaintiff's presidents.

The Commissioner of Internal Revenue determined that the fair rental value of the House should have been included in the gross income of the various presidents, and that plaintiff should have withheld income and F.I.C.A. taxes thereon for the years 1959 and 1960. The parties agreed that the fair rental value of the House during these years was $125 per month. The Commissioner of Internal Revenue thereupon assessed such withholding and F.I.C.A. taxes against plaintiff in the amount of $705, together with interest thereon in the amount of $42.89. No part of this $747.89 in taxes and interest was actually deducted or withheld by plaintiff. After plaintiff paid these assessments and its claims for refund were disallowed, the present suit was timely filed.

It was found by our trial commissioner that plaintiff's presidents traveled extensively throughout the United States, visiting local and state organizations, in carrying out their responsibilities for supervision of all of plaintiff's affairs. During the years here in issue, roughly one-half of a president's time was spent in Tulsa actively directing plaintiff's various programs and the other half of his time was spent in traveling. While in Tulsa, plaintiff's presidents worked during both the day and night. There is an office in the House which the presidents used at night for the purpose of conducting staff meetings and briefings by subordinate officials. In addition, the presidents used the House for official entertainment connected with plaintiff's business.

The trial commissioner concluded that the evidence established that for the convenience of plaintiff, and as a condition of a president's tenure, he was, as a practical matter, required to live in the House. The trial commissioner further found that the House constituted a part of the business premises of plaintiff. Defendant disputes each and every one of these conclusions. However, we agree with the conclusions of the trial commissioner.

The Government contends that, because of the broad scope of § 61 of the 1954 Code, the fair rental value of the House constituted income to plaintiff's presidents unless such income was excludable under § 119. It is the Government's position that the fair rental value of the House was not excludable under § 119 because none of the three requirements under that section was met. Therefore, the Government concludes that the fair rental value of the House constituted income to plaintiff's presidents and that plaintiff should have withheld income and F.I.C.A. taxes thereon.

Section 119 of the Internal Revenue Code of 1954 provides in part:

> "There shall be excluded from gross income of an employee the value of any meals or lodging furnished to him by his employer for the convenience of the employer, but only if—
>
> *   *   *   *   *   *   *   *   *   *
>
> "(2) in the case of lodging, the employee is required to accept such lodging on the business premises of his employer as a condition of his employment."

Thus, there are three conditions which must be met if the value of the lodging furnished an employee by his employer are to be excluded from the employee's gross income: The lodging must be furnished for the convenience of the employer; the employee is required to accept such lodging as a condition of his employment; and the lodging must be on the business premises of the employer. In determining the applicability of § 119, the intention of the employer (whether or not he regarded the fair rental value of the lodging furnished to be compensation) is not particularly important. Indeed, both the Senate and House Committee Reports in discussing § 119 of the 1954 Code contain an example, which is now Example 3 in Treas.Regs. § 1.119–1(d), showing that even when the employer regarded the lodging furnished to be a part of the employee's compensation, the employee would nevertheless be entitled to exclude the value of such lodging from his gross income if the conditions of § 119 are otherwise met. Further, § 119 itself provides that in determining whether meals or lodging are furnished for the convenience of the employer, "the provisions of an employment contract or of a State statute fixing terms of employment shall not be determinative of whether the meals or lodging are intended as compensation." Therefore, we conclude that the Congress intended that an objective test should be used in applying § 119.

There does not appear to be any substantial difference between the first two conditions of § 119: The "convenience of the employer" test and the "required as a condition of his employment" test. The Senate Committee Report accompanying the 1954 Code defined the phrase "required as a condition of his employment" to mean "required in order for the employee to properly perform the duties of his employment." S.Rep.No.1622, 83d Cong., 2d Sess. 190 (1954), 3 U.S.C.Cong. & Ad.News (1954), pp. 4621, 4825. On the other hand, the Commissioner of Internal Revenue has said that:[2]

> "As a general rule, the test of 'convenience of the employer' is satisfied if living quarters or meals are furnished to an employee who is required to accept such quarters and meals in order to perform properly his duties."

See Diamond v. Sturr, 221 F.2d 264, 266 (2d Cir. 1955); and Stone v. Commissioner, 32 T.C. 1021, 1024 (1959). Although the last quoted definition was issued before the promulgation of the 1954 Code, it is at least indicative of the meaning of the phrase used by the Congress. Furthermore, the only post-1954 case cited by the Government as bearing on the "convenience of the employer" test supports the above interpretation of the 1954 Code. Olkjer v. Commissioner, 32 T.C. 464 (1959).

The issue of whether or not the lodging was furnished for the convenience of the employer, or whether the employee was required to accept the lodging in order to properly perform his duties, is primarily a question of fact to be resolved by a consideration of all the facts and circumstances of the case. Olkjer v. Commissioner, supra; Stone v. Commissioner, supra. Under the facts of the present case we believe that the use of the House was furnished to plaintiff's presidents for the convenience of plaintiff. These presidents were elected for a term of one year each, and they may not succeed themselves in office. They came from all parts of the country. During their one year in Tulsa they were away half of the time. In these circumstances, it is not unreasonable to suppose that some of them would, for their temporary stay in Tulsa, rent living quarters not suitable for purposes of plaintiff's official activities.

Plaintiff's business is devoted primarily to organizing and promoting interest and activity on the part of young men in the affairs of their community, state and Nation. It is common knowledge that such a business requires constant staff meetings and official entertainment. Furthermore, plaintiff's presidents were away from Tulsa half of the time during their term in office. Consequently, when a president is back in Tulsa he must quickly catch up with his administrative duties and plan his future trips. These appear to be the reasons why the presidents frequently worked and entertained at night.

2. Mim. 5023, 1940–1, Cum.Bull. 14.

Since the work and entertainment were plaintiff's business activities, plaintiff was responsible for providing suitable space for their proper execution. In light of these facts we believe that it was not unreasonable for plaintiff to permanently rid itself of the problem by furnishing its presidents with quarters where they could carry out the required work and entertainment at night.

The Government apparently does not dispute that plaintiff's official functions required access to a place such as the House. What the Government seems to be saying is that other suitable residences were available in the Tulsa area and so it was not necessary for plaintiff to furnish its presidents with the House for the proper performance of plaintiff's functions. The Government appears to be contending that § 119 does not apply unless *the* furnished lodging was so necessary to the performance of the duties of the employment that the absence of the specific lodging would render the performance virtually impossible.

We do not think that such a strict construction of § 119 is warranted. There are few instances in life where such an abstract concept of necessity would be met. Even in the cases cited by the Government,[3] where the employment was at a construction jobsite 40 miles from Anchorage and so the meals and lodging furnished to the employees were allowed to be excluded, it would presumably be possible for the employer to require the employees to furnish their own housetrailers to live near the jobsite. We believe that § 119 should be given a reasonable interpretation. It seems to us that the "required as a condition of his employment" test is met if, due to the nature of the employer's business, a certain type of residence for the employee is required and that it would not be reasonable to suppose that the employee would normally have available such lodging for the use of his employer. Of course, the employee is incidentally benefited by the furnished lodging, but as the Tax Court has observed in the Olkjer and Stone cases, supra, this is true in all cases where desirable working facilities as well as living quarters are concededly furnished "for the convenience of the employer."

Finally, § 119 requires that the lodging furnished must be on the business premises of the employer. The trial commissioner found that the House constituted a part of the business premises of plaintiff because plaintiff's official functions were carried out there at night. The Government argues that the residential character of the House is not transformed by the limited use of the House for purposes connected with plaintiff's activities. We think that the business premises of § 119 means premises of the employer on which the duties of

3. Olkjer v. Commissioner, 32 T.C. 464 (1959); Stone v. Commissioner, 32 T.C. 1021 (1959).

the employee are to be performed. Thus, a domestic servant who lives in the residence of this employer, and who is required to be available for duty at any time, may exclude the value of his lodging from his gross income even though the residence may or may not be the employer's "business premises." I.T. 2253, V–1 Cum.Bull. 32 (1926). In the present case, part of plaintiff's official activities were carried out at the House which it owned. We believe that the House is part of the business premises of plaintiff within the meaning of § 119 of the 1954 Code. See Anderson v. Commissioner, 42 T.C. No. 25, decided May 20, 1964.*

During the oral argument the Government's counsel cited the cases of John L. Nolen, P–H Tax Ct.Mem. ¶ 64,099 (1964); and Atlanta Biltmore Hotel Corporation, P–H Tax Ct.Mem. ¶ 63,255 (1963).[4] The Nolen case involved a medical receptionist who was required to live on the second floor of the office of her employer so that she could answer telephone calls from patients and pharmacists after the normal office hours and perform other duties on the employer's premises, including storing and caring for perishable medicines. The Tax Court held that Mrs. Nolen was entitled to exclude the fair rental value of the lodging from her gross income. Similarly, in our present case, the use of suitable space is essential to the proper performance of the job. In the Atlanta Biltmore case, supra, the Tax Court held that an apartment with a fair rental value of $550 per month furnished to an employee of the hotel does not qualify under § 119. The facts of that case are clearly distinguishable from the instant case in that the employee in Atlanta Biltmore performed no services for the employer by residing in the apartment.

For the above reasons we hold that the fair rental value of the House was excludable, under § 119 of the 1954 Code, from the gross income of plaintiff's presidents. Plaintiff is therefore entitled to

* The 3rd Circuit reversed *Anderson* in 1966, 371 F.2d 59, cert. den., 387 U.S. 906 (1967). In that case as well as this the residence in question was geographically separated from the main business premises of the employer, a finding rejected in a close (across the street) situation later in Jack B. Lindeman, 60 T.C. 609 (1973), acq. 1973–2 C.B. 2. In *Anderson*, although a motel manager was always "on call," his residence two blocks from the motel was held not to be *on* the employer's premises, as the court held that mere "on call" status did not constitute the performance of duties. The court in the instant case properly takes that hurdle on the basis of meetings held and other work regularly done at the residence. (Accord, Rev.Rul. 75–540, 1975–50 I.R.B. 7, state governor not taxed on fair rental value of state mansion.) The court had to face the convenience of the employer test; but it is a question of how far I.R.C. § 119 should be stretched. Ed.

4. The Government also cited the case of Leonard F. Longo, P–H Tax Ct. Mem. ¶ 64,054 (1964). That case concerned the deductibility of certain moving and relocation expenses paid by an employer to a new employee, and it is not pertinent to the issues in the present case.

recover.   The amount of recovery will be determined under Rule 47 (c)(2).

[Findings of Fact and Conclusion of Law are omitted.   Ed.]

NOTE

Housing benefits provided to a "minister of the gospel" [1] are excluded from the minister's gross income by section 107 but, somewhat anomalously, they must be furnished to him "as compensation." The exclusion applies not only to the fair rental value of a home actually provided for the minister's use, similar to I.R.C. § 119, but also to a rental allowance.   In order to qualify an allowance must be specifically earmarked in the minister's employment contract, the church minutes, or some similar document,[2] and then it is excluded only to the extent that it is actually used to rent or provide a home. Congress may have made § 107 more liberal than section 119, because ministers are more likely to use their homes in conjunction with church activities than are other employees in their business activities.

Sec 119

PROBLEMS

1.   Employer provides Employee and wife and child a residence on Employer's premises, having a rental value of $4000 per year, but charging Employee only $2000.

2000, Includable

(a)   What result if the nature of Employee's work does not require him to live on the premises?

Includable, in income

(b)   What result if Employer and Employee simply agreed to a clause in the employment contract requiring Employee to live in the residence?

(c)   If Employee's work does require him to live on the premises, do you see any additional problems?

(d)   What result if Employee's work and contract require him to live on the premises and Employer furnishes Employee and family $3000 worth of groceries during the year?

Compensation

(e)   What result if Employer transferred the residence to Employee in fee simple in the year that Employee accepted the position and commenced work?   Does the value of the residence constitute excluded lodging?

1.   Reg. § 1.107–1(a).   Compare Silverman v. Comm'r, 1973–2 USTC para. 9546 (8th Cir. 1973), § 107 applied to a cantor in the Jewish faith who, although unordained, had duties essentially the same as a minister in non-Jewish faith, with Marc H. Tanenbaum, 58 T.C. 1 (1972), ordained rabbi employed as the National Director of Interreligious Affairs by the American Jewish Committee who did not have sacerdotal duties and was not a minister.   See Block, "Who is a 'Minister of the Gospel' for Purposes of the Parsonage Exclusion?" 51 Taxes 47 (1973).

2.   Reg. § 1.107–1(a).   See Rev.Rul. 72–462, 1972–2 C.B. 76.

2. Planner incorporated his motel business and the corporation purchased a piece of residential property adjacent to the motel. The corporation by contract "required" Planner to use the residence and also furnished him food. Planner worked at the motel and was on call 24 hours a day. May Planner exclude the value of the residence or the meals or both from his gross income?

3. State highway patrolman is required to be on duty from 8 a. m. to 5 p. m. At noon he eats lunch at various privately owned restaurants which are adjacent to the state highway. At the end of each month the state reimburses him for his luncheon expenses. Are such cash reimbursements included in his gross income? Compare United States v. Barrett, 321 F.2d 911 (5th Cir. 1963), United States v. Morelan, 356 F.2d 199 (8th Cir. 1966), and United States v. Keeton, 383 F.2d 429 (10th Cir. 1967) with Wilson v. United States, 412 F. 2d 694 (1st Cir. 1969), Burl J. Ghastin, 60 T.C. 264 (1973), and Robert J. Kowalski, 65 T.C. 44 (1975). But, perhaps more importantly, what do you yourself perceive to be the two principal legal questions presented, and how do you think they should be answered?

Cash reimbursements are not allowable. Sec 119 Does not apply requirement is for meals

CHAPTER 6. AWARDS

A. PRIZES

Internal Revenue Code: Section 74.
Regulations: Section 1.74–1.

EXCERPT FROM SENATE FINANCE COMMITTEE REPORT NO. 1622, 83RD CONGRESS, 2D SESSION (1954)

Pp. 178–179.

Section 74. Prizes and awards

This section is identical with section 74 of the bill as passed by the House. It is a new section which includes in gross income all prizes and awards with certain specified exceptions. It is intended to eliminate some existing confusion in court decisions over whether a prize is income or a gift and would overrule both the *Pot O'Gold* case (Washburn v. Commissioner (1945) 5 T.C. 1333) and the *Ross Essay Contest* case (McDermott v. Commissioner (C.A.D.C.1945) 150 F. 2d 585) insofar as each held prizes were not income under the 1939 Code. A cross reference to section 117 (relating to scholarships and fellowship grants) is inserted to preclude taxing such awards under this section.

Subsection (b) excludes from income those prizes and awards which are made primarily to recognize past achievements of the recipient in one of the specified fields, provided the recipient was selected without any action on his part to enter the contest or to submit his works in the proceeding and provided he is not required to render any substantial future services as a condition to receiving the prize or award. Thus, such awards as the Nobel prize would be excluded under this section. Subsection (b) is not intended to exclude prizes or awards from an employer to an employee in recognition of some achievement in connection with his employment, such as having the largest sales record or best production record during a certain period. Amounts received from radio and television giveaway shows, or as door prizes, or in any similar type contest would also not be covered by subsection (b).

ALLEN J. McDONELL

Tax Court of the United States, 1967.
26 T.C.M. 115.

Memorandum Findings of Fact and Opinion

TANNENWALD, JUDGE: Respondent determined a deficiency in income tax and an addition to tax under section 6653(a) [1] for 1960 in the amounts of $246.83 and $12.34, respectively.

Because of concessions by respondent, the only issue remaining for decision is whether all or any portion of expenses of a trip taken by petitioners and paid for by petitioner Allen's employer are includable in petitioners' income, or, if so, are deductible in arriving at adjusted gross income.

Findings of Fact

Some of the facts are stipulated and are found accordingly.

Allen J. and Jeanne M. McDonell, husband and wife, residing at 5505 Russett Road, Madison, Wisconsin, filed their joint tax return for 1960 with the district director of internal revenue, Milwaukee, Wisconsin.

Allen was employed by Dairy Equipment Co. (hereinafter referred to as DECO) in 1956 as assistant sales manager and he continued in that position through the taxable year in question. At the time of hiring Allen DECO pursuant to established policy, interviewed Jeanne. The purpose of interviewing the wife of a potential home office salesman was to be sure the wife understood that her husband would be required to do considerable traveling for the company and to evaluate her capacity to discharge social responsibilities required in connection with the company's business activities.

At no time did either of the petitioners own any stock in DECO.

DECO is a sales company, distributing bulk milk coolers manufactured for it on a subcontract basis. During the period in question, DECO coolers were sold through territorial salesmen and independent distributors. They handled other products dissimilar to those of DECO but competitive in terms of demand upon their time and effort.

Sales supervision was provided by home office salesmen. Allen, as assistant sales manager, was one of eight home office salesmen. None of the home office salesmen was assigned to a specific territory; each would be sent into the field when and where needed.

Beginning in 1959, DECO initiated an incentive sales contest for its 31 distributors and 9 territorial salesmen. The prize in 1959 for achieving an established sales quota was a trip to Hawaii for each winner and his wife. Home office salesmen did not participate.

---

1. All references are to the Internal Revenue Code of 1954.

There were 11 winners. They had produced $3,929,690.62 in gross sales, representing 56 percent of the total sales volume generated by the company during the period of the contest. Of the 11 winners in 1959, 10 decided to take the trip.

At the time of initiating the contest, DECO management decided to send one home office salesman and his wife for each three contest winners. This decision was based upon the company's past experience that unguided gatherings of salesmen and distributors often turned into complaint sessions and were otherwise damaging to the company's business interests. DECO assigned four home office salesmen and their wives to the trip. They were selected by placing the names of all the home office salesmen in a hat and drawing out four names. This random method was used to avoid discontent and dissatisfaction. The same random method was used for selecting home office personnel to represent the company on subsequent similar trips. A home office salesman chosen one year was eligible the next year. Those selected to go on a particular trip received no cut in pay and did not lose vacation time. Those not chosen received no substitute benefit.

Allen was one of the four chosen. At the time of drawing the names, the home office salesmen were told that those selected and their wives were expected to go, although they would have been excused for good reasons. They were instructed that they should consider the trip as an assignment and not as a vacation and that their job was to stay constantly with the contest winners, to participate in all the scheduled activities, and not to go off alone. Their objective was not only to make sure that every winner enjoyed himself but to guide anticipated informal discussion relating to DECO's business in order to protect and enhance DECO's image with its distributors and territorial salesmen. The wives were considered essential participants in the achievement of this objective. DECO felt it would be impossible for stag salesmen to host a trip for couples.

The contest winners and the home office personnel departed from Madison, Wisconsin, on February 4, 1960, arriving in Honolulu on February 5. They left Hawaii on February 14, returning to Madison on February 15. Aside from one day which was devoted to a sales meeting, there were no direct business activities on the trip.

Petitioners performed their assigned duties, which consumed substantially all of the trip time. Neither had any spare time, as they had hoped to have, to go swimming or shopping.

The portion of the trip costs paid by DECO and attributable to petitioners was $1,121.96.

Petitioners reported $600 as miscellaneous commissions in their tax return for 1960 as the estimated cost to DECO attributable to Jeanne's presence on the trip.

Respondent determined a deficiency based on the entire cost of the trip.[2] Petitioners now claim that they erroneously reported the $600 and seek a refund in addition to the determination that respondent's deficiency was in error.

Opinion

The battle lines in this case are clearly drawn. Petitioners assert that they took the trip in order to carry out duties required of them by virtue of Allen's employment by DECO. Respondent counters that the trip represented an award, taxable to petitioners under section 74, or additional compensation, taxable under section 61. We agree with petitioners.

The mere fact that petitioners were selected by a random drawing does not make the trip a taxable prize or award under section 74. Surely there would have been no question if the drawing had been designed to choose a home office salesman to take a trip without his wife to handle a disgruntled customer. The method of selection was founded on a sound business reason, namely, to choose those who were to serve DECO's business objectives on a basis which would obviate any feeling of discrimination. The situation of petitioners is to be distinguished from that of the contest winners, whose tax liability is not before us and for whom the trip was both a reward and an incentive.

Similarly, the fact that the trip was a vacation for the contest winners does not necessarily make it a vacation for petitioners. Unlike the contest winners, petitioners were expected to go as an essential part of Allen's employment. The right to go carried with it the duty to go. The trip was not a vacation for the petitioners. It was realistically a command performance to work. What was a social benefit to the contest winners was a work obligation to these petitioners. More importantly, petitioners herein were expected to devote substantially all of their time on the trip to the performance of duties on behalf of DECO in order to achieve, albeit subtly, DECO's well-defined business objectives. In this respect, the situation is unlike that in Patterson v. Thomas, 289 F.2d 108 (C.A. 5, 1961), certiorari denied 368 U.S. 837 (1961), where the Court found that, although the taxpayer had an obligation to attend the convention, his work responsibility was minimal.

Nor do we consider it material that petitioners enjoyed the trip. Pleasure and business, unlike oil and water, can sometimes be mixed. See Wilson v. Eisner, 282 F. 38, 42 (C.A. 2, 1922). Similarly, although the fact that the trip involved a resort area is an element to be taken into account, cf. Patterson v. Thomas, supra, it is not con-

---

2. Respondent concedes that the deficiency is partially in error because of the amount reported by petitioners.

clusive. A resort may be heaven to certain people but something less than that to others, depending on the circumstances. See Mr. Justice Douglas dissenting in Rudolph v. United States, 370 U.S. 269, 280 (1962). It is noteworthy that neither of petitioners went swimming or shopping during their entire stay, two activities for which Hawaii is famous.

Again, unlike the taxpayer in Patterson v. Thomas, supra, petitioners' right to go on the trip was not determined by any standard of work performance. In addition, home office salesmen who did not go on the trip received no substitute compensation and those who did go were not eliminated from consideration for trips in subsequent years. There is not the slightest suggestion that the trip which the petitioners took was conceived of as disguised remuneration to them. On the contrary, DECO had sound business reasons for them to go. We recognize that the presence of an employer business purpose does not thereby preclude a finding of compensation to the employee. Patterson v. Thomas, supra. But such business reasons, when coupled with the equally compelling business circumstances involving these petitioners' participation, made the trip no different from any other business trip requiring their services—including Jeanne, whose duties were substantial and could not have been performed by stag men. Cf. Gotcher v. United States, 259 F.Supp. 340 (E.D.Tex.1966); Warwick v. United States, 236 F.Supp. 761 (E.D.Va.1964).

We hold that, under all the facts and circumstances herein, the expenses of the trip are not includable in the gross income of petitioners. In view of this holding, we need not consider an alternative argument of petitioners that the trip had no fair market value to them. See, e. g., Lawrence W. McCoy, 38 T.C. 841 (1962).

Decision will be entered under Rule 50.

WILLS v. COMMISSIONER

United States Court of Appeals, Ninth Circuit, 1969.
411 F.2d 537.

BARNES, CIRCUIT JUDGE: This case arises upon a petition to review a decision of the Tax Court sustaining the Commissioner's determination of deficiencies in the taxpayers' income taxes paid for the years 1962 and 1963. The opinion of the court below is reported at 48 T.C. 308 (1967). Jurisdiction is conferred on this court by 26 U.S.C. § 7482.

Taxpayers Maurice M. Wills and Gertrude E. Wills are husband and wife. They filed joint income tax returns on a cash basis for the calendar years 1962 and 1963. Taxpayer Maurice M. Wills has been a professional baseball player since 1951. From June 1959 through November 1966, he played baseball for the Los Angeles Dodgers, whose club home is Los Angeles, California.

* * *

In 1962, taxpayer broke the major league baseball record for the most stolen bases in one season. He played in the 1962 All Star game and was voted "player of the game." He was also voted "most valuable player" of the National League, and received awards from the Associated Press as "Athlete of the Year," the Sport Magazine as "Man of the Year," the Baseball Writers as "Athlete of the Year," and California as "Athlete of the Year."

Following the final Dodger game of the 1962 season, taxpayer was also awarded an MG automobile with a fair market value of $1,731. This award was made by an automobile agency in Los Angeles after Wills was elected "most popular Dodger" by the patrons of that last game.

In January 1963, taxpayer received the S. Rae Hickok belt, stipulated to have had a fair market value of $6,038.19 at the time of receipt. The belt is awarded annually to the outstanding professional athlete of the prior year, and the predominant criterion for selecting each recipient is excellence in athletics. Ballots for electing the winner of the belt were sent to over 250 sportswriters and sportscasters throughout the United States, and the outcome of that vote determined who received the award. The belt was presented to Wills without any restrictions upon its disposition.

In his notice of deficiency, the Commissioner asserted that . . . the fair market value of the MG automobile received by taxpayer as a prize or award was taxable as ordinary income under 26 U.S.C. § 74(a); and . . . the fair market value of the Hickok belt received by taxpayer as a prize or award was taxable as ordinary income under 26 U.S.C. § 74(a). The Tax Court upheld the Commissioner's determination with regard to each of these * * * items, and the correctness of that decision is now before us.

* * *

We next consider the taxability of the automobile and the belt received by taxpayer. With regard to prizes and awards, 26 U.S.C. § 74 provides:

"(a) *General rule.*—Except as provided in subsection (b) and in section 117 (relating to scholarships and fellowship grants), gross income includes amounts received as prizes and awards.

"(b) *Exception.*—Gross income does not include amounts received as prizes and awards made primarily in recognition of religious, charitable, scientific, educational, artistic, literary, or civic achievement, but only if—

"(1) the recipient was selected without any action on his part to enter the contest or proceeding; and

"(2) the recipient is not required to render substantial future services as a condition to receiving the prize or award."

It is clear that Wills received the two awards without any action on his part to enter any contest, and that he was not required to render any future services. Thus Wills is not barred by (1) and (2) above, if he falls within (b), supra. The difficult question we must decide is whether the two awards come within any exception listed in subsection (b) or whether they are taxable under subsection (a). In order to recover, the taxpayer must show that his award comes within one of the specified exceptions. Griggs v. United States, 314 F.2d 515, 161 Ct.Cl. 84 (1963).

The Tax Court found that the award of the MG automobile was made for taxpayer's popularity alone, and that there was no indication that it was given for religious, charitable, scientific, educational, artistic, or civic achievements. The Tax Court then concluded that this award for popularity did not fall within any of the categories listed in § 74(b) and, accordingly held that the fair market value of the automobile was includible in taxpayer's taxable income.

The Tax Court further found that the Hickok belt was awarded to Wills primarily in recognition of athletic skills, and that excellence in sport is the predominant criterion for selecting the recipient. The court then held that the fair market value of the belt must be included in Wills' taxable income.

Taxpayer here contends that we should reverse the decision of the Tax Court with respect to the car and the belt, for the reason that these awards were made for civic and artistic achievement. He cites no legal authority in support of this proposition.

A firmly established principle of statutory interpretation is that the words of statutes, including revenue acts, should be interpreted in their ordinary and usual senses wherever possible. Malat v. Riddell, 383 U.S. 569, 571, 86 S.Ct. 1030, 16 L.Ed.2d 102 (1966); Hanover Bank v. Commissioner of Internal Revenue, 369 U.S. 672, 687, 82 S.Ct. 1080, 8 L.Ed.2d 187 (1962); Commerce-Pacific, Inc. v. United States, 278 F.2d 651, 654 (9th Cir.), cert. denied, 364 U.S. 872, 81 S.Ct. 115, 5 L.Ed.2d 94 (1960). The Tax Court considered the taxpayer's contention that his awards were for civic achievement, and rejected this characterization of his achievement. In other cases also, courts have been urged to regard certain achievements as civic or artistic, and have rejected such arguments in favor of construing these terms in their ordinary and usual senses.

In Hornung v. Commissioner, 47 T.C. 428 (1967), for example, the petitioner was a well-known professional football player who was awarded a new Corvette automobile for being selected as the outstanding player in the National Football League championship game. He asserted that this award was made in recognition of educational, artistic, scientific and civic activity, but the court concluded that the car was received in recognition of athletic achievement—which was not encompassed by the terms of § 74(b), as those terms are ordinarily understood.

The court in *Hornung* relied in large part upon the decision in Simmons v. United States, 308 F.2d 160 (4th Cir. 1962). The court in *Simmons* rejected the contention that a prize presented for catching a particular fish was awarded for a "civic achievement" within the meaning of § 74(b), and held that the crucial test for exemption under the statute is the nature of the activity being awarded. The court further refused to adopt the suggestion that the prize was for a civic achievement since it rewarded the taxpayer's skill as a fisherman, and stated that a "civic achievement" implies positive action which is exemplary, unselfish and broadly advantageous to the community. It was also noted that all the fields of endeavor listed in § 74(b) represent activities enhancing in some way the public good.

In light of the above standards for characterizing an activity as a civic achievement, we cannot say that the Tax Court's finding that Wills received the car and belt for his popularity and athletic prowess and that these accomplishments did not constitute civic achievements, was clearly erroneous.

Nor can we hold that the Tax Court clearly erred in finding that Wills was not rewarded for artistic achievements. As the term "artistic" is ordinarily used, it connotes activities of an aesthetic nature, including, for example, painting, drawing, architecture, sculpture, poetry, music, dancing and dramatics. In normal parlance, athletic achievements are not regarded as "artistic," despite the great skill which is frequently necessary for athletic success.

We find further support for our decision in the fact that Congress has recently heard several proposals to add the word "athletic" to the list of exempted prizes in § 74(b), but has, thus far, refused to do so. For example, on September 13, 1967, Senator Smathers, referring to the decision of the Tax Court in the present case, proposed such an amendment. *See*, S. 2397, 90th Cong., 1st Sess., 113 Cong.Rec. 25384– 25385 (1967). When introducing his bill, he acknowledged that under the present statute there is a basis for taxing the recipient on the value of any award received for athletic achievement, and specifically stated that he did not mean to be critical of the Tax Court for the reason that the court correctly observed that Congress had not expressed itself on the question of athletic awards as it had with religious, charitable, scientific, educational, artistic, literary and civic awards. We note that had Senator Smathers' bill been enacted, it would have affected only awards received after the date of enactment. Thus, even if the amendment had been passed, it would not affect our decision in the present case. Similar bills were also introduced in the House of Representatives, but not passed. *See* H.R. 12453, 90th Cong., 1st Sess. (1967); H.R. 13190, 90th Cong., 1st Sess. (1967); H.R. 13823, 90th

Cong., 1st Sess. (1967); H.R. 13825, 90th Cong., 1st Sess. (1967); H.R. 13875, 90th Cong., 1st Sess. (1967); H.R. 13946, 90th Cong., 1st Sess. (1967); H.R. 13979, 90th Cong., 1st Sess. (1967).

The taxpayer here makes the further argument that the Hickok belt should not be taxed because it is a "trophy." This argument has some equitable appeal, for the reason that a trophy is not a utilitarian item (such as an automobile) which the taxpayer would ordinarily purchase with his earned income. Yet the argument has no basis in the Internal Revenue Code. To agree, as the taxpayer does, the belt could be sold for some amount is to agree that the belt is the "equivalent of cash" in which case it is taxable when received. 2 Mertens, Law of Federal Income Taxation, Ch. 11 (1967). As previously stated, the crucial criterion is the *nature of the activity* awarded. The Code draws no distinctions based on the *form* of the award.

If the award is in the form of property other than cash, the only problem is one of valuation—not taxability. Property thus received is to be taxed at its fair market value at the time of receipt. Treas.Reg. § 1.74–1(a) (2). Koons v. United States, 315 F.2d 542, 544–545 (9th Cir. 1963). Valuation is not an issue in the instant case, for the taxpayer has not disputed the Commissioner's evaluation.

Nor does the taxpayer here contend that the car and belt were received as gifts. Such a contention would seem to be precluded by Congress' intention in enacting § 74, and by the absence of the requisite disinterested generosity. *See* Commissioner of Internal Revenue v. Duberstein, *supra* 363 U.S. at 285, 290, 80 S.Ct. 1190; Simmons v. United States, *supra* 308 F.2d at 164.

The decision of the Tax Court is

Affirmed.

The law as it presently exists requires the foregoing conclusion. We dislike it, for we are convinced it is an inequitable result. The next step would be for the Internal Revenue Service to tax the gold and silver in the medals awarded to Olympic Games' winners. Unfortunately for the taxpayer in this case, the court has no authority to legislate equities into the Internal Revenue Code or the Treasury Regulations. Both the problem and the remedy lie with the Congress, not with the courts.[1]

---

1. "The regulation here in question represents an effort by the Commissioner to supply the definitions that Congress omitted. [footnote omitted] And it is fundamental, of course, that as 'contemporaneous constructions by those charged with administration of' the Code, the Regulations 'must be sustained unless unreasonable and plainly inconsistent with the revenue statutes,' and 'should not be overruled except for weighty reasons.' Commissioner of Internal Revenue v. South Texas Lumber Co., 333 U.S. 496, 501 [68 S.Ct. 695, 698, 92 L.Ed. 831]. In this respect our statement last Term in United States v. Correll, 389 U.S. 299 [88 S.Ct. 445, 19 L.Ed.2d 537], bears emphasis:

'[W]e do not sit as a committee of revision to perfect the administration of the tax laws. Congress has delegated to the Commissioner, not to the courts, the task of prescribing "all

PROBLEMS

1. Contestant was in the studio audience of the television show "Let's Make a Deal" and was selected to participate in the show. She was successful and won a color television set worth $500 and a vacation for two to Hawaii worth $1500. Would Contestant's winnings be excluded from gross income under I.R.C. § 74? Suppose she elected to take the Hawaii trip alone at a cost of $750?

2. The local bar association presents a $1000 award to the law student who writes the best student comment published in the school's Law Review during the year. The recipient of the award is expected to make a 30 minute talk about his comment when he accepts the award at a bar association luncheon. Should student report the $1000 as income? See Rev.Rul. 58–89, 1958–1 C.B. 40.

3. Maurice Wills is a professional athlete. Would the result be different if he were an amateur athlete who had won a gold medal at the Olympic games? Should it be? If Congress decided to exclude trophies, such as the Hickock belt, how should "trophy" be defined?

4. Each year Embraceable U. selects its outstanding professor based on a student poll and it awards him or her $1000 in cash. Does Professor who won the award in the current year have gross income? If you think you can win this one for Professor, how are you going to persuade the court (looks like you'll be there) that the award is not taxable under the last clause of Reg. § 1.74–1(a)(1)?

B. SCHOLARSHIPS AND FELLOWSHIPS

Internal Revenue Code: Section 117.
Regulations: Section 1.117–1, –2(a), –2(b)(1) and (2), –3, –4(c).

NOTE

If we may borrow from the classic "Gentlemen, start your engines," the phrase here is: "Gentlemen and ladies, pick up your spoons!" You are about to be fed. Although this is not characteristic of most portions of this book, the tax law on scholarships and fellowships is in a somewhat chaotic state. Even if the controlling

needful rules and regulations for the enforcement" of the Internal Revenue Code. 26 U.S.C. § 7805(a). In this area of limitless factual variations, "it is the province of Congress and the Commissioner, not the courts, to make the appropriate adjustments." *Id.*, at 306–307 [88 S.Ct. at 449]." Bingler, etc. v. Johnson et al., 394 U. S. 741, 89 S.Ct. 1439, 22 L.Ed.2d 695 (decided April 23, 1969).

legal principles are not utterly obscure, minor variations in factual
circumstances have spawned large numbers of reported judicial controversies. Unlitigated controversies must be prodigious. This area
may not be of extraordinary importance; but it does touch the affairs
of many taxpayers and can involve substantial amounts of money.
We expect not to devote class time to the area but here is some (dirty
word?) *information.*

Prior to the enactment of the 1954 Internal Revenue Code, there
was no statutory provision that dealt expressly with the taxability
of scholarships or fellowships. The basis for the sometimes exclusion of such grants from gross income under the 1939 Code was the
treatment accorded amounts received as "gifts". Outside of routine
matters, factual variations in the "gift" area required that the tax
status of scholarships and fellowships be determined largely on a case
by case approach. Congress enacted I.R.C. § 117 with the express
purpose of providing a clear-cut method for distinguishing between
taxable and nontaxable educational grants.[1] According to the Treasury Regulations, their tax status is now governed exclusively by
§ 117.[2] The specific Congressional carve-out of scholarships and
fellowships from § 74 [3] is of course a part of this package.

Section 117(a), as a general rule, excludes from gross income an
amount received as a scholarship at an educational institution or as a
fellowship grant [4] and the exclusion, not limited to dollars, extends
to the value of contributed services and accommodations, such as room
and board, provided in connection with the grant.[5] Amounts received
to cover incidental expenses for travel, research, clerical help or
equipment are also excluded from gross income if the funds are specifically designated to cover such expenses [6] and are in fact used for
the specified purposes.[7] The regulations provide that expenses are
"incidental" to the grant if incurred to carry out the purpose for
which the grant was awarded.[8] Reasonable enough? Lick that
spoon!

Section 117(b) imposes limitations on the excludability of some
amounts otherwise seemingly under the protective § 117(a) umbrella.
In doing so, it draws a distinction between an individual who is a

---

1. S.Rep.No.1622, 83rd Congress, 2d
Sess. 17 (1954).

2. Reg. § 1.117–1(a).

3. I.R.C. § 74(a), and S.Rep., supra
note 1.

4. I.R.C. § 117(a)(1)(A) as amended by
§ 1901(b) of TRA (1976) adopts the
definition of "educational organization" contained in § 170(b)(1)(A)(ii),
which provides that an "educational
organization" is an institution which

maintains a regular faculty and curriculum and has a regularly enrolled
body of students in attendance at a
place where the educational activities are regularly carried on.

5. Reg. § 1.117–3(d).

6. Reg. § 1.117–1(b)(1).

7. I.R.C. § 117(a)(2).

8. Reg. § 1.117–1(b)(1).

candidate for a degree at an educational institution with a regular faculty and student body and one who is not.[9] The regulations define the term "candidate for a degree" as one who is "pursuing studies or conducting research to meet the requirements for an academic or professional degree conferred by colleges or universities."[10] Individuals who are candidates for a degree find no limit on the size or duration of their grants. I.R.C. § 117(b)(1) does require the inclusion in gross income of otherwise excluded sums that are received as payment for "teaching, research, or other services in the nature of part-time employment required as a condition to receiving the scholarship or the fellowship grant." The compensation portion of a grant may be taxable. However, if the only services required are those required of all candidates for a particular degree as a condition of their receiving the degree, the services are not treated as "part-time employment,"[11] and no part of the grant is taxed.

If an individual is not a candidate for a degree at an educational institution, amounts received as a scholarship or fellowship will be excluded from gross income only if the grantor is an organization exempt from tax under I.R.C. § 501(c)(3) or is a governmental organization.[12] The amount of the exclusion in these cases is limited to $300 per month for the period for which amounts are received as a scholarship or fellowship during the taxable year. Once a non-degree candidate has received this kind of scholarship or fellowship money during 36 months, whether consecutive or not, any additional amounts received will be included in his gross income; and this is so even if he did not make use of the full $300 exclusion for some or all of the months.[13]

If "scholarships" and "fellowships" are to be excluded from the recipient's gross income, what is the meaning of those terms?[14] Although Congress did not provide a definition of either in I.R.C. § 117, the Regulations attempt to fill the statutory gap. They define a scholarship generally to mean an amount paid for the benefit of an undergraduate or graduate student to aid him in his studies, and a fellowship as an amount paid for the benefit of an individual, who may or may not be a student, to aid him in the pursuit of study or research.[15] Both "scholarships" and "fellowships" encompass the value of contributed services and accommodations, tuition, matriculation and other fees, as well as amounts received in the nature of a family allowance.[16] Ruled out, however, is any amount that repre-

9. I.R.C. § 117(b)(1) & (2).

10. Reg. § 1.117–3(e).

11. I.R.C. § 117(b)(1).

12. I.R.C. § 117(b)(2)(A).

13. Reg. § 1.117–2(b)(2)(ii).

14. See Tucker, "Federal Income Taxation of Scholarships and Fellowships: A Practical Analysis," 8 Ind.L.Rev. 749 (1975); Hutton, "Scholarships and Fellowships: What's in a Name?" 56 A.B.A.J. 592 (1970).

15. Reg. § 1.117–3(a) and (c).

16. Ibid.

sents either "compensation for past, present or future services or represents payment for services which are subject to the direction or supervision of the grantor" unless the services are required of all candidates for a degree.[17]   There must be a gratuity flavor to the grant similar to the gift concept as developed in the well-known *Duberstein*[18] opinion.   Accordingly, amounts paid to enable an individual to pursue his studies or research "primarily for the benefit of the grantor" reap no tax benefit under I.R.C. § 117.   Whereas, on the other hand, if the primary purpose of the studies or research is to enhance the training of the recipient and is noncompensatory in nature, the fact that the grantor derives an incidental benefit from the services will not result in taxation of the grant.[19]

The United States Supreme Court in Bingler v. Johnson [20] upheld the definitions of scholarships and fellowships which appear in the Regulations, specifically the compensation restrictions imposed by Reg. § 1.117–4(c).   The *Johnson* case involved a Westinghouse employee who received a stipend from Westinghouse, based on a percentage of his salary, to financially assist him while on a leave of absence to obtain a Ph.D. degree.   The stipend was part of a Westinghouse plan under which employees were required to return to Westinghouse for two years following their educational leave.   The Court rejected the notion that I.R.C. § 117 broadly encompassed all amounts given for the support of one who is a student and held the stipend taxable, stating that "the thrust of the [Reg. § 1.117–4(c) (1)] provision dealing with compensation is that bargained-for payments, given only as a 'quo' in return for the quid of services rendered —whether past, present, or future—should not be excludable from income as 'scholarship' funds." [21]

After the *Johnson* case supported the restrictions imposed by Reg. § 1.117–4(c), subsequent litigation has focused on their scope. The principal questions raised are whether the stipends represent compensation for services and whether they are "primarily for the benefit of the grantor" or primarily to further the education and training of the recipient.   In *Johnson* the Supreme Court accepted the government's contention that the "primarily for the benefit of the grantor" language of Reg. § 1.117–4(c)(2) is merely an adjunct to the "compensation" provision of Reg. § 1.117–4(c)(1).[22]   The "grantor" language was added to insure that "bargained for" arrangements, even outside the employer-employee relationship, would be taxed.   Thus, following the *Johnson* case the predominant issue

17. Reg. § 1.117–4(c)(1).

18. Comm'r v. Duberstein, 363 U.S. 278 (1960).

19. Reg. § 1.117–4(c)(2). See Rev.Rul. 57–560, 1957–2 C.B. 108.

20. 394 U.S. 741 (1969).

21. Id. at 757.

22. Id. at 758.

in determining "scholarship" status under § 117 has become whether a grant has the indicia of compensation.[23] The problem of distinguishing nontaxable scholarships from taxable compensation has been rife in several distinct circumstances.

Educational grants made by an employer to a current or former employee, as in the *Johnson* case, have generally been held taxable because they represent compensation for past, present or future services.[24] This result has been reached even in cases in which the employee has no contractual obligation to render future services if there is a "clear expectation" that the employment relationship will continue.[25]

Stipends for research and teaching assistants, to be excludable from income, must initially be found to have those "scholarship" characteristics that are set out in the regulations.[26] This involves a factual determination of whether the stipend is primarily to further the recipient's education and training, on the one hand, or is compensatory or primarily for the benefit of the grantor, on the other. Some of the factors considered are: (1) the degree of supervision of the student's work, (2) the relationship of the student's duties to his field of interest and educational objectives, (3) the basis on which the awards were made, and (4) whether academic credit is given for the work done.[27]

An area of difficulty has been that of grants awarded by a university to degree candidates who are research assistants in the applied sciences. The problem arises especially where the research contributes to performance by the university of a contract it has with a government agency. In an early case under § 117, the Tax Court held such payments excludable from gross income, as the grants were primarily to further the training of the recipient.[28] Despite the Commissioner's acquiescence in the case, the I.R.S. persisted for some time in questioning the character of similar grants on the ground that the primary purpose of the research was to benefit either the grantor university or the government.[29] A recent ruling that attempts to clarify the

23. Comment, "Excludability of Scholarship and Fellowship Grants Under Section 117 of the Internal Revenue Code of 1954," 31 Ohio St.L.J. 186, 192 (1970).

24. See, for example, Leonard T. Fielding, 57 T.C. 761 (1972).

25. John E. MacDonald, Jr., 52 T.C. 386 (1969); see also Ehrhart v. Comm'r, 470 F.2d 940 (1st Cir. 1973).

26. Elmer L. Reese, 45 T.C. 407, 411 (1966), aff'd. per curiam 373 F.2d 742 (4th Cir. 1967). But see Randall, "Teaching Assistants and Taxes—Paid to Study, or Paid to Work?" 8 Gonzaga L.Rev. 33 (1972).

27. See Clurman and Reiner, "Scholarship and Fellowship Grants: An Analysis of Factors Needed for Exclusion," 39 J.Tax. 150 (1973) and Stuart, "Tax Status of Scholarship and Fellowship Grants: Frustration of Legislative Purpose and Approaches to Obtain the Exclusion Granted by Congress," 25 Emory L.J. 357 (1976).

28. Chander P. Bhalla, 35 T.C. 13 (1960), acq. 1965–1 C.B. 4.

29. See Myers and Hopkins, "I.R.S. Is Limiting the Scope of the Exclusion for Fellowship and Scholarship Grants," 42 J.Tax. 212 (1975).

situation should serve to provide some certainty in the area.[30]   The ruling provides that the I.R.S. will assume the stipends are primarily to further the education and training of the recipient and therefore qualify as scholarships or fellowships if certain conditions are established.[31]

Much of the litigation under § 117 has involved payments of stipends to medical interns and residents.   The amount has generally been treated as compensation for services rendered even though the recipient derives significant benefit from the training.[32]   For example, in Parr v. U. S.,[33] the taxpayer, a resident physician who received a stipend from a hospital, was charged with patient care duties consisting of taking medical histories, seeing patients, proposing diagnoses, and assisting in the performance of surgery.   Noting the extensive nature of Dr. Parr's duties and that additional personnel would have been needed to perform the duties in his absence, the court found the stipend was "primarily for the benefit of the grantor" and thus not a fellowship.[34]   Nevertheless, (and it may sound paradoxical to express it this way) the taxpayer may prevail if he can demonstrate an absence of benefit to the hospital from his activities.[35]   In Frederick A. Bieberdorf,[36] the Tax Court distinguished, *Parr*, holding a stipend excludable from gross income because the medical resident's duties consisted primarily, perhaps as much as eighty percent, of non-grantor research and treatment of persons who were not regular patients of the grantor hospital.

The primary purpose for which the grantor hospital is operated may be a factor in determining whether a grant is a fellowship, but the cases are not in agreement.   In Hembree v. U. S.,[37] the Fourth Circuit held the primary purpose of the grantor institution is irrele-

30.   Rev.Rul. 75–280, 1975–29 I.R.B. 7.

31.   In general, the assumption will be made if the recipient is a degree candidate who performs services for the university, the services satisfy degree requirements, and equivalent services are required of all degree candidates. However, the assumption will not be made if (1) the services are performed for a party other than the grantor; (2) the grant is awarded in consideration of past or anticipated future services; (3) the degree requirements are not "reasonably appropriate" to the particular degree; and (4) to the extent that the recipient performs services in excess of the degree requirements.   With regard to (3) above, the statute obviously invites skullduggery, but even in hard times it is difficult to imagine academic institutions seeking to earn research contract money through the tax-shel-

tered efforts of students working outside the area of their academic interests.

32.   Aloysius J. Proskey, 51 T.C. 918, 925 (1969); William K. Rundell, Jr., 30 T.C.M. 177 (1971).

33.   469 F.2d 1156 (5th Cir. 1972).

34.   See also *Rundell,* supra note 32.

35.   Rev.Rul. 57–560, 1957–2 C.B. 108. Foundation grants to physicians who are advanced degree candidates constitute fellowships where the recipients' activities do not benefit the grantor or training institution and the grantees replace no salaried personnel.

36.   60 T.C. 114 (1973), acq. 1973–2 C.B. 1.

37.   464 F.2d 1262 (4th Cir. 1972).

vant, stating that under the regulations the primary purpose of the payment controls, not the purpose for which the facility is operated.[38] However, some courts have emphasized that the grantor hospital was primarily a teaching institution in favoring the taxpayer with a § 117 exclusion.[39]

When medical student recipients of state loans were subsequently relieved of their obligation to repay the loans in consideration for their agreement to work in state rural areas, they were held to have gross income.[40]   The Service ruled that the arrangement was not within § 117 because it required a substantial *quid pro quo* from the recipient and was primarily for the benefit of the grantor with the predictable adverse consequences for the taxpayer.[41]   However, an opposite rule applies to the discharge of some student loans by reason of congressional amnesty, effective until January 1, 1979, under § 2117 of the Tax Reform Act of 1976, a statutory tax rule not made a part of the Code.[42]

PROBLEMS

1. T graduated from high school but could not afford to attend college and therefore went to work as a sales clerk in a department store.   The next year she entered a contest conducted by a large oil refinery as part of its advertising campaign.   The prize, won by T, was in the form of two years of college tuition to be paid directly to Skidrock College on behalf of the winner, but only if the winner could meet the entrance requirements and could qualify as a degree candidate.   T met both requirements and entered Skidrock.   The tuition was $3400 per year.   Does T have gross income?

2. Second year Law Student working toward a J.D. degree was awarded a full tuition scholarship and room and board for the academic year, along with $1500 cash.   As a scholarship student, he is required to do about 300 hours of legal research for the professor to

38. See also *Parr*, supra note 33.

39. Wrobleski v. Bingler, 161 F.Supp. 901 (W.D.Pa.1958); Leathers v. U. S., 471 F.2d 856 (8th Cir. 1972), cert. denied, 412 U.S. 932 (1973); Cf. Gerald R. Faloona, 34 T.C.M. 265 (1975).

40. Rev.Rul. 73–256, 1973–1 C.B. 56. See Cattanach, "Scholarship and Fellowship Exclusion—Forgiveness of Education Loans," 1974 Wis.L.Rev. 237. *Rev.Rul. 73–256* will be applied only to loans made after the date of its issuance, June 11, 1973. Rev.Rul. 74–540, 1974–2 C.B. 38.

41. Technically this is not a straight § 117 issue. Ordinarily a loan is not income when received, because it is accompanied by a contemporaneously acknowledged obligation to repay; and of course this applies as much to loans to medical students as to others. In contrast, forgiveness of a loan may constitute the receipt of gross income. See United States v. Kirby Lumber Co., infra page 199. A recognized exception to the *Kirby Lumber* doctrine is the gift exception where a creditor has a Duberstein, supra note 18, donative intention with respect to the forgiveness. Here the state obviously did not intend a gift; and their conditions for discharge of the obligation clearly left the obligor doctors with taxable income.

42. The *Kirby Lumber* doctrine is explored in Chapter 9, infra.

whom he is assigned. Nonscholarship students, if hired, receive $5.00 per hour for such work.

    (a) What tax consequences to Law Student?

    (b) What tax consequences to Law Student if all second year J.D. students are required to do 300 hours of legal research, whether compensated or not, for faculty or for other lawyers in the state?

    (c) What tax consequences to Law Student if all second year J.D. students are required to do research work whether compensated or not but nonscholarship students are required to expend only 100 hours at such efforts?

    3. Career Diplomat takes a leave from his work to return to his alma mater as a "fellow" for the academic year with a view to writing a book. He has no specific responsibilities and may pursue independent research.

    (a) What result to Diplomat if his alma mater provides him a stipend of $1000 per month for the nine month academic year?

    (b) What result if the full $9000 is paid to Diplomat on September first when the school year commences? See Reg. § 1.117–2(b)(3) Ex. 2.

    (c) What result if financial troubles make it possible to pay Diplomat only $200 per month from September through December, but from January through May he is paid his full $1000 per month plus arrearages from the prior year. See Reg. § 1.117–2(b)(2)(i) and (ii).

    (d) What change in result in (a), above, if his alma mater also provides Diplomat with an additional $500 for expenses for him and his family to travel to alma mater and they incur $500 of traveling expenses?

    (e) What result if the award in (a), above, were made to Sci Poli, a regular member of the faculty of the university granting the fellowship?

CHAPTER 7. GAIN FROM DEALINGS IN PROPERTY

A. FACTORS IN THE DETERMINATION OF GAIN

Internal Revenue Code: Sections 1001(a), (b) first sentence, (c); 1012.
Regulations: Section 1.1001–1(a).

If T lends B money and later B pays it back no one would suppose that T has gross income upon the mere repayment of the principal amount of the loan. In tax parlance, the reason for this conclusion is that the repayment constitutes a mere *return of capital* to T. There is no element of gain in such a transaction and, consequently, this exclusionary rule has always been recognized just as if the principle were spelled out in the statutory provisions.

But the return-of-capital concept is by no means restricted to the loan repayment area. It arises in many more sophisticated ways, both as a kind of common law rule and as a statutory principle. In other circumstances, it may be more difficult to say to what extent the taxpayer's capital is merely being returned. In general the device adopted for aid in measuring this is "basis." Basis, unadjusted, essentially answers the question: How much have I got in it? Thus, if T buys property for $10,000, he has that amount in it, and his basis is $10,000. Basis and value must be carefully differentiated. If the property so acquired is securities that increase in *value* to $15,000, *basis* is still only $10,000. Avoid the student inclination to use these terms indiscriminately.

If the value of the property increases to $15,000 and T sells the property for $15,000 he has made $5,000 on his investment because the property has appreciated in value to that extent and because he has liquidated his investment. This rather obvious result is translated into tax terminology by I.R.C. (26 U.S.C.A.) § 1001(a), which identifies gain on the disposition of property as the excess of the "amount realized" over the "adjusted basis". The "amount realized" is defined in I.R.C. (26 U.S.C.A.) § 1001(b) as the amount of money received and the fair market value of property (other than money) received on the disposition. Here the amount realized by T is $15,000 (only money was received) and, if his basis is $10,000, his § 1001(a) gain is $5,000. Current attention is directed only to the "amount" of gain; Part Six of this book is addressed to the "character" of gain and the tax consequences of such characterization. What would be the result to T under § 1001(a) if, instead of appreciating, the property had declined in value and he had sold it for $8,000 cash? Again,

141

characterization and final tax consequences are intended to be deferred.

Determination of the "amount realized" on a disposition of property and of the property's "adjusted basis" are not always as simple as in the hypothetical posed above. The materials that follow suggest ways, other than by purchase, in which basis is established and circumstances calling for adjustment in basis, both upward and downward. They also present some less obvious circumstances in which the "amount realized" must be determined as a factor in the measurement of gain on a sale or other disposition of property.

B. DETERMINATION OF BASIS

---

1. COST AS BASIS *

Internal Revenue Code: Sections 1012; 1016(a)(1).
Regulations: Sections 1.61–2(d)(2)(i); 1.1012–1(a).

PHILADELPHIA PARK AMUSEMENT CO. v. UNITED STATES

Court of Claims of the United States, 1954.
130 Ct.Cl. 166, 126 F.Supp. 184.

[In 1889, the taxpayer had been granted a 50-year franchise to operate a passenger railway in Fairmount Park, Philadelphia. At a cost of $381,000, it built the Strawberry Bridge over the Schuylkill River, which was used by its streetcars. In 1934, it deeded the bridge to the city in exchange for a ten year extension of its franchise. In 1946 when the extended franchise still had several years to run, it was abandoned, and the taxpayer arranged bus transportation for visitors to its amusement park. The taxpayer's basis for the ten year extension of its franchise became important when the taxpayer asserted depreciation deductions based on the cost of the extension and a loss upon abandonment of the franchise. Basis questions for these purposes are essentially the same as those that arise in the determination of gain or loss on the disposition of an asset. Ed.]

LARAMORE, JUDGE.

* * *

This brings us to the question of what is the cost basis of the 10-year extension of taxpayer's franchise. Although defendant contends

---

* There is an early but comprehensive discussion of cost as basis in Greenbaum, "The Basis of Property Shall Be the Cost of Such Property: How is Cost Defined?" 3 Tax.L.Rev. 351 (1948).

that Strawberry Bridge was either worthless or not "exchanged" for the 10-year extension of the franchise, we believe that the bridge had some value, and that the contract under which the bridge was transferred to the City clearly indicates that the one was given in consideration of the other.   *   *   *

The gain or loss, whichever the case may have been, should have been recognized, and the cost basis under section 113(a)[4] of the Code, of the 10-year extension of the franchise was the cost to the taxpayer.   The succinct statement in section 113(a) that "the basis of property shall be the cost of such property" although clear in principle, is frequently difficult in application.   One view is that the cost basis of property received in a taxable exchange is the fair market value of the property *given* in the exchange.[5]   The other view is that the cost basis of property received in a taxable exchange is the fair market value of the property *received* in the exchange.[6]   As will be seen from the cases and some of the Commissioner's rulings[7] the Commissioner's position has not been altogether consistent on this question.   The view that "cost" is the fair market value of the property given is predicated on the theory that the cost to the taxpayer is the economic value relinquished.   The view that "cost" is the fair market value of the property received is based upon the theory that the term "cost" is a tax concept and must be considered in the light of the *   *   *   prime role that the basis of property plays in determining tax liability.   We believe that when the question is considered in the latter context that the cost basis of the property received in a taxable exchange is the fair market value of the property *received* in the exchange.

When property is exchanged for property in a taxable exchange the taxpayer is taxed on the difference between the adjusted basis of the property given in exchange and the fair market value of the property received in exchange.   For purposes of determining gain or loss the fair market value of the property received is treated as cash and taxed accordingly.   To maintain harmony with the fundamental purpose of these sections, it is necessary to consider the fair market value of the property received as the cost basis to the taxpayer.   The failure to do so would result in allowing the taxpayer a stepped-up basis, without paying a tax therefor, if the fair market value of the property received is less than the fair market value of the property given, and the taxpayer would be subjected to a double tax if the fair market value of the property received is more than the fair market value of the prop-

---

4. Section 113(a) provides: "Basis, (unadjusted) of property. The basis of property shall be the cost of such property; except that * * *." 26 U.S.C.A. § 113. [See I.R.C. § 1012. Ed.]

5. [Citations omitted. Ed.]

6. [Citations omitted. Ed.]

7. Compare I.T. 2212, IV–2 C.B. 118 with I.T. 3523, 1941–2 C.B. 124 and the Commissioner's equivocal acquiescence in Estate of Isadore L. Myers case, supra, 1943–1 C.B. 17.

erty given. By holding that the fair market value of the property received in a taxable exchange is the cost basis, the above discrepancy is avoided and the basis of the property received will equal the adjusted basis of the property given plus any gain recognized, or that should have been recognized, or minus any loss recognized, or that should have been recognized.

Therefore, the cost basis of the 10-year extension of the franchise was its fair market value on August 3, 1934, the date of the exchange. The determination of whether the cost basis of the property received is its fair market value or the fair market value of the property given in exchange therefor, although necessary to the decision of the case, is generally not of great practical significance because the value of the two properties exchanged in an arms-length transaction are either equal in fact, or are presumed to be equal.[8] The record in this case indicates that the 1934 exchange was an arms-length transaction and, therefore, if the value of the extended franchise cannot be determined with reasonable accuracy, it would be reasonable and fair to assume that the value of Strawberry Bridge was equal to the 10-year extension of the franchise. The fair market value of the 10-year extension of the franchise should be established but, if that value cannot be determined with reasonable certainty, the fair market value of Strawberry Bridge should be established and that will be presumed to be the value of the extended franchise. This value cannot be determined from the facts now before us since the case was prosecuted on a different theory.

The taxpayer contends that the market value of the extended franchise or Strawberry Bridge could not be ascertained and, therefore, it should be entitled to carry over the undepreciated cost basis of the bridge as the cost of the extended franchise under section 113(b) (2).[9] If the value of the extended franchise or bridge cannot be ascertained with a reasonable degree of accuracy, the taxpayer is entitled to carry over the undepreciated cost of the bridge as the cost basis of the extended franchise. Helvering v. Tex-Pen Oil Co., 300 U.S. 481, 499, 57 S.Ct. 569, 81 L.Ed. 755; Gould Securities Co. v. United States, 2 Cir., 96 F.2d 780. However, it is only in rare and extraordinary cases that the value of the property exchanged cannot be ascertained with reasonable accuracy. We are presently of the opinion that either the value of the extended franchise or the bridge can be determined with a reasonable degree of accuracy. Although the value of the extended franchise may be difficult or impossible to ascertain because of the nebulous and intangible characteristics inherent in such property, the value of the bridge is subject to more exact measurement. Consider-

---

8. [Reference omitted. Ed.]

9. Section 113(b) (2) provides: "Substituted basis. The term 'substituted basis' as used in this subsection means a basis determined under any provision of subsection (a) of this section or under any corresponding provision of a prior income tax law, providing that the basis shall be determined— (A) by reference to the basis in the hands of a transferor, donor, or grantor, or (B) by reference to other property held at any time by the person for whom the basis is to be determined."

ation may be given to expert testimony on the value of comparable bridges, Strawberry Bridge's reproduction cost and its undepreciated cost, as well as other relevant factors.

Therefore, because we deem it equitable, judgment should be suspended and the question of the value of the extended franchise on August 3, 1934, should be remanded to the Commissioner of this court for the taking of evidence and the filing of a report thereon.

The failure of taxpayer to properly record the transaction in 1934 and thereafter does not prevent the correction of the error, especially under the circumstances of this case. Countway v. Commissioner, 1 Cir., 127 F.2d 69.

* * *

We, therefore, conclude that the 1934 exchange was a taxable exchange and that the taxpayer is entitled to use as the cost basis of the 10-year extension of its franchise its fair market value on August 3, 1934, for purposes of determining depreciation and loss due to abandonment, as indicated in this opinion.

Accordingly, judgment will be suspended and the question of the value of the extended franchise on August 3, 1934, is remanded to the Commissioner of this court for the taking of evidence and the filing of a report thereon.

JONES, CHIEF JUDGE, and MADDEN, WHITAKER, and LITTLETON, JUDGES, concur.

PROBLEMS

1. Owner purchases some land for $10,000 and later sells it for $16,000.

(a) Determine the amount of Owner's gain on the sale.

(b) What difference in result if when the land had a value of $10,000 Owner, a real estate salesman, received it from his employer as a bonus for putting together a major real estate development, and Owner's income tax was increased $3,000 by reason of his receipt of the land.

(c) What difference in result in (a), above, if Owner who was a realtor had purchased the land from his employer but was required to pay only $9500 for it, instead of $10,000, because he would have earned a 5% sales commission if he had arranged a sale to a third party?

(d) What result in (a), above, if Owner purchased the land for $10,000, spent $2000 in clearing the land prior to its sale, and sold it for $18,000? (Consider generally how I.R.C. § 182 might affect your conclusion here.)

(e) What difference in result if in addition to the facts in (d), above, Owner had previously rented the land to Lessee for five years for $1000 per year cash rental and permitted

Lessee to expend $2000 clearing the property? Assume that, although Owner properly reported the cash rental payments as gross income, the $2000 expenditures were properly excluded under § 109. See § 1019.

(f) What difference in result in (a), above, if Owner purchased the land by paying $1000 for an option to purchase the land for an additional $9000 and subsequently exercised the option?

(g) What result to Owner in (f), above, if rather than ever actually acquiring the land Owner sold the option to investor for $1500?

2. PROPERTY ACQUIRED BY GIFT

Internal Revenue Code: Section 1015(a). See Section 1015(d)(1)(A), (d) (4), and (d)(6).

Regulations: Sections 1.1001–1(e); 1.1015–1(a),–4.

TAFT v. BOWERS

Supreme Court of the United States, 1929.
278 U.S. 470, 49 S.Ct. 199.

MR. JUSTICE McREYNOLDS delivered the opinion of the Court.

Petitioners, who are donees of stocks, seek to recover income taxes exacted because of advancement in the market value of those stocks while owned by the donors. The facts are not in dispute. Both causes must turn upon the effect of paragraph (2), § 202, Revenue Act, 1921, (c. 136, 42 Stat. 227) which prescribes the basis for estimating taxable gain when one disposes of property which came to him by gift. The records do not differ essentially and a statement of the material circumstances disclosed by No. 16 will suffice.

During the calendar years 1921 and 1922, the father of petitioner Elizabeth C. Taft, gave her certain shares of Nash Motors Company stock then more valuable than when acquired by him. She sold them during 1923 for more than their market value when the gift was made.

The United States demanded an income tax reckoned upon the difference between cost to the donor and price received by the donee. She paid accordingly and sued to recover the portion imposed because of the advance in value while the donor owned the stock. The right to tax the increase in value after the gift is not denied.

Abstractly stated, this is the problem—

In 1916 A purchased 100 shares of stock for $1,000 which he held until 1923 when their fair market value had become $2,000. He then gave them to B who sold them during the year 1923 for $5,000. The United States claim that, under the Revenue Act of 1921, B must pay income tax upon $4,000, as realized profits. B maintains that only $3,000—the appreciation during her ownership—can be regarded as income; that the increase during the donor's ownership is not income assessable against her within intendment of the Sixteenth Amendment.

The District Court ruled against the United States; the Circuit Court of Appeals held with them.

Act of Congress approved November 23, 1921, Chap. 136, 42 Stat. 227, 229, 237—

"Sec. 202.   (a) That the basis for ascertaining the gain derived or loss sustained from a sale or other disposition of property, real, personal, or mixed, acquired after February 28, 1913, shall be the cost of such property; except that—

"(1) * * *

"(2) In the case of such property, acquired by gift after December 31, 1920, the basis shall be the same as that which it would have in the hands of the donor or the last preceding owner by whom it was not acquired by gift. * * * [See I.R.C. (1954) § 1015(a). Ed.]

"Sec. 213.   That for the purposes of this title (except as otherwise provided in section 233) the term 'gross income'—

"(a) * * *

"(b) Does not include the following items, which shall be exempt from taxation under this title;

"(1) * * *   (2) * * *

"(3) The value of property acquired by gift, bequest, devise, or descent (but the income from such property shall be included in gross income); * * * *" [See I.R.C. (1954) § 102. Ed.]

We think the manifest purpose of Congress expressed in paragraph (2), Sec. 202, supra, was to require the petitioner to pay the exacted tax.

The only question subject to serious controversy is whether Congress had power to authorize the exaction.

It is said that the gift became a capital asset of the donee to the extent of its value when received and, therefore, when disposed of by her no part of that value could be treated as taxable income in her hands.

The Sixteenth Amendment provides—

"The Congress shall have power to lay and collect taxes on incomes from whatever source derived, without apportionment among the several States, and without regard to any census or enumeration."

Income is the thing which may be taxed—income from any source. The Amendment does not attempt to define income or to designate how taxes may be laid thereon, or how they may be enforced.

Under former decisions here the settled doctrine is that the Sixteenth Amendment confers no power upon Congress to define and tax as income without apportionment something which theretofore could not have been properly regarded as income.

Also, this Court has declared—"Income may be defined as the gain derived from capital, from labor, or from both combined, provided it be understood to include profit gained through a sale or conversion of capital assets." Eisner v. Macomber, 252 U.S. 189, 207. The "gain derived from capital," within the definition, is "not a gain accruing to capital, nor a growth or increment of value in the investment, but a gain, a profit, something of exchangeable value proceeding from the property, severed from the capital however invested, and coming in, that is, received or drawn by the claimant for his separate use, benefit and disposal." United States v. Phellis, 257 U.S. 156, 169.

If, instead of giving the stock to petitioner, the donor had sold it at market value, the excess over the capital he invested (cost) would have been income therefrom and subject to taxation under the Sixteenth Amendment. He would have been obliged to share the realized gain with the United States. He held the stock—the investment— subject to the right of the sovereign to take part of any increase in its value when separated through sale or conversion and reduced to his possession. Could he, contrary to the express will of Congress, by mere gift enable another to hold this stock free from such right, deprive the sovereign of the possibility of taxing the appreciation when actually severed, and convert the entire property into a capital asset of the donee, who invested nothing, as though the latter had purchased at the market price? And after a still further enhancement of the property, could the donee make a second gift with like effect, etc.? We think not.

In truth the stock represented only a single investment of capital—that made by the donor. And when through sale or conversion the increase was separated therefrom, it became income from that investment in the hands of the recipient subject to taxation according to the very words of the Sixteenth Amendment. By requiring the recipient of the entire increase to pay a part into the public treasury, Congress deprived her of no right and subjected her to no hardship. She accepted the gift with knowledge of the statute and, as to the property received, voluntarily assumed the position of her donor. When she sold the stock she actually got the original sum invested, plus the entire appreciation; and out of the latter only was she called on to pay the tax demanded.

The provision of the statute under consideration seems entirely appropriate for enforcing a general scheme of lawful taxation. To accept the view urged in behalf of petitioner undoubtedly would defeat, to some extent, the purpose of Congress to take part of all gain derived from capital investments. To prevent that result and insure enforcement of its proper policy, Congress had power to require that for purposes of taxation the donee should accept the position of the donor in respect of the thing received. And in so doing, it acted neither unreasonably nor arbitrarily.

* * *

There is nothing in the Constitution which lends support to the theory that gain actually resulting from the increased value of capital can be treated as taxable income in the hands of the recipient only so far as the increase occurred while he owned the property. And Irwin v. Gavit, 268 U.S. 161, 167, is to the contrary.

The judgments below are

Affirmed.

The CHIEF JUSTICE took no part in the consideration or decision of these causes.

FARID–ES–SULTANEH v. COMMISSIONER

United States Court of Appeals, Second Circuit, 1947.
160 F.2d 812.

CHASE, CIRCUIT JUDGE. The problem presented by this petition is to fix the cost basis to be used by the petitioner in determining the taxable gain on a sale she made in 1938 of shares of corporate stock. She contends that it is the adjusted value of the shares at the date she acquired them because her acquisition was by purchase. The Commissioner's position is that she must use the adjusted cost basis of her transferor because her acquisition was by gift. The Tax Court agreed with the Commissioner and redetermined the deficiency accordingly.

The pertinent facts are not in dispute and were found by the Tax Court as they were disclosed in the stipulation of the parties substantially as follows:

The petitioner is an American citizen who filed her income tax return for the calendar year 1938 with the Collector of Internal Revenue for the Third District of New York and in it reported sales during that year of 12,000 shares of the common stock of the S. S. Kresge Company at varying prices per share, for the total sum of $230,802.-36 which admittedly was in excess of their cost to her. How much this excess amounted to for tax purposes depends upon the legal significance of the facts now to be stated.

In December 1923 when the petitioner, then unmarried, and S. S. Kresge, then married, were contemplating their future marriage, he delivered to her 700 shares of the common stock of the S. S. Kresge Company which then had a fair market value of $290 per share. The shares were all in street form and were to be held by the petitioner "for her benefit and protection in the event that the said Kresge should die prior to the contemplated marriage between the petitioner and said Kresge." The latter was divorced from his wife on January 9, 1924, and on or about January 23, 1924 he delivered to the petitioner 1800 additional common shares of S. S. Kresge Company which were also in street form and were to be held by the petitioner for the same purposes as were the first 700 shares he had delivered to her. On April 24, 1924, and when the petitioner still retained the possession of the stock so delivered to her, she and Mr. Kresge executed a written ante-nuptial agreement wherein she acknowledged the receipt of the shares "as a gift made by the said Sebastian S. Kresge, pursuant to this indenture, and as an ante-nuptial settlement, and in consideration of said gift and said ante-nuptial settlement, in consideration of the promise of said Sebastian S. Kresge to marry her, and in further consideration of the consummation of said promised marriage" she released all dower and other marital rights, including the right to her support to which she otherwise would have been entitled as a matter of law when she became his wife. They were married in New York immediately after the ante-nuptial agreement was executed and continued to be husband and wife until the petitioner obtained a final decree of absolute divorce from him on, or about, May 18, 1928. No alimony was claimed by, or awarded to, her.

The stock so obtained by the petitioner from Mr. Kresge had a fair market value of $315 per share on April 24, 1924, and of $330 per share on, or about May 6, 1924, when it was transferred to her on the books of the corporation. She held all of it for about three years, but how much she continued to hold thereafter is not disclosed except as that may be shown by her sales in 1938. Meanwhile her holdings had been increased by a stock dividend of 50 per cent, declared on April 1, 1925; one of 10 to 1 declared on January 19, 1926; and one of 50 per cent, declared on March 1, 1929. Her adjusted basis for the stock she sold in 1938 was $10.66⅔ per share computed on the basis of the fair market value of the shares which she obtained from Mr. Kresge at the time of her acquisition. His adjusted basis for the shares she sold in 1938 would have been $0.159091.[1]

When the petitioner and Mr. Kresge were married he was 57 years old with a life expectancy of 16½ years. She was then 32 years of age with a life expectancy of 33¾ years. He was then worth ap-

---

1. Current rules for allocation of basis in the case of stock dividends appear in I.R.C. (26 U.S.C.A.) § 307. Ed.

proximately $375,000,000 and owned real estate of the approximate value of $100,000,000.

The Commissioner determined the deficiency on the ground that the petitioner's stock obtained as above stated was acquired by gift within the meaning of that word as used in § 113(a) (2) of the Revenue Act of 1938, 26 U.S.C.A. Int.Rev.Acts, page 1048, and, as the transfer to her was after December 31, 1920, used as the basis for determining the gain on her sale of it the basis it would have had in the hands of the donor.[2] This was correct if the just mentioned statute is applicable, and the Tax Court held it was on the authority of Wemyss v. Commissioner, 324 U.S. 303, 65 S.Ct. 652, 89 L.Ed. 958, 156 A.L.R. 1022, and Merrill v. Fahs, 324 U.S. 308, 65 S.Ct. 655, 89 L.Ed. 963.

The issue here presented cannot, however, be adequately dealt with quite so summarily. The Wemyss case determined the taxability to the transferor as a gift, under §§ 501 and 503 of the Revenue Act of 1932, 26 U.S.C.A. Int.Rev.Acts, pages 580, 585, and the applicable regulations, of property transferred in trust for the benefit of the prospective wife of the transferor pursuant to the terms of an ante-nuptial agreement. It was held that the transfer, being solely in consideration of her promise of marriage, and to compensate her for loss of trust income which would cease upon her marriage, was not for an adequate and full consideration in money or money's worth within the meaning of § 503 of the statute, the Tax Court having found that the transfer was not one at arm's length made in the ordinary course of business. But we find nothing in this decision to show that a transfer, taxable as a gift under the gift tax, is ipso facto to be treated as a gift in construing the income tax law.

In Merrill v. Fahs, supra, it was pointed out that the estate and gift tax statutes are in pari materia and are to be so construed. Estate of Sanford v. Commissioner of Internal Revenue, 308 U.S. 39, 44, 60 S.Ct. 51, 84 L.Ed. 20. The estate tax provisions in the Revenue Act of 1916 required the inclusion in a decedent's gross estate of transfers made in contemplation of death, or intended to take effect in possession and enjoyment at or after death except when a transfer was the result of "a bona fide sale for a fair consideration in money or money's worth." Sec. 202(b), 39 Stat. 756, 777. The first gift tax became effective in 1924, and provided inter alia, that where an exchange or sale of property was for less than a fair consideration in money or money's worth the excess should be taxed as a gift. Rev. Act of 1924, § 320, 43 Stat. 314, 26 U.S.C.A. Int.Rev.Acts, page 81. While both taxing statutes thus provided, it was held that a release of dower rights was a fair consideration in money or money's worth. Ferguson v. Dickson, 3 Cir., 300 F. 961, certiorari denied 266 U.S. 628, 45 S.Ct. 126, 69 L.Ed. 476; McCaughn v. Carver, 3 Cir., 19 F.2d 126.

2. See I.R.C. (1954) § 1015(a).   Ed.

Following that, Congress in 1926 replaced the words "fair consideration" in the 1924 Act limiting the deductibility of claims against an
estate with the words "adequate and full consideration in money or
money's worth" and in 1932 the gift tax statute as enacted limited
consideration in the same way. Rev.Act 1932, § 503. Although Congress in 1932 also expressly provided that the release of marital rights
should not be treated as a consideration in money or money's worth in
administering the estate tax law, Rev.Act of 1932, § 804, 26 U.S.C.A.
Int.Rev.Acts, page 642, and failed to include such a provision in the
gift tax statute, it was held that the gift tax law should be construed
to the same effect.[3] Merrill v. Fahs, supra.

We find in this decision no indication, however, that the term
"gift" as used in the income tax statute should be construed to include
a transfer which, if made when the gift tax were effective, would be
taxable to the transferor as a gift merely because of the special provisions in the gift tax statute defining and restricting consideration for
gift tax purposes. A fortiori, it would seem that limitations found in
the estate tax law upon according the usual legal effect to proof that a
transfer was made for a fair consideration should not be imported into
the income tax law except by action of Congress.

In our opinion the income tax provisions are not to be construed as
though they were in pari materia with either the estate tax law or the
gift tax statutes. They are aimed at the gathering of revenue by taking for public use given percentages of what the statute fixes as net
taxable income. Capital gains and losses are, to the required or permitted extent, factors in determining net taxable income. What is
known as the basis for computing gain or loss on transfers of property
is established by statute in those instances when the resulting gain or
loss is recognized for income tax purposes and the basis for succeeding
sales or exchanges will, theoretically at least, level off tax-wise any
hills and valleys in the consideration passing either way on previous
sales or exchanges. When Congress provided that gifts should not be
treated as taxable income to the donee there was, without any correla-
tive provisions fixing the basis of the gift to the donee, a loophole
which enabled the donee to make a subsequent transfer of the property
and take as the basis for computing gain or loss its value when the gift
was made. Thus it was possible to exclude from taxation any increment in value during the donor's holding and the donee might take advantage of any shrinkage in such increment after the acquisition by
gift in computing gain or loss upon a subsequent sale or exchange. It
was to close this loophole that Congress provided that the donee should
take the donor's basis when property was transferred by gift. Report of Ways and Means Committee (No. 350, P. 9, 67th Cong., 1st
Sess.). This change in the statute affected only the statutory net tax-

___

3. See I.R.C. (1954) §§ 2043(b) and
   2512(b). Ed.

able income. The altered statute prevented a transfer by gift from creating any change in the basis of the property in computing gain or loss on any future transfer. In any individual instance the change in the statute would but postpone taxation and presumably would have little effect on the total volume of income tax revenue derived over a long period of time and from many taxpayers. Because of this we think that a transfer which should be classed as a gift under the gift tax law is not necessarily to be treated as a gift income-tax-wise. Though such a consideration as this petitioner gave for the shares of stock she acquired from Mr. Kresge might not have relieved him from liability for a gift tax, had the present gift tax then been in effect, it was nevertheless a fair consideration which prevented her taking the shares as a gift under the income tax law since it precluded the existence of a donative intent.

Although the transfers of the stock made both in December 1923, and in the following January by Mr. Kresge to this taxpayer are called a gift in the ante-nuptial agreement later executed and were to be for the protection of his prospective bride if he died before the marriage was consummated, the "gift" was contingent upon his death before such marriage, an event that did not occur. Consequently, it would appear that no absolute gift was made before the ante-nuptial contract was executed and that she took title to the stock under its terms, viz: in consideration for her promise to marry him coupled with her promise to relinquish all rights in and to his property which she would otherwise acquire by the marriage. Her inchoate interest in the property of her affianced husband greatly exceeded the value of the stock transferred to her. It was a fair consideration under ordinary legal concepts of that term for the transfers of the stock by him. Ferguson v. Dickson, supra; McCaughn v. Carver, supra. She performed the contract under the terms of which the stock was transferred to her and held the shares not as a donee but as a purchaser for a fair consideration.

As the decisive issue is one of law only, the decision of the Tax Court interpreting the applicable statutory provisions has no peculiar finality and is reviewable. Bingham v. Commissioner, 325 U.S. 365, 65 S.Ct. 1232, 89 L.Ed. 1670.

Decision reversed.

[The dissenting opinion of CIRCUIT JUDGE CLARK has been omitted. Ed.]

PROBLEMS

1. Donor gave Donee property under circumstances that required no payment of gift tax. What gain or loss to Donee on the subsequent sale of the property if:

    (a) The property had cost Donor $20,000, had a $30,000 fair market value at the time of the gift, and Donee sold it for:

(1) $40,000?

(2) $15,000?

(3) $25,000?

(b) The property had cost Donor $30,000, had a $20,000 fair market value at the time of the gift, and Donee sold it for:

(1) $40,000?

(2) $15,000?

(3) $25,000?   *gift = fMU — AMt received*

2. Father had some land that he had purchased for $30,000 but which had increased in value to $60,000. He transferred it to Son for $30,000 in cash in a transaction properly identified as in part a gift and in part a sale.* Assume no gift tax was paid on the transfer.

(a) What gain to Father and what basis to Son under Reg. §§ 1.-1001–1(e) and 1.1015.4?

(b) Suppose the transaction were viewed as a sale of one half the land for full consideration and an outright gift of the other half. How would this affect Father's gain and Son's basis? Is it a more realistic view than that of the Regulations? Cf. I.R.C. (26 U.S.C.A.) § 1011(b), relating to bargain sales to charities.

---

3. PROPERTY ACQUIRED FROM A DECEDENT

Internal Revenue Code: Sections 1014(a), (b)(1) and (6), (d); 1023.
Regulations: Section 1.1014–1(a), –3(a).

Background

While property that is the subject of a gift receives what is commonly referred to as a carry-over or transferred basis, the same has not long been true of property acquired by inheritance. Until 1976 under I.R.C. (26 U.S.C.A.) § 1014(a) property acquired from a decedent received a basis equal to its fair market value on the date on which it was valued for federal estate tax purposes.[1] The effect of

---

* See Wurzel, "The Tax Basis for Assorted Bargain Purchases, or: The Inordinate Cost of 'Ersatz' Legislation," 20 Tax L.Rev. 165 (1964).

1. The estate tax is usually based on date of death value, but the executor may sometimes use an alternate valuation date which is a date within six months after decedent's death. I.R.C. (26 U.S.C.A.) §§ 2031 and 2032. The

date-of-death value basis rule was often criticized. See "Taxation of Appreciation of Assets Transferred at Death or by Gift," United States Treasury Dept., Tax Reform Studies and Proposals, 91st Cong., 1st Sess., Pt. 3, at 331–340 (1969), reprinted in Sander and Westfall, Readings in Federal Taxation 542 (Foundation Press 1970); see also Waterbury, "A Case for Realizing Gains at Death in Terms

this basis rule was to give property that appreciated during the decedent's ownership a "stepped-up" basis with no income tax cost to anyone. Of course a "stepped-down" basis resulted without deductible loss if property declined in value during decedent's ownership.

Section 1014 applied and in a limited way still applies not only to property held by the decedent at his death, but also to some property that he transferred during his life if the value of the property is nevertheless required to be included in his estate for federal estate tax purposes.[2] Thus, if a decedent had made an intervivos gift of property that was subsequently taxed as a part of his estate under the I.R.C. (26 U.S.C.A.) § 2035, which taxed lifetime transfers "in contemplation of death" (and which now taxes lifetime transfers made within three years of death), the property took a date-of-death value basis to the donee. Since an estate tax was paid on the value of such property, it is logical to treat it for basis purposes the same as property actually owned at death. But suppose one to whom property was given in contemplation of death sold it before the donor died. A close look at § 1014(a) will disclose that it generally did not purport to determine basis in such circumstances, i. e., in instances in which the property is "sold, exchanged, or otherwise disposed of before the decedent's death." If § 1014 did not apply, what did? Generally § 1015; the property was acquired by lifetime gift and, even if its value was going to be subjected to estate tax like property actually transferred at death, the donee could not wait until the donor's death to learn what his basis was. Thus § 1015 applied.[3]

The Revenue Act of 1948 brought into the Code a number of provisions designed, at least roughly, to equalize the tax status of persons in noncommunity property and community property states.[4] As

---

of Family Interests," 52 Minn.L.Rev. 1 (1967); Slawson, "Taxing as Ordinary Income the Appreciation of Publicly Held Stock," 76 Yale L.J. 623 (1967), reprinted in part in Sander and Westfall, Readings in Federal Taxation 495 (Foundation Press 1970); Castruccio, "Becoming More Inevitable? Death and Taxes * * * and Taxes," 17 U.C.L.A. L.Rev. 459 (1970); Heckerling, "The Death of the 'Stepped-Up' Basis at Death," 37 S.Cal.L.Rev. 247 (1964).

2. See I.R.C. (26 U.S.C.A.) § 1014(b) (2)–(9).

3. Generally property a donee acquired in exchange for, or by reinvestment after the sale of property acquired from a decedent but taxed in the decedent's gross estate took a new cost basis. However, the Regs. carried the § 1014 date-of-death basis over to newly acquired property if the value of the newly acquired property (not the value of the property actually transferred by the decedent) was included in the decedent's gross estate. It was rare, however, probably only in the case of lifetime transfers in trust, that the newly acquired property was accorded estate tax significance. See Stephens, Maxfield & Lind, *Federal Estate and Gift Taxation*, 4–72 (Warren, Gorham & Lamont, 1974), which criticizes different treatment of direct transfers from transfers in trust in this respect.

4. See Chapter 27, infra at page 947.

a part of that enactment Congress added I.R.C. (26 U.S.C.A.) § 1014 (b)(6), which gave a § 1014 basis to a surviving spouse's one-half share of community property, if at least one-half of the whole of the community interest in such property was included in the decedent spouse's estate (whether or not the estate was of sufficient size to require an estate tax return or payment of tax).[5] This was a somewhat perplexing provision, because the surviving spouse's share is not subjected to estate tax on the decedent's death. However, an examination of § 2056 will reveal that in a common law state a decedent's property that passes to his spouse, which automatically gets a § 1014 basis, also may escape tax by way of the estate tax marital deduction.

The § 1014 basis rule was an important element in estate planning. It meant that, although appreciated property was fully subjected to the estate tax, the appreciation itself entirely escaped the income tax. Thus, elderly people with substantially appreciated property often chose not to sell such property in order to avoid income taxation and were said to be "locked-in" to their positions. The step-up in basis was attacked both on economic and social policy grounds,[6] and there were many proposals for legislation either to provide a transferred basis at death or to subject the appreciation to income tax at death or for an estate tax surcharge measured by the amount of untaxed appreciation.[7] In 1976 Congress chose a compromise version of the carryover basis approach.

THE NEW BASIS RULE

By the enactment of new I.R.C. § 1023,[8] a carryover basis rule applies to property acquired from a decedent after December 31, 1976, which generally parallels the basis rule for property acquired by gift, § 1015. For purposes of determining loss, the basis for personal and household effects cannot exceed fair market value at the date of the decedent's death[9] but, as there is no such limitation on other types of property, a decedent's paper losses on investments, for example, may carry forward to the estate or other recipients through the carryover of a high basis. The aggregate assets of an estate are given a minimum basis of $60,000, whatever their basis to the decedent, if that amount does not exceed fair market value at death.[10] An upward adjustment in the carryover basis is made for state and

5. Reg. § 1.1014–2(a)(5).

6. See references cited at note 1, supra.

7. See Graetz, "Taxation of Unrealized Gains at Death—An Evaluation of the Current Proposals," 59 Virg.L.R. 830 (1973); but see G. Break and J. Pechman, Tax Reform: The Impossible Dream, pp. 13–18 (1975).

8. Tax Reform Act (1976) § 2005(a).

9. I.R.C. (26 U.S.C.A.) § 1023(a)(2). The executor may elect to value $10,000 worth of such property at its fair market value. See § 1023(b)(3)(A).

10. I.R.C. (26 U.S.C.A.) §§ 1023(d) and (f)(1).

federal death taxes attributable to net appreciation in property acquired from the decedent, limited again, however, so that the adjustments permitted do not push the basis above fair market value at death, even though the carryover basis itself *may* exceed such value.[11] This brief synopsis is obviously not all inclusive; the statute must be examined.[12] Moreover, for many years a special adjustment must be taken into account.

The Transitional Period

It is difficult to overstate the ultimate impact of new § 1023 on estate planning. However, it may be said to be creeping onto the scene. This is because of § 1023(h), the "fresh start" adjustment.[13] The general sense of this provision is that, if a decedent owned carryover basis property on December 31, 1976, *for purposes of determining gain* its fair market value on that date becomes its carryover basis. The affirmative aspect of this rule says, in effect, that Congress does not choose suddenly to make taxable all gain that has accrued to individuals through 1976 without having been realized, if the individual retains the property to the time of his death. To this extent old basis concepts (and reasonable expectations) prevail.

The negative aspect of the new rule is designed to foreclose artificial loss deductions. T buys property in 1975 for $100. On December 31, 1976 its value is $300. T dies in 1977 and his executor sells the property for $200. A loss deduction by way of the "fresh start" exception to the carryover basis rule? No indeed! Obviously, the family unit, if we may look at it this way, has an economic gain of $100. The "fresh start" rule permits escape from tax on that gain, but it does not convert the situation into a $100 tax loss. This is avoided by permitting a "fresh start" upward adjustment only for purposes of determining gain.[14] It will be recalled, however, there is no general restriction on the carryover basis for *loss* purposes. T buys property in 1975 for $300. On December 31, 1976, its value is

---

11. I.R.C. (26 U.S.C.A.) § 1023(c). But see the special rule on minimum basis for personal and household effects. I.R.C. (26 U.S.C.A.) § 1023(d)(2). A similar increase in basis (not in excess of fair market value) is made for state death taxes imposed on the transferee of such property. See § 1023(e).

12. Under § 1023 the order of adjustments to the basis of carryover basis property is provided by the statute as follows: § 1023(h) "fresh start" adjustment; § 1023(c) adjustment for estate taxes attributable to apprecia-

tion; § 1023(d) $60,000 minimum; and § 1023(e) adjustment for transferee's taxes paid. That order must be followed so as to reach the proper end result under the statute.

13. See also new I.R.C. § 1016(a)(23).

14. If the property involved were marketable securities and they were subsequently sold by the executor or legatee for $350, he would recognize only a $50 gain on the sale even though their fair market value at death was only $200. I.R.C. (26 U.S. C.A.) § 1023(h)(1).

$100. T dies in 1977 and his executor sells it for $200. A $100 deductible loss is allowed.[15]

It must now be conceded that the "fresh start" adjustment is not so simple as initially presented. Perhaps it is for marketable securities [16] for which December 31, 1976, values are easily ascertainable. As time goes on it will be more and more difficult to determine the December 31, 1976, value for other property, which has caused Congress to create an artificial rule for "fresh start" purposes. The artificial rule presumes that the decedent's time of acquisition and basis will be known, perhaps too hopefully,[17] and that value at death will be known. The essence of the adjustment, then, to take account of December 31, 1976, value is, in effect, an irrebuttable presumption that appreciation in value occurred at an even pace over the period the property was held.[18] The artificial "fresh start" rule of § 1023(h)(2)(B) is not especially difficult to apply to nondepreciable property but somewhat more complex where depreciation [19] is a factor. In Problems 2 and 3, below, apply the statute mechanically and then ask yourself where you have been and why.

Sec 1014(A) Property from Decedent FMV. date of death

PROBLEMS

1. On January 1, 1978, Elderly has two thousand shares of Solar Energy Corporation stock worth $10 per share. One thousand of the shares were purchased in 1970 by Elderly for $4 per share and the other one thousand shares in 1976 for $9 per share. The fair market value of Solar was $12 on December 31, 1976. In his estate planning Elderly decides to give one thousand shares to Son intervivos and to bequeath the other one thousand to Son at Elderly's death. Does it make any difference which one thousand shares Elderly transfers intervivos to Son?

Sec 1015
Sec 1014/b

2. Older purchased a home for $50,000 on January 1, 1976. Its value at his death on January 1, 1981, was $60,000.

    (a) Assuming his estate included other property sufficient to make § 1023(d) inapplicable but was small enough to incur no estate tax, what is the basis of the home in the hands of his executor?

1023 Repealed

    (b) What result in (a), above, if Older's total property subject to estate taxes under § 2001 was worth $320,000 and his total federal and state estate taxes were $40,000?

No adjustment

15. But see I.R.C. (26 U.S.C.A.) § 1023 (a)(2) providing a different rule here for personal and household effects.

16. See I.R.C. (26 U.S.C.A.) § 1023(h) (1).

17. See I.R.C. (26 U.S.C.A.) § 1023(g) (3).

18. This will work out to be a harsh assumption if property, say rural land, peaks in value in 1976, if a decedent who acquired it cheaply in 1970 dies in 1990.

19. Exhaustion, wear and tear, etc. in the sense of I.R.C. (26 U.S.C.A.) § 167.

(c) What results in (a) and (b), above, if Older had purchased the home on January 1, 1976 for $70,000?

3. Still Older purchased some equipment for $8000 on January 1, 1976. Its value at his death on January 1, 1979 was $12,000.

(a) Still Older had claimed straight-line depreciation on the equipment, using a useful life of 8 years and no salvage value. This resulted in $1000 of § 167 depreciation in each year and the equipment's adjusted basis at death was $5000. What is the basis of the equipment in the hands of his executor after the § 1023(h) adjustment? See § 1023(h)(2) (B).

(b) If Still Older had used the double declining accelerated depreciation method he would have taken $2000 of depreciation in 1976, $1500 of depreciation in 1977 and $1125 of depreciation in 1978 and the adjusted basis of the equipment would have been $3375. What is the basis of the equipment in the hands of his executor after the § 1023(h) adjustment? See § 1023(h)(2)(B).

C. THE AMOUNT REALIZED

Internal Revenue Code: Section 1001(b).
Regulations: Section 1.1001–1(a).

UNITED STATES v. DAVIS *

Supreme Court of the United States, 1962.
370 U.S. 65, 82 S.Ct. 1190.
Rehearing den., 371 U.S. 854, 83 S.Ct. 14.

MR. JUSTICE CLARK delivered the opinion of the Court.

These cases involve the tax consequences of a transfer of appreciated property by Thomas Crawley Davis[1] to his former wife pursuant to a property settlement agreement executed prior to divorce, as well as the deductibility of his payment of her legal expenses in connection therewith. The Court of Claims upset the Commissioner's determination that there was taxable gain on the transfer but upheld his ruling that the fees paid the wife's attorney were not deductible. 152 Ct.Cl. 805, 287 F.2d 168. We granted certiorari on a conflict in the Court of Appeals and the Court of Claims on the taxability of such

---

* See Solomon, "Property Transfer Pursuant to Divorce—Taxable Event?," 17 Stan.L.Rev. 478 (1965); Kilbourn; "Puzzling Problems in Property Settlements—The Tax, Anatomy of Divorce," 27 Mo.L.Rev. 354 (1962). Ed.]

1. Davis' present wife, Grace Ethel Davis, is also a party to these proceedings because a joint return was filed in the tax year in question.

transfers.[2] 368 U.S. 813. We have decided that the taxpayer did have a taxable gain on the transfer and that the wife's attorney's fees were not deductible.

In 1954 the taxpayer and his then wife made a voluntary property settlement and separation agreement calling for support payments to the wife and minor child in addition to the transfer of certain personal property to the wife. Under Delaware law all the property transferred was that of the taxpayer, subject to certain statutory marital rights of the wife including a right of intestate succession and a right upon divorce to a share of the husband's property.[3] Specifically as a "division in settlement of their property" the taxpayer agreed to transfer to his wife, *inter alia*, 1,000 shares of stock in the E. I. du Pont de Nemours & Co. The then Mrs. Davis agreed to accept this division "in full settlement and satisfaction of any and all claims and rights against the husband whatsoever (including but not by way of limitation, dower and all rights under the laws of testacy and intestacy) * * *." Pursuant to the above agreement which had been incorporated into the divorce decree, one-half of this stock was delivered in the tax year involved, 1955, and the balance thereafter. Davis' cost basis for the 1955 transfer was $74,775.37, and the fair market value of the 500 shares there transferred was $82,250. The taxpayer also agreed orally to pay the wife's legal expenses, and in 1955 he made payments to the wife's attorney, including $2,500 for services concerning tax matters relative to the property settlement.

I.

The determination of the income tax consequences of the stock transfer described above is basically a two-step analysis: (1) Was the transaction a taxable event? (2) If so, how much taxable gain resulted therefrom? Originally the Tax Court (at that time the Board of Tax Appeals) held that the accretion to property transferred pursuant to a divorce settlement could not be taxed as capital gain to the transferor because the amount realized by the satisfaction of the husband's marital obligations was indeterminable and because, even if such benefit were ascertainable, the transaction was a nontaxable division of property. Mesta v. Commissioner, 42 B.T.A. 933 (1940); Halliwell v. Commissioner, 44 B.T.A. 740 (1941). However, upon being reversed in quick succession by the Courts of Appeals of the Third and Second Circuits, Commissioner v. Mesta, 123 F.2d 986 (C.A.3d

---

2. The holding in the instant case is in accord with Commissioner v. Marshman, 279 F.2d 27 (C.A.6th Cir. 1960), but is contra to the holdings in Commissioner v. Halliwell, 131 F. 2d 642 (C.A.2d Cir. 1942), and Commissioner v. Mesta, 123 F.2d 986 (C.A. 3d Cir. 1941).

3. 12 Del.Code Ann. (Supp. 1960) § 512; 13 Del.Code Ann. § 1531. In the case of realty, the wife in addition to the above has rights of dower. 12 Del. Code Ann. §§ 502, 901, 904, 905.

Cir. 1941); Commissioner v. Halliwell, 131 F.2d 642 (C.A.2d Cir. 1942), the Tax Court accepted the position of these courts and has continued to apply these views in appropriate cases since that time, Hall v. Commissioner, 9 T.C. 53 (1947); Patino v. Commissioner, 13 T.C. 816 (1949); Estate of Stouffer v. Commissioner, 30 T.C. 1244 (1958); King v. Commissioner, 31 T.C. 108 (1958); Marshman v. Commissioner, 31 T.C. 269 (1958). In Mesta and Halliwell the Courts of Appeals reasoned that the accretion to the property was "realized" by the transfer and that this gain could be measured on the assumption that the relinquished marital rights were equal in value to the property transferred. The matter was considered settled until the Court of Appeals for the Sixth Circuit, in reversing the Tax Court, ruled that, although such a transfer might be a taxable event, the gain realized thereby could not be determined because of the impossibility of evaluating the fair market value of the wife's marital rights. Commissioner v. Marshman, 279 F.2d 27 (1960). In so holding that court specifically rejected the argument that these rights could be presumed to be equal in value to the property transferred for their release. This is essentially the position taken by the Court of Claims in the instant case.

II.

We now turn to the threshold question of whether the transfer in issue was an appropriate occasion for taxing the accretion to the stock. There can be no doubt that Congress, as evidenced by its inclusive definition of income subject to taxation, i. e., "all income from whatever source derived, including * * * [g]ains derived from dealings in property," [4] intended that the economic growth of this stock be taxed. The problem confronting us is simply *when* is such accretion to be taxed. Should the economic gain be presently assessed against taxpayer, or should this assessment await a subsequent transfer of the property by the wife? The controlling statutory language, which provides that gains from dealings in property are to be taxed upon "sale or other disposition," [5] is too general to include or exclude conclusively the transaction presently in issue. Recognizing this, the Government and the taxpayer argue by analogy with transactions more easily classified as within or without the ambient of taxable events. The taxpayer asserts that the present disposition is comparable to a nontaxable division of property between two co-owners,[6] while the Govern-

---

4. Internal Revenue Code of 1954 § 61 (a).

5. Internal Revenue Code of 1954 §§ 1001, 1002.

6. Any suggestion that the transaction in question was a gift is completely unrealistic. Property transferred pursuant to a negotiated settlement in return for the release of admittedly val-

uable rights is not a gift in any sense of the term. To intimate that there was a gift to the extent the value of the property exceeded that of the rights released not only invokes the erroneous premise that every exchange not precisely equal involves a gift but merely raises the measurement problem discussed in Part III, infra, p. 169. Cases in which this Court has held transfers of property in ex-

ment contends it more resembles a taxable transfer of property in exchange for the release of an independent legal obligation. Neither disputes the validity of the other's starting point.

In support of his analogy the taxpayer argues that to draw a distinction between a wife's interest in the property of her husband in a common-law jurisdiction such as Delaware and the property interest of a wife in a typical community property jurisdiction would commit a double sin; for such differentiation would depend upon "elusive and subtle casuistries which * * * possess no relevance for tax purposes," Helvering v. Hallock, 309 U.S. 106, 118 (1940), and would create disparities between common-law and community property jurisdictions in contradiction to Congress' general policy of equality between the two. The taxpayer's analogy, however, stumbles on its own premise, for the inchoate rights granted a wife in her husband's property by the Delaware law do not even remotely reach the dignity of co-ownership. The wife has no interest—passive or active—over the management or disposition of her husband's personal property. Her rights are not descendable, and she must survive him to share in his intestate estate. Upon dissolution of the marriage she shares in the property only to such extent as the court deems "reasonable." 13 Del. Code Ann. § 1531(a). What is "reasonable" might be ascertained independently of the extent of the husband's property by such criteria as the wife's financial condition, her needs in relation to her accustomed station in life, her age and health, the number of children and their ages, and the earning capacity of the husband. See, e. g., Beres v. Beres, 52 Del. 133, 154 A.2d 384 (1959).

This is not to say it would be completely illogical to consider the shearing off of the wife's rights in her husband's property as a division of that property, but we believe the contrary to be the more reasonable construction. Regardless of the tags, Delaware seems only to place a burden on the husband's property rather than to make the wife a part owner thereof. In the present context the rights of succession and reasonable share do not differ significantly from the husband's obligations of support and alimony. They all partake more of a personal liability of the husband than a property interest of the wife. The effectuation of these marital rights may ultimately result in the ownership of some of the husband's property as it did here, but certainly this happenstance does not equate the transaction with a division of property by co-owners. Although admittedly such a view may

change for the release of marital rights subject to gift taxes are based not on the premise that such transactions are inherently gifts but on the concept that in the contemplation of the gift tax statute they are to be taxed as gifts. Merrill v. Fahs, 324 U. S. 308 (1945); Commissioner v. Wemyss, 324 U.S. 303 (1945); see Harris v. Commissioner, 340 U.S. 106 (1950). In interpreting the particular income tax provisions here involved, we find ourselves unfettered by the language and considerations ingrained in the gift and estate tax statutes. See Farid-Es-Sultaneh v. Commissioner, 160 F.2d 812 (C.A.2d Cir. 1947).

permit different tax treatment among the several States, this Court in the past has not ignored the differing effects on the federal taxing scheme of substantive differences between community property and common-law systems.   E. g., Poe v. Seaborn, 282 U.S. 101 (1930). To be sure Congress has seen fit to alleviate this disparity in many areas, e. g., Revenue Act of 1948, 62 Stat. 110, but in other areas the facts of life are still with us.

Our interpretation of the general statutory language is fortified by the long-standing administrative practice as sounded and formalized by the settled state of law in the lower courts.   The Commissioner's position was adopted in the early 40's by the Second and Third Circuits and by 1947 the Tax Court had acquiesced in this view. This settled rule was not disturbed by the Court of Appeals for the Sixth Circuit in 1960 or the Court of Claims in the instant case, for these latter courts in holding the gain indeterminable assumed that the transaction was otherwise a taxable event. Such unanimity of views in support of a position representing a reasonable construction of an ambiguous statute will not lightly be put aside. It is quite possible that this notorious construction was relied upon by numerous taxpayers as well as the Congress itself, which not only refrained from making any changes in the statutory language during more than a score of years but re-enacted this same language in 1954.

III.

Having determined that the transaction was a taxable event, we now turn to the point on which the Court of Claims balked, viz., the measurement of the taxable gain realized by the taxpayer. The Code defines the taxable gain from the sale or disposition of property as being the "excess of the amount realized therefrom over the adjusted basis. * * * " I.R.C. (1954) § 1001(a). The "amount realized" is further defined as "the sum of any money received plus the fair market value of the property (other than money) received." I.R.C. (1954) § 1001(b). In the instant case the "property received" was the release of the wife's inchoate marital rights. The Court of Claims, following the Court of Appeals for the Sixth Circuit, found that there was no way to compute the fair market value of these marital rights and that it was thus impossible to determine the taxable gain realized by the taxpayer. We believe this conclusion was erroneous.

It must be assumed, we think, that the parties acted at arm's length and that they judged the marital rights to be equal in value to the property for which they were exchanged. There was no evidence to the contrary here. Absent a readily ascertainable value it is accepted practice where property is exchanged to hold, as did the Court of Claims in Philadelphia Park Amusement Co. v. United States, 130 Ct.Cl. 166, 172, 126 F.Supp. 184, 189 (1954), that the values "of the two properties exchanged in an arms-length transaction are either equal in fact, or are presumed to be equal." Accord, United States v. General Shoe Corp., 282 F.2d 9 (C.A.6th Cir. 1960); International Freighting Corp. v. Commissioner, 135 F.2d 310 (C.A.2d Cir. 1943). To be sure there is much to be said of the argument that such an assumption is weakened by the emotion, tension and practical necessities involved in divorce negotiations and the property settlements arising therefrom. However, once it is recognized that the transfer was a taxable event, it is more consistent with the general purpose and scheme of the taxing statutes to make a rough approximation of the gain realized thereby than to ignore altogether its tax consequences. Cf. Helvering v. Safe Deposit & Trust Co., 316 U.S. 56, 67 (1942).

Moreover, if the transaction is to be considered a taxable event as to the husband, the Court of Claims' position leaves up in the air the wife's basis for the property received. In the context of a taxable transfer by the husband,[7] all indicia point to a "cost" basis for this property in the hands of the wife.[8] Yet under the Court of Claims' position her cost for this property, i. e., the value of the marital rights relinquished therefor, would be indeterminable, and on subsequent disposition of the property she might suffer inordinately over the Commissioner's assessment which she would have the burden of proving erroneous, Commissioner v. Hansen, 360 U.S. 446, 468 (1959). Our present holding that the value of these rights is ascertainable eliminates this problem; for the same calculation that determines the amount received by the husband fixes the amount given up by the wife, and this figure, i. e., the market value of the property transferred by the husband, will be taken by her as her tax basis for the property received.

Finally, it must be noted that here, as well as in relation to the question of whether the event is taxable, we draw support from the prior administrative practice and judicial approval of that practice. See p. 163, supra. We therefore conclude that the Commissioner's assessment of a taxable gain based upon the value of the stock at the date of its transfer has not been shown erroneous.[9]

---

7. Under the present administrative practice, the release of marital rights in exchange for property or other consideration is not considered a taxable event as to the wife. For a discussion of the difficulties confronting a wife under a contrary approach, see Taylor and Schwartz, Tax Aspects of Marital Property Agreements, 7 Tax L.Rev. 19, 30 (1951); Comment, The Lump Sum Divorce Settlement as a Taxable Exchange, 8 U.C.L.A. L.Rev. 593, 601–602 (1961).

8. Section 1012 of the Internal Revenue Code of 1954 provides that:

"The basis of property shall be the cost of such property, except as otherwise provided in this subchapter and subchapters C (relating to corporate distributions and adjustments), K (relating to partners and partnerships), and P (relating to capital gains and losses). * * * "

9. We do not pass on the soundness of the taxpayer's other attacks upon this determination, for these contentions were not presented to the Commissioner or the Court of Claims.

IV.

The attorney-fee question is [omitted. Ed.]

Reversed in part and affirmed in part.

MR. JUSTICE FRANKFURTER took no part in the decision of these cases.

MR. JUSTICE WHITE took no part in the consideration or decision of these cases.

NOTE

The unscrambling of property interests in the case of divorce in a community property state may present a situation quite different from the *Davis* case. If one simply keeps that which is his or hers, no taxable event has occurred; and that would seem to be the effect of an *in kind* equal division of community property. This is indeed acknowledged in *Davis*. However, no reported cases reflect such equal in kind divisions, probably because they are a practical impossibility. That is, the bargaining will go: You take the business and I will take the farm and all the telephone stock, etc.; or the judge in the divorce case may make that decision. Even though all the property involved is community property, exchanges easily recognized by the tax lawyer are taking place; and there is no statutory exception to the recognition of gain or loss seemingly required by § 1001(c). Nevertheless, in cases that involve only a scattering of community property between the spouses the courts are refusing to recognize either gain at the Commissioner's prompting[1] or loss at the urging of the taxpayer.[2] In a recent Tax Court case,[3] Judge Cynthia Hall aptly identified this phenomenon as follows:[4]

> Usually, unless otherwise expressly provided in the Code, gain from the sale or exchange of property is recognized for tax purposes. Section 1002 [now Section 1001 (c)]. However, the judge-made, well-settled law concerning the division of community property upon a divorce makes exceptions to that general rule. In effect a nonstatutory nonrecognition rule has been created.

1. E. g., Osceola Heard Davenport, 12 T.C.M. 856 (1953); Clifford H. Wren, 24 T.C.M. 290 (1965).

2. E. g., Frances R. Walz, 32 B.T.A. 718 (1935).

3. Jean C. Carrieres, 64 T.C. 959 (1975).

4. Id. at 963.

And more recently the Service has accepted the result.[5] Probably anyone not seriously allergic to judicial legislation applauds this result. But the scope of the rule is obscure.[6]

Even before the rule could be accorded Judge Hall's "well-settled" classification, difficulties surfaced regarding the nature of the spouses' property interests under state law. After a long series of litigation, in 1969 the Tenth Circuit decided that Oklahoma law created marital co-ownership interests that *could* be the subject of a tax-free division at the time of divorce.[7] More recently a district court has differentiated *Davis* in a similar manner, finding that Colorado law also creates marital interests that fall on the community property rather than the common law side of the dividing line.[8] On the other hand, the Eighth Circuit has found that an Iowa wife's property interest in her husband's estate is inchoate, like the Delaware wife's interest in *Davis,* and treated the husband's transfer in satisfaction of the interest as a taxable event;[9] and more recently the Tenth Circuit (which had, in effect, placed Oklahoma in the community property category) refused to find that Kansas law (even though it called for an equitable division of property upon divorce) created marital property interests like those in community property states.[10] Thus, we have to concede that we reach Judge Hall's well-settled rule only after we have made sure we are dealing with interests that are, or at least are very like, community property interests. Of course, in common law states an equal division of property owned as tenants in common or as joint tenants is not a taxable event.[11]

When, even in a community property state, property that is not community property enters the picture, the unscrambling of marital

5. Rev.Rul. 76–83, 1976–1 C.B. 213. With respect to basis, the ruling holds that "the basis of each individual asset received in its entirety by one spouse or the other in the division will retain its present community basis in the hands of the spouse receiving it. The basis of each asset that will be partitioned will be the applicable percentage of the asset received multiplied by that asset's present basis to the community."

6. Hjorth, "Community Property Marital Settlements: The Problem and a Proposal," 50 Wash.L.Rev. 231 (1975); Schwartz, "Divorce and Taxes: New Aspects of the *Davis* Denouement," 15 U.C.L.A.L.Rev. 176 (1967); Brawerman, "A Practical Approach to Tax Problems in Divorce and Property Settlement Agreements," 12 U.S.C. Tax Inst. 753 (1960).

7. Collins v. Comm'r, 412 F.2d 211 (10th Cir. 1969).

8. Imel v. U. S., 375 F.Supp. 1102 (D. Colo.1974).

9. Wallace v. U. S., 439 F.2d 757 (8th Cir. 1971).

10. Wiles v. Comm'r, 499 F.2d 255 (10th Cir. 1974), cert. den. 95 S.Ct. 310, 42 L.Ed.2d 270 (1974). See Lawson, "Tax Implications of Using Appreciated Property in a Property Settlement," 42 J.Tax. 58 (1975) and Glickfeld, Rabow, and Schwartz, "Federal Income Tax Consequences of Marital Property Settlements," 26 U.S.C.T.I. 307 (1974).

11. Cf. Beth W. Corp. v. U. S., 350 F.Supp. 1190 (S.D.Fla.1972), aff'd per curiam 481 F.2d 1401 (5th Cir. 1973), cert. den. 415 U.S. 916 (1974), holding that the spouses receive such property with a transferred rather than stepped-up basis after a nontaxable division of property held as a tenancy by entirety.

interests is pretty certain to be a taxable event. It should be obvious that if one spouse acquires all the community property by compensating the other with noncommunity property, a taxable exchange has taken place. This is by no means within the judge-made nonrecognition rule.[12]

A more likely happening, however, is an unequal division of the community property made up by the spouse who receives more compensating the other with separate property or perhaps cash borrowed for the purpose. That was the situation in *Jean C. Carrieres*.[13] Is the magic spell of the judge-made nonrecognition rule broken so that the full tax consequences of a sale or exchange are encountered? In *Carrieres*, Judge Hall noted that this would create a "cliff effect," saying "the use of even $1 of separate property to remedy a disparity * * * would render entirely inapplicable the protection of the nonrecognition principle and would frustrate the beneficial policy underlying that principle."[14] Rejecting that, Judge Hall held that to the extent one spouse received cash or separate property for portions of his or her community property (but only to that extent), a taxable sale or exchange had taken place.[15]

The *Davis* case concerned the tax consequences to the transferor husband. But what about his former wife who received the stock? Does she have income? She received property with a fair market value and so the answer would appear to depend on the amount of her basis in the property interests she relinquished. Supported by footnote 7 of *Davis*, supra, Revenue Ruling 67–221 [16] states:

> Under the terms of a divorce decree and in accordance with a property settlement agreement, which was incorporated in the divorce decree, the husband transferred his interest in an apartment building to his former wife in consideration for and in discharge of her dower rights. The marital rights the former wife relinquished are equal in value to the value of the property she agreed to accept in exchange for those rights. *Held*, there is no gain or loss to the wife on the transfer and the basis of the property to the wife is its fair market value on the date of the transfer.

If Wife realizes no income, is this because her basis in her marital rights was equal to their value? Where could such basis come from?

---

12. See Jessie Lee Edwards, 22 T.C. 65 (1954).

13. Supra note 3. See also cases cited therein.

14. Id. at 965. Taxpayer has appealed the *Carrieres* decision to the Ninth Circuit.

15. There can well be an allocation problem, as is noted in the *Carrieres* opinion. If a spouse gives up his or her interest in both low basis and high basis property, which is a mere part of the tax-free division? And which is the portion of the transaction that reflects a taxable exchange? In *Carrieres*, the court felt able to identify the wife's interest in close corporation stock as the asset intended to be "sold" rather than divided.

16. 1967–2 C.B. 63.

This seems to be merely another judge-made rule but, again, one that appears fair when the *Davis* tax on the transferor is considered.

In view of the difference between community and noncommunity property states and the possible nonapplication of *Davis* in some noncommunity states one may question whether such a substantial difference in tax consequences should be left to be dependent upon state law. Certainly the *Davis* case imposes a tax in an already troubled divorce or legal separation situation where the transfer does not generate any liquidity, any funds with which to pay. Perhaps Congress should come to the rescue of noncommunity property states (as it did in 1948) and reverse the *Davis* result. If it does, it should also consider the consequences to the recipient spouse as well, expressly excluding receipts from income but providing suitable carry-over basis provisions.[17]

Recognize that the holding of the *Davis* case extends well beyond the context of a divorce property settlement situation. Whenever appreciated property is transferred to satisfy an obligation, a gain will result. Thus, if an employer owns some land with a basis of $8000 which is worth $10,000 and he transfers it to employee in discharge of employee's $10,000 salary, employer has a $2000 gain. What result to employer if he had purchased the land for $12,000?[18]

CRANE v. COMMISSIONER *

Supreme Court of the United States, 1947.
331 U.S. 1, 67 S.Ct. 1047.

[The Crane case, which follows, is hard going at best. One key to understanding the concepts that are developed in the opinion is some understanding of the income tax aspects of depreciation and consequent basis adjustments. If this is a new problem for you, as a student, you may benefit from a reading of the note on depreciation in Chapter 22 at page 721. Ed.]

MR. CHIEF JUSTICE VINSON delivered the opinion of the Court.

The question here is how a taxpayer who acquires depreciable property subject to an unassumed mortgage, holds it for a period, and finally sells it still so encumbered, must compute her taxable gain.

---

17. Cf. I.R.C. § 1015.

18. Cf. William E. Robertson, 55 T.C. 862 (1971); Worthy W. McKinney, 64 T.C. 263 (1975).

* See Del Cotto, "Basis and Amount Realized Under Crane: A Current View of Some Tax Effects in Mortgage Financing," 118 U. of Pa.L.Rev.

69 (1969); Adams, "Exploring the Outer Boundaries of the Crane Doctrine; An Imaginary Supreme Court Opinion," 21 Tax L.Rev. 159 (1966), reprinted in Sander and Westfall, Readings in Federal Taxation at page 325 (Foundation Press 1970); Cooper, "Negative Basis," 75 Harv.L.Rev. 1352 (1962). Ed.

Petitioner was the sole beneficiary and the executrix of the will of her husband, who died January 11, 1932. He then owned an apartment building and lot subject to a mortgage,[1] which secured a principal debt of $255,000.00 and interest in default of $7,042.50. As of that date, the property was appraised for federal estate tax purposes at a value exactly equal to the total amount of this encumbrance. Shortly after her husband's death, petitioner entered into an agreement with the mortgagee whereby she was to continue to operate the property— collecting the rents, paying for necessary repairs, labor, and other operating expenses, and reserving $200.00 monthly for taxes—and was to remit the net rentals to the mortgagee. This plan was followed for nearly seven years, during which period petitioner reported the gross rentals as income, and claimed and was allowed deductions for taxes and operating expenses paid on the property, for interest paid on the mortgage, and for the physical exhaustion of the building. Meanwhile, the arrearage of interest increased to $15,857.71. On November 29, 1938, with the mortgagee threatening foreclosure, petitioner sold to a third party for $3,000.00 cash, subject to the mortgage, and paid $500.-00 expenses of sale.

Petitioner reported a taxable gain of $1,250.00. Her theory was that the "property" which she had acquired in 1932 and sold in 1938 was only the equity, or the excess in the value of the apartment building and lot over the amount of the mortgage. This equity was of zero value when she acquired it. No depreciation could be taken on a zero value.[2] Neither she nor her vendee ever assumed the mortgage, so, when she sold the equity, the amount she realized on the sale was the net cash received, or $2,500.00. This sum less the zero basis constituted her gain, of which she reported half as taxable on the assumption that the entire property was a "capital asset." [3]

The Commissioner, however, determined that petitioner realized a net taxable gain of $23,767.03. His theory was that the "property" acquired and sold was not the equity, as petitioner claimed, but rather the physical property itself, or the owner's rights to possess, use, and dispose of it, undiminished by the mortgage. The original basis thereof was $262,042.50, its appraised value in 1932. Of this value $55,-000.00 was allocable to land and $207,042.50 to building.[4] During the period that petitioner held the property, there was an allowable depre-

---

1. The record does not show whether he was personally liable for the debt.

2. This position is, of course, inconsistent with her practice in claiming such deductions in each of the years the property was held. The deductions so claimed and allowed by the Commissioner were in the total amount of $25,500.00.

3. See § 117(a), (b), Revenue Act of 1938, c. 289, 52 Stat. 447. Under this provision only 50% of the gain realized on the sale of a "capital asset" need be taken into account, if the property had been held more than two years.

4. The parties stipulated as to the relative parts of the 1932 appraised value and of the 1938 sales price which were allocable to land and building.

ciation of $28,045.10 on the building,[5] so that the adjusted basis of the building at the time of sale was $178,997.40. The amount realized on the sale was said to include not only the $2,500.00 net cash receipts, but also the principal amount [6] of the mortgage subject to which the property was sold, both totaling $257,500.00. * * *

The Tax Court   *   *   *   [essentially] adopted petitioner's contentions, and expunged the deficiency.[9] * * * [T]he Circuit Court of Appeals reversed, one judge dissenting.[10] We granted certiorari because of the importance of the questions raised as to the proper construction of the gain and loss provisions of the Internal Revenue Code.[11]

The 1938 Act,[12] § 111(a), defines the gain from "the sale or other disposition of property" as "the excess of the amount realized therefrom over the adjusted basis provided in section 113(b) * * *." It proceeds, § 111(b), to define "the amount realized from the sale or other disposition of property" as "the sum of any money received plus the fair market value of the property (other than money) received." Further, in § 113(b), the "adjusted basis for determining the gain or loss from the sale or other disposition of property" is declared to be "the basis determined under subsection (a), adjusted * * * [(1) (B)] * * * for exhaustion, wear and tear, obsolescence, amortization * * * to the extent allowed (but not less than the amount allowable) * * *." The basis under subsection (a) "if the property was acquired by * * * devise * * * or by the decedent's estate from the decedent," § 113(a)(5), is "the fair market value of such property at the time of such acquisition." *

---

5. The parties stipulated that the rate of depreciation applicable to the building was 2% per annum.

6. The Commissioner explains that only the principal amount, rather than the total present debt secured by the mortgage, was deemed to be a measure of the amount realized, because the difference was attributable to interest due, a deductible item.

9. 3 T.C. 585. The Court held that the building was not a "capital asset" within the meaning of § 117(a) and that the entire gain on the building had to be taken into account under § 117(b), because it found that the building was of a character subject to physical exhaustion and that petitioner had used it in her trade or business.
But because the Court accepted petitioner's theory that the entire property had a zero basis, it held that she was not entitled to the 1938 depreciation deduction on the building which she had inconsistently claimed.

For these reasons, it did not expunge the deficiency in its entirety.

10. 153 F.2d 504.

11. 328 U.S. 826.

12. All subsequent references to a revenue act are to this Act unless otherwise indicated. The relevant parts of the gain and loss provisions of the Act and Code are identical.

* The basis rule expressed here, most recently found in I.R.C. (26 U.S.C.A.) § 1014, was of course altered by TRA (1976) which added § 1023, the carryover basis provision. Nevertheless, the principles of *Crane* have always applied to acquisitions other than by bequest, devise or inheritance. Consequently the case is of continuing importance. New § 1023(g)(4) purports to deal with adjustments to the carryover basis in the case of mortgaged property. In the vernacular, as enacted it is screwed up. See Reg. § 20.2053–7. A speedy change may be anticipated. Ed.

Logically, the first step under this scheme is to determine the unadjusted basis of the property, under § 113(a) (5), and the dispute in this case is as to the construction to be given the term "property." If "property," as used in that provision, means the same thing as "equity," it would necessarily follow that the basis of petitioner's property was zero, as she contends. If, on the contrary, it means the land and building themselves, or the owner's legal rights in them, undiminished by the mortgage, the basis was $262,042.50.

We think that the reasons for favoring one of the latter constructions are of overwhelming weight. In the first place, the words of statutes—including revenue acts—should be interpreted where possible in their ordinary, everyday senses.[13] The only relevant definitions of "property" to be found in the principal standard dictionaries [14] are the two favored by the Commissioner, i. e., either that "property" is the physical thing which is a subject of ownership, or that it is the aggregate of the owner's rights to control and dispose of that thing. "Equity" is not given as a synonym, nor do either of the foregoing definitions suggest that it could be correctly so used. Indeed, "equity" is defined as "the value of a property * * * above the total of the liens. * * * " [15]   The contradistinction could hardly be more pointed. Strong countervailing considerations would be required to support a contention that Congress, in using the word "property," meant "equity," or that we should impute to it the intent to convey that meaning.[16]

In the second place, the Commissioner's position has the approval of the administrative construction of § 113(a) (5). With respect to the valuation of property under that section, Reg. 101, Art. 113(a) (5)–1, promulgated under the 1938 Act, provided that "the value of property as of the date of the death of the decedent as appraised for the purpose of the Federal estate tax * * * shall be deemed to be its fair market value * * *." The land and building here involved were so appraised in 1932, and their appraised value—$262,042.50— was reported by petitioner as part of the gross estate. This was in accordance with the estate tax law [17] and regulations,[18] which had always required that the value of decedent's property, undiminished by liens, be so appraised and returned, and that mortgages be separately

13. Old Colony R. Co. v. Commissioner, 284 U.S. 552, 560.

14. See Webster's New International Dictionary, Unabridged, 2d Ed.; Funk & Wagnalls' New Standard Dictionary; Oxford English Dictionary.

15. See Webster's New International Dictionary, supra.

16. Crooks v. Harrelson, 282 U.S. 55, 59.

17. See §§ 202 and 203(a) (1) Revenue Act of 1916; §§ 402 and 403(a) (1), Revenue Acts of 1918 and 1921; §§ 302, 303(a) (1), Revenue Acts of 1924 and 1926; § 805, Revenue Act of 1932.

18. See Reg. 37, Arts. 13, 14, and 47; Reg. 63, Arts. 12, 13, and 41; Reg. 68, Arts. 11, 13, and 38; Reg. 70, Arts. 11, 13, and 38; Reg. 80, Arts. 11, 13, and 38.

deducted in computing the net estate.[19]   As the quoted provision of the Regulations has been in effect since 1918,[20] and as the relevant statutory provision has been repeatedly reenacted since then in substantially the same form,[21] the former may itself now be considered to have the force of law.[22]

Moreover, in the many instances in other parts of the Act in which Congress has used the word "property," or expressed the idea of "property" or "equity," we find no instances of a misuse of either word or of a confusion of the ideas.[23]   In some parts of the Act other than the gain and loss sections, we find "property" where it is unmistakably used in its ordinary sense.[24]   On the other hand, where either Congress or the Treasury intended to convey the meaning of "equity," it did so by the use of appropriate language.[25]

A further reason why the word "property" in § 113(a) should not be construed to mean "equity" is the bearing such construction would have on the allowance of deductions for depreciation and on the collateral adjustments of basis.

Section 23(*l*) permits deduction from gross income of "a reasonable allowance for the exhaustion, wear and tear of property. * * * * " Sections 23(n) and 114(a) declare that the "basis upon which exhaustion, wear and tear * * * are to be allowed" is the basis "provided in section 113(b) for the purpose of determining the gain upon the sale" of the property, which is the § 113(a) basis "adjusted * * * for exhaustion, wear and tear * * * to the extent allowed (but not less than the amount allowable). * * * " *

---

19. See City Bank Farmers' Trust Co. v. Bowers, 68 F.2d 909, cert. denied, 292 U.S. 644; Rodiek v. Helvering, 87 F.2d 328; Adriance v. Higgins, 113 F. 2d 1013.

20. [Citations omitted. Ed.]

21. [Citations omitted. Ed.]

22. Helvering v. Reynolds Co., 306 U. S. 110, 114.

23. Cf. Helvering v. Stockholms Bank, 293 U.S. 84, 87.

24. Sec. 23(a) (1) permits the deduction from gross income of "rentals * * * required to be made as a condition to the continued use * * * for purposes of the trade or business, of *property* * * * in which he [the taxpayer] has no *equity.*" (Italics supplied.)
Sec. 23(*l*) permits the deduction from gross income of "a reasonable allowance for the exhaustion, wear and tear of *property* used in the trade or business * * *." (Italics supplied.)

See also § 303(a) (1), Revenue Act of 1926, c. 27, 44 Stat. 9; § 805, Revenue Act of 1932, c. 209, 47 Stat. 280.

25. See § 23(a) (1), supra, note 24; § 805, Revenue Act of 1932, supra, note 24; § 3482, I.R.C.; Reg. 105, § 81.38. This provision of the Regulations, first appearing in 1937, T.D. 4729, 1937–1 Cum.Bull. 284, 289, permitted estates which were not liable on mortgages applicable to certain of decedent's property to return "only the value of the equity of redemption (or value of the property, less the indebtedness) * * *."

* In the Internal Revenue Code of 1954, as compared with earlier Acts cited here, the depreciation deduction is authorized by § 167(a); § 167(g) makes reference to § 1011 for a determination of the basis upon which deductions are to be claimed. Detailed differences are not of significance here. Ed.

Under these provisions, if the mortgagor's equity were the § 113 (a) basis, it would also be the original basis from which depreciation allowances are deducted. If it is, and if the amount of the annual allowances were to be computed on that value, as would then seem to be required,[26] they will represent only a fraction of the cost of the corresponding physical exhaustion, and any recoupment by the mortgagor of the remainder of that cost can be effected only by the reduction of his taxable gain in the year of sale.[27] If, however, the amount of the annual allowances were to be computed on the value of the property, and then deducted from an equity basis, we would in some instances have to accept deductions from a minus basis or deny deductions altogether.[28] The Commissioner also argues that taking the mortgagor's equity as the § 113(a) basis would require the basis to be changed with each payment on the mortgage,[29] and that the attendant problem of repeatedly recomputing basis and annual allowances would be a tremendous accounting burden on both the Commissioner and the taxpayer. Moreover, the mortgagor would acquire control over the timing of his depreciation allowances.

Thus it appears that the applicable provisions of the Act expressly preclude an equity basis, and the use of it is contrary to certain implicit principles of income tax depreciation, and entails very great administrative difficulties.[30] It may be added that the Treasury has never furnished a guide through the maze of problems that arise in connection with depreciating an equity basis, but, on the contrary, has consistently permitted the amount of depreciation allowances to be computed on the full value of the property, and sub-

---

26. Secs. 23(n) and 114(a), in defining the "basis upon which" depreciation is "to be allowed," do not distinguish between basis as the minuend from which the allowances are to be deducted, and as the dividend from which the amount of the allowance is to be computed. The Regulations indicate that the basis of property is the same for both purposes. Reg. 101, Art. 23(*l*)–4, 5.

27. This is contrary to Treasury practice, and to Reg. 101, Art. 23(*l*)–5, which provides in part:

"The capital sum to be recovered shall be charged off over the useful life of the property, either in equal annual installments or in accordance with any other recognized trade practice, such as an apportionment of the capital sum over units of production."

See Detroit Edison Co. v. Commissioner, 319 U.S. 98, 101.

28. So long as the mortgagor remains in possession, the mortgagee can not take depreciation deductions, even if he is the one who actually sustains the capital loss, as § 23(*l*) allows them only on property "used in the trade or business."

29. Sec. 113(b) (1) (A) requires adjustment of basis "for expenditures * * * properly chargeable to capital account * * *."

30. Obviously we are not considering a situation in which a taxpayer has acquired and sold an equity of redemption only, i. e., a right to redeem the property without a right to present possession. In that situation, the right to redeem would itself be the aggregate of the taxpayer's rights and would undoubtedly constitute "property" within the meaning of § 113(a). No depreciation problems would arise. See note 28.

tracted from it as a basis. Surely, Congress' long-continued acceptance of this situation gives it full legislative endorsement.[31]

We conclude that the proper basis under § 113(a) (5) is the value of the property, undiminished by mortgages thereon, and that the correct basis here was $262,042.50. The next step is to ascertain what adjustments are required under § 113(b). As the depreciation rate was stipulated, the only question at this point is whether the Commissioner was warranted in making any depreciation adjustments whatsoever.

Section 113(b)(1)(B) provides that "proper adjustment in respect of the property *shall in all cases be made* * * * for exhaustion, wear and tear * * * to the extent allowed (but not less than the amount allowable). * * * (Italics supplied.)** The Tax Court found on adequate evidence that the apartment house was property of a kind subject to physical exhaustion, that it was used in taxpayer's trade or business, and consequently that the taxpayer would have been entitled to a depreciation allowance under § 23(1), except that, in the opinion of that Court, the basis of the property was zero, and it was thought that depreciation could not be taken on a zero basis. As we have just decided that the correct basis of the property was not zero, but $262,042.50, we avoid this difficulty, and conclude that an adjustment should be made as the Commissioner determined.

Petitioner urges to the contrary that she was not entitled to depreciation deductions, whatever the basis of the property, because the law allows them only to one who actually bears the capital loss,[32] and here the loss was not hers but the mortgagee's. We do not see, however, that she has established her factual premise. There was no finding of the Tax Court to that effect, nor to the effect that the value of the property was ever less than the amount of the lien. Nor was there evidence in the record, or any indication that petitioner could produce evidence, that this was so. The facts that the value of the property was only equal to the lien in 1932 and that during the next six and one-half years the physical condition of the building deteriorated and the amount of the lien increased, are entirely inconclusive, particularly in the light of the buyer's willingness in 1938 to take subject to the increased lien and pay a substantial amount of cash to boot. Whatever may be the rule as to allowing depreciation to a mortgagor on property in his possession which is subject to an unassumed mortgage and clearly worth less than the lien, we are not faced with that problem and see no reason to decide it now.

---

31. See note 22.

** See I.R.C. (1954) § 1016(a)(2); refinements in the amounts of the adjustments in basis required do not affect the principles for which the case is studied here. Ed.

32. See Helvering v. Lazarus & Co., 308 U.S. 252; Duffy v. Central R. Co., 268 U.S. 55, 64.

At last we come to the problem of determining the "amount realized" on the 1938 sale. Section 111(b), it will be recalled, defines the "amount realized" from "the sale * * * of property" as "the sum of any money received plus the fair market value of the property (other than money) received," and § 111(a) defines the gain on "the sale * * * of property" as the excess of the amount realized over the basis. Quite obviously, the word "property," used here with reference to a sale, must mean "property" in the same ordinary sense intended by the use of the word with reference to acquisition and depreciation in § 113, both for certain of the reasons stated heretofore in discussing its meaning in § 113, and also because the functional relation of the two sections requires that the word mean the same in one section that it does in the other. If the "property" to be valued on the date of acquisition is the property free of liens, the "property" to be priced on a subsequent sale must be the same thing.[33]

Starting from this point, we could not accept petitioner's contention that the $2,500.00 net cash was all she realized on the sale except on the absurdity that she sold a quarter-of-a-million dollar property for roughly one per cent of its value, and took a 99 per cent loss. Actually, petitioner does not urge this. She argues, conversely, that because only $2,500.00 was realized on the sale, the "property" sold must have been the equity only, and that consequently we are forced to accept her contention as to the meaning of "property" in § 113. We adhere, however, to what we have already said on the meaning of "property," and we find that the absurdity is avoided by our conclusion that the amount of the mortgage is properly included in the "amount realized" on the sale.

Petitioner concedes that if she had been personally liable on the mortgage and the purchaser had either paid or assumed it, the amount so paid or assumed would be considered a part of the "amount realized" within the meaning of § 111(b).[34] The cases so deciding have already repudiated the notion that there must be an actual receipt by the seller himself of "money" or "other property," in their narrowest senses. It was thought to be decisive that one section of the Act must be construed so as not to defeat the intention of another or to frustrate the Act as a whole,[35] and that the taxpayer was the

---

33. See Maguire v. Commissioner, 313 U.S. 1, 8.

We are not troubled by petitioner's argument that her contract of sale expressly provided for the conveyance of the equity only. She actually conveyed title to the property, and the buyer took the same property that petitioner had acquired in 1932 and used in her trade or business until its sale.

34. United States v. Hendler, 303 U.S. 564; Brons Hotels, Inc., 34 B.T.A. 376; Walter F. Haass, 37 B.T.A. 948. See Douglas v. Willcuts, 296 U.S. 1, 8.

35. See Brons Hotels, Inc., supra, 34 B. T.A. at 381.

"beneficiary" of the payment in "as real and substantial [a sense] as if the money had been paid it and then paid over by it to its creditors." [36]

Both these points apply to this case. The first has been mentioned already. As for the second, we think that a mortgagor, not personally liable on the debt, who sells the property subject to the mortgage and for additional consideration, realizes a benefit in the amount of the mortgage as well as the boot.[37] If a purchaser pays boot, it is immaterial as to our problem whether the mortgagor is also to receive money from the purchaser to discharge the mortgage prior to sale, or whether he is merely to transfer subject to the mortgage—it may make a difference to the purchaser and to the mortgagee, but not to the mortgagor. Or put in another way, we are no more concerned with whether the mortgagor is, strictly speaking, a debtor on the mortgage, than we are with whether the benefit to him is, strictly speaking, a receipt of money or property. We are rather concerned with the reality that an owner of property, mortgaged at a figure less than that at which the property will sell, must and will treat the conditions of the mortgage exactly as if they were his personal obligations.[38] If he transfers subject to the mortgage, the benefit to him is as real and substantial as if the mortgage were discharged, or as if a personal debt in an equal amount had been assumed by another.

Therefore we conclude that the Commissioner was right in determining that petitioner realized $257,500.00 on the sale of this property.

The Tax Court's contrary determinations, that "property," as used in § 113(a) and related sections, means "equity," and that the amount of a mortgage subject to which property is sold is not the measure of a benefit realized, within the meaning of § 111(b), announced rules of general applicability on clear-cut questions of law.[39] The Circuit Court of Appeals therefore had jurisdiction to review them.[40]

36. See United States v. Hendler, supra, 303 U.S. at 566.

37. Obviously, if the value of the property is less than the amount of the mortgage, a mortgagor who is not personally liable cannot realize a benefit equal to the mortgage. Consequently, a different problem might be encountered where a mortgagor abandoned the property or transferred it subject to the mortgage without receiving boot. That is not this case. [But Cf. Rev.Rul. 76–111, 1976–1 C.B. 214 Ed.]

38. For instance, this petitioner returned the gross rentals as her own income, and out of them paid interest on the mortgage, on which she claimed and was allowed deductions. See Reg. 77, Art. 141; Reg. 86, Art. 23(b)–1; Reg. 94, Art. 23(b)–1; Reg. 101, Art. 23(b)–1.

39. See Commissioner v. Wilcox, 327 U.S. 404, 410; Trust of Bingham v. Commissioner, 325 U.S. 365, 369–372. Cf. John Kelley Co. v. Commissioner, 326 U.S. 521, 527; Dobson v. Commissioner, 320 U.S. 489.

40. Ibid; see also § 1141(a) and (c), I.R.C.

Petitioner contends that the result we have reached taxes her on what is not income within the meaning of the Sixteenth Amendment. If this is because only the direct receipt of cash is thought to be income in the constitutional sense, her contention is wholly without merit.[41] If it is because the entire transaction is thought to have been "by all dictates of common sense * * * a ruinous disaster," as it was termed in her brief, we disagree with her premise. She was entitled to depreciation deductions for a period of nearly seven years, and she actually took them in almost the allowable amount. The crux of this case, really, is whether the law permits her to exclude allowable deductions from consideration in computing gain.[42] We have already showed that, if it does, the taxpayer can enjoy a double deduction, in effect, on the same loss of assets. The Sixteenth Amendment does not require that result any more than does the Act itself.

Affirmed.

MR. JUSTICE JACKSON, dissenting.

The Tax Court concluded that this taxpayer acquired only an equity worth nothing. The mortgage was in default, the mortgage debt was equal to the value of the property, any possession by the taxpayer was forfeited and terminable immediately by foreclosure, and perhaps by a receiver *pendente lite*. Arguments can be advanced to support the theory that the taxpayer received the whole property and thereupon came to owe the whole debt. Likewise it is argued that when she sold she transferred the entire value of the property and received release from the whole debt. But we think these arguments are not so conclusive that it was not within the province of the Tax Court to find that she received an equity which at that time had a zero value. Dobson v. Commissioner, 320 U.S. 489; Commissioner v. Scottish American Investment Co., Ltd., 323 U.S. 119. The taxpayer never became personally liable for the debt, and hence when she sold she was released from no debt. The mortgage debt was simply a subtraction from the value of what she did receive, and from what she sold. The subtraction left her nothing when she acquired it and a small margin when she sold it. She acquired a property right equivalent to an equity of redemption and sold the same thing. It was the "property" bought and sold as the Tax Court considered it to be under the Revenue Laws. We are not required

---

41. Douglas v. Willcuts, supra, 296 U. S. at 9; Burnet v. Wells, 289 U.S. 670, 677.

42. In the course of the argument some reference was made, as by analogy, to a situation in which a taxpayer acquired by devise property subject to a mortgage in an amount greater than the then value of the property, and later transferred it to a third person, still subject to the mortgage, and for a cash boot. Whether or not the difference between the value of the property on acquisition and the amount of the mortgage would in that situation constitute either statutory or constitutional income is a question which is different from the one before us, and which we need not presently answer.

in this case to decide whether depreciation was properly taken, for there is no issue about it here.

We would reverse the Court of Appeals and sustain the decision of the Tax Court.

MR. JUSTICE FRANKFURTER and MR. JUSTICE DOUGLAS join in this opinion.

PROBLEMS

1. In view of the result in the *Davis* case, what was the tax status of S. S. Kresge, the husband in the *Farid-Es-Sultaneh* case?

2. In Delaware, the same state where the *Davis* case occurred, Husband transfers some land that he purchased for $20,000 which is worth $50,000 to Wife to satisfy her statutory (non-alimony) marital rights. What are the tax consequences to Husband and Wife on the transfer? *Husband has 30,000 gain*

3. Mortgagor owns some property with a $2000 adjusted basis and $10,000 fair market value. He borrows $4000, incurring no personal liability but the property is subject to the liability. Does he have income? See Woodsam Associates, Inc. v. Commissioner, 198 F.2d 357 (2d Cir. 1952).

D. DETERMINATION OF GAIN

Internal Revenue Code: Sections 1001(a); 1011(a); 1012; 1015(a), (d)(1)(A), (d)(4) and (6).
Regulations: Sections 1.61–6(a); 1.1001–1(a); 1.1011–1; 1.1012–2.

MALONE v. UNITED STATES *

District Court of the United States, Northern District of Mississippi (1971).
326 F.Supp. 106.
Affirmed per curiam, 455 F.2d 502, 5th Cir. 1972.

MEMORANDUM OPINION
Whole court

KEADY, CHIEF JUDGE. This action was instituted under 28 U.S.C. § 1346(a)(1) by R. C. Malone and Nettie A. Malone against the United States for recovery of $5,706.73 assessed against and collected from them as federal income taxes for the calendar year 1961, plus interest and costs.[1]

* See Lefter, "Income Tax Consequences of Encumbered Gifts: The Advent of Crane," 28 U.Fla.L.Rev. 935 (1976).

1. § 1346. *United States as defendant*

(a) The district courts shall have original jurisdiction, concurrent with the Court of Claims, of:

(1) Any civil action against the United States for the recovery of any

The case presents three questions: (1) whether plaintiff realized a * * * gain in 1961 as the result of a transfer of 546 acres of encumbered farm land to a trust for the benefit of his grandchildren; * * * Following briefing by counsel and the submission of a comprehensive pre-trial order stipulating the legal and factual issues, the parties consented to submit the entire case to the court for final judgment upon the pleadings, pre-trial order, exhibits and the deposition of R. C. Malone, without an evidentiary hearing.

As revealed by the pre-trial order and by plaintiff's deposition, the factual background of the case as to question (1) [is] as follows:

On or about January 25, 1940, plaintiff purchased, for $13,650, 546 acres of farm land, known as the Willis Place, in Bolivar County, Mississippi. On or about February 6, 1956, he obtained a loan of $21,000 from the Federal Land Bank of New Orleans, executing his personal note and deed of trust [2] on the Willis Place as security. The loan was to be repaid in 21 annual installments, the first to be due and payable on November 15, 1956.

On or about July 28, 1961, after having reduced the initial mortgage debt to $16,000, plaintiff obtained a second loan from the Federal Land Bank, this time procuring an additional $16,000. The second loan was also evidenced by his personal note and secured by deed of trust on the same land; the two loans were consolidated for purposes of payment and were to be repaid in 35 annual installments commencing on January 15,

* * *

On October 31, 1961, plaintiff established an irrevocable trust, known as the "Malone Trust", for the benefit of his four minor grandchildren and any afterborn grandchildren. On the same date he conveyed the Willis Place, subject to the two mortgages, to the trustees of the Malone Trust. The two trustees, who were plaintiff himself and The Cleveland State Bank of Cleveland, Mississippi, joined as grantees in the execution of the conveyance "to acknowledge and accept the property as trust property" and "to further acknowledge the acceptance and agreement of the terms and conditions expressed in * * * [the] Trust Agreement." The trust agreement itself

internal-revenue tax alleged to have been erroneously or illegally assessed or collected, or any penalty claimed to have been collected without authority or any sum alleged to have been excessive or in any manner wrongfully collected under the internal-revenue laws.

(The parties agree that Mrs. Malone joins as a plaintiff only because she filed a joint tax return with Mr. Malone for 1961. Unless the context requires otherwise, R. C. Malone will be referred to as the plaintiff in this action.)

2. Under Mississippi law, which is applicable here in determining the nature and existence of legal rights and interests, Morgan v. Commissioner of Internal Revenue, 309 U.S. 78, 626, 60 S.Ct. 424, 84 L.Ed. 585 (1940), a deed of trust executed to secure a debt, although in form a conveyance, passes no title but creates only a lien or mortgage, general ownership remaining in the mortgagor. Carpenter v. Bowen, 42 Miss. 28, 49–50; Buck v. Payne & Raines, 52 Miss. 271, 279.

provided that the Willis Place was "to be held by said Trustees in Trust, but subject to certain indebtedness [to the Federal Land Bank of New Orleans in the amount of $32,000] secured by the Trust Property." This agreement specifically directed the trustees to "hold the lands", and

> "manage and invest the Trust Property and shall collect and receive the income thereof; and after *deducting* all necessary expenses incident to the administration of the Trust and the installments of principal and interest due annually on the loan [from the Federal Land Bank of New Orleans] and secured by the Trust Property, shall dispose of the principal and income of the Trust as follows   *   *   *"
> [Here follow discretionary directions to pay remaining income to the grandchildren during their minority and mandatory directions to terminate the trust as each grandchild becomes 21 years of age and pay to him his share of the corpus and undistributed income.]   (Emphasis added).

The evidence reflects that plaintiff did not use the proceeds of either loan to improve or operate the trust property, but to conduct his personal farm operations on other lands and purchase farm machinery for his own use. It is clear that both loans were for plaintiff's personal use unrelated to the establishment or operation of the trust.

Since the formation of the trust in 1961, the trustees have received annual rent of $7,500 upon lease of the trust property and have paid the annual loan installments therefrom. Plaintiff has not been called upon to make any loan payment. The trust has also accumulated an undisclosed sum of money after meeting the annual mortgage payments and other expenses and making certain distributions to the trust beneficiaries.

On June 12, 1962, plaintiffs filed a joint United States gift tax return, reporting the aforesaid conveyance to the Malone Trust and listing its gross market value as $57,485. They listed the net value of the gift as $25,485, after deducting the $32,000 lien thereon; and plaintiffs paid no gift tax by claiming applicable exclusions and exemptions.

Following an audit of plaintiffs' 1961 joint federal income tax return, the Commissioner of Internal Revenue, by a ninety-day letter, gave them statutory notice that: (1) they had realized a   *   *   * gain of $18,616.30 in 1961 on account of the transfer to the Malone Trust of the 546 acres of debt-encumbered land;   *   *   *

Based on the Commissioner's determinations, Internal Revenue Service assessed additional taxes of $4,898.48, plus $808.25 interest, totaling $5,706.73, which plaintiffs promptly paid. They timely filed a claim for refund, waived statutory notice of disallowance, and instituted the present action.

I.

Plaintiff contends that the conveyance to the trust was wholly a gift, which resulted in no pecuniary benefit to him, and he therefore realized no gain taxable as income. The government disagrees, arguing that by the trust agreement the trustees assumed the mortgage debt, relieving the plaintiff of primary liability thereon, and since the mortgage debt was greater than his basis, the transaction was part gift and part sale. Conceding that the plaintiff made a valid gift of $25,485, the value of the land in excess of the debt, the government claims plaintiff also made a sale, or other disposition, whereby he realized a * * * gain of $18,650, or the difference between the $32,000 debt and $13,350, plaintiff's adjusted basis in the land.

Plaintiff insists that his conveyance to the Malone Trust fulfilled all requirements of law to constitute a valid gift.[4] Yet, the government urges that the transaction was not wholly gratuitous since plaintiff received a valuable consideration in the form of relief from his primary liability on a $32,000 debt, and that the transaction was, therefore, a partial sale resulting in a substantial taxable gain to plaintiff. This directly raises the question of whether the trust estate merely accepted title subject to the mortgage or assumed responsibility for its payment. It is settled state law "that a mortgagor may convey the mortgaged premises subject to the mortgage [in which case the grantee incurs no liability], or he may convey them in such manner that the grantee assumes the payment of the mortgage debt, and thus renders himself personally and primarily liable therefor." [5]

The government argues that the language of the trust instrument, although not cast in terms of a formal assumption, was sufficient under applicable Mississippi law to create an assumption of the taxpayer's debt by the trust. This argument is well-taken, since under the general law no particular form of words is necessary to create a binding assumption, and it is sufficient that the language shows a clear intent on the part of a grantee to assume the liability for paying the mortgage debt.[6] The general rule above stated was first recognized by the Mississippi court in 1925, and has been fol-

---

4. A valid inter vivos gift, under Mississippi law and generally, has the following elements: a competent donor who, freely intending to make a gift, delivers it absolutely and irrevocably to a donee capable of taking the gift, who accepts it. To consummate an effective gift, the transaction must be gratuitous and complete, with nothing left undone. McClellan v. McCauley, 158 Miss. 456, 130 So. 145 (1930); Allison v. Allison, 203 Miss. 20, 33 So.2d 619 (1948);

Maier v. Hill, 221 Miss. 120, 72 So.2d 209 (1954). Noel v. Parrott, 15 F.2d 669 (1926). Mertens, Laws of Federal Income Taxation, Vol. I, § 7.12, Chapter 7, p. 36.

5. Hodges v. Southern Building & Loan Association, 166 Miss. 677, 148 So. 223 (1933).

6. See 59 C.J.S. Mortgages § 406a, p. 571.

lowed consistently ever since.[7]   As the court stated in *Gilliam*, quoting from 3 Pomeroy's Equity Jurisprudence, ¶ 1206:

> "The mortgagor may not only convey the premises 'subject to' the mortgage; he may also convey them in such a manner that the grantee assumes the payment of the mortgage debt, and thus renders himself personally liable therefor. * * * No particular form of words is necessary to create a binding assumption; it is sufficient that the language shows unequivocally an intent on the part of the grantee to assume the liability of paying the mortgage debt, but this intent must clearly appear. When the deed executed by the grantor contains a clause sufficiently showing such an intent, the acceptance thereof by the grantee consummates the assumption, and creates a personal liability on his part, which inures to the benefit of the mortgagee as though he had himself executed the deed."

Here, plaintiff not only conveyed the lands to the Malone Trust subject to the mortgage, but he also directed that the trustees "deduct" the annual debt installments from the trust income. It is important to note that plaintiff, as settlor, neither reserved any portion of the income from the Willis Place for his own use in paying the debt, nor did he covenant with the trust that he would protect it against paying the mortgage. Necessarily, the directions to the trustees that they deduct from the trust income an amount equal to the annual installments of the loan's principal and interest can mean only a mandate to pay the deducted amount to the mortgagee, thereby enabling the trustees to protect the lands against foreclosure and secure its income for the trust, which was their duty under the trust instrument. The trustees expressly accepted this paramount obligation, which had to be satisfied before they could make any distribution to a beneficiary or otherwise fulfill the purposes of the trust. Such provisions clearly establish an intent on the plaintiff's part for the trust estate to bear the payment of the mortgage and also an intent on the trustees' part to accept responsibility for such payment. Of course, the trustees did not bind themselves individually, but they unequivocally committed the trust to use its income to pay the mortgage. It is also clear from the evidence that the trustees understood their obligations as to payment of the mortgage debt, since each subsequent installment to date has been paid direct to the mortgagee, Federal Land Bank of New Orleans, by a check drawn on the trust account.

As the Fifth Circuit, applying Mississippi law in *Hays' Estate*, supra, an estate tax case, has said:

7. Gilliam v. McLemore, 141 Miss. 253, 106 So. 99, 43 A.L.R. 79 (1925); Hays' Estate v. Commissioner of Internal Revenue, 181 F.2d 169 (5 Cir., Miss. 1950); Edwards v. Greenwald, 217 F.2d 632 (5 Cir., Ga.1954).

"It is elementary that the grantee in an instrument who accepts such a trust is bound by its obligations, and that *the form of the assumption is immaterial provided it casts upon the grantee the burden to pay the indebtedness.*" (Emphasis added).[8]

In *Hays' Estate,* the settlor conveyed certain farm lands, subject to outstanding mortgages, to the trust estate and, according to the Court's opinion, it authorized and directed the trustee to pay the lien indebtedness out of income derived from the property. The Court of Appeals held that this was sufficient to constitute an assumption of the debt and reversed the Tax Court's holding that under Mississippi law the trust agreement did not indicate that the trustee was to assume the mortgage debt. Plaintiff's counsel agreed that the *Hays'* trust provisions, construed by the Fifth Circuit as a direction to pay the debt, are substantially identical to the Malone provisions.

We hold that when the Malone trustees received the conveyance and trust instrument and accepted their duties thereunder, the trust estate assumed the debt and became primarily liable for its payment; and plaintiff was thereafter only secondarily liable as a surety.[9] Granting that the assumption of debt did not constitute either a cancellation or total discharge of plaintiff's debt liability, the chances that he would ever have to pay any portion of the debt were remote indeed. For even though the mortgagee under Mississippi law still had the option to proceed against either plaintiff or the trust estate if the mortgage installments were not paid,[10] plaintiff, as a surety, would be subrogated to the rights of the mortgagee if he were compelled to pay the mortgage, and could thereafter go against both the income and the corpus of the trust estate to recoup any amounts he might have paid to the mortgagee.[11]

Nor may we ignore the realities of the situation, i. e.: the debt installments amounted to only ⅓ of the annual trust income; the entire debt, $32,000, was considerably less than the admitted fair market value of the trust property, $57,485; plaintiff himself was one of the two trustees and in that capacity has made the annual

---

8. We note that although the part of *Hays'* decision concerning reservation of income for estate tax purposes has been overruled, Lober v. United States, 108 F.Supp. 731, 124 Ct.Cl. 44 (Ct.Cl.1952), aff'd 346 U.S. 335, 74 S.Ct. 98, 98 L.Ed. 15 (1952), the part of that decision on which we here rely is still good law. Barber v. United States, 251 F.2d 436 (5 Cir. 1958).

9. Edwards v. Greenwald, *supra;* Hays' Estate, *supra;* Gilliam v. McLemore, *supra.*

10. Smith v. General Investments, Inc., 246 Miss. 765, 150 So.2d 862 (1963); North American Life Ins. Co. v. Smith, 178 Miss. 238, 172 So. 135 (1937).

11. McLeod v. Building & Loan Ass'n of Jackson, 168 Miss. 457, 151 So. 151 (1933). Miss.Code Ann. § 253 et seq.; 59 C.J.S. Mortgages § 416, pp. 603–608.

debt payments regularly from 1961 to the present, the trust having excess income to bank thereafter; there is no evidence that the mortgagee has indicated an intention to demand payment by plaintiff personally. Thus it is apparent that the assumption of the plaintiff's debt by the trust estate resulted in a pecuniary benefit to him. This benefit was clearly a consideration extended by the trust to plaintiff for his "gift" of the Willis Place, and the transaction may not be considered a pure gift.

Having determined that the transfer to the trust resulted in pecuniary benefit to plaintiff, we next consider whether that benefit constituted a taxable gain, and if so, in what amount.

"Gain", for purposes of federal income taxation, is not limited to receipt of cash or tangible property.

> "While economic gain is not always taxable as income, realization of gain need not be in cash derived from sale of asset, and 'gain' may occur as the result of exchange of property, payment of a taxpayer's indebtedness, relief from a liability, or other profit realized from completion of a transaction." Helvering v. Bruun, 60 S.Ct. 631, 309 U.S. 461, 84 L.Ed. 864 at 869 (1940).

The cancellation, discharge or assumption of a debt has long been considered a taxable gain to the debtor where the debtor gives no consideration for the cancellation. A common type of transaction in which such gain by cancellation of debt occurs is the establishment of a trust with income in a low tax bracket by a settlor in a high tax bracket with directions that the trust pay his debts.[12]

* * *

The government relies on several statutes and administrative regulations to support its contention that the amount of the gain is the amount by which the assumed debt exceeds plaintiff's adjusted basis. § 1001(a) of the 1954 Internal Revenue Code provides that the gain from the sale or other disposition of property shall be the excess of the amount realized therefrom over the adjusted basis provided in § 1011 for determining gain. § 1001(b) of the Code explains that the amount realized from the sale or other disposition of property shall be the sum of any money received plus the fair market value of the property (other than money) received.[13] Treasury regulations also provide that where a transfer of property is in part a sale and in part a gift, the transferor has a gain to the extent that

---

12. Douglas v. Willcuts, 296 U.S. 1, 56 S.Ct. 59, 80 L.Ed. 3 (1935); Darling v. United States, 375 F.2d 843, 179 Ct. Cl. 891 (1967); see annotations at 101 A.L.R. 397, 109 A.L.R. 1048, 132 A.L.R. 819 and 158 A.L.R. 1315. We note that for federal income tax purposes, gain in the form of debt assumption is considered "money" received. Estate of Lipman v. United States, 376 F.2d 455 (6 Cir. 1967); Smith v. Commissioner of Internal Revenue, 324 F.2d 725 (9 Cir. 1963).

13. [The applicable Internal Revenue Statutes are omitted. Ed.]

the amount realized by him exceeds his adjusted basis in the property.[14]

Having concluded that there was an effective assumption, we need not consider the government's contention that taxable gain is always realized when a taxpayer disposes of property mortgaged in excess of the taxpayer's adjusted basis, even if he was not personally liable on the mortgage debt.[15] While it is doubtful that the noted cases establish the proposition which the government contends they do, we need not reach those broad questions in the case sub judice, where the taxpayer: (a) was personally liable on the mortgage debt before disposing of the property; (b) used the loan proceeds for his own purposes; and (c) then placed primary liability for repayment of the debt upon the trust income.[16]

Because plaintiff expended the mortgage funds for his own benefit and not on the trust property, we find the Fifth Circuit decision of Edwards v. Greenwald, supra, similarly inapposite. In *Greenwald* a brother and sister purchased interests in certain retail businesses, giving their notes and mortgages on the business property to secure their purchase price obligations. They then conveyed the property, subject to the encumbrances, to separate trusts for the benefit of their children and grandchildren, directing the trustees to pay the mortgage debts out of the trust income. Under applicable Georgia law the trusts then became primarily liable for the debts, and the settlors became mere sureties on the notes, liable only if the trustees failed to pay and a foreclosure sale of the property failed to satisfy the debts. The Fifth Circuit held that since the debts were incurred contemporaneously with the creation of the trusts and for the sole purpose of acquiring property to place in the trusts, and not for any personal benefit to the taxpayers-settlors, the transaction was a pure gift, not subject to federal income taxation. Since taxpayer here used the proceeds of the loan for his own purposes, and not for the benefit of the trust, *Greenwald* is clearly inapplicable here.[17]

---

14. 26 C.F.R. § 1.1001–1 *Computation of gain or loss.*

(e) *Transfers in part a sale and in part a gift.*

(1) Where a transfer of property is part a sale and in part a gift, the transferor has a gain to the extent that the amount realized by him exceeds his adjusted basis in the property.

15. Crane v. Commissioner of Internal Revenue, 331 U.S. 1, 67 S.Ct. 1047, 91 L.Ed. 1301 (1947); Parker v. Delaney, 186 F.2d 455 (1 Cir. 1950); O'Dell & Sons Co., Inc. v. Commissioner of Internal Revenue, 169 F.2d 247 (3 Cir. 1948); and Stamler v. Commissioner of Internal Revenue, 145 F.2d 37 (3 Cir. 1944).

16. Nor need we reach the government's alternate contention that in the absence of an assumption the plaintiff would realize ordinary income to the extent that the trust made payments on the mortgage debt. See Old Colony Trust Co. v. Commissioner of Internal Revenue, 279 U.S. 716, 49 S.Ct. 499, 73 L.Ed. 918 (1928).

17. See also Commissioner of Internal Revenue v. Turner, 410 F.2d 752, 753 (6 Cir. 1969), and Herff v. Rountree, 140 F.Supp. 201 (M.D.Tenn.1956), appeal dismissed 249 F.2d 958 (6 Cir. 1957).

Plaintiff argues that if his transfer to the trust is a disposition taxable to him, there will result double taxation on the gain upon the trustees' later disposition of the property, by asserting that the trust basis at that time will be $13,350, the same as plaintiff's basis under the provisions of 26 U.S.C. § 1015(a).[18] We find no merit in this contention since that statute is applicable only in the case of a pure gift, which is not the situation here. Instead, the provisions of 26 U.S.C. § 1015(b)[19] would control, making the basis of trust property acquired by transfer other than by gift the transferor's basis increased by the amount of gain recognized to the transferor in the year of the transfer. Thus, the basis of the Malone Trust in the Willis Place would be the transferor's basis, $13,350, increased by the amount of gain recognized to plaintiff on the transfer to the trust, $18,650, or a total basis in the trust property of $32,000.[20] Plaintiff's fears of double taxation are, therefore, unfounded in light of the donee's increased basis.

The government's position here is not contradictory to the position it took in Woodsam Associates Inc. v. Commissioner of Internal Revenue, 198 F.2d 357 (2 Cir. 1952), as plaintiff contends, because the property disposition in that case was pursuant to a tax-free exchange under a special statute, and not a partial sale, as here.

$2,000 gain   Unpaid Debt — Basis [handwritten]

PROBLEMS

1. Mortgagor owns property with a basis of $2000 and value of $10,000. Bank loans him $4000 on a loan in which he incurs no personal liability (although the property is subject to the liability). Two years later, having paid nothing on the loan and in circumstances that require payment of no gift tax, he transfers the property gratuitously to his Daughter.

2,000 gain [handwritten] (a) What tax consequences to Mortgagor on the transfer?

(b) What is Daughter's basis in the property?

(c) If Daughter immediately sells the property to Purchaser how much cash may she expect to receive?

(d) What is Daughter's gain on the sale?

(e) What is Purchaser's basis for the property?

---

18. (a) *Gifts after December 31, 1920.* —If the property was acquired by gift after December 31, 1920, the basis shall be the same as it would be in the hands of the donor.

19. (b) *Transfers in trust after December 31, 1920.*—If the property was acquired after December 31, 1920, by a transfer in trust (other than by a gift, bequest, or devise), the basis shall be the same as it would be in the hands of the grantor increased in the amount of gain or decreased in the amount of loss recognized to the grantor on such transfer under the law applicable to the year in which the transfer was made.

20. 26 U.S.C. § 1015(d); see also Treas. Regs. § 1.1015–4.

2. Investor purchased three acres of land, each acre worth $10,-000, for $30,000. Investor sold one of the acres in year one for $14,-000 and a second in year two for $16,000. The total amount realized by Investor was $30,000 which is not in excess of his total purchase price. Does Investor have any gain or loss on the sales?

3. In 1977 Gainer acquired an apartment in a condominium complex by intervivos gift from Relative. Both used it only as a residence. It had been purchased by Relative for $20,000 cash and was given to Gainer when it was worth $30,000. Relative paid a $6000 gift tax on the transfer. In 1978 Gainer sells the apartment to Shelterer.

(a) What gain or loss to Gainer on his sale to Shelterer for $32,-000?

(b) What is Shelterer's basis in the apartment?

(c) Same questions now assuming that Relative acquired the property for $8000 cash, but subject to a $12,000 mortgage on which neither he nor Gainer was ever personally liable or ever paid any amount of principal, and that Relative paid $3000 tax on the gift. See I.R.C. § 1015(d)(6) and cf. § 1023(g)(4). Upon purchase, Shelterer merely took the property subject to the mortgage, paying $20,000 cash for it.

CHAPTER 8. ANNUITIES AND LIFE INSURANCE PROCEEDS

Internal Revenue Code: Sections 72(a), (b), (c), (e) and (h); 101(a), (c) and (d).

Regulations: Sections 1.72–4(a), –7(a) and (b), –9 (Tables), –11(d)(1); 1.101–1(a)(1), (b)(1), –4(a)(1), (b)(1), (c).

It should be acknowledged at the beginning that the tax picture presented here of life insurance and annuities is no more than a long-range photograph taken without the benefit of a telephoto lens. This is for two reasons: (1) the presentation is in only one dimension ignoring, as it does, related estate and gift tax considerations that are likely to be of even more importance here than in other portions of this book; and (2) many details are set aside as out of keeping with the objective of this book to try to establish a good grounding in income tax fundamentals. The student should, nevertheless, emerge with an understanding of basic congressional policy in the area, an ability to apply the statute in routine circumstances, and a foundation for grappling with complexities that arise in other situations.

Insurance Proceeds. A common element of all life insurance policies is the agreement by the insurer to make payments upon the insured's death to his estate or to others whom he may designate as beneficiaries. The plain thrust of I.R.C. (26 U.S.C.A.) § 101(a) (1) is to exclude the proceeds of such policies from the gross income of the recipients.[1] There are, however, two important conditions to this result.

First of all, § 101(a) applies only to amounts "paid by reason of the death of the insured." It is possible, for example, that after a policy has been in effect for some time the cash surrender value of the policy (the amount the insurer will pay the policy owner *during* the insured's life in discharge of all rights under the policy) will ex-

---

1. One restriction on the exclusion arises in cases in which the policy has been the subject of a transfer for valuable consideration. See § 101(a)(2) which requires the excess of the proceeds received over the costs incurred (i. e. the gain on the policy) to be included in gross income. Congress enacted § 101(a)(2) to discourage speculation on the death of an insured. S.Rep.No.1622, 83d Cong., 2d Sess. 14 (1954). The § 101(a)(2) income rule does not apply if the transfer for consideration is to a transferee who acquired the policy with a carryover basis, § 101(a)(2)(A), or is to the insured, a partner of the insured, or a partnership or corporation in which the insured has an interest, § 101(a)(2)(B). See Lawthers, "Income Tax Aspects of Transfers of Life Insurance Policies and of Various Forms of Settlement Options," 22 N.Y.U.Inst. on Fed.Tax 1299 (1964).

ceed the net premiums paid. If the insured elects to take the cash surrender value, he may realize an amount in excess of basis, which is a taxable gain to him unprotected by the exclusionary rules of § 101(a), because it is an amount *not* paid by reason of his death. Perhaps more important, an insurance policy that guarantees payments on the insured's death often contains alternative lifetime benefits that may be elected. For example, the insured may be able to demand the payment of fixed annual sums for his life in lieu of and upon cancellation of any right to death benefits. If such a demand is made the receipts are obviously not paid by reason of the insured's death and, again, are not within the § 101(a) exclusion.[2]

Secondly, although it might appear § 101(a) excludes from gross income *whatever* amount is paid by reason of the insured's death, the introductory reference to subsection (d) calls attention to an important limitation. Usually an insurance policy will identify a fixed sum to be paid at death (the "face amount" of the policy). Essentially, it is this amount that is to be received tax-free. We might pause to wonder why this amount should not be taxed to the recipient. Consider the possibility that Young Married took out a $100,000 term policy on his life paying only the initial premium of $100. A week later he was killed in an automobile accident, and the insurer paid Mrs. Married $100,000. Neither of the Marrieds will ever be taxed on a clear gain (crass thought) of $99,900. Is this a reflection of a "suffered enough" notion?[3] The result indicated persists after the enactment of I.R.C. § 1023 by the Tax Reform Act of 1976,[4] and it no longer seems relevant to consider the relationship of the philosophy behind I.R.C. (26 U.S.C.A.) §§ 102 and 1014.

Under most life insurance policies Mrs. Married would have an option to accept something different from the $100,000, the face amount of the policy. She might, instead, be entitled to elect fixed monthly payments of amounts, determined with reference to her age and life expectancy, for the rest of her life. Without close regard to mortality tables and actuarial principles, let us assume that she can and does elect to be paid $250 each month ($3000 per year) for life and that her life expectancy is 50 years. If she should live just that long she will receive, overall, $150,000 (50 × $3000).[5] What, now, should be excluded? Until 1954, the entire $150,000 was excluded on these facts. But is this also consistent with the basic policy behind the exclusion? Congress has decided that it is not, and that is what I.R.C. (26 U.S.C.A.) § 101(d) is all about.

---

2. But see the comments below on the exclusionary rules of § 72.

3. See Note on § 104 at page 205, infra; see also Swihart, "Federal Taxation of Life Insurance Wealth," 37 Ind. L.J. 167 (1962).

4. I.R.C. (26 U.S.C.A.) § 1023(b)(2)(B).

5. Obviously, an insurer will agree to pay a larger sum over a long time than the amount to be paid as a lump sum immediately, because he has the use of much of the money over the long period.

If there are reasons for allowing an exclusion of $100,000 on the above facts, is it not just as clear that amounts that may be paid in excess of that sum represent amounts earned after the death of the insured on property of the beneficiary, much the same as on any other investment? With this much background, attack I.R.C. (26 U.S. C.A.) § 101(d) to determine the congressional answer to this problem. You should conclude that, if Mrs. Married were not the surviving spouse of the insured, she would in each of the 50 years of her remaining life exclude $2000 from and include $1000 in gross income. Logical? If she lived years beyond her life expectancy the same exclusionary rule would apply in all those years.[6] Supportable? As Mrs. Married *is* the surviving spouse of the insured all her receipts under the policy may come in tax-free.[7] Acceptable? How may this bear on a beneficiary's decision whether to take a lump sum or a periodic settlement where she has the option?

An insurance beneficiary may have the right to leave the entire proceeds with the insurer, drawing only interest on the amount which otherwise would be paid as a lump sum. I.R.C. (26 U.S.C.A.) § 101 (c) specifies that such interest payments are fully taxable. In general, sections 101(c) and (d) are mutually exclusive; whenever any recurring payments substantially eat into the principal amount of the insurance (d), not (c), applies.[8]

Annuity Payments. Broadly speaking, an annuity is an arrangement under which one buys a right to future money payments. Being a mere matter of contract, the variety of such arrangements is limited only by the scope of human ingenuity. But there are some common classes: (1) A single-life annuity calls for fixed money payments to the annuitant for his life after which all rights under the contract cease. (2) Under a self-and-survivor annuity, fixed payments are made to an annuitant during his life and are then continued to another (in the same or a different amount) after his death. (3) The joint-and-survivor type annuity pays amounts jointly to two annuitants while both are living, and then payments are continued (in the same or a different amount) to the survivor. It is also not uncommon for the agreement to contain a refund feature; the contract may guarantee the payment of a sum certain to assure against severe loss through the premature death of the annuitants. Moreover the payments may be for a term certain, rather than for the life or lives of individuals. That is, the purchaser may buy the right to receive $1000

---

6. Reg. § 1.101–4(c); and see Sen.Rep. No. 1622, 83rd Cong.2d Sess., 181 (1954).

7. I.R.C. (26 U.S.C.A.) § 101(d)(1)(B). See Rev.Rul. 72–164, 1972–1 C.B. 28, holding that the status of surviving spouse is determined at the time of the insured's death and is not altered by remarriage. See also Beausang, "Caveat: The Widow's $1000 Exclusion and the Option to Withdraw Principal," 43 Taxes 409 (1965).

8. Reg. § 1.101–3(a); but see § 1.101–4 (h).
See Irenas, "Life Insurance Interest Income Under the Federal Income Tax," 21 Tax L.Rev. 297 (1966).

per month for twenty years, in which case payments would continue to his designee in the event of his death before expiration of the term. Such arrangements are sometimes called endowment contracts, and at an earlier time they were differentiated from annuities for tax purposes,[9] but both types of arrangements are now treated alike under I.R.C. (26 U.S.C.A.) § 72.

In recent years the practice has developed of combining the annuity with the mutual fund concept to produce what is called the variable annuity.[10] Under one form of variable annuity, the annuitant in effect acquires an interest (generally described as a certain number of "units") in a diversified investment portfolio. When he starts receiving payments his rights are defined in terms of the number of units credited to him which are to be distributed to him or his survivors over the pay-out period. But the amount he receives each time varies with the investment experience of the fund—hence the term "variable". The use of variable annuities is becoming fairly common under qualified employee's pension plans [11] in an effort to provide against the ravages of inflation.[12] Variable annuities outside the qualified plan area present some tax difficulties not expressly answered in I.R.C. (26 U.S.C.A.) § 72 and are the subject of special rules in the Regulations [13] which, however, are not discussed here.

Most annuity arrangements are made with insurance companies, although the rules of I.R.C. (26 U.S.C.A.) § 72 are equally applicable to contracts between individuals.[14]

Even these brief remarks on annuities suggest the complexity of the area. Any attempt to explore the tax aspects of all the variations would of course be out of keeping with the objectives of this book. Accordingly, we turn now in as simple a setting as possible to the fundamental questions: How are annuities taxed and why? The

---

9. See I.R.C. (1939) § 22(b) (2) and Reg. § 39.22(b) (2)–2.

10. Cf. I.R.C. (26 U.S.C.A.) § 801(g) (1) (A). Earlier, some employees' annuities were made variable in accordance with the Cost of Living Index. See Kern, "The Income Taxation of Variable Annuities," 55 A.B.A.J. 369 (1969); and see, generally, Bartlett, "Variable Annuities: Evolution and Analysis," 19 Stan.L.Rev. 150 (1966), a non-tax treatment.

11. See Goodman, "Planning for Maximum Tax Benefits with Variable Annuities in Qualified Pension Plans," 30 J.Tax 300 (1969).

12. Employees' annuities are not further discussed here, but it might be noted that, except where an employee has contributed his own taxed dollars to the purchase of an annuity under a qualified plan, his receipts under the annuity whether variable or fixed will generally be fully taxable to him as ordinary income. I.R.C. (26 U.S.C.A.) §§ 72(d) and 402(a) (1); but see § 402(a) (2).

13. Reg. § 1.72–2(b)(3) and see Reg. § 1.72–4(d)(3) Ex.

14. So-called "private" annuities present some special tax considerations, which are explored in Ellis, Private Annuities, 195 Tax Management (1969); see also Vernava, "Tax Planning for the Not-so-Rich: Variable and Private Annuities," 11 Wm. and Mary L.Rev. 1 (1969).

keys to basic understanding are that (1) Income connotes gain and (2) A mere return of capital is not income. These are concepts that are familiar from the preceding chapter.

Assume now that Abouto Retire pays an insurance company $60,-000 for their agreement to pay him $5000 each year for the rest of his life. Payments begin and Retire receives $5000 in the current year. Does this, or some part of it, represent income? If there were no special statutory rule applicable, we might say that Retire has just received a partial return of his capital which should go untaxed. Indeed, that was the law until 1934. Of course its corollary was that after 12 years when Retire had fully recovered his capital (12 × $5000 = $60,000), any further payments he received would be fully taxable and, under facts such as these, Retire might have a life expectancy of twenty years when the annuity payments began.

The Revenue Act of 1934 [15] took account of a deficiency in this taxing plan. It was recognized that there was really an income element in *each* annuity payment from the outset. Somewhat arbitrarily, that element was identified as an amount equal to 3% of the cost of the contract. Congress decided to tax that amount and to exclude from gross income the balance of each year's receipts. Thus, one in Retire's circumstances became taxable, as to each $5000 payment, on $1800 (3% of $60,000) and could exclude from gross income $3200 ($5000 − $1800). Under this statutory approach the exclusions continued until the tax-free portions of his receipts equalled the cost of the contract. In Retire's case this might work out pretty well. That is, it would take about 19 years (19 × $3200 = $60,800) for him to recover his investment tax free, and we have assumed Retire might have a life expectancy of twenty years. But the 3% rule was subject to criticism in that it did not purport to fix the amount of the tax-free receipt with respect to the relationship of the cost of the annuity and the life expectancy and probable return to the annuitant. In some circumstances it was quite possible that one who had little or no chance for a full tax-free recovery of his investment was, nevertheless, taxed on portions of his annual receipts.[16]

The philosophy of present I.R.C. (26 U.S.C.A.) § 72, enacted in 1954, is not sharply different from the provision it replaced. Congress still attempts properly to accord tax neutrality to the taxpayer's return of capital. Examine the statute. It allows a recovery of capital over the expected life of the contract by excluding the portion of each payment which is in the ratio of the "investment in the contract" [17] to the "expected return under the contract." [18] The excess

---

15. § 22(b) (2), 48 Stat. 680, 686 (1934).

16. See Vernava, supra note 14, at 10.

17. § 72(c)(1) defines this term as cost less recoveries of such cost under the pre-1954 code.

18. § 72(c)(3).

receipt is taxed as the income element in each payment.[19] Assuming Abouto Retire, under the facts above, has a 20 year life expectancy,[20] he would include $2000 of each $5000 payment in income, excluding 60,000/100,000 of each $5000 payment.

But annuities are not all so simple. For example, if Abouto purchased again for $60,000 a self and survivor annuity which paid $5000 per year until the survivor of Abouto and his spouse died and we assume this creates a payment expectancy of 30 years,[21] then each $5000 payment would include $3000 of taxable income, after excluding 60,000/150,000 of each $5000 payment.[22] Some annuities contain what are known as "refund features." One example of a refund occurs if any annuity is paid to an annuitant for his life, but if the annuity payments made prior to the annuitant's death do not exceed the premiums paid for the contract, the excess is refunded.[23] In such a situation § 72(c)(2) requires that the potential refund (based on the annuitant's life expectancy) be subtracted from the "investment in the contract," which has of course the intended effect of increasing the income portion of each annuity payment.[24] The legislative history indicates that, as the refund itself is exempt from tax,[25] the purpose of § 72(c)(2) is to avoid a double exclusion from tax.[26]

That is not to imply that all refunds are exempt from tax. Refunds may be totally or partially included in income under § 72(e). For example, Les Abouto Retire at age 55 pays $60,000 for an annuity which is to begin payment of $6000 per year to him at age 65 but, after a time, he may cancel the contract prior to age 65 and receive back amounts in excess of $60,000, more the longer he waits. Les has purchased a single premium deferred life annuity with a refund feature and if he cancels at age 62 receiving $66,000 he has

---

19. § 72(a).

20. See Reg. § 1.72–9 Table I.

21. See Reg. § 1.72–9 Table II.

22. Another alternative here is an annuity in which the survivorship annuity payments are only one-half the regular payments ($2500). If such an assumption were cranked into our text hypothetical, obviously the "investment in the contract" and the "expected return" would be less. However, whatever exclusion ratio is established by those factors remains constant over the life of the contract, whether the full or reduced payments are being received.

23. Reg. § 1.72–7(a).

24. See Reg. § 1.72–7(b). Our friend Abouto, age 57 with a 20 year life expectancy might be entitled to receive $5000 per year under a single life annuity but, if he died prior to recovering the $60,000 premium paid, his estate would receive a payment equal to the excess of the premium over prior annuity payments received. As computed under Reg. §§ 1.72–7(b) Ex. and 1.72–9 Table III, the refund feature would amount to $6600. Abouto's "investment in the contract" would be reduced to $53,400 and his exclusion ratio would be 53,400/100,000. He would include 46.6% of each $5000 payment in income or $2330 (as compared with $2000 above).

25. It would be excluded from gross income under § 72(e) or as an insurance payment under § 101(a).

26. S.Rep.No.1622, 83rd Cong., 2d Sess. 11 (1954).

$6,000 of gross income.[27]   There are numerous other possible types of refunds.[28]

If a beneficiary who has a right to a lump sum refund not fully tax exempt, instead exercises an option to receive a second annuity in lieu of such refund and does so within 60 days of the lump sum refund becoming payable, then no part of the lump sum refund is included in income.[29]   The annuity payments are then included in income to the extent they constitute § 72 income.

Is the current plan for taxing annuities an improvement over prior law? Does it still have an inherent weakness? Hark back now to the treatment of life insurance proceeds paid over a period of time. Note that, while there is a different method of determining the amount that may be recovered tax-free (Why?), the plan for excluding such amounts from gross income is basically the same. The similarity includes the fact that in the case of annuities, just as was noted as regards life insurance, the annual exclusion determined by application of the exclusion ratio continues even if an annuitant outlives his life expectancy and, consequently, reaches a point where he has been permitted fully to recover his investment tax free.[30] On the other hand, no loss deduction is provided if an annuitant dies prematurely and all payments under the contract cease before he has effected a tax-free recovery of his investment. In this connection, consider the *Waller* case set out below.

Recall that life benefits under a life insurance policy are subject to tax under I.R.C. (26 U.S.C.A.) § 72, rather than § 101, because they are not received by reason of the death of the insured. But when § 101 applies, § 72 is inapplicable.[31]

Now, after a careful examination of the statute, test your grasp of the basic working of these principles by way of the problems at the end of the chapter.

WILLIAM WALLER

Tax Court of the United States, 1963.
39 T.C. 665.

ATKINS, JUDGE:

* * *

By an annuity policy dated September 15, 1933, the Sun Life Assurance Co. of Canada agreed to pay $50 to petitioner on September 2, 1958, and a like amount monthly thereafter on the second day of each succeeding month during the subsequent lifetime of the petitioner,

---

27. § 72(e)(1)(B).

28. See Reg. § 1.72–11(c)(2).

29. § 72(h).

30. Reg. § 1.72–4(a)(4).

31. Reg. § 1.72–2(b)(1).

in consideration of the payment by the petitioner to the company of $129.25 on September 2, 1933, and the payment of a like amount yearly thereafter on September 2 in every year until 25 full years' premiums should have been paid. The policy stated in part as follows:

> Payment of Annuity. The person or persons entitled to any payment under this policy shall be bound to produce proof, in writing, satisfactory to the Company, that the annuitant was alive on the day on which the said payment became due, and the Company will not be liable for any annuity payment under this policy, except on the production of such proof. No part of the purchase price shall be returnable by the Company at the death of the annuitant and no portion of the annuity shall be payable for any fractional period between the date on which the last, payment becomes due and the date of death.

The petitioner received a total of $200 from the company pursuant to this policy in 1958. He did not report any of this amount as income in his income tax return for the calendar year 1958. In the notice of deficiency the respondent determined that $59.18 of the $200 was excludable from the petitioner's income under section 72 of the 1954 Code and that the balance of $140.82 constituted taxable income to him.

Opinion.

* * *

The petitioner contends that the respondent erred in taxing to him in the taxable year 1958 any portion of the $200 received by him in that year under the annuity policy. * * * He concedes that the respondent's computation under section 72 of the Internal Revenue Code of 1954 is correct, but points out that if a taxpayer reports annuity payments under section 72 but dies before recouping his investment, he is not entitled to a deductible loss or other adjustment for tax purposes in the year of his death, and that an individual taxpayer may die long before recouping his investment after having paid income taxes on payments which constituted return of capital. It is his position that if section 72 be interpreted as requiring any part of the annuity payments to be included in his taxable income for 1958 and subsequent years, prior to the return in full to him of his investment, then the tax imposed is not upon income and is, to that extent, unconstitutional and void and is not authorized by the 16th amendment to the Constitution. He therefore contends that, to conform to constitutional requirements, section 72 must be construed as providing an election rather than as being mandatory.

At the outset it may be stated that we think there can be no question that section 72, by its terms, is mandatory, and does not provide annuitants with an election as to how they shall report annuity payments for income tax purposes.

An act of Congress is not lightly to be set aside; doubts must be resolved in its favor; and the presumption of validity is particularly strong in the case of a revenue measure. Nicol v. Ames, 173 U.S. 509; Penn Mutual Indemnity Co., 32 T.C. 653, affd. (C.A. 3) 277 F.2d 16; and Eleanor C. Shomaker, 38 T.C. 192, petition for review dismissed (C.A. 8) December 13, 1962. The taxing power of Congress was granted by article I of the Constitution and such power is exhaustive and embraces every conceivable power of taxation, subject only to certain constitutional restrictions, one of which is that direct taxes shall be apportioned among the States according to population. As pointed out in Penn Mutual Indemnity Co. v. Commissioner, supra, the requirement of apportionment is strictly limited to taxes on real and personal property and capitation taxes. The 16th amendment to the Constitution provides that income from any source may be taxed without apportionment. And as we pointed out in the *Penn Mutual Indemnity Co.* case, a tax upon gross receipts is not unconstitutional.

Clearly the tax imposed by section 72 is not a direct tax upon any property owned by taxpayers. Rather, it is a tax upon payments which taxpayers receive pursuant to annuity contracts. We think it clear that the taxation of such receipts is within the all-inclusive taxing power of Congress.

It may be added that in any event we think Congress has precluded any possible constitutional objections by providing that there shall be excluded from income that part of any annuity payment which bears the same ratio to the amount of the payment as the investment in the contract bears to the expected return under the contract. The expected return is computed, in the case of an annuity of the type here involved, upon the basis of the life expectancy of the annuitant ascertained by reference to actuarial tables. We see nothing unreasonable or capricious in this manner of computing the part of each payment which constitutes a return of the annuitant's cost and the part which constitutes gain. While in the case of the type of annuity here involved the annuitant might never recover his cost tax free, he might, on the other hand, under the statutory provision, receive a great deal more than his cost tax free, depending upon the actual length of his life.

It may be further pointed out that the constitutionality of section 22(b) (2) of the 1939 Code, predecessor of section 72 of the 1954 Code, has been upheld on numerous occasions. See Manne v. Commissioner, (C.A. 8) 155 F.2d 304, affirming a Memorandum Opinion of this Court; Florence M. Shelley, 10 T.C. 44; Title Guarantee & Trust Co., Executor, 40 B.T.A. 475; F. A. Gillespie, 38 B.T.A. 673;

and Egtvedt v. United States, 112 Ct.Cl. 80. While the provisions of section 72 of the 1954 Code and section 22(b) (2) of the 1939 Code are not the same, they are similar in that each provides for the taxation of portions of annuity payments prior to complete recovery of cost.

The petitioner relies principally upon Burnet v. Logan, 283 U.S. 404, in which the Supreme Court held that receipts from an inherited contract did not constitute income until the amount at which the contract was valued for estate tax purposes had been recouped. However that case did not involve a constitutional question; it merely held that payments there involved did not constitute income within the intendment of the income tax statute which was in effect at that time. Here section 72 of the Code clearly provides that annuity payments shall be considered as income to the extent provided therein.

We hold that section 72 of the 1954 Code is not unconstitutional and that the respondent did not err in taxing the petitioner upon the annuity payments received by him in the taxable year 1958.

* * *

PROBLEMS

1. Insured died in the current year owning a policy of insurance that would pay Beneficiary $100,000 but under which several alternatives were available to Beneficiary.

(a) What result if Beneficiary simply accepts the $100,000 in cash?

(b) What result in (a) above, if Beneficiary instead leaves all the proceeds with the company and they pay him $6000 interest in the current year?

(c) What result if Insured's Daughter is Beneficiary of the policy and in accordance with an option that she elects, the company pays her $5000 in the current year? Assume that such payments will be made annually for her life and that she has a 25 year life expectancy.

(d) What result in (c) above, if Beneficiary is Insured's husband, instead of her daughter, but the facts are otherwise the same? *Surviving Spouse gets an additional $1,000 exemption*

(e) What result under the facts of (d), above, if three years after Insured's death, Beneficiary (husband) remarries and he continues to receive the annual $5000 payment?

(f) What result in (d), above, if Insured's husband lives beyond his 25 year life expectancy and receives $5000 in the twenty-sixth year?

2. Jock agreed to play football for Pro Corporation. Pro, fearful that Jock might not survive, acquired a $1 million insurance policy

on Jock's life. If Jock dies during the term of the policy and the proceeds of the policy are paid to Pro, what different consequences will Pro incur under the following alternatives?

[handwritten margin: Non Tax b/o]

(a) With Jock's consent Pro took out and paid $20,000 for a two year term policy on Jock's life.

[handwritten margin: Taxable]

(b) Jock owned a paid-up two year term $1 million policy on his life which he sold to Pro for $20,000, Pro being named beneficiary of the policy.

[handwritten margin: Transfer charges / Taxability of gain]

(c) Same as (b), above, except that Jock was a shareholder of Pro Corporation. *[handwritten: Non Taxable — Sec. 101(A) — Transfer where stockholder transfers to corporation]*

3. In the current year, T, a 52 year old male taxpayer, purchases a single life annuity with no refund feature for $48,000. Under the contract T is to receive $3000 per year for life.

(a) To what extent, if at all, is T taxable on the $3000 received in the first year? See Reg. § 1.72–9, Table 1.

(b) If the law remains the same and T is still alive, how will T be taxed on the $3000 received in the thirtieth year of the annuity payments?

(c) If T dies within ten years will he or his estate be allowed an income tax deduction?

(d) To what extent is T taxable on the $3000 received in the current year if T (still 52) is married to a 50 year old wife and at a cost of $76,500 they purchase a joint and survivorship annuity to pay $3000 per year as long as either lives?

(e) Assume the same facts as in (a), above, except that if T dies prior to receiving $48,000 in annuity payments his estate will be given a refund equal to $48,000 less the amount of annuity payments received. To what extent, if at all, is T taxable on the $3000 received in the first year? See footnote 24 in the text, supra.

(f) At age 42 T purchased the annuity in part (a), above, which begins payment at age 52 under an agreement that he may terminate the contract in the first ten years of payments and receive $48,000 less $1500 for each year that payments have been made. If at the beginning of year six after receiving $15,000 in payments he terminates the contract and receives $40,500, does he have income? To what extent?

CHAPTER 9. DISCHARGE OF INDEBTEDNESS

Internal Revenue Code: Sections 61(a)(12); 102(a); 108(a); 1017. Regulations: Section 1.61–12(a). See Section 1.1017–1(a).

UNITED STATES v. KIRBY LUMBER CO.

Supreme Court of the United States, 1931.
284 U.S. 1, 52 S.Ct. 4.

MR. JUSTICE HOLMES delivered the opinion of the Court.

In July, 1923, the plaintiff, the Kirby Lumber Company, issued its own bonds for $12,126,800 for which it received their par value. Later in the same year it purchased in the open market some of the same bonds at less than par, the difference of price being $137,521.30. The question is whether this difference is a taxable gain or income of the plaintiff for the year 1923. By the Revenue Act of (November 23,) 1921, c. 136, § 213(a) gross income includes "gains or profits and income derived from any source whatever," and by the Treasury Regulations authorized by § 1303, that have been in force through repeated reënactments, "If the corporation purchases and retires any of such bonds at a price less than the issuing price or face value, the excess of the issuing price or face value over the purchase price is gain or income for the taxable year." Article 545(1) (c) of Regulations 62, under Revenue Act of 1921. See Article 544(1) (c) of Regulations 45, under Revenue Act of 1918; Article 545(1) (c) of Regulations 65, under Revenue Act of 1924; Article 545(1) (c) of Regulations 69, under Revenue Act of 1926; Article 68(1) (c) of Regulations 74, under Revenue Act of 1928. We see no reason why the Regulations should not be accepted as a correct statement of the law.

In Bowers v. Kerbaugh-Empire Co., 271 U.S. 170, the defendant in error owned the stock of another company that had borrowed money repayable in marks or their equivalent for an enterprise that failed. At the time of payment the marks had fallen in value, which so far as it went was a gain for the defendant in error, and it was contended by the plaintiff in error that the gain was taxable income. But the transaction as a whole was a loss, and the contention was denied. Here there was no shrinkage of assets and the taxpayer made a clear gain. As a result of its dealings it made available $137,521.30 assets previously offset by the obligation of bonds now extinct. We see nothing to be gained by the discussion of judicial definitions. The defendant in error has realized within the year an accession to income, if we take words in their plain popular meaning, as they should be taken here. Burnet v. Sanford & Brooks Co., 282 U.S. 359, 364.

Judgment reversed.

KIRBY LUMBER EXCEPTIONS

If Holmes, J., can be characteristically succinct, perhaps so can we. We seek to emulate him with some *brief* comments on the *Kirby* area.

The *Kirby Lumber* case accords some meaning to the cryptic language of I.R.C. (26 U.S.C.A.) § 61(a) (12), requiring that income from the discharge of indebtedness be included within gross income. The simplest view of *Kirby* is that it reflects the corollary of the 34th Street lullabye, "buy low-sell high;" with respect to one's obligations, if he sells high and then buys back low, he can profit equally. The receipt of money in the form of a loan has, by itself, no income tax consequences. To be sure, the taxpayer derives an economic benefit from the funds obtained through a loan; however, the obligation to repay, whether in the form of a note, account payable or a simple "I.O.U.", offsets the receipt of the loan proceeds, effecting a "wash" for tax purposes. No income is realized. But if a taxpayer pays off a debt for less than the amount owing, the difference constitutes income to him, because he realizes an economic benefit by way of an increase in his net worth much as if he had sold property at a profit. The taxable event is the freeing of assets that previously were held subject to the obligation. However, the *Kirby Lumber* doctrine is subject to exceptions, several of which are the subject of this note. More than one exception may apply in a single situation. In determining which exception to rely on, the taxpayer should determine which works to his overall tax advantage. Students should consider this in working problem three, below.

Gifts

If the cancellation of an indebtedness is motivated by a donative intent on the part of the creditor, the economic benefit to the debtor constitutes a gift. In such circumstances an amount that *could* be gross income is brought within the explicit statutory protection of I.R.C. (26 U.S.C.A.) § 102. Such a donative intent is more likely to be found in a family setting than in business or commercial situations. Before *Duberstein* [1] in Helvering v. American Dental Co.,[2] the Supreme Court expressed a liberal view of the gift exception to the *Kirby Lumber* doctrine, treating as a gift the "receipt of financial advantage gratuitously" without regard to any showing of donative intent. But, still before the decision in *Duberstein*, the Court retreated from that position. Since Comm'r v. Jacobson [3] was decided, commercial transactions have been placed generally outside the gift exception to the *Kirby Lumber* doctrine by the requirement that donative intent on the part of the creditor be shown if the discharge of indebtedness for less than the full amount is to escape tax as a gift within § 102. No donative intent is present if the creditor was merely

---

1. See Chapter 4, supra at page 66.   3. 336 U.S. 28, 69 S.Ct. 358 (1949).

2. 318 U.S. 322, 63 S.Ct. 577 (1943).

attempting to obtain the "best price available" [4] for the debtor's obligation.

Insolvency

Since the theory behind the *Kirby Lumber* doctrine is that advantageous cancellation of a debt results in an increase in the debtor's net worth in the form of freed assets, it is settled that a debtor who is insolvent both before and after the cancellation still has no freed assets available and therefore has received no economic benefit that may constitute gross income.[5] If, however, a debtor is made solvent by the cancellation of the debt, then assets are freed to the extent of his post-cancellation net worth, and he has gross income to that extent.[6] This exception, although long established, has been criticized on the ground that, with respect to other sources of income, the solvency of the taxpayer is not a factor in determining taxability.[7]

Contribution to Capital

If a corporation is indebted to one of its shareholders, a relinquishment of the debt may, rather than constituting income to the corporation, be regarded as a contribution to its capital by the shareholder.[8] The relinquishment must be voluntary or gratuitous, without consideration passing from the debtor corporation.[9] The effect of this exception is to convert the shareholder's debt interest in the corporation to an equity interest and increase his basis in his shares by the amount of his basis for the debt.

Adjustment of Purchase Price

This exception to the *Kirby Lumber* doctrine assumes a renegotiation of a sale of property between a debtor and creditor in a situation where the debtor still holds the property that has declined in value subsequent to the sale and the debtor is as a result of such negotiations relieved of all or part of his obligation. The negotiations are viewed as resulting in a reduction of the purchase price of the property *ab initio*. Two additional aspects of this exception should be emphasized. First, this exception should apply only if the creditor

---

4. Id. at 51, 69 S.Ct. at 370.

5. Madison Railways, 36 B.T.A. 1106 (1937); Reg. § 1.61–12(b). Taxpayer has the burden of proof of showing the validity of any claimed indebtedness. Yale Avenue Corp., 58 T.C. 1062 (1972).

6. Lakeland Grocery Co., 36 B.T.A. 289 (1937). See B. M. Marcus Estate, 34 T.C.M. 38 (1975), holding that in determining the extent of one's solvency, assets exempt from the claims of creditors under state law are not to be included.

7. See Eustice, "Cancellation of Indebtedness and the Federal Income Tax: A Problem of Creeping Confusion," 14 Tax L.Rev. 225, 246 (1959), which explores the *Kirby Lumber* doctrine in depth.

8. Reg. § 1.61–12(a); see also I.R.C. (26 U.S.C.A.) § 118 and Comm'r v. Auto Strop Safety Razor Co., Inc., 74 F.2d 226 (2d Cir. 1934).

9. Arlington Metal Industries, Inc., 57 T.C. 302 (1971).

is the one from whom the debtor made the acquisition giving rise to the indebtedness. That is if P bought property from S for which he paid by borrowing money from Bank B, and B later relieves P from a part of the obligation, the exception is inapplicable as P and B can hardly be viewed as renegotiating the contract between P and S. The exception contemplates in effect a renegotiation of price between buyer and seller and, of course, Bank B is neither.[10] Second a necessary corollary to the exception is an adjustment in the debtor's cost basis for the property. His basis is reduced to the adjusted purchase price, which will have an appropriate impact on the determination of gain or loss on any subsequent sale of the property.[11]

Specific Statutory Exceptions

Under I.R.C. (26 U.S.C.A.) § 108, a taxpayer may sometimes elect to exclude from gross income amounts otherwise taxable to him under the *Kirby Lumber* doctrine. However, the section applies only to debts incurred or assumed by a corporation or to individual debts incurred in connection with property used in the individual's trade or business. The price of exclusion under I.R.C. (26 U.S.C.A.) § 108 is set by I.R.C. (26 U.S.C.A.) § 1017 as a concurrent reduction in the basis of property in the amount that would have been taxed but for the application of § 108. The regulations provide priority rules as to which property of the taxpayer should be the subject of the basis reduction.[12] The statutory exception of §§ 108 and 1017 will be seen to be quite similar in scope and effect to the exception based on a fictitious renegotiation of the purchase price. This concept is illustrated in the problems below.

Under § 2117 of the Tax Reform Act of 1976, which is not made a part of the Internal Revenue Code, the forgiveness of some student loans will not result in any inclusion in gross income. The Service vacillated on this question in earlier revenue rulings.[13] When applicable the new exclusionary rule will be effective with respect to the discharge of indebtedness made before January 1, 1979.

PROBLEMS

1. Poor borrowed $10,000 from Rich several years ago. What tax consequences to Poor if he pays off the so far undiminished debt with:

   (a) A settlement of $7000 of cash?

---

10. Denman Tire & Rubber Co., 14 T.C. 706, 714 (1950), aff'd 192 F.2d 261 (6th Cir. 1951); but see Hirsch v. Comm'r, 115 F.2d 656 (7th Cir. 1940), and Charles L. Nutter, 7 T.C. 480 (1946), acq., 1946–2 C.B. 4.

11. Other *Kirby Lumber* variations are discussed in Eustice, supra note 7; see also Steutzer, "Discharge of In-

debtedness at a Discount," 7 N.Y.U. Inst. on Fed.Tax. 229 (1959) and Stone, "Cancellation of Indebtedness," 34 N.Y.U.Inst. on Fed.Tax. 555 (1976).

12. Reg. § 1.1017–1(a).

13. See Rev.Rul. 73–256, 1973–1 C.B. 56, and Rev.Rul. 74–540, 1974–2 C.B. 38.

(b) A painting with a basis and fair market value of $8000?

(c) A painting with a value of $8000 and a basis of $5000?

(d) Services, in the form of remodeling Rich's office, which are worth $10,000?

(e) Services that are worth $8000?

(f) Same as (a), above, except that Poor's Employer makes the $7000 payment to Rich, renouncing any claim to repayment by Poor.

2. Businessman borrows $25,000 from Creditor to purchase a piece of machinery from Dealer at a cost of $25,000 for use in Businessman's business. What result to Businessman in each of the following circumstances:

(a) Businessman is insolvent as his liabilities exceed his assets by $5000. Creditor agrees to discharge the debt for only $10,000. To what extent does the insolvency exception apply to Businessman?

(b) Assuming instead that Creditor sold the machinery, which has declined in value, to Businessman, what additional exceptions are applicable?

(c) Under the facts of (b), above, which overall result is preferable to Businessman?

3. Decedent owed Friend $5000 and Nephew owed Decedent $10,000.

(a) At Decedent's death Friend neglected to file a claim against Decedent's estate in the time allowed by state law and Friend's claim was barred by that statute of limitations. (Let's defer our concern for Nephew.) What result to Decedent's estate?

(b) What result to the estate in (a), above, (with Nephew still in cold storage) if instead Friend simply permitted the statute to run stating that he felt sorry for Decedent's widow, the residuary beneficiary of his estate?

(c) Now, what result to Nephew if Decedent's will provided that his estate not collect Nephew's debt to the estate?

CHAPTER 10. DAMAGES AND RELATED RECEIPTS

Internal Revenue Code: Sections 104–106.
Regulations: Sections 1.104–1(a), (c), (d); 1.105–1(a), –2, –3; 1.106–1.

INTRODUCTION

An on-going effort to enable students to determine what is and what is not gross income has indicated by this time that the identification of basic principles in tax law is much the same as in other fields of law. A tax *common law* rule may develop: Is there any element of gain in a receipt? If not, the receipt falls outside the income concept, as in the case of the payment of principal on a loan. There may be a controlling *statutory* rule: How sweet it is to receive a gift, the essence of gain! And yet by statutory proscription, I.R.C. § 102, property received by gift is excluded from gross income.

Amounts received as damages and as similar reimbursements are governed in part by statute. Code sections 104–106, discussed in Part A of this chapter immediately below, contain most of the tax rules on compensation for injuries and sickness.[1] But some other similar receipts are not accorded express congressional recognition and so their treatment must be worked out under more general tax principles. It is these general principles that, for example, add gloss to the phrase "income from whatever source derived" in I.R.C. § 61, which are referred to as the common law of federal taxation.[2] Of course, federal taxation is not a common law subject and the statute is "the thing." But when a statutory term is general a body of case law soon grows around it which is not unlike the growth of the common law and so it is with the kinds of receipts that are the subject of discussion in Parts B and C of this chapter.

A detailed study of the area covered by this chapter could well be justified. But by now an inescapable fact of life must be plain to the student: It is impossible in any course or even a series of courses to cover in detail *all* facets of federal taxation. Federal taxation is the life-size shadow of "life in all its fullness"; and who can ever know

---

1. A number of other Code sections deal with the includibility as gross income of damages or settled recoveries of other types or with other special rules regarding such recoveries. Not discussed in this note are: I.R.C. § 71, Alimony and separate maintenance payments; § 80, Restoration of value of certain securities; § 111, Recovery of bad debts, prior taxes and delinquency amounts; § 1342, Computation of tax where taxpayer recovers substantial amount held by another under a claim of right; § 1346, Recovery of nonconstitutional federal taxes; § 1347, Claims against the United States, involving acquisitions of property; § 1351, Recoveries of foreign expropriation losses.

2. See Ericksen, G., "The Common Law of Federal Taxation," 7 U. of Fla.L. Rev. 178 (1954).

all about life, much less its tax shadow? These comments of course again explain why there are scattered notes throughout this book which are intended to be read and to be informative without making the related statute the subject of detailed examination.

A. COMPENSATION FOR INJURIES OR SICKNESS:
STATUTORY EXCLUSIONS

Some benevolent provisions of the Internal Revenue Code rest simply on the compassionate thought that the taxpayer has suffered enough. Sections 104–106 are of this order. In broad outline they say that a taxpayer who has incurred bodily injury should not additionally suffer injury to his purse in the form of tax liability, if he achieves some financial recompense.

Section 104 is the principal provision. Its exclusionary rules are limited to amounts recovered for injuries to the person or for sickness. Thus damages for assault and battery, for example, are within its scope; damages for libel and slander likely are not.[3] Five areas of exclusion are expressly identified, covering amounts received (1) under workmen's compensation acts, (2) as damages for injury or sickness, (3) as benefits under health and accident insurance policies purchased by the taxpayer, and (4) as disability pensions arising out of some types of governmental service, recently limited by new subsection (b), and (5) disability income received by United States officials who are violently attacked outside the Country, an addition by the Tax Reform Act of 1976.

All exclusions under I.R.C. § 104 are restricted by an "except" clause which is echoed in § 105(b). It reads:

> Except in the case of amounts attributable to (and not in excess of) deductions allowed under section 213 (relating to medical, etc. expenses) for any prior taxable year, * * *

The general effect of this exception is to *include* in gross income any amount, otherwise excluded, which constitutes reimbursement of a medical expense that served as the basis of a § 213 deduction in a prior year. The obvious objective is to dovetail the exclusionary rule with the medical expense deduction. Assume in year one T incurred $500 of *deductible* medical expenses that were reimbursed in year two. If he were allowed to claim the deduction in year one and exclude the reimbursement in year two, he would have a *double* tax benefit, a $500 deduction with no out-of-pocket expense.[4]

---

3. Compare Rev.Rul. 58–418, 1958–2 C.B. 18, with Rev.Rul. 75–45, 1975–1 C.B. 47. But see Dudley G. Seay, infra note 11.

4. This disregards, as it seems we should, the 3% floor under the medical expense deduction, § 213(a), and the 1% rule on medicine and drugs, § 213 (b).

If reimbursement is received in the same year the expense is incurred, the exclusion applies, as there has been no deduction with respect to that amount in any "prior taxable year." This fits well, however, with § 213 which denies the deduction for expenses of medical care which are "compensated for by insurance or otherwise." That is, the medical expense deduction will not have been allowed for such reimbursed amounts. The §§ 104 and 105 exceptions are statutory expressions of the tax benefit doctrine, partially codified more broadly in I.R.C. § 111.[5] The related principles of §§ 104 and 105 and § 213 are rather well illustrated in the regulations.[6]

Section 104(a)(1). In most states, statutes assure employees compensation for injuries and illnesses arising out of and in the course of their employment. These are the classic "workmen's compensation acts" contemplated by § 104(a)(1). A comparable federal statute also within the scope of the section is the Longshoreman's and Harbor Workers' Compensation Act.[7] "Black lung" benefits legislation in 1969, the Federal Coal Mine Health and Safety Act, and the later Black Lung Benefits Act of 1972 are among similar federal statutes.[8] Section 104(a)(1) is interpreted literally to exclude benefits paid to an employee's survivors under workmen's compensation acts and similar statutes in the case of job-related death, not mere injury.[9] However, to be excluded under § 104(a)(1) the amount in question must be paid for death or injury that *is* job-related, not merely under a statute entitled "workmen's compensation law." Nonoccupational benefits, such as amounts paid for disability during employment but not caused by injury or sickness related to the employment, are not covered by § 104(a)(1).[10]

Section 104(a)(2). Here we find excluded from gross income recoveries for both intentional and unintentional torts resulting in bodily injury or sickness, and the statute makes it clear by a parenthetical phrase that an amount received by way of settlement is to be treated the same as damages judicially determined.[11] Of course very

---

5. See Chapter 20, infra.

6. See Reg. § 1.213–1(g)(1)–(3)(iii). Other portions of this regulation, which are more complex, may not be of much concern as they reflect the dollar limitation on the medical expense deduction which was repealed for years beginning in 1967 and later.

7. 33 U.S.C. chapter 18.

8. Rev.Rul. 72–400, 1972–2 C.B. 75.

9. Reg. § 1.104–1(b).

10. Compare Rev.Rul. 72–45, 1972–1 C.B. 34, with Rev.Rul. 72–191, 1972–1.

C.B. 45, amplified in Rev.Rul. 75–499, 1975–2 C.B. 43. These amounts may however qualify fully or partially for exclusion under § 105, discussed in Part B, below.

11. It was recognized in Dudley G. Seay, 58 T.C. 32 (1972), that damages awarded in a single case might be partly for breach of contract and unaffected by § 104(a)(2) and partly for personal injury and therefore within the exclusion. See Burken, "Tax Treatment of Post-Termination Personal Injury Settlements," 61 Calif.L.Rev. 1237 (1973).

large sums of money change hands in this way outside the reach of the tax gatherer; and question can be raised about the policy behind the provision.   On the one hand, one hardly thinks in terms of *gain* in connection with compensatory damages for injuries suffered, say, in an automobile accident that caused a broken leg or a whip-lash injury to the spine. But neither is there any *tax basis* for what is lost or relinquished, and cash flows in which it is difficult to identify as a return of capital.   The exclusions go back to a time when multi-million dollar damages were generally unknown and must be viewed as compassionate in nature. Would Congress adopt a different policy if the matter came up afresh? If damages were taxed, would the settlements and judgments soon increase (double?) to take account of the tax attrition? And how might that affect insurance rates that are already skyrocketing? The problem is further compounded by the fact that the subsection excludes *any* damages received, and the Service has ruled that this includes punitive damages as well as compensatory damages.[12]

One of the major problems of the day is the rising number and amount of medical malpractice recoveries which have generated hard questions for doctors practically required to purchase insurance against such recoveries, even though the premiums paid are deductible expenses under I.R.C. § 162. There is a surprising lack of authority on the tax consequences of such recoveries to the victim. Apparently they are excluded from gross income under § 104(a)(2). This would appear to be the case regardless of the nature of the claim of recovery, tort or contract;[13] although if the recovery were for breach of contract the application of § 104(a)(2) might be questioned on the ground that the damages are on account of breach of contract rather than "on account of personal injuries or sickness."[14] The forgotten surgical sponge sewed up in the victim rather clearly is a negligent "injury" of the kind contemplated by § 104. Negligent advice that the tumorous lump is innocuous and benign probably produces the kind of tortiously caused "sickness," recovery for which is intended to be excluded from gross income by the section.[15]

In recent years defendants have asked for jury instructions identifying the tax-free nature of the damages to be recovered. The majority of federal courts indicate that such instructions are proper but within the discretion of the trial judge. However, the instructions are rarely given.[16] One can rightly question the logic of denying a

12. Rev.Rul. 75-45, 1975-1 C.B. 47; and see note 55, infra.

13. See Epstein, "Medical Malpractice: The Case for Contract," 1976 Amer. Bar.Found.Research J. 87 (1976).

14. See Reg. § 1.104-1(c) stating that § 104(a)(2) applies to actions "based upon tort or tort-type rights."

15. This seems so, even though as is commonly said: "The physician did not *give* the patient cancer." Epstein, supra note 13.

16. E. g., Cunningham v. Bay Drilling Co., 421 F.2d 1398 (5th Cir. 1970); McWeeney v. N.Y., New Haven and Hartford R.R. Co., 282 F.2d 34 (2d Cir. 1960).

defendant's request. The theory behind recovery of compensatory damages is that the plaintiff should be put in as nearly as possible the same position he would have been in had the damage not occurred. Because of the § 104 exclusion a successful plaintiff is generally in a better after-tax financial position because of the injury. Even the British have recognized that income tax consequences should be considered in assessing damages.[17] A court may compute damages to be awarded on the basis of a net earnings concept (gross earnings minus income tax consequences).[18]

Whether damages are computed by judge or jury or merely by the parties in an out-of-court settlement, it may be important to allocate the total award among two or more causes of action. Dudley G. Seay [19] involved an allocation between alleged personal injuries and damages for breach of contract to which § 104 is inapplicable. In a personal injury suit it is just as likely that compensatory damages may be paid partly for the cost of medical care and partly for pain and suffering; that part allocated to medical care will not qualify for the exclusion to the extent it has been the subject of a prior medical expense deduction.[20]

If death is caused by the tortious act of another the theory on which damages may be recovered by the wrong-doer varies from state to state. For a time this created a recognized difference for estate tax purposes,[21] but damages to which a decedent was entitled that are collected by others after his death are within the exclusion of I.R.C. § 104(a)(2), and recoveries under wrongful death acts have simply been held not to be in the nature of income without the benefit of any express statutory provision.[22] The like treatment of like economic circumstances under the income tax seems preferable to the thin conceptional distinctions previously drawn for estate tax purposes.

Of course in a situation in which death is caused by the negligent or other wrongful act of another, such as in the case of an airplane accident, question may arise whether the recovery represents damages or insurance. The amount will be excluded in any event for

---

17. British Transp. Comm'n v. Gourly, 3 All E.R. 796 (1955).

18. E. g., in Furumizo v. U. S., 245 F. Supp. 981 (D.Hawaii 1965). But Cf., Brooks v. United States, 273 F.Supp. 619 (D.S.C.1967), where the court indicated that use of net earnings to award damages should be limited to wrongful death actions and not personal injury claims.

19. Supra, note 11.

20. See Rev.Rul. 75–230, 1975–1 C.B. 93, also pointing out that the medical expense portion of the award may

have a bearing on future § 213 deductions.

21. See Stephens, Maxfield and Lind, *Federal Estate and Gift Taxation*, 4–54 et. seq. (3d Ed. 1974), in general "survival statutes" sustain rights of the decedent, the value of which was at one time part of his gross estate, while "wrongful death acts" create new rights in survivors in which the decedent had no taxable interest. But see Rev.Rul. 75–126, 1975–1 C.B. 296, and Rev.Rul. 75–127, 1975–1 C.B. 297.

22. Rev.Rul. 54–19, 1954 C.B. 179.

income tax purposes either under I.R.C. § 104 or § 101, even though the details of the insurance arrangement can make a difference whether the amount is includible in the decedent's gross estate for estate tax purposes.[23]

Section 104(a)(3). The third paragraph of § 104(a) excludes from gross income amounts received under accident and health insurance policies for personal injuries or sickness.[24] However, this rule is limited to the proceeds of policies paid for by the individual himself and should be compared with the treatment of certain employee health and accident benefits under § 105, described below. Being subject to the general prefatory exception of § 104(a), the exclusion does not cover amounts attributable to medical expense deductions for prior years.[25]

It appears that § 104(a)(3) holds out an opportunity for a tax-free profit in health and accident insurance. Some policies pay a stated number of dollars per day for hospitalized illness and will pay even if other policies in effect have already defrayed the charges. It is curious that Congress invites this kind of tax-free profiteering, even if it may occur only infrequently.

Under I.R.C. § 106 the gross income of employees does not include an employer's contributions to accident and health plans set up by way of insurance or otherwise to pay compensation to his employees for injuries or sickness. However, § 105(e) does treat amounts *paid out* by such plans, as well as by sickness and disability funds of states and the District of Columbia as amounts received through accident and health insurance. This would be awkward and inappropriate except that the 105(e) rule does not bring such amounts under the protective umbrella of § 104(a)(3). See the parenthetical exception in paragraph (3). Both direct payments by employers of accident and health benefits to employees and indirect pay-

---

23. Compare Rev.Rul. 75–45, 1975–1 C.B. 47 with Rev.Rul. 57–54, 1957–1 C.B. 298.

24. This has been held to include "no fault" insurance disability benefits received for loss of income or earning capacity. Rev.Rul. 73–155, 1973–1 C.B. 50.

25. This exception is clear enough in one respect and fuzzy in another. It nails as includible in gross income insurance reimbursements for explicit previously deducted medical expenses. For example, if the proceeds are obtained only after having been deducted as a medical expense in a prior year, to the extent that they have been previously deducted they are knocked out of the exclusion by the exception and are includible in income. It may also be true that the proceeds *escape* tax (are not within the exception) if they are payable merely in case of certain injury or illness without regard to expenses incurred in connection therewith. This seems to be the Tax Court's view. Cf., Robert O. Deming, Jr., 9 T.C. 383 (1943). It is uncertain, however, whether premiums paid for the health and accident insurance and deducted in a prior year or years as medical expenses operate to reduce the exclusion. The insurance proceeds would probably be attributable to the deducted premiums and to that extent should not be excluded.

ments funded by amounts not taxed to the employees are placed outside § 104(a)(3). This is not to say they will always be taxed, but only that their tax status must be tested under § 105. It is realistic to differentiate insurance proceeds paid by policies bought with the recipient's own taxed or partially taxed dollars from amounts simply paid directly by employers or paid under arrangements that have been without cost, tax or otherwise, to the recipient.[26]

Section 106. This seems the best place to take brief further account of the enigmatic sentence which is § 106, excluding from an employee's gross income an employer's contributions to accident and health plans set up to pay compensation to employees for injuries or sickness. The function of I.R.C. (26 U.S.C.A.) § 106 is to equalize the tax status of employees (1) whose employers undertake to pay health or accident benefits to employees directly, and employees (2) whose employers accomplish the same results through the purchase of insurance or the funding of benefit plans. Before the enactment of the 1954 Code, an employer's payment of a premium for an individual health and accident policy for an employee resulted in income taxable to the employee.[27] But the employee was in the same situation as an employee whose employer himself would pay benefits like those purchased under the insurance contract and, in the second case, the employee realized no income from his employer's direct assumption of this obligation. There was no reason why one should incur tax liability and the other not, and § 106 eliminates the difference by way of its further exclusionary rule. It may be well to emphasize that the exclusion under § 106 relates, not to amounts paid to employees who are sick or injured, but to amounts paid by employers for insurance premiums or into funded plans to set up benefits for employees in case of future sickness or injury.

Sections 104(a)(4) and (5). Section 104(a)(4) excludes disability pensions of members of the armed forces and certain other governmental units.[28] Although subsection (b) of I.R.C. § 104 now limits the application of § 104(a)(4) in general, it "grandfathers"

---

26. In a highly technical fashion, the last sentence of § 104(a) fits quasi-employees (self-employed persons given employee status for purposes of tax benefits) into this scheme of things. See Reg. § 1.72–15(g). Although the self-employed person's payments would be deductible under § 404(a), making the introductory reference to § 213 irrelevant, the general effect, nevertheless, is again to deny the double benefit of an exclusion for amounts attributable to deductible payments.

27. See Sen.Rep.No.1622, 83rd Cong., 2d Sess., 185–186 (1954).

28. Although this note makes no pretense at being exhaustive, it may be well to note that § 1403 of Title 10 U.S.C. expressly provides: "That part of the retired pay of a member of an armed force computed * * * on the basis of years of service, which exceeds the retired pay that he would receive if it were computed on the basis of disability is not considered as a pension * * * under section 104(a) of Title 26."

in persons who were receiving benefits excluded under § 104(a)(4) in 1975 and continues its application to persons receiving compensation for combat-related injuries or who would, upon application, be entitled to disability compensation from the Veterans' Administration.

Section 104(a)(5), added by the Tax Reform Act of 1976, excludes disability income attributable to injuries incurred as a result of terrorist attacks on United States employees performing official duties outside the United States.

Section 105(a).   The question now is what about taxpayers who *as employees* receive some financial benefit arising out of their employer's concern for their health.   Some comments above, explaining the limited scope of § 104(a)(3) which generally excludes amounts received through accident and health plans, serve as an introduction to this provision.   Its first thrust is generally to label *includible* gross income amounts that an employee [29] receives through accident or health insurance.   They are expressly includible if (1) attributable to an employer's contributions to a plan which were not taxed to the employee or (2) simply paid by the employer.   It will be recalled that these are the very amounts that failed to be excluded under § 104(a) (3).   Is all lost?   No.   The main messages of § 105 are in subsections (b), (c), and (d) which back off from the generally includible rule of subsection (a).

Section 105(b).   If an employer directly or indirectly reimburses an employee for expenses of medical care [30] for himself, his spouse or his dependents,[31] the amount received is excluded from gross income under § 105(b).   Of course it was noted earlier in the chapter that the prefatory exception in § 104(a) is echoed in § 105(b).   Thus, an employee's medical expense deductions for a prior year may reduce the excludible amount of his later reimbursement, just as in the case of exclusions under § 104(a)(3).   The tax benefit concept requires this limitation on the exclusions.

Note that here it is the amount of medical care actually paid for which measures the exclusion, in contrast to the possibility (maybe even likelihood) under § 104(a)(3) that the *amounts received* under a health or accident policy, which measure the exclusions, may exceed the medical expenses incurred.   Under this scheme of things an obvious problem arises if an individual has two accident and health insurance policies, the premiums of one being paid by the individual and the other by his employer, and both compensate him for the same illness.   Assume, for example, that an employee had $900 of medical expenses related to an illness and that he received $800 from an employer funded policy and $400 from his own policy.   Under I.R.C. (26

---

29. Quasi-employees, see note 26, above, are not "employees" here. I.R.C. § 105(g).

30. The I.R.C. § 213(e) definition is expressly adopted.

31. The I.R.C. § 152 definition of dependent is expressly adopted.

U.S.C.A.) § 104(a)(3), all proceeds from his own policy are excluded from income, but I.R.C. (26 U.S.C.A.) § 105(b) limits the exclusion for his other benefit to amounts which reimburse him for his medical care. Thus, the question arises as to what amount of the $800 received from the employer funded policy may be excluded. *Revenue Ruling 69–154* [32] indicates that the amount of medical expense to be considered paid by each policy is proportionate to the benefits received from each policy. Under this approach, if the employee received $800 from the employer's policy and $400 from his own policy (a total of $1200), 800/1200 or two-thirds of the medical expense is deemed paid by the employer's policy. Therefore, two-thirds of the $900 of medical expenses, or $600, will be considered as paid for out of the proceeds of the employer policy. It follows that of the $800 received from the employer funded policy only $600 is excluded by I.R.C. § 105(b), because the exclusion under § 105(b) is limited to the amount of reimbursement for actual expenses. $200 of the $800 received is included in the employee's gross income.[33] Of course, the full $400 received from the employee's policy is excluded under § 104(a)(3) which has no such limitation. Even if the taxpayer who is self-supporting in this respect may deserve some kind of acclaim, the exclusion of "profits" on health and accident policies under § 104(a)(3) may still be questioned. More complex problems sometimes arise regarding the interrelationship of I.R.C. §§ 104(a)(3) and 105(b).[34]

Section 105(c). This subsection provides that, if an employee receives payments through health or accident insurance [35] provided by his employer without tax cost to him for loss of a member or function of the body or for disfigurement, not just of himself but also of his spouse or a dependent,[36] and if the amount is computed only with regard to the nature of the injury and not to the period the employee is absent from work,[37] the amount is excluded from gross income.[38] Of course, as a rule the employee himself will receive payment for casualties of this type under workmen's compensation legislation and can exclude the receipts under § 104(a)(1). When this is so § 104(a)(1) preempts § 105(c), according to the Service.[39] This seems to make little difference, however, because amounts that are of the type received under workmen's compensation acts but are outside § 104 because they exceed what is provided for *are* permitted

---

32. 1969–1 C.B. 46.

33. Rev.Rul. 69–154, Situation 3, supra note 32.

34. Rev.Rul. 69–154, Situation 4, supra note 32.

35. Recall the broad definition in I.R.C. § 105(e).

36. The § 152 definition of dependent is expressly adopted.

37. See Rev.Rul. 74–603, 1974–2 C.B. 35.

38. Receipts of this kind do not affect the amount of a taxpayer's medical expense deduction. See § 105(f).

39. Reg. § 1.105–3, last sentence.

to be excluded under § 105(c).[40] And of course nonoccupational injuries and disfigurement and also injuries and disfigurement of an employee's spouse and dependents may produce financial compensation outside § 104 which is excluded from gross income by § 105(c).[41]

Section 105(d). Before 1977, if an employee was ill and therefore absent from work and his employer had a plan that fully or partly continued his compensation, all or part of what he received under the plan was tax-free under § 105(d). But concern that abuses might creep in caused this essentially simple proposition to be made quite complex; and one might question the rhetoric as well. The Tax Reform Act of 1976 not only improved the language, it substituted a wholly new provision reflecting a different concept. Here is what is said about the new rules in the Summary of the Conference Agreement on H.R. 10612 prepared by the House Committee on Ways and Means on September 14, 1976:

> Under present law, an employee can exclude from gross income up to $100 a week of sick pay received under wage continuation plans when the employee is absent from work on account of injury or sickness. Individuals who incur additional or extraordinary medical expenses due to sickness or injury may deduct those medical expenses that exceed certain percentage of income limitations.
>
> The conference agreement generally repeals the present sick pay exclusion and substitutes a maximum annual exclusion of up to $5,200 a year for retirees under age 65 who have retired on disability and who are permanently and totally disabled. (After age 65, these retirees will be eligible for the revised elderly credit.)[42] The term "permanently and totally disabled" means unable to engage in any substantial gainful activity by reason of any medically determined physical or mental impairment which can be expected to result in death or which has lasted or can be expected to last for a continuous period of not less than 12 months. Proof of disability must be substantiated by the taxpayer's employer who is to certify this status under procedures approved in advance by the Internal Revenue Service. The IRS may also issue regulations requiring the taxpayer to provide proof from time to time that he is still disabled. The maximum amount excludable is to be reduced on a dollar-for-dollar basis by the individual's adjusted gross income (including disability income) in excess of $15,000 (this amount applies to both single and joint returns). Thus, the disability income exclusion is unavailable if the individual has adjusted gross income of $20,200. Persons who retired before

---

40. Reg. § 1.104–1(b).

41. Ibid.

42. [See Chapter 27, infra page 964. Ed.]

January 1, 1976 on disability and who were permanently and totally disabled on that date may claim the disability income exclusion, if they otherwise qualify, even though they may not have been permanently and totally disabled on their retirement date. These new rules apply equally to civilians and military personnel.

These provisions apply to taxable years beginning after December 31, 1975.

B. PERSONAL INJURIES NOT SUBJECT TO STATUTORY RULES

In a very early case,[43] the Board of Tax Appeals held that compensatory damages for defamation are not gross income. The gravamen of the opinion seems to be the lack of a profit element in an award of this type which seeks only "to make the plaintiff whole as before the injury." [44] The Board's decision found support in an earlier Solicitor's Opinion [45] which had been rested on the same grounds: "Without gain of some sort no income within the meaning of the sixteenth amendment can be said to be realized." [46] The Opinion gave like exempt status to damages received for alienation of affection.

Libel, slander, and alienation of affection might well be considered "personal injuries" within the protective rules of § 104. Indeed, a recent Tax Court case accepts the view that they are.[47] As a technical matter it seems incorrect to apply § 104(a)(2) to the non-physical torts. The provision entered the income tax statutes as § 213(b)(6) of the Revenue Act of 1918; and yet in 1922, as explained above, the Treasury's view was that the basis for excluding damages for defamation from gross income was not any statutory rule, but a more basic concept of what is "income." [48]

Similarly, after the Supreme Court's decision in *Glenshaw Glass*,[49] the Treasury asserted that punitive damages awarded in a libel suit are includible in gross income.[50] When that ruling is compared with the very recent ruling holding § 104(a)(2) excludes *all* damages, whether compensatory or punitive [51] awarded on account

---

43. C. A. Hawkins, 6 B.T.A. 1023 (1928).

44. Id. at 1025.

45. Sol.Op. 132, 1–1 C.B. 92 (1922).

46. Id. at 93.

47. Dudley G. Seay, 58 T.C. 32 (1972). Two earlier cases intimating that non-physical personal injuries may be "personal injuries" within § 104(a)(2) are Knuckles v. Comm'r, 349 F.2d 610 (10th Cir. 1965), and Agar v. Comm'r, 290 F.2d 283 (2d Cir. 1961).

However, as the courts found the payments in question to be for breach of contract and for job severance, respectively, neither squarely faced the issue of exclusion under § 104(a)(2).

48. Sol.Op. 132, supra, note 45. See also Rev.Rul. 74–72, 1974–1 C.B. 33; and Cf., Reg. § 1.105–4(g).

49. 348 U.S. 426 (1955).

50. Rev.Rul. 58–418, 1958–2 C.B. 18.

51. Rev.Rul. 75–45, 1975–1 C.B. 47.

of personal injuries, it is fairly clear that the Treasury and the courts may be slipping toward a coverage not originally supposed for § 104 (a)(2). Perhaps, however, we have arrived at that stage. The rulings just mentioned would point the other way only if reversed in time of promulgation; but it seems the Treasury should declare the earlier ruling obsolete, or perhaps better still, Congress should remove the uncertainty. In any event, compensatory damages for the non-physical torts escape tax either under common law or statutory principles, and exemplary or punitive damages for such torts *may* escape tax now; they will if these torts are finally held to effect the kind of "personal injuries" contemplated by § 104.

Damages for the invasion of a taxpayer's right of privacy are probably not taxable. Dictum in Meyer v. United States [52] indicates that § 22(b)(5) of the 1939 Code, which is like § 104(a)(2) of the 1954 Code, *could* exclude such payments, but the court holds it cannot be applied to prior payment for *anticipated* damages, the most that was alleged in the case. Runyon v. United States [53] might have squarely presented the issue, but the taxpayer's assertion that an amount received was paid for invasion of privacy was rejected there on the ground that relevant New York law recognized no such tort at that time. Other cases have gone off on the ground that no personal damages were in fact proven.[54]

There is an apparent need for some congressional tidying up but, if torts that result in physical injuries result in tax-exempt damages, there seems little reason to treat other types of personal injuries differently; and that seems to be the trend in the law.

C. RECOVERIES FOR INJURIES TO BUSINESS OR TO PROPERTY

It is not appropriate here, even though this chapter is entitled Damages and Related Receipts, to attempt a broad description of the tax treatment of recoveries for injuries to business and to property generally. The reason is that there are necessarily involved characterization questions.[55] All these matters are the subject of detailed

52. 173 F.Supp. 920 (D.C.Tenn.1959).

53. 281 F.2d 590 (5th Cir. 1960).

54. E. g., J. A. Fanelli, 20 T.C.M. 1617 (1961).

55. These include the capital gain or loss, ordinary income or loss dichotomy, see, e. g., I.R.C. §§ 1201–1223; special rules on sales or exchanges of business property and involuntary conversions of that and also capital assets, see the I.R.C. § 1231 "hotchpot"; the depreciation recapture concept, e. g., the I.R.C. §§ 1245 and 1250 "gotchas"; and nonrecognition principles, e. g., §§ 1033 and 1034.

consideration in Parts Six and Seven of this book and they cannot sensibly be anticipated here. For example, we can say that severance damages awarded in a condemnation proceeding (taxpayer may be paid compensation for what is taken and also damages for reduction of value of the property he retains) are applied against the basis of his retained property and to that extent escape tax.[56] But it is not a complete picture of the transaction, which may also involve taxable gain or loss on the principal taking and its recognition or characterization and, also, characterization of the severance damages to the extent they are taxable as amounts in excess of basis. Nevertheless, a few comments are advanced here.

As a general proposition, taxability of a recovery can be determined by an identification of the purpose for the award.[57] If an injured party receives damages for loss of profits in his business, the damages being a substitute for the profits are fairly easily identified as gross income.[58] Of course this basic principle may be altered by statute. In some instances if there is a recovery for patent infringement, breach of contract or of a fiduciary duty, or violations of the Clayton Act, a compensating deduction may nullify the inclusion in gross income.[59]

We have known since 1955, or maybe in your case since page 45,[60] that punitive or exemplary damages, even if properly characterized as a windfall, are fully taxable.[61]

Generally, damages or other recoveries for the improper taking of or injury to physical property operate simply to reduce the loss deduction otherwise potentially available,[62] but they become gross income subject to tax under special rules where the amounts received exceed the basis for the property.

As in the case of personal injuries, damages recovered in a single suit may rest on several grounds. Tax analysis requires allocation of the award in such circumstances.[63]

56. Rev.Rul. 68–37, 1968–1 C.B. 359.

57. Farmer's & Merchant's Bank v. Comm'r, 59 F.2d 912 (6th Cir. 1932): "In lieu of what were the damages awarded?" Cf. Hort v. Comm'r, 313 U.S. 28 (1941).

58. Taxable: recovery for average profits whaling vessel might have made if not detained by United States, J. R. Knowland, 29 B.T.A. 618 (1933); recovery for profits lost in sealing operations because of improper interference by the United States, Liebes & Co. v. Comm'r, 90 F.2d 932 (9th Cir. 1937).

59. See I.R.C. § 186.

60. Comm'r v. Glenshaw Glass Co., 348 U.S. 426, rehearing denied, 349 U.S. 925 (1955).

61. An exception under § 104(a)(2) is noted above.

62. See page 490, infra. Cf. I.R.C. § 123, considered page 494, infra.

63. Compare State Fish Corp., 48 T.C. 465 (1967), acq. 1968–2 C.B. 3, amounts received for damages to goodwill escaped tax as not in excess of taxpayer's basis for goodwill, with Raytheon Products Corp. v. Comm'r, 144 F.2d 110 (1st Cir. 1944), cert. den., 323 U.S. 779 (1944), recovery for destruction of business and good will fully taxable for failure to establish any basis for the business and good will of the company.

A contract for the sale of property may contain a clause anticipating the possibility of breach and expressing the consequences. If
amounts are then required to be paid as liquidated damages, not
penalties, do the recipients have income? While arguably the transaction represents a mere recovery of capital with a concurrent basis
reduction, nevertheless the recoveries are treated as income.[64] And
properly so, as the seller is left where he began, having given up no
property or property interests. The recovery is most appropriately
treated as a "windfall." [65]

Professional people these days are appropriately held to a reasonably high standard of performance and may incur liability for
failure to attain it, as mentioned above in the discussion of medical
malpractice. It is a shattering thought to a young tax lawyer that
his bad advice to a client might give rise to personal liability for tax
costs unnecessarily incurred by the client. Should such an event occur, Edward H. Clark [66] is authority for the client's exclusion from
gross income of his recovery from the lawyer. This old opinion seems
erroneously to rest on the notion that the recovery is not "derived
from capital or from labor or from both combined." While *Glenshaw
Glass* [67] repudiated this rationale, it may still be true that such awards
lack any element of gain, which is an essential characteristic of income.[68]

PROBLEMS

1. Plaintiff brought suit and unless otherwise indicated successfully recovered. Discuss the tax consequences in the following
alternative situations:

   (a) Plaintiff's suit was based on a claim of defamation of his
       professional reputation. He recovered $8000 of cash for
       compensatory damages and $4000 of cash for punitive dam-
       ages.

   (b) Plaintiff's suit was based on a claim of defamation of his
       personal reputation (as opposed to his business or profes-
       sional reputation) and he won a judgment for $8000 for
       compensatory damages. Defendant was short of cash and
       he satisfied the judgment by transferring some land worth
       $8000 to Plaintiff. Does Plaintiff have income and what
       is his basis in the land?

64. Harold S. Smith, 50 T.C. 273
(1968), aff'd per curiam, 418 F.2d 573
(9th Cir. 1969); Meyer Mittleman, 56
T.C. 171 (1971).

65. The recovery also has characterization consequences. If a "windfall",
the gain should be ordinary income,
Harold S. Smith and Meyer Mittleman, supra note 64. But see Alvin
G. Lowe, 44 T.C. 363 (1965).

66. 40 B.T.A. 333 (1939), acq., 1944
C.B. 5.

67. Supra, note 60.

68. If the award were made for a
medical malpractice recovery, it is
seemingly shielded from the Commissioner's grasp by § 104(a)(2). See
page 206, supra.

(c) Same questions as (b), above, except that the land is worth $12,000 but is subject to a $4000 mortgage which Plaintiff assumes.

(d) Plaintiff's suit was based on a claim of defamation to his personal reputation. He recovered $8000 of cash for compensatory damages and $4000 of cash for punitive damages.

(e) Plaintiff's suit was based on a recovery of an $8000 loan that he made to Debtor. Plaintiff recovered $8500 of cash, $8000 for the loan plus $500 in interest.

(f) Plaintiff's suit was based on a claim of injury to the goodwill of his business. Plaintiff had a $4000 cost basis for the goodwill of the business (the amount he paid for goodwill when he purchased the business). He recovered $10,000 damages for injury to goodwill which he had built up over the years.

(g) Plaintiff's suit was for a refund of a $2000 overpayment of his federal income taxes for a prior year. He received cash of $2240 which included the refund and $240 of interest.

2. Injured and Spouse were injured in an automobile accident. Their total medical expenses incurred were $2500.

(a) In the year of the accident they properly deducted $1500 of the expenses on their joint income tax return and filed suit against Wrongdoer. In the succeeding year they settled their claim against Wrongdoer for $2500. What income tax consequences on receipt of the settlement?

(b) What result under the facts of (a), above, if Injured and Spouse had used the standard deduction (see Chapter 18, infra at page 507) rather than taking a medical expense deduction in the year of the accident? See Reg. § 1.213–1 (g)(2).

(c) In the year of the settlement Spouse was ill but, happily, Injured carried medical insurance and additionally had insurance benefits under a policy provided by Injured's Employer. Spouse's medical expenses totalled $4000 and they received $3000 of benefits under Injured's policy and $2000 of benefits under Employer's policy. To what extent are the benefits included in their gross income?

(d) Under the facts of (c), above, may Injured and Spouse deduct the medical expenses? (See I.R.C. § 213(a) introductory clause.)

CHAPTER 11. SEPARATION AND DIVORCE

A. SUPPORT vs. PROPERTY SETTLEMENTS

Internal Revenue Code: Sections 71(a); 72(k); 215 (first sentence); 7701 (a)(17).
Regulations: Section 1.71–1(a), –1(b)(4).

Prior to 1942 in the absence of explicit statutory provisions, alimony payments were looked upon as nondeductible personal expenses of the husband,[1] like family expenses in an unbroken home. Similarly, alimony was not required to be included in a divorced wife's gross income, because it was considered merely an interest in the husband's property to which the wife was equitably entitled.[2] When World War II required a substantial escalation of income tax rates, it became possible for alimony and income taxes to exceed the entire net income of divorced husbands. Even in less extreme circumstances, nondeductible alimony payments were very burdensome. Consequently, it is not surprising that in the 1942 Revenue Act Congress effected a statutory reversal of previously established principles; alimony would be included within the wife's gross income and, to the extent so included, would be deductible by the husband.[3]

This is the first place in this book that the deduction concept is prominently encountered. For the most part, deductions are deferred to Part Four, beginning with Chapter 15. Still most people have some notion of the concept of taxable (net) income, if only from hearing their fathers complain that the really good things always seem to turn out to be either immoral, illegal, fattening, or at best *nondeductible*. In any event I.R.C. (26 U.S.C.A.) §§ 71 and 215 are so interrelated that they must be viewed together. In some of the materials below they are referred to as §§ 22(k) and 23(u), their 1939 Code designations. In general, deductibility by the paying spouse is made dependent upon includibility of the payment in the gross income of the recipient spouse. But this limited reciprocal principle should not be taken as a general rule applicable in other areas. For

---

1. See I.R.C. (26 U.S.C.A.) § 262.

2. Gould v. Gould, 245 U.S. 151, 38 S. Ct. 53, 62 L.Ed. 211 (1917).

3. The constitutional validity of the 1942 provision was sustained in Mahana v. U. S., 115 Ct.Cl. 716, 88 F. Supp. 285 (1950), which held that *Gould*, supra note 2, was not based on a decision that alimony was not income within the Sixteenth Amendment, but instead on a determination that the Income Tax Act of 1913 did not purport to tax it.

example, when Viewer pays a t.v. repairman $15, the repairman has $15 gross income even though Viewer has merely incurred a nondeductible personal expense.

The provisions of I.R.C. (26 U.S.C.A.) §§ 71 and 215 can well be viewed as a kind of income-splitting or tax allocation device.[4] That is, divorced or separated persons may in effect allocate taxability between them of some of the paying spouse's income by the wife assuming the tax burden for the amount received as alimony and the husband being accorded a deduction for that amount. Whether that is accomplished, however, depends upon how things are done. Thus, the manner in which interspousal payments are arranged becomes a bargaining matter in negotiations for any settlement, with a close eye on the tax consequences. Think of this in studying the materials in this Chapter. So you're not much interested in tax, because you plan to be a general practitioner? This is one of several areas in which federal tax law has come to dominate "general practice" law.

The student should, however, avoid thinking of alimony payments as coming "out of" the husband's income. If he makes the payments himself, their origin is immaterial in determining their taxability to the wife and their deductibility by him. A husband might have no job and hold all his wealth in the form of a checking account and unproductive, speculative real estate and thus have no gross income. Still, if he pays his divorced wife $1000 per month as alimony, she will be taxed on it; while it is deductible by him, the deduction would be wasted for lack of any income to be offset.

Congress intended that the 1942 Act and the current provisions apply only to alimony and support payments.[5] Not all transfers arising out of a divorce situation are alimony and support. Thus, if in a divorce one spouse pays off a debt to the other, the payment is not "because of the marital or family relationship" but because of the contractual obligation, and is not within the scope of §§ 71 and 215. Another example of a payment that is neither alimony nor support is considered in the *Bernatschke* case which follows.

Now, what do you know! Here is a large area that Congress left untouched in 1976. Well . . . almost. There is no change in I.R.C. §§ 71, 215, or even 682, mentioned later in this Chapter. However, Congress did add subsection (13) to § 62, permitting the deduction allowed by § 215 for alimony payments to be claimed in determining adjusted gross income.[6] This is more significant when we

---

4. In Chapters 13 and 27 of this book you will come across the concept of income-splitting for *married* taxpayers. Its origin and purpose are, however, quite different. Still, it is related to the present problem inasmuch as the effective income-splitting rules of § 71(a)(2) and (3) and § 215, applicable where the parties are still married, do not apply if the parties

achieve income-splitting advantages under I.R.C. § 1(a), as they can by way of electing to file a joint return under § 6013. See I.R.C. (26 U.S.C.A.) § 71(a)(2) and (3), last sentences.

5. S.Rep.No.1631, 77th Cong. 2d Sess. 1942, 1942–2 C.B. 504, 568.

6. TRA (1976) § 502(a).

look at Chapter 18, infra, but for now it may just be said that, for years beginning in 1977 and later, alimony becomes deductible by the paying spouse even if deductions are not itemized—in addition, that is, to the standard deduction.[7]

BERNATSCHKE v. UNITED STATES [*]

Court of Claims of the United States, 1966.
176 Ct.Cl. 1234, 364 F.2d 400.

Before COWEN, CHIEF JUDGE, and LARAMORE, DURFEE, DAVIS and COLLINS, JUDGES.

Opinion

PER CURIAM:

This case was referred to Trial Commissioner Herbert N. Maletz with directions to make findings of fact and recommendation for conclusions of law. The commissioner has done so in an opinion and report filed on January 20, 1966. On February 19, 1966, defendant filed a notice of intention to except. However, on June 6, 1966, defendant filed a motion to withdraw notice of intention to except to commissioner's report to which, on June 9, 1966, plaintiffs filed a response stating, among other things, that on the basis of plaintiffs' understanding that the case will be submitted to the court on the commissioner's report if defendant's motion is granted, plaintiffs have no objection to the granting of such motion. The case is thus submitted to the court on the trial commissioner's report filed January 20, 1966, without exception by the parties. Since the court agrees with the trial commissioner's opinion, findings and recommended conclusion of law, as hereinafter set forth, it hereby adopts the same as the basis for its judgment in this case without oral argument. Plaintiffs are, therefore, entitled to recover, together with interest as provided by law and judgment is entered for plaintiffs with the amount of recovery to be determined pursuant to Rule 47(c) (2).

OPINION OF COMMISSIONER

MALETZ, COMMISSIONER: That is a suit for refund of income taxes and assessed interest thereon paid by plaintiff [1] for the years 1956 through 1959 and 1961, together with statutory interest. The sole issue is whether Section 72 or Section 71(a) (1) of the Internal Revenue Code of 1954 governs the taxability of the sum of $25,000 received

---

7. See I.R.C. (26 U.S.C.A.) §§ 63(b) and 141.

* See Harris, "The Federal Income Tax Treatment of Alimony Payments—The 'Support' Requirement of the Regulations," 22 Hastings L.J. 53 (1970). Ed.

1. Plaintiff Cathalene Crane Bernatschke's present husband, Rudolf A. Bernatschke, is a party to the proceedings because joint returns were filed for the tax years in question. All references hereafter to plaintiff will refer to Cathalene Crane Bernatschke.

each year by plaintiff under certain annuity contracts for which the consideration was paid by her former husband, Cornelius Crane, pursuant to an Agreement of February 20, 1940 incident to a divorce.[2]

In general, annuity payments are taxable under the rules of Section 72 of the Code, with Section 72(b) providing for the exclusion from gross income of a portion of amounts received as an annuity, based on the ratio of the "investment in the contract" to the "expected return." These rules, however, are not applicable to payments under an annuity contract which are includible in the income of the wife under Section 71; such payments are wholly includible in the wife's gross income.[3] * * *

The substance of Section 71 was first enacted in 1942[4] to allow the husband to deduct "payments in the nature of or in lieu of alimony or an allowance for support" and to tax such payments to the

2. The Agreement recites that plaintiff had instituted a divorce action against Cornelius Crane; that each of the parties was possessed of separate property and estate; that each of the parties was fully appraised of the financial position of the other; that the parties were "desirous of making a complete adjustment and final settlement of all property rights and the respective interests of each of the parties in the properties of the other by virtue of their marital relation, and of releasing to the other all interest in the other's property"; and that Cornelius Crane was desirous of "satisfying and discharging his obligation to pay alimony to * * * [plaintiff]." The Agreement provides that in the event plaintiff was found by the court entitled to a divorce, Cornelius Crane agreed "in lieu of alimony, to deposit with one or more life insurance companies * * * a sum or sums of money sufficient to purchase annuity contracts which shall yield the sum of * * * $25,000 per year payable to * * * [plaintiff] during her lifetime, which sum of money is estimated to be approximately * * * $647,000. * * *" The Agreement states that the annuity contracts were to provide in substance that there was to be no power to revoke the annuities therein provided, nor any power to change the beneficiaries without the consent of both parties; that upon the death of plaintiff, any refund due under the policies was to be divided equally between the daughter of plaintiff (who had been adopted by Cornelius Crane) and Cornelius Crane; and that in the event of the prior decease of Cornelius Crane, any refund was to be distributed to plaintiff's daughter. The Agreement provides that plaintiff agreed to accept the payments "in lieu of all claims of alimony which she may by virtue of said decree have against him." It also provides that Cornelius Crane "does hereby waive, release, quitclaim, relinquish, sell, assign and convey" to plaintiff "all rights of dower, as well as all rights and claims as husband, widower or otherwise" in and to "all property and estate" of plaintiff, "both real, personal and mixed". In addition, plaintiff gave, in the same language, a release and conveyance to Cornelius Crane of "all rights of dower, as well as all rights and claims as wife, widow, or otherwise."

3. The parties have stipulated that if the annuity amount of $25,000 received by plaintiff is taxable under Section 72 rather than under Section 71, then the sum of $7,199.05 (rather than $25,000) was properly includible in her gross income for each of the years in issue.

4. The provision was enacted as a portion of Section 22(k) of the Internal Revenue Code of 1939, by Section 120(a) of the Revenue Act of 1942, 56 Stat. 816. When the Internal Revenue Code of 1954 was enacted, the language of Section 22(k) was "restated for purposes of clarity", but no substantive change was made. H.Rep. No. 1337, 83d Cong., 2d Sess., pp. A–20—A–21 (1954). See also S.Rep. No. 1662, 83d Cong., 2d Sess., p. 170 (1954), U.S.Code Cong. & Admin. News 1954, p. 4017.

wife who receives them.[5]   H.Rep.No.2333, 77th Cong., 2d Sess., p. 71 (1942).   See also S.Rep.No.1631, 77th Cong., 2d Sess., p. 83 (1942); 5 Mertens, Law of Federal Income Taxation, § 31A.01, pp. 1–2.   In conformity with this legislative purpose, Section [1.71–1] of the Treasury Regulations on Income Tax (1954) specifies that "Section 71 provides rules for treatment in certain cases of payments in the nature of or in lieu of alimony or an allowance for support as between spouses who are divorced or separated.   *   *   *"   In addition, Section 1.71–1(b) (4) of the Regulations states that "Section 71(a) applies only to payments made because of the family or marital relationship in recognition of the general obligation to support which is made specific by the decree, instrument, or agreement   *   *   *"   See also e. g. H.Rep.No.2333, 77th Cong., 2d Sess., p. 72 (1942).

Against this background, plaintiff contends that all or part of the cost of the annuity contracts was paid by Cornelius Crane for reasons other than his obligation to support plaintiff and hence that the annual payments of $25,000 received pursuant to the contracts were taxable in whole or in part under the rules set forth in Section 72 of the Code.   Defendant argues, on the other hand, that the annual payments of $25,000 received by plaintiff constituted periodic payments in discharge of a legal obligation incurred by her former husband because of the marital or family relationship, and not in settlement of any property rights, and thus were wholly includible in her gross income under Section 71(a) (1) of the Code.

The nub of the problem is thus to determine whether or not plaintiff's former husband, Cornelius Crane, paid the consideration for the annuities by virtue of an obligation to support plaintiff which was imposed on him by their marital relationship.   This is a question that depends upon the substance of the transaction and the true intent of the parties, rather than on the labels or formal provisions of the written contract or divorce decree.   [Citations omitted.]   Parol evidence may be considered in making this determination, particularly since the Agreement here is ambiguous at best, failing, for example, to afford any indication as to how or why the parties determined either the amount which Cornelius Crane would pay or the provisions applicable to the annuities to be purchased.   [Citations omitted.]   We therefore turn to the facts of the present case as established by the testimony in the record.

Plaintiff, who was born in 1906, is a housewife and has never been gainfully employed.   Her father was a naval medical officer who came from a family of well-to-do professional people;   her mother

---

5. Though the 1942 Act was adopted some two years after plaintiff's divorce from Cornelius Crane, the Act made these provisions applicable, in general, to amounts received in taxable years beginning after December 31, 1941, regardless of the date of the divorce or written instrument.   See Section 120(g) of the Revenue Act of 1942, 56 Stat. 818; Mahana v. United States, 88 F.Supp. 285, 115 Ct.Cl. 716 (1950), cert. den. 339 U.S. 978, 70 S.Ct. 1023, 94 L.Ed. 1383 (1950).

also had considerable means in her own right due largely to her skill as an investor. In 1922 plaintiff was married to a naval flyer but the marriage ended in divorce some seven years later. They had one child, a daughter.

In 1929 plaintiff married Cornelius Crane (hereafter referred to as "Cornelius"), the grandson of the founder of the Crane Company (a manufacturer of plumbing equipment and valves) and the only son of R. T. Crane, Jr., the president and controlling stockholder of that company. The Crane family was possessed of great wealth and its members—including Cornelius and plaintiff—lived on a lavish scale in family mansions in Chicago (their primary residence), Massachusetts and Georgia, and a family apartment at the Ritz in New York. Cornelius, who himself possessed substantial wealth through gifts and inheritance, and also received income from trusts established by his father, was not interested in the family business and at no time in his life held a position for which he received a salary. As a young man he decided he did not want to go to college, but would like to go around the world on a yacht and explore parts of the world which others had not reached. Accordingly, his father bought him a sailing ship which was about 140 feet in length and carried a crew of 26. From this trip he developed an interest in archeology and anthropology, and financed and conducted several expeditions in his vessel to the South Seas. His other interests consisted of hunting, fishing, walking through the woods and reading.

Cornelius' personal budget (as well as that of the entire Crane family) was managed by J. K. Prentice, who had been his father's private secretary, who served as a confidant to the entire family and who stood in place of a father to Cornelius after R. T. Crane, Jr. died. Cornelius had a different attitude toward money than most people. For example, very early in his marriage to plaintiff he became "sick" of Bermuda and suddenly sold for the extraordinarily low price of $25,000 a 26-acre island he owned at the entrance to the harbor in Bermuda, together with a restored house thereon and four boats. He purchased property in Tahiti without ever having seen it. Withal, Cornelius and plaintiff were more alike than different in various respects. Neither had ever been gainfully employed. While Cornelius occupied himself with his interests in archeology and anthropology, plaintiff occupied herself with giving singing concerts (which were artistic successes rather than profitable ventures) and with charitable endeavors. Both were unconcerned with, and uninterested in, finances and property. Thus, until her marriage to Cornelius, plaintiff relied on her mother completely to manage stocks and bonds which her mother and grandmother had given her; after the marriage she turned her investments over to the Crane family to manage. During her marriage to Cornelius, her stock and bond holdings were augmented by gifts from Cornelius and his father, and as of February 1940 had a market value of about $347,000, which produced a yield of about $13,000 in that year.

Throughout his marriage to plaintiff, Cornelius continued his sailing expeditions and was away for extended periods of time; plaintiff did not accompany him on these trips. After February 1936, Cornelius and plaintiff did not live together as man and wife, although he continued to support her and her daughter by her first marriage. By 1939, plaintiff was considering getting a divorce and retained an attorney, but did not pursue the matter further at that time. In the latter part of that year, Cornelius adopted plaintiff's daughter, the adoption being prompted at least in part by his desire to effect a reconciliation with plaintiff. (Plaintiff and Cornelius had no children of their own.) Thereafter, upon the happening of some incident, plaintiff finally reached a firm decision to go ahead with the divorce and filed a divorce action in the Circuit Court of Cook County, Illinois, on February 19, 1940. The divorce was granted on the ground of desertion on February 23, 1940. Up to the final day of the divorce, Cornelius tried to dissuade plaintiff from going through with it. Plaintiff and Cornelius remained friendly at all times during, before and after the divorce proceedings.

At the time that she finally decided to proceed with the divorce, plaintiff's attorney indicated to her that she had a dower right and that such right was a third of an estate. Plaintiff told her attorney that she wanted a lump-sum settlement and asked him to find out from Cornelius what would be fair. She felt that having been a good wife something was due her and she wanted any settlement in a lump sum so that she would never again have to go back to Cornelius and ask for anything—for household money and things like that in the future; she wanted all ties cut.

Meanwhile, Cornelius discussed the matter with his advisers and stated that he would be willing to make a reasonable property settlement, based on his assets, to take care of plaintiff and that he wanted to be, if anything, liberal in the amount of such settlement. He requested one of his advisers to ascertain the amount of income-producing assets he had under his control and it was determined that they were worth about $2,000,000. Cornelius thereupon indicated to his attorney that if he died without a will, plaintiff would get one-third of that amount. The attorney said that that would probably be right by virtue of her dower rights.[6] Cornelius then stated to his advisers that he and plaintiff had been married for ten years; that he thought he should make a property settlement which substantially represented her dower rights in his assets; and that he would give her $650,000, approximately one-third of his assets of $2,000,000. After having so

---

6. Under Chapter 3, Section 11 of the Illinois Code, effective January 1, 1940 (Ill.Rev.Stat.1941, Ch. 3, § 162), the surviving spouse of a resident intestate decedent was entitled to one-third of his real and personal property when there was also a surviving descendant of the decedent; under Chapter 3, Section 14, a lawfully adopted child was deemed a descendant for this purpose (Ill.Rev.Stat.1941, Ch. 3, § 165).

decided (and also determining what he would give to plaintiff's daughter whom he had adopted), he told his advisers to work out the details.

J. K. Prentice (who, as previously indicated, managed Cornelius' personal budget) approved of Cornelius' decision to make a liberal settlement for plaintiff, but opposed turning over liquid assets to her since he was afraid she might give them away or that someone might take them from her. Consequently, he felt strongly that the sum to be paid should be so invested that she could not dissipate her principal, and he urged that annuities be used for that purpose. He mentioned the subject to plaintiff; she respected and trusted Prentice and when he recommended annuities to her, she accepted this recommendation and asked Cornelius to take care of buying the annuities for her, insisting, however, that Cornelius be given a contingent right to receive refunds under the annuity contracts in the event of her death. The actual arrangements for the purchase of annuities were handled by Cornelius' advisers who made inquiries of insurance companies to ascertain how much of an annuity for a person of plaintiff's age and description could be bought for $650,000 and were informed by such insurance companies that approximately $647,000 would buy an exact or round amount of $25,000 per year. The amount of the income to be paid was the result of the determination of the approximate amount of the principal to be paid, not the cause of such amount.

In the discussions Cornelius had with his advisers there was no mention of alimony; Cornelius simply determined that he would give plaintiff part of his assets. Nor did anyone at any time mention alimony in the discussions in which plaintiff participated with her attorney, Cornelius or any of his advisers. During the course of the negotiations, Cornelius told her she would receive a lump sum and plaintiff understood that she would get a "one-time payment."

At the time of the divorce, plaintiff did not transfer any of her property to Cornelius, except for such items as primitive artifacts that had no great intrinsic value. Nor, with the exception of some household items, did Cornelius transfer any property to plaintiff at the time of the divorce other than the amount provided in the Agreement of February 20, 1940.

Following the divorce, plaintiff in March 1940 married her present husband, a portrait painter, who has been successful artistically though not financially.

Subsequently, in accordance with the Agreement of February 20, 1940, plaintiff (and her present husband) granted to Cornelius quitclaim deeds and released to him all rights in property Cornelius owned in Massachusetts and Tahiti. Cornelius fulfilled his obligations under the Agreement by liquidating a substantial portion of his income-producing assets and having one of his advisers in the months following the divorce purchase 13 annuity policies from various insurance companies to provide total annual payments of $25,000 to plaintiff.

Plaintiff's standard of living changed markedly after her divorce from Cornelius since she could no longer live in the kind of lavish luxury produced by the Crane family's great wealth. In the tax years here involved, plaintiff has received dividend and interest income from her stocks and bonds (which are now worth about $1,000,000) of from $23,000 to $30,000 a year, which income is over and above the $25,000 each year received under the annuity contracts. The $25,000 annuity is commingled with her dividend income and is used for normal living expenses, taxes, investments, savings, etc.

In summary, the record shows that at no time during the negotiation of the Agreement of February 20, 1940 was there any mention of alimony. Plaintiff did not request it and Cornelius did not mention it. Nor was there any attempt to determine the extent or the dollar value of Cornelius' obligation to support plaintiff or to pay alimony. The record shows, rather, that the amount which plaintiff received pursuant to the Agreement was derived solely on the basis of the income-producing property then owned outright by Cornelius and what the parties understood to be plaintiff's intestate share in his estate or "dower" rights; and that such amount was determined without reference to any obligation to support or pay alimony. Thus, it seems evident that the amounts paid by Cornelius for the annuity contracts were not based on the marital obligation to support and were not intended to be payments in discharge of such an obligation but rather were intended to be in the nature of a property settlement [7] under which plaintiff's inchoate interests in Cornelius' property under Illinois law were extinguished.[8]

In addition to these considerations, other factors present here provide further indication that the annuity payments to plaintiff do not have the usual characteristics of alimony or support.[9] See generally 5 Mertens, Law of Federal Income Taxation, § 31A.02, pp. 20–1. First, the fact that the payments were to continue for the lifetime of the plaintiff, without regard to her remarriage or the death

7. It is not necessary that there be an exact, mathematical division of property in order for a divorce agreement to constitute a property settlement. In Scott v. United States, 225 F.Supp. 257 (D.Oreg.1963), it was held that payments received by the wife were pursuant to a property settlement and not taxable under Section 71, even though neither the wife nor the husband knew what property stood in their individual names and what property stood in their joint names.

8. Even under the somewhat unusual facts of the present case, it would be unrealistic to regard the transaction here as a gift. "Property transferred pursuant to a negotiated settlement in return for the release of admittedly valuable [inchoate marital] rights is not a gift in any sense of the term." United States v. Davis, 370 U.S. 65, 69, fn. 6, 82 S.Ct. 1190, 1192, 8 L.Ed. 2d 335 (1962).

9. The concept of "alimony" and "support" under Section 71 is not governed by "the laws of different States concerning the existence and continuance of an obligation to pay alimony." H.Rep. 2333, 77th Cong., 2d Sess., p. 72 (1942). See also e. g., Taylor v. Campbell, 335 F.2d 841, 845–846 (5th Cir. 1964); Bardwell v. Commissioner of Internal Revenue, 318 F.2d 786, 789 (10th Cir. 1963).

of her ex-husband, tends to show that they were not intended as alimony or in discharge of a marital obligation to support. Soltermann v. United States, 272 F.2d 387, 390 (9th Cir. 1959); Campbell v. Lake, 220 F.2d 341, 343 (5th Cir. 1955); Scofield v. Greer, 185 F.2d 551, 552 (5th Cir. 1950). See also Anno. 39 A.L.R.2d 1406 (1955); 48 A.L.R.2d 270 (1956). Cf. Ada M. Dixon, 44 T.C. 709, 713 (1965). It is relevant, also, that plaintiff received and exercised the right to determine the beneficiary of refunds that might be payable after her death. It would appear that if the annuity payments had been intended as support payments for plaintiff, Cornelius, rather than plaintiff, would have retained and exercised the power to determine the recipient of any part of the sum not needed for that purpose.

In addition, it is customary for support payments to be related to the husband's income and, frequently, to vary if there is a substantial change in such income. See Ann Hairston Ryker, 33 T.C. 924, 929 (1960); Brown v. United States, 121 F.Supp. 106, 107 (N.D.Cal.1954). The wife is ordinarily entitled to be supported in the same style of living to which she was accustomed during the marriage. [Citations omitted.] The amount of the wife's own income is, obviously, also a factor in determining her need for support. Here the payments were not related in any way to Cornelius' substantial income. The parties agreed on a lump sum based entirely on assets which he owned outright, without reference to the trust income he received, and then fixed the amount of the annual payments on the basis of what annuities the lump sum would buy. There could be no variation, of course, because of changes in Cornelius' income (or because of any property which he might later inherit). Nor was plaintiff's income considered in any way as a factor in determining the amount to be paid. Furthermore, the amount of the annuity payments, even when combined with plaintiff's income from her stocks and bonds, could not possibly allow her to live in a style which would in any way approach that to which she had been accustomed as Cornelius' wife, and the record in fact shows that her standard of living changed markedly after the divorce.

Another factor of significance is whether or not there is a fixed sum the husband is required to pay; the absence of such a fixed sum is considered to indicate that support was intended. Taylor v. Campbell, 335 F.2d 841, 845 (5th Cir. 1964); Bardwell v. Commissioner of Internal Revenue, 318 F.2d 786, 789 (10th Cir. 1963); Campbell v. Lake, 220 F.2d 341, 343 (5th Cir. 1955); Ann Hairston Ryker, 33 T.C. 924, 929 (1960). Here the contract itself specifically provides the amount which the husband was required to pay and the record shows that the settlement was determined on the basis of his paying such amount.

In conclusion, the record establishes that Cornelius Crane did not pay the consideration for the annuity contracts because of any marital obligation to support plaintiff and, accordingly, the annuity payments

are not taxable under Section 71.[10]   Plaintiffs are entitled to a refund of income tax for the years involved based on the application
of the rules of Section 72 to the annuity payments received in each
year.

NOTE

The *Bernatschke* case illustrates a potential tax difficulty in any
separation or divorce.   The problem is one that can be resolved to the
mutual satisfaction of the parties, however, by an awareness of the issue and careful drafting of the separation and property settlement
agreements.   The regulations [1] state that the provisions of section 71
(a) apply only to payments "made because of the family or marital relationship *in recognition of the general obligation to support* which is
made specific by the decree, instrument or agreement."   The obvious
effect of this limitation on the scope of section 71(a) is that payments
which are not in the nature of support are neither includible in the recipient's gross income nor deductible by the payor.[2]   Although there
is no statutory authority for the "support" requirement, other than the
requirement that the obligation must rest "on the marital or family relationship", the legislative history [3] of the predecessor of section 71 indicates that Congress intended this construction and, as *Bernatschke* [4]
indicates, most courts have accepted it.[5]

It is well established that payments made to effect a division of
property between the spouses are not made for "support" and consequently are not within the provisions of section 71(a).[6]   The characterization of payments either as "alimony" (in the nature of support) or as part of a property settlement is a factual determination
which, like many tax factual questions, is dependent upon the intent
of the parties [7] to be determined by all facts and circumstances surrounding the agreement.[8]   The mere labeling of payments as "alimony" or "support" either in an agreement between the parties or in

10. In view of this conclusion, it is unnecessary to pass upon plaintiff's alternative contention that she in substance purchased the annuities with
her own money, with Cornelius acting, in effect, as her agent for that
purpose.

1. I.R.C. Reg. § 1.71–1(b)(4), emphasis added.

2. The tax consequences of such payments are considered in conjunction
with the *Davis* case at pages 159
through 165, supra.

3. H.Rep.No.2333, 77th Cong. 2d Sess.
72 (1942); S.Rep.No.1631, 77th Cong.
2d Sess. 83–85 (1942), 1942–2 C.B.
372, 409 and 504, 568, respectively.

4. Bernatschke v. U. S., the principal
case, supra p. 221.

5. See Harris, "The Federal Income
Tax Treatment of Alimony Payments
—The 'Support' Requirement of the
Regulations," 22 Hastings L.J. 53
(1970).

6. Ernest H. Mills, 442 F.2d 1149 (10th
Cir. 1971); Ann Hairston Ryker, 33
T.C. 924, 929 (1960).

7. Phinney v. Mauk, 411 F.2d 1196
(5th Cir. 1969).

8. Taylor v. Campbell, 335 F.2d 841
(5th Cir. 1964); Bardwell v. Comm'r,
318 F.2d 786, 789 (10th Cir. 1963).

a divorce decree will not control their status.[9] The *Bernatschke* court and others have recognized several factors that are relevant in ascertaining the intent of the parties as to the character of the payments.[10] In *Bernatschke,* the court put substantial emphasis on the discussions leading up to the payments, indicating that negotiations prior to the agreement ought to be considered. However, no one factor by itself is controlling.

The form of payment is often an important factor. An obligation discharged by a transfer of specific property or a lump sum of cash will not be held deductible alimony.[11] On the other hand, if there is a series of payments fairly uniform in size, the payments will probably be viewed as "support" [12] in absence of other factors indicating an intended property settlement. If an initial cash or other payment is disproportionately large in relation to subsequent payments, there is authority sensibly characterizing the payments separately, treating the former as a property division and the latter as support payments.[13]

Some contingencies modifying a payment obligation are factors bearing a strong indication that the payments represent "support" rather than a property division.[14] Contingencies of this type, either provided by agreement or imposed by state law, are those that would normally affect support expectations of the recipient spouse, such as the death of either the payor or the recipient, remarriage of the recipient, and change in economic status of either the payor or recipient.[15] Although the contingency factor is one of the most significant in determining the status of payments, the mere presence or absence of contingencies is not necessarily dispositive of the issue.

If periodic payments have been made prior to the divorce decree, whether voluntarily or pursuant to a formal separation agreement, and such payments are comparable in amount to payments specified in a subsequent separation agreement or the divorce decree, some courts have viewed this as a factor favoring "support" characterization for the later payments.[16] Similarly, where an agreement provides for

---

9. Lewis B. Jackson, Jr., 54 T.C. 125, 130 (1970).

10. See Ben C. Land, 61 T.C. 675, 683 (1974), for a brief discussion of these factors.

11. Schwab v. Comm'r, 442 F.2d 40 (7th Cir. 1971). Whether a lump sum payment is intended as a property settlement or for support the tax consequences are the same, no income to the recipient and no deduction by the payor, because such payments fail the periodicity requirement uniformly provided in each paragraph of § 71(a).

12. Hazel Porter, 25 T.C.M. 448 (1966), aff'd per curiam, 388 F.2d 670 (6th Cir. 1968).

13. *Schwab,* supra note 11 at 42.

14. Blanche C. Newbury, 46 T.C. 690, 695 (1966).

15. The contingency of the payments is also relevant in determining a separate issue, e. g., whether the payments meet the "periodic" requirement of § 71(a). Contingencies, as well as exceptions expressed in § 71 (c)(2), may avoid the rule of § 71(c) (1) that installment payments of a principal sum cannot be treated as periodic payments. See Part B, which follows.

16. Julia Nathan, 19 T.C. 865 (1953); Landa v. Comm'r, 93 U.S.App.D.C. 265, 211 F.2d 46 (1954).

more than one kind of payment and clearly separates one set of payments with "support" characteristics from another that resemble a property settlement, courts have tended to rely on inferences reasonably drawn from the agreement in resolving a dispute as to the character of the sets of payments.[17]

PROBLEM

Determine to what extent the following payments are likely in the nature of "support" and therefore potentially subject to the provisions of § 71(a):

(a) The divorce decree directs Husband to transfer Heartache Hill acres and $10,000 cash to Wife within one month after entry of the decree.

(b) The divorce decree directs Wife to pay Husband $5000 per year until Husband's death or remarriage.

(c) The divorce decree directs Husband to pay Wife $5000 per year plus interest for the next 11 years in repayment of a $55,000 loan.

(d) Husband and Wife were domiciled in California, a community property state, and obtained a divorce there. Wife's share of the community property was found to be $60,000. The divorce decree directed Husband to pay Wife $10,000 per year for 12 years.

(e) Husband and Wife obtain a divorce in a common law state. Husband agreed in the property settlement agreement to pay Wife $18,000 per year for 11 years, but on Wife's remarriage or death the payment is reduced to $6,000 per year, for any balance of the term.

B. PERIODIC ALIMONY PAYMENTS

Internal Revenue Code: Sections 71(a), (c); 215 (first sentence).
Regulations: Section 1.71–1(a), (b), (d).

The 1942 Act provided that alimony and support payments would be taxed to a wife only if she was "legally separated from her husband under a decree of divorce or of separate maintenance"[1] and therefore encompassed only payments currently within I.R.C. (26 U.S.C.A.) § 71 (a)(1). Thus prior to 1954, in the absence of the requisite judicial decree, previously established tax common law principles prevailed.

---

17. E. g., Van Orman v. Comm'r, 418   **1.** I.R.C. (1939) § 22(k).
F.2d 170 (7th Cir. 1969).

In 1954 I.R.C. (26 U.S.C.A.) § 71(a) was expanded to accord alimony treatment to certain payments under a written separation agreement, even though there had been no judicial proceeding,[2] and to certain temporary payments made under a judicial order for support, even though there had been neither a decree of divorce or separation nor any written separation agreement.[3]

The major prerequisite to the application of all paragraphs of I.R.C. (26 U.S.C.A.) § 71(a), and therefore a like condition to the application of § 215, is that the payments in question be "periodic".[4] The only *statutory* definition of periodic payments appears in I.R.C. (26 U.S.C.A.) § 71(c)(2). But that definition is not exclusive, and the true flavor of the concept is developed in the cases and administrative pronouncements.[5] The significance of this requirement, other basic tests under § 71(a), and related special rules expressed in I.R.C. (26 U.S.C.A.) § 71(c) may be examined in connection with the *Baker* case and the problems that follow it, immediately below. Payments that do not meet the § 71 requirements are outside I.R.C. (26 U.S.C.A.) § 71(a) and consequently are neither includible in gross income of the wife nor deductible by the husband under § 215. This is a tax factor that enters prominently into the bargaining process in divorce settlements.

BAKER v. COMMISSIONER

United States Court of Appeals, Second Circuit, 1953.
205 F.2d 369.

FRANK, CIRCUIT JUDGE. As the facts are stated in the opinion of the Tax Court, reported in 17 T.C. 1610, they will not be repeated here.

The separation agreement made between the taxpayer Mr. Baker and his former wife, and incorporated in the divorce decree, provided that he was to pay her $300 per month from September 1, 1946 to August 31, 1947, and $200 a month from September 1, 1947 to August 31, 1952, but that, should she die or remarry, his obligation to make any such payments thereafter would cease.[1] The Tax Court held that these were "installment payments"—within § 22(k) of the Internal

---

2. I.R.C. (26 U.S.C.A.) § 71(a)(2).

3. I.R.C. (26 U.S.C.A.) § 71(a)(3).

4. Note that the term "periodic payments" appears in all three paragraphs of I.R.C. (26 U.S.C.A.) § 71 (a). There is a general analysis of the alimony provisions in Rudick, "Tax Consequences of Marriage and Its Termination," (ALI–ABA 1964); Rosenkrantz, "Divorce and the Federal Income Tax," 16 U. of Fla.L.Rev. 1 (1963); see also Wren, "Tax Problems Incident to Divorce and Property Settlements," 49 Calif.L.Rev. 665 (1961); Holland, Piper, Bailey, and Sander, "Matrimony, Divorce, and Separation," 18 N.Y.U.Inst. on Fed. Tax. 901 (1960).

5. Reg. § 1.71–1(d)(3).

1. Provisions for reduction of these payments in certain circumstances need not here be considered, for, as the Tax Court said, their only relevant effect was to extend the prescribed period of payments from a period of six years to a maximum of seven years and eight months.

Revenue Code, 26 U.S.C.A.,—each discharging "a part of an obligation the principal sum of which is   *   *   *   specified in the decree". We do not agree.

Section 22(k) differentiates "periodic payments" and "installment payments." The latter, as the wording shows, must be parts of a "principal sum." Here no such sum was explicitly stated in figures. But the Tax Court said: "Simple arithmetic indicates that the principal sum to be paid was $15,600"—in other words, the addition of the several payments. Were there no contingencies, this conclusion might be sound. But there are contingencies which the Tax Court ignored. In doing so, it cited Steinel, 10 T.C. 409, at page 410, where it had said that "the word 'obligation' is used in § 22(k) in its general sense and includes obligations subject to contingencies where those contingencies have not arisen and have not avoided the obligation during the taxable years." [2] We see no justification for this interpretation.

We need not decide whether the words "principal sum" exclude all annuities, even those predictable actuarially, as would be the case here if the sole contingency reducing the payments were the wife's death. For here there was the further contingency of the wife's remarriage, and no proof of any actuarial computations in respect of such a contingency. Since a divorced wife's remarriage—in most instances in this respect unlike her death—depends upon some elements of her own seemingly unpredictable choosing, the computation seems as far beyond the reach of an educated guess as what will be the first name of the man or woman who will become President of the United States in 1983. True, in Commissioner of Internal Revenue v. Maresi, 2 Cir., 156 F.2d 929, we affirmed a decision of the Tax Court, 6 T.C. 582, which relied on American experience tables, relating to the chances of the continued celibacy of widows, in determining the chance that a particular divorced woman would take with a new spouse. [3] In the Maresi case, however, the question was whether we should appraise a concededly deductible estate at zero; we said, in effect, that there were means to guess at its value, unreliable perhaps, but still better than nothing, and that in such circumstances a poor guess was better than an almost certain mistake, i. e., to say that the estate was worth nothing. [4] And we there applied a statute dealing with the valuation of interests which, by their very nature, are guessy. [5] But the language of the statute before us in the instant case—"the principal sum *   *   *   specified in the decree"—clearly implies an amount of a fairly definite character, and thus carries with it no such suggestion

---

2. See to the same effect, Estate of Orsatti, 12 T.C. 188, and Fleming v. Commissioner, 14 T.C. 1308.

3. That here the wife in fact remarried in September, 1949 is irrelevant.

4. See Bankers Trust Co. v. Higgins, 2 Cir., 136 F.2d 477, 479.

5. See, e. g., Commissioner of Internal Revenue v. Marshall, 2 Cir., 125 F.2d 943, 946; cf. Andrews v. Commissioner, 2 Cir., 135 F.2d 314.

of uncertainty.[6] Consequently, in this respect, we reverse the decision of the Tax Court.

* * *

Reversed in part.

PROBLEMS

In each of the questions that follow, unless there is an express statement to the contrary, assume that the payments are "alimony or support" in the sense that they are made "because of the marital or family relationship" within § 71(a)(1) and (2), and that they can fall within § 71(a) if the other requirements of the subsection are met.

1.) Husband and Wife are divorced. Analyze the tax consequences to each in the following circumstances assuming in each case, except in 1(c), that the payment was required by the divorce decree.

(a) Husband pays Wife $2000 per month in alimony, as required by the decree until the death of either spouse or the remarriage of Wife.

(b) Husband pays Wife $2000 per month in alimony for five years, as required by the decree but his obligation ceases on the death of either spouse, or the remarriage of Wife.

(c) Same as (a), above, except that the decree provided that the $2000 payments terminated only on the death or remarriage of Wife. Several years subsequent to the decree, Husband and Wife enter into a written substitute agreement, valid although not approved by the court, that Husband will pay Wife $2500 per month but that the payments will terminate on the death of either or on her remarriage. Consider the consequences of the $2500 payments.

(d) Husband pays Wife $24,000 under a decree that calls for one $24,000 payment each year for ten years, the first payment to be made one month after the divorce decree becomes final and all later payments to be made on corresponding dates. The payments are to be made in all events, by Husband, or by his estate in the event of his death.

(e) Same as (d), above, except that the court retains the power to alter the amount of the payments in the event of a change of economic status of either of the parties.

(f) Husband pays Wife $24,000 under a decree that calls for $24,000 payments for ten years, the payments to begin one year and one day subsequent to the decree. The payments are to be made in all events, by Husband, or by his estate in the event of his death.

---

6. Cf. Rohmer v. Commissioner, 2 Cir., 153 F.2d 61, 65: "It is well to remember that the concepts employed in construing one section of a statute are not necessarily pertinent when construing another with a distinguishable background."

(g) Same as (f), above, except that the payments are to satisfy Wife's statutory rights in lieu of dower.

(h) Same as (f), above, except that in year two Husband prepays the full $240,000.

(i) Same as (f), above, except that in the first year of payments Husband is able to pay only $18,000, but in the second year of payments he makes up the arrearage and the current obligation with a payment of $30,000.

(j) Same as (a), above, except that Wife remarries and although his obligation has ceased, Husband continues to make the $2000 payments.

2. After many years of married life Husband and Wife separated. He agreed with her orally that she would get $2000 each month. Neither divorce nor reconciliation are in the wind. Husband has substantial salary and investment income; Wife is entirely dependent on Husband. One day, in the current year, Husband gets a call from Attorney, a friend of Wife's, who says he can suggest a way for Husband to increase his support of Wife to $2500 each month at no greater out-of-pocket expense to Husband.

(a) Is this quite likely so? Explain.

(b) What additional requirement must be met? Why is that requirement present?

3. Husband and Wife separate and agree to a divorce and, without making any formal property or support arrangements, Husband voluntarily pays Wife the $2000 a month they anticipate he will have to pay under the divorce decree when it is obtained the next year. If they file separate returns for the year of separation, will Wife be required to include the payments in her income under § 71(a)(3)?

C. OTHER ASPECTS OF ALIMONY PAYMENTS

---

1. CHILD SUPPORT

Internal Revenue Code: Section 71(b).
Regulations: Section 1.71–1(e).

COMMISSIONER v. LESTER *

Supreme Court of the United States, 1961.
366 U.S. 299, 81 S.Ct. 1343.

MR. JUSTICE CLARK delivered the opinion of the Court.

The sole question presented by this suit, in which the Government seeks to recover personal income tax deficiencies, involves the validity of respondent's deductions from his gross income for the taxable years 1951 and 1952 of the whole of his periodic payments during those years to his divorced wife pursuant to a written agreement entered into by them and approved by the divorce court. The Commissioner claims that language in this agreement providing "[i]n the event that any of the [three] children of the parties hereto shall marry, become emancipated, or die, then the payments herein specified shall * * * be reduced in a sum equal to one-sixth of the payments which would thereafter otherwise accrue" sufficiently identifies one-half of the periodic payments as having been "payable for the support" of the taxpayer's minor children under § 22(k) of the Internal Revenue Code of 1939 and, therefore, not deductible by him under § 23(u) of the Code.[1] The Tax Court approved the Commissioner's disallowance, 32 T.C. 1156, but the Court of Appeals reversed, 279 F.2d 354, holding that the agreement did not "fix" with requisite clarity any specific amount or portion of the periodic payments as payable for the support of the children and that all sums paid to the wife under the agreement were, therefore, deductible from respondent's gross income under the alimony provision of § 23(u). To resolve a conflict among the Courts of Appeals on the question,[2] we granted certiorari. 364 U.S. 890. We have concluded that the Congress intended that, to come within the exception portion of § 22(k), the agreement providing for the periodic payments must specifically state the amounts or parts thereof allocable

---

* See Miller, "Supreme Court in Lester Makes Form of Child-Support Agreement Controlling," 15 J.Tax. 208 (1961). Ed.

1. [I.R.C. (1939) §§ 22(k) and 23(u) are omitted. See I.R.C. (1954) §§ 71(b) and 215. Ed.]

2. Both Metcalf v. Commissioner, 271 F.2d 288 (C.A.1st Cir.1959), and Eisinger v. Commissioner, 250 F.2d 303 (C. A.9th Cir. 1957), have arrived at conclusions contrary to those of the court below.

to the support of the children. Accordingly, we affirm the judgment of the Court of Appeals.

Prior to 1942, a taxpayer was generally not entitled to deduct from gross income amounts payable to a former spouse as alimony, Douglas v. Willcuts, 296 U.S. 1 (1935), except in situations in which the divorce decree, the settlement agreement and state law operated as a complete discharge of the liability for support. Helvering v. Fitch, 309 U.S. 149 (1940). The hearings, Senate debates and the Report of the Ways and Means Committee of the House all indicate that it was the intention of Congress, in enacting § 22(k) and § 23(u) of the Code, to eliminate the uncertain and inconsistent tax consequences resulting from the many variations in state law. "[T]he amendments are designed to remove the uncertainty as to the tax consequences of payments made to a divorced spouse * * *." S.Rep. No. 673, Pt. 1, 77th Cong., 1st Sess. 32. They "will produce uniformity in the treatment of amounts paid * * * regardless of variance in the laws of different States * * *." H.R.Rep. No. 2333, 77th Cong., 2d Sess. 72. In addition, Congress realized that the "increased surtax rates[3] would intensify" the hardship on the husband who in many cases, "would not have sufficient income left after paying alimony to meet his income tax obligations," H.R.Rep. No. 2333, 77th Cong., 2d Sess. 46, and perhaps also that, on the other hand, the wife, generally being in a lower income tax bracket than the husband, could more easily protect herself in the agreement and in the final analysis receive a larger net payment from the husband if he could deduct the gross payment from his income.

The first version of § 22(k) was proposed by the Senate as an amendment to the Revenue Act of 1941. The sums going to child support were to be includible in the husband's gross income [sic] only if the amount thereof was "specifically designated as a sum payable for the support of minor children of the spouses." H.R. 5417, 77th Cong., 1st Sess., § 117. The proposed amendment thus drew a distinction between a case in which the amount for child support was "specifically designated" in the agreement, and one in which there was no such designation. In the latter event, "the whole of such amounts are includible in the income of the wife. * * *" S.Rep. No. 673, Pt. 1, 77th Cong., 1st Sess. 35. Action on the bill was deferred by the conference committee[4] and hearings on the measure were again held the following year. The subsequent Report of the Senate Finance Committee on § 22(k) carried forward the term "specifically designated," used in the 1941 Report (No. 673), with this observation:

"If, however, the periodic payments * * * are received by the wife for the support and maintenance of herself and of minor chil-

---

3. Sections 22(k) and 23(u) were enacted as part of the Revenue Act of 1942 which provided for greatly increased tax revenue to meet the expenses of World War II.

4. H.R.Rep. No. 1203, 77th Cong., 1st Sess. 11.

dren of the husband without such specific designation of the portion
for the support of such children, then the whole of such amounts is includible in the income of the wife as provided in section 22(k).   *   * "
S.Rep. No. 1631, 77th Cong., 2d Sess. 86.*

As finally enacted in 1942, the Congress used the word "fix" instead
of the term "specifically designated," but the change was explained
in the Senate hearings as "a little more streamlined language." Hearings before Senate Committee on Finance on H.R. 7378, 77th Cong.,
2d Sess. 48. As the Office of the Legislative Counsel reported to the
Senate Committee:

> "If an amount is specified in the decree of divorce attributable to
> the support of minor children, that amount is not income of the wife.
> *   *   * If, however, that amount paid the wife includes the support
> of children, *but no amount is specified for the support of the children*,
> the entire amount goes into the income of the wife.   *   *   * " *Ibid.*
> (Italics supplied.)

This language leaves no room for doubt. The agreement must expressly specify or "fix" a sum certain or percentage of the payment for
child support before any of the payment is excluded from the wife's
income. The statutory requirement is strict and carefully worded.
It does not say that "a sufficiently clear purpose" on the part of the
parties is sufficient to shift the tax. It says that the "written instrument" must "fix" that "portion of the payment" which is to go to the
support of the children. Otherwise, the wife must pay the tax on the
whole payment. We are obliged to enforce this mandate of the Congress.

One of the basic precepts of the income tax law is that "[t]he income that is subject to a man's unfettered command and that he is
free to enjoy at his own option may be taxed to him as his income,
whether he sees fit to enjoy it or not." Corliss v. Bowers, 281 U.S.
376, 378 (1930). Under the type of agreement here, the wife is free
to spend the monies paid under the agreement as she sees fit. "The
power to dispose of income is the equivalent of ownership of it." Helvering v. Horst, 311 U.S. 112, 118 (1940). Including the entire payments in the wife's gross income under such circumstances, therefore,
comports with the underlying philosophy of the Code. And, as we
have frequently stated, the Code must be given "as great an internal
symmetry and consistency as its words permit." United States v.
Olympic Radio & Television, 349 U.S. 232, 236 (1955).

It does not appear that the Congress was concerned with the perhaps restricted uses of unspecified child-support payments permitted
the wife by state law when it made those sums includible within the
wife's alimony income. Its concern was with a revenue measure and

* This Report and this quotation appear at 1942-2 C.B. 504, 570, respectively. Ed.

with the specificity, for income tax purposes, of the amount payable under the terms of the written agreement for support of the children. Therefore, in construing that revenue act, we too are unconcerned with the variant legal obligations, if any, which such an agreement, by construction of its nonspecific provisions under local rules, imposes upon the wife to use a certain portion of the payments solely for the support of the children. The Code merely affords the husband a deduction for any portion of such payment not specifically earmarked in the agreement as payable for the support of the children.

As we read § 22(k), the Congress was in effect giving the husband and wife the power to shift a portion of the tax burden from the wife to the husband by the use of a simple provision in the settlement agreement which fixed the specific portion of the periodic payment made to the wife as payable for the support of the children. Here the agreement does not so specifically provide. On the contrary, it calls merely for the payment of certain monies to the wife for the support of herself and the children. The Commissioner makes much of the fact that the agreement provides that as, if, and when any one of the children married, became emancipated or died the total payment would be reduced by one-sixth, saying that this provision did "fix" one-half (one-sixth multiplied by three, the number of children) of the total payment as payable for the support of the children. However, the agreement also pretermitted the entire payment in the event of the wife's remarriage and it is as consistent to say that this provision had just the opposite effect. It was just such uncertainty in tax consequences that the Congress intended to and, we believe, did eliminate when it said that the child-support payments should be "specifically designated" or, as the section finally directed, "fixed." It does not say that "a sufficiently clear purpose" on the part of the parties would satisfy. It says that the written instrument must "fix" that amount or "portion of the payment" which is to go to the support of the children.

The Commissioner contends that administrative interpretation has been consistently to the contrary. It appears, however, that there was such a contrariety of opinion among the Courts of Appeals that the Commissioner was obliged as late as 1959 to issue a Revenue Ruling which stated that the Service would follow the rationale of Eisinger v. Commissioner, 250 F.2d 303 (C.A.9th Cir. 1957),[5] but that Weil v. Commissioner, 240 F.2d 584 (C.A.2d Cir. 1957),[6] would be

---

5. The court there approved the rule that "when the settlement agreement, read as a whole, discloses that the parties have earmarked or designated * * * the payments to be made, one part to be payable for alimony, and another part to be payable for the support of children, with sufficient certainty and specificity to readily determine which is which, without reference to contingencies which may never come into being, then the 'part of any periodic payment' has been fixed 'by the terms of the decree or written instrument' * * *." 250 F. 2d, at 308.

6. In that case the agreement provided for reductions only in the event the divorced wife remarried. The court

followed "in cases involving similar facts and circumstances." Rev. Rul. 59–93, 1959–1 Cum.Bull. 22, 23.

All of these considerations lead to the conclusion that if there is to be certainty in the tax consequences of such agreements the allocations to child support made therein must be "specifically designated" and not left to determination by inference or conjecture. We believe that the Congress has so demanded in § 22(k). After all, the parties may for tax purposes act as their best interests dictate, provided, as that section requires, their action be clear and specific. Certainly the Congress has required no more and expects no less.

Affirmed.

MR. JUSTICE DOUGLAS, concurring.

While I join the opinion of the Court, I add a few words. In an early income tax case, Mr. Justice Holmes said "Men must turn square corners when they deal with the Government." Rock Island, A. & L. R. Co. v. United States, 254 U.S. 141, 143. The revenue laws have become so complicated and intricate that I think the Government in moving against the citizen should also turn square corners. The Act, 1939 I.R.C. § 22(k), makes taxable to the husband that part of alimony payments "which the terms of the decree or written instrument fix, in terms of an amount of money or a portion of the payment, as a sum" payable for support of minor children.

I agree with the Court that this agreement did not "fix" any such amount. To be sure, an amount payable in support of minor children may be inferred from the *proviso* that one-sixth of the payment shall no longer be due, if the children marry, become emancipated, or die. But Congress in enacting this law realized that some portion of alimony taxable to the wife might be used for support of the children, as the opinion of the Court makes clear.

The present agreement makes no specific designation of the portion that is intended for the support of the children. It is not enough to say that the sum can be computed. Congress drew a clear line when it used the word "fix." Resort to litigation, rather than to Congress, for a change in the law is too often the temptation of government which has a longer purse and more endurance than any taxpayer.

PROBLEMS

1. Husband and Wife enter into a support agreement which is approved by the court when they are divorced. They have one child who is in Wife's custody. Discuss the tax consequences to Husband and Wife in the following situations:

    (a) The agreement provides that Husband will pay Wife $2000 per month until her death or remarriage but that the amount

stated that "[t]he fortuitous or incidental mention of a figure in a provision meant to be inoperative, unless some more or less probable future event occurs, will not suffice to shift the tax burden from the wife to the husband." 240 F.2d, at 588.

will be reduced to $1500 per month in ten years when Child reaches majority. In the event that Wife dies or remarries, $500 per month will be paid to Child until majority. Husband makes the agreed payments in this taxable year.

(b) What rationale is behind the "hard-nosed" reasoning in (a), above?

(c) The agreement provides that Husband will pay Wife $1500 per month until her death or remarriage and an additional $500 per month for the support of Child which will terminate when Child reaches majority.

(d) What result in (c), above, if Husband pays only $12,000 of his $24,000 obligation in the current year?

---

2. INDIRECT BENEFITS

Internal Revenue Code: Section 101(e).

JAMES PARKS BRADLEY

30 T.C. 701 (1958).

Opinion

TIETJENS, JUDGE: The Commissioner determined the following deficiencies in income tax against petitioners:

Year	Deficiency
1952	$3,254.03
1953	3,501.28
1954	469.31

The several questions for decision are as follows: (1) Whether the rental value of the residence occupied rent-free by petitioner's former wife in the taxable years constitutes periodic alimony payments deductible by him within the meaning of sections 22(k) and 23(u) of the Internal Revenue Code of 1939 and sections 71 and 215 of the Internal Revenue Code of 1954; * * * and (4) whether premiums paid by petitioner on certain life insurance policies are deductible under those sections.

All of the facts are stipulated, are so found, and the stipulations together with the pertinent exhibits are incorporated herein by this reference.

James Parks Bradley and Jane L. Bradley are husband and wife. They filed joint income tax returns for the taxable years on a cash basis with the district director of internal revenue, San Francisco, California.

James was formerly married to Frances D. Bradley from whom he was divorced in 1946. James and Frances entered into a property settlement agreement on May 14, 1946, which was subsequently incorporated and approved in the divorce decree.

* * *

Record title to the premises located at 2750 Scott Street, San Francisco, at the time of the divorce, during the tax years involved, and as of March 1958, was and is vested in James.

In accordance with the terms of the property agreement petitioner removed his personal possessions from the residence and left Frances in sole possession of the premises. In 1948 Frances married Glenn Lane and during the years 1952, 1953, and 1954 they resided in the house. They paid no rent for the use of these premises. No rental income from this source was reported by James in his income tax returns.

* * *

At the time of the divorce decree, the fair market value of the building located at 2750 Scott Street, San Francisco, was $60,000 and at that time the building had a useful life of 25 years. Its fair rental value is stipulated to be $500 per month during the taxable years.

During the calendar years 1952, 1953, and 1954 petitioner paid premiums on the policies of life insurance referred to above, in the following respective amounts: $1,167.50, $1,164.20, and $1,155.30. These policies were ordinary life insurance as distinguished from term insurance or endowment policies.

The original beneficiary provision on policy No. 8–042–277 issued by Prudential Insurance Company provided in material part as follows:

> If this Policy matures at death, the proceeds then payable in accordance with the terms of the Policy shall be payable forthwith to Frances D. Bradley, Beneficiary, wife of the Insured, if living, otherwise in equal shares to the living children, if any, of the Insured, Beneficiaries, otherwise to the executors or administrators of the Insured.

On January 7, 1947, the said policy was amended under the "Provisions as to Rights Under Policy" as follows:

> This Policy is hereby amended to provide that the following right(s) under the Policy, viz.: to remove or replace Frances D. Bradley, former wife of the Insured, as Beneficiary, to assign the Policy against the interest of said Beneficiary

except as security for a loan made by the Company to pay premiums under the Policy, to designate settlement under the Provisions as to Modes of Settlement or to revoke any such designation, to obtain cash loans, cash surrender values, or to secure reduced paid-up insurance, may be exercised by the Insured during the lifetime of said Frances D. Bradley only with the written consent of said Frances D. Bradley any provision of the Policy to the contrary notwithstanding.

The beneficiary designation on policy No. 600540 and policy No. 600541, issued by the Lincoln National Life Insurance Company under date of April 23, 1941, provides in relevant part as follows:

Frances D. Bradley, wife of the Insured. If living, otherwise to any then living children that may be born of the marriage of the Insured and said wife and any then living children that may be legally adopted by said wife and the Insured during their marriage, the survivor or survivors equally, but if there be no survivor, to the Executors, Administrators or Assigns of the Insured, with right of revocation, subject to the terms and conditions of the policy.
* * *

On December 23, 1946, the beneficiary provision was changed by interlineation to read as follows:

Frances D. Bradley, *former* wife of the Insured, if living, *without right of revocation*, otherwise to any then living children * * * [Italics supplied to designate the changes made by interlineation.]

By letter of January 6, 1956, the Lincoln National Life Insurance Company advised James, with respect to the then present status of policies No. 600–540–A10 and No. 600–541–A10, as follows:

As the policies now stand, the signature of Frances D. Bradley is required for any request of the Insured in connection with the policies such as changing the beneficiary, making a policy loan, assigning the policies or surrendering the policies for cash.

James, prior to December 31, 1954, did not request consent from Frances to:

a. remove or replace Frances D. Bradley, former wife of petitioner, as beneficiary of any of the policies;

b. assign the interest of said beneficiary;

c. designate settlement under the provisions as to modes of settlement;

d. revoke any such designations;

   e.   obtain cash loans;

   f.   procure cash surrender values;

   g.   secure reduced paid-up insurance.

And James, prior to December 31, 1954, took none of the above-mentioned actions.

From the date of the divorce decree until the present time the insurance policies have been in the custody and possession of Frances.

On the Federal income tax returns filed by the petitioners for the taxable year 1952, petitioners claimed and deducted from income the amount of $5,967.50 as alimony. The Commissioner disallowed this deduction on the ground that it did not constitute an allowable deduction under the provisions of section 23(u).

On petitioners' Federal income tax return for the year 1953, the amount of $7,164.20 was claimed as an alimony deduction. The Commissioner disallowed this deduction as not allowable under the provisions of section 23(u).

On petitioners' Federal income tax return for the year 1954, the amount of $7,155.30 was claimed as an alimony deduction. The Commissioner, in explaining his adjustments to income, said:

    (a) The deductions claimed in your return for $6,000.-00, representing the rental value of a home furnished pursuant to a divorce decree and $1,155.30 representing life insurance premiums paid pursuant to a divorce decree are disallowed as not constituting allowable deductions under the provisions of Section 215(a) of the Internal Revenue Code (1954).

In substance, petitioners' contention is that the arrangement concerning the rent-free use of the residential premises conferred a monthly economic benefit of $500 on Frances during the time she occupied the residence; that this economic benefit was taxable to her as alimony and, accordingly, that James, her former husband, was entitled to deduct $6,000 in each of the taxable years as "periodic payments" received by the wife from him in discharge of a legal obligation incurred under a written agreement incident to divorce.

So far as we can ascertain this contention has never before been presented for decision to this Court. It has, however, been rejected by the Court of Appeals for the Fifth Circuit in Pappenheimer v. Allen, 164 F.2d 428, affirming 71 F.Supp. 788. The petitioners' arguments in attempting to show error in the decision of the Fifth Circuit are unconvincing. We are content to concur in the following reasoning from the *Pappenheimer* case:

    Pappenheimer urges that the monthly rental values of the home are "periodic payments" received in discharge of, or attributable to property transferred in discharge of, a legal marital obligation imposed on him by the divorce agreement and decree and made income to his wife by Section 22(k). The district judge held there were no periodic payments in any ordinary sense, and we agree. It is true that a payment may be made in property, and if the enjoyment of the residence be thought of as a payment of his alimony, it was a payment by transferring a property right in the home; but then it is not periodic, but is a single right to occupy until her death or remarriage, or until the children both leave her, or marry or reach the age of twenty-three. Nobody paid any monthly rent. She occupied under the right granted her, as a sort of estate. But if the rental values can be considered "periodic payments", they are attributable to property transferred and Section 22(k) goes on to say that although they are income to the wife, "Such amounts received as are attributable to property so transferred shall not be includible in the gross income of such husband", and the last sentence of Section 23(u) says that because of that provision in 22(k) the husband may have no deduction. The theory of the subsections is that the wife shall pay tax on what she periodically receives from the husband in money or property. If he pays money, it will ordinarily be from his taxed income, and he is granted a deduction to avoid double taxation to him and his former wife. If the payments are attributable to property transferred, the wife is to be taxed on them, but they are not to be taxed to the husband as income because he did not receive them; but he has no deduction because they did not form part of his taxed income. * * * [Footnote omitted.]

* * *

The remaining question is whether the premium payments on the life insurance policies described above are deductible as alimony. We think they are not. This question has been dealt with in a number of decisions by this Court and the Courts of Appeals in varying fact situations. See Anita Quimby Stewart, 9 T.C. 195; Lemuel Alexander Carmichael, 14 T.C. 1356; Smith's Estate v. Commissioner, (C.A. 3) 208 F.2d 349, reversing in part a Memorandum Opinion of this Court; Lilian Bond Smith, 21 T.C. 353; Raoul Walsh, 21 T.C. 1063. The cases stand for the proposition that where the wife's interest in the policies is simply that of a contingent beneficiary—that is, where the policies have not been assigned to her in such a way that she becomes the actual owner and where the proceeds of the policies become hers only if she outlives her husband—the premiums paid by the husband are not deductible by him. We think that is the situation here. The policies were never assigned to Frances. Under the agreement James bound himself to continue to pay the premiums and not to remove Frances as beneficiary so long as she should live. Although Frances held possession of the policies, that was not enough to make her their owner. Should she predecease James her interest ceased. Paraphrasing the language of Judge Black in *Raoul Walsh,* supra:

We think it also may be correctly said in the instant case that Frances' only interest in the policies of insurance on James' life is contingent and that the premiums on the policies were not paid for her sole benefit. She will only receive benefits from these policies in case she survives James. We sustain the Commissioner in his disallowance of the net premiums which James paid on the insurance policies in the taxable years. They did not represent periodic payments of alimony to Frances.

Decision will be entered for the respondent.

PROBLEMS

Husband and Wife are divorced and Wife has custody of their two minor children. Pursuant to a written separation agreement approved by the divorce court Husband is required:

(a) To pay Wife $1000 per month for the support of Wife and the children. The obligation is to be reduced by a stated amount on Wife's death or remarriage and by stated amounts as each of the children reaches majority.

(b) To provide medical insurance for Wife for the same period and for the children until majority.

(c) To transfer their family home worth $80,000 but subject to a $20,000 mortgage outright to Wife. The property has a monthly fair rental value of $500. Also, to make the mortgage payments of $250 per month on the property; this obligation ceases on the death of either party or on Wife's remarriage.

(d) To purchase a $50,000 ordinary life insurance policy on Husband's life and transfer it outright to Wife. Preferring to satisfy his obligation immediately, Husband buys a single premium paid-up policy of a face amount of $50,000 for which he pays $30,000.

(e) To purchase term insurance naming Wife as owner-beneficiary to satisfy his obligations in (a) and (b), above, in the event of Husband's death. The current annual premium on the term insurance is $1,000.

Discuss the tax consequences of the above provisions to both Husband and Wife.

3. DIVORCE

REVENUE RULING 67–442 *

1967–2 Cum.Bull. 65.

Advice has been requested whether an *ex parte* divorce is valid for Federal income tax purposes even though the divorce has been invalidated by a state court under the circumstances described below.

The taxpayer obtained an *ex parte* divorce in Mexico in 1961. His divorce was promptly challenged by his first wife and subsequently declared invalid in 1963 by a state court with personal jurisdiction of the parties and jurisdiction of the subject matter of the action. A marriage entered into by the husband following the Mexican divorce was also declared to be invalid.

G.C.M. 25250, C.B. 1947–2, 32, holds that a Mexican divorce decree of a couple domiciled in Connecticut will be recognized for Federal income tax purposes, even though it was doubtful that the Connecticut courts would recognize the validity of the Mexican decree. However, the Connecticut court was never presented with the issue of the validity of the particular Mexican decree. See Revenue Ruling 57–113, C.B. 1957–1, 106, which states that the position taken in G.C.M. 25250 was not intended to recognize the Mexican decree over subsequent decrees in other jurisdictions.

The Internal Revenue Service generally will not question for Federal income tax purposes the validity of any divorce decree until a court of competent jurisdiction declares the divorce to be invalid.** However, where a state court, in a proceeding in which there is personal jurisdiction of the parties or jurisdiction of the subject matter of the action, declares the prior divorce to be invalid, the Service will usually follow the later court decision rather than the divorce decree for Federal income tax purposes for such years as may not be barred by the statute of limitations. In this regard the Service will not follow the decisions in Estate of Herman Borax v. Commissioner, 349 F.2d 666 (1965), certiorari denied, 383 U.S. 935 (1966), and Harold E. Wondsel v. Commissioner, 350 F.2d 339 (1965), certiorari denied 383 U.S. 935 (1966).

Furthermore, the Service will not follow the Borax and Wondsel decisions in the disposition of cases involving questions of marital status for Federal estate and gift tax purposes, such as questions per-

---

* See Spolter, "Invalid Divorce Decrees," 24 Tax L.Rev. 163 (1969); Kapp, "Tax Aspects of Alimony Agreements and Divorce Decrees: The Effect of Conflicting Decrees," 27 N.Y.U.Inst. on Fed.Tax. 1231 (1969); the conflict of laws question is considered in detail in Currie, "Suitcase Divorce in the Conflict of Laws: Simons, Rosentiel, and Borax," 34 U.Chi.L.Rev. 26 (1966). Ed.

** This principle is further applied in Rev.Rul. 71–390, 1971–2 C.B. 82. Ed.

taining to the marital deductions allowed by sections 2056 and 2523 of the Internal Revenue Code of 1954.

G.C.M. 25250 is clarified to remove any possible implication that the Service will follow invalidated divorce decrees for Federal income tax purposes.

NOTE

In *Borax* the taxpayer had obtained a Mexican divorce. The decree provided for alimony payments to be made to his ex-wife. After the taxpayer had married another woman, his ex-wife obtained an ex parte decree in New York holding the Mexican divorce to be invalid. In *Wondsel* the facts were essentially the same as those in *Borax* except that the divorce decree was entered by a Florida court. In each case, the Court of Appeals for the Second Circuit held the divorce decrees to be valid for federal income tax purposes. Accordingly, the Court concluded that the respective taxpayers were entitled to deduct the alimony payments under § 215 and further, that they were entitled to file joint income tax returns with their current wives under § 6013.[1]

In the application of I.R.C. (26 U.S.C.A.) § 71, the courts, over the Commissioner's objection, have equated an annulment to a divorce with the usual inclusion and deduction consequences to the parties.[2] The Commissioner now agrees.[3]

D. NONDEDUCTIBLE ALIMONY

Internal Revenue Code: Sections 71(a), (d) ; 215, 682.
Regulations: Sections 1.71–1(c) ; 1.215–1.

The objective here in part is to pull together some peripheral problems that arise in connection with payments and property transfers occasioned by separation and divorce. A modest excursion into the area of trusts is inescapable, and these comments may be more

1. But see Harold K. Lee, 64 T.C. 552 (1975), limiting *Borax* and *Wondsel* to alimony situations, stating that marriage is authorized and defined by state law alone, and denying taxpayer the right to file a joint return with his current wife. Taxpayer has appealed. And see Estate of Wesley A. Steffke, 64 T.C. 530 (1975), and Estate of Leo J. Goldwater, 64 T.C. 540 (1975), again limiting *Borax* and *Wondsel* to alimony situations refusing to allow § 2056 marital deductions to taxpayers' current wives.

2. Anna E. Laster, 48 T.C. 178 (1967); George F. Reisman, 49 T.C. 570 (1968); Andrew M. Newburger, 61 T.C. 457 (1974).

3. Acquiescence in the *Laster* and *Reisman* cases, supra note 2, appears at 1971–2 C.B. 3.

meaningful after the student has explored the note in Chapter 14 at page 301, although even there the taxation of trusts is not considered in depth.

It is possible now to see an overall pattern in I.R.C. (26 U.S.C.A.) §§ 71 and 215. If a husband hangs on to his property and discharges his obligation to support a divorced wife piece-meal (by "periodic" payments), she is taxed on such payments and he may deduct them. If instead he discharges the obligation by giving his wife some of his property in one transfer (a payment that is not "periodic"), the transfer may be without tax significance to either.[1] But, of course, as the transferred property produces income it will be income taxable to the wife and not the husband. Thus no tax hardship such as prompted the 1942 legislative reversal of the *Gould* principle is presented. A lump sum settlement accomplishes an *actual* splitting of income (with tax liability in accord with the economic reality), making unnecessary the somewhat artificial splitting accomplished in other circumstances by the § 71 inclusion and § 215 deduction.[2]

The question dealt with here is: What are the consequences of a lump sum transfer by the husband that does not go directly to her but which results in periodic receipts to the wife? Some facets of this problem arose in connection with the *Bernatschke* case, in Part A, supra page 221, where, however, the emphasis was only on the tax status of the recipient wife. There was no question that she was in receipt of periodic payments ($25,000 per year under the annuity policies), but she escaped tax on the full amount under § 71(a), and was taxed under § 72, because the arrangement was considered in the nature of a property settlement, rather than in discharge of the support obligation arising out of the family relationship. Suppose the decision had gone the other way on this issue; would the husband then be entitled to a deduction for amounts received by the wife? The answer is no, based upon the last sentence of § 215 and § 71(d). Under the latter, the husband may exclude from his income amounts taxed to the wife which are attributable to property that he has transferred. And under § 215 amounts so excluded properly give rise to no deduction. Note again the essentially income-splitting objective of these provisions.[3]

1. Even gift tax neutrality can be assured. See I.R.C. (26 U.S.C.A.) § 2516. Recall, however, the possibility of taxable gain on a transfer of appreciated property, as in the *Davis* case, supra, page 159.

2. The 10-year rule of I.R.C. (26 U.S.C.A.) § 71(c)(2) can be seen to be a somewhat arbitrary classification of equivocal transfers as essentially lump sum and of neutral tax significance if paid over a short period or periodic taxable and deductible ali-

mony if spread over more than ten years.

3. To put it mildly, a number of tax concepts merge here to complicate this problem beyond the presentation in the text. For example, the exclusionary rule of § 71(d) is not needed in the *Bernatschke* setting to screen the husband from tax liability. While the principles of Old Colony Trust Co. v. Comm'r, 279 U.S. 716, 49 S.Ct. 499 (1929), may tax one on amounts paid in discharge of his obligation,

The student will quickly see a distinction between the purchase of annuity policies for the wife and the following arrangement, although the economic significance to the wife may not vary greatly. Suppose the husband opens a savings account, deposits half a million dollars in it, and directs the bank to pay the wife the interest, which might amount to $25,000 annually. This arrangement is unaffected by § 71(d) and the second sentence of § 215, because there is no "transferred property." That is, the half million dollars remains the property of the husband, even though he has directed the interest on it to be paid to his wife, whereas the annuities, as in *Bernatschke*, became the property of the wife and the annuity payments were attributable to such transferred property. The bank account arrangement would invoke the routine application of §§ 71(a) and 215. Under the *Horst* principle,[4] the interest income would be that of the husband and taxable to him, but § 71(a) would also tax the wife on such amounts as she received them, and § 215 would give the husband a corresponding deduction (not an exclusion). In other words the result is the same as if the husband had simply drawn the interest himself and made commensurate payments to the wife. If the payments in *Bernatschke* were in the nature of alimony would the husband have been better off having the annuity paid to him, he then paying the amount to wife? Why might wife not be agreeable to such an arrangement from a non-tax point of view?

Outside the annuity area, the most likely circumstances for the application of the rules of § 71(d) and the second sentence of § 215 involve trusts. Suppose, for example, the decree requires that the husband discharge his support obligation by the transfer of a specified amount of property to a trust under the terms of which the income is to be paid to the wife for her life or until her remarriage with provision for distribution of the remainder to the husband or to others upon the wife's death. Money or property placed in such a trust does constitute transferred property.[5] Thus, amounts paid to the wife are attributable to transferred property and are taxable to her under § 71(a) and, even though they operate to discharge a continuing obligation of the husband, the amounts are excluded from his gross income by § 71(d). He needs and gets no deduction for such payments under § 215, second sentence. We are talking about an "alimony trust." The beneficiaries of such trusts are taxed *outside* the regular taxation of trusts rules of Subchapter J and, even

the *annual* payments to the wife would discharge no such obligation; *that* obligation was eliminated with the *purchase* of the annuities. Of course, since the purchase had that effect it could have resulted in tax liability, if the purchase had involved the transfer of appreciated property, rather than a mere payment of cash.

Cf., U. S. v. Davis, 370 U.S. 65, 82 S. Ct. 1190 (1962).

4. Helvering v. Horst, 311 U.S. 112, 61 S.Ct. 144 (1940). See Chapter 13, infra at page 275.

5. Cf. Blair v. Comm'r, 300 U.S. 5, 57 S.Ct. 330 (1937).

if a wife receives amounts from the trust in excess of its income, she is taxed on the entire amount received as alimony under § 71(a).[6]

There is a possibility a husband has set up a trust for his wife's support, *not* in accordance with any separation agreement and *not* in accordance with a divorce decree or any instrument incident thereto. If the parties are then divorced and her rights under the trust continue, she is then receiving support payments that are *outside* the rules of § 71(a). Check the statute. Tax liability with respect to the income of such trusts *is* determined under the rules of Subchapter J, including the "grantor trust" provisions [7] and § 682 which is addressed to just this situation.

The big difference to the wife with respect to such "pre-existing trusts" (those not arising out of the separation) is that she is taxed in the same manner as any other trust beneficiary, except that, in keeping with § 71(b) which is a pervasive exception, she is relieved of tax on amounts fixed for support of minor children of the husband.[8] Prior to divorce, the income of a support trust of this sort would be taxed to the grantor husband.[9] These principles continue to leave him taxable on income used to discharge his obligation to support his children. But income used to support the wife herself after the divorce becomes *her* income in the tax sense, and the husband is relieved of tax on it, yielding an income-splitting effect similar to that which in other circumstances is achieved under I.R.C. (26 U.S. C.A.) §§ 71(a) and 215.

One might wonder about the difference in treatment of the "alimony" trust and the "pre-existing" trust. The answer is that in the case of a pre-existing trust any amounts to which the wife is entitled beyond income earned by the trust are acquired by gift. The usual trust rules accomplish this result by tagging such amounts as principal rather than income distributions.[10] However, if a trust is *set up* to discharge an alimony obligation, amounts received by the wife in excess of trust income keep their alimony flavor and logically are not treated as received by gift.[11] In effect, this prevents a husband from conferring a special tax favor on the divorced wife by, for example, setting up a trust for her with the income *and principal* to be paid out to her over twelve years. As such payments would be

---

6. In the case of trusts that are subject to the rules of Subchapter J, the amount on which a beneficiary can be taxed is limited to the trust's distributable net income. I.R.C. (26 U.S.C. A.) §§ 652, 662. Taxability of the alimony trust itself is determined under Subchapter J but, for this purpose, the recipient wife is treated as a beneficiary, I.R.C. (26 U.S.C.A.) § 682(b), so that in general such trusts escape actual tax liability by way of the distribution deduction. I.R.C. (26 U.S.C. A.) §§ 651, 661; see Ferguson, Freeland, and Stephens, Federal Income Taxation of Estates and Beneficiaries, 583–594 (Little, Brown 1970).

7. I.R.C. (26 U.S.C.A.) §§ 671–678.

8. I.R.C. (26 U.S.C.A.) § 682(a), second sentence.

9. I.R.C. (26 U.S.C.A.) § 677(a) and (b).

10. See I.R.C. (26 U.S.C.A.) §§ 102, 652, 662.

11. But see Ellis v. U. S., 416 F.2d 894 (6th Cir. 1969) and Anita Quinby Stewart, 9 T.C. 195 (1947).

fully taxed to the wife under § 71(a) if made directly, they are also taxed fully to her if made through the vehicle of a trust. However, if a trust vehicle is used, pursuant to which the amounts paid to the wife simply constitute installment payments of a principal sum then, since it is a § 71 trust, the provisions of § 71(c) apply. If such payments are within § 71(c) (1), the payments are not gross income to the wife.[12] In this circumstance, since the trust is used as a vehicle for discharging the husband's obligation, *he* is the taxpayer on the trust's income so used.[13]

12. See Richard T. Daniel, Jr., 56 T.C. 655 (1971).

13. I.R.C. (26 U.S.C.A.) § 677; see also Reg. § 1.643(c)–1. For a discussion of nondeductible alimony see Peschel, "Income Taxation of Alimony Payments Attributable to Transferred Property: Congressional Confusion," 44 Tulane L.Rev. 223 (1970).

CHAPTER 12. OTHER EXCLUSIONS FROM GROSS INCOME

A. MISCELLANEOUS STATUTORY EXCLUSIONS

Internal Revenue Code: See Sections 109; 112; 113; 116; 911; 1019.

There are several statutory exclusions from gross income, not identified elsewhere in the book, but of sufficient significance to warrant brief discussion. Not all exclusions from gross income occur as a result of a specific statutory provision in the Internal Revenue Code. In the case of fringe benefits we have already seen an example of administrative exclusions. Similarly benefits received under federal Social Security legislation are also administratively excluded from gross income.[1] Items may also be excluded from gross income by federal legislation not within the Internal Revenue Code. For example, payments of benefits under any law administered by the Veteran's Administration are excluded from gross income by Title 38 of the United States Code.[2] This chapter considers only statutory exclusions under the Internal Revenue Code and only those sections listed above.[3] I.R.C. (26 U.S.C.A.) § 103, excluding interest paid on some governmental obligations which has constitutional overtones is taken up, along with other constitutional concepts, at page 256, infra.

I.R.C. (26 U.S.C.A.) §§ 109 and 1019. Congress in 1942 enacted I.R.C. (26 U.S.C.A.) § 109 which provides that improvements, other than those intended as rent, made by a lessee on a lessor's real property are to be excluded from the lessor's gross income. A companion provision, § 1019, specifies that, if § 109 applies, the lessor receives no increase in the basis of his property as a result of the improvements.[4] The overall effect of I.R.C. (26 U.S.C.A.) §§ 109 and 1019

---

1. Old age and survivors insurance benefit payments are excluded by Rev.Rul. 70–217, 1970–1 C.B. 12, and medicare benefits by Rev.Rul. 70–341, 1970–2 C.B. 31. See Reg. § 1.61–11(b). This includes educational assistance allowances. See Rev.Rul. 71–536, 1971–2 C.B. 78. Compare Rev.Rul. 76–121, 1976–1 C.B. 24, holding social security benefits paid by the United Kingdom to a resident of the United States includible in gross income and Rev.Rul. 66–34, 1966–1 C.B. 22, involving a similar payment by Germany to a United States resident.

2. 38 U.S.C. § 3101(a). Cf. Strickland v. Comm'r, 540 F.2d 1196 (4th Cir. 1976).

3. I.R.C. (26 U.S.C.A.) §§ 110, 114, and 122 are not discussed in the book.

4. See Schlesinger, "Consequences to Lessor of Lessee Construction," 17 N. Y.U.Inst. on Fed.Tax. 697 (1959).

is that non-rental improvements are not required to be included in income at the time they are received but, when the lessor subsequently sells the property, they will generate income (or reduce loss) to the extent that they have increased the value of the property,[5] as illustrated in problem 1(e) at page 145 of the text.

I.R.C. (26 U.S.C.A.) §§ 112 and 113. Although payments to military personnel are generally included in gross income,[6] Congress has carved out some exceptions in limited circumstances. Under I.R.C. (26 U.S.C.A.) § 112 military personnel below the rank of commissioned officers, but including warrant officers, may exclude all compensation received for services in a combat zone and compensation for periods during which the serviceman is hospitalized as a result of wounds, disease, or injury incurred while serving in a combat zone. A similar exclusion for commissioned officers is limited to $500 per month. In addition, the section excludes compensation of members of the armed forces of the United States and of civilian governmental employees for periods during which they were prisoners of war, missing in action, or in a detained status during the Viet Nam conflict.[7] Under I.R.C. (26 U.S.C.A.) § 113, amounts received by military personnel as mustering-out payments are excluded from gross income.[8]

I.R.C. (26 U.S.C.A.) § 116. Since 1964, I.R.C. (26 U.S.C.A.) § 116 has permitted each taxpayer to exclude from gross income up to $100 received as dividends from domestic corporations.[9] What policy reason justifies this exclusion? Should it be either increased or abandoned? Are similar exclusions available for $100 of interest on savings accounts, or on bonds? Is interest properly differentiated from dividends for this purpose? [10]

Husbands and wives are treated separately under I.R.C. (26 U.S.C.A.) § 116. Each is entitled to a $100 exclusion but, if a husband receives $150 of domestic dividends and his wife receives only $50, they must include in gross income the $50 which is in excess of the husband's exclusion, even though they file a joint income tax return and their total dividends are only $200.[11] However, if husband

---

5. But see I.R.C. (26 U.S.C.A.) § 1023 and the discussion at page 156, supra. I.R.C. (26 U.S.C.A.) §§ 109 and 1019 would also in many circumstances convert the value of the improvements from ordinary income to capital gain. See generally Chapter 21, infra.

6. I.R.C. (26 U.S.C.A.) § 61(a)(1).

7. I.R.C. § 112(d).

8. Some tax benefits for military personnel, not limited to those expressed in the Internal Revenue Code, are discussed in Weiss, "Tax Problems of the Serviceman," 34 Taxes 277 (1956); on the deduction side, see also Behren, "Many Tax Deductions Are Overlooked by Military Reservists," 16 J. Tax. 232 (1962).

9. A pre-1965 exclusion of only $50 was coupled with a more meaningful tax credit measured by the entire amount of dividend income. See I.R.C. (26 U.S.C.A.) § 34 (repealed).

10. See I.R.C. (26 U.S.C.A. § 163 and the discussion at page 465, infra.

11. Reg. § 1.116–1(b).

and wife hold stock jointly and each has a right to one half of the dividends, or if they have similar income rights under a state's community property laws, they can secure the benefit of a full $200 exclusion whether they file jointly or separately.[12]

I.R.C. (26 U.S.C.A.) § 911. Finally, income earned abroad sometimes escapes the federal income tax. I.R.C. (26 U.S.C.A.) § 911 excludes from gross income certain "earned income," such as wages, salaries, and other compensation for personal services rendered by United States citizens outside of the United States.[13] If a taxpayer is engaged in a trade or business in which both personal services and capital are material income-producing factors, he may be able to treat as qualified compensation for services an amount not in excess of 30% of his net profits.[14] The exclusion does not apply to amounts paid by the United States or any of its agencies [15] but, otherwise, the source of the compensation, foreign or domestic, is immaterial.[16]

To qualify for the § 911 exclusion a taxpayer must either be a bona fide resident of a foreign country or countries for an uninterrupted period which includes the taxable year,[17] or he must be outside the United States for at least 510 full days during a period of 18 consecutive months.[18]

Even if other requirements of § 911 are met, § 911(c) provides numerous limitations upon the exclusion. Section 911 has been a favorite congressional plaything over the years and, as recently amended, it imposes now in general a $15,000 limitation on excluded income.[19] Here is what the House Ways and Means Committee said in summary of the 1976 changes:

> The conference agreement reduces the present exclusion for income earned abroad by U. S. citizens from $20,000 to $15,000. (Employees of U. S. charitable organizations (section 501(c)(3) organizations) who work abroad will retain the $20,000 earned income exclusion.) In addition, three modifications in the computation of the exclusion are provided. First, any individual entitled to the earned income exclusion may not credit or deduct foreign income taxes paid on excluded income. Second, any income derived by individuals beyond the income eligible for the earned income exclusion

12. Reg. § 1.116–1(c).

13. I.R.C. (26 U.S.C.A.) § 911(b). See Bittker and Ebb, United States Taxation of Foreign Income and Foreign Persons 193–209 (2d Ed. 1968); Note, "Section 911 Tax Reform," 54 Minn. L.Rev. 823 (1970).

14. I.R.C. § 911(b); Reg. § 1.911–2(c).

15. I.R.C. (26 U.S.C.A.) § 911(a).

16. Andrew O. Miller, Jr., 52 T.C. 752 (1969).

17. I.R.C. (26 U.S.C.A.) § 911(a) (1). Criteria for determining bona fide residence are indicated in Reg. §§ 1.911–1(a) (2) and 1.871–2(b).

18. I.R.C. (26 U.S.C.A.) § 911(a) (2). Reg. § 1.911–1(b) (8–11).

19. TRA (1976) § 1011(a).

is subject to U. S. tax at the higher rate brackets which would apply if no exclusion had been allowed. Third, income earned abroad which is received outside the country in which earned in order to avoid tax in that country is ineligible for the earned income exclusion. However, an individual may make a permanent election not to have the earned income exclusion apply at all. Once an election is made not to have the exclusion apply, it is binding for all subsequent years and may be revoked only with the consent of the Internal Revenue Service. The conference agreement also provides that individuals who claim the standard deduction may also claim the foreign tax credit.

These provisions apply to taxable years beginning after December 31, 1975.

A brief historical footnote on the development of the provisions now found in § 911 may be of interest. The exclusion of income earned abroad by nonresident citizens is of longstanding and, originally, was subject to no limitation. But much controversy was created by the addition of an alternative 510 day test, also originally with no limitation on the exclusion. This rule was immediately abused, perhaps especially by the movie industry which could make pictures abroad and pay their stars with tax exempt dollars, if the stars were willing to forsake home and hearth for most of an eighteen month period. So Congress imposed a ceiling on the exclusion for cases in which the taxpayer relied on the 510 day rule. A ceiling now is imposed also on the bona fide nonresident.

B. FEDERAL TAXES AND STATE ACTIVITIES

Internal Revenue Code: Sections 103(a) and (b); 115. See Section 103 (c) and (d).

"The power to tax involves the power to destroy." So said Chief Justice Marshall in 1819 in McCulloch v. Maryland.[1] This hypothesis is the foundation of a doctrine of intergovernmental immunity which imposes some restraint upon undertakings by the federal and local governments to impose taxes that impinge upon each other. The *McCulloch* case itself repudiated a *state* tax on the privilege of issuing bank notes but applicable in fact only to national banks. It was held invalid as an improper interference with powers expressly granted to the federal government. The doctrine finds no express support

---

1.   17 U.S. (4 Wheat.) 316, 431 (1819).

in the Constitution but rests instead upon an implied guarantee of governmental self-preservation. Over the years its scope has become very limited. But, even where the doctrine of intergovernmental immunity may impose no obstacles, there are important policy questions of the extent to which the federal government should exercise restraint in the imposition of taxes that have some impact on the activities of the states.

The philosophy adopted in the *McCulloch* case was applied in reverse in The Collector v. Day.[2] There the court held that a *federal* tax (the Civil War Income Tax) could not be validly imposed on the salary of a *state* judge, because to do so would threaten an essential function of the state. Some time later the reciprocal nature of the doctrine of intergovernmental immunity was expressed as follows:[3]

> As the States cannot tax the powers, the operations, or the property of the United States, nor the means which they employ to carry their powers into execution, so it has been held that the United States have no power under the Constitution to tax either the instrumentalities or the property of a State.

Despite its bold beginning and vigorous earlier life, the doctrine of intergovernmental immunity has suffered a marked decline over about the past half century. Much of its attrition occurred about the time of World War II. By 1939, Mr. Justice Frankfurter was able to refer to John Marshall's classic dictum, quoted above, as a mere "seductive cliche."[4] The reciprocal nature of the doctrine was rejected about this time:[5]

> [I]n laying a federal tax on federal instrumentalities the people of the states, acting through their representatives, are laying a tax on their own institutions and consequently are subject to political restraints which can be counted on to prevent abuse. State taxation of national instrumentalities is subject to no such restraint, for the people outside the state have no representatives who participate in the legislation; and in a real sense, as to them, the taxation is without representation.

See also New York v. U. S., 326 U.S. 572, 577, 66 S.Ct. 310, 312 (1940):

> The considerations bearing upon taxation by the states of activities or agencies of the Federal Government are not corre-

---

2. 78 U.S. (11 Wall.) 113 (1870).

3. Pollock v. Farmers' Loan & Trust Co., 157 U.S. 429, 584, 15 S.Ct. 673, 683 (1895).

4. Graves v. People of State of New York ex rel. O'Keefe, 306 U.S. 466, 489, 59 S.Ct. 595, 602 (1939). Earlier,

Mr. Justice Holmes had delivered the classic comment: "The power to tax is not the power to destroy while this Court sits." Panhandle Oil Co. v. Mississippi ex rel. Knox, 277 U.S. 218, 223, 48 S.Ct. 451, 453 (1928).

5. Helvering v. Gerhardt, 304 U.S. 405, 58 S.Ct. 969, 971 (1938).

lative with the considerations bearing upon federal taxation of state agencies and activities.

The question whether a tax might have an adverse impact on an essential governmental function [6] gave way to consideration whether the tax was imposed even-handedly in a non-discriminatory fashion. After first differentiating the *Day* case in a decision involving a federal tax on somewhat less essential state employees,[7] the court soon overruled it, saying: [8]

> So much of the burden of a non-discriminatory general tax upon the incomes of employees of a government, state or national, as may be passed on economically to that government, through the effect of the tax on the price level of labor or materials, is but the normal incident of the organization within the same territory of two governments, each possessing the taxing power.

Despite the nostalgic feeling it may generate in law professors at state universities, it has now long been settled that neither state nor federal employees enjoy immunity from state or federal income taxes.[9]

Possible application of the tattered doctrine of intergovernmental immunity to the taxation of interest paid on governmental obligations remains a matter of some uncertainty. One ground on which the Supreme Court nullified the 1894 federal income tax was that Congress could not validly tax the interest on state bonds.[11] However, developments since then which condone a federal tax on salaries of state employees go a long way, by analogy, to undermine the basis for this early decision. The argument can be made that a state's activities are no differently affected if it must pay higher (taxable) interest on its bonds than if it must pay higher (taxable) salaries to its employees. Moreover, it has been suggested that the basis for the immunity of state bond interest was obliterated when the Sixteenth Amendment authorized Congress to tax incomes "from whatever source derived." [12]

Nevertheless, the bond interest question has remained largely academic. The states do not tax interest paid on federal bonds [13] and, since its inception, the federal income tax has excluded interest on most state and municipal bonds under provisions now found in

---

6. See The Collector v. Day, supra note 2.

7. Helvering v. Gerhardt, supra note 5.

8. Graves v. People of State of New York ex rel. O'Keefe, supra note 4.

9. See the Public Salary Tax Act of 1939, 53 Stat. 574.

11. Pollock v. Farmers' Loan & Trust Co., supra note 3.

12. Black, J., concurring in Helvering v. Gerhardt, supra note 5 at 425.

13. New York Tax Law § 359(2) (d); A similar exemption is recognized in California which rests only on a statutory provision exempting from tax income which may not constitutionally be taxed. West's Ann.Cal.Rev. & T. Code § 17137.

I.R.C. (26 U.S.C.A.) § 103.[14] The Tax Reform Act of 1976 made no fundamental change in this arrangement.

There is of course an inherent unfairness in the exclusionary rules of § 103. *Should* Congress. continue a provision that generates a huge source of untaxed income?[15] Efforts in Congress to eliminate the inequity have been rebuffed.[16] One problem has been the extent to which such a change might be accorded retroactive effect to tax interest on outstanding state bonds. And of course an acute current problem is the extent to which the near-chaotic state fiscal situation would be further complicated by the increased cost of state borrowing, which would follow if the interest on state bonds were subject to the income tax. There is the possibility that state losses could be made up by the *states* extending their income taxes to interest on federal obligations.[17]

---

14. In recent years there have been some minor encroachments on the broad exclusion under § 103. In 1968, Congress taxed interest on bonds issued by a state or local government to finance private industrial development with some exceptions. See Spiegel, "Financing Private Ventures with Tax Exempt Bonds: A Developing 'Truckhole' in the Tax Law," 17 Stan. L.Rev. 224 (1965); Snodgrass, "Amended Section 103: The Industrial Development Bond Loophole Further Restricted," 30 U. of Pitt.L.Rev. 180 (1968). In 1969, states were issuing tax exempt bonds, paying low interest rates on them because of their exempt status, and investing the proceeds in other securities (generally taxable bonds) with a higher yield. As state income is generally not taxed, (see comments below) the states had a clear gain on the rate differential largely traceable to § 103. Congress provided in general that interest on the state or municipal bonds issued for such purposes (commonly referred to as "arbitrage bonds") is taxable income to the bond holders, although the provision is subject to limited exceptions. For an article prior to the enactment of this restriction see Lewis and Loftis, "The Tax Exempt Status of Local Government Bonds Used in Arbitrage Transactions," 35 Geo.Wash.L.Rev. 574 (1967). A private device for abuse of the § 103 exclusion has long been restrained by § 265(2) which, in general, denies a deduction for interest paid by a taxpayer to purchase or carry tax exempt obligations. See Leslie v. Comm'r, 413 F.2d 636 (2d Cir. 1969),

cert. den. 396 U.S. 1007, 90 S.Ct. 564 (1970). The scope and application of the § 265(2) limitation continues to present problems. See e. g., Phipps v. U. S., 515 F.2d 1099 (Ct.Cl.1975), and Levitt v. U. S., 517 F.2d 1339 (8th Cir. 1975); and see page 470, infra.

15. Note that to a taxpayer at the 50% bracket the yield on a 4% tax-exempt bond is worth the same amount as the yield on an 8% taxable bond; at the 20% bracket the differentials are only 4% and 5%, respectively. See generally, Surrey, "Federal Income Taxation of State and Local Government Obligations," 36 Tax Policy 3 (1969), reprinted in Sander and Westfall, Readings in Federal Taxation, page 277 (1970) and Morris, "Tax Exemption for State and Local Bonds," 42 Geo.Wash.L.Rev. 483 (1974).

16. See Maxwell, "Exclusion from Income of Interest on State and Local Government Obligations," House Comm. on Ways and Means, 86th Cong.2d Sess., 1 Tax Revision Compendium 701, 702–703 (1959). In 1969, an unsuccessful effort was made to bring such interest at least within the reach of the new Minimum Tax for Tax Preferences, I.R.C. (26 U.S.C.A.) §§ 56–58. H.Rep. No. 91–413 (Part 1), 91st Cong. 1st Sess. (1969), 1969–2 C.B. 249.

17. This is one to conjure with. It is likely Congress could by legislation prohibit the imposition of state income taxes on the interest paid on federal obligations. Congressional

It will be observed that the foregoing comments all concern circumstances in which federal income taxes may impinge on the states only indirectly, that is, by way of imposing a tax on an individual or other recipient with respect to amounts *paid* by a state, such as salary or bond interest. What about taxing the *state's* income? From a statutory point of view it is surprising how loosely this matter has been handled.

A great many organizations enjoy express statutory exemption from the federal income tax.[18] Nevertheless, while these provisions may encompass some state-owned instrumentalities, they do not embrace the states as such.[19] This does not mean, however, that the states are subject to tax on their net receipts. Instead, it reflects a generally assumed state exemption. At one time even the Treasury Department considered this exemption to rest on the constitutional doctrine of intergovernmental immunity.[20] But it changed its position and later considered the state's exemption to rest on an interpretation of the statute, which failed to make the state a taxpayer.[21]

As to some types of income, the state's exempt status is supported by I.R.C. (26 U.S.C.A.) § 115(a), which precludes tax on a state's receipts from any public utility and from the exercise of any "essential governmental function." At present, there is only one instance in which amounts received by states or state agencies are in fact subjected to federal income tax.[22] Obviously, as long as Congress and the Treasury did not attempt to subject a state's receipts to the federal income tax, actual questions regarding the scope of the federal power to do so could not arise. Should such questions arise, it now appears they probably will not be answered on a straight state immunity basis.

Among several decisions suggesting some state income may be vulnerable to the federal income tax is New York v. U. S.[23] There the court held that New York, in its sale of mineral waters from Saratoga Springs, was not immune from a federal excise on the sale of soft

---

power to protect its agencies and activities clearly extends beyond any automatic immunities inferred from the Constitution. See Graves v. New York ex rel. O'Keefe, supra note 4, at 478, and cases there cited. However, to do so would seem to lend support to the argument of the states that the imposition of federal income tax on interest paid on state obligations should be precluded under remnants of the constitutional doctrine of intergovernmental immunity on a kind of fair's fair principle.

18. See I.R.C. (26 U.S.C.A.) § 501(c) and (d).

19. See Rev.Rul. 60–351, 1960–2 C.B. 169, 173; but cf. Estate of Leslie E. Johnson, 56 T.C. 944 (1971).

20. G.C.M. 13745, XIII–2 C.B. 76 (1934).

21. G.C.M. 14407, XIV–1 C.B. 103 (1935); and see Rev.Rul. 71–132, 1971–1 C.B. 28, superseding G.C.M. 13745, supra note 20, reaching the same result as the earlier G.C.M. but *without* reference to the immunity doctrine.

22. See I.R.C. (26 U.S.C.A.) § 511(a) (2) (B) which taxes the "unrelated business income" of state colleges and universities.

23. 326 U.S. 572, 66 S.Ct. 310 (1946).

drinks. In the employee salary cases the court finally rejected as a criterion of taxability the question whether the activity in which the employee was engaged constituted an essential governmental function, but the question of essentiality may still have some relevance. Sustaining the excise tax in the *New York* case [24] the court said:

> There are, of course, state activities and state-owned property that partake of uniqueness from the point of view of inter-governmental relations. These inherently constitute a class by themselves. Only a state can own a statehouse; only a state can get income by taxing. These could not be included for purposes of federal taxation in any abstract category of taxpayers without taxing the state as a state. But so long as Congress generally taps a source of revenue by whomsoever earned and not uniquely capable of being earned only by a state, the Constitution of the United States does not forbid it merely because its incidence falls also on a state.

Consider the retail liquor business against this background. In State A liquor stores are state-owned and operated. In State B they are publicly licensed but privately owned and operated. Under present circumstances does this appear to give rise to an inequitable application of the federal income tax laws? [25] If you think so, what do you think should be done about it?

These are at best fragmentary comments on a tax area that has produced a very great amount of administrative, judicial and academic literature. Some of the important articles that examine the cases and competing philosophies in depth include: (1) The classic analysis of the intergovernmental immunities doctrine up to 1946, in Powell, "The Waning of Intergovernmental Tax Immunities," 58 Harv.L.Rev. 633 (1945), and Powell, "The Remnant of Intergovernmental Tax Immunities," 58 Harv.L.Rev. 757 (1945); (2) Frank, "Reciprocal Taxation of Governments," 40 Taxes 468 (1962); (3) Ratchford, "Intergovernmental Tax Immunities in the United States," 6 Nat.Tax.J. 305 (1953); (4) Surrey, "Federal Income Taxation of State and Local Government Obligations," 36 Tax Policy 3 (May–June 1969).

24. Supra note 23, 326 U.S. at 582, 66 S.Ct. at 314.

25. See Rev.Rul. 71–132, supra note 21.

PART THREE: IDENTIFICATION OF THE PROPER TAXPAYER

CHAPTER 13. ASSIGNMENT OF INCOME

A. INTRODUCTION

Internal Revenue Code: Sections 1(a), (c); 6013(a).

An examination of I.R.C. (26 U.S.C.A.) § 1(c), which provides the tax rates applicable to the "taxable income" [1] of unmarried individuals, indicates that a single person with taxable income of $10,000 pays $2090 in taxes; in other words, he is subject to an overall effective rate of roughly 20%. However, when his taxable income increases to $20,000 he pays $5230 in taxes, and the effective rate now exceeds 25%. At $100,000 he pays $53,090, and the effective rate has gone beyond the 50% mark. Even if the rate remained constant, one with more income would pay more tax but only *proportionately* more. The characteristic described of increasing *rates* applicable to additional increments of income stamps the federal income tax as a "progressive" tax. What policy reasons may support the accelerating rates? Are they persuasive? [2]

The progressive income tax rates provide a strong inducement to the fragmentization of income. In many instances it may be a matter of indifference to a taxpayer whether he himself actually receives an item of income or whether it goes instead to a related individual or an economically related artificial entity such as a trust or a corporation. In a sense, the game is have your cake and eat it too and the temptation is great to spread income among family members or entities or both in an effort to reduce total tax liability. As seen above, if an unmarried individual has taxable income of $100,000 he pays $53,090 in taxes; whereas five unmarried individuals each with $20,-000 of taxable income pay only $5,230 each, and the total tax on $100,-000 spread five ways is only $26,150. Thus, although the aggregate income is the same, the five individuals together pay less than one half the tax paid by the single individual. If, for example, a widower with

---

1. Taxable Income, defined in I.R.C. (26 U.S.C.A.) § 63, is essentially the taxpayer's gross income reduced by all allowable deductions. Credits are ignored here.

2. See Blum and Kalven, "The Uneasy Case for Progressive Taxation," 19 U. of Chi.L.Rev. 417 (1952), Smith "High Progressive Tax Rates: Inequity and Immorality?" 20 U. of Fla.L.Rev. 451 (1968).

$100,000 in income could divide that amount equally among himself and his four children, none of whom has other income, he could reduce the family's taxes by over 50%. And maybe he can! But he had better be careful about the method adopted. In the income tax area there are both statutory and judge-made restraints on the "assignment of income," the subject of this and the next Chapter. This Chapter deals with assignments of income to other individuals; Chapter 14 concerns assignments of income when artificial entities, as well as other individuals, enter the picture.

In some instances the Code itself offers either an elective or mandatory provision permitting assignment of income. A mandatory provision appears in I.R.C. (26 U.S.C.A.) § 73. Under some state laws income arising out of the services of a minor child is deemed to be the property of his parents. Conceivably, such income could be taxed to them as *theirs*.[3] However, § 73 provides that "amounts received in respect of the services of a child shall be included in *his* gross income. * * *" Thus, a uniform rule is provided for federal tax purposes, which operates independently of the vagaries of state property laws. Obviously, the rule is generally favorable to taxpayers.[4]

So-called "income-splitting" provisions available on an elective basis to married taxpayers are of greater significance. If they elect to file a joint return,[5] their combined taxable income is taxed at rates provided in § 1(a). If they file separately, each is taxed at rates provided in § 1(d). A comparison of the two rate tables will show that, the tax on the combined taxable income of husband and wife under § 1(a) is twice the tax on one-half their combined taxable income using § 1(d) rates. Consequently, the filing of a joint return, even where one spouse has all the income, produces the same tax as if the income were equally divided and each half were taxed under the § 1(d) rates.[6]

Lucas v. Earl, which follows immediately, is a landmark case. It involved a husband and wife but a tax year before 1948 when income splitting was enacted. What is the present importance of the case? Was the assignment in Lucas v. Earl effected for the tax reasons? Note the date of the contract in the case.

3. But compare Lucas v. Earl with Comm'r v. Giannini, both infra, this Chapter.

4. But see I.R.C. (26 U.S.C.A.) § 6201 (c), sometimes making a parent liable for tax on income included in a child's gross income by § 73.

5. I.R.C. (26 U.S.C.A.) § 6013 permits this, even if one of the spouses has no gross income.

6. This is an artificial splitting only for tax purposes. Before 1971, the statutory splitting device was more apparent in the statute. Pre-1971, I.R.C. (26 U.S.C.A.) § 2(a) provided that, if a joint return was filed, "the tax imposed by section 1 shall be twice the tax which would be imposed if the taxable income were cut in half." The change was required by a reduction in tax rates applicable to unmarried taxpayers. See § 1(c). The origin of this statutory income-splitting device and computation questions concerning the several § 1 rate tables are further explored in Chapter 27, infra.

B. INCOME FROM SERVICES

LUCAS v. EARL

Supreme Court of the United States, 1930.
281 U.S. 111, 50 S.Ct. 241.

MR. JUSTICE HOLMES delivered the opinion of the Court.

This case presents the question whether the respondent, Earl, could be taxed for the whole of the salary and attorney's fees earned by him in the years 1920 and 1921, or should be taxed for only a half of them in view of a contract with his wife which we shall mention. The Commissioner of Internal Revenue and the Board of Tax Appeals imposed a tax upon the whole, but their decision was reversed by the Circuit Court of Appeals, 30 F.2d 898. A writ of certiorari was granted by this Court.

By the contract, made in 1901, Earl and his wife agreed "that any property either of us now has or may hereafter acquire * * * in any way, either by earnings (including salaries, fees, etc.), or any rights by contract or otherwise, during the existence of our marriage, or which we or either of us may receive by gift, bequest, devise, or inheritance, and all the proceeds, issues, and profits of any and all such property shall be treated and considered and hereby is declared to be received, held, taken, and owned by us as joint tenants, and not otherwise, with the right of survivorship." The validity of the contract is not questioned, and we assume it to be unquestionable under the law of the State of California, in which the parties lived. Nevertheless we are of opinion that the Commissioner and Board of Tax Appeals were right.

The Revenue Act of 1918 approved February 24, 1919, c. 18, §§ 210, 211, 212(a), 213(a), 40 Stat. 1057, 1062, 1064, 1065, imposes a tax upon the net income of every individual including "income derived from salaries, wages, or compensation for personal service * * * of whatever kind and in whatever form paid," § 213(a). The provisions of the Revenue Act of 1921, c. 136, 42 Stat. 227, in sections bearing the same numbers are similar to those of the above. A very forcible argument is presented to the effect that the statute seeks to tax only income beneficially received, and that taking the question more technically the salary and fees became the joint property of Earl and his wife on the very first instant on which they were received. We well might hesitate upon the latter proposition, because however the matter might stand between husband and wife he was the only party to the contracts by which the salary and fees were earned, and it is somewhat hard to say that the last step in the performance of those contracts could be taken by anyone but himself alone. But this case is not to be decided by attenuated subtleties. It turns on the import and reasonable construction of the taxing act. There is no doubt that the statute could tax salaries to those who earned them and provide that the tax could not be escaped by anticipatory arrangements and contracts however skilfully devised to prevent the salary when paid from vesting even for a second in the man who earned it. That seems to us the import of the statute before us and we think that no distinction can be taken according to the motives leading to the arrangement by which the fruits are attributed to a different tree from that on which they grew.

Judgment reversed.

The CHIEF JUSTICE took no part in this case.

COMMISSIONER v. GIANNINI

United States Court of Appeals, Ninth Circuit, 1942.
129 F.2d 638.

STEPHENS, CIRCUIT JUDGE. Petition by the Commissioner of Internal Revenue for a review of a decision of the Board of Tax Appeals which is reported at 42 B.T.A. 546 to the effect that there is no deficiency in taxpayer's federal income tax for the year 1928.

The facts upon which the Commissioner relies in claiming a deficiency are as follows:

The taxpayer and his wife at all relevant times were husband and wife and were residents of California. The taxpayer was a Director and President of Bancitaly Corporation from 1919 until its dissolution after the tax year in question. From 1919 to 1925 he performed the services of these offices without compensation, and on January 22, 1925, the Board of Directors authorized a committee of three to devise a plan to compensate him, he in the meantime to have the privilege of drawing upon the corporation for his current expenditures.

On April 19th, 1927, the committee reported and on June 27th, 1927, the Directors unanimously approved the report. It was: "The committee as above met on Wednesday, April 13, 1927, at 2:00 o'clock, in Mr. Fagan's office, in the Crocker First National Bank, San Francisco, and unanimously agreed to, and hereby do, recommend to the directors of the Bancitaly Corporation that Mr. A. P. Giannini, for his services as President of your Corporation, be given 5% of the net profits each year, with a guaranteed minimum of $100,000 per year, commencing January 1, 1927, in lieu of salary." *

On November 20, 1927, the withdrawal account of taxpayer showed an indebtedness to the corporation of $215,603.76, and on that date his account was credited and the salary account on the books of the

---

* About twenty years earlier the directors had voted Mr. Giannini, as founder and vice-president, a salary of $200 a month. Thomas and Witts, the San Francisco Earthquake, 41 (1971). Ed.

corporation was debited with the amount of $445,704.20, being the equivalent of 5% of the corporation net profits from January 1, 1927, to July 22, 1927.

In 1927 after the taxpayer learned the amount of the profits from January to July of that year and that he would receive $445,704.20 as his 5% thereof, the taxpayer informed members of the Board of Directors of the corporation that he would not accept any further compensation for the year 1927, and suggested that the corporation do something worth while with the money. The finding of the Board in this respect is that the refusal was "definite" and "absolute", and there is ample evidence in the record to support such finding.

The corporation never credited to the taxpayer or his wife any portion of the 5% of the net profits for the year 1927, other than the $445,704.20 above referred to, nor did it set any part of the same aside for the use of the taxpayer or his wife. The only action of the corporation in this respect is as follows:

On January 20, 1928, the Board of Directors of Bancitaly Corporation adopted a resolution reading in part as follows:

"Whereas, this Corporation is prepared now to pay to Mr. A. P. Giannini for his services as its President and General Manager five per cent (5%) of the net profits of this Corporation computed from July 23, 1927 to the close of business January 20, 1928, which five percent (5%) amounts to the sum of One Million Five Hundred Thousand Dollars ($1,500,000.00); and

"Whereas, Mr. A. P. Giannini refuses to accept any part of said sum but has indicated that if the Corporation is so minded he would find keen satisfaction in seeing it devote such a sum or any lesser adequate sum to the objects below enumerated or kindred purposes; and

"Whereas, we believe that this Corporation would do a great good and derive a great benefit from the establishment of a Foundation of Agricultural Economics at the University of California, and we believe that something should be done by this Corporation to evidence its appreciation of the fact that without the general confidence and hearty cooperation of the people of the State of California the great success of this Corporation would not have been possible * * *;

*   *   *   *   *   *   *   *   *   *

"Now, Therefore, Be it Resolved, by the Board of Directors of this Corporation, that the aforesaid sum of One Million Five Hundred Thousand Dollars ($1,500,000.00) be set apart from the undivided profits of this Corporation in a Special Reserve Account for the purpose hereinafter described, and the whole of said sum be donated to the Regents of the University of California for the purpose of establishing a Foundation of Agricultural Economics; and

"Be it Further Resolved, that said donation be made in honor of Mr. A. P. Giannini, and that said Foundation shall be named after him; and

"Be it Further Resolved, that a Committee consisting of James A. Bacigalupi, P. C. Hale and A. Pedrini be appointed to confer with the President of the University of California, for the purpose of discussing and determining upon the general scope of said Foundation, and with full power of settling all details in connection therewith; * * * ".

In accordance with said resolution the Corporation in February, 1928, submitted a written offer of contribution to the Regents of the University of California, and the offer was accepted. One deviation occurred in carrying out the plan, however, in that 5% of the profits of the Bancitaly Corporation for the period January 1, 1927, to January 20, 1928, less the sum of $445,704.20 credited to taxpayer amounted to $1,357,607.40 instead of the estimated $1,500,000.00, and the difference of $142,392.60 was paid by the taxpayer personally. There is no question in this appeal concerning this $142,392.60.

The taxpayer and his wife in reporting their income for taxation purposes in 1928 did not report any portion of the $1,357,607.40 paid to the Regents of the University of California by the Bancitaly Corporation as aforesaid, and it is the Commissioner's contention that one-half of said sum should be reported by each.* Based upon this theory the Commissioner assessed a deficiency of $137,343.50 in the case of the taxpayer in this appeal and a deficiency of $123,402.71 in the case of his wife. Separate appeals have been taken by each party, but it is stipulated by the parties that the decision in the wife's case is to abide the final decision in the case now before this court.

The Commissioner's argument in support of the claimed deficiency may be summarized as follows: That actual receipt of money or property is not always necessary to constitute taxable income; that it is the "realization" of taxable income rather than actual receipt which gives rise to the tax; that a taxpayer "realizes" income when he directs the disposition thereof in a manner so that it reaches the object of his bounty; that in the instant case the taxpayer had a right to claim and receive the whole 5% of the corporation profit as compensation for his services; and that his waiver of that right with the suggestion that it be applied to some useful purpose was such a disposition thereof as to render the taxpayer taxable for income "realized" in the tax year in which the suggestion is carried out. In connection with this latter argument the Commissioner states in his opening brief that "For the purposes of income tax it would seem immaterial whether the taxpayer waived his compensation, thus in effect giving it to Bancitaly Corporation, with the suggestion that it be applied to some useful purpose, or whether he failed to waive the right to receive the

---

* Between the tax year involved in *Earl*, a principal case above, and this case, California became a community property state. The effect, reflected here, was actual income-splitting between husband and wife. Ed.

compensation and directed that it be paid to a donee of his choice."
Again it is stated by the Commissioner, "Insofar as the question of
taxation is concerned it would not seem to make much difference
whether he directed Bancitaly Corporation to pay his compensation to
the University of California or whether he merely told his employer
to keep it."

Supplemental to the argument as above summarized, the Commissioner urges that the Board's finding that the money paid to the Foundation of Agricultural Economics as above set forth "was the property of Bancitaly and the petitioner [taxpayer] had no right, title or
interest therein" is unsupported by the evidence; and that in any
event such finding is an "ultimate finding" and therefore reviewable
by this court under the rule announced in Commissioner v. Boeing, 9
Cir., 106 F.2d 305 and cases therein cited. We agree that the question
of the effect of the taxpayer's unqualified refusal to take the compensation for his services is a question of law subject to review by this
court. That question is the sole question presented by this appeal.

The taxpayer, on the other hand, urges that "A person has the
right to refuse property proffered to him, and if he does so, absolutely
and unconditionally, his refusal amounts to a renunciation of the proffered property, which, legally, is an abandonment of right to the property without a transfer of such right to another. Property which is
renounced (i. e. abandoned) cannot be 'diverted' or 'assigned' by the
renouncer, and cannot be taxed upon the theory that it was received."

The Commissioner takes issue with the argument of the taxpayer
as above quoted by arguing that the amount involved was more than
"property proffered to" the taxpayer, but was instead compensation
which the taxpayer had a contractual right to receive. The point is
that any disposition of this contractual right, whether it be by waiver,
transfer, assignment or any other means, and whether it be before or
after the rendition of the services involved, results in taxable income
under the rules announced in the cases of Lucas v. Earl, 281 U.S. 111,
50 S.Ct. 241, 74 L.Ed. 731; Helvering v. Horst, 311 U.S. 112, 61 S.Ct.
144, 85 L.Ed. 75, 131 A.L.R. 655; Helvering v. Eubank, 311 U.S. 122,
61 S.Ct. 149, 85 L.Ed. 81; and Harrison v. Schaffner, 312 U.S. 579,
61 S.Ct. 759, 85 L.Ed. 1055.

The *Earl* case arises out of an assignment of salary and attorneys
fees by a husband to his wife in advance of the rendition of the services. It was claimed that the husband never beneficially received
them, but the Court refused to follow this reasoning and held that "the
tax could not be escaped by anticipatory arrangements and contracts
however skillfully devised to prevent the salary when paid from vesting even for a second in the man who earned it". The gist of the decision appears to be that the salary was accepted, and the employee's
dominance over it amounted to his receipt of it.

In the *Horst* case the taxpayer gave away interest bearing coupons, and the donee collected the interest during the taxpayer's taxable year. A conflict was asserted between the Circuit Court decision and the case of Lucas v. Earl, supra. In commenting upon the rule that income is not taxable until "realized", the Court [311 U.S. 122, 61 S.Ct. 147, 85 L.Ed. 75, 131 A.L.R. 655] asserted that such rule is a rule of postponement of the tax to the final event of enjoyment, saying "income is 'realized' by the assignor * * * who owns or controls the source * * * controls the disposition * * * and diverts. * * * The donor [taxpayer] here, * * * has * * * by his act, procured payment of the interest, as a valuable gift * * *. Such a use * * * would seem to be the enjoyment of the income * * *."

In the *Eubank* case a life insurance agent, after terminating agency contracts, made assignments of renewal commissions payable to him for services rendered in procuring policies. The Court held the renewal commissions taxable to the assignor. Here again [in *Eubank*], the dominance over the fund by the assignor was shown.

In the Schaffner case the life beneficiary of a trust assigned to children income from the trust for the year following the assignment. In holding that the income was taxable to the assignor the Court analyzes and compares these three cited cases. The Court said [312 U.S. 579, 61 S.Ct. 760, 85 L.Ed. 1055],

"Since granting certiorari we have held, following the reasoning of Lucas v. Earl, supra, that one who is entitled to receive, at a future date, interest or compensation for services and who makes a gift of it by an anticipatory assignment, realizes taxable income quite as much as if he had collected the income and paid it over to the object of his bounty. Helvering v. Horst, 311 U.S. 112, 61 S.Ct. 144, 85 L.Ed. 75, 131 A.L.R. 655; Helvering v. Eubank, 311 U.S. 122, 61 S.Ct. 149, 85 L.Ed. 81."

Here again [in *Schaffner*] the dominance over the fund and taxpayer's direction show that he beneficially received the money by exercising his right to divert it to a use.

Now, turning again to the instant case. The findings of the Board, supported by the evidence, are to the effect that the taxpayer did not receive the money, and that he did not direct its disposition. All that he did was to unqualifiedly refuse to accept any further compensation for his services with the suggestion that the money be used for some worthwhile purpose. So far as the taxpayer was concerned, the corporation could have kept the money. All arrangements with the University of California regarding the donation to the Foundation were made by the corporation, the taxpayer participating therein only as an officer of the corporation.

In this circumstance we cannot say as a matter of law that the money was beneficially received by the taxpayer and therefore subject to the income tax provisions of the statute. It should be kept in mind that there is no charge of fraud in this case. It would be impossible to support the Commissioner in his contention that the money was received by the taxpayer without arriving at the conclusion that the taxpayer was acting in less than full and open frankness.[1] The Board rejects this suggestion and we see no occasion for drawing inferences from the evidence contrary to the plain intent of the testimony which is not disputed. To support the Commissioner's argument we should have to hold that only one reasonable inference could be drawn from the evidence, which is that the donation is but a donation of the taxpayer masquerading as a creature of the corporation to save the true donors [taxpayer and his wife] some tax money. The circumstances do not support this contention. In our opinion the inferences drawn by the Board are more reasonable and comport with that presumption of verity that every act of a citizen of good repute should be able to claim and receive.

Affirmed.

[The concurring opinion of CIRCUIT JUDGE HEALY is omitted. Ed.]

REVENUE RULING 66–167

1966–1 Cum.Bull. 20.

In the instant case, the taxpayer served as the sole executor of his deceased wife's estate pursuant to the terms of a will under which he and his adult son were each given a half interest in the net proceeds thereof. The laws of the state in which the will was executed and probated impose no limitation on the use of either principal or income for the payment of compensation to an executor and do not purport to deal with whether a failure to withdraw any particular fee or commission may properly be considered as a waiver thereof.

The taxpayer's administration of his wife's estate continued for a period of approximately three full years during which time he filed two annual accountings as well as the usual final accounting with the probate court, all of which reported the collection and disposition of a substantial amount of estate assets.

---

1. We say that the Commissioner's argument compels this conclusion for the reason that the claimed deficiency is for the tax year in which the donation was actually made to the Foundation. It should be recalled that the taxpayer's unqualified refusal to take any further compensation for his services in 1927 was made prior to December 31, 1927. If the Commissioner were earnestly taking the position that a waiver of compensation, with nothing more, is such an exercise of dominion over the moneys to be received as to render it taxable, it seems apparent that the deficiency if any would be in the year of the waiver, rather than some subsequent year in which the corporation disposes of the fund in some other manner.

At some point within a reasonable time after first entering upon the performance of his duties as executor, the taxpayer decided to make no charge for serving in such capacity, and each of the aforesaid accountings accordingly omitted any claim for statutory commissions and was so filed with the intention to waive the same. The taxpayer-executor likewise took no other action which was inconsistent with a fixed and continuing intention to serve on a gratuitous basis.

The specific questions presented are whether the amounts which the taxpayer-executor could have received as fees or commissions are includible in his gross income for Federal income tax purposes and whether his waiver of the right to receive these amounts results in a gift for Federal gift tax purposes.

In Revenue Ruling 56–472, the executor of an estate entered into an agreement to serve in such capacity for substantially less than all of the statutory commissions otherwise allowable to him and also formally waived his right to receive the remaining portion thereof. The basic agreement with respect to his acceptance of a reduced amount of compensation antedated the performance of any services and the related waiver of the disclaimed commissions was signed before he would otherwise have become entitled to receive them. Under these circumstances, the ruling held that the difference between the commissions which such executor could have otherwise acquired an unrestricted right to obtain and the lesser amount which he actually received was not includible in his income and that his disclaimer did not effect any gift thereof.

In Revenue Ruling 64–225, the trustees of a testamentary trust in the State of New York waived their rights to receive one particular class of statutory commissions. This waiver was effected by means of certain formal instruments that were not executed until long after the close of most of the years to which such commissions related. This circumstance, along with all the other facts described therein, indicated that such trustees had not intended to render their services on a gratuitous basis. The Revenue Ruling accordingly held that such commissions were includible in the trustees' gross income for the taxable year when so waived and that their execution of the waivers also effected a taxable gift of these commissions.

The crucial test of whether the executor of an estate or any other fiduciary in a similar situation may waive his right to receive statutory commissions without thereby incurring any income or gift tax liability is whether the waiver involved will at least primarily constitute evidence of an intent to render a gratuitous service. If the timing, purpose, and effect of the waiver make it serve any other important objective, it may then be proper to conclude that the fiduciary has thereby enjoyed a realization of income by means of controlling the disposition thereof, and at the same time, has also effected a taxable gift by means of any resulting transfer to a third party of his contingent beneficial interest in a part of the assets under his fiduciary control * * *.

The requisite intention to serve on a gratuitous basis will ordinarily be deemed to have been adequately manifested if the executor or administrator of an estate supplies one or more of the decedent's principal legatees or devisees, or of those principally entitled to distribution of decedent's intestate estate, within six months after his initial appointment as such fiduciary, with a formal waiver of any right to compensation for his services. Such an intention to serve on a gratuitous basis may also be adequately manifested through an implied waiver, if the fiduciary fails to claim fees or commissions at the time of filing the usual accountings and if all the other attendant facts and circumstances are consistent with a fixed and continuing intention to serve gratuitously. If the executor or administrator of an estate claims his statutory fees or commissions as a deduction on one or more of the estate, inheritance, or income tax returns which are filed on behalf of the estate, such action will ordinarily be considered inconsistent with any fixed or definite intention to serve on a gratuitous basis. No such claim was made in the instant case.

Accordingly, the amounts which the present taxpayer-executor would have otherwise become entitled to receive as fees or commissions are not includible in his gross income for Federal income tax purposes, and are not gifts for Federal gift tax purposes.

Revenue Ruling 56–472 is clarified to remove any implication that, although an executor effectively waives his right to receive commissions, such commissions are includible in his gross income unless the waiver is executed prior to performance of any service.

Revenue Ruling 64–225 is distinguished.

REVENUE RULING 74–581

1974–2 Cum.Bull. 25.

Advice has been requested concerning the Federal income tax treatment of payments received for services performed by a faculty member or a student of a university's school of law under the circumstances described below.

The university's school of law has as part of its regular teaching curriculum several clinical programs. The clinics include programs in Constitutional Litigation, Urban Legal Problems, Women's Rights, Prisoner's Rights and Corrections, and from time to time other clinical programs as well. Each program is supervised and conducted by full-time faculty members of the school of law's teaching staff.

At times, various clinics in the law school program handle criminal matters wherein faculty members are assigned as counsel. On occasion, the faculty member is appointed by a Federal District Court, * * * pursuant to the provisions of the Criminal Justice Act of 1964, as amended, 18 U.S.C. 3006A ("Criminal Justice Act"), which authorizes the payment of compensation of attorneys appointed to represent indigent defendants. In the cases for which an appointment under the Criminal Justice Act is made, the students in the clinical programs assist the attorney-faculty member in investigation of the case, research of the case, and preparation of the litigation papers as the case may require. In other circumstances, the individual student may be able to participate directly in the legal representation of the client pursuant to the newly promulgated rule of the United States Court of Appeals for the Third Circuit (Local Rule 9(2), Entry of Appearance by Eligible Law Students), or under similar rules in other jurisdictions.

When an attorney-faculty member is appointed in a criminal case by the Federal Courts pursuant to the Criminal Justice Act, the attorney is entitled to submit a voucher for the expenditure of time and for disbursements incident to the representation. With regard to the clinical programs of the law school, each faculty member has agreed, as a condition of participation in the program, that since the time spent in supervising work of students on these cases and in the representation of the client is part of the faculty member's teaching duties for which the faculty member is compensated by a total annual salary, all amounts received under the Criminal Justice Act will be endorsed over to the law school. The attorney-faculty members involved are working solely as agents of the law school, while supervising the law students within the scope of the clinical programs, and realize no personal gain from payments for their services in representing the indigent defendants.

Although the Criminal Justice Act itself does not specify that the monies may not be paid directly to the law school, the Clerk of the District Court has taken the generally acknowledged position that under the Criminal Justice Act payment cannot be arranged through the law school or its clinical programs. Therefore, as a matter of practice, the vouchers would be submitted by the attorney-faculty member to the appropriate Federal court in the name of the faculty member, and upon receipt of the check, he would endorse it over to the university's law school accounts.

Section 61(a) of the Internal Revenue Code of 1954 provides that, unless excluded by law, gross income means all income from whatever source derived including (but not limited to) compensation for services, including fees and similar items.

The Supreme Court of the United States has stated that the dominant purpose of the revenue laws is the taxation of income to those who earn or otherwise create the right to receive it and enjoy the benefit of it when paid. Helvering v. Horst, 311 U.S. 112 (1940), 1940–2 C.B. 296. Consistent with this, it is well established that a taxpayer's anticipatory assignment of a right to income derived from the ownership of property will not be effective to redirect that income to the assignee for tax purposes. See the *Horst* case and Lucas v. Earl, 281 U.S. 111 (1930).

However, the Internal Revenue Service has recognized that amounts that would otherwise be deemed income are not, in certain unique factual situations, subject to the broad rule of inclusion provided by section 61(a) of the Code.

For example, Rev.Rul. 65–282, 1965–2 C.B. 21, holds that statutory legal fees received by attorneys for representing indigent defendants are not includible in gross income where the attorneys, pursuant to their employment contracts, immediately turn the fees over to their employer, a legal aid society.

Rev.Rul. 58–220, 1958–1 C.B. 26, holds that the amount of the checks received by a physician from patients he has treated in the hospital by which he is employed full-time, which checks he is required to endorse over to the hospital, is not includible in his gross income.

Similarly, Rev.Rul. 58–515, 1958–2 C.B. 28, considers a situation where a police officer, in the performance of duties as an employee of the police department, entered into private employment for the purpose of obtaining certain information for the department. Pursuant to the rules and procedures of the department, the officer remitted to the police pension fund the compensation he received from the private employer. That Revenue Ruling holds that the officer was acting as an agent of the department while privately employed and that the compensation remitted to the pension fund is not includible in his gross income.

In similar circumstances, Rev.Rul. 69–274, 1969–1 C.B. 36, holds that faculty physicians of a medical school who provide medical services to indigent patients at a hospital are not required to include in their income fees collected and remitted to the university in accordance with the university policy and agreement.

Accordingly, in the instant case, amounts received for services performed by a faculty member or a student of the university's school of law under the clinical programs and turned over to the university are not includible in the recipient's income.

C. INCOME FROM PROPERTY

HELVERING v. HORST

Supreme Court of the United States, 1940.
311 U.S. 112, 61 S.Ct. 144.

MR. JUSTICE STONE delivered the opinion of the Court.

The sole question for decision is whether the gift, during the donor's taxable year, of interest coupons detached from the bonds, delivered to the donee and later in the year paid at maturity, is the realization of income taxable to the donor.

In 1934 and 1935 respondent, the owner of negotiable bonds, detached from them negotiable interest coupons shortly before their due date and delivered them as a gift to his son who in the same year collected them at maturity. The Commissioner ruled that under the applicable § 22 of the Revenue Act of 1934, 48 Stat. 680, 686, the interest payments were taxable, in the years when paid, to the respondent donor who reported his income on the cash receipts basis. The Circuit Court of Appeals reversed the order of the Board of Tax Appeals sustaining the tax. 107 F.2d 906; 39 B.T.A. 757. We granted certiorari, 309 U.S. 650, because of the importance of the question in the administration of the revenue laws and because of an asserted conflict in principle of the decision below with that of Lucas v. Earl, 281 U.S. 111, and with that of decisions by other circuit courts of appeals. See Bishop v. Commissioner, 54 F.2d 298; Dickey v. Burnet, 56 F.2d 917, 921; Van Meter v. Commissioner, 61 F.2d 817.

The court below thought that as the consideration for the coupons had passed to the obligor, the donor had, by the gift, parted with all control over them and their payment, and for that reason the case was distinguishable from Lucas v. Earl, supra, and Burnet v. Leininger, 285 U.S. 136, where the assignment of compensation for services had preceded the rendition of the services, and where the income was held taxable to the donor.

The holder of a coupon bond is the owner of two independent and separable kinds of right. One is the right to demand and receive at maturity the principal amount of the bond representing capital investment. The other is the right to demand and receive interim payments of interest on the investment in the amounts and on the dates specified by the coupons. Together they are an obligation to pay principal and interest given in exchange for money or property which was presumably the consideration for the obligation of the bond. Here respondent, as owner of the bonds, had acquired the legal right to demand payment at maturity of the interest specified by the coupons and the power to command its payment to others, which constituted an economic gain to him.

Admittedly not all economic gain of the taxpayer is taxable income. From the beginning the revenue laws have been interpreted as defining "realization" of income as the taxable event, rather than the acquisition of the right to receive it. And "realization" is not deemed to occur until the income is paid. But the decisions and regulations have consistently recognized that receipt in cash or property is not the only characteristic of realization of income to a taxpayer on the cash receipts basis. Where the taxpayer does not receive payment of income in money or property realization may occur when the last step is taken by which he obtains the fruition of the economic gain which has already accrued to him. Old Colony Trust Co. v. Commissioner, 279 U.S. 716; Corliss v. Bowers, 281 U.S. 376, 378. Cf. Burnet v. Wells, 289 U.S. 670.

In the ordinary case the taxpayer who acquires the right to receive income is taxed when he receives it, regardless of the time when his right to receive payment accrued. But the rule that income is not taxable until realized has never been taken to mean that the taxpayer, even on the cash receipts basis, who has fully enjoyed the benefit of the economic gain represented by his right to receive income, can escape taxation because he has not himself received payment of it from his obligor. The rule, founded on administrative convenience, is only one of postponement of the tax to the final event of enjoyment of the income, usually the receipt of it by the taxpayer, and not one of exemption from taxation where the enjoyment is consummated by some event other than the taxpayer's personal receipt of money or property. Cf. Aluminum Castings Co. v. Routzahn, 282 U.S. 92, 98. This may occur when he has made such use or disposition of his power to receive or control the income as to procure in its place other satisfactions which are of economic worth. The question here is, whether because one who in fact receives payment for services or interest payments is taxable only on his receipt of the payments, he can escape all tax by giving away his right to income in advance of payment. If the taxpayer procures payment directly to his creditors of the items of interest or earnings due him, see Old Colony Trust Co. v. Commissioner, supra; Bowers v. Kerbaugh-Empire Co., 271 U.S. 170; United States v. Kirby Lumber Co., 284 U.S. 1, or if he sets up a revocable trust with income payable to the objects of his bounty, §§ 166, 167, Revenue Act of 1934, Corliss v. Bowers, supra; cf. Dickey v. Burnet, 56 F.2d 917, 921, he does not escape taxation because he did not actually receive the money. Cf. Douglas v. Willcuts, 296 U.S. 1; Helvering v. Clifford, 309 U.S. 331.

Underlying the reasoning in these cases is the thought that income is "realized" by the assignor because he, who owns or controls the source of the income, also controls the disposition of that which he could have received himself and diverts the payment from himself to others as the means of procuring the satisfaction of his wants. The taxpayer has equally enjoyed the fruits of his labor or investment and obtained the satisfaction of his desires whether he collects and uses the income to procure those satisfactions, or whether he disposes of his right to collect it as the means of procuring them. Cf. Burnet v. Wells, supra.

Although the donor here, by the transfer of the coupons, has precluded any possibility of his collecting them himself, he has nevertheless, by his act, procured payment of the interest as a valuable gift to a member of his family. Such a use of his economic gain, the right to receive income, to procure a satisfaction which can be obtained only by the expenditure of money or property, would seem to be the enjoyment of the income whether the satisfaction is the purchase of goods at the corner grocery, the payment of his debt there, or such nonmaterial satisfactions as may result from the payment of a campaign or community chest contribution, or a gift to his favorite son. Even though he never receives the money, he derives money's worth from the disposition of the coupons which he has used as money or money's worth in the procuring of a satisfaction which is procurable only by the expenditure of money or money's worth. The enjoyment of the economic benefit accruing to him by virtue of his acquisition of the coupons is realized as completely as it would have been if he had collected the interest in dollars and expended them for any of the purposes named. Burnet v. Wells, supra.

In a real sense he has enjoyed compensation for money loaned or services rendered, and not any the less so because it is his only reward for them. To say that one who has made a gift thus derived from interest or earnings paid to his donee has never enjoyed or realized the fruits of his investment or labor, because he has assigned them instead of collecting them himself and then paying them over to the donee, is to affront common understanding and to deny the facts of common experience. Common understanding and experience are the touchstones for the interpretation of the revenue laws.

The power to dispose of income is the equivalent of ownership of it. The exercise of that power to procure the payment of income to another is the enjoyment, and hence the realization, of the income by him who exercises it. We have had no difficulty in applying that proposition where the assignment preceded the rendition of the services, Lucas v. Earl, supra; Burnet v. Leininger, supra, for it was recognized in the Leininger case that in such a case the rendition of the service by the assignor was the means by which the income was controlled by the donor and of making his assignment effective. But it is the assignment by which the disposition of income is controlled when the service precedes the assignment, and in both cases it is the exercise of the power of disposition of the interest or compensation, with the resulting payment to the donee, which is the enjoyment by the donor of income derived from them.

This was emphasized in Blair v. Commissioner, 300 U.S. 5, on which respondent relies, where the distinction was taken between a gift of income derived from an obligation to pay compensation and a gift of income-producing property. In the circumstances of that case, the right to income from the trust property was thought to be so identified with the equitable ownership of the property, from which alone the beneficiary derived his right to receive the income and his power to command disposition of it, that a gift of the income by the beneficiary became effective only as a gift of his ownership of the property producing it. Since the gift was deemed to be a gift of the property, the income from it was held to be the income of the owner of the property, who was the donee, not the donor—a refinement which was unnecessary if respondent's contention here is right, but one clearly inapplicable to gifts of interest or wages. Unlike income thus derived from an obligation to pay interest or compensation, the income of the trust was regarded as no more the income of the donor than would be the rent from a lease or a crop raised on a farm after the leasehold or the farm had been given away. Blair v. Commissioner, supra, 12, 13 and cases cited. See also Reinecke v. Smith, 289 U.S. 172, 177. We have held without deviation that where the donor retains control of the trust property the income is taxable to him although paid to the donee. Corliss v. Bowers, supra. Cf. Helvering v. Clifford, supra.

The dominant purpose of the revenue laws is the taxation of income to those who earn or otherwise create the right to receive it and enjoy the benefit of it when paid. See, Corliss v. Bowers, supra, 378; Burnet v. Guggenheim, 288 U.S. 280, 283. The tax laid by the 1934 Revenue Act upon income "derived from   *   *   *   wages, or compensation for personal service, of whatever kind and in whatever form paid,   *   *   *;   also from interest   *   *   *" therefore cannot fairly be interpreted as not applying to income derived from interest or compensation when he who is entitled to receive it makes use of his power to dispose of it in procuring satisfactions which he would otherwise procure only by the use of the money when received.

It is the statute which taxes the income to the donor although paid to his donee. Lucas v. Earl, supra; Burnet v. Leininger, supra. True, in those cases the service which created the right to income followed the assignment, and it was arguable that in point of legal theory the right to the compensation vested instantaneously in the assignor when paid, although he never received it; while here the right of the assignor to receive the income antedated the assignment which transferred the right and thus precluded such an instantaneous vesting. But the statute affords no basis for such "attenuated subtleties." The distinction was explicitly rejected as the basis of decision in Lucas v. Earl. It should be rejected here; for no more than in the Earl case can the purpose of the statute to tax the income to him who earns, or creates and enjoys it be escaped by "anticipatory arrangements however skilfully devised" to prevent the income from vesting even for a second in the donor.

Nor is it perceived that there is any adequate basis for distinguishing between the gift of interest coupons here and a gift of salary or commissions. The owner of a negotiable bond and of the investment which it represents, if not the lender, stands in the place of the lender. When, by the gift of the coupons, he has separated his right to interest payments from his investment and procured the payment of the interest to his donee, he has enjoyed the economic benefits of the income in the same manner and to the same extent as though the transfer were of earnings, and in both cases the import of the statute is that the fruit is not to be attributed to a different tree from that on which it grew. See Lucas v. Earl, supra, 115.

Reversed.

[The dissenting opinion of MR. JUSTICE REYNOLDS, in which the CHIEF JUSTICE and MR. JUSTICE ROBERTS concurred, has been omitted. Ed.]

BLAIR v. COMMISSIONER

Supreme Court of the United States, 1937.
300 U.S. 5, 57 U.S. 330.

MR. CHIEF JUSTICE HUGHES delivered the opinion of the Court.

This case presents the question of the liability of a beneficiary of a testamentary trust for a tax upon the income which he had assigned to his children prior to the tax years and which the trustees had paid to them accordingly.

The trust was created by the will of William Blair, a resident of Illinois who died in 1899, and was of property located in that State. One-half of the net income was to be paid to the donor's widow during her life. His son, the petitioner Edward Tyler Blair, was to receive the other one-half and, after the death of the widow, the whole of the net income during his life. In 1923, after the widow's death, petitioner assigned to his daughter, Lucy Blair Linn, an interest amounting to $6000 for the remainder of that calendar year, and to $9000 in each calendar year thereafter, in the net income which the petitioner was then or might thereafter be entitled to receive during his life. At about the same time, he made like assignments of interests, amounting to $9000 in each calendar year, in the net income of the trust to his daughter Edith Blair and to his son, Edward Seymour Blair, respectively. In later years, by similar instruments, he assigned to these children additional interests, and to his son William McCormick Blair other specified interests, in the net income. The trustees accepted the assignments and distributed the income directly to the assignees.

The question first arose with respect to the tax year 1923 and the Commissioner of Internal Revenue ruled that the income was taxable to the petitioner. The Board of Tax Appeals held the contrary. 18 B.T.A. 69. The Circuit Court of Appeals reversed the Board, holding that under the law of Illinois the trust was a spendthrift trust and the assignments were invalid. Commissioner v. Blair, 60 F.2d 340. We denied certiorari. 288 U.S. 602.

Thereupon the trustees brought suit in the Superior Court of Cook County, Illinois, to obtain a construction of the will with respect to the power of the beneficiary of the trust to assign a part of his equitable interest and to determine the validity of the assignments he had made. The petitioner and the assignees were made defendants. The Appellate Court of Illinois, First District, after a review of the Illinois decisions, decided that the trust was not a spendthrift trust and upheld the assignments. Blair v. Linn, 274 Ill.App. 23. Under the mandate of the appellate court, the Superior Court of Cook County entered its decree which found the assignments to be "voluntary assignments of a part of the interest of said Edward Tyler Blair in said trust estate" and as such adjudged them to be valid.

At that time there were pending before the Board of Tax Appeals proceedings involving the income of the trust for the years 1924, 1925, 1926 and 1929. The Board received in evidence the record in the suit in the state court and, applying the decision of that court, the Board overruled the Commissioner's determination as to the petitioner's liability. 31 B.T.A. 1192. The Circuit Court of Appeals again reversed the Board. That court recognized the binding effect of the decision of the state court as to the validity of the assignments but decided that the income was still taxable to the petitioner upon the ground that his interest was not attached to the corpus of the estate and that the income was not subject to his disposition until he received it. Commissioner v. Blair, 83 F.2d 655, 662.

Because of an asserted conflict with the decision of the state court, and also with decisions of circuit courts of appeals, we granted certiorari. October 12, 1936.

First. The Government contends that the judgment relating to the income for 1923 is conclusive in this proceeding as *res judicata.* Tait v. Western Maryland Ry. Co., 289 U.S. 620. Petitioner insists that this question was not raised before the Board of Tax Appeals and hence was not available before the Circuit Court of Appeals. General Utilities Co. v. Helvering, 296 U.S. 200, 206; Helvering v. Salvage, 297 U.S. 106, 109. The Government responds that the answers before the Board of Tax Appeals in the instant case had been filed before the first decision of the Circuit Court of Appeals was entered, and that, while the case was heard before the Board without amended pleadings, the whole matter was actually before the Board and the question of *res judicata* was raised by an assignment of error on the petition for review before the Circuit Court of Appeals.

It is not necessary to review the respective contentions upon this point, as we think that the ruling in the *Tait* case is not applicable. That ruling and the reasoning which underlies it apply where in the subsequent proceeding, although relating to a different tax year, the questions presented upon the facts and the law are essentially the same. Tait v. Western Maryland Ry. Co., supra, pp. 624, 626. Here, after the decision in the first proceeding, the opinion and decree of the state court created a new situation. The determination of petitioner's liability for the year 1923 had been rested entirely upon the local law. Commissioner v. Blair, 60 F.2d 340, 342, 344. The supervening decision of the state court interpreting that law in direct relation to this trust cannot justly be ignored in the present proceeding so far as it is found that the local law is determinative of any material point in controversy. Compare Freuler v. Helvering, 291 U.S. 35; Hubbell v. Helvering, 70 F.2d 668.

Second. The question of the validity of the assignments is a question of local law. The donor was a resident of Illinois and his disposition of the property in that State was subject to its law. By that law the character of the trust, the nature and extent of the interest of the beneficiary, and the power of the beneficiary to assign that interest in whole or in part, are to be determined. The decision of the state court upon these questions is final. Spindle v. Shreve, 111 U.S. 542, 547, 548; Uterhart v. United States, 240 U.S. 598, 603; Poe v. Seaborn, 282 U.S. 101, 110; Freuler v. Helvering, supra, p. 45. It matters not that the decision was by an intermediate appellate court. Compare Graham v. White-Phillips Co., 296 U.S. 27. In this instance, it is not necessary to go beyond the obvious point that the decision was in a suit between the trustees and the beneficiary and his assignees, and the decree which was entered in pursuance of the decision determined as between these parties the validity of the particular assignments. Nor is there any basis for a charge that the suit was collusive and the decree inoperative. Freuler v. Helvering, supra. The trustees were entitled to seek the instructions of the court having supervision of the trust. That court entertained the suit and the appellate court, with the first decision of the Circuit Court of Appeals before it, reviewed the decisions of the Supreme Court of the State and reached a deliberate conclusion. To derogate from the authority of that conclusion and of the decree it commanded, so far as the question is one of state law, would be wholly unwarranted in the exercise of federal jurisdiction.

In the face of this ruling of the state court it is not open to the Government to argue that the trust "was, under the Illinois law, a spendthrift trust." The point of the argument is that, the trust being of that character, the state law barred the voluntary alienation by the beneficiary of his interest. The state court held precisely the contrary. The ruling also determines the validity of the assignment by the beneficiary of parts of his interest. That question was necessarily presented and expressly decided.

Third. The question remains whether, treating the assignments as valid, the assignor was still taxable upon the income under the federal income tax act. That is a federal question.

Our decisions in Lucas v. Earl, 281 U.S. 111, and Burnet v. Leininger, 285 U.S. 136, are cited. In the Lucas case the question was whether an attorney was taxable for the whole of his salary and fees earned by him in the tax years or only upon one-half by reason of an agreement with his wife by which his earnings were to be received and owned by them jointly. We were of the opinion that the case turned upon the construction of the taxing act. We said that "the statute could tax salaries to those who earned them and provide that the tax could not be escaped by anticipatory arrangements and contracts however skilfully devised to prevent the same when paid from vesting even for a second in the man who earned it." That was deemed to be the meaning of the statute as to compensation for personal service, and the one who earned the income was held to be subject to the tax. In Burnet v. Leininger, supra, a husband, a member of a firm, assigned future partnership income to his wife. We found that the revenue act dealt explicitly with the liability of partners as such. The wife did not become a member of the firm; the act specifically taxed the distributive share of each partner in the net income of the firm; and the husband by the fair import of the act remained taxable upon his distributive share. These cases are not in point. The tax here is not upon earnings which are taxed to the one who earns them. Nor is it a case of income attributable to a taxpayer by reason of the application of the income to the discharge of his obligation. Old Colony Trust Co. v. Commissioner, 279 U.S. 716; Douglas v. Willcuts, 296 U.S. 1, 9; Helvering v. Stokes, 296 U.S. 551; Helvering v. Schweitzer, 296 U.S. 551; Helvering v. Coxey, 297 U.S. 694. See, also, Burnet v. Wells, 289 U.S. 670, 677. There is here no question of evasion or of giving effect to statutory provisions designed to forestall evasion; or of the taxpayer's retention of control. Corliss v. Bowers, 281 U.S. 376; Burnet v. Guggenheim, 288 U.S. 280.

In the instant case, the tax is upon income as to which, in the general application of the revenue acts, the tax liability attaches to ownership. See Poe v. Seaborn, supra; Hoeper v. Tax Commission, 284 U.S. 206.

The Government points to the provisions of the revenue acts imposing upon the beneficiary of a trust the liability for the tax upon the income distributable to the beneficiary.[1] But the term is merely descriptive of the one entitled to the beneficial interest. These provisions cannot be taken to preclude valid assignments of the beneficial interest, or to affect the duty of the trustee to distribute

---

1. Revenue Acts of 1921, § 219(a) (d); 1924 and 1926, § 219(a) (b); 1928, §   162(a) (b). [See I.R.C. (1954) §§ 652 (a) and 662(a) (1). Ed.]

income to the owner of the beneficial interest, whether he was such initially or becomes such by valid assignment. The one who is to receive the income as the owner of the beneficial interest is to pay the tax. If under the law governing the trust the beneficial interest is assignable, and if it has been assigned without reservation, the assignee thus becomes the beneficiary and is entitled to rights and remedies accordingly. We find nothing in the revenue acts which denies him that status.

The decision of the Circuit Court of Appeals turned upon the effect to be ascribed to the assignments. The court held that the petitioner had no interest in the corpus of the estate and could not dispose of the income until he received it. Hence it was said that "the income was *his*" and his assignment was merely a direction to pay over to others what was due to himself. The question was considered to involve "the date when the income became transferable." 83 F.2d, p. 662. The Government refers to the terms of the assignment,—that it was of the interest in the income "which the said party of the first part now is, or may hereafter be, entitled to receive during his life from the trustees." From this it is urged that the assignments "dealt only with a right to receive the income" and that "no attempt was made to assign any equitable right, title or interest in the trust itself." This construction seems to us to be a strained one. We think it apparent that the conveyancer was not seeking to limit the assignment so as to make it anything less than a complete transfer of the specified interest of the petitioner as the life beneficiary of the trust, but that with ample caution he was using words to effect such a transfer. That the state court so construed the assignments appears from the final decree which described them as voluntary assignments of interests of the petitioner "in said trust estate," and it was in that aspect that petitioner's right to make the assignments was sustained.

The will creating the trust entitled the petitioner during his life to the net income of the property held in trust. He thus became the owner of an equitable interest in the corpus of the property. Brown v. Fletcher, 235 U.S. 589, 598, 599; Irwin v. Gavit, 268 U.S. 161, 167, 168; Senior v. Braden, 295 U.S. 422, 432, 433; Merchants' Loan & Trust Co. v. Patterson, 308 Ill. 519, 530, 139 N.E. 912. By virtue of that interest he was entitled to enforce the trust, to have a breach of trust enjoined and to obtain redress in case of breach. The interest was present property alienable like any other, in the absence of a valid restraint upon alienation. Commissioner v. Field, 42 F.2d 820, 822; Shanley v. Bowers, 81 F.2d 13, 15. The beneficiary may thus transfer a part of his interest as well as the whole. See Restatement of the Law of Trusts, §§ 130, 132 et seq. The assignment of the beneficial interest is not the assignment of a chose in action but of the "right, title and estate in and to property." Brown v. Fletcher, supra; Senior v. Braden, supra. See Bogert,

"Trusts and Trustees," vol. 1, § 183, pp. 516, 517; 17 Columbia Law Review, 269, 273, 289, 290.

We conclude that the assignments were valid, that the assignees thereby became the owners of the specified beneficial interests in the income, and that as to these interests they and not the petitioner were taxable for the tax years in question. The judgment of the Circuit Court of Appeals is reversed and the cause is remanded with direction to affirm the decision of the Board of Tax Appeals.

Reversed.

NOTE

The court's discussion in *Blair* on the effect in a tax controversy of a local court's determination of a related property issue has been substantially modified by later decisions in Comm'r v. Estate of Bosch and Second Nat. Bank of New Haven, Executor v. U. S., 387 U.S. 456, 87 S.Ct. 1776 (1967). See Ferguson, Freeland, and Stephens, Federal Income Taxation of Estates and Beneficiaries, c. 2, "Local Law and Local Adjudications in Federal Tax Cases," 25–47 (1970).

SUSIE SALVATORE

Tax Court of the United States, 1970.
29 T.C.M. 89.

FEATHERSTON, JUDGE: Respondent determined a deficiency in petitioner's income tax for 1963 in the amount of $31,016.60. The only issue presented for decision is whether petitioner is taxable on all or only one-half of the gain realized on the sale of certain real property in 1963.

Findings of Fact

Petitioner was a legal resident of Greenwich, Connecticut, at the time her petition was filed. She filed an individual Federal income tax return for 1963 with the district director of internal revenue, Hartford, Connecticut.

Petitioner's husband operated an oil and gas service station in Greenwich, Connecticut, for a number of years prior to his death on October 7, 1948. His will, dated December 6, 1941, contained the following pertinent provisions:

SECOND: I give devise and bequeath all of my estate both real and personal of whatsoever the same may consist and wheresoever the same may be situated of which I may die possessed or be entitled to at the time of my decease, to my beloved wife, SUSIE SALVATORE, to be hers absolutely and forever.

I make no provision herein for my beloved children because I am confident that their needs and support will be provided for by my beloved wife.

* * *

FOURTH: I hereby give my Executors full power to sell any and all of my property in their discretion and to execute any and all necessary deed or deeds of conveyance of my said property or any part or parts thereof, and which said deed or deeds, conveyance or assignment so executed by my Executors shall be as good and effectual to pass the title to the property therein described and conveyed as if the same had been executed by me in my lifetime.

For several years after her husband's death petitioner's three sons, Amedeo, Eugene, and Michael, continued operating the service station with the help of her daughter Irene, who kept the books of the business. Sometime prior to 1958, however, Michael left the service station to undertake other business endeavors; and in 1958 Eugene left to enter the real estate business, leaving Amedeo alone to manage and operate the service station.

During this period and until 1963, petitioner received $100 per week from the income of the service station. This sum was not based on the fair rental of the property, but was geared to petitioner's needs for her support. The remaining income was divided among the family members who worked in the business.

The land on which the service station was located became increasingly valuable. Several major oil companies from time to time made purchase proposals, which were considered by members of the family. Finally, in the early summer of 1963 representatives of Texaco, Inc. (hereinafter Texaco), approached Amedeo regarding the purchase of the service station property. Petitioner called a family conference and asked for advice on whether the property should be sold. Realizing that Amedeo alone could not operate the station at peak efficiency, petitioner and her children decided to sell the property if a reasonable offer could be obtained.

Amedeo continued his negotiations with Texaco and ultimately received an offer of $295,000. During the course of the negotiations Eugene discovered that tax liens in the amount of $8,000 were outstanding against the property. In addition, there was an outstanding mortgage, securing a note held by Texaco, on which approximately $50,000 remained unpaid. The family met again to consider Texaco's offer.

As a result of the family meeting (including consultation with petitioner's daughter Geraldine, who lived in Florida), it was decided that the proposal should be accepted and that the proceeds should be used, first, to satisfy the tax liens and any other outstanding liabilities. Second, petitioner was to receive $100,000, the estimated amount needed to generate income for her life of about $5,000 per year—the approximate equivalent of the $100 per week she previously received out of the service station income. Third, the balance was to be divided equally among the five children. To effectuate this family understanding, it was agreed that petitioner would first convey a one-half interest in the property to the children and that deeds would then be executed by petitioner and the children conveying the property to Texaco.

On July 24, 1963, petitioner formally accepted Texaco's offer by executing an agreement to sell the property to Texaco for $295,000, the latter making a down payment of $29,500. Subsequently, on August 28, 1963, petitioner executed a warranty deed conveying an undivided one-half interest in the property to her five children. This deed was received for record on September 6, 1963. By warranty deeds dated August 28 and 30, 1963, and received for record on September 6, 1963, petitioner and her five children conveyed their interest in the property to Texaco; Texaco thereupon tendered $215,-582.12, the remainder of the purchase price less the amount due on the outstanding mortgage.

Petitioner filed a Federal gift tax return for 1963, reporting gifts made to each of her five children on August 1, 1963, of a ⅟₁₀ interest in the property and disclosing a gift tax due in the amount of $10,744.35.

After discharge of the mortgage and the tax liens the remaining proceeds of the sale (including the down payment) amounted to $237,082, of which one-half, $118,541, was paid to petitioner. From the other half of the proceeds the gift tax of $10,744.35 was paid and the balance was distributed to the children.

In her income tax return for 1963 petitioner reported as her share of the gain from the sale of the service station property a long-term capital gain of $115,063 plus an ordinary gain of $665. Each of the children reported in his 1963 return a proportionate share of the balance of the gain.

In the notice of deficiency respondent determined that petitioner's gain on the sale of the service station property was $238,856, all of which was taxable as long-term capital gain. Thereafter each of petitioner's children filed protective claims for refund of the taxes which they had paid on their gains from the sale of the service station property.

Opinion

The only question is whether petitioner is taxable on all or only one-half of the gain realized from the sale of the service station property. This issue must be resolved in accordance with the following principle stated by the Supreme Court in Commissioner v. Court Holding Co., 324 U.S. 331, 334 (1945):

"The incidence of taxation depends upon the substance of a transaction. The tax consequences which arise from gains from a sale of property are not finally to be determined solely by the means employed to transfer legal title. Rather, the transaction must be viewed as a whole, and each step, from the commencement of negotiations to the consummation of the sale, is relevant. *A sale by one person cannot be transformed for tax purposes into a sale by another by using the latter as a conduit through which to pass title.* To permit the true nature of a transaction to be disguised by mere formalisms, which exist solely to alter tax liabilities, would seriously impair the effective administration of the tax policies of Congress." [Footnote omitted. Emphasis added.]

See Harry C. Usher, Sr., 45 T.C. 205 (1965); John E. Palmer, 44 T.C. 92 (1965), affirmed per curiam 354 F.2d 974 (C.A.1, 1965).

The evidence is unmistakably clear that petitioner owned the service station property prior to July 24, 1963, when she contracted to sell it to Texaco. Her children doubtless expected ultimately to receive the property or its proceeds, either through gifts or inheritance, and petitioner may have felt morally obligated to pass it on to them. But at that time the children "held" no property interest therein.[1] Petitioner's subsequent conveyance, unsupported by consideration, of an undivided one-half interest in the property to her children—all of whom were fully aware of her prior agreement to sell the property—was merely an intermediate step in the transfer of legal title from petitioner to Texaco; petitioner's children were only "conduit[s] through which to pass title." That petitioner's conveyance to the children may have been a bona fide completed gift prior to the transfer of title to Texaco, as she contends, is immaterial in determining the income tax consequences of the sale, for the form of a transaction cannot be permitted to prevail over its substance. In substance, petitioner made an anticipatory assignment to her children of one-half of the income from the sale of the property.

The artificiality of treating the transaction as a sale in part by the children is confirmed by the testimony by petitioner's witnesses that the sum retained by her from the sale was a computed amount— an amount sufficient to assure that she would receive income in the amount of approximately $5,000 annually. If the sales price had been less, petitioner would have retained a larger percentage of the proceeds; if more, we infer, she would have received a smaller percentage.[2] While the children's desire to provide for their mother's care

---

1. Sec. 1221, I.R.C.1954, defines the term "capital asset" to mean "property held by the taxpayer."

2. Eugene Salvatore testified as follows:

Q. You stated that you wanted one hundred thousand dollars for your mother. That is, this was to be her share, more or less?

A. Yes.

Q. If the property was sold for one hundred thousand dollars would your mother have kept all the money?

A. She had to.

Q. She would have?

A. She would have kept all the money.

Q. Because she needed the money to live on the interest?

A. Because we felt she needed it to live on.

Q. The children would have got nothing?

A. If she got $90 a week the five children would have made up the difference. We felt she needed the money to live on.

and petitioner's willingness to share the proceeds of her property with her children during her lifetime may be laudable, her tax liabilities cannot be altered by a rearrangement of the legal title after she had already contracted to sell the property to Texaco.

All the gain from sale of the service station property was taxable to petitioner. We find nothing in Oscar Deinert, 11 B.T.A. 651 (1928), or Charles W. Walworth, 6 B.T.A. 788 (1927), cited by petitioner, which requires an opposite conclusion.

Decision will be entered for the respondent.

NOTE

The "fruit-tree" tax area is a very large orchard indeed, stretching out over many acres not visible from the vantage point of materials included in this Chapter. The classic work in the orchard is Lyon and Eustice, "Assignment of Income: Fruit and Tree as Irrigated by the P. G. Lake Case," 17 Tax L.Rev. 293 (1962); supplemented in Eustice, "Contract Rights, Capital Gain, and Assignment of Income—The Ferrer Case," 20 Tax L.Rev. 1 (1964).

At this point of time the *Horst* case seems easy. The owner of the tree picks some fruit and gives it to another who converts it to cash. As the owner has kept the tree that produces the fruit, the tree's produce (interest later paid) remains his for tax purposes, even though economically it has become the property of another. Rev.Rul. 69–102, set out below at page 296, is illuminating as to the period for which the owner must report the income thus attributed to him.

If the owner gives away the tree (the bond itself in the *Horst* setting), the donee in general is taxable on fruit subsequently produced (later interest payments), because he has become the owner of the income-producing property itself. But what if there is ripe fruit hanging on the tree at the time of the gift? Rev.Rul. 69–102, set out below at page 296, has a message here, also, and see Austin v. Comm'r.[1] In many instances, however, it is difficult to say what should be regarded as fruit. Mere appreciation in the value of the property (the tree) is not fruit until it is realized. What further concept was applied, then, to tax Susie Salvatore on the gain on the sale of the property? Can appreciation ripen into fruit?

In Campbell v. Prothro [2] the taxpayer raised calves. On May 7 he transferred 100 head of calves by written instrument to a charitable donee.[3] The donated calves were never physically separated from the rest of the calves. On June 8 taxpayer and the charitable donee en-

---

1. 161 F.2d 666 (6th Cir. 1947), cert. den., 332 U.S. 767, 68 S.Ct. 75 (1947).

2. 209 F.2d 331 (5th Cir. 1954).

3. The fact that the donee was a charity makes no difference with respect to the ripeness of income issue raised by the case. However, since 1969 the charitable deduction question in cases of this sort is sharply affected by I.R. C. (26 U.S.C.A.) § 170(e) (1) (A).

tered into a contract to sell the entire calf crop to a third party. The court held that gain on the sale of the calves given to the charity could not be attributed to the donor. Rejecting the Commissioner's argument that no gift in fact occurred prior to the sale, the court went on to say: [4]

"We find ourselves in agreement with appellees' views. In the Horst case, the father, when the coupons on the bonds involved had become, or were about to become due, gave them to his son who collected them, and the court there properly held that the gift constituted an anticipatory assignment of the interest as income, within the Lucas-Earl rule (Lucas v. Earl, 281 U.S. 111, 50 S.Ct. 241, 74 L.Ed. 731). It was not there held, nor has any case cited to or found by us held that if both principal and interest are given, and the principal matures in the year of the assignment, there would be an anticipatory assignment of income as to the principal, so as to make the giver taxable on unrealized appreciation in its value, or on interest accruing in successive years. Indeed, the contrary has been held in Austin v. Commissioner of Internal Revenue, 6 Cir., 161 F.2d 666.

"Here the facts are entirely different from those of any of the cited cases. Here not interest due on choses in action in the year in which the assignment is made, but calves, chattels, whose value could be realized only by a sale, were given. We have found no case, we have been referred to none holding that unrealized appreciation in the value of cattle given away would be regarded as ordinary income merely because they had no base, were kept for sale in the ordinary course of business, and when sold by the taxpayer would have been ordinary income. Cf. Visintainer v. Commissioner of Internal Revenue, 10 Cir., 187 F.2d 519 and White v. Brodrick, D.C., 104 F.Supp. 213 to the contrary.

　　*　　　*　　　*　　　*　　　*　　　*　　　*　　　*　　　*　　　*

"Were the calves when transferred by gift to the Y.M.C.A. realized income to the appellees in the taxable sense? We think it clear that they were not. If they were, then every appreciation in value of property passing by gift is realized income. We know that this is not so, and that, though it is and has been the contention of the Bureau that it ought to be, Congress has never enacted legislation so providing.

"If appellant's position is sustained here, it must be because the calves were already income to the taxpayers. If in their hands the calves were then their income, of course the making of the gift did not change this status. If they were not income in taxpayers' hands, their gift of them could not, in the present state of the law, result in the receipt of income by them. It is true that efforts have been made to procure the enactment of statutes to change the rule that a gift does not make the donor taxable on unrealized appreciation in the value of

4.　Campbell v. Prothro, supra note 2 at 335–336.

the property given. Congress has so far not adopted, indeed has declined to adopt that view. Under the statutes as they exist, the court may not do so. The judgment is right. It is affirmed."

The opposite result was reached in the distinguishable case of *Tatum v. Commissioner.*[5] In *Tatum* taxpayers owned land which they leased to sharecroppers who paid their rent in the form of a portion of the crops produced. Had the rent been payable in cash or in any form other than crop shares, the landlord would have had to report the rent as gross income for the year of receipt. However, Reg. § 1.61–4(a), a reporting regulation, permits a landlord to defer reporting crop share rent until the year in which such crops are reduced to money or the equivalent of money. Taxpayer landlords upon receiving the crops immediately transferred them to a charitable donee, which sold them in the same year. The court agreed with the Commissioner that the value of the crops was required to be included in taxpayers' income and differentiated Campbell v. Prothro, saying: [6]

"Turning to the question of law we conclude that crop shares in the hands of the landlord essentially are income assets, taxable when reduced to money or the equivalent of money, rather than, like crops in the hands of a farmer, appreciated property items not taxable if assigned to a third party prior to the realization of any income.

"An operating farmer who donates crops to a third party prior to a taxable event, and prior to the point at which he must recognize income, is not required to include the value of the crops in gross income. Rev.Rul. 55–138, supra; Rev.Rul. 55–531, supra. The farmer has done nothing more than assign to another a property asset which has appreciated in value. There has been no taxable event. Neither the harvesting of the crop nor the donative transfer is a taxable event. E. g., Campbell v. Prothro, supra. Thus far Congress has not seen fit to tax unrealized appreciation in property value.

"The share-crop landlord, on the other hand, enters an agreement with his tenant whereby the tenant is given the use of the land in return for a share of the crops produced. When the crops are harvested and delivered the landlord has been paid in kind for the use of his land. Crop shares representing payment by the tenant for the use of the land are rental income assets no less than money paid for the same purpose.

*   *   *   *   *   *   *   *   *   *

"For present purposes it is enough to say that crop shares are potential income assets, not property, and that a landlord may not avoid taxation by assigning his rights to the income prior to the reduction of the crop shares to money or its equivalent. The assignment of income principles of Helvering v. Horst, supra, and the rule of Treas.Reg. § 1.61(a) are applicable to this case and dispositive of the issues it presents."

---

5. 400 F.2d 242 (5th Cir. 1968).   **6.** Id. at 246–248.

The *Tatum* case was followed in Parmer v. Comm'r; [7] and now the Treasury also accepts the timing principles expressed in *Tatum*.[8] Usually, of course, realization of income by the donee fixes the donor's time of reporting in assignment of income cases. The *Tatum* case and its followers differentiate *Horst* on this issue, which at least subsumed that the donor of income (ripe fruit) property should take it into income just as and when he would if he had made no gift and had in fact received the income. The difference lies in the peculiar nature of crop shares which *are* realized income but which, as a matter of administrative convenience, are not required to be reported until converted into money or its equivalent.

Under an extension of the fruit-tree metaphor, it is not just fruit but *ripe* fruit that may leave a donor taxable on post-transfer income. Generally a determination of ripeness is simple, at least once we get the hang of it. Thus in *Tatum*, crop shares in hand represent realized income just waiting around to be taxed. If the income generated by property accrues ratably over time, that portion accrued at the time of the gift is likewise ripe. For example, if interest on a coupon bond is payable semi-annually on January 1 and July 1 and a donor transfers the bond (not just the coupon) on April 1 midway between payment dates, one-half of the current interest coupon is "ripe" as of the time of the transfer and one-half the amount of the coupon is taxed to the donor and the other one-half is taxed to the donee, generally upon payment.[9] This same principle applies to rents, interest on bank accounts and other items that accrue or are generated merely by the passage of time. Dividends on stock create a more difficult problem. They do not automatically accrue with time but are dependent on a decision by the Board of Directors to issue dividends. Consequently, for business purposes a relevant date must be determined on which ownership of the stock fixes the right to the dividend, the so-called "record" date. There are normally four important dates with respect to the issuance of dividends: the declaration date, the record date, the payment date and the date of actual receipt. Sometimes, especially in a closely held corporation,[10] two dates, possibly the record and payment dates, coincide. In one such case [11] the court held that the fruit ripened on the declaration date, taxing the dividend to a donor who made a gift of the stock the day before the record date. But the case involved a small, closely held corporation. In contrast, in Bishop v. Shaughnessy,[12] involving a minority shareholder of a more widely held

7.   468 F.2d 705 (10th Cir. 1972); cf. Sheldon v. Comm'r, 62 T.C. 96 (1974).

8.   Rev.Rul. 75–11, 1975–1 C.B. 27, partially repudiating Rev.Rul. 63–66, 1963–1 C.B. 13.

9.   The timing depends upon the donor's and donee's accounting methods. See Ch. 19, infra.

10.   E. g. Estate of Smith v. Comm'r, 292 F.2d 478 (3rd Cir. 1961).

11.   Ibid.

12.   195 F.2d 683 (2d Cir. 1962). C. (26 U.S.C.A.) §§ 665–668.

corporation, the court reached the conclusion that the fruit ripened on the record date because no enforceable right accrued to any shareholder at the time of the dividend declaration. Is this distinction between closely held and more widely held corporations justified? Are we confronted with conflicting doctrines on assignment of dividend income or merely with divergent tax results sometimes called for, especially in close family circumstances, under the broad rubric of sham transactions?

D. ANTICIPATORY ASSIGNMENT FOR VALUE

ESTATE OF STRANAHAN v. COMMISSIONER

472 F.2d 867 (6th Cir. 1973)*

PECK, CIRCUIT JUDGE: This appeal comes from the United States Tax Court, which partially denied appellant estate's petition for a redetermination of a deficiency in the decedent's income tax for the taxable period January 1, 1965 through November 10, 1965, the date of decedent's death.

The facts before us are briefly recounted as follows: On March 11, 1964, the decedent, Frank D. Stranahan, entered into a closing agreement with the Commissioner of Internal Revenue Service (IRS) under which it was agreed that decedent owed the IRS $754,815.72 for interest due to deficiencies in federal income, estate and gift taxes regarding several trusts created in 1932. Decedent, a cash-basis taxpayer, paid the amount during his 1964 tax year. Because his personal income for the 1964 tax year would not normally have been high enough to fully absorb the large interest deduction, decedent accelerated his future income to avoid losing the tax benefit of the interest deduction. To accelerate the income, decedent executed an agreement dated December 22, 1964, under which he assigned to his son, Duane Stranahan, $122,820 in anticipated stock dividends from decedent's Champion Spark Plug Company common stock (12,500 shares). At the time both decedent and his son were employees and shareholders of Champion. As consideration for this assignment of future stock dividends, decedent's son paid the decedent $115,000 by check dated December 22, 1964. The decedent thereafter directed the transfer agent for Champion to issue all future dividend checks to his son, Duane, until the aggregate amount of $122,820 had been paid to him. Decedent reported this $115,000 payment as ordinary income for the 1964 tax year and thus was able to deduct the full interest payment from the sum of this payment and his other income. During decedent's taxable year in question, dividends in the total amount of $40,050 were paid to and received by decedent's son. No

* Some footnotes omitted.

part of the $40,050 was reported as income in the return filed by decedent's estate for this period. Decedent's son reported this dividend income on his own return as ordinary income subject to the offset of his basis of $115,000, resulting in a net amount of $7,282 of taxable income.

Subsequently, the Commissioner sent appellant (decedent's estate) a notice of deficiency claiming that the $40,050 received by the decedent's son was actually income attributable to the decedent. After making an adjustment which is not relevant here, the Tax Court upheld the deficiency in the amount of $50,916.78. The Tax Court concluded that decedent's assignment of future dividends in exchange for the present discounted cash value of those dividends "though conducted in the form of an assignment of a property right, was in reality a loan to [decedent] masquerading as a sale and so disguised lacked any business purpose; and, therefore, decedent realized taxable income in the year 1965 when the dividend was declared paid."

As pointed out by the Tax Court, several long-standing principles must be recognized. First, under Section 451(a) of the Internal Revenue Code of 1954, a cash basis taxpayer ordinarily realizes income in the year of receipt rather than the year when earned. Second, a taxpayer who assigns future income for consideration in a bona fide commercial transaction will ordinarily realize ordinary income in the year of receipt. Commissioner v. P. G. Lake, Inc., 356 U.S. 260, 78 S.Ct. 691, 2 L.Ed.2d 743 (1958); Hort v. Commissioner, 313 U.S. 28, 61 S.Ct. 757, 85 L.Ed. 1168 (1941). Third, a taxpayer is free to arrange his financial affairs to minimize his tax liability;[1] thus, the presence of tax avoidance motives will not nullify an otherwise bona fide transaction.[2] We also note there are no claims that the transaction was a sham, the purchase price was inadequate or that decedent did not actually receive the full payment of $115,000 in tax year 1964. And it is agreed decedent had the right to enter into a binding contract to sell his right to future dividends. 12 Ohio Jur. 2d, Corporations, Sec. 604.

The Commissioner's view regards the transaction as merely a temporary shift of funds, with an appropriate interest factor, within

1. "Any one may so arrange his affairs that his taxes shall be as low as possible; he is not bound to choose that pattern which will best pay the Treasury; there is not even a patriotic duty to increase one's taxes." Helvering v. Gregory, 69 F.2d 809, 810 (2d Cir. 1934) (Hand, J. Learned), aff'd 293 U.S. 465, 55 S.Ct. 266, 79 L.Ed. 596 (1935).

2. "As to the astuteness of taxpayers in ordering their affairs so as to minimize taxes, we have said that 'the very meaning of a line in the law is that you intentionally may go as close to it as you can if you do not pass it.' Superior Oil Co. v. Mississippi, 280 U.S. 390, 395–396, [50 S.Ct. 169, 74 L.Ed. 504]. This is so because 'nobody owes any public duty to pay more than the law demands; taxes are enforced exactions, not voluntary contributions.'" Atlantic Coast Line v. Phillips, 332 U.S. 168, 172–173, 67 S.Ct. 1584, 1587, 91 L.Ed. 1977 (1947) (Frankfurter, J.).

the family unit. He argues that no change in the beneficial ownership of the stock was effected and no real risks of ownership were assumed by the son. Therefore, the Commissioner concludes, taxable income was realized not on the formal assignment but rather on the actual payment of the dividends.

It is conceded by taxpayer that the sole aim of the assignment was the acceleration of income so as to fully utilize the interest deduction. Gregory v. Helvering, 293 U.S. 465, 55 S.Ct. 266, 79 L.Ed. 596 (1935), established the landmark principle that the substance of a transaction, and not the form, determines the taxable consequences of that transaction. See also Higgins v. Smith, 308 U.S. 473, 60 S.Ct. 355, 84 L.Ed. 406 (1940). In the present transaction, however, it appears that both the form and the substance of the agreement assigned the right to receive future income. What was received by the decedent was the present value of that income the son could expect in the future. On the basis of the stock's past performance, the future income could have been (and was) estimated with reasonable accuracy. Essentially, decedent's son paid consideration to receive future income. Of course, the fact of a family transaction does not vitiate the transaction but merely subjects it to special scrutiny. Helvering v. Clifford, 309 U.S. 331, 60 S.Ct. 554, 84 L.Ed. 788 (1940).

We recognize the oft-stated principle that a taxpayer cannot escape taxation by legally assigning or giving away a portion of the income derived from income producing property retained by the taxpayer. Lucas v. Earl, 281 U.S. 111, 50 S.Ct. 241, 74 L.Ed. 731 (1930); Helvering v. Horst, 311 U.S. 112, 61 S.Ct. 144, 85 L.Ed. 75 (1940); Commissioner v. P. G. Lake, Inc., supra. Here, however, the acceleration of income was not designed to avoid or escape recognition of the dividends but rather to reduce taxation by fully utilizing a substantial interest deduction which was available. As stated previously, tax avoidance motives alone will not serve to obviate the tax benefits of a transaction. Further, the fact that this was a transaction for good and sufficient consideration, and not merely gratuitous, distinguishes the instant case from the line of authority beginning with Helvering v. Horst, supra.

The Tax Court in its opinion relied on three cases. In Fred W. Warner, 5 B.T.A. 963 (1926), which involved an assignment by taxpayer to his wife of all dividend income respecting his 12,500 shares of General Motors Corporation stock, it was held the dividends were income to the taxpayer and were not diverted to the wife through the purported assignment. However, this was a mere gratuitous assignment of income since apparently the only consideration for the assignment was ten dollars. Alfred LeBlanc, 7 B.T.A. 256 (1927), involved a shareholder-father assigning dividends to his son for as long as the son remained with the father's corporation. The Court held that in effect the father postdated his assignment to the dates when he was to receive dividends and hence the dividends were income to the father. However, here again it is apparent that at the time of the assignment there was no consideration.

* * *

[The third case is omitted. Ed.]

Hence the fact that valuable consideration was an integral part of the transaction distinguishes this case from those where the simple expedient of drawing up legal papers and assigning income to others is used. The Tax Court uses the celebrated metaphor of Justice Holmes regarding the "fruit" and the "tree", and concludes there has been no effective separation of the fruit from the tree. Judge Cardozo's comment that "[m]etaphors in law are to be narrowly watched, for starting as devices to liberate thought, they end often by enslaving it" (Berkey v. Third Avenue Railway Co., 244 N.Y. 84, 94, 155 N.E. 58, 61 (1926)) is appropriate here, as the genesis of the metaphor lies in a gratuitous transaction, while the instant situation concerns a transaction for a valuable consideration.

The Commissioner also argues that the possibility of not receiving the dividends was remote, and that since this was particularly known to the parties as shareholders and employees of the corporation, no risks inured to the son. The Commissioner attempts to bolster this argument by pointing out that consideration was computed merely as a discount based on a prevailing interest rate and that the dividends were in fact paid at a rate faster than anticipated. However, it seems clear that risks, however remote, did in fact exist. The fact that the risks did not materialize is irrelevant. Assessment of the risks is a matter of negotiation between the parties and is usually reflected in the terms of the agreement. Since we are not in a position to evaluate those terms, and since we are not aware of any terms which dilute the son's dependence on the dividends alone to return his investment, we cannot say he does not bear the risks of ownership.

Accordingly, we conclude the transaction to be economically realistic, with substance, and therefore should be recognized for tax purposes even though the consequences may be unfavorable to the Commissioner. The facts established decedent did in fact receive payment. Decedent deposited his son's check for $115,000 to his personal account on December 23, 1964, the day after the agreement was signed. The agreement is unquestionably a complete and valid assignment to decedent's son of all dividends up to $122,820. The son acquired an independent right against the corporation since the latter was notified of the private agreement. Decedent completely divested himself of any interest in the dividends and vested the interest on the day of execution of the agreement with his son.

The Commissioner cites J. A. Martin, 56 T.C. 1255 (1972), aff'd No. 72–1416 (5th Cir., August 18, 1972), to show how similar attempts to accelerate income have been rejected by the courts. There taxpayer assigned future rents in return for a stated cash advance. Taxpayer agreed to repay the principal advanced plus a 7% per annum interest. These facts distinguish this situation from the instant case as there the premises were required to remain open for two years' full rental operation, suggesting a guarantee toward repayment. No such commitment is apparent here.

The judgment is reversed and the cause remanded for further proceedings consistent with this opinion.

REVENUE RULING 69–102

1969–1 Cum.Bull. 32.

Advice has been requested by an individual with respect to the Federal income tax consequences to him upon the maturity and surrender for their cash surrender values of an endowment life insurance contract and an annuity contract under the circumstances described below.

In the instant case, the taxpayer sold an unencumbered endowment life insurance contract to a charitable organization described in section 170(c) of the Internal Revenue Code of 1954 for an amount equal to his basis therein, net aggregate of premiums or other consideration paid less dividends received, donating his remaining interest to the charity. [Since 1969 such a transaction would require an allocation of taxpayer's basis between the portion sold to a charity and the portion given so that there would be a taxable gain on these facts at the time of the transfer. I.R.C. (26 U.S.C.A.) § 1011(b). See I.R.C. (26 U.S.C.A.) § 1011(b) and Chapter 23, infra at page 835. Ed.] At the same time he made a gift of an unencumbered annuity contract to his son. In the donor's succeeding taxable year both contracts matured and were surrendered by the donees to the insurance company for their then cash surrender values. The cash surrender value of each contract at the time of the transfers to the donees exceeded the amount of the donor's basis. In accordance with the terms of the policy, the insurance company was notified of its assignment and provided with the name and address of the new owners.

Section 1.61–1 of the Income Tax Regulations provides, in part, that gross income includes income realized in any form. It is well established that income is taxable to the person who realizes it, the incidence of the tax not being shifted by a gift thereof to another. Lucas v. Guy C. Earl, 281 U.S. 111 (1930). Also, it has been pointed out that "one who is entitled to receive at a future date, interest or compensation for services and who makes a gift of it by an anticipatory assignment, realizes taxable income quite as much as if he had collected the income and paid it over to the object of his bounty" and "the power to dispose of income is the equivalent of ownership of it and   *   *   *   the exercise of the power to procure its payment to another, whether to pay a debt or to make a gift, is within the reach of the statute taxing income 'derived from any source whatever.'" Harrison v. Sarah H. Schaffner, 312 U.S. 579 (1941), Ct.D. 1503, C.B. 1941-1, 321, 322. The Tax Court of the United States has held that "The theory of the cases dealing with anticipatory assignment of income by gift has not been concerned with when the income was accrued in a legal sense of accrual but rather with whether the income has been earned so that the right to the payment at a future date existed when the gift was made.   *   *   *   It is the giving away of this right to income in advance of payments which has been held not to change the *incidence* of the tax." (Emphasis added.) S. M. Friedman v. Commissioner, 41 T.C. 428, 435, affirmed 346 F.2d 506 (1965).

As to the time of realization, the Supreme Court of the United States has said, "Where the taxpayer does not receive payment of income in money or property realization may occur when the last step is taken by which he obtains the fruition of the economic gain *which has already accrued to him.*" (Emphasis added.) Helvering v. Paul R. G. Horst, 311 U.S. 112, 115 (1940), Ct.D. 1472, C.B. 1940-2, 206, 207. It follows that the time of the gift is not determinative of the time when income is realized. It has been consistently held that a gift of income does not operate to accelerate the year of taxability. See the *Friedman* case, above, wherein the following was said (p. 436):

"A cash basis taxpayer is not taxable on income until he receives it actually or constructively. The making of a gift of his right to receive income does not cause such income to be received until the donor derives the economic benefit of having the income received by his donee.   *   *   *"

See also Helvering v. Gerald A. Eubank, 311 U.S. 122 (1940), Ct.D. 1473, C.B. 1940-2, 209; Abraham E. Duran et al., v. Commissioner, 123 F.2d 324 (1941); and Annie A. Colby v. Commissioner, 45 B.T.A. 536 (1941), acquiescence C.B. 1942-2, 4.

In the instant case, it is held that the taxpayer is in receipt of taxable income for the taxable year in which the endowment and annuity contracts were surrendered for their cash surrender values by the recipients, the amount of such income being the excess of the cash surrender value of each contract at the time of gift over the taxpayer's basis in that contract. The gain realized through the transfer of the contracts is ordinary income. Commissioner v. Percy W. Phillips, et al., 275 F.2d 33 (1960).

The excess of the fair market value of the endowment contract sold to the charitable organization over the amount received therefor is the measure of the charitable contribution for the taxable year in which the contract was transferred.

*   *   *

PROBLEMS

1. Executive has a salaried position with Hi Rolling Corporation under which he earns $80,000 each calendar year.

   (a) Who is taxed if Executive, at the beginning of the year, directs that $20,000 of his salary be paid to his aged parents?

   (b) Who is taxed if Executive at the beginning of the year directs that $20,000 of his salary be paid to any charity the Board of Directors of Hi Rolling selects? (Executive is not a member of the Board.)

   (c) Same as (b), above, except that Executive makes the same request with respect to a $10,000 year end bonus which Corporation has announced toward the end of the year, based on services rendered during the year?

   (d) Who is taxed if Executive, in his corporate role, gives a series of lectures on corporate finance at a local business school, and, pursuant to his contract with Hi Rolling, turns his $1000 honorarium over to Corporation?

2. Father owns a corporate coupon bond which he purchased several years ago for $8000. It has a $10,000 face amount and is to be paid off in 1984. The current fair market value of the bond is $9,000. The bond pays 6% interest, semi-annually April 1st and October 1st (i. e., $300 each payment). What tax consequences to Father and Daughter in the following alternative situations?

   (a) On April 2 of the current year, Father gives Daughter all the interest coupons.

   (b) On April 2, Father gives Daughter the bond with all interest coupons attached.

   (c) On April 2, Father gives Daughter a one-half interest in the bond and all the interest coupons.

   (d) On April 2, Father sells Daughter two succeeding interest coupons for $500, their fair market value as of the time of sale.

   (e) On December 31, Father gives Daughter the bond with all interest coupons attached.

   (f) On April 2, Father sells the bond and directs that the $9,000 sale price be paid to Daughter.

   (g) Prior to April 2, Father negotiates the above sale and on April 2 he transfers the bond to Daughter who transfers the bond to Buyer who pays Daughter the $9,000.

3. In a recent clipping from the financial page of the San Francisco *CHRONICLE* it was reported:

   Playboy Enterprises Inc. declared a semiannual dividend of six cents a share Tuesday, but the company said its president, Hugh Hefner, decided to give his back.

A spokesman said Hefner's dividend would have totaled more than $380,000. He holds more than six million of the total shares in the company, or 72 percent of the stock.

"It was a gesture of his faith in the company," the spokesman said. "It will go back to the company for its use."

How will Mr. Hefner's gesture be treated by the Commissioner? What additional facts do you want to know?

4. Inventor develops a new electric switch which he patents. Who is taxed on the proceeds of its subsequent sale if:

(a) The patent is transferred gratuitously to Son who sells it to Buyer?

(b) Inventor transfers all his interest in the patent to Buyer for a royalty contract and then transfers the contract gratuitously to Son prior to receiving any royalties? See Heim v. Fitzpatrick, 262 F.2d 887 (2d Cir. 1959).

CHAPTER 14. INCOME PRODUCING ENTITIES

A. INTRODUCTION

The Internal Revenue Code recognizes three principal types of income producing entities: partnerships, corporations, and trusts. To what extent do they lend themselves to income fragmentization with an eye toward graduated tax rates? Only partial answers are suggested here. The routine tax treatment of, and detailed measures designed to prevent the tax abuse of each entity are large areas of study usually relegated to separate courses. This part of this Chapter describes the basic tax character of each entity, and the parts that follow explore some income assignment questions with respect to each.

Partnerships. The Internal Revenue Code provisions that present special rules for income earned by partnerships appear in Subchapter K, §§ 701 through 771. A partnership is essentially a conduit for income tax purposes, because it is required to file only an information return reporting its annual income or loss,[1] and the income is taxed to, or the loss deducted by the various partners, individually.[2] A partnership's "taxable income" is computed under I.R.C. (26 U.S. C.A.) § 703, but this is for the purpose of allocating taxable amounts among the members, as "[p]ersons carrying on business as partners shall be liable for income tax only in their separate or individual capacities." [3] In general, the tax impact of partnership transactions on each individual partner is determined by the partnership agreement. With some exceptions, such private agreements fix a "partner's distributive share of income, gain, loss, deduction, or credit   *   *   *." [4] The partnership form of doing business is of course very flexible; almost everything depends upon what is agreed to by the members. The tax laws take account of such flexibility and, to a great extent, give effect to the private agreements made. When transactions are at arm's length, this works rather well. But the obvious question here is to what extent family members may make agreements at variance with economic reality and then seek to insist that such agreements be accorded tax recognition. Is there, at least at first blush, an invitation to income assignment?

Corporations. The Internal Revenue Code provisions that provide special rules for the income taxation of corporations and shareholders appear in Subchapter C, §§ 301 through 395. A corporation is at the opposite end of the tax spectrum from a partnership. A corporation is an entity that is taxed, at special rates applicable only to

1. Form 1065.

2. I.R.C. (26 U.S.C.A.) § 701.

3. Ibid.

4. I.R.C. (26 U.S.C.A.) § 704(a).

corporations.[5] When corporate after-tax income is distributed as dividends to shareholders, it is taxed (again?) to the shareholders, in their individual capacities.[6] Dividends are taxed as ordinary income, however, only to the extent of the corporation's "earnings and profits," earnings of the current year or accumulated from prior years.[7]

While a partner is not insulated from partnership income for tax purposes, a shareholder usually is insulated from the income of a corporation. In general, a corporation is an entity separate and apart from its shareholders.[8] Therefore, the incorporation of a partnership or sole proprietorship is itself a fragmentation device, because a new taxpayer has come upon the scene. But is this invariably a tax advantage? Recall the tax treatment of corporate distributions. In any event, corporate distributions are generally taxed to the owners of the stock on which the dividends are paid. Are there, then, double fragmentization possibilities with respect to income earned by corporations?[9]

Trusts. For tax purposes a trust falls between a partnership and a corporation. Depending upon the circumstances, the income from a trust may be taxed to the beneficiaries, to the trust, or in part to each. The Internal Revenue Code provisions that present special rules for the determination of tax liability on income earned by trusts (and decedent's estates) appear in Subchapter J, I.R.C. (26 U.S.C.A.) §§ 641 through 692. While quite successful in fitting trusts and estates into a comprehensive scheme of federal taxation, the provisions are highly complex. But this is not to say the area should be completely ignored in a course on tax fundamentals. The objectives here are two-fold: first, to describe very generally the way in which trust and estate income is taxed and second, as in the partnership and corporate area, to look in just a little more detail at specified circumstances in which Congress prescribes a departure from the usual trust rules in order to prevent tax abuses that could arise out of questionable income assignment devices.

Congress has identified a trust as a tax-paying entity whose tax liability is generally determined in a manner similar to that of individuals.[10] On the other hand, a basic aspect of congressional policy is

---

5. I.R.C. (26 U.S.C.A.) § 11.

6. I.R.C. (26 U.S.C.A.) §§ 61(a) (7), 301.

7. I.R.C. (26 U.S.C.A.) § 316.

8. The exceptions are a corporation that is treated as a mere sham and ignored, U. S. v. McGuire, 249 F.Supp. 43 (S.D.N.Y.1965), and a so-called "tax-option" corporation. Tax option corporations that elect Subchapter S achieve more nearly conduit status. I.R.C. (26 U.S.C.A.) §§ 1371–1379.

9. The student should be fully aware that many assignment of income problems in the business area are largely ignored here. E. g., I.R.C. (26 U.S.C.A.) § 482, authorizing the commissioner to reallocate income, deductions, etc., among related taxpayers; § 269, disallowing some expected tax benefits questionably sought by way of corporate acquisitions and transfers; § 1551, denying surtax exemptions to some multiple incorporations.

10. I.R.C. (26 U.S.C.A.) § 641.

that trust income is to be taxed only once on its way into the hands of its beneficial owners. A further aspect of the plan, seemingly inconsistent with the objective of taxing trust income but once, is to tax trust beneficiaries on amounts of trust income to which they are entitled or which are in fact properly distributed to them.[11] If income may be taxed to the beneficiaries *and* to the trust, how is the one tax objective to be accomplished? The answer is a distribution deduction for the trust, commensurate with the amount of its income which is distributed and taxed to the beneficiaries.[12] In determining the *taxable* income of the trust, a deduction is allowed generally for amounts required to be, or otherwise properly paid to beneficiaries. In effect, *such* income escapes tax at the trust level but is taxed to the beneficiaries.[13]

It will be observed that in the case of what is called a "simple" trust (essentially one required to distribute all its income currently) the trust, while a *potential* taxable entity, serves as little more than a conduit for both tax and non-tax purposes, simply funneling income to the trust beneficiaries. In other trusts, known as "complex" trusts, where all or a part of the trust income may be accumulated, all or a part of the income may be taxed to the trust and none or only a part of the income to beneficiaries. Consider, then, how a trust appears to present a double fragmentization opportunity somewhat similar to that noted with respect to corporations.

This general description can be extended without getting into too much detail. Outside the "throw-back" area,[14] the statute operates with regard to trust income for the taxable year of the trust. The objective is a division of the tax on such *annual* income between the trust and its beneficiaries. Some students will see a difference from the corporate approach in which previously accumulated (not just current) earnings and profits affect the taxability of corporate distributions.

In another respect, however, the trust provisions resemble the corporate rules. For trust purposes a "distributable net income" of the trust is determined annually,[15] which is somewhat similar to *current* corporate earnings and profits in its regulation of the *amount* on which distributees may be subject to tax.[16] In effect D.N.I., as it is often called, identifies a kind of net income for the year, which could be taxed entirely to the trust or partly or entirely to beneficiaries. However, in the trust (and estate) area, this quantitative objective is not the sole function of D.N.I. In keeping with an essentially conduit

---

11. I.R.C. (26 U.S.C.A.) §§ 652, 662.

12. I.R.C. (26 U.S.C.A.) §§ 651, 661.

13. These broad comments apply equally to the income of estates and their beneficiaries. See I.R.C. (26 U.S.C.A.) § 641.

14. There are possible abusive uses of the trust not discussed here. See I.R. C. (26 U.S.C.A.) §§ 665–668.

15. I.R.C. (26 U.S.C.A.) § 643(a).

16. I.R.C. (26 U.S.C.A.) §§ 651(b), 652 (a), 661(a), 662(a).

approach to the taxation of trust income, D.N.I. is seen as made up of the various *kinds* of income received by the trust, and distributions are considered to consist of ratable portions of each *kind* of income.[17] In this respect, D.N.I. serves a characterization or *qualitative* function in addition to its quantitative function. Thus, if a trust properly distributes half its income to a beneficiary and if half of the trust's income is tax-exempt interest, one half of what the beneficiary receives retains its tax-exempt character in his hands.[18]

One laudable objective of the D.N.I. device is to eliminate the need for tracing. There are circumstances in which a trust instrument may direct income of a particular kind to a specified beneficiary;[19] but, in the ordinary case, where income is simply to be divided no tracing is required; instead, each beneficiary reports a ratable share of all trust income items.[20] Similarly, it is no longer open to argument whether a particular distribution was of principal or of income; the question is immaterial, in the determination of tax liability, as a distribution is deemed to be out of distributable net income to the extent of D.N.I. Distributions that exceed D.N.I. are generally received as tax-free gifts or, in case of an estate, bequests.[21]

A detailed description of the federal income tax characteristics of each of these three types of entities is beyond the scope of this book. Such details, however, are well supplied in Willis, *Partnership Taxation* (2nd Edition, McGraw-Hill, 1976); Bittker and Eustice, *Federal Income Taxation of Corporations and Shareholders* (3rd Edition, Warren, Gorham, and Lamont, 1971); Ferguson, Freeland, and Stephens, *Federal Income Taxation of Estates and Beneficiaries* (Little, Brown and Company, 1970), in large part as applicable to trusts as to estates.

---

17. I.R.C. (26 U.S.C.A.) §§ 652(b), 662 (b); see also § 661(b) and Reg. § 1.651 (b)–1.

18. Recall, e. g., the tax-exempt nature of some bond interest under I.R.C. (26 U.S.C.A.) § 103.

19. See Reg. §§ 1.652(b)–2, 1.662(b)–1.

20. I.R.C. (26 U.S.C.A.) §§ 652(b), 662 (b).

21. See I.R.C. (26 U.S.C.A.) § 102.

B.   TRUSTS AND ESTATES

Internal Revenue Code: Sections 671;   672(a), (b);   673;   676;   677.   See
    Sections 644;   672(c), (d);   674;   675;   678;   679.
Regulations: Sections   1.671–1;   1.673(a)–1   (omit 1.673(a)–1(a)   (2));
    1.676(a)–1;   1.676(b)–1.

CORLISS v. BOWERS

Supreme Court of the United States, 1930.
281 U.S. 376, 50 S.Ct. 336.

MR. JUSTICE HOLMES delivered the opinion of the Court.

This is a suit to recover the amount of an income tax paid by the plaintiff, the petitioner, under the Revenue Act of 1924, June 2, 1924, c. 234, § 219, (g) (h), 43 Stat. 253, 277.   (U.S.C., Tit. 26, § 960.)   The complaint was dismissed by the District Court, 30 F.2d 135, and the judgment was affirmed by the Circuit Court of Appeals, 34 F.2d 656. A writ of certiorari was granted by this Court.

The question raised by the petitioner is whether the above section of the Revenue Act can be applied constitutionally to him upon the following facts.   In 1922 he transferred the fund from which arose the income in respect of which the petitioner was taxed, to trustees, in trust to pay the income to his wife for life with remainder over to their children.   By the instrument creating the trust the petitioner reserved power "to modify or alter in any manner, or revoke in whole or in part, this indenture and the trusts then existing, and the estates and interests in property hereby created" &c.   It is not necessary to quote more words because there can be no doubt that the petitioner fully reserved the power at any moment to abolish or change the trust at his will.   The statute referred to provides that "when the grantor of a trust has, at any time during the taxable year,   *   *   *   the power to revest in himself title to any part of the corpus of the trust then the income of such part of the trust for such taxable year shall be included in computing the net income of the grantor."   § 219(g) with other similar provisions as to income in § 219(h).   [See I.R.C. §§ 676 and 677.   Ed.]   There can be no doubt either that the statute purports to tax the plaintiff in this case.   But the net income for 1924 was paid over to the petitioner's wife and the petitioner's argument is that however it might have been in different circumstances the income never was his and he cannot be taxed for it.   The legal estate was in the trustee and the equitable interest in the wife.

But taxation is not so much concerned with the refinements of title as it is with actual command over the property taxed—the actual benefit for which the tax is paid.   If a man directed his bank to pay over income as received to a servant or friend, until further orders, no one would doubt that he could be taxed upon the amounts so paid. It is answered that in that case he would have a title, whereas here he did not. But from the point of view of taxation there would be no difference. The title would merely mean a right to stop the payment before it took place. The same right existed here although it is not called a title but is called a power. The acquisition by the wife of the income became complete only when the plaintiff failed to exercise the power that he reserved. Saltonstall v. Saltonstall, 276 U.S. 260, 271. Chase National Bank v. United States, 278 U.S. 327. Reinecke v. Northern Trust Co., 278 U.S. 339. Still speaking with reference to taxation, if a man disposes of a fund in such a way that another is allowed to enjoy the income which it is in the power of the first to appropriate it does not matter whether the permission is given by assent or by failure to express dissent. The income that is subject to a man's unfettered command and that he is free to enjoy at his own option may be taxed to him as his income whether he sees fit to enjoy it or not. We consider the case too clear to need help from the local law of New York or from arguments based on the power of Congress to prevent escape from taxes or surtaxes by devices that easily might be applied to that end.

Judgment affirmed.

The CHIEF JUSTICE took no part in this case.

MORRILL v. UNITED STATES

District Court of the United States, Southern District of Maine, 1964.
228 F.Supp. 734.

GIGNOUX, DISTRICT JUDGE. This is an action for refund of federal income taxes for the years 1959, 1960 and 1961 in the amounts of $1,736.75, $2,344.50 and $3,064.63, respectively. The only question presented is whether the amounts of the income of four trusts established by George B. Morrill, Jr., which the trustees applied to the payment of the tuition and room charges of the taxpayers' four minor children at private schools and colleges, were taxable as income to him under the provisions of Section 677(a) of the Internal Revenue Code of 1954, 26 U.S.C.A. § 677(a).

The relevant facts, which have been stipulated, may be briefly stated: In April, 1959 Mr. Morrill established four short-term trusts, one for the benefit of each of his four minor children, and named a corporate trustee of each trust. The income of each trust was to be accumulated until the child became 21 years of age, at which time the accumulated income, and thereafter during the remaining term of the trust any current income, was to be distributed to the beneficiary. Ten years after the date of their creation, the trusts were to terminate and the corpus of each was to revert to Mr. Morrill. Each of the trusts also provided that during the minority of the beneficiary, the trustee might, in its discretion, use the trust income "for the payment of room, tuition, books and travel to and from any private school, college or other institution of learning at home or abroad."

During the tax years in question, the taxpayers' children attended Vassar College, Connecticut College, Brown University, The Holderness School and The Waynflete School. Mr. Morrill expressly assumed responsibility for the payment of the tuition, room, board and other expenses of his children at Vassar College and Connecticut College.[1] There was no express agreement between Mr. Morrill and Brown University, The Holderness School, or The Waynflete School regarding the payment of the expenses of his children at those schools. However, each school submitted its bills to Mr. Morrill. He then wrote out a personal check to the institution for that portion of the bill other than room and tuition, sent the bill with his personal check to the trustee of the appropriate trust, and requested the trustee to pay from the trust the room and tuition charges on the bill. The trustee then mailed to the institution its check in payment of the room and tuition charges, together with Mr. Morrill's check for the balance of the bill involved.

George B. Morrill, Jr. and Elizabeth H. Morrill, as husband and wife, filed joint federal income tax returns for the calendar years 1959, 1960 and 1961. They did not include in the returns any of the income of the four children's trusts. Upon audit of the returns, the Commissioner determined that the amounts of trust income which had been applied in payment of the children's tuition and room charges had been used to satisfy legal obligations of Mr. Morrill, as father of the children, and were therefore taxable as income to him under Section 677 of the 1954 Code.[2] Plaintiffs paid under protest the resulting de-

1. Mr. Morrill signed the following agreement with Vassar College: "In consideration of the acceptance by Vassar College of Bonnie Elizabeth Morrill I agree to be responsible for her tuition, room and board, and other incidental expenses, in accordance with the terms and conditions stated in the current catalogue." He signed the following agreement with Connecticut College: "Bills may be sent to me and I assume responsibility for their payment until further notice."

2. The Commissioner initially based his assessment on Section 677(b). The Government later shifted its ground for asserting taxability to Section 677(a). During legal argument before the Court, counsel for the Government and for the taxpayers conceded that Section 677(b) has no application to the facts of this case. In this they were correct because Sub-

section (b) merely limits the tax, imposed by Subsection (a), on trust income which may be applied for the support or maintenance of a beneficiary whom the grantor is legally obligated to support or maintain, to that portion of the trust income which is so applied. Here the Government has not attempted to tax that part of the trust income which was not used to pay the school and college bills in issue. Congress enacted what is now Subsection (b), 58 Stat. 51 (1944), to change the law established by the holding in Helvering v. Stuart, 317 U.S. 154, 63 S.Ct. 140, 87 L.Ed. 154 (1942). See 6 Mertens, Federal Income Taxation § 37.21 (1948).

Despite the Government's change of theory, the burden of proof in this tax refund suit remains on the taxpayers to show that they have overpaid their taxes for the years in question. Lewis v. Reynolds, 284 U.S.

ficiency assessments, and instituted this suit after their claims for refund were disallowed. For reasons which it will state briefly, this Court has concluded that the Commissioner was correct.

Section 671 of the Internal Revenue Code of 1954, 26 U.S.C. § 671, provides that the income of a trust is taxable to the person specified in the Code as the owner of the trust. Section 677(a) of the Code provides in relevant part:

"§ 677. Income for benefit of grantor

"(a) General rule.—The grantor shall be treated as the owner of any portion of a trust ` * * *` whose income without the approval or consent of any adverse party is, or, in the discretion of the grantor or a nonadverse party, or both, may be—

   "(1) distributed to the grantor [or the grantor's spouse * * *; (as amended in 1969). Ed.]"

A long line of judicial decisions applying Section 677(a) and its predecessor statutes has established that trust income which is used to satisfy a legal obligation of the grantor is, in effect, distributed to him and is, therefore, taxable to him. Douglas v. Willcuts, 296 U.S. 1, 56 S.Ct. 59, 80 L.Ed. 3 (1935) (trust income used to discharge divorced settlor's alimony obligation); Helvering v. Stokes, 296 U.S. 551, 56 S.Ct. 308, 80 L.Ed. 389 (1935), reversing, C. I. R. v. Stokes, 3 Cir., 79 F.2d 256 (trust income used to discharge settlor's legal obligation to support, educate and maintain his minor children); Helvering v. Schweitzer, 296 U.S. 551, 56 S.Ct. 304, 80 L.Ed. 389 (1935), reversing 7 Cir., 75 F.2d 702 (trust income used to discharge settlor's legal obligation to support, educate and maintain his minor children); Helvering v. Blumenthal, 296 U.S. 552, 56 S.Ct. 305, 80 L.Ed. 390 (1935), reversing 2 Cir., 76 F.2d 507 (trust income used to discharge settlor's debt); Helvering v. Coxey, 297 U.S. 694, 56 S.Ct. 498, 80 L.Ed. 986 (1936), reversing 3 Cir., 79 F.2d 661 (trust income used to discharge settlor's alimony and support obligation); Helvering v. Fitch, 309 U.S. 149, 60 S.Ct. 427, 84 L.Ed. 665 (1940) (trust income used to discharge divorced settlor's alimony obligation); Helvering v. Stuart, 317 U.S. 154, 63 S.Ct. 140, 87 L.Ed. 154 (1942) (trust income used to discharge settlor's legal obligation to support, educate and maintain his minor children); Mairs v. Reynolds, 120 F.2d 857 (8th Cir. 1941) (trust income used to discharge settlor's legal obligation to support and educate his minor children); Hamiel's Estate v. Comm'r, 253 F.2d 787 (6th Cir. 1958) (trust income used for the support, maintenance and education of settlor's minor child); Sheaffer's Estate v. Comm'r, 313 F.2d 738 (8th Cir.), cert. denied, 375 U.S. 818, 84 S.Ct. 55, 11 L.Ed.2d 53 (1963) (trust income used to discharge settlor's primary obligation to pay gift taxes arising from transfers in creation of the trust.) The Treasury Regulations reflect this fundamental

281, 52 S.Ct. 145, 76 L.Ed. 293 (1932); Roybark v. United States, 218 F.2d 164 (9th Cir. 1954); Maine Steel, Inc. v. United States, 174 F.Supp. 702, 715 (D.Me.1959).

principle. Treas.Reg. § 1.677(a)–1(d). The transaction is regarded "as being the same in substance as if the money had been paid to the taxpayer and he had transmitted it to his creditor." Douglas v. Willcuts, supra, 296 U.S. at 9, 56 S.Ct. at 63, 80 L.Ed. 3. The income is taxable to the grantor when used to discharge his individual obligation, whether imposed by law or by contract. 6 Mertens, Federal Income Taxation § 37.06 at 434 (1948); compare Douglas v. Willcuts, supra with Helvering v. Blumenthal, supra.

In the present case, the trust income paid to each of the schools and colleges was used to defray expenses for which Mr. Morrill was legally liable. The taxpayers concede that Mr. Morrill was personally obligated for payment of his children's expenses at Vassar College and Connecticut College, because he had expressly assumed that responsibility. It also seems very evident that Mr. Morrill had impliedly obligated himself to pay his children's bills at Brown University, The Holderness School and The Waynflete School. It is a settled principle of contract law that when one renders services to another at the request, or with the knowledge and consent, of the other, and the surrounding circumstances make it reasonable for him to believe that he will receive payment therefor from the other, and he does so believe, a promise to pay will be inferred, and there is an implied contract. 3 Corbin, Contracts, § 566 (1960); Restatement, Contracts § 72 (1932); Saunders v. Saunders, 90 Me. 284, 38 A. 172 (1897); Leighton v. Nash, 111 Me. 525, 90 A. 385 (1914); Gordon v. Keene, 118 Me. 269, 107 A. 849 (1919); Stinson v. Bridges, 152 Me. 306, 129 A.2d 203 (1957). The implied obligation to pay arises whether the services are rendered directly to the other person or to a third person at the request of the other. 3 Corbin, op. cit. supra, § 566 at 312–14. The application of this principle to the determination of Mr. Morrill's obligations with reference to payment of the children's expenses at Brown University, The Holderness School and The Waynflete School is clear. Mr. Morrill was the parent and natural guardian of the children, and insofar as the record shows, approved of their enrollment in these institutions. The record is devoid of evidence that the schools were asked, or agreed, to accept the children with the understanding that they would look only to the trusts for the payment of their room and tuition charges—in fact, there is no evidence that the schools were even aware of the existence of the trusts when they accepted the children. Nor is there any suggestion that the schools looked to the children themselves for the payment of these bills. In each instance the institutions sent their bills to Mr. Morrill. Not once did they submit their bills to the trustees or to the children. Under these circumstances, the only reasonable conclusion is that the schools believed that Mr. Morrill was to be responsible for payment of any bills incurred on behalf of his children. In this they were clearly justified, as it was reasonable for them to expect, in the absence of an express disclaimer by him of an intention to be responsible for the bills, that he would pay for his children's education.

Plaintiffs argue that Mr. Morrill at most undertook, as a party secondarily liable, to guarantee payment of the schools' bills by the children, as the primary obligors. In this view, they assert that the payments by each trustee satisfied the child's obligation and merely extinguished that of Mr. Morrill. The fallacy in this argument is that it presupposes the existence of contracts between the schools and the children. There is no indication that there were any such express contracts; nor is there any showing of circumstances from which a court could imply such contracts. Indeed, it is incredible that these institutions were looking to the children, all of whom were minors without any apparent assets of their own, for payment of these bills. The facts of the case clearly establish that Mr. Morrill, rather than his children, expressly or impliedly undertook to assume primary responsibility for the payment of the school bills here in issue, and that he, and he alone, was legally liable therefor.

The Court holds that the amounts of trust income which the trustees applied in payment of the tuition and room charges of the taxpayers' four minor children at the private schools and colleges which they attended during the tax years in question were used to satisfy express or implied contractual obligations of Mr. Morrill, the grantor of the trusts, and were therefore taxable as income to him under the provisions of Section 677(a) of the 1954 Code. In view of this disposition of the case, it is unnecessary for the Court to consider the Government's alternative contention that such income was taxable to Mr. Morrill, also under Section 677(a), on the theory that Mr. Morrill, as a parent, was under a duty imposed by Maine law to pay the school and college bills of his children. Compare Mairs v. Reynolds, supra.

Judgment will be entered for the defendant against the plaintiffs, with costs.

HELVERING v. CLIFFORD

Supreme Court of the United States, 1940.
309 U.S. 331, 60 S.Ct. 554.

MR. JUSTICE DOUGLAS delivered the opinion of the Court.

In 1934, respondent declared himself trustee of certain securities which he owned. All net income from the trust was to be held for the "exclusive benefit" of respondent's wife. The trust was for a term of five years, except that it would terminate earlier on the death of either respondent or his wife. On termination of the trust the entire corpus was to go to respondent, while all "accrued or undistributed net income" and "any proceeds from the investment of such net income" was to be treated as property owned absolutely by the wife. During the continuance of the trust respondent was to pay over to his wife the whole or such part of the net income as he in his "absolute discretion" might determine. And during that period he had full power (a) to exercise all voting powers incident to the trusteed shares of stock; (b) to "sell, exchange, mortgage, or pledge" any of the securities under the declaration of trust "whether as part of the corpus or principal thereof or as investments or proceeds and any income therefrom, upon such terms and for such consideration" as respondent in his "absolute discretion may deem fitting"; (c) to invest "any cash or money in the trust estate or any income therefrom" by loans, secured or unsecured, by deposits in banks, or by purchase of securities or other personal property "without restriction" because of their "speculative character" or "rate of return" or any "laws pertaining to the investment of trust funds"; (d) to collect all income; (e) to compromise, etc., any claims held by him as trustee; (f) to hold any property in the trust estate in the names of "other persons or in my own name as an individual" except as otherwise provided. Extraordinary cash dividends, stock dividends, proceeds from the sale of unexercised subscription rights, or any enhancement, realized or not, in the value of the securities were to be treated as principal, not income. An exculpatory clause purported to protect him from all losses except those occasioned by his "own wilful and deliberate" breach of duties as trustee. And finally it was provided that neither the principal nor any future or accrued income should be liable for the debts of the wife; and that the wife could not transfer, encumber, or anticipate any interest in the trust or any income therefrom prior to actual payment thereof to her.

It was stipulated that while the "tax effects" of this trust were considered by respondent they were not the "sole consideration" involved in his decision to set it up, as by this and other gifts he intended to give "security and economic independence" to his wife and children. It was also stipulated that respondent's wife had substantial income of her own from other sources; that there was no restriction on her use of the trust income, all of which income was placed in her personal checking account, intermingled with her other funds, and expended by her on herself, her children and relatives; that the trust was not designed to relieve respondent from liability for family or household expenses and that after execution of the trust he paid large sums from his personal funds for such purposes.

Respondent paid a federal gift tax on this transfer. During the year 1934 all income from the trust was distributed to the wife who included it in her individual return for that year. The Commissioner, however, determined a deficiency in respondent's return for that year on the theory that income from the trust was taxable to him. The Board of Tax Appeals sustained that redetermination. 38 B.T.A. 1532. The Circuit Court of Appeals reversed. 105 F.2d 586. We granted certiorari because of the importance to the revenue of the use of such short term trusts in the reduction of surtaxes.

Sec. 22(a) of the Revenue Act of 1934, 48 Stat. 680, includes among "gross income" all "gains, profits, and income derived * * * from professions, vocations, trades, businesses, commerce, or sales, or dealings in property, whether real or personal, growing out of the ownership or use of or interest in such property; also from interest, rent, dividends, securities, or the transaction of any business carried on for gain or profit, or gains or profits and income derived from any source whatever." The broad sweep of this language indicates the purpose of Congress to use the full measure of its taxing power within those definable categories. Cf. Helvering v. Midland Mutual Life Insurance Co., 300 U.S. 216. Hence our construction of the statute should be consonant with that purpose. Technical considerations, niceties of the law of trusts or conveyances, or the legal paraphernalia which inventive genius may construct as a refuge from surtaxes should not obscure the basic issue. That issue is whether the grantor after the trust has been established may still be treated, under this statutory scheme, as the owner of the corpus. See Blair v. Commissioner, 300 U.S. 5, 12. In absence of more precise standards or guides supplied by statute or appropriate regulations,[1] the answer to that question must depend on an analysis of the terms of the trust and all the circumstances attendant on its creation and operation. And where the grantor is the trustee and the beneficiaries are members of his family group, special scrutiny of the arrangement is necessary lest what is in reality but one economic unit be multiplied into two or more [2] by devices which, though valid under state law, are not conclusive so far as § 22(a) is concerned.

In this case we cannot conclude, as a matter of law that respondent ceased to be the owner of the corpus after the trust was created. Rather, the short duration of the trust, the fact that the wife was the beneficiary, and the retention of control over the corpus by respondent all lead irresistibly to the conclusion that respondent continued to be the owner for purposes of § 22(a).

So far as his dominion and control were concerned it seems clear that the trust did not effect any substantial change. In substance his control over the corpus was in all essential respects the same after the trust was created, as before. The wide powers which he retained included for all practical purposes most of the control which he as an individual would have. There were, we may assume, exceptions, such as his disability to make a gift of the corpus to others during the term of the trust and to make loans to himself. But this dilution in his control would seem to be insignificant and immaterial, since control over

---

1. We have not considered here Art. 166–1 of Treasury Regulations 86 promulgated under § 166 of the 1934 Act and in 1936 amended (T.D. 4629) so as to rest on § 22(a) also, since the tax in question arose prior to that amendment.

2. See Paul, The Background of the Revenue Act of 1937, 5 Univ.Chic.L. Rev. 41.

investment remained. If it be said that such control is the type of dominion exercised by any trustee, the answer is simple. We have at best a temporary reallocation of income within an intimate family group. Since the income remains in the family and since the husband retains control over the investment, he has rather complete assurance that the trust will not effect any substantial change in his economic position. It is hard to imagine that respondent felt himself the poorer after this trust had been executed or, if he did, that it had any rational foundation in fact. For as a result of the terms of the trust and the intimacy of the familial relationship respondent retained the substance of full enjoyment of all the rights which previously he had in the property. That might not be true if only strictly legal rights were considered. But when the benefits flowing to him indirectly through the wife are added to the legal rights he retained, the aggregate may be said to be a fair equivalent of what he previously had. To exclude from the aggregate those indirect benefits would be to deprive § 22 (a) of considerable vitality and to treat as immaterial what may be highly relevant considerations in the creation of such family trusts. For where the head of the household has income in excess of normal needs, it may well make but little difference to him (except income-tax-wise) where portions of that income are routed—so long as it stays in the family group. In those circumstances the all-important factor might be retention by him of control over the principal. With that control in his hands he would keep direct command over all that he needed to remain in substantially the same financial situation as before. Our point here is that no one fact is normally decisive but that all considerations and circumstances of the kind we have mentioned are relevant to the question of ownership and are appropriate foundations for findings on that issue. Thus, where, as in this case, the benefits directly or indirectly retained blend so imperceptibly with the normal concepts of full ownership, we cannot say that the triers of fact committed reversible error when they found that the husband was the owner of the corpus for the purposes of § 22(a). To hold otherwise would be to treat the wife as a complete stranger; to let mere formalism obscure the normal consequences of family solidarity; and to force concepts of ownership to be fashioned out of legal niceties which may have little or no significance in such household arrangements.

The bundle of rights which he retained was so substantial that respondent cannot be heard to complain that he is the "victim of despotic power when for the purpose of taxation he is treated as owner altogether." See DuPont v. Commissioner, 289 U.S. 685, 689.

We should add that liability under § 22(a) is not foreclosed by reason of the fact that Congress made specific provision in § 166 for revocable trusts [I.R.C. § 676. Ed.], but failed to adopt the Treasury recommendation in 1934, Helvering v. Wood, post, p. 344, that similar specific treatment should be accorded income from short term trusts. [See I.R.C. § 673, not added until 1954. Ed.] Such choice, while relevant to the scope of § 166, Helvering v. Wood, supra, cannot be said to have subtracted from § 22(a) what was already there. Rather, on this evidence it must be assumed that the choice was between a generalized treatment under § 22(a) or specific treatment under a separate provision [3] (such as was accorded revocable trusts under § 166); not between taxing or not taxing grantors of short term trusts. In view of the broad and sweeping language of § 22(a), a specific provision covering short term trusts might well do no more than to carve out of § 22(a) a defined group of cases to which a rule of thumb would be applied. The failure of Congress to adopt any such rule of thumb for that type of trust must be taken to do no more than to leave to the triers of fact the initial determination of whether or not on the facts of each case the grantor remains the owner for purposes of § 22(a).

In view of this result we need not examine the contention that the trust device falls within the rule of Lucas v. Earl, 281 U.S. 111 and Burnet v. Leininger, 285 U.S. 136, relating to the assignment of future income; or that respondent is liable under § 166, taxing grantors on the income of revocable trusts.

The judgment of the Circuit Court of Appeals is reversed and that of the Board of Tax Appeals is affirmed.

Reversed.

MR. JUSTICE ROBERTS, dissenting:

I think the judgment should be affirmed.

The decision of the court disregards the fundamental principle that legislation is not the function of the judiciary but of Congress.
* * *

MR. JUSTICE MCREYNOLDS joins in this opinion.

NOTE

The student should note that in *Clifford* the settlor assigned *property* to the trust, not mere naked rights to income as was the case involving an outright assignment in Helvering v. Horst.[1] The trust was irrevocable; otherwise I.R.C. (26 U.S.C.A.) § 676 would have been enough to tax the settlor on the trust income.[2] Also, in *Clifford* the

3. As to the disadvantage of a specific statutory formula over more generalized treatment see Vol. I, Report, Income Tax Codification Committee (1936), a committee appointed by the Chancellor of the Exchequer in 1927. In discussing revocable settlements the Committee stated, p. 298:
"This and the three following clauses reproduce section 20 of the Finance Act, 1922, an enactment which has been the subject of much litigation, is unsatisfactory in many respects, and is plainly inadequate to fulfil the apparent intention to prevent avoidance of liability to tax by revocable dispositions of income or other devices. We think the matter one which is worthy of the attention of Parliament."

1. 311 U.S. 112, 61 S.Ct. 144 (1940), Chapter 13, supra at page 275.

2. Cf., Corliss v. Bowers, 281 U.S. 376, 50 S.Ct. 336 (1930), supra at page 304.

government stipulated that the income of the trust was not used for the support of the settlor's wife; for, if the income were so used, it would have been taxable to Clifford under I.R.C. (26 U.S.C.A.) § 677, and it is doubtful the case would have reached the Supreme Court.[3] Thus one can surmise that, in frustration resulting from the failure of Congress to enact specific Code provisions dealing with short-term, family control trusts, the government, in a calculated risk, sought to combat such devices in a maneuver relying solely on the vagueness of I.R.C. (26 U.S.C.A.) § 61; and it paid off. It is clear that the settlor's retention of control over the property was the basis for the court's decision. The short duration of the trust is properly regarded as one of the settlor's retained strings of control. Following *Clifford*, the question became how many and what strings of control could a settlor of a trust retain without incurring tax liability on income that is payable to others. Its immediate sequel, however, was confusion because, while Clifford himself may have retained enough of the bundle of rights to be held to "own" the trust property, the outer limits of the *Clifford* doctrine were very obscure. In 1945, the Treasury sought to accord some definition to the doctrine by elaborate and expansive regulations. A look at a few pages in the case citator will indicate the extent to which uncertainty continued. Finally, in the enactment of the Internal Revenue Code of 1954, Congress undertook to give the grantor trust area a more substantial statutory underpinning by the enactment of I.R.C. (26 U.S.C.A.) §§ 671–675 and 678. The Tax Reform Act of 1976 added § 679 to deal with problems arising under some foreign trusts. As indicated in *Clifford*, I.R.C. (26 U.S.C.A. §§ 676 and 677 had a much earlier origin.[4] What is the scope and effect of the restrictive language in the last sentence of § 671?

Some feel for the grantor trust area can be attained by a look at I.R.C. (26 U.S.C.A.) §§ 673, 676, and 677. That is all that is attempted by the problems in this book. However, here are a few comments on the so-called "grantor trust" provisions, which may help to round out the broad picture.

Under I.R.C. (26 U.S.C.A.) § 673, the grantor of a trust is taxed on the income from the trust (see § 671) if he retains a reversionary interest in corpus or income which may reasonably be expected to revert to him within ten years of his transfer. An exception is created under § 673(c) if the expectation of short-term reversion rests only on the anticipated early death of the income beneficiary.

---

3. See George B. Morrill, Jr. v. U. S., 228 F.Supp. 734 (D.C.Me.1964), supra page 305.

4. See Revenue Act of 1924, §§ 219(g) and (h), 43 Stat. 253, 277 (1942); and see Corliss v. Bowers set out, supra at page 287. An early basic discus-

sion of the 1954 legislative changes appears in Greenberger, "Changes in the Income Taxation of Clifford Type Trusts," 13 N.Y.U.Inst. on Fed.Tax. 165 (1955); and see Yohlin, "The Short-Term Trust—A Respectable Tax-Saving Device," 14 Tax L.Rev. 109 (1958).

Under § 674(a), the grantor of a trust is taxed on the income from the trust if he or a nonadverse party [5] holds a power to determine who, other than the grantor,[6] will receive the income or the corpus of the trust. Subsections (b), (c) and (d) provide exceptions to the general rule of § 674(a) identifying groups of situations in which the grantor is not taxed even though such powers are held. The exceptions look to two factors, the nature of the power held and the person holding the power. Generally very indirect or weak powers to alter the beneficial enjoyment may be held by anyone, including the grantor, without invoking § 674(a).[7] As the scope of the power increases, it will render the grantor taxable unless it is held by someone not closely associated with him.[8]

I.R.C. (26 U.S.C.A.) § 675 may apply if a grantor or a nonadverse party holds merely administrative powers over the trust corpus. For example, a power to dispose of trust property for less than full consideration is proscribed; and so is a power to borrow trust corpus or income without payment of adequate interest or the posting of adequate security. Generally, § 675 may apply in situations in which normal stringent fiduciary standards are waived by the trust instrument.

The income from a trust need not be actually paid to the grantor to provide benefits to him and if the income from a trust may benefit the grantor, directly or indirectly, Congress has provided in I.R.C. (26 U.S.C.A.) § 677 that he may be taxed on the income. In 1969, Congress decided that the same result should follow if the income may be used directly or indirectly for the grantor's spouse.[9] In general, the provisions of § 677 apply if the income "may be" used for the proscribed purposes, regardless of how it is in fact used.[10]

I.R.C. (26 U.S.C.A.) § 678 presents a new twist to the so-called grantor provisions. Under this section a third person (not the grantor), not necessarily a beneficiary, may be taxed on the income of a trust, if the grantor escapes the other grantor trust provisions [11] and the third person has a power to obtain the income or corpus for his own benefit.[12]

5. See I.R.C. (26 U.S.C.A.) § 672(a) and (b).

6. I.R.C. (26 U.S.C.A.) § 677(a) controls if the income may be used for the grantor's benefit.

7. I.R.C. (26 U.S.C.A.) § 674(b).

8. I.R.C. (26 U.S.C.A.) § 674(c) and (d). See Westfall, "Trust Grantors and Section 674: Adventures in Income Tax Avoidance," 60 Colum.L.Rev. 326 (1960), reprinted in Sander and Westfall, Readings in Federal Taxation 471 (Foundation Press 1970).

9. Tax Reform Act of 1969, § 332.

10. But see I.R.C. (26 U.S.C.A.) § 677 (b), relieving the grantor of tax on income that may be used to support a dependent (other than his spouse) except to the extent it is so used; and see Morrill v. U. S., supra at page 305.

11. See I.R.C. (26 U.S.C.A.) § 678(b).

12. A person's possession of a power, as a fiduciary, merely to have trust income used for the support of his dependents does not invite tax, ex-

The new (1976) rules on foreign trusts enacted as § 679 obviously are not fundamentals such as are considered in this book. However, here is a portion of the comment on the new section, which appeared in the Summary of the Conference Agreement on H.R. 10612 by the House Ways and Means Committee, September 14, 1976:

> The conference agreement provides a new grantor trust rule for foreign trusts. Under this rule, a U.S. person who transfers property to a foreign trust is treated as the owner of the trust and is taxed currently on the income of the trust for each taxable year during which the trust has a U.S. beneficiary. Employee trusts described in Code section 404(a) (4) are excluded from this rule * * *.

The foreign trusts rules are not to be considered in the problems that follow.

PROBLEMS

1. Grantor who is a lawyer creates a trust for the benefit of his adult Son with income to Son for life, remainder to Son's children. Who is taxed on the income paid to Son in the following circumstances:

(a) Grantor transfers to the trust accounts receivable for services which have never been included in his gross income. The clients pay the fees represented by the receivables in the succeeding year.

(b) Grantor owns a building subject to a long term lease. He transfers the right to future rentals under the lease to the trust.

(c) Same as (b), above, except that he transfers the building along with the right to the rentals at a time when no rent has accrued.

(d) Same as (c), above, except that six months' rent has accrued on the lease at the time of Grantor's transfer.

(e) Same as (c), above, except that Grantor retains the right to revoke the trust at any time.

(f) Same as (c), above, except that Grantor holds liberal powers to change the income beneficiary of the trust from Son to anyone other than Grantor.

(g) Same as (c), above, except that at Son's death the property reverts to Grantor if Grantor is then living.

cept to the extent the income is so used. I.R.C. (26 U.S.C.A.) § 678(c); and cf. § 677(b). One might escape § 678 by reason of a trust requirement that *another* person join in the exercise of his power. Reg. § 1.678 (c)–1(b). However, the Treasury holds that one whose obligations are discharged by trust distributions is taxable as a beneficiary under §§ 652 or 662. See Reg. § 1.662(a)–4.

(h) Same as (c), above, except that Grantor may direct the sale of the trust corpus to any person including himself for any price he wishes.

(i) Same as (c), above, except that Son is a minor and the income from the trust while Son is a student is used to pay Son's tuition at a private high school which Son attends.

(j) Same as (c), above, except that under the terms of the trust, Wife may require the trustee to pay the income from the trust to her in any year.

2. Do you see a relationship betwen the results in problem one and the messages of the *Earl, Horst,* and other cases of Chapter 13? What additional concept does the Grantor trust provisions add?

Income in Respect of Decedents

Questions arise upon the death of a taxpayer which involve, not only the issue of *who* is taxable on income (the major question in this Chapter) but also *when* the income is taxed and the *character* of the income; and there are related issues with respect to deductions. Fundamental consideration is given later in this book to questions of timing, characterization, and deductions, but these phenomena cannot properly be injected here. Moreover, more knowledge on the income taxation of trusts and estates than is presented in this book is needed for a full grasp of the area. Nevertheless a brief note on income in respect of decedents is presented here. It might, at most, be skimmed at this time. Later, it might be reviewed as a general introduction to a very difficult area.

I.R.C. (26 U.S.C.A.) § 691 addresses itself to some of the transitional problems that arise because a person's financial affairs, instead of terminating neatly at the time of his death, linger on, sometimes for a considerable period after his demise. An executor marshalling the decedent's assets will usually find that his efforts involve the collection of amounts that would have been gross income to the decedent had he collected them and the payment of amounts that would have been tax deductions if paid by the decedent. What should be the post-death tax consequences of such transactions? *Possible* answers to this question are suggested by a brief review of three legislative approaches that Congress has, at different times, taken to the matter of income and deductions in respect of decedents.

From the inception of the individual income tax in 1913 to 1934, Congress did not legislate specifically on the subject. But of course such inaction itself had important tax consequences. The principal result was for much income constitutionally subject to tax to escape the federal exaction. This came about by way of the treatment of income rights as a part of the corpus of a decedent's estate entitled, along with all other property owned by him, to a new date-of-death value basis, which foreclosed the imposition of income tax upon its post-death collection. It must be kept in mind (See Chapter 7, supra) that § 1023 did not alter this basis rule until 1976. Of course, at the same time, expenses incurred before death that could not under the decedent's accounting method be deducted on his final return also lost their potential for tax reduction when paid.

The two main problems with the pre-1934 approach were: (1) substantial revenue loss through the escape from income taxation of transitional income items and (2) quite unequal treatment of accrual and cash method taxpayers. With regard to the second difficulty, it is obvious that some transitional income items, such as a decedent's unpaid salary, interest, and gain on the sale of property, were either *taxed or not* according to the decedent's accounting method,[1] whereas in the case of living taxpayers accounting methods generally affect only timing and do not govern whether an item is subject to tax at all.

To overcome these problems, Congress in 1934 in effect put all final returns of decedents on the accrual method. Thus, notwithstanding the fact that a decedent had been a cash method taxpayer, his *final* return included accrued items of income and deduction. This stemmed the revenue loss and eliminated the discriminatory advantage previously enjoyed by estates and beneficiaries of cash method taxpayers. But it was soon evident that there were equally strong objections to the new approach. Especially when the courts gave support to a broad administrative interpretation of what income items could be treated as accrued by reason of death, there was great possibility that substantial previously untaxed income would be bunched in the final return of a cash method taxpayer.[2]

The origin of the present congressional approach to the problem was the Revenue Act of 1942, which first presented the concept of income and deductions in respect of decedents. If it can be capsulized, the intended thrust of I.R.C. (26 U.S.C.A.) § 691 is insofar as possible to neutralize the tax consequences of a person's death. Thus, income generated by him, but untaxed to him, is to be taxed to others when received by them, not in the decedent's final return. And some potential deductions of the decedent may be claimed by others when they pay the related pre-death expenses of the decedent. In general, this will be seen: (1) To prevent revenue loss which, pre-1934, was a sometimes result of death, (2) To let accounting method continue to affect the timing of income and deductions, but not to affect the questions whether income would be taxed or whether deductions could be

1. See Chapter 19, infra.

2. It is a question whether this would have been regarded as serious if there had then been in existence an income averaging provision as broad as I.R.C. (26 U.S.C.A.) §§ 1301–1305, as amended by the Tax Reform Act of 1969. See Chapter 20, infra at page 615. But there was not.

claimed, also pre-1934 inequities, and (3) To avoid the bunching problem inherent in the 1934 legislation.[3]

Together with I.R.C. (26 U.S.C.A.) §§ 451, 1014(c) and 1023(b) (2)(A), which excludes I.R.D. from the definition of "carryover basis property," § 691(a) taxes a decedent's transitional income items to the one who receives the item after a decedent's death. When death terminates his taxable year, income inclusions in the decedent's final return are determined by his established accounting method under § 451(a).[4] The full income component of post death receipts is preserved by §§ 1014(c) and 1023(b), which deny any change in basis to any right to receive income in respect of a decedent.

I.R.D. items[5] are to be included "when received," which makes the recipient's accounting method immaterial with respect to such items.[6] The statute is explicit as regards who may be taxed upon receipt of I.R.D. If, as is usually the case with respect to unpaid salary, the executor collects the amount, it is an item of gross income to the estate.[7]

Finally, upon acquisition of an I.R.D. item as a part of the decedent's estate, the executor or administrator may transmit it, before collection, to one who is entitled to it by reason of bequest, devise, or

---

3. There are estate tax problems intimately related to the question of income in respect of decedents. At a time when the statute was silent on this income tax matter, it was apparently deemed inappropriate to impose both income and estate taxes with respect to the same transitional income items. Perhaps it was sound not to assume a congressional intent to impose such "double taxation" in the absence of a clear congressional mandate. Nevertheless, a decedent's untaxed right to income is clearly an interest in property subject to estate tax under I.R.C. (26 U.S.C.A.) § 2033. And there is no good reason why estate taxation should turn on whether the right has been subjected to income tax in a return of the decedent or is only to be taxed to another after the decedent's death. In fact, section 691 now carries the clear inference that such "double taxation" *is* intended. The inference is found in provisions of § 691 allowing a deduction for estate taxes that are attributable to the inclusion in the gross estate of items of income in respect of decedents, and it is no longer open to question that income in respect of decedents can be subjected to both income and estate taxes after death. There is a comprehensive examination of § 691 in Ferguson, Freeland,

and Stephens, Federal Income Taxation of Estates and Beneficiaries, c. 4, "Income in Respect of Decedents," 139–300 (1970).

4. Thus, receipt prior to death (or constructive receipt) is the test for inclusions for cash method taxpayers. In the case of accrual method decedents, the usual "all events" test will control, especially since § 451(b) forecloses accrual only by reason of death in the case of such taxpayers.

5. The examples in Reg. § 1.691(a)–2 are helpful as illustrations of what constitutes an I.R.D. item.

6. Some variations in the "when received" rule, such as may be necessary in the case of the death of a partner, see Reg. § 1.753–1(b), are not discussed here.

7. I.R.C. (26 U.S.C.A.) § 691(a) (1) (A). This of course does not answer the ultimate question regarding the incidence of the tax, however, which will depend in part on distributions by the executor and the usual deduction and inclusion rules for estates and beneficiaries under §§ 661 and 662. Thus, even when the executor collects the item, the tax bite may fall on estate beneficiaries.

inheritance. In such a case, the one to whom it is transmitted takes it into account as I.R.D. when payment is received.[8] However, some transmissions of I.R.D. items are far from neutral events. Instant tax liability results to the transferor if, for example, the executor sells an I.R.D. item or a beneficiary who acquired it innocuously from the executor makes a gift of it.[9]

The neutralization objective of § 691 is further carried out by provisions that *characterize* I.R.D. when received in accordance with the nature of the income that would have been realized by the decedent had he collected the item during life.[10] Thus, gain on the sale of a capital asset, taxed as I.R.D. when the proceeds are collected after death, is capital gain to the recipient. Salary collected after death is ordinary income. Dividends, if collected as I.R.D., qualify for the $100 exclusion under § 116. And so forth.

The deductions side of I.R.C. (26 U.S.C.A.) § 691 in effect passes through to the decedent's estate or beneficiaries the tax benefit of certain deductible expenses incurred by the decedent but not properly taken into account in his final, or any earlier return. However, only expenses that are of a business nature within § 162 or are non-trade expenses within § 212, plus interest under § 163 and taxes under § 164, qualify as deductions in respect of decedents for this purpose.[11] In general as regards expenses that may be deducted as deductions in respect to decedents, a "when paid" test parallels the "when received" test that applies to I.R.D. I.R.C. (26 U.S.C.A.) § 691(b) (1) (A) accords the right to the deduction to the estate but, under subparagraph (B), if the estate is not liable to discharge the obligation, one who by

---

8. I.R.C. (26 U.S.C.A.) § 691(a) (1) (C). It should be noted that such transmission of an I.R.D. item takes place outside the usual distribution rules of §§ 661 and 662. That is, it does not give rise to a distribution deduction for the estate, and it is not regarded as an "amount properly paid" (not a distribution in kind) such as would cause tax liability to the beneficiary within limitations of the estate's distributable net income. While authority for this proposition, statutory or otherwise, is skimpy (would an addition to § 663 be in order?), the matter seems settled. See Ferguson, Freeland and Stephens, Federal Income Taxation of Estates and Beneficiaries, c. 7, p. 533 (Little, Brown 1970). The result is in keeping with the § 691 objective to neutralize the effect of death with respect to I.R.D. items.

9. I.R.C. (26 U.S.C.A.) § 691(a) (2). These acceleration rules are some-

what analogous to the more familiar principles that apply to the disposition of installment obligations under § 453(d). See Chapter 24, *infra* at page 882.

10. I.R.C. (26 U.S.C.A.) § 691(a) (3). See Chapter 21, *infra*.

11. The omission of depreciation from this list is logical. Depreciation is not an expense to be paid; and pre-death depreciation on the decedent's property will be taken into account on the final return. Post-death depreciation will be allocated between the estate and beneficiaries in accordance with § 167(h). However, § 691 (b) (2) undertakes to match a depletion deduction with related I.R.D. that is taxed to the one who receives it. And § 691(b) also attempts to match the § 33 credit for tax on foreign income against such income taxed as I.R.D. when received.

bequest, devise or inheritance acquires property subject to the obligation, succeeds to the right to the deduction.

A minor breakdown in the neutralization objective of § 691 occurs with respect to estate taxes. When the value of an I.R.D. item included in the decedent's gross estate is later subjected to an income tax imposed on someone else, the estate tax on the decedent's estate may be larger than it would have been if the decedent had collected the item himself. Had he collected the item, his taxable estate would have been smaller by the amount of income tax *he* paid upon the receipt, or by the amount of deduction for income tax due that could have been claimed for estate tax purposes under § 2053. It might appear that some adjustment could be made in estate tax liability to take into account this phenomenon. But that is not practicable. In fact, a hypothetical determination of the income tax that the decedent might have paid is at odds with the objective of § 691 *not* to tax him on I.R.D. items. Congress has settled for an acceptable rough and ready answer to this recognized problem.

Section 691(c) allows one who is taxed on an I.R.D. item, upon receipt, an *income* tax deduction for *estate* tax attributable to the inclusion of the item in the decedent's estate. This is obviously not precisely responsive to the problem that seems to call for some adjustment; but is there any better way to handle the problem? [12] The I.R.C. (26 U.S.C.A.) § 691(c) deduction creates a situation where it is sometimes advantageous to the taxpayer to have an income item classified as I.R.D. Why? Should the § 691(c) concept be extended to unrealized appreciation reflected in the carryover basis now prescribed under § 1023? See § 1023(c).

---

12. The general principle of § 691(c) can be expressed quite simply. The complexities of the provision, not discussed here in detail, are needed to answer questions such as (1) What portion of the estate tax is attributable to all I.R.D. items? § 691(c) (2). (2) How is that amount to be allocated as deductions available to each recipient of I.R.D.? § 691(c) (1) (A), formula. (3) If the deduction becomes available to an estate or a trust, how is it to be divided between the estate or trust and its beneficiaries? § 691(c) (1) (B).

C. PARTNERSHIPS *

Internal Revenue Code: Sections 701; 704(e); 707(c).
Regulations: Sections 1.704–1(e)(1), –1(e)(2)(i), (viii), –1(e)(3)(i).

COMMISSIONER v. CULBERTSON

Supreme Court of the United States, 1949.
337 U.S. 733, 69 S.Ct. 1210.

MR. CHIEF JUSTICE VINSON delivered the opinion of the Court.

This case requires our further consideration of the family partnership problem. The Commissioner of Internal Revenue ruled that the entire income from a partnership allegedly entered into by respondent and his four sons must be taxed to respondent,[1] and the Tax Court sustained that determination. The Court of Appeals for the Fifth Circuit reversed. 168 F.2d 979. We granted certiorari, 335 U.S. 883, to consider the Commissioner's claim that the principles of Commissioner v. Tower, 327 U.S. 280 (1946), and Lusthaus v. Commissioner, 327 U.S. 293 (1946), have been departed from in this and other courts of appeals decisions.

Respondent taxpayer is a rancher. From 1915 until October 1939, he had operated a cattle business in partnership with R. S. Coon. Coon, who had numerous business interests in the Southwest and had largely financed the partnership, was 79 years old in 1939 and desired to dissolve the partnership because of ill health. To that end, the bulk of the partnership herd was sold until, in October of that year, only about 1,500 head remained. These cattle were all registered Herefords, the brood or foundation herd. Culbertson wished to keep these cattle and approached Coon with an offer of $65 a head. Coon agreed to sell at that price, but only upon condition that Culbertson would sell an undivided one-half interest in the herd to his four sons at the same price. His reasons for imposing this condition were his intense interest in maintaining the Hereford strain which he and Culbertson had developed, his conviction that Culbertson was too old to carry on the work alone, and his personal interest in the Culbertson boys. Culbertson's sons were enthusiastic about the proposition, so respondent thereupon bought the remaining cattle from the Coon and Culbertson partnership for $99,440. Two days later Culbertson sold an undivided one-half interest to the four boys, and the following day they gave their father a note for $49,720 at 4 per cent interest due one

---

* See Note, "Family Partnerships and the Federal Income Tax," 41 Ind.L.J. 684 (1966); Lifton, "The Family Partnership: Here We Go Again," 7 Tax L.Rev. 461 (1952).

1. Gladys Culbertson, the wife of W. O. Culbertson, Sr., is joined as a party because of her community of interest in the property and income of her husband under Texas law.

year from date. Several months later a new note for $57,674 was executed by the boys to replace the earlier note. The increase in amount covered the purchase by Culbertson and his sons of other properties formerly owned by Coon and Culbertson. This note was paid by the boys in the following manner:

Credit for overcharge .... $ 5,930
Gifts from respondent 21,744
One-half of a loan procured by Culbert-
      son & Sons partnership 30,000

The loan was repaid from the proceeds from operation of the ranch.

The partnership agreement between taxpayer and his sons was oral. The local paper announced the dissolution of the Coon and Culbertson partnership and the continuation of the business by respondent and his boys under the name of Culbertson & Sons. A bank account was opened in this name, upon which taxpayer, his four sons and a bookkeeper could check. At the time of formation of the new partnership, Culbertson's oldest son was 24 years old, married, and living on the ranch, of which he had for two years been foreman under the Coon and Culbertson partnership. He was a college graduate and received $100 a month plus board and lodging for himself and his wife both before and after formation of Culbertson & Sons and until entering the Army. The second son was 22 years old, was married and finished college in 1940, the first year during which the new partnership operated. He went directly into the Army following graduation and rendered no services to the partnership. The two younger sons, who were 18 and 16 years old respectively in 1940, went to school during the winter and worked on the ranch during the summer.[2]

The tax years here involved are 1940 and 1941. A partnership return was filed for both years indicating a division of income approximating the capital attributed to each partner. It is the disallowance of this division of the income from the ranch that brings this case into the courts.

First. The Tax Court read our decisions in Commissioner v. Tower, supra, and Lusthaus v. Commissioner, supra, as setting out two essential tests of partnership for income-tax purposes: that each partner contribute to the partnership either vital services or capital originating with him. Its decision was based upon a finding that none of respondent's sons had satisfied those requirements during the tax years in question. Sanction for the use of these "tests" of partnership is sought in this paragraph from our opinion in the *Tower* case:

"There can be no question that a wife and a husband may, under certain circumstances, become partners for tax, as for other, purposes.

2. A daughter was also made a member of the partnership some time after its formation upon the gift by respondent of one-quarter of his one-half interest in the partnership. Respondent did not contend before the Tax Court that she was a partner for tax purposes.

If she either invests capital originating with her or substantially contributes to the control and management of the business, or otherwise performs vital additional services, or does all of these things she may be a partner as contemplated by 26 U.S.C. §§ 181, 182. The Tax Court has recognized that under such circumstances the income belongs to the wife. A wife may become a general or a limited partner with her husband. But when she does not share in the management and control of the business, contributes no vital additional service, and where the husband purports in some way to have given her a partnership interest, the Tax Court may properly take these circumstances into consideration in determining whether the partnership is real within the meaning of the federal revenue laws." 327 U.S. at 290.

It is the Commissioner's contention that the Tax Court's decision can and should be reinstated upon the mere reaffirmation of the quoted paragraph.

The Court of Appeals, on the other hand, was of the opinion that a family partnership entered into without thought of tax avoidance should be given recognition tax-wise whether or not it was intended that some of the partners contribute either capital or services during the tax year and whether or not they actually made such contributions, since it was formed "with the full expectation and purpose that the boys would, in the future, contribute their time and services to the partnership." [3] We must consider, therefore, whether an intention to contribute capital or services sometime in the future is sufficient to satisfy ordinary concepts of partnership, as required by the *Tower* case. The sections of the Internal Revenue Code involved are §§ 181 and 182,[4] which set out the method of taxing partnership income, and §§ 11 and 22(a),[5] which relate to the taxation of individual incomes.

In the *Tower* case we held that, despite the claimed partnership, the evidence fully justified the Tax Court's holding that the husband, through his ownership of the capital and his management of the business, actually created the right to receive and enjoy the benefit of the income and was thus taxable upon that entire income under §§ 11 and 22(a). In such case, other members of the partnership cannot be considered "Individuals carrying on business in partnership" and thus "liable for income tax * * * in their individual capacity" within the meaning of § 181. If it is conceded that some of the partners contributed neither capital nor services to the partnership during the tax years in question, as the Court of Appeals was apparently

3.   168 F.2d 979 at 982. The court further said: "Neither statute, common sense, nor impelling precedent requires the holding that a partner must contribute capital or render services to the partnership prior to the time that he is taken into it. These tests are equally effective whether the capital and the services are presently contributed and rendered or are later to be contributed or to be rendered." Id. at 983. See Note, 47 Mich.L.Rev. 595.

4.   26 U.S.C. §§ 181, 182.

5.   26 U.S.C. §§ 11, 22(a).

willing to do in the present case, it can hardly be contended that they are in any way responsible for the production of income during those years.[6] The partnership sections of the Code are, of course, geared to the sections relating to taxation of individual income, since no tax is imposed upon partnership income as such. To hold that "Individuals carrying on business in partnership" includes persons who contribute nothing during the tax period would violate the first principle of income taxation: that income must be taxed to him who earns it. Lucas v. Earl, 281 U.S. 111 (1930); Helvering v. Clifford, 309 U.S. 331 (1940); National Carbide Corp. v. Commissioner, 336 U.S. 422 (1949).

Furthermore, our decision in Commissioner v. Tower, supra, clearly indicates the importance of participation in the business by the partners during the tax year. We there said that a partnership is created "when persons join together their money, goods, labor, or skill for the purpose of carrying on a trade, profession, or business and when there is community of interest in the profits and losses." Id. at 286. This is, after all, but the application of an often iterated definition of income—the gain derived from capital, from labor, or from both combined [7]—to a particular form of business organization. A partnership is, in other words, an organization for the production of income to which each partner contributes one or both of the ingredients of income—capital or services. Ward v. Thompson, 22 How. 330, 334 (1859). The intent to provide money, goods, labor or skill sometime in the future cannot meet the demands of §§ 11 and 22(a) of the Code that he who presently earns the income through his own labor and skill and the utilization of his own capital be taxed therefor. The vagaries of human experience preclude reliance upon even good faith intent as to future conduct as a basis for the present taxation of income.[8]

Second. We turn next to a consideration of the Tax Court's approach to the family partnership problem. It treated as essential to membership in a family partnership for tax purposes the contribution of either "vital services" or "original capital." [9] Use of these "tests"

---

6. Of course one who has been a bona fide partner does not lose that status when he is called into military or government service, and the Commissioner has not so contended. On the other hand, one hardly becomes a partner in the conventional sense merely because he might have done so had he not been called.

7. Eisner v. Macomber, 252 U.S. 189, 207 (1920); Merchants Loan & Trust Co. v. Smietanka, 255 U.S. 509, 519 (1921). See Treas.Reg. 101, Art. 22 (a)–1. See 1 Mertens, Law of Federal Income Taxation, 159 et seq.

8. The *reductio ad absurdum* of the theory that children may be partners with their parents before they are capable of being entrusted with the disposition of partnership funds or of contributing substantial services occurred in Tinkoff v. Commissioner, 120 F.2d 564, where a taxpayer made his son a partner in his accounting firm the day the son was born.

9. While the Tax Court went on to consider other factors, it is clear from its opinion that a contribution of either "vital services" or "original capital" was considered essential to

of partnership indicates, at best, an error in emphasis. It ignores what we said is the ultimate question for decision, namely, "whether the partnership is real within the meaning of the federal revenue laws" and makes decisive what we described as "circumstances [to be taken] into consideration" in making that determination.[10]

The *Tower* case thus provides no support for such an approach. We there said that the question whether the family partnership is real for income-tax purposes depends upon

"whether the partners really and truly intended to join together for the purpose of carrying on business and sharing in the profits or losses or both. And their intention in this respect is a question of fact, to be determined from testimony disclosed by their 'agreement, considered as a whole, and by their conduct in execution of its provisions.' Drennen v. London Assurance Co., 113 U.S. 51, 56; Cox v. Hickman, 8 H.L.Cas. 268. We see no reason why this general rule should not apply in tax cases where the Government challenges the existence of a partnership for tax purposes." 327 U.S. at 287.

The question is not whether the services or capital contributed by a partner are of sufficient importance to meet some objective standard supposedly established by the *Tower* case, but whether, considering all the facts—the agreement, the conduct of the parties in execution of its provisions, their statements, the testimony of disinterested persons, the relationship of the parties, their respective abilities and capital contributions, the actual control of income and the purposes for which it is used, and any other facts throwing light on their true intent—the parties in good faith and acting with a business purpose intended to join together in the present conduct of the enterprise.[11] There is noth-

membership in the partnership. After finding that none of respondent's sons had, in the court's opinion, contributed either, the court continued: "In addition to the above inquiry as to the presence of those elements deemed by the *Tower* case essential to partnerships recognizable for Federal tax purposes, * * *." 6 CCH TCM 692, 699. Again, the court commented:

"Though, the petitioner urges that many cattle businesses are composed of fathers and sons, and that the nature of the industry so requires, we think the same is probably equally true of other industries where men wish to take children into business with them. Nevertheless, we think that fact does not override the many decisions to the general effect that partners must contribute capital originating with them, or vital services." Id. at 700.

10. See Mannheimer and Mook, A Taxwise Evaluation of Family Partnerships, 32 Iowa L.Rev. 436, 447–48.

11. This is not, as we understand it, contrary to the approach taken by the Bureau of Internal Revenue in its most recent statement of policy. I.T. 3845, 1947 Cum.Bull. 66, states at p. 67:

"Where persons who are closely related by blood or marriage enter into an agreement purporting to create a so-called family partnership or other arrangement with respect to the operation of a business or income-producing venture, under which agreement all of the parties are accorded substantially the same treatment and consideration with respect to their designated interests and prescribed responsibilities in the business as if they were strangers dealing at arm's length; where the actions of the parties as legally responsible persons evidence an intent to carry on a business in a partnership relation; and where the terms of such agreement are substantially followed in the operation of the business or venture, as well as in the dealings of the partners or mem-ing new or particularly difficult about such a test. Triers of fact are constantly called upon to determine the intent with which a person acted.[12] The Tax Court, for example, must make such a determination in every estate tax case in which it is contended that a transfer was made in contemplation of death, for "The question, necessarily, is as to the state of mind of the donor." United States v. Wells, 283 U.S. 102, 117 (1931). See Allen v. Trust Co. of Georgia, 326 U.S. 630 (1946). Whether the parties really intended to carry on business as partners is not, we think, any more difficult of determination or the manifestations of such intent any less perceptible than is ordinarily true of inquiries into the subjective.

But the Tax Court did not view the question as one concerning the bona fide intent of the parties to join together as partners. Not once in its opinion is there even an oblique reference to any lack of intent on the part of respondent and his sons to combine their capital and services "for the purpose of carrying on the business." Instead, the court, focusing entirely upon concepts of "vital services" and "original capital," simply decided that the alleged partners had not satisfied those tests when the facts were compared with those in the *Tower* case. The court's opinion is replete with such statements as "we discern nothing constituting what we think is a requisite contribution to a real partnership," "we find no son adding 'vital additional service' which would take the place of capital contributed because of formation of a partnership," and "the sons made no capital contribution, within the sense of the *Tower* case." [13]   6 CCH TCM 698, 699.

Unquestionably a court's determination that the services contributed by a partner are not "vital" and that he has not participated

bers with each other, it is the policy of the Bureau to disregard the close family relationship existing between the parties and to recognize, for Federal income tax purposes, the division of profits as prescribed by such agreement. However, where the instrument purporting to create the family partnership expressly provides that the wife or child or other member of the family shall not be required to participate in the management of the business, or is merely silent on that point, the extent and nature of the services of such individual in the actual conduct of the business will be given appropriate evidentiary weight as to the question of intent to carry on the business as partners."

12. Nearly three-quarters of a century ago, Bowen, L. J., made the classic statement that "the state of a man's mind is as much a fact as the state of his digestion." Edgington v. Fitzmaurice, 29 L.R.Ch.Div. 459, 483. State of mind has always been determinative of the question whether a partnership has been formed as between the parties. See, e. g., Drennen v. London Assurance Co., 113 U.S. 51, 56 (1885); Meehen v. Valentine, 145 U.S. 611, 621 (1892); Barker v. Kraft, 259 Mich. 70, 242 N.W. 841 (1932); Zuback v. Bakmaz, 346 Pa. 279, 29 A.2d 473 (1943); Kennedy v. Mullins, 155 Va. 166, 154 S.E. 568 (1930).

13. In the *Tower* case the taxpayer argued that he had a right to reduce his taxes by any legal means, to which this Court agreed. We said, however, that existence of a tax avoidance motive gives some indication that there was no bona fide intent to carry on business as a partnership. If *Tower* had set up objective requirements of membership in a family partnership, such as "vital services" and "original capital," the motives behind adoption of the partnership form would have been irrelevant.

in "management and control of the business" [14] or contributed "original capital" has the effect of placing a heavy burden on the taxpayer to show the bona fide intent of the parties to join together as partners. But such a determination is not conclusive, and that is the vice in the "tests" adopted by the Tax Court. It assumes that there is no room for an honest difference of opinion as to whether the services or capital furnished by the alleged partner are of sufficient importance to justify his inclusion in the partnership. If, upon a consideration of all the facts, it is found that the partners joined together in good faith to conduct a business, having agreed that the services or capital to be contributed presently by each is of such value to the partnership that the contributor should participate in the distribution of profits, that is sufficient. The *Tower* case did not purport to authorize the Tax Court to substitute its judgment for that of the parties; it simply furnished some guides to the determination of their true intent. Even though it was admitted in the *Tower* case that the wife contributed no original capital, management of the business, or other vital services, this Court did not say as a matter of law that there was no valid partnership. We said, instead, that "There was, thus, more than ample evidence to support the Tax Court's finding that no genuine union for partnership business purposes *was ever intended* and that the husband earned the income." 327 U.S. at 292. (Italics added.)

Third. The Tax Court's isolation of "original capital" as an essential of membership in a family partnership also indicates an erroneous reading of the *Tower* opinion. We did not say that the donee of an intra-family gift could never become a partner through investment of the capital in the family partnership, any more than we said that all family trusts are invalid for tax purposes in Helvering v. Clifford, supra. The facts may indicate, on the contrary, that the amount thus contributed and the income therefrom should be considered the property of the donee for tax, as well as general law, purposes. In the *Tower* and *Lusthaus* cases this Court, applying the principles of Lucas v. Earl, supra; Helvering v. Clifford, supra; and Helvering v. Horst, 311 U.S. 112, found that the purported gift, whether or not technically complete, had made no substantial change in the economic relation of members of the family to the income. In each case the husband continued to manage and control the business as before, and income from the property given to the wife and invested by her in the partnership continued to be used in the business or expended for family purposes. We characterized the results of the transactions entered into between husband and wife as "a mere paper reallocation of income among the family members," noting that "The actualities of their relation to the income did not change." 327 U.S. at 292. This, we thought, provided ample grounds for the finding that no true part-

---

14. Although "management and control of the business" was one of the circumstances emphasized by the *Tower* case, along with "vital services" and "original capital," the Tax Court did not consider it an alternative "test" of partnership. See discussion, infra, at part *Third*, and note 17.

nership was intended; that the husband was still the true earner of the income.

But application of the *Clifford-Horst* principle does not follow automatically upon a gift to a member of one's family, followed by its investment in the family partnership. If it did, it would be necessary to define "family" and to set precise limits of membership therein. We have not done so for the obvious reason that existence of the family relationship does not create a status which itself determines tax questions,[15] but is simply a warning that things may not be what they seem. It is frequently stated that transactions between members of a family will be carefully scrutinized. But, more particularly, the family relationship often makes it possible for one to shift tax incidence by surface changes of ownership without disturbing in the least his dominion and control over the subject of the gift or the purposes for which the income from the property is used. He is able, in other words, to retain "the substance of full enjoyment of all the rights which previously he had in the property." Helvering v. Clifford, supra, at 336.[16]

The fact that transfers to members of the family group may be mere camouflage does not, however, mean that they invariably are. The *Tower* case recognized that one's participation in control and management of the business is a circumstance indicating an intent to be a bona fide partner despite the fact that the capital contributed originated elsewhere in the family.[17] If the donee of property who then invests it in the family partnership exercises dominion and control over that property—and through that control influences the conduct of the partnership and the disposition of its income—he may well be a true partner. Whether he is free to, and does, enjoy the fruits

---

15. Except, of course, when Congress defines "family" and attaches tax consequences thereto. See, e. g. 26 U.S. C. § 503(a) (2).

16. It is not enough to say in this case, as we did in the *Clifford* case, that "It is hard to imagine that respondent felt himself the poorer after this [partnership agreement] had been executed or, if he did, that it had any rational foundation in fact." 309 U.S. at 336. Culbertson's interest in his partnership with Coon was worth about $50,-000 immediately prior to dissolution of the partnership. In order to sustain the Tax Court, we would have to conclude that he felt himself worth approximately twice that much upon his purchase of Coon's interest, even though he had agreed to sell that interest to his sons at the same price.

17. As noted above (note 13), participation in control and management of the business, although given equal prominence with contributions of "vital services" and "original capital" as circumstances indicating an intent to enter into a partnership relation, was discarded by the Tax Court as a "test" of partnership. This indicates a basic and erroneous assumption that one can never make a gift to a member of one's family without retaining the essentials of ownership, if the gift is then invested in a family partnership. We included participation in management and control of the business as a circumstance indicative of intent to carry on business as a partner to cover the situation in which active dominion and control of the subject of the gift had actually passed to the donee. It is a circumstance of prime importance.

of the partnership is strongly indicative of the reality of his participation in the enterprise. In the *Tower* and *Lusthaus* cases we distinguished between active participation in the affairs of the business by a donee of a share in the partnership on the one hand, and his passive acquiescence to the will of the donor on the other.[18] This distinction is of obvious importance to a determination of the true intent of the parties. It is meaningless if "original capital" is an essential test of membership in a family partnership.

The cause must therefore be remanded to the Tax Court for a decision as to which, if any, of respondent's sons were partners with him in the operation of the ranch during 1940 and 1941. As to which of them, in other words, was there a bona fide intent that they be partners in the conduct of the cattle business, either because of services to be performed during those years, or because of contributions of capital of which they were the true owners, as we have defined that term in the *Clifford, Horst,* and *Tower* cases? No question as to the allocation of income between capital and services is presented in this case, and we intimate no opinion on that subject.

The decision of the Court of Appeals is reversed with directions to remand the cause to the Tax Court for further proceedings in conformity with this opinion.

Reversed and remanded.

[The separate concurring opinions of JUSTICES BLACK and RUTLEDGE, BURTON, JACKSON, and FRANKFURTER have been omitted. Ed.]

PROBLEMS

1. Section 704(e)(1) recognizes as a partner in a family partnership one who "owns a capital interest in a partnership in which capital is a material income-producing factor." Consider whether the following situations meet the statutory requirement:

(a) Father is a doctor who makes his Son (a law student) a partner in his practice, assuming applicable state law does not prohibit such associations.

(b) Father is a doctor who makes his Daughter (a recent medical school graduate) a partner in his practice.

(c) Father owns a shopping center where the stores are subject to long-term leases and he transfers the leases to a partnership with Son and Daughter.

18. There is testimony in the record as to the participation by respondent's sons in the management of the ranch. Since such evidence did not fall within either of the "tests" adopted by the Tax Court, it failed to consider this testimony. Without intimating any opinion as to its probative value, we think that it is clearly relevant evidence of the intent to carry on business as partners.

(d) Father transfers both the shopping center and the leases in (c), above, to the partnership with Son and Daughter.

(e) Same as (d), above, except that Father retains the right to make all business decisions with respect to the shopping center and to use income from the center to expand the center.

(f) Do you see a relationship between § 704(e) and both the messages in Chapter 13 and the *Clifford* case in Chapter 14?

2.　Father owns a group of apartments which he transfers to a partnership with Son and two Daughters who provide no consideration for their ¼ interests in the partnership.　The income from the partnership is $100,000.

(a) What result if Father renders services worth $20,000 to the partnership, but the partnership agreement merely calls for splitting the income ¼ each and each partner actually receives $25,000?

(b) What result if Father renders no services but the agreement provides the income is to be divided 10% to Father and 30% each to Son and each of his Daughters?

(c) What result if Father and Son both render services worth $20,000 and the agreement is the same as in part (b), above. See Reg. § 1.704–1(e)(3)(i)(b).

D.　CORPORATIONS

Internal Revenue Code:　Sections 11(a); 482.

OVERTON v. COMMISSIONER

United States Court of Appeals, Second Circuit, 1947.
162 F.2d 155.

SWAN, CIRCUIT JUDGE.　These appeals involve gift tax liability of petitioner Overton for the years 1936 and 1937 and income tax liability of petitioner Oliphant for the year 1941.　Each petitioner was held liable on the theory that dividends received by his wife in the year in question on stock registered in her name on the books of Castle & Overton, Inc., a New York corporation, were income of the husband for tax purposes.　No gift tax return with respect to such dividends was filed by Mr. Overton in 1936 or 1937, and the dividends received by Mrs. Oliphant in 1941 were not included in her husband's return for that year.

There is no dispute as to the evidentiary facts.　They are stated in detail in the opinion of the Tax Court, 6 T.C. 304, and will be here repeated only so far as may be necessary to render intelligible the discussion which follows. On May 26, 1936 the corporation had outstanding 1,000 shares of common stock without par value but having a liquidating value of at least $120 per share. On that date, pursuant to a plan devised to lessen taxes, the certificate of incorporation was amended to provide for changing the outstanding common stock into 2,000 shares without par value, of which 1,000 were denominated Class A and 1,000 Class B. The old stock was exchanged for the new, the shareholders then gave the B stock to their respective wives, and new certificates therefor were issued to the wives. The B stock had a liquidating value of one dollar per share; everything else on liquidation was to belong to the holders of the A stock, who had also the sole voting rights for directors and on all ordinary matters.[1] By virtue of an agreement made in April 1937 restricting alienation of their stock, the wives were precluded from realizing more than one dollar a share by selling their shares. The A stock was to receive noncumulative dividends at the rate of $10 a share per year before payment of any dividend on the B stock; if dividends in excess of $10 per share were paid on the A stock in any year, such excess dividends were to be shared by both classes of stock in the ratio of one-fifth thereof for the A stock and four-fifths for the B stock. During the six year period ending in December 1941, the dividends paid on B stock totaled $150.-40 a share as against $77.60 a share paid on A stock. In 1941 the A stock had a book value of $155 per share.

The Tax Court was of opinion that the 1936 arrangement, though made in the form of a gift of stock, was in reality an assignment of part of the taxpayers' future dividends. Unless form is to be exalted above substance this conclusion is inescapable. Since the total issue of B stock represented only $1,000 of the corporate assets, it is plain that the property which earned the large dividends received by the B shareholders was the property represented by the A stock held by the husbands. In transferring the B shares to their wives they parted with no substantial part of their interest in the corporate property. Had they been content to transfer some of the original common stock, they could have accomplished their purpose of lessening taxes on the family group,[2] but they would then have made substantial gifts of capital. The arrangement they put into effect gave the wives nothing, or substantially nothing, but the right to future earnings flowing from property retained by the husbands. That anticipatory assignments of income, whatever their formal cloak, are ineffective taxwise is a principle too firmly established to be subject to question. See Lucas v. Earl, 281 U.S. 111, 50 S.Ct. 241, 74 L.Ed. 731; Helvering v.

---

1. Whether the amendment of the certificate of incorporation excluded B shareholders from voting on extraordinary matters specified in section 51 of the Stock Corporation Law of New York, McK.Consol.Laws, c. 59, in effect on May 26, 1937, the Tax Court did not find it necessary to determine; nor do we.

2. See Blair v. Commissioner, 300 U.S. 5, 57 S.Ct. 330, 81 L.Ed. 465.

Horst, 311 U.S. 112, 61 S.Ct. 144, 85 L.Ed. 75, 131 A.L.R. 655; Helvering v. Eubank, 311 U.S. 122, 61 S.Ct. 149, 85 L.Ed. 81; Harrison v. Schaffner, 312 U.S. 579, 61 S.Ct. 759, 85 L.Ed. 1055; Commissioner v. Tower, 327 U.S. 280, 66 S.Ct. 532, 90 L.Ed. 670; Lusthaus v. Commissioner, 327 U.S. 293, 66 S.Ct. 539, 90 L.Ed. 679; Hyman v. Nunan, 2 Cir., 143 F.2d 425. We think the Tax Court correctly applied this principle to the facts of the case at bar.

Orders affirmed.

McGUIRE v. UNITED STATES

District Court of the United States, Southern District of New York (1969),
1969–1 USTC para. 9279.
Aff'd 1971–1 USTC para. 9304, 2d Cir. 1971.

TYLER, JR., DISTRICT JUDGE. The Court: Miss McBryant and ladies and gentlemen, now that you have heard the arguments of the lawyers, Mr. Cohen and Mr. Hering in this case, the time has come for me, as you know, to give you the rules of law which will be applicable to your deliberations here.

* * *

Now as you are well aware from the submissions of counsel, the plaintiffs, the three McGuire sisters, sue here for refund of income taxes paid by them as individuals for the tax years of 1955 and 1956.

As I recall it, the combined total refunds claimed by the three sisters for each of these tax years is the sum of $33,232.95.

As you know, they paid their taxes, which include these claims, under protest; and under the law they filed this civil suit to collect these sums by way of refunds when their protests, copies of which, by the way, are in evidence, were rejected by the Commissioner of Internal Revenue.

Simply stated, this case, that is, the claims of the plaintiffs and the defenses thereto by the government, can be simply summarized as presenting the question of whether or not certain income earned by the group known as the McGuire Sisters, was income earned by them as individuals or was it properly earned by two corporations which were set up by them in 1955, which, as you know, had the names of McGuire Sisters Corporation and McGuire Sisters Productions, Inc.

That is a simple statement of the basic dispute between the parties.

However, of course, as I think you are also aware, the specific claims of the plaintiffs and the defense thereto of the government raise a number of questions. * * * I have determined to put these * * * basic questions, if you will, to you in the form of special questions which are susceptible of a simple yes-or-no answer.

Thus your verdict in this case will take the form of a simple yes-or-no answer to these * * * basic questions, which I now intend to articulate for you, and beyond that, to discuss in relation to those questions the rules of law and other considerations which either are or may be relevant to your deliberations in an effort to answer these * * * questions.

The first of these * * * questions cast up by this case can be posed essentially as follows:

Were the corporations formed by the plaintiffs actually engaged in a valid business or commercial or industrial activity as opposed to some non-business or non-commercial activity, as, for example, merely to avoid paying certain taxes or to save certain taxes?

Now on this question plaintiffs, at least initially, as I understand them, argue that the two corporations which they formed in September of 1955 or at least caused to be formed in that month, were valid firms actually engaged in a valid business.

Specifically, as I understand the plaintiffs, they contend that those corporations were formed for the business purpose of realizing, at least initially, income from the entertainment services of the three sisters, and then taking that income and investing it in income-producing real estate properties.

But the United States, as you know, argues that the evidence shows that the corporations never got close to investing in any income-producing real estate or in any commercial real estate, as it is sometimes called; or doing any other valid business or commercial activities.

Thus, this first question can be simply related thus:

Did the two corporations in fact engage in any business or were they just depositories for the income earned by the plaintiffs as the well-known entertainers that they were in the years in question?

Keep in mind, ladies and gentlemen, that here the plaintiffs have the burden by the preponderance of the evidence of proving to your satisfaction that these two corporations in fact engaged in some valid business or commercial purpose.

Now in considering this first question there are some rules and considerations which are or may be relevant here and indeed on the other questions which I am going to discuss with you in a few moments.

I start out, for example, by observing that under our law it is true a taxpayer has the right to organize and run his business in a way which will avoid certain taxes or minimize federal income taxes.

However, a taxpayer is not permitted by our law to use the corporate organization or the corporate form, if you will, for no other activity than tax avoidance or tax reduction or tax minimization.

Now in considering this first question I pose to you and which we are going to ask you to answer, and the contentions of the parties on this first question which you have just heard from Mr. Cohen and Mr. Hering, bear in mind that corporate or business or commercial formalities and labels are not necessarily determinative of this first question, or indeed any other basic question in this case.

That is, ladies and gentlemen, you should examine entire transactions as they are shown by the evidence during the trial in order to get the substance of the transaction, that is to say, in order to determine what really happened in a particular activity or transaction.

For example, you should, of course, consider documents which were put in evidence here, such as the corporate records of these two corporations formed by the ladies McGuire. You should consider the books and records of these two corporations, and the facsimile stock certificates, for example, which I recall were placed in evidence.

However, you may also consider other things about these corporations, again as shown by the evidence.

To illustrate, how did these corporations operate? Or in fact did they operate at all?

How did the suppliers of goods and services to these corporations or to the McGuire sisters deal with the corporations or the McGuire sisters?

For example, did the suppliers think they were dealing with the sisters as individuals? Or did they think they were dealing with two corporations or one corporation?

Another question you might ask yourself is: Did these corporations have a place of business? And, if so, what kind of place of business was it?

Did these corporations have employees? If they did, how were these employees compensated?

Who were the stockholders of these corporations? Who were the officers of these corporations? What were the activities of these officers and stockholders, as shown by the evidence?

The point I am trying to get across is a simple one. These and similar questions are the kind of questions to ask yourselves in the course of deciding whether or not the two corporations formed in September, 1955, were engaged in a valid business or commercial purpose.

I should say before I conclude on this first question, by the way, ladies and gentlemen, that the intention or purpose of the three McGuire sisters, is, strictly speaking, not really too important or important at all here.

That is to say, the main point raised by this first question is: What in fact did these two corporations do or what in fact did they not do?

* * *

[L]et me pose the [final] question [this way] : Was the Internal Revenue Service, or, as it is sometimes put, the Commissioner of Internal Revenue, arbitrary or capricious in allocating or apportioning income from the corporation contracts with the Copacabana Club, for example, and all those other clubs as shown in the evidence, in 1955 and 1956 to the three plaintiffs rather than to the two corporations?

Now, ladies and gentlemen, let me explain that this question comes up in this case because of one of the government's arguments, which is based upon the statute known to lawyers at least as Section 482 of the Internal Revenue Code of 1954.

Very simply, that statute states in words or substance, that where two or more organizations, or businesses, if you will, whether or not incorporated, are owned and controlled by the same person or persons, the Commissioner or the Internal Revenue Service is authorized to apportion or allocate gross income for tax purposes between or among such businesses or entities or persons as the Commissioner deems necessary to clearly reflect income as it was actually earned or to prevent improper avoidance of income tax.

Now in certain respects, as some of you may have divined, this question does cast up similar issues as were implicit in the first two basic questions.

However, there are some other elements here involved and the emphasis is somewhat different.

To explain, I start off by observing that plaintiffs here must prove by a preponderance of the evidence that the Internal Revenue Service was arbitrary or capricious, that is to say, that the Internal Revenue Service acted without any factual basis whatsoever in allocating income from the singing engagements, not to the corporations or one of them, but to the three ladies McGuire as individual taxpayers.

In other words, if you find from the evidence before you that the Internal Revenue Service had justification, factually, for deciding that it was the plaintiffs rather than the corporations who were the real earners of the income in question, or for deciding that the corporations were set up solely to avoid paying income taxes at a higher personal rate, then the plaintiffs would not have carried their burden on this issue and you would be obliged to answer this third and last question "No."

On the other hand, if you determine that the corporations and not the ladies McGuire, as individuals, earned these engagement fees at such clubs as, for example, the Copacabana here in New York City, then you would be entitled to find further that the Internal Revenue Service acted arbitrarily, that is, without foundation in fact, in allocating this income to the plaintiffs, and not to the two corporations.

Now from what I have just been saying, ladies and gentlemen, you should note that the question here is not whether you would have allocated the income as the Commissioner did; rather, it is [did] the Commissioner have factual justification for making the allocation he did even though you might decide you would have done it otherwise?

* * *

Written Questions and Jury's Answers

1. Q. Were the two corporations formed by plaintiffs actually engaged in a valid business or commercial activity, as opposed to merely a tax-saving activity?

A. NO.

* * *

BORGE v. COMMISSIONER *

United States Court of Appeals, Second Circuit, 1968.
405 F.2d 673.
Cert. denied, 395 U.S. 933, 89 S.Ct. 1994, 1969.

HAYS, CIRCUIT JUDGE: Petitioners seek review of a decision of the Tax Court sustaining the Commissioner's determination of deficiencies in their income tax payments for the years 1958 through 1962, inclusive. The Tax Court upheld * * * the Commissioner's allocation to Borge [1] under Section 482 of the Internal Revenue Code of 1954, 26 U.S.C. § 482 (1964), of a portion of the compensation received by Danica Enterprises, Inc., Borge's wholly owned corporation, for services performed by Borge as an entertainer. * * * We affirm.

[From 1952 to 1958 Borge, as an individual, operated ViBo Farms where he developed, produced, processed and sold quality chickens known as rock cornish hens. He had substantial losses each year which he deducted against the substantial income he earned as an entertainer. Ed.]

* * *

* * * Borge organized Danica, and, on March 1, 1958, transferred to the corporation, in exchange for all of its stock and a loan payable, the assets of the poultry business (except the farm real property).

Borge is a well-known professional entertainer. During the years preceding the organization of Danica he made large sums from television, stage and motion picture engagements.

---

* See Katz, "Can Section 482 Be Used to Negate the Tax Effect of a Bona Fide Corporation?" 28 J.Tax. 2 (1968). Ed.

1. "Borge" refers herein to Victor Borge. His wife has been included as a party to the action solely because of the filing of joint returns. [Discussion in the opinion of an alternative issue of tax liability under I.R.C. § 269 has been deleted. Ed.]

Since Danica had no means of meeting the expected losses from the poultry business, Borge and Danica entered into a contract at the time of the organization of the corporation under which Borge agreed to perform entertainment and promotional services for the corporation for a 5-year period for compensation from Danica of $50,000 per year. Danica offset the poultry losses [3] against the entertainment profits, which far exceeded the $50,000 per year it had contracted to pay Borge.[4] Borge obviously would not have entered into such a contract with an unrelated party.

Danica did nothing to aid Borge in his entertainment business. Those who contracted with Danica for Borge's entertainment services required Borge personally to guarantee the contracts. Danica's entertainment earnings were attributable solely to the services of Borge, and Danica's only profits were from the entertainment business.

The only year during the period in dispute in which Danica actually paid Borge anything for his services was 1962, when Borge was paid the full $50,000.

The issues in controversy are (1) whether the Commissioner, acting under Section 482 of the Internal Revenue Code of 1954, 26 U.S.C. § 482 (1964), properly allocated to Borge from Danica $75,000 per year from 1958 through 1961 and $25,000 for 1962, * * *

I.

When two or more organizations, trades or businesses, whether or not incorporated, are owned or controlled by the same interests, Section 482 of the Internal Revenue Code of 1954, 26 U.S.C. § 482 (1964), authorizes the Commissioner to apportion gross income between or among such organizations, trades or businesses if he deems that apportionment is necessary clearly to reflect income or to prevent evasion of tax.[5] We conclude that the Commissioner could properly have found that for purposes of Section 482 Borge owned or controlled two businesses, an entertainment business and a poultry business, and that the allocation to Borge of part of the entertainment compensation paid to the corporation was not error.[6]

We accept, as supported by the record, the Tax Court's finding: that Borge operated an entertainment business and merely assigned to Danica a portion of his income from that business; that Danica did nothing to earn or to assist in the earning of the entertainment income; that Borge would not have contracted for $50,000 per year

3. [Details of the poultry losses are omitted. Ed.]

4. [Details of Danica's net entertainment income are omitted. Ed.]

5. [I.R.C. § 482 is omitted. Ed.]

6. We agree with petitioners' contention that since Borge's employment contract with Danica went into effect on March 1, 1958, the 1958 allocation should have been only $62,500 (⅚ of $75,000). A recomputation of Borge's deficiency to this extent should be made.

with an unrelated party to perform the services referred to in his contract with Danica. Thus Borge was correctly held to be in the entertainment business.

At the same time Danica, Borge's wholly owned corporation, was in the poultry business.

Petitioners, relying primarily on Whipple v. Commissioner, 373 U.S. 193, 83 S.Ct. 1168, 10 L.Ed.2d 288 (1963), argue that Borge is not an "organization, trade or business" and that Section 482 is therefore inapposite.

In *Whipple* the Supreme Court held only that where one renders services to a corporation as an investment, he is not engaging in a trade or business:

"Devoting one's time and energies to the affairs of a corporation is not of itself, and without more, a trade or business of the person so engaged. Though such activities may produce income, profit or gain in the form of dividends or enhancement in the value of an investment, this return is distinctive to the process of investing and is generated by the successful operation of the corporation's business as distinguished from the trade or business of the taxpayer himself. When the only return is that of an investor, the taxpayer has not satisfied his burden of demonstrating that he is engaged in a trade or business since investing is not a trade or business and the return to the taxpayer, though substantially the product of his services, legally arises not from his own trade or business but from that of the corporation." 373 U.S. at 202, 83 S.Ct. at 1174.

Here, however, Borge was in the business of entertaining. He was not devoting his time and energies to the corporation; he was carrying on his career as an entertainer, and merely channeling a part of his entertainment income through the corporation.

Moreover, in *Whipple* petitioner was devoting his time and energies to a corporation in the hope of realizing capital gains treatment from the sale of appreciated stock. When the hoped-for appreciation did not materialize he attempted to deduct his losses as ordinary losses. The Court decided that where one stands to achieve capital gains through an investment, any losses incurred in connection with the investment are capital losses. Borge is clearly earning ordinary income; the only question is who should pay the taxes on it. Thus, *Whipple* is not apposite.

For somewhat similar reasons we find Commissioner v. Gross, 236 F.2d 612 (2d Cir. 1956), on which petitioner also seeks to rely, also inapposite.

Nor do we consider the other cases cited by petitioners persuasive. The Commissioner is not arguing here, as he did, for example, in Charles Laughton, 40 B.T.A. 101 (1939), remanded, 113 F.2d 103 (9th Cir. 1940), that the taxpayer should be taxed on the entire amount paid into the wholly owned corporation, i. e. that the corporation should be ignored. See also Pat O'Brien, 25 T.C. 376 (1955); Fontaine Fox, 37 B.T.A. 271 (1938). Instead he recognizes the existence of the corporation, but under Section 482 allocates a portion of its income to its sole shareholder who alone was responsible for the production of such income.

Petitioner contends that the Congress, in enacting the personal holding company and collapsible corporation provisions of the Code, precluded the Commissioner's action in this case under Section 482. We do not read those provisions, however, as the only available methods for dealing with the situations there involved. As the Third Circuit said in National Sec. Corp. v. Commissioner, 137 F.2d 600, 602 (3d Cir.), cert. denied, 320 U.S. 794, 64 S.Ct. 262, 88 L.Ed. 479 (1943):

"In every case in which [Section 482] is applied its application will necessarily result in an apparent conflict with the literal requirements of some other provision of the [Internal Revenue Code]. If this were not so Section [482] would be wholly superfluous."

The fact that similar, but not identical, factual situations have been dealt with by legislation does not mean that this situation, because it was not also specifically dealt with by legislation, cannot be reached even by a general code provision.

We thus conclude that the Tax Court was correct in upholding the Commissioner's ruling that Borge controlled two separate businesses. See Pauline W. Ach, 42 T.C. 114 (1964), aff'd, 358 F.2d 342 (6th Cir.), cert. denied, 385 U.S. 899, 87 S.Ct. 205, 17 L.Ed.2d 131 (1966).

The Commissioner's action in allocating a part of Danica's income to Borge was based upon his conclusion that such allocation was necessary in order clearly to reflect the income of the two businesses under Borge's common control. The Commissioner's allocation has received the approval of the Tax Court. As this Court held in dealing with the predecessor of Section 482, "Whether the Tax Court was correct in allocating income to the petitioner under § 45 [of the Internal Revenue Code of 1939] is essentially one of fact and the decision below must be affirmed if supported by substantial evidence." Advance Mach. Exch. v. Commissioner, 196 F.2d 1006, 1007–08 (2d Cir.), cert. denied, 344 U.S. 835, 73 S.Ct. 45, 97 L.Ed. 650 (1952). See Int.Rev.Code of 1954, § 7482(a), 26 U.S.C. § 7482(a) (1964). Here the determination of the Commissioner and the decision of the Tax Court are supported by substantial evidence that the income of Borge's two businesses has been distorted through Borge's having arranged for Danica to receive a large part of his entertainment income although Danica did nothing to earn that income, and the sole purpose of the arrangement was to permit Danica to offset losses from the poultry business with income from the entertainment business. The amount allocated by the Commissioner ($75,000 per year) was entirely reasonable—indeed, generous—in view of the fact that

Danica's annual net income from Borge's entertainment services averaged $166,465 during the years in question.

*   *   *

PROBLEMS

1.   Attorney who is a sole practitioner incorporates his law practice under his state's Professional Incorporation Act.   In Rev.Rul. 70–101, 1970–1 C.B. 278, the I.R.S. announced that it will recognize such corporations as corporate entities for federal tax classification purposes.   Nevertheless, the rationale of the *McGuire* case might be used to set aside such a corporation.   Attorney is the sole shareholder of the corporation; however, corporation employs clerical help and contracts out and makes collections on Attorney's services.   Prior to incorporation Attorney netted $75,000 per year.   In the first year of incorporation, Corporation nets $100,000 before taking account of Attorney's $40,000 prearranged salary.   Assuming the Commissioner recognizes Corporation as valid under the *McGuire* test, what tool would he likely use to assert that Attorney should have paid tax on more of the corporate income?

2.   Father runs his own hardware store and has income far in excess of his needs.   Several years ago he started, as an investment, a small manufacturing company that produces "frisbees."   For the first few years of operation, the business operated at a loss, but with the recent frisbee craze, business is booming.   Father has no need for all of this income and in fact has considered transferring the business to Son and Daughter.   Father ultimately decides that by incorporating the frisbee business, and retaining 51% of the stock, he can maintain control of the business and still transfer part of the business (and hence the income in dividend form) to Son and Daughter.   Will Father's plan successfully rid him of the surplus income? Is there another vehicle (other than a corporation) that Father can use to effectuate his plan?

PART FOUR: DEDUCTIONS IN COMPUTING TAXABLE INCOME

CHAPTER 15.　BUSINESS DEDUCTIONS

A.　INTRODUCTION

Internal Revenue Code: Sections 1; 63(a).

There is no constitutional obstacle to a tax on *gross* income. This is not to say the 16th Amendment would support an unapportioned tax on gross receipts, for the term "incomes" as used there connotes "gain," at least to the extent that a mere return of capital is not "income." But expenses incurred earning income might constitutionally be disregarded in the computation of the tax. For this reason, deductions are spoken of as a matter of "legislative grace;" and it is at least true that, as a taxpayer has no constitutional right to a deduction,[1] he must find a statutory provision that specifically allows the deduction claimed.

Is the "grace" aspect of deduction provisions of importance in their interpretation? There may be some notion that by allowing a deduction Congress bestows a *special* benefit that should be narrowly construed. Consider whether this is a proper view of any or all the deduction provisions presented in this Part. At least where it is not, should not the courts seek to give meaning to a deduction provision in the same manner as they approach any other congressional product?[2]

Since the statute is all-important in the deduction area, its basic design should be noted. The individual income tax rates[3] are applied to "taxable income."[4] In general, under I.R.C. (26 U.S.C.A.) § 63 (a) taxable income is gross income minus the deductions provided in the statute.[5]

1. First National Bank & Trust Co. v. U. S., 115 F.2d 194 (5th Cir. 1940).

2. See Griswold, "An Argument Against the Doctrine that Deductions Should Be Narrowly Construed as a Matter of Legislative Grace," 56 Harv. L.Rev. 1142 (1943).

3. I.R.C. (26 U.S.C.A.) § 1.

4. See I.R.C. (26 U.S.C.A.) § 63. Consideration must be given later to (1) computation of tax in the case of joint returns, I.R.C. (26 U.S.C.A.) § 1(a), and certain other special circumstances, and (2) to the tax tables for low-income taxpayers, I.R.C. (26 U.S. C.A.) § 3.

5. It will be necessary later to take account of the "standard" deduction,

This Part of the book divides deductions allowed in computing taxable income into four groups. Chapter 15 is concerned with trade and business deductions; and these provisions apply alike to individuals and corporations, although sometimes with variations. For individuals only, Congress identifies a kind of sub-business category in which some expenditures that are not incurred in "business" are considered sufficiently connected with income or profit-seeking activities to warrant their deduction. Chapter 16 is addressed to the deductibility of these expenditures.

A general appreciation of the dichotomy recognized in Chapters 15 and 16 can be gleaned from an examination of some of the Code sections making use of the differing concepts. For example, sections 162 (expenses), 165(c)(1) (losses), and 167(a)(1) (depreciation) all relate specifically to "trade or business" activities. In contrast, sections 165(c)(2) (losses), 167(a)(2) (depreciation) and 212(1) and (2) are all concerned with activities directed toward the "production of income," the "collection of income" or "transactions entered into for profit" without regard to whether the activity involved can be classified as a trade or business.

A third group of deductions available alike to individuals and corporations are allowed without regard to whether they have a business, or income, or profit connection. These are presented in Chapter 17. Finally, Chapter 18 identifies a group of deductions, also outside the business, or income, or profit area which, however, are available only to individuals.

In the deduction area, there are some negative provisions that sometimes countermand what seems to be clear statutory allowance. Thus a practitioner (and of course a student) must be on the alert for congressional finger-crossing. Throughout these Chapters, references are made to these negative provisions, many of which (but not all, see, e. g., § 183) are grouped in the Code at §§ 261–281. A glance at the headings of those sections might be in order at this point.

This Chapter begins with section 162 which is the most comprehensive of the sections concerning business deductions. By this stage a student knows that he does not read the Code the way he does a novel and will appreciate therefore a kind of pondering analysis of the opening clause of section 162(a). Significant words and phrases will light up as if electrified by the push of a button. For example, it will appear that it is "expenses" that are allowed as deductions by the section. What kinds of expenditures are properly classified as expenses? It will appear further that it is only "ordinary and necessary" expenses that are to be deducted. Does "ordi-

I.R.C. (26 U.S.C.A.) § 141, which is in lieu of some deductions that individuals may otherwise claim and which brings into consideration the concept "adjusted gross income," defined in

I.R.C. (26 U.S.C.A.) § 62. When the standard deduction is used, I.R.C. (26 U.S.C.A.) § 63(b) defines taxable income.

nary" have its ordinary meaning here? And does "necessary" mean absolutely necessary? Further, the expenses that are deductible are only those that relate to "carrying on" a trade or business. Are we "carrying on" when we are getting ready to do business?

The next three segments of this Chapter are addressed directly to the questions just raised. Of course, that does not exhaust the interesting words and phrases of the introductory clause of section 162(a). For example, it is expenses "paid or incurred" that may be deducted and of course the question further arises whether an expense was paid or incurred "during the taxable year." These are timing questions and, while they necessarily arise here in some circumstances, their development is reserved for later treatment in Chapter 19.

Obviously, deduction under section 162 also hinges on the expenses involved being related to a "trade or business." This Chapter devotes no separate treatment to that concept because, as indicated above, it arises in numerous contexts throughout the tax areas to which this book is addressed. Accordingly, Part B of this Chapter develops three crucial factors in the application of section 162 ("ordinary and necessary," "expenses," and "carrying on") and then examines specific expenditures that the statute identifies as deductible business expenses when all requirements of section 162 are met.

B. THE ANATOMY OF THE BUSINESS DEDUCTION WORKHORSE: SECTION 162

---

1. "ORDINARY AND NECESSARY"

Internal Revenue Code: Section 162(a).
Regulations: Section 1.162–1(a).

WELCH v. HELVERING

Supreme Court of the United States, 1933.
290 U.S. 111, 54 S.Ct. 8.

MR. JUSTICE CARDOZO delivered the opinion of the Court.

The question to be determined is whether payments by a taxpayer, who is in business as a commission agent, are allowable deductions in the computation of his income if made to the creditors of a bankrupt corporation in an endeavor to strengthen his own standing and credit.

In 1922 petitioner was the secretary of the E. L. Welch Company, a Minnesota corporation, engaged in the grain business. The company was adjudged an involuntary bankrupt, and had a discharge from its debts. Thereafter the petitioner made a contract with the Kellogg Company to purchase grain for it on a commission. In order to reëstablish his relations with customers whom he had known when acting for the Welch Company and to solidify his credit and standing, he decided to pay the debts of the Welch business so far as he was able. In fulfilment of that resolve, he made payments of substantial amounts during five successive years. In 1924, the commissions were $18,028.20; the payments $3,975.97; in 1923, the commissions $31,-377.07; the payments $11,968.20; in 1926, the commissions $20,925.-25, the payments $12,815.72; in 1927, the commissions $22,119.61, the payments $7,379.72; and in 1928, the commissions $26,177.56, the payments $11,068.25. The Commissioner ruled that these payments were not deductible from income as ordinary and necessary expenses, but were rather in the nature of capital expenditures, an outlay for the development of reputation and good will. The Board of Tax Appeals sustained the action of the Commissioner (25 B.T.A. 117), and the Court of Appeals for the Eighth Circuit affirmed. 63 F.2d 976. The case is here on certiorari.

"In computing net income there shall be allowed as deductions * * * all the ordinary and necessary expenses paid or incurred during the taxable year in carrying on any trade or business." Revenue Act of 1924, c. 234, 43 Stat. 253, 269, § 214; 26 U.S.C. § 955; Revenue Act of 1926, c. 27, 44 Stat. 9, 26, § 214; 26 U.S.C.App. § 955; Revenue Act of 1928, c. 852, 45 Stat. 791, 799, § 23; cf. Treasury Regulations 65, Arts. 101, 292, under the Revenue Act of 1924, and similar regulations under the Acts of 1926 and 1928.

We may assume that the payments to creditors of the Welch Company were necessary for the development of the petitioner's business, at least in the sense that they were appropriate and helpful. McCulloch v. Maryland, 4 Wheat. 316. He certainly thought they were, and we should be slow to override his judgment. But the problem is not solved when the payments are characterized as necessary. Many necessary payments are charges upon capital. There is need to determine whether they are both necessary and ordinary. Now, what is ordinary, though there must always be a strain of constancy within it, is none the less a variable affected by time and place and circumstance. Ordinary in this context does not mean that the payments must be habitual or normal in the sense that the same taxpayer will have to make them often. A lawsuit affecting the safety of a business may happen once in a lifetime. The counsel fees may be so heavy that repetition is unlikely. None the less, the expense is an ordinary one because we know from experience that payments for such a purpose, whether the amount is large or small, are the common and accepted means of defense against attack. Cf. Kornhauser v. United States,

276 U.S. 145. The situation is unique in the life of the individual affected, but not in the life of the group, the community, of which he is a part. At such times there are norms of conduct that help to stabilize our judgment, and make it certain and objective. The instance is not erratic, but is brought within a known type.

The line of demarcation is now visible between the case that is here and the one supposed for illustration. We try to classify this act as ordinary or the opposite, and the norms of conduct fail us. No longer can we have recourse to any fund of business experience, to any known business practice. Men do at times pay the debts of others without legal obligation or the lighter obligation imposed by the usages of trade or by neighborly amenities, but they do not do so ordinarily, not even though the result might be to heighten their reputation for generosity and opulence. Indeed, if language is to be read in its natural and common meaning (Old Colony R. Co. v. Commissioner, 284 U.S. 552, 560; Woolford Realty Co. v. Rose, 286 U.S. 319, 327), we should have to say that payment in such circumstances, instead of being ordinary is in a high degree extraordinary. There is nothing ordinary in the stimulus evoking it, and none in the response. Here, indeed, as so often in other branches of the law, the decisive distinctions are those of degree and not of kind. One struggles in vain for any verbal formula that will supply a ready touchstone. The standard set up by the statute is not a rule of law; it is rather a way of life. Life in all its fullness must supply the answer to the riddle.

The Commissioner of Internal Revenue resorted to that standard in assessing the petitioner's income, and found that the payments in controversy came closer to capital outlays than to ordinary and necessary expenses in the operation of a business. His ruling has the support of a presumption of correctness, and the petitioner has the burden of proving it to be wrong. Wickwire v. Reinecke, 275 U.S. 101; Jones v. Commissioner, 38 F.2d 550, 552. Unless we can say from facts within our knowledge that these are ordinary and necessary expenses according to the ways of conduct and the forms of speech prevailing in the business world, the tax must be confirmed. But nothing told us by this record or within the sphere of our judicial notice permits us to give that extension to what is ordinary and necessary. Indeed, to do so would open the door to many bizarre analogies. One man has a family name that is clouded by thefts committed by an ancestor. To add to his own standing he repays the stolen money, wiping off, it may be, his income for the year. The payments figure in his tax return as ordinary expenses. Another man conceives the notion that he will be able to practice his vocation with greater ease and profit if he has an opportunity to enrich his culture. Forthwith the price of his education becomes an expense of the business, reducing the income subject to taxation. There is little difference between these expenses and those in controversy here. Reputation and

learning are akin to capital assets, like the good will of an old partnership. Cf. Colony Coal & Coke Corp. v. Commissioner, 52 F.2d 923.
For many, they are the only tools with which to hew a pathway to
success. The money spent in acquiring them is well and wisely spent.
It is not an ordinary expense of the operation of a business.

Many cases in the federal courts deal with phases of the problem
presented in the case at bar. To attempt to harmonize them would be
a futile task. They involve the appreciation of particular situations,
at times with borderline conclusions. Typical illustrations are cited
in the margin.[1]

The decree should be

Affirmed.

PROBLEMS

1. Taxpayer is a businessman, local politician who is also an of-
ficer-director of a savings and loan association of which he was a
founder. When, partially due to his mismanagement, the savings
and loan began to go under, he voluntarily donated nearly one half
a million dollars to help bail it out. Is the payment deductible under
I.R.C. § 162? See Elmer W. Conti, 31 T.C.M. 348 (1972).

2. Employee incurred ordinary and necessary expenses on a
business trip for which he was entitled to reimbursement upon filing
a voucher. However, Employee did not file a voucher and was not

---

1. Ordinary expenses: Commissioner v. People's-Pittsburgh Trust Co., 60 F.2d 187, expenses incurred in the defense of a criminal charge growing out of the business of the taxpayer; American Rolling Mill Co. v. Commissioner, 41 F.2d 314, contributions to a civic improvement fund by a corporation employing half of the wage earning population of the city, the payments being made, not for charity, but to add to the skill and productivity of the workmen (cf. the decisions collated in 30 Columbia Law Review 1211, 1212, and the distinctions there drawn); Corning Glass Works v. Lucas, 59 App.D.C. 168; 37 F.2d 798, donations to a hospital by a corporation whose employes with their dependents made up two thirds of the population of the city; Harris v. Lucas, 48 F.2d 187, payments of debts discharged in bankruptcy, but subject to be revived by force of a new promise. Cf. Lucas v. Ox Fibre Brush Co., 281 U.S. 115, where additional compensation, reasonable in amount, was allowed to the officers of a cor-poration for services previously ren-dered.

Not ordinary expenses: Hubinger v. Commissioner, 36 F.2d 724, payments by the taxpayer for the repair of fire damage, such payments being distin-guished from those for wear and tear; Lloyd v. Commissioner, 55 F.2d 842, counsel fees incurred by the taxpayer, the president of a corporation, in prosecuting a slander suit to protect his reputation and that of his busi-ness; 105 West 55th Street v. Com-missioner, 42 F.2d 849, and Blackwell Oil & Gas Co. v. Commissioner, 60 F. 2d 257, gratuitous payments to stock-holders in settlement of disputes be-tween them, or to assume the expense of a lawsuit in which they had been made defendants; White v. Commis-sioner, 61 F.2d 726, payments in set-tlement of a lawsuit against a mem-ber of a partnership, the effect being to enable him to devote his undivided efforts to the partnership business and also to protect its credit.

reimbursed but, instead, deducted his costs on his income tax return. Is Employee entitled to a § 162 deduction? See Heidt v. Comm'r, 274 F.2d 25 (7th Cir. 1954).

3. Suppose on the facts of problem 2, above, Employee, having accounted to Employer for the expenses incurred, was fully reimbursed by Employer.

(a) How may he treat this expense and the reimbursement? See Reg. § 1.162–17(b)(1).

(b) What if the amount paid to the Employee as reimbursement exceeds his actual expenses? See Reg. § 1.162–17(b)(2).

(c) What if actual expenses exceed his reimbursement? See Reg. § 1.162–17(b)(3).

---

2. "EXPENSES"

Internal Revenue Code: Sections 162(a); 263(a).
Regulations: Sections 1.162–4; 1.263(a)–2.

MIDLAND EMPIRE PACKING CO.

Tax Court of the United States, 1950.
14 T.C. 635(A).

ARUNDELL, JUDGE: The issue in this case is whether an expenditure for a concrete lining in petitioner's basement to oilproof it against an oil nuisance created by a neighboring refinery is deductible as an ordinary and necessary expense under section 23(a) of the Internal Revenue Code, on the theory it was an expenditure for a repair, or, in the alternative, whether the expenditure may be treated as the measure of the loss sustained during the taxable year and not compensated for by insurance or otherwise within the meaning of section 23 (f) of the Internal Revenue Code.

The respondent has contended, in part, that the expenditure is for a capital improvement and should be recovered through depreciation charges and is, therefore, not deductible as an ordinary and necessary business expense or as a loss.

It is none too easy to determine on which side of the line certain expenditures fall so that they may be accorded their proper treatment for tax purposes. Treasury Regulations 111,* from which we quote in

---

* Sec. 29.23(a)–4. Repairs.—The cost of incidental repairs which neither materially add to the value of the property nor appreciably prolong its life, but keep it in an ordinarily efficient operating condition, may be deducted as expense, provided the plant or property account is not increased by the amount of such expenditures. Repairs in the nature of replacements, to the extent that they arrest deterioration and appreciably prolong the

the margin, is helpful in distinguishing between an expenditure to be classed as a repair and one to be treated as a captial outlay. In Illinois Merchants Trust Co., Executor, 4 B.T.A. 103, at page 106, we discussed this subject in some detail and in our opinion said:

"It will be noted that the first sentence of the article [now Regulations 111, sec. 29.23(a)–4] relates to repairs, while the second sentence deals in effect with replacements. In determining whether an expenditure is a capital one or is chargeable against operating income, it is necessary to bear in mind the purpose for which the expenditure was made. To repair is to restore to a sound state or to mend, while a replacement connotes a substitution. A repair is an expenditure for the purpose of keeping the property in an ordinarily efficient operating condition. It does not add to the value of the property, nor does it appreciably prolong its life. It merely keeps the property in an operating condition over its probable useful life for the uses for which it was acquired. Expenditures for that purpose are distinguishable from those for replacements, alterations, improvements, or additions which prolong the life of the property, increase its value, or make it adaptable to a different use. The one is a maintenance charge, while the others are additions to capital investment which should not be applied against current earnings."

It will be seen from our findings of fact that for some 25 years prior to the taxable year petitioner had used the basement rooms of its plant as a place for the curing of hams and bacon and for the storage of meat and hides. The basement had been entirely satisfactory for this purpose over the entire period in spite of the fact that there was some seepage of water into the rooms from time to time. In the taxable year it was found that not only water, but oil, was seeping through the concrete walls of the basement of the packing plant and, while the water would soon drain out, the oil would not, and there was left on the basement floor a thick scum of oil which gave off a strong odor that permeated the air of the entire plant, and the fumes from the oil created a fire hazard. It appears that the oil which came from a nearby refinery had also gotten into the water wells which served to furnish water for petitioner's plant, and as a result of this whole condition the Federal meat inspectors advised petitioner that it must discontinue the use of the water from the wells and oilproof the basement, or else shut down its plant.

To meet this situation, petitioner during the taxable year undertook steps to oilproof the basement by adding a concrete lining to the walls from the floor to a height of about four feet and also added concrete to the floor of the basement. It is the cost of this work which

life of the property, should be charged against the depreciation reserve if such account is kept. (See sections 29.23(1)–1 to 29.23(1)–10, inclusive.) [The similar current provision is Reg. § 1.162–4. Ed.]

it seeks to deduct as a repair. The basement was not enlarged by this work nor did the oilproofing serve to make it more desirable for the purpose for which it had been used through the years prior to the time that the oil nuisance had occurred. The evidence is that the expenditure did not add to the value or prolong the expected life of the property over what they were before the event occurred which made the repairs necessary. It is true that after the work was done the seepage of water, as well as oil, was stopped, but, as already stated, the presence of the water had never been found objectionable. The repairs merely served to keep the property in an operating condition over its probable useful life for the purpose for which it was used.

While it is conceded on brief that the expenditure was "necessary," respondent contends that the encroachment of the oil nuisance on petitioner's property was not an "ordinary" expense in petitioner's particular business. But the fact that petitioner had not theretofore been called upon to make a similar expenditure to prevent damage and disaster to its property does not remove that expense from the classification of "ordinary" for, as stated in Welch v. Helvering, 290 U.S. 111, "ordinary in this context does not mean that the payments must be habitual or normal in the sense that the same taxpayer will have to make them often. * * * the expense is an ordinary one because we know from experience that payments for such a purpose, whether the amount is large or small, are the common and accepted means of defense against attack. Cf. Kornhauser v. United States, 276 U.S. 145. The situation is unique in the life of the individual affected, but not in the life of the group, the community, of which he is a part." Steps to protect a business building from the seepage of oil from a nearby refinery, which had been erected long subsequent to the time petitioner started to operate its plant, would seem to us to be a normal thing to do, and in certain sections of the country it must be a common experience to protect one's property from the seepage of oil. Expenditures to accomplish this result are likewise normal.

In American Bemberg Corporation, 10 T.C. 361, we allowed as deductions, on the ground that they were ordinary and necessary expenses, extensive expenditures made to prevent disaster, although the repairs were of a type which had never been needed before and were unlikely to recur. In that case the taxpayer, to stop cave-ins of soil which were threatening destruction of its manufacturing plant, hired an engineering firm which drilled to the bedrock and injected grout to fill the cavities where practicable, and made incidental replacements and repairs, including tightening of the fluid carriers. In two successive years the taxpayer expended $734,316.76 and $199,154.33, respectively, for such drilling and grouting and $153,474.20 and $79,-687.29, respectively, for capital replacements. We found that the cost (other than replacement) of this program did not make good the depreciation previously allowed, and stated in our opinion:

"In connection with the purpose of the work, the Proctor program was intended to avert a plant-wide disaster and avoid forced abandonment of the plant. The purpose was not to improve, better, extend, or increase the original plant, nor to prolong its original useful life. Its continued operation was endangered; the purpose of the expenditures was to enable petitioner to continue the plant in operation not on any new or better scale, but on the same scale and, so far as possible, as efficiently as it had operated before. The purpose was not to rebuild or replace the plant in whole or in part, but to keep the same plant as it was and where it was."

The petitioner here made the repairs in question in order that it might continue to operate its plant. Not only was there danger of fire from the oil and fumes, but the presence of the oil led the Federal meat inspectors to declare the basement an unsuitable place for the purpose for which it had been used for a quarter of a century. After the expenditures were made, the plant did not operate on a changed or larger scale, nor was it thereafter suitable for new or additional uses. The expenditure served only to permit petitioner to continue the use of the plant, and particularly the basement for its normal operations.

In our opinion, the expenditure of $4,868.81 for lining the basement walls and floor was essentially a repair and, as such, it is deductible as an ordinary and necessary business expense. This holding makes unnecessary a consideration of petitioner's alternative contention that the expenditure is deductible as a business loss, nor need we heed the respondent's argument that any loss suffered was compensated for by "insurance or otherwise."

Decision will be entered under Rule 50.

NOTE

Tax Lawyer (T.L.) kept at the side of his bed a collection of cases carefully selected for him by his law clerk to be used by him as a substitute for Nytol when sleep was elusive. He had just finished reading *Midland Empire Packing Co.* and was comfortably close to dozing when he eye caught *Mt. Morris Drive-In Theatre Co.*[1] Hastily scanning the one-page Tax Court opinion, he discovered that when the Theatre Company was required by threat of a lawsuit by adjacent property owners to expend money for a drainage system that would protect the Company's neighbors from the flow of water from its

1. Mt. Morris Drive-In Theatre Co. v. Comm'r, 25 T.C. 272, aff'd, 238 F.2d 85 (6th Cir. 1956).

land, it had made a nondeductible capital expenditure. He noticed also that when the Tax Court opinion was reviewed, one judge concurred in two sentences, to which when read by another he said, "uh huh." On the other hand, another judge spent four sentences dissenting and picked up four of his brethren as followers. But T.L. was not sure he could see a difference in the expenditures to prevent liquid incursion by an offended flowee from those of an offending flow-er.

T.L. had a bad night. He *could* see, as did the concurring Tax Court judge, that if the drainage expenditure had been undertaken initially when the drive-in theatre had been first built, it certainly would have been a capital cost of construction, not an expense. However, he felt most frustrated by not being able to ask the concurring Tax Court judge how the *Midland Empire* expenditure would have been treated if it, too, had been made at the time the packing plant was being built. He found very little tranquility in the comment in the Tax Court opinion that in the business expense, capital expenditure area, "The decisive test is * * * the character of the transaction which gives rise to the payment."

After a wholly sleepless night, T.L.'s first action at the office in the morning was to dictate a memorandum to his law clerk directing him to select no more cases for him dealing with the question whether an expenditure is an expense or one to be capitalized.[2]

And so it is with equivocal expenditures such as those in *Midland Empire* and *Mt. Morris.* We are here of course only beginning to examine the way in which costs are taken into account in arriving at the *net* figure now called "taxable income" to which income tax rates are applied. We should say, therefore, that the present problem is really only one of timing because, as a rule the cost incurred will be either deducted immediately, "expensed" as the accountants say, or capitalized and written off over a period of time by way of depreciation or amortization deductions. But of course timing is important. Here it determines whether the taxpayer will continue to have the use of dollars at least momentarily saved by way of a deduction for an expense or whether he must let the government have

---

2. The dilemma reflected in *Midland Empire* and *Mt. Morris Drive-In* can be elaborated to present a possible *three-way* tax view of a single expenditure. In Hochschild v. Comm'r, 161 F.2d 817 (2d Cir. 1947), a taxpayer had paid attorneys' fees defending a stockholders' derivative suit. The Tax Court in the later income tax case treated the fees in part as capital expenditures, a cost of defending title to the taxpayer's stock (see page 432, infra) and in part as deductible expense incurred for the collection of income (see I.R.C. § 212 (1) and the text infra at page 431). Could at least a part, as the taxpayer argued, have been treated as a § 162 business expense, sufficiently related to the taxpayer's business as a corporate employee? Indeed, it does not upset the purpose of this example to state that in reversing the Tax Court the Second Circuit, noting the taxpayer was defending a charge of malfeasance in his position as a director and officer, treated the *entire* fee as a § 162 expense.

the use of the money paid as tax when the expense deduction is disallowed and get back his costs piecemeal by way of deductions in future years. It is therefore not surprising, although it is unfortunate, to discover much controversy and expensive litigation in this area and too little light for sound prediction.

The regulations[3] attempt to differentiate deductible expenses from capital expenditures somewhat enigmatically. Thus they place in the immediately deductible "expense" category of § 162 "repairs which neither materially add to the value of the property nor appreciably prolong its life, but keep it in efficient operating condition * * *" This is certain to be perplexing to the neophyte. For example, in *Midland Empire* one asks himself: (1) Was not the property more valuable when the basement was lined? (2) Would not use of the basement have ceased, shortening its useful life, except for the expenditure which thus "prolonged" useful life? These questions misconstrue the controlling concepts. Consider this comment in a very early B.T.A. opinion:[4]

> In determining whether an expenditure is a capital one or is chargeable against operating income, it is necessary to bear in mind the purpose for which the expenditure was made. To repair is to restore to a sound state or to mend, while a replacement connotes a substitution. A repair is an expenditure for the purpose of keeping the property in an ordinarily efficient operating condition. It does not add to the value of the property nor does it appreciably prolong its life. It merely keeps the property in an operating condition over its probable useful life for the uses for which it was acquired. Expenditures for that purpose are distinguishable from those for replacements, alterations, improvements or additions which prolong the life of the property, increase its value, or make it adaptable to a different use. The one is a maintenance charge, while the others are additions to capital investment which should not be applied against current earnings.

This may be somewhat enlightening but, even so, we are dealing with concepts with edges no more sharp than those of "fraud", "proximate cause" or "reasonably prudent person". Decisions in the area often defy reconciliation. Should we throw up our hands and seek academic fun and satisfaction in a parade of judicial inconsistencies?[5]

3. § 1.162–4.

4. Illinois Merchants Trust Co., Executor, 4 B.T.A. 103, 106 (1926).

5. Compare Zimmern v. Comm'r, 28 F.2d 769 (5th Cir. 1928), cert. den. 300 U.S. 671 (1937), reversing 9 B.T.A. 1382 (1928), allowing business expense deductions of $20,000 for refurbishing a barge that had been sunk in a storm, with P. Dougherty Co. v. Comm'r, 159 F.2d 269 (4th Cir. 1947), affirming 5 T.C. 791 (1945), requiring capitalization of $17,000 spent to rebuild the stern of a barge where timbers and planks had rotted out.

Even if specific cases are difficult to analyze, it seems more profitable to strive for an understanding of the basic criteria for decision.

I.R.C. Section 263(a), one of the negative Code provisions, is somewhat more precise then the section 162 regulations in disallowing deductions for "permanent improvement or betterments" and for "any amount expended in restoring property or making good the exhaustion thereof for which an allowance is or has been made." The § 263 regulations [6] also nail as capital expenditures amounts spent "to adapt property to a new or different use."

The general idea is that the cost of property acquired for business use is a charge against income that it helps to earn, ratably over the expected useful life of the property.[7] Expenditures made to enable the taxpayer to use the property for *that* expected period and for the planned purpose are deductible expenses. Thus he can paint and patch and repaper and add some new shingles to the roof and charge the costs against ordinary income;[8] but if he undertakes the same activities as a part of the overall restoration of a building, which will extend its use beyond the period originally expected, he must capitalize these and related expenditures.[9]

Perhaps it is a mistake to attempt to talk about property generally in this context. If the property concerned is complex, like a building consisting of walls and floors and roof and foundation and fixtures and elevators and heating and cooling equipment and so forth, it is probably necessary to think in terms of the various components. Shoring up a floor to achieve continuing utility *may* be a deductible expense, but the replacement of a floor, or possibly even of an important door, is a capital expenditure.[10]

In thinking of the useful life of a building, does one anticipate only the replacement of a few shingles or that the entire roof may have to be renewed? This *question* may be wrong, if we should think in terms of the roof as one component. In thinking of the life of a roof, one expects to replace a few shingles.

Do we get some better idea now of what is meant by prolonging useful life as that concept is expressed in the regulations? If so, what about increases in value? Have you increased the value of your car when you put in a new set of spark plugs? Certainly, in a sense; but not in the sense of the section 162 and 263 regulations. Nor is that an "improvement" or "betterment" in the sense in which those terms are used in section 263(a)(1). But if a building that was improperly built is given a going over by shoring up the walls with

6. § 1.263(a)–1(b).

7. See text at page 721, infra.

8. Chesapeake Corp. of Virginia, 17 T.C. 668, acq. Rev.Rul. 65–13, 1965–1 C.B. 87.

9. Regenstein v. Edwards, 121 F.Supp. 952 (M.D.Ga.1954).

10. See Alabama-Georgia Syrup Co., 36 T.C. 747 (1961), rev'd on other issue, sub. nom. L. B. Whitfield, Jr., 31 F.2d 640 (5th Cir. 1962).

steel rods, inserting new beams to support the roof, and replacing an inadequate foundation with cinder block, it is "improved", and the costs must be capitalized.[11]

Nor is it material that the work is done under compulsion, as pursuant to the order of the city building commissioner,[12] or under threat of an injunction.[13]

Attention should be drawn to the fact that some Code sections make expensing or capitalizing expenditures elective. These provisions are conveniently collected in the regulations.[14]

Much more could be said here about the expense, capital expenditure dichotomy. But it would probably not be profitable. Many matters are crisp and clean, as just a little research will show. The gray areas are best approached by a wide reading of the cases; it may be more a matter of developing a "feel" for the problems than just acquiring some knowledge.[15]

Happily a recent development sometimes reduces the repair expense deduction question to a mathematical formula. I.R.C. § 167(m) now permits a taxpayer to depreciate property without direct regard to its useful life in *his* business; instead he may write it off with some expressed flexibility over the "class lives" for various kinds of property in his industry or other business group.[16] A companion to the adoption of class life depreciation under § 167(m) is the elective "Reasonable Repair Allowance" provided by § 263(f). In general, an administratively determined percentage of the cost of each class of property is deemed annually to be within the "repair" and therefore "expense" category; and amounts in excess of that are required to be capitalized.[17] It is obvious that this automatic classification of some equivocal expenditures will reduce uncertainty and controversy and litigation.[18]

11. J. L. Boland, 19 T.C.M. 1030 (1960).

12. Ibid.

13. See Woolrich Woolen Mills v. U. S., 289 F.2d 444 (3rd Cir. 1961), addition of filtration plant required by state anti-pollution law.

14. Reg. § 1.263(a)–3. See also I.R.C. § 190, Expenditures to remove architectural and transportation barriers to the handicapped and elderly, added by TRA (1976) § 2122.

15. This note deals with the expense, capital expenditure dichotomy largely on the basis of whether something is a repair or an improvement. The problem is of course very much broader as the *Welch* case, supra page 344 indicates. And compare, e. g., Zim-

merman & Sons, Inc. v. U. S., 1972–2 USTC para. 9585 (E.D.Wis.1972), subscription lists costs expensed, with Manhattan Co. of Va., 50 T.C. 78 (1968), purchased customer lists were partly nondepreciable goodwill that could not be expensed and partly intangibles with useful lives subject only to the allowance for depreciation.

16. This depreciation concept, a legislative sequel to the administratively developed Asset Depreciation Range system, is given some further consideration in Chapter 22, infra.

17. Reg. § 1.167(a)–11(d)(2); Rev.Proc. 72–10, 1972–1 C.B. 721.

18. Some property is placed outside the scope of the reasonable repair allowance rule; e. g., "if a taxpayer

3. "CARRYING ON" BUSINESS

Internal Revenue Code: Sections 162(a); 262.
Regulations: Section 1.162–6.

MORTON FRANK

Tax Court of the United States, 1953.
20 T.C. 511.

The respondent determined an income tax deficiency against the petitioners for the year 1946 in the amount of $2,914.92. The only issue presented is whether the petitioners are entitled to deduct traveling expenses and legal fees in the amount of $5,965 in the taxable year.

Findings of Fact

Morton Frank and Agnes Dodds Frank, the petitioners, are husband and wife who filed a joint income tax return for 1946 with the collector of internal revenue for the eighteenth district of Ohio. In November 1945, Morton Frank was released from the Navy. His place of residence during the period of his service was Pittsburgh, Pennsylvania. Prior to the war, he had been employed by such newspapers as The Pittsburgh Press, The Braddock Free Press, The Braddock Daily News Herald, and The Michigan Daily. His wife, an attorney, had no experience in the newspaper business and during the war had been employed by several government agencies. During and prior to his service in the Navy, Morton Frank was interested in purchasing and operating a newspaper or radio station. Near the end of November 1945, the petitioners began a trip to examine newspapers and radio properties throughout the country. The purpose of the trip was to investigate, and, if possible, acquire a newspaper or radio enterprise to operate.

The trip took both petitioners westward from Pittsburgh through Ohio, Indiana, Michigan, Minnesota, Wisconsin, Oklahoma, and New Mexico. They interviewed persons in these states with respect to local newspapers and radio stations. On January 1, 1946, the petitioners were in San Diego, California. They then traveled through California, New Mexico, Texas, and Arizona. They arrived in Phoenix, Arizona, on February 12, 1946. The taxpayers estimated that their travel and communication expenses from January 1 to February 12, 1946, aggregated $1,596.44.

follows the practice of acquiring for his own use property (in need of repair * * *) and of making expenditures to repair * * * such property in order to take advantage of [the repair allowance rule], the asset guideline class repair allowance * * * shall not apply to such expenditures." Reg. § 1.167(a)–11(d)(2)(v).

The petitioners took employment in Phoenix with The Arizona Times and remained in that city from February to mid-July 1946. While working in Phoenix, the petitioners made several trips to various cities throughout the country in search of a newspaper plant to purchase. They traveled to Los Angeles and Santa Barbara, California, Yuma, Arizona, Pittsburgh, Pennsylvania, and Wilmington, Delaware. Offers of purchase were made to the owners of several newspapers. While in Phoenix, the petitioners lived first in a hotel and later in a house which they acquired. The petitioners estimated their traveling, telephone, and telegraph expenses from March through December 1946, at $5,027.94. Included within this total was a legal fee of $1,000 paid to an attorney for services rendered in connection with unsuccessful negotiations to purchase a newspaper in Wilmington, Delaware. None of these claimed expenses were incurred in connection with the petitioners' employment in Phoenix, Arizona. A portion of it was based on estimated allowances of mileage at 6 cents per mile, lodging at $5 per day per person, and other costs at comparable rates, the whole expenditures reasonably aggregating $5,027.-94. In November 1946, the petitioners purchased a newspaper in Canton, Ohio, and commenced publication of the Canton Economist in that month.

Opinion

VAN FOSSAN, JUDGE: The only question presented is whether the petitioners may deduct $5,965 in the determination of their net income for the year 1946 as ordinary and necessary business expenses or as losses. The petitioners base their claim for deductions upon section 23(a) (1) and (2) and (e) (2) of the Internal Revenue Code.[1] The evidence reasonably establishes that the petitioners expended the amount of expenses stated in our Findings of Fact during the taxable year in traveling, telephone, telegraph, and legal expenses in the search for and investigation of newspaper and radio properties. This total amount was spent by the petitioners in their travels through various states in an endeavor to find a business which they could purchase and operate. These expenses do not include amounts spent while living in Phoenix, Arizona.

The travel expenses and legal fees spent in searching for a newspaper business with a view to purchasing the same cannot be deducted under the provisions of section 23(a) (1), Internal Revenue Code. The petitioners were not engaged in any trade or business at the time the expenses were incurred. The trips made by the taxpayers from Phoenix, Arizona, were not related to the conduct of the business that they were then engaged in but were preparatory to locating a busi-

---

1. [The 1939 Code section cited is omitted. See I.R.C. (1954) §§ 162(a), 165(a) and (c)(2), 212. The portion of the opinion dealing with §§ 165 and 212 has been deleted. Ed.]

ness venture of their own. The expenses of investigating and looking for a new business and trips preparatory to entering a business are not deductible as an ordinary and necessary business expense incurred in carrying on a trade or business. George C. Westervelt, 8 T.C. 1248. The word "pursuit" in the statutory phrase "in pursuit of a trade or business" is not used in the sense of "searching for" or "following after," but in the sense of "in connection with" or "in the course of" a trade or business. It presupposes an existing business with which petitioner is connected. The fact that petitioners had no established home during the period of their travels further complicates the question and alone may be fatal to petitioners' case. If they had no home, how could they have expenses "away from home"? The issue whether all or part of the expenses so incurred were capital expenditures is not raised or argued and we do not pass judgment on such question.

* * *

We conclude that the petitioners may not deduct the expenses claimed for 1946 under the applicable provisions of the Internal Revenue Code.

Decision will be entered for the respondent.

NOTE

I.R.C. section 162(a) provides: "There shall be allowed as a deduction all the ordinary and necessary expenses paid or incurred during the taxable year in carrying on any trade or business * * * " The corresponding clause in § 23(a)(1) of the Internal Revenue Code of 1939, which controlled in *Morton Frank*, supra, was identical. Reference in the opinion to the phrase "in pursuit of a trade or business" may be confusing. It appears in § 162(a)(2) and its predecessor, § 23(a)(1)(A) of the 1939 Code, in connection with the specific provision on business travel. Even so, the "pursuit" phrase takes color from the more general "carrying on" expression and, as the opinion in *Frank* suggests, both phrases have about the same meaning.

It seems almost axiomatic that one cannot be "carrying on" a business unless he *has* a business, a frailty in the *Frank* circumstances which, among other factors,[1] foreclosed any § 162 deduction. Nevertheless, the opinion should not be read so broadly as to suggest all costs incurred in seeking employment can never give rise to a § 162 deduction. If *Frank* had been in a trade or business and was seeking to expand that business or some branch of it, his position would have been stronger.[2]

1. See the discussion of the meaning of "away from home", infra page 369.
2. First National Bank of South Carolina, 1976–1 USTC para. 9397 (D.C.

S.C.1976); Colorado Springs Nat. Bank v. U. S., 505 F.2d 1185 (10th Cir. 1974).

The Tax Court has also distinguished *Frank* in situations where the taxpayer has proceeded beyond an initial investigation stage and has entered a transactional stage.[3] The transactional stage is reached at the point where the preliminary investigation has led to the decision to purchase a specific business, but further investigation of the business continues.[4] If subsequent developments compel the taxpayer to abandon the venture, this is not necessarily a bar to a deduction but the deduction claimed should be for a loss on a transaction entered into for profit allowed by I.R.C. section 165(c)(2), not a business expense under section 162.[5] Would such transactional stage expenses be deductible if taxpayer did not abandon the project?[6]

The above cases involved a self-employed or about to be self-employed taxpayer. It is well settled that being an employee constitutes carrying on a trade or business,[7] but in recent years question has arisen whether a prospective employee is in a trade or business and whether new employment, perhaps of short duration, prevents one from continuing to be considered as carrying on his former trade, and whether lack of employment ends a trade altogether. Since the statutory language is the same for an employee as a self-employed person, the deductibility of expenses ought to be the same. A person who has never "carried on" a trade or business as an employee should not be permitted a deduction for expenses incurred in entering a trade or business.[8]

Although it might seem that pre-employment expenses could never be deductible because not incurred in carrying on a trade or business, the Tax Court sensibly made an exception in a situation where services were rendered to a prospective employee prior to the commencement of his employment but payment for those services was contingent upon his becoming employed,[9] as he later did. In *Hundley*, the petitioner who later became a major league baseball player, was earlier taught the tools of his trade by his father, a former semiprofessional baseball player. As compensation for those services, it had been agreed that the father would receive fifty percent of any bonus that might be paid to the petitioner under the terms of a professional baseball contract if one should later be signed.[10] The petitioner even-

3. John Domenie, 34 T.C.M. 469 (1975); Harris W. Seed, 52 T.C. 880 (1969).

4. Id. at 472 and 885, respectively.

5. See page 455, infra.

6. See problem 1(d) at page 362, infra.

7. David J. Primuth v. Comm'r, 54 T.C. 374 (1970); U. S. v. Generes, 405 U.S. 93 (1972).

8. Rev.Rul. 75–120, 1975–1 C.B. 55, 56. Cf. Reg. § 1.162–5(b)(2)(i) and 3(i).

The Service had previously ruled that fees paid to employment agencies for actually securing an initial employment (as distinguished from merely seeking employment) were deductible. Rev.Rul. 60–223, 1960–1 C.B. 57. The Ruling, conditioning deductibility on success, not properly a condition to the deduction, was revoked in Rev. Rul. 75–120.

9. C. R. Hundley, Jr., 48 T.C. 339 (1967).

10. Id. at 340.

tually signed a bonus contract with a professional baseball club and paid one half of the bonus to his father. The Tax Court found that this expense was not paid or incurred prior to petitioner's entering into the business of baseball, because the payment of compensation to the father was not due or incurred or payable until the petitioner was engaged in the business of baseball.[11] The court concluded that the payments made under the terms of the agreement were paid for services actually rendered in carrying on a trade or business and thus were deductible,[12] and the Commissioner has acquiesced.[13] The rationale of the *Hundley* decision could extend to any situation in which payment for employment-seeking services is contingent upon employment and does not become due until employment is secured.

Once an employee has entered a trade or business one issue is: How long does one remain in that trade or business during periods of unemployment or diversification into other businesses? It is becoming clear that once having entered a trade or business being unemployed does not prevent one from still being considered as in a trade or business,[14] but there are qualifications. A prolonged length of time away from one's usual employment is a factor that may be considered in determining he is no longer carrying on that employment as a trade or business. In *James D. Protiva*,[15] the Tax Court held that the petitioner was not entitled to deduct the cost of newspaper advertisements that were unsuccessful in locating him a new teaching position. He had previously held a teaching position for several years, but not during the year of the advertisements, and the court found that he was not in that trade or business at any time during the year at issue. The Tax Court also denied a taxpayer a deduction for education expenses where over a four year period up to the time of litigation, the taxpayer did no teaching while obtaining a graduate degree.[16]

The Treasury states the position in Revenue Ruling 75-120 [17] that it will not allow deductions for expenses incurred by individuals who have been unemployed for such a period of time that there is a substantial lack of continuity between their past employments and their endeavors to find new employments, but the length of time necessary to establish this substantial lack of continuity remains uncertain.

Another factor bearing on whether an unemployed person is in a trade or business is the length of time he has been employed before becoming unemployed. In *Albert Ruehmann, III*,[18] a law student who had passed his state's bar examination and had worked as an attorney

11. Id. at 348.

12. Id. at 349.

13. 1967-2 C.B. 2.

14. Furner v. Comm'r, 393 F.2d 292 (7th Cir. 1968); Harold Haft, 40 T.C. 2 (1963); Rev.Rul. 75-120, supra note 8.

15. 29 T.C.M. 1318 (1970).

16. Corbett v. Comm'r, 55 T.C. 884 (1971).

17. Supra note 8 at 56.

18. 30 T.C.M. 675 (1971).

for three months with a law firm was (surprisingly?) held to be carrying on a trade or business when he went back to graduate school. In contrast, an engineering student who worked for a year after graduation prior to doing graduate work in engineering was found not to have entered a trade or business that he could be carrying on to make his education expenses deductible.[19]

Even if it is clear an individual is engaged in a trade or business, question may be raised whether his expenses were incurred in carrying on *that* trade or business, which of course they must be to be deductible.

After some extensive judicial battering,[20] the Treasury has conceded [21] that an employee's expenses in seeking employment elsewhere but in the same trade are deductible whether or not successful. This determination does not of course extend to first jobs, lengthy unemployment, or new trades or businesses.[22] This concession by the Treasury followed on the heels of several cases holding that success is not an element in the deductibility of employment-seeking expenses,[23] the Commissioner finally conceding the issue by acquiescing in *Leonard Cremona*.

Although Revenue Ruling 75–120 appears to clear the air with regard to the question of deductibility of employment-seeking expenses, some trouble spots remain. The courts have taken the position that in the case of a position obtained by public election, the incumbent's trade or business is concluded at the end of the elective term. Under this view, election and re-election expenses are not differentiated, and neither are deductible. Thus, in *McDonald v. United States*, the Supreme Court of the United States disallowed a deduction for a judge's re-election expenses because the expenses were not incurred in being a judge but "in trying to be a judge." [24] The Commissioner distinguishes political campaign expenses from other employment-seeking expenses in Revenue Ruling 75–120 [25] and continues successfully to challenge the deductibility of campaign expenses.[26] In con-

---

19. Barry Reisine, 29 T.C.M. 1429 (1970). Business deductions for education expenses are considered further, infra at page 396.

20. David J. Primuth, 54 T.C. 374 (1970); Kenneth R. Kenfield, 54 T.C. 1197 (1970); Roy E. Blewitt, Jr., 31 T.C.M. 1225 (1972); Leonard Cremona, 58 T.C. 291 (1972).

21. Leonard Cremona, supra note 20, acq., 1975–15 I.R.B. 5.

22. Ibid.

23. Ibid., see note 8, supra.

24. McDonald v. Comm'r, 323 U.S. 57, 60 (1944).

25. Supra note 8 at 56.

26. Nichols v. Comm'r, 1975–1 USTC para. 9404 (CA–5); Joseph Martino, 62 T.C. 840 (1974); Carey v. Comm'r, 460 F.2d 1259 (4th Cir. 1972), cert. den. 93 S.Ct. 325 (1972). Court decisions have not only denied a § 162 deduction for campaign expenses but also have held that these expenses may not be amortized over the term of office, Maness v. U. S., 367 F.2d 357 (5th Cir. 1966); Levy v. U. S., 1976–1 USTC para. 9405 (Ct.Cls. 1976), although capitalized replace-

trast, Rev.Rul. 71–470 [27] properly allows a deduction for expenses incurred in fighting a recall procedure which would have removed a judge from office, obviously keeping him from carrying on his judicial duties.

PROBLEMS

1. Determine the deductibility of expenses incurred in the following situations.

   (a) Tycoon, a salesman, unexpectedly inherited a sizeable amount of money from an eccentric millionaire. Tycoon decided to invest a part of his fortune in the development of industrial properties and he incurred expenses in making a preliminary investigation.

   (b) The facts are the same as in (a), above, except that Tycoon, rather than having been a salesman, was a successful developer of residential and shopping center properties.

   (c) The facts are the same as in (b), above, except that Tycoon, desiring to diversify his investments, incurs expenses in investigating the possibility of purchasing a professional sports team.

   (d) The facts are the same as in (a), above, except that the preliminary investigation results in Tycoon's decision to purchase a real estate development business. He then incurs further expenses in preparing to consummate the purchase. Are these further expenses deductible?

2. Law student's Spouse completed secretarial school just prior to student entering law school. Consider whether Spouse's employment agency fees are deductible in the following circumstances:

   (a) Agency is unsuccessful in finding Spouse a job.

   (b) Agency is successful in finding Spouse a job.

   (c) Same as (b), above, except that agency's fee was contingent upon its securing employment for Spouse and the payments will not become due until Spouse has begun working.

   (d) Same as (a) and (b), above, except that Spouse previously worked as a secretary in Old Town and seeks employment in New Town where student attends law school.

   (e) Same as (d), above, except that Agency is successful in finding Spouse a job in New Town as a bank teller.

ments of a physical nature are depreciable. See page 721, infra.

27. 1971–2 C.B. 121; and see I.R.C. § 7701(a)(26).

C. SPECIFIC BUSINESS DEDUCTIONS

---

1. "REASONABLE" SALARIES

Internal Revenue Code: Section 162(a)(1).
Regulations: Section 1.162–7, –8, –9.

HAROLDS CLUB v. COMMISSIONER *

United States Court of Appeals, Ninth Circuit, 1965.
340 F.2d 861.

HAMLEY, CIRCUIT JUDGE.

[In the years 1952 to 1956 Harolds Club, an incorporated gaming establishment in Nevada, paid Raymond I. Smith salary in annual amounts ranging from about $350,000 to $560,000. The Commissioner disallowed in part the corporation's deductions based on these payments. Smith was not a shareholder in the corporation all the stock of which was owned by his two sons. However, the business was essentially a continuation of one that Smith had earlier operated illegally in California but which, upon the move to Nevada, became at first that of son Harold, as a proprietorship, and later in 1938 a partnership owned by Harold and another son of Smith. The partnership was incorporated in 1946. The scope of the business is suggested by the fact that by 1952 there were seven bars in the Club. Harolds Club did not prosper initially but in 1935 Smith, while not an owner as indicated, agreed to take over management of the Club. Ed.]

* * *

At the outset, Smith was paid a salary, plus a bonus which was determined at the end of each year. In the early part of January, 1941, Smith and his sons decided upon a fixed percentage arrangement, Smith suggesting that he be paid twenty percent of the profits. Since Smith was running the club at this time and was the "brains" of the organization, his sons had no objection. Percentage employment contracts were not uncommon in the gaming business. On January 15, 1941, Smith and his sons entered into a formal written contract, under which Smith would receive an annual salary of ten thousand dollars plus twenty percent of the yearly net profits accruing from the operation of the club.

* * *

By 1952, Harolds Club was employing approximately eight hundred people. Harold was then an assistant manager and Raymond was

---

* See **Sugarman**, "Contingent Compensation Agreement Leads to Disallowance of Corporate Deduction," 53 Calif.L.Rev. 1544 (1965). **Ed.**

in the bookkeeping department. The club also employed a business manager and a casino manager, both of whom reported directly to Smith. On several occasions between 1941 and 1956, one or the other of the three Smiths proposed to expand gaming activities into other areas. A majority vote decided against each of the proposals, Smith sometimes thereby getting his way, and sometimes not.

*   *   *

For the tax years 1952 through 1956 the annual net income of Harolds Club ranged from $1,367,029.88 to $2,098,906.01. The amounts paid to Smith for those years have already been indicated. Harold and Raymond each received salaries of from sixty thousand to seventy-five thousand dollars a year during this period.

Competitors testified that, in their opinion, the salary contract between Smith and Harolds Club was reasonable, and that he was worth all that was paid to him. As before noted however, Harolds Club does not here challenge the Tax Court's implicit finding that annual amounts paid to Smith in excess of ten thousand dollars plus fifteen percent of yearly net profits constituted unreasonable compensation for the years 1952 to 1956.

Petitioner predicates its claimed business expense deductions for the entire amounts paid to Smith during these years upon section 162 (a) of the 1954 Code and section 23(a) (1) (A) of the 1939 Code.[1] Since the amount of compensation was contingent upon the amount of net profits of the business, petitioner also relied on Treasury Regulations 111, § 29.23(a) 6 and Treasury Regulations 118, § 39.23(a) (6) for the years 1952 and 1953, and Treasury Regulations § 1.162–7(b) for the remaining years.[2]

Under the quoted regulations contingent compensation, generally speaking, should be allowed as a deduction even though it may prove to be greater than the amount which would ordinarily be paid, if paid pursuant to a "free bargain" between the employer and the individual, and if the contract for compensation was reasonable under the circumstances "existing at the date when the contract for services was made."

The Tax Court determined that the amount paid to Smith as compensation in the years 1952 to 1956, under the contract for contingent compensation, was greater than the amount which would ordinarily be paid in those years, a conclusion which is not here disputed. The Court then proceeded to determine whether the deduction was nevertheless allowable under Regulation § 1.162–7(b), because such compensation resulted from a "free bargain" which, when entered into, was reasonable. It concluded that the 1941 salary agreement was not the result of a "free bargain" within the meaning of the quoted regulation, and that therefore reasonableness must be judged as of the time the compensation was paid. In reaching this conclusion the Court placed

1. [I.R.C. § 162(a) (1) is omitted. Ed.]   2. [Reg. § 1.162–7(b) (2) and (3) are omitted. Ed.]

primary reliance upon the family relationship between Smith and his employers in 1941, and circumstances indicating that he dominated them at that time.[3]

In contesting this conclusion petitioner first points out that the Commissioner, after audit, agreed that the salaries paid to Smith under the 1941 formula in the years 1941 through 1949 were reasonable. Petitioner reasons from this that if the contract was reasonable and entitled to recognition when the owners-sons were younger and more likely to be dominated by their father than when they themselves were over forty, " * * * it would seem that logically the contract would not become unreasonable as the domination abated."

The precise question before us, however, is not as to the Tax Court determination concerning the reasonableness of the contract at any particular time, but as to its determination that the contract was not the result of a "free bargain" in 1941. The Internal Revenue Service had no occasion to look into the latter question until it first determined that the compensation was unreasonable for a particular tax year. Since the agency determined that the compensation was in fact reasonable for the years 1941 through 1949, it made no determination for those years as to whether the 1941 contract resulted from a "free bargain."[4]

Petitioner next contends that the Tax Court erred in attributing adverse significance to the family relationship between Smith and the 1941 owners of the business, in view of the fact that the owners-sons were adults and legally competent.

The question of whether the 1941 compensation agreement resulted from a "free bargain," is one of fact. In determining that question all circumstances bearing upon the ability of the employer to exercise a free and independent judgment are relevant.

One such circumstance is family relationship. The fact that Harold and Raymond were competent adults at the time they entered into the 1941 contract tends to minimize the significance which should be attached to the fact, standing alone, that they were the sons of

---

3. The Tax Court said, in part:
"In view of the family relationship existing between Harold and Raymond, the employers, and Smith, the employee; the ages and experience of the employers; Smith's domination over his sons in the past; the respective roles and duties of the sons and Smith in Harolds Club's creation and organization; and the reasons offered by Harold and Raymond for agreeing to Smith's 'suggested' compensation, we cannot say that petitioner has established that the original employment contract (1941) between Harolds Club and Smith was the product of a free bargain or arm's-length transaction."

4. Even if the reasonableness of Smith's compensation were here in question we fail to see how its solution is promoted by considering the likelihood that Smith's domination decreased as the years went by. Reasonableness of compensation for services depends upon the value of the services rendered. Under that test, compensation could be reasonable or unreasonable wholly apart from any factor of domination.

Smith. But that fact did not stand alone. The record fully supports the Tax Court's finding that Smith dominated the sons, notwithstanding their adulthood and competency. Indeed, the latter finding is not challenged on this review. Where there is such domination, lack of ability to bargain freely may exist even as between competent adults.

Petitioner asserts that in concluding that the 1941 agreement did not result from a free bargain, the Tax Court applied a standard which is the exact and precise opposite of the correct standard. Petitioner asserts that the statute permitting business expense deductions is designed to prevent deduction for salaries in excess of the employee's true worth. The Tax Court therefore erred, petitioner urges, in accepting the Commissioner's argument that Smith's services were so essential to the success of his sons' business that the sons could not bargain with him on equal terms, hence the "bargain" was not "free." Under this reasoning, petitioner argues, only drones can bargain freely for their compensation.

Whatever the Commissioner may have argued in the Tax Court, we find no indication that the Court predicated its resolution of the "free bargain" question upon the theory that the sons felt obliged to enter into the 1941 agreement because of their belief that Smith's services were indispensable. The only court finding which might imply such a view is the statement that since Smith was running the club in 1941 and was the "brains" of the organization, his sons had no objection to the percentage arrangement. In our opinion this finding tends more to show that the sons surrendered their judgments to that of their father's because he exerted control rather than because he was indispensable.[5]

The Tax Court did consider the value of Smith's services in deciding what compensation for the years in question was reasonable. But the question now under discussion is the entirely different one of whether the 1941 contract resulted from a free bargain.

Petitioner argues, additionally, that apart from the above-discussed regulation pertaining to contingent compensation, the statute does not authorize the "double taxation" of payments made solely as compensation for personal services and not as disguised dividends or as the purchase price of property. By "double taxation" petitioner refers to the fact that Smith has paid personal income taxes on the full amount paid to him and, to the extent that such compen-

5. As indicated in the Tax Court findings quoted in note 3, one of the factors which the Court took into account in determining that the 1941 bargain was not "free," was " * * * the reasons offered by Harold and Raymond for agreeing to Smith's 'suggested' compensation, * * * " We have examined that part of Harold's and Raymond's testimony contained in the excerpted record before us and find nothing therein to indicate that they agreed to the 1941 arrangement because of Smith's indispensability.

sation is not allowed as a business expense deduction, petitioner must also pay a corporate income tax thereon.

Petitioner acknowledges that there is good reason to set reasonable bounds upon ostensible salaries paid to employees who are also shareholders or who are selling property to the corporation. Regulation § 1.162–7(b) (1), quoted in the margin, gives recognition to this need.[6] But petitioner argues that Congress did not intend to authorize the Commissioner to sit in judgment on salaries paid to non-shareholders. This is true, petitioner reasons, because such salaries are, unless the disguised purchase price of property, paid solely to obtain personal services. No revenue purpose is served, petitioner urges, because the progressive tax structure on individuals goes higher than the corporate tax rate, consequently what is gained in corporate income taxes will be more than lost in reduced personal income taxes.

Whatever practical effect the disallowance of salary as a corporate business expense deduction may have upon the tax revenue,[7] the statute in question admits of no such qualification. Under section 162(a) (1) of the 1954 Code, only "reasonable" compensation is made deductible. Petitioner's thesis would read "reasonable" out of the statute, for it would sanction disallowance only where the payment was not compensation at all, but was really disguised dividends, property payments or gifts. The Tax Court, however, has been sustained in disallowing what was held to be unreasonable compensation which could not have been a dividend or purchase price of property. See Patton v. Commissioner, 6 Cir., 168 F.2d 28.

The fact that the regulation quoted in note 6 singles out cases where a salary is disallowed in part because it is a disguised dividend or payment for property does not alter the requirement that the salary must be reasonable to be deductible. The regulation purports only to give illustrative examples of the practical application of the Code and not to define the limits of its application.

Petitioner contends that to interpret and apply the Code section as is here done makes it a regulatory provision to control salary and wage scales. Congress, petitioner argues, intended no such regulation.

Section 162(a) (1) is designed to define which expenses are deductible. To the extent that a salary is unreasonable it is not deductible. The disallowance of a deduction for an unreasonable

6. [Reg. § 1.162–7(b) (1) is omitted. Ed.]

7. Petitioner's argument as to the practical effect of the Tax Court ruling is open to question. Corporate net income withheld from disbursement as compensation for services, because in excess of reasonable compensation, would ordinarily be distributed, to a large extent, as dividends. To this extent it would be subject to both corporate and personal income taxes, whereas if disbursed as compensation for services, with an off-setting business expense deduction, it would be subject only to personal income taxes.

salary with resulting adverse tax effects to the business has a regulatory effect to the extent that it discourages the employer from disbursing, as salaries to employees what, if disbursed at all, should be distributed to such employees or others as dividends or gifts. But this regulatory effect is unavoidably incident to the tax scheme whereby only necessary business expenses may be deducted in calculating the employer's income tax.

Other arguments advanced by petitioner have been examined but are without merit.

The Tax Court's construction of the Code provisions and regulations is correct and its determination based thereon is affirmed.

PROBLEMS

Employee is the majority shareholder (248 of 250 outstanding shares) and president of Corporation. Shortly after Corporation was incorporated, its Directors adopted a resolution establishing a contingent compensation contract for Employee. The plan provided for Corporation to pay Employee a nominal salary plus an annual bonus based on a percentage of Corporation's net income. In the early years of the plan, payments to Employee averaged $50,000 annually. In recent years, Corporation's profits have increased substantially and, as a consequence, Employee has received payments averaging more than $200,000 per year.

(a) What are the alternative tax treatments for the payments by Corporation to Employee?

(b) What factors should be considered in determining the proper tax treatment for the payments?

(c) The problem assumes Employee *always* owned 248 of the Corporation's 250 shares. Might it be important to learn that the compensation contract was made at a time when Employee held only 10 out of the 250 outstanding shares?

2. TRAVEL "AWAY FROM HOME" *

Internal Revenue Code: Section 162(a)(2). See Section 274(c).
Regulations: Sections 1.162–2; 1.262–1(b)(5).

ROSENSPAN v. UNITED STATES

United States Court of Appeals, Second Circuit, 1971.
438 F.2d 905.
Cert. den., 404 U.S. 864, 92 S.Ct. 54, 1971.

FRIENDLY, CIRCUIT JUDGE: This appeal is from the dismissal on the merits of an action for refund of income taxes, brought in the District Court for the Eastern District of New York. The taxes were paid as a result of the Commissioner's disallowance of deductions for unreimbursed expenses for meals and lodging allegedly incurred "while away from home in the pursuit of a trade or business," I.R.C. § 162(a) (2), in 1962 and 1964.

Plaintiff, Robert Rosenspan, was a jewelry salesman who worked on a commission basis, paying his own traveling expenses without reimbursement. In 1962 he was employed by one and in 1964 by two New York City jewelry manufacturers. For some 300 days a year he traveled by automobile through an extensive sales territory in the Middle West, where he would stay at hotels and motels and eat at restaurants. Five or six times a year he would return to New York and spend several days at his employers' offices. There he would perform a variety of services essential to his work—cleaning up his sample case, checking orders, discussing customers' credit problems, recommending changes in stock, attending annual staff meetings, and the like.

Rosenspan had grown in Brooklyn and during his marriage, had maintained a family home there. After his wife's death in 1948, he abandoned this. From that time through the tax years in question he used his brother's Brooklyn home as a personal residential address, keeping some clothing and other belongings there, and registering, voting, and filing his income tax returns from that address. The stipulation of facts states that, on his trips to New York City, "out of a desire not to abuse his welcome at his brother's home, he stayed more often" at an inn near the John F. Kennedy Airport. It recites also that "he generally spent his annual vacations in Brooklyn, where

---

* See Tallant, Logan, and Milton, "The Travelling Taxpayer: A Rational Framework for His Deductions," 29 U.Fla.L.R. 119 (1976); Klein, "Income Taxation and Commuting Expenses: Tax Policy and the Need for Nonsimplistic Analysis of 'Simple' Problems," 54 Cornell L.Rev. 871 (1969); Klein, "The Deductibility of Transportation Expenses of a Combination Business and Pleasure Trip— A Conceptual Analysis," 18 Stan.L. Rev. 1099 (1966).

his children resided, and made an effort to return to Brooklyn whenever possible," but affords no further indication where he stayed on such visits. In 1961 he changed the registration of his automobile from New York to Ohio, giving as his address the address of a cousin in Cincinnati, where he also received mail, in order to obtain cheaper automobile insurance. Rosenspan does not contend that he had a permanent abode or residence in Brooklyn or anywhere else.

The basis for the Commissioner's disallowance of a deduction for Rosenspan's meals and lodging while in his sales territory was that he had no "home" to be "away from" while traveling. Not denying that this would be true if the language of § 162(a) (2) were given its ordinary meaning, Rosenspan claimed that for tax purposes his home was his "business headquarters," to wit, New York City where his employers maintained their offices, and relied upon the Commissioner's long advocacy of this concept of a "tax home," see e. g., G.C.M. 23672, 1943 Cum.Bull. 66–67. The Commissioner responded that although in most circumstances "home" means "business headquarters," it should be given its natural meaning of a permanent abode or residence for purposes of the problem here presented. Rosenspan says the Commissioner is thus trying to have it both ways.

The provision of the Internal Revenue Code applicable for 1962 read:

"SEC. 162. TRADE OR BUSINESS EXPENSES.

(a) In general.—There shall be allowed as a deduction all the ordinary and necessary expenses paid or incurred during the taxable year in carrying on any trade or business, including—

* * *

(2) traveling expenses (including the entire amount expended for meals and lodging) while away from home in the pursuit of a trade or business; * * * "

For 1964 the statute remained the same except for the interpolation in the parenthesis after "lodging" of the words "other than amounts which are lavish or extravagant under the circumstances"—a change not relevant in this case.

What is now § 162(a) (2) was brought into the tax structure by § 214 of the Revenue Act of 1921, 42 Stat. 239. Prior to that date, § 214 had permitted the deduction of "ordinary and necessary expenses paid or incurred . . . in carrying on any trade or business," Revenue Act of 1918, 40 Stat. 1066 (1918), without further specification. In a regulation, the Treasury interpreted the statute to allow deduction of "traveling expenses, including railroad fares, and meals and lodging *in an amount in excess of any expenditures ordinarily required for such purposes when at home*," T.D. 3101, amending Article 292 of Regulations 45, 3 Cum.Bull. 191 (1920) (emphasis supplied). A formula was provided for determining what expenditures were thus "ordinarily required"; the taxpayer was to compute such items as rent, grocery bills, light, etc. and servant hire for the periods when he was away from home, and divide this by the number of members of his family. Mim. 2688, 4 Cum.Bull. 209–11 (1921). The puzzlement of the man without a home was dealt with in a cryptic pronouncement, O.D. 905, 4 Cum. Bull. 212 (1921):

Living expenses paid by a single taxpayer who has no home and is continuously employed on the road may not be deducted in computing net income.

The 1921 amendment, inserting what is now § 162(a) (2)'s allowance of a deduction for the entire amount of qualified meals and lodging, stemmed from a request of the Treasury based on the difficulty of administering the "excess" provision of its regulation. See United States v. Correll, 389 U.S. 299, 301 n. 6 (1967). While the taxpayer cites statements of legislators in the 1921 Congress that the amendment would provide "a measure of justice" to commercial travelers,[1] there is nothing to indicate that the members making or hearing these remarks were thinking of the unusual situation of the traveler without a home. There is likewise nothing to indicate that the Treasury sought, or that Congress meant to require, any change in the ruling that disallowed deductions for living expenses in such a case. The objective was to eliminate the need for computing the expenses "ordinarily required" at home by a taxpayer who had one, and the words used were appropriate to that end. If we were to make the unlikely assumption that the problem of the homeless commercial traveler ever entered the legislators' minds, the language they adopted was singularly inept to resolve it in the way for which plaintiff contends. Thus, if the literal words of the statute were decisive, the Government would clearly prevail on the simple ground that a taxpayer cannot be "away from home" unless he has a home from which to be away, cf. Haddleton, Traveling Expenses "Away from Home," 17 Tax.L.Rev. 261, 263, 286 (1962); 49 Va.L.Rev. 125, 126–28 (1963). Although that is our ultimate conclusion, the Supreme Court has wisely admonished that "More than a dictionary is thus required to understand the provision here involved, and no appeal to the 'plain language' of the section can obviate the need for further statutory construction," United States v. Correll, supra, 389 U.S. at 304 n. 16. We turn, therefore, in the first instance to the Court's decisions.

The initial Supreme Court decision bearing on our problem is C. I. R. v. Flowers, 326 U.S. 465 (1946). Flowers, a lawyer, had

1. Representative Hawley, a member of the Committee on Ways and Means, 61 Cong.Rec. 5201 (1921); see also the remarks of Senator Walsh, a member of the Committee on Finance, 61 Cong.Rec. 6673 (1921).

a "home" in the conventional sense in Jackson, Mississippi, but his principal post of business was at the main office of his employer, the Gulf, Mobile & Ohio Railroad in Mobile, Alabama. Flowers sought to deduct the cost of transportation for his trips to Mobile and the meal and lodging expenses which he incurred in that city. In upholding the Commissioner's disallowance of these deductions, the Court said that "three conditions must thus be satisfied before a traveling expense deduction may be made" under what was substantially the present statute, 326 U.S. at 470. These were:

(1). The expense must be a reasonable and necessary traveling expense, as that term is generally understood. This includes such items as transportation fares and food and lodging expenses incurred while traveling.

(2) The expense must be incurred "while away from home."

(3) The expense must be incurred in pursuit of business. This means that there must be a direct connection between the expenditure and the carrying on of the trade or business of the taxpayer or of his employer. Moreover, such an expenditure must be necessary or appropriate to the development and pursuit of the business or trade.

It noted that "The meaning of the word 'home' * * * with reference to a taxpayer residing in one city and working in another has engendered much difficulty and litigation," with the Tax Court and the administrative officials having "consistently defined it as the equivalent of the taxpayer's place of business" and two courts of appeals having rejected that view and "confined the term to the taxpayer's actual residence," 326 U.S. at 471–72. The Court found it "unnecessary here to enter into or to decide this conflict," 326 U.S. at 472. This was because the Tax Court had properly concluded "that the necessary relationship between the expenditures and the railroad's business was lacking." The railroad's interest was in having Mr. Flowers at its headquarters in Mobile; it "gained nothing" from his decision to continue living in Jackson, 326 U.S. at 472–74; hence, the third condition the *Flowers* Court had enunciated as a prerequisite to deductibility was absent. Mr. Justice Rutledge dissented. He did not believe that when Congress used the word "home," it meant "business headquarters," and thought the case presented no other question, 326 U.S. at 474. The most that Rosenspan can extract from *Flowers* is that it did not decide *against* his contention that the employer's business headquarters is the employee's tax home.

The Court's next venture into this area was in Peurifoy v. C. I. R., 358 U.S. 59 (1958). That case dealt with three construction workers employed at a site in Kinston, North Carolina, for periods of 20½, 12½, and 8½ months respectively, who maintained permanent residences elsewhere in the state. The Tax Court had allowed them deductions for board and lodging during the employment at Kinston and expenses in regaining their residences when they left, apparently of their own volition and before completion of the project.[2] The Fourth Circuit had reversed, C. I. R. v. Peurifoy, 254 F.2d 483 (1957). After having granted certiorari "to consider certain questions as to the application of § 23(a) (1) (A) of the Internal Revenue Code of 1939 raised by the course of decisions in the lower courts since our decision in Commissioner v. Flowers," 358 U.S. at 59–60, the Court announced in a *per curiam* opinion that it had "found it inappropriate to consider such questions." It read *Flowers* as establishing that "a taxpayer is entitled to deduct unreimbursed travel expenses * * * only when they are required by 'the exigencies of business,' " a "general rule" which the majority seemed to feel would mandate disallowance of the deductions under consideration. However, the Court went on to acknowledge an exception to this rule engrafted by the Tax Court, which would have allowed the claimed deductions if the taxpayer's employment were shown to be "temporary" rather than "indefinite" or "indeterminate." Nevertheless, even within this framework, the majority thought that the Court of Appeals had been justified in holding the Tax Court's finding of temporary employment to be clearly erroneous. Mr. Justice Douglas, joined by Justices Black and Whittaker, dissented. Adopting Mr. Justice Rutledge's position in *Flowers*, they disagreed "with the Commissioner's contention that 'home' is synonymous with the situs of the employer's business." While adhering to "the exigencies of business" test announced in *Flowers* they thought this requirement was satisfied by the fact that, in view of the impracticability of construction workers' moving their homes from job to job, "the expenses incurred were necessary, not to the business of the contractor for whom the taxpayers worked, but for the taxpayers themselves in order to carry on their chosen trade," 358 U.S. at 62–63 n. 6. While the three dissenting Justices thus rejected the Commissioner's identification of "home" with "the situs of the employer's business," the majority did not adopt it and, so far as our problem is concerned, that matter remained in the state of indecision where *Flowers* had left it.

We come finally to C. I. R. v. Stidger, 386 U.S. 287 (1967), where the Court sustained the disallowance of the expense for meals incurred by a Marine Corps captain who had been assigned to a base in Japan, while his wife and children—prohibited from accompanying him to that post—remained near his previous duty station in California. After noting that in this case there could be no question of the "direct connection between the expenditure and the carrying on of the trade or business of the taxpayer or of his employer," 386 U.S. at 289–90, the Court reviewed the continuing disagreement among the circuits over the Commissioner's view "that 'home' meant the taxpayer's principal place of business or employment whether

---

2. The Court of Appeals explicitly so found with respect to two of the three. 254 F.2d 483, 485 (4 Cir. 1957).

or not it coincided with his place of residence," [3] and took note of a ruling of the Board of Tax Appeals that members of Congress could not deduct living expenses incurred in Washington, D. C.,[4] and of Congress' response by enacting a special provision making the legislator's place of residence within the district that he represents his home but limiting the amount of deductible living expenses to $3,000, 66 Stat. 467 (1952), now codified in I.R.C. § 162(a). However, the Court again found it unnecessary either to approve or to disapprove the Commissioner's interpretation of "home," since it found that "in the context of the military taxpayer, the Commissioner's position has a firmer foundation." 386 U.S. at 292. This built "on the terminology employed by the military services to categorize various assignments and tours of duty, and also on the language and policy of the statutory provisions prescribing travel and transportation allowance for military personnel," id. The Court particularly stressed "the fact that Congress traditionally has provided a special system of tax-free allowances for military personnel," 386 U.S. at 294. Mr. Justice Douglas, who had written the dissent in *Peurifoy*, again joined by Justice Black and now by Justice Fortas, dissented. He thought it was "clear that home means residence, with the qualification that a taxpayer should establish his residence as near to his place of employment as is reasonable," 386 U.S. at 297.[5] The fact that Congress provides special allowances for military personnel did not, in Justice Douglas' view, call for what he deemed an unnatural reading of § 162(a) (2) even in that context.

Proper analysis of the problem has been beclouded, and the Government's position in this case has been made more difficult than it need be, by the Commissioner's insistence that "home" means "business headquarters," despite the Supreme Court's having thrice declined to endorse this, and its rejection by several courts of appeals, see Flowers v. C. I. R., 148 F.2d 163 (5 Cir. 1945), rev'd on other grounds, 326 U.S. 465 (1946); United States v. LeBlanc, 278 F.2d 571 (5 Cir. 1960); Burns v. Gray, 287 F.2d 698 (6 Cir. 1961); James v. United States, 308 F.2d 204 (9 Cir. 1962). But cf. C. I. R. v. Mooneyhan, 404 F.2d 522 (6 Cir. 1968), cert. denied, 394 U.S. 1001 (1969); Wills v. C. I. R., 411 F.2d 537, 540 (9 Cir. 1969). When Congress uses such a non-technical word in a tax statute, presumably it wants administrators and courts to read it in the way that ordinary people would understand, and not "to draw on some unexpressed

3. Although the opinion lists this circuit as having subscribed to the Commissioner's definition of "home," citing O'Toole v. C. I. R., 243 F.2d 302 (2 Cir. 1957), and a sentence in our per curiam opinion does read that way, the facts of O'Toole presented a typical Flowers situation and the ratio decidendi was the same as in that case, namely, that "The job, not the taxpayer's pattern of living, must require the traveling expenses," 243 F.2d at 303.

4. Lindsay v. C. I. R., 34 B.T.A. 840 (1936). This had long been the Commissioner's position. O.D. 864, 4 Cum.Bull. 211 (1921).

5. Perhaps more accurately, he should be treated as if he had done so.

spirit outside the bounds of the normal meaning of words," Addison v. Holly Hill Fruit Prods., Inc., 322 U.S. 607, 617 (1944). The construction which the Commissioner has long advocated not only violates this principle but is unnecessary for the protection of the revenue that he seeks. That purpose is served, without any such distortion of language, by the third condition laid down in *Flowers, supra,* 326 U.S. at 470, namely, "that there must be a direct connection between the expenditure and the carrying on of the trade or business of the taxpayer or of his employer" and that "such an expenditure must be necessary or appropriate to the development and pursuit of the business or trade." These requirements were enough to rule out a deduction for Flowers' lodging and meals while in Mobile even if he was "away from home" while there. The deduction would not have been available to his fellow workers living in that city who obtained similar amenities in their homes or even in the very restaurants that Flowers patronized, and Flowers was no more compelled by business to be away from his home while in Mobile than were other employees of the railroad who lived there.

Since the Commissioner's definition of "home" as "business headquarters" will produce the same result as the third *Flowers* condition in the overwhelming bulk of cases arising under § 162(a) (2), courts have often fallen into the habit of referring to it as a ground or an alternate ground of decision, as this court did in O'Toole v. C. I. R., 243 F.2d 302 (1957), see fn. 3. But examination of the string of cases cited by plaintiff as endorsing the "business headquarters" test has revealed almost none, aside from the unique situations involving military personnel considered above, which cannot be explained on the basis that the taxpayer had no permanent residence, or was not away from it, or maintained it in a locale apart from where he regularly worked as a matter of personal choice rather than business necessity.[6] This principle likewise affords a satisfactory rationale for the "temporary" employment cases, see 49 Va.L.Rev., supra, at 162–63. When

---

6. Whether the "personal choice" principle has not sometimes been pressed too far is another matter. The case of a Congressman, see fn. 4, may have been one such instance. It is also hard to be completely satisfied with the distinction between Barhill v. C. I. R., 148 F.2d 913 (4 Cir. 1945), disallowing meals and lodging deductions while in the state capital to justices of the Supreme Court of North Carolina who spent approximately 7 months a year there, but maintained their residences elsewhere, in deference to a custom that, at the time of selection, the justices should be fairly distributed throughout the state and a decision allowing such a deduction in the case of a justice of the Supreme Court of Louisiana who spent 9 months at the Court's headquarters in New Orleans but who, in contrast to the unwritten North Carolina practice, was required by the state constitution to maintain his residence in his own parish. United States v. LeBlanc, 278 F.2d 571 (5 Cir. 1960). England v. United States, 345 F.2d 414 (7 Cir. 1965), cert. denied, 382 U.S. 986 (1966), is another case in which the "personal choice" principle scarcely provides a satisfactory basis of decision if it suffices that the expenses be necessary to the taxpayer-employee's "trade or business" as distinguished from his employer's. As to this, see the discussion in the text, infra.

an assignment is truly temporary, it would be unreasonable to expect the taxpayer to move his home, and the expenses are thus compelled by the "exigencies of business"; when the assignment is "indefinite" or "indeterminate," the situation is different and, if the taxpayer decides to leave his home where it was, disallowance is appropriate, not because he has acquired a "tax home" in some lodging house or hotel at the worksite but because his failure to move his home was for his personal convenience and not compelled by business necessity. Under the facts here presented, we need not decide whether in the case of a taxpayer who is not self-employed the "exigencies of business" which compel the traveling expenses away from home refer solely to the business of his employer or to the business of the taxpayer as well. We note only that the latter contention is surely not foreclosed by decisions to date. See Peurifoy v. C. I. R., 358 U.S., supra, at 62–63 n. 6 (Douglas, J., dissenting); Rev.Rul. 60–189, 1960–1 Cum.Bull. 60; see generally 49 Va.L.Rev., supra, at 136–45; and Trent v. C. I. R., 291 F.2d 669, and cases cited, especially at 674 (2 Cir. 1961).

Shifting the thrust of analysis from the search for a fictional "tax home" to a questioning of the business necessity for incurring the expense away from the taxpayer's permanent residence thus does not upset the basic structure of the decisions which have dealt with this problem. Compare 49 Va.L.Rev., supra, at 162–63, with Haddleton, supra, at 286. It merely adopts an approach that better effectuates the congressional intent in establishing the deduction and thus provides a sounder conceptual framework for analysis while following the ordinary meaning of language. Cf. 19 U.Chi.L.Rev. 534, 545 (1952); 49 Va.L.Rev., supra, at 163. We see no basis whatever for believing that when the 1921 Congress eliminated the requirement for determining the excess of the costs of meals and lodging while on the road over what they would have been at home, it meant to disallow a deduction to someone who had the expense of maintaining a home from which business took him away but possessed no business headquarters. By the same token we find it impossible to read the words "away from home" out of the statute, as Rosenspan, in effect, would have us do and allow a deduction to a taxpayer who had no "home" in the ordinary sense. The limitation reflects congressional recognition of the rational distinction between the taxpayer with a permanent residence—whose travel costs represent a duplication of expense or at least an incidence of expense which the existence of his permanent residence demonstrates he would not incur absent business compulsion—and the taxpayer without such a residence. Cf. James v. United States, supra, 308 F.2d at 207. We fail to see how Rosenspan's occasional trips to New York City, assuming for the sake of argument that his "business headquarters" was in New York rather than in his sales territory, differentiate him economically from the homeless traveling salesman without even the modicum of a business headquarters Rosenspan is claimed to have possessed. Yet we approved disallowance of the deduction in such a case many years ago. Duncan v. C. I. R., 17 B.T.A. 1088 (1929), aff'd per curiam, 47 F.2d 1082 (2 Cir. 1931), as the Ninth Circuit has done more recently, James v. United States, supra, 308 F.2d 204.

It is enough to decide this case that "home" means "home" and Rosenspan had none. He satisfied the first and third conditions of Flowers, supra, 326 U.S. at 470, but not, on our reading of the statute, the second. The judgment dismissing the complaint must therefore be affirmed.

REVENUE RULING 75–432 [1]

1975–2 Cum.Bull. 60.

The purpose of this Revenue Ruling is to update and restate, under the current statute and regulations, the position set forth in Rev. Rul. 54–497, 1954–2 C.B. 75, at 77–81, with regard to the principles applicable in determining when an employee may deduct expenses for meals and lodging incurred while traveling on business.

The courts in considering questions involving deductions for traveling expenses have frequently stated that each case must be decided on its own particular facts. Furthermore, there appears to be no single rule that will produce the correct result in all situations.

Section 162(a)(2) of the Internal Revenue Code of 1954 provides that a deduction shall be allowed for all the ordinary and necessary expenses paid or incurred during the taxable year in carrying on any trade or business, including traveling expenses (including amounts expended for meals and lodging other than amounts which are lavish or extravagant under the circumstances) while away from home in the pursuit of a trade or business. On the other hand, section 262 of the Code states that, except as otherwise expressly provided, no deduction shall be allowed for personal, living, or family expenses.

A taxpayer cannot deduct the cost of meals and lodging while performing duties at a principal place of business, even though the taxpayer maintains a permanent residence elsewhere. Congress did not intend to allow as a business expense those outlays that are not caused by the exigencies of the business but by the action of the taxpayer in having a home, for the taxpayer's convenience, at a distance from the business. Such expenditures are not essential for the conduct of the business and were not within the contemplation of Congress, which proceeded on the assumption that a person engaged in business would live within reasonable proximity of the business. See Barnhill v. Commissioner, 148 F.2d 913 (4th Cir. 1945), 1945 C.B. 96; Commissioner v. Stidger, 386 U.S. 237 (1967), 1967–1 C.B. 32.

---

1. Prepared pursuant to Rev.Proc. 67–6, 1967–1 C.B. 576.

It is therefore the long-established position of the Internal Revenue Service that the "home" referred to in section 162(a)(2) of the Code as the place away from which traveling expenses must be incurred to be deductible is, as a general rule, the place at which the taxpayer conducts the trade or business. If the taxpayer is engaged in business at two or more separate locations, the "tax home" for purposes of section 162(a)(2) is located at the principal place of business during the taxable year. Markey v. Commissioner, 490 F.2d 1249 (6th Cir. 1974); Rev.Rul. 60–189, 1960–1 C.B. 60. It should, of course, be emphasized that the location of an employee's tax home is necessarily a question of fact that must be determined on the basis of the particular circumstances of each case.

In the rare case in which the employee has no identifiable principal place of business, but does maintain a regular place of abode in a real or substantial sense in a particular city from which the taxpayer is sent on temporary assignments, the tax home will be regarded as being that place of abode. This should be distinguished from the case of an itinerant worker with neither a regular place of business nor a regular place of abode. In such case, the home is considered to go along with the worker and therefore the worker does not travel away from home for purposes of section 162(a)(2) of the Code, and may not deduct the cost of meals or lodging. Rev.Rul. 73–529, 1973–C.B. 37; Rev.Rul. 71–247, 1971–1 C.B. 54.

The tax home rule may be illustrated by its application to railroad employees. The principal or regular post of duty of a member of a train crew is not regarded as being aboard the train, but at the terminal where such member ordinarily, or for an indefinite period (as distinguished from a temporary period, discussed below), begins and ends actual train runs. This terminal is referred to, for tax purposes, as that employee's tax home, the location of which may or may not coincide with the railroad's designation of the home terminal for a particular run.

Whether an employee's current post of duty is that employee's tax home depends on whether that individual is assigned there temporarily or permanently (an assignment for an indefinite period is regarded as a permanent assignment for section 162(a)(2) of the Code purposes). The basic principle is that an employee is considered to maintain a residence at or in the vicinity of that employee's principal place of business. See *Markey*. An employee who is temporarily transferred to a different area is not expected to move to the new area, and is therefore considered away from home and "in a travel status" while at his temporary post. Truman C. Tucker, 55 T.C. 783 (1971); Rev.Rul. 60–189. However, an employee who is permanently transferred to a new area is considered to have shifted the home to the new post, which is the employee's new tax home. See Commissioner v. Mooneyhan, 404 F.2d 522 (6th Cir. 1968), cert. denied, 394 U.S. 1001. The maintenance of the old residence where the taxpayer's family resides, and the taxpayer's travel back and forth, are strictly personal expenses that, under the provisions of section 262, are not deductible. See Commissioner v. Flowers, 326 U.S. 465, 1946–1 C.B. 57.

An exception to this rule exists in those unusual situations when the employee maintains a permanent residence for that employee's family at or near the minor or temporary post of duty, and another residence at or near the principal post of duty. Since the employee is traveling away from the principal post of duty on business where the employee also maintains a residence, the cost of meals and lodging at the minor or temporary post of duty is allowed as a deduction. Of course, the deduction is limited to that portion of the family expenses for meals and lodging that is properly attributable to the employee's presence there in the actual performance of business duties. Rev. Rul. 61–67, 1961–1 C.B. 25; Rev.Rul. 54–147, 1954–1 C.B. 51, 53.

An employee whose assignment away from that employee's principal place of business is strictly temporary (that is, its termination is anticipated within a fixed or reasonably short period of time) is considered to be in a travel status for the entire period during which duties require the employee to remain away from the regular post of duty. For example, if a member of a railroad train crew receives a temporary assignment to a run (whether or not "overnight," a rule discussed below) that begins and ends at a terminal situated at a distance from the tax home, the member may deduct not only the expenses for meals and lodging while making runs from and to that terminal, but all such expenses for the entire time during which duties prevent such member from returning to the regular post of duty. Typical of temporary assignments necessitating such an absence from the employee's regular post of duty are replacement or relief jobs during sick or vacation leave of the employees who regularly perform those duties.

Another kind of temporary assignment away from an employee's regular post of duty is a seasonal job that is not ordinarily filled by the same individual year after year. For example, during seasonal shipping periods for the marketing of crops, an employee may be assigned for several months to one or more places that are located at a distance from the regular place of employment. Such an employee is generally regarded as being in a travel status for the duration of such a temporary assignment.

The same rule would be true even if the seasonal job is not temporary, but a regularly recurring post of duty. A seasonal job to which an employee regularly returns, year after year, is regarded as being permanent rather than temporary employment. For example, a railroad employee might habitually work eight or nine months each year transporting ore from the same terminal, maintaining a residence for the employee's family at or near such work location. During the winter, when the ore-hauling service is suspended, the same employee might also be employed for three or four months each year at another regular seasonal post of duty, taking up residence at or near such employment. The ordinary rule is that when an employee leaves one permanent job to accept another permanent job, such employee is regarded as abandoning the first job for the second, and the principal post of duty shifts from the old to the new place of employment. The employee in the above example, however, is not regarded as having abandoned the ore-hauling assignment during the period in which that service is suspended, since the employee reasonably expects to return to it during the appropriate following season. The employee is conducting a trade or business each year at the same two recurring, seasonal places of employment, and under these circumstances the tax home does not shift during alternate seasons from one business location to the other, but remains stationary at the principal post of duty throughout the taxable year. In each case of this nature, a factual determination must be made in order to establish which of the seasonal posts of duty is the principal post of duty. Of course, the employee may only deduct the cost of the meals and lodging at the minor place of employment while duties there require such employee to remain away from the principal post of duty.

The rule known as the "overnight rule" or the "sleep or rest rule" is used to determine whether an employee whose duties require that employee to leave the principal post of duty during all or part of actual working hours is considered to be in a travel status. An employee may deduct the expenses for meals and lodging on a business trip away from the principal post of duty only when the trip lasts substantially longer than an ordinary day's work, the employee cannot reasonably be expected to make the trip without being released from duty for sufficient time to obtain substantial sleep or rest while away from the principal post of duty, and the release from duty is with the employer's tacit or express acquiescence, or is required by regulations of a governmental agency regulating the activity involved. The overnight rule is discussed in Rev.Rul. 75–170, 1975–19 I.R.B. 14, as are the requirements for substantiating claims for deductions for the cost of meals and lodging under section 274 of the Code.

When expenses are incurred for meals and lodging by an employee "while away from home" in the course of business duties, they are deductible as traveling expenses under section 162(a)(2) of the Code, subject to the substantiation requirements of section 274. Since such expenses are deductible under section 62(2)(B) in computing adjusted gross income, the deduction of such expenses does not prevent the employee from electing to compute the tax either by using the tax table or the optional standard deduction, instead of itemizing actual deductions.

The portion of Rev.Rul. 54–497 regarding the principles applicable in determining when an employee may deduct expenses for meals and lodging incurred while traveling on business is superseded.

PROBLEMS

1. Commuter owns a home in Suburb of City and drives to work in City each day. He eats lunch in various restaurants in City.

(a) May Commuter deduct his costs of transportation and/or meals? See Reg. § 1.162–2(e).

(b) Same as (a), above, but Commuter is an attorney and often must travel between his office and the City Court House to file papers, try cases, etc. May Commuter deduct all or any of his costs of transportation and meals?

(c) Commuter resides and works in City, but occasionally must fly to Other City on business for his employer. He eats lunch in Other City and returns home in the later afternoon or early evening. May he deduct all or a part of his costs?

(d) Commuter is a carpenter who works in various areas of City and takes his tools home to Suburb each night when it is impossible for him to store them at job site. Commuter uses his personal automobile to travel to work when he cannot store his tools at job sites and incurs expenses attributable to his commuting by car of $5.00 per day. When working on jobs where he is not required to carry his tools, Commuter uses public transportation at a daily cost of $2.50. May Commuter deduct all or any part of his commuting expenses? See Fausner v. Comm'r, 413 U.S. 838 (1973), and Rev.Rul. 75–380, 1975–2 C.B. 59.

2.

(a) Taxpayer lives with her family in City and works there. However, her employer sends her to Metro on business for two days and one night each week. If Taxpayer is not reimbursed for her expenses, what may she deduct?

(b) Same as (a), above, except that she works three days and spends two nights each week in Metro and maintains an apartment there.

(c) Taxpayer operates a consulting business as a sole proprietorship in City and also works as an Employee of Employer in Metro. She spends 5 days per week in Metro and earns approximately $12,000 per year from Employer. Each weekend Taxpayer returns to City to attend to her business and substantial investments there. What expenses may Taxpayer deduct if her net income from the consulting business and investments in City is $100? $5000? $25,000? See Markey v. Comm'r, 490 F.2d 1249 (6th Cir. 1974).

(d) Taxpayer and husband own a home in Metro and husband works there. Taxpayer works in City, maintaining an apartment there, and travels to Metro each weekend to visit her husband and family. See Robert A. Coerver, 36 T.C. 252 (1961), aff'd per curiam, 297 F.2d 837 (3d Cir. 1962), and John R. Masline, 30 T.C.M. 850 (1971).

3.

(a) Burly is a professional football player for the City Stompers. He and his wife own a home in Metro where they reside during the 7-month "off season". Burly's only source of income is his salary from the Stompers. May Burly deduct any of his City living expenses which he incurs during the football season? See Ronald L. Gardin, 64 T.C. 1079 (1975).

(b) Would there be any difference in result in (a), above, if during the 7-month "off season" Burly worked as an insurance salesman in Metro? See George R. Lanning, 34 T.C.M. 1366 (1975).

4. Temporary works for Employer in City where he and his family live.

(a) Employer has trouble in Branch City office in another state. He asks Temporary to supervise the Branch City office for nine months. Temporary's family stays in City and he rents an apartment in Branch City. Are Temporary's expenses in Branch City deductible?

(b) What result in (a), above, if Employer asks Temporary to remain in Branch City for "as long as it takes to clear up the mess over there", if it is likely at the time that it will take only three months? See Harvey v. Comm'r, 283 F.2d 491 (1960), and Rev.Rul. 61–95, 1961–1 C.B. 749.

(c) What result in (a), above, if Temporary rents to another the home he owns in City and he and family move to Branch City for the nine months?

(d) What result in (c), above, if Temporary and his family had lived in a furnished apartment in City and they gave that up merely to live in a furnished apartment in Branch City? Compare J. B. Stewart, 30 T.C.M. 1316 (1971), with Alvin L. Goldman, 32 T.C.M. 574 (1973).

5. Traveler goes from his personal and tax home in New York to a business meeting in Florida on Monday. The meeting ends late Wednesday and he flies home on Friday afternoon after two days in the sunshine.

(a) To what extent are Traveler's transportation, meals, and lodging deductible? See Reg. § 1.162–2(a) and (b).

(b) May Traveler deduct any of Wife's expenses if she joins him on the trip? See Reg. § 1.162–2(c) and U. S. v. Disney, 413 F.2d 783 (9th Cir. 1969).

(c) What result in (a), above, if Traveler stays in Florida until Sunday afternoon?

(d) What result in (a), above, if Traveler's trip is to Mexico City rather than Florida? See § 274(c).

(e) What result in (d), above, if Traveler went to Mexico City on Thursday and conducted business on Thursday, Friday, Monday, and Tuesday, and returned to New York on the succeeding Friday night? See Reg. § 1.274–4(d)(2)(v).

(f) What result in (d), above if Traveler's trip to Mexico City is to attend a business convention? See I.R.C. 274(h) added by TRA (1976) § 602(a).

---

3. NECESSARY RENTAL AND SIMILAR PAYMENTS

Internal Revenue Code: Section 162(a)(3).
Regulations: Section 1.162–11.

ESTATE OF STARR v. COMMISSIONER

United States Court of Appeals, Ninth Circuit, 1959.
274 F.2d 294.

CHAMBERS, CIRCUIT JUDGE. Yesterday's equities in personal property seem to have become today's leases. This has been generated not a little by the circumstance that one who leases as a lessee usually has less trouble with the federal tax collector. At least taxpayers think so.

But the lease still can go too far and get one into tax trouble. While according to state law the instrument will probably be taken (with the consequent legal incidents) by the name the parties give it, the internal revenue service is not always bound and can often recast it according to what the service may consider the practical realities.[1] We have so held in Oesterreich v. Commissioner, 9 Cir., 226 F.2d 798, and Commissioner of Internal Revenue v. Wilshire Holding Corporation, 9 Cir., 244 F.2d 904, certiorari denied 355 U.S. 815, 78 S.Ct. 16, 2 L.Ed.2d 32. The principal case concerns a fire sprinkler system installed at the taxpayer's plant at Monrovia, California, where Delano T. Starr,[2] now deceased, did business as the Gross Manufacturing Company. The "lessor" was "Automatic" Sprinklers of the Pacific, Inc., a California corporation. The instrument entitled "Lease Form

---

1. Thus it shifts rental payments of a business (fully deductible) to a capital purchase for the business. If the nature of the property is wasting, then depreciation may be taken, but usually not all in one year.

2. Presumably the plant and the business were California community property of Starr and his wife, Mary W. Starr. For each of the calendar years 1951 and 1952, they filed joint tax returns.

of Contract" (hereafter "contract") is just about perfectly couched in terms of a lease for five years with annual rentals of $1,240. But it is the last paragraph thereof, providing for nominal rental for five years, that has caused the trouble. It reads as follows:

"28. At the termination of the period of this lease, if Lessee has faithfully performed all of the terms and conditions required of it under this lease, it shall have the privilege of renewing this lease for an additional period of five years at a rental of $32.00 per year. If Lessee does not elect to renew this lease, then the Lessor is hereby granted the period of six months in which to remove the system from the premises of the Lessee."

Obviously, one renewal for a period of five years is provided at $32.00 per year, if Starr so desired. Note, though, that the paragraph is silent as to status of the system beginning with the eleventh year. Likewise the whole contract is similarly silent.

The tax court sustained the commissioner of internal revenue, holding that the five payments of $1,240, or the total of $6,200, were capital expenditures and not pure deductible rental.[3] Depreciation of $269.60 was allowed for each year. Generally, we agree.

Taxpayers took the deduction as a rental expense under trade or business pursuant to Section 23(a) of the Internal Revenue Code, as amended by Section 121(a) of the Revenue Act of 1942.[4]

The law in this field for this circuit is established in Oesterreich v. Commissioner, supra, and Robinson v. Elliot, 9 Cir., 262 F.2d 383. There we held that for tax purposes form can be disregarded for substance and, where the foreordained practical effect of the rent is to produce title eventually, the rental agreement can be treated as a sale.

In this, Starr's case, we do have the troublesome circumstance that the contract does not by its terms ever pass title to the system to the "lessee." Most sprinkler systems have to be tailor-made for a specific piece of property and, if removal is required, the salvageable value is negligible. Also, it stretches credulity to believe that the "lessor" ever intended to or would "come after" the system. And the "lessee" would be an exceedingly careless businessman who would enter into such contract with the practical possibility that the "lessor" would reclaim the installation. He could have believed only that he was getting the system for the rental money. And we think the commissioner was entitled to take into consideration the practical effect rather than the legal, especially when there was a record that on other such installations the "lessor", after the term of the lease was over, had not reclaimed from those who had met their agreed payments. It is obvious that the nominal rental payments after five years of $32.00 per year were just a service charge for inspection.[5]

3. Starr, Estate of, v. Commissioner, 30 T.C. 856.

4. [I.R.C. (1939) § 23(a) is omitted. See I.R.C. (1954) § 162(a). Ed.]

5. It is true that the normal inspection fee would be $64.00. However, the difference between $32.00 and $64.00 would not seem to ruin the tax court's

Recently the Court of Appeals for the Eighth Circuit has decided Western Contracting Corporation v. Commissioner, 1959, 271 F.2d 694, reversing the tax court in its determination that the commissioner could convert leases of contractor's equipment into installment purchases of heavy equipment. The taxpayer believes that case strongly supports him here. We think not.[6]

There are a number of facts there which make a difference. For example, in the contracts of Western there is no evidence that the payments on the substituted basis of rent would produce for the "lessor" the equivalent of his normal sales price plus interest. There was no right to acquire for a nominal amount at the end of the term as in Oesterreich and the value to the "lessor" in the personalty had not been exhausted as in Starr's case. And there was no basis for inferring that Western would just keep the equipment for what it had paid. It appears that Western paid substantial amounts to acquire the equipment at the end of the term. There was just one compelling circumstance against Western in its case: What it had paid as "rent" was apparently always taken into full account in computing the end purchase price. But on the other hand, there was almost a certainty that the "lessor" would come after his property if the purchase was not eventually made for a substantial amount. This was not even much of a possibility in Oesterreich and not a probability in Starr's case.

In Wilshire Holding Corporation v. Commissioner, 9 Cir., 262 F. 2d 51, we referred the case back to the tax court to consider interest as a deductible item for the lessee. We think it is clearly called for here. Two yardsticks are present. The first is found in that the normal selling price of the system was $4,960 while the total rental payments for five years were $6,200. The difference could be regarded as interest for the five years on an amortized basis. The second measure is in clause 16 (loss by fire), where the figure of six per cent per annum discount is used. An allowance might be made on either basis, division of the difference (for the five years) between "rental payments" and "normal purchase price" of $1,240, or six per cent per annum on the normal purchase price of $4,960, converting the annual payments into amortization. We do not believe that the "lessee" should suffer the pains of a loss for what really was paid for the use of another's money, even though for tax purposes his lease collapses.

We do not criticize the commissioner. It is his duty to collect the revenue and it is a tough one. If he resolves all questions in favor of the taxpayers, we soon would have little revenue. However, we do

determination for income tax purposes that there was a sale.

6. It is unnecessary to determine here whether the Ninth Circuit would follow the decision of the Eighth Circuit or the decision of the tax court. (Western Contracting Corp. v. Commissioner, 17 TCM 371, T.C.Memo. 1958–77, CCH. Dec. 22, 1960 [M]). It is enough here to say that the Ninth Circuit regards the Eighth Circuit's opinion distinguishable from Starr's case and not inconsistent with the holding herein.

suggest that after he has made allowance for depreciation, which he concedes, and an allowance for interest, the attack on many of the "leases" may not be worth while in terms of revenue.

Decision reversed for proceedings consistent herewith.

WHITE v. FITZPATRICK

United States Court of Appeals, Second Circuit, 1951.
193 F.2d 398.
Cert. denied, 343 U.S. 928, 72 S.Ct. 762.

CLARK, CIRCUIT JUDGE. Involved in this appeal is the recurring problem of tax savings claimed as a consequence of a transfer of property from husband to wife with resulting lease or license back. Here neither the Commissioner of Internal Revenue nor the district court has accepted the taxpayer's view of the transactions; and he now appeals from the judgment against him in his action for a refund of the deficiency assessed against him by the Commissioner upon his income and victory taxes for the years 1941, 1943, and 1944.

The following are the facts of the case as stipulated by the parties and found by the trial court. During the years in question and for some time prior thereto, plaintiff engaged in the manufacture of chokes for use on the barrels of shotguns, as sole proprietor of the Poly Choke Company, an unincorporated business. Beginning in 1939 the company occupied certain properties—land, three factories, a garage, and an office—under a lease coupled with a nontransferable option to purchase for $15,370. Plaintiff had developed the basic invention for this device himself and obtained a United States patent for it on December 27, 1932.

On January 21, 1941, he entered into a written agreement with his wife, transferring "the entire right, title and interest in and to" the patent, "to the full end of the term of said patent," for a stated consideration of $10. The following day his wife licensed the exclusive manufacturing right back to him "to the full end of the entire term of said patent." The assignment back was subject to cancellation only if (a) payments fell into sixty days' arrears, or (b) receivership, bankruptcy, forced assignment, or other financial difficulty made it impossible for her husband to carry on his manufacturing concern. It provided for royalties of $1 on each product marketed. Plaintiff filed a gift tax return for the year declaring the fair market value of the patent to be $10,000 and for the next four years, 1941–1944 inclusive, paid his wife some $60,000 as royalties.

At about the same time, December 27, 1940, plaintiff's wife also purchased the property on which the company was located for $16,800 and immediately leased it to her husband orally. On the next day plaintiff made a gift to his wife of $16,175 to cover the purchase price and filed a gift tax return for that amount. Rental payments for the years 1941–1944 inclusive were $1,500 a year, which was the amount that plaintiff had been paying to the original lessor; in 1944, plaintiff in addition paid his wife some $5,000 as "an adjustment in rent."

During the years in question plaintiff deducted both rental payments and royalties as business expenses. After investigation and audit, the Commissioner of Internal Revenue issued a deficiency notice disallowing the deductions in 1948. Plaintiff paid the total deficiency of about $47,000 thus assessed and brought this action for refund. The district court found (1) that the plaintiff's motivation was to make good certain losses in the value of securities held by his wife and to minimize income taxes for the family group, but (2) that "it was the taxpayer's expectation that no action would be taken by the wife in exercise of her rights of ownership of the patent or real property which would be detrimental to the plaintiff's interests." The court then concluded that by the gifts and license and lease back "by reason of the family relationship the husband retains effective control of the patent and real property, while valid transfers for other purposes, will not form a valid basis for deduction of royalties and rent paid by the husband to the wife as business expenses in arriving at the taxpayer's net income for income tax purposes."

The bare assignment of the patent was legally adequate to transfer all rights adhering thereto to the wife. Likewise the land was purchased in the name of the wife alone. From this plaintiff contends on appeal that the wife's legal title and power were absolute and subject to no conditions or future claims whatsoever. Moreover, there is no evidence, nor does defendant contend, that the plaintiff derived any direct benefit in the form of income from these transactions. Therefore, plaintiff argues that, since the royalties and rents were both ordinary in nature for his type of business and reasonable in amount, they constitute valid business expenses under I.R.C. § 23(a) (1) (A), 26 U.S.C.A. § 23(a) (1) (A), which authorizes the deduction from gross income of "ordinary and necessary expenses" paid "in carrying on any trade or business." See Welch v. Helvering, 290 U.S. 111, 54 S.Ct. 8, 78 L.Ed. 212; Deputy v. DuPont, 308 U.S. 488, 60 S.Ct. 363, 84 L.Ed. 416.

Underlying reality, however, contradicts this appearance of a complete assignment. "Title" to the patent and land may legally reside in the plaintiff's wife; practically and actually, as the district court concluded, control rests with the husband as effectively as if he had never made the gift of the patent to his wife or given her the money with which to buy the property. Assignment and gift cannot be divorced for tax purposes from their accompanying agreements whereby the husband retained dominion. And in fact plaintiff never intended that it should be; he admitted the impossibility of conducting the business without this basic patent or of finding a comparable factory site in Connecticut. His wife was neither equipped nor evinced any desire to exercise or transfer any rights to the use of either of the properties; in the case of the patent at least, it is clear that she had no legal right to do so, save in the unlikely event of the husband's default. The sole practical effect of these transactions, therefore, was to create a right to income in the wife, while leaving untouched in all practical reality the husband-donor's effective dominion and control over the properties in question. It is not without significance on this point that the arrangement made was actually disadvantageous to the business. For it passed over the reduction of land charges which the taxpayer might have made by taking up his option to purchase in order to create the income right in the donor's wife, and that, too, at a greater capital cost. For the statutory purposes, the mere creation of a legal obligation to pay is not controlling. Interstate Transit Lines v. C. I. R., 8 Cir., 130 F.2d 136, affirmed 319 U.S. 590, 63 S.Ct. 1279, 87 L.Ed. 1607.

In this respect, then, the case before us does not involve the definite problem presented by the completed assignment of a created product which divided our court and the Fourth Circuit, both inter- and extra-murally, in the two cases of Wodehouse v. C. I. R., 2 Cir., 177 F. 2d 881, Id., 4 Cir., 178 F.2d 987. Gift and retained control must be regarded as inseparable parts of a single transaction, especially since it was only in their sum total that they had any reality in regard to the conduct of plaintiff's business. To isolate them, as would be necessary to bring them within the rationale of our own majority ruling in Wodehouse v. C. I. R., supra, is to hide business reality behind paper pretense.

For the question here is as to the tax consequences of a formal gift of certain income-producing properties by the husband to his wife coupled with the informal retention of administrative control—the transfer, in effect, of the right to receive income and the retention of those complex of "use rights" which are usually compressed in the term "ownership." In the context of I.R.C. § 23(a) (1) (A), the question is a rather new one; under I.R.C. § 22(a), 26 U.S.C.A. § 22(a), [See I.R.C. (1954) § 61. Ed.] where it arises in the definition of gross income problems, it is not. And we think the line drawn in the precedents under the latter section is the same as that in the field of deductibility of business expenses. Plaintiff here, for example, accepts as his own the income he has received on the patent equivalent to the royalties he is paying his wife, but then seeks to deduct it as a business expense; in effect this is not different from claiming that the gift itself made the original income hers in the first place.

We think, therefore, that the principles governing the intermarital transfer of income enunciated in Helvering v. Clifford, 309 U.S. 331, 60 S.Ct. 554, 84 L.Ed. 788, and re-enforced by later cases, are also decisive here. In the case at bar, plaintiff assigned the "legal title" to the patent and provided for his wife's assumption of the "legal title" to the land; but he retained, by formal agreement in the first case, by informal arrangement in the second, the administrative control of these properties. His wife had the right to income, but he had a right to the use of the patent and land. Henson v. C. I. R., 5 Cir., 174 F.2d 846, is thus distinguishable. The Clifford rule is clear, that this direct control, when fused with the indirect control which we must imply from a formal but unsubstantial assignment within the closed family group displaying no obvious business purpose, renders the assignment ineffective for federal tax purposes. The same result should obtain whether the question arises under § 22(a) or 23(a) (1) (A) of the Internal Revenue Code.

Plaintiff relies heavily on Skemp v. C. I. R., 7 Cir., 168 F.2d 598, and Brown v. C. I. R., 3 Cir., 180 F.2d 926, certiorari denied C. I. R. v. Brown, 340 U.S. 814, 71 S.Ct. 42, 95 L.Ed. 598. These cases, which are criticized in reasoned discussions in 51 Col.L.Rev. 247 and 59 Yale L.J. 1529, may be thought to go to the verge of the law in support of what are essentially intrafamily transfers. But both, being to trustees, were sufficiently outright, to be distinguishable from our present case. Both involved claimed deductions under I.R.C. § 23(a) (1) (A). In the first, a plaintiff-physician had deeded the building in which he had his office in irrevocable trust for twenty years or until the prior deaths of both himself and his wife, with their children as beneficiaries. He then leased the building back for ten years. In the second, there were two trusts, also irrevocable, terminating on the majority of the beneficiaries who were children of the settlor, coupled with an immediate leaseback of the corpus properties. In upholding the deductions, both courts expressly emphasized the independence of the trustees. It is probable that a like result would probably have obtained had the question been one of gross income under I.R.C. § 22(a). For three factors determine attributability of income to the settlor of a family trust. Whether these are conjunctive tests, see Helvering v. Clifford, supra, 309 U.S. at page 335, 60 S.Ct. 554, or alternative, under the new Clifford regulations, U.S.Treas.Reg. No. 111, § 29.22 (a)–21; Kay v. C. I. R., 3 Cir., 178 F.2d 772, it seems likely that in both the cases relied on, income would have been attributable to the trusts and thus to the beneficiaries, rather than the settlors. For (1) the settlors retained no reversionary interests; (2) they retained no dispositive power over either corpus or income;[1] and (3) administrative control was not exercisable primarily for the benefit of the settlors.[2] See Alexandre, Case Method Restatement of the New Clifford Regulations, 3 Tax.L.Rev. 189.

1. In the Skemp case, 7 Cir., 168 F.2d 598, 599, the "taxpayer * * * did reserve the right to rent all or a part of the building 'at a rental to be determined by the trustee' "; but this does not constitute "beneficial enjoyment" of the property in the Clifford sense. Moreover, both leases back were for a term and were not coextensive with the life of the trust.

2. Here the factor of independent trusteeship is crucial. And it is in this respect that the instant case differs on its facts from the Skemp and Brown results.

The Supreme Court has long emphasized the test of retention of practical ownership in passing on the tax consequences of intra-family assignment. Soll, Intra-Family Assignments: Attribution and Realization of Income, 6 Tax L.Rev. 435. In the recent case of C. I. R. v. Sunnen, 333 U.S. 591, 68 S.Ct. 715, 92 L.Ed. 898, involving the assignment by the inventor-husband of patent licensing contracts to his wife, the court said, "The crucial question remains whether the assignor retains sufficient power and control over the assigned property or over receipt of the income to make it reasonable to treat him as the recipient of the income for tax purposes," 333 U.S. at page 604, 68 S.Ct. at page 722, and went on to note that "The taxpayer's controlling position in the corporation also permitted him to regulate the amount of royalties payable to his wife." 333 U.S. at page 609, 68 S.Ct. at page 725. In essence the assignment in the present case was effective only to the extent of transferring the single right to receive income. It is now too late to question the well-established proposition that mere assignment of such a right will not suffice to insulate the grantor from tax liability under § 22(a), and we think like tax results must obtain under § 23(a) (1) (A). See Lucas v. Earl, 281 U.S. 111, 50 S.Ct. 241, 74 L.Ed. 731; Helvering v. Horst, 311 U.S. 112, 61 S.Ct. 144, 85 L.Ed. 75; Helvering v. Eubank, 311 U.S. 122, 61 S.Ct. 149, 85 L.Ed. 81. The recent case of C. I. R. v. Culbertson, 337 U.S. 733, 69 S.Ct. 1210, 93 L.Ed. 1659, has established the test in the family-partnership field, whether or not there existed as part of the arrangement a "bona fide intent" to have the donee exercise a real part in management, thus giving a final blessing to the doctrine that "true ownership" is decisive in matters of federal taxation. See also C. I. R. v. Tower, 327 U.S. 280, 66 S.Ct. 532, 90 L.Ed. 670, 164 A.L.R. 1135; Harrison v. Schaffner, 312 U.S. 579, 61 S.Ct. 759, 85 L.Ed. 1055; Ingle Coal Corp. v. C. I. R., 7 Cir., 174 F.2d 569.

Since here we find no evidence of a potential exercise of "control and management" on the part of the donee, only of "passive acquiescence to the will of the donor," C. I. R. v. Culbertson, supra, 337 U.S. at pages 747, 748, 69 S.Ct. at page 1217, since the transaction is in all practical respects a "mere paper reallocation of income among the family members," C. I. R. v. Tower, supra, 327 U.S. at page 292, 66 S.Ct. at page 538, and since the husband has remained the actual enjoyer and owner of the property, payments to the wife do not constitute valid business deductions within the statute. See Johnson v. C. I. R., 2 Cir., 86 F.2d 710; W. H. Armston Co. v. C. I. R., 5 Cir., 188 F.2d 531.

Affirmed.

CHASE, CIRCUIT JUDGE (dissenting). Perhaps it would be desirable to protect the revenue by amending Sec. 23(a) (1) (A) to exclude from the business expense deductions now allowed those which become necessary only because of intrafamily gifts of property used, or to be used, in the business. But that is a matter to be determined by Congress and, until it acts, I think courts are bound to give effect taxwise to gifts which are fully effective otherwise.

There is, I think, some distinction between the disallowance of the royalty and the disallowance of the rent deductions. It is that the transfer of the patent by gift to the wife was a transfer of needed business property already owned by the taxpayer which was intended to, and did, make it necessary to pay her the royalties. The gift of the money, however, which she used together with some of her own to buy the building never owned by the taxpayer was not shown to have been of money which had any connection with the business at all and the net result from the standpoint of the taxpayer and his business was merely a change in landlord. However, as I view this case, it is not necessary to rely upon this distinction.

In respect to the claimed deductions, the decisive factor as the statute is now, is whether the rent and royalty payments were "required to be made as a condition to the continued use or possession, for purposes of the trade or business, of property to which the taxpayer has not taken or is not taking title or in which he had no equity." Sec. 23(a) (1) (A). The findings, based on evidence adequately supporting them, show that everything was done to transfer the legal and equitable titles both to the patent and to the building absolutely to the wife, and the ownership she thereby acquired gave her the right to whatever she could get by way of royalties and rents which were, of course, taxable to her as income. And, as Sec. 23(a) (1) (A) is now so broad that no exception is made because of the way in which business expenses become necessary, i. e., by gift or otherwise, the reasonable royalties and rents the husband paid her were, I think, well within the scope of the statute, being "required" by the license and lease arrangements, and therefore deductible. Skemp v. Commissioner, 7 Cir., 168 F.2d 598; Brown v. Commissioner, 3 Cir., 180 F.2d 926, certiorari denied, 340 U.S. 814, 71 S.Ct. 42, 95 L.Ed. 598. See also Henson v. Commissioner, 5 Cir., 174 F.2d 846. The fact that in the Skemp and Brown cases the transfers were to independent trustees for the benefit of family members is a distinction without a difference since that bore only on the completeness of the gifts and reasonableness of the royalties and rentals paid, both here shown and found. W. H. Armston Co. v. Commissioner, 5 Cir., 188 F.2d 531, is distinguishable as an instance of a disguised transfer of dividends to a large stockholder of the corporation.

The cases dealing with problems arising under Sec. 22(a), I.R.C. as to the identity of the taxpayer liable for taxes payable by some one, on which my brothers so much rely, help little, if any, in determining what deductions an identified taxpayer may take under Sec. 23(a) (1) (A) in computing his net income. Assuming, arguendo, that these cases are relevant [1] factually they are inapplicable. The only basis

---

1. The only issue to which these cases could be relevant is whether or not the taxpayer was "required" to pay the royalties and rents as a condition to using the property since that is the test set forth in the statute. In order

pointed out by the majority for applying these cases to the facts before us is that the license of the patent and the lease of the buildings given to the taxpayer left "untouched in all practical reality the husband-donor's effective dominion and control over the properties in question." But whatever control the taxpayer received was the control of a licensee and lessee and was conditioned upon making the payments here claimed to be deductible. It would seem erroneous, therefore, to deny the claimed deduction on this basis.

One other point warrants brief mention. My brothers apparently think that the taxpayer is no longer entitled to any rent deduction because, presumably, he could have used the money he gave his wife to buy the building himself and then he would have had no rent to pay. If he had done so, no doubt he would have been allowed as deductions the maintenance costs, taxes, etc., which must have been included in the rent he paid his wife to make it reasonable over all but the effect of this decision may deprive him of even them. I cannot help but think that my brothers have mistakenly applied the business purpose rule of cases like Gregory v. Helvering, 293 U.S. 465, 55 S.Ct. 266, 79 L.Ed. 596, to a situation where what the taxpayer did was merely to use permissible business judgment as to whether he would increase his business investment or continue to pay reasonable rent.

I would reverse and remand for a judgment for the appellant.

NOTE

A thoughtful student when he reads *White v. Fitzpatrick* will see, not an isolated business deduction issue, but a new facet of the assignment of income problem to which attention is directed principally in Chapters 13 and 14. Income may be fragmented among an intimate group as much by way of deductible payments that are taxable to the recipients as by more direct devices suggested by the familiar *Earl, Horst*, and *Clifford* cases. The analogy is so pat that one might confidently expect like administrative, judicial, and legislative attacks on the problem. In contrast, however,[1] Congress has been relatively inactive in the deduction sector, which has encouraged an aggressive posture by the Commissioner; and some courts at least have been led far afield by a spurious but aromatic red herring.[2]

to be relevant to this issue, and to hold as the majority does, it would seem that one must accept the premise that a donor who retains sufficient control over property transferred by him so as to make any income from that property includible in the donor's gross income under Sec. 22(a), is not, as a matter of law, "required" to pay the donee for its use even though he has entered into a firm,

and legally enforceable, obligation so to do.

1. Compare, e. g., I.R.C. §§ 671–678 and 704(e), dealing with income assignment, with § 267(a)(2), mildly restraining deduction for some intrafamily payments.

2. E. g., Mathews v. Comm'r, 520 F.2d 323 (5th Cir. 1975), reflecting one court's enchantment with a questionable "business purpose" doctrine.

In the typical or at least *early* typical case,[3] where a plan was prepared to yield maximum tax benefits, possibly though with a high risk of failure, a doctor, say, would transfer his office and equipment to a trust under which Doctor was trustee for his child as the income beneficiary and provide for a reversion to Doctor in 122 months,[4] carefully avoiding also any control or other arrangement that would offend the grantor trust sections. The trust as owner would then lease office and equipment to Doctor for its fair rental value. As rent was paid it would be distributed to and taxed to Child, with the usual attending deduction for the trust.[5] Meanwhile, Doctor would claim a § 162(a)(3) deduction for rent. Abstractly, the matter would look like this:

BEFORE

Doctor: Income, $40,000 (Ignoring depreciation deductions).

AFTER

Doctor		Trust		Child	
Income	$40,000	Income	$10,000		
Rent	–10,000	Distribution			
Income		Deduction	–10,000	Income	$10,000
Taxed	$30,000	Income			
		Taxed	–0–		

With $10,000 peeled off the top of Doctor's income, escaping tax to the trust by way of I.R.C. §§ 651 or 661, and subjected to lower rates as income of Child, the scene would be:

Doctor: Taxable Income, $30,000. *Child*: Taxable Income, $10,000.[6]

The viability of this type of arrangement should be tested against the rules, statutory and now quite specific, for more direct income assignment through the use of trusts[7] or under the *Horst* doctrine which addresses directly the taxation of income from property.[8]

---

3. See VanZandt v. Comm'r, 341 F.2d 440 (5th Cir. 1965), cert. denied 382 U.S. 814.

4. See I.R.C. § 673.

5. I.R.C. §§ 651 and 652, 661 and 662.

6. In the typical case, Child's taxable income will be reduced by deprecia- tion deductions on the trust property which would have been available to Doctor if the trust had not been created. I.R.C. § 167(a) and (h).

7. I.R.C. §§ 671–678.

8. Cf., I.R.C. § 704(e).

Of course, taxation is properly interested in things only as they *are*, not as they *seem*. Consequently, an alleged transfer and leaseback that lacked reality, possibly shown to be a sham by unrealistic rental payments, could properly be disregarded merely by refusing to exalt form over substance.[9] But assuming that all *t*'s are crossed and all *i*'s dotted, and that judicial supervision of a trustee under local law assures regularity, it is difficult to see from a policy point of view why the asserted rental deduction is vulnerable. At present, however, results in this area are not uniform.[10]

It seems that the major difficulties stem from a failure to recognize that it is the owner of property who should be taxed on the income from the property. Sham transactions should always be disregarded. But if one effectively transfers ownership of his property to another, the other becomes the taxpayer on the property's income. This is what makes relevant in this case the preoccupation in the trust, partnership and corporate area with determination of ownership for tax purposes. The trust rules are most elaborate and should control when a trust is involved.[11] Partnership provisions recognize that an interest carrying income sharing rights in a partnership, where capital is a substantial income-producing factor, may arise by gift;[12] but the regulations caution against purported transfers of interests which lack reality.[13] And although no *Clifford* trust or family partnership doctrine has developed formally in the corporate area, assignments of interests in corporate businesses which are mere sham and lack substance are not accorded recognition.[14]

Assuming that a *real* ownership interest is created in another of property that a taxpayer uses in his business, payment of fair rental for his use of the property should accord the taxpayer a business deduction under I.R.C. § 162. Only one respectable question can be raised about this conclusion. Section 162 permits the deduction of "necessary" expenses: Is an expense unnecessary if it arises only because the taxpayer gives away (directly or to a trust) or sells[15] the property to one to whom it must *then* pay rent for its use.

In *Mathews*,[16] fusing the gift and the lease agreement, the Fifth Circuit has found a lack of necessity for the rental payments in the

---

9. Kirschenmann v. Westover, 255 F.2d 69 (9th Cir. 1955), cert. denied 350 U.S. 834 (1955); and cf. Armston Co. v. Comm'r, 188 F.2d 531 (5th Cir. 1951).

10. Compare Brooke v. U. S., 468 F.2d 1155 (9th Cir. 1972), allowing the deduction, with Mathews v. Comm'r (reversing T.C.) 520 F.2d 323 (5th Cir. 1975), deduction disallowed.

11. I.R.C. §§ 671–678 are given some consideration in Chapter 14.

12. I.R.C. § 704(e).

13. Reg. § 1.704–1(e)(2)(i)–(iii).

14. E. g., Overton v. Comm'r, 162 F.2d 155 (2d Cir. 1947).

15. See Sun Oil Company, 35 T.C.M. 173 (1976).

16. Supra note 2; accord, Perry v. U. S., 520 F.2d 235 (4th Cir. 1975).

absence of any "business purpose" for the arrangement.[17]　Other courts, viewing the gift and the rental agreement as separate transactions have been willing to find the requisite necessity for the rental payment after the property in question has been placed in the hands of a trustee for the benefit of others.[18]　Whether the unified or separate view is more appropriate seems a better question for Congress than for the courts.　Nevertheless, as there are several clear ways to skin this very cat and apt analogies regarding the treatment of *income* from property that has been the subject of a gift, it seems the unified view of the Fifth Circuit should be rejected and the deduction more freely allowed.　It would be well for Congress to so specify along the lines of the language in § 704(e).

Within the history of this litigious area are distinctions based on whether (1) more property was transferred than was leased back by the taxpayer, (2) the transferor retained a reversionary interest or, when a trust was used, put the remainder in others, (3) whether, when the transfer was in trust, the trustee was independent and (4) whether the transferor-lessee had an equity interest in the property.[19] There is no agreement, however, on the effect of these various factors and they might all well be regarded as irrelevant.

One may validly make a direct gift of property to a relative and thereafter lease it from him, paying deductible rent.　One may also effectively transfer the income from property to another who will be taxed on it, if he does it by giving the other person a trust interest that does not run afoul of the grantor trust provisions.　Other income splitting possibilities arise through the use of partnerships and corporations, as seen in Chapter 14.　All these possibilities are within the teachings of the *Horst* case, as embellished in some instances by statute.　Consequently, one may well ask: What's the big deal about some similar income splitting by way of deductions?　Clearly Congress should answer this question but, until it does, controversy should be resolved with a clear view of the analogy between the income and deduction areas.

17.　Accord, Frank L. Butler, 65 T.C. 327 (1975), denying the rental deduction, but under the *Golsen* principle requiring the court merely to analyze and apply the teachings of the Fifth Circuit; contra, Albert T. Felix, 21 T.C. 794 (1954).

18.　E. g. Skemp v. Comm'r, 168 F.2d 598 (7th Cir. 1948); Brown v. Comm'r, 180 F.2d 926 (3rd Cir. 1950).

19.　This last issue rests on the express statutory proscription that a lessee who would claim a deduction for rent may do so only with respect to property "in which he has no equity." I.R.C. § 162(a)(3).　Although there is some authority for the notion that a reversionary interest may be an "equity", e. g. dictum in Alden B. Oaks, 44 T.C. 524, 531 (1965), the phrase is properly applied only in cases such as Estate of Starr v. Comm'r supra page 383, in which it is uncertain whether one making payments for the use of property is paying deductible rent or is purchasing the property.

One final point should be made. The *Clifford* or Grantor Trust area of the statute is fairly well worked out to answer related questions. When its provisions bite in, § 671 treats the grantor as the *owner* of the property involved. The expressed consequence is to tax him on the income from the trust property and to allow him deductions otherwise available to the trust. The income beneficiary is treated as receiving amounts free of tax by way of the gift exclusion.[20] Thus, a trust grantor taxed on income under the grantor trust provisions is entitled to depreciation on the trust property. It is fairly clear that in cases such as *Mathews* [21] the Commissioner will not seek to tax the trust beneficiary when the grantor's rental deduction is denied.[22] It seems clear too that, if the transferor-lessee is to be treated as owner under Rev.Rul. 54–9,[23] it is he who will be entitled to depreciation and maintenance expense deductions for the property,[24] which is only fair.[25]

---

4. EXPENSES FOR EDUCATION *

Internal Revenue Code: Sections 162(a); 262.
Regulations: Section 1.162–5.

INTRODUCTION

There are two cases presented in this segment, *Hill* and *Coughlin*. They were decided by the Fourth Circuit and the Second Circuit in 1950 and 1953, respectively. Each seems to clash with a dictum in Justice Cardozo's 1933 opinion in *Welch v. Helvering*, set out above at page 344:

> [A] man conceives the notion that he will be able to practice his vocation with greater ease and profit if he has an opportunity to enrich his culture. Forthwith the price of his education becomes [the Justice is being facetious] an ex-

---

20. See § 102(a) and the negative inference of § 102(b).

21. Supra note 2.

22. See Rev.Rul. 54–9, 1954–1 C.B. 20; and cf. Rev.Rul. 57–315, 1957–2 C.B. 624 which, while specifically addressed to gift tax liability and modifying the earlier ruling in this respect, leaves intact the income tax rulings of Rev. Rul. 54–9.

23. See note 22, supra.

24. Cf. Lyon Co. v. U. S., 536 F.2d 746 (8th Cir. 1976).

25. The authors have had the use of a research paper prepared by Peter J. Losavio, Jr., an LL.M. student at the University of Florida, in the writing of this Note. His thoughts were helpful; responsibility for comments appearing here, however, is assumed by the authors.

* See McNulty, "Tax Policy and Tuition Credit Legislation: Federal Income Tax Allowances for Personal Costs of Higher Education," 61 Calif.L.Rev. 1 (1973).

pense of the business, reducing the income subject to taxation.

The clash is apparent only, and *Hill* and *Coughlin* can now be found in distilled form as paragraphs (1) and (2) (but in reverse order) of Reg. § 1.162–5(a), an affirmative general rule on the deductibility of expenses for education.

The two basic concepts expressed in the general rule of the regulations are fairly simple and forthright and answer a great many questions. Even so, nice distinctions have been drawn in numerous circumstances: How do we decide whether an Internal Revenue Agent should be allowed to deduct the expenses he incurs in obtaining a law degree? [1]

Recent developments have made the area one of greater concern to lawyers with respect to their own personal tax liability not just that of their clients. Some states are now requiring continuing education for the bar. Others are permitting specialty designation by lawyers who can establish expertise in various areas of the law, either by way of experience or education.[2] As more lawyers will be getting more formal education and spending more for it, and as similar developments are taking place in other disciplines, the importance of studying the tax aspects of education expenses is obvious.

HILL v. COMMISSIONER

United States Court of Appeals, Fourth Circuit, 1950.
181 F.2d 906.

DOBIE, CIRCUIT JUDGE. This is an appeal by Nora Payne Hill (hereinafter called taxpayer) from a decision of the Tax Court of the United States entered on September 7, 1949, affirming a determination of the Commissioner of Internal Revenue that there is a deficiency in the income tax due by taxpayer in the amount of $57.52 for the calendar year 1945.

During the taxable year and for twenty-seven years prior thereto, taxpayer was engaged in the business of teaching school in the State of Virginia. During the taxable year in question, she attended summer school at Columbia University in New York City, for which she incurred expenses in an amount of $239.50, which she deducted in computing her net income on her federal income tax return for the year 1945. These expenses were disallowed upon the grounds that

1. See Melnik v. U. S., 521 F.2d 1065 (9th Cir. 1975), cert. requested by taxpayer.

2. See Kalb and Roberts, "The Deductibility of Post-graduate Legal Education Expenses," 27 U.Fla.L.Rev. 995 (1975), written in partial satisfaction of requirements for the LL.M. degree at the University of Florida and Mock "Deductibility of Educational Expenses for Full Time Graduate Study," 25 Okla.L.R. 582 (1972).

they were personal expenses and were not deductible for federal income tax purposes. The only question for decision by us is: Was the taxpayer correct in deducting those expenses as ordinary and necessary expenses incurred in carrying on her trade or business? We think this question must be answered in the affirmative. The reasonableness of the amount of these expenses is not disputed.

* * *

[The Court quotes here I.R.C. (1939) §§ 23(a)(1)(A), 23(a)(2) and 24(a)(1) which for purposes of this case are essentially the same as I.R.C. (1954) § 162(a), concerning trade or business expenses, § 212, concurring expenses for the production of income, and § 262, disallowing any deduction for personal expenses. Ed.]

The pertinent provisions of the Virginia Code Annotated, 1942, applicable to the issues before us, are as follows:

Title 11, Chapter 33, Section 660

* * * No teacher shall be employed or paid from the public funds unless such teacher holds a certificate in full force in accordance with the rules of certification laid down by the State Board of Education, provided, that, where a teacher holding a certificate in force is not available, a former teacher holding an expired certificate may be employed temporarily as a substitute teacher to meet an emergency * * *.

Title 11, Chapter 35, Section 786(b)(3)

* * * provided, that no school board shall employ or pay any teacher from the public funds unless the teacher shall hold a certificate in full force, according to the provisions of section six hundred and sixty of the laws relating to the public free schools in counties; * * *.

The Regulations Governing the Certification of Teachers and the Qualifications of Administrators and Supervisors in Virginia required for the renewal of a teacher's certificate that taxpayer present evidence that she had been a successful teacher, had read at least five books on the Teachers' Reading Course during the life of her certificate and also must either (a) present evidence of college credits in professional or academic subjects earned during the life of the certificate or (b) pass an examination on five books selected by the State Department of Education from the Teachers' Reading Course for the year in which her license expired.

In 1945, taxpayer was head of the Department of English and a teacher of English and Journalism at the George Washington High School in Danville, Virginia. A Master of Arts of Columbia University, she held the Collegiate Professional Certificate, the highest certificate issued to public school teachers by the Virginia State Board of Education. She was notified of the expiration of her certificate and that the certificate could not be renewed unless she complied with the Regulations set out above.

The alternatives required for the renewal of taxpayer's certificate were: (a) acquiring college credits or (b) passing an examination on five selected books. She elected (a) and attended the Summer School of Columbia University. We hardly think it open to question that she chose the alternative which would most effectively add to her efficiency as a teacher. At Columbia she took two courses: one on the technique of short story writing, which was right in her alley; another in abnormal psychology, which would be most useful to a teacher whose pupils were adolescents.

It is clear that to be deductible as a business expense the item must be—(a) "paid or incurred" within the taxable year; (b) incurred in carrying on a "trade or business"; and (c) both "ordinary and necessary." As a corollary, the expenses must not be personal in their nature. We think taxpayer has completely satisfied all these requisites, so that the decision of the Tax Court must be reversed.

In its opinion, the Tax Court stated:

> We cannot assume that public school teachers *ordinarily* attend summer school to renew their certificates when alternative methods are available. The record does not show that the course pursued by petitioner was the usual method followed by teachers in obtaining renewals of their certificates or that it was necessary so to do. * * *

> The record is devoid of any showing that petitioner was employed to continue in her position as teacher at the time she attended summer school in 1945 and made the expenditures in connection therewith for which she seeks a deduction. The inference may well be that she took the summer course to obtain a renewal of her certificate that would qualify her for reemployment. The expense incurred was more in the nature of a preparation to qualify her for teaching in the High School in Danville, Virginia.

> Also, in support of its decision, the Tax Court quoted O.D. 892, 4 C.B. 209 (1921): "The expenses incurred by school-teachers in attending summer school are in the nature of personal expenses incurred in advancing their education and are not deductible in computing net income.

As to the first of these statements, we think it is quite unreasonable to require a statistical showing by taxpayer of the comparative number of Virginia teachers who elect, for a renewal of their certificates, the acquisition of college credits rather than the much less desirable alternative of standing an examination on the five selected books. The existence of two methods for the renewal of these certificates, one or the other of which is compulsory, is not in itself vital in this connection. If the particular course adopted by the taxpayer is a response that a reasonable person would normally and naturally make under the specific circumstances, that would suffice. Even if a statistical study actually revealed that a majority of Virginia teachers adopted the examination on the selected books, in order to renew their certificates, rather than the method of acquiring college credits, our conclusion here would be the same. Manifestly, the added expense of attending a summer school, in the light of the slender salaries paid to teachers, would deter many teachers from such a course, however strong might be their predilections in favor of such a procedure. We note that the statistical requirement does not seem to have been enforced in the cases subsequently cited in this opinion—cases, we think, far less meritorious than the one before us.

Nor do we approve the reasoning of the Tax Court that the taxpayer's failure to show by positive evidence that she was employed to continue in her position as teacher when she incurred the summer school expenses should negative the deduction of these expenses. She did prove to the Tax Court that she had been continuously so engaged for consecutive decades. She had not resigned her position and no practical advantage would accrue to her upon a renewal of her certificate other than the privilege and power to continue as a teacher. Clearly, the very logic of the situation here shows that she went to Columbia to maintain her present position, not to attain a new position; to preserve, not to expand or increase; to carry on, not to commence. Any other view seems to us unreal and hypercritical. And taxpayer, in her petition to the Tax Court for a review of its decision, showed conclusively that when she went to Columbia University in the summer of 1945, she was then under contract with the Danville School Board to teach for the ensuing session of 1945–1946 and that to carry out this existing contract, she was obligated to renew her certificate by complying with the pertinent regulations.

* * *

Dictionary definitions of the words "ordinary," "necessary," and "personal" afford scant assistance in the solution of our problem. Quite helpful, though, are the opinions in the decided cases. Frequently quoted is the observation of Mr. Justice Cardozo, in Welch v. Helvering, 290 U.S. 111, 113, 54 S.Ct. 8, 9, 78 L.Ed. 212: "Now, what is ordinary, though there must always be a strain of constancy within it, is none the less a variable affected by time and place and circumstance. Ordinary in this context does not mean that the payments must be habitual or normal in the sense that the same taxpayer will have to make them often. A lawsuit affecting the safety of a business may happen once in a lifetime. The counsel fees may be so heavy that repetition is unlikely. None the less, the expense is an ordinary one because we know from experience that payments for such a purpose, whether the amount is large or small, are the common and accepted means of defense against attack. Cf. Kornhauser v.

United States, 276 U.S. 145, 48 S.Ct. 219, 72 L.Ed. 505. The situation is unique in the life of the individual affected, but not in the life of the group, the community, of which he is a part. At such times there are norms of conduct that help to stabilize our judgment, and make it certain and objective. The instance is not erratic, but is brought within a known type."

* * *

Said Mr. Justice Douglas, in Deputy v. Du Pont, 308 U.S. 488, 496, 60 S.Ct. 363, 367, 84 L.Ed. 416: "One of the extremely relevant circumstances is the nature and scope of the particular business out of which the expense in question accrued. The fact that an obligation to pay has arisen is not sufficient. It is the kind of transaction out of which the obligation arose and its *normalcy in the particular business* which are crucial and controlling." (Italics ours.)

* * *

We quote a trenchant critique on the decision of the Tax Court from Maguire, Individual Federal Income Tax in 1950, 35 American Association of University Professors Bulletin, 748, 762: "As to the matters just discussed, Nora P. Hill, 13 T.C. [291] No. 41 (1949), is an interesting decision, if scarcely an encouragement. The taxpayer, a Virginia public school teacher, sought to deduct as an ordinary and necessary business expense for 1945 the cost of attending summer courses in Columbia University. Her teaching certificate, the highest granted by the State Board of Education, came up for renewal in 1945. Virginia law required for renewal of teaching certificates either the taking of professional or academic courses for credit or the passing of examinations on prescribed reading. The Tax Court denied the claim of deduction. Part of its reasoning was that because the Virginia legal requirements might be satisfied by pursuing either of the two alternatives, the showing was insufficient that what the taxpayer had done was the ordinary method of satisfaction. Another part of the reasoning was that the taxpayer had not explicitly shown she was employed to continue as a teacher at the time she took the summer school courses. Hence, said the Court, it might be inferred that the taxpayer was seeking to qualify for reemployment as distinguished from merely maintaining an employed status. While these views seem hypercritical and are an invitation to the same teacher or another teacher to try again with more carefully detailed proof, the tone of the opinion hints at strong distaste for this sort of deduction."

Our conclusion is that the expenses incurred by the taxpayer here were incurred in carrying on a trade or business, were ordinary and necessary, and were not personal in nature. She has, we think, showed that she has complied with both the letter and the spirit of the law which permits such expenses to be deducted for federal income tax purposes. We do not hold (and it is not necessary for us to hold) that all expenses incurred by teachers in attending summer schools are deductible. Our decision is limited to the facts of the case before us. The decision of the Tax Court of the United States is, accordingly, reversed and the case is remanded to that Court with instructions to allow taxpayer as a deduction the expenses which she claims.

Reversed.

COUGHLIN v. COMMISSIONER *

United States Court of Appeals, Second Circuit, 1953.
203 F.2d 307.

CHASE, CIRCUIT JUDGE. The petitioner has been a member of the bar for many years and in 1944 was admitted to practice before the Treasury Department. In 1946 he was in active practice in Binghamton, N. Y., as a member of a firm of lawyers there. The firm engaged in general practice but did considerable work which required at least one member to be skilled in matters pertaining to Federal taxation and to maintain such skill by keeping informed as to changes in the tax laws and the significance of pertinent court decisions when made. His partners relied on him to keep advised on that subject and he accepted that responsibility. One of the various ways in which he discharged it was by attending, in the above mentioned year, the Fifth Annual Institute on Federal Taxation which was conducted in New York City under the sponsorship of the Division of General Education of New York University. In so doing he incurred expenses for tuition, travel, board and lodging of $305, which he claimed as an allowable deduction under section 23(a) (1) (A) I.R.C., as ordinary and necessary expenses incurred in carrying on a trade or business and no question is raised as to their reasonableness in amount. The Commission[er] disallowed the deduction and the Tax Court, four judges dissenting, upheld the disallowance on the ground that the expenses were non-business ones "because of the educational and personal nature of the object pursued by the petitioner."

The Tax Court found that the Institute on Federal Taxation was not conducted for the benefit of those unversed in the subject Federal taxation and students were warned away. In 1946, it was attended by 408 attorneys, accountants, trust officers, executives of corporations and the like. In 1947, over 1500 of such people from many states were in attendance. It was "designed by its sponsors to provide a place and atmosphere where practitioners could gather trends, thinking and developments in the field of Federal taxation from experts accomplished in that field."

Thus there is posed for solution a problem which involves no dispute as to the basic facts but is, indeed, baffling because, as is so

---

* See Niswander, "Tax Aspects of Education: When Ordinary and Necessary; When Personal," 26 N.Y.U.Inst. on Fed.Tax. 27 (1968). Ed.

often true of legal problems, the correct result depends upon how to give the facts the right order of importance.

We may start by noticing that the petitioner does not rely upon section 23(a) (2) which permits the deduction of certain non-trade or non-business expenses, but rests entirely upon his contention that the deduction he took was allowable as an ordinary and necessary expense incurred in the practice of his profession. The expenses were deductible under section 23(a) (1) (A) if they were "directly connected with" or "proximately resulted from" the practice of his profession. Kornhauser v. United States, 276 U.S. 145, 153, 48 S.Ct. 219, 220, 72 L.Ed. 505. And if it were usual for lawyers in practice similar to his to incur such expenses they were "ordinary." Deputy v. DuPont, 308 U.S. 488, 495, 60 S.Ct. 363, 84 L.Ed. 416. They were also "necessary" if appropriate and helpful. Welch v. Helvering, 290 U.S. 111, 54 S.Ct. 8, 78 L.Ed. 212. But this is an instance emphasizing how dim a line is drawn between expenses which are deductible because incurred in trade or business, i. e., because professional, and those which are non-deductible because personal. Section 24(a) (1) of Title 26.

The respondent relies upon T.R. 111, § 29.23(a)–15, which provides that "expenses of taking special courses or training" are not allowable as deductions under section 23(a) (2). But section 23(a) (2) concerns non-trade or non-business expenses. It is not necessary to decide whether, in the light of the regulation, an expense of the nature here involved would be deductible if incurred in connection with a profit-making venture that is not a trade or business. It will suffice to say that, since the expense was incurred in a trade or business within the meaning of section 23(a) (1) (A), the regulation interpreting section 23(a) (2) is not a bar to allowance here.

In Welch v. Helvering, supra 290 U.S. at page 115, 54 S.Ct. at page 9, there is a dictum that the cost of acquiring learning is a personal expense. But the issue decided in that case is far removed from the one involved here. There the taxpayer paid debts for which he was not legally liable whose payment enhanced his reputation for personal integrity and consequently the value of the good will of his business, and it was held that these payments were personal expenses. The general reference to the cost of education as a personal expense was made by way of illustrating the point then under decision, and it related to that knowledge which is obtained for its own sake as an addition to one's cultural background or for possible use in some work which might be started in the future. There was no indication that an exception is not to be made where the information acquired was needed for use in a lawyer's established practice.

T.R. 111, § 29.23(a)–5, makes clear that among the expenses which a professional man may deduct under Section 23(a) (1) (A) are dues to professional societies, subscriptions to professional journals, and amounts currently expended for books whose useful life is

short. Such expenses as are here in question are not expressly included or excluded, but they are analogous to those above stated which
are expressly characterized as allowable deductions.

This situation is closely akin to that in Hill v. Commissioner, 4
Cir., 181 F.2d 906, where the expenses incurred by a teacher in attending a summer school were held deductible. The only difference is in
the degree of necessity which prompted the incurrence of the expenses.
The teacher couldn't retain her position unless she complied with the
requirements for the renewal of her teaching certificate; and an
optional way to do that, and the one she chose, was to take courses in
education at a recognized institution of learning. Here the petitioner
did not need a renewal of his license to practice and it may be assumed
that he could have continued as a member of his firm whether or not
he kept currently informed as to the law of Federal taxation. But
he was morally bound to keep so informed and did so in part by means
of his attendance at this session of the Institute. It was a way well
adapted to fulfill his professional duty to keep sharp the tools he
actually used in his going trade or business. It may be that the
knowledge he thus gained incidentally increased his fund of learning
in general and, in that sense, the cost of acquiring it may have been a
personal expense; but we think that the immediate, over-all professional need to incur the expenses in order to perform his work with
due regard to the current status of the law so overshadows the personal aspect that it is the decisive feature.

It serves also to distinguish these expenditures from those made
to acquire a capital asset. Even if in its cultural aspect knowledge
should for tax purposes be considered in the nature of a capital asset
as was suggested in Welch v. Helvering, supra, the rather evanescent
character of that for which the petitioner spent his money deprives
it of the sort of permanency such a concept embraces.

Decision reversed and cause remanded for the allowance of the
deduction.

PROBLEMS

1. Alice, Barbara, Cathy, and Denise were college roommates
who after graduating in 1970 went on to become a doctor, a dentist, an
accountant (C.P.A.), and a lawyer, respectively. In 1977, after some
time in practice as an orthopedic surgeon, Alice, who was often called
upon to give medical testimony in malpractice suits, decided to go to
law school so as to better understand this aspect of her medical practice. Barbara enrolled in a course of postgraduate study in ortho-
dontics, intending to restrict her dental practice to that specialty in
the future. Cathy enrolled parttime in law school (with eventual
prospects of attaining a degree) so as better to perform her accounting duties in areas in which law and accounting tend to overlap. And
Denise took a leave of absence from her firm to enroll in an LL.M.

course in taxation, intending to practice exclusively in the tax area. Which, if any, is incurring deductible expenses of education?

2.   Don, Ben, and Carl were college roommates and each earned a bachelor's degree in education in 1970. Don took a position as a first grade teacher, teaching the usual subjects: reading, writing, arithmetic, science, and social studies. Ben became a high school Latin teacher. Carl undertook the teaching of romance languages, especially Spanish and French, in a junior high school. In 1977 they contemplate a summer European tour together and in planning it each wishes to do things that will be beneficial to his teaching efforts. Each also wishes to know the possibility that his expenses will be deductible. What can we say?

D.   MISCELLANEOUS BUSINESS DEDUCTIONS

1.   INTRODUCTION

Internal Revenue Code: Sections 162(a); 274(a), (d), (e). See Sections 162(b); 274(b), (c); 276.
Regulations: Section 1.162–14. See Sections 1.162–20; 1.274–2(a), (c), (d).

The three business expense deductions listed in paragraphs (1) through (3) of I.R.C. (26 U.S.C.A.) § 162(a) are illustrative only and by no means exclusive. The statute specifically states that *all* ordinary and necessary business expenses are deductible *including* those specifically listed, and it is similar in that regard to I.R.C. (26 U.S. C.A.) § 61.[1] It would be impossible to list every conceivable type of deduction within the section, especially since the test varies among different businesses. This note will, however, attempt to highlight some of the more important business expense deductions.

Entertainment. Entertainment expenses may be deductible. Waiters often overhear someone say: "Have another—it's deductible!" or "Don't worry, I can write it off on my income tax!" Certainly entertainment is an accepted practice and expense in carrying on many businesses. But when such expenses fall within I.R.C. (26 U.S. C.A.) § 162(a) are there not obvious possibilities for abuse? Prior to 1962 there were few restrictions on the deductibility of entertainment expenses, either as to the scope of items which were considered within

1. On the Code meaning of "including," see I.R.C. (26 U.S.C.A.) § 7701 (b).

permissible entertainment or as to the amount of proof or substantiation of expenses incurred. The question of substantiation was raised in the case of Cohan v. Comm'r,[2] in which the actor, George M. Cohan, attempted to deduct large unsubstantiated travel and entertainment expenses. The Second Circuit instructed that in such cases the trial court should approximate the expenses stating:[3]

"In the production of his plays Cohan was obliged to be freehanded in entertaining actors, employees, and, as he naively adds dramatic critics. He had also to travel much, at times with his attorney. These expenses amounted to substantial sums but he kept no account and probably could not have done so. At the trial before the Board [Tax Court] he estimated that he had spent eleven thousand dollars in this fashion during the six months of 1921, twenty-two thousand dollars, between July 1, 1921 and June 30, 1922, and as much for his following fiscal year, fifty five thousand dollars in all. The Board refused to allow him any part of this, on the ground that it was impossible to tell how much he had in fact spent, in the absence of any items or details. The question is how far this refusal is justified, in view of the finding that he had spent much and that the sums were allowable expenses. Absolute certainty in such matters is usually impossible and is not necessary; the Board should make as close an approximation as it can, bearing heavily if it chooses upon the taxpayer whose inexactitude is of his own making. But to allow nothing at all appears to us inconsistent with saying that something was spent. True, we do not know how many trips Cohan made, nor how large his entertainments were; yet there was obviously some basis for computation, if necessary by drawing upon the Board's personal estimates of the minimum of such expenses. The amount may be trivial and unsatisfactory, but there was basis for some allowance, and it was wrong to refuse any, even though it were the travelling expenses of a single trip. It is not fatal that the result will inevitably be speculative; many important decisions must be such."

Prior to 1962, the *Cohan* rule was often applied to allow some deduction in the absence of proof.[4] A fairly easy attitude on the scope of deductions for entertainment and the fluidity of the *Cohan* rule caused many to wonder whether, by way of "business" deductions, taxpayers generally were being called upon to pay for the enjoyments of a relatively select few in the business community. The limiting concepts of "ordinary" and "necessary" under I.R.C. (26 U.S.C.A.) § 162 (a) and I.R.C. (26 U.S.C.A.) § 262 seemed not to do the job.[5]

2. 39 F.2d 540 (2d Cir. 1930).

3. Id. at 543–544.

4. See James Schulz, 16 T.C. 401 (1951); Harold A. Christensen, 17 T. C. 1456 (1952); Richard A. Sutter, 21 T.C. 170 (1953).

5. See Caplan, "The Travel and Entertainment Expense Problem," 30 Taxes 947 (1961).

In 1962, Congress enacted I.R.C. (26 U.S.C.A.) § 274 in an attempt to muffle the cry: "It's deductible!" The effect of § 274 is to narrow the scope of I.R.C. (26 U.S.C.A.) § 162 with respect to expenses for entertainment, gifts, and travel [6] by imposing some limitations and requiring substantiation.[7] As regards entertainment, one of the principal limitations of I.R.C. (26 U.S.C.A.) § 274 is the requirement that, for expenses related to any entertainment, amusement, or recreational *activity* to be deductible, the activity must be "directly related to" or "associated with" the taxpayer's trade or business.[8] The regulations grapple with these terms.[9] Essentially, the phrase "directly related to" requires an intention by the taxpayer that business go on *during* the entertainment for which an expense deduction is claimed (Sales pitch during the ball game?); and the phrase "associated with" requires that the entertainment be planned with a business purpose in mind, either immediately to precede or follow a bona fide business discussion (Lunch and ball game after office conference?).[10]

One problem with respect to business meals is the deductibility of the taxpayer's own meals and those of his wife. In pure theory, if a taxpayer takes a customer to dinner to talk business and taxpayer's wife goes along the amount that it would have cost husband and wife to eat anyway, is a nondeductible personal expense under I.R.C. § 262. Along this line, in Richard A. Sutter [11] the court sustained the Commissioner's disallowance of a deduction for the taxpayer's own meals at business lunches. However, the Service applies the *Sutter* doctrine "only to abuse cases where taxpayers claim deductions for substantial amounts of personal living expenses." [12] Would it be administratively feasible to apply the *Sutter* doctrine comprehensively? Similarly, the regulations under § 274 allow the taxpayer to deduct his wife's expenses if they are closely connected to the business activity.[13]

I.R.C. (26 U.S.C.A.) § 274(a) (1) (B) aims a direct blow at expenses incurred in connection with *facilities* that are of an entertainment nature, such as yachts, summer houses, and club memberships. In this area, not only must the expenditure be "directly related to" the taxpayer's trade or business, but actual use of the facility must be primarily for business purposes.[14] Even if the "primarily" test is met,

6. I.R.C. (26 U.S.C.A.) § 274 also limits deductions under § 212.

7. I.R.C. (26 U.S.C.A.) § 274(b), limitations on business gifts, and 274(c), limitations on deductibility of foreign travelling expenses, have previously been referred to in Chapters 4 and 15 at pages 87 and 383, respectively.

8. I.R.C. (26 U.S.C.A.) § 274(a) (1) (A).

9. Reg. § 1.274–2(c) and 2(d).

10. Under I.R.C. (26 U.S.C.A.) § 274 (e), various inherently business activities (typical business meals) and expenditures for employees are excepted from the requirements of I.R.C. (26 U.S.C.A.) § 274(a) (1).

11. Supra note 4.

12. Rev.Rul. 63–144, 1963–2 C.B. 129, 135.

13. Reg. § 1.274–2(d) (4).

14. In such instances the regulations prescribe a more than 50% test. Reg.

only the business portion of expenditures is of course deductible. Thus if a businessman belongs to a country club and he uses it 40% of the time for business purposes, he may deduct none of his dues. If he uses it 60% of the time for business purposes, he may deduct only 60% of his dues. We do not speak here, of course, of his total monthly bills; despite the restriction on dues, the full amount paid for business lunches would be deductible (as an activity) without regard to the (facility) "primarily" test.

In addition to classifying some expenses, possibly within I.R.C. (26 U.S.C.A.) § 162, as not deductible at all, subsection (d) of § 274 also imposes substantiation requirements with respect to expenditures that are allowable as deductions.[15] The substantiation requirements apply to travel expenses (both foreign and domestic) including meals and lodging,[16] as well as to expenditures for entertainment and gifts. The regulations under § 274(d),[17] which have received judicial blessing,[18] impose stringent documentation requirements, normally necessitating a receipt for expenditures in excess of $25. Rev.Rul. 63–144,[19] in the form of a detailed list of questions and answers, will aid in the understanding of the overall impact of I.R.C. (26 U.S.C.A.) § 274.[20]

§ 1.274–2(e) (4). It should be noted here that I.R.C. (26 U.S.C.A.) § 274 may thus deny a depreciation deduction under § 167.

15. In the areas affected by I.R.C. (26 U.S.C.A.) § 274 (but only those areas), § 274(d) overrules the long-established *Cohan* rule. With respect to substantiation of deductions not within the scope of § 274, the *Cohan* rule still applies. Ellery W. Newton, 57 T.C. 245 (1971), business use of an automobile other than in a travel status; William H. Green, 31 T.C.M. 592 (1972), wagering losses.

16. See Rev.Rul. 75–169, 1975–1 C.B. 59. See also I.R.C. § 274(h), added by TRA (1976) § 602, sometimes wholly denying deductions for expenses incurred in attending foreign conventions.

17. Reg. § 1.274–5.

18. Sanford v. Comm'r, 412 F.2d 201 (2d Cir. 1969), cert. den. 396 U.S. 841, 90 S.Ct. 104, 24 L.Ed.2d 92 (1970); Robert H. Alter, 50 T.C. 833 (1968); John Robinson, 51 T.C. 520 (1968), aff'd per curiam (this issue) 422 F.2d 873 (9th Cir. 1970). The Fifth Circuit has ruled that each and every element of each expenditure must be adequately substantiated. Dowell v. U. S., 522 F.2d 708 (5th Cir. 1975). There is a comment on the *Sanford* case by Aaron, "Substantiation Requirements for Travel, Entertainment and Gift Expenses," 35 Mo.L.Rev. 70 (1970); and see McNally, "Substantiation of Business Related Entertainment Expenses," 54 Marq.L.Rev. 347 (1971).

19. 1963–2 C.B. 129.

20. For further discussion of I.R.C. (26 U.S.C.A.) § 274, see Graichen, "Effect of T and E Disallowances Upon Employer, and Employee, Officer, Stockholder," 22 N.Y.U.Inst. on Fed. Tax. 843 (1964); Emmanuel and Lipoff, "Travel and Entertainment: The New World of Section 274," 18 Tax L.Rev. 487 (1963); Axelrad, "An Evaluation of the New Rules Relating to the Deductibility of Entertainment, Travel and Gifts: A Critical Look at Section 274," 16 U.S.C. Tax Inst. 345 (1964); Osborn, "Tax Problems of the Attorney and Other Professionals in Connection with Travel and Entertainment . . ." 11 Wake Forest L.Rev. 535 (1975).

Uniforms. Recall from prior consideration of the "carrying on" requirement that an employee is considered to be in a trade or business in his role as an employee.[21] Consequently, he may deduct unreimbursed expenses that he incurs which otherwise meet the I.R.C. (26 U.S.C.A.) § 162 requirements. A common deduction for employees is the cost of obtaining and maintaining their uniforms. Deductions for uniforms are allowed only if "(1) the uniforms are specifically required as a condition of employment and (2) are not of a type adaptable to general or continued usage to the extent that they take the place of ordinary clothing." [22] Thus, policemen, firemen, baseball players, jockeys, etc. may deduct their uniform costs, because their required uniforms are not adaptable to personal use.[23] In one case the Tax Court held that the most advanced styles and fashions which the taxpayer, a fashion coordinator, was required to wear were not suitable for her personal use and hence were deductible.[24] The Treasury takes the position that uniforms of military personnel are for general use and generate no deductions, but recognizes an exception for uniforms of reservists that are worn only occasionally and also for swords, which can hardly be considered available for general use.[25]

Advertising. Generally advertising expenses of a business are deductible in the year in which they are incurred or paid even though the benefits may extend over several years.[26] On the other hand, an expenditure related to advertising can be capital in nature and thus fail to qualify as a § 162 expense. For example, the purchase of a piece of property or the construction of a billboard or advertising sign which lasts several years involve capital expenditures, the latter to be written off by way of depreciation deductions under § 167.[27] Moreover, promotional expenditures that might produce deductible advertising expenses in some lines of endeavor may have to pass the § 274 tests for deductible entertainment expenses if, for example, they are incurred by an attorney the canons of whose profession prohibit advertising.[28] Generally, the cost of advertising in magazines, television, and sports programs is deductible. A limitation is imposed on such advertising if it borders on the area of political contributions. Contributions other than by individuals [29] directly or indirectly to po-

21. Supra page 359.

22. Mim. 6463, 1950–1 C.B. 29.

23. Rev.Ruls. 70–474, 475, and 476, 1970–2 C.B. 35. See also Robert C. Fryer, 33 T.C.M. 403 (1974) where a commercial airline pilot was allowed to deduct the cost of his shoeshines but not the cost of his haircuts.

24. Betsy Lusk Yeomans, 30 T.C. 757 (1958).

25. Reg. § 1.262–1(b)(8).

26. G. G. Ebner, 17 T.C.M. 550 (1958).

27. Cf. Alabama Coca-Cola Bottling Co., 29 T.C.M. 635 (1969).

28. Wm. Andress, Jr., 51 T.C. 863 (1969), aff'd per curiam, 423 F.2d 679 (5th Cir. 1970).

29. Cf. I.R.C. §§ 41 and 218 which provide either a limited credit or deduction for political contributions. See page 536 infra.

litical candidates and political parties are not allowed as deductions.[30] Consequently, to foreclose attempted subterfuge, deduction of the cost of advertising in convention programs or publications of political parties is expressly proscribed.[31]

Dues. In general dues paid to organizations directly related to one's business are deductible under I.R.C. (26 U.S.C.A.) § 162.[32] Thus, attorney's dues paid to the local bar are deductible and an employee's labor union dues are also deductible. Dues, like advertising, must be examined according to the substance of the payment to determine their deductibility. For example, dues to a social, athletic or sporting club are considered amounts paid for an entertainment facility under I.R.C. (26 U.S.C.A.) § 274(a)(1)(B) and must meet the requirements imposed by that section in order to be deductible.[33]

Some payments, such as those for interest and property taxes, which may occur in business, are deductible whether or not business oriented. These are reserved for consideration in Chapter 17.[34]

2. BUSINESS LOSSES

Internal Revenue Code: Section 165(c)(1).

If a transaction or event produces a "loss", the threshold question *whether* the loss may be deductible must always be answered on the basis of the rules in I.R.C. (26 U.S.C.A.) § 165. It is the Code's central switchboard for *all* losses. But statutory restrictions may be encountered elsewhere, and the *manner* in which the taxpayer may make use of loss deductions is the subject of a number of special provisions. The most recent restrictive developments are the subject of comment at the end of this brief note.

Although I.R.C. (26 U.S.C.A.) § 165(a) seems to make all losses deductible,[1] attention is directed to § 165(c). An individual taxpayer can deduct only such losses as are identified there. I.R.C. (26 U.S.

30. I.R.C. (26 U.S.C.A.) § 162(e) and see § 271; Reg. § 1.162–20; and Holzman, "That Advertising Expense Deduction," 40 Taxes 555 (1962).

31. I.R.C. (26 U.S.C.A.) § 276(a)(1). From 1968 through 1974 § 276(c) (now repealed) allowed deductions for advertising in programs at the presidential nominating conventions but only if certain qualifications were met.

32. Some restrictions on this general rule are expressed in Reg. § 1.162–20 (c)(3).

33. Ford S. Worthy, Jr., 62 T.C. 303 (1974).

34. Payments to organizations which may qualify for the charitable deduction under I.R.C. (26 U.S.C.A.) § 170 but for their connection with business are considered in Chapter 23.

1. In general, they are for corporate taxpayers.

C.A.) § 165(c)(1) permits the deduction by an individual of any loss "incurred in a trade or business." As this Chapter is addressed to business deductions, we defer for later consideration other individual losses that may be deducted under § 165(c)(2) or (3), and focus on business losses.[2]

What is a business "loss"?[3] At the outset, it must be stated that only "realized" losses are taken into account. The concept of realization is essentially the same here as in the income area. Just as mere appreciation in the value of property is not income subject to tax, so a mere decline in the value of the property is not a loss than can be deducted. To be deductible, a loss must be evidenced by a closed and completed transaction, such as a sale, or fixed by an identifiable event, such as a fire.[4]

Here are a few examples of deductible business losses. A buys a delivery truck for use in his business and sells it a year later for less than its adjusted basis. B buys a tractor for use on his farm and, when he determines it is completely worn out, abandons it—gives it to the junk man for no consideration. C pays $1000 for an option on a plant to be used in his business, but forfeits the $1000 when he decides not to exercise the option. D buys a Chriscraft which he operates for hire at a resort, but the boat which is not insured is demolished in a storm. The measurement of the loss deduction depends in part on the adjusted basis of the property.[5] Thus, A's loss will be the familiar difference between the amount realized and adjusted basis. In the other three cases the deductible loss will probably be the adjusted basis of the property.[6]

Each of the losses suggested above will ultimately have a direct impact on the taxable income reported by the individual. If the § 165(c) (1) losses incurred in a business during the year, along with its other expenses, exceed its income, the business will be unprofitable and the owner will have an overall business loss for the year.[7] The business loss can be deducted against other types of income on his return such as income from investments, other businesses, or salaries. If he has a business loss and no other income (or if the business loss exceeds his other income) so that the loss cannot be fully utilized to reduce taxable income, he will get the benefit of a net operating loss carryback or carryover to another taxable year.[8]

2. I.R.C. (26 U.S.C.A.) § 165(c) (2) and (3) losses are considered in Chapters 16 and 17, respectively.

3. The question whether the taxpayer is engaged in a "trade or business" is the same here as in I.R.C. (26 U.S.C.A.) § 162(a) (and § 167(a) (1)) and is not further explored at this point.

4. Reg. § 1.165–1(b).

5. I.R.C. (26 U.S.C.A.) § 165(b).

6. See, e. g., Reg. § 1.165–7(b)(1), last sentence.

7. Some gains and losses, even if incurred in a separate identifiable business, must be aggregated with the results of other transactions outside the business. See especially Chapter 21 at pages 640 and 650 and Chapter 22 at page 762.

8. See Chapter 20 at page 631.

Not every closed transaction that involves financial disadvantage qualifies as a loss. The point can be illustrated by some comments on the alternative tax consequences of the demolition of business property. In general, the demolition of a business building on real property is a form of abandonment of the building amounting to an identifiable event which will support a loss deduction in the amount of the unamortized basis of the building.[9] However, the taxpayer's intentions at the time of acquisition of the building demolished, and possibly as regards the reason for ultimate demolition may affect the result. It is settled that, if a building is demolished upon acquisition of the property in accordance with the taxpayer's intention at the time of purchase, no loss deduction is allowed.[10] Instead, the entire purchase price for the property is allocated to the land.[11] The rationale for this rule is as follows. Generally, upon an acquisition of improved realty the basis for land and building is determined by an allocation of a part of the purchase price to each in accordance with their respective values.[12] But, if the taxpayer plans simply to raze the building, its value to him is zero, and any allocation of basis to the building would be inappropriate. Finally, if no basis can be ascribed to the building, there can be no loss upon its demolition.[13] Struggle with the following hypothetical for a minute in light of the above comments, and then check your conclusions against Reg. § 1.165-3(a) (2). Purchaser buys improved property intending to rent the building to Lessee for three years and then, at the end of the lease term, to raze the building and to erect a new one. Consider allocation of the purchase price and the question of loss deduction if the building is razed during or at the end of the three years.

There is substantial authority for the proposition that, if there was no demolition intention at the time of the acquisition of the property, a conventional allocation of basis to land and building (proportionate to relative values) should be made and, upon a later demolition of the building, a loss deduction will be allowed in the amount of the building's unamortized basis.[14] However, there are some decisions to the effect that the loss deduction will not be allowed if, at the time of demolition, the taxpayer's purpose for demolishing the old building is to build a new one in its place.[15] The companion principle is that in such cases the unamortized basis for the old building should be added

9. Other improvements, such as railroad tracks, are treated the same way. Cf. Rev.Rul. 69–62, 1969–1 C.B. 58.

10. Reg. § 1.165–3(a)(1). Time of purchase means the time equitable title passes (signing of a contract) not the later date of transfer of the deed. If an intent to demolish arises between such dates, a demolition loss is allowed. The First National Bank & Trust Co. of Chickasha v. U. S., 462 F.2d 908 (10th Cir. 1972).

11. Ibid.

12. Reg. § 1.167(a)–5.

13. See I.R.C. (26 U.S.C.A.) § 165(b).

14. See, e. g., A. F. McBride, Jr., 50 T.C. 1 (1968), acq., 1969–1 C.B. 21; J. A. Rider, 30 T.C.M. 188 (1971).

15. Commissioner v. Appleby, 123 F.2d 700 (2d Cir. 1941), aff'g 41 B.T.A. 18 (1940), nonacq., 1940–2C.B. 9; Henry Phipps Estate, 5 T.C. 964 (1945), nonacq., 1946–2 C.B. 6.

to the basis for the new building. Except for special equities involved in the case, it is difficult to see any support for these decisions. If a business building becomes an obstacle to a taxpayer's plans, indeed less than valueless to him, and he abandons it, a loss deduction is warranted, and there is no identifiable fiscal alchemy that carries any of the old building's basis into the new.

In cases in which the taxpayer's intention properly bears on the loss deduction an obvious difficulty arises: How can intent be proved? Since direct proof is very difficult, the regulations list a number of objective factors from which inferences may be drawn regarding the taxpayer's intent.[16]

E. RESTRICTIONS ON DEDUCTIONS

1. ARTIFICIAL LOSSES

Internal Revenue Code: Sections 165; 183. See Section 465.

In 1975 and 1976 there was a lion-like roar in Congress to impose "limitations on artificial losses," LAL. However, the Tax Reform Act produced only a mouse-like squeak. A principal provision that was enacted is severely limited in scope. The Staff of the Joint Committee on Internal Revenue Taxation summarizes new I.R.C. § 465 [1] as follows:

> Under prior law, the only general restriction on the amount of losses a taxpayer could claim from any investment activity was that losses were limited to the taxpayer's cost or other basis in the activity. A taxpayer's basis in an investment activity includes not only his actual cash investment and liabilities he is obligated to pay but also nonrecourse liabilities of the activity for which he has no payment obligation. The taxpayer's actual risk of economic loss might also be further limited by other contractual arrangements (such as guarantees or repurchase agreements). As a result, in many situations, a taxpayer could deduct losses which substantially exceeded the amount he was actually "at risk" in an activity.

16. Reg. § 1.165–3(c). The demolition regulations are discussed in Knight, "New Regulations on Demolition Losses Formalize the Critical Intent Test," 12 J.Tax. 218 (1960); see also Chace, "Tax Problems in Demolition,

Retirement and Abandonment of Property," 13 U.S.C. Tax Inst. 63 (1961).

1. The new section was added by TRA (1976) § 204.

The Act provides that the amount of any loss (otherwise allowable for the year) which may be deducted in connection with any one of certain activities cannot exceed the aggregate amount with respect to which the taxpayer is at risk in each such activity at the close of the taxable year. This "at risk" limitation applied to the following activities: (1) farming (except farming operations involving trees other than fruit or nut trees); (2) exploring for, or exploiting, oil and gas resources; (3) holding, producing, or distributing motion picture films or video tapes; and (4) equipment leasing. The limitation applies to all taxpayers (other than corporations which are not subchapter S corporations or personal holding companies) including individuals and sole proprietorships, estates, trusts, shareholders in subchapter S corporations, and partners in a partnership which conducts an activity described in this provision.[2]

Under this provision, a taxpayer is generally to be considered "at risk" with respect to an activity to the extent of his cash and the adjusted basis of other property contributed to the activity, any amounts borrowed for use in the activity with respect to which the taxpayer has personal liability for payment from his personal assets, and his net fair market value of personal assets which secure nonrecourse borrowings. However, a taxpayer is not at risk in an activity, even as to the equity capital he has contributed, to the extent he is protected against economic loss of all or a part of his equity capital by reason of an agreement or arrangement for compensation or reimbursement to him of any loss which he may suffer.

In general, the at risk provision applies to losses attributable to amounts paid or incurred (and depreciation or amortization allowed or allowable) in taxable years beginning after December 31, 1975.

* * *

In applying the at risk provisions to activities which were begun in taxable years beginning before January 1, 1976 (and not exempted from this provision by the [omitted] transition rules), amounts paid or incurred in taxable years beginning prior to that date and deducted in such taxable years will generally be treated as reducing first that portion of the taxpayer's basis which is attributable to amounts not at risk. (On the other hand, withdrawals made in taxable

---

2. This provision will not apply, for example, to corporations (other than subchapter S corporations and personal holding companies) either where such taxpayers engage in these activities by themselves, with other such corporations through a partnership, or with other taxpayers which are subject to this at risk limitation.

years beginning before January 1, 1976, will be treated as reducing the amount which the taxpayer is at risk.)

So-called "Hobby Losses" have had earlier attention by Congress. A relatively unworkable provision [3] that was in the Code for a number of years was replaced in 1969 by § 183.[4] It is not strictly speaking a restriction on business losses, as new § 465 usually is. Instead, it seeks to differentiate essentially personal transactions from those which are engaged in for profit and to disallow deductions in the personal setting, except for those that are designed by the Code to be allowed without regard to their business or profit-making connection. It is sometimes difficult to say whether an activity that produces *some* gross income should be viewed as generating business losses deductible from income earned in other ways, or whether the expenditures in excess of revenue really only pay for the taxpayer's purely personal pleasure.[5] The following quotation reflects the congressional approach to this problem.

EXCERPT FROM THE GENERAL EXPLANATION OF THE
TAX REFORM ACT OF 1969

Staff of the Joint Committee on Internal Revenue Taxation.
Pp. 94–95 (1970).

5. **Hobby Losses (sec. 213 of the Act and secs. 183 and 270 of the code)**

Prior law.—Prior law contained a so-called "hobby loss" provision (section 270) which limited to $50,000 per year the amount of losses from a trade or business carried on by an individual that could be used to offset other income. This limitation only applied, however, where the losses from the business exceeded $50,000 per year for a period of at least 5 consecutive years. In computing the amount of a loss for purposes of this provision, certain specially treated deductions were disregarded. These disregarded deductions were taxes, interest, casualty and abandonment losses connected with a trade or business, farm drought losses, net operating loss carryovers, and expenditures which may either be capitalized or currently deducted.

General reasons for change.—The hobby loss provision generally was of limited application because it usually was possible to break the required string of five loss years. In addition, where the provision applied to disallow the deduction of a loss, the taxpayer was faced in one year with a combined additional tax attributable to a five-year period.

---

3. I.R.C. (26 U.S.C.A.) § 270.

4. See Lee, "A Blend of Old Wines in a New Wineskin: Section 183 and Beyond," 29 Tax L.R. 347 (1974).

5. E. g., Imbesi v. Comm'r, 361 F.2d 640 (3d Cir. 1966).

Explanation of provision.—The Act provides in general that an individual (or a subchapter S corporation) is not allowed to deduct losses (to the extent attributable to business deductions) arising from an activity which is not engaged in for profit. This rule does not apply to corporate taxpayers (other than subchapter S corporations). No inference should be drawn from the inapplicability of this rule in the case of a corporation, however, as to whether or not any activity of the corporation is a business, or is engaged in for profit, for purposes of the tax laws.

An activity is not engaged in for profit if deductions with respect to the activity are not allowable as trade or business expenses or as expenses incurred for the production of income or in connection with property held for the production of income. In making the determination of whether an activity is not engaged in for profit, it is intended that an objective rather than a subjective approach be employed. Thus, although a reasonable expectation of profit is not required, the facts and circumstances (without regard to the taxpayer's subjective intent) have to indicate that the taxpayer entered the activity, or continued the activity, with the objective of making a profit. A taxpayer who engaged in an activity in which there was a small chance of a large profit, for example, a person who invested in a wildcat oil well or an inventor, could qualify under this test even though the expectation of profit might be considered unreasonable.

Even where an activity is not engaged in for profit, however, the Act specifically provides that a deduction is allowed for items which are of the type which may be deducted without regard to whether they are incurred in a trade or business or for the production of income. This would include the deductions allowed for interest and state and local property taxes, and the long-term capital gains deduction. It further provides that, in the case of an activity not engaged in for profit, a deduction is nevertheless allowed for the trade or business or production of income items which could be deducted if the activity were engaged in for profit, but only to the extent these items do not exceed the amount of gross income derived from the activity reduced by the deductions which are allowed in any event such as interest and certain state and local taxes.

A taxpayer is presumed to be engaged in an activity for profit for the current taxable year, unless established to the contrary by the Secretary of the Treasury or his delegate, if in two or more years of the period of five consecutive taxable years (seven consecutive years in the case of an activity which consists in major part of the breeding, training, showing, or racing of horses) ending with the current taxable year, the activity was carried on at a profit (i. e., if the gross income from the activity exceeds the deductions attributable to the activity which would be allowed if it were engaged in for profit). For purposes of this presumption, all deductions attributable to the activity other than that allowed for net operating loss carryovers are taken into account. [An amendment in 1971 added § 183(e) under which a taxpayer may defer the time for determination whether the statutory presumption applies. With respect to any such deferral, TRA (1976) § 214 added new paragraph 183(e)(4) to protect the government against inappropriate running of limitation periods on deficiency assessments. Ed.]

Prior to 1976 only the general rules of I.R.C. § 183 were applicable in determining the extent to which expenses incurred in connection with the rental of vacation homes were deductible.[6] I.R.C. § 280A added by T.R.A.1976[7] provides more restrictive rules limiting the deduction of such expenses.[8] The Staff of the Joint Committee on Internal Revenue Taxation summarized the new provision as follows:

> Under prior law, there were no definitive rules relating to how much personal use of vacation property would result in the disallowance of deductions because the rental activities are not engaged in for profit. The act provides a limitation on deductions for expenses attributable to the rental of a vacation home if the home is used by a taxpayer for personal purposes in excess of the greater of 2 weeks or 10 percent of the actual business use (that is, its rental time) during a year. In this case, the deductions allowed in connection with a vacation home cannot exceed the gross income from the business use of the vacation home, less expenses which are allowable in any event (such as interest and taxes).[9] In addition, if a vacation home is actually rented for less than 15 days during the year, then no business deductions nor income derived from the use of the vacation home are to be taken into account in the taxpayer's return for the year. The provision applies to taxable years beginning after December 31, 1975.

If a taxpayer is limited by § 280A then § 183 is inapplicable,[10] but for any year in which § 280A does not apply the rules of § 183 may apply.[11]

6. See Reg. § 1.183–1(d)(3) and Rev. Rul. 73–219, 1973–1 C.B. 134.

7. T.R.A. (1976) § 601(a).

8. I.R.C. § 280A also applies to deductions for expenses attributable to *business* use of homes. See page 420, infra.

9. [Note the § 280A(e) limitation as well. Ed.]

10. I.R.C. § 280A(f)(3)(A) and (g).

11. See I.R.C. § 280A(f)(3) and note 7, supra.

2. OTHER STATUTORY RESTRICTIONS ON DEDUCTIONS

Internal Revenue Code: See Sections 162(e); 267(a)(2); 271; 276; 278; 280A.

Regulations: See Section 1.162–20.

That which Congress giveth Congress may also take away. And so it is with deductions, as recently indicated in this Chapter, for example, with respect to deductions for losses and for generally deductible expenditures or charges incurred in a hobby circumstance. In this book an effort is made to present the negative deduction rules along with the affirmative provisions to which they relate. But here are brief comments on some restrictive provisions that do not appear prominently elsewhere.

Unpaid Expenses and Interest. Generally an accounting provision, but going beyond timing questions to the point of disallowance, I.R.C. (26 U.S.C.A.) § 267(a) (2) sometimes overrides I.R.C. § 162 (and §§ 163 and 212 as well) to deny deductions for expenses (and for interest) when the payor and payee are related taxpayers.[1] The congressional concern is that taxpayer A may deduct the expense without making payment, as a proper *accrued* item, but that taxpayer B to whom payment is to be made will not then have to report it as income because, if he is on the *cash* method, the amount has not been either actually or constructively received.[2] The possibility for hanky-panky is obvious if, for example, payor and payee are father and son. In fact, beyond convenient timing of the deduction for the payor (early) and income to the payee (late, when paid) lies the possibility the amount will never in fact be paid. Draconically, rather than merely deferring the deduction to the year of payment, Congress denies any deduction, ever, in these circumstances, unless payment is made within two and one half months of the end of the year in which the deduction would otherwise be allowed.[3] However, payment by note to the extent of its cash equivalence is adequate to support the deduction.[4]

Certain Horticultural Development Costs. Under liberal accounting rules for farmers, it became accepted practice over the years to "expense" (currently deduct) the costs of developing a citrus grove,[5]

---

1. I.R.C. (26 U.S.C.A.) § 267(b) describes the family, financial, or business relationships that invoke the negative rule.

2. See Chapter 19 on fundamental timing principles.

3. Note that the deduction issue is thus settled at least a month before the payor's return must be filed. I.R.C. (26 U.S.C.A.) § 6072.

4. Musselman Hub-Brake Co. v. Comm'r, 139 F.2d 65 (6th Cir. 1943); Rev. Rul. 55–608, 1955–2 C.B. 546.

5. Reg. § 1.162–12 (1961).

expenditures that would be capitalized in other businesses. By adding I.R.C. (26 U.S.C.A.) § 278, Congress terminated this special advantage for years after 1969, except for trees replaced after casualties or planted before the statutory change was made.[6] A year later the same proscription was applied to the development costs of almond groves, by way of amendment of § 278, effective as to taxable years beginning after January 12, 1971.[7]

Bad Debts of Political Parties. Generally, a taxpayer may claim a deduction for an obligation owing to him which becomes worthless.[8] If he lends money to a political party which defaults, does he get a bad debt deduction? No. This is now foreclosed by I.R.C. (26 U.S. C.A.) § 271. Contributions to political parties are deductible only to a limited extent,[9] and the § 271 limitation on bad debt deductions precludes what might otherwise appear to be a way *indirectly* to make a deductible political contribution.[10]

Lobbying Expenses. Generally expenses incurred to promote or defeat legislation are not deductible.[11] But some such expenses may now be deducted under I.R.C. (26 U.S.C.A.) § 162(e), specifically those which involve business related appearances before legislative bodies in support of or opposition to legislation or dues paid to organizations to the extent attributable to such appearances.[12]

Interest On Indebtedness Incurred by a Corporation to Acquire Stock or Assets of Another Corporation. Recently, there has been an increasing use of bonds and debentures by corporations to acquire the stock or assets of other corporations. The acquiring corporation has been entitled to a deduction under I.R.C. § 163 for the interest paid on this debt. In order to discourage the use of debt financing of corporate acquisitions, Congress has enacted I.R.C. § 279 imposing limitations on the deductibility of interest on this type of indebtedness, but it applies only when the stakes are high.

Evasion or Avoidance of Income Tax. Ordinarily, a taxpayer is entitled to a deduction whenever authorized by statute. However, Congress has promulgated legislation denying statutorily authorized deductions when necessary to prevent the avoidance or evasion of taxes. Where a person or persons acquires control of a corporation, or where a corporation acquires the property of another corporation, and

---

6. Tax Reform Act of 1969, § 216(a).

7. P.L. 91–172, § 216(a) (1971), 84 Stat. 2064.

8. See Chapter 23 at page 808.

9. I.R.C. (26 U.S.C.A.) §§ 41, 162(e), and 218.

10. TRA (1976) § 2104(a) added I.R.C. § 271(c), corrected a flaw in the provision by guardedly allowing certain accrual method taxpayers to claim bad debt deductions for unpaid obligations arising out of their furnishing of goods or services.

11. The origin of this rule is administrative, not legislative. See Cammarano v. U. S., 358 U.S. 498, 79 S. Ct. 524 (1959).

12. See Reg. § 1.162–20(c) (2) (ii) (b); and see Boehm, "Taxes and Politics," 22 Tax L.Rev. 369 (1967).

the principal purpose for the acquisition is the evasion or avoidance of Federal income tax by securing the benefit of a deduction or some other tax allowance that would not otherwise be available, I.R.C. § 269 authorizes the Treasury to disallow the deduction, credit, or other allowance. This and the immediately preceding comment are of course the proper subject of more detailed study in a course on corporate taxation.

Business Use of the Home. On a more mundane level, controversy has raged in recent years over a taxpayer's right to claim deductions for expenses connected with his home, if he uses it in part for business purposes.[13] The Tax Reform Act of 1976 [14] added new I.R.C. § 280A sharply restricting such deductions. Here is what the Staff of the Joint Committee on Internal Revenue had to say about the new provision:

> The Act provides definitive rules relating to deductions for expenses attributable to the business use of homes. Under the Act, a taxpayer is not permitted to deduct any expenses attributable to the use of his home for business purposes except to the extent attributable to the portion of the home used exclusively on a regular basis: (a) as the taxpayer's principal place of business, (b) as a place of business which is used for patients, clients, or customers in meeting or dealing with the taxpayer in the normal course of business, or (c) in the case of a separate structure which is not attached to a dwelling, in connection with the taxpayer's trade or business. Further, in the case of an employee, the business use of the home must be for the convenience of his employer. An exception to the exclusive use test is provided where the dwelling unit is the sole fixed location of a trade or business which consists of selling products at retail or wholesale and the taxpayer regularly uses a separate identifiable portion of the residence for inventory storage. An overall limitation is provided which limits the amount of the deductions to the gross income generated by the business activity of the taxpayer in his home. The provision applies to taxable years beginning after December 31, 1975.

---

3. ILLEGALITY OR IMPROPRIETY

Internal Revenue Code: Section 162. See Sections 2; 152(b)(5); 6013.

Although the first modern (post-16th Amendment) income tax act taxed income from the transaction of any "lawful" business, the

---

13. E. g. Stephen A. Bodzin, 60 T.C. 820 (1973), rev'd 509 F.2d 679 (4th Cir. 1975).   **14.** TRA (1976) § 601.

term "lawful" was dropped quickly in 1916 and, since that time, the fact that income may somehow be tainted has had no bearing on its taxability. Thus, the Supreme Court early sustained a tax on the bootlegger's profits.[1] And much later the extortionist's plunder was held taxable.[2] Although the Supreme Court once refused to sustain a tax on embezzled income,[3] it was not because the income had a shady origin but, essentially, because such receipts were likened to loans. In any event, development of an "economic benefit" theory of income in James v. United States [4] enabled the Court to bring embezzled income into the area of taxability. It is unnecessary here to extend the discussion to other kinds of ill-gotten gains.

On the other hand, when the deduction question arises the propriety of an expenditure may be significant. Generally, the statute itself is free from moralizing restrictions, and the income tax is not a sanction against wrong-doing. Senator Williams, manager of the 1913 act, said to the Senate:[5]

> The object of this bill is to tax a man's net income; that is to say, what he has at the end of the year after deducting from his receipts his expenditures or losses. It is not to reform men's moral characters. * * * The tax is not levied for the purpose of restraining people from betting on horse races or upon "futures", but the tax is framed for the purpose of making a man pay upon his net income, his actual profit during the year.

Of course, over the years a little moralizing has crept in. Curiously, against the background of the Williams statement, Congress has decided to limit the deduction for wagering losses to an amount not in excess of gains from such transactions, possibly imposing a mild restraint on betting on the ponies.[6] Also, a man may find that Congress has expressly foreclosed a dependency deduction for his mistress, certainly a mild fiscal attack against living in sin.[7] It might be added, borrowing from Dorothy Parker, that the benefits of the joint return go along with the solid comforts of the double bed, not the hurly-burly of the chaise-lounge.[8] Perhaps more concretely, Congress also expressly disallows any deduction for bribes to government officials and, in some circumstances, for illegal bribes or kickbacks to anyone.[9] Fines and similar penalties are also now expressly proscribed

1. U. S. v. Sullivan, 274 U.S. 259, 47 S.Ct. 607 (1927).

2. Rutkin v. U. S., 343 U.S. 130, 72 S. Ct. 571 (1952).

3. Comm'r v. Wilcox, 327 U.S. 404, 66 S.Ct. 546 (1946).

4. 366 U.S. 213, 81 S.Ct. 1052 (1961). See page 564, infra.

5. 50 (Part 4) Cong.Rec. 3849, 63d Cong., 2d Sess. (1913).

6. I.R.C. (26 U.S.C.A.) § 165(d).

7. I.R.C. (26 U.S.C.A.) § 152(b)(5). But see page 497, infra, indicating that living in sin may be more advantageous taxwise!

8. See I.R.C. (26 U.S.C.A.) §§ 2 and 6013.

9. I.R.C. (26 U.S.C.A.) § 162(c). See Lycan, "Public Policy and the Deductibility of Kickbacks Under § 162(c) (2)," 35 Ohio State L.J. 686 (1974).

as nondeductible,[10] as are certain payments required as sanctions under the antitrust laws.[11] But these statutory provisions are the exception rather than the rule.

The foregoing comments on the statute suggest a simplicity in this area which, however, does not exist. The courts have found that public policy (that "notoriously unruly horse, likely to carry its rider off in any direction") sometimes stands in the way of a deduction which, otherwise, would appear to be authorized by the statute. As a general proposition it may be said that expenditures that are against the law and others whose deduction would tend to frustrate sharply defined public policy are not deductible.[12] While there is still substantial uncertainty, confusion in the area shrinks as provisions such as those mentioned in the preceding paragraph are added to the Code. A few words of history may be enlightening.

The first Supreme Court decision in which a claimed business expense deduction was denied on public policy grounds was Textile Mills Securities Corp. v. Commissioner.[13] The expenditures in question included amounts paid to a publicist and lawyers to seek legislation that would enable German textile interests to recover properties seized during World War I. In part the decision was rested on a long-continued (since 1915) regulation denying any deduction for lobbying expenses. The court noted the lack of precision in the "ordinary and necessary" requirement of the statute which, it held, left room for administrative interpretation. And it accepted the interpretation denying deductions for lobbying expenses on public policy grounds, saying:[14]

> Contracts to spread such insidious influences through legislative halls have long been condemned. * * * Whether the precise arrangement here in question would violate the rule of [such] cases is not material. The point is that the general policy indicated by those cases need not be disregarded by the rule-making authority in its segregation of non-deductible expenses.

---

10. I.R.C. (26 U.S.C.A.) § 162(f).

11. I.R.C. (26 U.S.C.A.) § 162(g); but see earlier Rev.Rul. 64–224, 1964–2 C. B. 52.

12. Although there is language in the legislative histories of the Code sections cited in footnotes 9–11, supra, indicating the statutory disallowances are "all inclusive" and are under the "control of Congress", [the most relevant comments can be found at 1972–1 C.B. 599 and 1969–3 C.B. 597.] nevertheless such statutory proscriptions have been held not to preclude a consideration whether public policy should stand in the way of a claimed § 165 deduction for theft where the claiming taxpayer was footsie with the thieves who were seemingly engaged in an illegal activity, counterfeiting currency. Raymond Mazzei, 61 T.C. 497 (1974), infra page 481.

13. 314 U.S. 326, 62 S.Ct. 272 (1941). Pre-1964 "public policy" cases are collected in Lamont, "Controversial Aspects of Ordinary and Necessary Business Expenses," 42 Taxes 808, 819–835 (1964).

14. Id. at 338–339, 62 S.Ct. at 279–280.

From that point on the question has been to what extent administrative and judicial moralizing can be expected when Congress has engaged in none.

The fact that *Textile Mills* involved efforts on behalf of alien Germans and that it was decided just prior to the full-scale conflagration of World War II might leave its present effect in some doubt. However, in 1959, the Supreme Court refused to give a restrictive interpretation to its *Textile Mills* opinion. Expenses involved in an attempt to protect the business of bars and liquor wholesalers from threatening state action in the form of an initiative and referendum measure, which would have created a state monopoly for retail sales, were held non-deductible.[15] To the supporting factors of a long-standing regulation and the Court's own decision in *Textile Mills*, the Court could now add that the reenactment in 1954 of the "ordinary and necessary" rule without change was "significant as indicating [congressional] satisfaction with the interpretation consistently given the statute by the regulations * * * and in demonstrating its [Congress'] prior intent." [16]

The lobbying expense area is interesting in reflecting administrative, judicial, and legislative participation in the development of tax law. In 1962, Congress marked off a limited area in which lobbying expenses may now be deducted,[17] without however adopting a rule that would make deductible efforts to shape legislation through broad appeals to the public.

In some other cases the Commissioner has asserted different public policy reasons for the disallowance of deductions for attorneys fees incurred in connection with business activities. A reference to two Supreme Court cases will suffice. In Commissioner v. Heininger,[18] the taxpayer, a Chicago dentist, was in the false teeth business. The teeth were advertised, ordered, delivered and paid for by mail. Challenging his claims for his product, the Postmaster General issued a fraud order to the Chicago postmaster, interrupting the taxpayer's business. The taxpayer sought an injunction against enforcement of the order but, while initially successful, he lost an appeal. The *tax* litigation arose out of the Commissioner's disallowance of a claimed deduction for $36,000 representing admittedly reasonable attorney's fees incurred in contesting the fraud order. The Board of Tax Appeals agreed with the Commissioner's assertion that these were not "ordinary and necessary" business expenses. The idea seemed to be that dentists do not "ordinarily" seek to sell false teeth fraudulently; therefore, expenses related to such activity (the legal expenses incurred) are not ordinary and not deductible. But the Supreme Court agreed with the Seventh Circuit's reversal, allowing the deduction, saying: [19]

15. Cammarano v. U. S., 358 U.S. 498, 79 S.Ct. 524 (1959).

16. Id. at 510, 79 S.Ct. at 532.

17. I.R.C. (26 U.S.C.A.) § 162(e).

18. 320 U.S. 467, 64 S.Ct. 249 (1943).

19. Id. at 474, 64 S.Ct. at 253, 254.

It has never been thought * * * that the mere fact that an expenditure bears a remote relation to an illegal act makes it non-deductible.   The language (of the statute) contains no express reference to the lawful or unlawful character of the business expenses which are declared to be deductible.   And the brief of the government in the instant case expressly disclaims any contention that the purpose of the tax laws is to penalize illegal business by taxing gross income instead of net income. * * *

* * *

If the respondent's litigation expenses are to be denied deduction, it must be because allowance of the deduction would frustrate the sharply defined policies of [the statutes] which authorize the Postmaster General to issue fraud orders.

The Court found no such threatened frustration.

Heininger of course involved expenses incurred in an unsuccessful effort to resist a civil sanction, no matter how penal it might be in nature.   The Commissioner thought it was still open to him to challenge a deduction for attorney's fees incurred in unsuccessfully attempting to defend a criminal prosecution that grew out of misconduct in the course of the taxpayer's business.   But, although the Tax Court agreed, neither the Court of Appeals nor the Supreme Court did.   One Tellier was convicted on several counts, including charges under the mail fraud provisions of the Securities Act of 1933, and sentenced to pay an $18,000 fine and to serve four and one half years in prison.   En route, he incurred $23,000 in legal expenses which he sought to deduct.   It is now settled that the legal expenses are deductible.[20]   In the *Tellier* case the court said:[21]

"No public policy is offended when a man faced with serious criminal charges employs a lawyer to help in his defense.   That is not 'proscribed conduct'.   It is his constitutional right."

Note that this is not to say all legal expenses are deductible but only that, if otherwise within section 162 or possibly section 212, the fact that they relate to the defense of a criminal charge,[22] successful or unsuccessful, will not foreclose the deduction.

Meanwhile, between the decisions in *Heininger* and *Tellier*, some other more difficult public policy cases worked their way to the Supreme Court.   In Lilly v. Commissioner,[23] the issue was the deductibility of kickbacks made by an optician to eye doctors who sent patients to him to have their prescriptions filled.   Probably most people would agree that such payments are contrary to public policy,

20. Comm'r v. Tellier, 383 U.S. 687, 86 S.Ct. 1118 (1966).

21. Id. at 694, 86 S.Ct. at 1122.

22. John Kurkjian, 65 T.C. 862 (1976).

23. 343 U.S. 90, 72 S.Ct. 497 (1952).

and perhaps further, that it violates generally accepted notions of public policy to allow a tax deduction for such payments. However, differing with the Commissioner and both lower courts, the Supreme Court held such payments to be deductible. The reason advanced was that public policies that might preclude a deduction may do so only if they are "national or state policies evidenced by some governmental declaration of them." [24] Finding no such declaration applicable to the payments in *Lilly*, the amounts were held to be deductible.[25] The general effect of the decision, at least outside the lobbying area, is to relieve the taxpayer from the obligation of having to comply with the Commissioner's appraisal of public policy in order to justify a deduction.[26]

Dictum appears in *Lilly* to the effect that expenditures which themselves violate a federal or state law could be argued, by virtue of their illegality, not to be "ordinary and necessary." As a matter of fact in a later case Mr. Justice Clark said directly: "Certainly the frustration of state policy is most complete and direct when the expenditure for which deduction is sought is itself prohibited by statute." [27] Still, it is not the law that an illegal expenditure is never deductible. In Commissioner v. Sullivan,[28] salary and rental payments made in carrying on an illegal gambling business, which payments were themselves in violation of Illinois law, were held to be deductible. The case cannot easily be reconciled with other "public policy" decisions. In support, if not in logical explanation, of the result reached Mr. Justice Douglas said for the Court:[29]

> If we enforce as federal policy the rule espoused by the Commissioner in this case [denying the deductions], we would come close to making this type of business taxable on the basis of its gross receipts, while all other business would be taxable on the basis of net income.

On the other hand, this does seem consistent with the amoral role ascribed to the income tax statute by Senator Williams in 1913.

An understanding of *Sullivan* is rendered even more difficult by the decisions in two cases decided at the same time. Each involved the deductibility of state fines incurred by trucking companies for violation of state laws against overweight loads on the highways.

24. Id. at 97, 72 S.Ct. at 501.

25. But see United Draperies v. Comm'r, 340 F.2d 936 (7th Cir. 1964), cert. den., 382 U.S. 813, 86 S.Ct. 30 (1965), denying a deduction for kickbacks found to be not "ordinary" in the industry.

26. Note that the new provision on kickbacks continues this philosophy by its requirement of a conviction or a plea of nolo contendere in a criminal proceeding. I.R.C. (26 U.S.C.A.) § 162(c) (2).

27. Tank Truck Rentals, Inc. v. Comm'r, 356 U.S. 30, 78 S.Ct. 507 (1958).

28. 356 U.S. 27, 78 S.Ct. 512 (1958).

29. Id. at 29, 78 S.Ct. at 514.

Such fines, whether incurred wilfully or inadvertently, were held non-deductible.[30] The rationale of these cases is that to allow the deduction would frustrate state policy by diluting the penalty for violation of the law. The penalty is less if the amount paid reduces income otherwise taxable. Said Mr. Justice Clark for the Court:[31]

> Deduction of fines and penalties uniformly has been held to frustrate state policy in severe and direct fashion by reducing the "sting" of the penalty prescribed by the state legislature.

Thus, if in the case of the corporations involved their income was effectively taxed at about a 50% rate, allowance of the deduction would reduce each $1.00 of fine to 50 cents, net cost after taxes. A seeming answer on these facts would be to say that the state could double the fine in order, after allowance of the deduction, to exact the full penalty. But this is an inadequate answer; consider in other circumstances how a low bracket individual (or a corporation subject only to the normal corporate tax) would incur a higher after tax penalty than a taxpayer whose deduction was in a sense more valuable because it would offset income otherwise to be subjected to higher rates.

In any event, fines are not deductible and Congress has now expressly said so.[32] In *Tellier* it was not contended that the taxpayer could deduct his $18,000 fine, only attorney's fees paid in seeking to avoid it. But this is another area of the law in which it is not always easy to differentiate an administrative requirement that is remedial in nature from the imposition of a fine or penalty, a sanction against wrongdoing. If fines may confidently be said generally to be non-deductible, what *is* a fine?[33] Congress, of course, has sought to avoid the "tyranny of labels" by disallowing deductions for "any fine *or similar penalty*."[34] Does this eliminate the problem?

Public policy problems such as are discussed in this note have evoked a substantial addition to the legal literature. There are perceptive discussions in Taggart, "Fines, Penalties, Bribes and Damage Payments," 25 Tax L.Rev. 611 (1970); Scallen, "The Deductibility of Antitrust Treble Damage Payments," 52 Minn.L.Rev. 1149 (1968); Wright, "Tax Formula to Restore the Historical Effects of Antitrust Treble Damages Provisions," 65 Mich.L.Rev. 245 (1966); Tyler, "Disallowance of Deductions on Public Policy Grounds," 20 Tax L.Rev. 665 (1965). See also Note, "Cost of Unsuccessful Criminal Defense," 64 Mich.L.Rev. 161 (1965); Note, "Business Expenses,

---

30. Tank Truck Rentals, Inc. v. Comm'r, supra note 27; Hoover Motor Express Co. v. U. S., 356 U.S. 38, 78 S.Ct. 511 (1958).

31. Tank Truck Rentals, Inc. v. Comm'r, supra note 27 at 35–36, 78 S.Ct. at 510.

32. I.R.C. (26 U.S.C.A.) § 162(f).

33. Compare Rossman Corp. v. Comm'r, 175 F.2d 711 (2d Cir. 1949), with Lentin v. Comm'r, 226 F.2d 695 (7th Cir. 1955), cert. den., 350 U.S. 934, 76 S.Ct. 305 (1956).

34. I.R.C. (26 U.S.C.A.) § 162(f).

Disallowance, and Public Policy: Some Problems of Sanctioning with the Internal Revenue Code," 72 Yale L.J. 108 (1962).

---

4. DEPRECIATION, DEPLETION, AND AMORTIZATION

Because these concepts are intimately related to the subject matter of Part Six their analysis is deferred to Chapter 22, which is in that Part.

CHAPTER 16. DEDUCTIONS FOR PROFIT–MAKING, NONBUSINESS ACTIVITIES

A. SECTION 212 EXPENSES

Internal Revenue Code: Section 212.
Regulations: Sections 1.212–1(g), (k), (l), (m); 1.262–1(b) (7).

HIGGINS v. COMMISSIONER

Supreme Court of the United States, 1941.
312 U.S. 212, 61 S.Ct. 475.

MR. JUSTICE REED delivered the opinion of the Court.

Petitioner, the taxpayer, with extensive investments in real estate, bonds and stocks, devoted a considerable portion of his time to the oversight of his interests and hired others to assist him in offices rented for that purpose. For the tax years in question, 1932 and 1933, he claimed the salaries and expenses incident to looking after his properties were deductible under § 23(a) of the Revenue Act of 1932.[1] The Commissioner refused the deductions. The applicable phrases are: "In computing net income there shall be allowed as deductions: (a) *Expenses.*—All the ordinary and necessary expenses paid or incurred during the taxable year in carrying on any trade or business * * *." There is no dispute over whether the claimed deductions are ordinary and necessary expenses. As the Commissioner also conceded before the Board of Tax Appeals that the real estate activities of the petitioner in renting buildings[2] constituted a business, the Board allowed such portions of the claimed deductions as were fairly allocable to the handling of the real estate. The same offices and staffs handled both real estate and security matters. After this adjustment there remained for the year 1932 over twenty and for the year 1933 over sixteen thousand dollars expended for managing the stocks and bonds.

Petitioner's financial affairs were conducted through his New York office pursuant to his personal detailed instructions. His residence was in Paris, France, where he had a second office. By cable, telephone and mail, petitioner kept a watchful eye over his securities. While he sought permanent investments, changes, redemptions, maturities and accumulations caused limited shiftings in his portfolio. These were made under his own orders. The offices kept records,

1. 47 Stat. 169, c. 209 [The parallel language in the 1954 Internal Revenue Code is of course found in § 162 (a). Ed.]

2. Cf. Pinchot v. Comm'r, 113 F.2d 718.

received securities, interest and dividend checks, made deposits, forwarded weekly and annual reports and undertook generally the care of the investments as instructed by the owner. Purchases were made by a financial institution. Petitioner did not participate directly or indirectly in the management of the corporations in which he held stock or bonds. The method of handling his affairs under examination had been employed by petitioner for more than thirty years. No objection to the deductions had previously been made by the Government.

The Board of Tax Appeals [3] held that these activities did not constitute carrying on a business and that the expenses were capable of apportionment between the real estate and the investments. The Circuit Court of Appeals affirmed,[4] and we granted certiorari because of conflict.[5]

Petitioner urges that the "elements of continuity, constant repetition, regularity and extent" differentiate his activities from the occasional like actions of the small investor. His activity is and the occasional action is not "carrying on business." On the other hand, the respondent urges that "mere personal investment activities never constitute carrying on a trade or business, no matter how much of one's time or of one's employees' time they may occupy."

Since the first income tax act, the provisions authorizing business deductions have varied only slightly. The Revenue Act of 1913 [6] allowed as a deduction "the necessary expenses actually paid in carrying on any business." By 1918 the present form was fixed and has so continued.[7] No regulation has ever been promulgated which interprets the meaning of "carrying on a business," nor any rulings approved by the Secretary of the Treasury, i. e., Treasury Decisions.[8] Certain rulings of less dignity, favorable to petitioner,[9] appeared in individual cases but they are not determinative.[10] Even acquiescence [11] in some Board rulings after defeat does not amount to settled administrative practice.[12] Unless the administrative practice

3. 39 B.T.A. 1005.

4. 111 F.2d 795.

5. Kales v. Commissioner, 101 F.2d 35; DuPont v. Deputy, 103 F.2d 257.

6. 38 Stat. 167, § II B.

7. 40 Stat. 1066, § 214(a) (1).

8. Cf. Helvering v. New York Trust Co., 292 U.S. 455, 467–468.

9. O.D. 537, 2 C.B. 175 (1920); O.D. 877, 4 C.B. 123 (1921); I.T. 2751, XIII–1 C.B. 43 (1934). See also 1934 C.C.H. Federal Tax Service, Vol. 3, ¶ 6035, p. 8027.

10. Biddle v. Commissioner, 302 U.S. 573, 582. Cf. Estate of Sanford v. Commissioner, 308 U.S. 39, 52. But see Helvering v. Bliss, 293 U.S. 144, 151, and McFeely v. Commissioner, 296 U.S. 102, 108.

11. Kissel v. Commissioner, 15 B.T.A. 1270, acquiesced in VIII–2 C.B. 28 (1929); Croker v. Commissioner, 27 B.T.A. 588, acquiesced in XII–1 C.B. 4 (1933).

12. Higgins v. Smith, 308 U.S. 473, 478–479.

is long continued and substantially uniform in the Bureau and without challenge by the Government in the Board and courts, it should not be assumed, from rulings of this class, that Congressional reënactment of the language which they construed was an adoption of their interpretation.

While the Commissioner has combated views similar to petitioner's in the courts, sometimes successfully [13] and sometimes unsuccessfully,[14] the petitioner urges that the Bureau accepted for years the doctrine that the management of one's own securities might be a business where there was sufficient extent, continuity, variety and regularity. We fail to find such a fixed administrative construction in the examples cited. It is true that the decisions are frequently put on the ground that the taxpayer's activities were sporadic but it does not follow that had those activities been continuous the Commissioner would not have used the argument advanced here, i. e., that no amount of personal investment management would turn those activities into a business. Evidently such was the Government's contention in the *Kales* case,[15] where the things the taxpayer did met petitioner's tests, and in Foss v. Commissioner [16] and Washburn v. Commissioner [17] where the opinions turned on the extent of the taxpayer's participation in the management of the corporations in which investments were held.[18]

Petitioner relies strongly on the definition of business in Flint v. Stone Tracy Company: [19] " 'Business' is a very comprehensive term and embraces everything about which a person can be employed." This definition was given in considering whether certain corporations came under the Corporation Tax law which levies a tax on corporations engaged in business. The immediate issue was whether corporations engaged principally in the "holding and management of real estate" [20] were subject to the act. A definition given for such an issue is not controlling in this dissimilar inquiry.[21]

To determine whether the activities of a taxpayer are "carrying on a business" requires an examination of the facts in each case. As the Circuit Court of Appeals observed, all expenses of every business transaction are not deductible. Only those are deductible which re-

13. Bedell v. Commissioner, 30 F.2d 622, 624; Monell v. Helvering, 70 F.2d 631; Kane v. Commissioner, 100 F.2d 382.

14. Kales v. Commissioner, 101 F.2d 35; DuPont v. Deputy, 103 F.2d 257, 259, reversed on other grounds, 308 U.S. 488.

15. Kales v. Commissioner, 34 B.T.A. 1046, 101 F.2d 35.

16. 75 F.2d 326.

17. 51 F.2d 949, 953.

18. Cf. Roebling v. Commissioner, 37 B.T.A. 82; Heilbroner v. Commissioner, 34 B.T.A. 1200.

19. 220 U.S. 107, 171.

20. Id. 169.

21. Cohens v. Virginia, 6 Wheat. 264, 399; Puerto Rico v. Shell Co., 302 U. S. 253, 269.

late to carrying on a business. The Bureau of Internal Revenue has this duty of determining what is carrying on a business, subject to reëxamination of the facts by the Board of Tax Appeals [22] and ultimately to review on the law by the courts on which jurisdiction is conferred.[23] The Commissioner and the Board appraised the evidence here as insufficient to establish petitioner's activities as those of carrying on a business. The petitioner merely kept records and collected interest and dividends from his securities, through managerial attention for his investments. No matter how large the estate or how continuous or extended the work required may be, such facts are not sufficient as a matter of law to permit the courts to reverse the decision of the Board. Its conclusion is adequately supported by this record, and rests upon a conception of carrying on business similar to that expressed by this Court for an antecedent section.[24]

The petitioner makes the point that his activities in managing his estate, both realty and personalty, were a unified business. Since it was admittedly a business in so far as the realty is concerned, he urges, there is no statutory authority to sever expenses allocable to the securities. But we see no reason why expenses not attributable, as we have just held these are not, to carrying on business cannot be apportioned. It is not unusual to allocate expenses paid for services partly personal and partly business.[25]

Affirmed.

NOTE

The congressional reaction to the *Higgins* decision was negative. But, instead of attempting to mitigate the problem by defining a trade or business as including income-producing activity, Congress enacted what is now I.R.C. (26 U.S.C.A.) § 212(1) and (2) as part of the Revenue Act of 1942.[1] Subparagraph (3) of § 212 first appeared with the enactment of the Internal Revenue Code of 1954.[2]

If a bridge is needed here from a preoccupation with trade or business problems in Chapter 15, it is the question: All right, we do not fit the trade or business requirements of I.R.C. (26 U.S.C.A.) § 162; so what? Is there, nevertheless a proper basis for asserting deductibility? Our inquiry here carries us primarily into § 212 [3]

---

22. Revenue Act of 1932, 47 Stat. 169, § 272; Internal Revenue Code, § 272.

23. Internal Revenue Code, § 1141.

24. Van Wart v. Commissioner, 295 U. S. 112, 115.

25. 3 Paul & Mertens, Law of Federal Income Taxation § 23.65; cf. National Outdoor Advertising Bureau v. Helvering, 89 F.2d 878, 881.

1. § 121, 55 Stat. 798, 819 (1942).

2. Paragraph (3) was prompted by the decision in Lykes v. U. S., 343 U.S. 118, 72 S.Ct. 585 (1952) which, essentially, it overruled.

3. Further possibilities are explored in Chapters 17 and 18.

where "the production [or collection] of income" test replaces that of the "trade or business" concept of § 162. The *Higgins* background of § 212 supports the other similarities of §§ 162 and 212; note especially that in either case it is only "expenses" that are "ordinary and necessary" which are deductible.

Other quasi-business deductions crop up in this chapter as well. A question may be whether a loss is one that, if not in business, arises out of a "transaction entered into for profit" as that phrase is used in § 165(c) (2). If one is seeking income (§ 212), is he engaged in a transaction entered into for profit (§ 165(c) (2)), and vice versa? It is worth noting here that in other respects § 165 clearly differs from § 212 (and § 162), not being concerned with "expenses" or the question whether what occurred was "ordinary" or "necessary." A related problem that appears somewhat prematurely here [4] is whether property is "held for the production of income" so as to be subject to depreciation under § 167(a) (2), even if not used in a trade or business. These related concepts are ably discussed by Professor Kilbourn in an article entitled "Deductible Expenses: Transactions Entered into for Profit; Income-Producing Property." [5]

Problems of the kind dealt with here cover a wide range of human activity and, thinking in terms of two of the cases that follow, it may be difficult to see that Mr. Surasky's proxy expenses (he won) have very much in common with those involved in Mr. Fleischman's divorce (he lost). However, if the following materials are approached with the underlying statutory concepts in mind they will not only appear less fragmentary, but they will also supply a basis for dealing with many other problems not specifically presented here.

BOWERS v. LUMPKIN

United States Court of Appeals, Fourth Circuit, 1944.
140 F.2d 927.
Cert. denied, 322 U.S. 755, 64 S.Ct. 1266, 1944.

SOPER, CIRCUIT JUDGE. This suit was brought by Mrs. Lumpkin to recover individual federal income taxes alleged to have been overpaid for the years 1936 and 1937. It was tried before the District Judge without a jury and resulted in a judgment for the plaintiff in the sum of $22,680.10. The taxpayer had a life interest under a trust created for her benefit by the will of her former husband in one-half of the stock of a corporation which owned valuable rights in the sale and distribution of coca cola syrup in South Carolina. She purchased the remaining stock of the corporation for $255,885 from trustees to whom it had been bequeathed to establish and maintain an orphanage. The Attorney General of South Carolina instituted an action to in-

---

4. See Note, "Depreciation," in Chapter 22, at page 721, infra.

5. 21 N.Y.U. Inst. on Fed. Tax. 19? (1963).

validate the sale and require the taxpayer to account for profits and the taxpayer was obliged to defend the suit in the courts of South Carolina where she finally won a decision upholding the sale. In connection with this litigation she incurred expenses of $250 in 1936 and $26,798.22 in 1937 which she deducted from gross income in preparing her income tax returns for these years. The Commissioner of Internal Revenue disallowed the deductions and assessed additional taxes and interest of $155 for 1936 and $19,187.72 for 1937, which were paid under protest and form the basis of the instant suit.

The taxpayer relies upon § 121 (a) of the Revenue Act of 1942, 56 Stat. 798, 819, 26 U.S.C.A. Int.Rev.Code, § 23 (a), which amended § 23 (a) of the Internal Revenue Code, 53 Stat. 12, whereby all the ordinary and necessary expenses of carrying on a trade or business were allowed as deductions from gross income. The Act of 1942 broadened the scope of allowable deductions by adding amongst others the following subsection to § 23 (a):

"(2) Non-trade or non-business expenses. In the case of an individual, all the ordinary and necessary expenses paid or incurred during the taxable year for the production or collection of income, or for the management, conservation, or maintenance of property held for the production of income." *

This amendment was made retroactive by the following provision:

"(e) Retroactive Amendment to Prior Revenue Acts.—For the purposes of the Revenue Act of 1938 or any prior revenue Act the amendments made to the Internal Revenue Code by this section shall be effective as if they were a part of such revenue Act on the date of its enactment." 56 Stat. 819, 26 U.S.C.A. Int.Rev.Code, § 23 note.

The purpose of this amendment was to permit deductions for certain non-trade and non-business expenses and thereby enlarge the allowable deduction for expenses which under previous revenue acts had been confined to expenses paid or incurred in carrying on any trade or business. Under the earlier statutes it had been held that investors not engaged in the investment business could not deduct expenses such as salaries, clerk hire or office rent incurred in connection with the earning or collection of taxable income, or in looking after one's own investments in stocks and bonds. See, Higgins v. Commissioner, 312 U.S. 212, 61 S.Ct. 475, 85 L.Ed. 783, decided February 3, 1941. To mitigate the harshness of this rule Congress in 1942 eliminated the requirement that the expenses to be deductible must be incurred in connection with a trade or business. But, as the reports of Congressional committees show, it was not the intention of Congress to remove the other restrictions and limitations applicable to deductions under § 23 (a) of the act. See S.Rep. No. 1683, 77th Cong., 2d Sess., 88; H. Rep. No. 2333, 77th Cong., 2d Sess., 75.

* See I.R.C. (1954) § 212(1) and (2).
Ed.

Under § 23(a), as it was prior to the amendment, it was firmly established that legal expenses involved in defending or protecting title to property are not "ordinary and necessary expenses" and are not deductible from gross income in order to compute the taxable net income, but constitute a capital charge which should be added to the cost of the property and taken into account in computing the capital gain or loss in case of a subsequent sale. The Treasury regulations throughout the years have consistently so provided;[1] the decisions of the courts have been to the same effect;[2] and Congress has retained the same language in repeated reenactments with this interpretation in mind.

Hence it may not be doubted that Congress, in amending § 23 of the Internal Revenue Code by the Revenue Act of 1942, used the phrase "all the ordinary and necessary expenses" under the caption "Non-Trade or Non-Business Expenses" in the same sense and with the same limitations that it had previously used in connection with trade and business expenses. It is contended that the phrase "all the ordinary and necessary expenses" in the amendment covers more ground than it did in the original act because the amendment expressly authorizes a deduction for expenses paid "for the management, conservation, or maintenance of property held for the production of income"; and the word "conservation" is said to be particularly pertinent in the pending case where the expenses were incurred in the protection of income producing stock from adverse attack. But the term "conservation" can be given effect if it is limited to expenses ordinarily and necessarily incurred during the taxable year for the safeguarding of the property, such as the cost of a safe deposit box for securities. The term cannot be given the meaning contended for by the taxpayer without losing sight of the purpose which Congress intended to accomplish and the settled meaning that the phrase "ordinary and necessary expenses" has been given in the administration and re-enactment of the federal income tax statutes.

Treasury Regulations 103, as amended by T.D. 5196, 1942-2 "C.B." 96, 97-100, which were promulgated to cover the 1942 amend-

---

1. Article 293 of Regulations 45 (1919 Ed.), and 62 (1922 Ed.), promulgated under the Revenue Acts of 1918 and 1921; Article 292 of Regulations 65 and 69, promulgated under the Revenue Acts of 1924 and 1926; Article 282 of Regulations 74 and 77, promulgated under the Revenue Acts of 1928 and 1932; Article 24-2 of Regulations 94 and 101, promulgated under the Revenue Acts of 1936 and 1938; Section 19, 24-2 of Regulations 103 (1940 Ed.) promulgated under the Internal Revenue Code.

2. Jones' Estate v. Commissioner, 5 Cir., 127 F.2d 231; Murphy Oil Co. v. Burnett, 9 Cir., 55 F.2d 17, 26, affirmed 287 U.S. 299, 53 S.Ct. 161, 77 L.Ed. 318; Brawner v. Burnett, 61 App.D.C. 352, 63 F.2d 129, 131; Farmer v. Commissioner, 10 Cir., 126 F.2d 542, 544; Crowley v. Commissioner, 6 Cir., 89 F.2d 715, 718. Cf. Welch v. Helvering, 290 U.S. 111, 113, 114, 54 S.Ct. 8, 78 L.Ed. 212.

ments, preserve the established interpretation. Section 19.23(a)–15 provides in part:

"(b) Except for the requirement of being incurred in connection with a trade or business, a deduction under this section is subject to all the restrictions and limitations that apply in the case of the deductions under section 23(a) (1) (A) of an expense paid or incurred in carrying on any trade or business. This includes restrictions and limitations contained in section 24, as amended. * * *

"Capital expenditures, and expenses of carrying on transactions which do not constitute a trade or business of the taxpayer and are not carried on for the production or collection of income or for the management, conservation, or maintenance of property held for the production of income, but which are carried on primarily as a sport, hobby, or recreation are not allowable as non-trade or non-business expenses.

*   *   *   *   *   *   *   *   *   *

"Expenditures incurred in defending or perfecting title to property, in recovering property (other than investment property and amounts of income which, if and when recovered, must be included in income), or in developing or improving property, constitute a part of the cost of the property and are not deductible expenses."

The judgment of the District Court must be

Reversed.

ESTATE OF BAIER v. COMMISSIONER

United States Court of Appeals, Third Circuit, 1976.
533 F.2d 117.

Opinion of the Court

VAN DUSEN, CIRCUIT JUDGE. The sole question presented on this appeal from the Tax Court is whether certain legal expenses incurred by the taxpayer during calendar years 1969–1971 qualify as an ordinary expense under § 212 of the Internal Revenue Code of 1954,[1] or whether those expenses must be treated as capital expenditures. The Tax Court held that the expenses have their origin in the disposition of a capital asset and, therefore, must be used to offset the realized capital gains. Baier v. Commissioner of Internal Revenue, 63 T.C. 513 (1975). We affirm.

Richard Baier was first employed by American Smelting and Refining Company (American) in 1933. In 1953, he became the chief engineer in a division of American's central research department. In conjunction with his promotion to this position, Baier signed an employment contract which contained the following provisions:

"7. [Employee] agrees that he will forthwith disclose and assign to the Company all discoveries, processes and in-

---

1. [26 U.S.C. (I.R.C.) § 212 is omitted. Ed.]

ventions made or conceived in whole or in part by him
. . . during his employment, relative to or useful in any
business carried on by the Company . . . and the said
discoveries, processes and inventions shall become and remain the property of the Company . . . Upon request
of the Company . . . the [employee] agrees to make application . . . for letters patent of the United States and
of any other countries where obtainable, on said discoveries,
processes and inventions, and forthwith to assign all such applications and the letters patent thereon to the Company
. . .

"8. Under the provisions of the Executive Committee
Circular No. 605 . . . employees of the Company making inventions in the course of their employment useful in
the business of the Company, may derive certain benefits
therefrom in accordance with the terms and conditions in
said circular set forth; but the granting of such benefits is
discretionary with the Company and the provisions of such
circular are subject to withdrawal or change without notice."

App. at 54a–55a. Circular No. 605, incorporated by reference into
the contract, provided that, if American should grant to any person
or corporation other than itself the right to make, use or vend the discovery, process, or invention, then the company would give to the employee or employees responsible a 15% share in the net proceeds realized.

In August 1961, Baier and a co-inventor reduced to practice a
method and apparatus for melting copper which had a tremendous
commercial potential. In May 1962, American amended Circular No.
605 by issuing Executive Committee Circular Letter No. 995. Circular No. 995 was identical to Circular No. 605 in all material respects
except that the payments made to employees under its terms would
be limited to $20,000 per year and would be paid only while the em-
ployee was actively employed by American. Baier was asked to sign
a new employment contract incorporating Circular No. 995, but he
refused.

In accordance with the terms of the 1953 employment contract,
Baier applied for a patent to cover the method and apparatus for melting copper, and assigned this application to American. Beginning in
November 1962, American licensed the invention to various unrelated
corporations.

A dispute arose between American and Baier over whether the
payments to Baier for the invention were to be determined under the
terms of Circular No. 605 or under the terms of Circular No. 995.
The licensing fees realized by American were of such magnitude that
the difference to Baier was extremely large. To protect his interests,
Baier retained legal counsel and then commenced suit. In February

1964, a settlement was reached, the terms of which were substantially more favorable to Baier than the terms of Circular No. 995.

The payments received from American have been properly reported by Baier as long-term capital gains. See Treas.Reg. § 1.1235–1(c)(2). His legal counsel was retained on a contingent fee basis, entitling such counsel to a percentage of the payments made by American to Baier. Payments were made by Baier to his attorney in the years 1969, 1970 and 1971 were claimed as an ordinary deduction for each year under 26 U.S.C. § 212. The Commissioner disallowed these payments as ordinary deductions and recharacterized them as capital expenditures, and ruled on the basis of 26 U.S.C. § 263 [2] that they were not deductible. Accordingly, the Commissioner assessed a deficiency for the years 1969–1971. Baier petitioned the Tax Court for a redetermination of the deficiencies. After the Tax Court upheld the Commissioner, Baier filed a timely notice of appeal.

Baier contends that he incurred legal fees to enforce a fully executed contract, complete as to its terms, and not incident to the disposition of a capital asset (the invention underlying the patent). "Litigation was required not to fill in any missing terms [such as price] but to enforce the contract as written" (taxpayer's brief at p. 31). The Tax Court found that the terms of the contract were not final with respect to the invention disposition price, and therefore the legal expenses were incurred as the cost of setting that price. See United States v. Hilton Hotels Corp., 397 U.S. 580 (1970). We believe it is unnecessary in this case to resolve the dispute over the construction of the employment contract.

It is clear that § 263 modifies § 212. See 26 U.S.C. § 211; Commissioner v. Idaho Power Co., 418 U.S. 1, 17 (1974). The test for determining what a § 263 capital expenditure is has been described by the Supreme Court in Woodward v. Commissioner, 397 U.S. 572 (1970), and United States v. Hilton Hotels Corp., supra:

> "[U]ncertainty is not called for in applying the regulation that makes the 'cost of acquisition' of a capital asset a capital expense. In our view application of [that] regulation to litigation expenses involves the simpler inquiry whether the origin of the claim litigated is in the process of acquisition itself."

2. 26 U.S.C. [I.R.C.] § 263 provides:

"(a) General rule.—No deduction shall be allowed for—

(1) Any amount paid out for new buildings or for permanent improvements or betterments made to increase the value of any property or estate. . . ."

This section has consistently been interpreted as requiring the capitalization of the costs incident to the acquisition or disposition of a capital asset. See Commissioner v. Idaho Power Co., 418 U.S. 1, 12–19 (1974); Woodward v. Commissioner, 397 U.S. 572, 575 (1970); United States v. General Bancshares Corp., 388 F.2d 184, 187 (8th Cir. 1968).

Woodward, supra at 577.

"The whole process of acquisition required both legal operations—fixing the price, and conveying title to the property—and we cannot see why the order in which these operations occurred . . . should make any difference in the characterization of the expenses . . ."

Hilton Hotels, supra, at 584. We are satisfied that the "origin of the claim test" applies to expenses incident to the disposition of property, as well as to the acquisition of property. See Munn v. United States, 455 F.2d 1028 (Ct.Cl.1972); Helgerson v. United States, 426 F.2d 1293 (8th Cir. 1970). The origin of the litigation expenses at issue in this case was the disposition of a capital asset—the patent.[3] We hold that the costs of disposition include legal fees incurred incident to a dispute over what the terms of the disposition are. See Munn, supra at 1032.[*]

To make the federal tax treatment of legal expenses turn on the underlying merits of the dispute giving rise to the legal expenses in a case such as this would involve the Commissioner in an area of the law far from his field of expertise. We can perceive no reason in law or policy to make the deductibility of legal expenses dependent upon the correct interpretation of a contract such as this involving the application of numerous rules of construction, see Restatement of Contracts §§ 235 and 236 (1932); Restatement of Contracts §§ 228 and 229 (Tent. Draft No. 5, 1970). See Galewitz v. Commissioner of Internal Revenue, 411 F.2d 1374, 1377–78 (2d Cir. 1969).

Appellants argue, however, that the Commissioner's interpretation of § 263 to encompass the legal fees involved in this case ignores the language and purpose of Treas.Reg. § 1–212–1(b). The text of this regulation is set out in the margin.[4] Reading the regulation as a whole, we are convinced that the regulation is not inconsistent with the Commissioner's position. We understand the regulation to mean that expenses which would be deductible from ordinary income if they were incurred in the maintenance or management of property ordinarily held for the production of income are deductible, even though the expenses were incurred in the management or maintenance of property not in fact producing ordinary income and not purchased

3. See 26 U.S.C. [I.R.C.] § 1235(a); Treas.Reg. § 1.1235–1(c)(2). [The cited regulation is omitted. Ed.]

* In a recent case an employee received an Invention Achievement Award which was held to constitute ordinary income as compensation for services rather than a capital gain from the transfer of inventions under § 1235. The Award was held to be separate from the transfer of the inventions. William F. Beausoleil, 66 T.C. 244 (1976). If the taxpayer in *Beausoleil* had incurred legal expenses in recovering the award would his expenses have been deductible? And from an *income* standpoint, is not the employment agreement involved in *Baier* much more favorable to the employee? Ed.

4. [Treas.Reg. § 1.212–1(b) is omitted. Ed.]

for the purpose of producing ordinary income. The function of the regulation is to make unnecessary any investigation into the taxpayer's subjective purpose in procuring any property or in incurring any expense. We have concluded that the regulation was not intended to overcome the injunction of § 263 that capital expenditures are not deductible expenses.

The decision of the Tax Court will be Affirmed.

SURASKY v. UNITED STATES

United States Court of Appeals, Fifth Circuit, 1963.
325 F.2d 191.

TUTTLE, CHIEF JUDGE. This appeal challenges the correctness of the judgment of the district court holding that the sum of $17,000 contributed by the taxpayer to the Wolfson-Montgomery Ward Stockholders Committee as a part of a proxy battle during 1955 was not allowable as a deduction as an ordinary and necessary non-business expense.[1]

The facts are not in dispute since substantially all of the facts were either stipulated between the parties or proved by undisputed affidavit and a deposition which was not in any way countered.

The taxpayer purchased 4000 shares of stock of Montgomery Ward & Co. in 1954 and 1955, at a total cost of $296,870.20. In making the purchase, he acted on the recommendation of Louis E. Wolfson after he made a personal investigation of the financial condition of Montgomery Ward & Co. Taxpayer purchased the stock for the sole reason that he thought it was a good chance to make money, in that it was a good long term investment because of anticipated increased dividends and appreciation in the value of the stock through improvements in the condition of the company. Mr. Wolfson, who had purchased more than 50,000 shares of the stock, had laid out what he believed to be an aggressive program which he testified he thought would improve the company and greatly enhance the value of the stock. In pursuing his plans he attempted, without success, to discuss his proposals with the management. Thereafter, the taxpayer and other stockholders formed a Committee known as the Wolfson-Montgomery Ward Stockholders Committee. The objectives of the Stockholders Committee were set out in a document entitled "Let's Rebuild Montgomery Ward."[2] This document made it clear that the Stockholders

1. [I.R.C. § 212 is omitted. Ed.]

2. Although the parties stipulated: "The objectives of this Committee were set forth in a document entitled 'Let's Rebuild Montgomery Ward', * * * which the Committee circulated, together with other similar material, to the stockholders of Montgomery Ward & Co. * * *," and although the document clearly stated the objectives to include the establishment of new stores, the relocating, modernizing or repairing of others, expanding manufacturing operations, improving employee morale, and mak-

Committee advocated far-reaching changes in the management of the company. It expressly called for the establishment of new stores; relocating and modernizing or repairing others; expanding manufacturing operations; developing private brands; increasing inventory turnovers; obtaining the services of outstanding merchandising personnel; improving employee morale; and generally revamping and bringing up to date all policies touching on advertising, merchandising, sales and corporate financing. The Committee expressly sought increased dividends and a stock split. The Stockholders Committee sought to accomplish these objectives by means of electing a new Board of Directors, or at least a majority of the Board which would then provide new management. It started a proxy campaign for the regular annual meeting of stockholders scheduled for April 22, 1955. In this effort, it incurred substantial expense which was financed by payments made from members of the Committee and other stockholders.

The taxpayer paid the Stockholders Committee $17,000 in 1955, which was expended for the purpose of the Committee during that year. The taxpayer was not an officer, director or employee and did not seek a position either as a director or as an officer or employee of the company. His stated purpose for making the payments was that he believed his opportunity to make more money from his stock investment was much greater if the purposes of the Committee could be accomplished.

It turned out that, while the drive was unsuccessful in placing a majority of the Stockholders Committees' candidates on the Board of Directors, it was at least partially successful in that three of its nominees were placed on the board of nine directors. Also, immediately after the election the Chairman of the Board and the President resigned. The Chairman of the Board and President were the focus of the attack by the Committee in challenging the current management policies of the company. It also eventuated that sales and earnings of the company increased during the latter half of the fiscal year ended January 31, 1956; the regular quarterly dividend was increased by the Directors at a meeting held on November 28, 1955,

ing changes generally in advertising, merchandising, sales, financial and personnel policies for the purpose of seeking increased dividends and a stock split, the Government, in its brief, states, "The object of the Wolfson Committee was to displace a majority of the Board of Directors and the existing management of Ward and replace them with its own nine candidates for the Board and new management."

The court also, in its finding No. 4 stated, "The object of the Wolfson Committee was to displace a majority of the Board of Directors and the existing management of Ward and replace them with its own nine candidates for the Board and new management."

The stipulation further provides, "The Committee proposed to *accomplish its objectives* by displacing a majority of the Board of Directors and existing management of the corporation with its own candidates for the Board and new management."

from $.75 per share to $1.00 per share, and an extra dividend of $1.25 per share was voted on the common stock. At the same meeting, the Board recommended a two-for-one split of the common stock, which was accomplished the following year. The market quotations of the stock increased substantially during 1955.

The taxpayer's venture in Montgomery Ward stock was a profitable one in that he received dividends totalling $30,000 on the stock purchased by him in less than a two year period, and he sold his stock in the first eight months of 1956, realizing a capital gain of $50,929.55.

Trying the case without a jury, the trial court based its legal conclusion that the expenditures were not deductible on the following summarization of the facts:

"To summarize the facts, the plaintiff herein contributed $17,000 to a committee which was to use the money to solicit proxies from other shareholders of a large, publicly-held corporation, in the hope that the committee would be able to seat a sufficient number of its candidates on the board of directors so that new management policies could be carried out which might result in larger profits and larger dividends to the shareholders.

"The plaintiff had clear title to his Ward stock and was receiving dividend income therefrom. It was certainly most speculative whether his contribution to the Wolfson Committee would touch off a series of events culminating in the production of increased income to the plaintiff. Furthermore, the plaintiff was not a candidate for the board of directors nor does the record reflect that he anticipated obtaining a position in Ward's management.

*　　*　　*

"The Court specifically finds lacking the necessary proximate relationship between the expenditure and the production of income or the management of income producing property. At the time the plaintiff contributed his funds to the committee, it was pure speculation whether he would derive any monetary reward therefrom. At the time the expenditure was made, the Court could certainly not find that it was necessary, nor was it even ordinary, within the common meaning of that word.

"The Court is not unmindful of the fact that the plaintiff, at the time he contributed the $17,000 to the committee, did so with hopes of realizing a profit and that, as a matter of fact, the dividends on his stock increased following the election of three of the Wolfson Committee's candidates. However, it is necessary to view the instant transaction as of the time it occurred, without the benefit of hindsight. The record is completely devoid of any evidence of a direct proximate relationship between the plaintiff's expenditure and the increased dividends; the latter could have been caused by any one of a myriad of factors. As for the plaintiff's desire to make a profit, there are any number of transactions entered into by the parties with a profit motive which are not accorded preferential tax treatment. The Treasury cannot be expected to underwrite all profit seeking speculations."

The appellant here urges that in its stressing of the "speculative" nature of the expenditure and the court's apparent reliance on the theory that for an expense, to be deductible under subparagraph 2 of Section 212, i. e., "for the management, conservation, or maintenance of property held for the production of income," there must be some threat of the loss of the property by the taxpayer, the court has imposed too rigid a requirement. We agree.

There is one thing both parties here agree upon, that is, that it was to change the result of the distinction between "business" and "personal" expenses that Section 212 was added to the Internal Revenue Code in 1942. The United States, in its brief, cites the decision by the Supreme Court in McDonald v. Commissioner, 323 U.S. 57, 61, 65 S.Ct. 96, 89 L.Ed. 68, as authority for the following statement: "In order to correct the inequity of making non-trade or non-business income taxable, but not allowing non-trade or non-business expenses to be deducted, Congress allowed a deduction in the new subsection (a) (2) for 'all the ordinary and necessary expenses paid or incurred' (1) 'for the production or collection of income' or (2) 'for the management, conservation, or maintenance of property held for the production or collection of income.' "

The parties also agree that in construing the language of Section 212, it is to be taken in *pari materia* with Section 162 so far as relates to the language "ordinary and necessary business expenses." [3]

From the manner in which the trial court stressed the terms "speculative" and "speculation" it is apparent that the court may have been too greatly persuaded by the language of the income tax regulations declaring, in Section 1.212–1(d), that "expenses to be deductible under Section 212, must be 'ordinary and necessary'. Thus, such expenses must be reasonable in amount and must bear a reasonable and proximate relation to the production or collection of taxable income or to the management, conservation, or maintenance of property held for the production of income." While we do not determine that this regulation is not warranted by the section of the statute with which we are involved, we think that it has been construed by the trial court to require much too difficult a showing of proximate cause in the common-law tort concept than is required by the statute.

It will be noted that nothing in the statute expressly requires a showing of a "proximate relation to the production or collection of taxable income." None of the cases cited to us by the United States contain such language. We think Congress had in mind allowing deduction of expenses genuinely incurred in the exercise of reasonable

3. [I.R.C. § 162(a) is omitted. Ed.]

business judgment in an effort to produce income that may fall far short of satisfying the common law definition of proximate cause. Thus, we think the use of the term "speculative" is not an apt expression that would describe the determining factor in deciding this issue.

This Court has held in Harris & Co. v. Lucas, Commissioner, 5th Cir., 48 F.2d 187,

"It is evident that the words 'ordinary' and 'necessary' in the statute are not used conjunctively, and are not to be construed as requiring that an expense of a business to be deductible must be both ordinary and necessary in a narrow, technical sense. On the contrary, it is clear that Congress intended the statute to be broadly construed to facilitate business generally, so that any necessary expense, not actually a capital investment, incurred in good faith in a particular business, is to be considered an ordinary expense of that business. This in effect is the construction given the statute by the Treasury Department and the courts. * * * " 48 F.2d 187, 188.

This Court has cited the Harris case a number of times with approval, most recently in Lutz v. Commissioner of Internal Revenue, 5 Cir., 282 F.2d 614, 617.[4]

In dealing with the "necessary" part of the formula, the Supreme Court has indicated in Welch v. Helvering, 290 U.S. 111, at page 113, 54 S.Ct. 8, at page 9, 78 L.Ed. 212, that this requirement may be satisfied if the expenditures "were appropriate and helpful", saying as to the taxpayer, Welch, "He certainly thought they were, and we should be slow to override his judgment."

Then, dealing with the question of what expenses are "ordinary" the Supreme Court in the same opinion said, "Here, indeed, as so often in other branches of the law, the decisive distinctions are those of degree and not of kind. One struggles in vain for any verbal formula that will supply a ready touchstone. The standard set up by the statute is not a rule of law; it is rather a way of life. Life in all its fullness must supply the answer to the riddle."

Here, it seems incontestable that the payments made by the taxpayer were made with the anticipation that profit to the taxpayer would result. It may have been a long chance that Mr. Surasky was taking. However, he testified he knew Mr. Wolfson well enough to know his ability and believed that there was reasonable likelihood of success. This testimony is undisputed. In point of fact, the activity resulting from the expenditures by the taxpayer and his associates did produce direct and tangible results in that three nominees of the Committee were elected to the Board of Directors, the President, who

4. The entire paragraph from the Harris & Co. case is quoted above although it is clear that the Supreme Court in Welch v. Helvering, 290 U.S. 111, 54 S.Ct. 8, 78 L.Ed. 212, has held that in order to qualify as a business deduction an expenditure must be *both* necessary *and* ordinary. However, we still believe that they need not be "both ordinary and necessary in a narrow, technical sense," as stated in the Harris & Co. case.

had been severely criticized by the Committee was caused to resign as was the Chairman of the Board, and many other actions which parallel those sought for by the Committee were undertaken by the corporation. Profits were increased; dividends were increased; the stock enhanced in value. We think that for a trial court to conclude that there was not sufficient connection between the expenditure to assist the Committee in its activities and the achievement of so many of its objectives was too remote to meet the test of what is reasonable and ordinary in this particular type of investor activity is to apply too rigid a standard in the application of a remedial statute.

While there are differences in the facts, as there must always be in different cases, we think that the Tax Court decision in Alleghany Corporation, 28 T.C. 298, acq. 1957–2 C.B. 3, points the direction in which the statute should be applied. The expenditures there sought to be deducted were for proxy solicitation and other committee activities in a railroad reorganization. To be sure, the proposal that was fought successfully in that case would have resulted in diluting the taxpayer's common stock possibly to the vanishing point. However, we think it immaterial whether the expenditure is directed towards an effort to prevent the loss or dilution of an equity interest or to cause an enhancement or increase of the equity value, as was the undoubted purpose in the case before us. The Tax Court there said, 28 T.C. page 304, "We think it is clear that the expenditures in question were made for no other purpose than to protect petitioner's business." See also Shoe Corporation of America, 29 T.C. 297, 1957, acq. 1958–2 C.B. 7, and Allied Chemical Corp. v. United States (Ct.Cl.1962), 305 F.2d 433.

It appearing, as we have noted above, that the decision of this case was based on undisputed evidence, most of which was stipulated, our review of the decision of the trial court is somewhat freed from the "clearly erroneous" rule. See Patterson v. Belcher, 5th Cir., 302 F.2d 289, 292, cert. denied, 371 U.S. 921, 83 S.Ct. 289, 9 L.Ed.2d 230; Galena Oaks Corporation v. Scofield, 5th Cir., 218 F.2d 217, 219.

The judgment is reversed and the case is remanded to the trial court for the entry of a judgment in favor of the appellant, taxpayer.

REVENUE RULING 64–236 [1]

1964–2 Cum.Bull. 64.

The Internal Revenue Service will follow the decision of the U. S. Court of Appeals for the Fourth Circuit in the case of R. Walter Graham, et ux. v. Commissioner, 326 F.2d 878 (1964).

---

1. Based on Technical Information Release 613, dated July 23, 1964.

This decision held that proxy fight expenditures are deductible by a stockholder under section 212 of the Internal Revenue Code of 1954, if such expenditures are proximately related to either the production or collection of income or to the management, conservation or maintenance of property held for the production of income.

The Service will also follow the decision of the U. S. Court of Appeals for the Fifth Circuit in Jack Surasky v. United States, 325 F.2d 191 (1963), a case involving a similar issue. Internal Revenue will not, however, follow this decision to the extent that the court in its opinion indicates that to be deductible proxy fight expenditures need not be proximately related to either the production or collection of income or to the management, conservation, or maintenance of property held for the production of income.

MEYER J. FLEISCHMAN *

Tax Court of the United States, 1966.
45 T.C. 439.

SIMPSON, JUDGE: The Commissioner has determined a deficiency in the petitioner's income tax for 1962 in the amount of $725.60. The issue in this case is whether the petitioner may deduct legal expenses incurred in defending his wife's lawsuit to set aside their antenuptial contract.

Findings of Fact

Meyer J. Fleischman, the petitioner, is a physician in Cincinnati, Ohio. He reported his income on the cash method of accounting and filed his 1962 income tax return with the district director of internal revenue at Cincinnati, Ohio.

On February 25, 1955, petitioner entered into an antenuptial agreement with Joan Ruth Francis. That agreement was made in contemplation of marriage and provided: [that in case of divorce Meyer would pay Joan $5000, in consideration for which Joan released all interest in Meyer's property.]

Petitioner and Joan R. Francis were married on February 26, 1955. On December 20, 1961, Joan filed for a divorce in the Court of Common Pleas, Division of Domestic Relations, Hamilton County, Ohio. In her suit for divorce the wife made the following prayer: [*inter alia*] That plaintiff be awarded a fair and equitable division of all properties, real and personal, of the defendant Meyer J. Fleisch-

---

* Two articles covering but ranging beyond the problems in *Fleischman* are Barton, "The Aspects of Divorce and Property Settlement Agreements— The *Davis*, *Gilmore*, and *Patrick* Cas- es," 16 U.S.C. Tax Inst. 421 (1964); Barton, "Current Tax Problems in Marriage and Divorce," 19 U.S.C. Tax Inst. 609 (1967). Ed.

man, and for all such other and further relief to which she may be entitled in the premises, including her attorney fees and expenses.

On December 26, 1961, she filed another action in the Court of Common Pleas, Hamilton County, Ohio. The latter suit was instituted to set aside the antenuptial agreement and was necessary because the domestic relations division had no jurisdiction to declare the contract void and invalid. In her petition, she alleged that her husband had deceived her by false representations concerning the validity of the agreement, and that at the time of the agreement and at the time of filing suit she had no idea of the nature and extent of the defendant's property. She asserted that the provisions made for her under the agreement were grossly disproportionate to her husband's means.

A decree of divorce was entered on October 19, 1962. The suit to rescind and invalidate the antenuptial agreement was dismissed with prejudice on the plaintiff's application October 22, 1962.

Petitioner did not deduct the legal expenses incurred in connection with the divorce proceeding. Petitioner did deduct on his 1962 return $3,000 for legal expenses incurred in defending the suit to invalidate the antenuptial agreement signed on February 25, 1955. Respondent disallowed this deduction and determined a deficiency of $725.60. This deficiency is in issue here.

Opinion

The sole question in this case is whether petitioner is entitled to deduct $3,000 in legal expenses incurred in defending his wife's suit to set aside an antenuptial agreement.

We hold that he is barred from deducting these expenses by section 262 of the Internal Revenue Code of 1954 [1] and the decision of the Supreme Court in United States v. Gilmore, 372 U.S. 39 (1963).

The petitioner's brief asserts first that his position was adequately set forth in the opinion of Carpenter v. United States, 338 F.2d 366 (Ct.Cl.1964). Second, he argues that Erdman v. Commissioner, 315 F.2d 762 (C.A.7, 1963), affirming 37 T.C. 1119 (1962), supports his position. Lastly, petitioner suggests that the litigation giving rise to the legal expenses here in issue did not grow out of the marriage relationship, but sprang from rights excluded from that relationship. The respondent has countered that the Carpenter case is distinguishable; that Erdman is inapposite; and that the suggested distinction between rights flowing from the marriage relationship and rights flowing from an antenuptial agreement is one of form and should be rejected. In the alternative, respondent urges that the expenses were incurred in defending title to property and should be capitalized, not allowed as a deduction.

---

1. All statutory references are to the Internal Revenue Code of 1954 unless otherwise indicated.

We agree with all three of respondent's arguments and, therefore, do not reach his alternative proposition.

Petitioner's first contention, that his position is sustained by *Carpenter* is untenable. *Carpenter* involved a deduction for legal expenses paid for tax counsel in the course of a divorce proceeding. The court found these payments to be deductible under section 212(3) as an ordinary and necessary expense paid in connection with the determination of a tax. In Fleischman's case, there is no suggestion in the record that the legal expenses involved were for consultation and advice on tax matters. The stipulation clearly states that the expenses were incurred in defending a suit to set aside and declare void an antenuptial contract.

If petitioner means to rely on *Carpenter* to sustain his case under section 212(2) or 212(1), he is left with the liability that the case did not deal with those paragraphs. Paragraph (3) of section 212, as the *Carpenter* case holds, expresses a policy and has a meaning quite different from paragraphs (1) and (2). In fact, the court pointed out in *Carpenter* that the legal fees would not be deductible under section 212(2).

If petitioner cites *Carpenter* for the proposition that certain legal fees can be deducted even though incurred in connection with a divorce, he is certainly correct. This Court has so held in the case of Ruth K. Wild, 42 T.C. 706 (1964). The question in the case before us, however, is whether *these* legal expenses are deductible, and in resolving that issue, the *Carpenter* case is of no assistance.

The petitioner's second argument is that the case of Erdman v. Commissioner, may be pertinent. We do not agree. *Erdman* concerned the deductibility of legal expenses incurred by taxpayers defending their title to property as beneficiaries of a testamentary trust. In the alternative, it was contended that the trust was entitled to deduct these expenses. This Court held that the attorney's fees were an expenditure of the trust, not of the taxpayer. In addition, the trust was not permitted to deduct the fee currently as it was charged to trust corpus, not income. Calvin Pardee Erdman, 37 T.C. 1119 (1962).

On appeal, the Seventh Circuit upheld the Tax Court on both grounds and added that the taxpayer's expenses were capital in nature, being in defense of title, and not deductible for that reason as well. Erdman v. Commissioner, supra. It is our view that the factual and legal issues in *Erdman* are so significantly different from those in this case that it is of no assistance in reaching our decision.

The expenditures in question are deductible, if at all, only under section 212.[2] Since there is not the slightest indication in the record that the counsel fees concerned taxes, we do not consider this case

2.　[I.R.C. § 212 is omitted. Ed.]

under section 212(3). In addition, there is no support for the view that the petitioner incurred the legal expenses for the production or collection of income, nor does he argue that he did; therefore, section 212(1) is not raised. The petition alleges that the expense was for the preservation and protection of taxpayer's real property inherited from his mother. This leaves only the suggestion that the expenses are deductible under section 212(2) as paid for the management, conservation, or maintenance of property held for the production of income.

In approaching the issue thus presented, it is helpful to consider the general purpose and history of section 212. Prior to 1942, legal expenses were deductible only if the suit occasioning them was directly connected with or proximately related to the taxpayer's trade or business. Sarah Backer, et al., Executors, 1 B.T.A. 214 (1924). Legal costs which were simply personal expenses were not deductible, although the line between personal and business expenses was sometimes difficult to draw. Kornhauser v. United States, 276 U.S. 145 (1928).

Certain investment activities conducted by the taxpayer might generate taxable income; however, the expenses attributable to these activities were not deductible where the activities did not constitute a trade or business. Higgins v. Commissioner, 312 U.S. 212 (1941). In order to equalize the treatment of these expenses with business expenses,[3] both of which produced taxable income, Congress added section 23(a) (2) to the 1939 Code by the Revenue Act of 1942 (56 Stat. 798, 819). That section provided as follows:

SEC. 23. DEDUCTIONS FROM GROSS INCOME.

In computing net income there shall be allowed as deductions:

(a) EXPENSES.—

*   *   *   *   *   *   *   *   *   *

(2) NON-TRADE OR NON-BUSINESS EXPENSES.—In the case of an individual, all the ordinary and necessary expenses paid or incurred during the taxable year for the production or collection of income, or for the management, conservation, or maintenance of property held for the production of income.

At the same time that Congress enacted section 23(a) (2), it also added sections 22(k) and 23(u) to the 1939 Code. In general, those sections required a divorced spouse to include alimony payments in her gross income and permitted the paying spouse to deduct the amounts paid from his taxable income. Thus, while the Congress increased the range of deductions by section 23(a) (2), it also provided for a new kind of taxable income to a divorced spouse. How-

3. H.Rept. No. 2333, 77th Cong., 2d Sess., p. 75 (1942), 1942–2 C.B. 372, 429.

ever, Congress left us with no guidance in the legislative history as to the relationship between the alimony provisions and section 23(a) (2).

Section 23(a) (2) was construed as enlarging the category of incomes with respect to which expenses were deductible. Deductions under that section were analogous to business expenses and were allowable or not in accordance with principles which had long controlled these expenses. McDonald v. Commissioner, 323 U.S. 57 (1944). In particular, legal expenses were allowable as investment expenses subject to the same limitations imposed on legal fees incurred in a trade or business. Trust of Bingham v. Commissioner, 325 U.S. 365 (1945).

Great difficulty was experienced in distinguishing deductible legal expenses from those which were purely personal. This Court found that a wife could deduct legal fees incurred to obtain alimony included in her gross income under the Revenue Act of 1942. Elsie B. Gale, 13 T.C. 661 (1949), affd. 191 F.2d 79 (C.A.2, 1951), acq. 1952-1 C.B. 2; Barbara B. LeMond, 13 T.C. 670 (1949), acq. 1952-1 C.B. 3. On the other hand, the husband's legal expenses were regarded as personal even if he was compelled to pay his wife's counsel fees, or if his income-producing property was threatened with sequestration to pay alimony. Lindsay C. Howard, 16 T.C. 157 (1951), affd. 202 F.2d 28 (C.A.9, 1953); Robert A. McKinney, 16 T.C. 916 (1951); Thorne Donnelley, 16 T.C. 1196 (1951).

The Supreme Court in construing the new section found that Congress did not intend to permit taxpayers to deduct personal, living, or family expenses. Lykes v. United States, 343 U.S. 118, 125 (1952). In applying this rationale, the Court stated as follows:

* * * Legal expenses do not become deductible merely because they are paid for services which relieve a taxpayer of liability. That argument would carry us too far. It would mean that the expense of defending almost any claim would be deductible by a taxpayer on the ground that such defense was made to help him keep clear of liens whatever income-producing property he might have. * * * Section 23(a) (2) never has been so interpreted by us. It has been applied to expenses on the basis of their immediate purposes rather than upon the basis of the remote contributions they might make to the conservation of a taxpayer's income-producing assets by reducing his general liabilities. See McDonald v. Commissioner, supra, * * *

In 1963, the Court undertook to explain the application of this rationale to a husband's legal expenses incurred in a divorce action. United States v. Gilmore, 372 U.S. 39 (1963).

The taxpayer in *Gilmore* owned a controlling interest in three corporations. The dividends and salary from these companies were his major source of income. In a divorce proceeding, his wife alleged that much of this property was community property and that more than half of the community property should be awarded to her. The taxpayer incurred substantial legal expenses in the course of successfully resisting these claims. He sought to deduct the expenses attributable to his defense against his wife's property claims under section 23(a) (2) of the 1939 Code. The Supreme Court sustained the Government's contention that deductibility depended upon the origin and nature of the claim giving rise to the legal expenses, rather than upon the consequences of such a claim to income-producing property.[4]

The Supreme Court reached this result for two basic reasons. First, the language of the statute "conservation of property" was said to refer to operations performed with respect to the property itself rather than the taxpayer's retention of ownership in it. Secondly, the Court examined the legislative history and discerned a congressional purpose to equalize treatment of expenditures for profit-seeking activities with those related to a trade or business. In order to achieve this result, any limitation or restriction imposed upon a business expense must be applied to section 23(a) (2) expenses. Among those restrictions was the rule, now embodied in section 262, that personal, living, or family expenses are not deductible. The characterization of litigation costs as personal or business depends upon whether the claim involved in the litigation arises in connection with the profit-seeking activities. A suit against a taxpayer must be directly connected with or proximately result from his business before it is a business expense. This being so, the "origin of claim" test used in the business deduction cases was selected as most consistent with the meaning of section 23(a) (2). The claim against the property in a divorce suit arises only from the marital relationship and is therefore personal. The wife's rights, if any, must have their source in the marriage.

Dispelling all doubts that the Supreme Court was passing only on community property claims was United States v. Patrick, 372 U.S. 53 (1963), decided the same day as *Gilmore*. The *Patrick* case dealt with a property settlement which was made prior to divorce and which was supposed to have preserved the husband's income-producing property. The Supreme Court found little or no difference between that situation and *Gilmore* where the issue concerned community property and the wife's claim to an award of more than her existing share of such property.

Gilmore was decided under the 1939 Code and *Patrick* under the 1954 Code. There was no suggestion in these cases that enactment of the 1954 Code changed the meaning of the statutory language.

---

4. The Commissioner's regulations have long provided that expenses do not become deductible merely because incurred in defense of a claim which may result in income-producing property being sold or used to satisfy taxpayer's liability. Sec. 39.23(a)–15(k), Regs. 118; sec. 1.212–1(m), Income Tax Regs.

The 1954 Code divides the provisions formerly contained in section 23(a) (2) of the 1939 Code into two paragraphs. The first deals with expenses for the production of income, and the second with expenses for the management, conservation, or maintenance of property held for the production of income. In connection with section 212(1) and (2), the legislative history specifically states that no substantive change from section 23(a) (2) of the Internal Revenue Code of 1939 was made. Thus, the Code simply puts in separate paragraphs what was once one sentence.

Scarcely had the *Gilmore* case been decided, when the Tax Court was again confronted with the issue of the deductibility of the wife's attorney fees expended to collect defaulted alimony payments. Jane U. Elliott, 40 T.C. 304 (1963), acq. 1964–1 C.B. (Part 1) 4. In accordance with prior law, the wife was allowed a deduction under section 212(1). The Court held that the legal fees in question were incurred for the production of her taxable income. *Gilmore* and *Patrick* were not cited in this opinion.

The following year the case of Ruth K. Wild, 42 T.C. 706 (1964), was presented for review by the whole Court. The wife sought a deduction for counsel fees under section 212(1) in reliance upon the *Elliott* case for expenses incurred in negotiating an alimony agreement and in hearings concerning this agreement. The respondent contended that *Gilmore* and *Patrick* required a contrary result since the expenses were attributable to a claim which was based on her marital rights and not on a profit-seeking activity. This Court distinguished *Gilmore* and *Patrick* upon the basis that both of those cases were decided under paragraph (2) of section 212 and the contention in the *Wild* case was that the legal fees were deductible under paragraph (1). The Commissioner's regulations permitting a deduction for legal costs attributable to the collection of taxable alimony had not been changed following the *Gilmore* decision. Neither had his acquiescence in *Elliott* been withdrawn. These two factors influenced the Court in holding that the wife could continue to deduct legal expenses related to alimony. Thus, she retained a deduction under section 212(1).

This Court has made it clear that the wife's deduction under section 212(1) is limited to expenses incurred in obtaining alimony includable in her gross income. There is no deduction for expenses related to property claims, even when incurred by the wife. Those claims grow out of the marital relationship and are covered by the rule in *Gilmore*. Georgia Leary Neill, 42 T.C. 793 (1964).

Turning to the case at hand, both petitioner and respondent have argued the case under section 212(2). In order to prevail, the petitioner must demonstrate how his expenses differ from those in *Gilmore* and *Patrick*. We find that he has failed in this task.

Petitioner suggests that his expenses differ from those at issue in *Gilmore* because his were caused by a separate suit to rescind a contract. In Joan Fleischman's second suit, she alleged that the provisions of the antenuptial agreement were disproportionate to her husband's means at the time the agreement was made and at the time of suit. Simultaneously, she had a divorce suit pending requesting support payments. Viewed in its entirety, her effort was one directed at obtaining support payments greater than those provided in the antenuptial agreement. In part, her claim to greater rights was founded upon facts existing or arising during the marriage. In this respect her claim was not unlike that involved in the *Gilmore* case. There, the claim was that certain community property belonging one-half to the husband should be awarded to the wife because of wrongs committed during the marital relationship. The Supreme Court rejected any distinction between legal expenses related to the issue of whether assets were community property and those related to an award of such property. Both issues have a common origin. In both *Gilmore* and here, the wife was requesting an award of property and her right was founded only upon the consequences that State law attaches to marriage. In petitioner's case, his wife made no claim to specific property except as a source of payment, hence his position is even weaker than that of the taxpayer in *Gilmore*.

The fact that Fleischman's wife first had to file a separate suit to invalidate the antenuptial agreement is solely the result of the restricted jurisdiction of the Ohio divorce courts. That fact alone is not a sound basis for a distinction in the field of Federal taxation.

For ascertaining the source of claims giving rise to legal expenses, the Supreme Court suggested a "but for" test. If the claim could not have existed but for the marriage relationship, the expense of defending it is a personal expense and not deductible. Applying that test, it is clear that but for her marriage to petitioner, the wife could have no claim to the property sought to be protected.

In deciding that the antenuptial agreement in this case is not significantly different from a property settlement incident to a divorce, we are aided in our reasoning by United States v. Patrick. In that case, complicated property adjustments were required so that the husband could retain controlling interest in a publishing business owned jointly with his wife. The legal fees involved were spent arranging a transfer of various stocks, leasing real property, and creating a trust, rather than conducting divorce litigation. The Supreme Court found no legal significance in these differences from *Gilmore*. The Court found that the transfers were incidental to the litigation which had its origin in taxpayer's personal life. It could be argued that we should take a narrow view and say that the suit to set aside petitioner's antenuptial agreement concerned contract rights. However, that view ignores the fact that marital rights were the subject of this contract and the fact that the second lawsuit was intimately bound up with the divorce litigation. In *Patrick*, the settlement agreement stated that it settled "rights growing out of the marital relationship." In the case at hand, the agreement states that the parties desire to agree to a distribution of property should their marriage be dissolved by divorce or annulment. We can perceive little or no difference between the two agreements when the question of deducting legal expenses is in issue.

A similar question was presented in David G. Joyce, 3 B.T.A. 393 (1926). The taxpayer there sought a deduction for legal expenses incurred in defending a postnuptial agreement from attack by his wife. The agreement was made in 1913 and governed rights upon death or divorce. In 1920 the wife instituted an action for divorce and for an award of maintenance in addition to the provisions of the postnuptial contract. The taxpayer sought to deduct the expenses related to defending the agreement as a business expense. He argued that the contract gave him greater freedom in managing his business property and that such property was the subject of the contract.

In holding that the expenses were personal, the Board stated that the husband's argument ignored the genesis of the rights he attempted to settle and limit by the postnuptial agreement. Those rights existed and would exist only by virtue of the marriage.[5]

In conclusion, we find no significant distinction between this case and the *Gilmore* and *Patrick* cases, and accordingly, we hold that the legal expenses incurred by the petitioner are not deductible.

Decision will be entered for the respondent.

PROBLEMS

1. Speculator buys 100 shares of Sound Company stock for $3000, paying his broker a commission of $50 on the purchase. Fourteen months later he sells the shares for $4000 paying a commission of $60 on the sale.

  (a) He would like to treat $110 paid as commissions as I.R.C. § 212 expenses. Why? Can he? See Spreckles v. Helvering, 315 U.S. 626, 62 S.Ct. 777 (1942).

  (b) What result in (a), above, if instead he sells the shares for $2500 paying a $45 commission on the sale? See I.R.C. § 165(c)(2).

  (c) Speculator owned only one-tenth of one percent of the Sound Company stock but being an eager investor during the time he owned the stock, he incurred $500 of transportation, meals and lodging expenses in traveling 1000 miles to New York City to attend Sound's annual shareholder meeting. May he deduct his costs under § 212(2)?

5. "It is hardly necessary to allude to the fact that marriage is a personal relationship, except for the purpose of pointing out that the legal rights and obligations annexed to the relationship are also personal and the expenses connected therewith would, we think, come within the classification of personal or family expenses." (David G. Joyce, 3 B.T.A. 393, 397.)

(d) What result in (c), above, if instead Speculator owned 10% of the total outstanding Sound stock worth $300,000?

(e) Speculator owns 10% of Sound's stock worth $300,000 and he incurs $10,000 in legal fees and personal costs investigating the operation of the business after the business has some serious setbacks. Is the $10,000 deductible?

(f) Speculator (a 10% shareholder) agrees to sell his stock in installments to Buyer at its price on the market at the time of each sale, but subject to changes in valuation for blockage. A dispute arises over the "blockage" effects on value. May Speculator deduct his Attorney's fees incurred in determining the "blockage" effect on his stock's value?

2.   After reading the *Fleischman* case, consider in what situations:

(a) Husband's attorneys' fees incurred in getting a divorce are deductible by him.

(b) Wife's attorneys' fees incurred in getting a divorce are deductible by her.

(c) Wife's attorneys' fees incurred in getting a divorce are deductible by Husband if he pays them.

3.   Planner consults his attorneys with respect to his estate plan. They decide to make various intervivos gifts and draft his will. To what extent, if any, are Planner's legal fees deductible under § 212 (3)?   Under § 212(2)?   See Rev.Rul. 72–545, 1972–2 C.B. 179, and Sidney Merians, 60 T.C. 187 (1973), acq., 1973–2 C.B. 2.

B. CHARGES ARISING OUT OF TRANSACTIONS ENTERED INTO FOR PROFIT

Internal Revenue Code: Sections 165(a), (b), (c)(2); 167(a)(2); 212.
Regulations: Sections 1.165–9(b); 1.167(g)–1; 1.212–1(h).

WILLIAM C. HORRMANN *

Tax Court of the United States, 1951.
171 T.C. 903(A).

[The Findings of Fact have been omitted.]

Opinion

BLACK, JUDGE: Three issues are presented in this proceeding. All issues relate to the real property, residence and garage, at 189 Howard Avenue, Staten Island, New York, which was acquired by petitioner by a devise from his mother upon her death in February 1940.

Petitioner redecorated the house and moved into it about October 1940. Shortly thereafter petitioner sold the residence in which he was living prior to October 1940. The property at 189 Howard Avenue was used by petitioner as his personal residence until October 1942, at which time petitioner abandoned the house. Petitioner, after living in the residence for awhile, considered the property too large and too expensive and when he left he planned never to use it again as his personal residence.

Petitioner considered converting the building into apartments, but this was found to be impractical. Numerous efforts were made to rent and to sell the property. The property was sold in June 1945, and the net proceeds from the sale were $20,800. At the time petitioner acquired the property its value was $60,000, and at the time it was abandoned by petitioner as a personal residence the value was $45,000, with $35,000 allocated to land and $10,000 to the buildings.

The issue which we shall first consider is whether petitioner is entitled to a deduction for depreciation on the property during the taxable years 1943, 1944, and 1945. The applicable provision of the Internal Revenue Code is set forth in the margin.[1]

---

* Problems such as those presented here and in *Lowry,* infra page ——, are discussed in Erck, "And You Thought Moving Was Bad—Try Deducting Depreciation and Maintenance Expenses on Your Unsold Residence," 26 U.Fla.L.R. 587 (1974); Reese, "Maintenance and Depreciation Deductions Are Not Available on a Residence Vacated and Offered for Sale But Not for Rent Unless Taxpayer Intends to Profit," 49 Texas L. Rev. 581 (1971); and Fasan, "Maintenance and Depreciation Deductions for a Personal Residence Offered for Sale," 25 Tax L.Rev. 269 (1970). Ed.

1. [I.R.C. (1939) § 23(*l*) (2) is omitted. See I.R.C. (1954) § 167(a) (2). Ed.]

Petitioner is entitled to a deduction for depreciation at the rate of $500 per year provided the property was *held for the production of income*. In determining whether the test prescribed by statute is satisfied the use made of the property and the owner's intent in respect to the future use or disposition of the property are generally controlling. Until November 1942, the property was used by petitioner solely as a personal residence, but thereafter that use was abandoned. The mere abandonment of such use does not mean that thereafter the property was held for the production of income. But when efforts are made to rent the property as were made by petitioner herein, the property is then being held for the production of income and this may be so even though no income is in fact received from the property, Mary Laughlin Robinson, 2 T.C. 305, and even though the property is at the same time offered for sale. While an intention not to rent the house was indicated in May 1943, on the brochure of the real estate clearing house, efforts to rent the property were made subsequent to that time. The evidence, when considered in its entirety, supports the conclusion that petitioner continuously offered to rent the property until it was sold. In the recomputation of tax for the years 1943, 1944, and 1945, petitioner is to be allowed depreciation at the rate of $500 per year until June 1945, when the property was sold.

The second issue is whether petitioner is entitled to a deduction for expenses incurred during the taxable years for the maintenance and conservation of the property. The applicable provision of the Internal Revenue Code is set forth in the margin.[2] The same phrase appearing in section 23(1) (2) of the Code, see footnote 1 of this Opinion, appears also in section 23(a) (2) of the Code, the requirement being that the property be *held for the production of income*. The taxpayer in Mary Laughlin Robinson, supra, claimed a deduction for depreciation on the property and expenses for services of a caretaker. Although the taxable year there was 1937, the sections of the Code applicable there (see footnote 1 of that Opinion) contain the same standard, *property held for the production of income*, as is applicable here. We there held that the taxpayer was entitled to both the deductions at issue. In accordance with that Opinion, we hold that petitioner in the recomputation of tax for the years 1943 and 1944, is entitled to deductions for maintenance and conservation expenses of the property as itemized in our Findings of Fact.

The third issue is whether petitioner is entitled to a deduction for a long term capital loss arising from the sale in 1945 of the property at 189 Howard Avenue. Petitioner claims a deduction under the provisions of section 23(e) (2) of the Code which are set forth in the margin,[3] and he has computed the deduction in accordance with the limitations provisions of section 117 of the Code.

---

2. [I.R.C. (1939) § 23(a) (2) is omitted. See I.R.C. (1954) § 212(2). Ed.]

3. [I.R.C. (1939) § 23(e) (2) is omitted. See I.R.C. (1954) § 165(c) (2). Ed.]

The language of the Code sections applicable in issues one and two was *property held for the production of income,* and the language of section 23(e) (2) of the Code is different. In order for a loss to be deductible under that section it must be incurred *in any transaction entered into for profit.* In a situation where the use of the property as a personal residence has been abandoned, and where the owner has offered the property for sale or for rent and finally sells the property at a loss, that distinction in language may result in allowing a deduction in one case and not allowing a deduction of another type. At least the cases have distinguished between the two statutory provisions, Warner v. Commissioner, 167 F.2d 633, affirming per curiam a Memorandum Opinion of this Court. We think that the facts in respect to this issue are not materially different from those in Allen L. Grammer, 12 T.C. 34, and those in Morgan v. Commissioner, 76 F.2d 390. When property has been used as a personal residence, in order to convert the transaction into one entered into for profit the owner must do more than abandon the property and list it for sale or rent, Allen L. Grammer, supra. See also Rumsey v. Commissioner, 82 F.2d 158. In that case, in denying the taxpayer any deduction for the loss so incurred, the Court said:

The taxpayer argues with considerable persuasive force that the fact that a man first rents his house before selling it is only significant as evidentiary of his purpose to abandon it as a residence and to devote the property to business uses; that renting is not the sole criterion of such purpose, as the regulations themselves imply by the words "rented or otherwise appropriated" to income producing purposes. But we think the argument cannot prevail over counter considerations. If an owner rents, his decision is irrevocable, at least for the term of the lease; and if he remodels to fit the building for business purposes, he has likewise made it impossible to resume residential uses by a mere change of mind. When, however, he only instructs an agent to sell or rent the property, its change of character remains subject to his unfettered will; he may revoke the agency at any moment. Certainly it strains the language of Article 171, Regulations 74, to find that the property is "appropriated to" and "used for" income producing purposes by merely listing it with a broker for sale or rental.   *   *   *

We have held that an actual rental of the property is not always essential to a conversion, Estate of Maria Assmann, 16 T.C. 632, but that case is not controlling here for the taxpayer there abandoned the residence only a few days after it was inherited, and then later demolished the residence. In Mary E. Crawford, 16 T.C. 678, which involved only the question of whether the loss was a section 23(e) (1) loss or a section 23(e) (2) loss, the owner-taxpayer had also demolished the residence. While we held in both cases that such action constituted an appropriation or conversion, in both cases the facts indicate that from the moment the properties were inherited the taxpayers did not intend to continue to occupy the property as their personal residence.

Here the situation is different. The petitioners in the instant case soon after the death of petitioner's mother took immediate and decisive action, fixing the character of the property in their hands as residential. The surrounding circumstances point to this conclusion; their expenditure of approximately $9,000 in redecorating the house in preparation for their use of it as a home; their moving into the property within nine months after they acquired it; the sale of their former residence at Ocean Terrace shortly after they had moved into the Howard Avenue property; and finally, their occupancy of the Howard Avenue property for a period of about two years as a home and residence. They could hardly have gone further more decisively to fix the character of this property, originally neutral in their hands, as personal residential property.

As to the third issue, we think there was no conversion of the property into a transaction entered into for profit. Respondent did not err in determining that petitioner was not entitled to the benefits of a capital loss carry-over to 1946 for the loss sustained upon the sale in 1945 of the property at 189 Howard Avenue. Allen L. Grammer, supra.

Decision will be entered under Rule 50.

LOWRY v. UNITED STATES

District Court of the United States, District of New Hampshire, 1974.
384 F.Supp. 257.

Opinion

BOWNES, DISTRICT JUDGE. Plaintiffs bring this action to recover federal income taxes and interest, in the amount of $1,072, which they allege were erroneously or illegally assessed and collected. Jurisdiction is based on 28 U.S.C. § 1346(a)(1).

The issue is whether plaintiffs, who ceased to use their summer house as residential property in 1967 and immediately offered it for sale without attempting to rent the property, converted it into "income producing property," thereby entitling them to deduct the maintenance expenses incurred after it was put on the market and prior to its sale in 1973. The Internal Revenue Service allowed plaintiffs to take maintenance deductions in the tax years 1968 and 1969. They disallowed similar maintenance deductions in the tax year 1970. The only year in issue is 1970.[1]

Plaintiffs are husband and wife domiciled in Peterborough, New Hampshire. (Since Edward G. Lowry, Jr., is the principal party in

---

1. Plaintiff, due to his own mistake, failed to take the allowable deprecia- tion deductions and that matter is not before this court.

this case, he alone will hereinafter be referred to as plaintiff.)   Plaintiff filed a joint federal income tax return for 1970 with the District Director of Internal Revenue in Portsmouth, New Hampshire.   On his 1970 income tax return, plaintiff deducted expenditures made for the care and maintenance of his former summer residence.   He based these deductions upon the premise that the summer residence was no longer personal property, but was property "held for the production of income."   Int.Rev.Code of 1954 § 212.   The Internal Revenue Service disagreed with plaintiff and disallowed the deduction basing its decision on Internal Revenue Code of 1954 § 262 which provides:

> Except as otherwise expressly provided in this chapter, no deductions shall be allowed for personal, living, or family expenses.

On November 27, 1971, plaintiff paid the disputed $1,072 under written protest.

The property in question is plaintiff's former summer residence on Martha's Vineyard (hereinafter referred to as Vineyard property).   The Vineyard property is part of a cooperative community known as Seven Gates Farm Corporation.

Seven Gates was formed in 1921 by five persons, one of whom was plaintiff's father.   Upon forming the corporation, plaintiff's father acquired the Vineyard property.   In 1942, plaintiff acquired "title" to the property by gift from his father.

Legal title to the Vineyard property is held by Seven Gates.   In 1970, plaintiff had a lease for the Vineyard property and was a 3% stockholder in the corporation.   The leasing arrangement treated plaintiff as the de facto owner of the property.   It ran for the life of the corporation with the proviso that, upon dissolution of the corporation, it would automatically be converted into a fee title.   No stockholder-lessee, however, could sell his stock and lease without the prior consent of 75% of the stockholder-lessees.   Each lease further provided that a rental for a year or less required the prior consent of the Committee on Admissions and that a lease for more than a year required the prior consent of 75% of the other stockholder-lessees.

In 1966, plaintiff owned three residential properties: he maintained his legal residence in Maryland; he had a winter residence in Florida; and the Vineyard property.   During 1966, plaintiff sold his Maryland home and purchased a house in Peterborough, New Hampshire.   Because the Peterborough house did "all the things that the house in Martha's Vineyard did," plaintiff decided, in 1967, to sell the Vineyard property and put a sales price on it of $150,000.   From 1921 through 1967, plaintiff had spent nearly all of his summers at the Vineyard property.

After it was put on the market, the house was never again used as residential property.   Each spring plaintiff went to Martha's

Vineyard, opened the house, put up curtains, pruned the shrubbery, generally cleaned and spruced up the property, and then left. This took two or three days and plaintiff occupied the house during this period. Each fall plaintiff returned and closed the house for the winter. The closing also took two to three days and plaintiff stayed in the house. The only other time that plaintiff occupied the property was once a year, when the corporation had its annual meeting of stockholders. As evidence of his intent to treat the Vineyard property as a business asset, plaintiff testified that in 1971 his daughter, after returning from abroad, requested the use of the property. Plaintiff refused, stating that the property was a business proposition. As a fatherly gesture, however, he rented a summer home in Maine for her use.

Plaintiff made no attempt to rent the house for the following reasons: He believed that it would be easier to sell a clean empty house than one occupied by tenants; the house being suitable for summer occupancy only, would have had to have been rented completely equipped, which would have required the plaintiff to purchase linen, silver, blankets, and recreational equipment at a cost which would not have been justified by any possible rental; rental prices bore no reasonable relation to the value of the property and the expected sales price; and rental was complicated by the restrictive provisions of the corporation's bylaws.

In 1968, a prospective purchaser offered to buy the property for $150,000. Plaintiff, however, could not obtain the necessary 75% approval of the stockholders of Seven Gates and the sale was not completed. In 1973, plaintiff received a cash offer of $150,000 for the property and the sale was closed in September of 1973. Plaintiff's 1973 tax return showed a net long-term capital gain of $100,-536.50, as a result of the sale.

Rulings of Law

The tax issue in this case is: When and how does residential property become converted into income producing property?

The Tax Court, in attempting to establish a clear guideline in a murky area, created a simple test: The taxpayer had to make a bona fide offer to rent in order to convert residential property into "income producing property." [2] The Tax Court's *sine qua non* was a product of administrative reality. There are three basic reasons why the Government established a rental prerequisite. First, it stemmed from a fear that taxpayers would countermand the listing for sale after taking a series of deductions and reoccupy the house on a personal basis. Mary Laughlin Robinson, 2 T.C. 305, 309 (1943). Second, the rental requisite provided a clear and convenient administrative test. Warren Leslie, Sr., 6 T.C. 488, 494 (1946). Third, the rental re-

---

2. *See* Note, Recent Developments, Hulet P. Smith, 66 Mich.L.Rev. 562, 564– 65 n. 14 (1968), and numerous cases cited therein.

quirement found some implied support in Treas.Reg. § 1.212–1(h) (1954), which provides:

> Ordinary and necessary expenses paid or incurred in connection with the management, conservation, or maintenance of property held for use as a residence by the taxpayer are not deductible. However, ordinary and necessary expenses paid or incurred in connection with the management, conservation, or maintenance of property held by the taxpayer as rental property are deductible even though such property was formerly held by the taxpayer for use as a home.[3]

In Hulet P. Smith, 26 T.C.M. 149 (1967), aff'd 397 F.2d 804 (9th Cir. 1968), the Tax Court abandoned the rental test and held that an offer for sale plus an abandonment transformed the property into an investment asset. The Court of Appeals, in affirming, circumspectly stated:

> The Government makes a strong case for reversal. See Recent Development, Hulet P. Smith, 66 Mich.L.Rev. 562 (1968). Unusual circumstances are present, however, and we are not persuaded that the Tax Court's factual finding and its consequent conclusions are clearly wrong.[4] *Smith,* supra, 397 F.2d 804.

In a subsequent decision, the Tax Court was presented with a fact pattern which was similar to the one presented in *Smith* and came to the opposite conclusion. Frank A. Newcombe, 54 T.C. 1298 (1970). The court stated that *Smith* was "of little precedential value." *Id.* at 1303.

In *Newcombe* the taxpayers moved out of their personal residence and immediately offered it for sale. At no time was the property offered for rent. The taxpayers argued that, under the *Smith* doctrine, the property was being held for the production of income. The Government contended that the *Smith* case was erroneous and that property can only be converted into income producing property use when there has been a bona fide offer to rent.

In rejecting both parties' positions, the court stated:

> We do not share the penchant for polarization which the arguments of the parties reflect. Rather, we believe that a variety of factors must be weighed. . . . *Newcombe,* supra, 54 T.C. at 1299–1300.

3. *Id.* at 566 where "[b]y implication, then the regulations require a rental offer to convert a former residence to income producing property."

4. It is unclear as to what "unusual circumstances" the Court of Appeals was referring to. *See* Note, 25 Tax L.Rev. 269, 272 (1970):

[O]ne would especially like to know what "unusual circumstances" the appellate court thought were present, since this does not appear to be such a situation.

The *Newcombe* court found that "[t]he key question, in cases of the type involved herein, is the purpose or intention of the taxpayer in light of all the facts and circumstances." *Id.* at 1303. The critical inquiry is, therefore, whether the taxpayer had or intended an "expectation of profit." To aid in its inquiry, the court took into account the following considerations: length of time the taxpayer occupied his former residence prior to abandonment; the availability of the house for the taxpayer's personal use while it was unoccupied; the recreational character of the property; attempts to rent the property; and, whether the offer to sell was an attempt to realize post-conversion appreciation. The court explained its final criterion as follows:

> The placing of property on the market for immediate sale, at or shortly after the time of its abandonment as a residence, will ordinarily be strong evidence that a taxpayer is not holding the property for post conversion appreciation in value. Under such circumstances, only a most exceptional situation will permit a finding that the statutory requirement has been satisfied. *On the other hand, if a taxpayer believes that the value of the property may appreciate and decides to hold it for some period in order to realize upon such anticipated appreciation, as well as an excess over his investment, it can be said that the property is being "held for the production of income."* *Id.* at 1302–1303 (emphasis added).

I rule that the Vineyard property was converted into income producing property in 1967 and that plaintiff was entitled to deduct his maintenance expenses. In ruling in plaintiff's favor, I adopt the approach taken by the *Newcombe* court and do not regard renting as the "litmus test" for conversion.[5]

Administrative difficulty in determining when personal property is transformed into investment property should not create a rigid and inflexible barrier to the benefits of conversion.[6] Plaintiff gave sound and substantial business reasons for his failure to rent. I also note that the rental rule does not provide an elixir to administrative ills, for it must be determined that the offer to rent is bona fide and not a sham. Paul H. Stutz, 1965 P–H Tax Ct.Mem. ¶ 65,-166; S. Wise, 1945 P–H Tax Ct.Mem. ¶ 45,298. Finally, I do not believe that Treas.Reg. § 1.212–1(h) (1954) commands a rental offer as a prerequisite to converting a prior residence into income produc-

---

5. I. J. Wagner, 33 T.C.M. 201 (February 19, 1974); Charles D. Mayes, 30 T.C.M. 363 (April 28, 1973); Raymond L. Opper, 31 T.C.M. 48 (May 25, 1972); Richard R. Riss, Sr., 56 T.C. 388 (May 24, 1971); Richard N. New-bre, 30 T.C.M. 705 (July 15, 1971); James J. Sherlock, 31 T.C.M. 383 (April 27, 1971).

6. *See* note 2, supra at 568.

ing property. I find the language contained therein, with regard to renting, to be illustrative and not an explicit statement of law.

In fact, another regulation provides that: "[t]he term 'income' for the purpose of section 212 . . . is not confined to recurring income but applies as well to gains from the disposition of property." Treas.Reg. § 1.212–1(b) (1954). The regulation further provides that the maintenance expenses of property held for investment are deductible; even if the property is not producing income, there is no likelihood of current income, and there is no likelihood of gain upon the sale of the property.

The determination of whether plaintiff's prior residence has been converted into income producing property is made by examining the taxpayer's purpose in light of all the facts and circumstances. Treas. Reg. § 1.212–1(c) (1954). I find that the facts and circumstances presented clearly indicate that plaintiff intended to benefit from post-abandonment appreciation.

I take judicial notice that the price for recreational property on Martha's Vineyard and everywhere else in New England has sky-rocketted in the past decade. Plaintiff has had wide exposure to financial and real estate transactions. He was thoroughly exposed to the real estate world from 1934 to 1943. During that period, he liquidated about 15,000 properties in about 1,200 communities located in thirty-six states. He was specifically aware of Martha's Vineyard land values, having spent nearly all of his summers there. Plaintiff also testified that he was aware, during the latter half of the 1960's of changing economic conditions. As administrator of a large New York insurance company, he saw increasing cash flow and rising prosperity. He testified that, as a result of this exposure, he came to the conclusion, during the latter part of 1967, that we were in the beginning of an inflationary trend and that the value of land would appreciate markedly. Although the 1967 market value of the Vine-yard property was $50,000, plaintiff's business acumen and experience suggested that he could obtain his list price of $150,000 if he kept the property visible and in good condition and waited for the anticipated real estate boom coupled with the anticipated inflation. After a period of five and one-half years, plaintiff did, in fact, sell the property in September of 1973, for his original list price. A capital gain of $100,536.50 appeared on his 1973 income tax return as a consequence of the sale.

The fact that plaintiff immediately listed the property does not negate his contention that he intended to capitalize on post-abandonment appreciation in land values. By an immediate listing, plaintiff made the property a visible commodity on a demanding market. He patiently waited until the economic forces pushed the market value of his property up to his list price.

Based on all the facts and circumstances, I find that plaintiff had a reasonable "expectation of profit" and that the Vineyard property was held as income producing property during 1967. Accordingly, I rule that plaintiff was entitled to deduct the property's maintenance expenses incurred during 1970.

Judgment for the plaintiffs.

So ordered.

PROBLEMS

1. Recall the *Morton Frank* case in Chapter 15 at page 356 supra.

    (a) Should Frank's expenses have been deductible under §§ 212 or 165(c)(2)?

    (b) If Frank had decided to buy the newspaper and incurred capital expenditures to begin operations, but then abandoned his plans, would he have been allowed a deduction? See Johan Domenie, 34 T.C.M. 469 (1975).

2. Homeowners purchased their residence for $80,000 ($10,000 of which was allocable to the land). When it was worth $60,000 ($10,000 of which was allocable to the land), they moved out and put it up for sale, but not rent, for $70,000.

    (a) May they take deductions for expenses and depreciation on the residence? If so, what types of expenses would qualify?

    (b) Assume instead that they rented the property and properly took $10,000 of depreciation on it. What result when they subsequently sell the property for

        (1) $45,000?

        (2) $75,000?

        (3) $65,000?

CHAPTER 17. DEDUCTIONS NOT LIMITED TO BUSINESS OR PROFIT–SEEKING ACTIVITIES

A. INTEREST *

Internal Revenue Code: Sections 163(a), (b); 265(2); 461(g). See Sections 163(d); 189; 483.

Regulations: Section 1.163–1.

REVENUE RULING 69–188

1969–1 Cum.Bull. 54.

Advice has been requested whether for Federal income tax purposes, a payment made under the circumstances set forth below is considered to be interest.

A taxpayer on the cash receipts and disbursements method of accounting who wished to purchase a building, arranged with a lender to finance the transaction. A conventional mortgage loan of $1,000x$ dollars was negotiated, secured by a deed of trust on the building, and repayable in monthly installments over a ten-year period at a stated annual interest rate of 7.2 percent. In addition to the annual interest rate the parties agreed that the borrower would pay a "loan processing fee" of $70x$ dollars (sometimes referred to as "points") prior to receipt of the loan proceeds. The borrower established that this fee was not paid for any specific services that the lender had performed or had agreed to perform in connection with the borrower's account under the loan contract. The loan agreement provided for separate charges for these services. For example, separate charges were made for a preliminary title report, a title report, an escrow fee, the drawing of the deed and other papers, and insurance.

In determining the amount of this "loan processing fee" the lender considered the economic factors that usually dictate an acceptable rate of interest. That is, he considered the general availability of money, the character of the property offered as security, the degree of success that the borrower had enjoyed in his prior business activities, and the outcome of previous transactions between the borrower and his creditors.

* See Bedell, "The Interest Deduction: Its Current Status," 32 N.Y.U.Inst. on Fed.Tax. 1117 (1974) and Kanter, "Interest Deduction: Use, Ruse, and Refuse," 46 Taxes 794 (1968); a brief- er discussion appears in Kanter, "The Interest Deduction: When and How Does It Work," 26 N.Y.U.Inst. on Fed.Tax. 87 (1968).

The taxpayer tendered a check for 70x dollars drawn on a bank account owned by him, which contained a sufficient balance, in payment of the fee. The monies in this account were not originally obtained from the lender.

Section 163(a) of the Internal Revenue Code of 1954 provides that there shall be allowed as a deduction all interest paid or accrued within the taxable year on indebtedness.

Section 446(a) of the Code provides that taxable income shall be computed under the method of accounting on the basis of which the taxpayer regularly computes his income in keeping his books. Section 446(b) of the Code provides, in part, that if the method used does not clearly reflect income, the computation of taxable income shall be made under such method as, in the opinion of the Secretary of the Treasury or his delegate, does clearly reflect income.

For tax purposes, interest has been defined by the Supreme Court of the United States as the amount one has contracted to pay for the use of borrowed money, and as the compensation paid for the use or forbearance of money. See Old Colony Railroad Co. v. Commissioner, 284 U.S. 552 (1932), Ct.D. 456, C.B. XI-1, 274 (1932); Deputy v. Dupont, 308 U.S. 488 (1940), Ct.D. 1435, C.B. 1940-1, 118. The Board of Tax Appeals has stated that interest is the compensation allowed by law or fixed by the parties for the use, forbearance, or detention of money. Fall River Electric Light Co. v. Commissioner, 23 B.T.A. 168 (1931). A negotiated bonus or premium paid by a borrower to a lender in order to obtain a loan has been held to be interest for Federal income tax purposes. L-R Heat Treating Co. v. Commissioner, 28 T.C. 894 (1957).

The payment or accrual of interest for tax purposes must be incidental to an unconditional and legally enforceable obligation of the taxpayer claiming the deduction. Paul Autenreith v. Commissioner, 115 F.2d 856 (1940). There need not, however, be a legally enforceable indebtedness already in existence when the payment of interest is made. It is sufficient that the payment be a "prerequisite to obtaining borrowed capital." L-R Heat Treating Co. The fee of 70x dollars in the instant case was paid prior to the receipt of the borrowed funds; however, this does not preclude the payment from being classified as interest.

It is not necessary that the parties to a transaction label a payment made for the use of money as interest for it to be so treated. See L-R Heat Treating Co. The mere fact that the parties in the instant case agreed to call the 70x dollars a "loan processing fee" does not in itself preclude this payment from being interest under section 163(a) of the Code. Further, this conclusion would not be affected by the fact that this payment is sometimes referred to as "points." Compare Revenue Ruling 67-297, C.B. 1967-2, 87, relating to the deductibility as interest of a loan origination fee paid by the purchaser of a residence to a lending institution in connection with the acquisition of a home mortgage. Also, compare Revenue Ruling 68–650, C.B. 1968–2, 78, relating to the deductibility as interest of the payment of a loan charge paid by the seller of a residence to assist the purchaser in obtaining a mortgage loan.

The method of computation also does not control its deductibility, so long as the amount in question is an ascertainable sum contracted for the use of borrowed money. See Kena, Inc. v. Commissioner, 44 B.T.A. 217 (1941). The fact that the amount paid in the instant case is a flat sum paid in addition to a stated annual interest rate does not preclude a deduction under section 163 of the Code.

To qualify as interest for tax purposes, the payment, by whatever name called, must be compensation for the use or forbearance of money per se and not a payment for specific services which the lender performs in connection with the borrower's account. For example, interest would not include separate charges made for investigating the prospective borrower and his security, closing costs of the loan and papers drawn in connection therewith, or fees paid to a third party for servicing and collecting that particular loan. See Workingmen's Loan Ass'n v. United States, 142 F.2d 359 (1944); Rev.Rul. 57–541, C.B. 1957–2, 319. Compare Revenue Ruling 57–540, C.B. 1957–2, 318, relating to the classification as interest of the fees imposed on borrowers by a mortgage finance company. Also, even where service charges are not stated separately on the borrower's account, interest would not include amounts attributable to such services. See Rev.Rul. 67–297; compare Norman L. Noteman, et al., Trustees v. Welch, 108 F.2d 206 (1939) relating to the classification as interest of the charges paid by borrowers to a personal finance company.

Accordingly, in the instant case, because the taxpayer was able to establish that the fee of $70x$ dollars was paid as compensation to the lender solely for the use or forbearance of money, and because he did not initially obtain the funds to pay this fee from the lender, the $70x$ dollars is considered to be interest.

NOTE

If interest is deductible, a question is: What is "interest"? Rev. Rul. 69–188, set out above, presents a basic definition. As the Ruling suggests, interest, like the rose, by any other name smells as sweet. If a corporation sells its own bonds at a discount (face $1000, price $970), the discount is disguised interest, for the $30 represents a price the corporation will have to pay, along with current interest, as the cost of using the money.[1] Similarly, where an individual borrows

1. Reg. § 1.163–4(a)(1). The Supreme Court has recognized that the charge made for the use of money is "interest." Deputy v. duPont, 308 U.S. 488, 498 (1940); but see Comm'r v. Nat'l Alfalfa Dehydrating & Milling Co., 417 U.S. 134 (1974), disallowing deductions where bonds were issued for previously outstanding preferred stock.

money and agrees to accept less than the stated amount of the loan but to repay the stated amount at a later date, the difference, again, may be interest.[2] In both instances the proper year for claiming the interest deduction depends in part on the taxpayer's accounting method and on other timing principles that are the subject of Chapter 19.[3]

A different kind of problem arises when one obligated to another for an interest-bearing loan pays an amount not designated either as principal or as interest. The parties may agree on the allocation, or the payor may designate the nature of the payment; otherwise there is generally a presumption that payments discharge any interest due before being applied against principal.[4]

Congress also "finds" deductible interest in other obscure places. Section 163(c) places redeemable ground rents in that category.[5] Section 483 finds an interest component in installment payments where no interest is stated [6] and, while this is normally thought of as resulting in ordinary income to the seller of the property who receives the "unstated interest" and may have other implications for him,[7] it also affords the paying purchaser a § 163 deductions. And § 163(b) itself separates out for treatment as interest a part of some confusing installment payments in which carrying charges are stated but the interest charge is not ascertainable.

Other than by express statute, such as sections 163(b) and 483, the tax law has been chary of finding imputed interest, either as a gross income inclusion [8] or as a deduction.[9] However, it will be recalled [10] that I.R.C. § 482 gives the Commissioner limited authority to allocate gross income, deductions, credits, or allowances among organizations controlled by the same persons. Although it may stretch the statute, this authority has been used to generate (a mere allocation?) interest payments on otherwise interest-free loans between such organizations.[11] However, when one is *taxed* on interest imputed to him by this strained application of § 482, the other party gains a corresponding interest *deduction*.[12]

2. Rev.Rul. 75–12, 1975–1 C.B. 62.

3. See page 557 infra. The proper treatment of prepaid interest is importantly affected by I.R.C. § 461(g) added by T.R.A. (1976) § 208.

4. See George R. Newhouse, 59 T.C. 783, 788 (1973).

5. See also I.R.C. (26 U.S.C.A.) § 1055.

6. But see § 483(f)(2), excluding installments subject to § 163(b).

7. See Chapter 24, page 880 infra.

8. E. g., J. Simpson Dean, 35 T.C. 1083 (1961).

9. Rainbow Gasoline Corp., 31 B.T.A. 1050 (1935).

10. See Chapter 14, supra page 337.

11. See, e. g., B. Forman Co. v. Comm'r, 453 F.2d 1144 (2d Cir. 1972), cert. den., 407 U.S. 934 (1972).

12. See Gerald F. Paduano, 34 TCM 368, 370 note 9 (1975).

Shifting to the negative side, there are many obstacles to the deduction for interest. One limiting rule, expressed in section 163 itself, is really of interest only to the so-called "fat cat" usually depicted with a comparably fat cigar. If his investment interest payments otherwise deductible under § 163 exceed $10,000 (he need not be quite so fat as before 1976 when the critical figure was $25,000), he may find them pared down. Why? In general because Congress thinks the rest of us taxpayers should not have to bear a part of another's large investment expenditures that are not presently productive of comparable amounts of taxable income. Thus, when "margin" rules permit it, a very large investment in "growth" stock, relatively unproductive of current dividends but expected to appreciate substantially in value, if paid for by borrowing money, may result in some of the interest paid on the loan being disallowed as a deduction.[13] Section 163(d) is *wonderfully* complex (seemingly Professor Bittker's idea of a student's idea of how professors view difficult statutes) and not right in the mainstream, and so its mysteries are not further explored here.

As in many areas the Commissioner and the courts have refused to let taxpayers exalt form over substance. Elaborate schemes have been attempted to generate an interest deduction in order to reduce taxes without the usual economic pain attached to paying for borrowed money. But not successfully if the device is tabbed a mere artifice.[14] In the corporate area, the "thin incorporation" has produced substantial litigation. Especially in a close corporation, if indebtedness is greatly disproportionate to equity capital, evidences of debt may be viewed instead as evidences of ownership and hoped for deductible interest may become nondeductible dividends.[15]

Even if amounts are paid as "interest," seemingly deductible under I.R.C. (26 U.S.C.A.) § 163, there are several other statutory restrictions. For example, § 264(a)(2) precludes a deduction for interest paid on debt incurred or continued to buy a "single premium" life insurance or endowment or annuity contract.[16] The reasons may

---

13. This concept first crept into the Code when in 1969, in I.R.C. (26 U. S.C.A.) § 57(a)(1) and (b) Congress identified "excess investment interest" as an item of tax preference "subject to the newly enacted minimum tax." See General Explanation of the Tax Reform Act of 1969, prepared by the Staff of the Joint Committee, page 104 et seq. (1970). It was incorporated into § 163 as a limitation on the interest deduction by the 1969 Act, but only effective for years beginning after December 31, 1971, until which time it was to be treated as an item of tax preference. Conf.Rep. 91–782, 1969–3 C.B. 659. TRA (1976) § 209 amended I.R.C. § 163(d) in several respects, one of which is indicated in the trust. The

philosophy behind the § 163(d) limitation will be better understood when capital gains have been explored in Chapter 21, infra.

14. See Knetsch v. U. S., 364 U.S. 361, 81 S.Ct. 132 (1960), and Jack E. Golsen, 54 T.C. 742 (1970), aff'd 445 F.2d 985 (10th Cir. 1971), both involving tax years unaffected by § 264(a)(3), briefly discussed infra.

15. E. g., Gooding Amusement Co. v. Comm'r, 236 F.2d 159 (6th Cir. 1956), cert. den., 352 U.S. 1031, 77 S.Ct. 595 (1957). See I.R.C. § 385.

16. The "single premium" limitation is not so restrictive as it sounds. See I.R.C. (26 U.S.C.A.) § 264(b).

be obvious. As regards life insurance, the purchaser is buying proceeds that will be received tax-free by beneficiaries.[17] It seems inappropriate to Congress to allow a deduction for interest paid on money used to purchase tax-free gain.[18] Annuity and endowment contracts produce funds also only partially taxed.[19] An offset against likely current high income (otherwise taxed at high rates) might be inappropriate looking ahead to the favorable tax treatment of the proceeds. At least so it seems to Congress.

More recently [20] § 264(a)(3) has emerged, no doubt prompted by some artful but unsuccessful efforts to abuse the interest deduction.[21] A bootstrap operation may be possible, at relatively little cost, to borrow from an insurer the periodic increases in cash surrender value (which mere increases are not taxed as income) and to pay only slightly higher interest than that in effect paid by the insurer. If this can be done *and* the interest paid can be deducted, it is a very nice plan indeed.[22] Subject to some details and to some thoughtful exceptions expressed in § 264(c), Congress now by § 264(a)(3) expressly disallows the interest deduction in these circumstances.

Suppose I borrow $1000 at the bank and use it to buy a municipal bond that pays tax-exempt [23] interest at 7%. If I also pay 7% interest at the bank, will the receipts on the bond and the interest paid merely wash? Not if I can deduct the interest from the income otherwise taxed, say, at 50%.

Interest received		$70
Less interest paid	$70	
Reduced by tax saved	− 35	
After tax cost		35
Gain after tax		$35

But a long time ago Congress appropriately stopped this. Section 265(2) disallows any deduction claimed for interest on indebtedness incurred or continued to purchase or carry tax-exempt obligations. Whether indebtedness is "incurred or carried" for the proscribed purpose is a question that has recently produced much litigation. The basic problem is: How much of a connection need be shown between the loan and tax-exempt interest in order to invoke the proscription against the deduction of the interest on the loan?

17. Recall I.R.C. (26 U.S.C.A.) § 101.

18. Cf. § 265(2), noted below.

19. Recall I.R.C. (26 U.S.C.A.) § 72.

20. See P.L. 88–272, 88th Cong., 2d Sess. § 215(b) (1964).

21. See, e. g., *Knetsch* and *Golsen,* supra note 14.

22. Ibid.

23. Recall I.R.C. (26 U.S.C.A.) § 103. Regulated investment companies may pay exempt-interest dividends which I.R.C. § 852(b)(5)(B) treats as tax exempt interest. See § 103(g)(24). TRA (1976) § 2137(e) added I.R.C. § 265(4) generally disallowing deductions for interest paid to purchase or carry securities in such companies.

It is settled that to disallow the interest deduction the Commissioner must show that "the relationship between the indebtedness and the tax-exempt securities involves more than their mere simultaneous existence in respect of a single taxpayer. * * *[24] [S]ection 265(2) applies only when 'the purpose for which the indebtedness is incurred or continued is to purchase or carry tax-exempt obligations.' (Emphasis supplied.)"[25] Nevertheless, the courts appear to be more and more willing to find the required nexus. Of course direct evidence of purpose to buy tax-exempts with a loan is sufficient; and pledging currently owned tax-exempts for the loan has been held to be the equivalent of such direct evidence.[26] Beyond that several courts of appeal have found the connection in less compelling circumstances.[27]

In some instances a taxpayer has the option of deducting an expenditure or charging it to capital account so that it has a favorable impact ultimately on his tax liability by way of increasing his basis for property. If he elects to capitalize a deductible expenditure the obvious counterpart is a denial of any deduction.[28] Interest paid on money borrowed to purchase property is one of the deductible casualties, if the taxpayer elects to capitalize the interest.[29]

Finally, an otherwise allowable interest deduction may be foreclosed by § 267(a)(2) which concerns transactions between related taxpayers. The issue raised is one of *timing* and, as problems of this sort are reserved for Chapters 19 and 20, infra, only a word about the matter here. Essentially, Congress is concerned about possible distortion of tax liability if an accrual method taxpayer owes interest to a related cash method taxpayer and claims a deduction in year one for accrued but unpaid interest. The cash method lender will not

24. Swenson Land and Cattle Co., 64 T.C. 686, 695 (1975).

25. Id. at 696, quoting Leslie v. Comm'r, 413 F.2d 636, 638 (2d Cir. 1969), 396 U.S. 1007 (1970). Further, a broker-dealer exception is recognized in Rev.Rul. 74–294, 1974–1 C.B. 71.

26. Wisconsin Cheeseman v. U. S., 388 F.2d 420 (7th Cir. 1968); and see Rev. Proc. 72–18, 1972–1 C.B. 740.

27. Levitt v. U. S., 517 F.2d 1339 (8th Cir. 1975); Israelson v. U. S., 508 F.2d 838 (4th Cir. 1974); aff'g per curiam, 367 F.Supp. 1104 (D.Md.1973); Mariorenzi v. Comm'r, 490 F.2d 92 (1st Cir. 1974), aff'g per curiam 32 TCM 681 (1973); Indian Trail Trading Post, Inc. v. Comm'r, 506 F.2d 102 (6th Cir. 1974); but see Handy Button Machine Co., 61 T.C. 846 (1974), where tax-exempts purchased were held to meet recognized business needs, and Rev. Proc. 72–18, supra, indicating the required nexus will not be found if investment in tax-exempts is insubstantial. See Note, "The Deductibility of Interest Costs by a Taxpayer Holding Tax-Exempt Obligations: A Neutral Principle of Allocation," 61 Virg.L.R. 211 (1975).

28. I.R.C. (26 U.S.C.A.) § 266. Although phrased negatively, "no deduction * * * etc.", it is interpreted affirmatively to permit capitalization, as provided by the regulations.

29. Reg. § 1.266–1(b)(1). The regulations properly emphasize, § 1.266–1 (b)(2), that "an item not otherwise deductible may not be capitalized under § 266." Thus, for example, the section does not apply to interest on money borrowed to buy tax-exempts.

treat it as income for year one. Indeed, if borrower and lender are related,[30] there is some chance the interest will never be paid and thus *never* reported as income. A stiff disallowance rule sometimes forecloses the deduction for accrued interest not seasonably paid; but it is examined, along with a parallel rule on salaries, in Chapter 19 at page 597, infra.

The Tax Reform Act of 1976, § 201, added I.R.C. § 189 disallowing "real property construction period" interest and taxes, requiring that they be capitalized. The restriction applies only to business or investment property (e. g. not a home) where amounts capitalized may later be charged off. The new provision expressly permits amortization of the capitalized amounts over ten years. A phase-in to the ten year period (Faster amortization is at first allowed.) and other transitional rules render the provision momentarily complex.

B. TAXES

Internal Revenue Code: Sections 164(a), (b), (c), (d)(1); 275; 1001(b) (2). See § 189.
Regulations: Section 1.164–1(a), –2, –3, –5.

TAX SUBSIDIES AS A DEVICE FOR IMPLEMENTING GOVERNMENT POLICY: A COMPARISON WITH DIRECT GOVERNMENT EXPENDITURES *

Stanley S. Surrey.

* * *

1. THE NATURE AND EXTENT OF EXISTING TAX SUBSIDIES * * *

A. The tax expenditure budget

The Federal Income tax system consists really of two parts: one part comprises the structural provisions necessary to implement the income tax on individual and corporate net income; the second part comprises a system of tax expenditures under which governmental financial assistance programs are carried out through special tax provisions rather than through direct government expenditures. The second system is simply grafted on to the structure of the income tax proper; it has no basic relation to that structure and is not necessary to its operation.

---

30. See I.R.C. (26 U.S.C.A.) § 267(b).

* Excerpts from Hearings before the Subcommittee on Priorities and Economy in Government of the Joint Economic Committee, 92d Cong., 1st Sess. pp. 49–51 (1972).

Instead, the system of tax expenditures provides a vast subsidy apparatus that uses the mechanics of the income tax as a method of paying the subsidies. The special provisions under which this subsidy apparatus functions take a variety of forms, covering exclusions from income, exemptions, deductions, credits against tax, preferential rates of tax, and deferrals of tax. The Tax Expenditure Budget * * * identifies and qualifies the existing tax expenditures. This Tax Expenditure Budget is essentially an enumeration of the present "tax incentives" or "tax subsidies" contained in our income tax system.

* * *

The Tax Expenditure Budget enables us to look at the income tax provisions reflected in that Budget in a new light. Once these tax provisions are seen not as inherent parts of an income tax structure but as carrying out programs of financial assistance for particular groups and activities, a number of questions immediately come into focus. Once we see that we are not evaluating technical tax provisions but rather expenditure programs, we are able to ask the traditional questions and use the analytical tools that make up the intellectual apparatus of expenditure experts.

We thus can put the basic question of whether we desire to provide that financial assistance at all, and if so in what amount—a stock question any budget expert would normally ask of any item in the regular Budget. We can inquire whether the program is working well, how its benefits compare with its costs, is it accomplishing its objectives—indeed, what are its objectives? Who is actually being assisted by the program and is that assistance too much or too little? Again, these are stock questions directed by any budget expert at existing programs. They all equally must be asked of the items and programs in the Tax Expenditure Budget.

* * *

The translation and consequent restatement of a tax expenditure program in direct expenditure terms generally show an upside-down result utterly at variance with usual expenditure policies. Thus, if cast in direct expenditure language, the present assistance for owner-occupied homes under the tax deductions for mortgage interest and property taxes would look as follows, envisioned as a HUD program:

> For a married couple with more than $200,000 in income, HUD would, for each $100 of mortgage interest on the couple's home, pay $70 to the bank holding the mortgage, leaving the couple to pay $30. It would also pay a similar portion of the couple's property tax to the State or city levying the tax.

> For a married couple with income of $10,000, HUD would pay the bank on the couple's mortgage $19 per each $100 interest unit, with the couple paying $81. It would also

pay a similar portion of the couple's property tax to the State or city levying the tax.

For a married couple too poor to pay an income tax, HUD would pay nothing to the bank, leaving the couple to pay the entire interest cost. The couple would also have to pay the entire property tax.

One can assume that no HUD Secretary would ever have presented to Congress a direct housing program with this upside-down effect.

PROBLEMS

1.   Which of the following taxes would be deductible *as such* under I.R.C. (26 U.S.C.A.) § 164?

(a) A state sales tax imposed at a single rate on sellers but required to be separately stated and paid by purchasers to sellers, applicable to retail sales of any property except food, clothing, and medicine.

(b) A state real property tax of $1000 for which A became liable as owner of Blackacre on January 1st but which B agreed to pay half of when he acquired Blackacre from A on July 1st.

(c) A state income tax.

(d) The federal income tax.

(e) A state tax on the sale of automobiles imposed at 3%, whereas the state's general sales tax is at a 5% rate.

(f) If the 3% rate mentioned in question (e), above, is also applicable to items of food, clothing and medicine, and sales of all other items are taxed at 5%, does the state have a general sales tax?

2.   Which of the following expenditures would be deductible as taxes incurred as § 162 or § 212 expenses within the second sentence of § 164(a)?

(a) A state tax on cigarettes (imposed on their sale at a rate five times the rate of the general sales tax) paid for cigarettes provided by the taxpayer gratuitously to customers.

(b) A filing fee required to be paid to the State Democratic Party by candidates entering state primary elections. See Horace E. Nichols, 60 T.C. 236 (1973).

3.   Son who is still in college owns substantial securities. Father, when paying his own intangibles tax to State X, pays the intangibles tax due by Son.

(a) May Father deduct the tax paid?

(b) Is it deductible by Son?

4.   Dr. Medic employs Charles to work for her as receptionist. She pays Charles's salary but withholds X dollars to which she adds Y

dollars all of which she pays to the federal government under the Federal Insurance Contributions Act (for "social security").

    (a) Can Dr. Medic deduct amount X? Amount Y? X plus Y?

    (b) Is Charles entitled to a deduction for the payments?

    5. The City of Oz constructs a yellow brick road that runs past Woodman's property. He and other property owners adjacent to the road are assessed varying amounts by Oz, based on the relative values of their properties. Woodman elects to pay off the assessment over five years and pays $400 in the taxable year. Deductible?

C. CASUALTY AND THEFT LOSSES

---

1. NATURE OF LOSSES ALLOWED *

Internal Revenue Code: Section 165(a), (c).
Regulations: Section 1.165–1(e), –7(a)(1), (3), (5), –8(a)(1), (d).

    Losses incurred by a taxpayer may have an impact on his tax liability. As indicated in Chapter 15, losses are generally deductible under I.R.C. § 165(a). Subsection (c) imposes some limitations regarding individuals. Losses incurred in the taxpayer's trade or business are deductible under § 165(a) and (c)(1) without regard to how they arise. Deductions claimed in this category may be challenged as not really incurred in business, a problem to which I.R.C. § 183 is addressed. Chapter 16 reflects another possible ground on which a taxpayer may claim a loss deduction without regard to how the loss arises, namely that the loss is within § 165(a) and (c)(2) as one incurred in a transaction entered into for profit, although not in a trade or business.

    Although deductible, both business and profit-seeking activity losses are restricted sometimes, as hinted by § 165(g), suggesting that §§ 1211 and 1212 be consulted for limitations in the case of capital losses. The limitations are examined along with the treatment of capital gains in Chapter 21, infra.

    A loss may of course occur outside the taxpayer's business and in a transaction not entered into for profit. Generally these losses

---

* See Note, "The Casualty Loss Deduction and Consumer Expectation: Section 165(c)(3) of the Internal Revenue Code," 36 U.Chi.L.Rev. 220 (1968); the statutory concepts are attacked in Epstein, "The Consumption and Loss of Personal Property under the Internal Revenue Code," 23 Stan.L.Rev. 454 (1971). The actual impact of the deduction on tax liability is dependent upon characterization principles that are the subject of Chapters 21 and 22. See page 762, infra.

are not deductible, in keeping with the philosophy of § 262 which forecloses deductions for personal, living or family expenses. The statute does not expressly foreclose these deductions; it simply does not provide for them. It will be recalled that a taxpayer gets no deduction for a loss on the sale of his residence unless he converts it to property held for profit and thereafter sustains the loss. However, § 165(c)(3) permits a deduction for some losses unconnected with business and not involved in an attempt to make a profit. What losses? "Casualty" and "theft" losses. Casualty or theft business losses or profit seeking losses may and should be treated under § 165 (c)(1) or § 165(c)(2), respectively, without regard to § 162(c)(3). But all casualty and theft losses do bear one thing in common, whether they arise in business, in a transaction entered into for profit or otherwise. Tucked away in the middle of the Code without so much as a cross reference in § 165(c) lurks § 1231, often determinative of the manner in which a casualty or theft loss actually plays its role. However, § 1231 applies to other transactions as well and is directly related to the provisions on capital gains and losses. For these reasons the consideration of § 1231 is reserved for Chapter 22, infra, and for the moment conclusions on casualty and theft losses must be viewed as only tentative.

Nevertheless, we are concerned here with losses arising out of a casualty or by theft which *need* § 165(c)(3) to make the scene. They are losses with respect to purely personal items of property. These losses raise first a question of the scope of the statutory concepts of "casualty" and "theft." We must also then consider: Second, the time at which (taxable year within which) these losses are to be deducted, and Third, the measurement of casualty and theft losses. For the most part, the answers to these questions are the same whether the losses concern business or profit-seeking or merely personal property.

REVENUE RULING 63–232
1963–2 Cum.Bull. 97.

The Internal Revenue Service has re-examined its position with regard to the deductibility of losses resulting from termite damage, as set forth in Revenue Ruling 59–277, C.B. 1959–2, 73.

Revenue Ruling 59–277 stated that the Service would follow the rule of George L. Buist, et ux. v. United States, 164 F.Supp. 218 (1958); Martin A. Rosenberg v. Commissioner, 198 F.2d 46 (1952); and Joseph Shopmaker et al. v. United States, 119 F.Supp. 705 (1953), only in those cases where the facts were substantially the same. The courts in these cases held that damage caused by termites over periods up to 15 months after infestation constituted a deductible casualty loss under section 165 of the Internal Revenue Code of 1954.

Revenue Ruling 59–277 further stated that in other cases, the Service would follow the rule announced in Charles J. Fay et al. v. Helvering, 120 F.2d 253 (1941); United States v. Betty Rogers, et al., 120 F.2d 244 (1941); and Leslie C. Dodge et ux. v. Commissioner, 25 T.C. 1022 (1956). In the latter cases the termite infestation and subsequent damage occurred over periods of several years.

An extensive examination of scientific data regarding the habits, destructive power and other factors peculiar to termites discloses that the biological background of all termites found in the United States is generally the same, with one notable exception. The subterranean or ground dwelling termite attacks only wood which is in contact with the ground, while the other types of termites attack wood directly from the air.

Leading authorities on the subject have concluded that little or no structural damage can be caused by termites during the first two years after the initial infestation. It has been estimated that under normal conditions, if left unchecked, depending upon climate and other factors, an infestation of three to eight years would be required to necessitate extensive repairs. Even under extreme conditions, the period would be from one to six years. See "Our Enemy the Termite" by Thomas Elliott Snyder; "Termite and Termite Control" by Charles A. Kofoid; "Insects Their Ways and Means of Living" by Robert Evans Snodgrass; and other authorities.

Such authorities agree that termite infestation and the resulting damage cannot be inflicted with the suddenness comparable to that caused by fire, storm or shipwreck.

Accordingly, it is the position of the Service, based on the scientific data available in this area, that damage caused by termites to property not connected with the trade or business does not constitute an allowable deduction as a casualty loss within the meaning of section 165(c) (3) of the Code. Such damage is the result of gradual deterioration through a steadily operating cause and is not the result of an identifiable event of a sudden, unusual or unexpected nature. Further, time elapsed between the incurrence of damage and its ultimate discovery is not a proper measure to determine whether the damage resulted from a casualty. Time of discovery of the damage, in some situations, may affect the extent of the damage, but this does not change the form or the nature of the event, the mode of its operation, or the character of the result. These characteristics are determinative when applying section 165(c) (3) of the Code.

The Internal Revenue Service will no longer follow the decisions of *Buist, Rosenberg,* and *Shopmaker,* supra. The only real distinction between these cases and the decisions of *Rogers, Fay* and *Dodge,* supra, is the time in which the loss was discovered.

Under the authority contained in section 7805(b) of the Code, Revenue Ruling 59–277, C.B. 1959–2, 73, is revoked for all taxable years beginning after November 12, 1963.

PULVERS v. COMMISSIONER

United States Court of Appeals, Ninth Circuit, 1969.
407 F.2d 838.

CHAMBERS, CIRCUIT JUDGE. Can taxpayers on their federal income tax return take a deduction for an "other casualty loss" when as a consequence of a nearby landslide that ruined three nearby homes, but did no physical damage to the property of taxpayers, with a resultant loss of value because of common fear the mountain might attack their residence and lot next? (There is yet no substantial impairment of ingress or egress on the street serving their home.) We agree with the tax court that they cannot.

* * *

The tax court affirmed the commissioner's determination that the taxpayers incurred no actual loss: that they suffered a hypothetical loss or a mere fluctuation in value.

It may be that the loss is all in the heads of taxpayers and of prospective purchasers, but that circumstance has resulted in a very substantial depreciation of value. (Of course, if the rest of the hill or mountain remains quiet for many years, some or most of the value would come back.) But we would agree with the Los Angeles County assessor that the value certainly went down. And, the finding that the loss was a "mere" fluctuation in value is enough to aggravate any taxpayer.

We think their loss is one that the Congress could not have intended to include in Sec. 165(c) (3). The specific losses named are fire, storm, shipwreck, and theft. Each of those surely involves physical damage or loss of the physical property. Thus, we read "or other casualty," in para materia, meaning "something like those specifically mentioned." The first things that one thinks of as "other casualty losses" are earthquakes and automobile collision losses, both involving physical damage losses.

One trouble with the construction of taxpayers on "other casualty" is that the consequences are limitless. Think of the thousands of claims that could be made for loss of value because of shift of highways, but still involving no lack of ingress.

If one is over the San Andreas fault in California, an authentic report (if one could be had) that it is about to slip would depreciate one's property value before the event.* A notorious gangster buying the house next door would depreciate the value of one's property.

It is difficult to imagine the consequences of taxpayers' reading of the statute. The internal revenue service now has an army of tax gatherers and it always claims it does not have enough. Think of the number this door, if opened, would add. We will not imply that

---

* Cf. Lewis F. Ford, 33 TCM 496 (1974), denying deduction for loss in value because of fear of future storms. Ed.

the Congress intended such a thing. Of course, if the courts would so imply, the Congress would straighten us out very quickly.

We agree with the Fourth Circuit case of Citizens Bank of Weston v. Commissioner, 252 F.2d 425. Also, our reading of United States v. White Dental Co., 274 U.S. 398, 47 S.Ct. 598, 71 L.Ed. 1120, indicates the result we reach here.

Some day we may get a case where a condition has arisen of such certain future consequences that the taxpayer in good sense has absolutely abandoned his property. It might call for a different result, but we shall not reach it here. Neither do we reach the case where egress and ingress have been lost for the foreseeable future or materially impaired.

The taxpayers' argument is appealing. The ingenuity is admirable. But the language is such that we do not think the Congress intended the contended for construction.

The decision of the Tax Court is affirmed.

MARY FRANCES ALLEN

Tax Court of the United States, 1951.
16 T.C. 163.

Petitioner contests respondent's adjustment disallowing a deduction for loss by theft, accounting for a deficiency of $1,800.16 in income tax for 1945.

* * *

Opinion

VAN FOSSAN, JUDGE: * * * Stripped to essentials, the facts are that petitioner owned a brooch which she lost in some manner while visiting the Metropolitan Museum of Art in New York. She does not, and cannot, prove that the pin was stolen. All we know is that the brooch disappeared and was never found by, or returned to, petitioner.

Petitioner has the burden of proof. This includes presentation of proof which, absent positive proof, reasonably leads us to conclude that the article was stolen. If the reasonable inferences from the evidence point to theft, the proponent is entitled to prevail. If the contrary be true and reasonable inferences point to another conclusion, the proponent must fail. If the evidence is in equipoise preponderating neither to the one nor the other conclusion, petitioner has not carried her burden.

In the case at bar we cannot find as a fact that a theft occurred. The reasonable inferences from the evidence point otherwise. It is noted that there is no evidence as to the nature of the clasp by which the pin was fastened to petitioner's dress. We do not know whether it was a "safety clasp" or merely a simple clasp. Nor is there any evidence that petitioner was jostled in the crowd (the usual occurrence when a theft from the person is attempted). If the pin was properly equipped (as may be assumed from its value) with a safety clasp and securely fastened to petitioner's dress, the question arises as to how it could have been removed without damage to the dress, there being no testimony as to any such damage. If it were essential to the disposition of this case that we find either that the pin was lost by theft or was lost by inadvertence, our finding on the record made would be that it was lost by some mischance or inadvertence— not by theft. The inference that such was true is the more readily drawn. However, we need not go so far. We need only hold that petitioner, who had the burden of proof, has not established that the loss was occasioned by theft, a *sine qua non* to a decision in her favor under section 23(e) (3).

We see no merit in petitioner's argument based on the New York Criminal Statutes which hold that the finder of a lost article shall report the finding and make certain efforts toward locating the owner. These statutes are neither binding nor persuasive here. There is no evidence that the pin was ever found and thus the New York statute could not be invoked against anyone. This argument but emphasizes the lack of proof which characterizes the record in this case.

We sustain the respondent's determination.

Reviewed by the Court.

Decision will be entered for the respondent.

OPPER, J., dissenting: As the hearer of the evidence, I would find the fact to be that petitioner's brooch was stolen. I would do so for the very reason that the Court now finds otherwise; that is, that of all the possibilities, the most probable is a loss by theft.

This conclusion presupposes that we believe the testimony of the witnesses. Having heard them testify, I have no reservations in this respect. If the evidence is believed, petitioner had the brooch pinned on her dress at about 4:30 in the afternoon. She was present only in well lighted rooms so constructed that no article could reasonably be lost—especially in view of the subsequent search which the record shows. At 5 o'clock she discovered that the brooch was missing, having in the meantime mingled with a crowd of 5,000 people preparing to leave the museum.

Accepting this evidence, the three possibilities are thus: that the brooch dropped off and has never been found; that it was found but not turned in, and that it was stolen by some person in the crowd. The first may be disregarded as not a reasonable probability; the second would be impossible if the finder were honest. It assumes a virtual concealment which in the case of so valuable an object would actually amount to a theft. Taken with the third, it necessarily points to theft as the only reasonable cause of disappearance.

The suggestion that failure to show the condition of the clasp is fatal to petitioner's case seems to me to prove too much. If the clasp were so difficult to open as to make its removal unlikely, it is even more improbable that it could have fallen off by itself; and if it could open accidentally so as to allow the brooch to fall off, it must have been easy game for a competent sneak thief. Since the clasp in any condition would make removal more likely than mere accidental opening, it is only on the assumption that she was not being candid that petitioner's failure to produce such evidence could be the ground for the result now reached.

Absolute proof by an eye witness is so improbable that the burden now being imposed upon taxpayers virtually repeals *pro tanto* section 23(e) (3). Ever since Appeal of Howard J. Simons, in 1 B.T.A. at page 351, the rule has been otherwise. Without regard to the New York penal law, to which, however, resort would appear to be authorized by the precedents,[1] the probabilities of theft have been demonstrated as completely as such circumstances could ever permit. I see no reason now for departing from principles so well settled and so long established.

LEECH and TIETJENS, JJ., agree with this dissent.

RAYMOND MAZZEI

Tax Court of the United States, 1970.
61 T.C. 497.

QUEALY, JUDGE: Respondent determined a deficiency in income tax against petitioners for the taxable year 1965 in the amount of $7,676.86. As a result of certain concessions by the parties, the sole question presented for decision is whether the petitioners are entitled to deduct a loss in the taxable year 1965 on account of being defrauded in a scheme to reproduce United States currency. Petitioners claim the deduction under section 165(c) (2) [1] or section 165(c) (3).[2]

* * *

Opinion

Petitioner contends that the fact that he incurred a loss is substantiated by the evidence and that such loss is deductible under sec-

1. Morris Plan Co. of St. Joseph, 42 B.T.A. 1190, 1195; Earle v. Commissioner, (CCA–2) 72 F.2d 366.

1. Unless otherwise indicated, all section references are to the Internal Revenue Code of 1954, as amended.

2. [The quoted portion of I.R.C. § 165 (c) has been omitted. Also omitted are the Court's Findings of Fact. Ed.]

tion 165(c)(2) or section 165(c)(3). Respondent contends initially that petitioner has failed to prove that a loss was in fact suffered, and, further, that even if a loss were proven in fact, a deduction for such loss would not be allowed under section 165(c)(2) or section 165(c)(3) on the grounds that allowance of such a deduction would be contrary to public policy. As our findings of fact indicate, the Court is convinced that petitioner, in fact, incurred a loss in the sum of $20,000, as the result of being defrauded. However, the deductibility of such loss is precluded by our decision in Luther M. Richey, Jr., 33 T.C. 272 (1959).

In the *Richey* case, the taxpayer became involved with two other men in a scheme to counterfeit United States currency. The taxpayer observed a reproduction process involving the bleaching out of $1 bills and the transferring of the excess ink from $100 bills onto the bleached-out bills. Upon observing this demonstration, the taxpayer became convinced that the process could reproduce money. When the taxpayer later met with the other men in a hotel room to carry out the scheme, the taxpayer turned over to one of the other men $15,000 which was to be used in the duplication process. Before the process was completed, one of the other men to whom the taxpayer had given the $15,000 left the room under the pretext of going to get something and never returned. The taxpayer later discovered that his money was gone and was not able to recover it. We disallowed the taxpayer's claimed loss deduction under section 165(c)(2) and section 165(c)(3), on the grounds that to allow the loss deduction would constitute an immediate and severe frustration of the clearly defined policy against counterfeiting obligations of the United States as enunciated by title 18, U.S.C., sec. 471.[3] This Court said:

> The record establishes that petitioner's conduct constituted an attempt to counterfeit, an actual start in the counterfeiting activity, and overt acts looking to consummation of the counterfeiting scheme. Petitioner actively participated in the venture. He withdrew money from the bank and changed it into high denomination bills with the full knowledge and intention that the money would be used to duplicate other bills. He was physically present at the place of alteration, and assisted in the process by washing the bills and otherwise aiding Randall and Johnson in their chores. He was part and parcel of the attempt to duplicate the money. Petitioner's actions are no less a violation of public policy because there was another scheme involved, namely, that of swindling the petitioner. From the facts, we hold that to allow the loss deduction in the instant case would

3. 18 U.S.C., sec. 471:
Whoever, with intent to defraud, falsely makes, forges, counterfeits, or alters any obligation or other security of the United States, shall be fined not more than $5,000 or imprisoned not more than fifteen years, or both.

constitute a severe and immediate frustration of the clearly defined policy against counterfeiting obligations of the United States. [33 T.C. at 276–277.]

Petitioner would distinguish the *Richey* case on the grounds that there the taxpayer was involved in an actual scheme to duplicate money where the process was actually begun, only to have the taxpayer swindled when his cohorts made off with his money, whereas in the instant case there never was any real plan to counterfeit money, it being impossible to duplicate currency with the black box.* Petitioner contends that, from the inception, the only actual illegal scheme was the scheme to relieve petitioner of his money, and petitioner was a victim and not a perpetrator of the scheme.

In our opinion, the fact that the petitioner was victimized in what he thought was a plan or conspiracy to produce counterfeit currency does not make his participation in what he considered to be a criminal act any less violative of a clearly declared public policy. Not only was the result sought by the petitioner contrary to such policy, but the conspiracy itself constituted a violation of law.[4] The petitioner conspired with his covictim to commit criminal act, namely, the counterfeiting of United States currency and his theft loss was directly related to that act. If there was a transaction entered into for profit, as petitioner argues, it was a conspiracy to counterfeit.[5]

While it is also recognized that the Supreme Court in Commissioner v. Tellier, 383 U.S. 687 (1966), may have redefined the criteria for the disallowance on grounds of public policy of an otherwise deductible business expense under section 162(a), we do not have that type of case. The loss claimed by the petitioner here had a direct relationship to the purported illegal act which the petitioner conspired to commit. Compare Commissioner v. Heininger, 320 U.S. 467 (1943).

We also do not feel constrained to follow Edwards v. Bromberg, 232 F.2d 107 (C.A. 5, 1956), wherein the court allowed a deduction for a loss incurred by the taxpayer when money, which he thought

---

* Petitioner had been led to believe that one $100 bill could be placed with special paper in a buzzing, black box and then two $100 bills withdrawn. Ed.

4. 18 U.S.C., sec. 371:

If two or more persons conspire either to commit any offense against the United States, or to defraud the United States, or any agency thereof in any manner or for any purpose, and one or more of such persons do any act to effect the object of the conspiracy, each shall be fined not more than $10,000 or imprisoned not more than five years, or both.

If, however, the offense, the commission of which is the object of the conspiracy, is a misdemeanor only, the punishment for such conspiracy shall not exceed the maximum punishment provided for such misdemeanor.

5. While *legal impossibility* may constitute a defense to a criminal prosecution, the *factual impossibility* of a completed crime may not be a defense to a criminal prosecution under a separate conspiracy or attempt statute. 16 Am.Jur.2d, sec. 7; 15A C.J.S., sec. 44. See also Elkind, "Impossibility in Criminal Attempts: A Theorist's Headache," 54 Va.L.Rev. 20 (1968).

was being bet on a "fixed" race, was stolen from him. The taxpayer never intended to participate in "fixing" the race.

The ultimate question for decision in this case is whether considerations of public policy should enter into the allowance of a theft loss under section 165(c)(3) where there is a "theft"—and the loss by the petitioner of his money would certainly qualify as such—the statute imposes no limitation on the deductibility of the loss. Nevertheless, in Luther M. Richey, Jr., supra, this Court held that the deduction of an admitted theft was properly disallowed on grounds of public policy in a factual situation which we find indistinguishable. We would follow that case.

Reviewed by the Court.

Decision will be entered for the respondent.

* * *

STERRETT, J. I respectfully dissent from the majority opinion for the following reasons:

In Tank Truck Rentals v. Comm'r, 356 U.S. 30, 33, 35 (1958), the Supreme Court laid down the test for denying a deduction on the grounds of public policy. An otherwise allowable deduction may be denied if allowance would "severely and immediately" frustrate "sharply defined national or State policies proscribing particular types of conduct, evidenced by some governmental declaration thereof." Frustration of a particular State policy "is most complete and direct when the expenditure for which deduction is sought is itself prohibited by statute." Tank Truck Rentals v. Comm'r, supra at 35. If the expenditure is payment of a penalty imposed by the State because of an illegal act, allowance of a deduction would clearly frustrate State policy by reducing the "sting" of the penalty imposed. Accordingly, the Supreme Court disallowed the deduction of fines the taxpayer had paid during the course of its trucking operations. The Court said, "To allow the deduction sought here would but encourage continued violations of State law by increasing the odds in favor of noncompliance." Tank Truck Rentals v. Comm'r, supra at 35.

In Commissioner v. Sullivan, 356 U.S. 27 (1958), decided the same day as *Tank Truck Rentals,* the Court refused to disallow the deduction of rent and wage expenses in operating an illegal bookmaking establishment. The Court stated, "The fact that an expenditure bears a remote relation to an illegal act does not make it nondeductible." Comm'r v. Sullivan, supra at 29. See also Comm'r v. Heininger, 320 U.S. 467 (1943); Lilly v. Comm'r, 343 U.S. 90 (1952). Once again in Comm'r v. Tellier, 383 U.S. 687, 694 (1966), the Supreme Court reiterated and emphasized its position that an otherwise allowable deduction should only be disallowed when in violation of a public policy that is sharply limited and carefully defined.

Against this background, Congress as part of the Tax Reform Acts of 1969 and 1971 attempted to set forth categories of expenditures within the purview of section 162 which were to be denied on the grounds of public policy. The Senate Finance Committee report for the 1969 Tax Reform Act states "The provision for the denial of the deduction for payments in these situations [1] which are deemed to violate public policy is intended to be *all inclusive*. Public policy, in other circumstances, generally is not sufficiently clearly defined to justify the disallowance of deductions." (Emphasis added.) S. Rept. No. 91–552, 91st Cong., 1st Sess. (1969), 1969–3 C.B. 597. In expanding the category of nondeductible expenditures, the legislative history of the 1971 Tax Reform Act states, "The committee continues to believe that the determination of when a *deduction* should be *denied* should remain under the *control* of *Congress*." (Emphasis added.) S.Rept. No. 92–437, 92d Cong., 1st Sess. (1971), 1972–1 C.B. 599.

While the above statements have direct effect under section 162, where most of the public policy decisions have arisen, it does seem to call for judicial restraint in other areas where Congress has not specifically limited deductions. Moreover, such statements may have been a reaction to widely varied decisions such as those in Edwards v. Bromberg, 232 F.2d 107 (C.A. 5, 1956), and Luther M. Richey, Jr., 33 T.C. 272 (1959), which we think are not fairly distinguishable, and have led to the disparate results so inimical to the uniform administration of the tax laws.[2]

Despite the above, the majority seeks to invoke public policy as the tool to deny the petitioner an otherwise allowable theft loss. While congressional intent could logicaly be read to remove public policy considerations from the Internal Revenue Code where not specifically included,[3] at a minimum the strict test laid down by the Supreme Court must be met.

In the majority opinion, as in *Richey*, we apparently pay lip service to the Supreme Court by stating "that to allow the loss deduction would constitute an immediate and severe frustration of the clearly defined policy against counterfeiting obligations of the United States." Unfortunately in both cases we fail to discuss precisely how that frustration will occur. In the case of illegal payments such as bribes and kickbacks, and the payment of fines, we are able to see a direct relationship between the allowance of the deduction and encouragement of continued violations of the law. In essence, the Government underwrites a portion of the expenses. However in the instant case we cannot see how counterfeiting will be encouraged in any manner

---

1. Fines, a portion of treble damages under antitrust laws, bribes to public officials, and other unlawful bribes and kickbacks.

2. We note that our decision in *Richey* did not mention or discuss Edwards v. Bromberg, 232 F.2d 107 (C.A. 5, 1956), decided 3½ years earlier.

3. Sec. 902, Tax Reform Act of 1969 had retroactive effect with respect to fines, penalties, and bribes and kickbacks to Government officials. See sec. 902(c), Pub.L. 91–172 (Dec. 30, 1969), 1969–3 C.B. 147.

by allowing the petitioner a theft loss deduction arising out of a distinctly different act. At best, the relationship is more remote than that in *Sullivan*, for the term "theft" presupposes that the victim has not voluntarily parted with his property.[4]

The majority seems to indicate that a deduction can be denied where there is *any* relationship between the loss or expense and the illegal activity, a position specifically rejected by *Sullivan*. Such reasoning does not readily lend itself to being "sharply limited" or "carefully defined." Had petitioner contracted pneumonia on his New York excursion, would the majority also deny him a medical expense deduction?

Or assume that customers on the premises of the bookmaking establishment involved in *Sullivan* were robbed by an outside intruder. Would the majority deny them a theft loss because they were engaged in an illegal activity? Or would the majority have this Court of special jurisdiction add to its assigned duties of interpreting the Internal Revenue Code the task of grading criminal activity, a task for which we obviously have no particular expertise. The authority for undertaking such additional duties remains obscure to me and would also be, I suspect, obscure to Congress.

Congress has authorized the imposition of severe punishment upon those found guilty of counterfeiting United States currency. It is designed to repress such criminal conduct. In the interest of uniform application of the Internal Revenue Code, where the frustration of State or national policy is neither severe nor immediate, we must not be tempted to impose a "clean hands doctrine" as a prerequisite to deductibility. To hold otherwise, especially in light of the broad brush-stroke of public policy applied by the majority opinion, makes the taxing statute an unwarranted instrument of further punishment.

FORRESTER, FEATHERSTON, HALL, and WILES, JJ., agree with this dissent.*

---

4. This should be contrasted with the situation where a counterfeiter has money and equipment confiscated during a legal search by police. Allowance of a casualty loss would frustrate public policy by lessening the adverse effect of proper governmental action directly related to the counterfeiting. Cf. Hopka v. U. S., 195 F. Supp. 474 (N.D.Iowa 1961).

* Other concurring and dissenting opinions have been omitted. Ed.

2. TIMING CASUALTY LOSSES

Internal Revenue Code: Section 165(c)(3), (e), (h).
Regulations: Section 1.165–1(d)(3), –8(a)(2), –11(a) through (d).

Once it is determined that there is a casualty or theft loss, the questions arise: When did the loss occur and for what year is a deduction allowed?[1] Casualty losses are deductible for the year in which the loss is sustained.[2] This may be the year of the casualty or a later year in which the amount of the loss is ascertained, in a case where the full extent of the loss was not or by its very nature could not be known until a subsequent year.[3]

Under a limited statutory alternative, the deduction may be allowed for a year prior to the casualty. Under I.R.C. (26 U.S.C.A.) § 165(h) if a casualty loss is attributable to a disaster in an area subsequently declared by the President to warrant assistance under the Disaster Relief Act of 1974, the taxpayer may elect to claim the deduction for the year immediately before the year in which the casualty occurred.

Theft losses are generally a deduction for the year in which the theft is discovered.[4] It has been held that when a theft is discovered in year one the loss must be deducted in year one and, if in subsequent years the taxpayer recalls additional items that were taken, their loss must be deducted in year one by means of an amended return or refund claim, rather than in the subsequent years.[5] However, the timing rule is generally helpful to taxpayers. For example, an embezzlement that occurred in 1960 but which is discovered in 1970, gives rise to a 1970 deduction. If the reverse were true, use of the 1960 deduction might be foreclosed by statutes of limitation.[6]

The Regulations recognize an exception to the general timing rules for both casualties and thefts. If in the year of the casualty or discovery of the theft there exists a reasonable prospect of recovery of the loss, the portion of the loss with respect to which there is a recovery prospect is not deductible unless or until it becomes clear there will be no recovery.[7] It is possible, however, that a loss is properly claimed for year one because no "reasonable prospect of re-

1. The broad treatment of tax timing principles appears in this book at Chapters 19 and 20, infra.

2. Reg. § 1.165–7(a)(1).

3. Rose Licht, 37 B.T.A. 1096 (1938), acq., 1963–2 C.B. 4; Donald H. Kunsman, 49 T.C. 63 (1967).

4. I.R.C. (26 U.S.C.A.) § 165(e).

5. Jane U. Elliot, 40 T.C. 304 (1963), acq., 1964–1 (Part 1) C.B. 4.

6. See Chapter 29, infra.

7. Reg. §§ 1.165–1(d)(2), 1.165–1(d)(3). See Katherine Ander, 47 T.C. 592 (1967); Ramsey Scarlett Co., Inc., 61 T.C. 795 (1974); Frank Hudock, 65 T.C. 351 (1976).

covery" exists in that year. In year two reimbursement is unexpectedly received. With what consequences? The amount recovered is treated as income when received in year two; the tax for year one is *not* recomputed.[8] This is a part of the tax benefit doctrine developed more fully in Chapter 20, infra.

---

3. MEASURING THE LOSS

Internal Revenue Code: Sections 123; 165(b), (c)(3).
Regulations: Section 1.165–7(a)(2), (b), –8(c).

HELVERING v. OWENS

Supreme Court of the United States, 1939.
305 U.S. 468, 59 S.Ct. 260.

MR. JUSTICE ROBERTS delivered the opinion of the Court.

The courts below have given opposing answers to the question whether the basis for determining the amount of a loss sustained during the taxable year through injury to property not used in a trade or business, and therefore not the subject of an annual depreciation allowance, should be original cost or value immediately before the casualty.[1] To resolve this conflict we granted certiorari in both cases.

In No. 180 the facts are that the respondent Donald H. Owens purchased an automobile at a date subsequent to March 1, 1913, and prior to 1934, for $1825, and used it for pleasure until June 1934 when it was damaged in a collision. The car was not insured. Prior to the accident its fair market value was $225; after that event the fair market value was $190. The respondents filed a joint income tax return for the calendar year 1934 in which they claimed a deduction of $1635, the difference between cost and fair market value after the casualty. The Commissioner reduced the deduction to $35, the difference in market value before and after the collision. The Board of Tax Appeals sustained the taxpayers' claim and the Circuit Court of Appeals affirmed its ruling.

In No. 318 it appears that the taxpayers acquired a boat, boathouse, and pier in 1926 at a cost of $5,325. In August 1933 the property, which had been used solely for pleasure, and was uninsured, was totally destroyed by a storm. Its actual value immediately prior to destruction was $3905. The taxpayers claimed the right to deduct cost in the computation of taxable income. The Commissioner allowed only value at date of destruction. The Board of Tax Appeals held with the taxpayers but the Circuit Court of Appeals reversed the Board's ruling.

---

8. John E. Montgomery, 65 T.C. 511 (1975).

1. Helvering v. Owens, 95 F.2d 318; Helvering v. Obici, 97 F.2d 431.

Decision in No. 180 is governed by the Revenue Act of 1934;[2] in No. 318 by the Revenue Act of 1932.[3] The provisions of both statutes touching the question presented are substantially the same and we shall refer only to those of the 1934 Act.* Section 23(e)(3) permits deduction from gross income of losses "of property not connected with the trade or business" of the taxpayer, "if the loss arises from * * * casualty." Subsection (h) declares that "The basis for determining the amount of deduction for losses sustained, to be allowed under subsection (e) * * *, shall be the adjusted basis provided in section 113(b)." Section 113 is entitled "Adjusted basis for determining gain or loss"; in subsection (a) it provides that "The basis of property shall be the cost of such property," with exceptions not material. Subsection (b), to which 23(h) refers, is: *"Adjusted basis.*—The adjusted basis for determining the gain or loss from the sale or other disposition of property, whenever acquired, shall be the basis determined under subsection (a), adjusted as hereinafter provided. (1) *General rule.*—Proper adjustment in respect of the property shall in all cases be made—(B) in respect of any period since February 28, 1913, for exhaustion, wear and tear, obsolescence, amortization, and depletion, to the extent allowed (but not less than the amount allowable) under this Act or prior income tax laws."

The income tax acts have consistently allowed deduction for exhaustion, wear and tear, or obsolescence only in the case of "property used in the trade or business." The taxpayers in these cases could not, therefore, have claimed any deduction on this account for years prior to that in which the casualty occurred. For this reason they claim they may deduct upon the unadjusted basis,—that is,—cost. As the income tax laws call for accounting on an annual basis; as they provide for deductions for "losses sustained during the taxable year"; as the taxpayer is not allowed annual deductions for depreciation of nonbusiness property; as § 23(h) requires that the deduction shall be on "the adjusted basis provided in section 113(b)," thus contemplating an adjustment of value consequent on depreciation; and as the property involved was subject to depreciation and of less value in the taxable year, than its original cost, we think § 113(b)(1)(B) must be read as a limitation upon the amount of the deduction so that it may not exceed cost, and in the case of depreciable non-business property may not exceed the amount of the loss actually sustained in the taxable year, measured by the then depreciated value of the prop-

2.　c. 277, 48 Stat. 680, §§ 23(a) (f) (h) (l), 24(a) 1, 41, 113; 26 U.S.C. §§ 23, 24, 41, 113.

3.　c. 209, 47 Stat. 169, §§ 23(e) (f) (g) (h), 24(a) 1, 113.

* The parallel current provisions are I. R.C. (1954) §§ 165(c) (3), 165(b), 1012, 1011, and 1016(a) (2), respectively. Ed.

erty. The Treasury rulings have not been consistent, but this construction is the one which has finally been adopted.[4]

In No. 180 judgment reversed.

In No. 318 judgment affirmed.

NOTE

The basic amount of a loss arising out of theft is of course the value of the thing stolen. If the item stolen was property other than money, the usual property valuation questions arise.[1] It may be even more difficult to establish the amount of cash that was feloniously taken; but see Bernard Eiferman [2] where the taxpayer was able to meet the challenge.

Reg. § 1.165–7(b) presents a fairly clear picture of the determination of the amount of more common casualty loss deductions. Study it. As the regulation indicates, the amount is generally the same whether the loss is incurred in a trade or business or in a transaction entered into for profit or is merely personal. There are two important differences however. First, business or profit classification makes inapplicable the $100 floor [3] which, on a de minimis principle and to avoid insurance claims, disallows the first $100 of loss from a casualty regarding purely personal assets. This is because these losses can be claimed under § 165(c)(1) or (2), escaping the limitation. Second, losses of a purely personal nature never exceed the difference in value of the property before and after the casualty. However, in the case of business or profit making property that is totally destroyed the loss deduction is for the full adjusted basis of the property (less reimbursements) even if that amount exceeds the *value* of the property before the casualty. Why this distinction?

Recently some question has been raised whether financial aid under federal disaster relief legislation constitutes compensation "by insurance or otherwise,"[4] reducing otherwise allowable loss deductions. It seems pretty clearly to have the same effect as reimbursement by way of insurance. For example, in James A. Shanahan [5] the taxpayers' home was damaged by an earthquake in 1971. Thereafter, in the same year they applied for and received a Small Business Administration unsecured disaster loan of $1600. Still in 1971 in accordance with the applicable federal statute, $1100 of the loan was cancelled. The Tax Court sustained the Commissioner's requirement that the taxpayer treat the $1100 as compensation for the loss under

4. Treasury Regulations 86, Arts. 23 (e)–1, 23(h) 1, 113(b) 1; G.C.M. XV 1, Cumulative Bulletin 115–118.

1. Cf. Est. of Smith v. Comm'r, 510 F. 2d 479 (2d Cir. 1975), cert. den. 423 U.S. 827 (1975), valuing nonrepresentational art objects for estate tax purposes.

2. 35 TCM 790 (1976).

3. See I.R.C. § 165(c)(3) and Reg. § 1.-165–7(b)(4).

4. I.R.C. § 165(a).

5. 63 T.C. 21 (1974).

§ 165(a). In so doing, the Tax Court expressed its agreement with Kroon v. United States,[6] which it described as follows:[7]

> In Kroon v. United States, —— F.Supp. —— (D.Alaska 1974), the taxpayers' residence was destroyed by an earthquake in 1964 and they filed an amended Federal income tax return for 1963 in which they claimed a casualty loss deduction in the amount of $54,800. The taxpayers obtained loans guaranteed by the SBA, for the purpose of refinancing the mortgages on the destroyed residence. They then applied to the Alaskan Mortgage Adjustment Agency for assistance and that agency made payments in 1968 which were applied against the taxpayers' mortgage obligations. The taxpayers contended that the payments were gifts and need not be reported in income. * * *

In both cases the courts rejected the taxpayers' assertions that the I.R.C. § 102 gift exclusion relieved them from a downward adjustment of their casualty loss deductions. And properly so.[8]

REVENUE RULING 68–531

1968–2 Cum.Bull. 80.

Advice has been requested concerning the computation of the casualty loss deduction under the circumstances stated below.

The taxpayer owns a citrus grove and is engaged in the business of growing and selling citrus fruit. In 1967 a hurricane damaged all of the citrus trees in the grove and totally destroyed the fruit ripening on the trees. The taxpayer's basis in the trees was $100x$ dollars. The trees had a value of $200x$ dollars (including the value of the fruit) immediately before the casualty. Immediately after the casualty the trees had a value of $120x$ dollars. The ripening fruit had a value immediately before the casualty of $20x$ dollars. The specific question is whether the value of the fruit may be included in determining the amount of the casualty loss deduction.

Section 165(a) of the Internal Revenue Code of 1954 provides that there shall be allowed as a deduction any loss sustained during the taxable year and not compensated for by insurance or otherwise.

Section 165(c) of the Code provides that in the case of an individual the deduction under subsection (a) shall be limited to certain classes of losses, including losses incurred in a trade or business.

Section 1.165–7(b) (1) of the Income Tax Regulations requires casualty losses to be measured by the lesser of (1) the amount equal to

---

6. 74–2 USTC para. 9641 (D. Alaska 1974).

7. Shanahan, supra note 5 at 23.

8. See Comm'r v. Duberstein, Ch. 4, supra p. 66.

the fair market value of the property immediately before the casualty reduced by the fair market value of the property immediately after the casualty, or (2) the amount of the adjusted basis for determining the loss from the sale or other disposition of the property involved. Section 1.165–7(b) (2) of the regulations requires in the case of property used in a trade or business that a separate computation be made with respect to each identifiable property damaged or destroyed.

Section 1.165–6(c) of the regulations provides that the total loss by frost, storm, flood or fire of a prospective crop being grown in the business of farming shall not be allowed as a deduction under section 165(a) of the Code.

In the instant case, since the cost of growing the fruit was deductible by the taxpayer as a business expense, he had no basis in the ripening fruit. Further, the difference between the cost of a growing crop and its prospective sales price is only anticipated income and the loss of anticipated income is not deductible.

Accordingly, the value of the fruit is to be excluded in determining, under section 165(a) of the Code, the amount of the casualty loss deduction.

However, with respect to the citrus trees damaged by the hurricane, the amount of the deductible loss is measured by the difference between the fair market value of the trees (not including the fruit) immediately before the casualty and the fair market value of the trees (not including the fruit) immediately after the casualty, but that amount may not exceed the adjusted basis of the trees for determining loss. In the instant case, the amount deductible for the damage to the trees is limited to $60x$ dollars, which is the difference between the fair market value of the trees immediately before the casualty ($200x$ dollars less $20x$ dollars) and their fair market value immediately after the casualty ($120x$ dollars).

KENTUCKY UTILITIES CO. v. GLENN

United States Court of Appeals, Sixth Circuit, 1968.
394 F.2d 631.

EDWARDS, CIRCUIT JUDGE. These are three entirely separate tax cases between the same parties raising somewhat complex issues of fact and law. The corporate parties in these tax cases are Kentucky Utilities Co., a major private supplier of electrical power in Kentucky and adjoining states, henceforth to be referred to as KU, . . .

The issues will be discussed under three headings: Generator Damage, Social Security Tax Deductions, and Preferred Stock Premiums and Dividends. [The second and third issues are omitted here. Ed.]

GENERATOR DAMAGE

KU claimed a right to deduct the sum of $44,486.77 on its 1953 corporate tax return, either as an uninsured loss or an ordinary and necessary business expense.[1] This was the sum which KU did not recover out of approximately $150,000 of damage to a turbo generator, located at Pineville, Kentucky, which was partially destroyed by accident on September 12, 1951. The turbo generator had been insured with Lloyds of London for $200,000, subject to a $10,000 deductible provision.

Lloyds never disputed its coverage of the loss, but did insist on its right of subrogation to KU's rights against Westinghouse, the supplier of the turbo generator. Westinghouse disputed any liability under its warranty of the generator.

Ultimately, as between the three disputing parties, Westinghouse paid $65,550.93 of the total cost of repairs; Lloyds paid $37,500, relinquishing any right of subrogation against Westinghouse, and KU assumed responsibility for the remaining $44,486.67 worth of damage.

The District Judge held that KU had sustained an uninsured loss of $10,000 because of the deductible feature of the policy. 250 F.Supp. 265. He found as a fact:

"6. For business reasons, K-U did not want any litigation brought against Westinghouse. Moreover, because of possible difficulty in retaining insurance of this character on its equipment, K-U did not want Lloyds to pay all of the loss except the $10,000.00 deductible under the policy.

* * * * * * * * * *

"8. K-U voluntarily assumed $34,486.67 of the cost of repairs to the generator to protect Westinghouse from suit by Lloyds and to avoid difficulty in obtaining insurance with Lloyds. The expenditure of $34,486.67 in this manner does not constitute a loss or an ordinary and necessary business expense."

This record convinces us that the District Judge's quoted findings of fact are not clearly erroneous. KU's loss over and above the $10,000 allowed by the District Judge was not an "uninsured loss." Sam P. Wallingford Grain Corp. v. Commissioner of Internal Revenue, 74 F.2d 453 (10th Cir. 1934).

Nor does KU's voluntary assumption of the loss for the reasons found by the District Judge seem to be either "necessary" or "ordinary" within the meaning of the tax statute. Welch v. Helvering, 290 U.S. 111, 54 S.Ct. 8, 78 L.Ed. 212 (1933).

On this issue we affirm the judgment of the District Court.

* * *

1. [Quotations from I.R.C. (1939) § 23 (a) and (f) are omitted. Ed.]

PROBLEMS

1. Prone slammed the car door on his wife's hand. Quick examination showed a slightly injured pinky but her diamond ring seemingly intact. Later that night they discovered the diamond had slipped out of its prongs, seemingly damaged by the car door. It was never found and the ring was uninsured. May Prone claim a casualty loss deduction? See J. P. White, 48 T.C. 430 (1967), and Rev.Rul. 72–592, 1972–2 C.B. 101.

2. Sleepy purchased a car in 1975 for $6000 which he thereafter used only for personal purposes, not business. In 1977 he dozed off one night while driving and the car attached itself to a tree. Before, it was worth $3000 but, after the accident, only $1000. It was partially insured and in 1977 Sleepy settled with the insurer for $1000.

(a) What is the amount of Sleepy's casualty loss deduction for 1977?

(b) What would be his deduction if the car had been totalled and Sleepy still received only $1000 insurance?

(c) Assume now that at the end of 1976, Sleepy converted the car to business use and that in fact he used it in his business for six months. At the time of conversion the car's fair market value was $4000 and Sleepy properly claimed $500 depreciation on the car for 1977. However, on July 1st he dozed off while driving the car and it attached itself to a tree inextricably. Value before $3000, value after zero. Still only $1000 insurance. Is the amount of Sleepy's deduction more than in (b), above? Should it be? What are the considerations?

(d) In any of the above circumstances would it make any difference if Sleepy collected no insurance (although entitled to $1000) for fear that if he reported the accident his insurer would no longer insure him?

(e) What difference would it make in any of the above cases if the insurer disputed liability and the $1000 insurance settlement was not made until January 10, 1978?

(f) Suppose the car in part (a), above, was one owned by Trusting which Sleepy had agreed to drive from New York to Miami for Trusting so that it would be there for Trusting's vacation. Trusting sued Sleepy for the car's value less insurance received, and Sleepy paid $1000 in damages. Can Sleepy claim a $1000 casualty loss deduction?

3. Shaky's house is damaged in an earthquake and he and his family are required to live in a motel and eat their meals in a restaurant while repairs are made. Shaky's insurance policy pays the total cost of the repairs and, additionally, pays $1200 of the family's meals

and lodging expenses which total $1800 during the repair period. Normally Shaky would pay only $1000 for these expenses during the period. What tax consequences to Shaky?

D. BAD DEBTS AND CHARITABLE CONTRIBUTIONS

Because these types of deductions are intimately related to characterization principles, their analysis is deferred to Chapter 23 in Part Six of this book. Admittedly, as indicated at the beginning of C, above, casualty and theft losses may also encounter characterization concepts under § 1231. That aspect of such losses is considered along with other § 1231 problems in Chapter 22.

CHAPTER 18. DEDUCTIONS FOR INDIVIDUALS ONLY

A. PERSONAL AND DEPENDENCY EXEMPTIONS

Internal Revenue Code: Sections 151; 152. See Sections 71(a), (b); 143; 215; 6013(a), (d).

Every individual taxpayer has at least one automatic deduction, the so-called "personal exemption."[1] Since 1972 the amount has been fixed at $750. Although the statute speaks somewhat confusingly of "allowance," "deduction" and "exemption," the amounts discussed here are simply subtractions from gross income or "adjusted gross income" (a term considered later in this chapter) in arriving at taxable income, the same as other deductions.

The $750 figure is the amount of each exemption for which one qualifies regardless of whether it is a personal or dependency exemption. Every individual taxpayer is allowed a personal exemption, even though another taxpayer may have properly claimed the individual as a dependent. A husband and wife filing a joint return constitute two taxpayers and they therefore are allowed two personal exemptions.[2] If they do not file a joint return, a spouse may claim an allowance for the other spouse only if the other has no gross income and is not the dependent of any other taxpayer.[3] Additional personal exemptions are allowed for the taxpayer (and the taxpayer's spouse also if the above qualification is met), if the spouse is over the age of sixty-five before the close of the taxable year or is blind at the close of the taxable year. Thus, if a married blind couple each of whom is over 65 years old files a joint return, they qualify for a total of six personal exemptions and, if the year, is after 1972, they will be allowed deductions of $4500 under I.R.C. (26 U.S.C.A.) § 151.

Students should note that the deduction provisions of I.R.C. (26 U.S.C.A.) § 151 can be broken down into two main parts. The first segment of § 151, subsections (a) through (d), concerns the *personal* exemption including special allowances for old age and blindness. The second part of the statute, § 151(e), governs the *dependency* exemption. I.R.C. (26 U.S.C.A.) § 152, defining the term "dependent" is not a deduction provision; it merely sets out precise rules for de-

1. See also the "standard deduction," discussed infra, this chapter.

2. Reg. § 1.151–1(b). President Ford's 1976 campaign oratory included a proposal to increase the $750 figure to $1000.

3. I.R.C. (26 U.S.C.A.) § 151(b).

termining who is a dependent. Neither a husband nor a wife is ever a "dependent" of the other for federal tax purposes. Right? Right!

There are two principal requirements for "dependent" status and a third basic prerequisite for the dependency deduction. First, the taxpayer and the person to be claimed as a dependent must bear one of the relationships specifically listed under I.R.C. (26 U.S.C.A.) § 152(a).[4] Although generally those relationships are by blood, nevertheless the section treats adopted or foster children the same as blood relatives [5] and includes as a dependent a non-related individual who lives in the taxpayer's house as a member of the household.[6] However, I.R.C. (26 U.S.C.A.) § 152(b)(5) provides that if at any time during the taxable year the relationship between the taxpayer and an individual is in violation of local law the individual does not qualify as a dependent.[7]

Secondly, the taxpayer claiming the dependent must provide over one-half of the support for the person during the year.[8] Support in these circumstances may be difficult to determine. It includes clothing, meals, lodging, and other necessities furnished to the dependent but does not include the value of personal services rendered to the dependent by the taxpayer,[9] or non-necessities such as a boat or an automobile.[10] The Code provides that a scholarship received by a student will not be considered as support in determining whether parents furnish sufficient support.[11] On the other hand, the statutory scholarship exclusion does not encompass student loans.[12]

In some situations, especially with respect to elderly persons, several members of a family may jointly contribute to the support of an individual. I.R.C. (26 U.S.C.A.) § 152(c) provides that, if certain requirements are met, those supporting the individual may agree that one of the group will be treated as though he provided over half of the individual's support for the year for purposes of § 152(a). Some of the Problems presented below call for close examination of § 152(c).

Support problems also arise with respect to the children of divorced or legally separated parents. Amounts received by a divorced

---

4. TRA (1976) § 1901(a)(24) lopped off paragraph 152(a)(10), possibly because of newly enacted I.R.C. § 44A, credit for dependent care expenses. Special rules relating to the listed relationships are found in I.R.C. (26 U.S.C.A.) § 152(b). See Glassberg, "Who Is a Dependent and How to Support Him Taxwise," 26 N.Y.U. Inst. on Fed.Tax 1 (1968).

5. I.R.C. (26 U.S.C.A.) § 152(b)(2).

6. I.R.C. (26 U.S.C.A.) § 152(a)(9). Household membership also sometimes brings an individual within the classification "child of the taxpayer" for purposes of § 151(e). § 152(b)(2).

7. Leonard J. Eichbauer, 30 TCM 581 (1971). See also Leon Turnipseed, 27 T.C. 758 (1957), reaching this result before the enactment of § 152(b)(5).

8. I.R.C. (26 U.S.C.A.) § 152(a).

9. Reg. § 1.152–1(a).

10. Rev.Rul. 56–399, 1956–2 C.B. 114; Flowers v. U. S., unreported, 1957–1 U.S.T.C. ¶ 9655 (D.C.Pa.1957).

11. I.R.C. (26 U.S.C.A.) § 152(d).

12. P. McCauley, 56 T.C. 48 (1971).

spouse which are included in gross income under I.R.C. (26 U.S.C.A.) § 71(a) and are used for the support of the children are deemed support contributions by that spouse. If, however, the payments are not within the recipient's income because of I.R.C. (26 U.S.C.A.) § 71(b), then the payments are support provided by the paying spouse. Under I.R.C. (26 U.S.C.A.) § 152(e) generally the custodial parent is entitled to the dependency deduction. If, however, the decree or an agreement provides that the non-custodial parent is entitled to the deduction and that parent provides at least $600 of support for the child, then the non-custodial parent can qualify for the deduction.[13] In the alternative, notwithstanding any provision in the decree or agreement, if the non-custodial parent proves that he provides $1200 or more in support of each child then that parent may claim them as dependents unless the custodial parent proves that more support was provided by the custodial than the non-custodial parent.[14] These rules apply only if the parents have custody of the child for at least one half of the year, if they provide more than one half of the child's support, if they do not file a joint return, and if the child is not the subject of a multiple support agreement.[15] As the divorced parents rules of § 152(e) are the subject of detailed examination in Rev.Rul. 73–175, set forth immediately below, no Problems at the end of this segment deal with that provision.

The third basic requirement for a dependency exemption is that the person claimed as a dependent may not have as much as $750 of *gross income*. For purposes of § 151(e) gross income is defined the same as under I.R.C. (26 U.S.C.A.) § 61, and therefore the income inclusion and exclusion sections apply in the determination of gross income.[16] The gross income limitation does not apply, however, if the dependent is a child of the taxpayer [17] *and* is either under the age of 19 at the close of the calendar year in which the taxpayer's taxable year begins or is a full-time student.[18]

No dependency exemption is allowed, even though the three requirements are met, if the dependent is married and files a joint return with his or her spouse.[19] The problems following the Ruling illustrate the statutory requirements presented above. In working them the student must scrutinize the statutory language.

---

13. I.R.C. (26 U.S.C.A.) § 152(e)(2)(A).

14. I.R.C. (26 U.S.C.A.) §§ 151(e)(1)(A) and 152(e)(2)(B). TRA (1976) § 2139 altered the subparagraph (B) test from $1200 for all to $1200 for each child.

15. Reg. § 1.152–4(a). See, generally, Sander, "Dependency Exemptions for Children of Divorced or Separated Spouses—the New Amendments to the Internal Revenue Code?" 45 Taxes 710 (1967), reprinted in 1967 Family Law Quarterly 114.

16. Reg. § 1.151–2(a).

17. I.R.C. (26 U.S.C.A.) §§ 151(e)(1)(B) and (e)(3).

18. I.R.C. (26 U.S.C.A.) §§ 151(e)(1)(B) and (e)(4).

19. I.R.C. (26 U.S.C.A.) § 151(e)(2).

REVENUE RULING 73–175

1973–1 Cum.Bull. 58.

Advice has been requested as to which parent is entitled to the dependency exemption deductions for their children under the circumstances described below.

A mother and a father, M and F, are the divorced parents of C, D, and E, who were in custody of M for the entire calendar year of 1968. M and the three children lived together with M's new husband, NH, in a home owned jointly by M and NH. M and NH filed a joint Federal individual income tax return for 1968 reporting gross income of $15,000, of which $7,000 represented wages earned by M and $8,000 represented wages earned by NH. F filed a separate Federal individual income tax return for 1968, reporting $16,000 of gross income. There was no provision in the decree of divorce, nor was there a written agreement between M and F, as to which parent would be entitled to the dependency exemptions for C, D, and E.

Support for C, D, and E during 1968 amounted to $7,300, that for C was $2,700, for D was $2,300, and for E was $2,300. This support was furnished to the children from the following sources: F made support payments of $960 for each child, gave presents costing $100 to each, and paid medical insurance premiums of $40 for each child; C paid $400 of his own expenses; and M and NH furnished the remaining support for the children, consisting of lodging valued at $500 for each, and general support items costing $700 for each.

Section 151(e) of the Internal Revenue Code of 1954 allows a dependency exemption for a dependent as defined in section 152 of the Code.

Section 152 of the Code defines the term "dependent" as one who meets certain requirements as to citizenship, relationship to the taxpayer, and support. Thus, under section 152 of the Code, a dependent includes a child of the taxpayer over half of whose support, for the calendar year in which the taxable year of the taxpayer begins, was received from the taxpayer (or is treated under subsection (c) or (e) as received from the taxpayer).

Section 152(c) of the Code provides that, under a multiple support agreement, a taxpayer who furnishes more than 10 percent but less than half of a dependent's total support will be treated as providing over half of the dependent's support under certain circumstances.

Section 152(c) of the Code contains the rules by which the divorced or separated parents of any child who both (1) receives over half of his total support during the calendar year from his parents, and (2) is in the custody of one or both of them for more than half of the calendar year, must determine which of them shall be treated as providing over half of the child's support. It is important to note that the rules of section 152(e) of the Code must be applied to determine which divorced parent shall be treated as providing over half of the support of such child, regardless of which parent actually provided over half of such support.

Section 152(e) of the Code provides the "general rule" that such a child is treated as receiving over half of his support from the parent who has custody of him for the greater part of the year unless his dependency exemption is claimed under a multiple support agreement pursuant to the provisions of section 152(c), or unless his circumstances place him within the exceptions set out in section 152(e)(2) (A) and (B) of the Code.

The exception set out in section 152(e)(2)(A) of the Code is that such a child is treated as receiving over half of his support from the noncustodial parent if (i) the decree of divorce or of separate maintenance, or a written agreement between the parents applicable to the taxable year beginning in such calendar year, provides that the parent not having custody shall be entitled to the child's dependency exemption, and (ii) the noncustodial parent provides at least $600 for the support of such child during the calendar year.

The exception set out in section 152(e)(2)(B) of the Code is that a child is treated as receiving over half of his support from the noncustodial parent if (i) that parent provides $1,200 or more for the support of such child (or if there is more than one such child, $1,200 or more for all of such children) for the calendar year, and (ii) the custodial parent does not clearly establish that he provided more for the support of such child during the calendar year than the parent not having custody.

In the instant case, the rules provided in section 152(e) of the Code are clearly applicable inasmuch as each child (1) received over half of his total support during the year from his parents, and (2) was in the custody of one or both of them for more than half of the calendar year. Therefore, the parent having custody of each child for the greater part of the calendar year is treated as providing over half of his support under section 152(e)(1) of the Code, unless the child's dependency exemption is claimed under a multiple support agreement pursuant to section 152(c) of the Code, or unless his circumstances place him within the exceptions of section 152(e)(2)(A) or (B) of the Code.

The taxpayers in this case did not, in fact, file multiple support agreements pursuant to section 152(c) of the Code so the exception for multiple support agreements does not apply here. Also, since there was no provision in the divorce decree or other written agreement as to which parent is entitled to the dependency exemption of any of the children, the exception set out in section 152(e)(2)(A) of the Code does not apply.

However, the exception provided in section 152(e)(2)(B) of the Code is applicable inasmuch as the noncustodial parent did provide the $1,200 required by that section for support of all of the children for the calendar year (*F* provided $1,100 of support for each child, totaling $3,300 for all the children). Therefore, *F* will be treated as providing over half of the support of each child unless it is established that the custodial parent provided more for the support of such child during the calendar year than did *F*.

Since *M* and *NH* together (but not *M* alone) provided $1,200 for each child, as compared with the $1,100 furnished for each by *F* individually, *M* can establish that she provided more for their support than did *F* only if the support provided by her and her new husband is treated as being provided by her for purposes of section 152(e) of the Code.

The legislative history of section 152(e) of the Code is silent as to the intent of Congress with regard to support furnished by a divorced parent's new spouse. However, the section was specifically enacted to alleviate the burden imposed on divorced parents and on the Internal Revenue Service by section 152 of the Code in determining which divorced parent was entitled to claim the children as dependents. See H.Rept. No. 102, 90th Cong., (1967) at 1967-2 C.B. 590-594.

In Martin and Yvonne Colton v. Commissioner, 56 T.C. 471 (1971), an analogous situation, the custodial parent (Mrs. Colton) claimed that her former husband had not provided at least $600 for the support of each child during the calendar year as required by section 152(e)(2)(A)(ii) of the Code and that he was not entitled to the exemption deductions allowable for them. Mrs. Colton's argument was based on the theory that half of the amount of support furnished by her former husband was attributable to his new wife since they resided in a community property state. The Court, however, held it was immaterial whether the support payments were from the former husband's funds alone, from jointly owned funds or from his new wife's funds. In rejecting Mrs. Colton's argument, the Court said:

> * * * Such an interpretation would introduce a whole new set of complexities—the necessity for distinguishing community from separate property—and would thus frustrate the congressional quest for simplicity and certainty. An interpretation so completely at variance with the declared legislative purpose should not be adopted unless required by the plain terms of the statute.
>
> *   *   *   *   *   *   *   *
>
> * * * The emphasis in section 152(e)(2)(A)(ii) was not upon the technical ownership of the $600 to be furnished by the 'parent not having custody' but rather was designed, we think, to require a support contribution 'for

the support' of the child at least equal to the personal exemption deduction then allowable.

Under the facts of this Revenue Ruling, if the support payments provided by *M* and *NH* are not treated as if they were all provided by *M*, taxpayers as well as the Service would have the additional burden of tracing the source of support payments made by the custodial parent and her spouse. Section 152 of the Code is a remedial statute and as such should be given a liberal construction. Accordingly, under the circumstances of this case, the support furnished by the divorced parent's new spouse will be treated as being furnished by the divorced parent. *M* and *NH*, therefore, are entitled to claim the dependency exemptions for *C*, *D*, and *E* on their joint Federal income tax return for 1968.

Revenue Ruling 71–19, 1971–1 C.B. 43, which concluded that for purposes of section 152(e) of the Code, the support furnished by a divorced parent is determined separately from that furnished by her or his new husband or wife, as the case may be, and that the support furnished by the new husband or wife may not be aggregated with and attributed to the parent to whom he or she is married, is hereby revoked.

Pursuant to the authority contained in section 7805(b) of the Code, to the extent this Revenue Ruling produces adverse tax effects, it will be applied without retroactive effect to taxable years ending on or before April 16, 1973, the date this Revenue Ruling is published in the Internal Revenue Bulletin. Thus, an adjustment in the tax liability of a taxpayer where the allowance of a dependency exemption was determined in accordance with Revenue Ruling 71–19 will not be required for taxable years ending on or before April 16, 1973, the date this Revenue Ruling is published.

PROBLEMS

1. In the following parts of this question, state the number of deductions for personal exemptions available. The following facts may be assumed unless otherwise indicated: T was married; T's spouse had no gross income during the year and was not a dependent of any other person; both T and his spouse were under 65 and had good eyesight; and T files a separate return. Treat each part separately unless otherwise indicated.

   (a) T married W on December 31, and W's only income for the year was $50 of dividends on some domestic stock she owns.

   (b) Same as (a) except that on December 31 W also received $100 as a wedding present from Uncle U.

   (c) Same as (a), above, except that the $50 was interest on a savings account.

   (d) Under the facts of (c), above, may T claim a dependency exemption for W if a personal exemption is foreclosed?

(e) Same as (c), above, except that T and W file a joint return.

(f) Same as (e), above, except that T's 65th Birthday falls on January 1 of the next year.

2.   A and B were husband and wife and calendar year taxpayers.   A died in 1976 and B married C that year six months after A's death.   B had no gross income for the year.

(a) When A's executor files A's final return as a separate return of A, may he claim an exemption for B even though C does too? See Rev.Rul. 71–159, 1971–1 C.B. 50.

(b) If it were B (who had no income) who had died and A (who had lots of income) had married D, could A on a separate return (D also filing separately) claim an exemption for B? See Rev.Rul. 71–158, 1971–1 C.B. 50.

3.   In each of the following parts state whether T was entitled to a "dependency" exemption for the particular person (i. e., X) involved.   Assume the following facts for each of these parts, unless otherwise indicated: the taxable year is after 1972; T was married but filed a separate return; and T furnished over one-half of the support for the particular person involved. Also assume, unless otherwise indicated, that such person earned less than $750 gross income during the year, and did not live with T.   Treat each part separately unless otherwise indicated.

(a) X was T's wife's brother.

(b) Same as (a), above, but assume further that:

    (1) T's wife died the year before.

    (2) T and W were divorced the year before. Cf. Steele v. Suwalski, 75 F.2d 885 (7th Cir. 1935).

(c) X was T's wife's sister's husband.

(d) Same as (c), above, except that X lived with T the entire year.

(e) X is T's son who will be 19 next January 1st and who earned $2000 from summer jobs during the year but who is a full-time college student, except in the summer.

(f) X is T's 18 year old daughter who had only $500 of gross income during the year, but who married Y during the year with whom she files a joint return.

(g) Same as (f), above, but Y also had relatively little income from which tax was withheld and their return was filed only for purposes of obtaining a refund. See Rev.Rul. 65–34, 1965–1 C.B. 86.

(h) X was T's 18 year old son for whom T contributed $2000 in support while X, who had no gross income, applied $3000 out of gifts from Uncle U to his support.

(i) Same as (h), above, except that X's only contribution to his own support was a $3000 scholarship enabling him to attend Embraceable U.

4. T's father X, who has no gross income, was supported in 1976 by T, T's two brothers (A and B), and C, an unrelated friend. A total of $4000 was spent for the father's support which was contributed in the following proportions by the above persons: X, 15%; T, 25%; A, 20%; B, 10%; and C, 30%. Which of these persons, if any, is entitled to claim X as a dependent and what procedures must they follow?

5. H and W were married for several years. On January 1st of the current year they are separated and execute a written separation agreement pursuant to which H agrees to pay W $200 per month. W has no other income. If H is in a high tax bracket would you advise him to deduct these payments under § 215? What alternative may be available to H? See § 71(a)(2); but see also § 62(13), Part B, infra.

B. THE CONCEPT OF ADJUSTED GROSS INCOME

Internal Revenue Code: Section 62.
Regulations: Section 1.62–1(a), (b), (c) and (d).

EXCERPT FROM SENATE FINANCE COMMITTEE REPORT NO. 885.

78th Congress, 2d Session (1944).
1944 Cum.Bull. 858, 877.

Fundamentally, the deductions * * * permitted to be made from gross income in arriving at adjusted gross income are those which are necessary to make as nearly equivalent as practicable the concept of adjusted gross income, when that concept is applied to different types of taxpayers deriving their income from varying sources. Such equivalence is necessary for equitable application of a mechanical tax table or a standard deduction which does not depend upon the source of income. For example, in the case of an individual merchant or store proprietor, gross income under the law is gross receipts less the cost of goods sold; it is necessary to reduce this amount by the amount of business expenses before it becomes comparable, for the purposes of such a tax table or the standard deduction, to the salary or wages of an employee in the usual case. Similarly, the gross income derived from rents and royalties is reduced by the deductions attributable thereto * * * in order that the resulting adjusted gross income will be on a parity with the income from interest and dividends in respect of which latter items no deductions are permitted in computing adjusted gross income.

The deductions [attributable to a trade or business] are limited to those which fall within the category of expenses directly incurred in the carrying on of a trade or business. The connection contemplated by the statute is a direct one rather than a remote one. For example, property taxes paid or incurred on real property used in the trade or business will be deductible whereas State income taxes, incurred on business profits, would clearly not be deductible for the purpose of computing adjusted gross income. Similarly, with respect to the deductions [attributable to rents and royalties] the term "attributable" shall be taken in its restricted sense; only such deductions as are, in the accounting sense, deemed to be expenses directly incurred in the rental of property or in the production of royalties. Thus, for this purpose, charitable contributions would not be deemed to be expenses directly incurred in the operation of a trade or business, or in the rental of property or the production of royalties. * * *.

This section creates no new deductions; the only deductions permitted are such of those allowed in Chapter 1 of the Code as are specified in any of the clauses [now (1) through (13) of § 62] above. The circumstance that a particular item is specified in one of the clauses and is also includible in another does not enable the item to be twice subtracted in determining adjusted gross income.

* * *

NOTE

The concept of adjusted gross income has relevance only with respect to individual taxpayers. It has no significance with respect to corporate taxpayers, or to estates, trusts or partnerships. With respect to individuals, it serves as a measuring device for computing the percentage standard deduction,[1] for computing the ceiling limitation on allowable charitable deductions,[2] for computing the amount of deductible medical expenses[3] and, although it used to affect the deduction for dependent care expenses, it does not enter into the computation of the new credit for dependent care expenses.[4]

In a very broad sense all deductions are from gross income and result in taxable income. However, in the statutory scheme, some items of deduction are spoken of as allowable "above the line" (those described in § 62), while some are deductible "below the line" (those outside § 62). In this regard, § 62 does not *authorize* any deduction. It simply *identifies* deductions, authorized elsewhere in the statute,

1. I.R.C. (26 U.S.C.A.) §§ 141–144.

2. I.R.C. (26 U.S.C.A.) § 170(b). This ceiling is now expressed in terms of "contribution base," but that term is defined with reference to adjusted gross income. § 170(b)(1)(F).

3. I.R.C. (26 U.S.C.A.) § 213(a)(1) and (b).

4. TRA (1976) § 504 replaced the old I.R.C. § 214 dependent care *deduction* with a new *credit* found in § 44A.

which may be taken in arriving at adjusted gross income. Deductions that are not mentioned in § 62 are deductible, but these deductions are *from* adjusted gross income (so-called itemized deductions) and can be taken only in lieu of the standard deduction.⁵ Deductions described in § 62 are not in lieu of the standard deduction but in addition to that deduction and in this light they are especially favorable deductions. Clear?

These brief comments identify a matter of major significance which must be given some thought. The thinking process will be aided by the Problems that follow and the segment on the standard deduction which follows the Problems.

PROBLEMS

Assume the following expenses are properly deductible. Does the deduction fall under I.R.C. (26 U.S.C.A.) § 62, or may it be claimed only by foregoing the standard deduction? See § 63(b).

1. Employee pays for his meals, lodging, and transportation to attend a business convention and is not reimbursed by Employer.

2. Employee, a policeman, purchases a new uniform at his own expense.

3. Employee Salesman (not "outside") pays the cost of entertaining purchasers in social circumstances that are directly related to his trade or business and is not reimbursed by Employer.

4. Same as 3, above, except that Employer reimburses Employee for the exact cost incurred. How should Employee treat the expenses and reimbursement on his return? See Reg. § 1.162–17.

5. Same as 3, above, except that Employer, an individual, rather than Employee, entertained the purchasers.

6. Same as 3, above, except that Employee incurs the expenses in his role as an outside salesman of Employer.

7. Employee, at his own expense, pays $500 tuition for a refresher course in Home Town to bring himself up to date on current business techniques relating to his employment.

8. Same as 7, above, except that Employee goes to Remote Town for the course and also incurs $500 in expenses for transportation, meals, and lodging.

9. Employee makes payments for medical expenses and charitable contributions and for taxes on his residence and interest on a note secured by a mortgage on the residence.

10. Same as 9, above, except that the taxes and interest relate to a residence that Employee rents to Tenant.

5. I.R.C. (26 U.S.C.A.) §§ 63(b), 141–144.

11.   Employee has a loss on the sale of some stock that he held for investment.

12.   Employer, whose business is unincorporated, pays his state income taxes.

13.   Single pays his ex-wife Jingle $6000 in alimony.

C. THE STANDARD DEDUCTION

Internal Revenue Code: Sections 63; 141; 142; 143; 144(a).
Regulations: Sections 1.141–1(a), (f); 1.142; 1.143; 1.144–1(a).

The standard deduction came into the Code in 1944 [1] to simplify tax returns by according individuals an election to deduct an amount equal to 10% of their adjusted gross incomes (but not more than $1,000, or $500 in the case of a married individual filing a separate return) in lieu of some deductions otherwise to be itemized. This permitted taxpayers to deduct a specified amount without keeping records of various expenditures and without specifically reporting a large group of deductions. The corresponding reduction in the administrative burden of the Internal Revenue Service is obvious. The standard deduction is usually an alternative to claiming deductions for items such as taxes, interest, medical expenses, charitable contributions, and any others not specified under I.R.C. (26 U.S.C.A.) § 62.

In the 1950's and 1960's inflation and the congressional addition of some itemized expenditures to the deductible list operated to reduce the percentage of individual returns using the elective standard deduction from 82.2% in 1944 to an estimated 58.2% in 1969.[2] Recognition of this prompted Congress, in enacting the Tax Reform Act of 1969, to increase both the percentage and ceiling limitations on the standard deduction over the next few years as follows:

Year	%	Maximum Deduction	
1970 (and before)	10%	$1000	(½ if married
1971	13%	$1500	and file
1972	14%	$2000	separate
1973	15%	$2000	returns)

---

1. Individual Income Tax Act of 1944, § 9, 58 Stat. 231, 236 (1944).

2. Staff of the Joint Committee on Internal Revenue Taxation, General Explanation of the Tax Reform Act of 1969, p. 216 (1970).

But the beat goes on, and further changes have been considered necessary. An extension of the above table to reflect changes initially considered "temporary" looks as follows:

Maximum Deduction

		Married		Single	
Year	*%*	*Joint*	*Separate*	*Surv. Spouse*	*No Special Status*
1975	16%	2600	1300	2600	2300
1976	16%	2800	1400	2800	2400

Reversion to the figures shown for 1973 after 1976 was contemplated, but the Tax Reform Act made the figures shown for 1976 permanent.

In corporate reorganization and other commercial settings we have become accustomed to look for "sham" and "step transactions" and cautioned not to exalt "form over substance." Encouraged now by an easier attitude on virtue, by graduated tax rates, *and* by the differences recorded above in the standard deduction, these terms are creeping into the domestic scene. For example, A and B, husband and wife are both doctors; both have incomes of about $30,000; and neither has consequential itemized deductions. Rather than file a joint return, they take a late December vacation trip to Barataria (Where is it? Maybe Gilbert could tell Sullivan.) and, while there, get a "quickie" divorce, intending to remarry in January, which they do. Each asserts a $2400 standard deduction for a total of $4800 vs. a $2800 standard on a joint return (and of course they are escaping high rate brackets applicable to their combined income, too.) [3] Mrs. Gregory, what did you start? [4] The Commissioner now says the divorce is a "sham," of no more substance than "The Gondoliers," and that A and B are tax mates, even if Baratarian singles. [5] Of course taxpayers of still easier virtue may elect not to marry or to adopt a permanently single status, for *tax* reasons! [6]

The Revenue Act of 1964 added a floor to the standard deduction in the form of the minimum standard deduction. [7] If the standard deduction was elected, the minimum standard deduction was to be used if it exceeded the amount of the 10% standard deduction. The $1000 maximum limitation applied to both. The minimum standard deduction was enacted especially to benefit large, low-income families,

---

3. Compare also the I.R.C. § 1(a) and 1(c) rates applicable to married and single taxpayers, respectively, with those in 1(d) applicable if married taxpayers file separately.

4. The court found her corporate reorganization to be a sham transaction in Gregory v. Helvering, 293 U.S. 465 (1935).

5. Rev.Rul. 76–255, 1976–2 C.B. ——.

6. Ibid. Annulment accorded full retrospective effect. Of course in other circumstances taxpayers with uneven incomes might seek to avoid high rates by a late December marriage to be followed by early January divorce.

7. Revenue Act of 1964, § 112, 78 Stat. 19, 23 (1964).

and it increased as the number of exemptions available to the taxpayer increased.[8]

The Tax Reform Act of 1969 changed both the designation and the amount of the minimum standard deduction. It is now the "low-income allowance" and, in conjunction with increased personal exemptions, it insures that persons who fall well below the poverty level will not be subject to any federal income tax. For years beginning in 1972 the low income allowance was a flat $1000 ($500 in the case of married individuals filing separate returns), and it was the standard deduction if it was larger than the amount of the percentage standard deduction.[9] Recent changes in the low income allowance are reflected in the following table:

	Married		Single	No Special
Year	Joint	Separate	Surv. Spouse	Status
1974	1300	650	1300	1300
1975	1900	950	1900	1600
1976	2100	1050	2100	1700

Again, the figures shown for 1975 and 1976 were to revert to those shown for 1974 after 1976, but the Tax Reform Act made the figures shown for 1976 permanent.

PROBLEMS

1. Husband and Wife, both under 65 and with good eyesight, have one dependent child. For 1977 they file a joint return showing gross income of $6000. They have no I.R.C. (26 U.S.CA.) § 62 deductions, but they do have $800 in itemized deductions.

   (a) What is their taxable income for the year if they itemize their deductions, and, in the alternative, if they elect the standard deduction?

   (b) Same question as (a), above, except that their itemized deductions amount to $2300.

   (c) Same question as in (a), above, except that they show gross income of $15,000.

---

8. The minimum standard deduction was never less than $200 ($100 in the case of a married individual filing a separate return) and it increased $100 for each exemption allowed to the taxpayer.

9. I.R.C. (26 U.S.C.A.) § 141(a) and (c). For the years 1970 and 1971 the amount of the low income allowance, like the amount of the minimum standard deduction, varied and its ceiling was $1100 for 1970 and $1050 for 1971. The somewhat lower allowance for 1972 takes account of a simultaneous increase in the personal exemption. The transitional rules applicable to years 1970 and 1971 are illustrated in Reg. § 1.141–1(e). For comments on a proposal that would go beyond the point of mere *relief from tax* for the poor, see Cohen, "Administrative Aspects of a Negative Income Tax," 117 U. of Pa.L.Rev. 678 (1969).

2. A lives in New York and B in Florida. Both are married and file joint returns properly claiming two exemptions, and both have very substantial all-salary incomes of identical amounts. For 1977 A pays state income tax in the amount of $3000. B pays no state income tax. Assume (quite artificially) that neither has any other cost, expense, or expenditure that could be claimed as a deduction. Which, if either, should claim the standard deduction? Explain and evaluate. Would your answer be different if the $3000 paid by A was fee paid an attorney for collection of rent on a house owned by A, instead of state income tax?

3. Husband and Wife file separate returns. Husband has substantial itemized deductions, but Wife has very few.

(a) Why does Congress proscribe the use of the standard deduction by Wife if Husband itemizes his deductions?

(b) May Wife use the low income allowance on her separate return, even if it is smaller than the percentage standard deduction, so that Husband may also use the low income allowance, which is larger than his percentage standard and itemized deductions?

4. Husband and Wife, both of whom have very substantial incomes, are living apart and their children reside with Wife who pays all the household expenses from her own income. Wife files a separate return for 1977, claiming a standard deduction of $2400. Properly? If husband also has substantial income, what is the ceiling on *his* standard deduction? See I.R.C. (26 U.S.C.A.) § 143(b) for both questions.

D. EXTRAORDINARY MEDICAL EXPENSES

Internal Revenue Code: Sections 152(c); 213(a), (b), (e), and (f). See
    Section 44A.
Regulations: Section 1.213–1(a)(1), (b)(1)(i), (e).

RAYMON GERARD

Tax Court of the United States, 1962.
37 T.C. 826(A).

MULRONEY, JUDGE:

[The Findings of Fact have been omitted. Ed.]

Opinion

Section 213(a)[1] as here applicable allows "as a deduction the
* * * amounts of the expenses paid during the taxable year,
* * * for medical care of the taxpayer, his spouse, or a dependent."
Section 213(e) defines the term "medical care" as follows:

SEC. 213. MEDICAL, DENTAL, ETC., EXPENSES.

(e) DEFINITIONS.—For purposes of this section—

(1) The term "medical care" means amounts paid—

(A) for the diagnosis, cure, mitigation, treatment,
or prevention of disease, or for the purpose of affecting any structure or function of the body (including
amounts paid for accident or health insurance), or

(B) for transportation primarily for and essential
to medical care referred to in subparagraph (A).

It is well established that some form of control of temperature and
humidity was a medical necessity in petitioners' home. Their daughter's illness made it dangerous for her to be exposed to dry, dusty air.
The evidence shows petitioners had tried a room air-conditioning unit
in their home in New Jersey but it was not satisfactory.[2] This restricted the child to one room for the entire day in order to get the
beneficial effects and it was bad for her psychologically. It was the

1. All section references are to the Internal Revenue Code of 1954, as
amended.

2. Petitioner testified he took a medical
deduction for this room air conditioner. Respondent's regulation sec.

1.213–1(e) (1) (iii) lists some capital
expenditures which can be medical
deductions and the list includes an expenditure for "an air conditioner
which is detachable from the property
and purchased only for the use of a
sick person."

doctor who advised petitioners it would be better for the child to have the central unit so she could have the whole home as her restricted area. Children afflicted with cystic fibrosis have a special diet and they are treated with antibiotics given by mouth and by aerosols and they sleep every night in a tent which has additional antibiotics.

We think the expenditure of $1,300 for installing the air-conditioning unit was an expenditure for medical care for petitioners' dependent, within the scope of the above-quoted statute. But there is another statute which must be considered because of the nature of this expenditure.

Section 263(a) (1) provides in part: "No deduction shall be allowed for * * * Any amount paid out * * * for permanent improvements or betterments made to increase the value of any property."

The general rule, expressed in respondent's regulation and numerous cases, is that a medical care expenditure for what is a capital expenditure in the nature of a permanent improvement to the taxpayer's home is not deductible as medical expense. Frank S. Delp, 30 T.C. 1230; John L. Seymour, 14 T.C. 1111; sec. 1.213–1(e) (1) (iii), Income Tax Regs. However, it has been held, and respondent admits, that the mere fact that a medical care expenditure is also a capital expenditure is not always sufficient to disqualify it for medical deduction. When the medical care expenditure is for a permanent addition to the taxpayer's home, deductibility as a medical expense depends upon whether it increases the value of the home. In Berry v. Wiseman, 174 F.Supp. 748 (W.D.Okla.1958), the court held the cost ($4,400) of installing an elevator in taxpayer's home was deductible as medical expense. There the housewife petitioner suffered from acute coronary insufficiency and the elevator was installed upon the advice of her physician. The court found that the elevator was permanent but "that it did not have the effect of increasing the value of the property." In Rev.Rul. 59–411, 1959–2 C.B. 100,[3] respondent announced he would follow the case of Berry v. Wiseman, supra, and his ruling indicates

---

3. The said ruling states in part:

The Internal Revenue Service will follow the decision of the United States District Court for the Western District of Oklahoma in the case of James E. Berry et ux. v. Earl R. Wiseman (W.D. Okla.1958), 174 F.Supp. 748.

The court ruled that the cost of an elevator installed in the taxpayers' residence was deductible as a medical expense. The elevator had been installed at a cost of some $4,400 on the advice of a doctor to alleviate an acute coronary insufficiency of Mrs. Berry.

Accordingly, expenditures made for medical purposes will not be disallow-

ed merely because they are of a capital nature. However, it is the position of the Service that the capital nature of an expenditure will be a consideration in determining its deductibility. If such expenditures constitute amounts paid out for permanent improvements which *increase the value* of any property or estate, they will not be allowed as medical expense deductions.

Steps will be taken to modify outstanding rulings contrary to this court decision and to conform Treasury regulations promulgated under section 213 of the Internal Revenue Code of 1954.

the significant fact in that case was the finding that the installation of the elevator did not increase the value of the house.

Prior to the above ruling, we had decided the *Delp* case in 1958. While the issue in Frank S. Delp, supra, was different (whether the electric air cleaner was permanently affixed to the home), there is an expression in the opinion indicating the extent of value increase is to measure medical deductibility. There we said speaking generally of medical care expenditures that represent permanent improvements to property:

Such expenditures, to the extent the permanent improvement of the asset increases the value of the property, at least in a sense compensate for the expense of such improvement.

Respondent admits on brief where the taxpayer is able to show the medical care expenditure in the nature of a permanent addition to the residence does not increase the value of the home, it qualifies for medical deduction. We think it necessarily follows that where the taxpayer is able to show such increase in value is less than the expenditure, the amount in excess of value enhancement is deductible as medical expense. Here the parties stipulate the cost of installing the air-conditioning unit was $1,300 and the unit increased the value of the home in the sum of $800. It follows that the balance, or $500, qualifies for medical deduction. We so hold.

Reviewed by the Court.

Decision will be entered under Rule 50.

COMMISSIONER v. BILDER

Supreme Court of the United States, 1962.
369 U.S. 499, 82 S.Ct. 881.

MR. JUSTICE HARLAN delivered the opinion of the Court.

This case concerns the deductibility as an expense for "medical care," under § 213 of the Internal Revenue Code of 1954, 26 U.S.C. § 213, of rent paid by a taxpayer for an apartment in Florida, where he was ordered by his physician, as part of a regimen of medical treatment, to spend the winter months.[1]

The taxpayer, now deceased, was an attorney practicing law in Newark, New Jersey. In December 1953, when he was 43 years of age and had suffered four heart attacks during the previous eight years, he was advised by a heart specialist to spend the winter season

1. [Quotations from I.R.C. § 213 are omitted. Ed.]

in a warm climate. The taxpayer, his wife, and his three-year-old daughter proceeded immediately to Fort Lauderdale, Florida, where they resided for the ensuing three months in an apartment rented for $1,500. Two months of the succeeding winter were also spent in Fort Lauderdale in an apartment rented for $829.

The taxpayer claimed the two rental payments as deductible medical expenses in his 1954 and 1955 income tax returns. These deductions were disallowed in their entirety by the Commissioner.[2] The Tax Court reversed the Commissioner's determination to the extent of one-third of the deductions, finding that proportion of the total claimed attributable to the taxpayer's own living accommodations. The remaining two-thirds it attributed to the accommodations of his wife and child, whose presence, the Tax Court concluded, had not been shown to be necessary to the medical treatment of the taxpayer's illness. 33 T.C. 155.

On cross-appeals from the decision of the Tax Court, the Court of Appeals held, by a divided vote, that the full rental payments were deductible as expenses for "medical care" within the meaning of § 213. 289 F.2d 291. Because of a subsequent contrary holding by the Court of Appeals for the Second Circuit, Carasso v. Commissioner, 292 F.2d 367, and the need for a uniform rule on the point, we granted certiorari to resolve the conflict. 368 U.S. 912.

The Commissioner concedes that prior to the enactment of the Internal Revenue Code of 1954 rental payments of the sort made by the taxpayer were recognized as deductible medical expenses. This was because § 23(x) of the Internal Revenue Code of 1939, though expressly authorizing deductions only for "amounts paid for the diagnosis, cure, mitigation, treatment, or prevention of disease," [3] had been construed to include "travel primarily for and essential to . . . the prevention or alleviation of a physical or mental defect or illness," Treasury Regulations 111, § 29.23(x)–1, and the cost of meals and lodging during such travel, I.T. 3786, 1946–1 Cum.Bull. 76.

---

2. The Commissioner concedes that the taxpayer's sojourn in Florida was not for vacation purposes but was "a medical necessity and . . . a primary part of necessary medical treatment of a disease" from which the taxpayer was suffering, i. e., atherosclerosis. 33 T.C., at 157. The taxpayer also claimed in each of his tax returns a $250 deduction for his transportation between Newark and Fort Lauderdale. Although the Commissioner initially disallowed this deduction he thereafter acquiesced in its allowance by the Tax Court.

3. Section 23(x) was added to the Internal Revenue Code of 1939 by § 127

(a) of the Revenue Act of 1942, 56 Stat. 825. It provided, in pertinent part:

"[In computing net income there shall be allowed as deductions] * * * expenses paid during the taxable year, not compensated for by insurance or otherwise, for medical care of the taxpayer, his spouse, or a dependent * * * of the taxpayer. The term 'medical care,' as used in this subsection, shall include amounts paid for the diagnosis, cure, mitigation, treatment, or prevention of disease, or for the purpose of affecting any structure or function of the body (including amounts paid for accident or health insurance)."

See, e. g., Stringham v. Commissioner, 12 T.C. 580, aff'd, 183 F.2d 597; Rev.Rule 55–261, 1955–1 Cum.Bull. 307.

The Commissioner maintains, however, that it was the purpose of Congress, in enacting § 213(e) (1) (A) of the 1954 Code, albeit in language identical to that used in § 23(x) of the 1939 Code (. . . see note 3, supra), to deny deductions for all personal or living expenses incidental to medical treatment other than the cost of transportation of the patient alone, that exception having been expressly added by subdivision (B) to the definition of "medical care" in § 213(e) (1).

We consider the Commissioner's position unassailable in light of the congressional purpose explicitly revealed in the House and Senate Committee Reports on the bill. These reports, anticipating the precise situation now before us, state:

"Subsection (e) defines medical care to mean amounts paid for the diagnosis, cure, mitigation, treatment, or prevention of diseases or for the purpose of affecting any structure or function of the body (including amounts paid for accident or health insurance), or for transportation primarily for and essential to medical care. The deduction permitted for 'transportation primarily for and essential to medical care' *clarifies existing law* in that it specifically *excludes deduction of any meals and lodging while away from home receiving medical treatment.* For example, if a doctor prescribes that a patient must go to Florida in order to alleviate specific chronic ailments and to escape unfavorable climatic conditions which have proven injurious to the health of the taxpayer, and the travel is prescribed for reasons other than the general improvement of a patient's health, the cost of the patient's transportation to Florida would be deductible *but not his living expenses while there.* However, if a doctor prescribed an appendectomy and the taxpayer chose to go to Florida for the operation not even his transportation costs would be deductible. The subsection is not intended otherwise to *change* the existing definitions of medical care, to deny the cost of ordinary ambulance transportation nor to deny the cost of food or lodging provided as part of a hospital bill." H.R.Rep.No.1337, 83d Cong., 2d Sess. A60 (1954); S.Rep.No.1622, 83d Cong., 2d Sess. 219–220 (1954).[4] (Emphasis supplied.)

Since under the predecessor statute, as it had been construed, expenses for meals and lodging *were* deductible as expenses for "medical care," it may well be true that the Committee Reports spoke in part inartistically when they referred to subsection (e) as a mere clarification of "existing law," although it will be noted that the report also referred to what was being done as a *pro tanto* "change" in "the existing definitions of medical care." Yet Congress' purpose to exclude such expenses as medical deductions under the new bill is un-

---

4. The substance of the rule set forth in both Reports has been embodied in the Treasury Regulations interpreting § 213. [See Reg. § 1.213–1(e) (1) (iv). Ed.]

mistakable in these authoritative pronouncements, ibid.; cf. Budget Message of the President for the Fiscal Year 1955, H.R.Doc.No. 264, 83d Cong., 2d Sess. M17 (1954); Memorandum of Joint Committee on Internal Revenue Taxation, 1 Senate Hearings on the Internal Revenue Code of 1954, 83d Cong., 2d Sess. 24 (1954); Memorandum of the Under Secretary of the Treasury, id., at 103. It is that factor which is of controlling importance here.[5]

We need not consider whether we would be warranted in disregarding these unequivocal expressions of legislative intent if the statute were so written as to permit no reasonable construction other than that urged on behalf of the taxpayer. Compare Boston Sand & Gravel Co. v. United States, 278 U.S. 41, 48; United States v. Dickerson, 310 U.S. 554, 561–562; Harrison v. Northern Trust Co., 317 U.S. 476, 479. See also Association of Westinghouse Salaried Employees v. Westinghouse Elec. Corp., 348 U.S. 437, 444. Even the initial decision of the Tax Court under the 1939 Code respecting the deductibility of similar expenses under § 23(x) recognized that the language of that statute was "susceptible to a variety of conflicting interpretations," Stringham v. Commissioner, 12 T.C. 580, 583. The Tax Court's conclusion as to the meaning of § 23(x) of the earlier statute which was affirmed by the Court of Appeals, 183 F.2d 579, and acquiesced in by the Commissioner, necessarily rested on what emerged from a study of the legislative history of that enactment. So too the conclusion in this case, which turns on the construction of the identical words re-enacted as part of § 213, must be based on an examination of the legislative history of this provision of the 1954 Code. The Committee Reports foreclose any reading of that provision which would permit this taxpayer to take the rental payments for his Florida apartment as "medical care" deductions.

Reversed.

MR. JUSTICE DOUGLAS would affirm the judgment below for the reasons given by Judge Kalodner, 289 F.2d 291.

MR. JUSTICE FRANKFURTER took no part in the decision of this case.

MR. JUSTICE WHITE took no part in the consideration or decision of this case.

5. The explicitness of the Committee Reports renders it unnecessary to consider the Commissioner's alternative argument that the statute on its face precludes these deductions because (1) § 262 of the 1954 Code, 26 U.S.C. § 262, allows no deductions for "personal, living, or family expenses" "[e]xcept as otherwise expressly provided in this chapter," and (2) apart from the medical "transportation" expense provided in § 213(e) (1) (B), no other *express* exception can be found in the statute. And the equitable considerations which the respondent brings to bear in support of her construction of § 213 are of course beside the point in this Court, since we must give the statute effect in accordance with the purpose so clearly manifested by Congress.

MONTGOMERY v. COMMISSIONER *

United States Court of Appeals, Sixth Circuit, 1970.
428 F.2d 243.

CELEBREZZE, CIRCUIT JUDGE. This is an appeal from a judgment of the Tax Court of the United States by the Commissioner of Internal Revenue [hereinafter "Commissioner"] against Morris C. Montgomery [hereinafter "Taxpayer"] and his wife, who had filed a joint return for the taxable year 1961. The Tax Court held, four judges dissenting, that the cost of meals and lodging of the Taxpayer and his wife, while en route from their home in Lawrenceburg, Kentucky, to Rochester, Minnesota, and return, on trips in 1961 for bona fide medical reasons, is included within the meaning of "transportation" expenses as used in Section 213(e) (1) (B) of the Internal Revenue Code of 1954; and therefore, such costs were deductible expenses for "medical care."

During 1961, the Taxpayer and his wife made three round trips to the Mayo Clinic, Rochester, Minnesota, from their legal residence in Lawrenceburg, Kentucky. Each of these trips was for admittedly medical purposes and the Commissioner concedes that although the later two trips were for the medical treatment of Taxpayer's wife, the Taxpayer's accompaniment of his wife was required for medical reasons. The Taxpayer and his wife made their first round trip by automobile and incurred certain itemized expenses, during their transportation, for food and lodging. Subsequently, Taxpayer's wife traveled by train, pullman accommodations, and bus to the Mayo Clinic for an operation; and the Taxpayer traveled by automobile to the Clinic after the operation and accompanied his convalescing wife on her return to Lawrenceburg. Thereafter, Taxpayer's wife made a final trip by plane to the Mayo Clinic where she was hospitalized. At the time of her discharge from the Clinic, her husband again traveled by automobile to bring her home. During these various trips, Taxpayer and his wife incurred a total expense for meals and lodging between Lawrenceburg and Rochester of $162.39.

The sole issue in the appeal is whether this $162.39 in expenses are deductible as expenses for "medical care" pursuant to Section 213 of the Internal Revenue Code of 1954.

The term "medical care" is defined under Section 213(e) (1) as amounts paid:

"(B) for transportation primarily for and essential to medical care referred to in subparagraph (A) [1], * * *."

---

* There is a comment on this case in Johnson, "Medical Travel Expense," 16 S.Dak.L.Rev. 326 (1971). Ed.

1. Subparagraph (a) reads: "for the diagnosis, cure, mitigation, treatment or prevention of disease, or for the purpose of affecting any structure or function of the body."

The Commissioner contends that moneys paid for food and lodging en route to a place of medication are "traveling" expenses in excess of the mere cost of "transporting" the person and baggage of the taxpayers to their place of destination. The Commissioner maintains that the use of the more narrow phrase "expenses for transportation," rather than "expenses * * * for traveling [to the place of medication]" indicates a plain intention to deny the deductibility of in-transit expenses for food and lodging. The Commissioner further contends that the cost of meals and lodging are "personal, living or family expenses" for which "no deduction shall be allowed, * * * [e]xcept as otherwise expressly provided." Internal Revenue Code, Section 262.

In response, the Taxpayer contends that "expenses * * * for transportation" includes, as the Tax Court held below, all expenses "required to bring the patient to the place of medication." 51 T.C. 410. Such expenses were deductible under the prior Internal Revenue Code of 1939, and the Tax Court found that the legislative history of the present Code, as well as the present Treasury Regulations, permit their continued deductibility. We agree.

Under the Internal Revenue Code of 1939, all food and lodging expenses of a patient on the way to the place of medication and at the place of medication were deductible. In Commissioner of Internal Revenue v. Bilder, 369 U.S. 499, 501, 82 S.Ct. 881, 8 L.Ed.2d 65 (1962), the United States Supreme Court denied the deductibility under the 1954 Code of lodging expenses at the place of medication. In doing so, it observed:

"The Commissioner concedes that prior to the enactment of the Internal Revenue Code of 1954 rental payments of the sort made by the taxpayer were recognized as deductible medical expenses. This was because § 23(x) of the Internal Revenue Code of 1939, 26 U.S. C.A. 23(x) though expressly authorizing deductions only for 'amounts paid for the diagnosis, cure, mitigation, treatment, or prevention of disease,' had been construed to include 'travel primarily for and essential to * * * the prevention or alleviation of a physical or mental defect or illness,' Treasury Regulations 111, § 29.23(x)–1, and the cost of meals and lodging during such travel, I.T. 3786, 1946–1 Cum.Bull. 76. *See,* e. g. Stringham v. Commissioner, 12 T.C. 580, aff'd, 183 F.2d 579; Rev.Rule 55–261, 1955–1 Cum.Bull. 307."

Unfortunately, the liberal provisions of the 1939 Code for deductibility of "travel" expenses led to very significant abuses. Taxpayers would travel on doctors' orders to resort areas for the alleviation of a specific ailment and deduct all of the costs of their food and lodging while on such medical vacations. The legislative history of the Internal Revenue Code of 1954 indicates a specific intent to eliminate the resort area medication abuse. Both the House and

Senate Committee Reports on the 1954 Code discuss the deductibility of medical care expenses. They state:

"The deduction permitted for 'transportation primarily for and essential to medical care' clarifies existing law in that it specifically *excludes deduction of any meals and lodging while away from home receiving medical treatment.* For example, if a doctor prescribes that a patient must go to Florida in order to alleviate specific chronic ailments and to escape unfavorable climate conditions which have proven injurious to the health of the taxpayer, and the travel is prescribed for reasons other than the general improvement of a patient's health, *the cost of the patient's transportation to Florida would be deductible but not his living expenses while there.* (Emphasis added) H.R.Rep.No.1337, 83d Cong. 2nd Sess. A 60 (1954); S.Rep.No.1622, 83d Cong., 2nd Sess. 219–220 (1954) U.S.Code Cong. & Admin. News, p. 4856."

The Treasury Department incorporated the substance of the above Reports in its Regulations interpreting Section 213. [See Reg. § 1.213–1(e) (1) (iv). Ed.]

* * *

It is apparent that the concern of Congress and the Treasury was to eliminate the abuse of "resort area" medication. Thus Congress eliminated the deductibility of food and lodging expenses at the actual place of medication.[2] Congress did not, however, eliminate the cost of transporting the patient to the place of medication.[3]

We believe that the legislative history and the accompanying regulations indicate a Congressional intent to maintain "existing law" with regard to the deduction of all costs required to transport the patient to the critical place of medication.

The abuse Congress sought to eliminate—the taking of ordinary living expenses "while there"—did not occur until after the patient arrived at the place of care. The effect of the regulations which deny deductibility for food and lodging expenses "while * * * receiving medical treatment" is to allow a deduction while traveling to the place of medical attention. If Congress had wished to exclude the costs for

2. Of course, expenses of meals and lodging incurred "as part of a hospital bill" are deductible. House and Senate Reports, infra, n. 3. Income Tax Regulations 1.213–1(e) (1) (iv) and (v).

3. As the House and Senate Reports state, the "cost of the patient's transportation to Florida would be deductible." H.R.Rep.No.1337, 83rd Congress, 2nd Sess. A60 (1954); S.Rep.No.1628, 83rd Cong., 2nd Sess., 219–220 (1954).

Similarly, if a patient required a professional ambulance service to transport him to the place of medication, that portion of the professional fee attributable to the food and lodging expenses of the driver would be a deductible transportation expense. The Treasury Regulations also provide that nurse's services, "including nurses' board" paid by the taxpayer, are a deductible expense. Treasury Regulations 1–213–1(e) (1) (ii).

food and lodgings incurred in traveling to the place of medication, it could have so provided. The legislative history nowhere indicates an intention to exclude "all ordinary food and lodging expenses," nor does it limit transportation expenses "to the cost of transporting the patient and his baggage."

Food and lodging expenses incurred while traveling are likely to be substantially higher than the cost of living at home. We believe that Congress intended that these higher costs, required by the transportation of a patient to the place of medical care, are to be deductible expenses for medical care under Section 213 of the 1954 Code.

Finally, we are not unmindful of the opinions of the four dissenting judges on the Tax Court. They correctly indicate that the word "transportation" has historically been given a narrower meaning than "travel." The former word has generally been used to cover the costs of transporting the person and his baggage, while the latter has been used in conjunction with the allowance of such amenities as food and lodging. See Internal Revenue Code of 1954 §§ 62(2) (B) (C), 162(a) (2), 217(b) (1) (B) and 274(d) (1). Further, it is clear that in passing the 1954 Code, Congress intended to retreat somewhat from its prior liberal attitude towards medical expenses. This is indicated by the inclusion of Section 262 requiring that "personal, living or family expenses" shall not be deductible "except as otherwise expressly provided," and the present regulations which state "deductions for expenditures for medical care * * * will be confined strictly to expenses incurred primarily for the prevention or alleviation of a physical or mental defect or illness." Treasury Regulations § 1.213–1(e) (1) (ii).

These two factors would be of great influence, but for our belief that the legislative history of Section 213(e) is clear in its import. Food and lodging expense while traveling to the place of medication and incurred prior to "receiving medical treatment" were to be maintained as deductible expenses. The use of the narrow term "transportation," rather than "travel" was indicative of Congress' intent to preclude food and lodging expenses after arrival at the place of medication. Cf. Commissioner v. Bilder, 369 U.S. 499, 82 S.Ct. 881 (1962). The phrase "expenses for traveling" might well have been construed to cover food and lodging expenses during periods of stay at the place of medical treatment; precisely the "abuse" Congress sought to eliminate by the 1954 Code.

We hold that the Taxpayer and his wife properly deducted under Section 213 food and lodging expenses required to bring them to the critical point of medical treatment. The judgment of the Tax Court is affirmed.

NOTE

Under the Internal Revenue Code of 1939, all food and lodging expenses of a patient en route to and from a place for medical care and at the place of medical care were deductible expenses. Off to Tucson for the winter?! No. The legislative history of the Internal Revenue Code of 1954 indicates congressional awareness of the prevalent abuses and an intention to deny a deduction for meals and lodging while away from home for medical treatment.[1]

Although Section 213(e) of the 1954 Code does not specifically exclude meals and lodging, in Commissioner v. Bilder [2] the Supreme Court denied the deductibility of mere lodging expenses at the place of medical care. Of course expenses for meals and "lodging" incurred as an in-patient in a hospital or similar institution are deductible.[3] But it is just as clear that the cost of noninstitutional expenses at the place of medical care are not deductible.[4] A close question exists as to the deductibility of the cost of meals and lodging incurred while traveling to and from the place where medical care is received. In Montgomery v. Commissioner,[5] the Sixth Circuit, affirming the Tax Court, held that the cost of meals and lodging is included within the meaning of "transportation" expenses as used in Section 213(e)(1) (B) and therefore is a deductible expense for medical care.[6] In Winoma Bell Hunt [7] it was held that meals and lodging expenses incurred during travel for medical reasons were not deductible, but it is unclear whether the expenses were incurred at or en route to the place of care. The issue is not settled. It seems equitable to allow a deduction for food and lodging expenses incurred while traveling to and from a place to receive medical care, as these expenses are likely to be substantially higher than the cost of living at home. However, meals and lodging are not easily squeezed into the meaning of transportation and there is express language in the legislative history [8] that indicates these expenses are not to be allowed as deductions. When the issue is raised again, it seems likely that *Montgomery* will not be followed.

Meals and lodging expenses are not the only borderline expenditures that may or may not be deemed medical expenses. A large number of questionable items have been placed within the deductible category. Here are some examples: The cost of a wig was ruled deductible when as a result of disease a woman lost all of her hair, and

1. H.R.Rep.No.1337, 83d Cong. 2d Sess. A60 (1954); S.Rep.No.1662, 83d Cong. 2d Sess. 219–220 (1954).

2. 369 U.S. 499 (1962).

3. Reg. § 1.213–1(e)(1)(v).

4. Max Carasso, 34 T.C. 1139, aff'd, 292 F.2d 367 (2d Cir. 1961), cert. den. 369 U.S. 874 (1962) and Rose v. Comm'r, 485 F.2d 581 (5th Cir. 1973).

5. 428 F.2d 243 (6th Cir. 1970).

6. In Kelly v. Comm'r, 440 F.2d 307 (7th Cir. 1971), although the deducti-bility of meals and lodging while traveling to the place of treatment was not at issue, the court indicated that the congressional purpose behind the changes in Section 213 was to prevent "resort area" abuses and not absolutely to prohibit the deductibility of meals and lodging while traveling to a place for medical attention.

7. 31 T.C.M. 1119 (1972).

8. Supra note 1.

a physician recommended the wig as needed to restore her mental health.[9] The costs of a son's clarinet and lessons to play it were ruled deductible when his orthodontist recommended them in order to alleviate a severe malocclusion of the son's teeth.[10] The cost of birth control pills prescribed by a physician [11] and the cost of a legal vasectomy [12] qualify as deductible medical expenses. Although not all our criminal courts recognize drug addiction as an illness, amounts paid by a taxpayer to maintain a dependent in a therapeutic center for drug addicts have been held deductible.[13] Similarly, transportation costs incurred in attending meetings of Alcoholics Anonymous may be so treated.[14]

Some borderline expenses have been disallowed. The cost of dancing lessons taken to benefit varicose veins in taxpayer's legs but without the advice of a physician is not deductible expense for medical care.[15] And a deduction for dancing lessons even recommended by a physician and admittedly beneficial to the taxpayer was denied because the activity was too personal.[16]

Amounts expended for the "prevention" of disease also involve close questions. Where a dentist recommended the installation of a device for adding fluoride to a home water supply as an aid in the prevention of tooth decay, the expenses of installation and the monthly rental charges thereon were treated as deductible medical expenses.[17] But the taxpayer was too optimistic, and no deduction was permitted, where he purchased and drank bottled distilled water merely to avoid drinking city fluoridated water.[18] Since the possibility of disease from nuclear fallout is very remote, the cost of a fallout shelter is probably a nondeductible personal expense.[19]

Where doctors recommended guardianship proceedings and hospitalization of the taxpayer, the fees of an attorney for services performed in connection with the initiation and termination of the guardianship proceedings were held deductible under Section 213.[20] But a legal fee paid by a taxpayer to obtain a divorce recommended by his psychiatrist was not a deductible medical expense.[21] Although amounts paid by taxpayers for psychiatric treatment for sexual inadequacy are considered by the Commissioner to be deductible medical

9. Rev.Rul. 62–189, 1962–2 C.B. 88.

10. Rev.Rul. 62–210, 1962–2 C.B. 89.

11. Rev.Rul. 73–200, 1973–1 C.B. 140.

12. Rev.Rul. 73–201, 1973–1 C.B. 140.

13. Rev.Rul. 72–226, 1972–1 C.B. 96.

14. Rev.Rul. 63–273, 1963–2 C.B. 112.

15. Adler v. Comm'r, 330 F.2d 91 (9th Cir. 1964).

16. J. J. Thoene, 33 T.C. 62 (1959).

17. Rev.Rul. 64–267, 1964–2 C.B. 69.

18. Rev.Rul. 56–19, 1956–1 C.B. 135.

19. F. H. Daniels, 41 T.C. 324 (1963).

20. Gerstacker v. Comm'r, 414 F.2d 448 (6th Cir. 1969).

21. J. H. Jacobs, 62 T.C. 813 (1974).

expenses,[22] fees paid to a clergyman to improve a taxpayer's marriage are not.[23]

The deductibility of various educational costs as medical expenses has been frequently litigated. In a case in which the taxpayer sent his two children to a boarding school to alleviate his wife's nervous condition and help her to recuperate from an illness, the tuition was held nondeductible as a medical expense, because it was considered a mere family expense analogous to wages paid to cook.[24] Tuition paid by parents for their blind son to attend a private school was held not deductible, because the school did not have a direct or proximate therapeutic effect on his blindness.[25] However, an individual's condition may be such that the primary reason for his being in an institution is the availability of "medical care." In these circumstances a deduction for tuition should be permitted, as it was where an ear specialist recommended a school designed to mitigate and alleviate a deafness handicap of the taxpayer's son.[26]

A deduction for tuition expenses was allowed where a child of average or above average intelligence but with psychiatric problems was sent to a private school because she was incapable of functioning normally at a public school.[27] However, in a case in which the taxpayer's son was sent to a private school, to help cure his "neurotic block against learning," and to get an education, the cost was allocated between nondeductible tuition and deductible mental therapy.[28] If university tuition and other charges are broken down, an identifiable fee for medical care is deductible.[29]

That which is an uncertain I.R.C. (26 U.S.C.A.) § 213 medical expense deduction may in some circumstances constitute an ordinary and necessary business expense under § 162. If a taxpayer on a business trip undergoes an operation and is required, upon discharge from the hospital, to remain at a hotel in the vicinity for a time for post-operative care prior to returning home,[30] it may be argued that the additional costs are a part of his deductible travel expenses under § 162, without regard to § 213 limitations. When an actor's teeth were knocked out while filming a movie the cost of the dental work to replace them was held deductible as a business expense under § 162.[31] Amounts paid for reader's services performed in connection with work of a blind individual are deductible under § 162, not § 213.[32]

22. Rev.Rul. 75–187, 1975–1 C.B. 92.

23. Rev.Rul. 75–319, 1975–2 C.B. 88.

24. Ochs v. Comm'r, 195 F.2d 692 (2d Cir. 1952), cert. den. 344 U.S. 827 (1952).

25. Arnold P. Grunwald, 51 T.C. 108 (1968).

26. Donovan v. Campbell, Jr., unreported, 61–1 USTC ¶ 9357 (N.D.Tex. 1961).

27. L. D. Greisdorf, 54 T.C. 1684 (1970), acq. 1970–2 C.B. XIX.

28. C. Fink Fischer, 50 T.C. 164 (1968), acq. 1969–2 C.B. XXIV.

29. Rev.Rul. 54–457, 1954–2 C.B. 100.

30. See Kelly v. Comm'r, supra note 6.

31. Reginald Denny, 33 B.T.A. 738 (1935), nonacq., XV–1 C.B. 30 (1936).

32. Rev.Rul. 75–316, 1975–2 C.B. 54.

Where it is questionable whether an expense is deductible as a business expense rather than a medical expense. Rev.Rul. 75–316 [33] indicates the expense may be deducted under § 162 if the following three elements are present: (1) the nature of the taxpayer's work clearly requires that he incur a particular expense to satisfactorily perform such work, (2) the goods or services purchased by such expense are clearly not required or used, other than incidentally, in the conduct of the individual's personal activities, and (3) the Code and Regulations are otherwise silent as to the treatment of such expense.

On October 18, 1967, Herb Caen reported in the San Francisco Chronicle the inflationary fact that topless dancer Carol Doda was attempting to deduct the cost of silicone injections to retain her title as Fastest Bust in the West. Are her expenses deductible, and if so, under I.R.C. (26 U.S.C.A.) § 162 or § 213?

PROBLEMS

1. Divorced Homeowner, who received neither alimony nor other support payments from her former husband, fully supported 20 year old Daughter who had no income and lived with her mother. In 1977, Homeowner installed a central air conditioning system at a cost of $4000, which Dr. Watson said was an elementary requirement in caring for Daughter's respiratory problems. After installation, Homeowner's home had increased in value by $2000. Other medical expenses incurred during 1977 by Homeowner and Daughter consisted of medicine in the amount of $320 and doctors' bills in the amount of $400. Late in 1977, she also paid $300 in premiums for health and accident insurance but received no reimbursements under the policy that year.

(a) If Homeowner's adjusted gross income is $12,000 for 1977, what will be the amount of her medical expense deduction?

(b) Would it make better sense and, if so, be possible under the present statute to allow a deduction of $200 per year for the air conditioning expenditure, assuming the system has a 10 year life expectancy?

(c) If in 1977 Homeowner incurs maintenance expenses of $300 on the air conditioning system can that be taken into account as a medical expense? Would a $150 deduction for those expenses be more supportable assuming, of course, Daughter is still there and still asthmatic? And what about an estimate that $400 of the year's electricity bill is attributable to running the air conditioning system?

2. A and B both went from their hometowns to Big City on business, each planning to return the next day, which A did. A incurred costs for transportation, meals and lodging in the amount of

$200. B, however, became ill at the end of his business day and remained in his hotel for two extra days until he was well enough to return home. His expenses, which without the illness would have been the same as A's, came to $300. What may B deduct, and on what authority?

3. X, Y, and Z supported their father F who lived alone but had no income. In 1977 X paid $2000 for Father's food, Y paid $2000 for Father's lodging, and Z paid $2000 for doctor and hospital expenses for Father. Under a multiple support agreement, X claimed Father as a dependent. What do you need to know to determine whether that was a serious mistake?

4. Sickly made frequent visits to his Psychiatrist. Late in 1977 when it was clear he would "itemize" for that year, he sent the doctor $6000, indicating it was to apply against future charges for services. Wobbly checked into a retirement home in the same year. He paid the home $20,000 for the lifetime right to live in the home and receive care, including medical care. The home gave him a statement indicating, appropriately, that $6000 of the charge was for medical care. May either Sickly or Wobbly deduct the $6000 payments? Compare Robert S. Bassett, 26 T.C. 619 (1956), with Rev. Rul. 75–302, 1975–2 C.B. 86.

E. MOVING EXPENSES*

Internal Revenue Code: Sections 82; 217.
Proposed Regulations: Sections 1.82–1(a); 1.217–1, –2(b), (c), (d) (1).

EXCERPT FROM THE GENERAL EXPLANATION OF THE TAX REFORM ACT OF 1969

Staff of the Joint Committee on Internal Revenue Taxation.
Pp. 101–104 (1970).

MOVING EXPENSES

(Sec. 231 of the Act and secs. 217 and 82 of the code)

Prior law.—Prior law allowed, under specified conditions, a deduction from gross income for the following job-related moving expenses: (1) the cost of transporting the taxpayer and members of his household from the old to the new residence; (2) the cost of transporting their belongings; and (3) the cost of meals and lodging

---

* See Allington, "Moving Expenses and Reimbursements," 56 A.B.A.J. 495 (1970); Youngman, "New Law Broad- ens Scope of Moving Expenses and Extends It to Self-Employed Individuals," 32 J.Tax. 292 (1970).

en route. The deduction was available to new employees (whether or not reimbursed) and to unreimbursed transferred employees, but not to self-employed individuals.

For a deduction for moving expenses to be allowed, the taxpayer's new principal place of work had to be located at least 20 miles farther from his former residence than was his former principal place of work (if the taxpayer had no former place of work, then at least 20 miles from his former residence). In addition, to obtain the deduction the taxpayer had to be employed full-time during at least 39 weeks of the 52 weeks immediately following his arrival at the new place of work.

The position of the Service under prior law also allowed existing employees whose moving expenses were reimbursed to exclude reimbursements for the above categories of expense (to the extent of the expenses) whether or not they satisfied the tests prescribed by the law for the deduction of moving expenses by other employees.

Prior law did not specifically deal with other reimbursed moving expenses; [1] however, the courts generally held that reimbursements for moving expenses, other than those which were deductible, had to be included in gross income.

General reasons for change.—The mobility of labor is an important and necessary part of the nation's economy, since it reduces unemployment and increases productive capacity. It has been estimated that approximately one-half million employees are requested by their employers to move to new job locations each year. In addition, self-employed individuals relocate to find more attractive or useful employment. Substantial moving expenses often are incurred by taxpayers in connection with employment-related relocations, and these expenses may be regarded as a cost of earning income.

The Congress believed that more adequate recognition should be given in the tax law to expenses connected with job-related moves. In addition, the Congress concluded that equity required that the moving expense deduction be made available on a comparable basis for self-employed persons who move to a new work location. Finally, it was desired to equalize fully the tax treatment for the moving expenses of new employees and unreimbursed transferred employees with the treatment accorded reimbursed employees.

Explanation of provision.—The Act broadens the categories of deductible moving expenses, provides that reimbursed taxpayers are to be treated in the same manner as unreimbursed taxpayers, increases

1. Prior law provided that no deduction was allowable for moving expenses for any item to the extent that the taxpayer received reimbursement or other expense allowance for such item unless the amount of the reimbursement or other expense allowance was included in the taxpayer's gross income. Thus, if an employee had claimed a deduction for moving expenses and subsequently received a reimbursement for those expenses which he did not include in his gross income, then he had to file an amended return for the taxable year in which the deduction was claimed.

the minimum 20-mile test to 50 [Reduced to 35 by TRA (1976). Ed.] miles, extends the moving expense deduction to the self-employed, and refines the application of the 39-week test which must be satisfied for the deduction to be available.

A moving expense deduction is allowed by the Act for three additional categories of expenses: (1) pre-move house-hunting trips; (2) temporary living expenses at the new job location; and (3) qualified expenses of selling, purchasing or leasing a residence. These additional moving expense deductions are subject to an overall limit of $2,500, with a $1,000 limit on the first two categories. [These figures became $3000 and $1500 under TRA (1976). Ed.]

The pre-move house-hunting trip expenses include the cost of transportation, meals, and lodging for the taxpayer and members of his household paid for the principal purpose of searching for a new residence. The deduction is not available, however, unless the taxpayer (a) has obtained employment at a new principal place of work before the trip begins, and (b) travels from his former residence to the general area of his new principal place of work and returns.

The temporary living expenses at the new job location include costs of meals and lodging for the taxpayer and members of his household at the new job location while waiting to move into permanent quarters. However, only those expenses incurred within 30 consecutive days after obtaining employment are deductible.

Residence sale and purchase expenses which qualify for the deduction are those reasonable expenses incident to the sale or exchange by the taxpayer (or his spouse) of his former residence and also expenses incident to his purchase of the new residence. Reasonable expenses incurred in settling an unexpired lease on an old residence or acquiring a lease on a new residence (except any amounts representing security deposits or payments or prepayments of rent) also may be deducted. The expenses related to the sale of the former residence include a real estate agent's commission, escrow fees, and similar expenses reasonably necessary to effect the sale or exchange of the residence. Expenses for fixing up a residence to assist in its sale are not in this category. The expenses related to purchasing the new residence include attorney's fees, escrow fees, appraisal fees, title costs, loan placement charges (which do not represent interest) and similar expenses reasonably necessary to effect the purchase of the new residence. These expenses do not include any portion of real estate taxes, any payments which represent interest, or any portion of the purchase price of the residence. A residence for this purpose includes a house, an apartment, a cooperative or condominium dwelling unit, or other similar dwelling.

The selling expenses on the former residence which are deductible under this provision do not reduce the amount realized on the sale of the residence for purposes of determining gain. Similarly, the expenses of purchasing a residence which have been deducted may not be added to the cost basis of the new residence for purposes of determining gain. These adjustments were necessary to prevent double tax benefits.

If a husband and wife both commence work at a new principal place of employment within the same general location, the $2,500 [now $3000] limit rule is to be applied as if there were only one commencement of work. Where a married couple files separate returns, the overall limit for these additional moving expenses is $1,250 [now $1500] for each, and the house-hunting trip and temporary living expenses are limited to $500 [now $750] out of the $1,250 [now $1500]. In those cases where the moving expenses (both those deductible under prior law and those for which a deduction is provided by the Act) relate to an individual other than the taxpayer, a deduction is to be allowed only if the individual lives in both the former and the new residence and is a member of the taxpayer's household.

The Act also provides that the reimbursement of expenses of moving from one residence to another are to be included in the taxpayer's gross income (as compensation for services). Under this provision, taxpayers include the reimbursements in gross income but then are permitted to take deductions to the extent permitted under the provisions for the deduction of moving expenses.

Since compensation for services is generally subject to the withholding of income tax, moving expense reimbursements are subject to the general withholding rules. However, the withholding provisions (sec. 3401(a)) do not apply to reimbursements to the extent it is reasonable to believe that a moving expense deduction will be allowable (under sec. 217).

The Act replaces the 20-mile test of prior law with a 50-mile [now 35-mile] test. Under the 50-mile [35-mile] rule, no deduction is allowed unless the taxpayer's new principal place of work is at least 50 miles [35 miles] farther from his former residence than was his former principal place of work. If the taxpayer has no former principal place of work, the deduction is allowed only if the distance between the new principal place of work and his former residence is at least 50 miles [35 miles]. In applying the 50-mile [35-mile] test, the distance between the two points is to be the shortest of the more commonly traveled routes between these two points.

Deductions are allowed under this provision only if the taxpayer during the 12-month period immediately following his arrival at his new principal place of work is a full-time employee for at least 39 weeks. However, in the case of self-employed persons (who did not qualify for any moving expense deduction under prior law) deductions are allowed if during the 24-month period immediately following their arrival at the new principal place of work they perform services on a full-time basis during at least 78 weeks, of which not less than 39 weeks occur during the 12-month period immediately following the arrival at their new place of work.[2] Whether a self-employed taxpayer performs services on a full-time basis depends upon the customary practices of his occupation. (These provisions do not include the semi-retired, part-time students, or other similarly situated self-employed taxpayers who work only a few hours each week.)

If a taxpayer has not satisfied his 39-week or 78-week test before the time for filing his income tax return for the year during which the moving expenses would be deductible, he may (as under prior law) nevertheless claim a deduction for these expenses incurred during the earlier taxable year if it is possible for him at the time of filing his return to still satisfy the test. If this condition is not satisfied at the close of the subsequent year in which the test period of time ends, an amount equal to the expenses which were deducted in the earlier taxable year must be included in the taxpayer's gross income for that subsequent year.

The 39-week test is waived if the employee is unable to satisfy it as a result of death, disability, or involuntary separation (other than for willful misconduct) from the service of, or transfer for the benefit of, an employer after obtaining full-time employment in which the taxpayer could reasonably have been expected to satisfy the requirement. The new 78-week test is waived for self-employed individuals in the case of death or disability.

The term "self-employed individual" is defined as an individual who performs personal services as the owner of an entire interest in an unincorporated trade or business, or as a partner in a partnership carrying on a trade or business. Under the Act, an individual who commences work at a new principal place of work as a self-employed individual is treated as having obtained employment when he has made substantial arrangements to commence such work.

Effective date.—These provisions generally apply with respect to taxable years beginning after December 31, 1969. However, no deduction is allowed for an item to the extent the taxpayer received (or accrued) reimbursement or other expense allowance for such item in a taxable year beginning on or before December 31, 1969, which was not included in his gross income. In addition, a taxpayer may elect to have these amendments not apply with respect to moving expenses paid or incurred before July 1, 1970, in connection with the commencement of work by the taxpayer as an employee at a new principal place of work of which the taxpayer had been notified by his employer on or before December 19, 1969.

---

2. The self-employed rule also applies to a person who has served both as an employee and in a self-employed capacity but who is unable to meet the 39-week employee test. [TRA (1976) added I.R.C. § 217(g), a special moving expense rule for members of the armed forces. See also Rev.Rul. 76–2, 1976–1 C.B. 82, Ed.]

Revenue effect.—The changes in the tax treatment of moving expenses adopted in the Act are expected to provide tax relief amounting to an estimated $110 million a year to individual income taxpayers.

REVENUE RULING 75–85

1975–1 Cum.Bull. 239.

Advice has been requested as to the proper treatment for Federal income tax purposes of moving expenses under the circumstances described below.

A, a citizen of the United States who files his Federal income tax return on a calendar year basis and uses the cash receipts and disbursements method of accounting, left the United States on November 1, 1970, and arrived in foreign country *X* on the same day for the purpose of seeking employment as an employee at a new principal place of work in that country. During 1970 *A*, for this purpose, incurred and paid unreimbursed moving expenses, as defined in section 217(b)(1) of the Internal Revenue Code of 1954, in the amount of $6,000.

A remained abroad during November and December of 1970, arriving in the general location of his new principal place of work and becoming a bona fide resident of country *X* on December 1, 1970. He commenced work as a full-time employee at his new principal place of work on January 4, 1971, and remained so employed during the entire 1971 taxable year. *A* had no earned income from sources without the United States during 1970. His earned income from employment in country *X* during 1971 amounted to $60,000, $20,000 of which is excludable from gross income under section 911(a)(1) of the Code.

Section 217(a) of the Code allows as a deduction moving expenses (as defined in section 217(b)) paid or incurred during the taxable year in connection with the commencement of work by the taxpayer as an employee or as a self-employed individual at a new principal place of work, provided certain requirements are met. One of these requirements, as set forth in Section 217(c)(2)(A), is that the taxpayer, if an employee during the 12-month period immediately following his arrival in the general location of his new principal place of work, must be a full-time employee in such general location during at least 39 weeks.

Section 217(d)(2) of the Code and section 1.217–2(d)(2)(i) of the Income Tax Regulations provide that if a taxpayer has not satisfied the 39-week period of employment requirement before the time prescribed by law (including extensions thereof) for filing the return for the taxable year during which he paid or incurred moving expenses which would otherwise be deductible under section 217, but may still satisfy such requirement, then such expenses may (at the election of the taxpayer) be deducted for such taxable year notwithstanding the minimum period of employment requirement.

Section 1.217–2(d)(2)(ii) of the regulations provides that where the above election is not made and the minimum period of employment requirement is subsequently satisfied, the taxpayer may file an amended return or a claim for refund for the taxable year in which such moving expenses were paid or incurred.

Section 911(a) of the Code allows an individual United States citizen employed abroad, who is either a bona fide resident of a foreign country or countries for an uninterrupted period which includes an entire taxable year (section 911(a)(1)), or present in a foreign country or countries for 510 days during a period of 18 consecutive months (section 911(a)(2)), to exclude from gross income amounts received from sources without the United States which constitute earned income (as defined in section 911(b)) attributable to services performed during such period.

Section 911(a) of the Code also provides that an individual citizen of the United States shall not be allowed, as a deduction from his gross income, any deductions (other than those allowed by section 151, relating to personal exemptions) properly allocable to or chargeable against amounts excluded from gross income thereunder.

Section 911(c)(1) of the Code provides, in part, that the amount of exclusion under section 911(a) for any taxable year shall not exceed an amount which shall be computed on a daily basis at an annual rate of $20,000.

Section 1.911–2(d)(6) of the regulations provides, in part, that in any case in which any amount is excluded from the gross income of an individual on account of residence or presence in a foreign country, there shall be disallowed as a deduction any expenses, losses, or other items otherwise deductible (other than those allowed by section 151 of the Code, relating to personal exemptions) properly allocable to or chargeable against the amount so excluded from gross income. If the earned income excludable under section 911(a)(1) or 911(a)(2) (determined without regard to the applicable dollar limitation) exceeds the earned income excludable under section 911(a)(1) or section 911(a)(2), the amount disallowed as a deduction shall be limited to an amount which bears the same ratio to the total of such items properly allocable to or chargeable against such earned income so excludable (determined without regard to the applicable dollar limitation) as the amount excluded from gross income under section 911(a)(1) or section 911(a)(2) bears to such earned income (determined without regard to the applicable dollar limitation).

Section 1.911–2(e)(1) of the regulations provides, in part, that any income tax return filed before the completion of the period necessary to qualify a citizen for the section 911 exclusion shall be filed without regard to such exclusion, but claim for credit or refund of any overpayment of tax may be filed if the taxpayer subsequently qualifies for the exclusion. Section 1.911-2(e)(1) further provides, that a taxpayer desiring an extension of time (in addition to the automatic extension of time granted by section 1.6081-2) for filing the return until after the completion of the qualifying period shall make application therefor on Form 2350, Application for Extension of Time for Filing U.S. Income Tax Return.

Section 1.6081-2 of the Regulations grants an automatic extension of time for filing returns of income to and including the fifteenth day of the sixth month following the close of the taxable year in the case of a United States citizen residing or traveling outside the United States and Puerto Rico.

For moving expenses to be deductible under section 217 of the Code, they must be incurred by a taxpayer in connection with the *commencement* of work by him at a new principal place of work. When such new principal place of work is in a foreign country, deductible expenses incurred in moving there are properly allocable to or chargeable against section 911 earned income. See Hartung v. Commissioner, 484 F.2d 953 (9th Cir. 1973), rev'g 55 T.C. 1 (1970), nonacquiescence page 3, this Bulletin; and Markus v. Commissioner, 486 F.2d 1314 (D.C.Cir. 1973), rev'g 30 CCH Tax Ct.Mem. 1346 (1971). In such cases, the Internal Revenue Service will view those expenses as allocable to or chargeable against earned income in the taxable year of the move and if the taxpayer's period of qualification under section 911 does not include the entire taxable year in which the move took place, then the moving expenses will also be considered allocable to the following taxable year or portion thereof during which the taxpayer qualifies under section 911.

Since *A* had no earned income from sources without the United States during 1970, he may claim in accordance with the election procedures of section 217(d)(2) of the Code and section 1.217-2(d)(2)(i) of the regulations, the $6,000 moving expense deduction on his 1970 Federal income tax return without regard to the exclusion provision of section 911. See section 1.911-2(e)(1).

Upon subsequently satisfying the section 911(a)(1) bona fide residence test on December 31, 1971, the income tax return filed by *A* for 1970 under the election procedures of section 217(d)(2) of the Code and section 1.217-2(d)(2)(i) of the regulations would have to be amended by eliminating, in accordance with section 1.911-2(d)(6), that portion of the previously deducted moving expenses which is allocable to the $20,000 excludable under section 911(a) from *A*'s gross income in 1971. The portion of *A*'s total moving expense deduction ($6,000) allocable to such excludable income is $2,000, computed pursuant to section 1.911–2(d)(6) as follows:

$$\frac{\text{Amount excludable under section 911}}{\text{Earned income for 1971}} \frac{\text{(a)(1) for 1971} - \$20,000 \times \$6,000}{\$60,000} = \$2,000 *$$

The remaining $4,000 ($6,000 minus $2,000) is allowable as moving expenses for 1970.

If A did not follow the election procedures under section 217 of the Code and section 1.217–2(d)(2)(i) of the regulations, but instead filed an amended return or a claim for refund for taxable year 1970 pursuant to section 1.217–2(d)(2)(ii), subsequent to the time required to file such return (or extension thereof) the same elimination of the $2,000 portion of the moving expense deduction must be made by him either (1) when filing such amended return or refund claim, or (2) in a second amended return or refund claim if he has not met the section 911(a)(1) requirements when filing pursuant to section 1.217–2(d)(2)(ii).

If A had received earned income from sources without the United States during 1970, the possible applicability of the section 911(a) exclusion provision to that year's earned income would exist. Thus, pursuant to section 1.911–2(e)(1) of the regulations, A could have requested an extension of time for filing his Federal income tax return for 1970 until after the completion of the section 911(a)(1) qualifying period on December 31, 1971. By that time, A's satisfaction of the minimum full-time employment period of 39 weeks required by section 217(c)(2)(A) of the Code would also have been determinable, and the proper allocation of the moving expense deduction, allocable to or chargeable against section 911 excludable earned income pursuant to section 1.911–2(d)(6) and thus nondeductible, could have been made on his return for 1970 filed in accordance with such requested extension of time, if granted. See the holding in Situation (1) of Rev.Rul. 75–84,** page 236, this Bulletin, for the computation of the allocation of moving expenses under this situation.

If A had received earned income from sources without the United States during 1970 and did not request an extension of time for filing

---

* This formula might better be depicted

$$\frac{\text{Excluded earned income} \quad \$20,000}{\text{All earned income} \quad \$60,000} \times \frac{\$6000}{\text{Expense}} = \frac{\$2000}{\text{Nondeductible expense}} \quad \text{Ed.}$$

** This ruling also deals with the possible application of I.R.C. § 217 to one who moves to the United States from a foreign country. Ed.

his Federal income tax return for 1970 pursuant to section 1.911–2(e) (1) of the regulations, he must file such return without regard to the exclusion that would apply through his subsequent satisfaction of the requirements of section 911(a)(1) of the Code. Thus, he would have to include such 1970 earned income from sources without the United States in gross income on his 1970 return, and would be allowed to claim the $6,000 moving expense deduction provided by section 217 and the regulations thereunder without regard to the possible future applicability of section 911(a)(1). Upon subsequent satisfaction of the bona fide residence test of section 911(a)(1), he would file an appropriate amended return or refund claim for the amount excludable under section 911(a)(1) and adjusting the moving expense previously deducted on the return in accordance with Situation (1) of Rev.Rul. 75–84.

The principles and procedures set forth herein with respect to an individual citizen of the United States who satisfies the section 911(a)(1) of the Code "bona fide residence" test are equally applicable to an individual citizen of the United States who satisfies the section 911(a)(2) "presence" test.

NOTE

For some time the Tax Court held that moving expenses are not disallowed as allocable to income exempt from tax under § 911, on the ground they are merely personal expenses made deductible by I.R.C. § 217. See Hartung v. Comm'r, 55 T.C. 1 (1970), rev'd. 484 F.2d 953 (9th Cir. 1973); Markus v. Comm'r, 30 TCM 1346 (1971), rev'd. 486 F.2d 1314 (D.C.Cir. 1973), both cited in the above Ruling. However, the Tax Court reversed its position in William Hughes, 65 T.C. 566 (1975), without the compulsion of *Golsen*, as *Hughes* is appealable to the 3rd Circuit which has not passed on the issue. Thus, the applicability of § 911 seems settled in accordance with the above Revenue Ruling.

PROBLEMS

1. Lawyer has been practicing law in Town X and he and his family live in Suburb of Town X ten miles away. He decides to open an office in Town Y. Consequently he moves himself and his family to a home in Town Y.

    (a) How far away from Suburb must Town Y be located in order for Lawyer to be allowed a moving expense deduction?

    (b) How far away from Suburb must Town Y be located in order for Lawyer to be allowed a moving expense deduction if Lawyer has just graduated from law school in Town X and he was not employed?

    (c) Assuming Lawyer is a sole practitioner what time requirements are imposed on him in order for § 217 to apply?

(d) What difference in result in (c), above, if Lawyer joins a firm in Town Y as a partner?

(e) What difference in result in (c), above, if Lawyer goes to work for a firm in Town Y but as an associate rather than a partner?

(f) Assuming the necessary time and distance requirements are met, and that a joint return is filed, what is the amount of Lawyer's § 217 deduction if he incurs the following expenses: $400 in moving his family's belongings; $250 in transporting his family, including meals and lodging en route; $400 on an unsuccessful house hunting trip to Town Y and back prior to acquiring a job; $1200 in motel and meal expenses for a period of 25 days two months after finding his job and moving to Town Y, but prior to locating permanent housing; and $700 to buy out of his lease on their apartment in Suburb; $1200 in closing costs on their newly purchased home; and $400 in "points" (interest) on their mortgage on their new home?

(g) Is there any difference in the result in (f), above, if Lawyer's wife also takes a job in Town Y and meets the necessary time and distance requirements?

(h) If Lawyer's firm reimburses Lawyer for $1000 of his expenses what tax consequences will the reimbursement have?

2. Tardy closed his law practice in Chicago on May 1, 1971, to seek greener pastures in Springfield, Illinois. He began work there on July 1, 1971, and has been there in active practice ever since, meeting the 78 week test of I.R.C. § 217(c)(2)(B) late in 1972. In his return for 1972 he claimed a deduction for his moving expenses in the amount of $4000. On April 10, 1975, the Commissioner issued a deficiency notice disallowing the claimed deduction. Any likely need at that time for speedy action by Tardy? See I.R.C. §§ 6072, 6511(a); and see Della M. Meadows, 66 T.C. 51 (1976).

3. When Employer moved her to Indianapolis, Ms. Keen bought a house for $40,000. Several years later her Employer asked her to move to San Francisco which she did. The best offer Ms. Keen could get for her house was $35,000 so, under her employment contract, Employer bought the house from her for $40,000 (her cost). He later resold it for $35,000. What are the tax consequences to Ms. Keen *and* to Employer. See Seth E. Keener, 59 T.C. 302 (1972).

4. Professor Bionic took a year's leave of absence from the Biology Department at a Louisiana college to teach biology at a college in Vermont. As planned, he left Louisiana in June, 1975, and returned in September, 1976. At a cost of $3000 he moved his modest apartment furnishings to Vermont and back, saving an estimated $1000 additional expense in Vermont. May he deduct the $3000 (and

some other unidentified costs as well) under I.R.C. § 217? See Alvin L. Goldman, 32 TCM 574 (1973).

5. A and B both leave the United States by air on December 27, 1976, planning permanently to reside thereafter in England. Each takes up residence in England on December 27th and goes to work for a new employer on January 2, 1977. Each incurs moving expenses within I.R.C. § 217 in the amount of $5000. In 1977, A has earned income of $20,000, $15,000 of which is exempt from tax under I.R.C. § 911(a). In the same year B has like earned income of $100,000 but of course only $15,000 of it is excluded. How much may each deduct as moving expenses under § 217? Is the lower income taxpayer afforded appropriate treatment? Do your answers have any bearing on the struggle the Tax Court has had with this issue?

F. POLITICAL CONTRIBUTIONS*

I.R.C. § 218 gives each individual a $100 ($200 on a joint return) deduction for political contributions; "newsletter fund" contributions are taken into account along with political contributions and both are defined in § 41(c). The remote location of the governing definition is not surprising; § 41 offers an *alternative* $25 ($50 on a joint return) credit. Only either the credit or the deduction may be claimed, not both. § 218(c). "Credit" may be a relatively new concept to you although you have encountered § 44A. A credit is differentiated from a deduction in Chapter 27, infra, at page 962.

* See Golden, "Federal Taxation and the Political Process," 24 U.Kans.L.R. 221 (1976).

PART FIVE: THE YEAR OF INCLUSION OR DEDUCTION

CHAPTER 19. FUNDAMENTAL TIMING PRINCIPLES

A. INTRODUCTION

Internal Revenue Code: Sections 441(a) through (e); 442; 446; 451(a); 461(a).
Regulations: Section 1.446–1(a) through (c)(1).

Federal income taxes are computed on the basis of a net income figure (taxable income) for a twelve month period (the taxable year).[1] Preceding chapters have developed some of the principles under which it is determined whether and how various items may bear on the computation of taxable income. Assuming an item is significant in this respect, our question now is: When, for what taxable year, is the item taken into account? The taxable year is usually a twelve month period ending on the last day of a month.[2] A taxpayer may use the calendar year which of course ends on December 31st, or he may elect a fiscal taxable year which ends on the last day of any other month.[3] After a taxpayer has chosen an accounting period, approval of the Commissioner is required for a change of his accounting period.[4] Why does Congress require such approval?

Identification of the proper taxable year for reporting an item of income or for claiming a deduction can bear importantly on the taxpayer's tax liability. Obviously, it is not just a question whether he is taxed on an item in 1972 or 1973. Substantive changes in the law, changes in the tax rates, changes in the taxpayer's status, changes in who the taxpayer is, the running of the statute of limitations, and other financial activities of the taxpayer all may bear on

---

1. I.R.C. (26 U.S.C.A.) § 441.

2. Sometimes a shorter period is treated as if it were a full taxable year, as upon the death of a taxpayer or the creation of a new taxable entity such as a corporation or a trust. I.R.C. (26 U.S.C.A.) § 443(a)(2). But, if a short period arises out of a change in a taxpayer's accounting pe-

riod, income must be "annualized." I.R.C. (26 U.S.C.A.) § 443(b).

3. If a taxpayer fails to adopt a proper fiscal period he must use the calendar year. I.R.C. (26 U.S.C.A.) § 441(b)(2) and (g).

4. I.R.C. (26 U.S.C.A.) § 442. Cf. § 443(b).

the amount of liability if the item falls into one year rather than another.

Whether a taxpayer uses the calendar year or a fiscal year, the period for which he reports items of income or deduction is affected by the method of accounting that he has adopted. The principal accounting methods, which are examined in this chapter, are the cash receipts and disbursements method and the accrual method. The cash method of accounting, normally used by individuals, measures tax liability by including an item in income or allowing a deduction at the time that cash or its equivalent is received or paid. The accrual method of accounting is normally used and sometimes must be used by businesses, and it measures tax liability by including an item in income at the time the taxpayer becomes entitled to it and allowing a deduction at the time a deductible obligation becomes fixed and certain, that is, when the income or deduction item "accrues".

Although the cash and accrual methods are the principal accounting methods, they are not the exclusive methods. The code approves some statutory variations in methods of accounting.[5] Approved variations include special rules relating to reporting income from installment sales under I.R.C. § 453[6] and special treatment of certain types of income and expense.[7]

With regard to the detailed implementation of any accounting method, the regulations state:[8]

> It is recognized that no uniform method of accounting can be prescribed for all taxpayers. Each taxpayer shall adopt such forms and systems as here, in his judgment, best suited to his need. However, no method of accounting is acceptable unless, in the opinion of the Commissioner, it clearly reflects income. A method of accounting which reflects the consistent application of generally accepted accounting principles in a particular trade or business in accordance with accepted conditions or practices in that trade or business will ordinarily be regarded as clearly reflecting income, provided all items of gross income and expense are treated consistently from year to year.

The student will find his analysis of tax accounting problems more interesting and less mechanical if he keeps in mind a "matching" concept familiar to accountants. We seek a net income figure for a specified period. But events and transactions affecting the computation do not all fall neatly within the beginning and end of the period like episodes in a three-act play. And so, ideally, we at-

5. The use of unspecified accounting methods is also permitted, subject to approval of the Commissioner. I.R.C. (26 U.S.C.A.) § 446(c).

6. See Chapter 24 at page 874.

7. Statutory references appear at Reg. § 1.446–1(c) (1) (iii).

8. Reg. § 1.446–1(a) (2).

tempt to take account of expenses incurred in producing income reportable for 1977 in the 1977 computations, even though such expenses represent expenditures actually made in 1976 or 1978. The cash method of accounting often fails miserably in this respect, but it is permitted to be used in most situations because of its essential simplicity. Other failures of tax accounting in this respect appear subsequently in this chapter.

As an introductory thought, consider this problem. T, a merchant, purchases 1000 widgets for sale in his business agreeing to pay $10,000 for them but not until 1978. He receives the widgets in 1977 and sells all of them that year for $20,000. In 1978 he pays the supplier the $10,000. Does he have gross income of $20,000 in 1977 (and maybe a $10,000 loss in 1978 if he goes out of business at the end of 1977)? or should the $10,000 cost of the widgets reduce T's gross income for 1977 to $10,000, even though he made payment for the widgets in 1978? Actually, T is not permitted a cash method approach here,[9] and the latter approach is required. But the point here is that an expenditure related to the production of 1977 income is "matched" against income to be reported in that year.

The matching concept is behind some accepted departures from straight cash or accrual method accounting. For example, a business activity may involve the building and sale of major structures, such as hotels or bridges, work on which may extend over several years. Under the approved "completed contract method" of accounting the taxpayer may be permitted to determine and report his net profit on the project upon completion of the entire contract.[10] The "percentage of completion method" may also be used in the case of long-term contracts. Under this method items of income and deduction are taken into account proportionately as work on the contract progresses.[11]

Various hybrid methods of accounting, even combining cash and accrual concepts, may be used.[12] However, a basic statutory requirement is that the method used must clearly reflect income.[13] Materials that follow in this chapter reflect the kinds of controversies that are engendered by this requirement.

A taxpayer is not limited to the use of a single accounting method in computing his tax liability. He may use one accounting method for his trade or business and another for computing taxable income on items not connected with his trade or business,[14] and he may use different accounting methods for separate trades or businesses in which he is involved.[15]

9. See note on Inventories, infra, this Chapter at page 580.

10. Reg. § 1.451–3(b) (2).

11. Reg. § 1.451–3(b) (1).

12. See I.R.C. (26 U.S.C.A.) § 446(c) (4).

13. I.R.C. (26 U.S.C.A.) § 446(b).

14. Reg. § 1.446–1(c)(1)(iv)(b).

15. Reg. § 1.446–1(d).

Although a taxpayer may initially adopt any accounting method that clearly reflects income, nevertheless the consent of the Commissioner must be obtained in order to change accounting methods.[16] Approval is required so as to avoid distortion of one's income by means of an accounting method change, and one must generally show a business purpose for making the change. The definition of what constitutes a change in accounting method and the procedures to be followed in seeking approval are stated in the Regulations.[17]

As a general principle each taxable year stands alone and each year's tax liability is computed separately, a concept spoken of as preserving the integrity of the taxable year.[18] Thus, if one reported an item of income as accrued in 1977, and in 1978 it became apparent that collection would never be made, taxable income for 1977 is not to be adjusted (the year is not reopened) and, if uncollectibility is to affect tax liability, it will affect liability for 1978, rather than 1977. Some exceptions to this strict approach to the taxable year concept are examined in Chapter 20, along with the related statutory provisions for income averaging and for the carryover or carryback to another year of some items of deduction.

In general, substantive provisions of the Code allowing deductions take account of both the cash and accrual method of accounting. See I.R.C. (26 U.S.C.A.) § 162(a) allowing a deduction for business expenses " *   *   *   paid or incurred during the taxable year *   *   *;" § 163(a) authorizing a deduction for   *   *   *   "interest paid or accrued within the taxable year   *   *   *;"   § 164(a) authorizing a deduction for certain taxes " *   *   *   paid or accrued *   *   *;" and similar language appears in § 212. There are other examples. In contrast, other provisions of the statute force the cash method, even though the taxpayer may have properly adopted the accrual method of accounting. See I.R.C. (26 U.S.C.A.) § 170(a) concerning the charitable deduction, requiring *payment*, and § 213(a) authorizing the deduction for medical expenses " *   *   *   paid during the taxable year   *   *   *." Alimony inclusion and deduction is also put on a cash basis. §§ 71(a), 215. There are other examples. But generally in most other cases, the Code accepts the taxpayer's cash or accrual method of accounting.

---

16. I.R.C. (26 U.S.C.A.) § 446(e).

17. Regs. § 1.446–1(e). See also Rev. Proc. 72–52, 1972–2 C.B. 833.

18. See Burnet v. Sanford & Brooks Co., 282 U.S. 359, 51 S.Ct. 150 (1931).

B. THE CASH RECEIPTS AND DISBURSEMENTS METHOD*

1.   RECEIPTS

Internal Revenue Code: Sections 446; 451(a).
Regulations: Sections 1.446–1(c)(1)(i); 1.451–1(a), –2.**

LAVERY v. COMMISSIONER ***

United States Court of Appeals, Seventh Circuit, 1946.
158 F.2d 859.

EVANS, CIRCUIT JUDGE. This appeal involves a dispute over the year a sum received by Lavery, the taxpayer, appellant herein, was taxable under the federal income tax law.

Mr. Lavery, the taxpayer, had been managing editor of the American Bar Association Journal. He was paid in full for his 1941 services. He terminated his services and the Board of Editors tendered him an honorarium, a check for $2,666.67, which he accepted as "payment in full satisfaction of all his claims against the said Association and the members of the said Board of Editors on account of his said employment as such Managing Editor and the termination of that position." The check represented four months' pay at the rate of $8,000 per annum.

The check was received December 30, 1941, and cashed January 2, 1942. December 30th fell on Tuesday.

Taxpayer reported on the cash receipts and disbursements basis.

[After quoting relevant provisions of the 1939 Code and corresponding regulations, not materially different from their current counterparts, the opinion continued.]

* * *

Taxpayer relies upon the case of Avery v. Commissioner, 292 U.S. 210, 54 S.Ct. 674, 78 L.Ed. 1216. In the later case of Putnam v. Commissioner, 324 U.S. 393, 65 S.Ct. 811, 814, 89 L.Ed. 1023, 158 A.L.R. 1426, the Court referred to its holding in the Avery case as follows: "Avery v. Commissioner * * * holds that dividends of a living taxpayer on the cash basis would not become his income on mere declaration but only when 'received,' that is, unqualifiedly made subject to the stockholder's demand *as by check* * * *." (Italics ours.)

---

* See Schapiro, "Prepayments and Distortion of Income Under Cash Basis Tax Accounting," 30 Tax L.R. 117 (1975).

** The doctrine of constructive receipt presented in this provision of the Regulations and involved in the Ross case, infra this Chapter, is broadly discussed in Finnegan, "Constructive Receipt of Income," 22 N.Y.U.Inst. on Fed.Tax. 367 (1964).

*** See generally Note, "Checks and Notes as Income When Received by a Cash Basis Taxpayer," 73 Harv.L.Rev. 1199 (1960). Ed.

The Court inferentially holds that receipt of a check is equivalent to the receipt of cash. The Avery case was decided on the fact hypothesis that the check was not received until January, following its execution in December.

There might perhaps be a distinction between the date of receipt of cash and the date of the receipt of a check which arrived the last day of the year and too late to be cashed by the payee on that day. In the instant case the taxpayer could have cashed the check on the day it was received by him, or at least on the next day. There was no doubt about the validity of the check or the solvency of the drawer.

Our conclusion is that the check was the equivalent of cash in this case, and this being so, we must hold it was received in 1941. Magill, Taxable Income, Rev.Ed., 1945, p. 179; Hedrick v. Commissioner, 2 Cir., 154 F.2d 90, 91.

Taxpayer also argues that the check was in payment of services by him rendered in 1942. While the fact assertion on which this argument is predicated is disputed, we dispose of this appeal on the theory that the date of the payment, not the date of the rendition of the services, is the determinative fact.

The decision of the Tax Court is affirmed.

CHARLES F. KAHLER

Tax Court of the United States, 1952.
18 T.C. 31.

[The Findings of Fact have been omitted. Ed.]

Opinion

RICE, JUDGE: The sole issue is when did the petitioner realize the income represented by the commission check delivered December 31, 1946. Was it in 1946, as determined by respondent, or in 1947, as claimed by petitioner? This, in turn, is based on the question whether the receipt of a check by a cash basis taxpayer after banking hours on the last day of the taxable period constitutes a realization of income.

Applicable provisions of the statute are set forth in the margin.[1]

In his brief, petitioner argues that "the mere receipt of a check does not give rise to income within the taxable year of receipt unless the check is received in sufficient time before the end of the taxable year so the check may be converted into cash within the taxable year." In support of such result, petitioner relies upon L. M. Fischer, 14 T.C. 792 (1950); Urban A. Lavery, 5 T.C. 1283 (1945), affd. (C.A.7, 1946) 158 F.2d 859; and Harvey H. Ostenberg, 17 B.T.A. 738 (1929).

1. [The quoted sections of the 1939 Code, not materially different from their current counterparts, are omitted. Ed.]

In the *Fischer* case, we held that a check delivered to the taxpayer on December 31, 1942, which was not deposited until 1943, was not income in 1942 but in 1943, since the check was subject to a substantial restriction. At the time of delivery of such check, there was an oral agreement made between the drawer and the taxpayer that the latter would hold the check for a few days before he cashed it since the drawer was short of money in the bank. Such a situation is completely distinguishable from that in the instant case.

The *Lavery* and *Ostenberg* cases both decided that checks delivered to the taxpayers were income in the year of delivery. In the *Lavery* case delivery was on December 30, and in the *Ostenberg* case delivery was on December 31. Petitioner relies on the dicta appearing in these cases to the effect that the result might have been different had the petitioner in either case been able to show that he could not have cashed the check in the year drawn. We fail to see where there should be any difference in result just because it might be impossible to cash a check in the year in which drawn, where delivery actually took place in such year. Respondent's regulations provide that all items of gross income shall be included in the taxable year in which received by the taxpayer, and that where services are paid for other than by money, the amount to be included as income is the fair market value of the thing taken in payment.[2]

Analogous cases to the instant case are those which were concerned with the proper year in which deductions might be taken where a check was drawn and delivered in one year and cashed in a subsequent year. Under the negotiable instruments law, payment by check is a conditional payment subject to the condition that it will be honored upon presentation; and once such presentation is made and the check is honored, the date of payment relates back to the time of delivery. See Estelle Broussard, 16 T.C. 23 (1951); Estate of Modie J. Spiegel, 12 T.C. 524 (1949); and cases cited therein. In the *Spiegel* case we said, at page 529:

It would seem to us unfortunate for the Tax Court to fail to recognize what has so frequently been suggested, that as a practical matter, in everyday personal and commercial usage, the transfer of funds by check is an accepted procedure. The parties almost without exception think and deal in terms of payment except in the unusual circumstance, not involved here, that the check is dishonored upon presentation, or that it was delivered in the first place subject to some condition or infirmity which intervenes between delivery and presentation.

2. Treasury Regulations 111, sec. 29.22 (a)-3, and sec. 29.41-2. [See Reg. §§ 1.61-2(d) and 1.446-1(a) and (c). Ed.]

Under such circumstances, we feel that it is immaterial that delivery of a check is made too late in the taxable year for the check to be cashed in that year. The petitioner realized income upon receipt of the commission check on December 31, 1946.

Reviewed by the Court.

Decision will be entered for the respondent.

MURDOCK, J., concurring: I agree with the result reached that the receipt of a check is regarded as payment and income unless it is subject to some restriction but feel that the petitioner's case is weaker in some respects than the majority opinion might indicate. A finding is made that the check in question was received by the petitioner "sometime after 5 p. m. on December 31, 1946." There is also evidence that he could not have obtained cash for the check at the drawee bank but he could have deposited the check in that bank, later on December 31, 1946. There was another bank in the town and the evidence does not show whether or not he could have cashed the check in that bank after regular banking hours. Furthermore he might have made some other use of the check during 1946. For example, he might have cashed it at some place other than at a bank or he might have used it to discharge some obligation, within the year 1946.

HARRON, J., agrees with this concurring opinion.

JAY A. WILLIAMS

Tax Court of the United States, 1957.
28 T.C. 1000(A).

WITHEY, JUDGE: The respondent determined a deficiency in petitioners' income tax for 1951 and additions to tax for that year under sections 291(a) and 294(d) (1) (A) and (d) (2) of the Internal Revenue Code of 1939 as follows:

		Additions to tax		
	Deficiency	Sec. 291(a)	Sec. 294(d) (1) (A)	Sec. 294(d) (2)
$1,443.10		$360.78	$169.44	$101.67

The sole issue presented for our decision is the correctness of the respondent's action in determining that a promissory note received by petitioner Jay A. Williams during 1951 constituted income taxable to petitioners in that year.

Findings of Fact

Some of the facts have been stipulated and are found accordingly.

Petitioners, husband and wife, residing in Portland, Oregon, filed their joint income tax return for 1951 with the director of internal revenue for the district of Oregon. Inasmuch as the activities of Jay

A. Williams are those with which we are here primarily concerned, "petitioner" or "Williams" as hereinafter used has reference to him.

The petitioner kept his accounts and prepared his returns on a cash basis.

During 1951, and prior thereto, petitioner was engaged in the business of locating marketable parcels of timberland for prospective purchasers of timber. Williams compiled information concerning certain stands of timber for Lester McConkey and J. M. Housley. Petitioner received nothing from McConkey and Housley at the time he turned over to them the desired information. Subsequently, on May 5, 1951, J. M. Housley issued to Williams an unsecured, non-interest-bearing promissory note in the amount of $7,166.60, payable 240 days thereafter.

At the time of issuance of the foregoing note, the maker was unable to pay anything on it because of his lack of funds. Further, it was understood by petitioner that Housley would be unable to make any payments on the note until he had first acquired and sold at least part of the available timber property which Williams had located.

Upon receipt of the note in 1951, petitioner attempted on 10 or 15 occasions to sell it to various banks or finance companies but was unable to realize any money thereon until 1954 when he collected proceeds from J. M. Housley to the extent of $6,666.66 in discharge of the debt represented by the note.

Petitioners did not report on their income tax return for 1951 any income resulting from the receipt of the note during that year, but reported income in the amount of $6,666.66 received in 1954 upon the discharge of the indebtedness.

The note received by petitioner on May 5, 1951, was not intended as payment of the indebtedness of J. M. Housley and had no fair market value at that time or at any time during 1951.

Opinion

The petitioners have taken the position that the receipt of the promissory note by Williams in 1951 was not intended as payment of the indebtedness of J. M. Housley and therefore did not result in the receipt of income during that year. In addition, the petitioners contend that if the foregoing note was received in payment of the debt, it nevertheless had no ascertainable fair market value and consequently cannot be considered the equivalent of cash.

The respondent has determined that the receipt by Williams of the note in question on May 5, 1951, constituted taxable income in that year under section 22(a) of the 1939 Code.

It is unquestioned here that promissory notes or other evidences of indebtedness received as payment for services constitute income, within the meaning of section 22(a) of the 1939 Code, to the extent of their fair market value. Regs. 118, sec. 39.22 (a)–4. Cf. Schlemmer v. United States, 94 F.2d 77; Robert J. Dial, 24 T.C. 117; San Jacinto Life Insurance Co., 34 B.T.A. 186; Great Southern Life Insurance Co., 33 B.T.A. 512, affd. 89 F.2d 54, certiorari denied 302 U.S. 698.

Petitioners contend that the note in question was not received by Williams as payment, but merely as an evidence of indebtedness. Petitioner's testimony to the effect that the note was not payable until the maker, J. M. Housley, realized income from the sale of the timber property located by Williams supports his contention. The petitioner stated categorically that the note in question was not given to him in payment of the indebtedness of the maker.

The respondent points out that petitioners rely solely on the self-serving declarations of Williams and insists that without supporting evidence the foregoing testimony is not worthy of belief. However, it is not within our province arbitrarily to disregard the unimpeached and uncontradicted testimony of a taxpayer. A. & A. Tool & Supply Co. v. Commissioner, 182 F.2d 300; Capitol-Barg Dry Cleaning Co. v. Commissioner, 131 F.2d 712; Wright-Bernet v. Commissioner, 172 F.2d 343. Inasmuch as no conflicting evidence is apparent from the record herein, petitioners have established to our satisfaction that the note received by Williams on May 5, 1951, was not received in payment of the outstanding debt due him for the performance of his services. A note received only as security, or as an evidence of indebtedness, and not as payment, may not be regarded as income at the time of receipt. Schlemmer v. United States, supra; Robert J. Dial, supra. A simple change in the form of indebtedness from an account payable to a note payable is insufficient to cause the realization of income by the creditor.

In the event that petitioners had failed to show that the promissory note here in issue was not intended as payment, we still would be unable to sustain the respondent's determination. The note bore no interest and was unsecured. It was not payable until 1952. The maker of the note, J. M. Housley, was without funds at the time of its execution. Petitioner testified that he was in need of immediate cash in 1951 and upon receipt of the note on May 5 of that year he attempted on 10 or 15 occasions to sell it to various banks or finance companies, but was unable to realize any money thereon. Accordingly, petitioners have demonstrated that the note in question had no fair market value in 1951 and consequently it cannot be held to be the equivalent of cash during the year of receipt. Cf. J. F. Weinmann, 5 B.T.A. 885. The receipt by petitioner of the promissory note in 1951 does not constitute taxable income realized during that year.

Decision will be entered under Rule 50.

PAUL V. HORNUNG

Tax Court of the United States, 1967.
47 T.C. 428(A).

HOYT, JUDGE: Respondent determined an income tax deficiency against petitioner in the amount of $3,163.76 for the taxable year 1962. Petitioner having conceded an issue relating to a travel expense deduction, the questions remaining for decision are:

(1) Whether the value of a 1962 Corvette automobile which was won by petitioner for his performance in a professional football game should be included in his gross income for the taxable year 1962.

* * *

Findings of Fact

The stipulated facts are found accordingly and adopted as our findings.

Petitioner is a cash basis taxpayer residing in Louisville, Ky. For the taxable year 1962, petitioner filed his Federal individual income tax return (Form 1040) with the district director of internal revenue, Louisville, Ky. Petitioner is a well-known professional football player who was employed by the Green Bay Packers in 1962. Prior to becoming a professional, petitioner attended the University of Notre Dame and was an All-American quarterback on the university football team.

Issue 1. *The Corvette*

Sport Magazine is a publication of the McFadden-Bartell Corp., with business offices in New York City. Each year Sport Magazine (hereinafter sometimes referred to as Sport or the magazine) awards a new Corvette automobile to the player selected by its editors (primarily by its editor in chief) as the outstanding player in the National Football League championship game. This award was won by John Unitas of the Baltimore Colts in 1958 and 1959 and by Norm Van Brocklin of the Philadelphia Eagles in 1960. A similar annual award is made to outstanding professional athletes in baseball, hockey, and basketball. The existence of the award is announced several days prior to the sporting event in question, and the selection and announcement of the winner is made immediately following the athletic contest. The Corvette automobiles are generally presented to the recipients at a luncheon or dinner several days subsequent to the sporting event and a photograph of the athlete receiving the car is published in the magazine, together with an article relating to his performance during the particular athletic event. The Corvette awards are intended to promote the sale of Sport Magazine and their cost is deducted by the publisher for Federal income tax purposes as promotion and advertising expense.

The Corvette which is to be awarded to the most valuable player in the National Football League championship game is generally purchased by the magazine several months prior to the date the game is played, and it is held by a New York area Chevrolet dealer until delivered to the recipient of the award. In some years when the game is played in New York the magazine has had the car on display at the stadium on the day of the game.

On December 31, 1961, petitioner played in the National Football League championship game between the Green Bay Packers and the New York Giants. The game was played in Green Bay, Wis. Petitioner scored a total of 19 points during this game and thereby established a new league record. At the end of this game petitioner was selected by the editors of Sport as the most valuable player and winner of the Corvette, and press releases were issued announcing the award. At approximately 4:30 on the afternoon of December 31, 1961, following the game, the editor in chief of Sport informed petitioner that he had been selected as the most valuable player of the game. The editor in chief did not have the key or the title to the Corvette with him in Green Bay and petitioner did not request or demand immediate possession of the car at that time but he accepted the award.

The Corvette which was to be awarded in connection with this 1961 championship game had been purchased by Sport in September of 1961. However, since the game was played in Green Bay, Wis., the car was not on display at the stadium on the day of the game, but was in New York in the hands of a Chevrolet dealership. As far as Sport was concerned the car was "available" to petitioner on December 31, 1961, as soon as the award was announced. However, December 31, 1961, was a Sunday and the New York dealership at which the car was located was closed. Although the National Football League championship game is always played on a Sunday, Sport is prepared to make prior arrangements to have the car available in New York for the recipient of the award on that Sunday afternoon if the circumstances appear to warrant such arrangements—particularly if the game is played in New York. Such arrangements were not made in 1961 because the game was played in Green Bay, and, in the words of Sport's editor in chief, "it seemed a hundred-to-one that * * * [the recipient of the award] would want to come in [to New York] on New Year's Eve to take possession" of the prize.

On December 31, 1961, when petitioner was informed that he had won the Corvette, he was also informed that a luncheon was to be held for him in New York City on the following Wednesday by the publisher of Sport, at which luncheon his award would be presented. At that time petitioner consented to attend the luncheon in order to receive the Corvette. There was no discussion that he would obtain the car prior to the presentation ceremony previously announced. The lunch was held as scheduled on Wednesday, January 3, 1962, in a New York restaurant. Petitioner attended and was photographed during the course of the presentation of the automobile to him. A photograph of petitioner sitting in the car outside of the restaurant was published in the April 1962 issue of Sport, together with an article regarding his achievements in the championship game and the Corvette prize award. Petitioner was not required to attend the lunch or to pose for photographs or perform any other service for Sport as a condition or as consideration for his receipt of the car.

The fair market value of the Corvette automobile received by petitioner was $3,331.04. Petitioner reported the sale of the Corvette in his 1962 Federal income tax return in Schedule D attached thereto as a * * * gain as follows:

Kind of property	Date acquired	Date sold	Gross sales price	Depreciation allowed	Cost	Gain
1962 Corvette gift— Sport Magazine___	1962	1962	3,331.04	0.00	0.00	None

* * *

Petitioner did not include the fair market value of this car in his gross income for 1962, or for any other year. McFadden-Bartell Corporation deducted its cost as a promotion and advertising expense.

* * *

Opinion
Issue 1. The Corvette

Petitioner alleged in his petition that the Corvette was received by him as a gift in 1962. However, at trial and on brief, he argues that the car was constructively received in 1961, prior to the taxable year for which the deficiency is being assessed. If this contention is upheld, the question of whether the car constituted a reportable item of gross income need not be considered. This argument is based upon the assertion that the announcement and acceptance of the award occurred at approximately 4:30 on the afternoon of December 31, 1961, following the game.

It is undisputed that petitioner was selected as the most valuable player of the National Football League championship game in Green Bay on December 31, 1961. It is also undisputed that petitioner actually received the car on January 3, 1962, in New York. Petitioner relies upon the statement at the trial by the editor in chief of Sport that as far as Sport was concerned the car was "available" to petitioner on December 31, 1961, as soon as the award was announced. It is therefore contended that the petitioner should be deemed to have received the value of the award in 1961 under the doctrine of constructive receipt.

The amount of any item of gross income is included in gross income for the taxable year in which received by the taxpayer unless such amount is properly accounted for as of a different period. Sec. 451

(a).[3] It is further provided in section 446(c) that the cash receipts method, which the petitioner utilized, is a permissible method of computing taxable income. The doctrine of constructive receipt is developed by regulations under section 446(c) which provides as follows: [4]

> Generally, under the cash receipts and disbursements method * * * all items which constitute gross income (whether in the form of cash, property, or services) are to be included for the taxable year in which actually or constructively received. * * *

The regulations under section 451 elaborate on the meaning of constructive receipt.[5]

> Income although not actually reduced to a taxpayer's possession is constructively received by him in the taxable year during which it is credited to his account, set apart for him, or otherwise made available so that he may draw upon it at any time, or so that he could have drawn upon it during the taxable year if notice of intention to withdraw had been given. However, income is not constructively received if the taxpayer's control of its receipt is subject to substantial limitations or restrictions. * * *

The probable purpose for development of the doctrine of constructive receipt was stated as follows in Ross v. Commissioner, 169 F.2d 483, 491 (C.A.1, 1948):

> The doctrine of constructive receipt was, no doubt, conceived by the Treasury in order to prevent a taxpayer from choosing the year in which to return income merely by choosing the year in which to reduce it to possession. Thereby the Treasury may subject income to taxation when the only thing preventing its reduction to possession is the volition of the taxpayer. * * *

However, it was held in the *Ross* case, at page 496, that the doctrine of constructive receipt could be asserted by a taxpayer as a defense to a deficiency assessment even though the item in controversy had not been reported for the taxable year of the alleged constructive receipt:

> if these items were constructively received when earned they cannot be treated as income in any later year, * * * and, in the absence of misstatement of fact, intentional or otherwise, the petitioner cannot be estopped from asserting that the items were taxable only in the years in which constructively received.

---

3. All section references are to the Internal Revenue Code of 1954 unless otherwise indicated.

4. Sec. 1.446–1(c)(1)(i), Income Tax Regs.

5. Sec. 1.451–2(a), Income Tax Regs.

The basis of constructive receipt is essentially unfettered control by the recipient over the date of actual receipt. Petitioner has failed to convince us that he possessed such control on December 31, 1961, over the receipt of the Corvette. The evidence establishes that the Corvette which was presented to petitioner on January 3, 1962, was in the possession of a Chevrolet dealer in New York City on December 31, 1961. At the time the award was announced in Green Bay, the editor in chief of Sport had neither the title nor keys to the car, and nothing was given or presented to petitioner to evidence his ownership or right to possession of the car at that time.

Moreover, since December 31, 1961, was a Sunday, it is doubtful whether the car could have been transferred to petitioner before Monday even with the cooperation of the editor in chief of Sport. The New York dealership at which the car was located was closed. The car had not been set aside for petitioner's use and delivery was not dependent solely upon the volition of petitioner. The doctrine of constructive receipt is therefore inapplicable, and we hold that petitioner received the Corvette for income tax purposes in 1962 as he originally alleged in his petition and as he reported in his 1962 income tax return.

* * *

[The Court held that the car was not received as a gift but was a prize or award specifically required to be included in ordinary income at its fair market value in 1962 under I.R.C. § 74; See Wills v. Comm'r, supra page 128. The subsequent sale of the car was a separate transaction. Ed.]

---

2. DISBURSEMENTS *

Internal Revenue Code: Section 461(a) and (g).
Regulations: Section 1.461–1(a)(1).

REVENUE RULING 54–465

1954–2 Cum.Bull. 93.

A charitable contribution in the form of a check is deductible, in the manner and to the extent provided by section 23(o) and (q) of the Internal Revenue Code of 1939 [See I.R.C. (1954) (26 U.S.C.A.) § 170(a).], in the taxable year in which the check is delivered provided the check is honored and paid and there are no restrictions as to time and manner of payment thereof. See Estate of Modie J. Spiegel v. Commissioner, 12 T.C. 524, acquiescence, C.B. 1949–2, 3.

* See Irwin, "Prepayments by a Cash
Basis Taxpayer," 15 U.S.C. Tax Inst.
547 (1963).

CREDIT CARD PAYMENTS

Over the years we have moved from a cash-paying society to a check-paying society to a credit card society. In the first transition the tax law kept pace by treating payment by check essentially the same as payment in cash.[1] From the standpoint of a cash method taxpayer, he has paid a deductible expense when he hands over a check. In fact payment is effected when he places a check in the mail;[2] but of couse this is qualified by the requirement that the check is honored and paid in due course when presented to the drawee bank.[3] If a purist can detect a departure from strict cash method doctrine here (recall for example that payment on a check may be stopped and its issuance does not constitute an irrevocable assignment of the drawer's funds), nevertheless the tax result comports with the way we all view things. We have "paid" the monthly bills when we mail out the checks. And it would be untidy to have to determine when a check was presented for payment.

Have we "paid" a bill when we sign a credit card chit? A doctrinal obstacle to an affirmative answer might seem to be that the card holder parts with no cash at that time. Nevertheless, he has "paid" the obligation to the principal creditor whose recourse thereafter is against the credit card company. At the same time he has incurred an obligation to the credit card company in accordance with his agreement with it. Should it not be viewed as if he had borrowed money and used it to pay his obligation, which would of course support an instant deduction? For purposes of determining when federal taxes are "paid," the Treasury has given qualified acceptance to this view.[4] On the other hand, the Treasury has taken the position in Rev.Rul. 71–216[5] that for purposes of the charitable deduction under I.R.C. (26 U.S.C.A.) § 170, "payment" does not occur when a contribution is made with the use of a credit card until the contributor pays the credit card company, even if the charity is in receipt of the funds at an earlier time.

The use of a credit card is not analogous to borrowing money at the bank and receiving less than the amount of the loan, the difference representing interest. Such interest is not considered paid at that time. But the use of a credit card presents a three party deal, and the obligation that is discharged is an obligation to a third party, not to the one who advances the money.

1. Witt Estate v. Fahs, 160 F.Supp. 521 (S.D.Fla.1956).

2. Id. and cf. Reg. § 1.170–1(b).

3. Cf. Reg. § 301.6311–1(a) (1). See Brooks Griffin, 49 T.C. 253 (1967).

4. I.R.S. News Release No. 1005 (Jan. 16, 1970) indicated that " * * * if a check or other document issued by a bank or credit card company used by a taxpayer in payment of taxes is acceptable by the Federal Reserve District concerned as a negotiable instrument for banking purposes, it will be accepted [as payment] by the I.R.S."

5. 1971–1 C.B. 96.

Of course in this respect it is necessary to look at the exact nature of the credit arrangement. If a department store issues a credit card for use in purchases only at the store, no payment occurs until the store's bill is paid. This is a two-party deal. Whether a charge on a credit card issued by an oil company falls into the two-party or three-party area depends upon whether the obligation runs to the company or to an independent dealer, the gas station from which merchandise was purchased. Indeed, it is not safe to try to generalize here, as credit card arrangements are largely a matter of contract, which suggests possible wide variations in the relationships of the parties, and the legal consequences of the use of credit cards are not fully settled.[6]

If the use of a credit card did not produce an instant deduction, what would be the alternatives? It might be said that payment occurs only when the credit card company pays the taxpayer's bill. But this is so impractical a view as to require rejection. The taxpayer will seldom know when his chits are presented for payment. It is also irrelevant, if we view the matter as involving a three-party deal in which the taxpayer's obligation to a supplier is discharged when he signs the chit. The credit card company does not pay as his agent.

Nor would it be proper to say that the taxpayer has paid only when he pays the credit card company's bill. He is certainly not then paying the supplier. He is, instead, repaying a loan made by the credit card company, which is not the obligation for which a deduction may be claimed. Moreover, if we accept the settled treatment of checks as payment, we seem to have an *a fortiori* argument here. After the check-maker hands over his check he can still stop payment on it; it is not so clear that the credit card user is in a position to recall his "payment" to a supplier.[7]

Finally, the instant deduction approach to credit card transactions again comports with the way our society views these transactions. We think of the *air line* as paid when they have accepted the credit card, even though we know we will be hearing from the *credit card company* at the end of the month. And so it seems the tax law *should* follow our move to a credit card society. Good theory and, even more important, practical considerations require it.

6. The non-tax aspects of credit card transactions are thoughtfully examined in Nordstrom, Law of Sales, pp. 353–360 (West Hornbook Series 1970); see also South, "Credit Cards: a Primer," 23 Business Lawyer 327 (1968).

7. See Brandel and Leonard, "Bank Charge Cards: New Cash or New Credit," 69 Mich.L.Rev. 1033 (1971).

VANDER POEL, FRANCIS & COMPANY, INC.

Tax Court of the United States, 1947.
8 T.C. 407.

Opinion

* * *

[This case involved the question whether a doctrine of "constructive payment" parallels the established doctrine of "constructive receipt." Some excerpts from the opinion will be informative. Ed.]

* * *

There is but one issue involved in this proceeding, and that is whether petitioner, a corporation which kept its books and made its income tax returns on the cash basis, is entitled to deduct the full amount of the salaries regularly and duly voted to its two officers, Vander Poel and Francis, and unconditionally credited to their respective accounts, notwithstanding it did not actually pay the full amount of these salaries in cash or other property during 1942.

* * *

They properly returned these salaries for taxation on their 1942 returns under the doctrine of "constructive receipt." * * * [T]he weight of authority as we interpret the authorities is against the doctrine that "constructive payment" is a necessary corollary of "constructive receipt." Mertens, in his Law of Federal Income Taxation, vol. 2, sec. 10.18, says:

> Constructive Payments as Deductions. Under the doctrine of constructive receipt a taxpayer on the cash basis is taxed upon income which he has not as yet actually received. Logically it would seem that where the payee is held to have constructively received an item as income, the payor should be entitled to deduct the same item as constructively paid, but the statute rather than logic is the controlling force in tax cases and so it is not surprising to find such reasoning often rejected. The difference is that the statute is presumed to reach and tax all income, and the doctrine of constructive receipt is an aid to that end. It must be remembered that the doctrine of constructive receipt is designed to effect a realistic concept of realization of income and to prevent abuses. Deductions, on the other hand, are a matter of legislative grace, and the terms of the statute permitting the particular deduction must be fully met without the aid of assumptions. "What may be income to the one may not be a deductible payment by the other." A review of the cases indicates that the courts will seldom support a doctrine of constructive payment in the sense in which it is used in this chapter, i. e., to determine when an item has been paid rather than who has paid it.

* * * If in any of our decisions, memorandum opinions or otherwise, we have said anything to the contrary of the above holdings, we think it is against the weight of authority and should not be followed. Therefore, following Martinus & Sons v. Commissioner [1] and other cases above cited, we sustain the Commissioner. See also our recent decision in Claude Patterson Noble,[2] in which among other things, we said:

> * * * No payment was made in 1942 by petitioner to her husband for his services; but the payment for services rendered in that year was made in 1943. Likewise the payment for 1943 services was not made until February 1944. It is argued that the custom was that petitioner's husband prepare all checks for her signature and that had he seen fit to do so, he could have received payment of the full amount of the salary at the close of each year for which the service was rendered. Thus it is said to follow that petitioner constructively paid and her husband constructively received payment of the salary for 1942 and 1943 at the close of each of those years. The fact remains, however, these checks were not prepared, signed, or delivered until after the close of those respective years. Accordingly there was no such payment or receipt in either case until after the close of the year. Massachusetts Mutual Insurance Co. v. United States, 288 U. S. 269; Martinus & Sons v. Commissioner, 116 F.2d 732; Cox Motor Sales Co., 42 B.T.A. 192; Sanford Corporation v. Commissioner, 106 F.2d 882.

* * *

COMMISSIONER v. BOYLSTON MARKET ASS'N

United States Court of Appeals, First Circuit, 1942.
131 F.2d 966.

MAHONEY, CIRCUIT JUDGE. The Board of Tax Appeals reversed a determination by the Commissioner of Internal Revenue of deficiencies in the Boylston Market Association's income tax of $835.34 for the year 1936, and $431.84 for the year 1938, and the Commissioner has appealed.

The taxpayer in the course of its business, which is the management of real estate owned by it, purchased from time to time fire and other insurance policies covering periods of three or more years. It keeps its books and makes its returns on a cash receipts and disbursements basis. The taxpayer has since 1915 deducted each year as insurance expenses the amount of insurance premiums applicable to carrying insurance for that year regardless of the year in which the premium was actually paid. This method was required by the Treasury

1. 116 F.2d 732, affirming B.T.A. memorandum opinion.   2. 7 T.C. 960.

Department prior to 1938 by G.C.M. 13148, XIII–1 Cum.Bull. 67 (1934). Prior to January 1, 1936, the taxpayer had prepaid insurance premiums in the amount of $6,690.75 and during that year it paid premiums in an amount of $1082.77. The amount of insurance premiums prorated by the taxpayer in 1936 was $4421.76. Prior to January 1, 1938, it had prepaid insurance premiums in the amount of $6148.42 and during that year paid premiums in the amount of $890.-47. The taxpayer took a deduction of $3284.25, which was the amount prorated for the year 1938. The Commissioner in his notice of deficiency for the year 1936 allowed only $1082.77 and for the year 1938 only $890.47, being the amounts actually paid in those years, on the basis that deductions for insurance expense of a taxpayer on the cash receipts and disbursements basis is limited to premiums paid during the taxable year.

We are asked to determine whether a taxpayer who keeps his books and files his returns on a cash basis is limited to the deduction of the insurance premiums actually paid in any year or whether he should deduct for each tax year the pro rata portion of the prepaid insurance applicable to that year. The pertinent provisions of the statute are Sections 23 and 43 of the Revenue Act of 1936,[1] 49 Stat. 1648, 26 U.S.C.A.Int.Rev.Acts, pages 813, 827, 839.

This court in Welch v. De Blois, 1 Cir., 1938, 94 F.2d 842, held that a taxpayer on the cash receipts and disbursements basis who made prepayments of insurance premiums was entitled to take a full deduction for these payments as ordinary and necessary business expenses in the year in which payment was made despite the fact that the insurance covered a three-year period. The government on the basis of that decision changed its earlier G.C.M. rule, supra, which had required the taxpayer to prorate prepaid insurance premiums. The Board of Tax Appeals has refused to follow that case in George S. Jephson v. Com'r, 37 B.T.A. 1117; Frank Real Estate & Investment Co., 40 B.T.A. 1382, unreported memorandum decision Nov. 15, 1939, and in the instant case. The arguments in that case in favor of treating prepaid insurance as an ordinary and necessary business expense are persuasive. We are, nevertheless, unable to find a real basis for distinguishing between prepayment of rentals, Baton Coal Co. v. Commissioner, 3 Cir., 1931, 51 F.2d 469, certiorari denied 284 U.S. 674, 52 S.Ct. 129, 76 L.Ed. 570; Galatoire Bros. v. Lines, 5 Cir., 1928, 23 F.2d 676; See Main & McKinney Building Co. v. Commissioner, 5 Cir., 1940, 113 F.2d 81, 82, certiorari denied 311 U.S. 688, 61 S.Ct. 66, 85 L.Ed. 444; bonuses for the acquisition of leases, Home Trust Co. v. Commissioner, 8 Cir., 1933, 65 F.2d 532; J. Alland & Bro., Inc. v. United States, D.C.Mass.1928, 28 F.2d 792; bonuses for the cancellation of leases, Steele-Wedeles Co. v. Commissioner, 30 B.T.A. 841, 842; Borland v. Commissioner, 27 B.T.A. 538, 542; commissions

---

1. [§ 23, not materially different from I.R.C. (1954) § 162(a), and § 43, similar   to I.R.C. (1954) § 461(a), are omitted. Ed.]

for negotiating leases, see Bonwit Teller & Co. v. Commissioner, 2 Cir., 1931, 53 F.2d 381, 384, 82 A.L.R. 325, and prepaid insurance. Some distinctions may be drawn in the cases cited on the basis of the facts contained therein, but we are of the opinion that there is no justification for treating them differently insofar as deductions are concerned. All of the cases cited are readily distinguishable from such a clear cut case as a permanent improvement to a building. This latter is clearly a capital expenditure. See Parkersburg Iron & Steel Co. v. Burnet, 4 Cir., 1931, 48 F.2d 163, 165. In such a case there is the creation of a capital asset which has a life extending beyond the taxable year and which depreciates over a period of years. The taxpayer regardless of his method of accounting can only take deductions for depreciation over the life of the asset. Advance rentals, payments of bonuses for acquisition and cancellation of leases, and commissions for negotiating leases are all matters which the taxpayer amortizes over the life of the lease. Whether we consider these payments to be the cost of the exhaustible asset, as in the case of advance rentals, or the cost of acquiring the asset, as in the case of bonuses, the payments are prorated primarily because the life of the asset extends beyond the taxable year. To permit the taxpayer to take a full deduction in the year of payment would distort his income. Prepaid insurance presents the same problem and should be solved in the same way. Prepaid insurance for a period of three years may be easily allocated. It is protection for the entire period and the taxpayer may, if he desires, at any time surrender the insurance policy. It thus is clearly an asset having a longer life than a single taxable year. The line to be drawn between capital expenditures and ordinary and necessary business expenses is not always an easy one, but we are satisfied that in treating prepaid insurance as a capital expense we are obtaining some degree of consistency in these matters. We are, therefore, of the opinion that Welch v. DeBlois, supra, is incorrect and should be overruled.

The decision of Board of Tax Appeals is affirmed.

NOTE

If cash method taxpayers generally deduct deductible amounts in the year in which paid, what about prepayment of interest on a loan? Until recently it would have been necessary to struggle with this question without specific statutory guidance.[1] However, § 208(a) of the Tax Reform Act of 1976 added subsection (g) to I.R.C. § 461 requiring cash method taxpayers to allocate deductions for prepaid interest

1. See e. g. John D. Fackler 39 BTA 395 (1939), nonacq., 1968–2 C.B. 3, allowing the deduction for prepaid interest, Burck v. Comm'r, 533 F.2d 768 (2d Cir. 1976), contra, and Rev.Rul. 68–643, 1968–2 C.B. 76, generally limiting the deduction to interest for twelve months beyond the year of payment.

to the periods to which they relate by way of capitalization and amortization.

The statute makes an exception for "points", a loan processing fee paid at the inception of a loan, which is treated as a payment of interest.[2] However, the exception is limited to customary arrangements in connection with indebtedness incurred to purchase or improve a residence. A taxpayer cannot easily manipulate these payments in a way to distort his income for a particular period.

Question may be raised whether Congress has gone far enough in new § 461(g). There is some possibility of distortion by way of deferring the payment of interest to a convenient later date when the corresponding tax deduction may be more beneficial. No statutory or common law rule forecloses this practice. However it may be substantially restricted in a self-policing manner by impatient creditors.

PROBLEMS

1. Lender lends out money at a legal interest rate to Debtor. Debtor is required to pay $5000 interest each year on the loan which extends over a five year period with no reduction in the obligation to make the interest payments even if payment of the principal is accelerated. The agreement calls for payment of each year's interest on December 31 of the year. Both parties are calendar year, cash method taxpayers. Discuss the tax consequences to both parties under the following alternatives:

(a) Debtor mails a check for $5000 interest to Lender on December 31 of year one. It is delivered to Lender on January 2 of year two.

(b) Debtor mails the check in (a), above, on December 30 of year one. It is delivered to Lender on December 31 of year one but after the banks are closed.

(c) Debtor pays all five years' interest ($25,000) to Lender in cash on December 31 of year one.

(d) Same as (c), above, but Debtor does so because Lender makes it a condition of extending Debtor another loan.

(e) Debtor pays year one's $5000 of interest in cash on January 2nd of year two and, as agreed, pays year two's interest on December 31 of year two.

(f) Debtor offers to pay Lender the $5000 interest due on December 31 of year one but Lender suggests that he pay it on January 2nd of year two, which he does.

(g) Debtor gives Lender a promissory note on December 31 of year one agreeing to pay year one's interest plus $50 on January 30 of year two. Debtor pays off the note on January 30 of year two.

2. See Rev.Rul. 69–188, 1969–1 C.B. 54.

2.   Lawyer renders services to Client which are deductible to Client under I.R.C. § 162. What result to both Lawyer and Client if both are cash method, calendar year taxpayers in each of the following circumstances:

(a) Lawyer sends out a bill for $1000 on December 24 of year one. Client pays the bill on January 5 of year two.

(b) Lawyer sends out a bill for $1000 on November 15 of year one. Client immediately pays the bill using his American Express credit card and American Express pays Lawyer the $1000 on December 15 of year one. Client pays American Express the $1000 credit card bill on January 15 of year two.

(c) Prior to rendering the services Lawyer and Client agree that Lawyer will be paid $500 in year one and $500 in year two. Client pays Lawyer $500 of cash on December 24 of year one and $500 of cash on January 5 of year two.

(d) Client calls Lawyer at 4:00 p. m., December 31 of year one, saying he has Lawyer's fee statement, has made out check in full payment and, as he is about to leave for Europe, will leave check with desk clerk at Client's apartment. Lawyer is ill, has no one to send to pick up check, and finally picks it up January 2 of year two. See Loose v. United States, 74 F. 2d 147 (8th Cir. 1934).

C. THE ACCRUAL METHOD

---

1. INCOME ITEMS

Internal Revenue Code: Section 451(a). See Sections 455 and 456.
Regulations: Section 1.451–1(a). See Section 1.455–1.

SPRING CITY FOUNDRY CO. v. COMMISSIONER

Supreme Court of the United States, 1934.
292 U.S. 182, 54 S.Ct. 644.
Rehearing den., 292 U.S. 613, 54 S.Ct. 857.

MR. CHIEF JUSTICE HUGHES delivered the opinion of the Court.

[The taxpayer, petitioner in the Supreme Court, using the calendar year, accrual method of accounting, had sold goods in 1920 on open account. Before the end of the year the purchaser went bankrupt and a receiver was appointed. By the end of the year it was clear the taxpayer would not be paid in full for the goods. The question was how, if at all, the post-sale events affected the taxpayer's taxable income for the year.

In a portion of the opinion not reproduced here, the court upheld the Commissioner's disallowance of any bad debt deduction for the year. As now, under I.R.C. § 166, the statute provided a bad debt deduction but only for debts that became worthless during the taxable year. There was then no provision for a deduction for *partially* worthless debts as is now provided by § 166(a) (2), and the purchaser's obligation had not become wholly worthless in 1920. The bad debt deduction is considered in Chapter 23, infra.

The alternate contention of the taxpayer was that the partial worthlessness of the purchaser's obligations in 1920 affected its *gross* income for that year. This contention was also rejected in the portion of the opinion that follows. Ed.]

* * *

Petitioner first contends that the debt, to the extent that it was ascertained in 1920 to be worthless, was not returnable as gross income in that year, that is, apart from any question of deductions, it was not to be regarded as taxable income at all. We see no merit in this contention. Keeping accounts and making returns on the accrual basis, as distinguished from the cash basis, import that it is the *right* to receive and not the actual receipt that determines the inclusion of the amount in gross income. When the right to receive an amount becomes fixed, the right accrues. When a merchandising concern makes sales, its inventory is reduced and a claim for the purchase price arises. Article 35 of Regulations 45 under the Revenue Act of 1918 provided: "In the case of a manufacturing, merchandising, or mining business 'gross income' means the total sales, less the cost of goods sold, plus any income from investments and from incidental or outside operations or sources." [1]

On an accrual basis, the "total sales," to which the regulation refers, are manifestly the accounts receivable arising from the sales, and these accounts receivable, less the cost of the goods sold, figure in the statement of gross income. If such accounts receivable become uncollectible, in whole or part, the question is one of the deduction which may be taken according to the applicable statute. See United States v. Anderson, 269 U.S. 422, 440, 441; American National Co. v. United States, 274 U.S. 99, 102, 103; Brown v. Helvering, 291 U.S. 193, 199; Rouss v. Bowers, 30 F.2d 628, 629. That is the question here. It is not altered by the fact that the claim of loss relates to an item of gross income which had accrued in the same year.

* * *

1. This provision has been carried forward in the regulations under the later revenue acts. See Regulations 77, Article 55.

REVENUE RULING 70–151

1970–1 Cum.Bull. 116.

The purpose of this Revenue Ruling is to update and restate, under the current statute and regulations, the position set forth in I.T. 3165, C.B. 1938–1, 158.

The question presented is when income accrues under the circumstances described below.

The taxpayer, a domestic corporation reporting its income under the accrual method of accounting for Federal income tax purposes, instituted a suit against the United States in the United States Court of Claims for damages for alleged breach of contract. The taxpayer was awarded a judgment in 1968. A petition for writ of certiorari was filed by the United States and denied by the Supreme Court of the United States in 1969. No petition for rehearing was filed by the United States. No appropriation was made by Congress for the amount of the judgment in 1969.

Section 451 of the Internal Revenue Code of 1954 provides, in part, that any item of gross income shall be included in gross income for the taxable year in which received by the taxpayer unless, under the method of accounting used in computing taxable income, such amount is to be properly accounted for as of a different period.

Section 1.451–1(a) of the Income Tax Regulations provide, in pertinent part, that under the accrual method of accounting, income is includible in gross income when all events have occurred that fix the right to receive such income and the amount thereof can be determined with reasonable accuracy.

In the instant case the right to receive the sum due as a result of the judgment was determined in 1969. The fact that Congress did not make an appropriation for the payment of such sum in 1969 does not govern since the judgment became an acknowledged liability of the United States in 1969.

Accordingly, the amount of the judgment must be included in the taxpayer's gross income in 1969 under the taxpayer's method of accounting.

I.T. 3165 is superseded, since the position set forth therein is restated under current law in this Revenue Ruling.

NORTH AMERICAN OIL CONSOLIDATED v. BURNET

Supreme Court of the United States, 1932.
286 U.S. 417, 52 S.Ct. 631.

MR. JUSTICE BRANDEIS delivered the opinion of the Court.

The question for decision is whether the sum of $171,979.22 received by the North American Oil Consolidated in 1917, was taxable to it as income of that year.

The money was paid to the company under the following circumstances. Among many properties operated by it in 1916 was a section of oil land, the legal title to which stood in the name of the United States. Prior to that year, the Government, claiming also the beneficial ownership, had instituted a suit to oust the company from possession; and on February 2, 1916, it secured the appointment of a receiver to operate the property, or supervise its operations, and to hold the net income thereof. The money paid to the company in 1917 represented the net profits which had been earned from that property in 1916 during the receivership. The money was paid to the receiver as earned. After entry by the District Court in 1917 of the final decree dismissing the bill, the money was paid, in that year, by the receiver to the company. United States v. North American Oil Consolidated, 242 F. 723. The Government took an appeal (without supersedeas) to the Circuit Court of Appeals. In 1920, that Court affirmed the decree. 264 F. 336. In 1922, a further appeal to this Court was dismissed by stipulation. 258 U.S. 633.

The income earned from the property in 1916 had been entered on the books of the company as its income. It had not been included in its original return of income for 1916; but it was included in an amended return for that year which was filed in 1918. Upon auditing the company's income and profits tax returns for 1917, the Commissioner of Internal Revenue determined a deficiency based on other items. The company appealed to the Board of Tax Appeals. There, in 1927 the Commissioner prayed that the deficiency already claimed should be increased so as to include a tax on the amount paid by the receiver to the company in 1917. The Board held that the profits were taxable to the receiver as income of 1916; and hence made no finding whether the company's accounts were kept on the cash receipts and disbursements basis or on the accrual basis. 12 B.T.A. 68. The Circuit Court of Appeals held that the profits were taxable to the company as income of 1917, regardless of whether the company's returns were made on the cash or on the accrual basis. 50 F.2d 752. This Court granted a writ of certiorari. 284 U.S. 614.

It is conceded that the net profits earned by the property during the receivership constituted income. The company contends that they should have been reported by the receiver for taxation in 1916; that if not returnable by him, they should have been returned by the company for 1916, because they constitute income of the company accrued in that year; and that if not taxable as income of the company for 1916, they were taxable to it as income for 1922, since the litigation was not finally terminated in its favor until 1922.

First. The income earned in 1916 and impounded by the receiver in that year was not taxable to him, because he was the receiver of only a part of the properties operated by the company. Under § 13(c) of the Revenue Act of 1916,[1] receivers who "are operating the property or business of corporations" were obliged to make returns "of net income as and for such corporations," and "any income tax due" was to be "assessed and collected in the same manner as if assessed directly against the organization of whose business or properties they have custody and control." The phraseology of this section was adopted without change in the Revenue Act of 1918, 40 Stat. 1057, 1081, c. 18, § 239. The regulations of the Treasury Department have consistently construed these statutes as applying only to receivers in charge of the entire property or business of a corporation; and in all other cases have required the corporations themselves to report their income. Treas.Regs. 33, arts. 26, 209; Treas.Regs. 45, arts. 424, 622. That construction is clearly correct. The language of the section contemplates a substitution of the receiver for the corporation; and there can be such substitution only when the receiver is in complete control of the properties and business of the corporation. Moreover, there is no provision for the consolidation of the return of a receiver of part of a corporation's property or business with the return of the corporation itself. It may not be assumed that Congress intended to require the filing of two separate returns for the same year, each covering only a part of the corporate income, without making provision for consolidation so that the tax could be based upon the income as a whole.

Second. The net profits were not taxable to the company as income of 1916. For the company was not required in 1916 to report as income an amount which it might never receive. See Burnet v. Logan, 283 U.S. 404, 413. Compare Lucas v. American Code Co., 280 U.S. 445, 452; Burnet v. Sanford & Brooks Co., 282 U.S. 359, 363. There was no constructive receipt of the profits by the company in that year, because at no time during the year was there a right in the company to demand that the receiver pay over the money. Throughout 1916 it was uncertain who would be declared entitled to the profits. It was not until 1917, when the District Court entered a final decree vacating the receivership and dismissing the bill, that the company became entitled to receive the money. Nor is it material, for the purposes of this case, whether the company's return was filed on the cash receipts and disbursements basis, or on the accrual basis. In neither event was it taxable in 1916 on account of income which it had not yet received and which it might never receive.

---

1. Act of September 8, 1916, 39 Stat. 756, 771, c. 463: "In cases wherein receivers, trustees in bankruptcy, or assignees are operating the property or business of corporations * * *, subject to tax imposed by this title, such receivers, trustees or assignees shall make returns of net income as and for such corporations * * *, in the same manner and form as such organizations are hereinbefore required to make returns, and any income tax due on the basis of such returns made by receivers, trustees, or assignees shall be assessed and collected in the same manner as if assessed directly against the organizations of whose business or properties they have custody and control." [See I.R. C. (1954) § 6012(b) (3). Ed.]

Third. The net profits earned by the property in 1916 were not income of the year 1922—the year in which the litigation with the Government was finally terminated. They became income of the company in 1917, when it first became entitled to them and when it actually received them. If a taxpayer receives earnings under a claim of right and without restriction as to its disposition, he has received income which he is required to return, even though it may still be claimed that he is not entitled to retain the money, and even though he may still be adjudged liable to restore its equivalent. See Board v. Commissioner, 51 F.2d 73, 75, 76. Compare United States v. S. S. White Dental Mfg. Co., 274 U.S. 398, 403. If in 1922 the Government had prevailed, and the company had been obliged to refund the profits received in 1917, it would have been entitled to a deduction from the profits of 1922, not from those of any earlier year. Compare Lucas v. American Code Co., supra.

Affirmed.

JAMES v. UNITED STATES *

Supreme Court of the United States, 1961.
366 U.S. 213, 81 S.Ct. 1052.

MR. CHIEF JUSTICE WARREN announced the judgment of the Court and an opinion in which MR. JUSTICE BRENNAN and MR. JUSTICE STEWART concur.

The issue before us in this case is whether embezzled funds are to be included in the "gross income" of the embezzler in the year in which the funds are misappropriated under § 22(a) of the Internal Revenue Code of 1939 [1] and § 61(a) of the Internal Revenue Code of 1954.[2]

The facts are not in dispute. The petitioner is a union official who, with another person, embezzled in excess of $738,000 during the years 1951 through 1954 from his employer union and from an insurance company with which the union was doing business.[3] Petitioner failed to report these amounts in his gross income in those years and was convicted for willfully attempting to evade the federal income tax due for each of the years 1951 through 1954 in violation of § 145(b) of the Internal Revenue Code of 1939 [4] and § 7201 of the Internal Revenue Code of 1954.[5] He was sentenced to a total of three years' impris-

---

* See Libin and Haydon, "Embezzled Funds as Taxable Income: A Study in Judicial Footwork," 61 Mich.L.Rev. 425 (1963); Hoffron, "Ill-Gotten Gains, Intent and the Revenue Laws," 20 N.Y.U.Inst. on Fed.Tax. 1105 (1962). Ed.

1. [I.R.C. (1939) § 22 has been omitted. Ed.]

2. [I.R.C. (1954) § 61 has been omitted. Ed.]

3. Petitioner has pleaded guilty to the offense of conspiracy to embezzle in the Court of Essex County, New Jersey.

4. [I.R.C. (1939) § 145(b) has been omitted. Ed.]

5. [I.R.C. (1954) § 7201 has been omitted. Ed.]

onment. The Court of Appeals affirmed. 273 F.2d 5. Because of a
conflict with this Court's decision in Commissioner v. Wilcox, 327 U.S.
404, a case whose relevant facts are concededly the same as those in
the case now before us, we granted certiorari, 362 U.S. 974.

In *Wilcox,* the Court held that embezzled money does not constitute taxable income to the embezzler in the year of the embezzlement
under § 22(a) of the Internal Revenue Code of 1939. Six years later,
this Court held, in Rutkin v. United States, 343 U.S. 130, that extorted
money does constitute taxable income to the extortionist in the year
that the money is received under § 22(a) of the Internal Revenue
Code of 1939. In *Rutkin,* the Court did not overrule *Wilcox,* but
stated:

> "We do not reach in this case the factual situation involved in
> Commissioner v. Wilcox, 327 U.S. 404. We limit that case to its
> facts. There embezzled funds were held not to constitute taxable in-
> come to the embezzler under § 22(a)." Id., at 138.[6]

However, examination of the reasoning used in *Rutkin* leads us inescapably to the conclusion that *Wilcox* was thoroughly devitalized.

The basis for the *Wilcox* decision was "that a taxable gain is
conditioned upon (1) the presence of a claim of right to the alleged
gain and (2) the absence of a definite, unconditional obligation to repay or return that which would otherwise constitute a gain. Without
some bona fide legal or equitable claim, even though it be contingent
or contested in nature, the taxpayer cannot be said to have received
any gain or profit within the reach of § 22(a)." Commissioner v. Wilcox, supra, at p. 408. Since Wilcox embezzled the money, held it
"without any semblance of a bona fide claim of right," ibid., and therefore "was at all times under an unqualified duty and obligation to repay the money to his employer," ibid., the Court found that the money
embezzled was not includible within "gross income." But, Rutkin's
legal claim was no greater than that of Wilcox. It was specifically
found "that petitioner had no basis for his claim * * * and that
he obtained it by extortion." Rutkin v. United States, supra, at p.
135. Both Wilcox and Rutkin obtained the money by means of a criminal act; neither had a bona fide claim of right to the funds.[7] Nor

---

6. The dissenters in *Rutkin* stated that
the Court had rejected the *Wilcox*
interpretation of § 22(a). Id., at 140.

7. The Government contends that the
adoption in *Wilcox* of a claim of right
test as a touchstone of taxability had
no support in the prior cases of this
Court; that the claim of right test
was a doctrine invoked by the Court
in aid of the concept of annual accounting, to determine *when, not
whether,* receipts constituted income.

See North American Oil v. Burnet,
286 U.S. 417; United States v. Lewis,
340 U.S. 590; Healy v. Commissioner,
345 U.S. 278. In view of our reasoning set forth below, we need not pass
on this contention. The use to which
we put the claim of right test here is
only to demonstrate that, whatever
its validity as a test of *whether* certain receipts constitute income, it
calls for no distinction between *Wilcox and Rutkin.*

was Rutkin's obligation to repay the extorted money to the victim any less than that of Wilcox. The victim of an extortion, like the victim of an embezzlement, has a right to restitution. Furthermore, it is inconsequential that an embezzler may lack title to the sums he appropriates while an extortionist may gain a voidable title. Questions of federal income taxation are not determined by such "attenuated subtleties." Lucas v. Earl, 281 U.S. 111, 114; Corliss v. Bowers, 281 U.S. 376, 378. Thus, the fact that Rutkin secured the money with the consent of his victim, Rutkin v. United States, supra, at p. 138, is irrelevant. Likewise unimportant is the fact that the sufferer of an extortion is less likely to seek restitution than one whose funds are embezzled. What is important is that the right to recoupment exists in both situations.

Examination of the relevant cases in the courts of appeals lends credence to our conclusion that the *Wilcox* rationale was effectively vitiated by this Court's decision in *Rutkin*.[8] Although this case appears to be the first to arise that is "on all fours" with *Wilcox*, the lower federal courts, in deference to the undisturbed *Wilcox* holding, have earnestly endeavored to find distinguishing facts in the cases before them which would enable them to include sundry unlawful gains within "gross income." [9]

It had been a well-established principle, long before either Rutkin or Wilcox, that unlawful, as well as lawful, gains are comprehended within the term "gross income." Section IIB of the Income Tax Act of 1913 provided that "the net income of a taxable person shall include gains, profits, and income * * * from * * * the transaction of any *lawful* business carried on for gain or profit, or gains or profits and income derived from any source whatever. * * *"

8. In Marienfeld v. United States, 214 F.2d 632, the Eighth Circuit stated, "We find it difficult to reconcile the Wilcox case with the later opinion of the Supreme Court in Rutkin . . . ." Id., at 636. The Second Circuit announced, in United States v. Bruswitz, 219 F.2d 59, "It is difficult to perceive what, if anything, is left of the Wilcox holding after Rutkin. * * *" Id., at 61. The Seventh Circuit's prior decision in Macias v. Commissioner, 255 F.2d 23, observed, "If this reasoning [of *Rutkin*] had been employed in Wilcox, we see no escape from the conclusion that the decision in that case would have been different. In our view, the Court in Rutkin repudiated its holding in Wilcox; certainly it repudiated the reasoning by which the result was reached in that case." Id., at 26.

9. For example, Kann v. Commissioner, 210 F.2d 247, was differentiated on the following grounds: the taxpayer was never indicted or convicted of embezzlement; there was no adequate proof that the victim did not forgive the misappropriation; the taxpayer was financially able to both pay the income tax and make restitution; the taxpayer would have likely received most of the misappropriated money as dividends. In Marienfeld v. United States, supra, the court believed that the victim was not likely to repudiate. In United States v. Wyss, 239 F.2d 658, the distinguishing factors were that the district judge had not found as a fact that the taxpayer embezzled the funds and the money had not as yet been reclaimed by the victim. See also Briggs v. United States, 214 F.2d 699, 702; Prokop v. Commissioner, 254 F.2d 544, 554–555. Cf. J. J. Dix, Inc. v. Commissioner, 223 F.2d 436.

(Emphasis supplied.)   38 Stat. 167.   When the statute was amended in 1916, the one word "lawful" was omitted.   This revealed, we think, the obvious intent of that Congress to tax income derived from both legal and illegal sources, to remove the incongruity of having the gains of the honest laborer taxed and the gains of the dishonest immune.   Rutkin v. United States, supra, at p. 138; United States v. Sullivan, 274 U.S. 259, 263.   Thereafter, the Court held that gains from illicit traffic in liquor are includible within "gross income."   Ibid. See also Johnson v. United States, 318 U.S. 189; United States v. Johnson, 319 U.S. 503.   And, the Court has pointed out, with approval, that there "has been a widespread and settled administrative and judicial recognition of the taxability of unlawful gains of many kinds," Rutkin v. United States, supra, at p. 137.   These include protection payments made to racketeers, ransom payments paid to kidnappers, bribes, money derived from the sale of unlawful insurance policies, graft, black market gains, funds obtained from the operation of lotteries, income from race track bookmaking and illegal prize fight pictures.   Ibid.

The starting point in all cases dealing with the question of the scope of what is included in "gross income" begins with the basic premise that the purpose of Congress was "to use the full measure of its taxing power."   Helvering v. Clifford, 309 U.S. 331, 334.   And the Court has given a liberal construction to the broad phraseology of the "gross income" definition statutes in recognition of the intention of Congress to tax all gains except those specifically exempted.   Commissioner v. Jacobson, 336 U.S. 28, 49; Helvering v. Stockholms Enskilda Bank, 293 U.S. 84, 87–91.   The language of § 22(a) of the 1939 Code, "gains or profits and income derived from any source whatever," and the more simplified language of § 61(a) of the 1954 Code, "all income from whatever source derived," have been held to encompass all "accessions to wealth, clearly realized, and over which the taxpayers have complete dominion."   Commissioner v. Glenshaw Glass Co., 348 U.S. 426, 431.   A gain "constitutes taxable income when its recipient has such control over it that, as a practical matter, he derives readily realizable economic value from it."   Rutkin v. United States, supra, at p. 137.   Under these broad principles, we believe that petitioner's contention, that all unlawful gains are taxable except those resulting from embezzlement, should fail.

When a taxpayer acquires earnings, lawfully or unlawfully, without the consensual recognition, express or implied, of an obligation to repay and without restriction as to their disposition, "he has received income which he is required to return, even though it may still be claimed that he is not entitled to retain the money, and even though he may still be adjudged liable to restore its equivalent." *

---

* [As is evident here, the question *whether* an item is gross income may merge with the question *when* it is to be so treated. The timing issue is considered more fully in Chapter 19, infra.   Ed.]

North American Oil v. Burnet, supra, at p. 424. In such case, the taxpayer has "actual command over the property taxed—the actual benefit for which the tax is paid," Corliss v. Bowers, supra. This standard brings wrongful appropriations within the broad sweep of "gross income"; it excludes loans. When a law-abiding taxpayer mistakenly receives income in one year, which receipt is assailed and found to be invalid in a subsequent year, the taxpayer must nonetheless report the amount as "gross income" in the year received. United States v. Lewis, supra; Healy v. Commissioner, supra. We do not believe that Congress intended to treat a law-breaking taxpayer differently. Just as the honest taxpayer may deduct any amount repaid in the year in which the repayment is made, the Government points out that, "If, when, and to the extent that the victim recovers back the misappropriated funds, there is of course a reduction in the embezzler's income." Brief for the United States, p. 24.[10]

Petitioner contends that the *Wilcox* rule has been in existence since 1946; that if Congress had intended to change the rule, it would have done so; that there was a general revision of the income tax laws in 1954 without mention of the rule; that a bill to change it [11] was introduced in the Eighty-sixth Congress but was not acted upon; that, therefore, we may not change the rule now. But the fact that Congress has remained silent or has re-enacted a statute which we have construed, or that congressional attempts to amend a rule announced by this Court have failed, does not necessarily debar us from re-examining and correcting the Court's own errors. Girouard v. United States, 328 U.S. 61, 69–70; Helvering v. Hallock, 309 U.S. 106, 119–122. There may have been any number of reasons why Congress acted as it did. Helvering v. Hallock, supra. One of the reasons could well be our subsequent decision in *Rutkin* which has been thought by many to have repudiated *Wilcox*. Particularly might this be true in light of the decisions of the Courts of Appeals which have been riding a narrow rail between the two cases and further distinguishing them to the disparagement of *Wilcox*. See notes 8 and 9, supra.

We believe that *Wilcox* was wrongly decided and we find nothing in congressional history since then to persuade us that Congress intended to legislate the rule. Thus, we believe that we should now correct the error and the confusion resulting from it, certainly if we do so in a manner that will not prejudice those who might have relied

---

10. Petitioner urges upon us the case of Alison v. United States, 344 U.S. 167. But that case dealt with the right of the victim of an embezzlement to take a deduction, under § 23 (e) and (f) of the 1939 Code, in the year of the discovery of the embezzlement rather than the year in which the embezzlement occurred. The Court held only "that the special factual circumstances found by the Dis-trict Courts in both these cases justify deductions under I.R.C. §§ 23(e) and (f) and the long-standing Treasury Regulations applicable to embezzlement losses." Id., at 170. The question of inclusion of embezzled funds in "gross income" was not presented in Alison.

11. H.R. 8854, 86th Cong., 1st Sess.

on it. Cf. Helvering v. Hallock, supra, at 119. We should not continue to confound confusion, particularly when the result would be to perpetuate the injustice of relieving embezzlers of the duty of paying income taxes on the money they enrich themselves with through theft while honest people pay their taxes on every conceivable type of income.

But, we are dealing here with a felony conviction under statutes which apply to any person who "willfully" fails to account for his tax or who "willfully" attempts to evade his obligation. In Spies v. United States, 317 U.S. 492, 499, the Court said that § 145(b) of the 1939 Code embodied "the gravest of offenses against the revenues," and stated that willfulness must therefore include an evil motive and want of justification in view of all the circumstances. Id., at 498. Willfulness "involves a specific intent which must be proven by independent evidence and which cannot be inferred from the mere understatement of income." Holland v. United States, 348 U.S. 121, 139.

We believe that the element of willfulness could not be proven in a criminal prosecution for failing to include embezzled funds in gross income in the year of misappropriation so long as the statute contained the gloss placed upon it by *Wilcox* at the time the alleged crime was committed. Therefore, we feel that petitioner's conviction may not stand and that the indictment against him must be dismissed.

Since MR. JUSTICE HARLAN, MR. JUSTICE FRANKFURTER, and MR. JUSTICE CLARK agree with us concerning *Wilcox*, that case is overruled. MR. JUSTICE BLACK, MR. JUSTICE DOUGLAS, and MR. JUSTICE WHITTAKER believe that petitioner's conviction must be reversed and the case dismissed for the reasons stated in their opinions.

Accordingly, the judgment of the Court of Appeals is reversed and the case is remanded to the District Court with directions to dismiss the indictment.

It is so ordered.

[The separate opinions of BLACK, J. (DOUGLAS, J., joining); CLARK, J.; WHITTAKER, J.; and HARLAN, J. (FRANKFURTER, J., joining) have been omitted.]

NEW CAPITAL HOTEL, INC.

Tax Court of the United States, 1957.
28 T.C. 706.
Aff'd per curiam, 261 F.2d 437 (6th Cir. 1958).

The respondent determined a deficiency in petitioner's income tax for the year 1949 in the amount of $11,724.50.

The sole issue is whether a $30,000 advance payment received in 1949 by the petitioner lessor, an accrual basis taxpayer, pursuant to lease contract is includible in gross income in 1949, as determined by the respondent, or in 1959, the year in which the advance payment is to be applied as rent.

[The findings of fact are omitted. Ed.]

Opinion

BLACK, JUDGE: The sole question involved here is whether the $30,000 advance payment received in 1949 by the petitioner is includible in its gross income for that year.

The petitioner lessor leased certain hotel property, which it owned, for a period of 10 years from January 1, 1950, to December 31, 1959. The lease contract provided that the lessee would pay rents as follows: $30,000 during each year of the lease and "for the last year of this lease, Lessee agrees to pay in advance the sum of Thirty Thousand Dollars ($30,000.00), the receipt of which is hereby acknowledged. Said sum, however, shall apply only on the rental for the last year of this lease." The lease also provided that if the building should be substantially destroyed during the period of the lease the lessor shall refund to the lessee all or part of the $30,000 as may not cover the rental of the property up to the time of such destruction, provided, however, that no rental is then in arrears.

The petitioner's president testified that the lessee preferred paying the last year's rent in advance rather than executing a performance bond, which the lessor was demanding. The lessee, during 1949, paid the above-mentioned $30,000 to the petitioner. There were no restrictions on the use of the $30,000; the petitioner had unfettered control over it.

The petitioner, an accrual basis taxpayer, reflected the advance rental payment in a liability account entitled "Deposit on lease contract" and contends that it should be reported as income in 1959, the year in which petitioner contends it would be considered as earned. The respondent determined that the $30,000 constituted gross income in 1949, the year of receipt, under section 22(a), Internal Revenue Code of 1939.[1]

It is clear from the record that the advance payment, although securing the lessee's performance of the covenants, was intended to be rent, was described in the lease contract as rent, and was primarily rent. Gilken Corporation, 10 T.C. 445, 451–456 (1948), affd. (C.A. 6, 1949) 176 F.2d 141, 144–145. Since the rent was received in 1949, it would be includible in gross income in that year even though the rent is to be applied for the use of the property in 1959. Hirsch Improvement Co. v. Commissioner (C.A.2, 1944) 143 F.2d 912, affirming a Memorandum Opinion of this Court. This is so regardless of whether the taxpayer keeps his books and computes his income on a cash basis, see Edwin B. De Golia, 40 B.T.A. 845 (1939), or on an accrual basis, see Palm Beach Aero Corporation, 17 T.C. 1169, 1170,

1. SEC. 22. GROSS INCOME.

    (a) General Definition.—"Gross income" includes gains, profits, and income derived from * * * rent, * * *

1177–1178 (1952); Hyde Park Realty, Inc. v. Commissioner (C.A. 2, 1954) 211 F.2d 462, affirming 20 T.C. 43 (1953).

The petitioner argues that its method of accounting clearly reflects its income and that the inclusion of the rent in gross income for the year 1949, rather than 1959, will distort its income for the 2 years because in 1959 it will incur approximately $23,000 in expenses incident to the earning of the $30,000 rent.[2]

We have recognized that the inclusion of prepaid income in gross income in the year of receipt of the item representing it, rather than in a subsequent year when it is considered earned, is not in accord with principles of commercial accounting. See Curtis R. Andrews, 23 T.C. 1026, 1033–1034 (1955); E. W. Schuessler, 24 T.C. 247, 249 (1955), reversed (C.A. 5, 1956) 230 F.2d 722. We have, however, consistently held that the Commissioner has acted within the discretion granted him under section 41 of the 1939 Code in holding that prepaid income must be returned in the year received in order to clearly reflect income. Cf. Automobile Club of Michigan v. Commissioner, 353 U.S. 180, 188–190 (1957). In the instant case the petitioner seeks to defer a nonrecurring advance rental payment[3] for a period of 10 years.[4] Under the circumstances detailed in our Findings of Fact we cannot say that the Commissioner abused the discretion granted him in section 41, Internal Revenue Code of 1939,[*] in determining that the $30,000 was includible in the petitioner's gross income in 1949.

Among the decisions which petitioner relies on in its brief in support of its contention that the $30,000 is not taxable in 1949, is John Mantell, 17 T.C. 1143 (1952). We think the facts of the instant case are clearly distinguishable from those present in the *Mantell* case. In the *Mantell* case our Findings of Fact made clear that the $33,320, which was involved there, was not meant to be paid as advance rental. It was paid primarily to be held as security to guarantee the performance by the lessees of the obligations and covenants contained in the lease. The next to the last paragraph of our Findings of Fact in the *Mantell* case enumerates the several things for which the $33,320 was

---

2. The petitioner, in its reply brief, apparently also contends that if the $30,000 is includible in its 1949 gross income it should be allowed a deduction of $23,000 for expenses to be incurred in 1959 in connection with the earning of the rent. This issue has not been properly pleaded and is not properly before us. Regardless, it has no merit. See Bressner Radio, Inc., 28 T.C. 378 (1957).

3. There is no contention that the Commissioner's action in this case will upset a consistent accounting system of long standing. Cf. Pacific Grape Products Co., 17 T.C. 1097

(1952), revd. (C.A.9, 1955) 219 F.2d 862.

4. Even under the liberalized provisions for reporting prepaid income under the short-lived section 452(b), Internal Revenue Code of 1954, a prepayment 10 years in advance, such as the one involved herein, would be includible in gross income ratably in the year of receipt and the next succeeding 5 years unless the Secretary or his delegate prescribed otherwise. See S.Rept.No.1622, 83d Cong., 2d Sess. (1954), pp. 301, 302.

* See I.R.C. (1954) § 446(b). Ed.

to act as security to guarantee that the lessees would perform. Our Findings of Fact then conclude with the following final paragraph (p. 1147):

> The sum of $33,320 received by the petitioner upon the execution of the lease in 1946 was intended to be and was in fact a security deposit. It was not paid as prepaid rent and was not taxable income when received.

Manifestly, we could make no such finding in the instant case because the lease agreement itself provides:

> And, for the last year of this lease, Lessee agrees to pay in advance the sum of Thirty Thousand Dollars ($30,000.00), the receipt of which is hereby acknowledged. Said sum, however, shall apply only on the rental for the last year of this lease.

That the $30,000 in question was paid by the lessee as advance rental for the year 1959 seems too clear for argument and, under the authorities cited, we must hold that it was taxable income to petitioner in the year 1949, when it was received.

Decision will be entered for the respondent.

ARTNELL CO. v. COMMISSIONER

United States Court of Appeals, Seventh Circuit, 1968.
400 F.2d 981.

FAIRCHILD, CIRCUIT JUDGE. The tax court upheld the commissioner's determination of deficiencies,[1] and Artnell Company, transferee taxpayer, seeks review. The main question is whether prepayments for services (proceeds of advance sales of tickets for baseball games and revenues for related future services) must be treated as income when received or whether such treatment could be deferred by the accrual basis taxpayer until the games were played and other services rendered.

Early in the 1962 baseball season, as in previous seasons, the White Sox team was operated by Chicago White Sox, Inc. It sold season tickets and single admissions for later games. It received revenues for broadcasting and televising future games, and it sold season parking books. Its taxable year would normally have run to October 31, 1962. It employed the accrual method of accounting for its own and for income tax purposes.

Before May 31, 1962, Artnell Company had acquired all the stock in White Sox. On that date White Sox was liquidated. Artnell

---

1. 48 T.C. 411.

became the owner of all the assets and subject to all the liabilities. It continued to operate the team.

As of May 31, the balance sheet of White Sox showed as deferred unearned income that part of the amount received for season tickets, advance single admissions, radio, television, and season parking books, allocable to games to be played after May 31. As the games were played Artnell took into income the amounts of deferred unearned income allocated to each.

The White Sox income tax return for the taxable year ending May 31, 1962 (because of the liquidation) was filed by Artnell as transferee. The return did not include the deferred unearned income as gross income. The commissioner decided it must be included and determined deficiencies accordingly.

When a business receives money in exchange for its obligation to render service or deliver goods and the costs of performance are incurred in a later accounting period, treatment of the receipt as income tends to reflect an illusory or partially illusory gain for the period of receipt. Accountancy has techniques (e. g. deferral of income, reserves for expenses) for achieving a more realistic reflection. The degree to which such techniques are available under income tax statutes is a vexing question.[2]

The commissioner urges the simple answer "that deferral of income is a matter for Congress to permit and, until Congress acts, deferral must be disallowed." He stands on "the established rule that an accrual basis taxpayer must include in gross income in the year of receipt prepaid items for which services will be performed in a later year. The rule implements the annual accounting principle which is at the heart of the federal taxing statute and which forbids transactional accounting for income tax purposes, however sound such methods might be for financial and other purposes under commercial accounting practice." [3]

Artnell relies upon statutory language which requires computation of taxable income under the accrual method of accounting regularly used by the taxpayer unless such method "does not clearly reflect income." [4] This language could call for a factual determination in the individual case whether an accrual system which employs the deferral of income technique clearly reflects income. Artnell contends that the White Sox system does so.

The commissioner's principal contention, which was sustained by the tax court, is that there is a rule of law which rejects deferral of income. Presumably he believes that any system in which prepaid

2. See Aland, Prepaid Income and Estimated Future Expenses, Jan. 1968 ABA Journal 84; Annotation: Income Taxes—Prepayment—When Income, 9 L.Ed.2d 1191.

3. The quotations are from the commissioner's brief.

4. 26 U.S.C. sec. 446.

income is deferred "does not clearly reflect income" and would consider the present statutory provisions for deferral in the case of prepaid subscription income [5] and prepaid dues of certain membership organizations [6] extensions of legislative grace.

One could reason from the statutory language that any deferral of prepaid income which fulfills standards of sound accounting practice could be employed by an accrual basis taxpayer, and the commissioner would not have power to reject it. Three Supreme Court decisions, *Automobile Club of Michigan*,[7] *American Automobile Association*,[8] and *Schlude*[9] have made it clear that this is not the law.

There are two other lines of reasoning reflected in the three decisions cited. All three held, upon consideration of the particular facts, that the commissioner did not abuse his discretion in rejecting a deferral of income where the time and extent of performance of future services were uncertain. Thus in *Automobile Club of Michigan:* "The pro rata allocation of the membership dues in monthly amounts is purely artificial and bears no relation to the services which petitioner may in fact be called upon to render for the member." In *American Automobile Association:* "That 'irregularity,' however, is highly relevant to the clarity of an accounting system which defers receipt, as earned income, of dues to a taxable period in which no, some or all the services paid for by those dues may or may not be rendered." In *Schlude:* "The American Automobile Association Case rested upon an additional ground which is also controlling here. Relying upon Automobile Club of Michigan * * *, the Court rejected the taxpayer's system as artificial since the advance payments related to services which were to be performed only upon customers' demands without relation to fixed dates in the future. The system employed here suffers from that very same vice * * *." In *Schlude* the Court also found that certain expenses were deducted in the year the payments were received even though related income had been deferred to later periods.

The uncertainty stressed in those decisions is not present here. The deferred income was allocable to games which were to be played on a fixed schedule. Except for rain dates, there was certainty. We would have no difficulty distinguishing the instant case in this respect.

A second consideration is reflected in *American Automobile Association* and *Schlude*. It is that Congress is aware of the problem

5. 26 U.S.C. sec. 455.

6. 26 U.S.C. sec. 456.

7. Automobile Club of Michigan v. Commissioner of Internal Revenue (1957), 353 U.S. 180, 77 S.Ct. 707, 1 L. Ed.2d 746.

8. American Auto. Ass'n v. United States (1961), 367 U.S. 687, 81 S.Ct. 1727, 6 L.Ed.2d 1109.

9. Schlude v. Commissioner of Internal Revenue (1963), 372 U.S. 128, 83 S.Ct. 601, 9 L.Ed.2d 633.

and that it is the policy of the Supreme Court to defer, where possible, to congressional procedures in the tax field. Thus in *American Automobile Association:* "At the very least, this background indicates congressional recognition of the complications inherent in the problem and its seriousness to the general revenues. We must leave to the Congress the fashioning of a rule which, in any event, must have wide ramifications. * * * Finding only that, in light of existing provisions not specifically authorizing it, the exercise of the Commissioner's discretion in rejecting the Association's accounting system was not unsound, we need not anticipate what will be the product of further 'study of this entire problem.' " In *Schlude:* "Plainly, the considerations expressed in American Automobile Association are apposite here. We need only add here that since the American Automobile Association decision, a specific provision extending the deferral practice to certain membership corporations was enacted * * * continuing, at least so far, the congressional policy of treating this problem by precise provisions of narrow applicability. Consequently, as in the American Automobile Association Case, we invoke the 'long-established policy of the Court in deferring, where possible, to congressional procedures in the tax field,' and, as in that case, we cannot say that the Commissioner's rejection of the studio's deferral system was unsound."

Has the Supreme Court left an opening for a decision that under the facts of a particular case, the extent and time of future performance are so certain, and related items properly accounted for with such clarity, that a system of accounting involving deferral of prepaid income is found clearly to reflect income, and the commissioner's rejection deemed an abuse of discretion? Or has it decided that the commissioner has complete and unreviewable discretion to reject deferral of prepaid income where Congress has made no provision? The tax court apparently adopted the latter view, for it concluded "that the Supreme Court would reach the same decision regardless of the method used by the taxpayer for deferring prepaid income."

It is our best judgment that, although the policy of deferring, where possible, to congressional procedures in the tax field will cause the Supreme Court to accord the widest possible latitude to the commissioner's discretion, there must be situations where the deferral technique will so clearly reflect income that the Court will find an abuse of discretion if the commissioner rejects it.

Prior to 1955 the commissioner permitted accrual basis publishers to defer unearned income from magazine subscriptions if they had consistently done so in the past. He refused to allow others to adopt the method.[10] In 1955 his refusal was held, by the tenth

---

10. See I.T. 3369, 1940–1 Cum.Bull. 46, modified, Rev.Rul. 57–87, 1957–1 Cum. Bull. 507. See also Anno., 9 L.Ed.2d 1191, at 1201–03.

circuit, in *Beacon*,[11] to be an abuse of discretion. In *Automobile Club of Michigan*, the Supreme Court distinguished *Beacon*, on its facts, because "performance of the subscription, in most instances, was, in part, necessarily deferred until the publication dates after the tax year." The Court, however, expressed no opinion upon the correctness of *Beacon*. In 1958, Congress dealt specifically with the *Beacon* problem.[12] It is at least arguable that the deferral as income of prepaid admissions to events which will take place on a fixed schedule in a different taxable year is so similar to deferral of prepaid subscriptions that it would be an abuse of discretion to reject similar accounting treatment.

In any event the prepaid admission situation approaches much closer to certainty than the situations considered in *Automobile Club of Michigan*, *American Automobile Association*, or *Schlude*.

The instant case was presented to the tax court on a stipulation of facts. The parties agreed as to the amounts of prepaid revenue allocated to the games played after May 31. The stipulation does not set forth other facts from which it could be determined that all other relevant items were so treated in the White Sox method of accounting that the income attributable to the first seven months of its normal fiscal and taxable year was clearly reflected.

The commissioner now points out that Artnell failed to produce this evidence and argues here that we must affirm on that ground even if we disagree with the commissioner's primary contention.

We think, however, that the commissioner shares responsibility for the failure of proof, for he seems to have let the tax court judge believe that this was not an issue. The judge wrote: "Since the respondent does not contend that the petitioner's method for deferring the advance receipts fails to match properly income and related expenses, we must therefore decide whether prepaid income is taxable in the year received, regardless of the merits of the proposed method for deferring it."

We choose, however, not to base our decision on an inferred waiver of this issue by the commissioner. It is specially important in this area to have the facts carefully developed.

We conclude that the tax court erred in deciding that these revenues were income when received regardless of the merits of the method employed. There must be further hearing in the tax court to determine whether the White Sox method of accounting did clearly reflect its income in its final, seven month, taxable year.

* * *

11. Beacon Publishing Company v. Commissioner of Internal Revenue (10th Cir., 1955), 218 F.2d 697.   12. 26 U.S.C. sec. 455.

The decision of the tax court is reversed and the cause remanded for further hearing consistent with this opinion.

[See note below for result on remand. Ed.]

DEFERRED INCOME

As can be discerned from the opinion, the *Artnell* case delivered a major jolt to long-standing and generally accepted Treasury policy requiring taxpayers, whether on the cash or accrual method, to include amounts received for goods and services to be furnished in a later year in income in the year of receipt. In *Artnell* on remand, the Tax Court concluded that the White Sox' method of accounting, while not perfect in matching income with related expenses, was more supportable than that proposed by the Commissioner and up-- held the taxpayer's deferred reporting of a portion of its income.[1]

Undeniably, the immediate inclusion policy challenged by *Artnell* is at variance with business accounting principles. It is tempting therefore simply to say that it is wrong. Nevertheless, there is some respectable support for it, both as a practical matter and as regards precedent. From the practical point of view, while both business and tax accounting principles are designed to yield an annual net income figure, their objectives are not identical. The business world wants a periodic net income figure for purposes of determining profitability of the business and comparative profitability for various accounting periods. Congress wants a steady flow of tax revenue and assurance that taxpayers in fact pay tax on all elements of gain. With this second objective in mind a momentary gain, even if it may later be offset by related expenses in a later period, *can* be identified as income. Thus, the issue is one of statutory interpretation: Has Congress compelled this result? On the other hand, with an eye toward the graduated rate tables, there is a question whether the business accounting purpose of identifying net income for the critical period, reasonably taking account of subsequent related costs or expenditures, is not as important for tax accounting as for business accounting. These thoughts have a direct bearing both on the interpretation of the Code's accounting sections as they stand and on the congressional question whether present provisions need revision, and they are reflected in the history of the Treasury's immediate reporting policy.

The Treasury's strict inclusion policy appeared as early as 1938 in a memorandum [2] which, relying upon "claim of right" language in *North American Oil Consolidated,* stated that "amounts received * * * within the taxable year without restriction as to disposition, use, or enjoyment, for subscription service to be rendered in a succeed-

---

1. 29 T.C.M. 403 (1970).   2. GCM 20021, 1938–1 C.B. 157, 158.

ing year or years constitute income for the year in which received regardless of the fact that the taxpayer's books of account are kept on the accrual basis." The proposition received judicial support both before and after publication of the memorandum.[3]

In the enactment of the 1954 Code, Congress undertook to change the immediate inclusion rule to a tax accounting rule in keeping with business accounting principles. Under I.R.C. (26 U.S.C.A.) § 452, accrual method taxpayers were permitted to report prepaid income from services or goods over the period in which the services were rendered or the goods were delivered up to a maximum period of five years subsequent to the year of receipt. At the same time, I.R.C. (26 U.S.C.A.) § 462 was added to allow, at the Commissioner's discretion, accrual method taxpayers to establish a reserve for estimated future expenses.[4] Because of congressional fear that a substantial temporary loss of revenue would occur in the period immediately following enactment of the sections as a result of taxpayers deferring recognition of their prepaid income under I.R.C. (26 U.S.C.A.) § 452 and accelerating deductions under § 462,[5] both sections were retroactively repealed in 1955.[6]

Subsequent to the repeal of I.R.C. (26 U.S.C.A.) §§ 452 and 462 and until *Artnell*, the Commissioner has been largely successful in maintaining that, in order clearly to reflect income under I.R.C. (26 U.S.C.A.) § 446, prepaid income of accrual method taxpayers for both goods and services must be included within income in the year of prepayment. In fairly recent times, several Supreme Court cases have endorsed this view, namely Automobile Club of Michigan v. Comm'r,[7] American Automobile Ass'n v. United States,[8] and Schlude v. Comm'r,[9] all of which are discussed and distinguished in *Artnell*.[10] In the meantime, limited statutory exceptions to the im-

3. E. g., Brown v. Helvering, 291 U.S. 193, 54 S.Ct. 356 (1934); South Dade Farms v. Comm'r, 138 F.2d 818 (5th Cir. 1943); South Tacoma Motor Co., 3 T.C. 411 (1944); Your Health Club, Inc., 4 T.C. 385 (1944), acq., 1945 C.B. 7; Curtis R. Andrews, 23 T.C. 1026 (1955). But see I.T. 3369, 1940–1 C.B. 46, and Beacon Publishing Co. v. Comm'r, 218 F.2d 697 (10th Cir. 1955).

4. See note following *Schuessler* case, page 559, infra, this chapter.

5. See H.Rep.No.293, 84th Cong. 1st Sess. (1955), 1955–2 C.B. 852, 853.

6. P.L. 74, 84th Cong. 1st Sess. (1955).

7. 353 U.S. 180, 77 S.Ct. 707 (1957).

8. 367 U.S. 687, 81 S.Ct. 1727 (1961).

9. 372 U.S. 128, 83 S.Ct. 601 (1963).

10. Lower court decisions to the same effect include, e. g., Services: Popular Library, Inc., 39 T.C. 1092 (1963); W. O. McMahon, Inc., 45 T.C. 221 (1965); Decision, Inc., 47 T.C. 58 (1966); Prichard Funeral Home, 25 T.C.M. 1434 (1966); Wide Acres Rest Home, Inc., 26 T.C.M. 391 (1967); Travis v. Comm'r, 406 F.2d 987 (6th Cir. 1969). Goods: Fifth & York Co. v. U. S., 234 F.Supp. 421 (W.D.Ky. 1964); Chester Farrara, 44 T.C. 189 (1965); Modernaire Interiors, Inc., 27 T.C.M. 1334 (1968); Hagen Advertising Displays, Inc. v. Comm'r, 407 F.2d 1105 (6th Cir. 1969); S. Garber, Inc., 51 T.C. 733 (1969). But see Veenstra and De Haan Coal Co., 11 T.C. 964 (1948), holding that the prepayment was a mere deposit.

mediate inclusion rule were made in the case of income from newspaper, magazine, and periodical subscriptions under I.R.C. § 455 and prepaid club dues under I.R.C. § 456.

It seems certain that *Artnell* has already had an impact on tax accounting principles and that it will play a role in subsequent developments. For one thing, the Government did not petition for certiorari in *Artnell*. Moreover, since the decision the promulgation of a Revenue Procedure concerning prepayment for services and a change in the accounting regulations relating to prepayment for goods reflect a kind of hesitant and creeping move toward the adoption of business accounting principles. In Rev.Proc. 70–21 [11] the Commissioner announced a new policy with respect to prepaid services.[12] The Procedure provides that, if there is a prepayment to an accrual method taxpayer for services to be rendered in the current and a succeeding year, income is required to be included in the current year only to the extent that services are rendered in that year and the remaining income need not be reported until the subsequent year. However, the ruling is restrictive in that no postponement is allowed if the prepayment is for services to be rendered beyond the end of the succeeding year or at an unspecified future date.[13] If the services were to have been rendered by the end of the succeeding year but they are not rendered by that time, any prepayment not previously reported is treated as gross income for the succeeding year. The Procedure is expressly inapplicable to prepaid interest or rent.[14]

Going back to *Artnell*, the continued immediate inclusion rule for interest and rent seems curious. The key question in *Artnell* was properly identified as whether the taxpayer's accounting method clearly reflects income.[15] Prepaid interest and rent are precisely allocable among accounting periods on the basis of elapsed time and thus are seemingly likely prospects for deferred reporting. Consider the new statutory amortization rule for the deduction of prepaid interest, I.R.C. § 461(g). On the other hand, what dollar amounts might be involved? And what impact on the revenue would result if the treatment generally allowed under Rev.Proc. 70–21 were applied to interest and rents?

The reasoning in *Artnell* likewise raises a question about the two-year rule of Rev.Proc. 70–21. If two-year spreading by way of deferral is within the statutes, why is three-year (or more) deferral

---

11. 1970–2 C.B. 501 (1970).

12. Rev.Proc. 71–21, 1971–2 C.B. 549, superseded Rev.Proc. 70–21, providing essentially the same rules.

13. The two-year limitation does not apply to prepayments for bus and streetcar tokens and photographic services.

14. For this purpose "rent" does not include payment for the use of property where significant services are rendered as in the case of hotels, boarding houses, and motels.

15. I.R.C. (26 U.S.C.A.) § 446(b).

not? One wonders whether restrictions in Rev.Proc. 70–21 may not
rest more on concern for the revenue than on any nice legal distinctions and, if so, whether the restrictions can stand if the basic break-
through in *Artnell* is accepted. One wonders further whether changes
of this type, even if highly desirable, cannot be better engineered to
accommodate all interests by Congress, rather than the administration
and the courts.[16]

A companion development to Rev.Proc. 70–21 is an amendment to
the accounting regulations which relates to prepayments for goods.[17]
Under the new provision a taxpayer may defer amounts received
as prepayment for goods sold in the ordinary course of his trade or
business until the year in which the payments are ordinarily ac-
cruable under the taxpayer's regular method of accounting.[18] There
is a complex two-year limitation, like that in Rev.Proc. 70–21, with
respect to prepayments for goods that the taxpayer has in inventory
or which are readily available through normal sources of supply.[19]

If services are to be performed in conjunction with the sale of
goods, the regulations still apply if the performance of the services
is an integral part of the sale.[20] If the amount allocable to payment
for services is less than 5% of the total price, the services obligation
will automatically be considered an integral part of the sale of the
goods.[21]

INVENTORIES

Whenever tax computations require the use of inventories, the
accrual method of accounting must be used, at least with regard to

16. Rev.Proc. 70–21 is discussed in Bat-
tle, "Advance Payments for Services:
Limited Deferral Permitted" 57 A.B.A.
J. 182 (1971). Prepayments for both
services and goods are discussed in
Sobeloff, "New Prepaid Income Rule:
IRS Reversal of Position will Aid
Many Taxpayers," 33 J.Tax. 194
(1970).

17. See Reg. § 1.451–5, proposed
August 7, 1970, and adopted March 3,
1971. The basic tax accounting problems in this area are interestingly discussed in Pacific Grape Products Co.
v. Comm'r, 219 F.2d 862 (9th Cir.
1955); and see Poole, "The Taxation
of Prepaid Sales of Goods," 24 Tax L.
Rev. 375 (1969), which also preceded
the amendment of the Regulations.

18. Regs. § 1.451–5(a)(1) and –5(b)(2).

See Rev.Rul. 72–208, 1972–1 C.B. 129.

19. Regs. § 1.451–5(c). The exception
seems another part of the Treasury's

reluctance to go too far too fast, perhaps again with the revenue in mind.
As a practical matter, however, if the
goods sold for future delivery are in
inventory, there may be a basis for
recognizing the cost of goods sold pri-
or to their later delivery, which over-
comes a problem involving the treatment of gross receipts as gross income
where goods sold for future delivery
are not in any way identifiable. See
Veenstra and De Haan Coal Co., supra note 10, at 967.

20. Regs. § 1.451–5(a) (2).

21. Reg. § 1.451–5(a) (3). Application
of the regulations is illustrated at Reg.
§ 1.451–5(c) (4). The history of tax
problems in the sale of goods and an
analysis of the new regulations is presented in Brody, "Advance Payment
for Sales of Goods: New Regulations
Permit Deferral" 57 A.B.A.J. 707
(1971).

purchases and sales.[1] When must inventories be used? Whenever "production, purchase, or sale of merchandise is an income-producing factor." [2] Consequently, inventory accounting plays a very large role in the federal income tax. It is required of the butcher, the baker, and the candlestick maker, but not of the attorney or the accountant.

The political science major who is frightened to death by mere mention of the term "inventory" can learn a comforting lot by a study of Amory and Hardee (Herwitz and Trautman revision), Materials on Accounting, c. 1, pp. 33–36, and c. 4, pp. 170–212 (Foundation Press, 1959).[3] The accounting profession worries a great deal about proper treatment of inventories in its effort to develop generally accepted accounting principles.[4] We eschew all the details that titillate accountants and attempt here only a very basic explanation of inventories and their general relationship to the determination of gross income and to the accounting period in which gross income must be reported, the subject of this chapter.

We already know that the general formula for determining gross income from the sale of property can be expressed as:

	Amount realized
Less	Adjusted basis
Equals	Realized gain

The parallel expression of this concept where property is sold in the course of a business, such as a haberdashery, is:

	Gross sales
Less	Cost of goods sold
Equals	Gross profit from sales

Gross sales is obviously a fairly automatic figure, but how does a merchant (or a manufacturer) determine the cost of the goods that he has sold during an accounting period? It is here that inventories play their principal role. It is usually impracticable for a merchant separately to determine his gain or loss on each sale.[5] A device is needed that will produce the correct overall result by way of a kind of aggregate approach.

To overcome the problem suggested, the figure used for cost of goods sold is determined by (1) ascertaining the cost of goods on hand at the start of the accounting period, which is called "opening inventory;" (2) adding to that the cost of goods acquired during the

---

1. Reg. § 1.446–1(c) (2).

2. Reg. § 1.471–1.

3. See also Fiflis and Kripke, Accounting for Business Lawyers, c. 1, pp. 43–54, and c. VI, pp. 234–278 (West 1971).

4. E. g., Accounting Research Bulletin No. 43, c. 4 "Inventory Pricing," set out in Amory and Hardee, supra, App. A, at 480–484.

5. The used car dealer and others who make relatively few sales of large items are exceptions.

accounting period, referred to in an abbreviated way as "purchases;" and (3) subtracting from that sum the cost of the goods still on hand at the end of the accounting period, "closing inventory." Thus:

	Opening inventory
Plus	Purchases
Less	Closing inventory
Equals	Cost of goods sold

Some assurance that in the long run all gain or loss will be taken into account is achieved by the fact that the figure to be used as opening inventory for a particular period is the figure that was used for closing inventory for the preceding period. Play with the formula enough to see that, if an improperly low figure were used for closing inventory in 1972, it would tend to show a higher cost of goods sold and lower profit for that year; but in 1973 the improperly low opening inventory figure (which is closing inventory for 1972) would result in a lower cost of goods sold and higher profit for 1973. This is not intended to suggest that the taxpayer has the option to juggle these figures.[6]

In this inventory approach the most uncertain figure is closing inventory. "Opening inventory" is somewhat automatic, simply being carried over as closing inventory of the last year.[7] "Purchases" is likewise somewhat automatic.[8] But closing inventory involves both a determination of the quantity of goods (or each item of goods) on hand [9] and then properly "pricing" it.

The quantity of goods on hand at the end of an accounting period can be determined by observation—"taking inventory." [10] However, the quantitative figure must be converted to a dollar figure, representing the *cost* of what is on hand.[11] In a hardware store the brass

---

6. There are legitimate juggling opportunities which can be achieved, e. g., by selling down (i. e., not replacing) high cost Lifo inventories; but this is rare.

7. But see footnote comments below on uncertainties regarding what is included in closing inventory.

8. A significant problem arises here as to when a purchase is taken into account; for example, does purchases include an item merely ordered or in transit to the taxpayer, or must it be received prior to the end of the accounting period? Must it be paid for? Note the parallel problems on sales and closing inventory.

9. As in the case of purchases, question arises here whether goods should be treated as no longer on hand if ordered or en route to the buyer or only

if delivered or paid for. There is some flexibility, but the answer must be meshed with the approach taken to the question when a sale is included in gross sales. A moment's reflection should indicate that distortion would result if goods considered to have passed out of closing inventory were not treated as sold for purposes of determining gross sales.

10. The student should not envisage the calendar year haberdasher having to forego New Year's Eve revels to take inventory. The job is accomplished at another time with suitable adjustment to achieve the year-end objective, or these days it may even be achieved electronically.

11. A conservative business accounting maxim of never over-stating income has generated a "cost or market" variation here, under which inventory is

screws in a box may have been purchased at several different times, some recently and some a year or more ago. What was their price when purchased? Nobody knows, but conventions answer the question. If it is assumed that the earliest purchased screws were the one's first sold (the "first in-first out" convention), then those on hand are treated as the most recently purchased and are "priced" for inventory purposes in accordance with this assumption. That is, if the last ten gross of screws acquired cost $14.40 and there are 1440 screws on hand, then each screw is included in closing inventory at one cent. If there are 1500 on hand, 60 of them are priced in accordance with the cost of the next-to-last batch of screws acquired, and so forth.[12]

A less common alternative pricing convention is the "last in-first out" approach. These conventions are commonly referred to as "Lifo" or "Fifo." Work out for yourself the basic consequences of inventory pricing under the Lifo convention.

A businessman may wish to show high earnings to creditors and shareholders but low earnings to employees and the Commissioner of Internal Revenue. He can't of course do both, and *consistency* is a key requirement in accounting matters.[13] Nevertheless, the gross profit on sales for any given year is affected by the pricing convention adopted. Try this: Assume a merchandising business makes substantial purchases of goods annually but maintains a fairly steady stock of goods, quantitatively. If over a period of time prices are rising, will the business report more income for a particular period under the Fifo approach or under the Lifo approach?

It will now be seen that inventories play a timing role as well as a measuring role for gross income. If the inventory pricing method followed tends to show a low *closing* inventory for the prior year, and the effect of the low figure is a greater cost of goods sold and a correspondingly lower profit on sales for that year, the effect is also to shift reportable income to a future year. That is because the lower *opening* inventory for the next year will result in a lower cost of goods sold and a correspondingly higher profit on sales in a subsequent period. In effect, given required consistency, the whole scheme operates within a kind of closed circle, and advantage now is bought only at the cost of disadvantage later, or vice versa.

Students should share the authors' recognition that even a thoughtful reading of the foregoing comments leaves them relatively

---

priced at market, if that is less than cost, and this variation is permitted for tax accounting. See Reg. § 1.471–2 and –4.

12. Note that inventory pricing is vastly more complicated in the case of a manufacturing rather than a mere merchandising business. This gets into the area of "cost accounting" in which there must be added to materials costs both labor and other direct and indirect expenses, as regards finished products and so-called "work in progress" as well.

13. See Reg. § 1.471–2(b). It should be noted that differences in business and tax accounting often do require the keeping of two sets of books.

uninformed about the intricacies of inventory accounting. Nevertheless, it may prepare them for further study as and if required or at least facilitate dialogue with members of the accounting profession.

2.   DEDUCTION ITEMS

Internal Revenue Code: Sections 267(a)(2); 461(a) and (f).
Regulations: Section 1.461–1(a)(2).

REVENUE RULING 57–463

1957–2 Cum.Bull. 303.

Advice has been requested concerning the period in which interest is deductible by a taxpayer using the accrual method of accounting where, after consenting to an assessment for income taxes, penalties, and interest, the taxpayer, in a subsequent year, entered into a compromise agreement providing for deferred installment payments of the amount assessed plus additional interest on the deferred payments.

Section 461 of the Internal Revenue Code of 1954 provides the general rule that the amount of any deduction or credit allowed by Subtitle A shall be taken for the taxable year which is the proper taxable year under the method of accounting used in computing taxable income. A taxpayer keeping his accounts and filing his returns on the accrual method of accounting is entitled to deduct interest in the taxable year in which liability accrues. I.T. 3740, C.B.1945, 109. Interest on a deficiency in tax should be accrued in the year in which the liability for the deficiency is finally determined. G.C.M. 9575, C.B. X–1, 381 (1931).

In the instant case, the taxpayer's liability for the deficiencies became determined at the time the taxpayer consented to the assessment, and a deduction for interest to that date may be allowed for that taxable year. The compromise agreement merely fixed the rate of payment of the assessed amounts. Interest accruing on the deferred payments may be allowed as a deduction ratably as the taxpayer's liability for such interest accrues.

SCHUESSLER v. COMMISSIONER

United States Court of Appeals, Fifth Circuit, 1956.
230 F.2d 722.

TUTTLE, CIRCUIT JUDGE.   This is a petition for review of a decision by the Tax Court disallowing a deduction in 1946 of an item of $13,300.00, representing a reserve set up by taxpayers while keeping their books on the accrual basis, to represent their estimated cost of carrying out a guarantee, given with each of the furnaces sold by them during the year, to turn the furnace on and off each year for five years.

The opinion of the Tax Court treats the matter as though ample proof was offered by the taxpayer (hereafter the husband will be called "taxpayer") to raise the legal issue and we find the record warrants this treatment. Taxpayer was in the gas furnace business in 1946, during which he sold 665 furnaces, each with a guarantee that he would turn the furnace on and off each year for five years. The fact that such service, if performed, would cost $2.00 per call was amply established. The taxpayer, himself a bookkeeper and accountant prior to entering this business, testified to his keeping his books on the accrual method and claimed that the only way his income could be accurately reported was by charging against the cost of furnaces sold in 1946 the reserve representing the amount which he became legally liable to expend in subsequent years in connection with the sales. The proof was clear that he actually sold the furnaces for $20.00 to $25.00 more than his competitors because of his guarantee, which they did not give.

We think it quite clear that petitioner's method of accounting comes much closer to giving a correct picture of his income than would a system in which he sold equipment in one year and received an inflated price because he obligated himself, in effect, to refund part of it in services later but was required to report the total receipts as income on the high level of the sales year and take deductions on the low level of the service years. The reasonableness of taxpayer's action, however, is not the test if it runs counter to requirements of the statute.

We find that not only does it not offend any statutory requirement, but, in fact, we think it is in accord with the language and intent of the law.[1] Clearly what is sought by this statute is an accounting method that most accurately reflects the taxpayer's income on an annual accounting basis.[2]

The decisions of the Tax Court and of the several Courts of Appeals are not uniform on this subject, some circuits requiring a mathematical certainty as to the exact amount of the future expenditures that cannot be satisfied in the usual case. Other circuits, seemingly more concerned with the underlying principle of charging to each year's income reasonably ascertainable future expenses necessary to earn or retain the income, have permitted the accrual of restricted items of future expenses. Two of this latter category are Harrold v. Commissioner[3] and Pacific Grape Products Co. v. Commissioner.[4]

---

1. [I.R.C. §§ 41 and 43 (1939), and Reg. 111 § 29.41–1 are omitted. Ed.]

2. This principle was early recognized in United States v. Anderson, 269 U.S. 422, 46 S.Ct. 131, 70 L.Ed. 347.

3. 4 Cir., 192 F.2d 1002.

4. 9 Cir., 219 F.2d 862, 869.

In the Harrold case the taxpayer was permitted to deduct from its gross income in 1945 the estimated cost of back filling a tract of land which would be done under state law requirements in the year 1946. The Court there said:

" * * * when all the facts have occurred which determine that the taxpayer has incurred a liability in the tax year, and neither the fact nor the amount of the liability is contested, and the amount, although not definitely ascertained, is susceptible of estimate with reasonable accuracy in the tax year, deduction thereof from income may be taken by a taxpayer on an accrual basis." Harrold v. Commissioner, 4 Cir., 192 F.2d 1002, 1006.

The Pacific Grape Products case is also, it seems to us, indistinguishable in principle from the case before us. There the taxpayer accrued the sales price of canned goods sold on December 31, and at the same time deducted the estimated cost of labeling and preparing the goods for shipping and brokerage fees to be paid the following year. The Tax Court, with six judges dissenting, accepted the Commissioner's view that the deductions should be disallowed. 17 T.C. 1097. The Court of Appeals reversed, saying:

"Not only do we have here a system of accounting which for years has been adopted and carried into effect by substantially all members of a large industry, but the system is one which appeals to us as so much in line with plain common sense that we are at a loss to understand what could have prompted the Commissioner to disapprove it. Contrary to his suggestion that petitioner's method did not reflect its true income it seems to us that the alterations demanded by the Commissioner would wholly distort that income."

The case of Beacon Publishing Co. v. Commissioner [5] is considered by both parties here and was noted by the Tax Court as of especial significance. That case involved the treatment of prepaid income received by the Beacon Publishing Co. covering subscriptions to be furnished in subsequent years. The Tax Court in its decision here said:

" * * * This is essentially the same problem as the reporting of prepaid income in the year in which received for services to be performed in following years. The petitioner in fact, on brief, recognizes that the two problems are identical and cites Beacon Publishing Co. v. Commissioner, 10 Cir., 1955, 218 F.2d 697, in support of his argument that the reserve here in issue was a proper deduction in computing his income in 1946."

The Tax Court then simply declined to follow the Court in the Beacon case, preferring to adhere to its own views as expressed in Curtis A. Andrews v. Commissioner, 23 T.C. 1026. We prefer the reasoning as well as the conclusion reached by the Court in the Tenth Circuit. There the opinion correctly, we think, disposed of the "claim

5.   10 Cir., 218 F.2d 697.

of right" theory advanced by the Commissioner and adopted by the Tax Court in this type of case.[6]

Finally we think the enactment in 1954 of Section 462 of the Internal Revenue Code of 1954 [7] and its subsequent repeal constitute no legislative history bearing on the construction of the provisions of the Internal Revenue Code of 1939.[8]

The record below amply supports the contention of the taxpayer that there was a legal liability created in 1946, when the purchase price was paid for the gas furnaces, for the taxpayer to turn the furnaces on and off for the succeeding five years; that the cost of such service as reasonably established at a minimum of $2.00 per visit; and that the payment of $20.00 to $25.00 extra by the purchasers fully proved their intention to call upon the taxpayer each year for the service. These facts authorized the setting up of a reserve out of the 1946 income to enable the taxpayer to meet these established charges in future years. The decision of the Tax Court is therefore in error and must be reversed.

Reversed with directions to enter judgment for the taxpayer.

RESERVE ACCOUNTING

There is more than one way to skin a cat. If an accounting objective is to match revenue with costs related to its production, one way to achieve it is the deferred income approach suggested by *Artnell* and grudging administrative changes reflected in the new rulings and regulation amendments previously considered. But it should be obvious that much the same thing can be accomplished by the immediate recognition of an item as income (even though something remains to be done to earn it), if anticipated future costs are taken into account at the same time, even if not actually incurred or paid until a later period, a concept known as reserve accounting. Of course, while these alternative matching possibilities may help to meet a fundamental objective, they do not answer the question for what period the net income resulting from the matching should be taken into account. (Do we push income forward or pull expenses back?) Nevertheless, if immediate reporting of revenue is the usual rule for tax purposes, it would be comforting to think that anticipated future costs could be pulled back into the early period, the result permitted in *Schuessler* and generally in keeping with accepted business accounting principles.

---

6. See Beacon Publishing Co. v. Commissioner, 218 F.2d 697, 699.

7. 26 U.S.C.A. § 462.

8. For an interesting discussion of the history of this legislation see Sen. Rep. No. 372, 84 Cong., 1st Sess., 1955 U.S.Code Congressional and Administrative News, p. 2046–2051. See also Sporrer, The Past and Future of Deferring Income and Reserving for Expenses, TAXES (Mag.) January 1956, 45.

Despite *Schuessler,* the federal income tax law has been just as slow to allow reserve accounting as it has to permit the deferral of income. Prior to the enactment of the 1954 Code there were other cases in which the costs of future services and goods were reasonably ascertainable and reserves were allowed.[1] Moreover, the Code has long permitted reserve accounting for business bad debts.[2] However, these exceptions merely tend to prove the rule against general reserve accounting. Perhaps on less compelling facts than those in *Schuessler,* decisions disallowing reserves have been reached in numerous cases.[3]

Whether or not regrettable, the divergence of business and tax accounting principles on reserves is somewhat understandable. Conservative business reporting, seeking not to overstate income for a period, seems to require anticipation of future costs. For tax purposes, the government is much less concerned that income may be overstated. If for business purposes one is pessimistic as to future costs he is only presenting a careful indication of his profitability. But for tax purposes, such pessimism carries with it an avoidance of current tax liability. Indeed, it is arguable that if one presently has the economic use of revenue undiminished by later charges that may arise, that full sum is a good measure of his income for tax purposes, even though he may later incur costs relating to it.[4] In any event, the case of Simplified Tax Records, Inc., which is reproduced following this note, is more representative of the tax approach to reserve accounting than *Schuessler* which appears above.[5] Notice how, in a manner analogous to the time-of-earning issue in *Artnell,* the certainty of the future expense has been a factor in limited judicial sanction of reserve accounting.

Again, an episode that occurred in connection with the enactment of the 1954 Code has been an obstacle to developments toward the adoption of business accounting principles for tax accounting. At the same time Congress undertook to provide for deferred reporting

1. E. g., Harrold v. Comm'r, 192 F.2d 1002 (4th Cir. 1951); Pacific Grape Products Co. v. Comm'r, 219 F.2d 862 (9th Cir. 1955).

2. I.R.C. (26 U.S.C.A.) § 166(c); Reg. § 1.166–4; and see § 166(g). The deduction for bad debts is considered in Chapter 23, infra at page 767.

3. E. g., *Services*: Frederick J. Villafranca, 24 T.C.M. 76 (1965); aff'd per curiam, 359 F.2d 849 (6th Cir. 1966), cert. den., 385 U.S. 840, 87 S.Ct. 91 (1966); Bell Electric Co., 45 T.C. 158 (1965); and *Goods*: Hamilton Memorial Gardens, Inc. v. Comm'r, 394 F.2d 905 (6th Cir. 1968), cert. den., 393 U.S. 936, 89 S.Ct. 298 (1968); S.

Garber, Inc., 51 T.C. 733 (1969). But see Hagen Advertising Displays, Inc. v. Comm'r, 407 F.2d 1105 (6th Cir. 1969), in which the court implies that it would have allowed a reserve for cost of goods sold if the taxpayer had made a showing of such costs. See Llewellyn, "Prepaid Income: Can a Deduction be taken for Reserve for Related Expenses". 30 J. Tax 330 (1969).

4. In this respect, consider the philosophy in the opinion in James v. U. S., 366 U.S. 213, 81 S.Ct. 1052 (1961), which caused the court to overrule its prior decision in Comm'r v. Wilcox, 327 U.S. 404, 66 S.Ct. 546 (1946).

5. See also, e. g., World Airways, Inc., 62 T.C. 786 (1974).

of income under I.R.C. (26 U.S.C.A.) § 452, provision was made for general reserve accounting under § 462. Both these sections were repealed retroactively when heavy, temporary revenue losses threatened.[6] Although the enactment and repeal of I.R.C. (26 U.S.C.A.) §§ 452 and 462 are not a complete obstacle to the development of common law tax principles on deferral and reserve accounting,[7] the events are in the nature of a negative expression of congressional policy which no doubt has had some bearing on administrative and judicial action. And it is a question whether the *Artnell* chink in the immediate-reporting armor will be followed by significant incursion into similarly fixed tax principles against reserve accounting, at least until Congress acts again.

The strong judicial position against the use of reserves is somewhat alleviated by the Commissioner's recent change in policy, after *Artnell*, to allow a partial deferral of income for prepaid services and goods. In instances in which income may be deferred, the deferral will provide a clearer annual net income picture more in accord with business accounting principles. In those situations reserve accounting is less likely to be needed. But with respect to situations in which the Commissioner's new policies are inapplicable, the need for leniency in establishing reserves remains, if a clear annual net income picture is to be presented.

SIMPLIFIED TAX RECORDS, INC.

Tax Court of the United States, 1963.
41 T.C. 75.

DRENNEN, JUDGE: Respondent determined deficiencies in petitioner's income tax for the taxable years 1954 and 1956 in the respective amounts of $6,843.39 and $30,040.24.

The only issue for decision is whether petitioner is entitled to accrue and deduct, as of the end of its fiscal years ended September 30, 1954, and September 30, 1956, additions to a reserve for estimated future expenses to be incurred in preparing tax returns for petitioner's subscribers.

Findings of Fact

Some of the facts have been stipulated and are so found.

Petitioner is a corporation organized in 1937 under the laws of New York. Its principal office during the period in controversy was located in New York, N. Y. Petitioner maintained its books on the accrual method of accounting using a fiscal year ending September 30. It filed timely Federal corporation income tax returns for the tax-

---

6. P.L. 74, 84th Cong. 1st Sess. (1955).   **7.** See H.Rep.No.293, 84th Cong. 1st Sess. (1955), 1955–2 C.B. 852, 855.

able years ended September 30, 1954, and September 30, 1956, with the district director of internal revenue for the Lower Manhattan district of New York.

During the period here involved petitioner was engaged in the business of selling an accounting service designed for small businesses. The service consisted of an accounting system, which included single entry books, bookkeeping forms, and supplemental records, together with an agreement that petitioner would prepare the income tax returns of the subscriber for 2 years. The service was sold to small businesses throughout the country through regional distributors at a cost of $79.50 covering a 2-year period.

Petitioner prepared returns for its subscribers only upon the request of subscribers. In order to have its returns prepared, a subscriber was required to submit a completed "Income Tax Information Sheet" no later than February 1 of the year in which its returns were to be prepared. Petitioner was not obligated to prepare a subscriber's returns unless this information sheet was received.

The years for which petitioner agreed to prepare a subscriber's income tax returns were not specified in the subscription agreement. All subscribers did not request petitioner to prepare their returns during the years of the subscription and sometimes a subscriber would request petitioner to prepare its returns after its 2-year subscription period had expired. If such a subscriber had not availed itself of petitioner's services during the 2-year period of its subscription, petitioner would usually prepare its returns although the subscription period had expired.

From 1943 through early 1956 petitioner contracted with a public accounting firm for the latter to prepare subscribers' income tax returns on a fixed-fee-per-return basis. The amount of this fee was agreed upon from year to year. During a filing period a representative of the accounting firm would go to petitioner's office and pick up any information sheets which had been sent in by subscribers. Based on the information contained on the information sheets the firm prepared subscribers' returns in pencil and delivered the penciled copies to petitioner. Petitioner typed the returns in final form and mailed them from its office. Petitioner hired typists and clerical help for this purpose during a filing period.

During its taxable year 1954 petitioner paid the accounting firm $2.10 for each Federal return and $1 for each State return prepared by the firm in penciled form. At the end of each week the accounting firm presented a bill to petitioner for the returns prepared during that week and received a check in payment. The accounting firm never received payments for preparing returns in advance of preparation and submission of a bill to petitioner, and had not billed petitioner by September 30, 1954, for any returns which they might prepare subsequent to that date. Petitioner's contract with the accountants did not call for any specified number of returns. On its income tax return for fiscal 1954, and for years prior thereto, petitioner deducted as a portion of its cost of goods sold the actual cost incurred during that year for the preparation of subscribers' income tax returns, including payments to the accounting firm and salaries for typing, clerical, and mailing employees.

The accounting firm which prepared the subscribers' returns for petitioner was retained by petitioner in 1954 to audit its books and prepare its own tax returns. As of September 30, 1954, the accountants set up on petitioner's books a reserve in the amount of $26,981.33, representing the estimated cost of preparing subscribers' income tax returns during its taxable year 1955. Petitioner reported this amount on its return for its fiscal year 1954 as a portion of its cost of goods sold for that year.

The amount of $26,981.33 added to petitioner's reserve as of the end of its fiscal year 1954 was arrived at by the accounting firm retained by petitioner by the following method: The number of systems sold in each of the taxable years 1950, 1951, 1952, and 1953 were determined, together with the total number of tax returns prepared in those years; the average number of sales of systems and the average number of returns prepared were calculated. The percentage of tax returns prepared to the number of systems sold was computed by dividing the average number of returns prepared by the average number of systems sold. The percentage was found to be 68.9 percent for Federal returns and 35.3 percent for State returns. It was found that 8,348 systems had been sold in the taxable year 1954, and the accounting firm estimated that 68.9 percent of the sales figure, or 5,779, would be the number of Federal income tax returns to be prepared in 1955 and that 35.3 percent of the sales figure, or 2,947, would be the number of State income tax returns to be prepared in 1955. The accounting firm multiplied the resulting figure by $2.10 to get its estimated charge to petitioner for preparing Federal returns during 1955 and multiplied the number of estimated State income tax returns by $1 to arrive at the estimated cost of its preparation of State returns. The total estimated cost for preparing returns in 1955 was $15,377.-60.[1] The accounting firm then computed the extra clerical payroll for the filing periods for the 4 previous years and arrived at an average figure for this payroll. This average payroll expense, in the amount of $11,603.73, was added to the estimated charges for preparation of the returns, and the resulting total was $26,981.33, which was the amount added to the reserve for the estimated expenses of preparing returns in 1955. The accounting firm actually prepared 6,314 Federal returns and 3,002 State returns during the 1955 tax-reporting season.

---

1. This figure is accurate. The number of returns estimated was taken from oral testimony which was apparently not entirely accurate.

Prior to the preparation of petitioner's 1954 returns, no reserve for this purpose had ever been established on its books. Petitioner reported all the income from sales of the systems in the years such sales were made. No request was ever made to the Commissioner of Internal Revenue for petitioner to change its method of accounting, nor was the Commissioner's consent to a change ever received by petitioner.

In 1956 petitioner retained another accounting firm and decided to prepare returns for its subscribers itself under a mass production system devised by these accountants. At September 30, 1955, the reserve for the expenses of preparing subscribers' income tax returns was $22,229.98.[2] In arriving at the amount to be added to the reserve as of the end of petitioner's taxable year 1956, petitioner's accountant estimated the clerical costs (including extra payroll, typewriter rental, and supplies) involved in preparing, typing, and mailing the returns which petitioner would have to prepare for its subscribers in the year 1957. Based upon the number of returns prepared in the year 1956 and the fact that petitioner's sales were holding up, the accountant estimated that 8,700 returns, Federal and State, would be prepared in 1957. The estimated cost of preparing 8,700 returns was approximately $40,000 and the accountant decided that since petitioner's obligation to prepare returns extended over a 2-year period, the reserve for the expenses of the future preparation of returns should be $80,000 as of the end of the taxable year 1956. Because the amount of $22,229.98 was then reflected in the reserve, petitioner added to the reserve as of September 30, 1956, the amount of $57,770.02, and this amount was deducted as a part of its cost of goods sold on its return for fiscal 1956.

During the 1957 tax season petitioner actually prepared about 11,000 returns. The actual cost of preparing subscribers' returns in 1957 was about $115,000, which included extra accounting fees as a result of a breakdown in the internal operation of the mass production system.

In the statutory notice of deficiency issued herein respondent has disallowed as a deduction in arriving at taxable income for the years 1954 and 1956 the respective amounts of $26,981.33 and $57,770.02, with the explanation that "deductions for estimated expenses claimed as part of the cost of goods sold in your returns for the taxable years * * * 1954 and * * * 1956, are not allowable under any provision of the Internal Revenue Code of 1939 with respect to your taxable year * * * 1954 or under any provision of the Internal Revenue Code of 1954 with respect to the taxable year * * * 1956."

---

2. Fiscal year 1955 is not before us. The actual expenses of preparing returns for 1955 charged against the reserve were apparently greater than the amounts credited to it.

Petitioner stated at the trial that should a deduction be allowed for the addition to its reserve in 1954, then the amount deducted on its return for that year for expenses actually incurred and paid for preparation of 1953 returns should be disallowed.

Opinion

The principal issue is whether respondent erred in disallowing a deduction for estimated future expenses of preparing subscribers' income tax returns which petitioner had claimed as a part of its cost of goods sold on its income tax returns for 1954 and 1956.

This is another of the plethora of cases coming before the courts in recent years involving the deferral of income or the accrual of expenses to cover the estimated cost of rendering services in the future. We think the issue here is controlled by the recent decisions of the Supreme Court in Schlude v. Commissioner, 372 U.S. 128 (1963), American Automobile Assn. v. United States, 367 U.S. 687 (1961), and Commissioner v. Milwaukee & Suburban Transport Corp., 367 U.S. 906 (1961), which require a decision against the taxpayer herein. While it is true that the *Schlude* and *American Automobile* cases were concerned with the deferral of income rather than the deduction of estimated future expenses, the Court remanded the *Milwaukee & Suburban Transport* case, which did involve the deductibility of estimated expenses, "in the light" of the *American Automobile* case, and on remand the Court of Appeals for the Seventh Circuit vacated its prior decision permitting the deduction of anticipated damage claims and reinstated the decision of this Court denying such deduction on the authority of the *American Automobile* case. See Milwaukee & Suburban Transport Corporation v. Commissioner, 293 F.2d 628 (C.A.7, 1961). While it can be argued that there are technical distinctions in deferring prepaid income and deducting estimated future expenses in cases like this the net result is the same and we think the same principles of tax accounting and the Commissioner's authority should be applied to both techniques.[3] As said in American Automobile Assn. v. United States, supra, the prepaid dues were credited to a reserve "as deferred or unearned income reflecting an estimated future service expense to members."

In Automobile Club of Michigan v. Commissioner, 353 U.S. 180 (1957), the Supreme Court held that the taxpayer could not defer its membership dues ratably over the year for which they were paid because the pro rata allocation of dues in monthly amounts was "purely artificial" and bore no relationship to the services which the taxpayer in fact might be called on to render its members, and therefore the Commissioner had not abused his discretion in determining that taxpayer's system of accounting did not clearly reflect its in-

---

3. Compare secs. 451(a) and 461(a), and see sec. 446, I.R.C. 1954.

come. In American Automobile Assn. v. United States, supra, under similar facts but with evidence that the pro rata deferral of income did correspond substantially with the cost and time of rendering services to its members, the Court said that, although it was admitted that the method used by taxpayer was in accord with generally accepted commercial and accounting principles, it failed to "respect the criteria of annual tax accounting and may be rejected by the Commissioner." The Court emphasized that the services were rendered solely upon a member's demand. It also discussed at length the enactment and repeal of sections 452 [4] and 462 [5] of the 1954 Code, which specifically permitted deferral of income and accrual of estimated future expenses, and the implications thereof, and concluded by saying, "Finding only that, in light of existing provisions not specifically authorizing it, the exercise of the Commissioner's discretion in rejecting the Association's accounting system was not unsound."

In its most recent decision in Schlude v. Commissioner, supra, the Court framed the question for decision as being, "Was it proper for the Commissioner, exercising his discretion under § 41, 1939 Code, and § 446(b), 1954 Code, to reject the studio's accounting system as not clearly reflecting income and to include as income in a particular year advance payments." The Court found the issue to be squarely controlled by American Automobile Assn. v. United States, supra, and answered the question in the affirmative. Again the Court discussed the implications of the repeal of section 452 of the 1954 Code, and the recent enactment of section 456, 1954 Code, and also emphasized that the taxpayer's system of accounting was artificial since the advance payments related to services which were to be performed only upon customers' demands without relation to fixed dates in the future.

Whether these more recent decisions of the Supreme Court will lay these problems to rest is problematical because the Court speaks in broad terms and it is not always clear just what the fundamental bases for the decisions are—hence other cases may be distinguished. See Automobile Club of New York v. Commissioner, 304 F.2d 781 (1962), affirming 32 T.C. 906 (1959), wherein the Court of Appeals for the Second Circuit, while relying on American Automobile Assn. v. United States, supra, to hold against the taxpayer, distinguished its own prior decision in favor of the taxpayer in Bressner Radio, Inc. v. Commissioner, 267 F.2d 520 (1959), reversing and remanding 28 T.C. 378 (1957).[6]

---

4. and 5. [I.R.C. §§ 452 and 462, both retroactively repealed in 1955, as indicated in the preceding textual note, have been omitted. Ed.]

6. We suspect, because of its repeated emphasis on the Commissioner's discretion under sec. 41 of the 1939 Code and sec. 446 of the 1954 Code, and the legislative history of secs. 452 and 462, that the majority of the Supreme Court stand for the principle that, absent statutory sanction for it, unless the taxpayer can show that the Commissioner clearly abused his discretion in disallowing deferral of prepaid income or accrual of estimated future expenses, this exercise of the Commissioner's discretion will not be disturbed by the Court even though the

But in any event we think these recent decisions of the Supreme Court are clearly dispositive of the issue in this case on narrower and more specific grounds.   Here the petitioner changed its long-established treatment of these expenses in 1954; the services which would give rise to the expenses were to be rendered only on the demand of the subscribers; and petitioner's method of estimating expenses was purely artificial and bore no relationship to the actual expenses incurred in rendering the services in the subsequent years.   All of these factors have been specifically mentioned by the Court in the above cases in disallowing deferral of income to cover the estimated cost of future expenses.

There can be no question that the first two factors mentioned above were present here.   And the latter factor is well established by the petitioner's experience.   In 1954 it established a reserve for the estimated cost of preparing subscribers' returns for only 1 year, although the contract obligated it to prepare them for 2 years.   The actual cost of preparing returns in 1955 exceeded the reserve established.   Then in 1956 petitioner not only changed its method of computing a reserve, estimating it on the basis of the cost of preparing returns for 2 years instead of 1, but also changed the method of having the returns prepared; it began preparing the returns itself instead of having accountants prepare them, which would seem necessarily to change the cost of preparing them.   Also its actual cost of preparing returns in 1957 was far in excess of the amount set up in its reserve for 2 years' returns.

Petitioner's reliance on such cases as Schuessler v. Commissioner, 230 F.2d 722 (C.A.5, 1956), reversing 24 T.C. 247 (1955); Pacific Grape Prod. Co. v. Commissioner, 219 F.2d 862 (C.A.9, 1955), reversing 17 T.C. 1097 (1952); and Denise Coal Co. v. Commissioner, 271 F.2d 930 (C.A.3, 1959), affirming in part and reversing in part 29 T.C. 528 (1957), is misplaced.   Whether or not those cases are all distinguishable from the *American Automobile* and *Schlude* cases, they are all distinguishable from this case.   In each of those cases the "operative facts" which gave rise to the future expenses had occurred in the year of accrual; in *Schuessler* the furnaces had been installed and there was a fixed obligation to turn them on and off;

taxpayer's method of accounting is in accord with generally accepted principles of commercial accounting. We also suspect that this principle, if such it be, will meet with some resistance in the courts. See the dissenting opinions of Mr. Justice Stewart in American Automobile Assn. v. United States, 367 U.S. 687, 698 (1961), and Schlude v. Commissioner, 372 U.S. 128, 137 (1963), and the opinions of various Courts of Appeals in Bressner Radio, Inc. v. Commissioner, 267 F.2d 520 (C.A. 2, 1959), reversing and remanding 28 T.C. 378 (1957), Beacon Publishing Co. v. Commissioner, 218 F.2d 697 (C.A. 10, 1955), reversing 21 T.C. 610 (1954), Schuessler v. Commissioner, 230 F.2d 722 (C.A. 5, 1956), reversing 24 T.C. 247 (1955), and Pacific Grape Prod. Co. v. Commissioner, 219 F.2d 862 (C.A. 9, 1955), reversing 17 T.C. 1097 (1952). The application of such a principle to the facts here would certainly require a decision for respondent on this issue.

in *Pacific Grape Products* the fruit had been sold and there was a fixed obligation to pack and ship the merchandise to the customers; and in *Denise* the land had been stripped and there was a statutory obligation to rehabilitate the land. But here, as in the *Automobile Club* cases and the *Schlude* case, the operative facts which gave rise to the obligation, i. e., the demands by the subscribers for the service, had not occurred in the years of accrual. Where the operative facts giving rise to the future expenses have not occurred in the year of accrual, the estimated expenses cannot be deducted even though they can be estimated with reasonable certainty and even though prudent business requires that a reserve be set up. Brown v. Helvering, 291 U.S. 193 (1934).

We conclude that respondent did not err in disallowing the deductions claimed by petitioner on its returns for 1954 and 1956 for additions to reserves for estimated future expenses of preparing subscribers' income tax returns.

Our conclusion above makes it unnecessary for us to decide whether petitioner's change in its method of treating these expenses constituted a change in its method of accounting, which would require the consent of the Commissioner, or was merely a correction of the prior erroneous treatment of these expenses under the accrual method of accounting, as claimed by petitioner. See American Can Co., 37 T.C. 198 (1961), affirmed in part and reversed in part 317 F.2d 604 (C.A.2, 1963).

Decision will be entered for the respondent.

PROBLEMS

1. Lawyer renders services for Client and sends him a bill for $500 on December 20 of year one. Client pays the bill on January 10 of year two. Discuss the tax consequences to Lawyer and Client assuming, even if unlikely, that both are calendar year, accrual method taxpayers.

2. Lender lends out money at a legal rate to Debtor. Debtor is required to pay $5,000 interest each year on the loan which extends over a five year period with no reduction in the obligation to make the interest payments even if payment of the principal is accelerated. The agreement calls for payment of each year's interest on December 31 of the year. Both parties are calendar year, accrual method taxpayers. Discuss the tax consequences to both parties under the following alternatives:

(a) Debtor pays all five years' interest ($25,000) to Lender in cash on December 31 of year one.

(b) Debtor pays the first two years' interest ($10,000) to Lender in cash on December 31 of year one.

(c) Debtor pays year one's $5,000 of interest in cash on January 2d of year two.

   (d) On December 31 of year one Debtor who is having "serious financial trouble" fails to pay Lender.

   (e) On December 31 of year one Debtor does not pay the interest because of a legitimate dispute over his obligation to pay the first year's interest.

   (f) On December 15 of year one Debtor legitimately disputes his obligation to pay year one's interest but he does pay it, and in year two he sues to recover it.

   3. Accrue, a calendar year, accrual method taxpayer, runs a dance school which offers lessons over 30 months with one lesson in each month. No make-up lessons are offered nor is the 30-month period extended for a participant who misses any scheduled lessons. The cost of the lessons is $300 which is required to be prepaid in January of the first year. Based on prior experience, Accrue has found that each lesson (including salaries, rent, utilities) costs her $4.00 per person. On January 1st of year one, 100 students sign up and pay for lessons which commence in January of year one. Discuss Accrue's tax consequences.

   4. All of the stock of Accrual Method Corporation is owned by Sole Shareholder who is a cash method taxpayer. Both Corporation and Shareholder are calendar year taxpayers. Shareholder has loaned money to Corporation at interest. Bookkeeper, who is unrelated to Shareholder, is responsible for paying Shareholder the interest which is due at the end of each year.

   (a) What result to Corporation and Shareholder if on December 15 of year one Bookkeeper informs Shareholder that the money to pay the interest for year one is available but Shareholder fails to collect it until March 30 of year two? See I.R.C. (26 U.S.C.A.) § 267(a)(2), which is discussed at page 471, and Fetzer Refrigerator Co. v. United States, 437 F.2d 577 (6th Cir. 1971).

   (b) What result to Corporation and Shareholder if on December 15 of year one Bookkeeper informs Shareholder that there is a shortage of cash and the interest will not be paid when due, but it is paid to Shareholder on March 30 of year two?

   (c) What result in (b), above, if Bookkeeper informs Shareholder the cash will be available on February 1st of year two and it is in fact paid to Shareholder at that time?

CHAPTER 20. HOW INELUCTABLE IS THE INTEGRITY OF THE TAXABLE YEAR?

A. TAXPAYER'S RESTORATION OF PREVIOUSLY TAXED INCOME

Internal Revenue Code: Section 1341(a) and (b)(1) and (2) (first sentence).

Regulations: Section 1.1341–1(a), (b)(1)(i) and (ii).

UNITED STATES v. LEWIS

Supreme Court of the United States, 1951.
340 U.S. 590, 71 S.Ct. 522.

MR. JUSTICE BLACK delivered the opinion of the Court.

Respondent Lewis brought this action in the Court of Claims seeking a refund of an alleged overpayment of his 1944 income tax. The facts found by the Court of Claims are: In his 1944 income tax return, respondent reported about $22,000 which he had received that year as an employee's bonus. As a result of subsequent litigation in a state court, however, it was decided that respondent's bonus had been improperly computed; under compulsion of the state court's judgment he returned approximately $11,000 to his employer. Until payment of the judgment in 1946, respondent had at all times claimed and used the full $22,000 unconditionally as his own, in the good faith though "mistaken" belief that he was entitled to the whole bonus.

On the foregoing facts the Government's position is that respondent's 1944 tax should not be recomputed, but that respondent should have deducted the $11,000 as a loss in his 1946 tax return. See G. C. M. 16730, XV–1 Cum.Bull. 179 (1936). The Court of Claims, however, relying on its own case, Greenwald v. United States, 102 Ct.Cl. 272, 57 F.Supp. 569, held that the excess bonus received "under a mistake of fact" was not income in 1944 and ordered a refund based on a recalculation of that year's tax. 117 Ct.Cl. 336, 91 F.Supp. 1017. We granted certiorari, 340 U.S. 903, because this holding conflicted with many decisions of the courts of appeals, see, e. g., Haberkorn v. United States, 173 F.2d 587, and with principles announced in North American Oil v. Burnet, 286 U.S. 417.

In the *North American Oil* case we said: "If a taxpayer receives earnings under a claim of right and without restriction as to its disposition, he has received income which he is required to return, even though it may still be claimed that he is not entitled to retain the money, and even though he may still be adjudged liable to restore its equivalent." 286 U.S. at 424. Nothing in this language permits an exception merely because a taxpayer is "mistaken" as to the validity of his claim. Nor has the "claim of right" doctrine been impaired, as the Court of Claims stated, by Freuler v. Helvering, 291 U.S. 35, or Commissioner v. Wilcox, 327 U.S. 404. The *Freuler* case involved an entirely different section of the Internal Revenue Code, and its holding is inapplicable here. 291 U.S. at 43. And in Commissioner v. Wilcox, supra, we held that receipts from embezzlement did not constitute income distinguishing *North American Oil* on the ground that an embezzler asserts no "bona fide legal or equitable claim." 327 U.S. at 408.

Income taxes must be paid on income received (or accrued) during an annual accounting period. Cf. I.R.C., §§ 41, 42; and see Burnet v. Sanford & Brooks Co., 282 U.S. 359, 363. The "claim of right" interpretation of the tax laws has long been used to give finality to that period, and is now deeply rooted in the federal tax system. See cases collected in 2 Mertens, Law of Federal Income Taxation, § 12.103. We see no reason why the Court should depart from this well-settled interpretation merely because it results in an advantage or disadvantage to a taxpayer.*

Reversed.

MR. JUSTICE DOUGLAS, dissenting.

The question in this case is not whether the bonus had to be included in 1944 income for purposes of the tax. Plainly it should have been because the taxpayer claimed it as of right. Some years later, however, it was judicially determined that he had no claim to the bonus. The question is whether he may then get back the tax which he paid on the money.

Many inequities are inherent in the income tax. We multiply them needlessly by nice distinctions which have no place in the practical administration of the law. If the refund were allowed, the integrity of the taxable year would not be violated. The tax would be paid when due; but the Government would not be permitted to maintain the unconscionable position that it can keep the tax after it is shown that payment was made on money which was not income to the taxpayer.

THE MECHANICS OF SECTION 1341

The student should study the economics of the example below and then try to work it out through the Code.

* It has been suggested that it would be more "equitable" to reopen respondent's 1944 tax return. While the suggestion might work to the advantage of this taxpayer, it could not be adopted as a general solution because, in many cases, the three-year statute of limitations would preclude recovery. I.R.C. § 322(b). [See I.R.C. (1954) § 6511(a). Ed.]

Assume that T, an unmarried taxpayer and not head of a household, in 1976 had gross income (all from commissions) in the amount of $38,000. His taxable income for the year 1976 was $32,000 on which T paid a tax of $10,290.

For the next year, 1977, T received gross income of $30,000 but, during the year, it was discovered that due to an accounting error on the employer's books, T's commissions for the prior year, 1976, were overstated by $10,000, meaning that T had been overpaid in the amount of $10,000 in 1976. T was required to and did repay $10,000 to his employer in 1977. Without regard to the repayment, T's taxable income for 1977 was (gross income $30,000 less $4,000 in deductions) $26,000.

Prior to the enactment of § 1341 (1954), T could *only* deduct the $10,000 repayment in 1977 in computing his tax for that year. (See United States v. Lewis, above). This he can still do (§ 1341(a) (4)) but another, and perhaps more favorable, alternative is open to T under § 1341(a) (5). That provision, by permitting the taxpayer to reduce his *tax* for the year of repayment by the amount of *tax* attributable to the amount repaid, effects a result essentially similar to the objective sought by the taxpayer in United States v. Lewis.

The following example, using the above facts, illustrates I. the deduction from year-of-repayment gross income and II. the reduction in tax alternative.

1976 Taxable income $32,000 and a tax of $10,290.
1977 Taxable income *without regard to repayment* is $26,000, but T repaid $10,000 received under claim of right in 1976.

T's tax liability for 1977, can be computed as follows:

I. Simply a deduction from 1977 income:
    Tax on ($26,000 – $10,000) $16,000 $3,830
                            or

II. Reduction in tax for 1977 by the amount of tax
    attributable to the $10,000 overpayment in 1976.
    (A) Tax on $26,000 (1977 taxable income,
        without regard to repayment) $7,590
    (B) Tax on (1976) $32,000 $10,290

    (C) *Less*: Tax payable on ($32,000–
        $10,000) $22,000 $5,990
    (D) Tax attributable to $10,000 repay-
        ment $4,300
The amount in (D) offsets the tax computed
                in (A) $4,300
    T's tax liability for 1977 _____ $3,290

CONCLUSION: Since the *reduction in tax* for 1977 by the amount of the 1976 *tax* attributable to the $10,000 repayment is of greater tax benefit than a deduction of the amount of the repayment from 1972 income (I, above), the taxpayer will use the reduction of tax method (II, above), effecting a tax saving of $540.00 ($3,830 minus $3,290). In other circumstances the deduction from income alternative (I in the above example) might prove to be more beneficial, effecting a greater tax saving. When would that occur?

JOSEPH P. PIKE

Tax Court of the United States, 1965.
44 T.C. 787(A).

[Petitioner was an attorney who handled legal matters before the Kentucky Department of Insurance. He was also a shareholder of the Cardinal Life Insurance Company. In 1957 he and other shareholders sold a part of their interest in the Company at a gain of about $20,000. An investigation of the transaction was conducted by a special counsel of the state (Wolford) who was of the opinion that the $20,000 gain properly belonged to the Cardinal Company. Although no suit was brought in 1958 several shareholders including petitioner paid their gains over to the Cardinal Company.]

FORRESTER, JUDGE:

* * *

Petitioner believed that any continued controversy over the sale of Cardinal contract stock or any litigation resulting from such controversy would damage his status and his reputation with the insurance industry. Petitioner was not entirely convinced that the profits legally belonged to Cardinal. However, petitioner realized the possibility that, when the attorney general's office and a prominent attorney like Wolford were contesting his position, his view of the law might have been erroneous. Rather than allow further controversy to endanger his professional career, petitioner decided to pay over his profit to Cardinal. Petitioner thereafter continued to engage in the private practice of law and to work for life insurance companies.

* * *

We next consider petitioner's contention that he is entitled to relief under section 1341 [1] on account of the payment to Cardinal in 1958 of his profits from the sale of contract stock. Respondent attacks this contention on two fronts: (1) Petitioner's payment to Cardinal is not deductible in 1958 because allowance of a deduction would frustrate sharply defined public policy and because the payment was personal in nature; (2) it was not "established" that petitioner was not en-

---

1. [I.R.C. § 1341(a) is omitted. Ed.]

titled to retain the profits.   As a corollary to his second approach, respondent contends that the payment was voluntary on the part of petitioner and for this reason not deductible.   We will deal with respondent's contentions in the order indicated.

Respondent asserts two separate reasons why petitioner's 1958 payment to Cardinal was not deductible.   Respondent first argues that allowance of a deduction would frustrate the sharply defined public policy of the Commonwealth of Kentucky, because, according to respondent, petitioner's actions with respect to the registration of the contract stock violated the criminal provisions of the Kentucky Securities Act.   Respondent cites Tank Truck Rentals v. Commissioner, 356 U.S. 30 (1958).   Even if we agreed with respondent that petitioner had committed a crime—and the evidence establishes no more than that the Kentucky attorney general had argued that the Securities Act had been violated—we would not for that reason disallow the deduction, because the payment in question was not made on account of and was not directly related to any such violation.   Rather, it was made in response to the claim by the department of insurance that the profits from the sale of contract stock rightfully belonged to Cardinal. Tank Truck Rentals v. Commissioner, supra, is clearly distinguishable, since the deductions there disallowed were payments of fines for violations of State law, and allowance of deductions would have diluted the intended penalties.   See Lawrence M. Marks, 27 T.C. 464 (1956); Rev.Rul. 61–115, 1961–1 C.B. 46.

Respondent's argument that petitioner's payment was a nondeductible personal expense is based upon the assertion that, in making the payment, petitioner was motivated by a desire to avoid criminal prosecution for violation of the Securities Act.   There is no support in the record for this assertion.   On the contrary, the evidence strongly supports petitioner's testimony that he paid over the money because he feared lest further controversy over the matter damage his status and reputation with the insurance industry and hence endanger his professional career, which was closely tied to that industry.   We have so found.   Nor do we think petitioner was unreasonable in his belief. No more is required for petitioner's payment to Cardinal to be deductible as an ordinary and necessary business expense under section 162(a).   Lawrence M. Marks, supra; Rev.Rul. 61–115, supra; see Old Town Corporation, 37 T.C. 845 (1962), acq. 1962–2 C.B. 5; C. Doris H. Pepper, 36 T.C. 886 (1961).

Respondent's second objection to granting relief under section 1341 is that it was not sufficiently "established," in 1958 or any other year, that petitioner "did not have an unrestricted right to" the profits from the sale of the contract stock.   Sec. 1341(a) (2).   Respondent urges that there must be a clear showing, under State statutes or decisions, of petitioner's liability to Cardinal, before section 1341(a) (2) can be satisfied.   Certainly, a judicial determination of liability is not required.   See Rev.Rul. 58–456, 1958–2 C.B. 415, 418.   However, we believe that it is necessary under section 1341(a) (2) for a taxpayer to demonstrate at least the probable validity of the adverse claim to the funds repaid. This position is supported by Rev.Rul. 58–456, supra, wherein the following language of the Court of Appeals for the Ninth Circuit is quoted with approval (Crellin's Estate v. Commissioner, 203 F.2d 812 (C.A.9, 1953), certiorari denied 346 U.S. 873, affirming 17 T.C. 781):

> In short, for tax purposes, it is that which the holding company could have compelled, not that in which the stockholders were willing to acquiesce, which controls. Otherwise, the taxpayers in this case could "lift the federal taxhand" to suit their convenience. * * *

Section 1341 was enacted to change the result reached in United States v. Lewis, 341 U.S. 590 (1951). See H.Rept. No. 1337, to accompany H.R. 8300 (Pub.L. 591), 83d Cong., 2d Sess., p. A294 (1954); Estate of Samuel Stein, 37 T.C. 945, 957 (1962). *Lewis* was a suit for refund of 1944 taxes paid on that part of an amount, received under claim of right as a bonus, which the taxpayer was required (under compulsion of a judgment) to restore in 1946. The Supreme Court held that no refund of the taxpayer's 1944 taxes was allowable. Consequently, the taxpayer was only entitled to a deduction in 1946, the year of the repayment.

We are of the opinion that, to become entitled to relief under section 1341, a taxpayer must prove by a preponderance of the evidence that he was not entitled to the unrestricted use of the amount received in the prior year. In other words (assuming that the Supreme Court had decided the *Lewis* case in taxpayer's favor) he must produce proof sufficient to have entitled him to an adjustment of the prior year's tax.

We do not believe that Congress intended to allow a credit based upon a recomputation of the prior year's tax in the absence of such a showing. This interpretation of the statute is supported by the use of the word "established" in section 1341(a) (2). For section 1341 to be applicable, it must be *"established* after the close of such prior taxable year (or years) that the taxpayer did not have an unrestricted right to such item." (Sec. 1341(a) (2). Emphasis supplied.) "Establish" means "to prove or make acceptable beyond a reasonable doubt." Webster's New International Dictionary (3d ed. 1961).

We are of the opinion that petitioner has not satisfied the requirements of section 1341(a) (2). Petitioner does not admit that he was not entitled to the profits he received in 1957. Indeed, he testified that he was not convinced the money belonged to Cardinal, though the formidable array of lawyers arguing the contrary raised some doubt in his mind. Petitioner was not compelled by legal process to make the payment. Finally, the record does not disclose the theory upon which Thurman and Wolford were basing their claim that the profits belonged to Cardinal; so we cannot say whether, under Kentucky law, such claim would have been upheld.

Petitioner relies upon Wetstone v. United States, an unreported case (D.Conn.1960, 5 A.F.T.R.2d 1486, 60–1 U.S.T.C. par. 9452), for the proposition that he need not prove the probable validity of the regulatory authorities' claim. The *Wetstone* case involved a year to which section 1341 was not applicable; it did not purport to construe section 1341. Although the court's reasoning seems questionable, we need not decide whether the case is correct on its own facts. Suffice it to say that the rule laid down therein is incompatible with our interpretation of the purpose and the language of section 1341. See Ernest H. Berger, 37 T.C. 1026, 1032.

Petitioner has not proved that he was not entitled to retain the profits from the sale of Cardinal contract stock. Accordingly, he does not meet the requirements for relief under section 1341. As previously pointed out, however, a bona fide claim was asserted against him, there was serious uncertainty as to the validity of the claim, and the payment in satisfaction of the claim was made for valid business reasons. The payment was not voluntary, in the sense of being gratuitous. It follows, then, that the payment is deductible under section 162(a) as an ordinary and necessary business expense. Lawrence M. Marks, supra.[2]

Decision will be entered under Rule 50.

NOTE

I.R.C. (26 U.S.C.A.) § 1341 may be a good place to take note of the rule of the seven barrel staves. Apparently, it took seven barrel staves to make a vessel that would hold water; if one was missing, it was just a case of nothing done. A statutory provision that requires the coincidence of several requirements presents the same problem; if one is not met the provision is inapplicable. Note the three prerequisites expressed in I.R.C. (26 U.S.C.A.) § 1341(a) ((1) through (3)).[1]

2. In his petition and amended petition, petitioner claimed a net operating loss carryback from 1958 to 1957. Respondent's objection to this claim was based upon the theory that the 1958 payment to Cardinal was not a deduction attributable to petitioner's trade or business. See sec. 172(d)(4). In view of our decision herein, respondent's objection is not well founded.

1. An additional limitation of § 1341 is found in § 1341(b)(2) which provides that the section "does not apply to any deduction allowable with respect to an item which was included in gross income by reason of the sale or other disposition of stock in trade of the taxpayer (or other property of a kind which would properly have been included in the inventory of the taxpayer if on hand at the close of the prior taxable year) or property held by the taxpayer primarily for sale to customers in the ordinary course of his trade or business."

In *Pike*, set out above, the taxpayer fulfilled the first requirement, which appears at § 1341(a) (1). He included an item in his gross income for 1957 because it appeared he had an unrestricted right to it. Indeed such inclusion was required under the *North American Oil Consolidated* doctrine.[2] Application of this first test may not be difficult.[3] For example, an embezzler who later returned misappropriated funds would obviously fail it.[4]

In *Pike* the taxpayer also met the third test, which appears at § 1341(a) (3); the amount in question exceeded $3000. One may wonder about this congressional insertion of a de minimis principle. But it probably does have the administrative advantage of relieving the Commissioner from the task of analyzing and cross-checking numerous Pike-like assertions that can have little impact on the revenue and are something less than cataclysmic to the taxpayer involved.

But the missing barrel stave in *Pike* was the requirement of § 1341(a) (2), (§ 1341 presents a three-stave barrel) and this is where the most controversy has arisen. Although, the taxpayer's act of turning over his gain to Cardinal was not wholly voluntary, it seems fair to say, as the Court did, that no obligation for him to do so was "established," as that term is used in the statute.

Note that the amount repaid must constitute an *allowable deduction* within the *Lewis* principle, if the § 1341 alternatives are to be available. In *Pike* this test was met but, where a repayment fails to fit within the requirements of I.R.C. (26 U.S.C.A.) § 162 or 212, it may not be.[5]

It is also clear that the taxpayer's lack of unrestricted right to the item must be established *after* the close of the year for which the item was included in gross income but on the basis of circumstances that existed *during* such prior year. The statutory test is whether the taxpayer "did not have" the right that was apparent in the year of receipt. Thus, a subsequent agreement to return an amount to which the taxpayer *was* entitled, no matter how binding on the taxpayer, will not invoke § 1341. In George L. Blanton,[6] *after* receiving corporate fees for three years, the taxpayer entered into an agreement that

2. The case is set out in the preceding chapter. See also Reg. § 1.1341–1(a) (2), treating income included under a claim of right as "an item included in gross income because it appeared from all the facts available in the year of inclusion that the taxpayer had an unrestricted right to such item." An early, basic analysis of § 1341 appears in Webster, "The Claim of Right Doctrine: 1954 Version," 10 Tax L.Rev. 381 (1955) and see Eman-

uel, "The Scope of Section 1341," 53 Taxes 644 (1975).

3. See Rev.Rul. 68–153, 1968–1 C.B. 371.

4. See Rev.Rul. 65–254, 1965–2 C.B. 50.

5. See Karl Hope, 55 T.C. 1020 (1971); and cf. U. S. v. Simon, 281 F.2d 520 (6th Cir. 1960).

6. 46 T.C. 527 (1966), aff'd per curiam, 379 F.2d 558 (5th Cir. 1967).

any fees held to be excessive by the Internal Revenue Service (and so not deductible by the corporation) would be returned by him to the corporation. When the first three years' fees were found to be excessive, taxpayer returned the excess to the corporation and asserted a right to the benefits of I.R.C. (26 U.S.C.A.) § 1341. The Tax Court held that the section did not apply because: [7]

> Under 1341(a) (2), the requisite lack of an unrestricted right to an income item permitting deduction must arise out of the circumstances, terms, and conditions of the *original* payment of such item to the taxpayer and not out of circumstances, terms, and conditions imposed upon such payment by reason of some subsequent agreement between payor and payee.

The *Blanton* result raises the question whether § 1341 would apply if *prior to receipt* a taxpayer, pursuant to a valid contract with the employer, agreed to repay amounts subsequently held not to be deductible by the employer. Is the answer indicated by Rev.Rul. 67–437, which follows, fully supported by the statute? Could an agreement of the type involved be drafted in a manner that would at least make the question closer?

REVENUE RULING 67–437

1967–2 Cum.Bull. 296.

The Internal Revenue Service has been asked whether the officer-stockholders of a closely held corporation who repay, under the circumstances described below, certain reimbursements they have received from the corporation may compute their tax for the year of the repayment in accordance with the provisions of section 1341 of the Internal Revenue Code of 1954 (relating to the restoration by a taxpayer of a substantial amount held under claim of right).

The taxpayers, father and son, own 51 percent and 43 percent, respectively, of the stock in a closely held corporation. The taxpayers are officers of the corporation and have executed agreements with it whereby the corporation will either pay, or reimburse them for, any and all travel, entertainment and other expenses paid or incurred by them on behalf of or for the benefit of the corporation, and they will repay to the corporation, promptly upon demand by it to do so, the amount of any such expenses paid or reimbursed to them by the corporation, which may be finally determined not to be deductible by the corporation for Federal income tax purposes.

---

7. Id. at 530. See Soled, "Reimbursement Agreements for Excessive Payments: Compensation and Other," 26 N.Y.U. Inst. on Fed. Tax. 1143 (1968).

The intent of this arrangement is to create a situation whereby the taxpayers can repay the disallowed amounts to the corporation and thus claim a deduction for the taxable year of repayment in accordance with the provisions of section 1341 of the Code.

That section provides rules for the computation of tax where a taxpayer is entitled to a deduction in excess of $3,000 as the result of restoring an amount included in gross income for a prior taxable year (or years) because it appeared that the taxpayer had an unrestricted right to such amount. However, section 1341 of the Code is not applicable when the taxpayer did, in fact, have an unrestricted right to receive the amount and where the obligation to repay arose as the result of subsequent events. If the instant taxpayers in a subsequent year should repay the disallowed amounts to the corporation, it will not be because it was established after the close of the prior taxable year in which the money was received that the taxpayers did not have an unrestricted right thereto in such prior year, but because a liability on their part has later accrued which does not in any way establish that they had no right to the money when received. See Revenue Ruling 58–226, C.B. 1958–1, 318, and Revenue Ruling 67–48, C.B. 1967–1, 50, relating to the applicability of the provisions of section 1341 of the Code.

Accordingly, the officer-stockholders may not compute their Federal income tax in accordance with section 1341 of the Code for the year in which the reimbursements were repaid to their closely held corporation.*

PROBLEMS

1. In 1976, Payer, an unmarried cash method taxpayer and not the head of a household, had $80,000 of gross income all in the form of advance and regular commissions on sales for Employer. His taxable income for the year was $60,000. In 1977 because some customers failed to pay their obligations Payer repaid Employer $10,000 of the commissions that were prepaid in 1976, as he was required to do under his contract. Without regard to the repayment, Payer's 1977 gross income was $65,000 and his taxable income was $50,000.

   (a) What result to Payer in 1977 under the *Lewis* case?

   (b) What result to Payer in 1977 under I.R.C. (26 U.S.C.A.) § 1341?

   (c) What result under § 1341 and why, if, without regard to the repayment, Payer's gross income in 1977 was $90,000 and his taxable income was $70,000?

* See Rev.Rul. 69–115, 1969–1 C.B. 50, which holds that the taxpayers would be allowed to deduct the payment as an I.R.C. § 162 deduction in the year of repayment. Ed.

2. Consider whether I.R.C. § 1341 would apply in problem 1, above, under the following changed circumstances:

   (a) Payer acquired the $10,000, which was subsequently returned, by embezzlement.

   (b) Payer acquired the $10,000 in the same manner as in problem 1, above; however, he was not required by contract to return the excess commissions, but did so voluntarily.

   (c) Payer returned the $10,000 based on a return of merchandise by a customer of Payer in 1977, under such circumstances that Payer's employer rescinded the contract with the customer, which, in turn, effected a reduced commission to Payer, requiring him to repay $10,000 to his employer.

B. THE TAX BENEFIT DOCTRINE *

Internal Revenue Code: Section 111(a) and (b).
Regulations: Section 1.111–1(a)(1), (2), –1(b)(1), (2)(i) and (ii).

ALICE PHELAN SULLIVAN CORP. v. COMMISSIONER *

Court of Claims of the United States, 1967.
381 F.2d 399.

COLLINS, JUDGE. Plaintiff, a California corporation, brings this action to recover an alleged overpayment in its 1957 income tax. During that year, there was returned to taxpayer two parcels of realty, each of which it had previously donated and claimed as a charitable contribution deduction. The first donation had been made in 1939; the second, in 1940. Under the then applicable corporate tax rates, the deductions claimed ($4,243.49 for 1939 and $4,463.44 for 1940) yielded plaintiff an aggregate tax benefit of $1,877.49.[1]

Each conveyance had been made subject to the condition that the property be used either for a religious or for an educational purpose. In 1957, the donee decided not to use the gifts; they were therefore reconveyed to plaintiff. Upon audit of taxpayer's income tax return, it was found that the recovered property was not reflected in its 1957 gross income. The Commissioner of Internal Revenue disagreed with plaintiff's characterization of the recovery as a nontaxable return of capital. He viewed the transaction as giving rise to taxable income

-----

* See Corlew, "The Tax Benefit Rule, Claim of Right Restorations, and Annual Accounting: A Cure for the Inconsistencies," 21 Vand.L.Rev. 995 (1968).

* There is a comment on *Sullivan* at 66 Mich.L.Rev. 381 (1967). Ed.

1. The tax rate in 1939 was 18 percent; in 1940, 24 percent.

and therefore adjusted plaintiff's income by adding to it $8,706.93—
the total of the charitable contribution deductions previously claimed
and allowed.   This addition to income, taxed at the 1957 corporate tax
rate of 52 percent, resulted in a deficiency assessment of $4,527.60.
After payment of the deficiency, plaintiff filed a claim for the refund
of $2,650.11, asserting this amount as overpayment on the theory that
a correct assessment could demand no more than the return of the tax
benefit originally enjoyed, *i. e.*, $1,877.49.   The claim was disallowed.

This court has had prior occasion to consider the question which
the present suit presents.   In Perry v. United States, 160 F.Supp. 270,
142 Ct.Cl. 7 (1958) (Judges Madden and Laramore dissenting), it was
recognized that a return to the donor of a prior charitable contribution
gave rise to income to the extent of the deduction previously allowed.
The court's point of division—which is likewise the division between
the instant parties—was whether the "gain" attributable to the recovery was to be taxed at the rate applicable at the time the deduction
was first claimed or whether the proper rate was that in effect at the
time of recovery.   The majority, concluding that the Government
should be entitled to recoup no more than that which it lost, held that
the tax liability arising upon the return of a charitable gift should
equal the tax benefit experienced at time of donation.   Taxpayer urges
that the *Perry* rationale dictates that a like result be reached in this
case.

The Government, of course, assumes the opposite stance.   Mind-
ful of the homage due the principle of stare decisis, it bids us first to
consider the criteria under which judicial reexamination of an earlier
decision is justifiable.   We are referred to Judge Davis' concurring
opinion in Mississippi River Fuel Corp. v. United States, 314 F.2d 953,
958, 161 Ct.Cl. 237, 246–247 (1963), wherein he states that:

* * *   The question is not what we would hold if we now took
a fresh look but whether we should take that fresh look.   * * *

[We] examine anew the issue which this case presents.

A transaction which returns to a taxpayer his own property cannot be considered as giving rise to "income"—at least where that term
is confined to its traditional sense of "gain derived from capital, from
labor, or from both combined."   Eisner v. Macomber, 252 U.S. 189,
207, 40 S.Ct. 189, 64 L.Ed. 521 (1920).   Yet the principle is well en-
grained in our tax law that the return or recovery of property that
was once the subject of an income tax deduction must be treated as income in the year of its recovery.   Rothensies v. Electric Storage Battery Co., 329 U.S. 296, 67 S.Ct. 271, 91 L.Ed. 296 (1946); Estate of
Black v. Commissioner, 39 B.T.A. 338 (1939), aff'd sub nom. Union
Trust Co. v. Commissioner, 111 F.2d 60 (7th Cir.), cert. denied, 311
U.S. 658, 61 S.Ct. 12, 85 L.Ed. 421 (1940).   The only limitation upon
that principle is the so-called "tax-benefit rule."   This rule permits

exclusion of the recovered item from income so long as its initial use as a deduction did not provide a tax saving. California & Hawaiian Sugar Ref. Corp. v. United States, supra; Central Loan & Inv. Co. v. Commissioner, 39 B.T.A. 981 (1939). But where full tax use of a deduction was made and a tax saving thereby obtained, then the extent of saving is considered immaterial. The recovery is viewed as income to the full extent of the deduction previously allowed.[2]

Formerly the exclusive province of judge-made law, the tax-benefit concept now finds expression both in statute and administrative regulations. Section 111 of the Internal Revenue Code of 1954 accords tax-benefit treatment to the recovery of bad debts, prior taxes, and delinquency amounts.[3] Treasury regulations have "broadened" the rule of exclusion by extending similar treatment to "all other losses, expenditures, and accruals made the basis of deductions from gross income for prior taxable years * * *."[4]

Drawing our attention to the broad language of this regulation, the Government insists that the present recovery must find its place within the scope of the regulation and, as such, should be taxed in a manner consistent with the treatment provided for like items of recovery, *i. e.*, that it be taxed at the rate prevailing in the year of recovery. We are compelled to agree.

Set in historical perspective, it is clear that the cited regulation may not be regarded as an unauthorized extension of the otherwise limited congressional approval given to the tax-benefit concept. While the statute, *(i. e.,* section 111) addresses itself only to bad debts, prior taxes, and delinquency amounts, it was, as noted in Dobson v. Commissioner, 320 U.S. 489, 64 S.Ct. 239, 88 L.Ed. 248 (1943), designed not to limit the application of the judicially designed tax-benefit rule, but rather to insure against its demise. "A specific statutory exception was necessary in bad debt cases only because the courts reversed the Tax Court and established as matter of law a 'theoretically proper' rule which distorted the taxpayer's income [*i. e.*, taxation of a recovery though no benefit may have been obtained through its earlier deduction]." 320 U.S. at 506, 64 S.Ct. at 249.

The *Dobson* decision insured the continued validity of the tax-benefit concept, and the regulation—being but the embodiment of that principle—is clearly adequate to embrace a recoverable charitable contribution. See California & Hawaiian Sugar Ref. Corp., supra, 311 F. 2d at 239, 159 Ct.Cl. at 567. But the regulation does not specify which tax rate is to be applied to the recouped deduction, and this consideration brings us to the matter here in issue.

---

2. The rationale which supports the principle, as well as its limitation, is that the property, having once served to offset taxable income (i. e., as a tax deduction) should be treated, upon its recoupment, as the recovery of that which had been previously deducted.

See Plumb, "The Tax Benefit Rule Today," 57 Harv.L.Rev. 129, 131 n. 10 (1943).

3. and 4. [I.R.C. § 111 and Reg. § 1.-111–1 are omitted. Ed.]

Ever since Burnet v. Sanford & Brooks Co., 282 U.S. 359, 51 S.Ct. 150, 75 L.Ed. 383 (1931),, the concept of accounting for items of income and expense on an annual basis has been accepted as the basic principle upon which our tax laws are structured. "It is the essence of any system of taxation that it should produce revenue ascertainable, and payable to the government, at regular intervals. Only by such a system is it practicable to produce a regular flow of income and apply methods of accounting, assessment, and collection capable of practical operation." 282 U.S. at 365, 51 S.Ct. at 152. To insure the vitality of the single-year concept, it is essential not only that annual income be ascertained without reference to losses experienced in an earlier accounting period, but also that income be taxed without reference to earlier tax rates. And absent specific statutory authority sanctioning a departure from this principle, it may only be said of *Perry* that it achieved a result which was more equitably just than legally correct.[5]

Since taxpayer in this case did obtain full tax benefit from its earlier deductions, those deductions were properly classified as income upon recoupment and must be taxed as such. This can mean nothing less than the application of that tax rate which is in effect during the year in which the recovered item is recognized as a factor of income. We therefore sustain the Government's position and grant its motion for summary judgment. Perry v. United States, supra, is hereby overruled, and plaintiff's petition is dismissed.

5. This opinion represents the views of the majority and complies with existing law and decisions. However, in the writer's personal opinion, it produces a harsh and inequitable result. Perhaps, it exemplifies a situation "where the letter of the law killeth; the spirit giveth life." The tax-benefit concept is an equitable doctrine which should be carried to an equitable conclusion. Since it is the declared public policy to encourage contributions to charitable and educational organizations, a donor, whose gift to such organizations is returned, should not be required to refund to the Government a greater amount than the tax benefit received when the deduction was made for the gift. Such a rule would avoid a penalty to the taxpayer and an unjust enrichment to the Government. However, the court cannot legislate and any change in the existing law rests within the wisdom and discretion of the Congress.

PROBLEMS

1.   In year one Recover, a cash method taxpayer, suffered a §
165(c)(3) casualty loss and properly deducted $1000 for that year,
because the insurance company denied liability and rejected all claims
as outside the coverage of Recover's policy. See John E. Montgomery,
65 T.C. 511 (1975) and Reg. § 1.165–1(d)(2)(i) and (iii). Recover's
gross income in year one was $10,000 and his total deductions includ-
ing the § 165(c)(3) loss were $10,600. Disregard here the possi-
bility of any net operating loss deduction under § 172, which is the
subject of a brief note later in this chapter. In year two the company
settled Recover's claim for $400.

   (a) What result to Recover in year two?

   (b) What result to Recover if the claim was settled in year two
        for $800 rather than $400?

   (c) What result to Recover in part (b), above, if $400 of the
        settlement was paid in year two and the other $400 in year
        three?

   (d) What result to Recover in (a), above, where he recovered
        $400 in year two if he had elected the standard deduction in
        year one?

2.   Compare I.R.C. § 111 with § 1341. Which is more beneficial?

C. INCOME AVERAGING

1. STATUTORY AVERAGING

Internal Revenue Code: Sections 1301; 1302(a)(1), (b)(1), (2) (disregard subparagraphs (A) and (B)), (c); 1303; 1304(a), (c)(2); 1305.
Regulations: Section § 1.1303–1(a) and (c).

EXCERPT FROM SENATE FINANCE COMMITTEE REPORT NO. 830

88th Congress, 2d Session 1964.
1964–1 (Part 2) C.B. 505, 643–645.

41. Income averaging (sec. 234 of the bill and secs. 1301–1305 of the code)

(*a*) *Present law.*—Present law does not provide any generally available income averaging provision for the persons whose income fluctuates widely from year to year. Instead, present law contains six specific averaging provisions dealing with special types of situations: Certain compensation for personal services, income from inventions or artistic work, certain income from backpay, compensation for damages for patent infringements, breach of contract damages, and damages for injuries under the antitrust laws. * * *

(*b*) *General reasons for provisions.*—A general averaging provision is needed to accord those whose incomes fluctuate widely from year to year the same treatment accorded those with relatively stable incomes. Because the individual income tax rates are progressive, over a period of years those whose incomes vary widely from year to year pay substantially more in income taxes than others with a comparable amount of total income but spread evenly over the years involved. This occurs because the progressive rates take a much larger proportion of the income in taxes from those whose incomes in some years are relatively high. The absence of any general averaging device has worked particular hardships on professions or types of work where incomes tend to fluctuate. This is true, for example, in the case of authors, professional artists, actors, and athletes as well as farmers, fishermen, attorneys, architects, and others.

The present averaging provisions have proved unsatisfactory, first because they are limited to a relatively small proportion of the situations where averaging is needed. Thus, while they presumably cover inventors and writers, they do not provide for actors, athletes, and in most cases do not provide for attorneys, architects, and others. * * *

The present averaging provisions also have proved unduly complicated in practice because of the requirement that the prior years' incomes and taxes must be recomputed as if the income had actually been received in those prior years.

Your committee agrees with the House that income averaging should be designed to treat everyone as nearly equally for tax purposes as possible, without regard to how their income is spread over a period of years and without regard to the type of income involved. At the same time, it is necessary to have any income averaging device in a form which is workable, both from the standpoint of the taxpayer and the Internal Revenue Service.

Although the bill generally repeals the averaging devices in present law (secs. 1301–1307), it is recognized that cases may arise where a person has entered into long-term contingent employments upon the assumption that the averaging device in present law applicable to compensation from an employment would be available. Since employments in some cases may last for extended periods of time, such as 20 years, the general 5-year averaging device might produce less favorable treatment than the present provision. As a result, the bill provides, in the case of these long-term employments which were already in being before 1963, for the taxpayers involved to continue the form of averaging available under present law if they elect to forgo the general 5-year averaging provided in this bill.

(c) *General explanation of provisions.*—In view of the considerations set forth above, the bill deletes all of the averaging provisions in present law referred to previously and substitutes instead an income averaging device available to individual taxpayers generally, substantially without regard to the source of the income. As indicated subsequently, however, in the case of the averaging device for compensation from an employment, the bill in certain cases permits the continuance of the application of this provision.

Under the averaging rule provided by the bill, once the amount of income to be averaged is determined—called averageable income in the bill—and assuming this amount is more than $3,000, the taxpayer is to compute a tentative tax on one-fifth of this amount. The tax on this one-fifth is determined by adding this one-fifth to $1\frac{1}{3}$ times the average income received in the prior 4 years, plus the average capital gains income in this same 4-year period. The tax attributable to this one-fifth is then multiplied by 5 to determine the final tax on this income.

Averaging is available only where the "averageable income" exceeds $3,000 because, with the present progressive rate structure with tax brackets usually of $2,000 to $4,000, smaller amounts achieve little if any benefit from averaging. The device of including one-fifth of the averageable income in the tentative tax base, computing the tax attributable to this amount, and then multiplying this result by 5, achieves a result which is substantially similar (except when there are rate changes during the 5 years) to including one-fifth of the income eligible for averaging in the taxable income base of each of the prior 4 years and of the current year. The advantage of making the computation in this manner is that it is not necessary to recompute the tax for each of the 4 prior years in order to obtain this result.

The "averageable income" referred to here is the excess of the taxable income in the current or computation year—with certain adjustments—over $1\frac{1}{3}$ times the average base period income. The average base period income is the average of the taxable income in the 4 prior years with certain adjustments specified below.

Averageable income is limited to that which is in excess of $1\frac{1}{3}$ times average income in the base period for two basic reasons. First, in any new provision of this type, it is necessary to limit the number of cases to which the new provision will apply to a manageable level from the administrative standpoint. In other words, it was necessary initially, at least, to limit the volume of cases where averaging will be applied. Moreover, it is clear that the greatest need for averaging occurs where the fluctuation in income levels varies widely. An increase of more than one-third from the prior average income was selected to make the new averaging rule available in those cases where it is needed the most.

* * *

EXCERPT FROM THE GENERAL EXPLANATION OF THE TAX REFORM ACT OF 1969

Staff of the Joint Committee on Internal Revenue Taxation, pp. 108–109 (1970).

H. INCOME AVERAGING

(Sec. 311 of the Act and secs. 1301–1305 of the code) *

Prior law.—Prior law provided a general averaging provision for an individual whose income fluctuates widely from year to year or increases rapidly over a short period. Generally, this averaging provision allowed the excess of the current year's taxable income over $1\frac{1}{3}$ times the average taxable income of the prior 4 years to be taxed at lower bracket rates than would otherwise apply, roughly approximating the tax which would have been imposed had the receipt of this excess income been spread evenly over the 5-year period.

* * *

Certain types of income such as long-term capital gains, wagering income, and income from gifts if in excess of $3,000 (as well as other relatively rare types of income) were not eligible for averaging under prior law. If a taxpayer had taxable income not eligible for aver-

---

* There is a basic analysis in Kearns, "Income Averaging—After the Tax Reform Act of 1969," 17 The Practical Lawyer 38 (1971). Ed.

aging, the tax computation required additional steps because it was necessary to divide the income into several segments in order to determine the tax attributable to one-fifth of averagable income as well as the tax on the nonaveragable income.

* * *

General reasons for change.—The 133⅓-percent test described above was considered too restrictive by the Congress in that it denied the benefits of averaging to taxpayers with a substantial increase in income and reduced the benefits of averaging for those who were eligible.

Denying averaging to certain types of income, particularly long-term capital gains, and permitting the alternative tax on capital gains for those who used averaging resulted in a complex provision and a complicated tax form. This complexity made it difficult for taxpayers to determine whether they would benefit from averaging and undoubtedly deterred some eligible taxpayers from making use of averaging. Simplifying the averaging provision should make it more generally available and usable.

In addition, Congress believed it was desirable to extend the benefits of averaging to long-term capital gains in order to maintain a better balance between taxation of capital gains and other types of income, especially in view of the increased tax on capital gains resulting from other provisions of the Tax Reform Act of 1969.

Explanation of provision.—The Act allows a taxpayer to average that part of his current year's taxable income (after adjustment for certain relatively rare items) which exceeds 120 percent of his average base period taxable income (if he meets the $3,000 test). Thus, for averaging to be available, the taxpayer's excess income in the current year now has to be only 20 percent greater than his average income for the prior 4 years rather than 33⅓ percent greater as under prior law.

The Act also provides that net long-term capital gains, income from gifts, and wagering income are to be eligible for averaging. Accordingly, for purposes of averaging, it is no longer necessary for the taxpayer to make adjustments to his current year's income for these items or to adjust his prior 4 years' income for capital gains or income from gifts.

* * *

REVENUE RULING 75–460

1975–2 C.B. 348.

Advice has been requested whether, under the circumstances described below, an individual qualifies for the limitation on tax provided in section 1301 of the Internal Revenue Code of 1954.

In 1969, 1970, and 1971 the taxpayer and spouse filed joint Federal income tax returns reporting taxable income in the amount of $20,000 each year. This income was entirely attributable to the spouse's earnings as a self-employed individual. In 1972 the taxpayer was divorced and reported $2,000 taxable income as a single individual. In 1973 and 1974 the taxpayer, filing as a single person, had taxable income of $8,000 and $20,000 respectively. During the years 1969 through 1974 the taxpayer was over 25 years of age and was not a full-time student. The taxpayer and spouse did not have earned income from sources outside the United States or from sources within United States possessions during this time.

Section 1301 of the Code provides that if an eligible individual has averagable income for the computation year, and if the amount of such income exceeds $3,000, then the tax imposed by section 1 for the computation year which is attributable to averagable income shall be five times the increase in tax under section 1 which would result from adding 20 percent of such income to 120 percent of average base period income.

Section 1302(a) of the Code provides that "averagable income" means the amount by which taxable income for the computation year (reduced as provided therein) exceeds 120 percent of average base period income.

Section 1302(b) of the Code provides, in part, that the term "average base period income" means one-fourth of the sum of the base period incomes for the base period, and that "base period income" for any taxable year is the taxable income for such year adjusted as provided therein.

Section 1302(c) of the Code defines the term "computation year" to mean the taxable year for which the taxpayer chooses the benefits of income averaging and the term "base period" to mean the four taxable years immediately preceding the computation year.

In the case of an individual who is not married in the computation year, but who was married during any of the base period years, section 1304(c)(2)(B) of the Code provides that the base period income of an individual for any base period year shall not be less than 50 percent of the base period income resulting from combining the individual's income and deductions for such year with the income and deductions for such year of the individual who was his spouse for such base period year.

The computations necessary to determine whether the individual in the instant case qualifies for the limitation on tax provided by section 1301 of the Code for the years 1973 and 1974 are shown below:

1.

	Computation Year	
Base Period Income	*1973*	*1974*
1969 (½ of taxpayer & spouse's	$10,000	—
1970 combined taxable	10,000	$10,000
1971 income of $20,000)	10,000	10,000
1972 (Taxpayer's taxable	2,000	2,000
1973 income as a single individual)	—	8,000
Total	$32,000	$30,000
Average base period income (Total ÷ 4)	$ 8,000	$ 7,500

2.

Determination of Averagable Income		
Taxable Income in Computation Year	$ 8,000	$20,000
Less: 120% of average base period income:		
(1973—$8,000 × 120%)	9,600	
(1974— 7,500 × 120%)		9,000
Averagable Income	—0—	$11,000

Accordingly, for the year 1973 the taxpayer does not qualify for the limitation on tax provided by section 1301 of the Code because the averagable income does not exceed $3,000. However, for the year 1974 the taxpayer does qualify for the section 1301 limitation on tax.

PROBLEMS

1. Looking at I.R.C. (26 U.S.C.A.) §§ 1301 and 1302 consider the following:

(a) Why is a year's taxable income made "averageable income" only to the extent that it exceeds average income from the preceding four years by 20%?

(b) Even if some taxable income is within the definition of "averagable income" (because taxable income exceeds %ths of average base period income), the "if" clause of § 1301 does not allow averaging unless such "averagable income" exceeds $3000. Why? Do these two requirements that are imposed for differing congressional purposes really impose a double qualification on a taxpayer? If they are met does the $3000 qualify for averaging?

(c) If a taxpayer has income that qualifies for averaging under § 1301, why does the statute require that the tax be computed on $\frac{1}{5}$ of such averagable income at a rate determined by *adding* 120% of base period income to it? The tax on averagable income is then 5 times the tax, as thus determined, on $\frac{1}{5}$ of the averagable income. What is the effect of all this?

(d) Would a provision such as § 1301 make any sense if individuals were taxed at a flat rate instead of at graduated rates? The section does not apply to corporations. Cf. I.R.C. (26 U.S.C.A.) § 11.

2. Based on the facts of *Revenue Ruling 75–460*, above:

(a) What is Taxpayer's 1974 tax liability under § 1(c) on $20,000 of taxable income if income averaging is not used?

(b) What is Taxpayer's 1974 tax liability using the income averaging provisions which the Ruling holds may be used in 1974?

3. Determine whether the following individuals are eligible for income averaging:

(a) Law Student, who has been in school, entirely supported by his family for seven years, earns $12,000 during his first year of practice.

(b) Law Student worked his way through college and law school using his earnings to provide $\frac{2}{3}$ of his support and receiving $\frac{1}{3}$ of his support from his family each year. In his first year of practice he earns $12,000 which is triple his average earnings in the prior four years.

(c) Married Law Student's wife supported herself and him through his last year of college and three years of law school with her $8000 per year income which they reported on a joint return. They both worked during his first year of practice when she continued to earn $8000 and he earned $12,000.

(d) Same as (c), above, except that Law Student was not married until he began law school and prior to that time his family supported him through college.

(e) Same as (d), above, except that Married Law Student wishes to average his income in his second year of practice when his and his wife's incomes are $16,000 and $8000 respectively.

(f) Same as (c), above, except that Law Student was not married until he began law school and prior to that time he provided $\frac{1}{3}$ of his support and received $\frac{2}{3}$ of his support on an athletic scholarship. See James B. Heidel, 56 T.C. 95 (1971).

(g) Upon graduating from law school Law Student, who has supported herself on $6000 per year for five years, marries Husband, a perennial academic who has always been supported by his parents. If Law Student gets a substantial increase in salary in her first year of practice and Husband does not work, can they benefit under § 1301 when they file a joint return for the year? See § 1303(c)(2)(C).

---

2. DO–IT–YOURSELF AVERAGING

REVENUE RULING 60–31

1960–1 Cum.Bull. 174.

Advice has been requested regarding the taxable year of inclusion in gross income of a taxpayer, using the cash receipts and disbursements method of accounting, of compensation for services received under the circumstances described below.

(1) On January 1, 1958, the taxpayer and corporation X executed an employment contract under which the taxpayer is to be employed by the corporation in an executive capacity for a period of five years. Under the contract, the taxpayer is entitled to a stated annual salary and to additional compensation of $10x$ dollars for each year. The additional compensation will be credited to a bookkeeping reserve account and will be deferred, accumulated, and paid in annual installments equal to one-fifth of the amount in the reserve as of the close of the year immediately preceding the year of first payment. The payments are to begin only upon (a) termination of the taxpayer's employment by the corporation; (b) the taxpayer's becoming a part-time employee of the corporation; or (c) the taxpayer's becoming partially or totally incapacitated. Under the terms of the agreement, corporation X is under a merely contractual obligation to make the payments when due, and the parties did not intend that the amounts in the reserve be held by the corporation in trust for the taxpayer.

The contract further provides that if the taxpayer should fail or refuse to perform his duties, the corporation will be relieved of any obligation to make further credits to the reserve (but not of the obligation to distribute amounts previously contributed); but, if the taxpayer should become incapacitated from performing his duties, then credits to the reserve will continue for one year from the date of the incapacity, but not beyond the expiration of the five-year term of the contract. There is no specific provision in the contract for forfeiture by the taxpayer of his right to distribution from the reserve; and, in the event he should die prior to his receipt in full of the balance in the account, the remaining balance is distributable to his personal representative at the rate of one-fifth per year for five years, beginning three months after his death.

(2) The taxpayer is an officer and director of corporation A, which has a plan for making future payments of additional compensation for current services to certain officers and key employees designated by its board of directors. This plan provides that a percentage of the annual net earnings (before Federal income taxes) in excess of $4,000x$ dollars is to be designated for division among the participants in proportion to their respective salaries. This amount is not currently paid to the participants; but, the corporation has set up on its books a separate account for each participant and each year it credits thereto the dollar amount of his participation for the year, reduced by a proportionate part of the corporation's income taxes attributable to the additional compensation. Each account is also credited with the net amount, if any, realized from investing any portion of the amount in the account.

Distributions are to be made from these accounts annually beginning when the employee (1) reaches age 60, (2) is no longer employed by the company, including cessation of employment due to death, or (3) becomes totally disabled to perform his duties, whichever occurs first. The annual distribution will equal a stated percentage of the balance in the employee's account at the close of the year immediately preceding the year of first payment, and distributions will continue until the account is exhausted. However, the corporation's liability to make these distributions is contingent upon the employee's (1) refraining from engaging in any business competitive to that of the corporation, (2) making himself available to the corporation for consultation and advice after retirement or termination of his services, unless disabled, and (3) retaining unencumbered any interest or benefit under the plan. In the event of his death, either before or after the beginning of payments, amounts in an employee's account are distributable in installments computed in the same way to his designated beneficiaries or heirs-at-law. Under the terms of the compensation plan, corporation A is under a merely contractual obligation to make the payments when due, and the parties did not intend that the amounts in each account be held by the corporation in trust for the participants.

(3) On October 1, 1957, the taxpayer, an author, and corporation Y, a publisher, executed an agreement under which the taxpayer granted to the publisher the exclusive right to print, publish and sell a book he had written. This agreement provides that the publisher will (1) pay the author specified royalties based on the actual cash received from the sale of the published work, (2) render semi-annual statements of the sales, and (3) at the time of rendering each statement make settlement for the amount due. On the same day, another agreement was signed by the same parties, mutually agreeing that, in consideration of, and notwithstanding any contrary provisions contained in the first contract, the publisher shall not pay the taxpayer more than $100x$ dollars in any one calendar year. Under

this supplemental contract, sums in excess of $100x$ dollars accruing in any one calendar year are to be carried over by the publisher into succeeding accounting periods; and the publisher shall not be required either to pay interest to the taxpayer on any such excess sums or to segregate any such sums in any manner.

(4) In June 1957, the taxpayer, a football player, entered into a two-year standard player's contract with a football club in which he agreed to play football and engage in activities related to football during the two-year term only for the club. In addition to a specified salary for the two-year term, it was mutually agreed that as an inducement for signing the contract the taxpayer would be paid a bonus of $150x$ dollars. The taxpayer could have demanded and received payment of this bonus at the time of signing the contract, but at his suggestion there was added to the standard contract form a paragraph providing substantially as follows:

The player shall receive the sum of $150x$ dollars upon signing of this contract, contingent upon the payment of this $150x$ dollars to an escrow agent designated by him. The escrow agreement shall be subject to approval by the legal representatives of the player, the Club, and the escrow agent.

Pursuant to this added provision, an escrow agreement was executed on June 25, 1957, in which the club agreed to pay $150x$ dollars on that date to the Y bank, as escrow agent; and the escrow agent agreed to pay this amount, plus interest, to the taxpayer in installments over a period of five years. The escrow agreement also provides that the account established by the escrow agent is to bear the taxpayer's name; that payments from such account may be made only in accordance with the terms of the agreement; that the agreement is binding upon the parties thereto and their successors or assigns; and that in the event of the taxpayer's death during the escrow period the balance due will become part of his estate.

(5) The taxpayer, a boxer, entered into an agreement with a boxing club to fight a particular opponent at a specified time and place. The place of the fight agreed to was decided upon because of the insistence of the taxpayer that it be held there. The agreement was on the standard form of contract required by the state athletic commission and provided, in part, that for his performance taxpayer was to receive $16x$ percent of the gross receipts derived from the match. Simultaneously, the same parties executed a separate agreement providing for payment of the taxpayer's share of the receipts from the match as follows: 25 percent thereof not later than two weeks after the bout, and 25 percent thereof during each of the three years following the year of the bout in equal semiannual installments. Such deferments are not customary in prize fighting contracts, and the supplemental agreement was executed at the demand of the taxpayer. Upon the taxpayer's insistence, the agreements also provided that any

telecast of the fight must receive his prior consent and that he was to approve or disapprove all proposed sales of radio and motion picture rights.

Section 1.451–1(a) of the Income Tax Regulations provides in part as follows:

> Gains, profits, and income are to be included in gross income for the taxable year in which they are actually or constructively received by the taxpayer unless includible for a different year in accordance with the taxpayer's method of accounting. * * *.

And, with respect to the cash receipts and disbursements method of accounting, section 1.446–1(c) (1) (i) provides in part—

> Generally, under the cash receipts and disbursements method in the computation of taxable income, all items which constitute gross income (whether in the form of cash, property, or services) are to be included for the taxable year in which actually or constructively received. * * *.

As previously stated, the individual concerned in each of the situations described above, employs the cash receipts and disbursements method of accounting. Under that method, as indicated by the above-quoted provisions of the regulations, he is required to include the compensation concerned in gross income only for the taxable year in which it is actually or constructively received. Consequently, the question for resolution is whether in each of the situations described the income in question was constructively received in a taxable year prior to the taxable year of actual receipt.

A mere promise to pay, not represented by notes or secured in any way, is not regarded as a receipt of income within the intendment of the cash receipts and disbursements method. See United States v. Christine Oil & Gas Co., 269 F. 458; William J. Jackson v. Smietanka, 272 F. 970, Ct.D. 5, C.B. 4, 96 (1921); and E. F. Cremin v. Commissioner, 5 B.T.A. 1164, acquiescence, C.B. VI–1, 2 (1927). Also C. Florian Zittel v. Commissioner, 12 B.T.A. 675, in which, holding a salary to be taxable when received, the Board said: "Taxpayers on a receipts and disbursements basis are required to report only income actually received no matter how binding any contracts they may have to receive more."

This should not be construed to mean that under the cash receipts and disbursements method income may be taxed only when realized in cash. For, under that method a taxpayer is required to include in income that which is received in cash or cash equivalent. W. P. Henritze v. Commissioner, 41 B.T.A. 505. And, as stated in the above-quoted provisions of the regulations, the "receipt" contemplated by the cash method may be actual or constructive.

With respect to the constructive receipt of income, section 1.451–2 (a) of the Income Tax Regulations (which accords with prior regulations extending back to, and including, Article 53 of Regulations 45 under the Revenue Act of 1918) provides, in part, as follows:

> Income although not actually reduced to a taxpayer's possession is constructively received by him in the taxable year during which it is credited to his account or set apart for him so that he may draw upon it at any time. However, income is not constructively received if the taxpayer's control of its receipt is subject to substantial limitations or restrictions. Thus, if a corporation credits its employees with bonus stock, but the stock is not available to such employees until some future date, the mere crediting on the books of the corporation does not constitute receipt.

Thus, under the doctrine of constructive receipt, a taxpayer may not deliberately turn his back upon income and thereby select the year for which he will report it. The Hamilton National Bank of Chattanooga, as Administrator of the Estate of S. Strang Nicklin, Deceased, v. Commissioner, 29 B.T.A. 63. Nor may a taxpayer, by a private agreement, postpone receipt of income from one taxable year to another. James E. Lewis v. Commissioner, 30 B.T.A. 318.

However, the statute cannot be administered by speculating whether the payor would have been willing to agree to an earlier payment. See, for example, J. D. Amend, et ux., v. Commissioner, 13 T.C. 178, acquiescence, C.B. 1950–1, 1; and C. E. Gullett, et al., v. Commissioner, 31 B.T.A. 1067, in which the court, citing a number of authorities for its holding stated:

> It is clear that the doctrine of constructive receipt is to be sparingly used; that amounts due from a corporation but unpaid, are not to be included in the income of an individual reporting his income on a cash receipts basis unless it appears that the money was available to him, that the corporation was able and ready to pay him, that his right to receive was not restricted, and that his failure to receive resulted from exercise of his own choice.

Consequently, it seems clear that in each case involving a deferral of compensation a determination of whether the doctrine of constructive receipt it applicable must be made upon the basis of the specific factual situation involved.

Applying the foregoing criteria to the situations described above, the following conclusions have been reached:

(1) The additional compensation to be received by the taxpayer under the employment contract concerned will be includible in his gross income only in the taxable years in which the taxpayer actually receives installment payments in cash or other property previously credited to his account. To hold otherwise would be contrary to the provisions of the regulations and the court decisions mentioned above.

(2) For the reasons in (1) above, it is held that the taxpayer here involved also will be required to include the deferred compensation concerned in his gross income only in the taxable years in which the taxpayer actually receives installment payments in cash or other property previously credited to his account.

In arriving at this conclusion and the conclusion reached in case "(1)," consideration has been given to section 1.402(b)–1 of the Income Tax Regulations and to Revenue Ruling 57–37, C.B. 1957–1, 18, as modified by Revenue Ruling 57–528, C.B. 1957–2, 263. Section 1.402(b)–1(a) (1) provides in part, with an exception not here relevant, that any contribution made by an employer on behalf of an employee to a trust during a taxable year of the employer which ends within or with a taxable year of the trust for which the trust is not exempt under section 501(a) of the Code, shall be included in income of the employee for his taxable year during which the contribution is made if his interest in the contribution is nonforfeitable at the time the contribution is made. Revenue Ruling 57–37, as modified by Revenue Ruling 57–528, held, *inter alia*, that certain contributions conveying fully vested and nonforfeitable interests made by an employer into separate independently controlled trusts for the purpose of furnishing unemployment and other benefits to its eligible employees constituted additional compensation to the employees includible, under section 402(b) of the Code and section 1.402(b)–1(a) (1) of the regulations, in their income for the taxable year in which such contributions were made. These Revenue Rulings are distinguishable from cases "(1)" and "(2)" in that, under all the facts and circumstances of these cases, no trusts for the benefit of the taxpayers were created and no contributions are to be made thereto. Consequently, section 402(b) of the Code and section 1.402(b)–1(a) (1) of the regulations are inapplicable.

(3) Here the principal agreement provided that the royalties were payable substantially as earned, and this agreement was supplemented by a further concurrent agreement which made the royalties payable over a period of years. This supplemental agreement, however, was made before the royalties were earned; in fact, it was made on the same day as the principal agreement and the two agreements were a part of the same transaction. Thus, for all practical purposes, the arrangement from the beginning is similar to that in (1) above. Therefore, it is also held that the author concerned will be required to include the royalties in his gross income only in the taxable years in which they are actually received in cash or other property.

(4) In arriving at a determination as to the includibility of the $150x$ dollars concerned in the gross income of the football player, under the circumstances described, in addition to the authorities cited above, consideration also has been given to Revenue Ruling 55–727, C.B. 1955–2, 25, and to the decision in E. T. Sproull v. Commissioner, 16 T.C. 244.

In Revenue Ruling 55–727, the taxpayer, a professional baseball player, entered into a contract in 1953 in which he agreed to render services for a baseball club and to refrain from playing baseball for any other club during the term of the contract. In addition to specified compensation, the contract provided for a bonus to the player or his estate, payable one-half in January 1954 and one-half in January 1955, whether or not he was able to render services. The primary question was whether the bonus was capital gain or ordinary income; and, in holding that the bonus payments constituted ordinary income, it was stated that they were taxable for the year in which received by the player. However, under the facts set forth in Revenue Ruling 55–727 there was no arrangement, as here, for placing the amount of the bonus in escrow. Consequently, the instant situation is distinguishable from that considered in Revenue Ruling 55–727.

In E. T. Sproull v. Commissioner, 16 T.C. 244, affirmed, 194 F. 2d 541, the petitioner's employer in 1945 transferred in trust for the petitioner the amount of $10,500. The trustee was directed to pay out of principal to the petitioner the sum of $5,250 in 1946 and the balance, including income, in 1947. In the event of the petitioner's prior death, the amounts were to be paid to his administrator, executor, or heirs. The petitioner contended that the Commissioner erred in including the sum of $10,500 in his taxable income for 1945. In this connection, the court stated:

> * * * it is undoubtedly true that the amount which the Commissioner has included in petitioner's income for 1945 was used in that year for his benefit * * * in setting up the trust of which petitioner, or, in the event of his death then his estate, was the sole beneficiary * * *.

> The question then becomes * * * was "any economic or financial benefit conferred on the employee as compensation" in the taxable year. If so, it was taxable to him in that year. This question we must answer in the affirmative. The employer's part of the transaction terminated in 1945. It was then that the amount of the compensation was fixed at $10,500 and irrevocably paid out for petitioner's sole benefit. * * *."

Applying the principles stated in the *Sproull* decision to the facts here, it is concluded that the 150x-dollar bonus is includible in the gross income of the football player concerned in 1957, the year in which the club unconditionally paid such amount to the escrow agent.

(5) In this case, the taxpayer and the boxing club, as well as the opponent whom taxpayer had agreed to meet, are each acting in his or its own right, the proposed match is a joint venture by all of these participants, and the taxpayer is not an employee of the boxing club. The taxpayer's share of the gross receipts from the match belong to him and never belonged to the boxing club. Thus, the taxpayer ac-

quired all of the benefits of his share of the receipts except the right of immediate physical possession; and, although the club retained physical possession, it was by virtue of an arrangement with the taxpayer who, in substance and effect, authorized the boxing club to take possession and hold for him. The receipts, therefore, were income to the taxpayer at the time they were paid to and retained by the boxing club by his agreement and, in substance, at his direction, and are includible in his gross income in the taxable year in which so paid to the club. See the *Sproull* case, supra, and Lucas v. Guy C. Earl, 281 U.S. 111.

As previously stated, in each case involving a deferral of compensation, a determination of whether the doctrine of constructive receipt is applicable must be made upon the basis of the specific factual situation involved.

Consistent with the foregoing, the nonacquiescence published in C.B. 1952-2, 5, with respect to the decision in Commissioner v. James F. Oates, 18 T.C. 570, affirmed, 207 F.2d 711, has been withdrawn and acquiescence substituted therefor at page 5 of this Bulletin.

With respect to deductions for payments made by an employer under a deferred compensation plan, see section 404(a) (5) of the 1954 Code and section 1.404(a)-12 of the Income Tax Regulations.

In the application of those sections to unfunded plans, no deduction is allowable for any compensation paid or accrued by an employer on account of any employee under such a plan except in the year when paid and then only to the extent allowable under section 404(a). Thus, under an unfunded plan, if compensation is paid by an employer directly to a former employee, such amounts are deductible under section 404(a) (5) when *actually* paid *in cash or other property to the employee,* provided that such amounts meet the requirements of section 162 or section 212.

Advance rulings will not be issued in specific cases involving deferred compensation arrangements.*

NOTE

Circumstance (5) in the foregoing Revenue Ruling is similar to that in a controversy involving Sugar Ray Robinson. When the *Robinson* case was litigated, the Tax Court rejected the Commissioner's "joint venture" theory and held, further, that amounts not received within the taxable year could not be treated as constructively received. Ray S. Robinson, 44 T.C. 20 (1965). The Commissioner has acquiesced in that decision. 1970-2 C.B. xxi. Moreover, the Commissioner has acknowledged that circumstance (5) in Rev.Rul. 60-31 does not reflect a joint venture and has proffered a modified circumstance (5) which does. Rev.Rul. 70-435, 1970-2 C.B. 100.

* Despite the last sentence of Rev.Rul. 60-31, the Treasury later announced that it will entertain requests for rulings on deferred compensation arrangements. Rev.Rul. 64-279, 1964-2 C.B. 121. Ed.

3. STATUTORY DO–IT–YOURSELF AVERAGING

Averaging under I.R.C. (26 U.S.C.A.) § 1301 does not rest primarily on planning by the taxpayer; instead, it involves automatic relief from bunched income by taxing unusual receipts in one year in accordance with the taxpayer's income experience in the four *preceding* years. In contrast, averaging efforts described in Rev.Rul. 60–31 do not involve any statutory dispensation; instead, they merely show how a taxpayer may order his affairs so that the actual receipt of income that might be bunched in one year can be spread *forward* with attending averaging consequences under general statutory and tax common law principles. There are some additional averaging possibilities that involve both statutory dispensations and careful planning.[1] A detailed analysis of this third category cannot reasonably be attempted in a course in fundamentals, but a general description of the area may be of interest.

The general averaging provisions of the Code do not aid an employee who receives steady salary increases over his working career.[2] Such an employee can arrange overall to pay less tax on his lifetime salary income if he makes an arrangement such as that described in circumstances (1) or (2) of Rev.Rul. 60–31 so that some of his compensation is deferred to and taxed in his retirement years when his lower annual income will attract lower tax rates. Can he *assure* such later payment, for example by having his employer irrevocably pay the deferred amounts into an irrevocable trust for the employee's benefit, and still get the hoped-for tax deferral? Generally not.[3] Here, even without regard to questions of constructive receipt, the trust benefits conferred on the employee would be taxed on contributions to the trust as they were made. But (and it is a *big but*) just such arrangements can be made *with* the desired tax deferral consequences, if they are made in connection with a "qualified" pension plan that meets the requirements of I.R.C. (26 U.S.C.A.) § 401(a). Contributions to a qualified plan may be made in an amount designed to achieve defined benefits. Other plans are geared directly to the employee's salary or in amounts varying with the profits of the business (a profit-sharing plan), and they may be made in cash or in securities of the employer. A glance at I.R.C. (26 U.S.C.A.) § 401 (a) will give at least a hint of the detailed factors that determine qualification of a plan. One key requirement is that the plan not discriminate in favor of "employees who are . . . officers, . . . shareholders, or . . . highly compensated." [4]

1. Actually a kind of averaging results from the application of number of Code provisions; e. g., the capital gains rules (See Chapter 21) and the installment sales provisions (See Chapter 24 at page 811), and even from the application of some tax common law principles, e. g., Burnet v.

Logan, 283 U.S. 404, 51 S.Ct. 550 (1931) (See Chapter 24 at page 799).

2. Review I.R.C. (26 U.S.C.A.) § 1302 (a), Averageable Income.

3. I.R.C. § 402(b).

4. I.R.C. (26 U.S.C.A.) § 401(a) (4).

From the point of view of the employee, two distinct tax advantages flow from participation in a qualified pension or profit-sharing plan:

1. The employee is not taxed on contributions for his benefit until amounts are distributed to him[5]. Thus he pays tax later on what is really current compensation and, very likely, at lower rates because distributions are received over his retirement years.

2. The trust to which contributions are made is exempt from tax.[6] Thus untaxed compensation grows while held in the trust, without usual tax attrition.

Compare the tax consequences to the employee of compensation paid directly to him and placed by him in a savings account or in a private trust of his own creation.

Notwithstanding deferral of the tax on the employee for contributions to a qualified plan, the employer can deduct the contributions when paid.[7]

The statute virtually forecloses a funded pension plan which does not qualify under § 401 and in which the employee's rights are forfeitable. It will be seen that this might be attractive, a way to reward specific employees outside the proscription against a discriminatory plan mentioned above. It would appear that the employee would get the benefit of deferral (if his rights are forfeitable, he would not have the equivalent of cash when contributions were made for his benefit), and it *might* seem the employer could claim a deduction for his contributions. The deferral is allowed, but if a plan of this type fails to qualify, and the employee's rights are forfeitable, the employer is allowed a deduction only at the time the employee reports gross income.[8] But if a plan is qualified, its overall advantages may be summarized as affording the employee the obvious advantages of tax deferral and growth of his savings without customary tax attrition,[9] while the employer secures the usual immediate deduction for compensation paid.

Deferred compensation arrangements of the type discussed above may be accomplished by way of an employer's purchase of annuities for employees.[10] And, under some additional limitations, annuities

---

5. I.R.C. (26 U.S.C.A.) § 402(a).

6. I.R.C. (26 U.S.C.A.) § 501(a) and (c)(17).

7. I.R.C. (26 U.S.C.A.) § 404(a). I.R.C. (26 U.S.C.A.) §§ 162 and 212 are made inapplicable to such contributions, but the qualifications of those sections are invoked by § 404(a), in addition to some further requirements.

8. I.R.C. (26 U.S.C.A.) § 404(a)(5).

9. In some circumstances, lump sum distributions from a qualified employees' trust are accorded long-term capital gain treatment notwithstanding the ordinary income nature of the compensation which they represent. I.R.C. (26 U.S.C.A.) § 404(a)(2). The significance of this will be apparent after a consideration of Chapter 21, infra.

10. I.R.C. (26 U.S.C.A.) § 403(a).

purchased by certain tax exempt organizations, including state educational institutions, are accorded similar deferral advantages even if not a part of a qualified pension plan.[11]

It will be observed that the foregoing comments all relate to taxpayers who enjoy *employee* status; what about the self-employed? The question opens up an area that has been fraught with controversy for many years. Shouldn't the self-employed lawyer or doctor, for example, have comparable deferred income opportunities? Indeed, professional people have sought such advantages, first by de facto incorporation enabling them to assert employee status.[12] Administrative attempts to thwart these devices have been unsuccessful [13] and special incorporation statutes, which have been enacted by all states, now afford some professional people the opportunity to achieve employment status (in effect to be employed by themselves) even though they are in professions that have previously rejected incorporation.[14]

In the meantime, Congress has afforded some limited relief from the employee-self-employed discrimination. Without seeking employment status, self-employed individuals may be able to secure a deduction for contributions to a pension plan that benefits them, which deduction has the effect of deferring earnings to the time when benefits under the plan are actually enjoyed.[15] However, in addition to limiting contributions to 15% of earned income of the business, deductions for such contributions are restricted by an annual ceiling of $7500.[16]

Recently Congress has made it possible for employees (not just self-employed persons) who are not covered by a deferred compensation plan by their employers [17] to make deductible payments into an "individual retirement account." [18] Such payments are deductible up

11. I.R.C. (26 U.S.C.A.) § 403(b). All these specially designated deferred compensation arrangements also are accorded estate and gift tax advantages. I.R.C. (26 U.S.C.A.) §§ 2039(c) and 2517; and see Estate of Leslie E. Johnson, 56 T.C. 944 (1971).

12. See U. S. v. Kintner, 216 F.2d 418 (9th Cir. 1954); and see the broad tax definition of corporation in I.R.C. (26 U.S.C.A.) § 7701(a) (3).

13. After losing a long line of cases, e. g., U. S. v. Empey, 406 F.2d 157 (10th Cir. 1969), U. S. v. O'Neill, 410 F.2d 888 (6th Cir. 1969), and Kurzner v. U. S., 413 F.2d 97 (5th Cir. 1969), in T.I. R. No. 1019, August 8, 1969, 7 CCH 1969 Stand. Fed. Tax Rep. ¶ 6867, the Commissioner conceded that organizations of professional people organized under state professional corporation acts will, generally, be treated as corporations for tax purposes.

14. Articles dealing with professional corporations include Eaton, "Professional Corporations and Associations in Perspective," 23 Tax L.Rev. 1 (1967); Scallen, "Federal Income Taxation of Professional Associations and Corporations," 49 Minn.L.Rev. 603 (1965); Bittker, "Professional Associations and Federal Income Taxation: Some Questions and Comments," 17 Tax L.Rev. 1 (1961).

15. I.R.C. (26 U.S.C.A.) § 404(a) (8) and (9).

16. I.R.C. (26 U.S.C.A.) § 404(e). A comprehensive treatise on deferred compensation is Holzman, Guide to Pension and Profit Sharing Plans (3rd ed. 1969).

17. See I.R.C. § 219(b).

18. See I.R.C. § 219(a), which also includes payments for retirement annuities and retirement bonds. These are favored deductions. See § 62(10).

to 15% of compensation included in gross income or $1500, whichever is less for the year. Such accounts (or annuities or bonds) are accorded a zero basis, because they are created out of untaxed dollars, and subsequent distributions (or redemption in the case of bonds), if they escape penalties imposed on early realization,[19] and are taxed fully when received.[20] Meanwhile, however, the account or annuity or bond may grow without usual tax attrition.[21]

A related deferred compensation device for corporate employees has been the stock option. The broad proposition is that an employee might be given an option to purchase stock in his corporate employer at a price below, at, or above current market. Instant income is discernible if he receives an unrestricted right to purchase below the market, because the spread is a taxable equivalent of cash. Nevertheless, special provisions of the Code have afforded relief here from the rigors of general tax principles.[22] Over the years, there has been some appropriate shrinkage in the benefits available by way of statutory stock options, and the Tax Reform Act of 1976 repealed the qualified stock option provisions, subject to some transitional rules.[23]

D. THE CARRYOVER AND CARRYBACK DEVICES

Internal Revenue Code: See Section 172.

Let us assume that a novelty merchandiser stocks up on Hoola Hoops, skate boards, or clackers (or some other symbol of a fleeting fad) and makes a killing in 1955, say $100,000 profit. In 1956, he redoubles his purchases, but the popular fancy has turned to yo-yos, and the Hoola Hoop and skate board have taken their places in history along side the buggy whip and the whiffle-tree. So perhaps he has a huge loss in 1956; let's say $50,000. Now, it's all very well to say that he *did* have $100,000 properly taxed in 1955 and that, as he had *no* taxable income for 1956, he should be grateful to be relieved of the obligation to pay any tax for that year. But our merchandiser, despite the much-touted integrity of the taxable year, can't help but take

---

19. See I.R.C. §§ 408(f) and 409(c).

20. I.R.C. §§ 408(d) and 409(b).

21. See I.R.C. § 408(e).

22. See I.R.C. (26 U.S.C.A.) §§ 421 through 425.

23. TRA (1976) § 603, and see I.R.C. (26 U.S.C.A.) § 83. There is an excel- lent discussion of non-statutory deferred compensation arrangements in Lefevre, Knight, and Danico, Tax Management Portfolio No. 20 3rd (BNA 1969), entitled "Deferred Compensation Arrangements" which, while stressing arrangements not within the special Code provisions, contains suitable references and some comment on the special statutory rules.

a little longer view of his operations. For the *two* years he sees aggregate net profits of $50,000 but especially with a view to graduated tax rates, the tax paid for the two years seems unconscionable. Congress agrees with his view and, by way of an exception to standard taxable year principles, we have long had statutory provisions that permit operating losses in one year to be utilized in a redetermination of tax liability for another year.

The device by which the relief suggested is accomplished is a provision that permits an operating loss in one year to be carried *back* and treated as a business deduction in one or more of three preceding taxable years; or, to the extent that income in such years will not absorb the loss, it is carried *forward* and treated as a business deduction in one or more of seven succeeding taxable years.[1] The year to which the loss is carried is not elective; of the ten years involved (three back and seven forward), the loss must be utilized, to the extent that it can be, in the earliest year, except that the Tax Reform Act of 1976 has provided for an elective relinquishment of the carryback period with respect to a net operating loss for any taxable year ending after 1975.[2]

What is the effect of a net operating loss that results in a carryback to a prior year. Generally speaking, it may result in a determination that the tax for the earlier year was overpaid and, if so, the happy consequence is a tax refund. There is a collateral consequence here which is not unintended. The operation of the net operating loss provision is not limited to the extreme situation suggested at the outset of this note. Many conventional businessmen suffer momentary setbacks. When an operating loss threatens continuation of the business, a refund of prior years' taxes may supply cash to meet payrolls and otherwise keep the business afloat until the storm is weathered. Refunds arising out of carrybacks are handled expeditiously, outside the procedures prescribed for regular claims for refund.[3]

A net operating loss that cannot be carried back (for lack of income in the preceding three years) or which a taxpayer elects not to carry back simply moves forwards as a deduction in the succeeding years. It is a momentary disaster but nearly money in the bank, because it represents an amount of otherwise taxable income that can be earned in effect tax free in later periods. Of course the potential

1. I.R.C. (26 U.S.C.A.) § 172(a) and (b) (1) (A and B), as amended by TRA (1976) § 806(a). There are some exceptions to the three year carryback, five year carryover rule found in § 172(b)(1)(A)(ii) and (C) through (G). See Asimow, "Detriment and Benefit of Net Operating Losses: A Unifying Theory," 24 Tax L.Rev. 1 (1968).

2. I.R.C. (26 U.S.C.A.) § 172(b)(2) and (b)(3)(E) as amended by TRA (1976) § 806(c).

3. See I.R.C. (26 U.S.C.A.) § 6411; and see Chapter 29, infra. See also § 6511(d)(2)(A) providing a special refund limitations period. Of course the government pays no interest on amounts refunded because of a net operating loss carryback. I.R.C. (26 U.S.C.A.) § 6611(f)(1).

advantage never reaches fruition unless the taxpayer in fact has commensurate earnings for later periods.

The foregoing comments present the net operating loss in broad outline, and no attempt is made here to deal with the many complexities of the provision. Nevertheless, it may be noted that a principal problem in working with I.R.C. (26 U.S.C.A.) § 172 is the computation of the net operating loss for the year. Generally speaking, there is such a loss when deductions exceed gross income.[4] However, the statute contains some refinements and, as the title of the section suggests, the objective is to identify the loss that is traceable to *business* operations. Thus, in the case of an individual the net operating loss for a year is essentially the excess of his trade or business deductions over gross income, including non-business income reduced by certain non-business deductions.[5]

It will be apparent that a net operating loss carryback may affect the computation of adjusted gross income for the year to which the loss is carried. And it will be recalled that some deductions are measured in part by adjusted gross income for the year. Whether a recomputation of the deductions so affected for purposes of measuring a refund or determining the net operating loss carryover to subsequent years [6] is required for the year to which the loss is carried depends upon the detailed provisions of the statute. The percentage limitation governing the medical expense deduction under I.R.C. § 213, for example, must be recomputed [7] but generally not the limitation on the charitable deduction.[8] The principal reason why the charitable deduction limitation for a year is not permitted to be affected by an operating loss carried back to such year is to assure the taxpayer of the expected deduction for charitable contributions without regard to subsequent events.

Overall, I.R.C. (26 U.S.C.A.) § 172 can properly be regarded as an income averaging device. While it does nothing to level off income when all the years are profitable years, it does at least permit a loss year to have a leveling effect on profit years within the nine year span. Should the deduction be designed to chip away at peak years first over the nine year period, instead of operating chronologically on an earliest-year-first basis? Or does general averaging under I.R.C. (26 U.S.C.A.) § 1301 now adequately cover that problem for individuals?

---

4. I.R.C. (26 U.S.C.A.) § 172(c).

5. The details are specified in I.R.C. (26 U.S.C.A.) § 172(d) where it will be seen, among other things, that neither the personal exemption under § 151 nor the capital gains deduction under § 1202 enter into the computation. I.R.C. (26 U.S.C.A.) § 172(d)(3) and (d)(2)(B), respectively. A corporation's normal deductions are modified under § 172(d)(5) and (6) in measuring its net operating loss.

6. See also I.R.C. (26 U.S.C.A.) § 172 (b)(2)(A).

7. Reg. § 1.172–5(a)(3)(ii). There is no special rule in § 213.

8. Ibid; and see I.R.C. (26 U.S.C.A.) § 170(b) (1) (F). An individual's charitable deduction carryover under § 170(d)(1) may be affected by the net operating loss deduction. See Reg. §§ 1.170A–8(e); 1.172–5(a)(3)(ii).

I.R.C. (26 U.S.C.A.) § 172 is by no means the only Code provision that makes use of the carryover concept as a kind of departure from strict annual accounting. It will be seen for example in Chapter 21 that, when limitations on the deductibility of capital losses preclude the full tax use of such a loss in one year, the unused portion may be utilized in later years. And in Chapter 23 it will become apparent that a similar opportunity is sometimes afforded for a later deduction for charitable contributions that exceed the statutory ceiling on the deduction for the year in which the contribution is made.

PART SIX: THE CHARACTERIZATION OF INCOME AND DEDUCTIONS

CHAPTER 21. CAPITAL GAINS AND LOSSES

A. INTRODUCTION

It must now be recognized that a mere quantitative approach to items of income and deduction is insufficient for federal income tax purposes; the quality of such items must also be considered. The thought is not entirely new at this point, for we have already recognized that some income which could be taxed escapes tax if it has a tax-exempt quality, such as interest on state or municipal bonds. We have also seen that some potential deductions are flatly disallowed. Here, however, we are concerned with income that is taxed but which, according to its character, is taxed under special rules, and with deductions which, while not flatly disallowed, are subject to important statutory limitations. In general it is "capital gain" that may qualify for special (favorable) tax treatment and "capital loss" that may encounter special (restrictive) rules as to deduction. Thus, we must look at items qualitatively as well as quantitatively, a process referred to as the "characterization" of income and deduction items.

Whether gain or loss is subject to special treatment, as "capital" as opposed to "ordinary", usually is dependent upon (1) whether it arises in a transaction involving a "capital asset," (2) whether the capital asset has been the subject of a "sale or exchange," and (3) how long the taxpayer has "held" the asset. But the student should be alert in addition for statutory provisions that may artificially accord capital gain or loss treatment to some transactions which do not actually involve the sale or exchange of a capital asset. Take a preliminary look at I.R.C. (26 U.S.C.A.) §§ 166(d) (1) (B) and 165(g) (1). See also the note at page 665, infra.

Parts D, E, and F of this Chapter deal with the basic problems of characterization of items of income and deduction. Parts B and C explore the statutory mechanics for the treatment of capital gains and losses. Before plunging into detail, brief consideration is given here to the history and general philosophy of the tax treatment accorded transactions in capital assets.

It has always been clear that a merchant's sale of his stock in trade gives rise to gain or loss to be taken into account for tax pur-

635

poses. However, when the individual income tax was first enacted in 1913,[1] it contained no specific reference to gains or losses from dealing in property. What then of a sale of plant or equipment? of land held for investment? of securities? and so forth. Taxpayers were prompted to argue that gain on the sale of such properties was not income within the meaning of the Sixteenth Amendment or the federal taxing statute. In part the thought was that if one sold, say, securities and merely reinvested the proceeds in other securities (or even put the money in the bank), his financial position was unaltered; he had merely substituted the new securities (or the cash) for the securities previously owned and his investment continued. The notion was bolstered by the further thought that if there was gain of some sort in such transactions it might be largely illusory anyway, often traceable to mere changes in the price structure. Perhaps these propositions seemed more cogent in the early 20th century when we were closer to the time when a man's wealth was gauged by the value of the property he owned without much regard to his income or instances of conspicuous consumption. These concepts gained substantial acceptance under the British Income Tax[2] and, strangely, substantial vestiges persisted until 1965 when capital gains were first formally subjected to tax in England.[3]

Under the modern federal income tax the proposition that capital gains should not be taxed was never accepted.[4] In Merchants' Loan & Trust Co. v. Smietanka,[5] the Supreme Court held that capital gains were income within the meaning of that term in the Sixteenth Amendment. Relying in part on cases under the Corporate Excise Tax Act of 1909, the Court, quoting its opinion in Eisner v. Macomber,[6] said:[7]

> Income may be defined as the gain derived from capital, from labor, or from both combined, *provided it be understood to include profit gained through a sale or conversion of capital assets.*

While *Merchants' Loan* was the end of the constitutional issue *whether* capital gains were subject to tax, it marked only the beginning of congressional consideration of *how* such gains should be taxed.[8] In 1921, Congress enacted the first provisions giving preferential treatment to capital gains by way of a tax rate on such gains

1. Revenue Act of 1916, 39 Stat. 756 (1916).

2. Magill, Taxable Income, 82–103 (1945).

3. Finance Act 1965, Part III.

4. Cf. Gray v. Darlington, 15 Wallace Rep. 63 (1872), where the proposition that capital gains should not be taxed was accepted under the Civil War Income Tax Act, 14 Stat. 477–8 (1867).

5. 255 U.S. 509, 41 S.Ct. 386 (1921).

6. 252 U.S. 189, 207, 40 S.Ct. 189, 193 (1920).

7. 255 U.S. 509, 518, 41 S.Ct. 386, 388 (1921), emphasis added.

8. See, generally, Magill, Taxable Income, 103–113 (1945).

below those applicable to other types of income.[9] Reporting the bill, the Ways and Means Committee said: [10]

> The sale of * * * capital assets is now seriously retarded by the fact that gains and profits earned over a series of years are under the present law taxed as a lump sum (and the amount of surtax greatly enhanced thereby) in the year in which the profit is realized. Many such sales, with their possible profit taking and consequent increase of the tax revenue, have been blocked by this feature of the present law. In order to permit such transactions to go forward without fear of a prohibitive tax, the proposed bill, * * * adds a new section * * * [placing a preferential rate on gains from the sale or dispositions of capital assets].

While it may be argued that capital gain is no different in kind from other income and is, perhaps, just as spendable, three factors have now been identified that seem to give it a different quality. That is, a disposition of a capital asset may involve only a continuation of an investment in a different form; gain said to be realized may merely or largely reflect only changes in the overall price structure; and the gain may have been some time in the making, raising the question whether it is fair to bunch it into a single taxable year with attending tax attrition through the progressive rate tables. Although no one of these factors, nor indeed all three in combination, has ever prompted Congress wholly to *relieve* capital gains from tax, all have played a part in the congressional deliberations on *how* to tax gains on the disposition of property. And the factors are relevant, not only in this Chapter which deals directly with capital gains and losses, but in other areas as well. Consider, for example, but not in detail at this point, the reasons for special provision for the taxation of installment sales (§ 453) and of gain on the disposition of property used in a trade or business (§ 1231), and for the nonrecognition of gain on certain exchanges (§ 1031) and involuntary conversions (§ 1033), and the addition in 1969 of capital gain to the income averaging provisions (§ 1301).

Over the years, Congress has seen fit on numerous occasions to alter the preferential treatment accorded capital gains. As originally enacted, the 1921 legislation imposed a maximum 12½% tax rate on gain from the disposition of capital assets held for more than two years. As the above committee report indicates, the principal policy reason prompting such preferential treatment was a recognition of the long period over which such gain accrued. This policy was more

9. Revenue Act of 1921, § 106(a) (6), 42 Stat. 227, 232 (1921).

10. House Rep. No. 350, 67th Cong. 1st Sess., pp. 10–11, (1921) as quoted in

Seidman, Legislative History of the Income Tax Laws, 1938–1861, 813, (1938).

strongly reflected in the 1934 Revenue Act,[11] in which Congress favored capital gains by providing that sometimes less than the entire gain had to be included in income; the longer the property had been held, the smaller percentage of the gain includible. Under the provisions of that Act, no preference was accorded gain on the disposition of capital assets held for only one year or less but, thereafter, the amount of capital gain subject to inclusion in income was reduced on a sliding scale which went as low as 30% if the property was held for more than 10 years. The Revenue Act of 1938,[12] shortened the holding periods. In 1942 Congress abolished the sliding scale inclusion approach in favor of a flat preferential ceiling rate on gain from the disposition of capital assets held for more than six months.[13] Although often challenged, the six months holding period remained in effect through 1976. It was increased to nine months for 1977 and to one year for 1978 and years thereafter.[14] Other parts of this chapter give substantial attention to the identification of "long-term" and "short-term" capital gains and losses and to the interrelationship of such gains and losses.

Changes in the treatment of capital gains have occurred, not only with regard to the holding period requirement, but also in the definition of capital assets and the maximum rates at which such gains may be taxed. These changes largely reflect shifts in congressional preoccupation with one or more of the factors that seem to set capital gains apart from other forms of income.[15]

The first limitation upon the deductibility of *capital losses* appeared in the Revenue Act of 1924.[16] The Ways and Means Committee, in suggesting a limitation on the rate and amount of deductions for capital losses, stated: [17]

> [Certain] considerations led Congress, in the revenue act of 1921, to provide that the tax on capital gains in the case of property acquired and held by the taxpayer for profit or investment for more than two years should be limited to 12½ per cent. But Congress failed to place a similar

11. Revenue Act of 1934, § 117(a), 48 Stat. 680, 714 (1934).

12. Revenue Act of 1938, § 117(b), 52 Stat. 447, 500 (1938).

13. Revenue Act of 1942, § 150(a), 56 Stat. 798, 843 (1942). Of and on these are indications that Congress may once again opt for a sliding scale.

14. See TRA (1976) § 1402. For a criticism of this aspect of capital gains see Lowndes, "The Taxation of Capital Gains and Losses Under the Federal Income Tax," 26 Texas L.Rev. 440, 442 (1948).

15. The policy arguments both for and against preferential treatment for capital gains, which have been advanced over the years, including some not stated here, are collected in Blum, "A Handy Summary of the Capital Gain Arguments," 35 Taxes 247 (1957) and see Kutsoris, "In Defense of Capital Gains," 42 Fordham L.R. 1 (1973).

16. Revenue Act of 1924, § 208(c), 43 Stat. 253, 262 (1924).

17. House Rep. No. 1388, 67th Cong. 4th Sess. (1923), as quoted in Seidman, Legislative History of the Income Tax Laws, 1938–1861, 721 (1938).

limitation on capital losses, so that to-day the taxpayer pays a maximum tax of 12½ per cent on gains derived from the sale of capital assets, but is allowed to deduct in full from his taxable income his net losses resulting from the sale of capital assets during the taxable year. The injustice to the Government is too obvious to require much comment. The taxpayer may refrain from taking his profits, or, if he does take them, pays but a 12½ per cent tax, whereas he is at liberty at any time to take advantage of any losses that may have been incurred and avail himself of a full deduction from his income. When we consider that the rate on the larger incomes runs as high as 58 per cent, it can readily be realized how great the advantage is. The Government can collect but 12½ per cent of a gain, but it is compelled to lighten the burden of the taxpayer to the extent of 58 per cent of his losses. Take, for example, the case of a man with an income of $350,000 a year. Assume that he bought in the year 1917 5,000 shares of stock X at par, and that he sells these shares in 1922 for $600,000, showing a profit of $100,-000. By reason of this transaction he would pay, in addition to the tax on his regular income, $12,500 to the Government. But assume that instead of selling this stock at a profit, he sold it in 1922 at a loss of $100,000. He would then be entitled to deduct the $100,000 from his income of $350,000, and the loss to the Government by reason of that deduction would be $58,000. Is there any further argument needed?

The Revenue Act of 1924 and successive acts through 1932 provided a limitation on the deductibility of capital losses. The device adopted was to foreclose any deduction from ordinary income for capital losses but to permit the tax, otherwise computed, to be reduced by an amount up to 12½% of qualified losses.[18] This produced a result more consonant with the maximum 12½% rate of tax on capital gains. Although changes have occurred, restrictions upon the deductibility of capital losses have continued to the present.[19]

The shifting congressional attitude toward the proper treatment of capital gains and losses prompts speculation regarding future congressional action. With minor exceptions the Tax Reform Acts of 1969 and 1976 reduced some of the advantages previously accorded capital transactions.[20] Should further reductions be anticipated? An answer to this question must take account of the fact that the favorable treatment accorded some capital gains and the steeply graduated

18. Revenue Act of 1924, supra, at § 208(c).

19. I.R.C. (26 U.S.C.A.) §§ 1211, 1212. An informative brief history of both the capital loss restrictions and the capital gains preferences appears in 3B Mertens, The Law of Federal Income Taxation, §§ 22.02–22.03 (1966 Rev.).

20. For an analysis of the changes under T.R.A. (1969) see Maxfield, "Capital Gains and Losses," 25 Tax L.R. 565 (1970).

income tax rates are, in combination, responsible in very large part for the complexity of the present income tax statute. Proper interest in the simplification of the tax laws therefore creates a strong pressure toward an elimination of the present bifurcation of income into "ordinary income" and "capital gain". In 1969, while narrowing the gap between ordinary and capital transactions, Congress brought capital gains within the income averaging provisions of I.R.C. § 1301. Could this be a step on the road to treating capital transactions identical to ordinary transactions for all tax purposes? Can such a pursuit of simplification be squared with policy reasons that, in the past, have seemed to require special treatment?

A philosophical consideration of the questions whether, when, and how capital gains should be taxed will be aided by a study of the following works: Surrey, "Definitional Problems in Capital Gains Taxation," 69 Harv.L.Rev. 985 (1956); Smith, Federal Tax Reform 151–155 (1961); Goode, The Individual Income Tax 199–207 (1964), all reprinted (the Surrey article with modifications) in Sander and Westfall, Readings in Federal Taxation (Foundation Press 1970) at pages 552–572, 537–541, and 529–537, respectively.

B. THE MECHANICS OF CAPITAL GAINS

Internal Revenue Code: Sections 1; 1201(b), (c); 1202; 1222. See Sections 1201(a); 1221.

Now the record reads that Ptolemy I, satrap of Egypt, desiring lore but not labor, demanded from his prize subject some shorter way in geometry than the *Elements*. Whereupon (so the record runs) Euclid replied: "There is no royal road to geometry" * * * or capital gains. Because the road is difficult, a map is provided here in the form of an explanatory note; and in Part C a similar map is provided with respect to capital losses. The notes must be used *with* the statute, *not* as a substitute for it. The novice will find both the notes and the statute hard going but, as usual, there are rewards for persistence.

1. Individuals

The Internal Revenue Code affords favorable tax treatment to "net capital gain," which § 1222(11) defines as the "excess of net long-term capital gain for the taxable year over net short-term capital loss for such year." And although in some circumstances the treatment is not as friendly since the enactment of the Tax Reform Acts of 1969 and 1976, it remains friendly enough with regard to most taxpayers. In general the Code retains the longstanding scheme, providing:

> (1) A basic method, § 1202, which accords the taxpayer a special deduction in the computation of his tax liability under § 1 rate tables. The § 1202 deduction, called the capital gains deduction, is an amount equal to one half of the "net capital

gain" which, as indicated above, is the excess of net long-term capital gain over net short-term capital loss for the year.

(2) An alternative method, § 1201(b), which provides for the computation at special rates of a partial tax on the *entire* "net capital gain" and a partial tax at § 1 rates on the taxpayer's other taxable income.[1] The sum of these partial taxes is the tax under the alternative method.

Whichever is lower, the tax under the basic method or the tax under the alternative method, is the taxpayer's tax for the year.

A. *The Basic Method*, § 1202.

Section 1202 was not altered substantially when major changes were made in 1969 and 1976, except as changes were made in the long-term holding periods in the later year. Under that section, if a taxpayer has net capital gain (§ 1222(11)), net long-term capital gain (§ 1222(7)) in excess of net short-term capital loss (§ 1222(6)), 50% of the net capital gain is required to be deducted from gross income. (It is a deduction in arriving at adjusted gross income. See § 62(3)). The effect of this 50% deduction is to cut the marginal rate in § 1 by one-half with respect to the net long-term gain that remains subject to tax after reduction by net short-term losses.[2] This is so because only half of such gain remains in taxable income and is taxed at the rates in § 1.

An example may be helpful. Assume T has a long-term capital gain (§ 1222(3)) of $20,000 and a long-term capital loss (§ 1222(4)) of $8,000. His net long-term capital gain is $12,000 (§ 1222(7)) and, if there are no short-term transactions for the year, § 1202 applies to the "net capital gain" of $12,000 (simply net long-term capital gain because there is no net short-term capital loss; it is zero). Assume T has other income, salary for example, of $10,000. Technically T's gross income is $30,000 computed as follows:

Salary	$10,000
Long-term gain	20,000
Gross income	$30,000

1. The other taxable income includes *ordinary* income and net short-term capital gains in excess of net long term capital losses.

2. While the foregoing statement is essentially accurate, it might be embroidered a bit for the benefit of the purist. After taking account of the § 1202 deduction, it is possible that the effective rate applicable to the entire gain may be less than one-half the rate that would have applied to the entire gain without the deduction. For example if a taxpayer had taxable ordinary income of $26,000 and a net long-term capital gain of $12,000 and there were no § 1202 deduction, his tax liability would be $13,290. (§ 1(c)) The tax on the excess over ordinary income is $5,700 ($13,290–$7,590) reflecting an overall rate on the capital gain of 47½%. When a § 1202 deduction is provided his tax liability is $10,290 (§ 1(c)), and the tax on the excess over ordinary income is $2,700 ($10,290–$7,590), reflecting an overall effective rate on the capital gain of 22½%. This is clearly less than one-half the overall 47½% rate that would have applied in the absence of a § 1202 deduction.

However the statute requires that long-term capital gains and losses and short-term capital gains and losses, respectively, be netted; the income tax return (Schedule D of Form 1040) and practice have separated the capital gains computations from the gross income computations, at least initially.[3] So in practice, we can say that T has gross income of $22,000, computed as follows:

Salary		$10,000
Long-term gain	$20,000	
Long-term loss	−8,000	
Net long-term gain (See §§ 1222(7) ; 62(4))		12,000
Gross income (after capital loss)		$22,000
Applying § 1202, T is *required* to deduct from gross income 50% of the amount of the net capital gain, (i. e., ½ of $12,000 as there were no short-term losses). See also § 62(3).		−6,000
Adjusted gross income		$16,000

If in this and in all subsequent examples we assume that T is a single individual and disregard all other deductions and credits to which T might be entitled (e. g., the § 141 optional standard and § 151 exemptions), then T's taxable income is $16,000 and T's tax is $3830. § 1 (c). The effective rate of tax on all T's taxable income is roughly 24%. But the point is that on the net capital gain the rate of tax is about 12%. This is so because only half of that gain is subjected to tax, and 24% of $6,000 is the equivalent of 12% of $12,000.

B. *The Alternative Method,* § 1201(b)

Initially it should be emphasized that the alternative tax is used *only* when the tax resulting from the basic method (§ 1202) exceeds the tax computed under § 1201(b). See the parenthetical clause of § 1201(b).

Prior to 1969, under the alternative provisions of § 1201(b) the excess of net long-term capital gain over net short-term capital loss (now called net capital gain) was taxed at a ceiling rate of 25%. If the basic method were the only provision affording favorable tax treatment to such gains, one can readily see that the ceiling rate of tax would be as high as 35%. This is so because the top rate in § 1 is 70% and, if a taxpayer had other income of sufficient amount, the

---

3. The procedure used on the income tax return and practice varies from the strict statutory formula which would require inclusion of all gains and deduction of losses. Although generally the variant procedure generates the same amount of adjusted gross income, it is sometimes necessary to establish "the gross income stated in the return." E. g., I.R.C. § 6501(e), sometimes extending limitation periods where gross income is substantially omitted. In such circumstances it seems clear the statutory formula would be applied rather than the short-cut generally permitted on the return.

50% deduction provided by § 1202 could result in an effective tax rate of 35% being applicable to the entire net capital gain. The alternative method, which prior to 1969 invariably applied a fixed 25% rate of tax to the entire amount of what we now call net capital gain, has been altered. Although the 25% top tax rate still appears in § 1201 (b), its application is limited to the first $50,000 of such gain.[4]

§ 1201(b) furnishes a recipe for computing a separate tax at special rates on the net capital gain. For a taxpayer having ordinary taxable income and net capital gain, a three-step computation may be required. The taxpayer using the alternative method is required to:

(1) Compute a tax on his other taxable income,[5] without regard to any net capital gain (§ 1201(b)(1));

(2) Compute a tax at 25% on net capital gain, but limited to $50,000 of such gain.[6] (§ 1201(b)(2));

(3) Compute a tax on net capital gain in excess of $50,000 in the manner it is taxed under the basic method at *rates* that take account of all the taxpayer's taxable income, including that taxed at the special 25% rate.[7] (§ 1201(b)(3) and (c)).

The sum of steps (1), (2) and (3), or of (1) and (2) when (3) is inapplicable, is the tax liability for the year. The above is only a summary; detailed discussion of the three steps follows.

First, all net capital gain is removed from taxable income. This is accomplished by deducting the remaining 50% of net capital gain from taxable income as computed under the basic method; it will be recalled that 50% of net capital gain has already been removed from taxable income by the § 1202 deduction. The remaining essentially ordinary taxable income[8] is then subjected to tax at § 1 rates under § 1201(b)(1). This is only a part of the taxpayer's tax liability, because as yet no tax has been computed on the net capital gain. The second and third steps operate to impose tax on the entire net capital gain.

Second, § 1201(b)(2) prescribes a flat tax rate of 25% for net capital gain not in excess of $50,000 ($25,000 in the case of a married taxpayer filing a separate return).[9]

4. Here is a simplification of the rule expressed in I.R.C. § 1201(b)(2), which is the way Congress should have enacted it:

  "(2) a tax of 25% of the lesser of—

   (A) $50,000 ($25,000 in the case of a married individual filing a separate return), or

   (B) the amount of the net capital gain, and . . . ."

5. See note 1, supra.

6. See note 4, supra.

7. In this computation the § 1202 deduction has the effect of imposing a 35% ceiling rate, one half the maximum tax rate, as explained in the text above.

8. See note 1, supra.

9. Transitional rules for the application of I.R.C. § 1201(b) to years following the enactment of the Tax Reform Act of 1969 are not discussed.

The 1969 legislation imposed a limitation on the familiar 25% tax rate and the 1976 legislation continues to limit that rate to net capital gain up to $50,000.[10] If all of a taxpayer's net capital gain is within the $50,000 limitation, he makes only the first two computations under the alternate method, and these are the same as long persisted under prior law. Most taxpayers will not reach the third step.

An example may be helpful. Assume taxpayer T has gross income of $250,000, consisting of $200,000 of ordinary income and $50,000 of net capital gain. If all other deductions are disregarded, except for the § 1202 deduction (basic method) T has taxable income of $225,000, computed as follows:

Basic Method: Ordinary income	$200,000
Net capital gain	50,000
Total gross income	$250,000
Less § 1202 deduction	−25,000
Taxable income	$225,000

Under § 1(c), T's tax is $140,590. However, T is eligible to use the alternative method tax rate of 25% with regard to the $50,000 net capital gain. In this case, T's tax will be $135,590, resulting in a tax saving to T of $5,000 ($140,590–$135,590). Thus:

Alternative Method:	
§ 1201(b)(1):	
Taxable income	$225,000
Less (§ 1201(b)(1))	−25,000
Taxable ordinary income	$200,000
Partial tax, at § 1(c) rates	
on $200,000	$123,090
§ 1201(b)(2):	
Partial tax, at 25% on $50,000	12,500
T's total tax liability:	$135,590

The reason for the $5,000 tax saving under the alternative method will be clear if it is noted that the capital gains that would be taxed at an effective rate of 35% under the basic method (one-half the § 1(c) maximum 70% rate) are taxed under § 1201(b)(2) at 25%. The difference, 10%, is $5,000 (10% times $50,000) which is the amount of the saving.[11] One should not lose sight of the fact that in other circumstances the basic method may effect greater tax savings

10. For a period after the enactment of the Tax Reform Act of 1969 it was possible for the 25% rate to apply to an amount in excess of $50,000. Again, this transitional possibility is not discussed.

11. This is the maximum saving under the alternative method. The saving under the alternative method is often less than $5,000. See problem 6 at page 649, infra.

than the alternative method. This is always the case when the taxpayer's effective marginal tax rate is less than 50%.

Third. The third step is required if the amount of net capital gain exceeds $50,000. (See § 1201(b)(3)), and it imposes a tax on that excess. (§ 1201(c)). In this event the congressional decision is that the excess will not be favored by the 25% rate. As to the excess (but only the excess), the alternative tax was abolished in 1969, leaving the amount of net capital gain that exceeds $50,000 to be taxed in the same manner as under the basic method at a maximum effective rate of 35% or, in other words, to benefit only from the § 1202 deduction. (§ 1201(b)(3)).

The tax on the excess under § 1201(c) applies the highest rates to which the taxpayer is subject under § 1 to one-half the excess. This is accomplished by layering half of the excess on top of ordinary taxable income, already taxed under § 1201(b)(1), plus $25,000, invariably half the amount already taxed under § 1201(b)(2), except for a married taxpayer filing separately.[12] The computation under § 1201(c) involves two steps. The first step reflects a straight application of the basic method, tax on "taxable income" from which § 1202 has removed one-half the net capital gain. The second step reflects an application of § 1 rates to taxable income from which one-half the net capital gain in excess of $50,000 has been removed. In this way half the net capital gain in excess of $50,000 is isolated so that the top § 1 rates can be applied to it.

Here is a graphic picture of § 1201(c):[13]

Step 1. Tax on: Ordinary income + $25,000 + ½ excess of net capital gain over $50,000

MINUS

Step 2. Tax on: Ordinary income + $25,000

———————

Difference in tax . . . . is . . . Tax on excess of net capital gain over $50,-000

The difference is the amount of tax under § 1201(b)(3).

The alternative tax, covering all three steps can now be illustrated by an example. In the example, all deductions (including the

———————

12. See note 4, supra.

13. This graphic picture is altered for a married taxpayer filing separately by substituting $12,500 and $25,000 for $25,000 and $50,000, respectively, wherever those figures appear.

personal exemption), except those which relate to capital gains, are ignored. T (unmarried) has ordinary taxable income of $200,000 plus net capital gain in the amount of $200,000.

Ordinary taxable income	$200,000
Net capital gain	200,000
Gross income	$400,000
Less § 1202 deduction	−100,000
Taxable income	$300,000
Tax (§ 1(c) rate) under basic method	$193,090

The capital gain is effectively taxed at the top rate of 35%. Because we have learned that under the alternative method the first $50,-000 of net capital gain is taxed at a 25% rate (§ 1201(b)(2)), we know that, here, T's tax will be smaller using the alternative. The following computation confirms this.

Alternative Method:

Step (1) Section 1201(b)(1):
Tax on $200,000, ordinary taxable income without regard to capital gain.
The tax under § 1(c) is: $123,090

Step (2) Section 1201(b)(2):
(A) LTCG up to $50,000: $50,000
(B) Net capital gain: $200,000
Tax rate of 25% on $50,000 (lesser of (A) or (B))
The tax is: 12,500

Step (3) Section 1201(b)(3), per § 1201(c)
(a) ordinary income $200,000
plus 50% of all
net capital gain
(½ of $200,000) 100,000
Taxable income (after the § 1202 deduction): $300,000
Tax on $300,000 (§ 1(c)) $193,090
(b) ordinary income $200,000
plus 25,000
$225,000
Tax on $225,000 (§ 1(c)) −140,590
(c) Tax on amount of net capital gain in excess of $50,000 (excess of (a) over (b)) 52,500
The tax is: 52,500
Total tax under alternative method is: $188,090

Note that, while the amount of the excess of net capital gain over $50,000 is $150,000, the tax is actually computed on half the excess ($75,000). Compare figures for income taxed in 3(a) with that in 3(b). Steps 3(a) and 3(b) simply kick the 50% of the excess into T's highest bracket. In effect the amount of net capital gain that exceeds $50,000 is taxed in this example at 35%.

Proof:

Excess net capital gain	$150,000
Tax rate	35%
Tax (see Step 3)	$ 52,500

But even so, the tax as thus computed ($188,090) is less than T's tax as computed under the Basic Method ($193,090). The Alternative Method effects a tax saving on these facts of $5000 ($193,090–188,090). This is not coincidental, it is because the first $50,000 is taxed at only 25%, while under the Basic Method the entire gain would be taxed effectively at 35%.

With the foregoing discussion in mind, two further comments should be made regarding the 1969 and 1976 [14] changes in the treatment of capital gains. First, while Congress saw fit to continue the 50% capital gains deduction under § 1202 (described above as the Basic Method), the alternate provision of § 1201(b), which used to tax a flat rate of 25% for *all* the net capital gain, was considered too big a break for high-bracket taxpayers and inconsistent with the progressive rate structure. This can be seen from the fact that, if a taxpayer was in the 60% bracket, the alternate computation gave him an advantage that would be the equivalent of a 58% § 1202 deduction. For example, on $100,000 of long-term capital gain the alternative tax would be *$25,000* at the flat 25% rate. It would take a 58% § 1202 deduction to yield this result if the taxpayer's rate was 60%. i. e.,

$100,000	
−58,000	(58% deduction)
42,000	addition to taxable income
.60	(assumed rate)
$25,200.00	Tax at 60% after 58% deduction.

The advantage of § 1201(b) with the old flat 25% rate was even greater for higher bracket taxpayers. Try some arithmetic. Congress rejected the regressive nature of the alternate provision, except for amounts up to $50,000.

14. The 1976 changes on gains are largely cosmetic except for the new holding period rules.

Second, in 1969 Congress added and in 1976 expanded a tax that will affect the total tax cost of capital gains to high income taxpayers. This is the so-called Minimum Tax For Tax Preferences, imposed by § 56. It is at a flat rate of 15% and is *in addition* to other federal taxes. Identified as an item of tax preference in the case of individuals is "an amount equal to one-half the net capital gain." § 57(a)(9)(A). This is of course the amount of the § 1202 deduction. However, the minimum tax has an exemption equal to the greater of $10,000 or one-half of the current year's tax liability. § 56(a). So it is only high bracket taxpayers who must add the minimum tax to tax conventionally determined in order to identify the full tax cost of long-term capital gains. See Chapter 27, Computations, infra at page 947.

2. Corporations

While § 1202 provides the basic method of taxing capital gains of individuals and other non-corporate taxpayers, the § 1202 basic method is inapplicable to corporations. I.R.C. § 1201(a) does, however, provide a method of taxing net capital gains to corporations, and that method is an alternative method to taxing net capital gains as ordinary income to the corporation under § 11 (the corporate income tax rate provision that is the counterpart of § 1 in the case of individuals). A corporation can, under § 1201(a), (1) compute a partial tax on its ordinary income with the net capital gain pulled out of such income and (2) compute an additional tax using a 30% rate on such net capital gains.

Since the taxable income of a corporation is taxed at stepped, not graduated rates, generally 22% for the first $25,000 and 48% on the excess over $25,000,[15] corporations with taxable income, including net capital gain, of $25,000 or less will clearly use § 11, instead of the higher alternative rate of 30% with respect to such gain.[16] In this case, such gain is treated no differently from ordinary income; but the rate (22%) is friendly enough.

If, however, a corporation has sizeable amounts of taxable income from operations, for example $100,000, and in addition has a net capital gain of $100,000, the § 1201(a) alternative method becomes

---

15. For the years 1974–1977 the § 11 rates are 20% for the first $25,000, 22% for the second $25,000 and 48% on the excess over $50,000.

16. For years 1974–1977 the statement applies to corporations having net § 1201 gain (now called net capital gain) of $50,000.

beneficial. Without § 1201(a), the net capital gain would be taxed at 48% under § 11. When § 1201(a) is applied the result is as follows:

Tax on $25,000 at 22% (so-called "normal tax")	$ 5,500
Tax on $75,000 at 48% (normal and surtax)	36,000
Partial tax on $100,000 taxable ordinary income (§§ 1201(a); 11)	$41,500
§ 1201(a)(1)(B) or (a)(2), net capital gain taxed at 30%	30,000
Corporate Tax	$71,500[17]

The tax figure of $41,500, above, is only a partial tax since it does not include a tax on the net capital gain. The tax on that gain is $30,000 (30% × $100,000). The total tax liability for the corporation is then $71,500 ($41,500 + $30,000) under the § 1201(a) method, as opposed to $89,500 (22% of $25,000 + 48% of $175,000), if there were no exception to the § 11 rates.

PROBLEMS

Cap Gainer has a $22,000 salary. Assuming that Cap is a single individual and disregarding all other deductions to which Cap might be entitled (e. g., the § 141 optional standard and § 151 exemptions), compute his tax liability for the year determining his gross income after netting his capital gains and losses and using, of course, the preferable alternative of § 1201(b) or § 1202 if applicable. Assume Cap has the following alternative additional capital gains and losses during the year:

1. A $20,000 long-term capital gain and a $12,000 long-term capital loss.

2. A $20,000 short-term capital gain and a $12,000 short-term capital loss.

3. A $50,000 long-term capital gain, an $8000 long-term capital loss, and a $2000 short-term capital loss. Note the top increment of his income is now subject to tax at a rate greater than 50%; does this mean the alternative method of § 1201 (b) will automatically be to his advantage?

4. A $50,000 long-term capital gain, an $8000 long-term capital loss, a $10,000 short-term capital gain, and a $2000 short-term capital loss.

5. An $80,000 long-term capital gain and a $20,000 long-term capital loss.

6. Same as 5, above, except that Cap Gainer has a $50,000 salary.

---

17. For 1974–1977 corporate tax liability would be $34,500 on ordinary income and $30,000 on net § 1201 gain or a total of $64,500.

C. THE MECHANICS OF CAPITAL LOSSES

Internal Revenue Code: Sections 165(f); 1211(b); 1212(b). See Sections 1211(a); 1212(a); 1221; 1222.

---

1. Individuals

The losses discussed here are only *deductible* losses. Under § 1222(2) and (4) the terms short-term capital loss and long-term capital loss are confined to encompass only such losses as are "taken into account in computing taxable income." What determines whether they are taken into account? In the case of individuals, primarily § 165(c), which should be reviewed. Thus, before we enter the area under discussion here there must be a decision *whether* loss is deductible. If it is, the provisions presently under examination determine *how* the deduction may be utilized.

In general, capital losses are deducted only from capital gains. Capital losses, whether long-term or short-term, offset capital gains, long-term or short-term, dollar for dollar. However, in the case of a taxpayer other than a corporation, capital losses in excess of capital gains can be deducted from ordinary income, but not always dollar for dollar and, after 1977, in any one year only to the maximum extent of $3000. If any loss balance remains it is carried forward into succeeding taxable years, retaining its character as long-term or short-term, as the case may be, to be applied against capital gains (and within the $3000 limitation against ordinary income) in each succeeding year until fully utilized. (§§ 1211(b); 1222(10); 1212 (b)).

The statutory mechanics require the taxpayer separately to net his long-term transactions and his short-term transactions. Net longs are then netted against net shorts. If there are overall net gains in each category, the net long-term capital gain becomes net capital gain and is afforded the special treatment described in Part B, above, and the net short-term capital gain is simply accorded ordinary income treatment. The possibility of net losses in both categories is considered later. If there is a net long-term gain and a net short-term loss, the loss reduces or eliminates dollar-for-dollar, the amount of net long-term gain accorded such special treatment. Likewise, if there is a net long-term loss and a net short-term gain, the long-term loss reduces or eliminates, dollar-for-dollar, the net short-term gain. There is, thus, a double netting process under which capital losses are always fully utilized in any year to the extent that there are capital gains for the year, but in accordance with priority which requires that long-term losses first be used against long-term gains and that short-term losses first be used against short-term gains. Implicit in all this is the principal distinction between short-term gain and ordinary income; short-term capital gain has a limit-less capacity for being offset by capital losses, subject only to the priority suggested, whereas the reduction of ordinary income by capi-tal losses is severely restricted. These restrictions and the possible deferred utilization of capital losses that run afoul of them, and which are accorded no immediate recognition, are the subject of this dis-cussion.

The starting point for the treatment of capital losses is § 1211(b). It provides, initially, that capital losses are deductible only to the ex-tent of capital gains. In addition, however, it permits the further use of capital losses against ordinary income in an amount not in excess of the smallest of three identifiable figures. First, the capital loss offsetting ordinary income may not exceed taxable income for the year, which simply precludes worthless utilization of the loss and is related to the matter of loss carryovers which is discussed further later on in this note. Second, it may not exceed $3000 in any year after 1977. The Tax Reform Act of 1976 increased this limitation from $1000 in 1976 and prior years to $2000 for 1977 and $3000 there-after. Third, a limitation introduced by the Tax Reform Act of 1969 differentiates the impact of short term losses from long term losses on taxable income. Recall that net capital gain is taxed only to the extent of 50% after application of the capital gain deduction. With this in mind, in 1969 Congress chose to dilute the capacity of long term losses to reduce ordinary income; and since 1969 it has required $1.00 of excess net long term loss over net short term gain to reduce ordinary income by 50¢. This further limitation on the utilization of capital losses against ordinary income is discernible in § 1211(b) (1)(C). Under that provision, for example, a taxpayer with sub-stantial income must use $2000 of net long term capital loss in excess of any net short term capital gain to deduct only $1000 from ordinary income.

In contrast to excess net long-term losses, net *short-term* losses in excess of net long-term gains can be deducted in full (dollar-for-dollar) from ordinary income up to the post-1977 ceiling limit of $3,000 or taxable income, whichever is less. § 1211(b)(1)(C)(i). Since net short-term capital *gains* (in excess of net long-term capital losses) are taxable in full as ordinary income, in contrast to the treat-ment accorded net long-term capital gains, there is no reason to dilute the deduction of excess net short-term capital losses from ordinary income.

At this point, an example may be helpful. In the example the year is 1978 and all deductions except those concerning capital losses are disregarded. Assume that T (a single taxpayer) has salary income of $12,000. During the same year, he has the following transactions:

Long-term capital gain	$800	Short-term capital gain	$ 300
Long-term capital loss	3200	Short-term capital loss	1,000
Net long-term capital loss	$(2400)	Net short-term capital loss	$(700)

Although the total of T's net long-term capital loss and net short-term capital loss is $3100, T can deduct only $1900 from ordinary income, computed as follows:

Tracking the statute, § 1211(b)(1), authorizes capital losses as deductions only from capital gains. This initial offset is reflected in the paragraph above. If such losses exceed such gains, as they do here, then after 1977 § 1211(b)(1) authorizes the deduction of the excess from ordinary income to the extent of the *smaller* of:

(A) the taxable income, or

(B) $3000, or

(C) the sum of

     (i) the excess net short-term loss, $700, and

     (ii) one-half the excess net long-term loss (½ × $2400) $1200.

The limitation in § 1211(b)(1)(A) comes into play only when taxable income (as specially computed, see § 1211(b)(3)) is less than $3000;[1] so that limitation is not applicable here. The result of apply-

---

1. In the example in the text, we assumed that T's gross income (and taxable income) was sufficient so as to use the ceiling limitation of § 1211 (b)(1)(C). On the other hand, if taxable income as defined in § 1211(b)(3) for the year is less than the amounts expressed in § 1211(b)(1)(B) and (C), § 1211(b)(1)(A) requires such smaller figure to be used as the ceiling. It is such an unusual circumstance, where one asserting a deduction for capital losses will have less than $3000 of taxable income, that no extended discussion of this limitation is warranted. It should be noted that the "taxable income" ceiling here is an adjusted figure which disregards capital gains and losses for the year and which also does not take account of the § 151 deductions for personal exemption and dependents. See § 1211(b)(3). These adjustments will not affect the taxpayer's tax liability for the year of the asserted loss, as his taxable income will be reduced to zero for such year in any event. But they do affect the amount of his loss carryover, a phenomenon discussed later in the text. In effect the § 151

deductions are wasted, because the loss carryover is reduced by the amount of such deductions without the taxpayer deriving any tax benefit from such deductions. For an example of the resulting reduction of the carryover see problem 5 at page 658, infra. Here is an example of the application of the taxable income ceiling.

Assume that T, a single taxpayer entitled to only one personal exemption, § 151, has *taxable income,* without regard to capital gains and losses (but taking account of his exemption) of only $175 in a year after 1977. In the same year, T has the following capital gains and losses:

Long-term gain	$800
Long-term loss	3200
Net long-term loss	($2400)
Short-term gain	$ 300
Short-term loss	$1,000
Net short-term loss	($ 700)

The amount potentially deductible from ordinary income is $1900; it is less than $3000, § 1211(b)(1)(B), and it is the sum of the excess of the net

ing § 1211(b)(1)(C)(i) and (ii) is $1900, $700 excess net short-term capital loss plus $1200, half the excess net long-term capital loss. This is less than the $3000 ceiling limitation of § 1211(b)(1)(B). Therefore, T's deduction from ordinary income is $1900 and his adjusted gross income is $10,100 computed as follows:

Salary	$12,000
Less: § 1211(b) deduction § 62(4)	1,900
Adjusted gross income	$10,100

Carryovers

In essence, capital losses, long-term or short-term, are deducted in full from capital gains and then utilized, subject to limitations described above, against ordinary income. In the case of net long-term losses, $2.00 of loss is consumed for every $1.00 deduction against ordinary income allowable under § 1211(b). Thus if a taxpayer has only excess net long-term losses of $2,000, he gets a $1,000 deduction from ordinary income but there is no amount to carry over to the next year. The carryover statute, § 1212(b) relating to non-corporate taxpayers, provides that capital losses not exhausted in the year incurred may be carried over into subsequent years and treated as long-term or short-term loss, depending upon their origin.[2] Such carried over losses are treated exactly the same as if they were losses actually arising in the year to which carried [3] and consequently may be carried forward into succeeding years indefinitely until finally used in accordance with the statute. They do, however, die with the taxpayer and are not passed along the way I.R.C. § 642(h) passes along losses of an estate or trust upon its termination.

short-term loss plus one-half the excess of net long-term loss. § 1211(b)(1)(C). But since taxable income is smaller, the deduction is limited to that. For purposes of this limitation, the statute requires taxable income to be recomputed without regard to the personal exemption. § 1211(b)(3). Thus T's taxable income for *this* purpose is $925, computed as follows:

Taxable Income exclusive of capital gains and losses	$175
Add: Personal exemption § 1211 (b)(3)	750
§ 1211(b) taxable income	$925

After claiming the appropriate capital loss deduction ($925) under § 1211(b)(1), T's taxable income is zero.

2. The "if" clause at the beginning of § 1212(b)(1) makes the carryover provisions dependent upon the taxpayer having a "net capital loss," which is defined in § 1222(10) as "the excess of the losses from the sales or exchanges of capital assets over the sum allowed under § 1211." This seems a useless bit of verbiage. The definition, which lumps short-term and long-term losses indiscriminately, does not measure either the amount or the character of the carryover, both of which remain to be determined under § 1212(b)(1) and (2). This statutory awkwardness might be noted in working the problems at the end of this Part.

3. A transitional rule, I.R.C. (U.S.C.A.) § 1212(b)(3), accords pre-1970 long-term losses that are carried over to 1970 or later years pre-1970 long-term loss treatment, i. e., dollar-for-dollar deduction from ordinary income within the statutory $1,000 limitation. Such carried over losses are used first and exhausted before the use of long-term losses for 1970 and later years. Rev.Rul. 71–195, 1971–1 C.B. 225.

Note in the preceding example T has a total of $3100 of net long-term and short-term losses, only $1900 of which has been deducted from ordinary income. Those familiar with carryover provisions might think that the entire excess of losses not deductible in the year in which they were realized could be carried over to the next year and used in that year to offset capital gains. Thus, here, in a sense T has *unused* capital losses of $1200 ($3100 − $1900). Prior to 1969 this was the law, and it is still the law with respect to net short-term losses that exceed the sum of net long-term gains plus (after 1977) $3000 of ordinary income or taxable income whichever is less. However, with respect to excess *net long-term losses*, recall that under § 1212 it takes $2.00 of net long-term loss to offset $1.00 of ordinary income. This required extravagant expenditure of long-term capital loss appears in the computation of the capital loss carryover. Thus, in the preceding example there is no carryover. Can you work this out under the precise language of the statute? See §§ 1212(b)(1)(B), 1212(b)(2)(B).

The character of a loss, long-term or short-term remains the same in the year to which it is carried. If a taxpayer has only net long-term loss unused in a particular year, it is obvious his carryover will be long-term capital loss. Just as obvious, if the taxpayer has only unused net short-term loss, his carryover will be short-term capital loss. But what if he has both net short-term and net long-term losses which may not be fully exhausted by § 1211(b) deductions from ordinary income? Which is used in the year incurred, and which remains to be carried over? § 1212(b)(2) answers this question by the effective but cryptic device of generating some constructive short-term capital gain. When it is recalled that the determination of a net short-term capital loss requires the netting of short-term gains and losses, it will be seen that the creation of constructive short-term gain reduces the amount of net short-term capital loss, initially. And, if short-term gain, real and constructive, exceeds short-term loss, only then will such gain reduce the amount of net long-term loss in excess of net short-term gain. These are the keys to the special rules of § 1212(b)(2) which govern the general carryover rules of § 1212(b)(1). See if you can unlock the statutory doors. Is it apparent Congress has decided that the allowable deduction against ordinary income under § 1211(b) consumes short-term capital loss first? [4]

4. Does the character (long or short) of a carried over capital loss really make a difference? It *might* appear not, as capital losses (long or short) offset capital gains (long or short) dollar-for-dollar. But consider this: In 1977 to which a $100 loss is carried from 1976, T has $100 of long-term capital gain and $100 of short-term capital gain. He has no actual capital losses for 1977. How will T fare if the carried over loss is long-term? If it is short-term?

On the other hand, the short-term-loss-first rule *can* work to the taxpayer's advantage. Short-term loss offsets ordinary income dollar-for-dollar, to the extent allowed under § 1211(b).

Consider the following examples of the operation of the carryover provisions.

T, a single taxpayer entered into transactions in 1978 with the following results (in all cases, it is assumed that taxable income is sufficient so as to permit the full $3000 deduction from ordinary income) :

(A)	Long-term gain	$20,000	Short-term gain	$ 8,000
	Long-term loss	15,000	Short-term loss	13,000
	Net long-term gain	$ 5,000	Net short-term loss	($ 5,000)

Here, there is no deduction from ordinary income and no capital loss carryover. The gains and losses offset each other. § 1211(b).

(B)	Long-term gain	$10,000	Short-term gain	$ 4,000
	Long-term loss	8,000	Short-term loss	22,000
	Net long-term gain	$ 2,000	Net short-term loss	($18,000)

Here, $2000 of the net short-term loss can be used against the net long-term gain. T can also deduct $3000 from ordinary gross income. § 1211(b), § 62(4). The unused balance of the loss ($13000) is carried into 1979 as a short-term capital loss (since the origin is short-term) to be used in that year to offset short-term gains, if any, and if none to offset *net* long-term gains, if any, and with up to $3000 of any remaining balance of the short-term loss to be applied against ordinary income under § 1211(b). See § 1212(b)(1)(A) and (2)(A). In short, the carryover of $13,000 is treated the same in 1979 as if it had been realized in 1979.

(C)	Still with reference to 1978:			
	Long-term gain	$ 3,000	Short-term gain	$ 1,000
	Long-term loss	20,000	Short-term loss	–0–
	Net long-term loss	($17,000)	Net short-term gain	$ 1,000

Here, the net short-term gain is absorbed by $1,000 of the net long-term loss, reducing the latter to $16,000. Applying § 1211(b) (1), T can deduct $3,000 from ordinary income, § 1211(b) (1) (B), at a cost of using an additional $6,000 of his net long-term loss. § 1212(b) (2) (B). This means that the long-term loss to be carried over to 1979 is $10,000. The carryover provision is consistent with the § 1211(b) (1) (C) (ii) ceiling as it relates to net long-term capital losses. In effect, the carryover computation eliminates from the carryover the portion (other half) of the excess net long-term loss which is *used* but not deducted from ordinary income. Thus, if a taxpayer had only a $6000 net long-term loss, he could deduct only $3000 from gross income, but the balance of the net long-term loss is not deductible

If the taxpayer were required to use long-term loss first, the *amount* of his carryover would be reduced $2.00 for each $1.00 allowed. Rather than squander his long-term loss this way, may he not be better off preserving it to a later year when it *may* offset, dollar-for-dollar, short-term gain of the later year, which would otherwise be taxed as ordinary income?

and forms no part of the carryover. This is accomplished by § 1212 (b) which requires a fresh computation.

Applying the precise language of the statute to the facts of Example (C) above, the starting point is the "if" clause of § 1212(b) (1).[5] "If the taxpayer * * * has a net capital loss for any taxable year * * *" Net capital loss, defined in § 1222(10), means the excess of capital losses over the sum allowed in § 1211. On our facts the figures are:

Capital losses	$20,000
sum allowed under § 1211	7,000
net capital loss	$13,000

Therefore, we meet the "if" clause of § 1212(b) (1).

Next, § 1212(b) (1) (B) identifies the long-term loss carryover as the excess of net long-term capital loss over the net short-term capital gain. But, looking at the facts stated in example (C), this is *not* $16,000, the difference between $17,000 and $1000. It is $10,000, after applying the special rules of § 1212(b) (2) (B). This provision generates some *constructive* short-term capital gain which must be taken into account in determining the excess of the net long-term capital loss over net short-term capital gain, which is the amount of the long-term capital loss carryover. Obviously § 1212(b) (1) is meaningless without taking account of § 1212(b) (2); thus one must first make a § 1212(b) (2) computation and plug that constructive short-term capital gain into § 1212(b) (1) in determining the § 1212(b) (1) carryover.[6] The results emerge as follows under the precise language of the statute:

Net long-term capital loss		$17,000
Actual short-term capital gain	$1000	
Constructive short-term capital gain		
(1) The amount allowed under § 1211 (b) (1) (B)	$3000	
(2) The amount by which the amount allowed under § 1211(b) (1) (B) exceeds the net short-term capital loss (zero in our case)	$3000	
Total (actual and constructive) short-term capital gain	$7000	
Less short-term capital loss (zero in our case)	0	
Net short-term capital gain taking into account § 1212(b) (2) (B)		$7000
Excess net long-term capital loss carried over		$10,000

---

5. See note 2, above.

6. The language the "amount *allowed*" in I.R.C. § 1212(b)(2)(B)(i) creates some uncertainty, but it is the Treasury's position that utilization of carryovers may not be deferred; the amount that *can* be used reduces the amount carried to the next year whether used or not. Rev.Rul. 76–177, 1976–1 C.B. 224.

In 1979 (the next year), the $10,000 is a long-term capital loss, just as if it had been actually realized in that year. § 1212(b) (1) (B).

To reach a correct result by way of a mechanical application of the statute requires the numerous steps shown in the above example (C). However, by this time you should be able to check such results by a shortcut computation, as follows:

1. We had a net short-term gain of $1000; there will be no deduction of short-term loss against ordinary income and no short-term carryover.

2. We had a net long-term loss of $17,000
    It will be partially used as follows:
    a. To offset net short-term gain $1000
    b. To offset ordinary income of $3000,
        at a $2 for $1 rate   6000

    Net long-term loss consumed   7000

    Long-term loss carried over to 1979 $10,000

(D) The year is still 1878, but now T has both net long-term and net short-term capital losses.

Long-term gain	$ 2,000	Short-term gain	$17,000
Long-term loss	40,000	Short-term loss	37,000
Net long-term loss ($38,000)		Net short-term loss ($20,000)	

The special rules of § 1212(b) (2) determine the amount of long-term and short-term loss, respectively, to be carried into 1979 under § 1212(b) (1). First, it is clear that the net short-term loss, accorded priority, is reduced to $17,000 when $3000 is deducted from ordinary income. § 1212(b) (2) (A). This is the consequence of the statute generating $3000 of constructive short-term gain. Therefore, the excess net short-term loss is $17,000 carried into 1979 as a short-term capital loss. This means then, with respect to the net long-term loss of $38,000, no amount was applied against ordinary income and the long-term capital loss carryover to 1979 should be and is $38,000. The statutory computation is as follows:

Net long-term loss		$38,000
Less (net short-term capital gains, if any)		
Actual short-term gain	$17,000	
Short-term gain § 1212(b) (2) (B) (i)	3,000	
Short-term gain § 1212(b) (2) (B) (ii)	–0–	
Total short-term gain	20,000	
Less: actual short-term loss	–37,000	
Net short-term loss	17,000	
There is no net short-term capital gain		–0–
Long-term capital loss carryover		$38,000

Again, $38,000 is treated in 1979 as a long-term capital loss realized in that year. § 1212(b) (1) (B). There is no time limit on the carryover, except as may be imposed by the taxpayer's death.[7] Capital losses, long-term or short-term may be carried over to succeeding years until exhausted.[8]

2. Corporations

The major difference in the treatment of capital losses of corporations and individuals is that § 1211(b), authorizing a limited deduction of excess capital losses from ordinary income, is not applicable to corporations. In the case of a corporation, § 1211(a) provides that losses from sales or exchanges of capital assets shall be allowed *only* to the extent of gains from such sales or exchanges. Would the code be simplified if the same rule applied to individuals? Why?

Further important differences are that § 1212(a) treats excess capital losses in a given year as a short-term capital loss carryback (regardless of its origin) to each of the three taxable years *preceding* the loss year and, to the extent not so used, as a short-term capital loss carryover (regardless of its origin) to each of the five taxable years *succeeding* the loss year. (§ 1212(a) (1).) The amount which is carried back may not increase or produce a net operating loss for the taxable year to which it is being carried back. (§ 1212(a) (1) (A) (ii).)

PROBLEMS

Here is a series of questions on capital losses incurred after 1977. The figure for taxable income given in Column A reflects the taxpayer's taxable income for each of five years *without* regard to his capital gains and losses and assumes that he was entitled to and claimed in each case only one personal exemption of $750. Note that in computing gross income (as adjusted) on the return (see page 642 of the text) since capital losses exceed capital gains no gains will be included. In addition, the § 1211(b) excess amount will be a deduction reducing other ordinary income.

7. Now that *potential* losses are passed on by a decedent by way of the new (1976) carryover basis rules of I.R.C. § 1023, perhaps Congress will reconsider the question of a pass-along of realized but unused losses.

8. A similar, somewhat briefer discussion of the mechanics of both capital gains and losses appears in

Andrews and Freeland, "Capital Gains and Losses of Individuals and Related Matters under the Tax Reform Act of 1969," 12 Ariz.L.Rev. 627, 630–645 (1970). And see Warren, "The Deductibility by Individuals of Capital Losses under the Federal Income Tax," 40 U.Chic.L.R. 291 (1973).

A. Taxable Income	B. LTCG	C. LTCL	D. STCG	E. STCL
1. $10,000	$2,000	$ 6,000	$ 600	$ 1,000
2. $10,000	$2,000	$10,000	$2,000	$ 1,000
3. $10,000	$2,000	$10,000	$2,000	$ 6,000
4. $10,000	$2,000	$10,000	$2,000	$ 4,000
5. $ 2,150	$2,000	$10,000	$2,000	$ 4,000

For each year separately, without regard to computations for other years, determine the amount of the taxpayer's capital loss that is allowed as a deduction from ordinary income under § 1211(b)(1)(A), (B), or (C) and the amount and character of his capital loss carryover, if any, under § 1212(b).

D. THE MEANING OF "CAPITAL ASSET"

---

1. THE STATUTORY DEFINITION

Internal Revenue Code: Section 1221.   See Sections 1234; 1236; 1237.

MAULDIN v. COMMISSIONER

United States Court of Appeals, 10th Circuit, 1952.
195 F.2d 714.

Before HUXMAN, MURRAH and PICKETT, CIRCUIT JUDGES.

MURRAH, CIRCUIT JUDGE.   This is an appeal from a decision of the Tax Court, holding that certain lots sold by petitioners during the taxable years 1944 and 1945, where "property held by the taxpayer primarily for sale to customers in the ordinary course of his trade or business" within the exclusionary clause of Section 117(a)(1) of the Internal Revenue Code, 26 U.S.C.A. § 117(a)(1).[1] If the gain from the sale of these lots was derived in this manner, it constituted ordinary income taxable under Section 22(a),[2] and not a capital gain taxable under Section 117(a)(1).[3] Petitioners, residents of the State of New Mexico, are husband and wife, and all income involved is community income.   The two cases were therefore consolidated for trial and disposition.   A summary of Mauldin's business activities is necessary to a determination of the issue presented.

C. E. Mauldin, a graduate veterinarian since 1904, who also engaged in some road contracting, moved to Albuquerque, New Mexico in 1916, where he organized a road construction company.   While in Clovis, New Mexico in 1920, to bid on a sewer project, he decided to move there and engage in the cattle business.   Later in the same year, he contracted to buy 160 acres of land one-half mile from the city limits of Clovis for $20,000.00.   This land was particularly suitable for cattle feeding, but was not at that time considered suitable for residential development, because the City, with a population of 5000, was not growing in that direction.

By the time Mauldin finally received title to the land in June 1921, he decided that it was not the time to go into the cattle business because of drought, crop and bank failures, and a decline in the cattle business which continued through 1924.   He tried to sell the entire tract in 1924 for less than he paid for it, but was unable to do so, partly because a highway had been surveyed diagonally across the land, splitting it into two tracts and rendering it less suitable for cattle

---

1. See I.R.C. § 1221(1) (1954). All footnotes in this opinion are by the editors.

2. See I.R.C. § 61(a).

3. See I.R.C. § 1221(1).

feeding.   A real estate agent with whom he listed the property for sale
advised him that they would have better success if he divided it into
small tracts and blocks.   The land was accordingly platted into 29
tracts and 4 blocks containing 88 lots each, and called the "Mauldin
Addition".   At the time the land was platted in 1924, there was still
no demand for residential property in the area.   In 1927, he built a
home for himself near the center of the Addition.

There were no sales of any consequence until the land commenced
to be included in the city limits of Clovis in 1931.   By 1939, it was
wholly within the city limits, and without Mauldin's request, the City
began a paving program in the area, for which he was assessed approximately $25,000.00.   When he was unable to pay this assessment,
the City instituted suits on its paving liens, and in order to save his
property, he divided some additional tracts into lots and devoted most
of his time to the sale of the lots in the Addition.   He listed the property with real estate agents and otherwise promoted sales through
personal solicitations, signs, newspaper advertisements, and gifts of
lots to a school and the builder of the first F.H.A. house in Clovis.
He stated that at times he would "chase" a prospective purchaser
"around the block".   During 1939 and 1940, he sold enough lots to
liquidate the paving indebtedness.

Mauldin testified that with the indebtedness to the City paid, he
decided to hold the remaining portions of the original tract for investment purposes, and after 1940, did nothing to promote sales.   He
stated, "I cut it up and tried my best to sell it to clear it, and when I
cleared it, I quit".   From 1940 until 1949, when his health failed,
Mauldin devoted full time to the lumber business he organized in 1939.
During this period, he had no real estate office, no license to sell real
estate, did not advertise the properties by newspapers or signs, had no
fixed price for lots, and at times refused to sell certain lots, either because the prospective purchaser would not pay the asked price, or
Mauldin did not wish to sell the particular property at that time.   The
only real estate purchased by Mauldin after acquiring the 160 acres
in 1920 was one "unsightly" block of lots near his residence, and some
commercial properties to be used in connection with his lumber business.

Due primarily to the location of war facilities nearby, the City of
Clovis grew in population to 14,000 in 1940 and to 20,000 to 25,000 in
1945, and the lots, Mauldin Addition, were in great demand.   By the
end of 1945, Mauldin had disposed of all but 20 acres of his original
160 acre tract.   This 20 acres was considered by him and real estate
dealers to be his most valuable property.   Mauldin's records show
that he sold 2 lots in 2 transactions in 1941; 11 in 1942 in 2 transactions (6 lots were given to his daughter as a wedding present); 5½
in 1943 in 3 transactions; 5½ in 1944 in 3 transactions; 44½ in
1945 in 15 transactions; 39 in 1946, 1 in 1947 and 2 in 1948.   For the

taxable years in 1939 and 1940, the taxpayers' income tax returns showed income from real estate only; for each of the years 1941 and 1944 (returns for 1942 and 1943 not shown) they showed net income of approximately $3,000.00 from sales of real estate and approximately $12,000.00 from the lumber business; for the year 1945, $20,484.84 from real estate and $12,339.80 from lumber; and in 1946, $21,942.88 from real estate and $25,005.07 from lumber. On his 1940 return, Mauldin stated that the nature of his business was "real estate"; in 1943 it was shown as "lumber business"; in 1944 he did not designate the nature of his business; and in 1945 it was shown as "lumber and real estate".

In their income tax returns for the years 1944 and 1945, petitioners showed the lots sold during those years as long-time capital assets, and computed the tax accordingly. The Commissioner determined that the profit realized was ordinary income within the meaning of Section 117(a)(1) [4] of the Internal Revenue Code, and assessed the additional tax. This appeal is from the judgment of the Tax Court sustaining the Commissioner, and the only question is whether its judgment on these facts can be said to be clearly erroneous.

It is admitted by taxpayer that during 1939 and 1940, he was engaged in the business of selling the tracts and lots in Mauldin Addition. He earnestly contends, however, that after 1940, his business status was changed; that his full time thereafter was devoted to the lumber business, and held the remaining lots for investment purposes, selling them only through unsolicited offers when the price was right.

There is no fixed formula or rule of thumb for determining whether property sold by the taxpayer was held by him primarily for sale to customers in the ordinary course of his trade or business. Each case must, in the last analysis, rest upon its own facts. There are a number of helpful factors, however, to point the way, among which are the purposes for which the property was acquired, whether for sale or investment; and continuity and frequency of sales as opposed to isolated transactions. Dunlap v. Oldham Lumber Co., 5 Cir., 178 F.2d 781; Annot. 106 A.L.R. 254; Mertens, Vol. 3, Sec. 22.08.[5] And, any other facts tending to indicate that the sales or transactions are in furtherance of an occupation of the taxpayer, recognizing however that one actively engaged in the business of real estate may discontinue such business and simply sell off the remnants of his holdings without further engaging in the business. Snell v. Commissioner, 5 Cir., 97 F.2d 891. Thus, where residents of New York bought land in Florida and elsewhere from time to time for investment, a part of which was platted and improved, it was held that the occasional sale of lots through local brokers was not sufficiently frequent or engrossing to give the taxpayers the vocation of real estate dealers. Phipps v. Commissioner, 2 Cir., 54 F.2d 469. And, in Foran v. Commissioner,

4. Ibid.   5. See Mertens, Vol. 3B, Sec. 22.15
                                            (1973).

5 Cir., 165 F.2d 705, a taxpayer admittedly engaged as a broker of nonproducing oil and gas leases and royalties purchased a producing property which he sold within eighteen months. The profit realized therefrom was held to be income from a long-time capital asset, the court reasoning that since this was the first producing property purchased by the taxpayer, there was no occasion to disbelieve his statement that he acquired it for investment or his motive for selling it.

On the other hand, sale and exchange of lots in 1939 and 1940 from a 92 acre tract of land, partially subdivided in 1932, was held to be in the ordinary course of business where the taxpayer had been continuously engaged in the real estate business since 1908, and had divided a part of the tract into lots in order to facilitate the sale of the land. Gruver v. Commissioner, 4 Cir., 142 F.2d 363. So too was the sale of lots from a tract of land which had been originally purchased for and used as a lettuce farm, but subdivided into lots when it became too valuable for truck farming operations. Richards v. Commissioner, 9 Cir., 81 F.2d 369, 106 A.L.R. 249. See also Oliver v. Commissioner, 4 Cir., 138 F.2d 910. And, lots sold through sales agencies after reacquisition at a trustee's sale, were held to be in the ordinary course of trade or business, as against the contention that they were sold in furtherance of an orderly liquidation in Ehrman v. Commissioner, 9 Cir., 120 F.2d 607. While the purpose for which the property was acquired is of some weight, the ultimate question is the purpose for which it was held. Rollingwood Corp. v. Commissioner, 9 Cir., 190 F.2d 263.

Admittedly, Mauldin originally purchased the property for purposes other than for sale in the ordinary course of trade or business. When, however, he subdivided and offered it for sale, he was undoubtedly engaged in the vocation of selling lots from this tract of land at least until 1940. As against his contention that he ceased to engage in the business after 1940, the record evidence shows that he sold more lots in 1945 on a sellers market without solicitation than he did in 1940 on a buyers market. It seems fairly inferable from the record that at all times he had lots for sale, and that the volume sold depended primarily upon the prevailing economic conditions, brought on by wartime activities and their aftermath. It is true that he was in the lumber business, but his returns plainly show that a substantial part of his income was derived from the sale of the lots. In these circumstances, we cannot say that the Tax Court's conclusions are without factual basis.

The decisions are Affirmed.

MALAT v. RIDDELL *

Supreme Court of the United States, 1966.
383 U.S. 569, 86 S.Ct. 1030.

PER CURIAM.   Petitioner [1] was a participant in a joint venture
which acquired a 45-acre parcel of land, the intended use for which is
somewhat in dispute.   Petitioner contends that the venturers' intention was to develop and operate an apartment project on the land;
the respondent's position is that there was a "dual purpose" of developing the property for rental purposes or selling, whichever proved to
be the more profitable.   In any event, difficulties in obtaining the
necessary financing were encountered, and the interior lots of the
tract were subdivided and sold.   The profit from those sales was reported and taxed as ordinary income.

The joint venturers continued to explore the possibility of com-
mercially developing the remaining exterior parcels.   Additional frus-
trations in the form of zoning restrictions were encountered.   These
difficulties persuaded petitioner and another of the joint venturers
of the desirability of terminating the venture; accordingly, they sold
out their interests in the remaining property.   Petitioner contends
that he is entitled to treat the profits from this last sale as capital
gains; the respondent takes the position that this was "property held
by the taxpayer primarily for sale to customers in the ordinary course
of his trade or business," [2] and thus subject to taxation as ordinary
income.

> The District Court made the following finding:
>
> The members of [the joint venture], as of the date the
> 44.901 acres were acquired, intended either to sell the prop-
> erty or develop it for rental, depending upon which course
> appeared to be most profitable.   The venturers realized that
> they had made a good purchase price-wise and, if they were
> unable to obtain acceptable construction financing or rezon-
> ing * * * which would be prerequisite to commercial de-
> velopment, they would sell the property in bulk so they
> wouldn't get hurt.   The purpose of either selling or develop-
> ing the property continued during the period in which [the
> joint venture] held the property.

The District Court ruled that petitioner had failed to establish that
the property was not held *primarily* for sale to customers in the ordinary course of business, and thus rejected petitioner's claim to capital
gain treatment for the profits derived from the property's resale.   The

---

* See Bernstein, " 'Primarily for Sale':
  A Semantic Snare," 20 Stan.L.Rev.
  1093 (1968).   Ed.

for simplicity are referred to throughout as "petitioner."

1. The taxpayer and his wife who filed
    a joint return are the petitioners, but

2. Internal Revenue Code of 1954, §
    1221(1), 26 U.S.C. § 1221(1). * * *

Court of Appeals affirmed, 347 F.2d 23. We granted certiorari (382 U.S. 900) to resolve a conflict among the courts of appeals [3] with regard to the meaning of the term "primarily" as it is used in § 1221(1) of the Internal Revenue Code of 1954.

The statute denies capital gain treatment to profits reaped from the sale of "property held by the taxpayer *primarily* for sale to customers in the ordinary course of his trade or business." (Emphasis added.) The respondent urges upon us a construction of "primarily" as meaning that a purpose may be "primary" if it is a "substantial" one.

As we have often said, "the words of statutes—including revenue acts—should be interpreted where possible in their ordinary, everyday senses." Crane v. Commissioner, 331 U.S. 1, 6. And see Hanover Bank v. Commissioner, 369 U.S. 672, 687–688; Commissioner v. Korell, 339 U.S. 619, 627–628. Departure from a literal reading of statutory language may, on occasion, be indicated by relevant internal evidence of the statute itself and necessary in order to effect the legislative purpose. See, e. g., Board of Governors v. Agnew, 329 U.S. 441, 446–448. But this is not such an occasion. The purpose of the statutory provision with which we deal is to differentiate between the "profits and losses arising from the everyday operation of a business" on the one hand (Corn Products Co. v. Commissioner, 350 U.S. 46, 52) and "the realization of appreciation in value accrued over a substantial period of time" on the other. (Commissioner v. Gillette Motor Co., 364 U.S. 130, 134.) A literal reading of the statute is consistent with this legislative purpose. We hold that, as used in § 1221(1), "primarily" means "of first importance" or "principally."

Since the courts below applied an incorrect legal standard, we do not consider whether the result would be supportable on the facts of this case had the correct one been applied. We believe, moreover, that the appropriate disposition is to remand the case to the District Court for fresh fact-findings, addressed to the statute as we have now construed it.

Vacated and remanded.

NOTE

The *Mauldin* case, above, is typical in paying little heed to whether real property may be said to be held for sale "to customers." Comparatively recently, we received the Supreme Court's exciting message that in I.R.C. § 1221(1), "primarily" means "of first impor-

---

3. Compare Rollingwood Corp. v. Commissioner, 190 F.2d 263, 266 (C.A.9th Cir.); American Can Co. v. Commissioner, 317 F.2d 604, 605 (C.A.2d Cir.), with United States v. Bennett, 186 F. 2d 407, 410–411 (C.A.5th Cir.); Munic-ipal Bond Corp. v. Commissioner, 341 F.2d 683, 688–689 (C.A.8th Cir.). Cf. Recordak Corp. v. United States, 163 Ct.Cl. 294, 300–301, 325 F.2d 460, 463–464.

tance" or "principally." [1] As time goes on our education expands. In International Shoe Machinery Corp. v. United States,[2] we discover that, even though rental income from property exceeds income from its sale, the property can be considered held primarily for sale. After *Malat* this is tough medicine to take, unless washed down with a good gulp of "corn." [3] In any event, the court in *Mauldin,* the principal case above, is discouragingly correct in suggesting that the question whether property is held primarily for sale is not answerable by a "fixed formula"; and the opinion does recite some factors that aid analysis.

The meaning of a term in the Internal Revenue Code is not always to be determined in the manner in which the Court approached the meaning of "primarily" in *Malat,* with reference to dictionary definitions and supposed common usage. Congress may provide its own definition for the terms used.[4] In the capital gain and loss area there are many instances in which, in order to achieve a desired result, Congress accords meanings to terms which are quite at variance from their "ordinary everyday senses." It seems desirable here to direct attention to some of this congressional game-playing; but the comments that follow are intended to be only generally informative and not to be used as a basis for detailed study at this point.

Recall that capital gain or loss consequences require: (1) a transaction involving a capital asset, (2) a sale or exchange of that capital asset, and (3) a determination of how long the taxpayer has held the capital asset. I.R.C. (26 U.S.C.A.) § 1221 defines the term capital asset but it is subject to both judicial and statutory exceptions.[5] The § 1221 definition has been amended several times, recently by adding a letter or memorandum (or a collection of such property) to other literary works that are excluded from the definition of a capital asset.[6]

If a transaction does not involve a capital asset, or if it does not constitute a sale or exchange, it will give rise only to ordinary income or to an ordinary deduction. It may be difficult to determine whether a transaction meets such tests. Consequently, at times Congress has seen fit to clarify the status of a transaction or artificially to accord to a transaction one or more of the essential elements. At other times Congress expressly deprives a capital asset transaction of its special

1. Malat v. Riddell, supra page 664.

2. 491 F.2d 157 (1st Cir. 1974), set out infra page 769.

3. See Corn Products Refining Co. v. Comm'r, set out infra page 680; *International Shoe,* supra, in the district court, 369 F.Supp. 588, 593 (D. Mass.1973); see also Rabinovitz and Shashy, "Indigestion from Corn Products," 27 (Number 4, 1st Annual Tax Issue) U. of Fla.L.Rev. 964, 972 (1975).

4. The student should be aware of a number of general definitions contained in I.R.C. (26 U.S.C.A.) § 7701.

5. See pages 680 and 698, infra.

6. The Tax Reform Act of 1976 added I.R.C. § 1221(6), excluding from "capital assets" government publications received by a taxpayer without charge or at a reduced price. Under § 170(e) this effectively precludes a deduction for charitable contributions of such items. See Chapter 23, infra.

characterization. Varying policy reasons, some of which are related to the reasons previously identified for special capital asset treatment, underlie such congressional decisions.

Instances in which Congress has seen fit to treat a transaction as though all three requirements are met, even though none or less than all may be met, include § 1235, according long-term capital gain consequences to certain dispositions of patent rights [7] and § 166(d), classifying nonbusiness bad debts as short-term capital losses.[8] Conversely, even though certain transactions meet all three requirements, §§ 1239, 1245, and 1250 through 1252 and 1254 [9] convert some potential capital gains to ordinary income, and §§ 1242 through 1244 accord ordinary loss treatment to some transactions which would generally produce capital losses.

In other situations Congress artificially supplies only one of the three requirements to a transaction. For example, the "sale or exchange" requirement is supplied by statute when securities become worthless and there is no actual sale or exchange that would normally be needed to make the resulting loss a capital loss. § 165(g).[10] Some casualties are similarly treated. § 1231.[11] The retirement of a bond may be "considered as" an exchange of the bond, § 1232, and a lessee's relinquishment of his lease may be "considered as" an exchange of the lease. § 1241.[12] In other instances, Congress prescribes artificial holding periods at variance with the time that property disposed of is actually held. § 1223.[13]

Similarly, there are times when Congress will treat property as a capital asset even though it is not within the § 1221 definition. For instance, under § 1231 property described in § 1221(2) may or may not be accorded capital asset status.[14] When one sells, exchanges, or has a loss on the failure to exercise an option, the characterization of the transaction depends, not upon whether the option itself is a capital asset, but upon whether the property to which it relates so qualifies. This is the prescription of § 1234, which was enacted to give the option itself a neutral status, recognizing that it is no more than a right to buy or sell property, and to make a more realistic characterization of the transaction on the basis of the character of the property subject to the option.[15]

Most of the provisions referred to above reappear for more detailed consideration in subsequent portions of this book. The two pro-

---

7. See page 699, infra.

8. See Chapter 23, infra at page 808.

9. See Chapter 22, infra at page 779.

10. See Chapter 23, infra at page 779.

11. See Chapter 22, infra at page 762.

12. See page 679, infra.

13. See page 718, infra.

14. See Chapter 22, infra at page 762.

15. See page 719, infra.

visions which are discussed below, §§ 1236 and 1237, are not reconsidered and therefore warrant brief analysis here.

Prior to 1951, it was often uncertain whether one who was a dealer in securities held particular securities in that capacity or as an investor.[16] Thus, the status of the securities in his hands, as non-capital or capital assets, was often the subject of controversy. A dealer would be tempted to shift securities from investment status to inventory status or vice versa, to support his contention that ordinary gain should be treated as capital gain or that capital loss should be treated as ordinary loss. I.R.C. § 1236 was addressed to the problem.[17] In effect it restricts classification changes that would be convenient for the taxpayer by requiring an identification of the status of the security at the time of its acquisition. Thus, Congress has attempted to clarify the character of a security as a capital asset or not when its actual classification may be equivocal. I.R.C. (26 U.S.C.A.) § 1236 provides that, if a dealer is to treat securities as capital assets, he must clearly indicate on his records within thirty days of their acquisition that the securities are held for investment purposes, and he cannot at anytime thereafter hold them for sale to customers. Once the purpose is identified under § 1236 as investment the classification may not in any event be changed if the security is subsequently sold at a loss. The statute does not expressly foreclose reclassification of securities originally classified as investments if they are sold at a gain. Why?

Another instance in which it may be difficult to determine whether one holding property is a dealer or an investor is when a landowner subdivides real property and sells it.[18] I.R.C. 26 U.S.C.A. § 1237 sometimes renders such a determination unnecessary; but the statute is limited in its application. First of all it is wholly unavailable to dealers or to persons who actually become dealers, a requirement creating factual uncertainties that tend to dilute the effectiveness of the clarification purpose of the statute. In addition under § 1237(a), the land in question (1) must never have been held primarily for sale to customers, (2) must not have been the subject of substantial improvement and (3) unless inherited, must have been held by the taxpayer for at least five years. For example in the *Mauldin* case, supra, there was no question but that in 1939 and 1940 the taxpayer held the "Mauldin Addition" for sale to customers in the ordi-

---

16. See Reg. § 1.1236–1(d)(1)(ii). David C. Fitch, 34 TCM 233 (1975), reflects a narrow definition of "dealer," resting in part on Higgins v. Comm'r, 312 U.S. 212 (1941).

17. Sen.Rep.No.781, 82d Cong. 1st Sess. (1951), 1951–2 C.B. 458 at 482.

18. See *Mauldin,* supra page 660. For further analysis of the relevant factors in making the dealer or investor determination in real estate transactions, see Emmanuel, "Capital Gains for Real Estate Operators," 12 U. of Fla.L.Rev. 280 (1959).

nary course of his business. This would in itself render § 1237 inapplicable under § 1237(a)(1).[19]

When § 1237 *is* applicable it provides only partial capital asset treatment. Five parcels may be sold at capital gains rates, but for any year in which a sixth sale occurs and thereafter, gain in an amount up to 5% of the sale price on each parcel will be ordinary income. § 1237(b)(1). Commissions paid to outside dealers may offset such ordinary income. § 1237(b)(2).

Although § 1237 is severely limited in application, nevertheless there are circumstances in which it can be of very great benefit to a taxpayer. For instance, one who has appreciated realty that he has held for many years may make minimal subdivisional improvements on it and sell it off piece-meal, himself or through a broker. The minimum but important assurance that § 1237 affords him is that his efforts in that transaction will not place him in a dealer category. Thus, except for the innocuous 5% rule, he may be able to count on capital gain treatment for all his sales. It should also be pointed out, however, that § 1237 is not exclusive [20] and, even if a taxpayer does not qualify for its benefits, he may still maintain he is an investor in an attempt to classify all of his gain as capital gain.[21] Some suggest that § 1237 is not available when needed and is not needed when available.

19. See also § 1237(a)(2)(C), disqualifying the Mauldin Addition (had § 1237 then been in effect) because of the substantial cost of the city paving which, because disqualified as a deductible tax by § 164(c)(2), would be a proscribed addition to the taxpayer's basis.

20. Reg. § 1.1237-1(a)(4); R. E. Gordy, 36 T.C. 855 (1961), acq., 1964-1 (part 1) C.B. 4.

21. His reason for making such an argument could be to avoid the 5% ordinary income characterization of § 1237(b)(1) or his failure to meet the requirements of § 1237(a). For cases treating subdivided land as a capital asset after the enactment of § 1237, see Bon v. U. S., unreported, 60-1 U.S. T.C. ¶ 9186 (D.Wyo.1960) and Barker v. U. S., unreported, 65-2 U.S.T.C. ¶ 9736 (S.D.Calif.1965). On § 1237 generally see Repetti, "What Makes a Dealer under Section 1237," 17 N.Y.U. Inst. on Fed.Tax. 651 (1959), and Weithorn, "Subdivisions of Real Estate-'Dealer' v. 'Investor' Problem," 11 Tax.L.Rev. 157 (1959).

2. "INCOME" PROPERTY *

Internal Revenue Code: Sections 102(b); 273; 1001(e); 1241.
Regulations: Sections 1.1014–4, –5; 1.1015–1(b), (c).

HORT v. COMMISSIONER

Supreme Court of the United States, 1941.
313 U.S. 28, 61 S.Ct. 757.

MR. JUSTICE MURPHY delivered the opinion of the Court.

We must determine whether the amount petitioner received as consideration for cancellation of a lease of realty in New York City was ordinary gross income as defined in § 22(a) of the Revenue Act of 1932 (47 Stat. 169, 178), and whether, in any event, petitioner sustained a loss through cancellation of the lease which is recognized in § 23(e) of the same Act (47 Stat. 169, 180).

Petitioner acquired the property, a lot and ten-story office building, by devise from his father in 1928. At the time he became owner, the premises were leased to a firm which had sublet the main floor to the Irving Trust Co. In 1927, five years before the head lease expired, the Irving Trust Co. and petitioner's father executed a contract in which the latter agreed to lease the main floor and basement to the former for a term of fifteen years at an annual rental of $25,000, the term to commence at the expiration of the head lease.

In 1933, the Irving Trust Co. found it unprofitable to maintain a branch in petitioner's building. After some negotiations, petitioner and the Trust Co. agreed to cancel the lease in consideration of a payment to petitioner of $140,000. Petitioner did not include this amount in gross income in his income tax return for 1933. On the contrary, he reported a loss of $21,494.75 on the theory that the amount he received as consideration for the cancellation was $21,494.75 less than the difference between the present value of the unmatured rental payments and the fair rental value of the main floor and basement for the unexpired term of the lease. He did not deduct this figure, however, because he reported other losses in excess of gross income.

The Commissioner included the entire $140,000 in gross income, disallowed the asserted loss, made certain other adjustments not material here, and assessed a deficiency. The Board of Tax Appeals, affirmed. 39 B.T.A. 922. The Circuit Court of Appeals affirmed per curiam on the authority of Warren Service Corp. v. Commissioner, 110 F.2d 723. 112 F.2d 167. Because of conflict with Commis-

---

* See Del Cotto, " 'Property' in the Capital Asset Definition: Influence of 'Fruit and Tree'," 15 Buffalo L.Rev. 1 (1965). See also the Classic Articles of Professors Eustice and Lyon cited in a note in Chapter 13, "Assignment of Income," at page 262, supra.

sioner v. Langwell Real Estate Corp., 47 F.2d 841, we granted certiorari limited to the question whether, "in computing net gain or loss for income tax purposes, a taxpayer [can] offset the value of the lease canceled against the consideration received by him for the cancellation." 311 U.S. 641.

Petitioner apparently contends that the amount received for cancellation of the lease was capital rather than ordinary income and that it was therefore subject to §§ 101, 111–113, and 117 (47 Stat. 169, 191, 195–202, 207) which govern capital gains and losses. Further, he argues that even if that amount must be reported as ordinary gross income he sustained a loss which § 23(e) authorizes him to deduct. We cannot agree.

The amount received by petitioner for cancellation of the lease must be included in his gross income in its entirety. Section 22(a), copied in the margin,[1] expressly defines gross income to include "gains, profits, and income derived from * * * rent, * * * or gains or profits and income derived from any source whatever." Plainly this definition reached the rent paid prior to cancellation just as it would have embraced subsequent payments if the lease had never been canceled. It would have included a prepayment of the discounted value of unmatured rental payments whether received at the inception of the lease or at any time thereafter. Similarly, it would have extended to the proceeds of a suit to recover damages had the Irving Trust Co. breached the lease instead of concluding a settlement. Compare United States v. Safety Car Heating Co., 297 U.S. 88; Burnet v. Sanford, 282 U.S. 359. That the amount petitioner received resulted from negotiations ending in cancellation of the lease rather than from a suit to enforce it cannot alter the fact that basically the payment was merely a substitute for the rent reserved in the lease. So far as the application of § 22(a) is concerned, it is immaterial that petitioner chose to accept an amount less than the strict present value of the unmatured rental payments rather than to engage in litigation, possibly uncertain and expensive.

The consideration received for cancellation of the lease was not a return of capital. We assume that the lease was "property," whatever that signifies abstractly. Presumably the bond in Helvering v. Horst, 311 U.S. 112, and the lease in Helvering v. Bruun, 309 U.S. 461, were also "property," but the interest coupon in *Horst* and the building in *Bruun* nevertheless were held to constitute items of gross income. Simply because the lease was "property" the amount received for its cancellation was not a return of capital, quite apart from the fact that "property" and "capital" are not necessarily synonymous in the Revenue Act of 1932 or in common usage. Where, as in this case, the disputed amount was essentially a substitute for rental payments

1. [I.R.C. (1939) § 22(a) is omitted. Ed.]

which § 22(a) expressly characterizes as gross income, it must be regarded as ordinary income, and it is immaterial that for some purposes the contract creating the right to such payments may be treated as "property" or "capital."

For the same reasons, that amount was not a return of capital because petitioner acquired the lease as an incident of the realty devised to him by his father. Theoretically, it might have been possible in such a case to value realty and lease separately and to label each a capital asset. Compare Maass v. Higgins, 312 U.S. 443; Appeal of Farmer, 1 B.T.A. 711. But that would not have converted into capital the amount petitioner received from the Trust Co., since § 22(b) (3) [2] of the 1932 Act (47 Stat. 169, 178) would have required him to include in gross income the rent derived from the property, and that section, like § 22(a), does not distinguish rental payments and a payment which is clearly a substitute for rental payments.

We conclude that petitioner must report as gross income the entire amount received for cancellation of the lease, without regard to the claimed disparity between that amount and the difference between the present value of the unmatured rental payments and the fair rental value of the property for the unexpired period of the lease. The cancellation of the lease involved nothing more than relinquishment of the right to future rental payments in return for a present substitute payment and possession of the leased premises. Undoubtedly it diminished the amount of gross income petitioner expected to realize, but to that extent he was relieved of the duty to pay income tax. Nothing in § 23(e) [3] indicates that Congress intended to allow petitioner to reduce ordinary income actually received and reported by the amount of income he failed to realize. See Warren Service Corp. v. Commissioner, supra; Josey v. Commissioner, 104 F.2d 453; Tiscornia v. Commissioner, 95 F.2d 678; Farrelly-Walsh, Inc. v. Commissioner, 13 B.T.A. 923; Goerke Co. v. Commissioner, 7 B.T.A. 860; Merckens v. Commissioner, 7 B.T.A. 32. Compare, United States v. Safety Car Heating Co., supra; Voliva v. Commissioner, 36 F.2d 212; Appeal of Denholm & McKay Co., 2 B.T.A. 444. We may assume that petitioner was injured insofar as the cancellation of the lease affected the value of the realty. But that would become a deductible loss only when its extent had been fixed by a closed transaction. Regulations No. 77, Art. 171, p. 46; United States v. White Dental Mfg. Co., 274 U.S. 398.

The judgment of the Circuit Court of Appeals is

Affirmed.

2. [I.R.C. (1939) § 22(b) (3) is omitted. See I.R.C. (1954) § 102(b) (1). Ed.]

3. [I.R.C. (1939) § 23(e) is omitted. See I.R.C. (1954) § 165(c). Ed.]

METROPOLITAN BUILDING CO. v. COMMISSIONER

United States Court of Appeals, Ninth Circuit, 1960.
282 F.2d 592.

MERRILL, CIRCUIT JUDGE. The question presented by this case involves the owner of real property, his lessee and a sublessee. The sublessee wished to enter into a desirable arrangement directly with the owner and to this end to eliminate the intervening interest of the lessee-sublessor. He paid a sum of money to the lessee, in consideration of which the lessee released to the owner, his lessor, all his right and interest under his lease.

The question presented is whether the sum so paid to the lessee is to be regarded entirely as the equivalent of rent owed to the lessee and taxable to the lessee as income or whether it is to be regarded entirely as a sale by the lessee of a capital asset and taxable as capital gain. The Commissioner of Internal Revenue ruled that the payment was the equivalent of rental and taxable as income.

At issue is the amount of tax from Metropolitan Building Company, the lessee, for the taxable year ending June 30, 1953. Following the ruling of the Commissioner, this proceeding was instituted in the Tax Court by Metropolitan for redetermination of deficiencies in income and excess profits taxes for that year. The Tax Court affirmed the ruling of the Commissioner. Metropolitan has petitioned this Court for review, contending that the payment in question should be held to be capital gain. We have concluded that petitioner is correct in its contention and that the judgment of the Tax Court must be reversed.

The University of Washington owns real estate comprising about four city blocks in the downtown area of Seattle. In 1907 it executed a lease upon this property extending to November 1, 1954. This lease was acquired by petitioner Metropolitan Building Company on December 3, 1907.

On August 1, 1922, Metropolitan executed a sublease of the greater portion of one city block, extending to October 31, 1954, one day prior to the termination of the main lease. Under the terms of the sublease the sublessee was to construct a hotel upon the leased premises. Rental provided was $25,000.00 a year. In addition, the sublessee agreed to pay its just proportion of any ad valorem personal property taxes assessed against Metropolitan's leasehold. The Olympic Hotel was constructed upon the leased premises. On March 31, 1936, the sublease was acquired by The Olympic, Inc.

During the year 1952, the University of Washington, as fee owner, was attempting to arrange a long-term disposition of the Olympic Hotel property for the period following the expiration of Metropolitan's lease in November, 1954. To this end the University invited proposals for the lease of the hotel, and a number of highly competitive proposals were submitted by various large hotel operators. All these proposals, except that of The Olympic, Inc., necessarily contemplated a lease commencing November 1, 1954.

The proposal made by The Olympic, Inc., offered, at no cost or expense to the University, to procure from Metropolitan a release to the University of all Metropolitan's right, title and interest in and to the Olympic Hotel property under its lease. Olympic then offered the University to take a new lease directly from it for a term of approximately twenty-two years commencing forthwith. Under this proposal, additional rentals of $725,000.00 would accrue to the University during the period prior to November 1, 1954, which otherwise would not have been forthcoming.

The University was favorably disposed to this proposal and negotiations were undertaken with Metropolitan for the acquisition by the University of Metropolitan's leasehold interest. A letter was written on August 18, 1952, by the Board of Regents of the University to Metropolitan requesting Metropolitan to release to the University its leasehold rights with respect to the Olympic Hotel property. At a meeting of the Board of Directors of Metropolitan, held August 19, 1952, the following resolution was adopted:

"Resolved, the President hereby is authorized to sell to the University of Washington our leasehold rights to that area of the Metropolitan Tract occupied by the Olympic Hotel, including the existing sub-lease, provided an agreement can be reached which is approved by the company's accounting and legal counsel."

On September 8, 1952, an agreement was reached between Metropolitan and the State of Washington, acting through the Board of Regents of the University, whereby petitioner conveyed, quitclaimed, assigned and released to the State of Washington all of the right, title and interest of Metropolitan in and to that portion of the leasehold upon which the Olympic Hotel was located. For this assignment and transfer Metropolitan received from The Olympic, Inc., the sum of $137,000.00. The University then proceeded in accordance with its understanding to lease the property to The Olympic, Inc.

Metropolitan's president, asked as to how the sum of $137,000.00 had been computed, testified that roughly it covered $53,000.00 ground rent, $44,000.00 as Metropolitan's just proportion of the ad valorem personal property tax assessed against Metropolitan's leasehold, and $40,000.00 for increased taxes.

The Commissioner contends that this payment is taxable to Metropolitan as ordinary income. He relies upon Hort v. Commissioner, 1940, 313 U.S. 28, 31, 61 S.Ct. 757, 85 L.Ed. 1168, where it is held:

"Where, as in this case, the disputed amount was essentially a substitute for rental payments which § 22(a) [26 U.S.C.A. § 22(a)] expressly characterizes as gross income, it must be regarded as ordinary income * * *."

In that case the petitioner owned a business building, a portion of which had been leased to the Irving Trust Company for a term of fifteen years at $25,000.00 a year. The Trust Company, finding it unprofitable to maintain a branch office at that location, paid the petitioner $140,000.00 for cancellation of the lease.

In that case the Trust Company did not acquire any interest of its lessor. It simply compromised and liquidated its rental obligation under the lease. The sum received by the lessor was in lieu of the rentals which the Trust Company otherwise was obligated to pay and was not compensation for acquisition of any interest of the lessor.

In the case before us, the sums paid to Metropolitan were not simply a discharge of Olympic's obligation to pay rental. They were paid for the purchase of Metropolitan's entire leasehold interest. The case is not one of a liquidation of a right to future income as is Hort, but rather it is one of a disposition of income-producing property itself. The giving up of a lease by a tenant fits the legal requirements of a sale or exchange under Internal Revenue Code 1939, 117(j) 26 U.S.C.A. § 117(j) and a gain realized by the tenant on such a transaction is capital gain. Commissioner of Internal Revenue v. Golonsky, 3 Cir., 1952, 200 F.2d 72, certiorari denied 345 U.S. 939, 73 S.Ct. 830, 97 L.Ed. 1366; Commissioner of Internal Revenue v. Ray, 5 Cir., 1954, 210 F.2d 300, certiorari denied 348 U.S. 829, 75 S.Ct. 53, 99 L.Ed. 654; Commissioner of Internal Revenue v. McCue Bros. & Drummond, Inc., 2 Cir., 1954, 210 F.2d 752, certiorari denied 348 U.S. 829, 75 S.Ct. 53, 99 L.Ed. 654; Walter H. Sutliff, 1942, 46 B.T.A. 446.

In Golonsky the court stated the problem of the case as follows:

"A tenant in possession of premises under a lease, upon receipt of payment by the landlord, and pursuant to an agreement made with the landlord, 'vacated and surrendered the premises' before the date at which the lease expired." 200 F.2d at page 73.

It was held that the proceeds of the transaction constituted capital gain.

The Commissioner would (and the Tax Court did) distinguish Golonsky upon the ground that in the instant case the consideration passed not from the lessor but from the sublessee, the very party obliged to pay rental to the recipient, and that such consideration represented the amount which the recipient felt it would otherwise have received under the sublease. Further, it is said, the value of the leasehold was fixed and limited by the rentals due under the sublease since the term of the sublease corresponded with that of the lease.

We are not impressed by this proposed distinction. The lease clearly had value over the amount of rentals due by virtue of the fact that its acquisition was of importance to Olympic. Irrespective of the method used by Metropolitan in arriving at the figure of $137,-000.00, it is clear that Metropolitan did profit to some extent by the transaction. The Commissioner seems to concede that if the consideration had been paid by the University or if the lease had been assigned to a third party the transaction would have constituted a sale by the lessee.

It is not the person of the payor which controls the nature of the transaction in our view. Rather, it is the fact that the transaction constituted a bona fide transfer, for a legitimate business purpose, of the leasehold in its entirety. It did not constitute a release or transfer only of the right to future income under the sublease and the business purpose of the transaction would not have been met by such a release.

We conclude that the sum of $137,000.00, received by petitioner for release of its leasehold, must be held taxable as capital gain and not as ordinary income.

Reversed and remanded for redetermination, in accordance with this opinion, of deficiencies in income and excess profits taxes of petitioner for its taxable year ended June 30, 1953.

NOTE

With *Hort* in mind (hopefully) as well as the modification of its message in *Metropolitan Building,* we approach the question of the tax consequences of the sale of a life or other term interest or of an income interest in a trust. For example, (and we shall use this example throughout this brief note) S transfers securities to T, as trustee, the income from the assets to be paid to L for life and then the securities to be distributed to R. We recall from Chapter 14, perhaps in a somewhat oversimplified way, that a trust of this type is viewed essentially as a conduit and that the income earned by the trust property which is distributable to L will be taxed to L. Suppose then that *L sells his interest to P.* Two questions are presented: (1) How is gain or loss to be measured? (2) How is gain or loss to be characterized?

Measurement of Gain. It may well be contended that L merely receives an advance payment of future income and, as in *Hort,* all that is received should be taxed. However, that argument runs into *Blair,*[1] which recognized an income interest in a trust as *property,* similar to the decision on the leasehold in *Metropolitan Building.* If this is a disposition of property and not simply an anticipatory assignment of income, then we must think in terms of basis as a subtraction from the amount realized to determine L's gain. And so we must, on good authority.[2]

1. Blair v. Comm'r, 300 U.S. 5 (1937). Supra page 279.

v. Comm'r, 157 F.2d 235 (2d Cir. 1946), cert. den. 330 U.S. 826 (1946).

2. E. g., Bell's Estate v. Comm'r, 137 F.2d 454 (8th Cir. 1943); McAllister

Three possibilities now appear. If one purchased a temporary interest, such as L's life interest, he would have a cost basis for it. The cost would be amortized, written off by way of deductions, over the expected duration of the interest. Upon sale of the interest, the adjusted basis would be subtracted from the amount received to determine gain. There is little doubt about this, but of course it does not answer L's question.

If a temporary interest in property is received by gift or bequest, it too is accorded a basis determined, as usual, with reference to § 1015 or § 1023, respectively. In a bequest situation the basis for the temporary interest is a part of the § 1023 basis for the underlying property. In the case of a lifetime gift, such as that received by L, the basis for the income interest is a part of the transferred basis of the donor under § 1015. Here (in both the bequest and the gift cases) we encounter the "uniform basis" concept and the phenomenon of a sharing of that basis in shifting percentages by those who have an interest in the property. The thought is that the basis of the property transferred remains uniform, except as it may be subject to adjustments such as for depreciation. But the separate interests in the property share the uniform basis in accordance with the changing *values* of their interests.[3]

Sections 273 and 102(b) are relevant here. The amortization deduction permitted one who *purchases* a temporary interest is denied to one such as L who acquires a life or other terminable interest by gift, and also to one acquiring a temporary interest by bequest or by inheritance. This is because Congress in § 102 expresses a policy to exclude from gross income a gift or bequest of *property*, but not the income therefrom. The entire exclusion finds its form in the uniform basis. That entire basis will ultimately be passed on to R, the remainderman. That being so, it would be inappropriate to allow L an amortization deduction using a part of the uniform basis. So, in general in these cases the uniform basis remains intact but the basis for the several interests in the property changes. When L's interest is worth 40% of the value of the property, the basis for this interest is 40% of the uniform basis and R's basis is the other 60%. As a life tenant grows older his interest diminishes in value. (Consider what you would pay for the right to income from a trust for the life of one 50 years of age and what you would pay if the life tenant were 80.) Thus, when L's interest declines to only 20% of the value of the property, his basis has also declined to only 20% of the uniform basis but R's basis (as he is now much closer to full ownership) has increased to 80%.

3. Reg. §§ 1.1015–1(b), 1.1014–5. I.R. C. § 1014 was not repealed by TRA (1976); indeed, new § 1023(b)(1) incorporates expressly principles expressed in § 1014(b). Nevertheless § 1014 withers, will ultimately be largely dead wood and may *then* be repealed. Meanwhile the uniform basis rules of the regulations may show up in a new place under the §§ 1015 and 1023 Regs.

Now, are we going to let L assert his share of the uniform basis when he sells his interest to P? Several cases have held that he may,[4] and quite properly in the absence of statutory proscription. But it does create a distortion. If L's interest has a relative value that gives him 40% of the uniform basis, which he subtracts in determining his gain, it is still true that R will have 100% of the uniform basis when L's interest which P purchased ends.[5] Thus we've used 140% of the uniform basis which is violative of the policy embodied in § 102(b). Yes, you say, but P invested new funds equal to the added basis. True, we say, *but* his amortization of that *cost* basis is not foreclosed by § 273 as it is for someone like L who acquires the interest by gift. So we *had* (note the past tense) a distortion here.

In 1969, Congress added § 1001(e) which requires L, upon the sale of his interest, to *disregard* his share of the § 1015 (or § 1023) uniform basis. Zero basis for L taxes him on *all* that he receives as gain.

Section 1001(e)(3) makes an exception to the zero basis rule of § 1001(e)(1) if there is a transfer of the entire interest in the property, such as a sale by L *and* R of their interests to P. In light of the preceding discussion, is the reason for this exception discernible?

Characterizing the Gain. If a life interest is property[6] and not within any of the exclusionary paragraphs of § 1221, it is a capital asset. If it is sold, the gain is capital gain. If it has been held for more than one year, it is long-term capital gain. *All* that L gets is gross income, but it is characterized as capital gain. So be it! *Should* that be it? There may be competing policies here. What L receives is essentially a substitute for what would probably have come to him as ordinary income.[7] While we veer back pretty close to *Hort* with this thought, we find shelter again (for L) in the *Metropolitan Building.* And as a policy matter we might feel that to telescope all of L's receipts into one year would be harsh if all were treated as ordinary income.[8]

4. See *Bell's Estate* and *McAllister,* supra note 2.

5. Notice that there is no similar problem with regard to a sale of R's remainder. His purchaser will take a cost basis unaffected by the uniform basis rules. Thus, § 1001(e) is not made applicable to the remainder interest, as the uniform basis will just expire with the life beneficiary, and R *may* use his share of the uniform basis upon the sale of this interest. Cf. § 1001(e)(3).

6. See Blair v. Comm'r, supra note 1.

7. Note, however, the characterization rules of I.R.C. §§ 652(b) and 662(b);

and see Ferguson, Freeland and Stephens, The Federal Income Taxation of Estates and Beneficiaries, c. 7, page 468, "The Qualitative Measure." Recall, too, that before 1978 the critical period for *long*-term gain was 9 months in 1977 and, before that, 6 months.

8. Consider, however, whether I.R.C. § 1301 relief (examined in Chapter 20) might now be sufficient comfort. Later consider also whether L might make use of the installment sales rules of § 453 (examined in Chapter 24).

In any event Congress left usual characterization rules intact at the time it changed the measuring device for gain or loss on sales of terminable interests.

PROBLEMS

1. Agent entered into a contract with a national insurance Company to manage its State office for a ten year period. After two years Company decides to discontinue its State operations and agrees to pay Agent $50,000 to terminate his contract. What result to Agent?

2. Landlord L owns two contiguous parcels of land. He leases both parcels to Tenant T for $1,000 per month per parcel or a total of $24,000 per year; the rent is payable at the end of each year. The lease is for a 10 year period. Upon the following events, which occur more than one year after the lease is signed, what are the results:

(a) To L if he sells the right to the rents on both parcels prior to any rental payments being due or paid to a third party for $200,000?

(b) To L if T pays him $20,000 to cancel the leases on both parcels?

(c) To T if L pays him $20,000 to cancel the leases on both parcels?

(d) To T, if after subleasing one of the parcels of land to S for $1200 per month for a five year period, S pays him $10,000 for all T's rights in his lease on that parcel and L releases T from the lease and accepts S as the new tenant?

(e) To T if S subleases one parcel of land from T at $1200 per month for the remainder of his ten year period?

3. Beneficiary B owns an income interest in a trust which he purchased several years ago. The remaining income interest has twenty years to run after the date of the sale described below and his adjusted basis in the remaining interest is $50,000. What result:

(a) If B sells the entire interest for $60,000?

(b) If B sells the right to one quarter of each year's income for $15,000?

(c) If B received the income interest as a gift (rather than by purchasing it, but assuming the same adjusted basis) and he sells his entire interest for $60,000?

(d) If B inherited the income interest and B and the remainderman R both sell their interests to a third party with B receiving $60,000 for his interest?

(e) If R sells his remainder interest when it has an adjusted basis of $100,000 for $150,000?

3. THE CORN PRODUCTS DOCTRINE

CORN PRODUCTS REFINING CO. v. COMMISSIONER *

Supreme Court of the United States, 1955.
350 U.S. 46, 76 S.Ct. 20.
Reh. den., 350 U.S. 943, 76 S.Ct. 297.

MR. JUSTICE CLARK delivered the opinion of the Court.

This case concerns the tax treatment to be accorded certain transactions in commodity futures.[1] In the Tax Court, petitioner Corn Products Refining Company contended that its purchases and sales of corn futures in 1940 and 1942 were capital-asset transactions under § 117(a) of the Internal Revenue Code of 1939. It further contended that its futures transactions came within the "wash sales" provisions of § 118. The 1940 claim was disposed of on the ground that § 118 did not apply, but for the year 1942 both the Tax Court and the Court of Appeals for the Second Circuit, 215 F.2d 513, held that the futures were not capital assets under § 117. We granted certiorari, 348 U.S. 911,[2] because of an asserted conflict with holdings in the Courts of Appeal for the Third, Fifth, and Sixth Circuits.[3] Since we hold that these futures do not constitute capital assets in petitioner's hands, we do not reach the issue of whether the transactions were "wash sales."

Petitioner is a nationally known manufacturer of products made from grain corn. It manufactures starch, syrup, sugar, and their by-products, feeds and oil. Its average yearly grind of raw corn during the period 1937 through 1942 varied from thirty-five to sixty million bushels. Most of its products were sold under contracts requiring shipment in thirty days at a set price or at market price on the date of

---

* See Rabinovitz and Shashy, "Properties of Property: Indigestion from Corn Products," 27 U. of Fla.L.Rev. 964 (1975) and Cunnane, "Acquiring Capital Items for Non-Capital Purposes, or When is a Capital Asset Not a Capital Asset?" 29 N.Y.U.Inst. on Fed. Tax. 705 (1971).

1. A commodity future is a contract to purchase some fixed amount of a commodity at a future date for a fixed price. Corn futures, involved in the present case, are in terms of some multiple of five thousand bushels to be delivered eleven months or less after the contract. Cf. Hoffman, Future Trading (1932), 118.

2. The grant was limited to the following two questions:

"1. Are transactions in commodity futures which are not 'true hedges' capital asset transactions and thus subject to the limitations of Section 117 of the Internal Revenue Code of 1939, or do the resulting gains and losses from such transactions give rise to ordinary income and ordinary deductions?

"2. Are commodity futures contracts 'securities' and thus subject to the 'wash sales' provisions of Section 118 of the Internal Revenue Code of 1939? "

3. Makransky's Estate v. Commissioner, 154 F.2d 59 (C.A.3d Cir.); Commissioner v. Farmers & Ginners Cotton Oil Co., 120 F.2d 772 (C.A.5th Cir.); Trenton Cotton Oil Co. v. Commissioner, 147 F.2d 33 (C.A.6th Cir.).

delivery, whichever was lower. It permitted cancellation of such contracts, but from experience it could calculate with some accuracy future orders that would remain firm. While it also sold to a few customers on long-term contracts involving substantial orders, these had little effect on the transactions here involved.[4]

In 1934 and again in 1936 droughts in the corn belt caused a sharp increase in the price of spot corn. With a storage capacity of only 2,300,000 bushels of corn, a bare three weeks' supply, Corn Products found itself unable to buy at a price which would permit its refined corn sugar, cerelose, to compete successfully with cane and beet sugar. To avoid a recurrence of this situation, petitioner, in 1937, began to establish a long position in corn futures "as a part of its corn buying program" and "as the most economical method of obtaining an adequate supply of raw corn" without entailing the expenditure of large sums for additional storage facilities. At harvest time each year it would buy futures when the price appeared favorable. It would take delivery on such contracts as it found necessary to its manufacturing operations and sell the remainder in early summer if no shortage was imminent. If shortages appeared, however, it sold futures only as it bought spot corn for grinding.[5] In this manner it reached a balanced position with reference to any increase in spot corn prices. It made no effort to protect itself against a decline in prices.

In 1940 it netted a profit of $680,587.39 in corn futures, but in 1942 it suffered a loss of $109,969.38. In computing its tax liability Corn Products reported these figures as ordinary profit and loss from its manufacturing operations for the respective years. It now contends that its futures were "capital assets" under § 117 and that gains and losses therefrom should have been treated as arising from the sale of a capital asset.[6] In support of this position it claims that its futures trading was separate and apart from its manufacturing operations and that in its futures transactions it was acting as a "legitimate capitalist." United States v. New York Coffee & Sugar Exchange, 263 U.S. 611, 619. It denies that its futures transactions were "hedges" or "speculative" dealings as covered by the ruling of General Counsel's Memorandum 17322, XV–2 Cum.Bull. 151, and claims that it is in truth "the forgotten man" of that administrative interpretation.

4. Petitioner had contracts with three consumers to furnish, for a period of ten years or more, large quantities of starch or feed. In January 1940, petitioner had sold 2,000,000 bags of corn sugar, delivery to be made several months in the future. Also, members of the canning industry on the Pacific Coast had contracts to purchase corn sugar for delivery in more than thirty days.

5. The dispositions of the corn futures during the period in dispute were as follows:

	Sales of futures thousand bushels	Delivery under futures thousand bushels
1938	17,400	4,975
1939	14,180	2,865
1940	14,595	250
1941	2,545	2,175
1942	5,695	4,460

6. [I.R.C. (1939) § 117(a)(1) is omitted. See I.R.C. (1954) § 1221. Ed.]

Both the Tax Court and the Court of Appeals found petitioner's futures transactions to be an integral part of its business designed to protect its manufacturing operations against a price increase in its principal raw material and to assure a ready supply for future manufacturing requirements. Corn Products does not level a direct attack on these two-court findings but insists that its futures were "property" entitled to capital-asset treatment under § 117 and as such were distinct from its manufacturing business. We cannot agree.

We find nothing in this record to support the contention that Corn Products' futures activity was separate and apart from its manufacturing operation. On the contrary, it appears that the transactions were vitally important to the company's business as a form of insurance against increases in the price of raw corn. Not only were the purchases initiated for just this reason, but the petitioner's sales policy, selling in the future at a fixed price or less, continued to leave it exceedingly vulnerable to rises in the price of corn. Further, the purchase of corn futures assured the company a source of supply which was admittedly cheaper than constructing additional storage facilities for raw corn. Under these facts it is difficult to imagine a program more closely geared to a company's manufacturing enterprise or more important to its successful operation.

Likewise the claim of Corn Products that it was dealing in the market as a "legitimate capitalist" lacks support in the record. There can be no quarrel with a manufacturer's desire to protect itself against increasing costs of raw materials. Transactions which provide such protection are considered a legitimate form of insurance. United States v. New York Coffee & Sugar Exchange, 263 U.S., at 619; Browne v. Thorn, 260 U.S. 137, 139–140. However, in labeling its activity as that of a "legitimate capitalist" exercising "good judgment" in the futures market, petitioner ignores the testimony of its own officers that in entering that market the company was "trying to protect a part of [its] manufacturing costs"; that its entry was not for the purpose of "speculating and buying and selling corn futures" but to fill an actual "need for the quantity of corn [bought] . . . in order to cover . . . what [products] we expected to market over a period of fifteen or eighteen months." It matters not whether the label be that of "legitimate capitalist" or "speculator"; this is not the talk of the capital investor but of the far-sighted manufacturer. For tax purposes petitioner's purchases have been found to "constitute an integral part of its manufacturing business" by both the Tax Court and the Court of Appeals, and on essentially factual questions the findings of two courts should not ordinarily be disturbed. Comstock v. Group of Investors, 335 U.S. 211, 214.

Petitioner also makes much of the conclusion by both the Tax Court and the Court of Appeals that its transactions did not constitute "true hedging." It is true that Corn Products did not secure complete protection from its market operations. Under its sales policy petitioner could not guard against a fall in prices. It is clear however, that petitioner feared the possibility of a price rise more than that of a price decline. It therefore purchased partial insurance against its principal risk, and hoped to retain sufficient flexibility to avoid serious losses on a declining market.

Nor can we find support for petitioner's contention that hedging is not within the exclusions of § 117(a). Admittedly, petitioner's corn futures do not come within the literal language of the exclusions set out in that section. They were not stock in trade, actual inventory, property held for sale to customers or depreciable property used in a trade or business. But the capital-asset provision of § 117 must not be so broadly applied as to defeat rather than further the purpose of Congress. Burnet v. Harmel, 287 U.S. 103, 108. Congress intended that profits and losses arising from the everyday operation of a business be considered as ordinary income or loss rather than capital gain or loss. The preferential treatment provided by § 117 applies to transactions in property which are not the normal source of business income. It was intended "to relieve the taxpayer from   .   .   .   excessive tax burdens on gains resulting from a conversion of capital investments, and to remove the deterrent effect of those burdens on such conversions." Burnet v. Harmel, 287 U.S., at 106. Since this section is an exception from the normal tax requirements of the Internal Revenue Code, the definition of a capital asset must be narrowly applied and its exclusions interpreted broadly. This is necessary to effectuate the basic congressional purpose. This Court has always construed narrowly the term "capital assets" in § 117. See Hort v. Commissioner, 313 U.S. 28, 31; Kieselbach v. Commissioner, 317 U.S. 399, 403.

The problem of the appropriate tax treatment of hedging transactions first arose under the 1934 Tax Code revision.[7] Thereafter the Treasury issued G.C.M. 17322, supra, distinguishing speculative transactions in commodity futures from hedging transactions. It held that hedging transactions were essentially to be regarded as insurance rather than a dealing in capital assets and that gains and losses therefrom were ordinary business gains and losses. The interpretation outlined in this memorandum has been consistently followed by the courts as well as by the Commissioner.[8] While it is true that this Court has not passed on its validity, it has been well recognized for 20 years; and

7. Section 208(8) of the Revenue Act of 1924 limited "capital assets" to property held more than two years. This definition was retained until the Act of 1934. Since the rules of the various commodity exchanges required that futures contracts be closed out in periods shorter than two years, these contracts could not qualify as capital assets.

8. Stewart Silk Corp. v. Commissioner, 9 T.C. 174; Battelle v. Commissioner, 47 B.T.A. 117; Grote v. Commissioner, 41 B.T.A. 247. See Estate of Makransky v. Commissioner, 5 T.C. 397, 412, aff'd per curiam, 154 F.2d 59; Trenton Cotton Oil Co. v. Commissioner, 147 F.2d 33, 35; Commissioner v. Farmers & Ginners Cotton Oil Co., 120 F.2d 772, 774; Tennessee Egg Co. v. Commissioner, 47 B.T.A. 558, 560; G.C.M. 18383, 1937-2 Cum.Bull. 244, 245; I.T. 3137, 1937-2 Cum.Bull. 164, 166. Cf. Commissioner v. Banfield, 122 F.2d 1017, 1019–1020; G.C.M. 18658, 1937-2 Cum.Bull. 77.

Congress has made no change in it though the Code has been re-enacted on three subsequent occasions. This bespeaks congressional approval. Helvering v. Winmill, 305 U.S. 79, 83. Furthermore, Congress has since specifically recognized the hedging exception here under consideration in the short-sale rule of § 1233(a) of the 1954 Code.[9]

We believe that the statute clearly refutes the contention of Corn Products. Moreover, it is significant to note that practical considerations lead to the same conclusion. To hold otherwise would permit those engaged in hedging transactions to transmute ordinary income into capital gain at will. The hedger may either sell the future and purchase in the spot market or take delivery under the future contract itself. But if a sale of the future created a capital transaction while delivery of the commodity under the same future did not, a loophole in the statute would be created and the purpose of Congress frustrated.

The judgment is

Affirmed.

MR. JUSTICE HARLAN took no part in the consideration or decision of this case.

NOTE

In Estate of Hazel S. Laughlin, 30 T.C.M. 227 (1971), it was the taxpayer who asserted the *Corn Products* doctrine in support of ordinary treatment for *losses* on commodity futures. However, the losses were characterized as capital losses when the futures transactions were held to be not an integral part of a deceased farmer's business, because they were not undertaken as insurance against any business risk.

COMMISSIONER v. BAGLEY & SEWALL CO.

United States Court of Appeals, Second Circuit, 1955.
221 F.2d 944.

BRENNAN, DISTRICT JUDGE.

Whether or not the loss incurred in the posting of U. S. Government bonds as security for the performance of a contract is a capital loss or a business expense is the question posed on this appeal.

---

9. Section 1233(a) provides that gain or loss from "the short sale of property, other than a hedging transaction in commodity futures," shall be treated as gain or loss from the sale of a capital asset to the extent "that the property, including a commodity future, used to close the short sale constitutes a capital asset in the hands of a taxpayer." The legislative history recognizes explicitly the hedging exception.

H.R.Rep. No. 1337, 83d Cong., 2d Sess., p. A278; S.Rep. No. 1622, 83d Cong., 2d Sess., p. 437: "Under existing law bona fide hedging transactions do not result in capital gains or losses. This result is based upon case law and regulations. To continue this result hedging transactions in commodity futures have been specifically excepted from the operation of this subsection."

A background of essential facts were submitted by stipulation to the Tax Court. The Bagley & Sewall Co. (hereinafter referred to as the taxpayer), is a New York corporation engaged in the manufacture and sale of paper making machinery. In 1946 the taxpayer entered into a contract with a corporation acting in behalf of the Government of Finland for the manufacture and delivery of two paper making machines at a cost of approximately $1,800,000. Payments were to be made periodically during the progress of manufacture. The Government of Finland required that U. S. 2½% Government bonds be deposited with a New York financial institution as security for the performance of the contract and in accordance with an agreement which provided for the return of the bonds to Bagley & Sewall upon receipt of the last payment due under the contract. The above provisions were incorporated in and made a part of the contract. The taxpayer did not have or own the required bonds and in order to carry out the provisions of the contract, U. S. Government bonds in a total face value of $800,000 were purchased by the taxpayer with moneys borrowed for that purpose and same were deposited as required by the contract, the total cost of same being $820,062.50. The interest earned upon the bonds during the period that they were held in escrow was reported as income received by the taxpayer. In accordance with the terms of the contract, the bonds were released in two lots, one of $400,000 face value on Sept. 7, 1948 and one of $400,000 face value on Sept. 22, 1948. The bonds were sold by the taxpayer in each instance a few days after their release resulting in a loss of approximately $15,000 which the taxpayer claimed, in its tax return for 1948, as an ordinary and necessary business expense. During the period that the bonds were held in escrow and until they were sold, they were carried in the general ledger of the taxpayer in an account entitled "U. S. Gov't. Bonds" and on its balance sheet of Dec. 31, 1946 and Dec. 31, 1947, the bonds were shown under the caption "U. S. Gov't. Bonds".

Upon re-audit, the Commissioner of Internal Revenue determined a deficiency in the taxpayer's 1948 return on the ground that the above loss was a capital loss under Section 117(a) (1) of the Internal Revenue Code of 1939, 26 U.S.C.A. The matter came on before the Tax Court and after making minor adjustments, which are not here in dispute, the Tax Court found in effect in accordance with the claim of the taxpayer that the sale of the bonds was of assets held for sale in the ordinary course of petitioner's business and the loss was deductible as an ordinary and reasonable business expense.

The findings made are substantially as outlined above with the following additions * * * that the taxpayer was not in the business of buying and selling securities, that its available cash reserve was necessary for working capital, that it is clear that no investment in U. S. bonds was intended by the petitioner, they were acquired solely to carry out a condition imposed by the contract. It was concluded that the purchase and sale of these bonds was merely an incident in the carrying on by the petitioner of its regular business of manufacturing and selling paper making machines. The Tax Court relied upon the decisions in Western Wine & Liquor Co., 18 T.C. 1090 and Charles A. Clark, 19 T.C. 48 and distinguished the case of Exposition Souvenir Corp. v. Commissioner, 2 Cir., 163 F.2d 283. This appeal followed.

Concisely stated, the contention by the Commissioner is that the bonds constituted capital assets, as the term is defined in Section 117(a) (1) of the Internal Revenue Code and that the loss sustained upon their sale is to be treated as a capital loss to the extent of offsetting capital gains, none of which are reported by the taxpayer and therefore the whole item is subject to elimination.

The taxpayer's contention is to the effect that the whole transaction is merely an incident required and made necessary in the performance of a contract undertaken in the regular course of the taxpayer's business and is deductible from gross income in its entirety by reason of the provision of Section 23(a) (1) (A) of the Internal Revenue Code of 1939.

The difficulty with the Commissioner's contention is that in effect he urges that the bond transaction should be considered independently of the contract of which it is a definite part. This circuit in Helvering v. New Haven & S. L. R. Co., 121 F.2d 985, at page 988 has held that a contract may not be thus atomized.

In Exposition Souvenir Corp. v. Commissioner, 2 Cir., 163 F.2d 283, the taxpayer was required to make an investment, related to, but not a part of the concession contract. This is not the situation here. The contract represents a complete business transaction, security of performance alone, not investment was required. The cost of procuring that security cannot be distinguished from ordinary premium expense of a surety company bond which is a usual item of contractor's costs. The Exposition case may be further distinguished by the fact that the debentures were treated as investments in the taxpayer's books and tax returns and in that case the Tax Court made a finding that the debentures were not held for sale in the ordinary course of business. There is no such treatment of this transaction in this taxpayer's tax return and no such finding. It is implicit that the Tax Court found that the bonds here were held for sale to purchasers as soon as released from escrow and available for sale. In the Exposition case, an investment was intended and the taxpayer relied upon the motive for the investment for relief. Here there is a clear finding that no investment was intended. The Taxpayer's lack of surplus capital, the interest return of the bonds, the interest obligation of the loan and the almost immediate sale of the bonds when available make such a finding imperative. The finding here in this respect is similar to that made in Gilbert v. Commissioner, 1 Cir., 56 F.2d 361.

In brief, it is urged that the all inclusive language of Section 117 requires that, since the bonds are "property", they must be treated as capital assets unless exempted by the specific language of the Section. The argument carries with it the necessary conclusion that the circumstances of the transaction, its factual background, the necessities of the business involved and the intentions of taxpayer are of no importance except in determining whether the bonds are exempted under the Section. We are not persuaded that Section 23 is so completely subordinate to Section 117 and we find no authority which goes so far.

"Whether an expenditure is directly related to a business and whether it is ordinary and necessary are doubtless pure questions of fact in most instances". Commissioner of Internal Revenue v. Heininger, 320 U.S. 467, at page 475, 64 S.Ct. 249, at page 254, 88 L.Ed. 171. The purchase of stock in order to terminate an agency contract was held to be business expense. Helvering v. Community Bond & Mortgage Corporation, 2 Cir., 74 F.2d 727. The purchase of stock in a non-profit corporation to aid business was held to be a business expense. Commissioner of Internal Revenue v. The Hub, 4 Cir., 68 F.2d 349. The purchase of stock of a liquor corporation in order to purchase liquor therefrom was held to be business expense. Hogg v. Allen, D.C., 105 F.Supp. 12, affirmed, Edwards v. Hogg, 5 Cir., 214 F.2d 640, 644. We find similar holdings by the Tax Court especially the two cases relied upon by that Court and referred to above. The above authorities are cited here not to show that we necessarily agree with the conclusions therein but as an indication that business expense, Section 23, has been many times determined by business necessity without a specific consideration of Section 117.

An appreciation of the particular situation, Welch v. Helvering, 290 U.S. 111, at page 116, 54 S.Ct. 8, 78 L.Ed. 212, to which is applied the pertinent sections of the law according to common understanding and experience, Helvering v. Horst, 311 U.S. 112, 61 S.Ct. 144, 85 L.Ed. 75, is the measure of the law's requirement.

We find no comparable authority wherein a contract is dissected and its separate parts are subjected to application of particular sections of the Revenue Law. The Tax Court was right in refusing to wrench this transaction from its setting and its finding and conclusion is amply supported by evidence. To decide otherwise is to apply the law so as to escape reality.

The decision is affirmed.

[The dissenting opinion of FRANK, CIRCUIT JUDGE, which has been largely omitted, concluded with the following paragraph. Ed.] :

My conclusion here derives from no ardent desire to add to the government's revenues by invariably interpreting statutes adverse to taxpayers; see, e. g., my dissenting opinion in Babcock & Wilcox Co.

v. Pedrick, 2 Cir., 212 F.2d 645. But I think that courts should not allow what they deem fairness to taxpayers to over-ride one of the most sensible canons of statutory construction, i. e., that, where a statute sets forth specific exceptions, further exceptions, by way of mere implication, are not permissible. Moreover, to hold for the taxpayer here may well mean unfairness to other taxpayers who, having acquired securities in situations just like this, but having made a gain on the sale of the securities, seek to claim that their taxable profits are capital gains, not ordinary income.

PROBLEMS

A student can make a reasonable attack on the questions presented here on the basis of the principal cases set out above. The authorities cited in each question afford an opportunity for optional closer analysis.

1. Taxpayer T was having difficulty obtaining a component part needed in his manufacturing process to produce a machine which he sells to customers. To assure a supply of the part, T purchased stock in Corporation X which produces it. The purchasing priority accorded Corporation X shareholders was T's principal purpose for purchasing the shares. Two years after the purchase of the shares at a cost of $200,000, T revamped his manufacturing process in such a way that the part was no longer needed.

   (a) What result to T if he immediately sold the Corporation X stock for $250,000? See Mansfield Journal Co. v. Comm'r, 274 F.2d 284 (6th Cir. 1960), and Revenue Ruling 58–40, 1958–1 C.B. 275. For $150,000? See Western Wine and Liquor Co., 18 T.C. 1090 (1952), acq., 1958–1 C.B. 6.

   (b) What result to T if at the time the part became unnecessary the stock was worth $250,000 but, rather than selling the stock immediately, T continued to hold it for five additional years and then sold it for $300,000? See Gulftex Drug Co., Inc., 29 T.C. 118 (1957), aff'd per curiam, 261 F.2d 238 (5th Cir. 1959).

   (c) Suppose that as well as strong business reasons for purchasing the X shares T regarded them as a good investment and had a secondary investment purpose for their purchase. Compare *Mansfield Journal* supra problem 1(a), with W. W. Windle Co., 65 T.C. 694 (1976).

2. T Corporation was engaged in both domestic and foreign transactions. To guard against possible adverse effects a devaluation of the British pound would have on a forthcoming financial statement (consolidated to include a British subsidiary), early in 1967 T entered into a contract to sell short (without owning) one million pounds

sterling at $2.77 per pound (just below the then rate), delivery and payment to be made on January 3, 1968. Late in 1967 T was able to sell the contract to a Belgian bank for $360,000 when the price of the pound had dropped to $2.40. The Belgian bank bought the pounds forthwith and made delivery to the other party to the contract in January, 1968, collecting at the $2.77 agreed price. Thus T had a profit of $360,000 on the deal (and the Belgian bank $10,000). Should T's profit be regarded as:

(a) A long-term capital gain?

(b) A *Corn Products* item of ordinary income?

See Int'l Flavors & Fragrances v. Comm'r, 524 F.2d 357 (2d Cir. 1975), in which the court remands the case to the Tax Court, but speculates further whether T merely closed a short sale through the Belgian bank as agent, giving rise to a short-term capital gain under I.R.C. § 1233, or possibly whether there was no "sale" by T (at least in 1967) but only a contract by T with the Belgian bank to purchase pounds on T's behalf.

E. THE SALE OR EXCHANGE REQUIREMENT

1. INTRODUCTION

Internal Revenue Code: Section 1222. See Sections 1040; 1232; 1235; 1241; 1253.

KENAN v. COMMISSIONER

United States Court of Appeals, Second Circuit, 1940.
114 F.2d 217.

AUGUSTUS N. HAND, CIRCUIT JUDGE. The testatrix, Mrs. Bingham, died on July 27, 1917, leaving a will under which she placed her residuary estate in trust and provided in item "Seventh" that her trustees should pay a certain amount annually to her niece, Louise Clisby Wise, until the latter reached the age of forty, "at which time or as soon thereafter as compatible with the interests of my estate they shall pay to her the sum of Five Million ($5,000,000.00) Dollars." The will provided in item "Eleventh" that the trustees, in the case of certain payments including that of the $5,000,000 under item "Seventh", should have the right "to substitute for the payment in money, payment in marketable securities of a value equal to the sum to be paid, the selection of the securities to be substituted in any instance, and the valuation of such securities to be done by the Trustees and their selection and valuation to be final."

Louise Clisby Wise became forty years of age on July 28, 1935. The trustees decided to pay her the $5,000,000 partly in cash and partly in securities. The greater part of the securities had been owned by the testator and transferred as part of her estate to the trustees; others had been purchased by the trustees. All had appreciated in value during the period for which they were held by the trustees, and the Commissioner determined that the distribution of the securities to the niece resulted in capital gains which were taxable to the trustees under the rates specified in Section 117 of the Revenue Act of 1934, which limits the percentage of gain to be treated as taxable income on the "sale or exchange" of capital assets. On this basis, the Commissioner determined a deficiency of $367,687.12 in the income tax for the year 1935.

The Board overruled the objections of the trustees to the imposition of any tax and denied a motion of the Commissioner to amend his answer in order to claim the full amount of the appreciation in value as ordinary income rather than a percentage of it as a capital gain, and confirmed the original deficiency determination. The taxpayers contend that the decision of the Board was erroneous because they realized neither gain from the sale or exchange of capital assets nor income of any character by delivering the securities to the legatee pursuant to the permissive terms of the will. The Commissioner contends that gain was realized by the delivery of the securities but that such gain was ordinary income not derived from a sale or exchange and therefore taxable in its entirety. The trustees have filed a petition to review the order of the Board determining the deficiency of $367,687.12 and the Commissioner has filed a cross-petition claiming a deficiency of $1,238,841.99, based on his contention that the gain was not governed by Section 117, and therefore not limited by the percentages therein specified.

The amount of gain is to be determined under Section 111 of the Revenue Act of 1934, which provides:

"(a) Computation of gain or loss. The gain from the sale or other disposition of property shall be the excess of the amount realized therefrom over the adjusted basis * * *.

"(b) Amount realized. The amount realized from the sale or other disposition of property shall be the sum of any money received plus the fair market value of the property (other than money) received."

Section 113, 26 U.S.C.A. Int.Rev.Code, § 113, is claimed by the taxpayers to be relevant and provides:

"(a) The basis of property shall be the cost of such property; except that—

*   *   *   *   *   *   *   *   *   *

"(5) Property transmitted at death. If the property was acquired by bequest, devise, or inheritance, or by the decedent's estate from the decedent, the basis shall be the fair market value of such property at the time of such acquisition."

The Taxpayer's Appeal.

In support of their petition the taxpayers contend that the delivery of the securities of the trust estate to the legatee was a donative disposition of property pursuant to the terms of the will, and that no gain was thereby realized. They argue that when they determined that the legacy should be one of securities, it became for all purposes a bequest of property, just as if the cash alternative had not been provided, and not taxable for the reason that no gain is realized on the transfer by a testamentary trustee of specific securities or other property bequeathed by will to a legatee.

We do not think that the situation here is the same as that of a legacy of specific property. The legatee was never in the position occupied by the recipient of specific securities under a will. She had a claim against the estate for $5,000,000, payable either in cash or securities of that value, but had no title or right to the securities, legal or equitable, until they were delivered to her by the trustees after the exercise of their option. She took none of the chances of a legatee of specific securities or of a share of a residue that the securities might appreciate or decline in value between the time of the death of the testator and the transfer to her by the trustees, but instead had at all times a claim for an unvarying amount in money or its equivalent.

If there had merely been a bequest to the legatee of $5,000,000 and she had agreed with the trustees to take securities of that value, the transaction would have been a "sale or other disposition" of the securities under Suisman v. Eaton, 15 F.Supp. 113, affirmed, 2 Cir., 83 F.2d 1019, certiorari denied 299 U.S. 573, 57 S.Ct. 37, 81 L.Ed. 422. There, a will creating a trust provided that each of the testator's children was to receive $50,000 on attaining the age of twenty-five. The trustee transferred stock of the value of $50,000 to one of the children, Minerva, in satisfaction of her legacy. Judge Hincks said in the district court (15 F.Supp. at page 115), that the "property which the trust estate received from the 'sale or other disposition' of said stocks was the discharge of the corpus from Minerva's equitable right to receive $50,000 therefrom; the amount realized, i. e., the 'fair market value of the property (other than money) received,' * * * was $50,000; and the excess of the amount realized over the basis was properly computed by the Commissioner, legally assessed as part of the taxable income of the trust estate, and the tax thereon was legally collected."

In the present case, the legatee had a claim which was a charge against the trust estate for $5,000,000 in cash or securities and the trustees had the power to determine whether the claim should be satisfied in one form or the other. The claim, though enforceable only in the alternative, was, like the claim in Suisman v. Eaton, supra, a charge against the entire trust estate. If it were satisfied by a cash payment securities might have to be sold on which (if those actually delivered in specie were selected) a taxable gain would necessarily have been realized. Instead of making such a sale the trustees delivered the securities and exchanged them pro tanto for the general claim of the legatee, which was thereby satisfied.

It is said that this transaction was not such a "sale or other disposition" as is intended by Section 111(a) or was dealt with in Suisman v. Eaton, because it was effectuated only by the will of the trustees and not, as in Suisman v. Eaton, through a mutual agreement between trustee and legatee. The Board made no such distinction, and we are not inclined to limit thus the meaning of the words "other disposition" used in Section 111(a), or of "exchange" used in Section 117. The word "exchange" does not necessarily have the connotation of a bilateral agreement which may be said to attach to the word "sale." Thus, should a person set up a trust and reserve to himself the power to substitute for the securities placed in trust other securities of equal value, there would seem no doubt that the exercise of this reserved power would be an "exchange" within the common meaning of the word, even though the settlor consulted no will other than his own, although, of course, we do not here advert to the problems of taxability in such a situation.

The Board alluded to the fact that both here and in Suisman v. Eaton the bequest was fixed at a definite amount in money, that in both cases there was no bequest of specific securities (nor of a share in the residue which might vary in value), that the rights of the legatee, like those in the Suisman case, were a charge upon the corpus of the trust, and that the trustees had to part either with $5,000,000 in cash or with securities worth that amount at the time of the transfer. It added that the increase in value of the securities was realized by the trust and benefited it to the full extent, since, except for the increase, it would have had to part with other property, and it cited in further support of its position United States v. Kirby Lumber Co., 284 U.S. 1, 52 S.Ct. 4, 76 L.Ed. 131. Under circumstances like those here, where the legatee did not take securities designated by the will or an interest in the corpus which might be more or less at the time of the transfer than at the time of decedent's death, it seems to us that the trustees realized a gain by using these securities to settle a claim worth $5,000,000, just as the trustee in Suisman v. Eaton realized one.

It seems reasonably clear that the property was not "transmitted at death" or "acquired by bequest * * * from the decedent." Section 113(a) (5). It follows that the fears of the taxpayers that double taxation of this appreciation will result because the legatee will take the basis of the decedent under Brewster v. Gage, 280 U.S. 327, 50 S.Ct. 115, 74 L.Ed. 457, are groundless. It is true that under Section 113(a) (5) the basis for property "acquired by bequest, devise, or inheritance" is "the fair market value of such property at the time of such acquisition" and that under Brewster v. Gage, supra, the date of acquisition has been defined as the date of death of the testator. But the holding of the present case is necessarily a determination that the property here acquired is acquired in an exchange and not "by bequest, devise or inheritance," since Sections 117 and 113(a) (5) seem to be mutually exclusive. The legatee's basis would seem to be the value of the claim surrendered in exchange for the securities; and the Board of Tax Appeals has so held. Sherman Ewing v. Commissioner of Internal Revenue, 40 B.T.A. 911.

The Commissioner's Appeal.

We have already held that a taxable gain was realized by the delivery of the securities. It follows from the reasons that support that conclusion that the appreciation was a capital gain, taxable at the rates specified in Section 117. Therefore, neither under Section 111(a) nor under Section 22(a), 26 U.S.C.A. Int.Rev.Acts, page 669, can the gain realized be taxed as ordinary income.

There can be no doubt that from an accounting standpoint the trustees realized a gain in the capital of their trust when they disposed of securities worth far more at the time of disposition than at the time of acquisition in order to settle (pro tanto) a claim of $5,000,000. It would seem to us a strange anomaly if a disposition of securities which were in fact a "capital asset" should not be taxed at the rates afforded by Section 117 to individuals who have sold or exchanged property which they had held for the specified periods. It is not without significance that the appeal of the Commissioner was plainly an afterthought. The original deficiency was determined on the theory that the capital gains rates were applicable and the Commissioner sought to amend his answer so as to claim that ordinary rates should be applied only after the case had been orally argued before the Board. The Board denied his motion to reopen the case for the consideration of this contention. Since we find that the Commissioner's cross-petition is unfounded on the merits, we have no reason to consider the technical question whether the denial of the motion to amend the answer was an abuse of discretion.

The purpose of the capital gains provisions of the Revenue Act of 1934 is so to treat an appreciation in value, arising over a period of years but realized in one year, that the tax thereon will roughly approximate what it would have been had a tax been paid each year upon the appreciation in value for that year. Cf. Burnet v. Harmel, 287 U.S. 103, 106, 53 S.Ct. 74, 77 L.Ed. 199. The appreciation in value in the present case took place between 1917 and 1935, whereas the Commissioner's theory would tax it as though it had all taken place in 1935. If the trustees had sold the securities, they would be taxed at capital gain rates. Both the trustees and the Commissioner, in their arguments as respondent and cross-respondents, draw the analogy between the transaction here and a sale, and no injustice is done to either by taxing the gain at the rates which would apply had a sale actually been made and the proceeds delivered to the legatee. It seems to us extraordinary that the exercise by the trustees of the option to deliver to the legatee securities, rather than cash, should be thought to result in an increased deficiency of enormous proportions.

Orders affirmed.

GALVIN HUDSON

Tax Court of the United States, 1953.
20 T.C. 734.
Aff'd sub. nom. Ogilvie v. Commissioner, 216 F.2d 748 (6th Cir. 1954).

Findings of Fact

All the facts are stipulated and are so found.

Petitioners, residents of Memphis, Tennessee, filed their income tax returns for the year 1945 with the collector of internal revenue for the district of Tennessee. Galvin Hudson is in the lumber and cooperage business, and Hillsman Taylor is a practicing attorney.

On November 23, 1929, Mary Mallory Harahan obtained a judgment against Howard Cole in the amount of $75,702.12 in the Supreme Court of the State of New York. This judgment will hereinafter be referred to as the Cole judgment.

On June 30, 1943, the petitioners purchased the Cole judgment from the residuary legatees of Mary Mallory Harahan's estate; each petitioner acquired a 50 per cent interest in the judgment. Their aggregate cost of the judgment was $11,004; this included attorney fees and expenses of $1,004.

In May 1945 Howard Cole paid petitioners the sum of $21,150 as a full settlement of the judgment against him.

Each of the petitioners reported his profit on the settlement of the Cole judgment for income tax purposes as a long-term capital gain for 1945.

Respondent explained the adjustment to petitioners' net income as follows:

(a) It is held that the profits realized on the collection of a judgment from Mr. Howard Cole is taxable as ordinary income. In your return you reported 50% of $5,073.00, or $2,536.50 as capital gain. Accordingly, ordinary net income is increased in the amount of $5,073.-00. * * *

The gain resulting to petitioners from the settlement of the Cole judgment is ordinary income, as distinguished from a capital gain.

JOHNSON, JUDGE: Simply, the issue is whether the gain realized from the settlement of a judgment is ordinary income or capital gain when the settlement was made between the judgment debtor and the assignee or transferee of a prior judgment creditor. Petitioners contend that they are entitled to the benefits of section 117(a), Internal Revenue Code, with regard to the gain from the settlement of a judgment. Respondent has determined that the gain is ordinary income and taxable as such. There is no question about the bona fides of the transaction, nor is there any disagreement about the fact that the judgment, when entered and transferred, was property and a capital asset. The parties differ, however, on the question of whether there was a "sale or exchange of a capital asset." Section 117(a)(4). Petitioners and respondent both adhere to the principle that the words "sale or exchange" should be given their ordinary meaning. Petitioners, citing authority, define the word "sale" as follows:

A sale is a contract whereby one acquires a property in the thing sold and the other parts with it for a valuable consideration * * * or a sale is generally understood to mean the transfer of property for money * * *.

Also, "Sell in its ordinary sense means a transfer of property for a fixed price in money or its equivalent."

We cannot see how there was a transfer of property, or how the judgment debtor acquired property as the result of the transaction wherein the judgment was settled. The most that can be said is that the judgment debtor paid a debt or extinguished a claim so as to preclude execution on the judgment outstanding against him. In a hypothetical case, if the judgment had been transferred to someone other than the judgment debtor, the property transferred would still be in existence after the transaction was completed. However, as it actually happened, when the judgment debtor settled the judgment, the claim arising from the judgment was extinguished without the transfer of any property or property right to the judgment debtor. In their day-to-day transactions, neither businessmen nor lawyers would call the settlement of a judgment a sale; we can see no reason to apply a strained interpretation to the transaction before us. When petitioners received the $21,150 in full settlement of the judgment, they did not recover the money as the result of any sale or exchange but only as a collection or settlement of the judgment.

It is well established that where the gain realized did not result from a sale or exchange of a capital asset, the gain is not within the provisions of section 117(a)(4). In R. W. Hale, 32 B.T.A. 356, affd. 85 F.2d 815, there was a compromise of notes for less than face value and the taxpayer claimed there was a sale or exchange of notes within the meaning of the capital gains provision of the Code. In deciding the issue against the taxpayer, we said:

The petitioners did not sell or exchange the mortgage notes, and consequently an essential condition expressly required by the statute has not been met and no capital loss has been suffered. * * *

The *Hale* case was cited with approval in Pat N. Fahey, 16 T.C. 105. There, the taxpayer, an attorney, was assigned, for a cash consideration, an interest in a fee. Upon a successful settlement of the litigation, the taxpayer was paid his part of the fee. We held that his share was not capital gain because he did not sell or exchange anything. In another situation, a redemption of bonds before maturity by the issuing corporation was not a sale or exchange of capital assets. Fairbanks v. United States, 306 U.S. 436. In a similar situation in Bingham v. Commissioner, 105 F.2d 971, 972, the court said:

What may have been property in the hands of the holder of the notes simply vanished when the surrender took place and the maker received them. He then had, at most, only his own obligations to pay himself. Any theoretical concept of a sale of the notes to the maker in return for what he gave up to get them back must yield before the hard fact that he received nothing which was property in his hands but had merely succeeded in extinguishing his liabilities by the amounts which were due on the notes. There was, therefore, no sale of the notes to him in the ordinary meaning of the word and no exchange of assets for assets since the notes could not, as assets, survive the transaction. That being so, such a settlement as the one this petitioner made involved neither a sale nor an exchange of capital assets within the meaning of the statute. * * *

See also, Jack Rosenzweig, 1 T.C. 24, and Matilda S. Puelicher, 6 T.C. 300.

We have carefully considered the many cases cited by petitioners but we have found none of them controlling the issue before us. Cf. Commissioner v. Bookstein, 123 F.2d 996; United States v. Adamson, 161 F.2d 942; Isadore Golonsky, 16 T.C. 1450, affd. 200 F.2d 72; Louis W. Ray, 18 T.C. 438; McCue Bros. & Drummond, Inc., 19 T.C. 667. The respondent, therefore, must be sustained on this issue.

Reviewed by the Court.

Decisions will be entered under Rule 50.

NOTE

The disparate results in the two principal cases above, *Kenan* and *Hudson*, point up a distinction that must be kept in mind here. In those cases no really effective argument could be advanced that the taxpayer had not made a "disposition of property." And § 1001 makes a disposition a taxable event. Moreover, the property disposed of was a capital asset, hopefully invoking preferential treatment that is now familiar. But in these cases the final crucial question is whether the disposition is in the nature of a "sale or exchange." Whether this requirement is met is clearly not determined by what the parties call the transaction; the answer will depend upon its substance.[1]

There is a superficial similarity between *Kenan* and *Hudson*. In one case a taxpayer obligor discharges his obligation and in the other a taxpayer obligee receives that to which he is entitled. However, in the former, the obligor is said to have made an exchange; in the latter the disposition by the obligee is not so characterized. The thought intrudes that we have come upon a unilateral exchange, where the goose's sauce is not for the gander. For the message of the cases is that, while a debt-discharging obligor may be engaged in an exchange, the payment-receiving obligee is not.

The rationale for this seeming anomaly, which is advanced in *Hudson*, rests on the extinguishment of the debt as it is received by the judgment debtor; thus, the taxpayer obligee is not involved in an exchange, because what he may be said to transfer ceases to exist in the transaction. But it might as well be said that in *Kenan* the taxpayer obligor received no property since the obligation disappears when he discharges it.

The rationale of *Hudson* fully applied could have yielded a rule that neither obligor nor obligee is engaged in a sale or exchange in transactions of this type. On the other hand, in both instances the obligation involved is property in the hands of the obligee and, if the courts had chosen to disregard the extinguishment of the obligation, both obligor and obligee might be viewed as engaged in an exchange. Either of these views might be easier to square doctrinally than the differentiation reflected in the principal cases. However there is some logic to the rules that have developed.

The doctrinal difficulty with these apparently conflicting results can probably best be eased by a realignment of the transactions. It is consistent with economic reality in *Kenan* to treat the transaction as if the obligor trustee had paid the obligation in cash and the obligee recipient, in turn, had used the cash to purchase the transferred property from the trustee. Thus, from the standpoint of the obligor trustee, the sale or exchange requirement is met. But the trust beneficiary obligee has made no sale or exchange, because he is seen as merely receiving a payment due and as using the receipt to make a purchase. Turning to *Hudson*, the obligee is seen to be in the same position as the recipient in *Kenan;* he has just received payment of the sum due. If we assume in a *Hudson* situation that

---

1.   Cf. Est. of Starr v. Comm'r, 274 F.2d
294 (9th Cir. 1959).

the judgment debtor satisfied his obligation with appreciated property, his position would be analogous to the *Kenan* trustee, supporting sale or exchange treatment of the transaction. But the obligee taxpayer could still be viewed as merely receiving payment of a debt and making a purchase of property, so that as to him the transaction still would not constitute a sale or exchange. Thus, even on a doctrinal level, it is possible to view the cases as not in conflict.

The *Davis* case [2] will be recalled, taxing a divorced husband upon his transfer of appreciated property in discharge of his wife's dower rights. The foregoing rationale supports sale or exchange treatment for his transfer, a point not at issue in *Davis*. Application of the *Kenan* principle can also produce a loss, if the amount of the obligation discharged is less than the basis of the property transferred to discharge it.[3]

The statute creates an interesting problem of identifying what constitutes a sale or exchange. The *Kenan* obligor's transfer, yes; the *Hudson* obligee's collection, no. However, question may be raised whether special preferential gain treatment or ordinary loss treatment should be made to turn on such an issue. If the *Hudson* creditor had sold the judgment debt to a third party, instead of collecting from the debtor, he would have reached the promised land.[4] Is sale to another really very different from what is in effect a sale to the debtor? Should characterization be governed, then, only by the nature of the asset and its holding period, rather than in part by the nature of its disposition? While Congress has not seen fit to go so far as a general rule, special statutory provisions sometimes take liberties with the usual sale or exchange requirement.

If a lessee relinquishes his lease in exchange for a payment by the lessor, is the character of his gain affected by the fact that the lease is extinguished so that the lessee has made no exchange? § 1241 specifically says no. Such receipts "are considered as amounts received in exchange for" the lease. Similarly, if a nonbusiness debt becomes bad or a security becomes worthless the creditor or shareholder has made no actual sale or exchange, but Congress characterizes the losses involved by a statutory pretention that there was an exchange. § 165(g), 166(d).[5] An uninsured, unreimbursed casualty loss involves no exchange, but § 1231 sometimes treats it as such.[6] Three other special statutory sale or exchange rules appear in §§ 1232, 1235, and 1253, which sections are singled out for brief discussion here.

In general, under § 1232 amounts paid upon the retirement of obligations issued by corporations and governmental units, which are

2. U. S. v. Davis, 370 U.S. 65, 82 S.Ct. 1190 (1962).

3. See Rev.Rul. 74–178, 1974–1 C.B. 196.

4. Paine v. Comm'r, 236 F.2d 398 (8th Cir. 1956).

5. See Chapter 23 at page 808, infra.

6. See Chapter 22 at page 762, infra.

capital assets in the recipient's hands, are treated as amounts received in exchange for such obligations. This is a statutory reversal of the *Hudson* principle, but only with respect to certain types of obligations. The reversal may well be applauded, even as we wonder whether the concept might be extended. However, even as an inequity is thus avoided, an additional problem is created, if the bond was issued at a discount. In such an instance some of the gain that accrues is essentially interest and should not be accorded capital gain consequences. The courts have recognized that fact [7] and, as amended by the Tax Reform Act of 1969, § 1232 expressly recognizes it as well, essentially by requiring all taxpayers (regardless of their accounting methods) to accrue (and report as ordinary income each year) a ratable portion of the original issue discount. Amounts so reported are added to the taxpayer's basis for the obligation.[8] Because all the original discount is taxed currently as interest over the life of the bond, there is no need to treat any portion of gain on a sale of the obligation as ordinary income. The above rules apply only to recently issued bonds. As to bonds issued prior to May 28, 1969, the gain which is essentially interest is also accorded ordinary income treatment but not until there is a disposition of the bond.[9]

Another provision that may artificially accord sale or exchange classification to a transaction is § 1235. An invention, whether patented or not, is usually within the § 1221 definition of capital assets.[10] A common method of exploiting an invention is for the inventor to license others to use it, often fixing the consideration in terms of a part of the proceeds from its use. Can this be regarded as a sale? For a "holder" [11] § 1235 says it can, and that section generates long-term capital gain (regardless of the length of time the invention was held) out of a licensing arrangement, if the "holder" transfers all his substantial rights in the property.[12]

---

7. In U. S. v. Midland Ross Corp., 381 U.S. 54, 58, 85 S.Ct. 1308 (1965), the court observed: "The $6 earned on a one year note for $106 issued for $100 is precisely like the $6 earned on a one-year loan of $100 at 6% stated interest."

8. I.R.C. (26 U.S.C.A.) § 1232(a)(3)(E).

9. I.R.C. (26 U.S.C.A.) § 1232(a)(2)(E). The corporate issuer of a bond also treats original issue discount as interest, deductible by way of amortization, but he may not generate a discount by allocating a part of the price to the convertible feature of a bond. Hunt Foods, Inc., 57 T.C. 633 (1972), aff'd per curiam 496 F.2d 592 (9th Cir. 1974).

10. However, note that a literary product of the inventive mind is not normally accorded capital asset treatment. § 1221(3). If a literary product is a capital asset the question whether its disposition is a sale or exchange as opposed to a mere royalty arrangement is subject to the same tests as a patent. Rev.Rul. 60–226, 1960–1 C.B. 26.

11. I.R.C. (26 U.S.C.A.) § 1235(b).

12. See Reg. § 1.1235–2(b). The retention of substantial rights, such as a right to terminate a license agreement after a period, Taylor-Winfield Corp., 57 T.C. 205 (1971), or the right to exploit the patent in geographical areas placed outside the agreement, Est. of Klein v. Comm'r, 507 F.2d 617, (7th Cir. 1974), may defeat the application of I.R.C. § 1235. However, one may, within the section, sell an undivided

If one who is not a "holder" disposes of a patent in a manner different from an outright sale or exchange, i. e. by way of an exclusive licensing arrangement for a period coterminus with the life of the patent or for consideration measured by the licensee's profit, he may have capital gain treatment also. For a time the Treasury held he would not,[13] but with judicial prompting the Treasury has changed its position,[14] and now a non-"holder" who disposes of a patent is in much the same position as one who is within § 1235, although he does not automatically satisfy the one year holding period for long-term gain.

Finally, the Tax Reform Act of 1969 added § 1253, concerning the disposition of franchises, trademarks, and trade names, which is aimed in part at a problem similar to that covered by § 1235, dealing with patents. The common problem is whether a disposition is a sale or exchange or whether instead it should be viewed as a mere license. In contrast to the affirmative approach of § 1235 (sale classification upon transfer of "all substantial rights"), § 1253 provides only a negative rule. The transfer of a franchise, trademark, or trade name is not to be treated as a sale or exchange if the transferor retains any significant power, right or continuing interest in the property. Moreover, and quite contrary to principles adopted in § 1235, under § 1253 any amounts received or accrued which are dependent on the productivity, use, or disposition of the property are expressly denied capital gain treatment. Dispositions of franchises, trademarks, or trade names which are not so proscribed may qualify as sales or exchanges and for capital gain characterization if, of course, the property is a capital asset in the hands of the taxpayer.[15]

The proposed regulations seem to promise a strict interpretation of I.R.C. § 1253. For example, among the listed agreement restrictions not expressed in the statute, which will defeat capital gain treatment on a transfer of a franchise, are: (1) "A right to prevent the transferee from removing equipment outside the territory in which the transferee is permitted to operate;" and (2) "Any other right which permits the transferor to exercise continuing, active, and operational control over the transferee's trade or business activities."[16]

interest, even a small interest, in *all* substantial rights. Reg. § 1.1235–2c; Allen G. Eickmeyer, 66 T.C. 109 (1976).

13. Mim. 6490, 1950–1, C.B. 9; Rev.Rul. 55–58, 1955–1 C.B. 97.

14. Rev.Rul. 58–353, 1958–2 C.B. 408.

15. The newness of § 1253 and its inherent obscurities foretell uncertainty and controversy in the area of its coverage for some time to come. An extensive critical analysis of the new section appears in Andrews and Freeland, "Capital Gains and Losses of Individuals and Related Matters under the Tax Reform Act of 1969," 12 Ariz. L.Rev. 627, 666–677 (1970); see also Hall and Smith, "Franchising Under The Tax Reform Act," 4 Ind. Legal Forum 305 (1970).

16. Proposed Reg. § 1.1253–2(d)(7) and (9); see also Resorts Int'l Inc. v. Comm'r, 511 F.2d 107, n. 7 (5th Cir. 1975), commenting on § 1253 although it did not apply to the tax years at issue.

EXCERPT FROM SENATE FINANCE COMMITTEE
REPORT NO. 91–552

91st Congress, 1st Session (1969).
1969–3 C.B. 423, 464–465.

1. *The "Clay Brown" provision or Debt-financed Property (sec. 121(d) of the bill and secs. 512 and 514 of the code)**

Present law.—Under present law, charities and some of the other types of exempt organizations are subject to tax on rental income from real property to the extent the property was acquired with borrowed money. However, this provision does not apply to all tax-exempt organizations, and there is an important exception which excludes rental income from a lease of 5 years or less. In addition, there is a question as to whether the tax applies to income from the leasing by a tax-exempt organization of assets constituting a going business.

General reasons for change.—During the past several years a device has been developing which exploits weaknesses in the taxation of unrelated business income of tax-exempt organizations. The net effect is the use of the tax exemption to reduce taxes for owners of a business by converting ordinary income to capital gain and eventually to the acquisition of the business by a tax-exempt organization entirely out of the earnings of that business. This device was challenged by the Government in the courts but existing law was construed by the Supreme Court to support it in *Clay B. Brown*.

The typical *Clay Brown* situation presents the following series of events: A sells an incorporated business to B, a charitable foundation, which makes a small (or no) down payment and agrees to pay the balance of the purchase price only out of profits to be derived from the property. B liquidates the corporation and then leases the business assets to C, a new corporation formed to operate the business. A (collectively, the stockholders of the original business) manages the business for C and frequently holds a substantial minority interest in C. C pays 80 percent of its business profits as "rent" to B, which then passes on 90 percent of those receipts to A until the original purchase price is paid in full. B has no obligation to pay A out of any funds other than the "rent" paid by C.

In this manner, in the *Clay Brown* case, the owners of the business (A in the above example) were able to realize increased after-tax income and the exempt organization was able to acquire the ownership of a business valued at $1.3 million without the investment of its own funds. In 1965 the Supreme Court held that the owners were entitled to treat as capital gains (reported on the installment basis) the money they received from the foundation).

---

* The circumstances that led to this legislation are discussed in Kinsey, "Bootstraps and Capital Gain. A Participant's View of Commissioner v. Clay Brown," 64 Mich.L.Rev. 581 (1966) Ed.

In the recent (1969) *University Hill Foundation* case, the Tax Court held that an organization engaged in essentially the Clay Brown type of operation on a large scale did not lose its tax exemption, nor did it have unrelated business income. This case involved a tax-exempt organization established for the purpose of raising funds for a church-supported university. Twenty-four businesses were acquired by the organization from 1945 to 1954. The economic effect of the acquisitions was to divide the net income of each business, 20 percent to the new operators, 8 percent to the exempt organization, and 72 percent as installments on the purchase price to the sellers of the business. As was true in the *Clay Brown* case, the 72 percent was taxable to the sellers at capital gain rates. The court found that the organization was entitled to exemption as a charitable organization (because it was not actively engaged in business); that the organization was not taxable as a "feeder organization" because for this purpose, trade or business does not include the rental of real property (including personal property leased with the realty) and because it was not a controlling factor that the real property was not the essential element in the transaction; and that the rent received from the lessees was not taxable as unrelated business income because this concept does not include "rentals from real property (including personal property leased with real property)."

Other variants of the debt-financed property problem have also been used.

Explanation of provision.—Both the House bill and the committee amendments provide that all exempt organizations' income from "debt-financed" property, which is unrelated to their exempt function, is to be subject to tax in the proportion in which the property is financed by the debt. Thus, for example, if a business or investment property is acquired subject to an 80 percent mortgage, 80 percent of the income and 80 percent of the deductions are to be taken into account for tax purposes. As the mortgage is paid off, the percentage taken into account diminishes. Capital gains on the sale of debt-financed property also are taxed in the same proportions.

The bill defines debt-financed property to be all property (e. g., rental real estate, tangible personal property, corporate stock) which is held to produce income and with respect to which there is an "acquisition indebtedness" at any time during the taxable year (or during the preceding 12 months, if the property is disposed of during the year).

* * *

NOTE

It will be apparent from the foregoing fragment of legislative history that the 1969 attack on the *Clay Brown* device was to tax the acquiring organization on income newly classified as "unrelated business income" or "unrelated debt financial income." [1] The seller in *Clay Brown* got long-term capital gain treatment, as the Supreme Court saw it,[2] and there has been no statutory change that affects such determinations. Of course, the tax burdens placed on potential acquiring organizations pretty well snip the bootstrap for the future. Some cases still come along from pre-1969 years. In Berenson v. Comm'r,[3] the *seller* got only *partial* capital gain treatment when the Second Circuit found the case distinguishable from *Clay Brown*. The purchase price was not inflated in *Brown*, but in *Berenson* it exceeded by 100% what would have been paid by a nonexempt purchaser. Although the Tax Court had held this difference characterized the entire gain as ordinary income,[4] the Court of Appeals held that an allocation should be made, based on the relationship of the taxpayer's basis to the appreciated value of the business (to a nonexempt purchaser) at the time of the sale. That ratio applied to each payment determined the amount to be accorded capital gain treatment.[5]

---

2. CORRELATION WITH PRIOR TRANSACTIONS

ARROWSMITH v. COMMISSIONER

Supreme Court of the United States, 1952.
344 U.S. 6, 73 S.Ct. 71, rehearing den., 344 U.S. 900, 73 S.Ct. 273.

MR. JUSTICE BLACK delivered the opinion of the Court.

This is an income tax controversy growing out of the following facts as shown by findings of the Tax Court. In 1937 two taxpayers, petitioners here, decided to liquidate and divide the proceeds of a corporation in which they had equal stock ownership.* Partial distributions made in 1937, 1938, and 1939 were followed by a final one in 1940. Petitioners reported the profits obtained from this transaction, classifying them as capital gains. They thereby paid less income tax than would have been required had the income been attributed to ordinary business transactions for profit. About the

1. I.R.C. (26 U.S.C.A.) §§ 512 and 514, respectively.

2. Comm'r v. Clay Brown, 380 U.S. 563 (1965).

3. 507 F.2d 262 (2d Cir. 1974).

4. 59 T.C. 412 (1972).

5. See also Aaron Kraut, 62 T.C. 420 (1974), in which, as in *Berenson*, which was then on appeal, the Tax Court applied the "sham" doctrine to deny a *Clay Brown* result. Here the Second Circuit affirmed, 527 F.2d 1014 (2d Cir. 1976), and the Supreme Court denied cert. 425 U.S. 973, 96 S.Ct. 2171 (1976).

* At dissolution the corporate stock was owned by Frederick P. Bauer and the executor of Davenport Pogue's estate. The parties here now are Pogue's widow, Bauer's widow, and the executor of Bauer's estate.

propriety of these 1937–1940 returns, there is no dispute. But in 1944 a judgment was rendered against the old corporation and against Frederick R. Bauer, individually. The two taxpayers were required to and did pay the judgment for the corporation, of whose assets they were transferees. See Phillips-Jones Corp. v. Parmley, 302 U.S. 233, 235–236. Cf. I.R.C. § 311(a). Classifying the loss as an ordinary business one, each took a tax deduction for 100% of the amount paid. Treatment of the loss as a capital one would have allowed deduction of a much smaller amount. See I.R.C. § 117(b), (d) (2) and (e). The Commissioner viewed the 1944 payment as part of the original liquidation transaction requiring classification as a capital loss, just as the taxpayers had treated the original dividends as capital gains. Disagreeing with the Commissioner the Tax Court classified the 1944 payment as an ordinary business loss. 15 T.C. 876. Disagreeing with the Tax Court the Court of Appeals reversed, treating the loss as "capital." 193 F.2d 734. This latter holding conflicts with the Third Circuit's holding in Commissioner v. Switlik, 184 F.2d 299. Because of this conflict, we granted certiorari. 343 U.S. 976.

I.R.C. § 23(g) treats losses from sales or exchanges of capital assets as "capital losses" and I.R.C. § 115(c) requires that liquidation distributions be treated as exchanges. [See I.R.C. (1954) § 331 (a). Ed.] The losses here fall squarely within the definition of "capital losses" contained in these sections. Taxpayers were required to pay the judgment because of liability imposed on them as transferees of liquidation distribution assets. And it is plain that their liability as transferees was not based on any ordinary business transaction of theirs apart from the liquidation proceedings. It is not even denied that had this judgment been paid after liquidation, but during the year 1940, the losses would have been properly treated as capital ones. For payment during 1940 would simply have reduced the amount of capital gains taxpayers received during that year.

It is contended, however, that this payment which would have been a capital transaction in 1940 was transformed into an ordinary business transaction in 1944 because of the well-established principle that each taxable year is a separate unit for tax accounting purposes. United States v. Lewis, 340 U.S. 590; North American Oil v. Burnet, 286 U.S. 417. But this principle is not breached by considering all the 1937–1944 liquidation transaction events in order properly to classify the nature of the 1944 loss for tax purposes. Such an examination is not an attempt to reopen and readjust the 1937 to 1940 tax returns, an action that would be inconsistent with the annual tax accounting principle.

The petitioner Bauer's executor presents an argument for reversal which applies to Bauer alone. He was liable not only by reason of being a transferee of the corporate assets. He was also held liable jointly with the original corporation, on findings that he had secretly profited because of a breach of his fiduciary relationship to the judgment creditor. Trounstine v. Bauer, Pogue & Co., 44 F.Supp. 767, 773; 144 F.2d 379, 382. The judgment was against both Bauer and the corporation. For this reason it is contended that the nature of Bauer's tax deduction should be considered on the basis of his liability as an individual who sustained a loss in an ordinary business transaction for profit. We agree with the Court of Appeals that this contention should not be sustained. While there was a liability against him in both capacities, the individual judgment against him was for the whole amount. His payment of only half the judgment indicates that both he and the other transferee were paying in their capacities as such. We see no reason for giving Bauer a preferred tax position.

Affirmed.

MR. JUSTICE DOUGLAS, dissenting.

I agree with MR. JUSTICE JACKSON that these losses should be treated as ordinary, not capital losses. There were no capital transactions in the year in which the losses were suffered. Those transactions occurred and were accounted for in earlier years in accord with the established principle that each year is a separate unit for tax accounting purposes. See United States v. Lewis, 340 U.S. 590. I have not felt, as my dissent in the *Lewis* case indicates, that the law made that an inexorable principle. But if it is the law, we should require observance of it—not merely by taxpayers but by the Government as well. We should force each year to stand on its own footing, whoever may gain or lose from it in a particular case. We impeach that principle when we treat this year's losses as if they diminished last year's gains.

MR. JUSTICE JACKSON, whom MR. JUSTICE FRANKFURTER joins, dissenting.

This problem arises only because the judgment was rendered in a taxable year subsequent to the liquidation.

Had the liability of the transferor-corporation been reduced to judgment during the taxable year in which liquidation occurred, or prior thereto, this problem, under the tax laws, would not arise. The amount of the judgment rendered against the corporation would have decreased the amount it had available for distribution, which would have reduced the liquidating dividends proportionately and diminished the capital gains taxes assessed against the stockholders. Probably it would also have decreased the corporation's own taxable income.

Congress might have allowed, under such circumstances, tax returns of the prior year to be reopened or readjusted so as to give the same tax results as would have obtained had the liability become known prior to liquidation. Such a solution is foreclosed to us and the alternatives left are to regard the judgment liability fastened by operation of law on the transferee as an ordinary loss for the year of adjudication or to regard it as a capital loss for such year.

This Court simplifies the choice to one of reading the English language, and declares that the losses here come "squarely within" the definition of capital losses contained within two sections of the Internal Revenue Code. What seems so clear to this Court was not seen at all by the Tax Court, in this case or in earlier consideration of the same issue; nor was it grasped by the Court of Appeals for the Third Circuit. Commissioner v. Switlik, 184 F.2d 299 (1950).

I find little aid in the choice of alternatives from arguments based on equities. One enables the taxpayer to deduct the amount of the judgment against his ordinary income which might be taxed as high as 87%, while if the liability had been assessed against the corporation prior to liquidation it would have reduced his capital gain which was taxable at only 25% (now 26%). The consequence may readily be characterized as a windfall (regarding a windfall as anything that is left to a taxpayer after the collector has finished with him).

On the other hand, adoption of the contrary alternative may penalize the taxpayer because of two factors: (1) since capital losses are deductible only against capital gains, plus $1,000, [See I.R.C. (1954) § 1211(b)(1)(B), prior to 1976 amendments. Ed.] a taxpayer having no net capital gains in the ensuing five years would have no opportunity to deduct anything beyond $5,000 [But see I.R.C. (1954) § 1212(b). Ed.]; and (2) had the liability been discharged by the corporation, a portion of it would probably in effect have been paid by the Government, since the corporation could have taken it as a deduction, while here the total liability comes out of the pockets of the stockholders.

Solicitude for the revenues is a plausible but treacherous basis upon which to decide a particular tax case. A victory may have implications which in future cases will cost the Treasury more than a defeat. This might be such a case, for anything I know. Suppose that subsequent to liquidation it is found that a corporation has undisclosed claims instead of liabilities and that under applicable state law they may be prosecuted for the benefit of the stockholders. The logic of the Court's decision here, if adhered to, would result in a lesser return to the Government than if the recoveries were considered ordinary income. Would it be so clear that this is a capital loss if the shoe were on the other foot?

Where the statute is so indecisive and the importance of a particular holding lies in its rational and harmonious relation to the general scheme of the tax law, I think great deference is due the twice-expressed judgment of the Tax Court. In spite of the gelding

of Dobson v. Commissioner, 320 U.S. 489, by the recent revision of
the Judicial Code, Act of June 25, 1948, § 36, 62 Stat. 991–992, I still
think the Tax Court is a more competent and steady influence toward
a systematic body of tax law than our sporadic omnipotence in a
field beset with invisible boomerangs. I should reverse, in reliance
upon the Tax Court's judgment more, perhaps, than my own.

<hr>

UNITED STATES v. SKELLY OIL CO.

Supreme Court of the United States, 1969.
394 U.S. 678, 89 S.Ct. 1379.

MR. JUSTICE MARSHALL delivered the opinion of the Court: During its tax year ending December 31, 1958, respondent refunded
$505,536.54 to two of its customers for overcharges during the six
preceding years. Respondent, an Oklahoma producer of natural gas,
had set its prices during the earlier years in accordance with a minimum price order of the Oklahoma Corporation Commission. After
that order was vacated as a result of a decision of this Court, Michigan Wisconsin Pipe Line Co. v. Corporation Comm'n of Oklahoma,
355 U.S. 425 (1958), respondent found it necessary to settle a number
of claims filed by its customers; the repayments in question represent settlements of two of those claims. Since respondent had claimed
an unrestricted right to its sales receipts during the years 1952
through 1957, it had included the $505,536.54 in its gross income in
those years. The amount was also included in respondent's "gross
income from the property" as defined in § 613 of the Internal Revenue
Code of 1954, the section which allows taxpayers to deduct a fixed
percentage of certain receipts to compensate for the depletion of
natural resources from which they derive income. Allowable percentage depletion for receipts from oil and gas wells is [was then]
fixed at 27½% of the "gross income from the property." Since
respondent claimed and the Commissioner allowed percentage depletion deductions during these years, 27½% of the receipts in question
was added to the depletion allowances to which respondent would
otherwise have been entitled. Accordingly, the actual increase in
respondent's taxable income attributable to the receipts in question
was not $505,536.54, but only $366,513.99. Yet, when respondent
made its refunds in 1958, it attempted to deduct the full $505,536.54.
The Commissioner objected and assessed a deficiency. Respondent
paid and, after its claim for a refund had been disallowed, began the
present suit. The Government won in the District Court, 255 F.Supp.
228 (D.C.N.D.Okla.1966), but the Court of Appeals for the Tenth
Circuit reversed, 392 F.2d 128 (1968). Upon petition by the Government, we granted certiorari, 393 U.S. 820 (1968), to consider
whether the Court of Appeals decision had allowed respondent "the
practical equivalent of double deduction," Charles Ilfeld Co. v. Her-

nandez, 292 U.S. 62, 68 (1934), in conflict with past decisions of this Court and sound principles of tax law. We reverse.

I. The present problem is an outgrowth of the so-called "claim-of-right" doctrine. Mr. Justice Brandeis, speaking for a unanimous Court in North American Oil Consolidated v. Burnet, 286 U.S. 417, 424 (1932), gave that doctrine its classic formulation. "If a taxpayer receives earnings under a claim of right and without restriction as to its disposition, he has received income which he is required to return, even though it may still be claimed that he is not entitled to retain the money, and even though he may still be adjudged to restore its equivalent." Should it later appear that the taxpayer was not entitled to keep the money, Mr. Justice Brandeis explained, he would be entitled to a deduction in the year of repayment; the taxes due for the year of receipt would not be affected. This approach was dictated by Congress' adoption of an annual accounting system as an integral part of the tax code. See Burnet v. Sanford & Brooks Co., 282 U.S. 359, 365–366 (1931). Of course, the tax benefit from the deduction in the year of repayment might differ from the increase in taxes attributable to the receipt; for example, tax rates might have changed, or the taxpayer might be in a different tax "bracket." See Healy v. Commissioner, 345 U.S. 278, 284–285 (1953). But as the doctrine was originally formulated, these discrepancies were accepted as an unavoidable consequence of the annual accounting system.

Section 1341 of the 1954 Code was enacted to alleviate some of the inequities which Congress felt existed in this area.[1] See H.R.Rep. No. 1337, 83d Cong., 2d Sess., 86–87 (1954); S.Rep. No. 1622, 83d Cong., 2d Sess., 118–119 (1954). As an alternative to the deduction in the year of repayment [2] which prior law allowed, § 1341(a)(5) permits certain taxpayers to recompute their taxes for the year of receipt. Whenever § 1341(a)(5) applies, taxes for the current year are to be reduced by the amount taxes were increased in the year or years of receipt because the disputed items were included in gross income. Nevertheless, it is clear that Congress did not intend to tamper with the underlying claim-of-right doctrine; it only provided an alternative for certain cases in which the new approach favored the taxpayer. When the new approach was not advantageous to the taxpayer, the old law was to apply under § 1341(a)(4).

1. [Section 1341(a) is omitted. Ed.] Section 1341(b)(2) contains an exclusion covering certain cases involving sales of stock in trade or inventory. However, because of special treatment given refunds made by regulated public utilities, both parties agree that § 1341(b)(2) is inapplicable to this case and that, accordingly, § 1341 (a) applies.

2. In the case of an accrual-basis taxpayer, the legislative history makes it clear that the deduction is allowable at the proper time for accrual. H.R. Rep.No.1337, 83d Cong., 2d Sess., A294 (1954); S.Rep.No.1622, 83d Cong., 2d Sess., 451–452 (1954).

In this case, the parties have stipulated that § 1341(a)(5) does not apply. Accordingly, as the courts below recognized, respondent's taxes must be computed under § 1341(a)(4) and thus, in effect, without regard to the special relief Congress provided through the enactment of § 1341. Nevertheless, respondent argues, and the Court of Appeals seems to have held, that the language used in § 1341 requires that respondent be allowed a deduction for the full amount it refunded to its customers. We think the section has no such significance.

In describing the situations in which the section applies, § 1341 (a)(2) talks of cases in which "a deduction is allowable for the taxable year because it was established after the close of [the year or years of receipt] that the taxpayer did not have an unrestricted right to such item . . . ." The "item" referred to is first mentioned in § 1341(a)(1); it is the item included in gross income in the year of receipt. The section does not imply in any way that the "deduction" and the "item" must necessarily be equal in amount. In fact, the use of the words "a deduction" and the placement of § 1341 in subchapter Q—the subchapter dealing largely with side-effects of the annual accounting system—make it clear that it is necessary to refer to other portions of the Code to discover how much of a deduction is allowable. The regulations promulgated under the section make the necessity for such a cross-reference clear. Treas. Reg. § 1.1341–1 (1957). Therefore, when § 1341(a)(4)—the subsection applicable here—speaks of "the tax . . . computed with such deduction," it is referring to the deduction mentioned in § 1341 (a)(2); and that deduction must be determined not by any mechanical equation with the "item" originally included in gross income, but by reference to the applicable sections of the Code and the case law developed under those sections.

II.   There is some dispute between the parties about whether the refunds in question are deductible as losses under § 165 of the 1954 Code or as business expenses under § 162.[3] Although in some situations the distinction may have relevance, cf. Equitable Life Ins. Co. of Iowa v. United States, 340 F.2d 9 (C.A.8th Cir. 1965), we do not think it makes any difference here. In either case, the Code should not be interpreted to allow respondent "the practical equivalent of double deduction," Charles Ilfeld Co. v. Hernandez, 292 U.S. 62, 68 (1934), absent a clear declaration of intent by Congress. See United States v. Ludey, 274 U.S. 295 (1927). Accordingly, to avoid that result in this case, the deduction allowable in the year of repayment must be reduced by the percentage depletion allowance which respondent claimed and the Commissioner allowed in the years of receipt as a result of the inclusion of the later-refunded items in respondent's "gross income from the property" in those years. Any

---

3. The Commissioner has long recognized that a deduction under some section is allowable. G.C.M. 16730, XV–1 Cum.Bull. 179 (1936).

other approach would allow respondent a total of $1.27½ in deductions for every $1 refunded to its customers.

Under the annual accounting system dictated by the Code, each year's tax must be definitively calculable at the end of the tax year. "It is the essence of any system of taxation that it should produce revenue ascertainable, and payable to the Government, at regular intervals." Burnet v. Sanford & Brooks Co., supra, at 365. In cases arising under the claim-of-right doctrine, this emphasis on the annual accounting period normally requires that the tax consequences of a receipt should not determine the size of the deduction allowable in the year of repayment. There is no requirement that the deduction save the taxpayer the exact amount of taxes he paid because of the inclusion of the item in income for a prior year. See Healy v. Commissioner, supra.

Nevertheless, the annual accounting concept does not require us to close our eyes to what happened in prior years. For instance, it is well settled that the prior year may be examined to determine whether the repayment gives rise to a regular loss or a capital loss. Arrowsmith v. Commissioner, 344 U.S. 6 (1952). The rationale for the *Arrowsmith* rule is easy to see; if money was taxed at a special lower rate when received, the taxpayer would be accorded an unfair tax windfall if repayments were generally deductible from receipts taxable at the higher rate applicable to ordinary income. The Court in *Arrowsmith* was unwilling to infer that Congress intended such a result.

This case is really no different.[4] In essence, oil and gas producers are taxed on only 72½% of their "gross income from the property" whenever they claim percentage depletion. The remainder of their oil and gas receipts is in reality tax exempt. We cannot believe that Congress intended to give taxpayers a deduction for refunding money that was not taxed when received. Cf. Maurice P. O'Meara, 8 T.C. 622, 634–635 (1947). Accordingly *Arrowsmith* teaches that the full amount of the repayment cannot, in the circumstances of this case, be allowed as a deduction.

This result does no violence to the annual accounting system. Here, as in *Arrowsmith*, the earlier returns are not being reopened.

---

4. The analogy would be even more striking if in *Arrowsmith* the individual taxpayer had not utilized the alternative tax for capital gains, as they were permitted to do by what is now § 1201 of the 1954 Code. Where the 25% alternative tax is not used, individual taxpayers are taxed at ordinary rates on 50% of their capital gains. See § 1202. In such a situation, the rule of the *Arrowsmith* case prevents taxpayers from deducting 100% of an item refunded when they were taxed on only 50% of it when it was received. Although *Arrowsmith* prevents this inequitable result by treating the repayment as a capital loss, rather than by disallowing 50% of the deduction, the policy behind the decision is applicable in this case. Here it would be inequitable to allow a 100% deduction when only 72½% was taxed on receipt.

And no attempt is being made to require the tax savings from the deduction to equal the tax consequences of the receipts in prior years.[5] In addition, the approach here adopted will affect only a few cases. The percentage depletion allowance is quite unusual; unlike most other deductions provided by the Code, it allows a fixed portion of gross income to go untaxed. As a result, the depletion allowance increases in years when disputed amounts are received under claim of right; there is no corresponding decrease in the allowance because of later deductions for repayments.[6] Therefore, if a deduction for 100% of the repayments were allowed, every time money is received and later repaid the taxpayer would make a profit equivalent to the taxes on 27½% of the amount refunded. In other situations when the taxes on a receipt do not equal the tax benefits of a repayment, either the taxpayer or the Government may, depending on circumstances, be the beneficiary. Here, the taxpayer always wins and the Government always loses. We cannot believe that Congress would have intended such an inequitable result.

The parties have stipulated that respondent is entitled to a judgment for $20,932.64 plus statutory interest for claims unrelated to the matter in controversy here; the District Court entered a judgment for that amount. Accordingly, the judgment of the Court of Appeals is reversed and the case is remanded to that court with instructions that it be returned to the District Court for re-entry of the original District Court judgment.

Reversed.

The dissenting opinions of STEWART, J. (DOUGLAS and HARLAN, J.J., joining), and DOUGLAS, J., are omitted. Ed.

NOTE

The scope of the *Arrowsmith* doctrine remains uncertain.[1] The parent decision involved a question of characterization, holding that loss quite arguably ordinary for lack of any sale or exchange in the

---

5. Compare the analogous approach utilized under the "tax benefit" rule. Alice Phelan Sullivan Corp. v. United States, 381 F.2d 399 (Ct.Cl.1967); see Internal Revenue Code of 1954 § 111. In keeping with the analogy, the Commissioner has indicated that the Government will only seek to reduce the deduction in the year of repayment to the extent that the depletion allowance attributable to the receipt directly or indirectly reduced taxable income. Proposed Treas.Reg. § 1.613–2(c)(8), 33 Fed.Reg. 10702–10703 (1968).

6. The 10% standard deduction mentioned by the dissent, post, at 6, differs in that it allows as a deduction a percentage of adjusted gross income, rather than of gross income. See § 141; cf. §§ 170, 213. As a result, repayments may in certain cases cause a decrease in the 10% standard deduction allowable in the year of repayment, assuming that the repayment is of the character to be deducted in calculating adjusted gross income. See § 62.

1. See Rabinovitz, "Effect of Prior Year's Transactions on Federal Income Tax Consequences of Current Receipts or Payments," 28 Tax L.Rev. 85 (1972).

taxable year, was *capital loss* because of its relationship to transactions in a prior year. There is little doubt that a similar approach can convert potential capital gain to *ordinary income*; and that was the result in David Bresler,[2] where part of a settlement in an antitrust suit compensated the taxpayer for a loss on the sale of business property claimed as an ordinary loss in a prior year.

Other applications of the *Arrowsmith* doctrine seem to extend its reach. For example, T made a gain on the sale of oil and gas leases, which he reported as long-term capital gain. Later, accused of fraud on the ground that some wells were illegally slanted, he settled the claim and treated the payment as a deductible business expense incurred to avoid litigation, to save legal expenses and to preserve his business reputation. Not so, said the Fifth Circuit, supporting the Commissioner and a prior district court decision. Under *Arrowsmith*, the payment was so related to the taxpayer's prior capital gain as to require capital loss treatment.[3]

The recapture of "insider's" profits under section 16(b) of the Securities and Exchange Act of 1934 has produced numerous *Arrowsmith* controversies. An insider who makes short swing profits on the purchase and sale (or sale and purchase) of stock in his corporation is required to disgorge and to pay the profits over to the corporation for the benefit of *all* shareholders. Can his payment qualify as a business expense deductible from ordinary income?

It is theoretically possible for a taxpayer to have a *tax* loss on transactions in which he has *S.E.C.* "insider's" profits. A buys 100 shares of his corporations' stock in year one for $1000. In March of year three he sells the 100 shares for $700, replacing them in June of year three for $600. He must pay the corporation $100 (or so it is alleged), but he has a $300 tax loss. If his corporate payment is to protect his business reputation and his job, certainly *Arrowsmith* is not an obstacle to an ordinary deduction. No known case deals with just this problem. In the *litigated* cases, the taxpayer has had a long-term capital gain on the sale. What then about the section 16(b) payment where respectable evidence is presented relating the payment and the taxpayer's business?

The Courts of Appeal have uniformly held, despite the Tax Court's insistence that the payments are a business expense generating an ordinary deduction, that *Arrowsmith* is overpowering, and the characterization of the deduction depends upon the prior tax treatment of the transaction generating the payment.[4] It has been sug-

2. 65 T.C. 182 (1975).

3. Kimbell v. United States, 490 F.2d 203 (5th Cir. 1974), cert. den. 419 U.S. 833, 95 S.Ct. 58 (1975).

4. Brown v. Commissioner, 529 F.2d 609 (10th Cir. 1976); Cummings v. Commissioner, 506 F.2d 449 (2nd Cir. 1974); Anderson v. Commissioner, 480 F.2d 1304 (7th Cir. 1973); Mitchell v. Commissioner, 428 F.2d 259 (6th Cir. 1970) reversing the Tax Court in each instance.

gested that the proper solution is to add the section 16(b) payment to the basis of the purchased shares,[5] but a court has yet to accept this alternative.[6] In this area the Tax Court looks rather like the nimble triple-threat back running out of running room [7] before he can reach the goal line. Zooks! Could it be the Tax Court is running the wrong way?

F. THE HOLDING PERIOD

Internal Revenue Code: Section 1223(1), (2), (11).
    See Sections 1014(a); 1015(a); 1023; 1222; 1233.

REVENUE RULING 66–7

1966–1 Cum.Bull. 188.

Advice has been requested as to when a capital asset will have been held for more than 6 * months within the meaning of sections 1222(3) and (4) of the Internal Revenue Code of 1954, particularly where the asset was acquired on the last day of a calendar month which has less than 31 days.

Section 1222(3) of the Code provides, in part, that the term "long-term capital gain" means gain from the sale or exchange of a capital asset *held for more than 6 months* and section 1222(4) of the Code provides, in part, that the "long-term capital loss" means loss from the sale or exchange of a capital asset *held for more than 6 months.*

It is well and long established that, in computing a period of "years" or "months" prescribed, in a contract or statute, "from" or "after" a designated day, date, act, or other event, the day thus designated is excluded and the last day of the prescribed period is included, unless a different intent is definitely evidenced. See I.T. 3287, C.B. 1939–1 (Part 1), 138.

---

5. Lokken, Tax Significance of Payments in Satisfaction of Liabilities Arising Under Section 16(b) of the Securities Exchange Act of 1934, 4 Ga.L.Rev. 298 (1970).

6. But see Drennen, J., agreeing in his dissent in Nathan Cummings, 61 T.C. 1, 4 (1973).

7. See Jack E. Golsen, 54 T.C. 742 (1970) in which the Tax Court indi-

cates that in a specific case it will follow the view of the court of appeals to which an appeal lies.

* This Ruling was promulgated prior to the amendment of I.R.C. § 1222(3) and (4) by TRA (1976) generally extending the critical period to 9 months for the year 1977 and to one year thereafter. Ed.

I.T. 3985, C.B. 1949–2, 51, states the position of the Internal Revenue Service that the determination of the holding period of "capital assets" under sections 117(a) (2), (3), (4), (5), and (h) (4), of the Internal Revenue Code of 1939, must be made with reference to calendar months and fractions thereof, rather than with reference to days. The ruling was concerned primarily with the determination of the total holding period of securities purchased and sold where the provisions of section 117(h) (4) of the 1939 Code, relating to "wash sales," were applicable. Although similar provisions are not involved in the instant case, the principles enunciated in that ruling apply here. Furthermore, although I.T. 3287 was not cited in I.T. 3985 the rule stated in the former was actually applied in all the appropriate illustrative examples of the latter, that is, in examples 1 through 6.

In view of the foregoing, it is concluded that the holding period of a capital asset begins to run on the day following the date of acquisition of the asset involved. Accordingly, a capital asset acquired on the last day of any calendar month, regardless of whether the month has 31 days or less, must not be disposed of until on or after the first day of the seventh succeeding month of the calendar in order to have been "held for more than 6 months" within the meaning of sections 1222(3) and (4) of the Code. For example, an asset acquired on April 30, 1963, must not have been disposed of before November 1, 1963, in order to have been held for more than 6 months.**

I.T. 3985, C.B. 1949–2, 51, is hereby amplified for the purpose of determining when a capital asset has been held for more than 6 months where the asset was acquired on the last day of a month having less than 31 days.

The same rule applies in determining holding periods of property for purposes of section 1231 of the Code.

Pursuant to authority contained in section 7805(b) of the Code the provisions of this Revenue Ruling will be applicable with respect to dispositions of property after April 10, 1966.

REVENUE RULING 66–97

1966–1 Cum.Bull. 190.

Advice has been requested regarding the holding period of debentures and as to whether there is a distinction between a trade effected on a registered securities exchange and a trade made in the "over-the-counter" market.

** In Lena M. Anderson, 33 TCM 234 (1974), the taxpayer had short-term capital gain on stock purchased December 2, 1966 and sold on June 2, 1967. Ed.

The taxpayer purchased for investment certain debentures on the same day in an "over-the-counter" trade and a trade effected on a registered securities exchange. There are two relevant dates in connection with such security transactions: (1) the "trade date"—the date on which the contract to buy or sell the security is made and (2) the "settlement date"—the date on which the security is delivered and payment is tendered. In many cases settlement takes place a fixed number of days after the trade. In transactions involving bonds, notes or other evidences of indebtedness, the buyer pays the interest accrued on the security to the date of settlement as a part of the consideration for the transfer. However, bonds as well as stocks are considered acquired or sold on the respective "trade dates." See I.T. 3442, C.B. 1941–1, 212. I.T. 3287, C.B. 1939–1, 138, states that the period during which an asset was held is to be computed by excluding the day on which the asset was acquired and including the day upon which it was sold. See also I.T. 3705, C.B. 1945, 174, and Revenue Ruling 66–7, page 188, this Bulletin. This rule applies whether the trade is made on a registered securities exchange or in the "over-the-counter" market.

Accordingly, the holding period for debentures acquired by purchase, whether on a registered securities exchange or in the "over-the-counter" market, is to be determined by excluding the "trade date" on which the debentures are acquired and including the "trade date" on which the debentures are sold.

The same rule applies generally in determining the holding periods of stocks and securities acquired by purchase.

NOTE

Close questions with respect to holding periods are most likely to arise in the purchase and sale of stocks and bonds. Anticipating the year 1978, in a broker's board room it will not be uncommon to hear someone say, "I don't yet have my year in." The inference is of course that he has a gain on a security which he hopes will be taxable as long-term capital gain. He is anxious to sell and fearful the price will decline but not quite willing to accept the tax attrition attending short-term gain. There is an obvious need for care in such cases.

Although the holding period is usually governed by the "trade dates," as indicated in Rev.Rul. 66–97, above, there is a different approach to the determination of the year for which the gain or loss on such transactions should be reported. If a trade is made in the regular way on December 31, the settlement date will be several days later. If a cash method, calendar year taxpayer has a gain on such a transaction, the trade date ends his holding period, but his gain is realized in and reportable for the next year.[1] On the other hand a loss on such a transaction is treated as realized and deductible for the year in which the trade date fell.[2]

These are settled principles fairly easily stated. But there are many transactions in securities that involve timing considerations not fully answered by these principles. For example, T buys 100 shares of A stock on February 1, 1977, and another 100 shares of A stock on July 1, 1977. On March 1, 1978, he sells 100 shares of A stock. Which 100 shares has he sold? This raises basically a question of identification but, if he is unable to identify which block was sold, the Regulations answer the question on a "first-in, first-out" basis.[3] Obviously, this has a bearing, not only on his holding period (Might he have been hoping for short-term treatment?), but on his basis as well, if the two blocks of A stock were acquired at different prices.

Suppose T thinks the price of B stock is going down. On January 5, 1978, he sells 100 shares of B stock "short." This means he sells the stock without owning it, borrowing it from someone else to whom he is obliged ultimately to repay the loan when he closes or "covers" the short sale. Of course he hopes to buy the stock later for this purpose at a price below that at which he sold and, thus, to realize a gain. The short sale itself is not a taxable transaction (What basis could he use to determine gain or loss?), but gain or loss is realized when the short sale is closed by delivery of the stock. In general, whether gain or loss is long-term or short-term is determined by the period for which the stock delivered has been held.[4] In the usual case, short-term gain or loss will therefore be the result.

Suppose now that T has 100 shares of C stock on which he has a substantial paper gain. He bought the stock November 1, 1977, and "now" is July 1, 1978. He is afraid the price might drop but disinclined to realize short-term gain, and in fact, not happy about adding to his 1978 income at all. (What advantages, apart from converting his gain to long-term, might arise from carrying the transaction over to 1979?) He decides upon what is termed a short sale "against the box." That is, he sells while "long" in (owning) C stock but with the idea that he will close the sale only later, delivering the C stock when he has held it more than one year. In pursuance of the plan he sells short July 1, 1978, and effects delivery January 2, 1979. To what extent has he accomplished his objective? 1. He has nailed down his gain; he can be indifferent to subsequent market fluctuations. 2. He has deferred realization of his gain until 1979,

---

1. Rev.Rul. 72–381, 1972–2 C.B. 233.

2. Rev.Rul. 70–344, 1970–2 C.B. 50. Although this proposition is doctrinally difficult to support, nevertheless the principle is well established. See G.C.M. 21503, 1939–2 C.B. 205.

3. Reg. § 1.1223–1(i). See Colgan, "Identification of Securities Sold or Transferred," 18 N.Y.U. Inst. on Fed. Tax. 323 (1960).

4. Reg. § 1.1233–1(a)(3).

not increasing his 1978 income, even though he assured his gain in that year. 3. But I.R.C. (26 U.S.C.A.) § 1233(b) classifies his gain as short-term. Aimed at just this kind of monkey business, that section specifies short-term treatment if on the day of a short sale a taxpayer owns property substantially identical to that sold short, which he has held for only one year or less.

Section 1233 has implications far beyond the problem presented in the preceding paragraph. And many securities transactions are much more sophisticated than those suggested above. The "put," the "call," and the "straddle," are exciting play-things for those whose securities dealings go beyond every-day investing. On April 8, 1974, the Internal Revenue Service issued a letter ruling dealing with numerous problems arising out of the burgeoning trading on the new option exchanges, of which the Chicago Board Options Exchange was the first. The ruling was published at 749 CCH Standard Federal Tax Reports para. 6597 and reproduced at 766 CCH Standard Federal Tax Reports para. 4739.20,[5] but no attempt is made here to consider holding period and related problems that arise with respect to these and related transactions.[6] Note, however, that in TRA (1976) Congress acted in one area of the option market by amending I.R.C. § 1234(b). In the case of a grantor of an option any gain or loss on a closing transaction with respect to the option or any gain on the lapse of an option is classified as short-term capital gain.

Close questions with respect to holding periods may arise in the purchase and sale of real estate, although the problem is not as crucial in this area as in the stock area, because real estate is normally held for a longer period of time. Wide variations in real estate transactions[7] suggest several points of time at which acquisition or disposition might be deemed to occur.[8] The Service has taken the position that, in the case of an unconditional contract for sale, the holding

---

5. A list of current articles dealing with "options," aptly identified as "The Newest Game in Town" appears at 31 Tax L.Rev. 362 (1976).

6. Analysis of some of the transactions appears in the following articles: Mintz, "How to Use Short Sales and Stock Option Contracts to Produce Tax Savings," 24 J.Tax. 66 (1966); Bennion, "Current Developments in Tax Planning with Securities Transactions: 'Puts'; 'Calls'; 'Straddles'; 'Short Sales'; 'Arbitrage'," 13 U.S.C. Tax Inst. 489 (1961); Hariton, "Puts, Calls and Straddles," 18 N.Y.U. Inst. on Fed.Tax. 357 (1960); Lippitz, "Tax Guide for a Seller of Puts and Calls," 38 Taxes 829 (1960); Esks, "Federal Tax Advantages to Investors in the Use of Put and Call Options," 31 Tax L.R. 1 (1975); Kennedy, "Selecting the Off-Beat Investments: Puts, Calls, Straddles, Warrants, Commodity Futures and Other Exotica," 32 N.Y.U. Inst. on Fed.Tax. 1093 (1974).

7. Vernon Hoven, 56 T.C. 50 (1971); Ted F. Merrill, 40 T.C. 66 (1963), aff'd per curiam, 336 F.2d 771 (9th Cir. 1964); Boykin v. Comm'r, 344 F.2d 889 (5th Cir. 1965).

8. Those possibilities include the date that an executory contract becomes binding, that title passes, that possession changes, and that the benefits and burdens of ownership pass. Withey, J., discusses this problem very well in Donald Borrelli, 31 TCM 876 (1972).

period for purposes of both acquisition and disposition is measured by the earlier of the date upon which title passes or the date upon which delivery of possession occurs and the burdens and privileges of ownership pass.[9]

Usually the actual dates on which a taxpayer acquires and disposes of property determine his holding period for the property. But, just as there are statutory exceptions to the general definition of capital assets and to the general requirement of a sale or exchange, so are there statutory exceptions to the general holding period concept. One, § 1233, was illustrated above. Attention is drawn to some other exceptions in the Problems that follow this note.

PROBLEMS

1. Taxpayer engaged in the following transactions in shares of stock. Consider the amount and character of his gain or loss in each transaction:

(a) T bought 100 shares of stock on February 28, 1977 at a cost of $50 per share. He sold them on November 30 of the same year for $60 per share.

(b) T bought 100 shares of stock on February 28, 1977 at a cost of $50 per share. He sold them on January 30, 1978 for $60 per share.

(c) Same as (b), above, except that the purchase and sale involve commodity futures rather than stock.

(d) T bought 100 shares of stock on February 28, 1979 at a cost of $50 per share. He sold them on February 29, 1980 for $60 per share.

(e) T bought 100 shares of stock on January 15, 1977 at a cost of $50 per share. He sold them on January 16, 1978 at $60 per share.

(f) T bought 100 shares at $50 per share on February 10, 1977 and another 100 shares at $50 per share on March 10, 1977. He sold 100 of the shares on February 15, 1978 for $60 per share. See Reg. § 1.1223–1(i).

(g) T told his broker to purchase 100 shares of stock on December 29, 1977 at a time when its price was $50 per share. The stock was delivered to T on January 3, 1978 when it was selling for $52 per share. T told his broker to sell the stock on December 30, 1978 when it sold for $60 per share, and it was delivered to Buyer on January 4, 1979 when it was selling for $63 per share.

9. Rev.Rul. 54–607, 1954–2 C.B. 177. The holding period is deemed to commence on the date following the earliest of the two dates and to cease on the earliest of the two dates. Rev. Rul. 54–607 expressly indicates that a mere purchase option contract, as opposed to an unconditional contract to sell, is not within these rules.

(h) Same as (g), above, except that the value of the stock on December 30, 1978 was $45 per share and on January 4, 1979 was $48 per share.

(i) T's father bought 100 shares of stock on January 10, 1977 at $30 per share. On March 10, 1977 when they were worth $40 per share he gave them to T who sold them on January 15, 1978 for $60 per share (see § 1223(2).)

(j) Same as (i), above, except that T sold them on January 15, 1978 for $20 per share.

(k) T's father also held 100 shares of stock in another corporation, which he had purchased on April 20, 1977 for $40 per share. He gave them to T on September 20, 1977 when they had a value of $30 per share. T subsequently sold them on May 20, 1978 for $25 per share. (See I.T. 3453, 1941–1 C.B. 254.)

(*l*) Same as (k), above, except that T sold them for $50 per share.

(m) Same as (k), above, except that T sold them for $35 per share.

(n) T's father purchased 1000 shares of stock for $10 per share several years ago. The stock was worth $50 per share on December 31, 1976 and on March 1, 1977, the date of Father's death. The stock was distributed to T by the executor on January 5, 1978 and T sold it for $60 per share on January 15, 1978.

(*o*) Same as (n), above, except that T was executor of his father's estate and as such he sold the stock on January 15, 1978 for $60 per share to pay the estate's administration expenses.

(p) Same as (n), above, except that T received the stock from father's estate on January 5, 1978 (when it was worth $55 per share) under a contract to render services to Father during his lifetime.

2. Owner owned four acres of urban land which he leased to Tacker for 99 years at an agreed rental of $10,000 per year. In addition, Tacker acquired an option under which he or his assignee could purchase the property at any time during the life of the lease for $250,000, the purchaser being permitted, upon exercise of the option to apply against the purchase price $1000 of prior rental for each year that rental payments had been made under the lease. Twenty-five years later Purchaser appeared on the scene ready, willing and able to buy the property for $300,000. What result to Tacker:

(a) If he exercises the option and sells to Purchaser for $300,000?

(b) If he sells Purchaser his option for $75,000?

3. T purchased unimproved land on April 1, 1978 and commenced construction of a house, which was completed on January 1, 1980. Before T even moved in, and on that date, B offered him $60,000 for the house and land. T's cost basis for the land is $20,000 and for the house is $30,000, and the proposed purchase price is allocable $25,000 for the land and $35,000 for the house. It can also be established that construction of the house was 50% completed on December 31, 1978. What would be the consequences to T if the sale is effected on January 1, 1980? (See Paul v. Comm'r, 206 F.2d 763 (3d Cir. 1953).)

CHAPTER 22. CHARACTERIZATION OF GAIN ON THE SALE OF DEPRECIABLE PROPERTY

A. DEPRECIATION

1. INTRODUCTION

Internal Revenue Code: Sections 167(a), (b), (c), (g); 1016(a)(2). See Sections 62(1), (5); 169; 189; 263(a).

Regulations: Sections 1.162–4; 1.167(a)–1, –3, –6, –9, –10; 1.167(b)–0, –1 (a), – 2(a), –3(a)(1); 1.167(c)–1(a)(1).

T leaves his position with a shoe manufacturing company to go into business by himself, making and selling shoes. He sets up shop in a garage on the back of his property and purchases an electric stitching machine for $1000, his only significant piece of equipment. For five years he purchases each year $2000 worth of leather and other supplies and electricity that cost him $500. Each year he makes 200 pairs of shoes and sells them at $22.50 each.

He sees the following results each year:

Receipts	$4500
Less materials and supplies	2500
Profit for the year	$2000

And over the five year period he considers he has made a profit of $10,000 (5 × $2000).

But now he learns that his stitching machine is worn out, has no salvage value, and must be replaced. Looking back he wonders about his profit. While it appears he made $10,000, he now sees that he has incurred another $1000 cost and has made only $9000. But did he make only $1000 for the first year (when he bought the machine) and $2000 each year for the next four years? Or maybe $2000 for each of the first four years and only $1000 for the fifth year when the machine finally wore out? Neither possibility makes good sense, if he wishes to think (or must for tax purposes) in terms of annual profit. The sensible thing is to allocate cost for something like the stitcher over the period it is useful to him. And this is what depreciation is all about. Under the simplest approach to the problem, T can quickly be made to see that if he used up his $1000 stitcher over

721

five years of work it has been an added manufacturing cost to him of $200 each year. He now sees each year's results as:

Receipts		$4500
Less:		
Materials & supplies	2500	
Depreciation	200	
		2700
Profit for year		$1800

And his profit for five years is $9000 (5 × $1800), as before, but more appropriately determined on the basis of a like amount of profit each year. Should he worry, too, that his garage is five years older?

For federal income tax purposes I.R.C. (26 U.S.C.A.) § 167 treats depreciation as if it were an operating expense by allowing an annual deduction for exhaustion and wear and tear (including predictable obsolescence) of property. The business community utilized the concept in the determination of annual profits even before there was a federal income tax.[1]

Prerequisites for Deduction. I.R.C. (26 U.S.C.A.) § 167 restricts the depreciation deduction to (1) property used in a trade or business and (2) property held for the production of income. Thus inventory and property held for sale to customers are placed outside the scope of the section. And so is property that is held for merely personal use, even though it too declines in value over a period of time. Why?

Only property that will be consumed, or will wear out, or will become obsolete, or will otherwise become useless to the taxpayer can qualify for the deduction. Thus, unimproved realty is said to be nondepreciable, meaning, in the tax sense, that it cannot be the subject of a depreciation deduction.[2] And if realty is improved, it is only the improvements that can qualify.[3]

The Useful Life Concept. It is only property that has an identifiable useful life to the taxpayer which can qualify for the § 167 deduction. As is apparent in the shoemaker illustration above, depreciation is a cost spreading device, and the concept anticipates that cost will be spread over the period the property is to be used. If

---

1. Knoxville v. Knoxville Water Co., 212 U.S. 1, 29 S.Ct. 148 (1908).

2. Reg. § 1.167(a)–2; but see comments on depletion under "Related Concepts," below and see Henderson, "Land Cost Expenditures: Recent Trend Shows Many Such Costs Are Now Depreciable," 38 J.Tax. 78 (1973). However, property need not be tangible to be depreciable. See Schenk, "Depreciation of Intangible Assets: The Uncertainty of Death

and Taxes," 13 Wayne L.Rev. 501 (1967).

3. See, for example, Rev.Rul. 74–265, 1974–1 C.B. 56, allowing depreciation of the cost of landscaping an apartment complex over the life of the apartment buildings if replacement of the buildings will destroy the landscaping. If not, landscaping has no useful life and is not depreciable. See "The Useful Life Concept," below.

property is such that no useful life is ascertainable it, too, is said to be nondepreciable. This requirement disqualifies goodwill which cannot be "written off" by way of depreciation[4] for lack of any ascertainable useful life, even though a taxpayer may have purchased goodwill along with the other assets of another's business.[5] Similarly, if one purchases a franchise or other contractual right which is to continue for a stated period, his cost may not be depreciable for lack of a useful life, if the right is renewable and it is uncertain whether the period will be extended.[6]

Other intangibles may have an "economic" useful life.[7]

Useful life is not only a requirement for the depreciation deduction, it also plays a role in measuring the amount of the deduction. As the Supreme Court has said:[8]

"The amount of the allowance for depreciation is the sum which should be set aside for the taxable year, in order that, at the end of the useful life of the [asset] in the business, the aggregate of the sums set aside will (with the salvage value) suffice to provide an amount equal to the original cost."

If, as in the shoemaker example, the simplest depreciation method is adopted, the useful life pegs the so-called depreciation rate. That is, if the machine is to be used for five years and if charges are to be spread equally over the five years, the rate must be 20% in order for the entire cost to be taken into account over the life of the asset $(20\% \times \$1000 = \$200;$ and $5 \times \$200 = \$1000)$.

It is obvious that the period of useful life with respect to any piece of property is speculative and a likely subject for disagreement

---

4. Reg. § 1.167(a)–3.

5. It is sometimes difficult to separate other assets from goodwill for depreciation purposes.   Nevertheless in KFOX, Inc. v. U. S., 510 F.2d 1365 (Ct. Cls.1975), the cost of a radio station's personal service contracts were allowed to be separated from its cost of goodwill.   The contracts were amortized over the life of the contract plus the period of the single renewal option.   Similarly in Computing and Software, Inc., 64 T.C. 223 (1975), a purchaser of a consumer credit information service was able to allocate part of the purchase price to credit information files (separate from goodwill).

6. Toledo TV Cable Co., 55 T.C. 1107 (1971) (renewable municipal franchises related to community antenna television); Westinghouse Broadcasting Co. v. Comm'r, 309 F.2d 279 (3d Cir.

1962), cert. den. 372 U.S. 935, 83 S.Ct. 881 (1963) (renewable television network affiliation contract); Nachman v. Comm'r, 191 F.2d 934 (5th Cir. 1951) (renewable liquor license).   But see I.R.C. § 1253(d).   Although the courts generally base these decisions on the useful life concept, it can be argued as well that salvage value may equal full initial cost, which would be an added reason for denial of any depreciation deduction.

7. In Computing and Software, Inc., supra note 5, credit information files were held to have an "economic" useful life of six years and in Rodeway Inns of America, 63 T.C. 414 (1974), acq., 1975–1 C.B. 2, an exclusive motel territorial agreement was determined to have a five year "economic" useful life.

8. U. S. v. Ludey, 274 U.S. 295, 300, 47 S.Ct. 608, 610 (1927).

between the Treasury and the taxpayer. In 1934 the burden of proving useful life was on the taxpayer,[9] and Treasury personnel took a restrictive approach to depreciation.[10] In 1942 the Treasury published revised Bulletin "F",[11] which stated for each industry, on an item by item basis, a guide to the normal useful lives of various assets. These estimates, while not binding on the taxpayer and often criticized for overestimating useful lives, provided the taxpayer with something of a shield against improper attack on audit.

In 1962, the Service adopted a new set of "guidelines" to be used in determining useful life, which superseded the Bulletin "F".[12] The guideline lives are "substantially shorter" than the Bulletin "F" lives.[13] Under the guidelines, which abandon the old item by item approach, average useful lives are expressed for classifications of assets.[14]

To insure that a businessman did not write off the cost of assets over a guideline useful life that turned out to be substantially shorter than his actual experience would warrant, the guidelines establish a check, expressed as the "reserve ratio test." [15] The test, not explained here,[16] is applicable only after the guidelines have been used for three years. The taxpayer is allowed to continue to use the guideline lives even if they turn out to be 20% shorter than the period reflected by his experience. As was true of Bulletin "F", the new guidelines are optional, not binding on the taxpayer.[17]

---

9. T.D. 4422, XIII–1 C.B. 58 (1934).

10. Stephens, "Tax Amortization is the Key to the Stable Door," 5 U. of Fla. L.Rev. 261, 266–271 (1952).

11. Bulletin "F", Bureau of Internal Revenue (1942). This Bulletin was a revision of a preliminary report on depreciation lives which had previously been published. Depreciation Studies —Preliminary Report of the Bureau of Internal Revenue, January, 1931.

12. Rev.Proc. 62–21, 1962–2 C.B. 418. The "guidelines" are discussed in: Romak, "Depreciation Reform: Using the New Guideline Lives," 22 N.Y.U. Inst. on Fed.Tax. 465 (1964); Michiels, "Pros and Cons of Adopting the Depreciation Guidelines," 13 Tulane Tax. Inst. 244 (1963).

13. Rev.Proc. 62–21, supra note 12 at 463. "According to the initial Treasury release, the guideline lives for machinery and equipment were, on the whole, 30 percent shorter than those previously suggested in Bulletin 'F' and would permit more rapid depreciation deductions than those presently taken on 70 percent to 80 percent of the machinery and equipment used in American business." Romak, supra note 12, at 466.

14. Examples of classifications are: office furniture, fixtures, plant, and equipment; various classifications of buildings; land improvements. Supplemental guidelines are added to Rev.Proc. 62–21, by Rev.Proc. 62–21, Supplements I, III, and IV at 1963–2 C.B. 740, 1964–1 (part 1) C.B. 639, and 1964–1 (part 1) C.B. 640, respectively.

15. The "reserve ratio test" is found in Rev.Proc. 62–21, 1962–2 C.B. 418 at 435–437 and 439–462. It was subsequently modified by Rev.Proc. 65–13, 1965–1 C.B. 759.

16. The "reserve ratio test" is discussed in: "How Workable is the Reserve Ratio Test? Here's What the Experts Say," 23 J.Tax. 333 (1965); Morris, "The Reserve Ratio Test," 22 N.Y.U. Inst. on Fed.Tax. 481 (1964).

17. Rev.Proc. 62–21, supra note 12 at 464. While it involves considerably more effort, a taxpayer may reject the guideline figures for a structure and calculate the depreciation allowance based on the useful lives of its separate components, most of which

The most recent governmental tinkering with the useful life concept is the asset depreciation range system commonly referred to as A.D.R. It was initially administratively introduced by the Treasury in 1971 without any Congressional action;[18] but later that year in the Revenue Act of 1971 Congress enacted I.R.C. § 167(m) legislatively adopting the system.[19]

The principal advantage of A.D.R. is that it allows the taxpayer to use a useful life of 80% to 120% of the useful life permitted under the Rev.Proc. 62–21 guidelines.[20] While this does not increase the amount of depreciation which may ultimately be taken, it does permit an acceleration of the rate at which it may by taken, which acts to increase deductions in the early years of the asset's life. Thus, again, a liberalization of depreciation rules is resorted to as a part of an attack on the sluggishness of the economy. If the shoemaker in the example above elected A.D.R. and the guideline life for his stitcher was five years, he would use four years and write off the machine at a rate of $250 per year, assuming no salvage value.[21]

The A.D.R. system also does away with the "reserve ratio test," with minor exception is currently available only with respect to tangible personal property,[22] and provides for a "repair allowance rule"

will be shorter than the class life of the structure as a whole. In this manner, the taxpayer's early depreciation deductions will be considerably greater than those allowable under normal calculations. This procedure was first approved by the Tax Court in Herbert Shainberg, 33 T.C. 241 (1959), acq. 1960–1 C.B. 5, where records of construction costs of the separate components of a building were maintained by the taxpayer, useful lives were calculated for each, and depreciation taken for each asset group. The I.R.S. limited its acquiescence to the decision, declaring that piecemeal depreciation would not be allowed for used buildings. Rev.Rul. 66–111, 1966–1 C.B. 46. However, in Harsh Investment Corp. v. U. S., 1971–1 U.S.T.C. para. 9183 (D.Ore. 1970), the taxpayer was allowed a depreciation deduction for a used building based on the component method since he had "presented competent expert testimony . . . [that the] values and the useful lives . . . assigned to each of the components [were] reasonable and proper." Id. at 85,798.

18. See Bittker, "Treasury Authority to Issue the Proposed 'Asset Depreciation Range System' Regulations," 49 Taxes 265 (1971).

19. The A.D.R. system is explained in great detail in Reg. § 1.167(a)–11. The legislation made some minor changes in the original administrative proposals such as tightening the rules on depreciation in the year of acquisition. See I.R.C. § 167(m)(2) and Reg. § 1.167(a)–11(c)(2)(ii) and (iii).

20. See Rev.Proc. 72–10, 1972–1 C.B. 721, which states class lives and acceptable depreciation ranges and revokes Rev.Proc. 62–21, supra note 12 except where Reg. § 1.167(a)–11 specifically retains it.

21. A.D.R. is summarily described in Announcement 71–76, 1971–2 C.B. 503 which also includes a very comprehensive historical and current analysis of the whole area of depreciation. And see Richman, "Class Life Asset Depreciation Range System," 25 U.S. C.T.I. 1 (1973); Monyek, "Asset Depreciation Range Regulations Adopted with No Major Changes," 35 J. Tax. 150 (1971); Coughlan and Steinmetz, "The New ADR Rules for Depreciation." 49 Taxes 725 (1971).

22. P.L. 93–625. The Treasury has not yet developed any regulations on a class life system for real estate and until they do so Congress has stated that real estate remains under Rev.

designed to reduce the repair-capital expenditure question to a mechanical computation.[23]

The Importance of Cost. In general aggregate depreciation deductions over the useful life of the asset should equal the cost of the asset. However, cost of the asset in the taxpayer's business operation must take account of what he may recover when he disposes of the asset, its salvage value. Thus, the deductions taken over the useful life should equal only cost, less salvage value. Suppose the shoemaker who acquires a stitcher for $1000 anticipates its sale five years later for $250. The 20% depreciation rate suggested above might properly be applied to $750 ($1000 cost, less $250 salvage value), yielding annual depreciation deductions of $150 which, over five years, will aggregate $750.[24]

Sometimes cost is difficult to determine when a lump sum is paid for several assets.[25] For example when a corporation purchased the Atlanta Falcons football team the I.R.S. contended that it was impossible to establish, except in an arbitrary manner, an allocation of the price between veteran player contracts, television rights, and other related assets. But the District Court made such an allocation; and although television rights were held non-amortizable because they had no determinable useful life, nevertheless player contracts were treated as amortizable over a useful life of five and one-half years.[26]

The word "cost" is used loosely here. One may have a machine that "cost" him nothing but which is subject to depreciation. If, for example, he acquired the machine by gift, § 1015 accords him a basis for the property. And he is entitled to write off *that* basis, less salvage value, by way of depreciation deductions.[27] Thus, it is cost or other basis which is deductible by way of depreciation.

Because cost or other basis (less salvage) fixes the overall limits of the depreciation deductions for any asset, an acquisition of a depreciable asset has the same ultimate impact on taxable income as

Proc. 62–21 supra note 12, or has its own separately determined life. See Sen.Rep.No.93–1357, 1975–1 C.B. 517, 518 (1974).

23. I.R.C. § 263(f). See Regs. §§ 1.263 (f)(1) and 1.167(a)–11(d)(2) and see page 351 supra.

24. In some circumstances, Congress permits a disregard or partial disregard of salvage value. § 167(f). See also Reg. § 1.167(a)–11(c)(1)(i), (which under the new asset depreciation range method allows depreciation to be taken against full cost (not cost less salvage value) although the property may not be depreciated below salvage value.)

25. See note 5, supra and cf. Williams v. McGowan, page 773, infra.

26. Laird v. U. S., 391 F.Supp. 656 (D. C.Ga.1975), on appeal to the Fifth Circuit. The court allocated over $3 million of the $8.5 million purchase price to the player contracts. See Weill, "Depreciation of Player Contracts— The Government is Ahead at the Half," 53 Taxes 581 (1975). But cf. I.R.C. § 1056(d), added by TRA (1976) § 212, which creates a rebuttable presumption that not more than 50% of the sales price of a sports enterprise franchise is allocable to player contracts.

27. See I.R.C. (26 U.S.C.A.) § 167(g).

any deductible expense; only the amount of the expenditure (less salvage) is deductible. When the depreciable cost of an asset is "recovered" (charged off by way of depreciation deductions) depreciation deductions stop.

It should now be possible to understand Justice Brandeis' recitation in a utility rate-making case of the principal purposes of the depreciation deduction:[28]

"It preserves the integrity of the investment. * * * It serves to distribute equitably throughout the several years of service life the only expense of plant retirement which is capable of reasonable ascertainment—the known cost less the estimated salvage value. And it enables those interested, through applying that plan of distribution, to ascertain, as nearly as possible, the actual financial results of the year's operation."

These remarks apply as well to § 167.

Depreciation Methods. With respect to property used in one's business or held for the production of income, once the property's basis, useful life, and salvage value are known, several different methods of depreciation may be available to the taxpayer. These methods regulate the timing of depreciation deductions within the cost (less salvage) limitations indicated above. The availability of several methods is made dependent upon the type of property, whether it is real or personal, whether it is tangible or intangible, whether it is new or used property, and upon its useful life. One can spread the depreciation deduction evenly over the life of his property, the so-called "straight-line" method used in the shoemaker illustration above. There are also several expressly authorized accelerated methods of depreciation which increase depreciation deductions in the early years of the asset's useful life and decrease them in later years. However, the total amount of depreciation that can ultimately be claimed is the same under each of the methods. In 1954, when the new accelerated depreciation methods were proposed the Senate Report stated:[29]

"The liberalized depreciation methods provided in the bills are to apply to all types of tangible depreciable assets, including farm equipment, machinery, and buildings, rental housing, and industrial and commercial buildings as well as machinery and equipment. They are limited however, to property new in use and therefore never before subject to depreciation allowances.

28. Brandeis, J., dissenting in United Rys. & Electrical Co. of Baltimore v. West, 280 U.S. 234, 264, 50 S.Ct. 123 (1930). The entire opinion is illuminating for one not previously well acquainted with depreciation concepts.

29. Sen.Fin.Comm.Rep. No. 1622, 83rd Cong. 3rd Sess., pp. 25–26 (1954).

"The bill limits the application of the liberalized depreciation methods to new assets acquired after the effective date of the bill primarily as a means of minimizing transitional revenue losses and obtaining maximum incentive effect. The application of the new methods to used property might artificially encourage transfers and exchanges of partially depreciated assets motivated only by tax considerations. The stimulus to investment through liberalized depreciation is most important with respect to the creation of new assets. Morever, the reality of faster depreciation in the early years is generally greater in the case of new than used property.

* * *

"More liberal depreciation allowances are anticipated to have far-reaching economic effects. The incentives resulting from the changes are well timed to help maintain the present high level of investment in plant and equipment. The acceleration in the speed of tax-free recovery of costs is of critical importance in the decision of management to incur risk. The faster tax writeoff would increase available working capital and materially aid growing businesses in the financing of their expansion. For all segments of the American economy, liberalized depreciation policies should assist modernization and expansion of industrial capacity, with resulting economic growth, increased production, and a higher standard of living.

"Small business and farmers particularly have a vital stake in a more liberal and constructive depreciation policy. They are especially dependent on their current earnings or short-term loans to obtain funds for expansion. The faster recovery of capital investment provided by this bill will permit them to secure short-term loans which would otherwise not be available."

The Senate Report went on to explain the three expressly authorized methods as follows:[30]

"Subsection (b) [of § 167] corresponds to the same provision of the House bill. Subsection (b) provides methods which, for taxable years ending after December 31, 1954, will be deemed to produce a reasonable allowance for depreciation of property described in subsection (c) so long as the useful life used in determining such allowance is accurate. Your committee has struck the word 'one' from the phrase 'an allowance computed in accordance with regulations prescribed by the Secretary of his delegate under one of the following methods:'. This word was deleted to make it clear that more than one method may be used on various property or classes of property of a taxpayer. For example, a taxpayer may use the straight-line method of deprecia-

---

30. Id. at 201–202.

tion on buildings while using the declining balance method on machinery. The methods described in subsection (b) are:

(1) The straight-line method—

"Under this method, the cost or other basis of the property, less its estimated salvage value, is deducted in equal annual installments over the period of its estimated useful life. The depreciation deduction is obtained by dividing the amount to be depreciated by the estimated useful life. This may be expressed as a rate of depreciation computed by dividing the estimated life into 1. The deduction per taxable year may be arrived at by multiplying the cost or other basis (less salvage value) by the resulting rate.

(2) Declining balance method—

"Under this method a uniform rate is applied to the unrecovered basis of the asset. Since the basis is always reduced by prior depreciation, the rate is applied to a constantly declining basis. The salvage value is not deducted from the basis prior to applying the rate, since under this method at the expiration of useful life there remains an undepreciated balance which represents salvage value. The rate to be used under this paragraph may never exceed twice the rate which would have been used had the deduction been computed under the method described in paragraph (1). Under section 23(1) of the 1939 Code the declining balance method was allowed in certain instances but the rate was generally limited to 1½ times of the rate used under the straight-line method. If this method has been used for property acquired prior to December 31, 1953, it may continue to be used but the rate provided for in paragraph (2) will not be presumed to be reasonable with respect to such property.

(3) The sum of the years-digits method—

"Your committee has added the sum of the years-digits method to those methods provided in the House bill which will be deemed to produce a reasonable allowance. Under this method the annual allowance is computed by applying a changing fraction to the taxpayer's cost of the property reduced by the estimated salvage value. The denominator of the fraction is the sum of the numbers representing the successive 12-month periods in the estimated life of the property * and the numerator of which is the number of 12-month periods, including that for which the allowance is being computed, remaining in the estimated useful life of the property. This method of depreciation can best be illustrated by an example. A acquires new property in 1954 which costs $175, has an estimated useful life of 5 years and an estimated

---

* A formula to compute the denominator if several years are involved is $X^2 + X$ divided by 2, with X as the number of years of useful life of the property to the taxpayer. Try it. Ed.

salvage value of $25. The depreciation schedule for the asset will be as follows:

Year	Fraction of cost less salvage ($175−25=$150)	Depreciation deduction	Total reserve	Adjusted basis
1	5/15	$50	$50	$125
2	4/15	40	90	85
3	3/15	30	120	55
4	2/15	20	140	35
5	1/15	10	150	25"

———

Below is a graphic illustration of the three depreciation methods expressly authorized by Code § 167, which assumes the same figures as the shoemaker's stitching machine illustrated above (i. e., a $1000 cost, five year life, and zero salvage value).

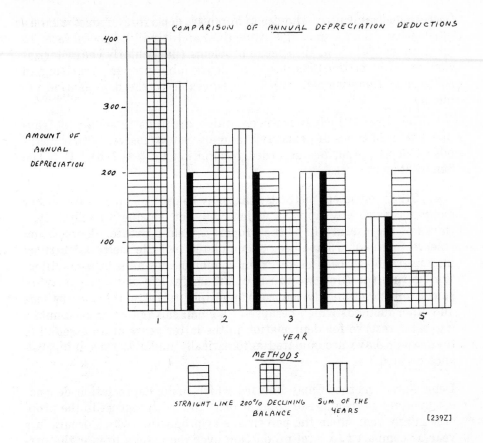

COMPARISON OF ANNUAL DEPRECIATION DEDUCTIONS

AMOUNT OF ANNUAL DEPRECIATION

YEAR

METHODS

STRAIGHT LINE   200% DECLINING   SUM OF THE
                    BALANCE   YEARS

[239Z]

	STRAIGHT LINE			200% DECLINING BALANCE			SUM OF THE YEARS		
YEAR	ANNUAL DEPREC	AGGREG DEPREC	ADJ BASIS	ANNUAL DEPREC	AGGREG DEPREC	ADJ BASIS	ANNUAL DEPREC	AGGREG DEPREC	ADJ BASIS
1	200	200	800	400	400	600	333	333	667
2	200	400	600	240	640	360	267	600	400
3	200	600	400	144	784	216	200	800	200
4	200	800	200	86	870	130	133	933	67
5	200	1000	0	52	922	78 *	67	1000	0

* Under this method, depreciation deductions would continue if the machine were used beyond its expected useful life.

In all instances, it is important to bear in mind, as explained above, that the depreciation deduction is merely a method of cost allocation which recognizes that to the extent buildings, equipment, and other items are consumed in profit-making activities, the value consumed represents a cost to be spread over the item's life and taken into account in determining a net income or loss for each year in the life of the item. Neither for business nor for tax accounting is any effort made to determine the exact value shrinkage in each accounting period as a means of determining an asset's cost for the period. Nor is it intended that cost less depreciation reflect *value* at any given point of time; "adjusted basis" and "value" are not synonymous. The cost-spreading methods described above are conventions, which operate mechanically and quite differently, depending upon the method selected. The graph illustrates this, and it will be useful later in an analysis of some of the special problems (particularly characterization of gain on the disposition of depreciable property) arising in subsequent assignments, which are traceable to the depreciation deduction.

The three principal methods which are illustrated are not applicable to all types of property [31] and are not exclusive. Other methods of depreciation are accorded recognition by § 167(b) (4). The Senate Report stated: [32]

"(4) Other consistent methods [that may be used include]—Any other method consistently applied which will not, during the first two-thirds of the useful life of the property, yield a greater depreciation reserve than would have been accumulated had the method described in paragraph (2) been used. Your committee has added the qualification 'during the first two-thirds of the useful life of the property' so as not to restrict unduly the use of multiple rate straight-line methods and other methods which because of a small salvage value accumulate a greater reserve for depreciation in the latter years of an asset's life than would have accumulated automatically under the declining balance method."

Depreciation methods may be used which make depreciation dependent upon the percentage of total income flow with respect to the property in any year, upon the percentage of production which occurs in a year as compared to total production over the asset's life, or the percentage of hours a machine is used in relation to the number of hours it will be used. [33]

The Relationship of Depreciation to Basis

As reflected in the chart, above, when a taxpayer claims depreciation on property, the deduction is attended by a commensurate reduction in his basis for the property. Thus, the cost or other basis for depreciable property may be likened to a limited supply of deductions from which the taxpayer may draw in accordance with various methods until the supply is used up. If the supply is to be tapped over a period of several years, there must be a device for keeping track of the supply. Basis is the device, although of course it serves other purposes as well. As deductions are claimed, downward basis adjustments effect a shrinkage of the supply, and "adjusted" basis reflects the remaining amount that can be claimed as deductions. In a tax sense the taxpayer thus achieves a "return" of his capital as he "ex-

---

31. I.R.C. (26 U.S.C.A.) § 167(c).

32. Sen.Fin.Comm.Rep. No. 1622, supra note 29 at 202.

33. The depreciation deduction is an ordinary deduction generally reducing gross income in arriving at adjusted gross income. I.R.C. (26 U.S.C.A.) § 62 (1) and (5).

penses" his capital expenditure piece-meal over the period during which depreciation deductions are claimed.

Basis adjustments arising out of depreciation are governed by § 1016(a) (2). The downward adjustment required is at least the amount of depreciation deduction permitted ("allowable") under the depreciation method employed by the taxpayer. This is because depreciation is in the nature of a continuing expense, unaffected by the success or failure of the taxpayer's business, and, especially with a view to the graduated tax rates, Congress does not permit a taxpayer to time his deductions for his own convenience. Thus, while depreciation does not involve a current pay-out, as salary expense may, it is properly viewed as a continuing each year, just as if it were salary expense paid or accrued. Consequently, basis is reduced even if the taxpayer claims no depreciation deduction. The amount of depreciation allowable is determined in accordance with the depreciation method that has been adopted by the taxpayer. If he has claimed no depreciation and has therefore adopted no method, the statute specifies that allowable depreciation is to be determined under the straight-line method.

It may be that a taxpayer will claim depreciation deductions in excess of those permitted. This could come about, for example, by his erroneous use of too high a basis for an asset, by his assumption of an improperly short useful life, by his inaccurate appraisal of too low a salvage value, or by his adoption of an accelerated method not permitted for the asset in question. What should be the effect on basis of his claiming excessive deductions? If the amount claimed is not challenged (and is therefore "allowed"), should the full amount claimed work to reduce basis, even though it exceeds the amount permitted by the statute (the amount "allowable")? Congress has said that it should, the sensible notion being that if the taxpayer's taxable income has been reduced by the deduction, even improperly, he has had the use of his capital expenditure to that extent. Thus, in general, the plan has been to call for downward basis adjustment for depreciation "allowed" but not less than the amount "allowable".

Before the statute took its present form a taxpayer unsuccessfully challenged the "allowed or allowable" approach in a case in which excessive deductions claimed and allowed had accorded the taxpayer no advantage, because losses left no potentially taxable income against which the excess deductions could be used.[34] Although the law at the time afforded no relief in such circumstances, Congress recognized the need for a modification of the "allowed" concept, which now appears in § 1016(a) (2) (B). With this change, while "allowable" depreciation always works a reduction in basis, depreciation allowed in excess of the amount allowable effects a basis reduction

_____

34. Virginian Hotel Corp. v. Helvering, 319 U.S. 523, 63 S.Ct. 1260 (1943).

only to the extent that such excess resulted in a reduction of the taxpayer's taxes.

Collateral Effects

Congressional adjustments in the depreciation deduction are by no means based solely on a search for the best way to determine a net income for the taxable year. The liberalizing changes in 1954 reflect, as the above excerpts from the Committee Reports indicate, an effort to stimulate the economy. Recently, Congress has made adjustments in the depreciation deduction in the hope of inducing sociological improvements and ecological advances. For example, changes made by the Tax Reform Act of 1969 were undertaken to stimulate investment in rehabilitating low income housing by allowing certain expenditures in that area to be deducted over a short sixty-month period. See § 167(k). In addition under the Revenue Act of 1971 Congress added § 188 providing for an elective sixty month amortization of capital expenditures relating to the acquisition, construction, or rehabilitation of on-the-job training and child care facilities. And in 1969 Congress also provided a rapid write-off for pollution control facilities, obviously with an eye toward our ecology. See § 169.[35] These provisions reflect a departure from the useful life concept, permitting cost "amortization" [36] over an artificial period.

Related Concepts

Those who drill oil, mine natural resources, or cut timber may encounter a phenomenon somewhat like the shoemaker's exhaustion of his stitcher. Or perhaps their situation should be likened to a merchant who gradually sells off his stock in trade. In either event, it is pretty clear that in a business operation they are using up or otherwise parting with something for which they probably have a tax basis. Question arises how the "depletion" of their resource should affect their tax liability.

The problem was not anticipated in the enactment of the Corporate Excise Tax Act of 1909.[37] Deciding a case under that Act on a procedural ground, the Supreme Court refused to permit any allowance for the wasting of gold and other precious metals in determining the net income from the taxpayer's mining operation.[38]

But Congress legislated specifically on the problem in the enactment of the first modern income tax statute. The Revenue Act of 1913 permitted "cost" depletion.[39] The effect of this provision was

---

35. Other rapid write-off sections include I.R.C. §§ 184 and 187.

36. Amortization is essentially the same as depreciation but it relates to intangible property or, as here, an accelerated life. It requires use of an equal annual write-off the same as straight line depreciation.

37. § 38, 36 Stat. 112 (1909).

38. Stratton's Independence, Ltd. v. Howbert, 231 U.S. 399, 34 S.Ct. 136 (1913). The opinion contains an inference that, had the amount been properly determined, an allowance might have been made under the statutory "depreciation" deduction.

39. Revenue Act of 1913, § 11B, 38 Stat. 166, 167 (1913).

very much like the current depreciation deduction, allowing a recovery
of cost or other basis as the wasting asset was consumed by its ex-
ploitation. The deduction was limited, however, to an amount not in
excess of 5% of the value of the product mined.[40] World War I
prompted a liberalization of the depletion deduction. To encourage
mining activities, Congress abandoned the cost approach to depletion
or, more accurately, added to it an alternative "discovery value" approach to the problem.[41]

In essence, what this meant was that, without regard to cost or
other basis, a taxpayer could establish a *value* for certain natural resources at the time of their discovery, or within thirty days thereafter,
and then write off that *value* as he exploited the resources. Although
there was thus a limit beyond which depletion deductions could not
be taken, the variation from the depreciation deduction, where allowances can never exceed cost or other basis, is apparent. Of course,
under either early method the depletion deduction had to be spread
differently from the depreciation deduction; no useful life concept
was relevant, but the recoverable amount was spread with reference
to the assumed portion of recoverable units recovered during the year.

Discovery value depletion persisted until 1954,[42] but was dropped
upon the enactment of the Internal Revenue Code of 1954. Cost
depletion is still a part of the tax law.[43] But a more controversial
depletion provision appeared in 1924, when Congress invented "percentage depletion." The concept gets its name from the fact that the
amount of the deduction, annually, is determined by a stated percentage of the "gross income from the property" subject to the allowance.[44] There is no ceiling on the amount of the deductions that can
be claimed over the years—no limitation to cost or other basis or even
to discovery value. Section 613(b) presents a long list of the types
of property that are subject to percentage depletion.[45] For each a
percentage of gross income is stated, which measures the amount of
the deduction. After some reduction in percentage figures in the Tax
Reform Act of 1969, the figures range from 5 percent to 22 percent.[46]

40. Ibid.

41. Revenue Act of 1918, § 214(a)(10), 40 Stat. 1057, 1067 (1918).

42. See I.R.C. (1939) § 23(M).

43. See I.R.C. (26 U.S.C.A.) §§ 611, 612.

44. I.R.C. (26 U.S.C.A.) § 613.

45. In Heisler v. U. S., 463 F.2d 375 (9th Cir. 1972), cert. den. 410 U.S. 927 (1972) the court denied percent-age depletion on taxpayers bodies be-cause they did not constitute "other natural deposits" within § 613(b).

46. A brief discussion of depletion, touching on problems not alluded to above, appears in Chommie, Federal Income Taxation, 185–197 (2d Ed. 1973). A more detailed analysis of some aspects of the depletion deduc-tion will be found in Menge, "The Role of Taxation in Providing for De-pletion of Mineral Reserves," House Committee on Ways and Means, 2 Tax Revision Compendium 967 (1959), reprinted in Sander and Westfall, Readings in Federal Taxation, 348–360 (1970), and Statement of Robert G. Dunlop (President, Sun Oil Com-pany), Hearings on T.R.A. 1969 before the Sen.Fin.Comm., 91st Cong. 1st Sess., pt. 5, at 4455–65 (1969), re-

Prior to 1975 oil and gas wells led the parade qualifying across the board for the maximum 22 percent depletion rate; but in 1975 Congress eliminated percentage depletion for major oil companies.[47] They did continue the 22 percent rate for some types of oil and gas [48] and they partially continued oil and gas depletion for independent producers,[49] although the percentage rate of depletion for independents gradually drops from 22 percent to 15 percent by 1984.[50]

JOEL A. SHARON

Tax Court of the United States, 1976.
66 T.C. 515.

SIMPSON, JUDGE: The Commissioner determined deficiencies in the petitioners' Federal income tax in the amounts of $235.56 for 1969 and $653.70 for 1970. Due to concessions, the following issues remain for decision: * * * (2) whether the petitioners are entitled to amortization deductions under section 167(a)(1) with respect to certain educational and other expenses incurred to enable the petitioner Joel A. Sharon to obtain a license to practice law in the State of New York; (3) whether the petitioners may deduct or amortize costs incurred by the petitioner Joel A. Sharon in taking the California bar examination and miscellaneous expenses incurred in obtaining admission to courts in that State; (4) whether the petitioners may deduct under section 162, or amortize pursuant to section 167, the cost of petitioner Joel A. Sharon's admission to the Supreme Court of the United States. * * *

Findings of Fact

Some of the facts have been stipulated, and those facts are so found.

During the years 1969 and 1970, and at the time of filing the petitions herein, Joel A. Sharon and Ann L. Sharon, husband and wife, resided in San Mateo, Calif. They filed their joint Federal income tax returns for the years 1969 and 1970 with the Internal Revenue Service Center, Ogden, Utah. Mr. Sharon will sometimes be referred to as the petitioner.

* * *

printed in Sander and Westfall, supra at 361.

47. I.R.C. § 613(d).

48. See I.R.C. § 613A(b).

49. Under I.R.C. § 613A(c)(3) independents may deplete their first 2000 barrels a day although that figure is gradually reduced to 1000 barrels a day by 1980.

50. I.R.C. § 613A(c)(5).

Bar Admission Expenses

The petitioner attended Brandeis University from September 1957 to June 1961 and received a bachelor of arts degree upon his graduation. During his years at Brandeis, the following expenses were paid by or on behalf of the petitioner in connection with his education:

| | | | *Academic year* | | |
	1957–58	1958–59	1959–60	1960–61	*Total*
Tuition and fees	$1,075	$1,080	$1,330	$1,330	$4,815
Room and board	1,340	1,340	1,340	1,480	5,500
Books	100	100	100	100	400
Miscellaneous	100	100	100	110	410
Total					11,125

After graduation from Brandeis University, the petitioner entered Columbia University School of Law, receiving a bachelor of laws degree in June 1964. While pursuing his law degree at Columbia University, the following expenses were paid by or on his behalf:

| | | *Academic year* | | |
	1961–62	1962–63	1963–64	*Total*
Tuition and fees	$1,360	$1,360	$1,510	$4,230
Room and board	2,130	0	0	2,130
Books	150	150	150	450
Miscellaneous	100	0	0	100
Total				6,910

In order to be eligible to take the New York bar examination, the petitioner was required to graduate from a fully accredited 4-year undergraduate institution and give evidence of his successful completion of 3 years of study at an accredited law school. The petitioner expended a total of $210.20 in gaining admission to practice law in the State of New York. This amount included $175.20 for bar review courses and materials related thereto and a New York State bar examination fee of $25.

The petitioner was admitted to practice law in the State of New York on December 22, 1964. Thereafter, he was employed as an attorney by a law firm in New York City until 1967, when he accepted a position in the Office of Regional Counsel, Internal Revenue Service, and moved to California.

Although not required by his employer to be a member of the California bar, the petitioner decided to become a member of that State's bar after moving here. However, he found that the study of California law, which he undertook in preparation for the California bar examination, was helpful in his practice of law as an attorney in the Regional Counsel's office. The petitioner spent the following amounts in order to gain membership in the California bar:

Registration as law student in California	$20
California bar review course	230
General bar examination fee	150
Attorney's bar examination fee	375
Admittance fee	26
Total	801

In 1969, the petitioner also spent a total of $11 in order to be admitted to practice before the U.S. District Court for the Northern District of California and the U.S. Court of Appeals for the Ninth Circuit.[2] The petitioner's employer required only that he be admitted to practice before the U.S. Tax Court.

In 1970, the petitioner incurred the following expenses in connection with his admission to the U.S. Supreme Court:

Round trip air fare, San Francisco to New York	$238.35
Round trip rail fare, New York to Washington, and miscellaneous expenses	75.00
Total	313.35

The petitioner's employer did not require that he be admitted to practice before the U.S. Supreme Court but did assist him in this matter. The Chief Counsel of the IRS personally moved the admission of a group of IRS attorneys, including the petitioner. Furthermore, two of his supervisors signed his application as personal references.

During 1970, the U.S. Supreme Court rules required a personal appearance before it in Washington, D.C., to be admitted to practice.

On their return for 1969, the petitioners claimed a deduction for "Dues and Professional Expenses" of $492. The Commissioner disallowed $385 of such deduction on the grounds that the disallowed portion was not a deductible business expense, but was a nondeductible capital expenditure. On their return for 1970, the petitioners claimed a deduction of $313.35 for the cost of petitioner Joel A. Sharon's admission to practice before the U.S. Supreme Court. The Commissioner also disallowed such deduction. In addition to challenging the disallowed deductions, the petitioners alleged in their petition that they were entitled to amortize or depreciate the cost of petitioner Joel A. Sharon's education. The Commissioner denied this allegation in his answer.

* * *

2. Although the parties stipulated that the total amount spent was $11, the petitioner testified that the total spent was $15. We find that the amount spent was $11.

Opinion

* * *

2. Amortization of License to Practice Law in New York

The next issue to be decided is whether the petitioner may amortize the cost of obtaining his license to practice law in New York. The petitioner contends that he is entitled under section 167 to amortize the cost of such license over the period from the date of his admission to the bar to the date on which he reaches age 65, when he expects to retire. In his cost basis of this "intangible asset," he included the costs of obtaining his college degree ($11,125), obtaining his law degree ($6,910), a bar review course and related materials ($175.-20), and the New York State bar examination fee ($25).[4] As justification for including these education expenses in the cost of his license, he points out that, in order to take the New York bar examination, he was required to have graduated from college and an accredited law school.

The petitioners rely upon section 1.167(a)–3 of the Income Tax Regulations, which provides in part:

> If an intangible asset is known from experience or other factors to be of use in the business or in the production of income for only a limited period, the length of which can be estimated with reasonable accuracy, such an intangible asset may be the subject of a depreciation allowance. * * *

There is no merit in the petitioner's claim to an amortization deduction for the cost of his education and related expenses in qualifying himself for the legal profession. His college and law school expenses provided him with a general education which will be beneficial to him in a wide variety of ways. See James A. Carroll, 51 T.C. 213, 216 (1968). The costs and responsibility for obtaining such education are personal. Section 1.262–1(b)(9) of the Income Tax Regulations provides that expenditures for education are deductible only if they qualify under section 162 and section 1.162–5 of the regulations. In the words of section 1.162–5(b), all costs of "minimum educational requirements for qualification in * * * employment" are "personal expenditures or constitute an inseparable aggregate of personal and capital expenditures." There is no "rational" or workable basis for any allocation of this inseparable aggregate between the nondeductible personal component and a deductible component of the total ex-

---

4. The parties stipulated that the petitioner expended a total of $210.20 in connection with gaining admission to practice law in New York. At the trial, the petitioner detailed the last two items listed above, but the record does not show for what specific purpose the other $10 was used.

The expenditures for the petitioner's college and law school education may have been furnished by his parents, but the Commissioner has not sought to deny the petitioners a deduction for that reason.

pense. Fausner v. Commissioner, 413 U.S. 838, 839 (1973). Such expenses are not made any less personal or any more separable from the aggregate by attempting to capitalize them for amortization purposes. David N. Bodley, 56 T.C. 1357, 1362 (1971); Nathaniel A. Denman, 48 T.C. 439, 446 (1967); Huene v. United States, 247 F. Supp. 564, 570 (S.D.N.Y.1965). Since the inseparable aggregate includes personal expenditures, the preeminence of section 262 over section 167 precludes any amortization deduction. Cf. Commissioner v. Idaho Power Co., 418 U.S. at 17; Bodzin v. Commissioner, 509 F. 2d at 681. The same reasoning applies to the costs of review courses and related expenses taken to qualify for the practice of a profession. William D. Glenn, 62 T.C. 270, 274–276 (1974).

In his brief, the petitioner attempts to distinguish our opinion in *Denman* by asserting that he is not attempting to capitalize his educational costs, but rather, the cost of his license to practice law. Despite the label which the petitioner would apply to such costs, they nonetheless constitute the costs of his education, which are personal and nondeductible. Moreover, in his petition, he alleged that the capital asset he was seeking to amortize was his education.

There remains the $25 fee paid for the petitioner's license to practice in New York.[5] This was not an educational expense but was a fee paid for the privilege of practicing law in New York, a nontransferable license which has value beyond the taxable years, and such fee is a capital expenditure. Cf. Arthur E. Ryman, Jr., 51 T.C. 799 (1969); Glenn L. Heigerick, 45 T.C. 475 (1966); S. M. Howard, 39 T.C. 833 (1963); O.D. 452, 2 C.B. 157 (1920). The Commissioner has limited his argument to the educational expenses and apparently concedes that the fee may be amortized. Since the amount of the fee is small, the petitioner might, ordinarily, be allowed to elect to deduct the full amount of the fee in the year of payment, despite its capital nature. Cf. sec. 1.162–12(a), Income Tax Regs., with respect to the treatment of inexpensive tools. However, since the fee was paid prior to the years in issue, we cannot allow a current deduction in this case. Therefore, in view of the Commissioner's concession and our conclusion with respect to the third and fourth issues, a proportionate part of such fee may be added to the amounts to be amortized in accordance with our resolution of the third issue.

3. License to Practice Law in California

The next issue to be decided is whether the petitioner may deduct or amortize the expenses he incurred in gaining admission to practice before the State and Federal courts of California. The Commissioner

---

5. In his petition, the petitioner only alleges that he should be allowed to amortize the cost of his education. However, the parties have tried and briefed this case as though the amor- tization of the petitioner's New York bar expenses were properly raised. Thus, we shall consider this issue. Rule 41(b)(1), Tax Court Rules of Practice and Procedure.

disallowed the amounts paid in 1969 to take the attorney's bar examination in California and the amounts paid for admission to the bar of the U.S. District Court for the Northern District of California and for admission to the U.S. Court of Appeals for the Ninth Circuit. He determined that such expenses were capital expenditures. In his brief, the petitioner argues for a current deduction only if the costs of his license to practice in California are not amortizable.

It is clear that the petitioner may not deduct under section 162 (a) the fees paid to take the California attorney's bar examination and to gain admission to practice before two Federal courts in California. In *Arthur E. Ryman, Jr.,* supra, an associate professor of law sought to deduct as an ordinary business expense the cost of his admission to the bar of the State in which he resided. We held that since the taxpayer could reasonably expect the useful life of his license to extend beyond 1 year, the cost of such license was a capital expenditure and not a currently deductible business expense. Unlike the small fee paid to New York, the aggregate amount of such payments in 1969 is too large to disregard their capital nature and allow the petitioners to deduct them currently.

In connection with his alternative claim that he be allowed to amortize the costs of acquiring his license to practice law in California, the petitioner asserts that such costs total $801. Such amount includes the cost of a California bar review course, registration fees, and other items specified in our Findings of Fact. However, the petitioner is in error in including the cost of his bar review course, $230, in the capital cost of his license to practice in California.

It is clear that the amount the petitioner paid for the bar review course was an expenditure "made by an individual for education" within the meaning of section 1.162–5(a) of the Income Tax Regulations. See William D. Glenn, 62 T.C. 270, 273–274 (1974); sec. 1.-162–5(b)(2)(iii), example (3), Income Tax Regs. Although the petitioner was authorized to practice law in some jurisdictions when he took the California bar review course, such course was nevertheless educational in the same sense as the first bar review course. The deductibility of such educational expenses is governed by the rules of section 1.162–5 of the regulations. The evidence indicates that the petitioner took the California bar examination twice, the latter time in early 1969, so that the payment for the California bar review course must have been made in a year prior to 1969. Thus, even if such payment is otherwise deductible, it may not be deducted in 1969.

Nor may the petitioner treat the payment for the California bar review course as a part of the costs of acquiring his license to practice in California. Educational expenses which are incurred to meet the minimum educational requirements for qualification in a taxpayer's trade or business or which qualify him for a new trade or business are "personal expenditures or constitute an inseparable aggregate of personal and capital expenditures." Sec. 1.162–5(b), Income Tax Regs. We find that the bar review course helped to qualify the petitioner for a new trade or business so that its costs are personal expenses.

We have previously adopted a "commonsense approach" in determining whether an educational expenditure qualifies a taxpayer for a "new trade or business." Kenneth C. Davis, 65 T.C. 1014, 1019 (1976); William D. Glenn, 62 T.C. at 275; Ronald F. Weiszmann, 52 T.C. 1106, 1110 (1969), affd. 443 F.2d 29 (9th Cir. 1971). If the education qualifies the taxpayer to perform significantly different tasks and activities than he could perform prior to the education, then the education qualifies him for a new trade or business. William D. Glenn, supra; Ronald F. Weiszmann, supra. Thus, we have held that a professor of social work is in a different trade or business than a social caseworker. Kenneth C. Davis, supra. A licensed public accountant is in a different trade or business than a certified public accountant. William D. Glenn, supra. A registered pharmacist is in a different trade or business than an intern pharmacist, even though an intern performs many of the same tasks as a registered pharmacist, but under supervision. Gary Antzoulatos, T.C. Memo. 1975–327.

Before taking the bar review course and passing the attorney's bar examination, the petitioner was an attorney licensed to practice law in New York. As an attorney for the Regional Counsel, he could represent the Commissioner in this Court. However, he could not appear in either the State courts of California, the Federal District Courts located there, nor otherwise act as an attorney outside the scope of his employment with the IRS. See Cal.Bus. & Prof.Code sec. 6125 (West 1974); 20 Op.Cal.Atty.Gen. 291 (1952). If he had done so, he would have been guilty of a misdemeanor. Cal.Bus. & Prof.Code sec. 6126 (West 1974). Yet, after receiving his license to practice law in California, he became a member of the State bar with all its accompanying privileges and obligations. He could appear and represent clients in all the courts of California. By comparing the tasks and activities that the petitioner was qualified to perform prior to receiving his license to practice in California with the tasks and activities he was able to perform after receiving such license, it is clear that he has qualified for a new trade or business. Consequently, the expenses of his bar review course were personal and are not includable in the cost of his license to practice law in California.

It is true that even before he became a member of the bar of California, the petitioner was engaged in the business of practicing law. Cf. David J. Primuth, 54 T.C. 374 (1970). However, in applying the provisions of section 1.162–5 of the regulations to determine whether educational expenses are personal or business in nature, it is not enough to find that the petitioner was already engaged in some business—we must ascertain the particular business in which he was previously engaged and whether the education qualified him to engage in a different business. Before taking the bar review course and becoming a member of the bar of California, the petitioner could not generally engage in the practice of law in that State, but the bar review course helped to qualify him to engage in such business.

The Commissioner does not argue that the capital expenditures incurred in obtaining his license to practice law in California may not be amortized. In a series of cases, the courts have held that the fees paid by physicians to acquire hospital privileges are not current business expenses but are capital expenditures amortizable over the doctor's life expectancy. Walters v. Commissioner, 383 F.2d 922, 924 (6th Cir. 1967), affg. a Memorandum Opinion of this Court, Glenn L. Heigerick, 45 T.C. 475, 478–479 (1966); S. M. Howard, 39 T.C. 833, 838–839 (1963) ; compare Wells-Lee v. Commissioner, 360 F.2d 665, 672–673 (8th Cir. 1966), revg. and remanding in part a Memorandum Opinion of this Court. We hold that the petitioner may treat the costs of acquiring his license to practice in California in a similar manner. Such costs include:

Registration fee	$20	U.S. District Court fee	$6
General bar exam fee	150	U.S. Court of Appeals fee	5
Attorney's bar exam fee	375	Total	582
Admittance fee	26		

Although the petitioner testified that he would retire at age 65 if he were financially able to do so, such testimony is not sufficient to establish the shorter useful life for which he argues.

We are aware that the petitioner's business as an employee of the Office of Regional Counsel did not require him to become a member of the California bar, and it may be argued that, within the meaning of section 167(a)(1), this intangible asset was not "used" in the petitioner's business during 1969 and 1970. However, the record does demonstrate that membership in the California bar was of some assistance to the petitioner in those years. Furthermore, when an attorney commences the practice of law, it is impossible to anticipate where his work will take him. He cannot with certainty establish what work he will receive and what bar memberships will be useful to him. Once he launches into the practice of law, he must decide what bars to join, and so long as there is some rational connection between his present or prospective work and those that he joins, we think that the expenses of joining them should be accepted as an appropriate cost of acquiring the necessary licenses to practice his profession. Since in 1969 and 1970, the petitioner was working in California, he had reason to anticipate that he might eventually leave the Government and enter into the private practice of law in that State; thus, when that possibility is considered together with the immediate benefit to be derived from membership in the California bar, there was ample reason for him to join such bar at that time. For these reasons, we are satisfied that in 1969 and 1970, the petitioner did make use of the tangible asset constituting the privilege of practicing law in California.

4. *Supreme Court Admission*

The fourth issue to be decided is whether the petitioner may either deduct or amortize the cost of gaining admission to practice before the U.S. Supreme Court. The petitioner deducted the travel costs he incurred in 1970 in traveling to Washington, D.C., to be personally present for the Supreme Court admission, as required by that Court's rules. The Commissioner disallowed the deduction and argued in his brief that such expenditures were capital in nature since the petitioner acquired an asset with a useful life beyond 1 year.

In his brief, the petitioner concedes that he may not deduct the costs he incurred if we find that his license to practice before the Supreme Court is an intangible asset with a useful life of more than 1 year. For the same reasons that we have concluded that the petitioner's New York and California licenses were intangible assets with a useful life of more than 1 year, we also hold that his Supreme Court license is an intangible asset with a useful life exceeding 1 year. Thus, the petitioner may not deduct under section 162 the cost of obtaining such license.

In order for such license to be amortizable pursuant to section 167, the petitioner must show that it was property used in his trade or business. There is little evidence concerning the petitioner's "use" in 1970 of his license to practice before the Supreme Court. However, he did testify that the admission to various bars was a factor used in evaluating attorneys for promotion by his employer, and the Commissioner never disputed such testimony. Furthermore, it is altogether appropriate for any attorney-at-law to become a member of the bar of the Supreme Court whenever it is convenient for him to do so. No one can know when the membership in such bar may be useful to him in the practice of law—it may bring tangible benefits today, tomorrow, on never; yet, if one holds himself out to practice law, there is ample reason for him to acquire membership in the bar of the Supreme Court. Under these circumstances, we find that the intangible asset acquired by becoming a member of such bar was used by the petitioner in 1970 and hold that he may amortize the costs of acquiring such asset over his life expectancy.

* * *

SCOTT, J., dissenting: I respectfully disagree with the conclusion of the majority that the $25 license fee paid by petitioner to New York, the $571 paid to take the California bar examination, the $11 for admission to practice before two Federal courts in California, and the $313.35 paid for travel to Washington, via New York, to practice before the United States Supreme Court are properly amortizable over petitioner's life expectancy. I agree that these expenditures, except for transportation to Washington, via New York, the place of the home of petitioner's family, are capital expenditures. However there is nothing in this record to show the reasonable useful life of these expenditures. How long petitioner will practice law and where are so conjectural as to cause there to be no way to ascertain the reasonable useful life of the asset petitioner acquired through his capital expenditures. Although respondent apparently makes no contention that the trip to Washington, via New York, when petitioner was admitted to practice before the Supreme Court was personal, the clear inference from the fact that he did go to New York where his family lived before coming to Washington and returned there after he came to Washington is that petitioner went to New York to visit his family and incidentally came to Washington to be admitted to practice before the Supreme Court. However, if the view of the majority, that the cost of travel to Washington, via New York, was properly part of the cost of petitioner's admission to practice before the Supreme Court, were proper, then this, as the other capital expenditures, should not be amortizable since the useful life of the asset acquired is not reasonably ascertainable.

STERRETT, J., agrees with this dissent.

IRWIN, J., dissenting: I disagree with that portion of the majority opinion which holds that petitioner may not treat the payment for the California bar review course as a part of the cost of acquiring his license to practice law in California. In the past, we have indeed adopted a "commonsense approach" in determining whether an educational expenditure qualifies a taxpayer for a new trade or business. Kenneth C. Davis, 65 T.C. 1014, 1019 (1976); William D. Glenn, 62 T.C. 270, 275 (1974); Donald F. Weiszmann, 52 T.C. 1106, 1110 (1969), affd. 443 F.2d 29 (9th Cir. 1971). However, I think we depart from that approach when we hold that an attorney, licensed to practice law in New York, qualifies for a new trade or business when he obtains a license to practice law in California. In William D. Glenn, supra at 275, we stated:

> We have not found a substantial case law suggesting criteria for determining when the acquisition of new titles or abilities constitutes the entry into a new trade or business for purposes of section 1.162–5(c)(1), Income Tax Regs. What has been suggested, and we uphold such suggestion as the only commonsense approach to a classification, is that a comparison be made between the *types of tasks and activities which the taxpayer was qualified to perform before the acquisition of a particular title or degree, and those which he is qualified to perform afterwards.* Ronald F. Weiszmann, 52 T.C. 1106, 1110 (1969), affd. 443 F.2d 29 (C.A. 9, 1971). Where we have found such activities and abilities to be significantly different, we have disallowed

an educational expense deduction, based on our finding that there had been qualification for a new trade or business. *Ronald F. Weiszmann*, supra. [Emphasis supplied.]

In my view there is no difference in the *types* of tasks and activities which petitioner was qualified to perform before and after he acquired his California license. By virtue of being licensed to practice in California, petitioner could perform the same types of tasks and activities in that state as he was already qualified to perform in New York. In this regard, respondent takes the position that once an individual is qualified to teach in State A, a college course taken in order to qualify for a teaching position in State B is neither a minimum educational requirement of his trade or business nor education qualifying him for a new trade or business. Rev.Rul. 71–58, 1971–1 C.B. 55. I would similarly conclude that once an individual is qualified to practice law in one State, a bar review course taken in preparation for the bar exam of another State is not education leading to qualification for a new trade or business.

STERRETT, J., dissenting: I disagree with the majority's conclusion that the costs incurred by petitioner in acquiring the licenses involved herein are amortizable over his life expectancy. Although the fees in question are undoubtedly business related, it seems clear to me that the realities of life preclude any rational method by which the useful life thereof can be estimated with any reasonable accuracy. As the majority recognizes at **page 743**, "Furthermore, when an attorney commences the practice of law, it is impossible to anticipate where his work will take him. He cannot with certainty establish what work he will receive and what bar memberships will be useful to him." What the licenses do is afford petitioner the opportunity to earn fees for appearances in court for an indefinite period of time; namely until his retirement or withdrawal from practice, his death, or in the case of the State licenses his commencement of practice in another State, whichever event occurs first. Such indefiniteness should preclude amortization of the cost of the licenses. Formico v. Commissioner, 491 F.2d 788 (9th Cir. 1974); Ralph Vander Hoek, 51 T.C. 203 (1968).

To allow the deductions for amortization of these fees is a triumph of the esoteric over the practical.

SCOTT, J., agrees with this dissent.

MASSEY MOTORS, INC. v. UNITED STATES

Supreme Court of the United States, 1960.
364 U.S. 92, 80 S.Ct. 1411.

MR. JUSTICE CLARK delivered the opinion of the Court.

These consolidated cases involve the depreciation allowance for automobiles used in rental and allied service, as claimed under § 23(*l*) of the Internal Revenue Code of 1939, which permits the deduction for income tax purposes of a "reasonable allowance for the exhaustion, wear and tear   *   *   *   of property used in the trade or business." *   *   *   The Courts of Appeals have divided on the method of depreciation which is permissible in relation to such assets, and we therefore granted certiorari to resolve this conflict. 361 U.S. 810, 812. We have concluded that the reasonable allowance for depreciation of the property in question used in the taxpayer's business is to be calculated over the estimated useful life of the asset while actually employed by the taxpayer, applying a depreciation base of the cost of the property to the taxpayer less its resale value at the estimated time of disposal.

In No. 143, Commissioner v. R. H. and J. M. Evans, the taxpayers are husband and wife. In 1950 and 1951, the husband, Robley Evans, was engaged in the business of leasing new automobiles to Evans U-Drive, Inc., at the rate of $45 per car per month. U-Drive in turn leased from 30% to 40% of the cars to its customers for long terms ranging from 18 to 36 months, while the remainder were rented to the public on a call basis for shorter periods. Robley Evans normally kept in stock a supply of new cars with which to service U-Drive and which he purchased at factory price from local automobile dealers. The latest model cars were required because of the demands of the rental business for a fleet of modern automobiles.

When the U-Drive service had an oversupply of cars that were used on short-term rental, it would return them to the taxpayer and he would sell them, disposing of the oldest and least desirable ones first. Normally the ones so disposed of had been used about 15 months and had been driven an average of 15,000 to 20,000 miles. They were ordinarily in first-class condition. It was likewise customary for the taxpayer to sell the long-term rental cars at the termination of their leases, ordinarily after about 50,000 miles of use. They also were usually in good condition. The taxpayer could have used the cars for a longer period, but customer demand for the latest model cars rendered the older styles of little value to the rental business.   *   *   *

In No. 141, Massey Motors, Inc. v. United States, the taxpayer, a franchised Chrysler dealer, withdrew from shipments to it a certain number of new cars which were assigned to company officials and employees for use in company business. Other new cars from these shipments were rented to an unaffiliated finance company at a substantial profit.

The cars assigned to company personnel were uniformly sold at the end of 8,000 to 10,000 miles' use or upon receipt of new models, whichever was earlier. The rental cars were sold after 40,000 miles or upon receipt of new models. For the most part, cars assigned to company personnel and the rental cars sold for more than they cost the taxpayer.

* * *

Some assets * * * are not acquired with intent to be employed in the business for their full economic life. It is this type of asset, where the experience of the taxpayers clearly indicates a utilization of the asset for a substantially shorter period than its full economic life, that we are concerned with in these cases. Admittedly, the automobiles are not retained by the taxpayers for their full economic life and, concededly, they do have substantial salvage, resale or second-hand value. Moreover, the application of the full-economic-life formula to taxpayers' businesses here results in the receipt of substantial "profits" from the resale or "salvage" of the automobiles, which contradicts the usual application of the full-economic-life concept. There, the salvage value if anything, is ordinarily nominal. Furthermore, the "profits" of the taxpayers here are capital gains and incur no more than a 25% tax rate. The depreciation, however, is deducted from ordinary income. By so translating the statute and the regulations, the taxpayers are able, through the deduction of this depreciation from ordinary income, to convert the inflated amounts from income taxable at ordinary rates to that taxable at the substantially lower capital gains rates. This, we believe, was not in the design of Congress.

It appears that the governing statute has at no time defined the terms "useful life" and "salvage value." * * *

It is true, as taxpayers contend and as we have indicated, that the language of the statute and the regulations * * * may not be precise and unambiguous as to the term "useful life." It may be that the administrative practice with regard thereto may not be pointed to as an example of clarity, and that in some cases the Commissioner has acquiesced in inconsistent holdings. But from the promulgation of the first regulation in 1919, he has made it clear that salvage had some value and that it was to be considered as something other than zero in the depreciation equation. In fact many of the cases cited by the parties involved controversies over the actual value of salvage, not as scrap but on resale.[1] The consistency of the Commissioner's position in this regard is evidenced by the fact that the definition of salvage as now incorporated in the regulations is identical with that

1. E. g., Davidson v. Commissioner, 12 CCH T.C.Mem. 1080 (1953); W. H. Norris Lumber Co. v. Commissioner, 7 CCH T.C.Mem. 728 (1948); Bolta Co. v. Commissioner, 4 CCH T.C.Mem. 1067 (1945); Wier Long Leaf Lumber Co. v. Commissioner, 9 T.C. 990 (1947), affirmed in part and reversed in part, 173 F.2d 549 (1949).

claimed at least since 1941. In the light of this, it appears that the struggle over the term "useful life" takes on less practical significance, for, if salvage is the resale value and a deduction of this amount from cost is required, the dollar-wise importance to the taxpayer of the breadth in years of "useful life" is diminished. It is only when he can successfully claim that salvage means junk and has no value that an interpretation of "useful life" as the functional, economic, physical life of the automobile brings money to his pocket. Moreover, in the consideration of the appropriate interpretation of the term, it must be admitted that there is administrative practice and judicial decision in its favor, as we shall point out. Furthermore, as we have said, Congress intended by the depreciation allowance not to make taxpayers a profit thereby, but merely to protect them from a loss. The concept is, as taxpayers say, but an accounting one and, we add, should not be exchangeable in the market place. Accuracy in accounting requires that correct tabulations, not artificial ones, be used. Certainly it is neither accurate nor correct to carry in the depreciation equation a value of nothing as salvage on the resale of the automobiles, when the taxpayers actually received substantial sums therefor. On balance, therefore, it appears clear that the weight of both fairness and argument is with the Commissioner.

* * *

* * * Congress was aware of * * * prior prevailing administrative practice as well as the concept of depreciation upon which it was based. Although the tax years involved here are 1950 and 1951, we believe that the action of Congress in adopting the 1954 Code should be noted, since it specifically recognized the existing depreciation equation. For the first time, the term "useful life" was inserted in the statutory provision. The accompanying House Report to the bill stated:

"Depreciation allowances are the method by which the capital invested in an asset is recovered tax-free over the years it is used in a business. The annual deduction is computed by spreading the cost of the property over its estimated useful life." H.R.Rep. No. 1337, 83d Cong., 2d Sess. 22.

It is also noteworthy that the report states that "The changes made by your committee's bill merely affect the timing and not the ultimate amount of depreciation deductions with respect to a property." Id., at 25.

* * *

Finally, it is the primary purpose of depreciation accounting to further the integrity of periodic income statements by making a meaningful allocation of the cost entailed in the use (excluding maintenance expense) of the asset to the periods to which it contributes. This accounting system has had the approval of this Court since United

States v. Ludey, 274 U.S. 295, 301 (1927), when Mr. Justice Brandeis said, "The theory underlying this allowance for depreciation is that by using up the plant, a gradual sale is made of it." The analogy applies equally to automobiles. Likewise in Detroit Edison Co. v. Commissioner, 319 U.S. 98, 101 (1943), this Court said:

"The end and purpose of it all [depreciation accounting] is to approximate and reflect the financial consequences to the taxpayer of the subtle effects of time and use on the value of his capital assets. For this purpose it is sound accounting practice annually to accrue * * * an amount which at the time it is retired will with its salvage value replace the original investment therein."

Obviously a meaningful annual accrual requires an accurate estimation of how much the depreciation will total. The failure to take into account a known estimate of salvage value prevents this, since it will result in an understatement of income during the years the asset is employed and an overstatement in the year of its disposition. The practice has therefore grown up of subtracting salvage value from the purchase price to determine the depreciation base.[2] On the other hand, to calculate arbitrarily the expected total expense entailed by the asset on the false assumption that the asset will be held until it has no value is to invite an erroneous depreciation base and depreciation rate, which may result in either an over- or an under-depreciation during the period of use. If the depreciation rate and base turn out to reflect the actual cost of employing the asset, it will be by accident only. The likelihood of presenting an inaccurate picture of yearly income from operations is particularly offensive where, as here, the taxpayers stoutly maintain that they are only in the business of renting and leasing automobiles, not of selling them. The alternative is to estimate the period the asset will be held in the business and the price that will be received for it on retirement. Of course, there is a risk of error in such projections, but prediction is the very essence of depreciation accounting. Besides, the possibility of error is significantly less where probabilities rather than accidents are relied upon to produce what is hoped to be an accurate estimation of the expense involved in utilizing the asset. Moreover, under a system where the real salvage price and actual duration of use are relevant, to further insure a correct depreciation base in the years after a mistake has been discovered, adjustments may be made when it appears that a miscalculation has been made.

2. This industry practice is emphasized by the *amicus curiae* brief of the American Automobile Leasing Association in Hillard v. Commissioner, 31 T.C. 961, now pending in the Court of Appeals for the Fifth Circuit. Comprising "about 65 per cent of the long-term leasing industry in motor vehicles in the country" the Association takes the position that the depreciation allowance "is designed to return to the taxpayer, tax-free, the cost of his capital asset over the period during which it is useful to the taxpayer in his business." A copy of the brief is on file in this case.

Accounting for financial management and accounting for federal income tax purposes both focus on the need for an accurate determination of the net income from operations of a given business for a fiscal period. The approach taken by the Commissioner computes depreciation expense in a manner which is far more likely to reflect correctly the actual cost over the years in which the asset is employed in the business.

We therefore conclude that the Congress intended that the taxpayer should, under the allowance for depreciation, recover only the cost of the asset less the estimated salvage, resale or second-hand value. This requires that the useful life of the asset be related to the period for which it may reasonably be expected to be employed in the taxpayer's business. Likewise salvage value must include estimated resale or second-hand value. It follows that No. 141, Massey Motors, Inc., v. United States, must be affirmed, and No. 143, Commissioner v. R. H. and J. M. Evans, reversed.

It is so ordered.

[The opinion of MR. JUSTICE HARLAN, dissenting in part and concurring in part, with which JUSTICES WHITTAKER and STEWART concur, and the dissenting opinion of MR. JUSTICE DOUGLAS have been omitted. Ed.]

NOTE

In Hertz Corp. v. United States,[1] decided the same day as the *Massey* case, the Supreme Court applied the useful life and salvage value to *the* taxpayer holding of *Massey* to preclude the use of accelerated depreciation by a taxpayer who held automobiles for less than three years.[2]

In addition with respect to property with a greater than three year life to the taxpayer the Court upheld regulations limiting depreciation under accelerated depreciation methods (here the declining balance method) to the taxpayer's reasonable salvage value. In reaching its conclusion the court stated:[3]

As we pointed out in the companion cases, the purpose of depreciation accounting is to allocate the expense of using an asset to the various periods which are benefited by that asset. The declining balance method permits a rapid rate of depreciation in the early years of an asset's life. The Congress has permitted under this method an allowance not to exceed twice the "straight line" rate, which rate was approved in *Massey* and *Evans*, supra. In applications, the taxpayer computes his straight-line percentage rate and

1. 364 U.S. 122 (1960).

2. See I.R.C. § 167(b)(2) through (4) and (c).

3. *Supra* note 1 at 126.

then doubles it for the first year. This doubled rate is then applied each subsequent year to the declining balance. Because of a belief that most assets do lose more value in the earlier years, this method is justified as an attempt to level off the total costs, including maintenance expense, which will generally be greater in the later years. This means, even under the Commissioner's theory, that if an asset is disposed of early in what was expected to be its useful life in the business, the depreciation taken may greatly exceed the difference between the purchase price of the asset and its retirement price; this is a result of the conscious choice to permit rapid depreciation. But this, by hypothesis, is an unusual situation. There is nothing inherent in the declining balance system which requires us to assume that depreciation should be allowed beyond what reasonably appears to be the price that will be received when the asset is retired. This would permit a knowing distortion of the expense of employing the asset in the years after that point is reached. It therefore appears that the interpretation contended for by the taxpayer does not comport with the overriding statutory requirement that the depreciation deduction be a *reasonable* allowance. § 167(a).

SHARP v. UNITED STATES

District Court of the United States, District of Delaware, 1961.
199 F.Supp. 743.
Aff'd, 303 F.2d 783, 3d Cir. 1962.

LAYTON, DISTRICT JUDGE. This is a ruling on cross motions for summary judgment under Rule 56 [1] by taxpayers and defendant in these two actions brought by taxpayers to recover alleged overpayments of federal income taxes for the calendar year 1954. The two actions were consolidated previously on stipulation of counsel.

Plaintiffs, Hugh R. Sharp, Jr., and Bayard Sharp, were equal partners in a partnership which on December 17, 1946, purchased a Beechcraft airplane at a cost of $45,875. From 1948 to 1953, additional capital expenditures were made with respect to the airplane in the amount of $8,398.50. Thus, the total cost of the airplane, including capital expenditures, was $54,273.50. Title was held by the partnership. During the period of ownership, the airplane was used by the partnership 73.654% for the personal use of the partners and 26.346% for business purposes.[2] Therefore, the partnership was allowed de-

---

1. 28 U.S.C.A. F.R.Civ.P. 56.

2. The stipulation is not precise as to the exact nature of the division into percentages of personal and business use. It was assumed in the briefs and at oral argument, and therefore it is assumed in this opinion, that the parties are agreed, for purposes of ruling on these motions, that the airplane was used from the beginning, and throughout its ownership by taxpay-

preciation on the basis of only $14,298.90, or 26.346% of the airplane's total cost. Depreciation taken by the partnership and allowed on this basis during the period totaled $13,777.92. During 1954, the airplane was sold by the partnership for $35,380. At issue here is the amount of gain or loss realized by the partnership on the sale of the airplane.

The taxpayers earnestly contend that, if anything, they suffered a loss on the sale, but certainly that they realized no gain. They contend that the relevant statutes permit no other conclusion. Taxpayers point out that the basis of property is its cost.[3] The total cost of the airplane was $54,273.50. For determining gain or loss, numerous adjustments in this basis are permissible, including subtracting from the cost basis the amount of depreciation allowed.[4] Since the depreciation allowed on the airplane was $13,777.92, taxpayers have subtracted this amount from $54,273.50, giving an adjusted basis of $40,495.58. The Code explicitly states that the loss recognized on the sale of property is the excess of the adjusted basis over the amount realized from the sale of the property.[5] The selling price of the airplane was $35,380. Accordingly, taxpayers subtracted this amount from the adjusted basis of $40,495.58 and compute their loss on the sale of the airplane as being $5,115.58. The taxpayers, as the Court understands their argument, do not seek to deduct any part of this loss. Their only claim is that no gain was realized on the sale.

The government theory is grounded in the fact that the airplane was used by the partnership 73.654% for pleasure and 26.346% for business purposes. Both the adjusted basis and the proceeds of sale of the plane are allocated in these proportions, giving in effect two sales. A gain on the business part of the sale is balanced against a non-deductible loss on the personal part, producing a net gain. More detail will clarify the government theory. It will be recalled that in computing depreciation, the cost basis was allocated so that depreciation was allowed on only 26.346% of the cost basis, i. e., $14,298.90.[6] The remainder of the cost basis, i. e., $39,974.60, was allocated to the personal use of the airplane and no depreciation was allowed. The government has adjusted only the business basis, by subtracting from $14,298.90 the depreciation allowed, i. e., $13,777.92, producing an adjusted business basis of $520.98. Now that the airplane is being sold, the government takes the view that this same allocation should

ers, approximately ¼ for business and ¾ for pleasure, without variations. Other considerations might apply if the nature of the ¼–¾ division of use had been different. Suppose, for example, during the total 8 years of ownership, that for the first 6 years the plane had been used exclusively for pleasure, and that for the last 2 years it had been used exclusively for business. Under such circumstances, gain or loss might depend not only on the original cost and the depreciation taken but also on the value of the plane when it was converted to a business use. See Treasury Regulations § 1.165–9(b).

3.   26 U.S.C.A. § 1012.

4.   26 U.S.C.A. § 1016(a) (2) (A).

5.   26 U.S.C.A. § 1001(a).

6.   See 26 U.S.C.A. § 167(a).

be continued for purposes of gain or loss computation on the sale. Accordingly, the proceeds from the sale of the airplane, i. e., $35,380, have been allocated in accordance with the percentages of past business and personal use into portions of $9,321.21 and $26,058.79, respectively. The government then subtracts the adjusted business basis of $520.98 from the proceeds of the sale which were allocated to the business use of the airplane, $9,321.21, and concludes that the taxpayers realized a gain of $8,800.23 on the sale. Any loss on the personal use of the airplane is not deductible because of its personal nature and is disregarded. The taxpayers, being equal partners, have each been assessed with a taxable gain on one-half of $8,800.23, or $4,400.11.

Counsel for the government have said this is the first challenge by a taxpayer to Rev.Rul. 286, 1953–2 Cum.Bull. 20,[7] and that if the position argued for by the taxpayers be sustained, it would "produce serious and far reaching inequities in the administration of the internal revenue laws."

While research has disclosed no decided case in which an allocation has been made in accordance with percentages of past business and personal use of property, taxpayers are clearly in error if it is their contention that courts will not regard a thing, normally accepted as an entity, as divisible for tax purposes. There are numerous decisions in which the sale proceeds from an orange grove, for instance, have been allocated between the trees (capital gain) and the unharvested crop (income),[8] or where the proceeds from the sale of an interest in a partnership have been allocated between the earned but uncollected fees,[9] or income producing property [10] (income), and the other assets of the business (capital gain). A different sort of allocation was ordered in a leading Third Circuit case, Paul v. Commissioner.[11] In Paul, taxpayer, who was in the business of holding rental property for investment purposes, bought a partially completed apartment building in May, which he sold more than six months later, in November. The issue was whether the taxpayer could treat the entire gain or any part thereof as long term capital gain, under Section

7. The relevant portion of Rev.Rule 286, 1953–2 Cum.Bull. 20, reads as follows:
"Only that part of a loss resulting from the sale of property used for both personal and income-producing purposes that can be allocated to the income-producing portion of the property constitutes a loss within the meaning of § 23(e) of the Internal Revenue Code [26 U.S.C.A. (I.R.C.1939), § 23(e)]. In determining the gain or loss on the sale, there must be an actual allocation of the amounts which represent cost, selling price, depreciation allowed or allowable, and selling expenses to the respective portions of property in the same manner as if there were two sparate transactions."

8. See e. g., Watson v. Commissioner, 345 U.S. 544, 73 S.Ct. 848, 97 L.Ed. 1232 (1953); Smyth v. Cole, 218 F.2d 667 (9th Cir. 1955).

9. Tunnell v. United States, 259 F.2d 916 (3d Cir. 1958); United States v. Snow, 223 F.2d 103 (9th Cir. 1955).

10. Williams v. McGowan, 152 F.2d 570 (2d Cir. 1945).

11. 206 F.2d 763 (3d Cir. 1953); see also Commissioner v. Williams, 256 F.2d 152 (5th Cir. 1958).

117(j) of the Internal Revenue Code of 1939.[12] The Court held that
a portion of the gain must be allocated to the part of the building
erected more than six months before the sale and given long term
treatment.[13] The remainder of the proceeds allocable to the construction between May and November was taxed as short term gain.

The closest analogy to the case at bar is the sale of depreciable and
non-depreciable property as a unit—the sale of a building and land
together, for instance. In United States v. Koshland,[14] a hotel caught
fire and was destroyed. At issue in the case was the amount of the
casualty loss deduction permissible under the circumstances. However, in the course of its opinion, the Court discussed the allocation
problem directly, noting that the hotel was depreciable whereas the
land on which it stood was not.

" *   *   * The result is that there is no single 'adjusted basis'
for the land and building as a unit. The depreciation allowed or allowable on the building reduces the basis of the building only. No depreciation is allowed on the land, and the original basis of the land
therefore remains unaffected. The adjusted basis of the building and
the basis of the land cannot be combined into a single 'adjusted basis'
for the property as a whole, for to do so would in effect be reducing the
basis of the whole by depreciation allowed or allowable only as against
the building, a part.

"Thus, for tax purposes, upon a sale of the property as a whole
the selling price must be allocated between the land and building and
the gain or loss separately determined upon each, by reference to the
adjusted basis of each." [15]

This principle has been recognized in other cases without discussion.[16]
The taxpayers point out that an airplane is not capable of separation
into business and personal uses in the same way that a hotel is separable from the land on which it stands, or in the same way that the
unharvested crop may be separated from the trees of the grove, or the
accounts receivable from the other partnership assets. There were
not two airplanes, say the taxpayers—a business airplane and a personal airplane—there was one airplane. There were not two sales;
there was but one sale, one adjusted basis and one selling price. Any
division or allocation, therefore, involves resorting to fiction, which is
anathema to the tax law.

The taxpayers' argument against allocation in this case has superficial appeal. The whole idea of allocation is lacking in explicit

12. 26 U.S.C.A. (1939) § 117(j).

13. 206 F.2d at 766.

14. 208 F.2d 636 (9th Cir. 1954).

15. 208 F.2d at 640.

16. See, e. g., Crane v. Commissioner,
331 U.S. 1, 4–5, 67 S.Ct. 1047, 91 L.

Ed. 1301 (1947); Tracy v. Commissioner, 53 F.2d 575, 577 (6th Cir. 1931);
Belle Isle Creamery Co. v. Commissioner, 14 B.T.A. 737, 738 (1928); C.
D. Johnson Lumber Corp. v. Commissioner, 12 T.C. 348, 356, 365 (1949).

authority from the literal words of the relevant sections in the Code. Since the situation here is not covered literally by the Statute, perhaps any interstices in statutory coverage should be filled by Congress not the Court. But this argument ignores the basic fact that no tax statute can encompass every situation which may arise. The Statute is phrased in general terms leaving it to the Commissioner by regulation or ruling and the Courts by interpretation to solve problems arising under unusual and novel facts. Merely because Congress did not specifically provide for the facts presented here does not mean it intended to exempt profits arising from the sale of property used both for business and pleasure. The taxpayers' argument also overlooks the fact that allocation has long been accepted by the courts in other cases. In dealing with another allocation problem, the Third Circuit Court of Appeals has said:

"The federal revenue laws are to be construed in the light of their general purpose 'so as to give a uniform application to a nation-wide scheme of taxation.' Burnet v. Harmel, 1932, 287 U.S. 103, 110, 53 S.Ct. 74, 77 L.Ed. 199; United States v. Pelzer, 1941, 312 U.S. 399, 402, 61 S.Ct. 659, 85 L.Ed. 913; Lyeth v. Hoey, 1938, 305 U.S. 188, 194, 59 S.Ct. 155, 83 L.Ed. 119." [17]

But if taxpayers' theory prevails, there will be lack of uniformity in tax treatment between those who use property partially for business and pleasure on the one hand, and those who use property exclusively for business on the other. To use round figures, if property used exclusively for business has an adjusted basis of $500 ($14,000 cost less $13,500 depreciation) and it is sold for $9,000, nobody will deny that a taxable gain of $8,500 has been realized. Now, suppose that a larger piece of property is used only $\frac{1}{4}$ for business purposes and $\frac{3}{4}$ for pleasure, but that the adjusted basis of the business part is the same as in the first example, namely $500, and that depreciation figures and cost of the business part are also the same. Taxes levied on the business segment of the larger property should not be different from taxes levied on the other property used exclusively for business. To put it another way, taxpayers having two business properties with the same cost and depreciation should pay the same taxes, if the properties are sold for the same price. The fact that one of the properties was also used for pleasure should make no difference.

Under the government's allocation theory, uniformity is achieved; under the taxpayers', it is not. If the government's theory involves, as the taxpayers suggest, "dividing" the plane up, it can only be replied that this is precisely what was done in calculating the depreciation deduction to which the taxpayers acquiesced. There is no greater peculiarity in doing the same thing when computing gain or loss on a sale. The depreciable business use and non-depreciable personal use

17. Paul v. Commissioner, 206 F.2d 763, 765–766 (3d Cir. 1953).

of the airplane are not essentially different from the depreciable hotel and non-depreciable land discussed in the Koshland case, supra.

The fairness of the government's theory can be seen more easily using a different analysis. This different analysis involves allocation of loss instead of sale proceeds and cost basis. Continuing the use of round numbers, the $20,000 loss on the sale of the airplane (cost of $55,000 less sale proceeds of $35,000) can be allocated ¾ to the personal use and ¼ to the business use. If the property had not been depreciable, but used in the same fashion, it would seem proper that the taxpayer should be allowed to deduct $5,000 as a business loss—no more, no less. Since depreciation deductions were taken in our case with respect to the business use of the airplane of about $13,500, and whereas the actual loss on this part of the plane's use was only $5,000, it would appear that taxpayer has received fortuitously the benefit of depreciation deductions equal to the difference between $13,500 and $5,000, or $8,500. Even though all depreciation was allowed or allowable, it is the government's position that the "excessive" depreciation should be taxed.[18] This Court agrees.

Application of the rationale and certain of the language of Paul v. Commissioner [19] to the instant case compels the following conclusion. Allocation of the proceeds from the sale of this plane in accordance with its percentages of business and personal use is "practical and fair." This Court believes that Rev.Rule 286, 1953–2 Cum.Bull. 20, as applied here, represents a reasonable exercise by the Commissioner of his rule making power. There is no reason to make this an "all or nothing proposition." It is realistic to recognize that there are "gradations" between the percentage of business and personal use of a piece of property. It is concluded here that it is "proper that those gradations have tax significance."

The taxpayers' motion for summary judgment is denied and the government's is granted. Let an order be submitted in conformity herewith.

PROBLEMS

1. If the *Sharp* "divided airplane" was purchased after 1962 and was used less than 50% of the time for business purposes, would I.R.C. § 274(a)(1)(B) deny the depreciation deduction? See John L. Beckley, 34 TCM 235 (1975).

2. I.R.C. § 263(a) provides "no deduction shall be allowed for any amount paid but for new buildings. . . . " Thus if one pays

---

18. Assuming that taxpayers are in a high tax bracket, it may be noted that complete equalization of tax benefits is not accomplished in the government's theory. Taxpayer took the $8,500 "excess" depreciation as ordinary deductions. Taxpayers are now being taxed on this amount at only capital gain rates. It would seem that taxpayers are still ahead.

19. 206 F.2d 763, 766 (3d Cir. 1953).

for salaries or for painting etc. in construction of a building, the expenses are capitalized and the total cost of the building is then depreciated assuming the § 167 requirements are met.

    (a) If Corporation owns trucks which are used during the year exclusively in constructing a new storage plant for the company, is Corporation allowed a depreciation deduction for the trucks during the current year? See Comm'r v. Idaho Power Company, 418 U.S. 1 (1974).

    (b) Are interests on loans connected with property and taxes on the property which are paid during the construction period currently deductible as paid? See I.R.C. § 189, added by T.R.A. 1976.

    3. Taxpayer acquires a depreciable asset which cost $100, has a five year life, and a $10 salvage value but will cost $20 to remove. Is taxpayer's salvage value for depreciation purposes $10, zero, or minus $10? Compare Portland General Electric Company v. U. S., 223 F.Supp. 111 (D.Ore.1963) with Rev.Rul. 75–150, 1975–1 C.B. 73.

2. SPECIAL RULES ON PERSONALTY

Internal Revenue Code: Sections 167(f); 179(a), (b), (c), (d)(1) and (9). See Section 1056(a) and (d).
Regulations: Sections 1.167(f)–1(a) and (b)(1); 1.179–1(a) through (d), –2(a), –3(a), (b), (f).

PROBLEMS

    1. On January 1, of year one Taxpayer purchases personal property new for use in his business at a cost of $10,000. The property is such that it could be used for ten years with an ultimate salvage value of $2,000, but Taxpayer plans to use it for only five years, when its salvage value is expected to be $3,000. Assume Taxpayer is a married calendar year taxpayer who files a joint return.

    (a) Determine whether Taxpayer may use the three principal depreciation methods of § 167(b) and whether he is entitled to the benefits of § 167(f) and § 179.

    (b) Assuming that all the above are available to him compute the amount of depreciation which he and Wife may take on the property in each year of its useful life to them under each of the three principal methods, using the benefits of § 167(f) and § 179.

    (c) How would the answer in (a), above, vary if the property were used, as opposed to new, property? (See Rev.Rul.

57–352, 1957–2 C.B. 150.)   Compute Taxpayer and Wife's depreciation deductions over the property's useful life to them under the principal methods available for used property, using the benefits of § 167(f) and § 179 only if they are available.

---

3.   SPECIAL RULES ON REALTY

Internal Revenue Code: Section 167(j) and (k). See Sections 167(n) and (o) and 191.

EXCERPT FROM THE GENERAL EXPLANATION OF THE TAX REFORM ACT OF 1969

Staff of the Joint Committee on Internal Revenue Taxation, pp. 181–182 (1970).

S. REAL ESTATE DEPRECIATION *

(Sec. 521 of the Act and secs. 167 and 1250 of the code)

Prior law.—Prior law (since 1954) provided that new real property and new tangible personal property could be depreciated by the first owner under either the double declining balance method or the sum of the years-digits method of depreciation. These methods generally permit large portions of an asset's total basis to be deducted in the first few years of the asset's useful life. A later owner was permitted to use the 150-percent declining balance method, which is significantly "faster" than straight line in the early years, but significantly "slower" than the two other methods referred to above. * * *

General reasons for change.—The prior tax treatment of real estate was used by some high-income individuals as a tax shelter to escape payment of tax on substantial portions of their economic income. The rapid depreciation methods allowed made it possible for taxpayers to deduct amounts in excess of those required to service the mortgage during the early life of the property. Moreover, because accelerated depreciation usually produced a deduction in excess of the actual decline in the usefulness of property, economically profitable real estate operations were normally converted into substantial tax losses, sheltering from income tax economic profits and permitting avoidance of income tax on the owner's other ordinary income, such as salary and dividends. Later, the property could be sold and the excess of the sale price over the remaining basis could be treated as a capital gain to the

---

* See Ritter and Sunley, "Real Estate and Tax Reform: An Analysis and Evaluation of the Real Estate Provisions of the Tax Reform Act of 1967," 30 Md.L.Rev. 5 (1970). Ed.

extent that the recapture provisions did not apply.   *   *   *   The tax advantages from such operations increased as a taxpayer's income moved into the higher tax brackets.

Because of the tax situation, when investment was solicited in a real estate venture it became the practice to promise a prospective investor substantial tax losses which could be used to diminish the tax on his income from other sources. Thus, there was, in effect, substantial dealing in "tax losses" produced by depreciable real property.

In addition to the tax shelter aspect of the prior law depreciation allowances in the case of individuals, problems were also raised as to whether these allowances constituted an undue incentive for commercial and industrial construction.

Explanation of provision.—The Act contains provisions designed to substantially reduce the opportunities to avoid taxes as a result of accelerated depreciation for real estate. It provides that new construction, other than residential housing, is to be limited to 150-percent declining balance depreciation. New residential housing continues to be eligible for the double declining balance or sum of the years-digits depreciation methods. For this purpose a building is considered to be residential housing only if 80 percent or more of the gross income from the building in the year is derived from rentals of residential units.

The new rules curtailing accelerated depreciation on new real estate construction apply unless (1) the construction of the building began before July 25, 1969, or (2) a written contract with respect to any part of the construction or for a substantial portion of the permanent financing was entered into before July 25, 1969.

The Act allows accelerated depreciation in the case of construction of residential housing in foreign countries only to the extent that the foreign country allows accelerated depreciation on similar housing.

To eliminate the repeated sale and resale of property for the purpose of tax minimization, used realty (other than used residential property) acquired after July 24, 1969, is generally limited to straight line or a comparable ratable method of depreciation. Used residential property with a useful life of 20 years or more, acquired after July 24, 1969, is limited to 125-percent declining balance depreciation. However, used property acquired after July 24, 1969, pursuant to a written contract for the acquisition of the property or for its permanent financing, which was binding on that date, continues to be eligible for the 150-percent declining balance depreciation permitted under prior law.

To encourage rehabilitation of buildings for low- and moderate-income rental housing, the Act allows taxpayers to elect to compute depreciation on rehabilitation expenditures which are made after July 24, 1969, under the straight line method over a period of 60 months,

if the additions or improvements have a useful life of 5 years or more.*
This rapid depreciation [was initially] limited to expenditures made
prior to January 1, 1975 [later extended to January 1, 1978] in order
to provide an opportunity for the Congress to evaluate the effectiveness and cost of the new incentive. It is available only for low-income
rental housing where the dwelling units are held for occupancy for
families or individuals of low or moderate income, consistent with
the policies of the Housing and Urban Development Act of 1968.
[The reference now is to "the Leased Housing Program" under section 8 of the United States Housing Act of 1937.]   The 60-month
rule does not apply to hotels, motels, inns, or other establishments,
where more than one-half of the units are used on a transient basis.

To qualify for the 60-month depreciation, the aggregate rehabilitation expenditures as to any housing may not exceed $15,000 [now
$20,000] per dwelling unit and the sum of the rehabilitation expendi-
tures for two consecutive taxable years—including the taxable year—
must exceed $3,000 per rental unit.   [The Editing in brackets re-
flects changes made by section 203(a) of the Tax Reform Act of
1976. Ed.]

* * *

PROBLEMS

1. In the current year Depreciator purchases a piece of new improved real property at a cost of $150,000, of which $110,000 is attributable to the building and $40,000 to the land. The building has
a useful life to Depreciator of 50 years and a salvage value to him of
$10,000. He rents the property to others.

(a) Are the benefits of § 167(f) or § 179 available to the tax-
    payer?

(b) The building has two floors; the bottom floor houses a pool
    hall and the top floor is used for residential apartments. He
    receives equal rents from both floors. What principal de-
    preciation methods are available to the taxpayer and how
    much depreciation would he be allowed in the first two years
    under those methods?

(c) Same as (b), above, except that both floors are rented exclu-
    sively for residential purposes.

(d) Same as (c), above, except that the building is a motel hous-
    ing transient guests.

(e) Same as (b), above, except that the building was acquired
    by Depreciator used, instead of new.

(f) Same as (c), above, except that the building was acquired by
    Depreciator used, instead of new.

* See Meir, "Tax Shelters and Real Estate: The Rehabilitation of Low Income Housing," 7 Suffolk U.L.R. 1
(1972) and Note, "Accelerated Depreciation for Housing Rehabilitation,"
79 Yale L.J. 961 (1970) Ed.

(g) Same as (e), above, except that the building is "substantially rehabilitated historic property" qualifying under § 167(*o*).

B. SALES AND EXCHANGES OF DEPRECIABLE PROPERTY

1. THE SECTION 1231 HOTCHPOT

Internal Revenue Code: Section 1231. See Sections 274(a)(1); 331; 741; 1221; 1222.
Regulations: Section 1.1231–1.

EXCERPT FROM SENATE FINANCE COMMITTEE REPORT NO. 91–552

91st Congress, 1st Session (1969).
1969–3 C.B. 423, 553–554.

Certain Casualty Losses Under Section 1231 (sec. 516(b) of the bill and sec. 1231(a) of the code) *

Present law.—Generally, under present law (sec. 1231(a) of the code), if the gains on the disposition of certain types of property exceed the losses on this same type of property, in effect, the excess is treated as long-term capital gain. On the other hand, if the losses exceed the gains, then the net loss is treated as an ordinary loss. The long-term gains or losses generally taken into account for purposes of this computation of net capital gains or net ordinary losses include recognized gains or losses from:

1. sales or exchanges of depreciable property and real estate used in a trade or business; and

2. the compulsory or involuntary conversion of capital assets held for 6 months and depreciable property and real estate used in a trade or business.

Other gains taken into account for this computation include certain gains from timber, coal, iron ore, livestock, and unharvested crops.

The Technical Amendments Act of 1958 [P.L. 85–866, C.B. 1958–3, 254] provided an exception to the rule described above. It provided that an uninsured loss on property (held for more than 6 months) resulting from fire, storm, shipwreck, or other casualty, or from theft, is not to be offset against gains treated as capital gains (that is, is not to be classified as a sec. 1231 loss) if the property was used in the

---

* See Andrews and Freeland, "Capital Gains and Losses of Individuals and Related Matters under the Tax Re- form Act of 1969," 12 Ariz.L.Rev. 627, 645 (1970). Ed.

taxpayer's trade or business (or was a capital asset held for the production of income). Thus, as a result of the 1958 amendment, these uninsured losses are deductible against ordinary income and are not required to be offset against gains which otherwise are treated as long-term capital gains. In other words, the 1958 amendment provided an exception to the general rule of section 1231 that the overall gain or loss position of the taxpayer under the section determines whether a loss is deductible against ordinary income or whether it must be used to offset what otherwise would be a capital gain.

General reasons for change.—The 1958 amendment was enacted to benefit business taxpayers who self-insure their business properties. Casualty losses on their business properties were excepted from section 1231 (and, thus, are fully deductible against ordinary income) in view of the fact that amounts added to their self-insurance reserves against casualty losses are not deductible although premiums paid to an outside insurance company for the same purpose by business taxpayers who are not self-insurers are deductible.

What may be considered somewhat anomalous results, however, have developed as a result of the 1958 amendment. On the one hand, a business taxpayer with a casualty loss on two similar business properties, one of which is insured and one of which is not, is allowed to deduct the loss on the uninsured property in full against ordinary income and at the same time is allowed to treat the gain on the insured property (the excess of the amount of insurance received over his adjusted basis in the property) as a capital gain. In other words, although this situation would appear to be squarely within the basic concept of section 1231 which requires losses to be netted against gains, such a netting is not required in this situation and, thus the loss rather than reducing the capital gain is deductible in full from ordinary income.

On the other hand, the basic offsetting of gains and losses is required where a business taxpayer only partially insures a business property. Thus, if a business taxpayer has a casualty loss on a business property which is only partially, perhaps 5 percent, insured, the deductibility of the loss against ordinary income is determined by the basic section 1231 rule which looks to the overall gain or loss position of the taxpayer. As indicated, however, if the property had not been insured at all, the loss would have been fully deductible against ordinary income without regard to the taxpayer's overall gain or loss position under section 1231.

The committee agrees with the House that the present distinction under section 1231 between insured and partially insured casualty losses is unrealistic. Moreover, the committee agrees that it is not appropriate to allow a business taxpayer to deduct an uninsured casualty loss on business property in full from ordinary income when he also has a larger casualty gain on insured business property which is treated as a capital gain.

Another problem which has arisen under section 1231 involves the basic scope of the section; namely, whether it is applicable to casualty losses on uninsured personal assets, such as a taxpayer's personal residence or nonbusiness automobile. The 1958 amendment does not apply if the destroyed property, whether or not completely uninsured, is a capital asset not held for the production of income or, in other words, a personal asset. In enacting this amendment, it appears Congress believed these uninsured casualty losses were subject to section 1231 and thus had to offset capital gains under the section, rather than being fully deductible against ordinary income. In initiating the 1958 amendment excluding uninsured casualty losses on business property from section 1231, this committee stated (S.Rept. 1983, 85th Cong., p. 204) : "On the other hand, the amendment does not apply to loss arising from the destruction or theft of the taxpayer's uninsured personal automobile." This would indicate that it was felt such a loss was otherwise included under section 1231.

Section 1231, however, has been interpreted by some courts to mean that a casualty loss is not subject to the provisions of that section unless the taxpayer receives some property or money as compensation for the loss. (See, for example, Maurer v. United States, 284 F.2d 122, where the 10th Circuit Court of Appeals held in 1960 that an uninsured casualty loss in 1954 did not give rise to a sec. 1231 loss; however, the Internal Revenue Service has announced it will not follow the decision and several courts since 1960 have refused to follow the *Maurer* decision.) The effect of the *Maurer* decision line of reasoning is to treat uninsured losses with respect to a taxpayer's personal assets, such as his residence or nonbusiness automobile, as fully deductible against ordinary income, rather than being required to offset under section 1231 what otherwise would be long-term capital gains.

Explanation of provision.—The House bill and the committee amendments modify the treatment of casualty losses and casualty gains under section 1231 to meet the problems discussed above. Under the bill, casualty (or theft) losses on depreciable property and real estate used in a trade or business and on capital assets held for 6 months [9 months as of 1977 and one year as of 1978. Ed.] are to be consolidated with casualty (or theft) gains on this type of property. If the casualty losses exceed the casualty gains, the net loss, in effect, will be treated as an ordinary loss (without regard to section 1231). On the other hand, if the casualty gains equal or exceed the casualty losses, then the gains and losses will be treated as section 1231 gains and losses which must then be consolidated with other gains and losses under section 1231.

This consolidation rule is to apply whether the casualty property is uninsured, partially insured, or totally insured. In addition, it is to apply in the case of casualty property which is a capital asset held for 6 months [9 months as of 1977 and one year as of 1978. Ed.] whether the property is business property, property held for the production of income or a personal asset. (Although the House clearly intended to include personal capital assets within this consolidation rule, they were inadvertently omitted from the House bill. The committee amendments correct this omission.)

The bill also clarifies the fact that uninsured casualty losses on a taxpayer's personal assets, such as his personal residence or nonbusiness automobile, are subject to the basic section 1231 provisions.

Effective date.—The committee amendments provide that this provision is to be effective with respect to taxable years beginning after December 31, 1969. Under the House bill, this provision would have been effective with respect to taxable years beginning after July 25, 1969.

STEPHEN P. WASNOK

Tax Court of the United States, 1971.
30 T.C.M. 39.

SACKS, COMMISSIONER: Respondent determined deficiencies in the income tax of petitioners for the taxable years and in the amounts set forth below:

Petitioner	Taxable Year	Amount
Stephen P. Wasnok	1967	$195.70
Mary Alice Wasnok	1967	158.66
Stephen P. and Mary Alice Wasnok	1968	54.46

The sole issue for decision is whether petitioners' disposition of certain real property at a loss constitutes an ordinary loss fully deductible in 1965, the year in which the loss was sustained, or a capital loss, deductible as a loss carryover in 1967 and 1968.

Findings of Fact

Most of the facts have been stipulated by the parties. Their stipulation, together with attached exhibits, is incorporated herein by this reference.

Stephen P. and Mary Alice Wasnok, sometimes hereinafter referred to as petitioners or as Stephen and Mary, are husband and wife who resided in Fullerton, California at the time of the filing of their petition herein. Their separate income tax returns for the taxable year 1967 and their joint income tax return for the taxable year 1968 were filed with the district director of internal revenue, Los Angeles, California.

In 1960 petitioners were residing in Cincinnati, Ohio. Sometime during that year they purchased a home there located at 5654 Sagecrest Drive, hereinafter referred to as the Sagecrest property. A substantial portion of the purchase price of this property was borrowed on a promissory note secured by a first mortgage on the property from Spring Grove Avenue Loan and Deposit Company (hereinafter referred to as Spring Grove Loan Co.).

Early in 1961 petitioners decided to move to California. They listed the Sagecrest property with its builder for sale, but without result since the market at the time was extremely poor. Finally, on June 15, 1961 petitioners leased the property for a monthly rental of $225.00 and thereafter departed for California.

Between June 15, 1961 and May 7, 1965 petitioners leased the Sagecrest property to various tenants at an average rental of $200.00 per month. Such tenants were located by advertising the property for rent in Cincinnati newspapers and by referrals from former neighbors. During this period petitioners on two occasions listed the property for sale with brokers, in each case, however, for only a ninety day period of time. Neither listing generated an offer for more than the amount due on the mortgage.

By 1965 petitioners found themselves unable to continue payments due on their note on the Sagecrest property to Spring Grove Loan Co. Spring Grove thereafter notified petitioners that they would either have to deed the property back or the company would have to institute foreclosure proceedings. On May 7, 1965 petitioners executed a deed conveying their interest in the Sagecrest property to Spring Grove Loan Co. in satisfaction of the then balance due on their note in the amount of $24,421.04.

For the taxable years 1961 through 1964 petitioners filed federal income tax returns reporting thereon rental income and claiming various expenses, including depreciation, on the Sagecrest property. Their return for 1961 was examined by the Internal Revenue Service and the cost basis of the land and improvements was agreed upon in the amount of $32,729.70. Total depreciation on the improvements claimed and allowed for the taxable years 1961 through 1964 was $4,697.42.

Petitioners did not file federal income tax returns for the taxable years 1965 and 1966 on the premise that no returns were required because no tax appeared to be due.

For 1965, however, petitioners had gross income in the amount of $5,603.21 and for 1966, in the amount of $3,180.00.

On their separate returns for the taxable year 1967, petitioners for the first time each claimed a capital loss carry-forward deduction in the amount of $1,000.00 which was predicated upon their disposition in 1965 of the Sagecrest property to Spring Grove Loan Co. Thereafter, on their joint return for 1968, petitioners claimed a further capital loss carry-forward deduction of $389.00, computed as follows:

Cost of Sagecrest property	$32,729.70
Less: depreciation taken	4,697.42
Adjusted basis	$28,032.28
Sale on May 7, 1965	24,421.04
Capital Loss	$ 3,611.24
Claimed in 1967 (separate return)	2,000.00
Sub-total	1,611.24
Claimed in 1968	$389.00 [1]
Balance to carry-over	$1,222.24

In his notices of deficiency, respondent disallowed to petitioners the claimed capital loss carry-over deductions for the taxable years 1967 and 1968 on the ground that the loss involved was an ordinary loss deductible in the year sustained (1965) rather than a capital loss subject to the carry-over provisions of the Internal Revenue Code of 1954.

Petitioners' disposition of the Sagecrest property at a loss constitutes an ordinary loss fully deductible in 1965, the year in which the loss was sustained and not a capital loss.

Opinion

It is petitioners' position herein that the Sagecrest property was a capital asset in their hands, and that its disposition at a loss resulted in a capital loss which they properly deferred deducting on their returns until 1967 and 1968 when they had sufficient income to file returns.

Respondent contends that the property in question was not a capital asset in petitioners' hands, but an asset of the type described in section 1231 of the Code [2] losses upon the disposition of which are ordinary in nature and required to be deducted, to the extent that there is gross income, in the year in which sustained. Since petitioners' gross income in 1965 was more than sufficient to absorb the loss in that year, no deduction of any kind is allowable in the years here at issue.

Section 1221 of the Code defines the term "capital asset" as any property held by the taxpayer, *excluding however*, "property used in his trade or business, of a character which is subject to the allowance for depreciation * * * or real property used in his trade or business." With respect to "property used in the trade or business"

---

1. The amount necessary to balance income with itemized deductions and exemptions for 1968.

2. [I.R.C. § 1231 is omitted. Ed.]

of a taxpayer, section 1231 provides that while net gains on sales or exchanges of such property shall be treated as capital gains, net losses are not to be treated as *capital* losses, but as *ordinary* losses.

The evidence presented to the Court is not complex. Simply stated, it shows that when petitioners moved from Ohio to California in 1961 they could not sell their residence in Ohio and therefore rented it to various tenants until May, 1965, when it was deeded back to the mortgagee because petitioners could no longer make the mortgage payments and did not desire the mortgagee to foreclose. It further shows that during the period 1961 through 1964 petitioners received rents of about two hundred dollars per month except for brief periods when the property was vacant. Their return for 1961 was examined by respondent and the tax basis for the property agreed upon. Depreciation was claimed on the improvements during the period 1961 to 1964 and, after reducing basis by the amount of depreciation claimed, the difference between the adjusted basis and mortgage balance produced a loss of $3,611.24.

In our view petitioners' activity in renting out the Sagecrest property for a fairly continuous period of four years between 1961 and 1965, at a substantial rental, together with the concurrent claiming on their income tax returns for these years of the expenses incurred in such rental activity, including depreciation, establishes the use of such property in a "trade or business." Leland Hazard, 7 T.C. 372 (1946).

We therefore find that the property in question was not a capital asset in petitioners' hands at the time of its disposition, but an asset of the kind described in section 1231. The loss sustained on the disposition of such an asset is an ordinary loss. Since such loss was sustained in 1965, when petitioners had gross income sufficient to entirely absorb it, no loss is allowable to petitioners in either 1967 or 1968.

Reviewed and adopted as the report of the Small Tax Case Division.

Decision will be entered for respondent.

NOTE

Stephen P. Wasnok is merely a current reaffirmation of a principle initially announced by the Tax Court in Leland Hazard [1], one of the "name" cases in this area. Whether it is a sound principle may be judged in part against the competing view of the Second Circuit, expressed as follows in Grier v. United States [2], another well-known case:

1. 7 T.C. 372 (1946), acq., 1946–2 C.B. 3.

2. 218 F.2d 603 (2d Cir. 1955); the quotation is from the opinion of the District Judge, 120 F.Supp. 395 (D.C. Conn.1954), adopted by the Court of Appeals in a per curiam affirmance.

In this case [quite similar to Wasnok Ed.] the activities with relation to this single dwelling, although of long duration, were minimal in nature. Activity to rent and re-rent was not required. No employees were regularly engaged for maintenance or repair.

Lacking the broader activities stressed in [cases other than Hazard which reached the 'business' result Ed.], the real estate in this case appears to partake more of the nature of property held for investment than property used in a trade or business. The property in this case, although used for the production of income, should not be considered as used in the taxpayer's trade or business.

Attention should be called as well to I.R.C. (26 U.S.C.A.) § 62(5) permitting an allowance in the determination of adjusted gross income of deductions, including losses, attributable to property held for the production of rent, even if such deductions do not come within § 62(1) as attributable to a trade or business of the taxpayer. Is there at least a negative inference here that not all rental activity constitutes business activity?

It would be a good time to reconsider the several classifications of profit-seeking activity as involving the conduct of a "trade or business," [3] property "held for the production of income," [4] or a "transaction entered into for profit." [5] For example, under the *Hazard* principle how would the taxpayer in *Horrmann* [6] have fared if he had been successful in attempts to rent the property in question?

And can you ever succeed in business (classification) only by really trying? If T opens up a new automobile dealership in December, 1977, but makes no sales until January, was he carrying on a trade or business in 1977? What about a young lawyer who hangs up his shingle in December but is carefully avoided by clients until the following year? [7]

INTERNATIONAL SHOE MACHINE CORPORATION v. U. S.

United States Court of Appeals, First Circuit, 1974.
491 F.2d 157.
Cert. den. 419 U.S. 834, 95 S.Ct. 59 (1974).

COFFIN, CHIEF JUDGE. Appellant taxpayer contends that the Commissioner of Internal Revenue erroneously treated income realiz-

3. See, e. g., Imbesi v. Comm'r, 361 F. 2d 640 (3rd Cir. 1966).

4. See, e. g., Bowers v. Lumpkin, supra, Chapter 16 at page 432.

5. See, e. g., William C. Horrmann, supra, Chapter 16 at page 454.

6. Supra note 5.

7. See, Cf., Morton Frank, supra, Chapter 15 at page 356.

ed from the appellant's sales of certain shoe machines as "property held by the taxpayer primarily for sale to customers in the ordinary course of his trade or business", 26 U.S.C. § 1231(b)(1)(B), thereby taxing it as ordinary income instead of treating it under the capital gains provisions of the Code, and assessing deficiencies against the taxpayer. After having paid the deficiencies, the appellant filed claims for refunds, which were denied, and then instituted the present case. The district court upheld the Commissioner's disposition.

It is undisputed that during the years in question, 1964 through 1966, appellant's main source of income derived from the leases of its shoe machinery equipment, rather than from their sales. The revenue from sales of the leased machinery comprised, respectively, only 7 per cent, 2 per cent, and 2 per cent of appellant's gross revenues. In fact, because the appellant preferred the more profitable route of leasing its machines, it never developed a sales force, never solicited purchases, set prices high to make purchasing unattractive, and even attempted to dissuade customers from purchasing them.

Yet the district court found that, beginning in 1964, when the investment tax credit made it more attractive for shoe manufacturers to buy shoe machinery rather than to lease it, the selling of machinery became an accepted and predictable, albeit small, part of appellant's business. Since appellant's chief competitor was selling leased shoe machines, it was necessary for appellant to offer its customers the same option. During the years in issue, appellant never declined to quote a price, nor did it ever decline to make a sale if the customer was persistent. Unlike previous years, purchase inquires were referred to the appellant's vice president for sales, normally charged with selling new, nonleased machines, whereupon a price was negotiated. A schedule was prepared, indicating the sales price of leased machines, based upon the number of years that the machines had been leased. In total, 271 machines were sold to customers who, at the time of the sales, had been leasing the machines for at least six months.

The case raises what has become a repeating source of difficulty in applying § 1231(b)(1)(B), which denies highly favored capital gains tax treatment to "property held . . . primarily for sale to customers in the ordinary course of his trade or business". In particular, does the word "primarily" invoke a contrast between sales and leases, as the appellant contends, or between sales made in the ordinary course of business and non-routine sales made as a liquidation of inventory? And, if the latter, how can sales made in the ordinary course of business be distinguished from a liquidation of inventory?

In support of its contention that "primarily" refers to a contrast between sales and leases, appellant relies upon Malat v. Riddell, 383 U.S. 569, 86 S.Ct. 1030, 16 L.Ed.2d 102 (1966). There, the taxpayer purchased a parcel of land, with the alleged intention of developing an apartment project. When the taxpayer confronted zoning restrictions, he decided to terminate the venture, and sold his interest in the property, claiming a capital gain. The lower courts found, however, that the taxpayer had had a "dual purpose" in acquiring the land, a "substantial" one of which was to sell if that were to prove more profitable than development. Therefore, since the taxpayer had failed to establish that the property was not held primarily for sale to customers in the ordinary course of his business, his gain was treated as ordinary income. The Supreme Court vacated and remanded the case, stating that the lower courts had applied an incorrect legal standard when they defined "primarily" as merely "substantially" rather than using it in its ordinary, everyday sense of "first importance" or "principally". Although the Court in *Malat* was dealing with § 1221, rather than § 1231, the same clause appears in both sections. Appellant argues that the present case is analogous, since the "first" and "principal" reason for holding the shoe machinery was clearly for lease rather than for sale.

We cannot agree that *Malat* is dispositive. Even if "primarily" is defined as "of first importance" or "principally", the word may still invoke a contrast between sales made in the "ordinary course of . . . business" and those made as liquidations of inventory, rather than between leases and sales. *Malat* itself concerned the dual purposes of developing an apartment complex on the land and selling the land. Although these two possible sources of income might be characterized as income from "lease" or "sale", a more meaningful distinction could be made between on-going income generated in the ordinary course of business and income from the termination and sale of the venture. See Continental Can Co. v. United States, 422 F.2d 405, 411 (Ct.Cl.1970); Recordak Corp. v. United States, 325 F.2d 460, 463 (Ct.Cl.1963).

We recognize that *Recordak*, invoking a contrast between "selling in the ordinary course of business and selling outside that normal course" was cited by the Supreme Court in *Malat* within a footnote which also listed the courts of appeals decisions then in conflict over the meaning of "primarily", supra, 383 U.S. at 571 n. 3, 86 S.Ct. 1030, 16 L.Ed.2d 102. Given, however, that *Recordak* was not directly included within the list, but merely cited as a case which had also addressed the question, we think that *Recordak's* interpretation of the contrast invoked by the word "primarily" remains undisturbed by the Court's opinion. Beyond semantics, an additional justification for the interpretation becomes obvious when one applies appellant's logic to a not unrealistic business situation: to rest the word "primarily" on the distinction between lease and sale income would lead to the absurd result that whenever lease income exceeded sale income on the same item, the sale income could be treated as capital gain.

The real question, therefore, concerns whether or not the income from the sales of appellant's shoe machinery should have been characterized as having been generated in the "ordinary course of . . . business". Appellant contests the conclusion of the district court that selling was "an accepted and predictable part of the business" by pointing out that sales were made only as a last resort, after attempts to dissuade the customer from purchasing had failed. We think that the district court was correct in its finding. While sales were made only as a last resort, it seems clear that after 1964 such sales were expected to occur, on an occasional basis, and policies and procedures were developed for handling them. Purchase inquiries were referred to the vice president for sales, a price schedule was drawn up, and discounts were offered to good customers. Appellant may not have desired such sales. It is likely that appellant would never have developed a sales policy for its leased machines had it not been forced to do so by the pressure of competition. But it was justifiable to find that such occasional sales were indeed "accepted and predictable".

Even "accepted and predictable" sales might not, however, occur in the "ordinary course of . . . business". For example, a final liquidation of inventory, although accepted and predictable, would normally be eligible for capital gains treatment. Appellant's final contention, therefore, is that the sales in question represented the liquidation of an investment. Appellant points out that the machines were leased for an average of eight and one half years before they were sold, during which time depreciation was taken on them and repairs were made. Thus, appellant seeks to bring itself within the scope of the "rental-obsolescence" decisions, which hold that the sale of rental equipment, no longer useful for renting, is taxable at capital gains rates. Hilliard v. Commissioner of Internal Revenue, 281 F.2d 279 (5th Cir. 1960) ; Philber Equipment Corporation v. Commissioner of Internal Revenue, 237 F.2d 129 (3d Cir. 1956) ; Davidson v. Tomlinson, 165 F.Supp. 455 (S.D.Fla.1958).

In the "rental obsolescence" decisions, however, equipment was sold only after its rental income-producing potential had ended and "such sales were . . . the natural conclusion of a vehicle rental business cycle". *Philber*, supra, 237 F.2d 132. Moreover, the equipment was specifically manufactured to fit the requirements of lessees; it was sold only when lessees no longer found the equipment useful. Id. In the present case, however, the shoe manufacturing equipment was sold, not as a final disposition of property that had ceased to produce rental income for the appellant, but, rather, as property that still retained a rental income producing potential for the appellant. Had appellant chosen not to sell the shoe machinery, the machinery would have continued to generate ordinary income in the form of lease revenue. Thus, the sale of such machinery, for a price which included the present value of that future ordinary income, cannot be considered the liquidation of an investment outside the scope of the "ordinary course of . . . business".

Affirmed.

WILLIAMS v. McGOWAN

United States Court of Appeals, Second Circuit, 1945.
152 F.2d 570.

L. HAND, CIRCUIT JUDGE. This is an appeal from a judgment dismissing the complaint in an action by a taxpayer to recover income taxes paid for the year 1940. [After holding that attorneys' fees incurred in obtaining an income tax refund were deductible under an earlier version of I.R.C. § 212, the opinion moved to a second issue. Ed.]

Williams, the taxpayer, and one, Reynolds, had for many years been engaged in the hardware business in the City of Corning, New York. On the 20th of January, 1926, they formed a partnership, of which Williams was entitled to two-thirds of the profits, and Reynolds, one-third. They agreed that on February 1, 1925, the capital invested in the business had been $118,082.05, of which Reynolds had a credit of $29,029.03, and Williams, the balance—$89,053.02. At the end of every business year, on February 1st, Reynolds was to pay to Williams, interest upon the amount of the difference between his share of the capital and one-third of the total as shown by the inventory; and upon withdrawal of one party the other was to have the privilege of buying the other's interest as it appeared on the books. The business was carried on through the firm's fiscal year, ending January 31, 1940, in accordance with this agreement, and thereafter until Reynolds' death on July 18th of that year. Williams settled with Reynolds' executrix on September 6th in an agreement by which he promised to pay her $12,187.90, and to assume all liabilities of the business; and he did pay her $2,187.98 in cash at once, and $10,000 on the 10th of the following October. On September 17th of the same year, Williams sold the business as a whole to the Corning Building Company for $63,926.28—its agreed value as of February 1, 1940— "plus an amount to be computed by multiplying the gross sales of the business from the first day of February, 1940 to the 28th day of September, 1940," by an agreed fraction. This value was made up of cash of about $8100, receivables of about $7000, fixtures of about $800, and a merchandise inventory of about $49,000, less some $1000 for bills payable. To this was added about $6,000 credited to Williams for profits under the language just quoted, making a total of nearly $70,000. Upon this sale Williams suffered a loss upon his original two-thirds of the business, but he made a small gain upon the one-third which he had bought from Reynolds' executrix; and in his income tax return he entered both as items of "ordinary income," and not as transactions in "capital assets." This the Commissioner disallowed and recomputed the tax accordingly; Williams paid the deficiency and sued to recover it in this action. The only question is whether the business was "capital assets" under § 117(a) (1) of the Internal Revenue Code, 26 U.S. C.A. Int.Rev.Code, § 117(a) (1).

It has been held that a partner's interest in a going firm is for tax purposes to be regarded as a "capital asset." Stilgenbaur v. United States, 9 Cir., 115 F.2d 283; Commissioner v. Shapiro, 6 Cir., 125 F.2d 532, 144 A.L.R. 349. We too accepted the doctrine in McClellan v. Commissioner, 2 Cir., 117 F.2d 988, although we had held the opposite in Helvering v. Smith, 2 Cir., 90 F.2d 590, 591, where the partnership articles had provided that a retiring partner should receive as his share only his percentage of the sums "actually collected" and "of all earnings * * * for services performed." Such a payment, we thought, was income; and we expressly repudiated the notion that the Uniform Partnership Act had, generally speaking, changed the firm into a juristic entity. See also Doyle v. Commissioner, 4 Cir., 102 F.2d 86. If a partner's interest in a going firm is "capital assets" perhaps a dead partner's interest is the same. New York Partnership Law §§ 61, 62(4), Consol.Laws N.Y. c. 39. We need not say. When Williams bought out Reynolds' interest, he became the sole owner of the business, the firm had ended upon any theory, and the situation for tax purposes was no other than if Reynolds had never been a partner at all, except that to the extent of one-third of the "amount realized" on Williams' sale to the Corning Company, his "basis" was different. The judge thought that, because upon that sale both parties fixed the price at the liquidation value of the business while Reynolds was alive, "plus" its estimated earnings thereafter, it was as though Williams had sold his interest in the firm during its existence. But the method by which the parties agreed upon the price was irrelevant to the computation of Williams' income. The Treasury, if that served its interest, need not heed any fiction which the parties found it convenient to adopt; nor need Williams do the same in his dealings with the Treasury. We have to decide only whether upon the sale of a going business it is to be comminuted into its fragments, and these are to be separately matched against the definition in § 117(a) (1), or whether the whole business is to be treated as if it were a single piece of property.

Our law has been sparing in the creation of juristic entities; it has never, for example, taken over the Roman "universitas facti"; [1] and indeed for many years it fumbled uncertainly with the concept of a corporation.[2] One might have supposed that partnership would have been an especially promising field in which to raise up an entity, particularly since merchants have always kept their accounts upon that basis. Yet there too our law resisted at the price of great and continuing confusion; and, even when it might be thought that a statute admitted, if it did not demand, recognition of the firm as an entity, the old concepts prevailed. Francis v. McNeal, 228 U.S. 695,

---

1. "By universitas facti is meant a number of things of the same kind which are regarded as a whole; e. g. a herd, a stock of wares." Mackeldey, Roman Law § 162.

2. "To the 'church' modern law owes its conception of a juristic person, and the clear line that it draws between 'the corporation aggregate' and the sum of its members." Pollack & Maitland, Vol. 1, p. 489.

33 S.Ct. 701, 57 L.Ed. 1029, L.R.A.1915E, 706. And so, even though we might agree that under the influence of the Uniform Partnership Act a partner's interest in the firm should be treated as indivisible, and for that reason a "capital asset" within § 117(a) (1), we should be chary about extending further so exotic a jural concept. Be that as it may, in this instance the section itself furnishes the answer. It starts in the broadest way by declaring that all "property" is "capital assets," and then makes three exceptions. The first is "stock in trade * * * or other property of a kind which would properly be included in the inventory"; next comes "property held * * * primarily for sale to customers"; and finally, property "used in the trade or business of a character which is subject to * * * allowance for depreciation." In the face of this language, although it may be true that a "stock in trade," taken by itself, should be treated as a "universitas facti," by no possibility can a whole business be so treated; and the same is true as to any property within the other exceptions. Congress plainly did mean to comminute the elements of a business; plainly it did not regard the whole as "capital assets."

As has already appeared, Williams transferred to the Corning Company "cash," "receivables," "fixtures" and a "merchandise inventory." "Fixtures" are not capital because they are subject to a depreciation allowance; the inventory, as we have just seen, is expressly excluded. So far as appears, no allowance was made for "goodwill"; but, even if there had been, we held in Haberle Crystal Springs Brewing Company v. Clarke, Collector, 2 Cir., 30 F.2d 219, that "goodwill" was a depreciable intangible. It is true that the Supreme Court reversed that judgment—280 U.S. 384, 50 S.Ct. 155, 74 L.Ed. 498—but it based its decision only upon the fact that there could be no allowance for the depreciation of "good-will" in a brewery, a business condemned by the Eighteenth Amendment. There can of course be no gain or loss in the transfer of cash; and, although Williams does appear to have made a gain of $1072.71 upon the "receivables," the point has not been argued that they are not subject to a depreciation allowance. That we leave open for decision by the district court, if the parties cannot agree. The gain or loss upon every other item should be computed as an item in ordinary income.

Judgment reversed.

FRANK, CIRCUIT JUDGE (dissenting in part).

I agree that it is irrelevant that the business was once owned by a partnership. For when the sale to the Corning Company occurred, the partnership was dead, had become merely a memory, a ghost. To say that the sale was of the partnership's assets would, then, be to indulge in animism.

But I do not agree that we should ignore what the parties to the sale, Williams and the Corning Company, actually did. They did not arrange for a transfer to the buyer, as if in separate bundles, of the several ingredients of the business. They contracted for the sale of the entire business as a going concern. Here is what they said in their agreement: "The party of the first part agrees to sell and the party of the second part agrees to buy, *all of the right, title and interest* of the said party of the first part *in and to the hardware business* now being conducted by the said party of the first part, *including* cash on hand and on deposit in the First National Bank & Trust Company of Corning in the A. F. Williams Hardware Store account, in accounts receivable, bills receivable, notes receivable, merchandise and fixtures, including two G. M. trucks, good will and all other assets of every kind and description used in and about said business.[1] * * * Said party of the first part agrees not to engage in the hardware business within a radius of twenty-five miles from the City of Corning, New York, for a period of ten years from the 1st day of October 1940."

To carve up this transaction into distinct sales—of cash, receivables, fixtures, trucks, merchandise, and good will—is to do violence to the realities. I do not think Congress intended any such artificial result. * * *

PROBLEMS

1. Hotchpot engaged in (or encountered) the following transactions (or events) in the current year, when he had a sizeable taxable income and apart from the transactions below no capital gains or losses. Determine separately for each part (a) through (f), how the matters indicated will affect Hotchpot's tax liability for the current year.

   (a) Hotchpot sells some land (#1) held for several years which was used in his business for $20,000. It had cost him $10,-000. The state condemns some other land (#2) he held as an investment for several years which was purchased for $18,000 and is sold for $16,000.

   (b) Same as (a), above, including same basis except that both pieces of land were inherited from Hotchpot's Uncle who died three months ago.

   (c) Hotchpot sells a building held for several years and used in his business which he depreciated using the straight line method. The sale price is $15,000 and the adjusted basis $5,000. His two year old family car is destroyed in a fire. The car, which had cost $10,000, was worth $8,100 prior to the fire and was totally destroyed. He received $6,000 in insurance proceeds.

   (d) In addition to the building and car in (c), above, assume that Hotchpot owned a painting, held as an investment, which he

---

1. Emphasis added.

purchased two years ago and which was also destroyed in the fire. The painting had been purchased for $4,000 and he received $8,000 in insurance proceeds for it.

(e) In addition to the building sale, car loss, and painting gain in (c) and (d), above, assume Hotchpot sells land used for several years in his business for $30,000. The land which had "hopefully" contained oil had been purchased for $50,000.

(f) Would Hotchpot be pleased if the Commissioner successfully alleged that the land in problem (e), above, was held as an investment rather than for use in Hotchpot's business?

2. Car Dealer uses some cars for demonstration purposes. Are those cars depreciable? Disregarding § 1245 if they are held more than a year does gain on their sale qualify for § 1231(a) main hotchpot treatment? See Rev.Rul. 75–538, 1975–2 C.B. 34.

3. Recall from Chapter 21, at page 680 of the text, that under the *Corn Products* doctrine if a transaction is an integral part of the taxpayer's trade or business the courts treat gains or losses on it as ordinary even though the specific property involved might appear to be within the definition of capital assets. Notice as well that both the *Corn Products* and *Sewall* cases involved such property. If a taxpayer sells depreciable property used in his trade or business at a gain, is that transaction such an integral part of his trade or business as to generate ordinary income? With respect to interrelationship of the *Corn Products* doctrine and § 1231, the Ninth Circuit Court has stated:

> "Whether property comes under § 1221 (and is therefore *defined* as a capital asset) or whether it comes under § 1231 (and is therefore *treated* as a capital asset even though it is excluded from the § 1221 definition) should make no difference, because the policy is the same—not to give preferential treatment to profits and losses arising from the everyday operation of the business. * * * We do not see why the fact that the property is subject to depreciation should make any difference." Hollywood Baseball Ass'n v. Comm'r, 423 F.2d 494, 498 (9th Cir. 1970), cert. den. 400 U.S. 848 (1970).

In the District Court opinion of the *International Shoe Machine Corporation* case, 369 F.Supp. 588 (D.Mass.1973), (the First Circuit affirmance which does not rely on the *Corn Products* doctrine appears at page 680) the Court stated:

> Recognizing the impact on its case that application of the *Corn Products* principles would have, plaintiff contends that *Corn Products* should not be applied to a case arising under § 1231 but should be restricted to § 1221 cases. We do

not agree. . . . . The general principles enumerated in *Corn Products* would be significant in any case where there is a question whether a business disposition of its products is to be accorded capital gain or ordinary income treatment. Secondly, the phrase in *Malat* that the Supreme Court construed, using *Corn Products* as one of its guides, is identical to the phrase in § 1231 which plaintiff invokes here. Sections 1221(1) and 1231(b)(1)(B) both exclude from capital gains treatment income realized from sales of "property held by the taxpayer primarily for sale to customers in the ordinary course of his trade or business. . . . " Thirdly, the Court of Appeals for the Ninth Circuit in Hollywood Baseball Ass'n v. C. I. R., 9 Cir. 1970, 423 F.2d 494, held that *Corn Products* applies to § 1231 assets in an opinion analyzing a contrary holding in Deltide Fishing & Rental Tools v. United States, (E.D.La.1968), 279 F.Supp. 661.

If the *Corn Products* doctrine can apply to withdraw property from the § 1231 category, just as in *Corn Products* itself it operated to withdraw property from the § 1221 category, when should that result be reached? It is possible that *use* of depreciable property can be an important facet of the taxpayer's business operation without the *sale* of such property being treated as an integral part of the business?

4. Merchant who has been in business for several years sells his sole proprietorship which has the following assets. Except for the inventory, all the assets have been held for more than one year.

	Adjusted Basis	*Fair Market Value*
Inventory	$ 8,000	$ 16,000
Goodwill	0	20,000
Land (used in business)	30,000	20,000
Building (used in business)	15,000	20,000
Machinery & Equipment		
(used in business)	12,000	14,000
Total	$ 65,000	$ 90,000

Merchant also agrees that for an additional $10,000 he will not compete in the same geographic area during the succeeding ten years.

(a) Disregarding any consideration of §§ 1245 and 1250, which are considered in the succeeding subchapters of the text, what are the tax consequences to Merchant on his sale of the Business for $100,000?

(b) What difference in result if Merchant's business is incorporated, he is the sole shareholder, and he has a $70,000 basis in the stock which he sells for $90,000, assuming that he is again paid an additional $10,000 for his covenant not to compete?

———————

2. CHARACTERIZATION UNDER SECTION 1239

Internal Revenue Code: Section 1239.

———————

UNITED STATES v. PARKER *

United States Court of Appeals, Fifth Circuit, 1967.
376 F.2d 402.

GOLDBERG, CIRCUIT JUDGE: The protesting and unhappy taxpayers, Curtis L. Parker and his wife, Martha, owned a wholesale and retail oil and gasoline business. On April 1, 1959, Parker and B. K. Eaves, a longtime employee, formed a Louisiana corporation incorporating Parker's business. The corporation had an authorized capital stock of 1,000 shares.

Parker subscribed to 800 shares and paid for them by transferring to the corporation certain property valued at $93,400.00 to be used in the corporation's business. Eaves subscribed to the remaining 200 shares. He paid $7,500.00 cash and agreed to pay the balance of $23,350.00 over a period of 5 years.

At the first meeting of the corporation's board of directors a resolution was passed accepting Eaves's subscription. He was issued stock certificates for the amount of stock paid for at that time (64.239 shares), and the board of directors resolved that the remainder of Eaves's stock certificates would be issued as their purchase price was paid. The Articles of Incorporation included a provision stating that none of the stock of the corporation might be transferred unless the stock were first offered to the corporation at the same price offered by the proposed transferee. (If the corporation did not accept the offer, another stockholder could.)

Parker and Eaves also entered into a stockholders' agreement which provided that whenever Eaves's employment should terminate for any reason, including death, his shares would then be purchased by Parker at a price to be governed by the fair market value per share of the corporation's assets, specifically excluding good will "or any other intangible asset." The value per share was set at $116.75 for the first year of the corporation's existence (until April 1, 1960), and thereafter the price was to be set by agreement between Parker and Eaves, with arbitration if they could not agree.

The face of all stock certificates issued to Parker and Eaves carried notice of the restriction on sale created by the Articles of In-

———————

* Some footnotes are omitted, others renumbered. Ed.

corporation. Only the stock certificates issued to Eaves carried a legend that they were subject to the Eaves-Parker buy-and-sell agreement.

Also, at the first meeting of the board of directors, Parker sold to the corporation certain other assets which were depreciable property (such as motor vehicles, furniture and fixtures, and other equipment which Parker had apparently used in the business before the incorporation) worth $95,738.70. The corporation was to pay for this property in ten annual installments with interest of 5 per cent. Parker elected to treat the sale as a capital transaction, and reported the gain from it as long term capital gain. IRC § 1231.

The present suit arises because the Internal Revenue Service treated the gain as ordinary income under IRC § 1239, based upon the contention that the taxpayers owned more than 80 per cent "in value" of all outstanding stock of the corporation at the time of sale. The Service assessed deficiencies for the calendar years 1959, 1960, and 1961. Taxpayers paid the assessments under protest and sued in district court for a refund. 28 U.S.C.A. § 1346(a). The district court granted summary judgment for the taxpayers, and the government appeals. We reverse.

* * *

[T]he government argues that even if the full 20 per cent of the shares allotted to Eaves was "outstanding" at the time of the sale, "the restrictions placed upon those shares and their inherent limitations made them worth less per share than Parker's." We * * * agree.

Section 1239 prevents capital gain treatment of a "sale or exchange" of depreciable property to a controlled corporation or a spouse. Without this section a taxpayer who had property which had been depreciated to a low basis could sell that property to a controlled corporation or spouse and pay only capital gains rates on the gain. The transferee (who is virtually identical to the transferor in the proscribed area) could then redepreciate the property, using the sale price as a new basis. The depreciation, of course, would be deducted from ordinary income.[1] Section 1239 renders such a scheme

1. The net effect may be shown graphically in a hypothetical case: R, the transferor, holds property depreciated to a value of $2,000. R sells the property for $6,000 to E, his controlled corporation. R pays a maximum capital gains tax of 25 per cent on the $4,000 gain, or a tax of $1,000. E, with a basis of $6,000 on the property takes depreciation deductions from ordinary income. After four or five years of these deductions E has depreciated the property back to the $2,000 basis. (See depreciation guidelines in Rev.Proc. 62–21; rates of depreciation in Rev.Proc. 65–13, Appendix I, Table A.) E has by then deducted $4,000 in depreciation from ordinary income. If E is in the 50 per cent bracket, the $4,000 in depreciation deductions has saved him $2,000 in income taxes. R has therefore paid a $1,000 capital gains tax and has saved E $2,000 in income taxes. If R and E are identical (and in cases covered by § 1239 they certainly may be considered so), then R has avoided $2,000 in taxes by paying only $1,000.

profitless by taxing the gain on the transfer at ordinary rather than capital rates.

The issue here, of course, is whether Parker's corporation is sufficiently Parker's slave to justify invocation of § 1239. We have concluded that Parker owned, for purposes of § 1239, exactly 80 per cent of the corporation's outstanding stock. The decisive question now is whether this 80 per cent is, under § 1239, "more than 80 per cent *in value* of the outstanding stock." [emphasis added]

We first note what § 1239 does not say. It does not use the standard of § 368(c) which is invoked by § 351 for transfers to a controlled corporation in exchange for that corporation's stock or securities. Control is defined by § 368(c) as

> "ownership of stock possessing at least 80 percent of the total combined *voting power* of all classes of stock entitled to vote and at least 80 percent of the total *number* of shares of all other classes of stock of the corporation." [emphasis added]

By contrast, § 1239 says "more than 80 per cent *in value*." The words "in value" in § 1239 must have some **meaning.** Trotz v. Commissioner of Internal Revenue, 10 Cir. 1966, 361 F.2d 927, 930. We cannot indulge in statutory interpretation by excision. Statutory explication may be an art, but it must not be artful. Further, we cannot say that by using "in value" Congress intended us to consider only the factors of voting power or number of shares. "If the 80% determination is to be [merely] on the basis of the number of shares outstanding, no reason exists for the use of the words 'in value'." Trotz v. Commissioner of Internal Revenue, supra, 361 F.2d at 930. Or, if number of shares and voting power were the sole indicia, Congress could have limited § 1239 by using terms similar to those which § 351 draws from § 368(c) in an analogous situation within the Code's framework. "In value" is a broader phrase, and we think that it calls for the familiar, though difficult, process of fair market valuation.[2]

"The value of property is an underlying factor in a great number of income tax cases, particularly in such areas of the law as those involving the receipt of income, the computation of gain or loss,

2. The district judge stated his findings of fact and conclusions of law with explicitness. He concluded, as do we, that market valuation was the proper test for § 1239. He found as a matter of law, however, that neither the restrictions on salability of the Eaves stock nor its minority position reduced its value per share, and it is here that we disagree. However, partly because of the peculiar circumstances of this case, but largely because the district judge stated his findings and conclusions so clearly and distinctly and isolated with precision the ground for his holding, we have been able to render unnecessary the remand which would usually be required. Even though we disagree on one point, the opinion of the district judge epitomizes the result sought by Rule 52(a), and thereby promotes the "just, speedy, and inexpensive determination of every action" sought by Rule 1.

depreciation and depletion." 10 Mertens, Law of Federal Income Taxation § 59.01 (1964 revision). Value is not a strange or alien concept in tax law, and we have held that "There is no distinction, for most purposes * * *, in the meaning of fair market value as used in an estate tax case and one involving income tax." Champion v. Commissioner, 5 Cir. 1962, 303 F.2d 887, 892–893.

We next note that in the present case Eaves owned exactly 20 per cent of the outstanding stock, and Parker owned exactly 80 per cent. Therefore, if any fact can be found which shows that the value per share of Parker's stock exceeded by any amount, no matter how small, the value per share of Eaves's, then Parker owned more than 80 per cent in value of the outstanding stock. While it is true that Parker and Eaves owned the same class of stock, Eaves's stock was burdened with impedimenta from which Parker's stock was free. We hold that as a matter of law these impedimenta must have decreased the value per share of Eaves's stock, and as we need only show that this value per share was lower by any indeterminate amount, no matter how miniscule, than the value per share of Parker's stock, we are able to render judgment here without remand.[3]

The impedimenta which depress the value spring from two sources.

A. *The restrictions on transfer of stock.* Eaves's stock was encumbered by two kinds of restrictions. First, the articles of incorporation stated that the corporation had the right of first refusal of any offer to sell to a third party. Second, Eaves's agreement with Parker stated that if Eaves left the employ of the corporation for any reason, he must sell all of his stock to Parker at a price representing the value per share of the assets, specifically excluding good will. Notice to the world of these restrictions, like the mark of Cain, was on the face of Eaves's stock certificates.

The practical effect of these restrictions was to reduce the number of opportunities for Eaves to sell or give away the stock and to place a limit (the duration of his employment) upon the period when he might hold the stock. "A commodity freely salable is obviously worth more on the market than a precisely similar commodity which cannot be freely sold." Judge Woodbury for the First Circuit in Worcester County Trust Co. v. Commissioner of Internal Revenue, 1 Cir. 1943, 134 F.2d 578, 582.

---

3. In this aspect the present case differs from Trotz v. Commissioner of Internal Revenue, supra. There, the taxpayer Trotz owned 79 per cent of the outstanding stock and the lesser shareholder owned 21 per cent. The Tenth Circuit remanded the case for a factual determination by the Tax Court of whether any difference between the values per share of the large and small blocks brought Trotz's holding above 80 per cent in value. In contrast, in the present case any extra value per share in Parker's stock will bring his holding above 80 per cent in value. No determination is needed of how much more per share Parker's stock is worth.

The alienability of Parker's stock was restricted only by the limitation imposed by the articles of incorporation. Whether this limitation, in the light of Parker's complete control, had any real effect on alienability we need not consider, for Eaves's stock was burdened not only by the articles but also by the extra and potent limitation of the buy-sell agreement. Even if we consider the Eaves and Parker stock as identically limited by the articles, Parker's stock was not affected by the buy-sell agreement; Eaves's was. "In our view it must be said that the restriction necessarily has a depressing effect upon the value of the stock in the market." Worcester County Trust Co., supra, 134 F.2d at 582. That such an extra limitation on alienability would depress market value to some greater extent is a well-recognized proposition: Mailloux v. Commissioner of Internal Revenue, 5 Cir. 1963, 320 F.2d 60; James v. Commissioner of Internal Revenue, 2 Cir. 1945, 148 F.2d 236; Kirby v. Commissioner of Internal Revenue, 5 Cir. 1939, 102 F.2d 115; Mathews v. United States, E.D.N.Y.1964, 226 F.Supp. 1003; Baltimore National Bank v. United States, D.Md.1955, 136 F.Supp. 642. "Separation of the power of alienation from the ownership of property, or other forms of restriction against transfer, have in numerous cases been held to lessen the value of property." 10 Mertens, Law of Federal Income Taxation § 59.20 (1964 Rev.).

B. *The lack of control.* Eaves owned only 20 per cent of the stock. This left Parker in sole control of the corporation's affairs. Parker could, without Eaves, elect and remove directors and officers, amend the articles, and promulgate by-laws. He could dissolve the corporation. 5 LSA–R.S. § 12:54. With these powers, Parker controlled without possibility of challenge the entire operation from the smallest detail to the largest. He exercised so much power that the corporation was his alter ego, or his slave. This is the situation at which § 1239 aims.

Any purchaser of Eaves's stock would not be buying any degree of control over the corporation. The voting power which technically inhered in Eaves's stock was in reality worthless; Parker owned all of the real voting stock.

We hold that this disability which inhered in Eaves's stock reduced its value per share below that of Parker's stock as a matter of law. Cravens v. Welch, S.D.Cal.1935, 10 F.Supp. 94; Irene de Guebriant, 14 T.C. 611 (1950), rev'd on other grounds sub nom. Clafin v. Commissioner of Internal Revenue, 2 Cir. 1951, 186 F.2d 307; Mathilde B. Hooper, 41 B.T.A. 114 (1940). See Mathews v. United States, supra; Worthen v. United States, D.Mass.1961, 192 F.Supp. 727.

> "Even absent any contemplated change in management, control increases the value of an investment by protecting it. The power to change the management, even while unexer-

cised, protects the investor with control against an abrupt change by someone else and against a gradual deterioration of the incumbent management. Therefore, in a sense, controlling shares are inherently worth more than noncontrolling shares for reasons relating solely to investment value. When control is diffused, the same reasoning establishes, to a lesser degree, that shares enabling their holder to participate in control are worth more than those that do not. This is the strongest part of any argument against a broad reading of [Perlman v. Feldmann, 2 Cir. 1955, 219 F.2d 173, cert. denied 349 U.S. 952, 75 S.Ct. 880, 99 L.Ed. 1277 (1955)]. It is the kernel of truth in the assertion that a premium paid for controlling shares only shows that controlling shares are inherently worth more than minority shares." Andrews, The Stockholder's Right to Equal Opportunity in the Sale of Shares, 78 Harvard L.Rev. 505, 526 (1965).[4]

In the vast majority of cases, courts of appeals have remanded where, as here, the lower courts failed to take into account all of the existing impedimenta on market value. For instance, in Kirby v. Commissioner of Internal Revenue, supra, we said:

"The Board [of Tax Appeals] * * * declined to make any allowance against the value [of the stock] for the burden of the contract under which the stock had been bought and held. The result was neither, a true nor a fair, [sic] determination of value. The finding which mirrors that result cannot stand.

"Therefore * * * we reverse the order of the Board, and remand * * * for a redetermination * * *." 102 F.2d at 118.

We reiterate that in the present case it is sufficient for the rendering of judgment to note that the restriction on Eaves's stock and its minority qualities combine to have some depressing effect, no matter how small, on its value per share. We hold, therefore, that Parker owned more than 80 per cent in value of the corporation's stock, and that any gain on the sale of the depreciable property was properly taxed at ordinary rates. We render judgment for the government.

Reversed and rendered.

---

4. This entire article is concerned with the inherent disparity of value between controlling and non-controlling shares. Professor Andrews proposes a remedy to allow minority shareholders to share in the premium paid for controlling stock, but that remedy is not part of the law of Louisiana; the article's call for a remedy demonstrates how real the problem is.

NOTE

The Tax Reform Act of 1976 made important changes in § 1239. For example, the ownership attribution rules of § 318 are now incorporated into § 1239 by § 1239(c). This alters the result properly reached under § 1239 in an important earlier case. In Mitchell v. Commissioner [1] a question was whether the stock held in trust for a minor child of the taxpayer could be attributed to the taxpayer to make applicable the 80 percent rule of § 1239. The court held it could not be under language that made reference to stock owned by "his minor children"; but under § 318 a taxpayer is treated as owning stock owned "directly or *indirectly*, by or *for*" his children. Stock held in trust for a child is obviously held indirectly for the child.

In Miller v. Commissioner [2] the court properly held § 1239 inapplicable to a sale between corporations owned by the same person. However under new § 1239(b)(3) corporations owned by the same person are now "related persons" between which sales and exchanges are affected by § 1239.

The result in United States v. Parker, the principal case above, is unaffected by the 1976 changes in § 1239. Nevertheless, the student should note a 1976 change in § 1239 from a "more than 80 percent" test to an "80 percent or more" test.[3]

PROBLEMS

1. Depreciator is a shareholder of Redepreciation Corporation and owns 30% of its stock. Depreciator's wife owns 20% of the stock, his adult son owns 20% and the remaining 30% is owned by unrelated persons. Depreciator sells a building used in his business and depreciated on the straight line method with a $40,000 adjusted basis and an $80,000 value and the land underlying it with a $10,000 adjusted basis and $30,000 value to Redepreciation for $110,000. The building will be used in the business of Redepreciation.

(a) What is the amount and character of the gain on the sale?

(b) What result if the 30% owned by outsiders was owned instead only 20% by outsiders and 10% by Depreciator's grandchildren?

(c) What result in (b), above, if grandchildren's stock is held in a trust for their benefit?

(d) What result if the property was Depreciator's residence and the sale was made by Depreciator to his wife? They rent an apartment and she rents the old residence out to Tenant?

1. 300 F.2d 533 (4th Cir. 1962).

2. 510 F.2d 230 (9th Cir. 1975).

3. See Beller, "The More—Than—80% Requirement of Section 1239: Identifying and Avoiding its Pitfalls," 43 J.Tax. 194 (1975).

(e) Do your answers suggest the purpose and scope of § 1239?

2. Depreciator owns 100% of both X and Y corporations and X corporation sells the building and land described in problem 1 to Y corporation, which will use them in its business. Is § 1239 applicable to any part of the sale?

---

3. RECAPTURE UNDER SECTION 1245

Internal Revenue Code: Section 1245(a), (b) (1) and (2), (c), (d). See Sections 64; 167; 1222; 1231.

Regulations: Section 1.1245–1(a) (1) through (3), (b) (1), (c), (d), –2(a) (1) through (3) (i) and (7).

The problem dealt with here comes about as follows: In § 167, Congress has authorized a deduction for depreciation on property used in a trade or business or held for the production of income. Under § 1016(a)(2), the price paid for such deductions is a reduction of basis. If depreciable property is sold at a gain, *quantitatively* the prior depreciation that reduced taxable income is offset at the time of sale by a corresponding increase in the gain on the sale. But § 1231 enters the picture with respect to property used in a trade or business. If in the year of sale § 1231 gains exceed such losses, the gain gets capital gains treatment. Gains on property held for the production of income also get capital gain treatment. Whereas the gains are normally *capital gains* the depreciation deductions previously taken reduced *ordinary* income. In this light the come-upance supposedly fostered by § 1016 basis adjustments succeeds quantitatively but fails *qualitatively*. A taxpayer will gladly accept an ordinary deduction now at a cost of a corresponding increase in capital gain later. And of course the scope of the problem is enlarged by express congressional approval of accelerated depreciation methods, as well as by salvage value reduction under § 167(f) and so-called bonus depreciation under § 179. The concept of recapture, the "Gotcha," is the principal congressional answer to this problem. To the extent that the recapture provisions apply they convert what would normally be § 1231 gain or capital gain to ordinary income. The Code sections providing for recapture, the most important of which are §§ 1245 and 1250, are complicated and far from flawless, both from a policy standpoint and with regard to drafting details. The strength of the congressional policy behind the sections is evidenced by the fact that they are made applicable notwithstanding any other Code section;[1] they simply override other Code

---

1. See I.R.C. (26 U.S.C.A.) §§ 1245(d) and 1250(i).

sections, except where the recapture provisions themselves specify an exception.[2]

Section 1245 must of course be carefully examined. Nevertheless, such an examination will be facilitated by a consideration of its scope and purpose as revealed in the legislative history of the section. The Senate Finance Committee Report stated in part: [3]

* * *

"In general, the new section provides for the inclusion in gross income (as ordinary income) of the gain from the disposition of certain depreciable property, to the extent of depreciation deductions taken in periods after December 31, 1961, which are reflected in the adjusted basis of such property.

Section 1245.   Gain from Dispositions of Certain Depreciable Property

"(a) *General rule*—Paragraph (1) of section 1245(a) provides the general rule that if 'section 1245 property' is disposed of, the amount by which the lower of 'recomputed basis' or the amount realized (or the fair market value in transactions in which no amount is realized) exceeds the adjusted basis of the property is to be treated as gain from the sale or exchange of property which is neither a capital asset nor property described in section 1231. [Amendments made by TRA (1976) now substitute 'ordinary income,' defined in I.R.C. § 64, for this cumbersome phrase. Ed.] The term 'disposed of' includes any transfer or involuntary conversion. The bill as passed by the House provided that paragraph (1) applies only to dispositions after the enactment of the Revenue Act of 1962. The bill as reported by your committee provides that paragraph (1) applies only to dispositions during taxable years beginning after December 31, 1962.

"Paragraph (2) of section 1245(a), under the bill as passed by the House, defined 'recomputed basis' as the adjusted basis of the property recomputed by adding thereto all adjustments, for taxable years beginning after December 31, 1961, reflected in such adjusted basis on account of deductions for depreciation, or for amortization under section 168,[4] whether in respect of the same or other property and whether allowed or allowable to the taxpayer or any other person. Your committee amendments provide that such adjustments shall be added thereto for all periods after December 31, 1961. For example, if a taxpayer, who reports his income on the basis of a

---

2. See I.R.C. (26 U.S.C.A.) §§ 1245(b) and 1250(d).

3. Sen.Fin.Comm.Rep.No.1881, 87th Cong. 2d Sess. (1962), 1962–3 C.B. 703, 984–985. See Schapiro, "Recapture of Depreciation and Section 1245 of the Internal Revenue Code," 72 Yale L.J. 1483 (1963).

4. Section 168, having expired, see § 168(i), was repealed in 1976. "Recomputed basis" has subsequently been expanded to include adjustments under §§ 169, 184, 185, 188, 190 and 191. Ed.

fiscal year ending November 30, purchases section 1245 property on January 1, 1962, at a cost of $10,000 and the taxpayer takes depreciation deductions of $2,000 (the amount allowable) before making a gift of the property to his son on October 31, 1962, the son's adjusted basis in the property for purposes of determining gain would, under the provisions of sections 1015 (relating to the basis of property acquired by gift) and 1016 (relating to adjustments to basis), be the same as his father's adjusted basis ($8,-000) and the recomputed basis of the property in the son's hands would be $10,000 since the $2,000 of depreciation deductions taken by the father are reflected in the son's basis in the property. Thus, if the son later sells the property during a taxable year of the son beginning after December 31, 1962, for $10,000, he would have $2,000 of gain to which section 1245(a) applies. Moreover, if the son himself takes $1,000 in depreciation deductions (the amount allowable) with respect to the property and then sells it for $10,000, he would have $3,000 of gain to which section 1245(a) applies.

"While recomputed basis is determined with respect to adjustments to basis for deductions for depreciation (and for amortization * * *) which were either allowed or allowable, if the taxpayer can establish by adequate records or other sufficient evidence that the amount allowed for any taxable year was less than the amount allowable, the amount to be added for such taxable year is the amount allowed. For example, assume that in the year 1967 it becomes necessary to determine the recomputed basis of property, the adjusted basis of which reflects an adjustment of $1,000 with respect to depreciation deductions allowable for the calendar year 1962. If the taxpayer can establish by adequate records or other sufficient evidence that he had been allowed a deduction of only $800 for 1962, then in determining the recomputed basis, the amount added to adjusted basis with respect to the $1,000 adjustment to basis for 1962 will be only $800.

"Paragraph (1) of section 1245(a) further provides that gain is to be recognized notwithstanding any other provision of substitle A of the 1954 Code. Thus, other nonrecognition sections of the code are overridden by the new section. For example, the gain under such paragraph (1) would be recognized to a corporation in the case of a distribution of section 1245 property by it to a shareholder, notwithstanding the provisions of section 311(a) or 336. Likewise, gain under such paragraph (1) would be recognized to a corporation on a sale or exchange of such property, notwithstanding the provisions of section 337. The operation of section 1245 may, however, be affected by the taxpayer's method of accounting. For example, the gain from a disposition to which section 1245 applies may be reported by the taxpayer under the installment method if such method is otherwise available under section 453 of the code. For another example, section 1245 does not require recognition of gain or loss upon normal retirement of an asset in a multiple asset account as long as the taxpayer's method of accounting, in accordance with Treasury regulations, does not require recognition of such gain or loss and clearly reflects income.

"In the case of a disposition of section 1245 property in which an amount is realized (a sale, exchange, or involuntary conversion), the gain to which section 1245(a) applies is the amount by which the amount realized or the recomputed basis, whichever is lower, exceeds the adjusted basis of the property. In the case of any other disposition, the gain to which section 1245(a) applies is the amount by which the fair market value of the property on the date of disposition or its recomputed basis, whichever is lower, exceeds its adjusted basis. [The recapture bite under § 1245(a) will be easily understood if it is recognized to the lower of two alternative amounts—viz:

(1) In case of a sale or exchange or involuntary conversion

Recomputed Basis		Amount Realized
-Adjusted Basis	or	-Adjusted Basis

(2) In case of other dispositions

Recomputed Basis		Fair Market Value
-Adjusted Basis	or	-Adjusted Basis

But carefully check these suggestions against the language of the statute. Ed.]

"For example, if section 1245 property has an adjusted basis of $2,000 and a recomputed basis of $3,300 and is sold for $2,900, the gain to which section 1245(a) applies is $900 ($2,900 minus $2,000). If the property is sold for $3,700, the gain is $1,700, of which $1,300 ($3,-300 minus $2,000) is gain to which section 1245(a) applies. If, on the other hand, the property is distributed by a corporation to a stockholder in a distribution to which section 1245(a) applies and at a time when the fair market value of the property is $3,100, the gain recognized to the corporation upon such disposition is $1,100 ($3,100 minus $2,000) ; if the fair market value is $3,800 at the time of such disposition, the gain to which section 1245(a) applies is $1,300 ($3,300 minus $2,000)."

Both the intrinsic nature and the use of property may have a bearing on whether it is subject to § 1245. Although Congress undertook to define § 1245 property in § 1245(a)(3), uncertainties inherent in the definition have been the subject of some of the sharpest criticism leveled at the provision. An aggravation is that § 1250 property, subject to different recapture rules considered later in this chapter, is defined residually as depreciable realty, other than § 1245 property.[5] The scope of the section in this respect is a serious problem for prac-

---

5. I.R.C. (26 U.S.C.A.) § 1250(c).

ticing lawyers and accountants.[6]   It is not a matter to which law students should address much attention, but it may be of some interest to see how the Senate Finance Committee viewed the definition.   The Committee Report stated:[7]

"Paragraph (3) of section 1245(a) defines 'section 1245 property.'   Section 1245 property is any property (other than livestock)[8] of a type described in subparagraph (A) or (B) of such paragraph (3) which is or has been property of a character subject to the allowance for depreciation provided in section 167.   Even though the property may not be subject to the allowance for depreciation in the hands of the taxpayer, such property is nevertheless subject to the provisions of section 1245(a) if the property was subject to the allowance for depreciation in the hands of any prior holder, and if such depreciation is taken into account in determining the adjusted basis of the property in the hands of the taxpayer.

" * * *   [T]he term 'personal property' in subparagraph (A) of section 1245(a) (3) is intended to include not only 'tangible personal property' * * * but also intangible personal property.

"Subparagraph (B) of section 1245(a) (3) describes other property (not including a building or its structural components) if such other property is tangible and has an adjusted basis in which there are reflected adjustments for depreciation or amortization under section 168 which would be taken into account in determining recomputed basis for a period in which such property (or other property) either (i) was used as an integral part of manufacturing, production, or extraction, or of furnishing transportation, communications, electrical energy, gas, water, or sewage disposal services, or (ii) constituted research or storage facilities used in connection with any such activities.   The language in clauses (i) and (ii) in section 1245(a) (3) (B) is intended to have the same meaning as when used in clauses (i) and (ii) in section 48(a) (1) (B) (relating to the definition of sec. 38 property subject to the investment credit).[9]   Even though the property is not used by the taxpayer as an integral part of an activity specified in clause (i), or does not constitute research or storage facilities within the meaning of clause (ii), such property in certain circumstances may, nevertheless, be section 1245 property under subparagraph (B).   An illustration of such a circumstance is when the adjusted basis of such property in the hands of the taxpayer reflects ad-

6. See "Depreciation Recapture Revisited: A Critique," 3 Real Property Probate, and Trust Journal, No. 4, Winter, 1968.

7. Sen.Fin.Comm.Rep.No.1881, supra note 3 at 985–986.

8. But see the 1969 change noted below. Ed.

9. See page 804, infra. Ed.

justments for depreciation with respect to such property taken for periods after December 31, 1961, at a time when such property was used as an integral part of manufacturing by the taxpayer or another taxpayer. Another illustration is when the adjusted basis of such property in the hands of the taxpayer reflects adjustments for depreciation with respect to *other* property (as, for example, in the case of a like kind exchange under sec. 1031) taken for periods after December 31, 1961, at a time when such other property was used as an integral part of manufacturing by the taxpayer."

The principal changes made in § 1245 since its enactment in 1962 have been to extend it to some property not within its original provisions. In 1963 elevators and escalators were added to the definition of § 1245 property under § 1245(a) (3) (C) and became subject to a special rule on recomputed basis under § 1245(a) (2) (B). In 1969 Congress added § 1245(a) (3) (D), bringing in certain real property subject to new amortization deductions, and § 1245(a) (2) (D), providing a special recomputed basis rule for it. In another 1969 change, Congress broadened the scope of the provision by deleting the exemption of livestock, now the subject of § 1245(a) (2) (C). With regard to livestock the Senate Committee Report stated:[10]

"In order to place livestock in the same position as other types of business property and to reduce the tax profit arising with respect to [depreciating livestock as an ordinary deduction at a later cost of only capital gain, Ed.] the House bill and the committee amendments eliminate the exception for livestock from the depreciation recapture rules. Thus, the gain on the sale or other disposition of purchased livestock with respect to which depreciation deductions have been claimed is to be treated as ordinary income rather than capital gain, to the extent of the depreciation deductions previously claimed, in the same manner as if any other type of tangible personal property used in a business were sold.

"This provision is to be effective with respect to taxable years beginning after December 31, 1969. The recapture rule, however, is to be applied only to the extent of depreciation deductions for periods after December 31, 1969."

The Tax Reform Act of 1976 added new § 1245(a)(4) providing a special rule for the determination of the recomputed basis of players' contracts for purposes of recapture upon the sale of a sports franchise.[11]

10. Sen.Fin.Comm.Rep.No.91–552, 91st Cong. 1st Sess. (1969), 1969–3 C.B. 423, 487–488.

11. Sales of player contracts were subjected to § 1245 gain prior to the 1976 T.R.A. Rev.Rul. 67–380, 1967–2 C.B. 291. The new provision has the effect of converting additional gain on the sale of a sports franchise to ordinary income to account for the greater of previously unrecaptured depreciation on player contracts acquired at the time of acquisition of the franchise or on player contracts involved in the transfer itself.

Section 1245 is not only a characterization provision. It may force a recognition of gain which, without it, would go unrecognized. But this is not the invariable result; there are some limited exceptions to its application found in § 1245(b). Some of the exceptions will be relevant only as subsequent chapters are considered, but their history is stated here. In explaining § 1245(b), the Senate Committee Report stated in part:[12]

"Subsection (b) of section 1245 sets forth certain exceptions and limitations to the general rule provided in subsection (a). Paragraph (1) provides that subsection (a) will not apply to a disposition by gift. Paragraph (2) provides that, except as provided in section 691, subsection (a) will not apply to a transfer at death.

* * *

"Paragraph (4) of section 1245(b) provides that if property is disposed of and gain (determined without regard to sec. 1245) is not recognized in whole or in part under section 1031 (relating to like kind exchanges) or 1033 (relating to involuntary conversions),[13] then the amount of gain taken into account under section 1245(a) is not to exceed the sum of the amount of gain recognized on such disposition (determined without regard to section 1245) plus the fair market value of property acquired which is not section 1245 property and which is not otherwise taken into account in determining the gain under section 1031 or 1033. For example, assume that a taxpayer owns section 1245 property with an adjusted basis of $100,000 and a recomputed basis of $116,000. The property is destroyed by fire and the taxpayer receives $117,000 of insurance proceeds. He uses $105,000 of the proceeds to purchase property similar or related in service or use to the property destroyed in an acquisition qualifying under section 1033(a)(3)(A), and he uses $9,000 of the proceeds to purchase stock in the acquisition of control of a corporation owning property similar or related in service or use to the converted property, which acquisition also qualifies under section 1033(a)(3)(A). The taxpayer properly elects under section 1033(a)(3)(A) and the regulations thereunder to limit recognition of gain to the amount by which the amount realized from the conversion exceeds the cost of the stock and other property acquired to replace the converted property. Since $3,000 of the gain is recognized (without regard to sec. 1245) under section 1033(a) (3) (that is, $117,000 minus $114,000), and since the stock purchased for $9,000 is not depreciable property and was not taken into account in determining the gain under section 1033, the amount of gain to be taken into account under section 1245(a) may not exceed $12,000. Thus, section 1245(a) applies to $12,000 of the $16,000 gain.

* * *

12. Sen.Fin.Comm.Rep.No.1881, supra   13. These sections are examined in
note 3 at 986–988 and 989.   later chapters. Ed.

"(d) *Application of section.*—Subsection (d) of section 1245 provides that the section is to apply notwithstanding any other provision of subtitle A of the code. Thus, section 1245 overrides any nonrecognition provision of subtitle A or any 'income characterizing' provision. For example, the gain to which section 1245(a) applies might otherwise be considered as gain from the sale or exchange of a capital asset under section 1231, (relating to property used in the trade or business and involuntary conversions). Since section 1245 overrides section 1231, the gain to which section 1245(a) applies will be treated as ordinary income, and only the remaining gain, if any, from the property may be considered as gain from the sale or exchange of a capital asset if section 1231 is applicable. For example, assume that a taxpayer sells for $130 section 1245 property with an adjusted basis of $40 and a recomputed basis of $100. The excess of the recomputed basis over adjusted basis, or $60, will be treated as gain under section 1245(a). The excess of the selling price over recomputed basis, or $30, may be considered under section 1231 as gain from the sale of a capital asset."

NOTE

Prior to the enactment of § 1245, the Supreme Court was asked to settle the issue whether the sale of a depreciable asset during a year for an amount in excess of its adjusted basis at the beginning of the year precludes a depreciation deduction for the year of sale. In Fribourg Navigation Co., Inc. v. Commissioner [1] the taxpayer had depreciated a ship using an acceptable reasonable life and salvage value in the years 1955 and 1956. In 1957 as a result of the Suez crisis ship prices soared and the taxpayer sold the ship for more than its original cost.[2] Allowing depreciation in the year of sale, the Court concluded:[3]

> Finally, the Commissioner's position contains inconsistencies. He contends that depreciation must be disallowed in 1957 since the amount received on sale shows that the use of the asset "cost" the taxpayer "nothing" in that year. But under this view, since the asset was sold at an amount greater than its original purchase price, it "cost" the taxpayer "nothing" in 1955 and 1956 as well. The Commissioner's reliance on the structure of the annual income tax reporting system does not cure the illogic of his theory. Further, the Commissioner apparently will not extend his

1. 383 U.S. 272 (1966). See Lewis, "Depreciation in Light of the Fribourg Case," 19 U.S.C. Tax Inst. 481 (1967).

2. The ship was purchased for $469,000. After 1955 and 1956 depreciation deductions it had an adjusted basis of $326,627.73 on January 1, 1957. It was sold for $695,500 late in 1957 and taxpayer attempted to take depreciation deductions of $135,367.24 for 1957.

3. 383 U.S. 272 at 286.

new theory to situations where it would benefit the taxpayer. If a depreciable asset is sold for *less* than its adjusted basis, it would seem to follow from the Commissioner's construction that the asset has "cost" the taxpayer an additional amount and that further depreciation should be permitted. * * *

The conclusion we have reached finds support among nearly all lower federal courts that have recently dealt with this issue. Upon consideration *en banc*, the Tax Court itself has concluded that the Commissioner's position is without authorization in the statute or the regulations.

In light of the foregoing, we conclude that the depreciation claimed by the taxpayer for 1957 was erroneously disallowed.

The Supreme Court also recognized that the question would have been moot had the litigation involved a year subsequent to 1962. Why? But the issue litigated in *Fribourg* is not moot in all circumstances. After studying I.R.C. § 1250, consider whether a taxpayer would now litigate a *Fribourg* type controversy if it involved straight line depreciation claimed on a building for the year of sale.

REVENUE RULING 69–487

1969–2 Cum.Bull. 165.

An individual taxpayer operating a business as a sole proprietorship converted to personal use an automobile that had been used solely for business purposes. At that time, the fair market value of the automobile was substantially higher than its adjusted basis.

Held, for the purposes of section 1245 of the Internal Revenue Code of 1954, the conversion to personal use is not a "disposition" of the automobile. Accordingly, there is no gain to be recognized by the taxpayer upon the conversion to personal use. However, the provisions of section 1245 of the Code would apply to any disposition of the automobile by the taxpayer at a later date.

PROBLEMS

1. Recap, a calendar year taxpayer, owns a trucking rig which he uses in his trucking business. The truck was purchased three years ago at a cost of $30,000 and has a five year life and reasonable salvage of $10,000 to Recap. Recap has depreciated it under the straight line method and without the benefit of I.R.C. § 167(f). I.R.C. § 179 was not electable by Recap. Why?

   (a) What result to Recap if he sells the trucking rig on December 31 of the current year for $20,000?

    (b) What result to Recap if as a result of higher production costs and a rail strike he is able to sell the rig for $32,000?

    (c) What result to Recap in (a), above, if he had failed to deduct depreciation on the rig? Would he be content to let things be or would he want to claim depreciation for the current year and seek a refund based on depreciation allowable for prior years?

    (d) What result to Recap in (b), above, if in addition he sold some land used for storage in his business and owned for three years with a $10,000 adjusted basis for a $6,000 sale price?

    (e) Same as (d), above, except that the land was sold for $9,000 rather than $6,000.

    2. Do you see a significant relationship between I.R.C. § 1245 (a)(2) and the carryover basis rules of I.R.C. §§ 1023 and 1015? Does the statute sanction assignment of "fruit" in these circumstances?

4. RECAPTURE UNDER SECTION 1250

Internal Revenue Code: Section 1250(a) (Study § 1250(a)(1)(B), (2)(B) and (3)(B), "applicable percentage," only as needed to work Problems in this chapter); (b)(1), (3) and (4); (c); (d)(1) and (2); (h); and (i). See Sections 167; 1222; 1231.

Regulations: Section 1.1250–1(a)(1) through (a)(3)(ii) (carefully taking account of a 1976 *statutory* change now reflected in *Code* Section 1.1250–(a)(1)), –1(c)(1) and (4); –1(e)(1) and (2); –2(a)(1); –2(b)(1).

Before beginning the battle with I.R.C. § 1250 it seems appropriate to comment on a phenomenon alluded to earlier, a new Code provision that has an obvious propensity for simplification, at least by way of a reduction in verbosity. Section 1901(a) of the Tax Reform Act of 1976 (a part of the "dead wood" provisions) adds § 64 to the Code to define "ordinary income." [1] The new provision is helpful in § 1250(a), because it makes it possible to say that § 1250 recapture (and of course § 1245 recapture, too) shall be treated as "gain which is ordinary income," [2] rather than as "gain from the sale or exchange of property which is neither a capital asset nor property described in § 1231." [3] The clause for which "ordinary income" is now substituted is of course approximately the "ordinary income" definition in new § 64.

----

1. "Ordinary loss" is defined, also, by new I.R.C. § 65.

2. See new §§ 1250(a) and 1245(a).

3. See old §§ 1250(a) and 1245(a).

Section 1245, dealing mainly with personal property, came into the Code in 1962; but it was not until 1964 that Congress enacted § 1250 which, with substantial differences, extends the recapture concept to dispositions of real property. The following excerpt from the 1964 Report of the Senate Finance Committee [4] reveals some of the reasons for the delay as well as for the different approach to the realty problem in § 1250.

"*(a) Present law*—Under present law, taxpayers may take depreciation on real property (other than land) used in a trade or business or held for the production of income. The depreciation methods available are the same as those applying to tangible personal property. They include (1) straight-line depreciation; (2) 150 percent declining balance depreciation; (3) double-declining balance depreciation; (4) sum-of-the-years-digits depreciation; and (5) any other consistent method of depreciation which does not during the first two-thirds of the useful life of the property result in greater depreciation than under the double-declining balance method. The 150-percent declining balance method is available with respect to used real property only under certain circumstances. The last three methods of depreciation referred to are available only for property with a useful life of 3 years or more and only if the property was new property in the hands of the taxpayer.[5]

"The depreciation is allowed as a deduction against ordinary income. As the depreciation deduction is taken the cost or other basis of the real property is reduced by a like amount. If the property subsequently is sold, any gain realized on the difference between the sales price (adjusted downward for selling expense) and the adjusted basis of the property is taxed as a capital gain if the total transactions in depreciable property and certain other property (referred to in sec. 1231) result in a gain for the year involved. On the other hand, where the aggregate of these transactions results in a loss, the net loss is an ordinary loss.

"*(b) General reasons for provisions*—Since the depreciation deductions are taken against ordinary income while any gain on the sale of the property is treated as a capital gain, there is an opportunity under present law in effect to convert ordinary income into capital gain. This occurs whenever the depreciation deductions allowed reduce the basis of the property faster than the actual decline in its value.

"Congress in the Revenue Act of 1962 recognized the existence of this same problem in the case of gains from the disposition of depreciable machinery and other personal property. In that act, the Congress provided that any gain realized on the sale of these assets in the future

---

4. Sen.Fin.Comm.Rep.No.830, 88th Cong. 2d Sess. (1964), 1964–1 (Part 2) C.B. 505, 635–637.

5. There have been some changes here since 1964. Ed.

would be ordinary income to the extent of any depreciation deductions taken in 1962 and subsequent years with respect to the property.

"In the case of real estate, this problem is magnified by the fact that real estate is usually acquired through debt financing and the depreciation deductions allowed relate not only to the taxpayer's equity investment but to the indebtedness as well. Since [under the gross basis concept of *Crane* (Ed.)] the depreciation deductions relate to the indebtedness as well as the equity in the property, this may permit the tax-free amortization of any mortgage on the property. As a result in such cases there is a tax-free cash return of a part of the investment which may in fact enable the taxpayer to show a loss for several years which he may offset against income for tax purposes.

"In 1962, Congress did not include real property in the recapture provision applicable to depreciable personal property because it recognized the problem in doing so where there is an appreciable rise in the value of real property attributable to a rise in the general price level over a long period of time. The bill this year takes this factor into account. It makes sure that the ordinary income treatment is applied upon the sale of the asset only to what may truly be called excess depreciation deductions. It does this first by providing that in no event is there to be a recapture of depreciation as ordinary income where the property is sold at a gain except to the extent the depreciation deductions taken exceed the deduction which would have been allowable had the taxpayer limited his deductions to those available under the straight-line method of depreciation.[6] Secondly, a provision has been added which in any event tapers off the proportion of any gain which will be treated as ordinary income so that it disappears gradually over a 10-year holding period for the real estate. As a result, under the bill, no ordinary income will be realized on the sale of real estate held for more than 10 years.

"*(c) General explanation of provisions*—In view of the considerations set forth above, the House and your committee have amended present law to provide that when depreciable real estate is sold after December 31, 1963, in certain cases a proportion of any gain realized upon the sale of the property is to be treated as ordinary income; that is, previous depreciation deductions against ordinary income are to be 'recaptured' from the capital gains category.

"The bill accomplishes this result by treating as ordinary income a certain percentage of what is called 'additional' depreciation or the amount of gain realized on the sale of the property, whichever is smaller. Generally, the 'additional' depreciation referred to here is that part of the depreciation deductions which exceeds the depreciation deductions allowable under the straight-line method. The deprecia-

---

6. This is technically incorrect. If property is sold within one year of its acquisition all depreciation deductions are recaptured as ordinary income. See I.R.C. § 1250(b)(1). Ed.

tion deductions taken into account, however, are only those taken after December 31, 1963. Thus, they are the excess of any depreciation deductions taken under the double-declining balance method, sum-of-the-years-digits method, or other method of rapid depreciation, over the depreciation which would have been taken under the straight-line method. In the case of property held for 1 year or less, however, the deductions recaptured are to include not only the excess over straight-line depreciation, but rather the entire depreciation deductions taken.

"The bill limits the depreciation recapture to the excess over straight-line depreciation because it is believed that only to this extent could the depreciation taken appropriately be considered in excess of the decline in the value of the property which occurs over time. If a gain still occurs, it is believed that this is attributable to a rise in price levels generally rather than to an absence of a decline in the value of the property. The portion representing the rise in value is comparable to other forms of gains which quite generally are treated as capital gains. Moreover, it is believed that when the property is held for an extended period of time, gains realized on the sale or other disposition of the property are more likely to be attributable to price rises generally than to an excess of depreciation deductions. For that reason, the bill also tapers off over a 10-year period the proportion of the additional depreciation (or gain where smaller) which is to be treated as ordinary income upon the sale of the property.

"This is accomplished by providing that the additional depreciation (or gain if smaller) which otherwise would be treated as ordinary income is to be decreased by 1 percentage point for each full month the property is held in excess of 20 full months. Thus, the amount which will be treated as ordinary income in the case of property held for a full 21 months would be 99 percent (the applicable percentage) of the amount which otherwise would be so treated. This decreases 1 percent for each succeeding month the property is held until the applicable percentage decreases to zero for property held for 10 years or more.

"The property which is to be given the type of treatment described above is depreciable real property other than real property which is eligible for the investment credit. Such property is already subject to the recapture rule provided by section 1245 which generally applies to tangible personal property. The types of real property, therefore, which are not subject to this provision are property other than buildings or structural components which are used as an integral part of manufacturing, production, or extraction, or of furnishing transportation, communications, electrical energy, gas, water, or sewage disposal services or represent research or storage facilities used in connection with these activities. Examples of the types of real property which, therefore, are not included under this provision are railroad track and bridges and blast furnaces.

"This provision applies only to the additional depreciation allowed or allowable. Consequently, the enactment of this provision is not intended to affect the question of whether all or any part of a claimed deduction for depreciation is in fact allowable. * * * "

In 1969 and 1976 Congress tightened the § 1250 screws. It will be recalled that the Tax Reform Act of 1969 also restricted the depreciation methods applicable to real property.[7] The Staff of the Joint Committee on Internal Revenue Taxation has summarized the principal 1969 changes in § 1250 and the congressional concerns that prompted them as follows: [8]

"In the case of sales of property used in the trade or business, net gains (with certain exceptions) were taxed as capital gains, and losses were treated as ordinary losses. In 1962, this was modified as to most personal property and certain real property to provide in general for taxing gain on sale as ordinary income to the extent of all the depreciation taken on that property after December 31, 1962. In 1964 the rules were modified as to buildings to provide in general for taxing gain on sale as ordinary income to the extent of certain depreciation taken after December 31, 1963; however, after the property was held for 12 months, only depreciation in excess of straight line was 'recaptured' and taxed as ordinary income and that amount was reduced after 20 months, at the rate of 1 percent per month for 100 months, after which nothing was recaptured.

"*General reasons for change*—The prior tax treatment of real estate was used by some high-income individuals as a tax shelter to escape payment of tax on substantial portions of their economic income. The rapid depreciation methods allowed made it possible for taxpayers to deduct amounts in excess of those required to service the mortgage during the early life of the property. Moreover, because accelerated depreciation usually produced a deduction in excess of the actual decline in the usefulness of property, economically profitable real estate operations were normally converted into substantial tax losses, sheltering from income tax economic profits and permitting avoidance of income tax on the owner's other ordinary income, such as salary and dividends. Later, the property could be sold and the excess of the sale price over the remaining basis could be treated as a capital gain to the extent that the recapture provisions did not apply. By holding the property for 10 years before sale, the taxpayer could arrange to have all the gain resulting from excess depreciation (which was previously offset against ordinary income) taxed as a capital gain without the recapture provisions coming into play. The tax advantages from such

---

7. See Chapter 22 at page 759.

8. General Explanation of the Tax Reform Act of 1969, Staff of the Joint Comm. on Int.Rev.Tax., 181–183 (1970). See also Grey, "How the New Proposed Depreciation Recapture Rules for 1250 Property will Operate," 35 J.Tax. 40 (1971); Nieman, "Real Estate Shelters and the Tax Reform Act of 1969," 34 Albany L.Rev. 579 (1970).

operations increased as a taxpayer's income moved into the higher tax brackets.

* * *

"The Act generally tightens the recapture rules applicable to the sale of real estate, which are designed to tax the gain from such sales as ordinary income rather than capital gain to the extent that they represent deductions taken under accelerated depreciation in excess of straight line depreciation. Except in the case of residential real property (and certain pre-existing contracts) gains from the sale of real property after December 31, 1969, are subject to recapture to the extent of the excess depreciation taken after Decembr 31, 1969, without any percentage reductions for the holding period. The recapture rules of previous law (which reduce the amount subject to recapture by one percentage point for each full month the property is held more than 20 months) are retained (1) for sales made under a written contract which was binding on July 24, 1969, and thereafter, (2) for Federal, State, and locally assisted projects, which are limited as to rate of return on the investment, such as the FHA 221(d) (3) and the FHA 236 programs, and which are constructed, reconstructed or acquired before January 1, 1975, and (3) with respect to excess depreciation taken for periods before January 1, 1970.

"For residential housing (other than that described in the preceding sentence), and also property with respect to which the rapid depreciation for rehabilitation expenditures has been allowed, the prior recapture rules are tightened to allow a one percent per month reduction in the amount to be recaptured as ordinary income after the property has been held for 100 full months.

"*Effective date*—The changes applicable to real estate are effective for taxable years ending after July 24, 1969."

The 1976 changes are reflected in I.R.C. § 1250(a)(1), newly enacted in that year, which further tightened the § 1250 screws by subjecting post-1976 additional depreciation on residential property (other than the exceptions under § 1250(a)(1)(B)) to a 100 percent applicable percentage.

PROBLEMS

1. On January 1, 1974 Owner purchased a new nonresidential building for use in his business for $460,000, of which $60,000 was properly allocated to the land and $400,000 to the building. The building had a 40 year useful life (with no salvage value), and Owner elected the straight line method of depreciation. On December 31, 1977 (four years later) Owner sold the building for $450,000 of which $80,000 was allocable to the land and $370,000 to the building. What is the amount and character of Owner's gain on the sale?

2. If on the facts of the first problem Owner had used the 150% declining balance method of depreciation, he would have taken the

following (rounded off to the nearest dollar) amounts of depreciation on the building: 1974: $15,000; 1975: $14,438; 1976: $13,896; 1977: $13,375; for total depreciation of $56,709. Assuming Owner had used the 150% declining balance method in those years, what would be the amount and character of Owner's gain on the sale of the property on December 31, 1977 for $450,000, $80,000 allocable to the land and $370,000 to the building?

3. Suppose now that Owner had purchased the property described in problem 1 on January 1, 1969, and had properly elected the double declining balance method of depreciation. Under that method Owner would have taken the following (rounded off to the nearest dollar) amounts of depreciation on the building: 1969: $20,-000; 1970: $19,000; 1971: $18,050; 1972: $17,148; 1973: $16,290; 1974: $15,476; 1975: $14,702; 1976: $13,967; 1977: $13,269; for total depreciation of $147,902. If Owner sold the property on December 31, 1977 for $450,000 ($80,000 for the land and $370,000 for the building) what would be the amount and character of Owner's gain on the sale?

4. At the beginning of year one (a post 1969 year) Rehabilitator made an $8,000 improvement to a piece of qualified rehabilitated low income rental housing. The improvement has an 8 year life and no salvage value. Rehabilitator properly elected the special depreciation deductions for the improvement under § 167(k). Due to unexpected difficulties, at the end of year three Rehabilitator sold the property. $6,000 of the purchase price was allocable to the rehabilitated property. Discuss the tax consequences to Rehabilitator on the sale. See I.R.C. §§ 1250(a) (1) (B) (iii) and (a) (2) (B) (iv) and 1250(b) (4).

5. Again assuming declining balance depreciation on facts otherwise the same as those in question one, what further difficulties would be presented if the building in question were a soft-drink bottling plant full of bottling equipment? Cf. Williams v. McGowan, Chapter 22 at page 773.

6. Especially in the light of the definitions of § 1245 and § 1250 property, confusion would be greatly reduced if the recapture principles of §§ 1245 and 1250 were identical. Would this be possible? If it were attempted by Congress, should the move be more toward § 1245 or toward § 1250 principles?

---

5. OTHER RECAPTURE CONCEPTS

Internal Revenue Code: See Sections 38; 46 through 50; 1238; 1251; 1252; 1254.

The recapture concept was not entirely new to the Code when Congress enacted §§ 1245 and 1250 in 1962 and 1964, respectively.

These provisions were preceded by § 1238, first enacted in 1950.[1] That section bore the same relationship to § 168 as §§ 1245 and 1250 bear to current depreciation and amortization provisions. During the Korean War as an incentive to production for the war effort, Congress permitted certified emergency facilities to be written off over a sixty-month period in lieu of conventional depreciation deductions.[2] The authorized accelerated write-off by way of amortization deductions raised the possibility of distortion, because deductions against ordinary income in excess of realistic depreciation were usually offset only by capital gain treatment of gain on a sale of the property. To prevent this § 1238 accorded ordinary income treatment to gain on the sale of such property (taking account of amortization and what the basis would have been if only conventional depreciation could have been claimed). The provision is of diminishing importance, because certification of such emergency facilities ceased December 31, 1959.[3]

In recent years Congress has extended the recapture concept, applying it to assumed past overcharges arising out of deductions other than the depreciation (or related amortization) deduction. § 1251, enacted in 1969, recaptures (for ordinary income treatment) gain on the sale of farm property, where, in the past, farm losses have offset non-farm income.

However, § 1251 is inapplicable to property that is within the scope of § 1250.[4] Thus, if barns and other farm buildings are sold, as to them § 1250, not § 1251, calls the recapture tune.

The legislative history of § 1251 emphasizes that the occupation of farming is subject to more liberal accounting rules than other occupations because farmers may deduct currently (i. e., "expense") some costs which persons in other occupations would be required to capitalize. In explaining the reasons for the new provision, the Staff of the Joint Committee on Internal Revenue Taxation indicated: [5]

"Although the special farm accounting rules were adopted to relieve farmers of bookkeeping burdens, these rules were used by some high-income taxpayers who were not primarily engaged in farming to obtain a tax, but not an economic, loss which was then deducted from

1. Rev.Act of 1950, § 216(c), 64 Stat. 906, 941 (1950).

2. I.R.C. (26 U.S.C.A.) § 168; I.R.C. (1939) §§ 23(t) and 124A. See also I.R.C. (1939) §§ 23(t) and 124, applicable during World War II. Compare current § 169, permitting amortization of pollution control facilities, and § 167(k), fixing a 60-month useful life for rehabilitation expenditures for low-income rental housing.

3. I.R.C. (26 U.S.C.A.) § 168(i).

4. I.R.C. (26 U.S.C.A.) § 1251(e)(1)(A).

5. General explanation of the Tax Reform Act of 1969, Staff of the Joint Comm. on Int.Rev.Tax, 90 (1970). See Koren, "Agricultural Taxation After the TRA: Unintended Results from an Ill-Sown Seed," 27 U.Fla.L.R. 97 (1974); see also O'Byrne, "New Law Greatly Limits the Tax Shelter Formerly Provided by Farming Operations," 32 J.Tax. 298 (1970); Hjorth, "Farm Losses and Related Provisions," 25 Tax L.Rev. 581 (1970).

their high-bracket, nonfarm income. In addition, when these high-income taxpayers sold their farm investment, they often received capital gains treatment on the sale. The combination of the current deduction against ordinary income for farm expenses of a capital nature and the capital gains treatment available on the sale of farm assets produced significant tax advantages and tax savings for these high-income taxpayers."

Section 1251 has required the taxpayer to maintain an excess deductions account in which are accumulated post-1959 but pre-1976 net losses on farming.[6] The account is reduced annually by any net farm income and by any net farm loss that is not used to reduce the taxpayer's tax liability.[7] Subject to various exceptions and limitations, the amount in the account fixes the amount of the gain on the sale or other disposition of the taxpayer's farm property which is to be taxed as ordinary income. If the balance in the account is greater than such gain, all the gain is treated as ordinary income; if it is lower only the lower amount is subject to recapture. If in any year § 1251 results in some tax at ordinary income rates, the amount in the excess deductions account which is carried over into the succeeding year is of course reduced by the amount of such recapture. However, § 1251 is being phased out by a provision in the Tax Reform Act of 1976, which adds new § 1251(b)(2)(E) providing that there shall be no additions to the excess deductions account for years beginning after 1975.

Section 1252, which bears a direct relationship to §§ 175 and 182, presents a somewhat simpler recapture rule. Section 175 permits expenditures for soil and water conservation and to prevent soil erosion to be expensed, not merely charged to capital account. Section 182 sometimes accords similar treatment to expenditures made for the purpose of clearing farm land. Thus, as explained by the Staff of the Joint Committee:[8]

"The current deduction allowed for soil and water conservation expenditures and land clearing expenditures with respect to farm land, combined with the capital gains treatment allowed under prior law on the sale of the farm land permitted high-income taxpayers to convert ordinary income into capital gains. These taxpayers could purchase farm land, deduct these expenditures from their high-bracket nonfarm income, and then receive capital gain treatment on the sale of the farm land."

---

6. Liberal exceptions in § 1251(b)(2)(B) make the section inapplicable if the taxpayer does not have substantial nonfarm income and substantial net farm losses.

7. See especially I.R.C. (26 U.S.C.A.) § 183.

8. General Explanation of the Tax Reform Act of 1969, supra note 5 at 95.

Under § 1252, if farm land is sold and it has been held for less than 10 years and has been the subject of deductions from ordinary income under §§ 175 and 182, gain on the sale to the extent of such deductions may be recaptured as ordinary income. If the land has been held for only five years or less, the amount of the §§ 175 and 182 deductions fixes the amount of the gain subject to ordinary income treatment. If a sale takes place in the sixth year only 80% of the amount of such deductions is recaptured; and there are corresponding 20% reductions in each succeeding year so that, in effect, § 1252 becomes inapplicable to land held for more than ten years. It should be noted, however, that § 1252 gives way to § 1251 where § 1251 applies.[9] Thus, in effect, a farmer with a relatively small balance in his excess deductions account under § 1251, but with larger recent § 175 and § 182 deductions, might find gain on the sale of farm land recaptured in part by § 1251, and in part by § 1252. And of course, while the expiration of ten years after acquisition makes § 1252 inapplicable, there is no complete amnesty for past § 175 and § 182 deductions; they may still result in some recapture to the extent that they operated to increase the excess deductions account under § 1251.

One of several recapture changes made in 1976 applies to a disposition of oil or gas property. New Code § 1254, added by § 205 of the Tax Reform Act, taxes as ordinary income some gain on the sale of oil and gas property if intangible drilling and development expenditures on the property, normally capital expenditures, have been expensed (currently deducted) as permitted by § 263(c). The new section, applicable to dispositions in 1976 or later, takes a form that will appear somewhat familiar from a prior study of §§ 1245 and 1250.

In recent years a tax device used to stimulate business has been the investment credit; not a mere deduction from gross income, the amount of the credit [10] (a percentage of the cost of certain newly acquired depreciable property) directly reduces the taxpayer's income tax bill.[11] Congress turns the investment credit on (at varying rates) and off to help stimulate or slow down business and in turn, the economy. The credit was terminated in 1969.[12] But in 1971 when the economy was lagging Congress enacted I.R.C. § 50 restoring and lib-

---

9. I.R.C. (26 U.S.C.A.) § 1252(a).

10. Although credits (which directly reduce the taxpayer's tax liability) are considered in Chapter 27, page 962, infra, nevertheless the investment credit is interrelated with the type of property that falls under § 1245 and the recapture of the investment credit is somewhat comparable to recapture under the general recapture provisions. Consequently the in-vestment credit, which was terminated by the 1969 T.R.A. but was restored by the 1971 Act in I.R.C. § 50, and the recapture of that credit are discussed in this Chapter. See Cragwell, "The Great Section 38 Property Muddle," 28 Vand.L.R. 1025 (1975).

11. See I.R.C. (26 U.S.C.A.) §§ 38, 46–48, and 50.

12. See I.R.C. (26 U.S.C.A.) § 49.

eralizing the credit.   The Staff of the Joint Committee explained the credit and its reenactment as follows:[13]

Prior to 1969, there was a 7-percent investment tax credit. . . . The Tax Reform Act of 1969 repealed this investment credit for property acquired after April 18, 1969, and for property the construction, reconstruction, or erection of which began after April 18, 1969.   In general terms, the investment credit under prior law was available with respect to: (1) tangible personal property; (2) other tangible property (not including buildings and structural components) which was an integral part of manufacturing production, etc., or which constituted a research or storage facility; and (3) elevators and escalators.   New property fully qualified for the credit, but in the case of used property, only an amount up to $50,000 could be taken into account in any one year.   In addition, the property had to be depreciable property with a useful life of at least 4 years.   Property with a useful life of from 4 to 6 years qualified for the credit to the extent of one-third of its cost.   Property with a useful life of 6 to 8 years qualified with respect to two-thirds of its cost, and property with an estimated useful life of 8 years or more qualified for the full amount.

The amount of the investment credit taken in any year could not exceed the first $25,000 of tax liability (as otherwise computed) plus 50 percent of the tax liability in excess of $25,000.   Investment credits which because of this limitation could not be used in the current year could be carried back to the 3 prior years and be used in those years to the extent permissible within the limitations applicable in those years, and then, to the extent of any amount still remaining, carried forward and used to the extent permissible under the applicable limitations in the succeeding 7 taxable years.

* * *

As indicated in the discussion of the reasons for the Act, the Congress concluded that the 7-percent investment credit should be restored as a means of providing stimulus to the lagging domestic economy by reducing the cost of capital to U.S. manufacturers.   This will also serve to place them in a more competitive position with foreign manufacturers and in that manner help improve our present serious balance-of-payments situations.

The Act provides for a 7-percent investment credit which is substantially similar to the investment credit previously allowed.   The three principal differences from the credit pre-

<hr>

13.   "General Explanation of the Revenue Act of 1971," Staff of the Joint Committee on Internal Revenue Taxation, pp. 20–22 (1972).

viously allowed are (1) the useful life brackets used in determining the amount of investment in property which is eligible for the credit are to be shortened by one year, (2) the credit is generally not to be allowed for foreign-produced machinery and equipment so long as the temporary import surcharge remains in effect (and may be limited after the additional duty is repealed at the discretion of the President),[14] and (3) public utility property is to be eligible for a 4-percent rather than a 3-percent credit.

The credit is to be available with respect to property acquired by the taxpayer after August 15, 1971, or in the case of property which is constructed, reconstructed, or erected by the taxpayer, where the construction is completed after August 15, 1971 (regardless of the time when construction, etc., began).

* * *

In order to more realistically reflect the useful lives of property in determining the amount of allowable investment credit, the Act shortens by one year the useful life brackets used in determining the portion of investment in property which qualifies for the credit. Under the Act, property with a useful life of 3 to 5 years is to qualify for the credit to the extent of one-third of its cost. Property with a useful life of 5 to 7 years is to qualify for the credit to the extent of two-thirds of its cost, and property with a useful life of 7 years or more is to qualify for the full amount. These replace brackets of 4 to 6 years for a one-third credit, 6 to 8 years for a two-thirds credit, and 8 years and over for a full credit.

In addition, the Act made minor changes in the definition of section 38 property, carryovers of the credit, and recapture of the credit.

In 1975 to further stimulate the economy the investment credit was generally increased to 10% for property placed in service after January 1, 1975.[15] Additionally the $50,000 limit on used property was increased to $100,000.[16] Although the 10% and $100,000 figures were at first of only very temporary applicability, Sections 801 and 802 of the Tax Reform Act of 1976 extend them to qualified acquisitions any time before January 1, 1981, along with other changes in the credit.

The Investment Credit is considered here because, if property qualifying for the credit is not held until the end of its estimated use-

---

14. The investment credit ban of foreign-produced goods applied only for the period August 15, 1971 through December 19, 1971. See Reg. 1.48–1 (o)(2). Ed.

15. I.R.C. (26 U.S.C.A.) § 46(a)(1)(A). In limited circumstances corporations are allowed an 11% credit. I.R.C. (26 U.S.C.A.) § 46(a)(1)(B).

16. I.R.C. (26 U.S.C.A.) § 48(c)(2)(A). The 1975 Reduction Act also enacted current § 46(d).

ful life, part or all of the credit must be recaptured as additional tax liability.[17]   Thus if investment credit property which had qualified for the credit is disposed of prior to its estimated useful life to the taxpayer, I.R.C. § 47(a) requires the taxpayer's tax for the taxable year of disposition to be increased by the amount of the decrease in the taxpayer's investment credit which results from deducting the amount of the investment credit based on the taxpayer's actual useful life of the property from the credit previously allowed on its estimated useful life.   The idea is that with hindsight that amount reflects excessive credit.   As the credit directly reduced tax liability, the recapture of the credit creates an actual additional tax (not just income) in the year of the property's early disposition.

If a taxpayer purchases $10,000 worth of qualifying property with an estimated useful life to him of more than seven years he is allowed a $1000 tax credit in the year of purchase.   If he disposes of the property after six years (in addition to tax on any gain or loss on the property) he is required to add an additional $333 to his tax liability for the year of the disposition.[18]   This is proper since taxpayer should have been allowed only a $667 credit in the first place (i. e. ⅔ × 10% × $10,000).   If the property were disposed of after only four years, taxpayer's recapture would be $667 resulting in increased tax liability to that extent.

---

17.   I.R.C. (26 U.S.C.A.) § 47(a).

18.   See I.R.C. (26 U.S.C.A.) § 47(b) which contains exceptions to the application of § 47.

CHAPTER 23. DEDUCTIONS AFFECTED BY CHARACTERIZATION PRINCIPLES

A. BAD DEBTS AND WORTHLESS SECURITIES

Internal Revenue Code: Sections 165(g)(1) and (2); 166(a) through (e). See Sections 62; 111(a), (b); 271(a); 6511(d)(1).
Regulations: Sections 1.165–5(a) through (c); 1.166–1, –2, –5.

Reconsider briefly the approach to deductions in general. If a deduction is to be claimed a Code section must specifically provide for it.[1] Even then, it must also be determined whether any other statutory or common law principle disallows or in some manner restricts the deduction.[2] If these hurdles are taken, question arises whether the deduction can be taken into account in the computation of adjusted gross income.[3] Finally the deduction, like an item of income, must be characterized as capital or ordinary, a process which may affect the other issues raised above.[4] Characterization presents a special problem under the bad debt deduction. As a similar problem arises with respect to the charitable deduction, § 170 is considered in the second part of this chapter.

HOWARD S. BUGBEE

Tax Court of the United States, 1975.
34 TCM 291.

Memorandum Findings of Fact and Opinion

STERRETT, JUDGE: The respondent determined a deficiency in petitioner's federal income tax for the taxable year 1966 in the amount of $7,242.68. Other issues having been conceded, the sole remaining issue [1] is whether petitioner has established the existence of a debtor-

---

1. I.R.C. (26 U.S.C.A.) § 63.

2. See, e. g., I.R.C. (26 U.S.C.A.) §§ 165(f), 262 through 279. The political party bad debt restriction of § 271 is referred to in Chapter 15, supra at page 419.

3. I.R.C. (26 U.S.C.A.) § 62.

4. I.R.C. (26 U.S.C.A.) §§ 1211, 1222.

1. Petitioner also avers respondent has erred in disallowing a medical expense deduction claimed on the same tax return. However, this disallowance was due solely to the increase in petitioner's adjusted gross income caused by the disallowance of the claimed short-term capital loss in issue. Petitioner has made no substantive allegations with respect to this disallowance.

creditor relationship with respect to funds advanced by petitioner to one Paul Billings and thereby validated his claim to a short-term capital loss under sections 166(a) and 166(d), Internal Revenue Code of 1954.[2]

Findings of Fact

Some of the facts have been stipulated and are so found. The stipulation of facts, together with the exhibits attached thereto, are incorporated herein by this reference.

Petitioner, Howard S. Bugbee (hereinafter petitioner), resided in Honolulu, Hawaii at the time of filing his petition herein. Petitioner filed a "married filing separately" federal income tax return for the taxable year 1966 with the district director of internal revenue at Los Angeles, California.

At all relevant times herein, petitioner was president and majority stockholder of Poop Deck, Inc., a California corporation operating a beer parlor in Hermosa Beach, California. The corporation's other shareholders were petitioner's then spouse Nancy Bugbee and William G. Garbade.

Petitioner first met Paul Billings (hereinafter Billings) at his beer parlor in 1957. Their relationship was first that of proprietor and customer. Over a period of time their friendship grew and they talked of business ventures that Billings might pursue. Billings became godfather to one of petitioner's children.

As a result of their conversations petitioner was impressed with Billings' abilities and thought he could turn his ideas into successful business ventures. Based on this impression, petitioner began to advance money to Billings. These advances were first evidenced by informal notes which were periodically consolidated into larger, more formal notes. There were 11 notes in all representing $19,750 advanced by petitioner to Billings.

These notes were all unconditional, unsecured demand notes signed by Billings between September, 1958 and December, 1960, and evidenced money actually received by Billings from petitioner.[3] The notes provided for interest at a rate of at least 6 percent, however no interest was ever actually paid. Billings has never repaid any part of the principal represented by these notes, although at trial he ac-

---

2. All statutory references are to the Internal Revenue Code of 1954 as amended, unless otherwise indicated.

3. A typical note provided as follows: $1000.00 September 30, 1959 ON DEMAND after date (without grace). I promise to pay to the order of Howard S. Bugbee One Thousand and no/100 ******* Dollars, for value received with interest at Six per cent per   from This Date until paid, interest payable Quarterly both principal and interest payable in lawful money of the United States.

(signed) Paul Billings
Paul Billings
1402 Strand
Hermosa Beach, Calif.
No. ——— Due On Demand.

knowledged these advances were still outstanding and evidenced an intention to repay them if possible.

During this period when the advances were made Billings was unemployed and he was basically unemployed between 1960 and 1966. Although petitioner knew Billings was unemployed between 1958 and 1960, petitioner neither investigated nor did he have any personal knowledge of Billings' financial position.

Billings used the funds received from the petitioner to investigate various business ventures, although in fact much of the money was used by Billings for personal living expenses.

Petitioner was aware of Billings' activities with respect to these ventures, but he did not participate in them. Petitioner's then spouse, Nancy Bugbee, was also aware that petitioner had advanced funds to Billings. Some of her personal funds represented the source of some of these advances. In 1966 petitioner and his spouse were divorced. In the interlocutory judgment of divorce entered June 23, 1966, by which the rights of the parties were established, no mention of the funds advanced by Nancy Bugbee was made.

Petitioner expected to be repaid after Billings established one of these ventures, but such repayment was not conditioned on the success of any of these ventures. Through 1967 petitioner had periodic personal contact with Billings and requested repayment of the notes without success.

Petitioner, on his 1966 tax return, reported a "Personal Bad Debt-Paul Billings" and claimed a $19,750 short-term capital loss. This loss was used in its entirety to offset long-term capital gain recognized that year from other sources. Respondent disallowed this loss as follows:

> (b) It is determined that the bad debt deduction which you
> claimed on your return resulting from loans to Paul Billings
> is not allowable under Section 166 of the Internal Revenue
> Code because it has not been established that a debtor-credi-
> tor relationship was intended by the loans, the amount of the
> loans have not been established and it has not been establish-
> ed that the money loaned was your property.

After the trial respondent filed a Motion for Leave to File Amended Answer to Conform the Pleadings to the Proof, pursuant to Rule 41(b) of the Rules of Practice and Procedure of this Court. In this motion respondent asserted that the testimony presented at trial raised the additional issue of whether the claimed bad debts became worthless in 1966. Respondent also filed an Amendment to Answer in which he requested that his original answer be amended to include the above issue of worthlessness as a ground for denying petitioner's claim.

Petitioner objected to this motion arguing that this issue was not raised at trial. Petitioner also objected on the grounds that this issue was not stated in the "Explanation of Adjustments" in the statutory notice received by the petitioner and that it should not be raised at this time. Petitioner asserted that if properly apprised of this issue, additional evidence with respect to it could have been presented at trial. Respondent's motion was denied by this Court.

In his reply brief, respondent has conceded that the amount of the advances has been established, and that the money advanced was the petitioner's property.

Opinion

The case at bar presents for our determination the sole issue of whether petitioner is entitled to claim a short-term capital loss within the terms of sections 166(a) and 166(d)[4] and the accompanying regulations as a result of Billings' failure to repay the funds he had advanced him. Other requirements of these provisions having been previously disposed of, the only remaining factual issue is whether a debtor-creditor relationship existed between Billings and petitioner at the time these advances were made.

To qualify under section 166 there first must exist a bona fide debt which arises from a debtor-creditor relationship based upon a valid and enforceable obligation to pay a fixed and determinable sum of money. Section 1.166–1(c), Income Tax Regs. "Whether a transfer of money creates a bona fide debt depends upon the existence of an intent by both parties, substantially contemporaneous to the time of such transfer, to establish an enforceable obligation of repayment". Delta Plastics Corp., 54 T.C. 1287, 1291 (1970). This determination then is a question of fact to which the substance and not the form of the relationship between petitioner and Billings must be applied. Delta Plastics Corp., supra.

Looking beyond the formal relationship between the petitioner and Billings, respondent has pointed out several factors that he believes amply illustrate his position. Respondent first argues that in reality these advances represented the money necessary to investigate prospective business ventures in which both men would share in the potential profits and as such do not represent loans.

Petitioner's testimony with respect to this matter is not entirely clear. At one point he stated that, if any of these ventures materialized, he "would be a part of it." Later, he stated that, although he expected to be repaid after one of these ventures was established, these advances were personal loans to Billings and that they were to be repaid from whatever sources Billings might have. Billings' testimony is more direct. He clearly stated that these advances were for his

---

4. [I.R.C. §§ 166(a) and 166(d) are omitted. Ed.]

personal business ventures and that petitioner was not involved in them. Billings also acknowledged liability for these advances and evidenced an intention to repay if possible. There is also no indication in the record of an agreement under which petitioner would be entitled to share in the profits of any of these ventures. We reject this contention of the respondent.

Respondent next argues that bona fide debts never existed since these advances were worthless when made and petitioner did not have a reasonable expectation that they would be repaid. In support respondent points out that during this period Billings was unemployed and had no independent means of support, that the loans were unsecured, that despite the failure of Billings to make interest payments on the first notes additional funds were advanced, that the nature of Billings' proposed ventures was purely speculative, and that petitioner never sought repayment in court.

Respondent does not question the wisdom of these advances. Anyway that determination could only be made with the use of hindsight, which in this instance is not an appropriate tool. As noted earlier our task is to determine the intent of the parties as it existed when the advances were made. *Delta Plastics Corp.*, supra. See Santa Anita Consolidated, Inc., 50 T.C. 536, 554 (1968).

The record in this case does indicate that Billings was in poor financial condition when these advances were made. However this Court has said that this factor does not preclude a finding of the existence of a bona fide debt. *Santa Anita Consolidated, Inc.*, supra, at 553; Richard M. Drachman, 23 T.C. 558 (1954). The use of unsecured notes reflects the nature of the risk involved that petitioner accepted. Any unsecured debt involves some risk, however this factor is not determinative. *Santa Anita Consolidated, Inc.*, supra at 552.

This Court has said, "For the advance to be a loan, it is not necessary that there be an unqualified expectation of repayment." *Richard M. Drachman,* supra at 562. In the final analysis the repayment of any loan depends on the success of the borrower. "The real differences lie in the debt-creating intention of the parties, and the genuineness of repayment prospects in the light of economic realities", *Santa Anita Consolidated, Inc.,* supra at 552. See also Earle v. W. J. Jones & Son, 200 F.2d 846, 851 (9th Cir. 1952).

We have found that petitioner made these advances because he believed Billings could be successful and that he would be subsequently repaid. After a careful review of the record, we believe petitioner's motives were genuine and that they existed throughout the period during which these advances were made.

Respondent maintains that, since Billings was in poor financial condition, in reality any repayment was conditioned on Billings' busiess success and, since that condition was never fulfilled, there never was an enforceable repayment obligation. For support respondent cites Zimmerman v. United States, 318 F.2d 611 (9th Cir. 1963). In that case the taxpayer advanced money to an organization he was initiating. Repayment was to be made out of the dues collected from the members of this new organization. The organization faltered and the taxpayer was not repaid. The court held that the contingent nature of the repayment obligation alone precluded the finding of a bona fide debt. See also Alexander & Baldwin v. Kanne, 190 F.2d 153, 154 (9th Cir. 1951) (repayment " 'only when, if and to the extent that,' after all the indebtedness and liquidation costs of Waterhouse Company had been paid, there remained an excess of assets.") ; Bercaw v. Commissioner, 165 F.2d 521, 525 (4th Cir. 1948), affirming a memorandum decision of this Court (" * * * oral agreement under which petitioner agreed to advance the money necessary to carry on the litigation and the guardian agreed to pay petitioner from any funds recovered * * *.")

The facts in the case at bar do not reveal that any repayments by Billings were conditioned on his ultimate success. Although petitioner expected to be repaid after Billings had established one of his ventures, we have found that petitioner was to be repaid from any assets that Billings might have. Billings himself testified that these advances were personal, unconditional loans for which he was liable.

Respondent finally argues that, since petitioner and Billings were close personal friends, these advances might be classified as gifts. Although the parties were friends, their relationship did not have a long history. There also was no blood relationship, although Billings was named godfather to one of the Bugbee children.

Although the record does not indicate petitioner's financial condition during the period 1958–1960, the divorce decree issued in 1966 only describes assets of moderate value. We do not believe that petitioner's financial condition was such that he could make these advances without expectation of repayment. The facts do not support respondent's contention that these advances were gifts. Commissioner v. Duberstein, 363 U.S. 278 (1960).

We believe that petitioner has established the existence of a debtor-creditor relationship and that respondent's determination must be denied.

Decision will be entered under Rule 155.

NOTE

The best approach to the bad debt deduction is to raise three questions: (1) Is there a debt? (2) Is it a bad debt? (3) Is it a business bad debt?

The first question which is raised in the *Bugbee* case, above, is most likely to arise with respect to individuals, although it has a corporate counterpart. There is a presumption that transfers between relatives or close friends do not constitute loans.[1] For example, if F "lends" $1000 to S, his son, this may or may not give rise to a debt, depending upon the subjective intention of the parties at the time of the "loan" and their ability to overcome the presumption. If there is no intention that the "debt" ever be repaid, that which takes the form of a loan is in fact a gift.[2] Of course, at the outset it makes no difference, as neither loan nor gift is deductible and neither is income to the recipient. But if a bad debt deduction is later asserted, it cannot be supported unless the original transaction was in fact a loan. The obvious uncertainties inherent in this situation are behind the restrictive treatment accorded nonbusiness debts. When the forerunner of § 166(d) was enacted in 1942, the committee reports indicated: [3]

> The present law gives the same treatment to bad debts incurred in nonbusiness transactions as it allows to business bad debts. An example of a nonbusiness bad debt would be an unrepaid loan to a friend or relative * * *. This liberal allowance for nonbusiness bad debts has suffered considerable abuse through taxpayers making loans which they do not expect to be repaid. This practice is particularly prevalent in the case of loans to persons with respect to whom the taxpayer is not entitled to a credit for dependents. The situation has presented serious administrative difficulties because of the requirement of proof.

Secondly, as regards the *bad* debt question, gratuitous forgiveness of a loan generates no deduction. A transaction that starts out as a loan may be converted to a mere non-deductible gift. The deduction arises only when the debt becomes uncollectible, "bad". This concept does not require proof of an unsatisfied judgment. The Regulations [4] indicate the degree of pessimism permitted the taxpayer in a determination that a debt is a bad debt.

Finally, the business or nonbusiness dichotomy of § 166 must be taken into account. Identify the three ways in which a business debt is or may be accorded different treatment from a nonbusiness debt when uncollectibility looms. The somewhat involved residual definition of a nonbusiness bad debt in § 166(d) (2) (A) and (B) will be better understood having in mind the following fragment of legislative history: [5]

> If a debt at the time it becomes worthless is not directly related to the taxpayer's trade or business, under present law

---

1. See Jacob Grossman, 9 B.T.A. 643 (1927); Carolyn C. Marlett, 35 TCM 456 (1976).

2. See note 1, supra.

3. House Rep.No.2333, 77th Cong. 1st Sess. (1942), 1942–2 C.B. 372, 408.

4. Reg. § 1.166–2.

5. Sen.Fin.Comm.Rep. No. 1622, 83rd Cong.2d Sess., p. 24 (1954).

it is treated as a nonbusiness bad debt. This rule is applied even though the debt was related to the taxpayer's trade or business at the time it was created. For example, a taxpayer is not permitted to treat as a business bad debt, which is fully deductible, an account receivable which proves uncollectible after the taxpayer has gone out of business. [See § 166(d)(2)(B). Ed.]

The bill eliminates this harsh treatment by permitting the taxpayer to deduct as a business bad debt an obligation which becomes worthless, whether or not it is directly related to the trade or business at that time, if it was a bona fide business asset at the time it was created or acquired. [See § 166(d)(2)(A). Ed.]

A policy reason for the business-nonbusiness bad debt classifications created by Congress in 1942 [6] was "to put nonbusiness investments in the form of loans on a footing with other nonbusiness investments." [7] With this reason in mind, the courts have been strict in interpreting the trade or business requirement. [8]

One problem has been that of loans by a shareholder-employee of a corporation to the corporation. In a leading case, Whipple v. Comm'r, [9] the taxpayer, who had for many years been promoting both corporate and noncorporate businesses, formed a corporation in which he was an 80% shareholder and subsequently made loans to it. The corporation failed and he attempted to treat the loans as business bad debts. Unsuccessful in the Tax Court [10] and the Court of Appeals, [11] he finally reached the Supreme Court where he fared no better. A corporation's business is of course not that of its shareholder, [12] and the business classification of the loan therefore depended upon the taxpayer's own business. Working from that premise, the Supreme Court said, in part: [13]

> Petitioner, therefore, must demonstrate that he is engaged in a trade or business, and lying at the heart of his

---

6. Revenue Act of 1942. § 124(a)(4), 56 Stat. 798, 821 (1942). There are other distinctions between business and nonbusiness bad debts. Partially worthless business bad debts are deductible to the extent property charged off (I.R.C. (26 U.S.C.A.) § 166(a)(2)), and a reserve may be established for business bad debts (I.R.C. (26 U.S.C.A.) § 166(c)).

7. Putnam v. Comm'r, 352 U.S. 82, 92, 77 S.Ct. 175 (1956). Cf. Bittker and Eustice, Federal Income Taxation of Corporations and Shareholders, 4–35 n. 72 (1971). For a consideration of the distinction between property held for investment and property used in a trade or business see Chapter 16 at page 428.

8. In addition to Putnam, supra note 7, see Comm'r v. Smith, 203 F.2d 310

(2d Cir. 1953), cert. den., 346 U.S. 816, 74 S.Ct. 27 (1953).

9. 373 U.S. 193, 83 S.Ct. 1168 (1963).

10. A. J. Whipple, 19 T.C.M. 187 (1960).

11. Whipple v. Comm'r, 301 F.2d 108 (5th Cir. 1962).

12. A. J. Whipple, supra note 10 at 192. See Knickerbocker, 'What Constitutes a Trade or Business for Bad Debt Purposes: 'Stockholder' as a Business," 23 N.Y.U. Inst. on Fed. Tax. 113 (1965).

13. 373 U.S. 193, 201–203, 83 S.Ct. 1168, 1173–1174 (1962). Footnotes omitted.

claim is the issue upon which the lower courts have divided and which brought the case here: That where a taxpayer furnishes regular services to one or many corporations, an independent trade or business of the taxpayer has been shown. But against the background of the 1943 amendments and the decisions of this Court in the *Dalton, Burnet, duPont* and *Higgins* cases, petitioner's claim must be rejected.

Devoting one's time and energies to the affairs of a corporation is not of itself, and without more, a trade or business of the person so engaged. Though such activities may produce income, profit or gain in the form of dividends or enhancement in the value of an investment, this return is distinctive to the process of investing and is generated by the successful operation of the corporation's business as distinguished from the trade or business of the taxpayer himself. When the only return is that of an investor, the taxpayer has not satisfied his burden of demonstrating that he is engaged in a trade or business since investing is not a trade or business and the return to the taxpayer, though substantially the product of his services, legally arises not from his own trade or business but from that of the corporation. Even if the taxpayer demonstrates an independent trade or business of his own, care must be taken to distinguish bad debts losses arising from his own business and those actually arising from activities peculiar to an investor concerned with, and participating in, the conduct of the corporate business.

If full-time service to one corporation does not alone amount to a trade or business, which it does not, it is difficult to understand how the same service to many corporations would suffice. To be sure, the presence of more than one corporation might lend support to a finding that the taxpayer was engaged in a regular course of promoting corporations for a fee or commission, see Ballantine, Corporations (rev. ed. 1946), 102, or for a profit on their sale, see Giblin v. Commissioner, 227 F.2d 692, (C.A.5th Cir.), but in such cases there is compensation other than the normal investor's return, income received directly for his own services rather than indirectly through the corporate enterprise, and the principles of *Burnet, Dalton, duPont* and *Higgins* are therefore not offended. On the other hand, since the Tax Court found, and the petitioner does not dispute, that there was no intention here of developing the corporations as going businesses for sale to customers in the ordinary course, the case before us inexorably rests upon the claim that one who actively engages in serving his own corporations for the purpose of creating future income through those enterprises is in a trade or business. That argument is untenable in light of *Burnet, Dalton, duPont* and *Higgins,* and we reject it. Absent substantial additional evidence, furnishing management and other services to corporations for a reward not different from that flowing to an investor in those corporations is not a trade or business under § 23 (k) (4). We are, therefore, fully in agreement with this aspect of the decision below.

Although the courts have held that loans by shareholder-employees are generally nonbusiness, investment-type loans, in some such circumstances business bad debt deductions have been allowed. A shareholder who is an employee of a corporation is engaged in business as an employee.[14] If such a taxpayer makes a loan to his corporation *to insure his continued employment*, the loan may properly be classified as one arising out of the conduct of his trade or business, that of performing services as an employee. In a leading case [15] adopting this rationale, the taxpayer was required by the majority shareholders of the corporation in which he was a minority shareholder to make loans to the corporation in order to retain his employment status. He was discharged later upon his refusal to make further loans. When the corporation subsequently failed and the loans become uncollectible, the taxpayer was allowed a business bad debt deduction.[16]

A loan to a corporation by a shareholder-employee, even if not made to preserve his job, may get business classification if it bears the required proximate relationship to a separate unincorporated business of the taxpayer.[17] In one case,[18] Abe Saperstein who, before his death, owned the Harlem Globetrotters outright, made loans to the now defunct American Basketball League, in which he owned an interest and for which he served, uncompensated, as commissioner. The loans later became worthless. The court held the loans were not mere investments but were proximately related to Mr. Saperstein's separate Globetrotter business. It was enough that the taxpayer had made the loans to the A.B.L. in the hope that it would provide competition and playing sites for the Globetrotter team.

It is generally accepted that business classification turns on the question whether loans are "proximately related" [19] to the taxpayer's trade or business. However, the application of this test has not been

---

14. Cf. I.R.C. (26 U.S.C.A.) § 62(1) and (2).

15 Trent v. Comm'r, 291 F.2d 669 (2d Cir. 1961).

16. Several recent cases have followed and extended this rationale. See B. A. Faucher, 29 T.C.M. 950 (1970); Maurice Artstein 29 T.C.M. 961 (1970).

17. In Whipple, supra note 9, the Supreme Court remanded the case to the Tax Court for a determination whether the loans bore the requisite relationship to a separate real estate business of the taxpayer. The case was settled prior to a decision on remand. See Knickerbocker, supra note 12.

18. Estate of A. M. Saperstein, 29 T.C. M. 919 (1970).

19. Reg. § 1.166–5(b).

uniform. The problem is that one can have both investment and business motives for making loans. In such cases is it enough that business is a significant motive for the loan? Or must it be the primary motive?

The Supreme Court has now set the requirement that business be the dominent motive for the loan.[20]

CHARLES J. HASLAM

Tax Court of the United States, 1974.
33 TCM 482.

Memorandum Findings of Fact and Opinion

FORRESTER, JUDGE: Respondent determined a deficiency in petitioners' Federal income tax for the taxable year 1967 in the amount of $979.01 and a penalty pursuant to section 6651(a)[1] in the amount of $244.75.

The only issue for our decision is whether petitioners are entitled to business or nonbusiness deductions for losses arising from their guarantee of debts of Charles J. Haslam's wholly owned corporation.[2]

Findings of Fact

Some of the facts have been stipulated and are so found.

Petitioners, Charles J. Haslam and Harriet S. Haslam, are husband and wife who, at the time of the filing of the petition herein, resided in Slingerlands, New York. They filed their Federal joint income tax return for 1967 on April 15, 1969, with the district director of internal revenue in Albany, New York.

From 1948 to 1954 Charles J. Haslam (hereinafter referred to as petitioner) was employed by the Dupont Company in their explosives division as a sales and technical representative. Prior to this time, he had worked a great deal with explosives in the army as a captain in the corps of combat engineers, and had received additional training in explosives at Michigan College of Mining and Technology where he received a bachelor of science degree in 1948.

In 1954 petitioner and Earl Canavan (Canavan) established Northern Explosives, Inc. (Northern), a corporation engaged in the sale and distribution of explosives. Petitioner and Canavan each owned 50 percent of the stock in Northern, each having an investment of $10,000.

Petitioner managed the corporate business of Northern and was also employed by the corporation as a salesman, while Canavan took no active part in the corporate operations. Northern had three em-

---

20. United States v. Generes, 405 U.S. 93 (1972).

1. All statutory references are to the Internal Revenue Code of 1954, as amended, unless otherwise specified.

2. Petitioners have conceded that the delinquency penalty imposed by respondent is warranted if there is a deficiency in their income tax for 1967.

ployees in addition to petitioner, two truck drivers and a part-time secretary.

In 1957, petitioner bought out Canavan's interest in Northern for $10,000, thereafter owning 100 percent of the stock with an investment of $20,000.

In 1960, Northern encountered financial difficulties and required additional cash to continue its operations. Thereafter petitioner guaranted loans in the total amount of $100,000 made to Northern by the National Commercial Bank and Trust Company of Albany, New York (Commercial). To secure these guarantees petitioner pledged certain marketable securities and his personal residence.

At the time petitioner guaranteed the loans, he was devoting his full time and effort to his employment with Northern. His salary was approximately $250 to $300 per week and, in addition, he received an automobile, funds for its maintenance and insurance, medical insurance, and other employee benefits. With the exception of stock dividends of $4,000 to $5,000 per year (said dividends from securities of petitioner other than his stock in Northern), petitioner had no other source of income.

Despite the loans to the corporation, Northern continued to experience financial difficulties. The corporation went into chapter XI status under the Federal Bankruptcy Act in 1961, and went bankrupt in 1964. Northern was unable to repay the loans guaranteed by petitioner, and in 1967 Commercial sold the securities pledged by petitioner for $70,464.58. Commercial applied $55,956 of this amount to the debt of Northern guaranteed by petitioner, and the remaining $14,508.58 to petitioner's liability on another debt obligation.

Petitioner remained an employee of Northern until it went bankrupt in 1964. In June 1964 he obtained employment as a salesman of steel castings for Falvey Steel Castings, Inc. (Falvey). Petitioner's gross income from his draw against commissions from Falvey during the years 1964 to 1968 are as follows:

Year	Draw Against Commissions
1964	$ 2,900.00
1965	14,025.00
1966	11,307.00
1967	10,704.06
1968	11,213.42

During the years 1965 and 1966 petitioner's actual earned commissions were only approximately $10,000 per year. Sums petitioner received in excess of these amounts were cash advances against future commissions.

On their joint Federal income tax return for 1967 petitioners claimed a business bad debt in the amount of $55,956 on the loss sustained on petitioner's guarantee of the Northern loans. Respondent disallowed petitioners' claimed loss as a business bad debt, determining that it was deductible only as a nonbusiness bad debt.

Opinion

The sole issue for our decision is whether petitioners are entitled to a business or nonbusiness bad debt deduction for losses arising from their guarantee of debts of a corporation in which petitioner Charles J. Haslam was both an employee and an investor.

A bad debt loss, deductible under section 166, is created where a taxpayer sustains a loss upon payment on the guarantee of a debt, and the debtor is unable to satisfy the guarantor. Putnam v. Commissioner, 352 U.S. 82 (1956); Stratmore v. United States, 420 F.2d 461 (C.A. 3, 1970); Estate of Martha M. Byers, 57 T.C. 568, 574 (1972), affirmed per curiam 472 F.2d 590 (C.A. 6, 1973); Robert E. Gillespie, 54 T.C. 1025, 1031, affirmed by an unpublished order [72–2 USTC ¶ 9742] (C.A. 9, 1972). Thus, petitioners sustained a bad debt loss upon payment of their guarantee of Northern debts subsequent to its bankruptcy.

Under section 166, business bad debt losses are deductible against ordinary income, while nonbusiness bad debt losses are deductible only as short-term capital losses. Petitioners argue that their bad debt loss is deductible as a business bad debt, while respondent argues that it is deductible only as a nonbusiness bad debt.

The character of a bad debt loss is determined by the relationship it bears to the taxpayer's trade or business. A debt will only qualify as a business bad debt if it bears a direct relationship to the taxpayer's trade or business (Hogue v. Commissioner, 459 F.2d 932, 939, fn. 11 (C.A. 10, 1972), affirming a Memorandum Opinion of this Court [Dec. 30,733(M)]; Estate of Martha M. Byers, 57 T.C. 568, 577 (1972); Oddee Smith, 55 T.C. 260, 268 (1970), vacated and remanded per curiam 457 F.2d 797 (C.A. 5, 1972), opinion on remand 60 T.C. 316 (1973)), and such relationship is a proximate one. I. Hal Millsap, Jr., 46 T.C. 751, 754, fn. 3 (1966), affd. 387 F.2d 420 (C.A. 8, 1968); Stratmore v. United States, 420 F.2d 461 (C.A. 3, 1970); sec. 1.166–5(b), Income Tax Regs. In the instant case, petitioners argue that their guarantees to Northern bear such a relationship to petitioner's trade or business as an employee of that corporation.

It is clear that being an employee may constitute a trade or business for the purposes of section 166. Trent v. Commissioner, 291 F.2d 669 (C.A. 2, 1961); cf. David J. Primuth, 54 T.C. 374 (1970). It is also clear that the debt obligations in the instant case were directly related to petitioner's trade or business as an employee, in that petitioners' guarantees were required for Northern to obtain the funds needed to continue its operations and petitioner's employment. The determination of whether the guarantees were proximately related to petitioner's trade or business as an employee, however, presents a more difficult question, in that petitioner also had an interest in Northern as its sole shareholder. Being an investor in a corporation does not constitute a trade or business, and losses resulting from guarantees made to protect a taxpayer's investment are not deductible as a business bad debt. Whipple v. Commissioner, 373 U.S. 193 (1963).

Where a taxpayer sustains a loss on a guarantee to a corporation in which he has both an employee and stockholder interest, a proximate relationship between the taxpayer's trade or business as an employee and his loss is established only if the taxpayer's dominant motivation in entering into the guarantees was to protect the employee interest. United States v. Generes, 405 U.S. 93 (1972). Petitioners, therefore, must prove that their dominant motivation in guaranteeing the loans to Northern was to protect petitioner's employment in order to establish the requisite proximate relationship.

The determination of taxpayer's dominant motivation is a factual question on which the taxpayer bears the burden of proof. Oddee Smith, 60 T.C. 316, 318 (1973). The trier of fact must determine the taxpayer's overriding reason for incurring the obligation and, in so doing "compare the risk against the potential reward and give proper emphasis to the objective rather than to the subjective." United States v. Generes, supra at 104.

In *Generes* the employee-shareholder had an initial investment of approximately $40,000 in his corporation. He worked six to eight hours a week for the corporation at an annual salary of $12,000, and had full-time employment outside of the corporation as the president of a savings and loan association at an annual salary of $19,000. His annual gross income was approximately $40,000 per year. Other members of the taxpayer's family also had employment and investment interests in the corporation. The Supreme Court held that these factors would not support a finding that the taxpayer's dominant motivation in guaranteeing loans to his corporation was to protect his employment with the corporation. In its holding, the Supreme Court disregarded the taxpayer's testimony that his dominant motivation was related to his employment, determining that his testimony was self-serving and not supported by the facts.

In the instant case, petitioner testified that his dominant motivation in guaranteeing loans to Northern was to protect his employment. It is our conclusion that the facts support his testimony, and accordingly we hold that petitioner's loss is deductible as a business bad debt.

Unlike the taxpayer in *Generes*, petitioner was a full-time employee of his corporation and he had no other employment. His salary from Northern was his major source of income. We note that petitioner's skills as an explosives' expert were not apparently readily marketable and that subsequent to Northern's bankruptcy petitioner obtained employment in a field unrelated to explosives at a salary less than he earned at Northern.

Viewing the facts in the record realistically, we think it much more likely that petitioner was more interested in preserving his position as an employee rather than as an investor in Northern. It is clear that petitioner made the guarantees in the hope of preserving Northern's corporate existence. From his position as an investor, it is clear that the preservation of the corporation would at best afford him some prospect of saving the $20,000 he had invested in the corporation. From his position as an employee however, such preservation would assure petitioner's continued employment at an annual salary of approximately $15,000. In our opinion, an assured salary of $15,000 per year over a period of years was a more valuable interest to petitioner than the mere possibility of recouping the already invested $20,000 in Northern, and the prospect of such continued employment was petitioner's dominant motivation in guaranteeing the loans to Northern. We thus decide the sole remaining issue for petitioner, but because of concessions.

Decision will be entered under Rule 155.

PROBLEMS

1. In year one Lawyer performs legal services for Client and bills him $1000. Client does not pay Lawyer. In year six it becomes evident the debt will never be paid.

   (a) What else must be known in order to determine whether Lawyer is entitled to a bad debt deduction? What will the character of any allowed deduction be?

   (b) Assuming that the Commissioner asserts (and Lawyer cannot show otherwise) that the debt in fact became worthless in year two, is Lawyer's use of the bad debt deduction necessarily foreclosed by the statute of limitations?

   (c) Assuming Lawyer was allowed a deduction for year six, what tax consequences to Lawyer if in year seven Client inherits some money and pays the $1000 obligation? What consequences upon payment in year seven if Lawyer properly was not allowed the deduction in year six?

2. Without regard to the transactions or events described below Cher Holder, who is a single taxpayer, has gross ordinary income of $60,000, ordinary deductions of $20,000, and taxable income of $40,000 in 1978. Consider *together* the following further facts and then answer questions (a) through (c) which follow:

   (1) Cher owns a $5,000 "note" of Flibinite Corporation which she got from the Corporation for a loan of that amount and which is supposed to pay nine percent interest each year. Flibinite goes bankrupt and Cher's "note" is worthless. The Commissioner successfully

asserts that Cher's "note" represents an equity contribution to Flibinite. Cher acquired the "note" two years ago.

(2) Cher owns common stock in Flibinite which also becomes worthless in the current year. She paid $3,000 for the stock the year before.

(3) Two years ago Cher loaned her friend Mooney $2600. That loan becomes worthless in the current year. (What factors would be considered in determining if the loan created a bona fide debt?) Assume the debt was bona fide.

(4) Cher owned some tax exempt state bonds which she purchased for $8,000 four years ago. When they were worth $12,000 they were stolen and Cher received $12,000 in insurance proceeds in the current year.

    (a) To what extent will the above transactions reduce Cher's taxable income for the year?

    (b) What, if any, is Cher's capital loss carryover to the succeeding year?

    (c) If, in addition, Cher had sold some stock for $20,000 which she had purchased one year earlier for $9,400, what is her tax liability for the current year? (Assume her other deductions, except for § 1202, are still $20,000.)

B. THE CHARITABLE DEDUCTION *

Internal Revenue Code: Sections 170(a)(1), (b)(1)(A), (B), (C), and (E), (c), (e)(1) and (2); 1011(b). See Sections 162(b); 170(b)(2), (d)(1)(A).

REVENUE RULING 73–113

1973–1 Cum.Bull. 65.

Advice has been requested whether payments to a special fund, under the circumstances described below, are deductible as ordinary and necessary business expenses.

* See Taggart, "The Charitable Deduction," 26 Tax L.Rev. 63–157 (1970); see also Livsey, "Charitable Deductions: Planning under the New Restrictions," 57 A.B.A.J. 236 (1971); Sorlien and Olsen, "Analyzing the New Charitable Contributions Rules: Planning, Pitfalls, Problems," 32 J. Tax. 218 (1970); Bittker, "Churches, Taxes, and the Constitution," 78 Yale L.J. 1285 (1969); McDaniel, "Federal Matching Grants for Charitable Contributions: A Substitute for the Income Tax Deduction," 27 Tax L.R. 377 (1972); Bittker, "Charitable Contributions: Tax Deductions or Matching Grants?" 28 Tax L.R. 37 (1972); Schwarz, "Limiting Religious Tax Exemptions: When Should the Church Render Unto Caesar?" 29 U. of Fla. L.Rev. 50 (1976).

The taxpayer is a corporation engaged in a retail business in a resort city, and derives a significant portion of its income from the tourist industry in that city. In 1969, an oil well blow-out occurred in the vicinity of the city's coast line, causing crude oil to pollute the channel waters and beaches. Even though the beaches were cleaned after the blow-out, the shifting of winds and tides periodically caused large quantities of crude oil to wash ashore and blacken the area's beaches.

The widespread publicity concerning the continuing pollution had a significant adverse effect on the city's business community and its tourist industry, and the taxpayer in particular suffered a considerable loss of business as a result of the oil blow-out. In addition, the pollution resulted in heavy loss of wildlife and damage to the beaches and other real and personal property. The steady upward trend in the city's tourist traffic was reversed in 1969, while other coastal communities continued to enjoy increasing traffic.

To reverse the detrimental effects described above, the City Council adopted a resolution which established a special fund for the protection of local business through an oil pollution control fund. The resolution limited expenditures of money from the fund to uses which were exclusively for the economic benefit of local trade and commerce and prohibited the use of the fund's money for lobbying efforts to influence public opinion with regard to legislation through advertising or otherwise, or any other political activity which seeks to influence legislation.

Amounts paid to the fund may be used for, but are not limited to, the following purposes:

(a) nonpartisan scientific research on the subject of oil pollution and publication of the results thereof,

(b) physical preservation of the city's natural beauty of its coastline and beaches, and

(c) advertising to counteract damaging publicity which threatened and continues to threaten the business community.

The taxpayer voluntarily paid an amount of money that was deposited in the fund administered by the city, and the amount thereof was commensurate with the financial return expected to be derived by the taxpayer. The specific question presented is whether the taxpayer may deduct the amount paid as an ordinary and necessary business expense.

Section 162(a) of the Internal Revenue Code of 1954 allows a deduction for all the ordinary and necessary expenses paid or incurred during the taxable year in carrying on any trade or business.

Section 162(b) of the Code provides that no deduction shall be allowed under subsection (a) for any contribution or gift which would be allowable as a deduction under section 170 were it not for the percentage limitations, the dollar limitations, or the requirements as to the time of payment, set forth in that section.

Section 1.162–15(a) (1) of the Income Tax Regulations provides, in part, that no deduction is allowable under section 162(a) of the Code for a contribution or gift by an individual or corporation if any part thereof is deductible under section 170.

Section 1.162–15(a) (2) of the regulations provides, in part, that the limitation in section 1.162–15(a) (1) of the regulations and the limitation in section 162(b) of the Code apply only to payments which are in fact contributions or gifts to organizations described in section 170.

Section 1.162–15(b) of the regulations provides that donations to organizations other than those described in section 170 of the Code, which bear a direct relationship to the taxpayer's business and are made with the reasonable expectation of a financial return commensurate with the amount of the donation, may constitute allowable deductions as business expenses.

Section 170 of the Code provides for the deductibility of charitable contributions as defined in subsection (c), payment of which is made within the taxable year. A charitable contribution is defined, in part, in section 170(c) (1) of the Code as meaning a contribution or gift to or for the use of a State or one of its political subdivisions, but only if the contribution is for an exclusively public purpose.

Sections 1.170–1(c) (1) and 1.170A–1(c) (5) of the regulations provide that transfers of property to an organization described in section 170(c) of the Code which bear a direct relationship to the taxpayer's business and which are made with a reasonable expectation of financial return commensurate with the amount of the transfer may constitute allowable deductions as trade or business expenses rather than as charitable contributions.

Thus, where a taxpayer engaged in trade or business makes a transfer of property with a reasonable expectation of financial return to himself in his trade or business, commensurate with the amount of the transfer, no deduction under section 170 of the Code is allowable with respect to such transfer and the transfer may constitute an ordinary and necessary business expense under section 162 of the Code. Conversely, where a taxpayer engaged in trade or business makes a voluntary contribution of property without a reasonable expectation of a financial return to him in his trade or business, the deductibility of the transfer is to be determined under section 170 of the Code and no deduction under section 162 of the Code will be allowable with respect to such transfer. These principles are applicable irrespective of whether the recipient of the payments is an organization described in section 170 of the Code.

826 CHARACTERIZATION Pt. 6

Whether a particular transfer was made with a reasonable expectation of a financial return, commensurate with the amount of the transfer, is a question of fact. In the circumstances described above, the taxpayer had suffered a considerable loss of business as a result of the oil blow-out. The payment made by the taxpayer to the fund was reasonably calculated to improve the taxpayer's future business and was commensurate with the financial return expected to be derived by the taxpayer.

Accordingly, the taxpayer's payments to the special fund are deductible as ordinary and necessary business expenses of carrying on his trade or business under section 162(a) of the Code.

Revenue Ruling 69-90, 1969-1 C.B. 63, concerning a situation where merchants and property owners voluntarily contributed money to enable the local government to acquire public parking facilities is distinguishable. In that Revenue Ruling, the taxpayers could not reasonably expect a financial return commensurate with the amount of payments, since the amount of the payments was not based on the proximity of the facilities to the taxpayer's property, nor on the probable use of the facilities by the taxpayers, their tenants, or customers.

REVENUE RULING 71-112

1971-9 Int.Rev.Bull. 16.

Advice has been requested whether, under the circumstances stated below, a deduction will be allowed for amounts paid to an educational organization described in section 170(c) of the Internal Revenue Code of 1954.

A private school that is an educational organization described in section 170(c) of the Code requires as a condition to enrollment payment of a $5x$ dollars "tuition fee" for each enrolling student and $10x$ dollars per family as a "donation."

Section 170 of the Code provides for allowance of a deduction for charitable contributions or gifts (subject to certain requirements and liimtations) to or for the use of certain specified types of organizations that include the educational institution described above.

The term "charitable contribution," as used in section 170 of the Code, has been held to be synonymous with the word "gift." Katherine M. Channing v. United States, 4 F.Supp. 33 (1933), affirmed per curiam 67 F.2d 986, certiorari denied 291 U.S. 686. A gift is generally defined as a voluntary transfer of property by its owner to another with donative intent and without consideration. If a payment proceeds primarily from the incentive of anticipated benefit to the payor beyond the satisfaction which flows from the performance of a generous act, it is not a gift. Commissioner v. Duberstein, 363 U.S. 278 (1960), Ct.D.1850, C.B. 1960-2, 428.

In this case, payments of both the tuition fee and the so-called "donation" represent consideration between the parties. Therefore, each lacks a donative intent and is not a gift for purposes of section 170 of the Code.

Accordingly, it is held that since the amounts paid under the circumstances described above are not gifts for the purposes of section 170 of the Code, no deduction for a charitable contribution is allowable under the provisions of that section.

REVENUE RULING 67–246

1967–2 Cum.Bull. 104.

Advice has been requested concerning certain fund-raising practices which are frequently employed by or on behalf of charitable organizations and which involve the deductibility, as charitable contributions under section 170 of the Internal Revenue Code of 1954, of payments in connection with admission to or other participation in fund-raising activities for charity such as charity balls, bazaars, banquets, shows, and athletic events.

Affairs of the type in question are commonly employed to raise funds for charity in two ways. One is from profit derived from sale of admissions or other privileges or benefits connected with the event at such prices as their value warrants. Another is through the use of the affair as an occasion for solicitation of gifts in combination with the sale of the admissions or other privileges or benefits involved. In cases of the latter type the sale of the privilege or benefit is combined with solicitation of a gift or donation of some amount in addition to the sale value of the admission or privilege.

The need for guidelines on the subject is indicated by the frequency of misunderstanding of the requirements for deductibility of such payments and increasing incidence of their erroneous treatment for income tax purposes.

In particular, an increasing number of instances are being reported in which the public has been erroneously advised in advertisements or solicitations by sponsors that the entire amounts paid for tickets or other privileges in connection with fund-raising affairs for charity are deductible. Audits of returns are revealing other instances of erroneous advice and misunderstanding as to what, if any, portion of such payments is deductible in various circumstances. There is evidence also of instances in which taxpayers are being misled by questionable solicitation practices which make it appear from the wording of the solicitation that taxpayer's payment is a "contribution," whereas the payment solicited is simply the purchase price of an item offered for sale by the organization.

Section 170 of the Code provides for allowance of deductions for charitable contributions, subject to certain requirements and limitations. To the extent here relevant a charitable contribution is defined by that section as "a contribution or gift to or for the use of" certain specified types of organizations.

To be deductible as a charitable contribution for Federal income tax purposes under section 170 of the Code, a payment to or for the use of a qualified charitable organization must be a gift. To be a gift for such purposes in the present context there must be, among other requirements, a payment of money or transfer of property without adequate consideration.

As a general rule, where a transaction involving a payment is in the form of a purchase of an item of value, the presumption arises that no gift has been made for charitable contribution purposes, the presumption being that the payment in such case is the purchase price.

Thus, where consideration in the form of admissions or other privileges or benefits is received in connection with payments by patrons of fund-raising affairs of the type in question, the presumption is that the payments are not gifts. In such case, therefore, if a charitable contribution deduction is claimed with respect to the payment, the burden is on the taxpayer to establish that the amount paid is not the purchase price of the privileges or benefits and that part of the payment, in fact, does qualify as a gift.

In showing that a gift has been made, an essential element is proof that the portion of the payment claimed as a gift represents the excess of the total amount paid over the value of the consideration received therefor. This may be established by evidence that the payment exceeds the fair market value of the privileges or other benefits received by the amount claimed to have been paid as a gift.

Another element which is important in establishing that a gift was made in such circumstances, is evidence that the payment in excess of the value received was made with the intention of making a gift. While proof of such intention may not be an essential requirement under all circumstances and may sometimes be inferred from surrounding circumstances, the intention to make a gift is, nevertheless, highly relevant in overcoming doubt in those cases in which there is a question whether an amount was in fact paid as a purchase price or as a gift.

Regardless of the intention of the parties, however, a payment of the type in question can in any event qualify as a deductible gift only to the extent that it is shown to exceed the fair market value of any consideration received in the form of privileges or other benefits.

In those cases in which a fund-raising activity is designed to solicit payments which are intended to be in part a gift and in part the purchase price of admission to or other participation in an event of the type in question, the organization conducting the activity should employ procedures which make clear not only that a gift is being solicited in connection with the sale of the admissions or other privileges related to the fund-raising event, but, also the amount of the gift being solicited. To do this, the amount properly attributable to the purchase of admissions or other privileges and the amount solicited as a gift should be determined in advance of solicitation. The respective amounts should be stated in making the solicitation and clearly indicated on any ticket, receipt, or other evidence issued in connection with the payment.

In making such a determination, the full fair market value of the admission and other benefits or privileges must be taken into account. Where the affair is reasonably comparable to events for which there are established charges for admission, such as theatrical or athletic performances, the established charges should be treated as fixing the fair market value of the admission or privilege. Where the amount paid is the same as the standard admission charge there is, of course, no deductible contribution, regardless of the intention of the parties. Where the event has no such counterpart, only that portion of the payment which exceeds a reasonable estimate of the fair market value of the admission or other privileges may be designated as a charitable contribution.

The fact that the full amount or a portion of the payment made by the taxpayer is used by the organization exclusively for charitable purposes has no bearing upon the determination to be made as to the value of the admission or other privileges and the amount qualifying as a contribution.

Also, the mere fact that tickets or other privileges are not utilized does not entitle the patron to any greater charitable contribution deduction than would otherwise be allowable. The test of deductibility is not whether the right to admission or privileges is exercised but whether the right was accepted or rejected by the taxpayer. If a patron desires to support an affair, but does not intend to use the tickets or exercise the other privileges being offered with the event, he can make an outright gift of the amount he wishes to contribute, in which event he would not accept or keep any ticket or other evidence of any of the privileges related to the event connected with the solicitation.

The foregoing summary is not intended to be all inclusive of the legal requirements relating to deductibility of payments as charitable contributions for Federal income tax purposes. Neither does it attempt to deal with many of the refinements and distinctions which sometimes arise in connection with questions of whether a gift for such purposes has been made in particular circumstances.

The principles stated are intended instead to summarize with as little complexity as possible, those basic rules which govern deductibility of payments in the majority of the circumstances involved.

They have their basis in section 170 of the Code, the regulations thereunder, and in court decisions. The observance of these provisions will provide greater assurance to taxpayer contributors that their claimed deductions in such cases are allowable.

Where it is disclosed that the public or the patrons of a fund-raising affair for charity have been erroneously informed concerning the extent of the deductibility of their payments in connection with the affair, it necessarily follows that all charitable contribution deductions claimed with respect to payments made in connection with the particular event or affair will be subject to special scrutiny and may be questioned in audit of returns.

In the following examples application of the principles discussed above is illustrated in connection with various types of fund-raising activities for charity. Again, the examples are drawn to illustrate the general rules involved without attempting to deal with distinctions that sometimes arise in special situations. In each instance, the charitable organization involved is assumed to be an organization previously determined to be qualified to receive deductible charitable contributions under section 170 of the Code, and the references to deductibility are to deductibility as charitable contributions for Federal income tax purposes.

Example 1:

The *M* Charity sponsors a symphony concert for the purpose of raising funds for *M*'s charitable programs. *M* agrees to pay a fee which is calculated to reimburse the symphony for hall rental, musicians' salaries, advertising costs, and printing of tickets. Under the agreement, *M* is entitled to all receipts from ticket sales. *M* sells tickets to the concert charging $5 for balcony seats and $10 for orchestra circle seats. These prices approximate the established admission charges for concert performances by the symphony orchestra. The tickets to the concert and the advertising material promoting ticket sales emphasize that the concert is sponsored by, and is for the benefit of *M* Charity.

Notwithstanding the fact that taxpayers who acquire tickets to the concert may think they are making a charitable contribution to or for the benefit of *M* Charity, no part of the payments made is deductible as a charitable contribution for Federal income tax purposes. Since the payments approximate the established admission charge for similar events, there is no gift. The result would be the same even if the advertising materials promoting ticket sales stated that amounts paid for tickets are "tax deductible" and tickets to the concert were purchased in reliance upon such statements. Acquisition of tickets or other privileges by a taxpayer in reliance upon statements made by a charitable organization that the amounts paid are deductible does not convert an otherwise nondeductible payment into a deductible charitable contribution.

Example 2:

The facts are the same as in *Example 1*, except that the *M* Charity desires to use the concert as an occasion for the solicitation of gifts. It indicates that fact in its advertising material promoting the event, and fixes the payments solicited in connection with each class of admission at $30 for orchestra circle seats and $15 for balcony seats. The advertising and the tickets clearly reflect the fact that the established admission charges for comparable performances by the symphony orchestra are $10 for orchestra circle seats and $5 for balcony seats, and that only the excess of the solicited amounts paid in connection with admission to the concert over the established prices is a contribution to *M*.

Under these circumstances a taxpayer who makes a payment of $60 and receives two orchestra circle seat tickets can show that his payment exceeds the established admission charge for similar tickets to comparable performances of the symphony orchestra by $40. The circumstances also confirm that that amount of the payment was solicited as, and intended to be, a gift to *M* Charity. The $40, therefore, is deductible as a charitable contribution.

* * *

EXCERPT FROM THE GENERAL EXPLANATION OF
THE TAX REFORM ACT OF 1969

Staff of the Joint Committee on Internal Revenue Taxation, pp. 75–79 (1970).

C. CHARITABLE CONTRIBUTIONS

1. Fifty-Percent Charitable Contribution Deduction (Sec. 201(a) of the Act and Sec. 170(b) of the Code)

Prior law.—Under prior law, the charitable contributions deduction allowed individuals generally was limited to 30 percent of the taxpayer's adjusted gross income. In the case of gifts to private foundations, however, the deduction was limited to 20 percent of the taxpayer's adjusted gross income. In addition, in limited circumstances, a taxpayer was allowed an unlimited charitable contributions deduction.

General reasons for change.—In order to strengthen the incentive effect of the charitable contributions deduction for taxpayers, the Act generally increases the 30-percent limitation to 50 percent. It is believed that the increase in the limitation will benefit taxpayers who donate substantial portions of their income to charity and for whom the incentive effect of the deduction is strong—primarily taxpayers in the middle- and upper-income ranges. In addition, the combination of the increase in the limitation to 50 percent with the repeal of the unlimited charitable deduction means, in effect, that charity can be an equal partner with respect to an individual's income; however, charitable contributions no longer will be allowed to reduce an individual's tax base by more than one-half.

Explanation of provision.—The Act generally increases the limitation on the charitable contributions deduction for individual taxpayers from 30 percent of adjusted gross income to 50 percent. The 30-percent limitation remains in effect, however, for gifts of appreciated property (see No. 3 below for discussion) unless in computing the amount of the contribution the appreciation element is reduced by one-half. Also, the 20-percent limitation remains for contributions to private foundations which are not operating foundations, unless within 2½ months after the year of receipt they distribute the contributions to an operating foundation or a public charity, school or college, etc., in which event the higher percentage limitations are applicable.

The 50-percent limit is generally not to be available with respect to gifts of property which have appreciated in value. However, where a taxpayer makes a contribution to a public charity of property which has appreciated in value, he may make use of the 50-percent limitation for such contributions if he elects to have these contributions reduced by one-half of the unrealized appreciation in value of the contributed property.

As indicated above, the 20-percent limitation of present law also is removed for contributions to private operating foundations, and for contributions to private nonoperating foundations which distribute the contributions they receive to public charities or private operating foundations within 2½ months following the year of receipt. Gifts to such foundations under the Act are to qualify for the 50-percent limitation (or the 30-percent limitation, as the case may be). The 50-percent (or the 30-percent) limitation is also made available with respect to contributions to private nonoperating foundations which qualify as "community foundations." Community foundations are those which pool the contributions they receive in a common fund but allow the donor (or his spouse) to retain the right to designate the organization (so long as it is the type qualifying for the 50-percent limitation) to whom the income from the contribution is given and also to whom the corpus of the contribution eventually is given. However, to qualify for this treatment the income must be paid out to "50-percent type charities" by the 15th of the third month after the year in which the income is earned, and the corpus must be distributed to such types of organizations within one year after the death of the donor or his spouse. Contributions to these three categories of private foundations are treated the same as contributions to public charities for purposes of the limitations.

Effective date.—The increase in the limit on the deductibility of contributions from 30 percent to 50 percent (including the change respecting private operating and nonoperating foundations and pooled community funds) is applicable with respect to contributions paid in taxable years beginning after December 31, 1969.

*   *   *

3. Charitable Contributions of Appreciated Property (Sec. 201(a) of the Act and Secs. 170(e) and 1011(b) of the Code)

Prior law.—Under prior law, a taxpayer who contributed property which had appreciated in value to charity generally was allowed a charitable contributions deduction for the fair market value of the property, and no tax was imposed on the appreciation in value of the property (nor was the appreciation in value taken into account in any other way for tax purposes). In a few areas, however, a special rule (sec. 170(e)) applied to gifts of certain property. In these cases, the amount of charitable contribution was reduced by the amount of gain which would have been treated as ordinary income under the recapture rules (had the property been sold at its fair market value) for certain mining property (sec. 617(d) (1)), depreciable tangible personal property (sec. 1245(a)), and certain depreciable real property (sec. 1250(a)).

For property sold to a charity at a price below its fair market value—a so-called bargain sale—the proceeds of the sale were considered to be a return of the cost and were not required to be allocated between the cost basis of the "sale" part of the transaction and the "gift" part of the transaction. The seller was allowed a charitable contributions deduction for the difference between the fair market value of the property and the selling price (often at his cost or other basis).

General reasons for change.—The combined effect of not taxing the appreciation in value and at the same time allowing a charitable contributions deduction for the fair market value of the property given produced tax benefits significantly greater than those available with respect to cash contributions. The tax saving resulting from not taxing the appreciation in the case of gifts of long-term capital assets was represented by the amount of the capital gains tax which would have been paid if the asset had been sold. In the case of ordinary income type assets, moreover, this tax saving was at the taxpayer's top marginal tax rate. In addition, the tax saving from not taxing the appreciation in value was combined with the tax saving of the charitable deduction at the taxpayer's top marginal rate. As a result, in some cases it was possible for a taxpayer to realize a greater after-tax profit by making a gift of appreciated property than by selling the property, paying the tax on the gain, and keeping the proceeds.

In the case of a so-called bargain sale to a charity (often at the taxpayer's cost or other basis), the taxpayer was allowed a charitable deduction for the appreciated value in excess of the sales price to the charity. No tax was payable on any of this excess appreciation, since the taxpayer was not required to allocate his cost or other basis between the part "sold" and the part "given" to the charity. As a result, in cases where the sales price equaled the cost or other basis, the entire appreciation was deductible and no tax was payable on any of the appreciation in value.

Explanation of provision.—The Act provides that the appreciation element in gifts of appreciated property is to be taken into account, or modified, for tax purposes in the case of four types of contributions. In those cases where appreciation is to be taken into account, the charitable deduction for gifts of ordinary income type property (or short-term capital gains property) is to be reduced by the full amount of the appreciation; and in the case of long-term capital gains property, the charitable deduction is to be reduced by 50 percent (62½ percent for corporations) of the appreciation which would have been a long-term capital gain had the property been sold at its fair market value.

(*1*) *Ordinary income property.*—In the case of gifts of appreciated property which (if sold) would have produced ordinary income or short-term capital gain, the amount of the appreciation in value is to result in a reduction of the contribution deduction to the extent of the appreciation (regardless of the type of charitable organization involved). Examples of the types of property giving rise to ordinary income are gifts of inventory, "section 306 stock" (stock acquired in a nontaxable transaction treated as ordinary income if sold), artistic works and letters, memorandums, etc., produced by the donor, and capital assets held for 6 months or less. The charitable deduction for gifts of property which to some extent at least would produce ordinary income if sold, as a result of the application of various recapture rules (those under secs. 617(d) (1), 1245(a), 1250(a), 1251(c), or 1252(a)), also is to be reduced by the amount subject to the recapture as ordinary income.

(*2*) *Certain tangible personal property.*—The charitable deduction for gifts of tangible personal property (long-term capital gains property) the use of which is unrelated to the purpose or function constituting the basis for the charitable donee's exemption (under sec. 501 or unrelated to the purpose or function of a governmental unit described in sec. 170(c)) is to be reduced. A clear example of where property is not being used for an organization's exempt purpose is where it is intended at the time of the donation that the exempt organization will sell the property. The amount of the reduction is to be 50 percent (62½ percent in the case of a corporation) of the amount of appreciation which would have been a long-term capital gain if the property contributed had been sold at its fair market value.

(*3*) *Certain private foundations.*—Appreciation is also to be taken into account for tax purposes in the case of gifts of appreciated property (even though it is property which would produce long-term capital gains if sold) to private foundations unless the foundation is (a) a private operating foundation, (b) a private nonoperating foundation which within 2½ months after the taxable year in which the gift is received distributes an amount equivalent to all contributions received during such taxable year to public charitable organizations or private operating foundations (such amounts distributed must be in addition to the income payout requirement), or (c) a private nonoperating foundation which qualifies as a "community foundation." Contributions to these three categories of private foundations are treated the same as contributions to public charities for purposes of the limitations.

(4) *Bargain sales.*—In the case of so-called bargain sales to charity—where a taxpayer sells property to a charitable organization for less than its fair market value (often at its cost or other basis)—the cost or other basis of the property is to be allocated (for purposes of determining taxable gain to the taxpayer) between the portion of the property "sold" and the portion of the property "given" to the charity, on the ratio of the fair market value of each portion to the total fair market value of the property.

Under cases (1), (2), and (3) above where the charitable contribution made represents less than the taxpayer's entire interest in the property contributed, the taxpayer's adjusted basis in the property is to be allocated between the interest contributed and any interest not contributed according to prescribed regulations.

Effective date.—The amendments made by this provision generally are to apply with respect to contributions paid (or treated as paid under sec. 170(a) (2)) after December 31, 1969; however, in the case of a contribution of a letter, memorandum, or similar property (to which sec. 514 of the Act applies), the amendments apply to such contributions after July 25, 1969. Further, the amendment with respect to bargain sales applies to sales made after December 19, 1969.

SARAH MARQUIS

Tax Court of the United States, 1968.
49 T.C. 695.

TANNENWALD, JUDGE: Respondent determined deficiencies in the Federal income tax of petitioner for the taxable years 1962 and 1963 in the respective amounts of $2,512.45 and $986.31. The sole issue for consideration is whether certain cash payments made by petitioner to customers who qualified as charitable organizations under section 170(c)[1] were deductible as business expenses without regard to the limitation contained in section 162(b).

1. All references hereinafter, unless otherwise stated, are to the Internal Revenue Code of 1954.

Findings of Fact

Some of the facts have been stipulated. Those facts and the exhibits attached thereto are incorporated herein by this reference.

Petitioner Sarah Marquis resided in and had business offices located in New York, N. Y., at the time the petition herein was filed. Her individual Federal income tax returns for the calendar years 1962 and 1963 were filed with the district directors of internal revenue in Newark, N. J., and New York, N. Y., respectively.

Since 1935, petitioner has conducted an unincorporated travel agency business in her own name. Such business entails the making of travel bookings for various organizational and individual clients, in exchange for which services petitioner receives commissions and fees based on total bookings. Since 1963 and for a period of 15 years prior thereto, petitioner's clientele has consisted largely of church organizations, religious groups, and other charitable and educational groups (hereinafter referred to as charitable clients). During 1962 and 1963, approximately 57 percent of petitioner's total billings resulted from organizational trips sponsored by some 30 clients of this type. The remainder were business firms and individuals, some of whom were referred to petitioner by her charitable clients. Such charitable clients accounted for total billings of $1,427,163.96 in 1962 and $1,473,534.12 in 1963.

For the most part, petitioner carried on all business with charitable clients by herself—either by direct meeting or over the telephone. Rather than promote such business via the use of salesmen (as her competitors did), she chose to solicit their patronage by means of annual cash payments which were geared to the amount of business which had been and/or was expected to be given to her agency by the particular client. Petitioner had found traditional commercial advertising ineffective with regard to charitable clients because their institutional journals or publications usually refrained from taking such advertising.

As a regular practice over a long period, including the taxable years involved herein, petitioner would, toward the close of each year, decide which organizations were to receive cash payments and the amount to be paid to each. In making such determination, she would consider various factors, including (1) the type and amount of business received from a particular client, (2) the nature of the recipient (i. e., group, conference, referral source), (3) the profitability of the business received, and (4) the prospects for continued patronage by the recipient. Checks drawn on petitioner's business account would be sent to each recipient, usually with an enclosed message to the effect such payments were "in lieu of a salesman's visit" and that petitioner appreciated the particular customer's patronage.[2]

---

2. All such checks were issued only in December of each year.

Petitioner had reason to believe that some of her charitable clients would have ceased doing business with her if she had not continued to make such payments. On the other hand, petitioner occasionally lost some or all of the business of organizations to which she made payments. If she felt that there was still a chance of regaining such business, she would continue—at least for a while—making the payments. Once a particular client actually switched over to a competing travel agent, however, payments would stop. Organizations which did only a very small amount of business with petitioner typically received no payments.

With one minor exception, where petitioner's client was the national organization with which her local church was affiliated, charitable clients included religious organizations of denominations different than her own. Aside from the business relationship, petitioner did not involve herself in the activities of her charitable clients.

During 1962, petitioner made cash disbursements totaling $7,570 to 31 of her charitable clients. During 1963, petitioner made similar disbursements totaling $7,360 to 29 of such clients. On her individual income tax returns for 1962 and 1963, petitioner claimed Schedule C deductions for "Promotion" in the amounts of $7,570 and $7,360, respectively. Respondent disallowed the claimed promotion deductions in their entirety for both years, but did allow portions of such expenses as charitable contributions—in the amounts of $2,281.61 and $5,734.04, respectively.

Separate and apart from such payments, petitioner made contributions to her own church and other charitable organizations (i. e., other than her charitable clients) in the respective amounts of $11,207 and $11,245 for 1962 and 1963.[3] Such contributions were made from her personal bank account and were reported as itemized individual deductions on petitioner's income tax returns for the years involved.

Schedule C of petitioner's tax returns for 1962 and 1963 reflects the following information:

	1962	1963
Receipts	$169,949.81	$184,932.90
Business expenses [1]	149,720.82	145,712.27
Net profit	22,228.99	39,220.63

[1] Including the following items:

	1962	1963
Advertising	$1,578.45	$817.57
Promotion	7,570.00	7,360.00
Promotion tours	2,615.27	1,588.22
Entertainment of clients	570.27	459.41

3. In both 1962 and 1963, petitioner contributed $10,000 to Coe College, her alma mater. Contributions to her Presbyterian Church in the amounts of $1,052 and $880 were also made in 1962 and 1963, respectively.

Opinion

The decision in this case turns upon a determination as to the scope of the limitation contained in section 162(b).[4] Petitioner contends that her cash payments to charitable clients were part and parcel of her travel agency business and therefore did not constitute contributions or gifts deductible only under section 170, with the result that the limitation does not apply. Respondent counters with the assertion that the legislative history of section 162(b) and its predecessor sections, his own regulations, and a prior decision of this Court in Wm. T. Stover Co., 27 T.C. 434 (1956), require that, in order to escape such limitations, payment must be made in exchange for a binding obligation on the part of the recipient. On all the facts and circumstances herein, we agree with the petitioner.

The genesis of section 162(b) is found in the area of contributions to charitable organizations by corporations. Prior to 1935, corporations were not permitted a deduction for charitable contributions as such. A deduction was allowed only if the test of an ordinary and necessary business expense was met. In this context, the courts evinced a lenient attitude in finding that the particular contributions had a business significance, merely requiring proof of "a benefit flowing directly to the corporation as an incident to its business." See Willcuts v. Minnesota Tribune Co., 103 F.2d 947, 952 (C.A.8, 1939), and cases therein cited. It was enough if the court was satisfied that the contribution would not have been made "but for" the existence of a business relationship.

In 1935, the income tax law was amended to limit deductions for charitable contributions by corporations to 5 percent of taxable income; no change was made in the subdivision allowing deductions for business expenses, seemingly because Congress thought that the specific 5-percent provision would control. When it appeared that the law needed clarification in this regard, it was recommended that "no deduction shall be allowed to corporations * * * [as a business expense] for any *contribution* * * * with respect to which a deduction is allowed * * * [as a charitable contribution]." (Emphasis supplied.) See Report of Subcommittee of Ways and Means Committee, 75th Cong., 3d Sess., p. 48 (Jan. 14, 1938), appearing in Seidman's Legislative History of Federal Income Tax Laws, 1938–1961, pp. 10, 11. This recommendation of the subcommittee was adopted by the full committee at the time of the enactment of section 23(a)(2) of the Revenue Act of 1938 (ch. 289, 52 Stat. 447), with the following comment, heavily relied upon by respondent:

> The limitations of section 23(a)(2) apply *only to payments which are contributions or gifts*. A deduction is not to be disallowed under section 23(a)(2) of the bill merely be-

4. [Sec. 162(b) is omitted. Ed.]

cause the recipient of amounts received from the corporation is a so-called charitable organization within the meaning of section 23(q), *as, for example,* in the case of a payment by a mining company to a local hospital *in consideration of an obligation assumed* by the hospital to provide hospital services and facilities for the employees of the company. [Emphasis supplied.]

See H.Rept. No. 1860, 75th Cong., 3d Sess., pp. 17–18 (1938) 1939–1 C.B. (Part 2) 740.

The provision of section 23(a)(2), which was codified the next year under the same section number in the Internal Revenue Code of 1939 and later designated section 23(a)(1)(B), is as follows:

> (2) CORPORATE CHARITABLE CONTRIBUTIONS.—No deduction shall be allowable under paragraph (1) [ordinary and necessary business expense] to a corporation for any *contribution* or *gift* which would be allowable as a deduction under subsection (q) [charitable contributions] were it not for the 5 per centum limitation therein contained and for the requirement therein that payment must be made within the taxable year. [Emphasis supplied.]

Respondent's Regulations 101 issued in 1939 is implementation of this provision specified (p. 61):

> Art. 23(a)–13. Corporate contributions.—No deduction is allowable under section 23(a) for a *contribution* or *gift* by a corporation if any part thereof is deductible under section 23(q). * * *
>
> *The limitations provided in paragraph (2) of section 23 (a) and in this article apply only to payments which are in fact contributions or gifts to organizations described in section 23(q).* For example, payments by a street railway corporation to a local hospital (which is a charitable organization within the meaning of section 23(q)) in consideration of a binding obligation on the part of the hospital to provide hospital services and facilities for the corporation's employees are not contributions or gifts within the meaning of section 23(q) and may be deductible under section 23(a) if the requirements of that section are otherwise satisfied. * * *

[Emphasis supplied.]

The foregoing provision was reissued *verbatim* as section 19.23 (a)–13 of Regulations 103 (1940), section 29.23(a)–13 of Regulations 111 (1943), and section 39.23(a)–13 of Regulations 118 (1953).

At the time of the enactment of the 1954 Code, the limitation of section 23(a)(1)(B) was incorporated into section 162(b) and extended to cover individuals as well as corporations. In so doing, the legislative committees made reference generally to the deductibility of "contributions" within a context of rendition of services (see H.Rept. No.1337, 83d Cong., 2d Sess., p. 20 (1954), S.Rept.No.1622, 83d Cong., 2d Sess., p. 22 (1954)), but went on to elaborate on their intention as follows:

Subsection (b) is derived from section 23(a) (1) (B) of the 1939 code. This section provides that no business deduction is available for any *contribution* which would be deductible as a charitable *gift,* were it not for the percentage *limitation on such gifts.* This was the rule for corporations under section 23(a) (1) (B) of the 1939 Code and this section now extends the rule to individuals. *No substantive change is made in the application of this rule. As under present law, it applies only to gifts, i. e., those contributions which are made with no expectation of a financial return commensurate with the amount of the gift. For example,* the limitation would not apply to a payment by an individual to a hospital in consideration of a binding obligation to provide medical treatment for the individual's employees. It would apply only if there were *no expectation of any quid pro quo* from the hospital. [Emphasis supplied. See H.Rept.No. 1337, 83d Cong., 2d Sess., p. A44 (1954); S.Rept.No.1622, supra.]

In promulgating new regulations under the 1954 Code, respondent merely republished its existing regulations, modified to reflect the new section numbers and the extension of the coverage of section 162(b) to individuals. Sec. 1.162–15(a), Income Tax Regs.

Respondent asserts that the foregoing legislative history, reinforced by its longstanding regulations, requires that, since the recipients herein were under no binding obligation to furnish any quid pro quo to petitioner, the payments in question must necessarily be considered contributions or gifts and therefore subject to the limitation of section 162(b).

We think respondent has interpreted both the legislative history and his own regulations too narrowly. The "hospital" situations— concededly obvious cases—are illustrative rather than definitive. If there were any doubt on this score, it is removed by the language of the legislative committee reports at the time of the enactment of section 162(b), which reports categorically stated that no substantive change in the law was intended, continued to emphasize that the limitation was to apply to "contributions," and added the clarifying standard of "no expectation of any quid pro quo." See H.Rept.No. 1337, supra; S.Rept.No.1622, supra.

The foregoing analysis leads to the conclusion that the limitation on the deduction of charitable contributions as business expenses was designed to tighten the "but for" test used in the earlier cases to determine the deductibility of such payments. Since 1938, that test has clearly not been the critical benchmark. On the other hand, neither the statute, the legislative history, nor respondent's regulations require the existence of a binding obligation on the part of the recipient organization as a precondition to deductibility.

Our decision in *Wm. T. Stover Co.*, supra, is clearly distinguishable. In the first place, there was a specific finding of fact, in that case, that the payments were "contributions." Secondly, the facts that the taxpayer therein did business with the recipients (three hospitals), that such business increased, and that the making of the apparently non-recurring contributions was "cold-blooded business" did no more than indicate [5] to the Court that the payments were "closely related to the corporate business" (see 27 T.C. at 442). Or, to put it another way, we did no more than indicate that the lenient "but for" test had been met—a test which, as we have already indicated, was an insufficient standard in the taxable years involved therein. See above. At no point did we delineate any requirement of a binding obligation as a prerequisite to escaping the clutches of the charitable contribution limitation on otherwise deductible business expenses.[6]

Against the foregoing background, we summarize the salient facts herein.

Petitioner's charitable clients were numerous (some 30 in all) and bookings in connection with their organizationally sponsored trips represented a very substantial part of her business (57 percent of her total billings). She had direct and continuous business dealings with them. Moreover, she contributed to the charities with which she was otherwise identified. On a recurring basis, she made payments of the type in question (including payments during the taxable years involved herein), not only in the expectation that she would continue to obtain business from the recipient, but because she could well have lost such business if she had stopped. The payments were directly keyed to the amount, character, and profitability of the business which petitioner obtained and expected to obtain from the charitable clients. Petitioner had no other feasible means of reaching these clients through normal advertising channels. Cf.

5. There is also no indication of the relationship of the amounts given to the amount or profitability of the business received.

6. Hartless Linen Service Co., 32 T.C. 1026 (1959), United States Potash Co., 29 T.C. 1071 (1958), and McDonnell Aircraft Corporation, 16 T.C. 189, 199 (1951), which also applied the limitation but which were not cited by respondent, are likewise distinguishable, either because there was not even an expectation of benefit or because payments were made to promote community projects where the taxpayers' businesses were located and the benefits to those businesses were peripheral at best. Moreover, in all of the foregoing cases, the contributions appear to have been nonrecurring and to have been made to only one or two recipients.

Hartless Linen Service Co., 32 T.C. 1026, 1030 (1959). In short, petitioner's charitable clients represented a substantial, continuing, integral part of her business.[7] They were in every sense petitioner's bread and butter.

As we see it, the key question is whether, in the words of section 162(b) itself, the payment is a "contribution or gift which would be allowable * * * under section 170." The same phrase, i. e., "contribution or gift," is used in section 170(c) and, in view of the express reference to section 170 in section 162(b), we perceive no valid reason for according it a different meaning in one place as against the other, a path which respondent's argument seemingly suggests that we follow.

In so concluding, we need not go so far as to suggest that the narrow test of "detached and disinterested generosity," often applied in cases involving the excludability of gifts from income, is the determinant of a charitable contribution. Compare Commissioner v. Duberstein, 363 U.S. 278 (1960), Publishers New Press, Inc., 42 T.C. 396 (1964), and Max Kralstein, 38 T.C. 810 (1962), with Channing v. United States, 4 F.Supp. 33 (D.Mass.1933), affirmed per curiam 67 F.2d 986 (C.A.1, 1933), DeJong v. Commissioner, 309 F.2d 373 (C.A.9, 1962), affirming 36 T.C. 896 (1961), and Crosby Valve & Gage Co., 46 T.C. 641 (1966), affirmed on other grounds 380 F.2d 146 (C.A.1, 1967). Indeed, as we have previously pointed out, the principles underlying the gift exclusion decisions may not be fully applicable in the area of charitable contributions. See United States v. Transamerica, 392 F.2d 522 (C.A.9, 1968); Jordon Perlmutter, 45 T.C. 311, 317 (1965). At the same time, we are unwilling to go to the other extreme and adopt respondent's standard that a payment must be considered a charitable contribution unless there is a binding obligation on the part of the recipient to furnish a quid pro quo. Such a standard would enlarge the area of allowable deductions for charitable contributions far beyond its present scope to include payments where elements of compulsion and anticipated benefit existed but a binding obligation on the part of the recipient organization was lacking. Jordon Perlmutter, supra; see Crosby Valve & Gage Co. v. Commissioner, 380 F.2d 146 (C.A. 1, 1967). We need go no further than to hold that, under all the circumstances herein, it would stretch credulity to characterize the payments at issue as "contributions."[8] See Jordon Perlmutter, supra at 317, cf. B. Manischewitz Co., 10 T.C. 1139 (1948).

Since petitioner has conceded other adjustments,

Decision will be entered under Rule 50.

Reviewed by the Court.

7. At no point herein has respondent questioned the reasonableness of the payments nor has he suggested that the payments be regarded as capital expenditures for goodwill.

8. We are aware that "Donations to organizations other than those described in section 170 which bear a direct relationship to the taxpayer's business and are made with a reason-

REVENUE RULING 75–358

1975–2 Cum.Bull. 76.

Advice has been requested concerning the deductibility under section 170 of the Internal Revenue Code of 1954 of a contribution of an easement to a state under the circumstances described below.

An individual who owned a mansion and the land on which it was situated granted an easement in gross in perpetuity in the property to the state in which the property was located. The mansion had previously been declared a state landmark by the state department of parks and recreation because of its outstanding and unique architecture. The deed conveying the easement to the state restricts the rights of the grantor as follows: The grantor may not alter the property from its historically significant appearance as a single family residence or modify in any way the unique architectural characteristics of the property. Further, the grantor may not subdivide the property and is prohibited from conducting industrial development and mining operations on and in the property. The grantee of the easement may inspect the property at any time and may exploit the easement only in such a manner as not to prevent the proper use and enjoyment of the property, including restoration of the property by the grantor.

Section 170 of the Code provides, subject to certain limitations, a deduction for gifts and contributions to or for the use of organizations described in section 170(c), payment of which is made within the taxable year.

Section 170(c) (1) of the Code provides, in part, that the term "charitable contribution" means a contribution or gift to or for the use of a state, a possession of the United States, or any political subdivision of any of the foregoing, or the United States or the District of Columbia, but only if the contribution or gift is made for exclusively public purposes.

Section 170(f) (3) (A) of the Code provides, in part, that in the case of a contribution (not made by a transfer in trust) of an interest in property which consists of less than the taxpayer's entire interest in such property, a deduction shall be allowed only to the extent that the value of the interest contributed would be allowable as a deduction under section 170 if such interest had been transferred in trust. A contribution by a taxpayer of the right to use property

able expectation of a financial return commensurate with the amount of the donation" may be allowable business deductions under sec. 1.162–15(b) of respondent's regulations. By our decision herein, we neither imply nor decide that the same standard would permit the avoidance of the limitation of sec. 162(b) with respect to payments to sec. 170 organizations in the course of a business relationship—at least where such payments are nonrecurring, the number of recipients is small, and the relationship to the amount of business transacted is not clearly defined.

shall be treated as a contribution of less than the taxpayer's entire interest in property.

Section 1.170A–7(b) (1) (ii) of the Income Tax Regulations provides that a charitable contribution of an open space easement in gross in perpetuity shall be considered a contribution of an undivided portion of the donor's entire interest in property to which section 170(f) (3) (A) of the Code does not apply. For this purpose an easement in gross is a mere personal interest in, or right to use, the land of another; it is not supported by a dominant estate but is attached to, and vested in, the person to whom it is granted. Thus, for example, a deduction is allowed under section 170 for the value of a restrictive easement gratuitously conveyed to the United States in perpetuity whereby the donor agrees to certain restrictions on the use of his property, such as restrictions on the type and height of buildings that may be erected, the removal of trees, the erection of utility lines, the dumping of trash, and the use of signs.

In the instant case, under the law of the state in which the property is located, a restrictive or scenic easement is a valuable property right or interest in favor of the party for whose benefit the easement is created and is enforceable by that party. The easement in gross in perpetuity herein described is a restrictive scenic easement. Thus, by the grant of such easement to the state, the individual made a contribution of a property right to the state. Furthermore, the easement is an open space easement within the meaning of section 1.170A–7(b) (1) (ii) of the regulations.

Accordingly, in the instant case, the individual is entitled to a charitable contribution deduction in the manner and to the extent provided by section 170 of the Code for the fair market value of the restrictive easement granted to the state. For the rules applicable in valuing the contribution, see Rev.Rul. 73–339, 1973–2 C.B. 68.

PROBLEMS

1. T's contribution base for the year of the following gifts is $150,000. During the year T makes contributions to Suntan U., an organization within § 170(b) (1) (A) (ii) and (c) (2), or to Private Foundation, which is within § 170(c) (2) but not within § 170(b) (1) (A) (ii). In each of the following circumstances determine T's § 170 deduction for the current year, and what effect, if any, § 170(d) (1) (A) will have:

(a) T gives $100,000 cash to Suntan U.

(b) T gives $100,000 cash to Private Foundation.

(c) T gives $60,000 cash to Suntan U. and $40,000 to Private Foundation.

(d) T gives $40,000 to Suntan U. and $60,000 to Private Foundation.

(e) T has a freshman daughter who attends Suntan U. and he pays $3,000 tuition for her and makes a $10,000 Sponsors' Club contribution. Children of members of the Sponsors' Club are automatically admitted to Suntan U.

2. This problem involves transfers of property by T, an individual, to Suntan U. and Private Foundation both as described in 1, above, in a year after 1977. Assume that in the current year T has a $200,000 "contribution base," and unless otherwise stated he makes no other charitable gifts. T owns property with a basis of $60,000 and a value of $80,000.

(a) If the property is inventory and he contributes it to Suntan U., what will T's charitable deduction be?

(b) If the property is inventory and he contributes it to Private Foundation, what will T's charitable contribution be?

(c) If the property is corporate stock held for more than one year and he contributes it to Suntan U. what will T's charitable contribution be?

(d) Same as (c), above, except the stock has been held only five months.

(e) Same as (c), above, except that the stock was given to Private Foundation rather than Suntan U.

(f) What result under the facts of (c), above, if T exercises the election proffered by § 170(b) (1) (C) (iii)?

(g) What result if T gives Suntan U. § 1250 property which if sold would be subject to $10,000 of § 1250 recapture?

3. After completing his term of office Publius Maximus who has been in a high office for several years donates his private working papers to Charity U. The papers are properly valued at $100,000.

(a) Will Publius be allowed a charitable deduction for the gift? See I.R.C. § 1221(3).

(b) Publius also teaches Sunday School at his church. Will he be allowed a charitable deduction for the value of his services? See Reg. § 1.170A–1(g).

(c) Publius donates blood (worth $100) during the year to the blood bank. Deductible? Consider Rev.Rul. 53–162, 1953–2 C.B. 127.

(d) Publius allows the United Way Crusade to use an office in a building that he owns; the office has a fair market value of $100 per month. Is he allowed a deduction for the value of the use of the office? See I.R.C. § 170(f) (3) (A) and note § 170(f) (2) (B). See also Rev.Rul. 70–477, 1970–2, C.B. 62, and new § 170(f) (3) (B) (iii) and (iv).

4. Planner has held for several years some stock that he purchased at a cost of $54,000. In the current year when his contribu-

tion base is $50,000 and the stock is now worth $80,000, he "sells" it for $60,000 to Charity U., an organization within § 170(b) (1) (A) (ii) and (c) (2).

(a) What is the amount of his gain or loss on the sale?

(b) What is his charitable deduction?

(c) Same questions as (a) and (b), above, except that the property is § 1250 property with a $54,000 adjusted basis and if the property were sold there would be $10,000 of § 1250 gain.

5.   Alumnus a § 1(c) taxpayer who has only ordinary income in the current year gives stock which he purchased five years ago for $10,000 to his alma mater. The stock is worth $20,000. Alumnus' total charitable gifts for the year are within the 50% § 170(b) (1) (A) limitation. Assuming without any gift or sale of the stock his taxable income would be $60,000, what result to Alumnus' net worth if:

(a) He gives the stock to charity?

(b) He sells the stock and keeps the proceeds?

PART SEVEN: DEFERRAL AND NONRECOGNITION OF INCOME AND DEDUCTIONS

CHAPTER 24. DEFERRED REPORTING OF GAINS

A. TIMING AND CHARACTER OF GAIN IN AN OPEN TRANSACTION

Internal Revenue Code: Sections 1001(a) through (c); 1011(a).
Regulations: Section 1.1001–1(a).

BURNET v. LOGAN

Supreme Court of the United States, 1931.
283 U.S. 404, 51 S.Ct. 550.

MR. JUSTICE MCREYNOLDS delivered the opinion of the Court.

These causes present the same questions. One opinion, stating the essential circumstances disclosed in No. 521, will suffice for both.

Prior to March, 1913, and until March 11, 1916, respondent, Mrs. Logan, owned 250 of the 4,000 capital shares issued by the Andrews & Hitchcock Iron Company. It held 12% of the stock of the Mahoning Ore & Steel Company, an operating concern. In 1895 the latter corporation procured a lease for 97 years upon the "Mahoning" mine and since then has regularly taken therefrom large, but varying, quantities of iron ore—in 1913, 1,515,428 tons; in 1914, 1,212,287 tons; in 1915, 2,311,940 tons; in 1919, 1,217,167 tons; in 1921, 303,020 tons; in 1923, 3,029,865 tons. The lease contract did not require production of either maximum or minimum tonnage or any definite payments. Through an agreement of stockholders (steel manufacturers) the Mahoning Company is obligated to apportion extracted ore among them according to their holdings.

On March 11, 1916, the owners of all the shares in Andrews & Hitchcock Company sold them to Youngstown Sheet & Tube Company, which thus acquired, among other things, 12% of the Mahoning Company's stock and the right to receive the same percentage of ore thereafter taken from the leased mine.

For the shares so acquired the Youngstown Company paid the holders $2,200,000 in money and agreed to pay annually thereafter for distribution among them 60 cents for each ton of ore apportioned to it. Of this cash Mrs. Logan received 250/4000ths—$137,500; and

847

she became entitled to the same fraction of any annual payment thereafter made by the purchaser under the terms of sale.

Mrs. Logan's mother had long owned 1100 shares of the Andrews & Hitchcock Company. She died in 1917, leaving to the daughter one-half of her interest in payments thereafter made by the Youngstown Company. This bequest was appraised for federal estate tax purposes at $277,164.50.

During 1917, 1918, 1919 and 1920 the Youngstown Company paid large sums under the agreement. Out of these respondent received on account of her 250 shares $9,900.00 in 1917, $11,250.00 in 1918, $8,995.50 in 1919, $5,444.30 in 1920—$35,589.80. By reason of the interest from her mother's estate she received $19,790.10 in 1919, and $11,977.49 in 1920.

Reports of income for 1918, 1919 and 1920 were made by Mrs. Logan upon the basis of cash receipts and disbursements. They included no part of what she had obtained from annual payments by the Youngstown Company. She maintains that until the total amount actually received by her from the sale of her shares equals their value on March 1, 1913, no taxable income will arise from the transaction. Also that until she actually receives by reason of the right bequeathed to her a sum equal to its appraised value, there will be no taxable income therefrom.

On March 1, 1913, the value of the 250 shares then held by Mrs. Logan *exceeded* $173,089.80—the total of all sums actually received by her prior to 1921 from their sale ($137,500.00 cash in 1916 plus four annual payments amounting to $35,589.80). That value also exceeded original cost of the shares. The amount received on the interest devised by her mother was less than its valuation for estate taxation; also less than the value when acquired by Mrs. Logan.

The Commissioner ruled that the obligation of the Youngstown Company to pay 60 cents per ton had a fair market value of $1,942,111.46 on March 11, 1916; that this value should be treated as so much cash and the sale of the stock regarded as a closed transaction with no profit in 1916. He also used this valuation as the basis for apportioning subsequent annual receipts between income and return of capital. His calculations, based upon estimates and assumptions, are too intricate for brief statement.* He made deficiency assess-

* In the brief for petitioner the following appears:

"The fair market value of the Youngstown contract on March 11, 1916, was found by the Commissioner to be $1,942,111.46. This was based upon an estimate that the ore reserves at the Mahoning mine amounted to 82,858,535 tons; that all such ore would be mined; that 12 per cent (or 9,942,564.2 tons) would be delivered to the Youngstown Company. The total amount to be received by all the vendors of stock would then be $5,965,814.52 at the rate of 60 cents per ton. The Commissioner's figure for the fair market value on March 11, 1916, was the then worth of $5,965,814.52, upon the assumption that the amount was to be received in equal annual installments during 45 years, discounted at 6 per cent,

ments according to the view just stated and the Board of Tax Appeals approved the result.

The Circuit Court of Appeals held that, in the circumstances, it was impossible to determine with fair certainty the market value of the agreement by the Youngstown Company to pay 60 cents per ton. Also, that respondent was entitled to the return of her capital—the value of 250 shares on March 1, 1913, and the assessed value of the interest derived from her mother—before she could be charged with any taxable income. As this had not in fact been returned, there was no taxable income.

We agree with the result reached by the Circuit Court of Appeals.

The 1916 transaction was a sale of stock—not an exchange of property. We are not dealing with royalties or deductions from gross income because of depletion of mining property. Nor does the situation demand that an effort be made to place according to the best available data some approximate value upon the contract for future payments. This probably was necessary in order to assess the mother's estate. As annual payments on account of extracted ore come in they can be readily apportioned first as return of capital and later as profit. The liability for income tax ultimately can be fairly determined without resort to mere estimates, assumptions and speculation. When the profit, if any, is actually realized, the taxpayer will be required to respond. The consideration for the sale was $2,200,000.00 in cash and the promise of future money payments wholly contingent upon facts and circumstances not possible to foretell with anything like fair certainty. The promise was in no proper sense equivalent to cash. It had no ascertainable fair market value. The transaction was not a closed one. Respondent might never recoup her capital investment from payments only conditionally promised. Prior to 1921 all receipts from the sale of her shares amounted to less than their value on March 1, 1913. She properly demanded the return of her capital investment before assessment of any taxable profit based on conjecture.

"In order to determine whether there has been gain or loss, and the amount of the gain, if any, we must withdraw from the gross proceeds an amount sufficient to restore the capital value that existed

with a provision for a sinking fund at 4 per cent. For lack of evidence to the contrary this value was approved by the Board. The value of the 550/4000 interest which each acquired by bequest was fixed at $277,164.50 for purposes of Federal estate tax at the time of the mother's death.

"During the years here involved the Youngstown Company made payments in accordance with the terms of the contract, and respondents respectively received sums proportionate to the interests in the contract which they acquired by exchange of property and by bequest.

"The Board held that respondents' receipts from the contract, during the years in question, represented 'gross income'; that respondents should be allowed to deduct from said gross income a reasonable allowance for exhaustion of their contract interests; and that the balance of the receipts should be regarded as taxable income."

at the commencement of the period under consideration." Doyle v. Mitchell Bros. Co., 247 U.S. 179, 184, 185. Rev.Act 1916, § 2, 39 Stat. 757, 758; Rev.Act 1918, c. 18, 40 Stat. 1057. Ordinarily, at least, a taxpayer may not deduct from gross receipts a supposed loss which in fact is represented by his outstanding note. Eckert v. Commissioner of Internal Revenue, ante, p. 140. And, conversely, a promise to pay indeterminate sums of money is not necessarily taxable income. "Generally speaking, the income tax law is concerned only with realized losses, as with realized gains." Lucas v. American Code Co., 280 U.S. 445, 449.

From her mother's estate Mrs. Logan obtained the right to share in possible proceeds of a contract thereafter to pay indefinite sums. The value of this was assumed to be $277,164.50 and its transfer was so taxed. Some valuation—speculative or otherwise—was necessary in order to close the estate. It may never yield as much, it may yield more. If a sum equal to the value thus ascertained had been invested in an annuity contract, payments thereunder would have been free from income tax until the owner had recouped his capital investment.* We think a like rule should be applied here. The statute definitely excepts bequests from receipts which go to make up taxable income. See Burnet v. Whitehouse, ante, p. 148.

The judgments below are affirmed.

NOTE

Recall from Chapter 7 that under I.R.C. § 1001(a) the measurement of gain or loss is determined by the difference between the "amount realized" on a disposition and the "adjusted basis" of the property relinquished. If either the "amount realized" or the "adjusted basis" is incapable of being measured then the gain or loss on a transaction is unknown as well. This simple concept is now well established as the doctrine of Burnet v. Logan,[1] or the "open transaction" doctrine.

An open transaction arises in two different types of situations. It may involve a situation like Burnet v. Logan where the amount

---

* Current statutory rules tax a portion of each annuity payment as received. See I.R.C. § 72, supra page 190. Moreover, a 1942 change would preclude the annuity-type treatment the court suggests for the disposition of the shares the taxpayer received from her mother. The mother's right to payment would be foreclosed from receiving a date-of-death basis by I.R.C. § 1014(c); and the recipient of payments attributable to the mother's rights would have income in respect of a decedent under § 691. See also § 1023(b)(2)(A) excluding § 691 items from the carryover basis rules enacted by TRA (1976); and see page 317, supra. None of this, however, affects the viability of the Logan principle regarding open transactions suggested by the treatment of payment for the shares owned originally by the taxpayer. Ed.

1. The doctrine is applicable to both cash and accrual method taxpayers. The open transaction doctrine is given statutory application in the limited area of patent sales. § 1235.

realized is unknown; the doctrine leaves these transactions "open" to see what is actually received in subsequent years. As amounts are received they initially constitute a recovery of capital. Once an amount equal to the adjusted basis of the transferred property is received capital has been recovered, and any further receipts constitute income in the year received. These are all concepts considered in Chapter 7 and a student may be asking: Why defer consideration of the open transaction doctrine until now? The answer is: The doctrine not only has measurement and timing consequences, it has characterization aspects as well. If the doctrine of Burnet v. Logan applies and a transaction is left open then subsequently recognized gain (or loss) is seen to arise out of the original transfer and is characterized by that transfer. Thus any gain Mrs. Logan subsequently recognized was long term capital gain. If, however, the doctrine is inapplicable because an "amount realized" can be determined then the transaction is "closed" and gain or loss based on that determination is immediately recognized. That gain is characterized by the original transaction but, if the amount actually realized over the years exceeds the initial determination, the excess is ordinary income and is not characterized by the nature of the original sale or exchange.[2] The rationale is that, while the initial gain arose out of the sale, the later gain is merely attributable to "payment" of an obligation with a basis less than the amount received.[3] Ironically, however, if the actual receipts are less than the estimate the loss that results takes its character from the original sale. Why?

The second situation in which the open transaction doctrine applies is where the "adjusted basis" of property disposed of is unknown, rather than the "amount realized" on its disposition. For example, in *Inaja Land Co., Ltd.*,[4] the taxpayer which owned some land with a basis of approximately $61,000 sold an easement for $50,000, giving the buyer the right to divert water across the taxpayer's property. The court concluded that, as it could not determine what portion of the property was being taken, there was no way to allocate a portion of the taxpayer's basis for use in the gain or loss formula. Accordingly gain or loss was impossible to compute, and the receipt of the $50,000 was treated as a mere recovery of capital, reducing the property's basis to $11,000 but giving rise to no gain. The court stated:[5]

* * *

> Capital recoveries in excess of cost do constitute taxable income. Petitioner has made no attempt to allocate a basis to that part of the property covered by the easements. It

2. Waring v. Comm'r, 412 F.2d 800 (3rd Cir. 1969); See Stephen H. Dorsey, 49 T.C. 606 (1968).

3. See Galvin Hudson, supra page 694.

4. 9 T.C. 727 (1947), Acq. 1948–1 C.B. 2.

5. Id. at 735–736.

is conceded that all of petitioner's lands were not affected by the easements conveyed. Petitioner does not contest the rule that, where property is acquired for a lump sum and subsequently disposed of a portion at a time, there must be an allocation of the cost or other basis over the several units and gain or loss computed on the disposition of each part, except where apportionment would be wholly impracticable or impossible. Nathan Blum, 5 T.C. 702, 709. Petitioner argues that it would be impracticable and impossible to apportion a definite basis to the easements here involved, since they could not be described by metes and bounds; that the flow of the water has changed and will change the course of the river; that the extent of the flood was and is not predictable; and that to date the city has not released the full measure of water to which it is entitled. In Strother v. Commissioner, 55 F.2d 626, the court says:

> * * * A taxpayer * * * should not be charged with gain on pure conjecture unsupported by any foundation of ascertainable fact. See Burnet v. Logan, 283 U.S. 404, 51 S.Ct. 550, 75 L.Ed. 1143.

This rule is approved in the recent case of Raytheon Production Corporation v. Commissioner, supra. Apportionment with reasonable accuracy of the amount received not being possible, and this amount being less than petitioner's cost basis for the property, it can not be determined that petitioner has, in fact, realized gain in any amount. Applying the rule as above set out, no portion of the payment in question should be considered as income, but the full amount must be treated as a return of capital and applied in reduction of petitioner's cost basis. Burnet v. Logan, 283 U.S. 404.

* * *

But some words of caution are needed. Although the doctrine of Burnet v. Logan is well-established in tax law, its importance should not be overemphasized. Section 1001(b) provides that the "amount realized" on a disposition of property is the amount of money received plus the fair market value of any property *received*. But recall from the *Philadelphia Amusement Park* case in Chapter 7 [6] that if the value of what is received cannot be ascertained in any arm's length transaction, it will be assumed that it is equal to the value of the property given up. Thus for the open transaction doctrine to apply on the ground that the amount realized cannot be ascertained, both the value of the property transferred and the value of the property received must be unknown.

---

6. See page 142, supra.

Additionally, the doctrine should not be overemphasized because, as the regulations properly state:[7] "The fair market value of property is a question of fact, but only in *rare and extraordinary* cases will property be considered to have no fair market value." Thus only in "rare and extraordinary circumstances" will courts cry "uncle" and give up on estimating fair market value. When they do, it does not mean it is completely impossible to make some sort of studied guess at value. Witness the fact that in the *Burnet v. Logan* case the mother's right to payment was in fact "valued" for estate tax purposes in 1917 even though her right then involved the amount of future payments to be expected which was the subject of controversy in the later income tax case. Nevertheless, the right to future payment was said to be incapable of being valued for income tax purposes. Why the difference?

A more recent example of an application of the open transaction doctrine occurred in Stephen H. Dorsey[8] where in return for their stock in a pinsetting company the taxpayers became entitled to receive one percent of all receipts by AMF from the sale or lease of its automatic pinsetting machines. The courts applied Burnet v. Logan because of the uncertainties and contingencies existing at the time of the transfer stating:[9]

* * *

> Here, as in Burnet v. Logan, supra, the petitioners received a "promise of future money payments wholly contingent upon facts and circumstances not possible to foretell with anything like fair certainty." A fair preponderance of the evidence in this record supports the position of petitioners that their contract rights with AMF had no ascertainable fair market value on September 16, 1954. Among the principal uncertainties and contingencies which existed on September 16, 1954, were:
>
> 1. *Conditions prevalent in the bowling industry,* particularly the unsavory past reputation of bowling and its unknown future potential.
>
> 2. *Obstacles to the success of automatic pinsetters within the bowling industry,* including the uncertainty as to their acceptance by the public and by bowling proprietors, their unproven status as a unique new product, and marketing problems.
>
> 3. *Problems facing the AMF pinsetter,* such as patent infringement suits, the quantity and quality of competition, especially from Brunswick Corp., the fact that AMF was a newcomer to the bowling industry in 1954, and the pinsetter's unproven character.

---

7.   Reg. § 1.1001–1(a); see also Reg. §   9.   Id. at 629.
      1.453–6(a)(2).

8.   Supra note 2.

4. *Difficulties of ascertaining how much of any success would actually redound to the participating certificate holders,* this being a consequence of AMF's control and constant changing of pinsetter prices, AMF's control of all marketing and management decisions, and the possibility that AMF could have operated its own pinsetting machines rather than sell or lease them, in which event the petitioners would have received no payments.

In short, without relying solely on any specific factor, we believe that the participating certificates had no ascertainable fair market value on September 16, 1954, and that the transaction before us must be treated as an 'open' transaction.

* * *

PROBLEMS

Taxpayer, a cash method taxpayer, owned all the stock in a company that owned all the rights in a new type of X-ray scanning device which had an extremely speculative value. She had owned the stock for several years and had a $100,000 cost basis in it. She sold the stock to a big electronics firm for $50,000 cash and 10 percent of the earnings generated by the scanning device over the succeeding 20 years. Although her right to earnings was speculative, she received $10,000 in each of the 20 succeeding years.

(a) What are the tax consequences to Taxpayer in each year?

(b) Would your result in (a), above, be altered if Taxpayer is an accrual method taxpayer?

(c) What are the consequences to Taxpayer in each of the years if she and the government agree that in the year of sale the total value of the cash received and the right to future payments is $200,000?

(d) What results to Taxpayer in each of the years if, instead of $200,000, they agree the total value is $300,000?

B.   TIMING AND CHARACTER OF GAIN IN A
CLOSED TRANSACTION

1.   TRANSACTIONS NOT INVOLVING A § 453
INSTALLMENT ELECTION
a.   Cash Method Taxpayers

ESTATE OF COID HURLBURT

Tax Court of the United States, 1956.
25 T.C. 1286 (NA).

Opinion

MULRONEY, JUDGE: The Commissioner determined a deficiency
in income tax in the amount of $4,555.07 for the calendar year 1947.
The sole issue is whether certain contracts entered into by Coid Hurlburt, decedent, in the sale of certain parcels of real estate in 1947
were includible in income as amounts realized under section 111(b)
of the 1939 Internal Revenue Code.

All of the facts have been stipulated and they are herein incorporated by this reference.

The decedent, Coid Hurlburt, and his wife, Merle Hurlburt, filed
a joint income tax return for the year 1947 with the then collector of
internal revenue for the district of Colorado.

In 1947 Coid Hurlburt sold three parcels of farm property located
in Washington County, Colorado. The sales were accomplished by
what we will call contracts of sale, which were documents entitled
"Receipt and Option." The contracts called for a downpayment
which was receipted for in the contract, one or two further payments
in 1947, and annual payments thereafter over the next 10 to 18 years
until the full purchase price, with interest, was paid. In one contract the vendor agreed to accept purchaser's $8,000 farm as a part
of the purchase price. It was provided in two of the contracts that
one copy of the contract, together with abstract and warranty deed,
be deposited with the Citizen's National Bank of Akron, Colorado,
"until payments have been completed as agreed." The other contract
did not have this provision but all three contracts, abstracts, and
warranty deeds were actually deposited with the bank. The purchasers all took immediate possession of the farms and there were
no defaults in the payments.

The taxpayer makes some argument that the receipt and option
documents were not contracts of sale but options. This is based on
the absence of express language in the instruments obligating the

purchasers to pay the purchase price—the language is that the purchasers were to receive the deeds when all of the payments were made. There is some language in some of the Colorado decisions cited in the brief interpreting similar instruments which might tend to support this argument of petitioner. But we do not go into the question for there is much general authority holding such a contract will be held to be one of purchase and sale when it appears the general intention was to consummate a sale. There is much law on the subject and it would be impossible to harmonize all of the decisions interpreting doubtful documents as contracts rather than options. The purchasers who signed the documents are not before us. We are content to assume the documents are valid contracts of sale and we will treat them as such for the purpose of this decision.

Section 111(a) of the 1939 Internal Revenue Code provides, in part: "The gain from the sale * * * of property shall be the excess of the amount realized therefrom over the adjusted basis * * *." Section 111(b) of the 1939 Internal Revenue Code provides: "The amount realized from the sale or other disposition of property shall be the sum of any money received plus the fair market value of the property (other than money) received."

There is no dispute over the vendor's adjusted base with regard to each of the three parcels and no dispute that in each instance it was more than the vendor received in money in the sale transaction in the year 1947, and no dispute that in each instance it was less than the full purchase price as stated in the contracts of sale. The vendor reported his income in 1947 on the cash basis without reporting any gain on the three contract sales. The Commissioner argues the sales were complete in 1947 when the contracts, abstracts, and warranty deeds were delivered to the bank, the initial payments made, and the purchasers took possession of the properties. The respondent then contends the contracts for the deferred payment of the purchase price had a fair market value in 1947 equal to the unpaid balances and the entire gain from the sale was realized in 1947 under section 111(b) of the 1939 Internal Revenue Code, supra.

The vital issue in this case is whether these contracts are to be valued in 1947 under section 111(b), supra, and that value included as "amount realized" by vendor in that year. It is stipulated that: "The purchasers executed no notes, bonds, and other evidence of indebtedness other than the 'Receipts and Options' hereinbefore mentioned and gave no additional security."

The contracts did nothing more than evidence the amounts due the vendor over a period of years and as such can be regarded as little more than accounts receivable. The vendor was a cash basis taxpayer and he did not receive any notes, bonds, mortgages, or other evidence of indebtedness such as normally would be considered amounts realized by a cash basis taxpayer.

In a like situation in Harold W. Johnston, 14 T.C. 560, where the only evidence of indebtedness was the contract for future payments, we held such a contract could not be valued by a cash basis taxpayer, and that value included in the "amount realized" under section 111 (b). Cf. Estate of Clarence W. Ennis, 23 T.C. 799, appeal dismissed C.A. 6; Nina J. Ennis, 17 T.C. 465.

In Harold W. Johnston, supra, we said:

"when the contract merely requires future payments and no notes, mortgages, or other evidence of indebtedness such as commonly change hands in commerce, which could be recognized as the equivalent of cash to some extent, are given and accepted as a part of the purchase price * * * [it] creates accounts payable by the purchasers and accounts receivable by the sellers which those two taxpayers would accrue if they were using an accrual method * * *. But such an agreement to pay the balance of the purchase price in the future has no tax significance to either purchaser or seller if he is using a cash system. * * * "

It was stipulated that when the vendor died in 1948 these contracts were valued at the unpaid balances for Colorado State inheritance tax purposes, in the vendor's estate. That evidence is without significance in determining whether the contracts had possessed a fair market value in the hands of a cash basis taxpayer. Admittedly the contract rights were assets in the deceased vendor's estate. As such, they would be valued as of the date of death and this would be true even though they were not the type of asset which would be includible in the income of a cash basis taxpayer.

We hold, therefore, that the contractual obligations were not amounts realized in 1947, and that the only "amount realized" in 1947 by the decedent was the total of the cash payments actually received in that year. These payments were not in excess of the decedent's basis for the property sold, and consequently no gain was realized on such sales in the year 1947.

Decision will be entered for the petitioners.

COWDEN v. COMMISSIONER

United States Court of Appeals, Fifth Circuit, 1961.
289 F.2d 20.

JONES, CIRCUIT JUDGE. We here review a decision of the Tax Court by which a determination was made of federal income tax liability of Frank Cowden, Sr., his wife and their children, for the years 1951 and 1952. In April 1951, Frank Cowden, Sr. and his wife made an oil, gas and mineral lease for themselves and their children upon described lands in Texas to Stanolind Oil and Gas Company. By related supplemental agreements, Stanolind agreed to make "bonus" or "advance royalty" payments in an aggregate amount of $511,-192.50. On execution of the instruments $10,223.85 was payable, the sum of $250,484.31 was due "no earlier than" January 5 "nor later than" January 10, 1952, and $250,484.34 was stipulated to be paid "no earlier than" January 5 "nor later than" January 10, 1953. One-half of the amounts was to be paid to Frank Cowden, Sr. and his wife, and one-sixth was payable to each of their children. In the deferred payments agreements it was provided that:

> "This contract evidences the obligation of Stanolind Oil and Gas Company to make the deferred payments referred to in subparagraphs (b) and (c) of the preceding paragraph hereof, and it is understood and agreed that the obligation of Stanolind Oil and Gas Company to make such payments is a firm and absolute personal obligation of said Company, which is not in any manner conditioned upon development or production from the demised premises, nor upon the continued ownership of the leasehold interest in such premises by Stanolind Oil and Gas Company, but that such payments shall be made in all events."

On November 30, 1951, the taxpayers assigned the payments due from Stanolind in 1952 to the First National Bank of Midland, of which Frank Cowden, Sr. was a director. Assignments of the payments due in 1953 were made to the bank on November 20, 1952. For the assignment of the 1952 payments the bank paid the face value of the amounts assigned discounted by $257.43 in the case of Frank Cowden, Sr. and his wife, and $85.81 in the case of each of their children. For the amounts due in 1953 the discounts were $313.14 for Frank Cowden, Sr. and his wife, and $104.38 for each of their children. The taxpayers reported the amounts received by them from the assignments as long-term capital gains. The Commissioner made a determination that the contractual obligations of Stanolind to make payments in future years represented ordinary income, subject to depletion, to the extent of the fair market value of the obligations at the time they were created. The Commissioner computed the fair market value of the Stanolind obligations, which were not interest bearing, by the deduction of a discount of four per cent. on the deferred payments from the date of the agreements until the respective maturities. Such computation fixed a 1951 equivalent of cash value of $487,647.46 for the bonus payments, paid in 1951 and agreed to be paid thereafter, aggregating $511,192.50. The Commissioner determined that the taxpayers should be taxed in 1951 on $487,647.46, as ordinary income.

A majority of the Tax Court was convinced that, under the particular facts of this case, the bonus payments were not only readily but immediately convertible to cash and were the equivalent of cash, and had a fair market value equal to their face value. The Tax Court decided that the entire amounts of the bonus payments, $511,192.50, were taxable in 1951, as ordinary income. Cowden v. Commissioner of Internal Revenue, 32 T.C. 853. Two judges of the Tax Court dissented.

The Tax Court stated, as a general proposition, "that executory contracts to make future payments in money do not have a fair market value." The particular facts by which the Tax Court distinguishes this case from the authorities by which the general proposition is established are, as stated in the opinion of the majority

> " * * * that the bonus payors were perfectly willing and able at the time of execution of the leases and bonus agreements to pay such bonus in an immediate lump sum payment; to pay the bonus immediately in a lump sum at all times thereafter until the due dates under the agreements; that Cowden, Sr., believed the bonus agreements had a market value at the time of their execution; that a bank in which he was an officer and depositor was willing to and in fact did purchase such rights at a nominal discount; that the bank considered such rights to be bankable and to represent direct obligations of the payor; that the bank generally dealt in such contracts where it was satisfied with the financial responsibility of the payor and looked solely to it for payment without recourse to the lessor and, in short, that the sole reason why the bonuses were not immediately paid in cash upon execution of the leases involved was the refusal of the lessor to receive such payments."

These findings are, in some respects, challenged by the taxpayers as being unsupported by the evidence. Our review of the record has led us to the conclusion that the findings of fact made by the Tax Court are sustained by substantial evidence. However, we must observe that the statement of Frank Cowden, Sr. that the contract obligations had "some market value" is not to be regarded as binding upon him and the other taxpayers with respect to the decisive issue in the case.

The dissenting opinion of the Tax Court minority states that the conclusion reached by the majority "is in effect that the taxpayers are not free to make the bargain of their choice," and one of the taxpayers' specifications of error is that the Tax Court "erred in holding that taxpayers are not free to make the bargain of their choice."

The Tax Court majority distinguishes the authorities cited and relied upon by the taxpayers upon several grounds. The Tax Court seemingly lays stress upon the fact, found to be here present, that the bonus payor was willing and able to make the entire bonus payment upon the execution of the agreement. It is said by the taxpayers that the Tax Court has held that a constructive receipt, under the equivalent of cash doctrine, resulted from the willingness of the lessee to pay the entire bonus on execution of the leases and the unwillingness of the taxpayers, for reasons of their own,[1] to receive the full amount. If this be the effect of the Tax Court's decision there may be some justification for the criticism appearing in the opinion of the minority and the concern expressed elsewhere.[2]

It was said in Gregory v. Helvering, 293 U.S. 465, 55 S.Ct. 266, 79 L.Ed. 596, 97 A.L.R. 1355, and recently repeated in Knetsch v. United States, 364 U.S. 361, 81 S.Ct. 132, 135, 5 L.Ed.2d 128, "The legal right of a taxpayer to decrease the amount of what otherwise would be his taxes, or altogether avoid them, by means which the law permits, cannot be doubted." See Rupe Investment Corporation v. Commissioner of Internal Revenue, 5 Cir., 1959, 266 F.2d 624; Williams v. United States, 5 Cir. 1955, 219 F.2d 523. As a general rule a tax avoidance motive is not to be considered in determining the tax liability resulting from a transaction. Sun Properties v. United States, 5 Cir., 220 F.2d 171; Caldwell v. Campbell, 5 Cir., 1955, 218 F.2d 567; Roscoe v. Commissioner of Internal Revenue, 5 Cir., 1954, 215 F.2d 478. The taxpayers had the right to decline to enter into a mineral lease of their lands except upon the condition that the lessee obligate itself for a bonus payable in part in installments in future years, and the doing so would not, of itself, subject the deferred payments to taxation during the year that the lease was made. Nor would a tax liability necessarily arise although the lease contract was made with a solvent lessee who had been willing and able to pay the entire bonus upon the execution of the lease.

While it is true that the parties may enter into any legal arrangement they see fit even though the particular form in which it was cast was selected with the hope of a reduction in taxes, it is also true that if a consideration for which one of the parties bargains is the equivalent of cash it will be subjected to taxation to the extent of its fair market value. Whether the undertaking of the lessee to make future bonus payments was, when made, the equivalent of cash and, as such, taxable as current income is the issue in this case. In a somewhat similar case, decided in 1941, the Board of Tax Appeals stated that "where no notes, bonds, or other evidences of indebtedness other than the contract were given, such contract had no fair market value." Kleberg v. Commissioner, 43 B.T.A. 277, quoting from Titus v. Commissioner, 33 B.T.A. 928. In 1959 the Tax Court held that where the deferred bonus payments were evidenced by promissory notes

---

1. It is not denied that a desire to save taxes was the sole purpose for the taxpayors' insistence that payment be postponed.

2. 9 Oil & Gas Tax Q. 122; 49 A.B.A.J. 1205; 59 Colum.L.Rev. 1237; 8 Tax

Fortnightor 835; 11th Ann.S.W.Leg. Found.Inst.Oil & Gas Law & Taxation 651.

the equivalent of cash doctrine might be applicable. Barnsley v. Commissioner, 31 T.C. 1260. There the Tax Court said:

> "It is, of course, possible under an oil and gas lease containing proper provisions to have a bonus payable and taxable in installments, Alice G. K. Kleberg, 43 B.T.A. 277. The case before us does not constitute such an arrangement. In the Kleberg case the contractual agreement was to pay a named amount in two payments as bonus. It was not a case like the one here where cash and negotiable notes, the latter being the equivalent of cash, representing the bonus were received in the same year by the taxpayer."

The test announced in Kleberg, from which Barnsley does not depart, seems to be whether the obligation to make the deferred payments is represented by "notes, bonds, or other evidences of indebtedness other than the contract". In this case, the literal test of Kleberg is met as the obligation of Stanolind to the Cowdens was evidenced by an instrument other than the contract of lease. This instrument is not, however, one of the kind which fall into the classification of notes or bonds. The taxpayers urge that there can be no "equivalent of cash" obligation unless it is a negotiable instrument. Such a test, to be determined by the form of the obligation, is as unrealistic as it is formalistic. The income tax law deals in economic realities, not legal abstractions,[3] and the reach of the income tax law is not to be delimited by technical refinements or mere formalism.[4]

A promissory note, negotiable in form, is not necessarily the equivalent of cash. Such an instrument may have been issued by a maker of doubtful solvency[5] or for other reasons such paper might be denied a ready acceptance in the market place. We think the converse of this principle ought to be applicable. We are convinced that if a promise to pay of a solvent obligor is unconditional and assignable, not subject to set-offs, and is of a kind that is frequently transferred to lenders or investors at a discount not substantially greater than the generally prevailing premium for the use of money, such promise is the equivalent of cash and taxable in like manner as cash would have been taxable had it been received by the taxpayer rather than the obligation. The principle that negotiability is not the test of taxability in an equivalent of cash case such as is before us, is consistent with the rule that men may, if they can, so order their affairs as to minimize taxes,[6] and points up the doctrine that substance and not form should control in the application of income tax laws.[7]

3. Commissioner of Internal Revenue v. Southwest Exploration Company, 350 U.S. 308, 76 S.Ct. 395, 100 L.Ed. 347.

4. United States v. Joliet & Chicago Railroad Company, 315 U.S. 44, 62 S. Ct. 442, 86 L.Ed. 658.

5. Board v. Commissioner, 18 B.T.A. 650.

6. Cf. Atlantic Coast Line Railroad Company v. Phillips, 332 U.S. 168, 67 S.Ct. 1584, 91 L.Ed. 1977, 173 A.L.R. 1; Bullen v. State of Wisconsin, 240 U.S. 625, 36 S.Ct. 473, 60 L.Ed. 830.

7. United States v. Phellis, 257 U.S. 156, 42 S.Ct. 63, 66 L.Ed. 180; Morsman v. Commissioner of Internal Rev-

The Tax Court stressed in its findings that the provisions for deferring a part of the bonus were made solely at the request of and for the benefit of the taxpayers and that the lessee was willing and able to make the bonus payments in cash upon execution of the agreements. It appears to us that the Tax Court, in reaching its decision that the taxpayers had received equivalent of cash bonuses in the year the leases were executed, gave as much and probably more weight to those findings than to the other facts found by it. We are persuaded of this not only by the language of its opinion but because, in its determination of the cash equivalent, it used the amounts which it determined the taxpayers could have received if they had made a different contract, rather than the fair market value cash equivalent [8] of the obligation for which the taxpayers had bargained in the contracts which they had a lawful right to make. We are unable to say whether or not the Tax Court, if it disregarded, as we think it should have done, the facts as it found them as to the willingness of the lessee to pay and the unwillingness of the taxpayers to receive a full bonus on execution of the leases, would have determined that the deferred bonus obligations were taxable in the year of the agreements as the equivalent of cash. This question is primarily a fact issue. Glenn v. Penn, 6 Cir., 1958, 250 F.2d 507; Kasper v. Banek, 8 Cir., 1954, 214 F.2d 125. There should be a remand to the Tax Court for a reconsideration of the questions submitted in the light of what has been said here.*

* * *

WARREN JONES CO. v. COMMISSIONER

United States Court of Appeals, Ninth Circuit, 1975.
524 F.2d 788.

ELY, CIRCUIT JUDGE: During its taxable year ending on October 31, 1968, the Warren Jones Company, a cash basis taxpayer, sold an apartment building for $153,000. In return, the taxpayer received a cash downpayment of $20,000 and the buyer's promise in a standard form real estate contract, to pay $133,000, plus interest, over the following fifteen years. The Tax Court held, with three judges dissenting, that the fair market value of the real estate contract did not constitute an "amount realized" by the taxpayer in the taxable year of sale under section 1001(b) of the Internal Revenue Code.[1] Warren Jones Co., 60 T.C. 663 (1973) (reviewed by the full Court). The Commissioner of Internal Revenue has appealed, and we reverse.

enue, 8 Cir., 1937, 90 F.2d 18, 113 A.L. R. 441.

8. Computed by the Commissioner by discounting the obligations at a 4 per cent rate.

* On remand the contractual obligations were held to be the equivalent of

cash. Frank Cowden, Sr., 20 TCM 1134 (1961).

1. Unless otherwise stated, all section references are to the Internal Revenue Code of 1954, 26 U.S.C. (1970).

I. Background

On May 27, 1968, the taxpayer, a family-held corporation chartered by the State of Washington, entered into a real estate contract for the sale of one of its Seattle apartment buildings, the Wallingford Court Apartments, to Bernard and Jo Ann Storey for $153,000. When the sale closed on June 15, 1968, the Storeys paid $20,000 in cash and took possession of the apartments. The Storeys were then obligated by the contract to pay the taxpayer $1,000 per month, plus 8 percent interest on the declining balance, for a period of fifteen years. The balance due at the end of fifteen years is to be payable in a lump sum. The contract was the only evidence of the Storeys' indebtedness, since no notes or other such instruments passed between the parties. Upon receipt of the full purchase price, the taxpayer is obligated by the contract to deed the Wallingford Apartments to the Storeys.

The Tax Court found, as facts, that the transaction between the taxpayer and the Storeys was a completed sale in the taxable year ending on October 31, 1968, and that in that year, the Storeys were solvent obligors. The court also found that real estate contracts such as that between the taxpayer and the Storeys were regularly bought and sold in the Seattle area. The court concluded, from the testimony before it, that in the taxable year of sale, the taxpayer could have sold its contract, which had a face value of $133,000, to a savings and loan association or a similar institutional buyer for approximately $117,980. The court found, however, that in accordance with prevailing business practices, any potential buyer for the contract would likely have required the taxpayer to deposit $41,000 of the proceeds from the sale of the contract in a savings account, assigned to the buyer, for the purpose of securing the first $41,000 of the Storeys' payments. Consequently, the court found that in the taxable year of sale, the contract had a fair market value of only $76,980 (the contract's selling price minus the amount deposited in the assigned savings account).

On the sale's closing date, the taxpayer had an adjusted basis of $61,913 in the Wallingford Apartments. In determining the amount it had realized from the sale, the taxpayer added only the $20,000 downpayment and the portion of the $4,000 in monthly payments it had received that was allocable to principal. Consequently, on its federal income tax return for the taxable year ending October 31, 1968, the taxpayer reported no gain from the apartment sale. The taxpayer's return explained that the corporation reported on the cash basis and that under the Tax Court's holding in Nina J. Ennis, 17 T.C. 465 (1951), it was not required to report gain on the sale until it had recovered its basis. The return also stated, however, that in the event the taxpayer was required to report gain in the taxable year of the sale, it elected to do so on the installment basis (I.R.C. § 453).

The Commissioner disagreed with the taxpayer's assertion that it had realized no gain on the sale, but he conceded that the sale qualified as an installment sale. Consequently, the Commissioner recalculated the taxpayer's gain in accordance with section 453 and notified the taxpayer that it had recognized an additional $12,098 in long term capital gain. The taxpayer then petitioned the Tax Court for a redetermination of its liability.

Section 1001 provides, in pertinent part, as follows:

(a) COMPUTATION OF GAIN OR LOSS.—The gain from the sale or other disposition of property shall be the excess of the amount realized therefrom over the adjusted basis . . . .

(b) AMOUNT REALIZED.—The amount realized from the sale or other disposition of property shall be the sum of any money received plus the fair market value of the property (other than money) received.[2]

The question presented is whether section 1001(b) requires the taxpayer to include the fair market value of its real estate contract with the Storeys in determining the "amount realized" during the taxable year of the sale.[3]

Holding that the fair market value of the contract was not includable in the amount realized from the sale, the Tax Court majority relied on the doctrine of "cash equivalency." Under that doctrine, the cash basis taxpayer must report income received in the form of property only if the property is the "equivalent of cash." See generally 2 J. Mertens, The Law of Federal Income Taxation §§ 11.01–11.05 (Malone rev. 1974).

The Tax Court majority adopted the following as its definition of the phrase, "equivalent of cash":

. . . if the promise to pay of a solvent obligor is unconditional and assignable, not subject to set-offs, and is of a kind that is frequently transferred to lenders or investors at a discount not substantially greater than the generally prevailing premium for the use of money, such promise is the equivalent of cash . . .

2. With certain exceptions not relevant here, section 1002 of the Code requires the full amount of gain determined under section 1001 to be recognized. The exceptions to section 1002 provide nonrecognition treatment for property received in an exchange that is "substantially a continuation of the old investment still unliquidated." Treas.Reg. §§ 1.1002–1(a)–(c).

3. Several commentators have addressed the question. See, e. g., 2 J. Mertens, The Law of Federal Income Taxation § 11.07 (Malone rev. 1974); J. Sneed, The Configurations of Gross Income 39–62 (1967); Levin & Javaras, Receipt of Notes and Other Rights to Future Payments by a Cash-Basis Taxpayer, 54 A.B.A.J. 405 (1968); Comment, *The Doctrine of Cash Equivalency*, 22 U.C.L.A.L.Rev. 219 (1974); Comment, *Realization of Income in Deferred-Payment Sales*, 34 Mo.L.Rev. 357 (1969).

Warren Jones Co., supra at 668–69, quoting, Cowden v. Commissioner, 289 F.2d 20, 24 (5th Cir. 1961). Applying the quoted definition, the Tax Court held that the taxpayer's contract, which had a face value of $133,000, was not the "equivalent of cash" since it had a fair market value of only $76,980. Had the taxpayer sold the contract, the discount from the face value, approximately 42 percent, would have been "substantially greater than the generally prevailing premium for the use of money." [4]

The Tax Court observed that requiring the taxpayer to realize the fair market value of the contract in the year of the sale could subject the taxpayer to substantial hardships. The taxpayer would be taxed in the initial year on a substantial portion of its gain from the sale of the property, even though it had received, in cash, only a small fraction of the purchase price. To raise funds to pay its taxes, the taxpayer might be forced to sell the contract at the contract's fair market value, even though such a sale might not otherwise be necessary or advantageous. Most importantly in the Tax Court's view, if the taxpayer were required to realize the fair market value of the contract in the year of the sale, the sale transaction would be closed for tax purposes in that year; hence, the taxpayer's capital gain on the transaction would be permanently limited to the difference between its adjusted basis and the contract's fair market value plus the cash payments received in the year of sale. If the taxpayer did retain the contract, so as to collect its face value, the amounts received in excess of the contract's fair market value would constitute ordinary income. The Tax Court also noted that requiring the cash basis taxpayer to realize the fair market value of the real estate contract would tend to obscure the differences between the cash and accrual methods of reporting.

The Commissioner does not dispute the Tax Court's conclusion that the taxpayer's contract with the Storeys had a fair market value of $76,980, or any other of the court's findings of fact. [5] Rather, the Commissioner contends that since, as found by the Tax Court, the contract had a fair market value, section 1001(b) requires the taxpayer to include the amount of that fair market value in determining the amount realized. [6]

4. The taxpayer's argument on appeal that to be a cash equivalent, a debt instrument must be negotiable is untenable. See, e. g., Heller Trust v. Comm'r, 382 F.2d 675, 681 (9th Cir. (1967); Cowden v. C.I.R., 289 F.2d 20, 24 (5th Cir. 1961).

5. Relying primarily on Bedell v. Comm'r, 30 F.2d 622 (2d Cir. 1929), the taxpayer disputes the Tax Court's finding that the sale of the Wallingford Apartments was a completed transaction in the taxable year ending

October 31, 1968. The question whether a particular sale is completed is ordinarily a question of fact, Clodfelter v. Comm'r, 426 F.2d 1391 (9th Cir. 1970), and the disputed finding in the present case is most assuredly not clearly erroneous.

6. The Commissioner's theoretical approach to the result for which he contends is not altogether clear. He may be rejecting the doctrine of cash equivalency altogether, cf. *Warren Jones Co.,* supra at 673–74 (Quealy, J., dis-

II.   *Statutory Analysis*

The first statutory predecessor of section 1001(b) was section 202(b) of the Revenue Act of February 24, 1919, which stated:

> When property is exchanged for other property, the property received in exchange shall for the purpose of determining gain or loss be treated as the equivalent of cash to the amount of its fair market value, if any .   . . .

Ch. 18, § 202(b), 40 Stat. 1060.   We have no doubt that under that statute, the taxpayer would have been required to include the fair market value of its real estate contract as an amount realized during the taxable year of sale.

Only three years later, however, in the Revenue Act of November 23, 1921, Congress replaced the language of the statute enacted in 1919 with the following:

> On an exchange of property, real, personal or mixed, for any other such property, no gain or loss shall be recognized unless the property received in exchange has a readily realizable market value .   . . .

Ch. 136, § 202(c), 42 Stat. 230.   The original statute had created "a presumption in favor of taxation."   H.R.Rep. No. 350, 67th Cong., 1st Sess. (1921), reproduced at 1939–1 Cum.Bull. (Part 2) 168, 175.   In the 1921 Act, Congress doubtless intended a policy more favorable to the taxpayer.   Interpreting the 1921 statute, the Treasury Regulations provided that

> [p]roperty has a readily realizable market value if it can be readily converted into an amount of cash or its equivalent substantially to the fair value of the property.

Treas.Reg. 62, Art. 1564 (1922 ed.).   The law established in 1921 appears to have been substantially in accord with the position taken in this case by the Tax Court majority.

Notwithstanding the foregoing, in the Revenue Act of 1924, ch. 234, § 202(c), 43 Stat. 256, Congress again changed the law, replacing the 1921 statute with the language that now appears in section 1001(b) of the current Code.   Of the 1921 statute, and its require-

senting), or he may be contending that any property with a fair market value is the equivalent of cash in the amount of its fair market value.   See Comment, *The Doctrine of Cash Equivalency*, supra n. 3 at 225–26; but see M. Levine, Real Estate Transactions, Tax Planning and Consequences § 731 (1973).   Since as to a cash basis taxpayer, with which we are here concerned, both theories would achieve the same result, we need not distinguish between them.

The taxpayer contends that the basic question before us is one of fact. We disagree.   The question is essentially one of statutory construction and it therefore presents an issue of law.

ment of a "readily realizable market value," the Senate Finance Committee wrote in 1924:

> The question whether, in a given case, the property received in exchange has a readily realizable market value is a most difficult one, and the rulings on this question in given cases have been far from satisfactory. * * * The provision can not be applied with accuracy or consistency.

S.Rep. No. 398, 68th Cong., 1st Sess. (1924), reproduced at 1939–1 Cum.Bull. (Part 2) 266, 275. See also H.R.Rep. No. 179, 68th Cong., 1st Sess. (1924), reproduced at 1939–1 Cum.Bull. (Part 2) 241, 251. Under the 1924 statute, "where income is realized in the form of property, the measure of the income is the fair market value of the property at the date of its receipt." H.R.Rep. No. 179, supra, 1939–1 Cum.Bull. (Part 2) at 250; S.Rep. No. 398, supra, 1939–1 Cum.Bull. (Part 2) at 275.[7]

There is no indication whatsoever that Congress intended to retain the "readily realizable market value" test from the 1921 statute as an unstated element of the 1924 Act. Indeed, as noted above, Congress sharply criticized that test. We cannot avoid the conclusion that in 1924 Congress intended to establish the more definite rule for which the Commissioner here contends and that consequently, if the fair market value of property received in an exchange can be ascertained, that fair market value must be reported as an amount realized.

Congress clearly understood that the 1924 statute might subject some taxpayers to the hardships discussed by the Tax Court majority. In the Revenue Act of 1926, ch. 27, § 212(d), 44 Stat. 23, Congress enacted the installment basis for reporting gain that is now reflected in section 453 of the current Code. Under section 453, a taxpayer who sells real property and receives payments in the year of sale totaling less than 30 percent of the selling price may elect to report as taxable income in any given year only

> that proportion of the installment payments actually received in that year which the gross profit, realized or to be realized when payment is completed, bears to the total contract price.

26 U.S.C. § 453(a) (1).

By providing the installment basis, Congress intended ". . . to relieve taxpayers who adopted it from having to pay an income tax in the year of sale based on the full amount of anticipated profits when in fact they had received in cash only a small portion of the sales price." Commissioner v. South Texas Lumber Co., 333 U.S. 496,

7. Section 203 of the Revenue Act of 1924, ch. 234, § 203, 43 Stat. 256, a forerunner of section 1002 of the current Code, required recognition of the entire amount of gain realized under the 1924 Act's section 202.

503, 68 S.Ct. 695, 700, 92 L.Ed. 831 (1948). For sales that qualify, the installment basis also eliminates the other potential disadvantages to which the Tax Court referred. Since taxation in the year of the sale is based on the value of the payments actually received, the taxpayer should not be required to sell his obligation in order to meet his tax liabilities. Furthermore, the installment basis does not change the character of the gain received. If gain on an exchange would otherwise be capital, it remains capital under section 453. Finally, the installment basis treats cash and accrual basis taxpayers equally.

We view section 453 as persuasive evidence in support of the interpretation of section 1001(b) for which the Commissioner contends. The installment basis is Congress's method of providing relief from the rigors of section 1001(b). In its report on the Revenue Act of 1926, the Senate Finance Committee expressly noted that in sales or exchanges not qualifying for the installment basis, "deferred-payment contracts"

> . . . are to be regarded as the equivalent of cash if such obligations have a fair market value. In consequence, that portion of the initial payment and of the fair market value of such obligations which represents profit is to be returned as income as of the taxable year of the sale.

S.Rep. No. 52, 69th Cong., 1st Sess. (1926), reproduced at 1939–1 Cum.Bull (Part 2) 332, 347.

On this appeal, however, the taxpayer has made another argument with respect to section 453. It contends that subsection (b) (3), added to section 453 in 1969, may be read as Congress's definition of the phrase "equivalent of cash." As noted above, taxpayers who sell property and receive "payments" in the year of sale that exceed 30 percent of the selling price may not report on the installment basis. Under section 453(b) (2) (A) (ii), "evidences of indebtedness of the purchaser" are not to be considered as "payments" in the year of sale in determining whether the payments constitute 30 percent of the selling price. Section 453(b) (3), added by the Tax Reform Act of 1969, provides that

> . . . a bond or other evidence of indebtedness which is payable on demand, or which is issued by a corporation or a government or a political subdivision thereof (A) with interest coupons attached or in registered form (other than one in registered form which the taxpayer establishes will not be readily tradable in an established securities market), or (B) in any other form designed to render such bond or other evidence of indebtedness readily tradable in an established securities market, shall not be treated as an evidence of indebtedness of the purchaser.

In the taxpayer's view, property received in a sale or exchange should not be considered the equivalent of cash under section 1001(b) unless the property is of the types described in section 453(b) (3).[8]

Congress added section 453(b) (3) to the Code for the purpose of excluding from the installment basis those taxpayers who sell property and receive more than 30 percent of the selling price in the form of highly liquid instruments of debt. Congress concluded that such taxpayers, like taxpayers receiving cash, would not suffer the hardships that the installment basis was designed to alleviate. See H.R. Rep. No. 413, 91st Cong., 1st Sess. 107–08 (1969) (1969–3 Cum.Bull. 200, 267), U.S.Code Cong. & Admin.News 1969, p. 1645. We find no indication that Congress intended that section 453(b) (3) should be given a broader application. If we were to adopt the taxpayer's argument, we would substantially nullify section 453 with respect to cash basis taxpayers receiving deferred payment obligations other than those described in section 453(b) (3). Such taxpayers, not required to include the fair market value of their obligations in determining the amount realized under section 1001(b), would rarely, if ever, elect to report on the installment basis. In the light of the other legislative history of section 453, hitherto discussed, it is clear to us that Congress, in 1969, did not contemplate, or intend, such a result.

III. Case Law

The prior decisions of our own court support the conclusion we have reached. On several occasions, we have held that if the fair market value of a deferred payment obligation received in a sale or other exchange can be ascertained, that fair market value must be included as an amount realized under section 1001(b). Most recently, in In re Steen, 509 F.2d 1398, 1404–05 (9th Cir. 1975), we held that the fair market value of an installment payment contract received in exchange for shares of stock was ascertainable and that consequently, that fair market value was an amount realized in the year of the sale. In Heller Trust v. Commissioner, 382 F.2d 675, 681 (9th Cir. 1967), our court affirmed a Tax Court decision requiring a taxpayer to include the fair market value of real estate contracts as an amount realized in the year of a sale, even though the fair market value of the contracts there involved was only 50 percent of their face value. See also Clodfelter v. Commissioner, 426 F.2d 1391 (9th Cir. 1970); Tombari v. Commissioner, 299 F.2d 889, 892–93 (9th Cir. 1962); Gersten v. Commissioner, 267 F.2d 195 (9th Cir. 1959).[9]

8. The argument upon which the taxpayer relies is fully developed in Comment, *The Doctrine of Cash Equivalency*, supra n. 3 at 233–38.

9. Accord, McCormac v. United States, 424 F.2d 607, 191 Ct.Cl. 483 (1970); Kaufman v. Comm'r, 372 F.2d 789, 793–94 (4th Cir. 1966); Campagna v. United States, 290 F.2d 682 (2d Cir. 1961); 2 J. Mertens, supra n. 3; J. Sneed, supra n. 3 at 48–49. The Tax Court adopted as its definition of "cash equivalency" certain language from the opinion in Cowden v. Comm'r, 289 F.2d 20 (5th Cir. 1961).

There are, of course, "rare and extraordinary" situations in which it is impossible to ascertain the fair market value of a deferred payment obligation in the year of sale. See Treas.Reg. § 1.1001-1(a). The total amount payable under an obligation may be so speculative, or the right to receive any payments at all so contingent, that the fair market value of the obligation cannot be fixed. See Burnet v. Logan, 283 U.S. 404, 51 S.Ct. 550, 75 L.Ed. 1143 (1931); In re Steen, 509 F. 2d 1398, 1403-04 (9th Cir. 1975) (right to payment depended on favorable judicial decision on novel question of state law); Westover v. Smith, 173 F.2d 90 (9th Cir. 1949). If an obligation is not marketable, it may be impossible to establish its fair market value. See Willhoit v. Commissioner, 308 F.2d 259 (9th Cir. 1962) (uncontradicted testimony that there was no market for high risk contracts); Phillips v. Frank, 295 F.2d 629 (9th Cir. 1961) (uncontradicted testimony that highly speculative contracts could not have been sold in the year of sale). But see United States v. Davis, 370 U.S. 65, 71-74, 82 S.Ct. 1190, 8 L.Ed.2d 335 (1962) (wife's release of her marital rights in a property settlement agreement held to have a fair market value equal to the value of property that her husband transferred to her in exchange); Gersten v. Commissioner, supra at 197 ("It is not necessary to find any actual sales of like articles to establish a fair market value.")

The Tax Court found, as a fact, that the taxpayer's real estate contract with the Storeys had a fair market value of $76,980 in the taxable year of sale. Consequently, the taxpayer must include $76,-980 in determining the amount realized under section 1001(b). As previously noted, however, the Commissioner has conceded that the taxpayer is eligible to report on the installment basis and has calculated the taxpayer's deficiency accordingly.

The decision of the Tax Court is reversed, and on remand, the Tax Court will enter judgment for the Commissioner.[10]

Reversed and remanded, with directions.

In our view, the holding in Cowden does not conflict with the prior decisions of our court or with our present decision. In Cowden, the Fifth Circuit held that the Tax Court had over-emphasized one of its findings of fact in reaching its decision and remanded the case for the Tax Court's reconsideration. The language adopted by the Tax Court appears within the context of the Fifth Circuit's discussion, in Cowden, of the taxpayer's contention that the deferred payment obligation he had received in exchange for an oil and gas lease could have no realizable value because it was not negotiable. In rejecting the taxpayer's contention, the Cowden court appears to have written the language adopted by the Tax Court principally as a description of the obligation involved in that case. See Dennis v. Comm'r, 473 F.2d 274, 285 (5th Cir. 1973), in which the Fifth Circuit, citing Cowden, states that when property received in a sale or exchange has a fair market value, that value constitutes an amount realized.

10. The taxpayer has not here challenged, and we have not examined, the Commissioner's calculation of the taxpayer's gain under section 453. The Tax Court may examine those calculations on remand, if the taxpayer so requests.

NOTE

If in a transaction seemingly closed a cash method taxpayer receives obligations that have no cash equivalence the transaction is again treated as open. The tax consequences are identical, as payments are received—a recovery of capital followed by a gain realized on any excess over the property's adjusted basis. The gain is characterized by the original transaction. As indicated in (c) and (d) of the "open transaction" Problems, supra page 854, if instead a cash method taxpayer in a *closed* transaction receives obligations that have a cash equivalent with a fair market value less than their face amount, only that fair market value is treated as an amount realized in the year of sale. What are the tax consequences on collection of the full amount of the obligations and what character will the amounts not previously taxed have?[1] Again, with a timing exception, we run parallel to a concept presented earlier.

The problem is perhaps best illustrated by a further example. Assume a cash method taxpayer sells a parcel of land, a capital asset held for more than one year in which he has a $20,000 basis, for a purchase price of $100,000. He receives from the buyer $50,000 cash in the year of sale and an interest bearing obligation under which the buyer agrees to pay $10,000 a year in each of the succeeding five years. Assume further that the obligation is the equivalent of cash to the extent of its $40,000 fair market value. The taxpayer would realize a $70,000 long term capital gain in the year of the sale, the difference between the $90,000 amount realized and the $20,000 adjusted basis. But what happens when he receives $10,000 as the first payment on the obligation in the year after the sale? The *Shafpa Realty Corp.* case[2] holds in effect that the difference between face and market which went untaxed in the year of the sale must be amortized over the life of the payments. The taxpayer has an obligation with a $40,000 basis (determined by the amount he previously included as a part of the amount realized) which may be amortized over the period during which payment is to be made. Thus in each of the five years the taxpayer will have an $8,000 recovery of capital and $2,000 of income.

If the obligation were to pay an indefinite amount for a specified period, say a percentage of income earned by the property for five years, but having an estimable fair market value of $40,000 (i. e., no Burnet v. Logan situation) then for the year of sale the amount realized would be $90,000 ($50,000 cash and other property worth $40,000) and taxpayer would have the same $70,000 long-term capital gain. However, since the total recovery is indefinite no income would be taxed as payments were made on the obligation itself until the $40,-000 tax cost basis was recovered. Any excess recovery over the $40,-

---

1. This note disregards discussion of any interest paid on such obligations.

2. 8 BTA 283 (1927).

000 would be income as received.[3] Consequently if (quite unrealistically) the percentage of the income came to $10,000 a year for five years, taxpayer would recover capital in the first four years and would have $10,000 of income in year five. This same rule has been applied in a situation where although the principal amount to be paid is definite, nevertheless it is highly speculative whether the payments under obligation will be made.[4]

Regardless of when the excess is taxed the remaining question is what is the character of the excess? Since the original transaction was closed in the year of sale, the receipt of any excess does not arise out of any sale or exchange. There is a mere extinction of the obligation and the excess regardless of when it is taxed is ordinary income.[5]

b. Accrual Method Taxpayers

Regulation: Section 1.453–6(a).

Under the accrual method of accounting there is no equivalency of cash question; the receipt of cash or its equivalent is not significant. As the Supreme Court stated in Spring City Foundry Co. v. Commissioner:[1]

> Keeping account and making returns on the accrual basis, as distinguished from the cash basis, import that it is the *right* to receive and not the actual receipt that determines the inclusion of the amount in gross income.

That quote dealt with a question of timing: When, for what period, is an item to be included? But it relates as well to the question of the amount of inclusion. Under § 1001(b) an "amount realized" is the "sum of any money received plus the fair market value of property (other than money) received." We are concerned with the right to receive something in the future; consequently it is the amount of money or the value of property *to be* received which is included in gross income. Thus if an accrual method taxpayer in the year of a sale receives the purchaser's obligation to pay $10,000 a year over a five year period, even if the obligation has a fair market value of only $40,000, he is required to treat the $50,000 face amount of the obligation, the amount *to be* received, as part of the amount realized

------

3. Cf. Stephen H. Dorsey, 49 T.C. 606 (1968).

4. Comm'r v. Liftin, 317 F.2d 234 (4th Cir. 1963).

5. Waring v. Comm'r, 412 F.2d 800 (3rd Cir. 1969); cf. Galvin Hudson, supra p. 694.

1. 292 U.S. 182 (1934).

in the year of the sale.[2] The Tax Court has stated this principle as follows:[3]

> Section 1001(b) of the Code provides that the amount realized from the sale or other disposition of property shall be the sum of any money received plus the fair market value of the property (other than money) received. However, an accrual basis taxpayer does not treat an unconditional right to receive money as property received, but rather as money received to the full extent of the face value of the right. See Key Homes, Inc., 30 T.C. 109, affirmed per curiam (C.A. 6) 271 F.2d 280. The fact that there is always the possibility that a purchaser or debtor may default in his obligation is not sufficient to defer the accruing of income that has been earned. Spring City Foundry Co. v. Commissioner, 292 U.S. 182.

This principle is well established. Nevertheless there is a possibly conflicting regulation, Reg. § 1.453–6(a), which provides in part:

> In * * * sales of real property involving deferred payments in which the payments received during the year of sale exceed 30 percent of the selling price, the obligations of the purchaser received by the vendor are to be considered as an amount realized to the extent of their fair market value in ascertaining the profit or loss from the transaction.

Technically this regulation should be limited to cash method taxpayers because it requires inclusion of only the fair market value rather than the face amount of an obligation in income. Dicta in one case has so limited it.[4] However, the regulation itself fails to make any such distinction and, as a policy matter, perhaps none should be made. With § 453 unavailable, except for the doctrinally questionable regulation accrual method taxpayers would be badly treated if they made major sales involving payments over a long period and received initially cash in excess of 30%[5] and the purchaser's notes with very little value.

2. George L. Castner Co., 30 T.C. 1061 (1958).

3. First Savings and Loan Association, 40 T.C. 474, 487 (1963).

4. Western Oaks Building Corp., 49 T. C. 365, 372, at fn. 4 (1968).

5. I.R.C. § 453(b)(2)(A).

2. TRANSACTIONS UNDER A § 453 ELECTION

Internal Revenue Code: Sections 453(a), (b), (d)(1) through (3). See Sections 483; 1038; 1245; 1250.

Regulations: Sections 1.453–1(a) through (c), 1.453–4, 1.453–9(a) and (b); 1.1245–6(d); 1.1250–1(c)(6). (The section 453 Reg. references are even more important than usual in working the Problems at the end of this segment.)

GEORGE L. CASTNER CO.

Tax Court of the United States, 1958.
30 T.C. 1061.

[The Court's findings of fact indicate that the taxpayer, an accrual method corporation, sold machinery and equipment on May 7, 1951. The sales price was $11,000 of which $3,000 was initially paid in cash, and the purchaser gave a secured note for $8000. In the same tax year two quarterly installments of $253.08 each were paid on the note of which in each case $200 represented payment on the principal of the note and the balance interest. On its return for the year the taxpayer elected the installment method of reporting its gain on the sale, under 1939 Code section 44(b), which corresponds to current section 453. Ed.]

Opinion

TURNER, JUDGE: In section 42(a) of the Internal Revenue Code of 1939, it is provided that all items of gross income are to be included in gross income for the taxable year in which received, unless under methods of accounting permitted under section 41, any such amounts are properly to be accounted for as of a different period. According to section 41, net income is to be computed upon the basis of the taxpayer's annual accounting period, fiscal or calendar year, "in accordance with the method of accounting regularly employed in keeping the books" of the taxpayer; provided, of course, it clearly reflects the income, in which case "it is to be followed with respect to the time as of which items of gross income and deductions are to be accounted for." Sec. 29.41–1, Regs. 111. And while "approved standard methods of accounting will ordinarily be regarded as clearly reflecting income," the method used must be such that "all items of gross income and all deductions are treated with consistency," and "in any case in which it is necessary to use an inventory, no method of accounting in regard to purchases and sales will correctly reflect income except an accrual method." Sec. 29.41–2, Regs. 111.

In section 44(b) of the Code, however, it is provided that in "the case (1) of a casual sale * * * of personal property (other than property of a kind which would properly be included in the inventory of the taxpayer if on hand at the close of the taxable year), for a price exceeding $1,000, or (2) of a sale or other disposition of real property, if in either case the initial payments do not exceed 30 per centum of the selling price, * * * the income may, under regulations prescribed * * * be returned on the basis and in the manner" prescribed in section 44(a) for the return of income from sales of personal property regularly made on the installment plan. Under the installment plan of reporting income, a taxpayer is permitted to return as the income from an installment sale in any taxable year "that proportion of the installment payments actually received in that year which the gross profit realized or to be realized when payment is completed, bears to the total contract price." As used in section 44(b), "the term 'initial payments' means the payments received in cash or property other than evidences of indebtedness of the purchaser during the taxable period in which the sale * * * is made."

Although section 44, supra, contains no provision covering the reporting of the gain from sales which are not installment sales under section 44(a), or the reporting of gain from casual sales of personal property or from sales of real property where in either case the initial payments exceed 30 per cent of the selling price, the respondent has nevertheless promulgated section 29.44–4 in his said Regulations 111, entitled "Deferred-Payment Sale of Real Property Not on Installment Plan," specifically covering the reporting of gain from sales of real property where some of the payments are deferred but the payments made during the taxable year exceed 30 per cent of the selling price. For the reporting of the gain from such sales, the regulation provides that the obligations of the purchaser received by the vendor are to be considered as the equivalent of cash to the extent of their fair market value, but if the said obligations received have no fair market value, the payments in cash or other property having a fair market value are to be applied against and reduce the basis of the property sold, and if in excess of such basis, are taxable to the extent of such excess.

There is no regulation carrying a similar provision with respect to casual sales of personal property, wherein the payments in cash or property other than evidences of indebtedness of the purchaser received during the year in which the sale is made exceed 30 per cent of the selling price, and under the provisions of section 41, it would thus appear that a taxpayer making such a casual sale of personal property would be required to report the results of the sale in accordance with the method of accounting regularly employed in the keeping of his books and reporting his income. And where the taxpayer reports his income on the cash basis, the rule for reporting the gain from sales of property, whether personal or real, is in substance the same as that prescribed by the above regulation section 29.44–4, namely, that the cash, plus other property and the evidences of indebtedness of the purchaser, such as notes or mortgages, to the extent of the fair market value thereof, is to be applied against the basis of the property sold, and if in excess of such basis, is taxable to the extent of such excess. For the case of a taxpayer reporting income on the cash basis and wherein the reporting of gain from deferred payment sales was discussed and decided, see Harold W. Johnston, 14 T.C. 560. See also Milton S. Yunker, 26 T.C. 161; Estate of Coid Hurlburt, 25 T.C. 1286; Curtis R. Andrews, 23 T.C. 1026; and Alice G. K. Kleberg, 43 B.T.A. 277.

The Castner Company, in reporting its 1951 gain from the sale of its machinery and equipment, and intending to take advantage of the provisions of section 44(b), reported its gain from the said sale on the installment basis. Since the initial payments received during the taxable year, and as defined in section 44(b), exceeded 30 per cent of the selling price of the property, it is now conceded that the gain from the sale was improperly reported as installment sale income. It is claimed, however, that the sale in question having been a deferred payment sale, the note evidencing the unpaid balance of the purchase price had no fair market value and the cash received being less than the Castner Company's basis for the property, the rule above outlined applies, and the Castner Company realized no taxable gain in 1951 on the sale of its machinery and equipment.

Aside from the fact that the evidence not only falls far short of any showing that the note had no fair market value when received, and further, is neither persuasive nor convincing that the value of the note was substantially, if any, less than face, the Castner Company was on an accrual basis of accounting, and the rule applicable to the reporting of gain by cash basis taxpayers from deferred payment sales of personal property where the initial payments exceed 30 per cent of the selling price does not apply. The evidence shows that the Castner Company computed and reported its profits for income tax purposes by the use of inventories, and as noted above, it is provided in section 29.41-2 of the regulations, a regulation of long standing, that where inventories are used by a taxpayer in computing its income, no method of accounting other than accrual will properly reflect income. See Aluminum Castings Co. v. Routzahn, 282 U.S. 92; Diamond A. Cattle Co. v. Commissioner, 233 F.2d 739, reversing on another point 21 T.C. 1; Caldwell v. Commissioner, 202 F.2d 112; Herberger v. Commissioner, 195 F.2d 293; Commissioner v. A & A Tool & Supply Co., 182 F.2d 300; Charles M. Kilborn, 29 T.C. 102; and Stern Brothers & Co., 16 T.C. 295. And under an accrual method of accounting, a receivable is accrued when the right to receive it becomes fixed. It is the right to receive and not the actual receipt that determines its inclusion in gross income. Spring City Foundry Co. v. Commissioner, 292 U.S. 182. It has been held, however, that where the facts are such that the item in question is uncollectible when the obligation therefor accrues, and there is little or no likelihood of collection in the future, a taxpayer on an accrual basis is not required to report such income. Corn Exchange Bank v. United States, 37 F.2d 34; Joy Manufacturing

Co., 23 T.C. 1082; O'Sullivan Rubber Co., 42 B.T.A. 721; Marguerite Hyde Suffolk & Berks, 40 B.T.A. 1121, 1133; American Fork & Hoe Co., 33 B.T.A. 1139; Atlantic Coast Line Railroad Co., 31 B.T.A. 730, 749; and Oregon Terminals Co., 29 B.T.A. 1332. Here, however, not only are there no facts which in any way support such a proposition, but to the contrary, the facts were such as to justify the belief that the payments would be made when they became due. The payments were in fact made on or before their due dates, and at the time of the trial only two payments remained to be paid and there was every prospect that the entire amount would be paid in full in some 3 years before the due date of the final payment. The entire $8,000 represented an accrued receivable from the date of sale on May 7, 1951, and the respondent did not err in taking the full amount into account in his determination of the deficiency against the Castner Company for that year.

*   *   *

REVENUE RULING 69–462

1969–2 Cum.Bull. 107.

Advice has been requested whether, under the circumstances described below, a taxpayer may elect to report income from the sale of real property on the installment method of accounting under section 453 of the Internal Revenue Code of 1954.

The taxpayer sold, at a gain, 60 acres of land. No payment was received in the year of sale. The contract of sale does not provide for multiple payments of the price by the purchaser. The entire purchase price, which is represented by the buyer's negotiable promissory note secured by a purchase money mortgage, is payable in a lump sum 10 years from the date of sale. Pursuant to the terms of the note, interest is paid annually on each anniversary date of the note.

*   *   *

Revenue Ruling 56–587, C.B. 1956–2, 303, holds that a taxpayer who is entitled, under terms of a sales contract with a dealer, to receive the sales price of goods upon the sale and delivery by the dealer, but not later than a particular date, may not treat such transactions as installment sales, since no provision was made in the contract for payment of fixed amounts at stated intervals. That Revenue Ruling states as follows:

"An installment sale is a sales arrangement whereby the selling price is collected in *periodical* installments." Finney and Miller, Principles of Accounting—Advanced, 4th Edition, p. 118 (Emphasis added) Installments are defined by Black's Law Dictionary, 4th Edition, as "*Different portions of the same debt payable at different successive periods as agreed.*" Webster's New International Dictionary states that: "The system of making *sales*, as in conditional sales, *for a sum made payable in portions* at stated intervals, is often called the installment plan." (Emphasis added.)

It is held that the taxpayer in the instant case may not elect to report the income from the sale of real property on the installment method of accounting since the total amount to be received for the property is to be received in a lump sum in a taxable year subsequent to his taxable year of sale. The installment method of reporting income is applicable only to those sales of real property that, by their terms and conditions, provide for two or more payments of portions of the purchase price in two or more taxable years.

REVENUE RULING 76–110

1976–1 Cum.Bull. 126.

Advice has been requested as to the proper treatment, for Federal income tax purposes, of the sale of real property under the circumstances described below.

The taxpayer sold three separate and unrelated parcels of real property, A, B, and C, under a single contract calling for a total selling price of $1,300x$ dollars. The total selling price of $1,300x$ dollars consisted of: (1) a cash payment of $200x$ dollars; (2) the buyer's assumption of a mortgage in the amount of $300x$ dollars on parcel B; and (3) an installment obligation in the amount of $800x$ dollars payable in eight annual installments with interest at the rate of six percent a year. The taxpayer's adjusted basis of each parcel, as determined under section 1011 of the Internal Revenue Code of 1954, was $150x$ dollars. Thus, the net gain to the taxpayer was $850x$ dollars ($1,300x$ dollars minus $450x$ dollars). Inasmuch as the $350x$ dollars payment received in the year of sale ($200x$ dollars cash and $150x$ dollars excess of the mortgage on parcel B over the adjusted basis in parcel B) was less than 30 percent of the selling price (30 percent of $1,300x=390x$ dollars), the taxpayer elected to report the gain on the installment method under section 453(b).

The fair market values of parcels A, B, and C were $600x$ dollars, $600x$ dollars, and $100x$ dollars, respectively. However, the contract of sale did not allocate the selling price or the cash payment received in the year of sale among the individual parcels.

The specific question presented is whether the taxpayer may treat the sale as one integrated transaction for purposes of section 453 of the Code or whether the taxpayer must first allocate the total selling price and cash payment among the parcels to determine whether the sale of a particular parcel would fail to qualify for the installment method of reporting.

Section 453(b) of the Code provides, in part, that income from the sale of real property may be reported on the installment method of accounting in the manner prescribed in section 453(a), if, in the year of sale, there are no payments, or the payments (exclusive of evidences of indebtedness of the purchaser) do not exceed 30 percent of the selling price. Section 453(a) (1) provides for the reporting of income on the installment method of accounting as the installment payments are actually received.

Section 1.453–1 of the Income Tax Regulations provides, in part, that the income to be returned by the seller in any taxable year is that proportion of the installment payments actually received in that year which the gross profit bears to the total contract price. The gross profit is equal to the selling price less the adjusted basis of the property sold.

Section 1.453–4(c) of the regulations provides, in part, that in the sale of mortgaged property the amount of the mortgage, whether the property is merely taken subject to the mortgage or whether the mortgage is assumed by the purchaser, shall, for the purpose of determining whether a sale is on the installment plan, be included as a part of the "selling price"; and for the purpose of determining the payments and the total contract price, as those terms are used in section 453 of the Code and sections 1.453–1 through 1.453–7 of the regulations, the amount of such mortgage shall be included only to the extent that it exceeds the basis of the property.

Rev.Rul. 70–430, 1970–2 C.B. 51, holds that a loss sustained on an installment sale of business assets is deductible only in the taxable year in which the sale is made. Such loss can not be distributed over the years during which the payments of the selling price are received.

Rev.Rul. 68–13, 1968–1 C.B. 195, which involves the question of whether gain on the sale of several assets in the sale of a business may be reported on the installment method, holds that the selling price and amounts received in the year of sale must be allocated to each class of assets for purposes of determining whether the sale of each separate class of assets qualifies for the installment method of reporting. That Revenue Ruling identifies the separate classes of assets as inventory, assets sold at a loss, real property, and the remaining personal property. The Revenue Ruling further holds that, since some of the gains that may be reported on the installment method may be ordinary income and others capital gains, as in the case of the disposition of section 1245 property, separate computations must be made to the extent necessary with respect to each individual asset in order that gains may be properly reported.

Accordingly, in the instant case, the taxpayer must allocate the total selling price and the amounts received in the year of sale between parcel C, which is separately treated because it was sold at a loss, and the remaining parcels as an aggregate to determine whether they qualify for installment reporting. The total selling price of 1,300x dollars should be allocated to the two classes of assets in the amount of 1,200x dollars for parcels A and B as an aggregate and 100x dollars for parcel C. The cash payment of 200x dollars received in the year of sale and the notes receivable of 800x dollars should be allocated to each class of assets on the basis of its proportionate net fair market value (the net fair market value of each class is its fair market value reduced by any encumbrance assumed or to which the property is subject). Thus, the allocation of the cash payment to each class of assets would be as follows: parcels A and B considered in the aggregate,

180x dollars $\left(200x \times \dfrac{1,200x-300x}{1,300x-300x}\right)$; parcel C, 20$x$ dollars $\left(\dfrac{200x \times 100x}{1,300x-300x}\right)$. The notes receivable would be allocated on the same basis, so that 720x dollars of the note would be allocated to parcels A and B considered in the aggregate $\left(\dfrac{800x \times 1,200x-300x}{1,300x-300x}\right)$, and 80$x$ dollars of the note would be allocated to parcel C $\left(800x \times \dfrac{100x}{1,300x-300x}\right)$.

Additional separate computations must be made with respect to parcel A and parcel B if necessary to determine the character of the gain (ordinary or capital) on those parcels.

Based upon the allocation of the selling price and amounts received in the year of sale described above, the 900x dollars gain on parcels A and B may be reported on the installment method because the payments received in the year of sale, 330x dollars (180x dollars cash and 150x dollars excess of mortgage over basis), are less than 30 percent of the selling price of 1,200x dollars. The sale of parcel C may not be reported on the installment method since the sale results in a loss. Such loss of 50x dollars must be reported in the year of sale.

ROBINSON v. COMMISSIONER

United States Court of Appeals, Eighth Circuit, 1971.
439 F.2d 767.

PER CURIAM: Petitioner and his wife seek to overturn a decision of the Tax Court which upheld a deficiency assessment against them for federal income tax liability for 1964.

Petitioner attempted to gain the beneficial income tax treatment of 26 U.S.C.A. § 453 by selling his insurance agency on an installment basis. Section 453(b) provides for deferred reporting of the gain from the installment sale of assets if in the year of the sale the payments received do not exceed 30% of the selling price. Before selling the business, petitioner spoke to the Internal Revenue Service and to his personal tax advisor in order to be sure that his proposed transaction would fall within this code provision. The parties have stipulated that on January 10, 1964, the date of the sale, petitioner had complied fully with § 453(b).

However, on February 26, 1964, Congress passed the Revenue Act of 1964 which added, inter alia, § 483 to the code. Section 483 provides that where property is sold with part of the payments due more than one year from the date of sale, and either no interest or interest below the rate prescribed by the Treasury Regulations is specified, a part of each payment due after the first six months from the date of sale shall be treated as interest. The provision, drawn to prohibit a seller from avoiding ordinary income liability by merely labeling receipts as selling price rather than interest, applies to payments made after December 31, 1963, on account of sales or exchanges of property after June 30, 1963, other than a sale or exchange pursuant to a written contract entered into before July 1, 1963. By regulations, the total imputed interest is not treated as part of the selling price of the asset. 26 CFR §§ 1.153–1(b) (2) and 1.483–2(a) (1). Thus, although petitioner's transaction occurred weeks before the statutory amendment was passed, it fell within the applicable dates and met the requisite conditions of the new enactment.

Pursuant to §§ 453 and 483 the Commissioner then reduced, for tax purposes, the agreed sale price of the petitioner's business by the total amount of imputed interest. Because the sale price had been reduced, the payment received by petitioner in the year of the sale was in excess of 30% of the selling price. Thus, the Commissioner determined that petitioner was not within the area protected by § 453 and assessed a deficiency for the unreported gain from the sale. The Tax Court upheld that determination, 54 T.C. No. 74, and petitioner asks this court to set that ruling aside.

Although the petitioner here and in the Tax Court argues against the retroactive application of § 483 to § 453 so as to affect the tax consequences of the sale, we note that in 1967 he filed an amended return for the year 1964 in which he reduced his reported capital gain from the initial payment. This reduction resulted from the petitioner's reducing the sale price by the amount of unstated interest required by § 483. Thus, for that purpose he did not question the retroactive application of § 483.

Basically, the Tax Court reasoned and held as follows:

1.   Even though § 483 does not specifically refer to § 453, the former provision is applicable to § 453 because § 483 is couched in the comprehensive and unambiguous language that it is to apply for "purposes of this title" (the Internal Revenue Code, Title 26).

2.   Congress intended that the provisions of § 483 apply to a taxpayer in petitioner's position, see Shanahan v. United States, D.C. Colo., 1970, 315 F.Supp. 3, appeal pending, 10th Cir., and that such retroactivity was not improper. See United States v. Hudson, 1937, 299 U.S. 498, 500–501; Gillmor v. Quinlivan, N.D.Ohio, 1956, 143 F. Supp. 440.

3. The Commissioner was not given the authority to limit the retroactive effect of this provision and his application of the section to petitioner was proper.

We agree with the thorough analysis and reasoned conclusion of the Tax Court and, on the basis of its opinion, we affirm.

NOTE

The installment sales provisions first became a part of the law in 1926.[1] With hindsight, one may now wonder why the original provision contained no rule concerning the tax consequences of the disposition of installment obligations. The possibility of various tax avoidance schemes based on such dispositions quickly became apparent. For example, the vendor of property, having made a sale on the installment method reporting only part of his gain, could make a gift of the purchaser's obligations to a third person, possibly a member of his family in a lower tax bracket. The result was that the vendor escaped tax and his donee was taxed less heavily.[2] Such avoidance possibilities prompted the enactment in 1928 of the forerunner of I.R.C. (26 U.S.C.A.) § 453(d).[3] This provision taxes the vendor on previously untaxed gain, upon his disposition of an installment obligation. The amount of gain so taxed is the difference between either the amount realized (in the case of a satisfaction, sale, or exchange) or the fair market value of the obligation (at the time of any other type of disposition) and the taxpayer's basis in the § 453 obligation.[4] The basis of an installment obligation is the face amount of the obligation less the amount of income that the taxpayer would have to report if the obligation were paid off in full.[5] Test the propriety of this basis rule in the light of the reporting rules of § 453(a).

In 1934 Congress added a characterization provision to § 453(d), which provides that the gain or loss on the disposition of an installment obligation is to be treated as arising from a sale or exchange of the property for which the obligation was received.[6] Initially de-

1. Revenue Act of 1926, § 212(d), 44 Stat. 9, 23 (1926).

2. Wallace Huntington, 15 B.T.A. 851 (1929). See House Rep. No. 2, 70th Cong. 1st Sess., p. 16 (1928) reported in Seidman, Legislative History of Income Tax Laws 1938–1861 at 521 (1938). Other avoidance possibilities were identified in the Report. Thus, in 1928, prior to the enactment of § 42 of the Revenue Act of 1934, and to the enactment of present § 691, which was first enacted in 1942, the death of one who had made an installment sale eliminated all income tax on gain on such a sale not previously reported. But see I.R.C. (1954) (26 U.S.C.A.) §§ 453(d) (3) and 691(a) (4). Moreover, in 1928, the same result would follow if a corporate vendor under the installment method made a dividend distribution of its installment obligations to an individual shareholder.

3. Revenue Act of 1928, § 44(d), 45 Stat. 791, 806 (1928). See Emory, "Disposition of Installment Obligations: Income Deferral, 'Thou Art Lost and Gone Forever'," 54 Iowa L. Rev. 945 (1969).

4. I.R.C. (26 U.S.C.A.) § 453(d) (1).

5. I.R.C. (26 U.S.C.A.) § 453(d) (2).

6. Revenue Act of 1934, § 44(d), 48 Stat. 680, 695 (1934).

signed to accord the taxpayer an advantage under the sliding scale approach to the inclusion of capital gains in income which was then in effect,[7] the provision is still important in some characterization situations under the 1954 code.[8]

The term "disposition" in § 453(d) is broadly interpreted. It includes gifts no matter the nature of the donee,[9] transfers to and from trusts,[10] and in rare circumstances even the assignment of the obligation as security for a loan,[11] but not mere changes in the terms of the obligation itself.[12] The statute removes from the disposition rules, however, the transmission of installment obligations at death [13] and their distribution in certain corporate liquidations.[14]

If real property is sold and the installment sales provisions of § 453 are elected, a repossession of the property by the vendor upon default by the purchaser constitutes a § 453(d) disposition of the installment obligations.[15] Absent other statutory provisions, the amount of gain to be reported would be the difference between the fair market value of the property, which is treated as the consideration received upon disposition of the obligations, and the vendor's basis for the obligations, with proper adjustment for any costs incurred by the vendor.[16] Still, in economic reality the vendor has only got his original property back, and it is fair to say that, with an interruption, there is essentially a continuation of the vendor's original investment, a circumstance that Congress has frequently treated as a situation in which gain should not be recognized. Section 1038, nonrecognition

7. Sen. Fin. Comm. Rep. No. 558, 73rd Cong. 2d Sess. (1934) as reported in Seidman, supra note 2 at 322. See Chapter 21, supra at page 608.

8. For example, the sale of an installment obligation held short term but received upon a sale of capital asset property held long term gets long term capital gain treatment. For a detailed study of the installment sales provisions, see Emory, "The Installment Method of Reporting Income: Its Election, Use, and Effect," 53 Cornell L.Rev. 181 (1968) and Solomon and Kirkelic, "The Installment Sale-Qualification," 26 U.S.C.T.I. 669 (1974).

9. Rev.Rul. 55–157, 1955–1 C.B. 293.

10. Cases and rulings dealing with transfers to a trust include Marshall v. U. S., 26 F.Supp. 580 (S.D.Cal. 1939); Springer v. U. S., unreported, 69–2 U.S.T.C. ¶9567 (N.D.Ala.1969); Rev.Rul. 67–167, 1967–1 C.B. 107. If the transfer is to a revocable trust it does not constitute a § 453(d) "disposi-

tion." Rev.Rul. 74–613, 1974–2 C.B. 153. On transfers from a trust to a beneficiary, see Rev.Rul. 55–159, 1955–1 C.B. 391.

11. Rev.Rul. 65–185, 1965–2 C.B. 153. But see Elmer v. Comm'r, 65 F.2d 568 (2d Cir. 1933); Town and Country Food Co., 51 T.C. 1049 (1969), acq., 1969–2 C.B. XXV; Rev.Rul. 68–246, 1968–1 C.B. 198.

12. Rev.Rul. 68–419, 1968–2 C.B. 196. Cf. Rev.Rul. 75–457, 1975–2 C.B. 196.

13. I.R.C. (26 U.S.C.A.) § 453(d) (3); but see § 691(a) (4).

14. I.R.C. (26 U.S.C.A.) § 453(d) (4).

15. Reg. § 1.453–5(b) (2).

16. The same result follows if, instead of a mere repossession, the vendor reacquires the property upon a foreclosure sale, applying the purchaser's obligation against the purchase price. Reg. § 1.453–5(b) (2).

provision, now applies here. However, the nonrecognition concept is reserved for Chapter 26, infra, and a brief note on § 1038 appears there at page 942.

PROBLEMS

1. Installer, a cash method calendar year taxpayer, sells land held several years as an investment with a basis of $10,000 and a value of $50,000. May § 453 be elected in the following situations:

(a) The payment is in the form of two $25,000 6% interest bearing notes both of which are to be paid in the fifth year after the sale, one on June 1 and the other on December 1.

(b) Same as (a), above, except the second note is due on June 1 of year six rather than December 1 of year five.

(c) Same as (b), above, except that the property has a $60,000 basis.

(d) Installer receives a $15,000 cash payment in the year of sale and seven noninterest bearing notes, one due in each of the succeeding seven years. Each note calls for a $5000 payment.

(e) Same as (d), above, except that the notes pay 8% simple interest.

(f) Same as (e), above, except the notes are worth only $4900 each (due to their low interest rate).

(g) Same as (e), above, except that Installer argues that the notes do not have the equivalency of cash; but if they do he alternatively elects § 453. The notes are later determined to have the equivalency of cash.

(h) Same as (e), above, except that Installer's land may contain oil and Buyer agrees in addition to pay Installer 10% of Buyer's oil profits. See In re Steen v. U. S., 509 F.2d 1398 (9th Cir. 1975).

2. Seller owns a parcel of land which he purchased five years ago for $2000. He sells it to Buyer under an arrangement where Buyer pays him $2000 cash in the current year and gives him four six percent interest bearing notes to be paid off in each of the succeeding four years. Each note has a $2000 face amount and a $1750 fair market value. Disregarding the tax consequences of any interest payments, what results to Seller in each of the five years if in the alternative:

(a) Seller is a cash method taxpayer and he makes no § 453 election.

(b) Seller is an accrual method taxpayer and he makes no § 453 election.

(c) Seller is a cash method taxpayer who makes a § 453 election.

(d) Seller is an accrual method taxpayer who makes a § 453 election.

(e) What result to Seller in (d), above, if the property was instead an office building on which Seller had claimed depreciation and the § 1250 recapture on the building amounted to $3000. See Reg. § 1.1250–1(c) (6) and Dunn Construction Co., Inc. v. U. S., 323 F.Supp. 440 (N.D.Ala.1971).

(f) What result to Seller in (d), above, if prior to collecting any of the notes he sells them to a third party for their fair market value of $7000?

(g) What result to Seller in (d), above, if prior to collecting any of the notes he gives them to his Daughter? Assume the notes are still worth $1750 each. What results to Daughter when she receives full payment of the notes?

(h) What results to Seller in part (d), above, if the property was subject to a $2000 mortgage which Buyer assumed and Buyer gave Seller only three of the $2000 notes. See Reg. § 1.453–4(c).

(i) What results to Seller in part (d), above, if the property was subject to a $3000 mortgage which Buyer assumed and Buyer gave Seller two $2000 notes to be paid in each of the succeeding two years and a $1000 note to be paid in the fourth year. See Reg. § 1.453–4(c)

CHAPTER 25. DISALLOWANCE OF LOSSES

A. LOSSES BETWEEN RELATED TAXPAYERS

Internal Revenue Code: Sections 267(a)(1), (b), (c), (d).
Regulations: Section 1.267(d)–1(a), (c)(3).

McWILLIAMS v. COMMISSIONER

Supreme Court of the United States, 1947.
331 U.S. 964, 67 S.Ct. 1477.

MR. CHIEF JUSTICE VINSON delivered the opinion of the Court.

The facts of these cases are not in dispute. John P. McWilliams, petitioner in No. 945, had for a number of years managed the large independent estate of his wife, petitioner in No. 947, as well as his own. On several occasions in 1940 and 1941 he ordered his broker to sell certain stock for the account of one of the two and to buy the same number of shares of the same stock for the other, at as nearly the same price as possible. He told the broker that his purpose was to establish tax losses. On each occasion the sale and purchase were promptly negotiated through the Stock Exchange, and the identity of the persons buying from the selling spouse and of the persons selling to the buying spouse was never known. Invariably, however, the buying spouse received stock certificates different from those which the other had sold. Petitioners filed separate income tax returns for these years, and claimed the losses which he or she sustained on the sales as deductions from gross income.

The Commissioner disallowed these deductions on the authority of § 24(b) of the Internal Revenue Code,[1] which prohibits deductions for losses from "sales or exchanges of property, directly or indirectly . . . Between members of a family," and between certain other closely related individuals and corporations.

On the taxpayers' applications to the Tax Court, it held § 24(b) inapplicable, following its own decision in Ickelheimer v. Commissioner,[2] and expunged the Commissioner's deficiency assessments.[3]

---

1. [I.R.C. (1939) § 24(b) is omitted. See I.R.C. (1954) § 267(a) (1), (b) (1), and (c) (4). Ed.]

2. 45 B.T.A. 478, affirmed, 132 F.2d 660 (C.C.A.2).

3. 5 T.C. 623.

The Circuit Court of Appeals reversed the Tax Court [4] and we granted certiorari [5] because of a conflict between circuits [6] and the importance of the question involved.

Petitioners contend that Congress could not have intended to disallow losses on transactions like those described above, which, having been made through a public market, were undoubtedly bona fide sales, both in the sense that title to property was actually transferred, and also in the sense that a fair consideration was paid in exchange. They contend that the disallowance of such losses would amount, *pro tanto*, to treating husband and wife as a single individual for tax purposes.

In support of this contention, they call our attention to the pre-1934 rule, which applied to all sales regardless of the relationship of seller and buyer, and made the deductibility of the resultant loss turn on the "good faith" of the sale, *i. e.*, whether the seller actually parted with title and control.[7] They point out that in the case of the usual intra-family sale, the evidence material to this issue was peculiarly within the knowledge and even the control of the taxpayer and those amenable to his wishes, and inaccessible to the Government.[8] They maintain that the only purpose of the provisions of the 1934 and 1937 Revenue Acts—the forerunners of § 24(b)[9]—was to overcome these evidentiary difficulties by disallowing losses on such sales irrespective of good faith. It seems to be petitioners' belief that the evidentiary difficulties so contemplated were only those relating to proof of the parties' observance of the formalities of a sale and of the fairness of the price, and consequently that the legislative remedy

---

4. 158 F.2d 637 (C.C.A.6).

5. 330 U.S. 814. In No. 946, the petition for certiorari of the Estate of Susan P. McWilliams, the deceased mother of John P. McWilliams, was granted at the same time as the petitions in Nos. 945 and 947, and the three cases were consolidated in this Court. As all three present the same material facts and raise precisely the same issues, no further reference will be made to the several cases separately.

6. The decision of the Circuit Court of Appeals for the Second Circuit in Commissioner v. Ickelheimer, supra, note 2, is in conflict on this point with the decision of the Circuit Court of Appeals for the Sixth Circuit in the present case, and also with that of the Circuit Court of Appeals for the Fourth Circuit in Commissioner v. Kohn, 158 F.2d 32.

7. Commissioner v. Hale, 67 F.2d 561 (C.C.A.1); Zimmermann v. Commissioner, 36 B.T.A. 279, reversed on other grounds, 100 F.2d 1023 (C.C.A.3); Uihlein v. Commissioner, 30 B.T.A. 399, affirmed, 82 F.2d 944 (C.C.A.7).

8. See H.Rep. No. 1546, 75th Cong., 1st Sess., p. 26 (1939–1 Cum.Bull. (Part 2) 704, 722–723). See also cases cited in note 7, supra.

9. The provisions of § 24(b) (1) (A) and (B) of the Internal Revenue Code originated in § 24(a) (6) of the Revenue Act of 1934, 48 Stat. 680, 691. These provisions were reenacted without change as § 24(a) (6) of the Revenue Act of 1936, 49 Stat. 1648, 1662, and the provisions of § 24(b) (1) (C), (D), (E), and (F) of the Code were added by § 301 of the 1937 Act, 50 Stat. 813, 827.

applied only to sales made immediately from one member of a family to another, or mediately through a controlled intermediary.

We are not persuaded that Congress had so limited an appreciation of this type of tax avoidance problem. Even assuming that the problem was thought to arise solely out of the taxpayer's inherent advantage in a contest concerning the good or bad faith of an intra-family sale, deception could obviously be practiced by a buying spouse's agreement or tacit readiness to hold the property sold at the disposal of a selling spouse, rather more easily than by a pretense of a sale where none actually occurred, or by an unfair price. The difficulty of determining the finality of an intra-family transfer was one with which the courts wrestled under the pre-1934 law,[10] and which Congress undoubtedly meant to overcome by enacting the provisions of § 24(b).[11]

It is clear, however, that this difficulty is one which arises out of the close relationship of the parties, and would be met whenever, by prearrangement, one spouse sells and another buys the same property at a common price, regardless of the mechanics of the transaction. Indeed, if the property is fungible, the possibility that a sale and purchase may be rendered nugatory by the buying spouse's agreement to hold for the benefit of the selling spouse, and the difficulty of proving that fact against the taxpayer, are equally great when the units of the property which the one buys are not the identical units which the other sells.

Securities transactions have been the most common vehicle for the creation of intra-family losses. Even if we should accept petitioners' premise that the only purpose of § 24(b) was to meet an evidentiary problem, we could agree that Congress did not mean to reach the transactions in this case only if we thought it completely indifferent to the effectuality of its solution.

Moreover, we think the evidentiary problem was not the only one which Congress intended to meet. Section 24(b) states an absolute prohibition—not a presumption—against the allowance of losses on any sales between the members of certain designated groups. The one common characteristic of these groups is that their members, although distinct legal entities, generally have a near-identity of economic interests.[12] It is a fair inference that even legally genuine intra-group transfers were not thought to result, usually, in economically genuine realizations of loss, and accordingly that Congress did not deem them to be appropriate occasions for the allowance of deductions.

10. Cf. Shoenberg v. Commissioner, 77 F.2d 446 (C.C.A.8); Cole v. Helburn, 4 F.Supp. 230; Zimmermann v. Commissioner, supra, note 7.

11. See H.Rep. No. 1546, 75th Cong., 1st Sess., p. 26, supra, note 8.

12. See the text of [§ 267(b). Ed.]

The pertinent legislative history lends support to this inference. The Congressional Committees, in reporting the provisions enacted in 1934, merely stated that "the practice of creating losses through transactions between members of a family and close corporations has been frequently utilized for avoiding the income tax," and that these provisions were proposed to "deny losses to be taken in the case of [such] sales" and "to close this loophole of tax avoidance." [13] Similar language was used in reporting the 1937 provisions.[14] Chairman Doughton of the Ways and Means Committee, in explaining the 1937 provisions to the House, spoke of "the artificial taking and establishment of losses where property was shuffled back and forth between various legal entities owned by the same persons or person," and stated that "these transactions seem to occur at moments remarkably opportune to the real party in interest in reducing his tax liability but, at the same time allowing him to keep substantial control of the assets being traded or exchanged." [15]

We conclude that the purpose of § 24(b) was to put an end to the right of taxpayers to choose, by intra-family transfers and other designated devices, their own time for realizing tax losses on investments which, for most practical purposes, are continued uninterrupted.

We are clear as to this purpose, too, that its effectuation obviously had to be made independent of the manner in which an intra-group transfer was accomplished. Congress, with such purpose in mind, could not have intended to include within the scope of § 24(b) only simple transfers made directly or through a dummy, or to exclude transfers of securities effected through the medium of the Stock Exchange, unless it wanted to leave a loop-hole almost as large as the one it had set out to close.

Petitioners suggest that Congress, if it truly intended to disallow losses on intra-family transactions through the market, would probably have done so by an amendment to the wash sales provisions,[16] making them applicable where the seller and buyer were members of the same family, as well as where they were one and the same individual. This

13. H.Rep. No. 704, 73d Cong., 2d Sess., p. 23 (1939–1 Cum.Bull. (Part 2) 554, 571); S.Rep. No. 558, 73d Cong., 2d Sess., p. 27 (1939–1 Cum. Bull. (Part 2) 586, 607).

14. The type of situations to which these provisions applied was described as being that "in which, due to family relationships or friendly control, artificial losses might be created for tax purposes." H.Rep. No. 1546, 75th Cong., 1st Sess., p. 28 (1939–1 Cum.Bull. (Part 2) 704, 724).

15. 81 Cong.Rec. 9019. Representative Hill, chairman of a House subcommittee on the income-tax laws, explained to the House with reference to the 1934 provisions that the Committee had "provided in this bill that transfers between members of the family for the purpose of creating a loss to be offset against ordinary income shall not be recognized for such deduction purposes." 78 Cong.Rec. 2662.

16. [I.R.C. (1939) § 118 is omitted. See I.R.C. (1954) § 1091. Ed.]

extension of the wash sales provisions, however, would bar only one particular means of accomplishing the evil at which § 24(b) was aimed, and the necessity for a comprehensive remedy would have remained.

Nor can we agree that Congress' omission from § 24(b) of any prescribed time interval, comparable in function to that in the wash sales provisions, indicates that § 24(b) was not intended to apply to intra-family transfers through the Exchange. Petitioners' argument is predicated on the difficulty which courts may have in determining whether the elapse of certain periods of time between one spouse's sale and the other's purchase of like securities on the Exchange is of great enough importance in itself to break the continuity of the investment and make § 24(b) inapplicable.

Precisely the same difficulty may arise, however, in the case of an intra-family transfer through an individual intermediary, who, by pre-arrangement, buys from one spouse at the market price and a short time later sells the identical certificates to the other at the price prevailing at the time of sale. The omission of a prescribed time interval negates the applicability of § 24(b) to the former type of transfer no more than it does to the latter. But if we should hold that it negated both, we would have converted the section into a mere trap for the unwary.[17]

Petitioners also urge that, whatever may have been Congress' intent, its designation in § 24(b) of sales "between" members of a family is not adequate to comprehend the transactions in this case, which consisted only of a sale of stock by one of the petitioners to an unknown stranger, and the purchase of different certificates of stock by the other petitioner, presumably from another stranger.

We can understand how this phraseology, if construed literally and out of context, might be thought to mean only direct intra-family transfers. But petitioners concede that the express statutory reference to sales made "directly or indirectly" precludes that construction. Moreover, we can discover in this language no implication whatsoever that an indirect intra-family sale of fungibles is outside the statute unless the units sold by one spouse and those bought by the other are identical. Indeed, if we accepted petitioners' construction of the statute, we think we would be reading into it a crippling exception which is not there.

---

17. We have noted petitioners' suggestion that a taxpayer is assured, under the wash sales provisions, of the right to deduct the loss incurred on a sale of securities, even though he himself buys similar securities thirty-one days later; and that he should certainly not be precluded by § 24(b) from claiming a similar loss if the taxpayer's spouse, instead of the taxpayer, makes the purchase under the same circumstances. We do not feel impelled to comment on these propositions, however, in a case in which the sale and purchase were practically simultaneous and the net consideration received by one spouse and that paid by the other differed only in the amount of brokers' commissions and excise taxes.

Finally, we must reject petitioners' assertion that the *Dobson* rule [18] controls this case. The Tax Court found the facts as we stated them, and then overruled the Commissioner's determination because it thought that § 24(b) had no application to a taxpayer's sale of securities on the Exchange to an unknown purchaser, regardless of what other circumstances accompanied the sale. We have decided otherwise, and on our construction of the statute, and the conceded facts, the Tax Court could not have reached a result contrary to our own.[19]

Affirmed.

MR. JUSTICE BURTON took no part in the consideration or decision of these cases.

NOTE

The application of § 267 may not depend entirely on the relationship between the seller and the one to whom title is transferred. In Julius Long Stern,[1] the Tax Court agreed with the Commissioner that § 24(b) (similar to present § 267) disallowed a loss deduction. The taxpayer had converted his residence to rental property and then, after a time, transferred it for consideration in an amount less than his basis to his daughter and son-in-law, as tenants by the entirety. The Court of Appeals reversed, allowing the claimed deduction,[2] saying, in part:

"Applying [the] statutory provisions to the case before us it will be seen that the loss, if any, which the taxpayer suffered upon the sale of the West River Street property was deductible by him for income tax purposes unless it was a sale between himself and his daughter, Claire Guttman. If it was a sale betwen himself and his son-in-law, Dr. Guttman, the loss was deductible, since a son-in-law is not within the class defined by section 24(b)(2)(D). We are in complete accord with views expressed by Judge Hill in his dissenting opinion that the sale in this case was between the taxpayer and Dr. Guttman and that no sale in fact took place to Claire Guttman who supplied no part of the consideration for the sale and received here interest in the property as a tenant by the entirety purely as a gift from her husband. Indeed the findings of fact of the Tax Court compel this conclusion for the court found: 'Dr. Guttman decided to, and did, purchase the house from the petitioner at a price of $30,000. * * * The petitioner's daughter did not participate in any of these negotiations, nor was she a party to them.'

18. Dobson v. Commissioner, 320 U.S. 489.

19. Cf. Trust of Bingham v. Commissioner, 325 U.S. 365.

1. 21 T.C. 155 (1953).

2. 215 F.2d 701 (3d Cir. 1954).

"The opinion filed by Judge Opper is based upon the proposition that under the law of Pennsylvania Claire Guttman became the owner of the entire property as a tenant by the entirety and accordingly was vendee of her father as to the whole property. The premise may be admitted but the conclusion sought to be drawn does not follow. For the fact that Mrs. Guttman acquired an estate by the entirety in the property under Pennsylvania law as a result of the direction of her husband that she be included as a grantee in the deed of conveyance did not make her, what in actual fact she was not, the purchaser of the property on a sale by her father, within the meaning of the Internal Revenue Code. As Judge Hill well said in his dissenting opinion, 21 T.C. 155, 'the majority relies upon legal fiction in the effort to establish that a sale between the petitioner and his daughter was accomplished as a matter of law. The fiction relied upon belongs to the law of real property. It had its roots in the common law and was born centuries before income taxation was a gleam in the fiscal eye of government. This fiction argues that husband and wife are one. In the enactment and administration of revenue laws, fact rather than fiction is made to prevail.' See Wisotzkey v. Commissioner of Internal Revenue, 3 Cir. 1944, 144 F.2d 632, 636.

"Moreover, the contention proves too much. For if Mrs. Guttman is to be regarded as grantee of the whole property under the Pennsylvania law of tenancy by the entirety and therefore as sole purchaser from the taxpayer, her husband, Dr. Guttman, must likewise under the same law be regarded as grantee of the whole and, therefore, likewise sole purchaser. It is obvious that at this point the fiction of the Pennsylvania law breaks down so far as concerns its usefulness to solve the tax question which is before us and that the question can only be solved upon a practical view of the actual facts of the case, disregarding the fictions of the ancient law of real property."

The student will recall that § 267 is by no means the only reason why a sale of property for a price less than basis may give rise to no tax deduction. The individual taxpayer's initial hurdles are to show that the loss was incurred either in his "trade or business," § 165(c) (1), or in "a transaction entered into for profit," § 165(c) (2). For these reasons two types of transactions yield no deduction even if § 267 is wholly inapplicable to them: (1) A sale of property held for merely personal use, such as the taxpayer's residence, fails the initial tests;[3] and (2) Even if the property is business or income-producing property, if the purported sale is in reality some sort of arrangement

---

3. David R. Pulliam, 39 T.C. 883 (1963), aff'd on other grounds, 329 F.2d 97 (10th Cir. 1964).

among parties with common interests which cannot be viewed as an arm's length transaction, again the initial tests are not met. Clearly not a loss in "business," such purported sales have also been held not to arise in a "transaction entered into for profit." [4]

PROBLEMS

1. Father purchased some corporate stock several years ago for $50,000. On January 15 of the current year he sells the stock to his Daughter for $40,000, its fair market value. What result if:

  (a) Daughter resells the stock to a third party for $45,000 on February 15 of the current year?

  (b) Daughter resells the stock to a third party for $55,000 on February 15 of the current year?

  (c) Daughter resells the stock to a third party for $35,000 on February 15 of the current year?

  (d) Daughter gives the stock to Spouse on February 15 of the current year when it is worth $45,000 and Spouse sells it on March 15 for $48,000?

2. Loser purchased corporate stock in 1960 for $90,000. Loser died on December 31, 1976 when the stock was worth $100,000. During the administration of the estate, the value of the stock declined to $50,000 and at that time in order to pay administration expenses the estate sold the stock to Loser's spouse for $50,000. What are the income tax consequences to the estate?

3. Taxpayer T owns some land that he purchased as an investment ten years ago for $10,000. In the current year he sells it to Corporation C for $5000, which is its fair market value. Will I.R.C. § 267 preclude a loss deduction for T if C is owned:

  (a) 10% by T.

     20% by T's son S.

     30% by equal partnership TX (X unrelated).

     40% by others?

  (b) 30% by T's son S.

     30% by equal partnership TX (X unrelated).

     40% by others?

  (c) 30% by T's son S.

     30% by equal partnership SX (X unrelated).

     40% by others?

4. Taxpayer owns stock which is seized by the government and sold at public auction at a loss to pay delinquent taxes. Taxpayer's

---

4. Estate of Minnie Miller v. Comm'r, 421 F.2d 1405 (4th Cir. 1970).

brother purchases the stock at the sale. Does § 267 apply to disallow the loss? Consider the Supreme Court's discussion of the legislative history of § 267 in *McWilliams* and compare Merritt v. Commissioner, 400 F.2d 417 (5th Cir. 1968) with McNeill v. Commissioner, 251 F. 2d 863 (4th Cir. 1968).

B. WASH SALES

Internal Revenue Code: Sections 1091(a), (d); 1223(4).
Regulations: Section 1.1091–1(g), –2.

PROBLEMS

1. On December 1 of the current year Taxpayer sold 1000 shares of X Corporation stock for $50,000. He had purchased the stock exactly two years earlier for $60,000. On December 15, he purchased another 1000 shares of identical X corporation stock for $55,-000.

(a) What are the tax consequences of the December 1 sale?

(b) What is Taxpayer's basis for the newly acquired shares?

(c) What is Taxpayer's holding period for the newly acquired shares as of January 1 of the next year?

(d) What result to Taxpayer in (a)–(c), above, (gain or loss, basis and new holding period), if the December 1 sale had been for $75,000 and he had repurchased 1000 shares of X stock on December 15 for $65,000?

(e) Is there any difference in result to Taxpayer in part (a), above, if he purchased the new shares on December 1 for $55,000 and sold the old shares on December 15 for $50,000?

(f) If the facts are the same as in (a), above, except that Taxpayer sold his original shares on December 1 to Wife, what result to Wife when she sells those shares on December 15 of the next year for $55,000? Consider the consequences to both Taxpayer and Wife. See § 267(d), last sentence.

(g) Are the Wash sale sanctions more or less stringent than those of § 267. Explain.

2. (a) On June 1 of the current year, Short borrowed 100 shares of B stock and sold it short for $9000. Owning no B shares, Short purchased 100 shares of identical B stock on June 15 for $10,000 and "closed" the sale. On July 5 of the same year, Short again purchased 100 shares of identical B stock at a price of $9500. Does § 1091 apply to disallow Short's loss? See Reg. 1.1091–1(g).

(b) Same as (a), above, except that Short closed the sale on June 15 with identical B stock which he had purchased on March 1 of the current year. What result?

CHAPTER 26. NONRECOGNITION PROVISIONS

A. INTRODUCTION

A precise use of language is an aid to, if not an outright prerequisite for, accurate thinking. And the precise use of language includes the proper use of terms, in accordance with their meaning in the context in which they are used. Thus, it is essential to avoid the use of the term "value" when "basis" is what is meant; and in installment sales matters one must differentiate "contract price" from "selling price." A new term now appears: "recognition" or, as the case may be, "nonrecognition." It crops up in the case of some transactions in which gain or loss is "realized;" but "realization" does not necessarily connote "recognition."

Gain (or loss) has no income tax significance as long as it is represented by a mere increase (or decrease) in the value of the taxpayer's property. Something more must occur, as for example a sale or an exchange of the property, before the gain (or loss), is said to be "realized." If gain is realized, is it subject to tax? Not necessarily. The message of the sections considered in this Chapter is that not all realized gains (or losses) are to be accorded immediate consideration in the determination of taxable income. Of course, that is the consequence of *deferred reporting* of gains, sometimes permitted under § 453, and of the *disallowance* of some losses, as in §§ 267 and 1091. But the sections presently under consideration provide that certain other gains and losses, although admittedly realized, shall simply go unrecognized, at least for the time being. The effect is that gain which clearly could be taxed is excluded from gross income, and loss that could be deducted loses its potential for reducing taxable income. The question must therefore always be raised whether a "realized" gain or loss is "recognized."

In approaching these provisions it would be well to keep in mind that § 453 is a mere timing device, that § 267 is an outright disallowance provision tempered only by the limited relief rules of § 267(d), and that § 1091 is a disallowance rule which is ameliorated substantially by the substitute basis provisions of § 1091(d). All the nonrecognition sections of this Chapter have related basis provisions, much like § 1091(d), which must be carefully examined in appraising the purpose and scope of these sections. The student should approach the nonrecognition rules of this Chapter curious as to why Congress spells out these additional exceptions to the usual treatment of realized gains and losses.

If a taxpayer who owns investment real estate with a basis of $100,000 and fair market value of $175,000 sells the property for cash, his realized gain of $75,000 is gross income and the tax consequences are immediate. Of course, if instead the sale qualifies as an installment sale under § 453, the gain may then be reported ratably over the years that payments are received, in that proportion which the profit on the sale bears to the contract price. But even so the entire gain is recognized. There is simply no way and no reason to apply the nonrecognition rules, because the taxpayer has closed out his investment by sale. Similarly, if the taxpayer exchanges his land for a yacht worth $175,000, his realized gain is all subject to immediate tax consequences. Although the yacht is property, it is clear that the taxpayer has closed out his real estate investment in exchange for the yacht. § 1001(a) and (c).

If in other circumstances the taxpayer should exchange his real estate for another parcel of real estate worth $175,000 to be held by him for investment, his realized gain is still $75,000. But can it be sensibly said that he has closed out his investment when the only changed circumstance is the different location of the new tract of land? In substance, the taxpayer's economic position after the exchange is the same as before. In these circumstances a special nonrecognition rule becomes applicable.

The non-recognition provisions are all predicated on the notion that realized gain, or a loss that otherwise would qualify as a deductible loss, is more sensibly deferred when the taxpayer has retained his investment in property that is essentially the same type as the originally held property. These rules are not universally applicable to all types of property. The statute provides nonrecognition to selective transactions, and it must be carefully examined. While the example here relates to an exchange that is accorded nonrecognition treatment under § 1031, some other types of transactions, not involving exchanges as such, also are accorded nonrecognition treatment under other sections. The philosophy underlying the nonrecognition rules of these other provisions will be seen to be similar to the philosophy underlying § 1031.

As a broad proposition, the nonrecognition rules and their attending basis provisions are so interrelated as to effect only a postponement of the tax on gain or the deduction of loss that initially goes unrecognized. The date-of-death value basis rule of § 1014 will no longer intervene to convert mere postponement to outright amnesty (or final disallowance) if, after a transaction in which gain (or loss) goes unrecognized, the taxpayer dies. Consequently, except for "fresh start" possibilities under new § 1023(h), the nonrecognition rules are largely rules of deferral. Take a further look at § 1231(a), which limits the hotchpot ingredients to *recognized* gains and losses. See again also § 1222, limiting the definition of short and long-term capital gains and losses to such gains and losses as are " * * * taken into account in computing taxable income."

B. LIKE KIND EXCHANGES

Internal Revenue Code: Sections 1001(c); 1031; 1223(1). See Sections
     1245(b)(4) and 1250(d)(4).
Regulations: Sections 1.1031(a)–1; 1.1031(b)–1(b) example (1); 1.1031
     (d)–(1).

At the outset, it should be stated that the "if" clause of § 1031
(a) is strewn with hurdles to be taken. First, with respect to the nature of the property transferred, it must be ". . . property held
for productive use in a trade or business or for investment . . .,"
expressly excluding inventory and the like and also excluding *inter
alia* stocks, bonds, certificates of trust and other securities.[1] Second,
the disposition must qualify as an *exchange*. Finally, the consideration received must be property of *like kind* to be held for productive
use in a trade or business or for investment.[2] All three criteria must
be met.

Depending on the nature of the controversy, taxpayer nonrecognition of gain or government effort to disallow loss,[3] the vast majority
of the cases has been concerned with the question whether the transaction constitutes an *exchange* of like kind properties.

BLOOMINGTON COCA–COLA BOTTLING CO. v. COMMISSIONER

United States Court of Appeals, Seventh Circuit, 1951.
189 F.2d 14.

* * *

A "sale" is a transfer of property for a price in money or its equivalent. "Exchange" means the giving of one thing for another. That
is to say, in a sale, the property is transferred in consideration of a
definite price expressed in terms of money, while in an exchange, the

1. Although the Tax Court has accepted an exchange of a general partnership interest in a real estate partnership for a similar interest in another
real estate partnership, Estate of
Meyer, 58 T.C. 311 (1972), aff'd per
curiam 503 F.2d 556 (9th Cir. 1974),
one wonders whether an exchange of
a limited partnership interest in partnership ABC for a similar interest in
partnership DFG would qualify regardless of the similarity of the respective partnership activities. If the
limited partnership interest is cate-
gorized as a "security," § 1031 cannot
apply.

2. If as part of a transaction otherwise
qualifying under § 1031, the taxpayer,
pursuant to pre-arranged plan, disposes of the property received in the
exchange, § 1031 does not apply.
This is so because the property received is not *to be held* for productive
use in his trade or business or for investment. See Rev.Rul. 75–292, 1975–
2 C.B. 333, and compare Rev.Rul. 75–
291, 1975–2 C.B. 332.

3. See e. g., 124 Front Street, Inc., 65
T.C. 6 (1975). To the extent that a
transaction falls within § 1031, no loss
on that transaction is *ever* recognized.
§ 1031(c). See e. g., Valley Title Co.,
34 TCM 312 (1975).

property is transferred in return for other property without the intervention of money. True, "Border-line cases arise where the money forms a substantial part of the adjustment of values in connection with the disposition of property and the acquisition of similar properties. The presence in a transaction of a small amount of cash, to adjust certain differences in value of the properties exchanged will not necessarily prevent the transaction from being considered an exchange. * * * Where cash is paid by the taxpayer, it may be considered as representing the purchase price of excess value of 'like property' received." 3 Mertens, Law of Federal Income Taxation, § 20.29, pp. 143, 144.

* * *

COMMISSIONER v. CRICHTON

United States Court of Appeals, Fifth Circuit, 1941.
122 F.2d 181.

HUTCHESON, CIRCUIT JUDGE. In 1936, respondent and her three children, owning, in undivided interests, a tract of unimproved country land and an improved city lot, effected an exchange of interests. Her children transferred to respondent their undivided interest in the city lot. Respondent transferred to her children, as of equal value, an undivided ¾₂ interest in the "oil, gas and other minerals, in, on and under, and that may be produced from" the country land. The ½ interest conveyed to respondent had a value of $15,357.77. The interest respondent transferred to her children had a cost basis of zero.

Respondent treating the exchange as one of property for property of like kind and therefore nontaxable under Section 112(b) (1),[1] Revenue Act of 1936, 26 U.S.C.A.Int.Rev.Acts, page 855, did not report any profit therefrom. The commissioner, of the opinion that the exchange resulted in a capital gain of $15,357.71, under Section 117, Revenue Act of 1936, 26 U.S.C.A.Int.Rev.Acts, page 873, determined a deficiency of $628.66 accordingly.

The Board [2] of the opinion that the exchange was "solely in kind", disagreed with the commissioner and on redetermination fixed the deficiency at $86.46. The commissioner is here insisting that the Board has wrongfully decided the question. We do not think so. We agree with the Board that whatever difficulty there might have been, if the statute stood alone, in determining the meaning of the very general words it uses, as applied to the facts of this case, that difficulty vanishes in the light of Treasury Regulation 94,[3] if that regulation is valid, and we think it quite clear that it is. As was the case with regard to the statute considered in Helvering v. Reynolds Tobacco Co., 306 U.S. 110, 113, 59 S.Ct. 423, 425, 83 L.Ed. 536, so here, the section "is

---

1. [I.R.C. (1939) § 112(b) is omitted. See I.R.C. (1954) § 1031(a). Ed.]

2. 42 B.T.A. 490.

3. [The provisions in the current regulations which correspond to earlier provisions quoted here are at Reg. § 1.1031–1 (b) and (c). Ed.]

so general in its terms as to render an interpretative regulation appropriate."

As was the case there, so here, "the administrative construction embodied in the regulation has [for many years], been uniform with respect to each of the revenue acts,   *   *   *,   as evidenced by Treasury rulings and regulations, and decisions of the Board of Tax Appeals."

The commissioner concedes, as he must, that under Louisiana law, mineral rights are interests not in personal but in real property, and that the rights exchanged were real rights.   In the light therefore of the rule the regulation lays down, of the examples given in the illustrations it puts forth, and of the construction which, under its interpretation, the statute has been given throughout this long period, it will not do for him to now marshal or parade the supposed dissimilarities in grade or quality, the unlikenesses, in attributes, appearance and capacities, between undivided real interests in a respectively small town hotel, and mineral properties.   For the regulation and the interpretation under it, leave in no doubt that no gain or loss is realized by one, other than a dealer, from an exchange of real estate for other real estate, and that the distinction intended and made by the statute is the broad one between classes and characters of properties, for instance, between real and personal property.   It was not intended to draw any distinction between parcels of real property however dissimilar they may be in location, in attributes and in capacities for profitable use.

The order of the Board was right.   It is affirmed.

CENTURY ELECTRIC CO. v. COMMISSIONER

United States Court of Appeals, Eighth Circuit, 1951.
192 F.2d 155.
Cert. denied, 342 U.S. 954, 72 S.Ct. 625, 1952.

RIDDICK, CIRCUIT JUDGE.   The petitioner, Century Electric Company, is a corporation engaged principally in the manufacture and sale of electric motors and generators in St. Louis, Missouri.   It is not a dealer in real estate.   As of December 1, 1943, petitioner transferred a foundry building owned and used by it in its manufacturing business and the land on which the foundry is situated to William Jewell College and claimed a deductible loss on the transaction in its tax return for the calendar year 1943.   The Commissioner of Internal Revenue denied the loss.   The Commissioner was affirmed by the Tax Court and this petition for review followed.

The opinion of the Tax Court and its findings of fact, stated in great detail, are reported in 15 T.C. 581.   Petitioner accepts the Tax Court's findings of fact as correct.

Since its organization in 1901 petitioner has been continuously successful in business.   In its income tax return for the year 1943 it reported gross sales of $17,004,839.73 and gross profits from sales of

$5,944,386.93. On December 31, 1942, petitioner owned land, buildings, and improvements of the total depreciated cost of $1,902,552.16. On December 31, 1943, its actual cash on hand amounted to $203,-123.70. During the year 1943 it distributed cash dividends of $226,-705.69 and made a contribution to Washington University of $42,500. It also held tax anticipation notes and Series G bonds totaling $2,000,-000, readily convertible into cash and sufficient to liquidate its outstanding 1943 tax liability and its two outstanding 90-day bank notes due January 20, 1944.

Petitioner has always operated its business in large part on borrowed capital. In 1943 it had open lines of credit with the Chase National Bank of New York of $300,000, with the Boatmen's National Bank of St. Louis of the same amount, and with the Mercantile-Commerce Bank and Trust Company of $400,000. At the end of 1943 its outstanding loans from the Mercantile bank amounted to $600,000 approved by the authorized officers of the bank. Petitioner has always been able to liquidate its outstanding 90-day bank loans as they become due either by payment or renewal.

The assessed value of petitioner's foundry building and land upon which it is located for 1943 was $205,780. There was evidence that in St. Louis real property is assessed at its actual value. There was also evidence introduced by petitioner before the Tax Court that the market value for unconditional sale of the foundry building, land, and appurtenances was not in excess of $250,000.

As of December 1, 1943, the adjusted cost basis for the foundry building, land, and appurtenances transferred to William Jewell College was $531,710.97. The building was a specially designed foundry situated in a highly desirable industrial location. It is undisputed in the evidence that the foundry property is necessary to the operation of petitioner's profitable business and that petitioner never at any time considered a sale of the foundry property on terms which would deprive petitioner of its use in its business.

Petitioner's explanation of the transaction with the William Jewell College is that in the spring of 1943 a vice-president of the Mercantile bank where petitioner deposited its money and transacted the most of its banking business suggested to petitioner the advisability of selling some of its real estate holdings for the purpose of improving the ratio of its current assets to current liabilities by the receipt of cash on the sale and the possible realization of a loss deductible for tax purposes. Petitioner's operating business was to be protected by an immediate long-term lease of the real property sold.

Petitioner's board of directors rejected this proposition as unsound. But in July 1943, when a vice-president of the Mercantile bank suggested to petitioner's treasurer that it would be a good idea for petitioner to pay off all its bank loans merely to show that it was able to do so, petitioner interpreted this advice as a call of its bank loans. Acting on this interpretation, petitioner borrowed from the First National Bank in St. Louis on the security of tax anticipation notes held by it, funds with which it discharged all its bank loans. Immediately thereafter it re-established its lines of bank credit and began consideration of a sale of the foundry property and contemporaneous lease from the purchaser.

On September 2, 1943, petitioner's board of directors adopted a resolution that the executive committee of the board study the situation "and present, if possible, a plan covering the sale and rental back by Century Electric Company of the foundry property." The decision to enter into the transaction described was communicated to the Mercantile bank, but petitioner never publicly offered or advertised its foundry property for sale. The Tax Court found that petitioner "was concerned with getting a friendly landlord to lease the property back to it, as there was never any intention on the part of petitioner to discontinue its foundry operations." Several offers to purchase the foundry property at prices ranging from $110,000 to $150,000 were received and rejected by petitioner.

At a special meeting of the board of directors of petitioner on December 9, 1943, the president of petitioner reported that the officers of petitioner had entered into negotiations for the sale of the foundry property to William Jewell College for the price of $150,000 with the agreement of said college; "that in addition thereto said Trustees of William Jewell College further have agreed to execute a lease of the property so purchased to Century Electric Company for the same time and on substantially the same terms and conditions which were authorized to be accepted by the special meeting of shareholders of this corporation, held on the 24th day of November, 1943." The stockholders at the November meeting had authorized the sale of the foundry property at not less than $150,000 cash, conditioned upon the purchaser executing its lease of the property sold for a term of not less than 25 and not more than 95 years. The Board by resolution approved the proposed transaction with the William Jewell College, but on condition that "this corporation will acquire from Trustees of William Jewell College, a Missouri Corporation, an Indenture of Lease * * * for a term of not less than twenty-five years and for not more than ninety-five years." The resolution set out in detail the terms of the lease from the college to petitioner, approved the form of the deed from the petitioner to the college, authorized the president and secretary of petitioner to execute the lease after its execution by the trustees of the college, and directed "that the president and secretary of this corporation be authorized to deliver said Warranty Deed to said purchaser upon receiving from said purchaser $150,000 in cash, and upon receiving from said purchaser duplicate executed Indenture of Lease on the forms exhibited to this Board." The resolution provided that the deed and lease should be dated December 1, 1943, and effective as of that date.

The deed and the lease were executed and delivered as provided by the resolution of petitioner's board of directors. Neither instrument referred to the other. The deed was in form a general warranty deed, reciting only the consideration of $150,000 in cash. The lease recited among others the respective covenants of the parties as to its term, its termination by either the lessor or lessee, and as to the rents reserved.

As of December 31, 1942, the ratio of petitioner's current assets to its current liabilities was 1.74. The $150,000 in cash received by petitioner on the transaction increased the ratio of current assets to current liabilities from 1.74 to 1.80. The loss deduction which petitioner claims on the transaction and its consequent tax savings would if allowed have increased the ratio approximately twice as much as the receipt of the $150,000.

The questions presented are:

1. Whether the transaction stated was for tax purposes a sale of the foundry property within the meaning of section 112 of the Internal Revenue Code, 26 U.S.C.A. § 112, on which petitioner realized in 1943 a deductible loss of $381,710.97 determined under section 111 of the code (the adjusted basis of the foundry property of $531,710.97 less $150,000) as petitioner contends; or, as the Tax Court held, an exchange of property held for productive use in a trade or business for property of a like kind to be held for productive use in trade or business in which no gain or loss is recognized under sections 112(b) (1) [1] and 112(e) [2] and Regulation 111, section 29.112(b) (1)–1.[3]

2. Whether if the claimed loss deduction is denied, its amount is deductible as depreciation over the 95-year term of the lease as the Tax Court held, or over the remaining life of the improvements on the foundry as the petitioner contends.

On the first question the Tax Court reached the right result. The answer to the question is not to be found by a resort to the dictionary for the meaning of the words "sales" and "exchanges" in other contexts, but in the purpose and policy of the revenue act as expressed in section 112. Compare Federal Deposit Insurance Corp. v. Tremaine, 2 Cir., 133 F.2d 827, 830; Cabell v. Markham, 2 Cir., 148 F.2d 737, 739; Markham v. Cabell, 326 U.S. 404, 409, 66 S.Ct. 193, 90 L.Ed. 165; Brooklyn National Corp. v. Commissioner, 2 Cir., 157 F.2d 450, 451; Emery v. Commissioner, 2 Cir., 166 F.2d 27, 30, 1 A.L.R.2d 409. In this section Congress was not defining the words "sales" and "exchanges". It was concerned with the administrative problem involved in the computation of gain or loss in transactions of the character with which the section deals. Subsections 112(b) (1) and 112(e) indicate the controlling policy and purpose of the section, that is, the nonrecognition of gain or loss in transactions where neither is readily measured in terms of money, where in theory the taxpayer may have real-

1. [I.R.C. (1939) § 112(b) (1) is omitted. See I.R.C. (1954) § 1031(a). Ed.]

2. [I.R.C. (1939) § 112(e) is omitted. See I.R.C. (1954) § 1031(c). Ed.]

3. [The provisions in the current regulations which correspond to earlier provisions quoted here are at Reg. § 1.1031–1(b) and (c). Ed.]

ized gain or loss but where in fact his economic situation is the same after as it was before the transaction. See Fairfield S. S. Corp. v. Commissioner, 2 Cir., 157 F.2d 321, 323; Trenton Cotton Oil Co. v. Commissioner, 6 Cir., 147 F.2d 33, 36. For tax purposes the question is whether the transaction falls within the category just defined. If it does, it is for tax purposes an exchange and not a sale. So much is indicated by subsection 112(b) (1) with regard to the exchange of securities of readily ascertainable market value measured in terms of money. Gain or loss on exchanges of the excepted securities is recognized. Under subsection 112(c) no loss is recognized on an exchange of property held for productive use in trade or business for like property to be held for the same use, although other property or money is also received by the taxpayer. Compare this subsection with subsection 112(c) (1) where in the same circumstances gain is recognized but only to the extent of the other property or money received in the transaction. The comparison clearly indicates that in the computation of gain or loss on a transfer of property held for productive use in trade or business for property of a like kind to be held for the same use, the market value of the properties of like kind involved in the transfer does not enter into the equation.

The transaction here involved may not be separated into its component parts for tax purposes. Tax consequences must depend on what actually was intended and accomplished rather than on the separate steps taken to reach the desired end. The end of the transaction between the petitioner and the college was that intended by the petitioner at its beginning, namely, the transfer of the fee in the foundry property for the 95-year lease on the same property and $150,000.

It is undisputed that the foundry property before the transaction was held by petitioner for productive use in petitioner's business. After the transaction the same property was held by the petitioner for the same use in the same business. Both before and after the transaction the property was necessary to the continued operation of petitioner's business. The only change brought by the transaction was in the estate or interest of petitioner in the foundry property. In Regulations 111, section 29.112(b) (1)–1, the Treasury has interpreted the words "like kind" as used in subsection 112(b) (1). Under the Treasury interpretation a lease with 30 years or more to run and real estate are properties of "like kind." With the controlling purpose of the applicable section of the revenue code in mind, we can not say that the words "like kind" are so definite and certain that interpretation is neither required nor permitted. The regulation, in force for many years, has survived successive reenactments of the internal revenue acts and has thus acquired the force of law. United States v. Dakota-Montana Oil Co., 288 U.S. 459, 466, 53 S.Ct. 435, 77 L.Ed. 893; Helvering v. R. J. Reynolds Tobacco Co., 306 U.S. 110, 116, 59 S.Ct. 423, 83 L.Ed. 536; and see Commissioner of Internal Revenue v. Crichton, 5 Cir., 122 F.2d 181.

On the second question the Tax Court held that petitioner was not entitled to depreciation on the improvements on the foundry property over their useful life after December 1, 1943. The answer to this question depends upon whether as a result of the transaction under consideration the petitioner has an identifiable capital investment in the improvements on the land covered by the lease. Petitioner contends that the amount of its claimed loss, $381,710.97, should be apportioned between the land and improvements in proportion to their respective cost bases as of November 30, 1943. This would result in an allocation of $277,076.68 of petitioner's investment in the leasehold to the improvements and $104,634.29 to the land. The difficulty with petitioner's position is that it involves assumptions and inferences which find no support in the record. What the petitioner has done is to exchange the foundry property having an adjusted basis of $531,710.97 on December 1, 1943, for a leasehold and $150,000 in cash. Its capital investment is in the leasehold and not its constituent properties. Accordingly, we agree with the Tax Court that petitioner is entitled to depreciation on the leasehold. The basis for depreciation of the leasehold on December 1, 1943 is, therefore, $381,710.97 under section 113 (a) (6) of the revenue code, deductible over the term of the lease.

The decision of the Tax Court is affirmed.

NOTE

The result in *Century Electric*, which is in accord with the Regulations,[1] may be open to challenge. In Jordan Marsh Co. v. Comm'r,[2] followed by *Leslie*, infra page 905, the Second Circuit distinguished *Century Electric* in a situation in which the taxpayer transferred two parcels of *loss* property for $2,300,000 in cash, representing the fair market value of the properties. At the same time he entered into a lease of the same property for 30 years with an option to renew for another 30 years. The Second Circuit concluded that the transaction was not a § 1031 exchange because it constituted a sale. The Commissioner has indicated he will not follow the *Jordan Marsh* decision, stating:[3]

> It is the position of the Service that a sale and leaseback under the circumstances here present constitute, in substance, a single integrated transaction under which there is an 'exchange' of property of like kind with cash as boot.

The Commissioner may assert the doctrine of substance over form in other circumstances to invoke the provisions of § 1031. In Rev.Rul. 61–119,[4] the taxpayer sold some old equipment used in his trade or business to a dealer at a gain. In a separate transaction he

1. Reg. § 1.1031(a)–1(c).

2. 269 F.2d 453 (2d Cir. 1959).

3. Rev.Rul. 60–43, 1960–1 C.B. 687, 688. See also Rev.Rul. 76–301, 1976–32 I.R.B. 12.

4. 61–1 C.B. 395.

purchased new equipment from the same dealer. The Service looked to the fact that the sale and purchase were reciprocal and mutually dependent transactions and concluded that, in substance, they constituted a § 1031 exchange. Why did the taxpayer set up two separate transactions? Would the Commissioner be as interested in § 1031 applying in the above circumstances today as he was in 1961? See Code §§ 1245(b) (4); 1250(d) (4) (A); see Reg. § 1.1245–2(c) (4).

LESLIE CO. v. COMMISSIONER

United States Court of Appeals, Third Circuit, 1976.
539 F.2d 943.

GARTH, CIRCUIT JUDGE: This appeal involves the tax consequences of a sale and leaseback arrangement. The question presented is whether the sale and leaseback arrangement constitutes an exchange of like-kind properties, on which no loss is recognized, or whether that transaction is governed by the general recognition provision of Int.Rev.Code § 1002.[1] The Tax Court, on taxpayer's petition for a redetermination of deficiencies assessed against it by the Commissioner, held that the fee conveyance aspect of the transaction was a sale entitled to recognition, and that the leaseback was merely a condition precedent to that sale. The Tax Court thereby allowed the loss claimed by the taxpayer. For the reasons given below, we affirm.

I. Leslie Company, the taxpayer, is a New Jersey corporation engaged in the manufacture and distribution of pressure and temperature regulators and instantaneous water heaters. Leslie, finding its *Lyndhurst*, New Jersey plant inadequate for its needs, decided to move to a new facility. To this end, in March 1967 Leslie purchased land in Parsippany, on which to construct a new manufacturing plant.

Leslie, however, was unable to acquire the necessary financing for the construction of its proposed $2,400,000 plant. Accordingly, on October 30, 1967, it entered into an agreement with the Prudential Life Insurance Company of America, whereby Leslie would erect a plant to specifications approved by Prudential and Prudential would then purchase the Parsippany property and building from Leslie. At the time of purchase Prudential would lease back the facility to Leslie. The property and improvements were to be conveyed to Prudential for $2,400,000 or the actual cost to Leslie, whichever amount was less.

The lease term was established at 30 years,[2] at an annual net rental of $190,560, which was 7.94% of the purchase price. The lease agreement gave Leslie two 10-year options to renew. The annual net rental during each option period was $72,000, or 3% of the

1. All references are to the Internal Revenue Code of 1954. [Footnotes have been edited and renumbered. Ed.]

2. The parties stipulated, and the Tax Court found accordingly, that the useful life of the building Leslie constructed was 30 years.

purchase price. The lease also provided that Leslie could offer to re-purchase the property [3] at five year intervals, beginning with the 15th year of the lease, at specified prices as follows:

	(15th year	$1,798,000
at the end of the	(20th year	1,592,000
	(25th year	1,386,000
	(30th year	1,180,000

Under the lease Prudential was entitled to all condemnation proceeds, net of any damages suffered by Leslie with respect to its trade fixtures and certain structural improvements, without any deduction for Leslie's leasehold interest.

Construction was completed in December, 1968, at a total cost to Leslie (including the purchase price of the land) of $3,187,414. On December 16, 1968 Leslie unconditionally conveyed the property to Prudential, as its contract required, for $2,400,000. At the same time, Leslie and Prudential executed a 30-year lease.

Leslie, on its 1968 corporate income tax return, reported and deducted a loss of $787,414 from the sale of the property.[4] The Commissioner of Internal Revenue disallowed the claimed loss on the ground that the sale and leaseback transaction constituted an exchange of like-kind properties within the scope of Int.Rev.Code § 1031. That section of the Code, if applicable, provides for nonrecognition (and hence nondeductibility) of such losses.[5] Rather than permitting Leslie to take the entire deduction of $787,414 in 1968, the Commissioner treated the $787,414 as Leslie's cost in obtaining the lease, and amortized that sum over the lease's 30-year term. Accordingly, Leslie was assessed deficiencies of $383,023.52 in its corporate income taxes for the years 1965, 1966 and 1968.

Leslie petitioned the Tax Court for a redetermination of the deficiencies assessed against it, contending that the conveyance of the Parsippany property constituted a sale, on which loss is recognized. The Tax Court agreed.[6]

Although the Tax Court found as a fact that Leslie would not have entered into the sale transaction without a leaseback guarantee, * * * it concluded that this finding was not dispositive of the character of the transaction. Rather, it held that to constitute an exchange under Int.Rev.Code § 1031 there must be a reciprocal transfer of properties, as distinguished from a transfer of property for a money consideration only, * * * *citing* Treas.Reg. § 1.1002–1(d).

---

3. See note 10 infra.

4. The $787,414 was the difference between Leslie's actual cost of $3,187,-414 and the $2,400,000 which Prudential paid Leslie for the property. This 1968 loss resulted in a net operating loss for that year of $366,907, which was carried back to 1965.

5. The Commissioner characterizes the instant transaction as an exchange of real property for a 30-year lease plus cash ($2,400,000). (Appellant's Brief at 2). Thus, in the Commissioner's view, Int.Rev.Code § 1031(c) applies.

6. 64 T.C. 247 (1975).

Based on its findings that the fair market value of the Parsippany property at the time of sale was "in the neighborhood of" the $2,-400,000 which Prudential paid, and that the annual net rental of $190,560 to be paid by Leslie was comparable to the fair rental value of similar types of property in the Northern New Jersey area,[7] the Tax Court majority reasoned that Leslie's leasehold had no separate capital value which could be properly viewed as part of the consideration paid. Accordingly, Leslie having received $2,400,000 from Prudential as the sole consideration for the property conveyed, the Tax Court held that the transaction was not an exchange of like-kind properties within the purview of Int.Rev.Code § 1031, but was rather a sale, and so governed by the general recognition provision of Int. Rev.Code § 1002.

Six judges of the Tax Court dissented from this holding. Judge Tannenwald, in an opinion in which Judges Raum, Drennen, Quealy and Hall joined, agreed with the Tax Court majority that the conveyance was a sale, but would have disallowed a loss deduction, reasoning that the leasehold had a premium value to Leslie equal to the $787,414 difference between cost and sales price.[8] This dissent reasoned that since Leslie would not have willingly incurred the loss but for the guaranteed lease, this amount should be treated as a bonus paid for the leasehold, and should be amortized over the leasehold's 30-year term.

Judge Wilbur, in a separate dissent with which Judges Tannenwald and Hall agreed, 64 T.C. at 257, declined to decide whether the conveyance was a sale or an exchange. His concern was that the Tax Court majority was permitting the taxpayer to "write off 25 per cent of the costs of acquiring the right to use a building for one-half a century that was constructed for its [Leslie's] own special purposes." He, like Judge Tannenwald, would hold the loss incurred was attributable to the acquisition of the leasehold interest rather than to the construction of the building.

---

7. These findings were based on the testimony of a witness presented by the Commissioner, who testified that the sale price of the property and the rental established by the lease were comparable to their respective fair market values. This testimony, as might be expected, was uncontroverted by the taxpayer.

8. Judge Quealy also filed a separate dissent, 64 T.C. at 257, in which he pointed to Leslie's reservation of a favorable option to repurchase the property as further support for the position that the petitioner incurred no loss upon sale.

We are hard pressed to agree with this characterization of Leslie's very limited rights of repurchase under the lease as "favorable." The repurchase right is set forth in * * * the lease * * *. Leslie is given the right to terminate the lease after the 15th, 20th, 25th and 30th years. To do so, however, it must make an offer to repurchase the property back from Prudential, at specified prices. * * * Prudential need not accept the offer, although nonacceptance does not prejudice Leslie's rights of termination. Thus Leslie's option to offer to repurchase may be exercised only at the risk of losing the right to use the property for the remainder of the lease term.

The Commissioner's appeal from the decision of the Tax Court followed.

II. The threshold question in any dispute involving the applicability of Int.Rev.Code § 1031 is whether the transaction constitutes an exchange. This is so because § 1031 nonrecognition applies only to exchanges. Section 1031 does not apply where, for example, a taxpayer sells business property for cash and immediately reinvests that cash in other business property even if that property is "like-kind" property. Bell Lines Inc. v. United States, 480 F.2d 710 (4th Cir. 1973). Hence, our inquiry must center on whether the Leslie-Prudential transaction was a sale, as Leslie contends, or an exchange, as the Commissioner argues. If a sale then, as stated, § 1031 is inapplicable and we need not be concerned further with ascertaining whether the other requirements of that section have been met. See Jordan Marsh Co. v. Commissioner, 269 F. 453, 455 (2d Cir. 1959). If an exchange, then of course we would be obliged to continue our inquiry to determine if the properties involved were "like-kind."

The Tax Court's conclusion that the Leslie conveyance resulted in a sale was predicated almost totally on an analysis of the applicable Treasury Regulations. Noting that Treas.Reg. § 1.1002–1(b) requires a strict construction of § 1031, the Tax Court tested the instant transaction against the definition of "exchange" contained in Treas. Reg. § 1.1002(d):

> (d) Exchange. Ordinarily, to constitute an exchange, the transaction must be a reciprocal transfer of property as distinguished from a transfer of property for a money consideration only.

Based on its conclusion that the leasehold had no capital value, the Tax Court held that it was not a part of the consideration received but was merely a condition precedent to the sale. Thus, the conveyance to Prudential was "solely for a money consideration" and therefore was not an "exchange." The Tax Court cited Jordan Marsh Co. v. Commissioner, supra, in support of its result. In light of its holding, it specifically declined to consider or resolve any possible conflict between *Jordan Marsh*, a decision of the Second Circuit, and the Eighth Circuit decision in Century Electric Co. v. Commissioner, 192 F.2d 155 (8th Cir. 1951), cert. denied 342 U.S. 954 (1952).

The Commissioner, relying on *Century Electric*, argues that the Tax Court erred in holding the Leslie-Prudential conveyance to be a sale. He could not, and does not, dispute the Tax Court's findings as to the fair market value and fair rental value of the property. Rather, he argues that value in this context is irrelevant and that the only appropriate consideration is whether the conveyance of the fee and the conveyance of the leasehold were reciprocal.[9] The Commis-

9. As noted above, the Tax Court found that this element of reciprocity *was* present.

sioner, without regard to his own regulations which define an "exchange," then seeks to support his position by reference to the legislative purpose giving rise to the enactment of the nonrecognition provision. He argues that this provision (§ 1031 and its predecessors) was adopted primarily to eliminate any requirement that the government value the property involved in such exchanges.[10] Alternatively, the Commissioner argues that even if the conveyance is held to be a sale and thereby not within Int.Rev.Code § 1031, any expenditure incurred by Leslie over and above the selling price of $2,-400,000 was not a loss as claimed, but rather a premium or bonus which Leslie paid to obtain the leasehold. Such an expenditure is a capital expenditure, the Commissioner argues, and therefore should be amortized over the 30-year lease term.

Leslie, on the other hand, urges affirmance of the Tax Court's holding, relying on Jordan Marsh Co. v. Commissioner, supra, and stresses, as does the Tax Court, that the initial issue to be resolved is the character of the transaction. * * *

In Century Electric Co. v. Commissioner, supra, the Eighth Circuit held a sale and leaseback arrangement to be a like-kind exchange governed by the nonrecognition provision. * * * Its holding that no loss was to be recognized was based solely on its finding that the sale and leaseback transactions were reciprocal. The Eighth Circuit read the legislative history of [§ 1031] as evidencing a Congressional purpose to relieve the government of the administrative burden of valuing properties received in like-kind exchanges. Thus the Court stated * * * that:

> the market value of the properties of like kind involved in the transfer does not enter into the equation.

By contrast, in Jordan Marsh v. Commissioner, supra, a case construing the same code provision as *Century Electric*, the Second Circuit held that a similar sale and leaseback transaction resulted in a *sale*, on which loss was recognized. The facts in *Jordan Marsh* were similar to the facts here. Jordan Marsh, the taxpayer, had sold two parcels of land for cash in the sum of $2.3 million an amount which was stipulated to be equal to the fair market value of the property. Simultaneously, the premises were leased back to Jordan Marsh for a term of 30-plus years, with options to renew. The rentals to be paid by Jordan Marsh were "full and normal rentals",

10. The Commissioner takes the position that:

"The statute was intended to be corrective legislation of three specific shortcomings of prior Revenue Acts, viz—(1) the administrative burden of valuing property received in a like-kind exchange; (2) the inequity, in the case of an exchange, of forcing a taxpayer to recognize a paper gain which was still tied up in a continuing investment; and (3) the prevention of taxpayer from taking colorable losses in wash sales and other fictitious exchanges. Preliminary Report of a Subcommittee of the House Committee on Ways and Means on Prevention of Tax Avoidance, 73d Cong., 2d Sess. (1933).

so that the Court found that the leasehold interest had no separate capital value.

The Court, in examining the legislative history of [§ 1031] took issue with the Eighth Circuit's interpretation of the Congressional purpose behind the nonrecognition provision. The Second Circuit said that:

> Congress was primarily concerned with the inequity, in the case of an exchange, of forcing a taxpayer to recognize a paper gain which was still tied up in a continuing investment of the same sort.

It reasoned further that, if gains were not to be recognized on the ground that they were theoretical, then neither should losses, which were equally theoretical, be recognized. Analyzing the *Jordan Marsh* transaction in the light of this interpretation of Congressional purpose, the Second Circuit, finding Jordan Marsh had liquidated its investment in realty for cash in an amount fully equal to the value of the fee, concluded that the taxpayer was not "still tied up in a continuing investment of the same sort." Accordingly, the Court held that there was no exchange within the purview of § 112(b), but rather a sale.

Thus we may interpret the essential difference between *Jordan Marsh* and *Century Electric* as centering on their respective views of the need to value property involved in a sale and leaseback.[11] *Jordan Marsh* viewing the Congressional purpose behind the nonrecognition provision as one of avoiding taxation of paper gains and losses, would value the properties involved in order to determine whether the requirements of an "exchange" have been met. *Century Electric,* on the other hand, viewing the legislative enactment as one to relieve the administrative burden of valuation, would regard the value of the properties involved as irrelevant.

We are persuaded that the *Jordan Marsh* approach is a more satisfactory one. First, it is supported by the Commissioner's own definition of "exchange" which distinguishes an exchange from a transfer of property *solely* for a money consideration. Treas.Reg. § 1.1002-1(d) (emphasis added).[12] Second, if resort is to be had to legislative history, it appears to us that the view of Congressional purpose taken by the *Jordan Marsh* court is sounder than that of the

---

11. The Court in *Jordan Marsh* also distinguished *Century Electric* on its facts, since in that case there had been no finding that the cash received by the taxpayer was the full equivalent of the value of the fee which had been conveyed. Nor had there been a finding that the leaseback was at a rental which was a fair rental for the premises.

Indeed, as noted in *Jordan Marsh*, the record in *Century Electric* indicated that the sales price was substantially less than the fair market value. There was also evidence from which the Court could have found that the leasehold had a separate capital value, since the conveyance to a nonprofit college avoided considerable tax liabilities on the property.

12. It was this definition on which the Tax Court relied in large part in holding the Leslie conveyance to be a sale for $2,400,000.

Eighth Circuit in *Century Electric*. As the Court in *Jordan Marsh* said in discounting the purpose attributed to Congress by the Commissioner and by *Century Electric:*

> Indeed, if these sections had been intended to obviate the necessity of making difficult valuations, one would have expected them to provide for nonrecognition of gains and losses in all exchanges, whether the property received in exchanges were 'of a like kind' or *not* of a like kind. And if such had been the legislative objective, [§ 1031] providing for the recognition of gain from exchanges not wholly in kind, would never have been enacted. * * *

It seems to us, therefore, that in order to determine whether money was the sole consideration for a transfer the fair market value of the properties involved must be ascertained. Here, the Tax Court found that Leslie had sold its property unconditionally for cash equal to its fair market value, and had acquired a leasehold for which it was obligated to pay fair rental value. These findings, not clearly erroneous, are binding on this Court. * * *

Nor do we think the Tax Court erred in concluding that the leasehold acquired by Leslie had no capital value. Among other considerations, the rental charged at fair market rates, the lack of compensation for the leasehold interest in the event of condemnation, and the absence of any substantial right of control over the property all support this conclusion. On this record, we agree with the Tax Court that the conveyance was not an exchange, "a reciprocal transfer of property," but was rather "a transfer of property for a money consideration only," and therefore a *sale.* * * *

The Commissioner's evidence that the rentals charged to Leslie under its lease were at fair market value, leading to our conclusion that the leasehold had no capital value, also disposes of the Commissioner's alternative argument on appeal that Leslie's excess cost of $787,414 was not a loss. * * *

The decision of the Tax Court will be affirmed.

NOTE

The underlying significant distinction between *Century Electric Company* and *Leslie* appears to be bona fide valuation. In *Century Electric*, if the taxpayer had won, it would have had a § 1231 loss of $381,710.97, resulting in an ordinary loss, plus cash of $150,000. The tax-motivated "sale", pegged at local property tax assessment valuation, was to a tax-exempt friendly purchaser-landlord.[1]

Sometimes taxpayers can avoid adverse tax consequences by way of what are commonly referred to as "three-cornered transac-

1. See Fischer, "Tax Free Exchanges of Real Property Under Section 1031 of the Internal Revenue Code of 1954," 78 Dickinson 615, 632–633 (1974).

tions." [2] As it requires an exchange, § 1031 does not apply if property is sold and the proceeds are reinvested in property of a like kind.[3] In the basic three-cornered transaction, A has property (property X) that B wants and C has property (property Y) that A wants. C's basis for his property Y is equal to its fair market value, but A's basis for his property X is much less than fair market value. Assume that the properties are of like kind and also that they are of equal value. Of course, A could sell property X to B and with the proceeds buy property Y from C. This would probably be all right with everyone except A who, in the process, would incur tax on his large gain on the sale of property X. So why not: (1) have B buy property Y from C (without adverse consequences to C because of his high basis for property Y) and (2) then have B exchange property Y with A for property X, tax-free under § 1031?

As regards A who has a large *realized* gain on the exchange the transaction *is* rendered tax-free by § 1031. The fact that B acquired property Y for the very purpose of making the exchange has no effect on A. A *has held* property X let's say for investment and he exchanges it for property Y *to be held* for investment, squarely within the statute. There is no doubt about this.[4]

It is just as clear, however, that B is not within § 1031. He does not have property *held* for productive use or for investment which he exchanges for property of a like kind. He has *newly purchased* property Y that he uses to effectuate the exchange. Thus § 1031 does not apply to him.[5] Of course on our facts B wouldn't give a four-letter-word whether he was within or without § 1031, because he has a new cost basis for property Y presumably equal to the fair market value of property X that he receives in the exchange. Consequently the transaction is neutral to him for tax purposes anyway. But consider the *Leslie* case, supra page 905. There on the exchange the taxpayer realized a loss on the exchange of newly acquired property. Of course the court winds up allowing the taxpayer's loss deduction; but do we not have a right to be impatient waiting for someone to say that § 1031, at least, is no obstacle?

In one case, property being disposed of by the taxpayer was transferred to another in exchange for other property. However, the property transferred by the taxpayer was subject to an option, and, when the optionholder exercised the option he, rather than the taxpayer's transferee, wound up with the property. The Tax Court held the taxpayer had sold his property and that § 1031 did not apply.[6]

2. W. D. Haden Co. v. Comm'r, 165 F. 2d 588 (5th Cir. 1948); see Dean, "Three-Party Exchanges of Real Estate," 17 Tulane Tax Inst. 131 (1967).

3. Compare § 1033, infra at page 914.

4. See Mercantile Trust Co. of Baltimore, 32 B.T.A. 82 (1935), acq. XIV–1

C.B. 13 (1935); Alderson v. Comm'r, 317 F.2d 790 (9th Cir. 1963); Rev. Rul. 75–291, 1975–2 C.B. 332.

5. See Rev.Rul. 75–292, 1975–2 C.B. 333.

6. John M. Rogers, 44 T.C. 126 (1965), aff'd. per curiam, 377 F.2d 534 (9th Cir. 1967).

Sham and "step transactions" are always with us in the tax law. In a recent case,[7] two brothers sought to arrange a tax-free § 1031 exchange that fell under such ancient hammers as Court Holding v. Commissioner [8] and Gregory v. Helvering.[9] It must be remembered, though, that § 1031 is two-edged and *not* elective. Both *Century Electric* and *Leslie* wished to escape its clutches so that realized *losses* would be recognized. One was successful, the other not. Probably more often the taxpayer seeks the protective covering of § 1031 to avoid immediate recognition of gain.

PROBLEMS

1. X leased a twenty story building, as lessee for a period of 60 years. The first five floors of the building are used by X as a retail clothing store. The balance of the building X subleases to others. X has a basis in the entire lease of $15,000. The fair market value of the lease is only $10,000. Z paid X $10,000 for the entire leasehold. Thereafter Z subleased the first five floors to X. What are the tax consequences to X? See Rev.Rul. 76–301, 2 C.B. ——.

2. Investor purchases 1000 gallons of new scotch grain whisky at a cost of $10,000. In six years it is expected to double in value at which time Investor will sell one half of it for $10,000 and trade the other one half, now aged and worth $10,000 for 1000 gallons of new whisky which costs $10,000. Discuss the tax consequences of Investor's transactions.

3. T has 100 acres of unimproved land which he farms. Its cost basis is $10,000 but its value much greater. He trades it to B for a city apartment building worth $70,000, which has a basis to B of $30,000, and B transfers to T, as well, $4000 in cash and 100 shares of X Corp. stock for which B's basis is $40,000 but which have a fair market value of $26,000. None of the property involved is mortgaged, and B always claimed straight line depreciation on the apartment.

(a) As regards T:

    (1) What is his realized gain on the exchange?

    (2) What is his *recognized* gain on the exchange?

    (3) What is his basis for the stock?

    (4) What is his basis for the apartment building?

    (5) Test whether your conclusions seem sensible by determining what the tax consequences to T would be if, immediately after the exchange, he sold the apartment building for $70,000 and the stock for $26,000 (taking account also of the amount on which he was taxed on the exchange), and comparing this with a straight sale of his farm land (instead of the exchange) for $100,000 cash.

7. Smith v. Comm'r, 537 F.2d 972 (8th Cir. 1976).

8. 324 U.S. 331 (1944).

9. 293 U.S. 465 (1934).

(b) As regards B:

   (1) What is his realized gain on the exchange?

   (2) What is his *recognized* gain or loss on the exchange?

   (3) What is his basis for the farm land acquired?

   (4) Could § 1250 affect B on these facts if, instead of straight line, B had claimed accelerated depreciation on the apartment?

   (5) Test your conclusions about B by seeing whether a sale of the farm by him for $100,000 immediately after the exchange (and taking account of the tax treatment of the disposition of the stock on the exchange) will yield the same overall results as if initially, instead of making the exchange, he had sold the apartment building for $70,000 and the stock for $26,000.

Note: B's problems are a bit more intricate than T's. It is apparent that he has realized $100,000, the *value* of the farm land. But this amount must be allocated $4000 to the cash paid, $26,000 to the stock (its value) and $70,000 to the apartment building (its value). See Reg. § 1.1031(d)–1(e), Example. Is it clear that the $4000 cash paid by B will affect his adjusted basis, as otherwise determined, for the farm land?

C. INVOLUNTARY CONVERSIONS*

Internal Revenue Code: Sections 1001(c); 1033(a)(1), (a)(2), (b) last sentence, (f)(1), (2) and (4); 1231. See Sections 1245(b)(4) and 1250 (d)(4).

Regulations: Section 1.1033(c)–1(b).

NOTE

The Tax Reform Act of 1976 made a few minor substantive amendments to § 1033. By deleting some deadwood provisions, Congress tinkered with the alphabet subsections. Thus by eliminating subparagraph (2) of § 1033(a), former subparagraph (3) is redesignated as subparagraph (2). Accordingly the essence of § 1033 nonrecognition rule now appears as § 1033(a)(2). The basis provision is now § 1033(b), and former § 1033(g) is now § 1033(f) with a

---

* Two general articles in this area are Schaff, "Tax Consequences of an Involuntary Conversion," 46 Taxes 323 (1968); Gannet, "Tax Advantages and Risks in Real Property Exchanges: Voluntary and Involuntary," 25 N.Y. U.Inst. on Fed.Tax. 1 (1967).

special three year replacement rule in lieu of the usual two year rule of § 1033(a).

In the preceding section of this chapter you encountered a special nonrecognition provision relating to like kind *exchanges*. The notion there and applicable here is that the taxpayer, although in possession of replacement property, has not changed his economic position. An exchange of like kind properties is a voluntary transaction. Section 1033 permits the nonrecognition of *gain* in certain circumstances in which property is *involuntarily* converted. The involuntary conversion may be the result of destruction, theft, seizure, requisition or condemnation or threat or imminence thereof. Earlier, in another chapter we considered virtually identical language in another Code section. Take another close look at § 1231.

The general message of § 1033 can be simply stated. When property is involuntarily converted into money, if the taxpayer so elects,[1] gain is recognized, only to the extent that the amount realized as a result of the conversion exceeds the cost of the replacement property.[2] The price of the nonrecognition ticket is that the replacement property must be "similar or related in service or use" to the converted property and the replacement must occur within the time limit of the statute.[3] The provision does not apply to losses resulting from involuntary conversions.[4] Students should be alert to a corresponding basis adjustment resulting from nonrecognition of gain. The basis of the replacement property is the cost of such property, reduced by the gain that is not recognized.[5] In view of § *1023*, this may be simply a deferral of tax to the future.

The complexity and controversy in the application of § 1033 has centered around the meaning of the phrase, "similar or related in service or use." [6]

1. In John McShain, 65 T.C. 686 (1976), the Tax Court held the § 1033 election to be irrevocable.

2. Moving expenses received as part of a lump sum condemnation award have been treated as a nonseverable part of the award itself and therefore as qualifying for § 1033 nonrecognition. E. R. Hitchcock Co. v. U. S., 514 F.2d 484 (2d Cir. 1975); Graphic Press, Inc. v. Comm'r, 523 F.2d 585 (9th Cir. 1975).

3. TRA (1976) § 1033(a)(2); § 1033(f) (4).

4. See §§ 165(c) and 1231.

5. I.R.C. § 1033(b), last sentence.

6. As to *condemned* real estate held for productive use in a trade or business or for investment, see § 1033(f) substituting "like kind" criteria. But see M.H.S. Company, Inc., 35 TCM 733 (1976) in which the taxpayer reinvested a real estate condemnation award in new real estate with a third party as tenants in common, as a joint venture. Under state law the interest is considered a partnership interest which again under state law is *personal* property. Therefore, domino fashion, the Tax Court concluded that the replacement property is not "like kind," holding § 1033 inapplicable. Cf. I.R.C. § 1033(a)(2)(E), as added by TRA (1976) § 1901(a)(128).

HARRY G. MASSER

Tax Court of the United States, 1958.
30 T.C. 741(A).

[The Findings of Fact have been omitted.   Ed.]

Opinion

KERN, JUDGE: The question presented by this case is whether section 112(f) (1) of the Internal Revenue Code of 1939 [1] is applicable to the facts here before us.   Those facts may be summarized as follows: Petitioner, who operated an interstate trucking business, bought at one time two pieces of property situated across a street from each other, one improved by a building (including offices and a bunkhouse) to be used for the loading and unloading of trucks, and the other to be used as space in which the trucks could be parked pending their loading and unloading.   The two pieces of property were used together as an economic unit, constituting petitioner's terminal facilities serving the New York metropolitan area.   It is conceded that the parking area was "involuntarily converted" by petitioner as the result of the threat or imminence of condemnation.   If petitioner retained the improved property, the closest available space for a parking area would have been approximately a mile and a half away.   For petitioner to have operated his truck terminal with his parking area that far from the building where the loading and unloading of his trucks took place and where his offices were located would have been physically possible, but would have been economically impractical because (1) it would have entailed considerable direct expense in connection with the additional labor required, (2) it would have resulted in increasing the hazards of traffic accidents and cargo thefts, (3) it would have resulted in such delays in deliveries as to have affected adversely petitioner's customer relations, and (4) it would have presented complicated problems in connection with traffic management. Because of the involuntary sale of the parking area as a result of the threat of condemnation, petitioner decided in good faith and in the exercise of prudent business judgment to sell the improved property also and to use the proceeds of both properties to buy property in the same general locality suitable for similar use as a truck terminal. Under these circumstances, was the sale of the improved property an involuntary conversion as a result of the threat or imminence of condemnation?

We are not aware of any authorities directly in point as to the question presented, and the legislative history of section 112(f) and its predecessor sections is not helpful.

Bearing in mind two basic principles, that "[t]axation * * * is eminently practical," Tyler v. United States, 281 U.S. 497, 503, and that a relief provision "should be liberally construed to effectuate its purpose," Massillon-Cleveland-Akron Sign Co., 15 T.C. 79, 83, we are of the opinion that when two pieces of property, practically adjacent to each other, were acquired for the purpose of being used and were used in a taxpayer's business as an economic unit, when one of the pieces of property was involuntarily sold as a result of the threat of condemnation, when it was apparent that the continuation of the business on the remaining piece of property was impractical, and as a result of the involuntary sale of the one piece of property the taxpayer in the exercise of good business judgment sold the other piece of property, and when the proceeds of both sales were expended in the acquisition of property similar to the economic unit consisting of the two properties sold, the transaction, considered as a whole, constitutes an involuntary conversion of one economic property unit withing the meaning of section 112(f).

Decision will be entered for petitioners.

CLIFTON INVESTMENT CO. v. COMMISSIONER

United States Court of Appeals, Sixth Circuit, 1963.
312 F.2d 719.
Cert. denied, 373 U.S. 921, 83 S.Ct. 1524, 1963.

BOYD, DISTRICT JUDGE. Petitioner is a real estate investment corporation organized and existing under the laws of the State of Ohio, with headquarters in Cincinnati. In 1956 the petitioner sold to the City of Cincinnati under its threat of exercising its power of eminent domain a six-story office building, known as the United Bank Building, located in the downtown section of that city, which building was held by petitioner for production of rental income from commercial tenants. The funds realized from the sale of this property to the city were used by the petitioner to purchase eighty percent of the outstanding stock of The Times Square Hotel of New York, Inc., also an Ohio corporation, which had as its sole asset a contract to buy the Times Square Hotel of New York City. The purchase of the hotel was effected by the corporation. The taxpayer-petitioner contends herein that the purchase of the controlling stock in the hotel corporation was an investment in property "similar or related in service or use" to the office building it had been forced to sell, thus deserving of the nonrecognition of gain provisions of Section 1033(a) (3) (A), Internal Revenue Code of 1954 (Title 26 U.S.C., Section 1033(a) (3) (A).[1] More specifically, the taxpayer contends that since both the properties herein were productive of rental income, the similarity contemplated by the statute aforesaid exists. The Commissioner ruled to the contrary, holding that any gain from the sale of the office building was recognizable and a deficiency was assessed against the tax-

---

1. See [I.R.C. § 1033(a)(2), as redesignated by TRA (1976). Ed.]

payer for the year 1956 in the amount of $19,057.09. The Tax Court agreed with the Commissioner, finding that the properties themselves were not "similar or related in service or use" as required by the statute. 36 T.C. 569. From the decision of the Tax Court this appeal was perfected.

In order to determine whether the requisite similarity existed under the statute between the properties herein, the Tax Court applied the so-called "functional test" or "end-use test." This it seems has been the Tax Court's traditional line of inquiry, when similar cases under the within statute have been considered by it. This approach takes into account only the actual physical end use to which the properties involved are put, whether that use be by the owner-taxpayer or by his tenant; that is, whether the taxpayer-owner is the actual user of the property or merely holds it for investment purposes, as in the case of a lessor. We reject the functional test as applied to the holder of investment property, who replaces such property with other investment property, as in the case at bar.

The Tax Court in this case relied in part on its earlier decision in Liant Record, Inc. v. Commissioner, 36 T.C. 224 and chiefly on the decision of the Court of Appeals for the Third Circuit in McCaffrey v. Commissioner, 275 F.2d 27, 1960, cert. denied 363 U.S. 828, 80 S.Ct. 1598, 4 L.Ed.2d 1523, the latter case approving and applying the aforesaid functional test in such a case as here presented. However, the Court of Appeals for the Second Circuit has since reversed the Tax Court's decision in Liant, 303 F.2d 326, 1962, and in so doing advanced what we consider to be the soundest approach among the number of decisions on this point. We need not here review all the relevant decisions, since this is done in the recent cases of Loco Realty Company v. Commissioner, 306 F.2d 207 (C.A.8) 1962, and Pohn v. Commissioner, 309 F.2d 427 (C.A.7) 1962, both of which decisions approved the Second Circuit Court's approach in Liant, the court in the Pohn case relying specifically on the Liant decision.

Congress must have intended that in order for the taxpayer to obtain the tax benefits of Section 1033 he must have continuity of interest as to the original property and its replacement in order that the taxpayer not be given a tax-free alteration of his interest. In short, the properties must be reasonably similar in their relation to the taxpayer. This reasonableness, as noted in the Liant case, is dependent upon a number of factors, all bearing on whether or not the relation of the taxpayer to the property has been changed. The ultimate use to which the properties are put, then, does not control the inquiry, when the taxpayer is not the user of the properties as in the case under consideration. As exemplary of the factors which are relevant the Liant decision mentions the following, after advancement of its "relation of the properties to the taxpayer" test:

"In applying such a test to a lessor, a court must compare, inter alia, the extent and type of the lessor's management activity, the amount and kind of services rendered by him to the tenants, and the nature of his business risks connected with the properties."

Thus, each case is dependent on its peculiar facts and the factors bearing on the service or use of the properties to the taxpayer must be closely examined. The Tax Court employed an erroneous test in this case, but on examination of the record, the correctness of the result is manifest.

The record before us discloses that the United Bank Building and the Times Square Hotel both produced rental income to the taxpayer. However, examination of what the properties required in the way of services to the tenants, management activity, and commercial tenancy considerations reveals an alteration of the taxpayer's interest. The record herein shows that the taxpayer corporation itself managed the United Bank Building, but deemed it necessary to procure professional management for the Times Square Hotel. There were primarily two employees for the United Bank Building, who afforded elevator and janitorial services to the tenants. In the Times Square Hotel between 130 and 140 employees were necessary to attend the hotel operation and offer services to the commercial tenants and hotel guests. Approximately 96% of the rental income from the hotel was from the guest room facilities and the large number of transients required daily services of varying kinds. Furniture, linens, personal services of every description were furnished the hotel guests, which were not furnished the commercial tenants of the United Bank Building. The hotel guests reside in the hotel rooms and that is obviously the only reason they are tenants. In the office building herein several tenants also used parts of the premises for living quarters, but were clearly not furnished the typical services the hotel guest demands. There was no great limitation placed on the types of commercial tenants to whom space was rented in the United Bank Building, but as the enumeration of commercial tenants of the hotel building reveals, space therein was leased for the most part and primarily with an eye to how such a business operation might fit in with the operation of a hotel, how it relates to the hotel guests. It is common experience that the services offered by a lessee of business premises in a hotel will reflect in the minds of its guests on the service they associate with the hotel itself. If a leased restaurant in a hotel offers good or bad service, there is a tendency to think of the food service at the hotel as good or bad. A number of unique business considerations enter when leasing commercial space in a hotel which do not apply to an office building.

We consider there to be, then, a material variance between the relation of the office building in question and the within hotel operation of the taxpayer, in the light of the relevant inquiry found in the Liant case. It is true that what the taxpayer derived from both properties herein was generally the same, rental income. But what the properties demanded of the taxpayer in the way of management, services, and relations to its tenants materially varied. That which the taxpayer receives from his properties and that which such properties demand of the taxpayer must both be considered in determining whether or not the properties are similar or related in service or use to the taxpayer.[2]

The decision of the Tax Court is affirmed.

SHACKELFORD MILLER, JR., CIRCUIT JUDGE (concurring).

I concur in the result reached in the majority opinion.

However, I am not willing to adopt, without some modification thereof, the test adopted and applied in Liant Record, Inc. v. Commissioner, 303 F.2d 326, C.A.2d, upon which the majority opinion relies. I think that the investment character of the properties involved should be given more consideration than what seems to me is given by the ruling in the Liant case, although I do not think that investment basis alone is sufficient to comply with the statute, as Steuart Brothers, Inc. v. Commissioner, 261 F.2d 580, C.A.4th, might be construed as holding. As pointed out in Loco Realty Co. v. Commissioner, 306 F.2d 207, 215, C.A.8th, the statute was not intended to penalize but to protect persons whose property may be taken on condemnation and, accordingly, should be construed liberally. I agree with the standard adopted in the opinion in that case, although for our present purposes I do not think that it results in a reversal of the decision of the Tax Court.

REVENUE RULING 64–237

1964–2 Cum.Bull. 319.

The Internal Revenue Service has reconsidered its position with respect to replacement property that is "similar or related in service or use" to involuntarily converted property within the meaning of section 112(f) of the Internal Revenue Code of 1939 and section 1033(a) of the Internal Revenue Code of 1954 in light of the decision of the United States Court of Appeals for the Second Circuit in the case of Liant Record, Inc. v. Commissioner, 303 Fed. (2d) 326 (1962), and other appellate court decisions.

In previous litigation, the Service has taken the position that the statutory phrase, "similar or related in service or use," means that the property acquired must have a close "functional" similarity to the property converted. Under this test, property was not considered

---

2. Congress has since provided that replacement of property held for productive use in trade or business or for investment purposes with property of "like kind" satisfies the "similar or related in service or use" requirement. However, the acquisition of controlling interest in stock of a corporation holding property was specifically excepted from the relaxation of the test. Title 26 U.S.C. Section 1033 (g) (1) and (2). (Technical Amendments Act of 1958). [TRA (1976) redesignated § 1033(g) as § 1033(f). Ed.]

similar or related in service or use to the converted property unless the physical characteristics and end uses of the converted and replacement properties were closely similar. Although this "functional use test" has been upheld in the lower courts, it has not been sustained in the appellate courts with respect to investors in property, such as lessors.

In conformity with the appellate court decisions, in considering whether replacement property acquired by an investor is similar in service or use to the converted property, attention will be directed primarily to the similarity in the relationship of the services or uses which the original and replacement properties have to the taxpayer-owner. In applying this test, a determination will be made as to whether the properties are of a similar service to the taxpayer, the nature of the business risks connected with the properties, and what such properties demand of the taxpayer in the way of management, services and relations to his tenants.

For example, where the taxpayer is a lessor, who rented out the converted property for a light manufacturing plant and then rents out the replacement property for a wholesale grocery warehouse, the nature of the taxpayer-owner's service or use of the properties may be similar although that of the end users change. The two properties will be considered as similar or related in service or use where, for example, both are rented and where there is a similarity in the extent and type of the taxpayer's management activities, the amount and kind of services rendered by him to his tenants, and the nature of his business risks connected with the properties.

In modifying its position with respect to the involuntary conversion of property held for investment, the Service will continue to adhere to the functional test in the case of owner-users of property. Thus, if the taxpayer-owner operates a light manufacturing plant on the converted property and then operates a wholesale grocery warehouse on the replacement property, by changing his end use he has so changed the nature of his relationship to the property as to be outside the nonrecognition of gain provisions.

REVENUE RULING 67–254

1967–2 Cum.Bull. 269.

Advice has been requested whether the nonrecognition-of-gain benefits under the provisions of section 1033 of the Internal Revenue Code of 1954 apply where the proceeds of a condemnation award are used to rearrange plant facilities on the remaining portion of the plant property. Additionally, the question is raised as to whether such benefits apply if the taxpayer uses part of the award to erect a building on land he presently owns.

A State condemned a portion of the land upon which the taxpayer's manufacturing plant was situated. The condemned portion had been used as a storage area for the taxpayer's product and also contained thereon a garage which housed the plant's delivery trucks. The taxpayer received an award for the condemned property, none of which was compensation for damages to the portion of the property which he retained.

Because of the prohibitive cost of acquiring land in the area suitable for storage, the taxpayer used part of the proceeds of the condemnation award in the year of its receipt to rearrange the layout of his plant facilities on the remainder of his land in order to create a new storage area. He used the remainder of the award to build a new garage (to house the plant's delivery trucks) on a small plot of land located nearby, which he had owned for several years.

Section 1033(a) (3) (A) * of the Code provides, in effect, that if property is compulsorily or involuntarily converted into money and the taxpayer, during the period specified, purchases other property similar or related in service or use to the property so converted, at the election of the taxpayer the gain shall be recognized only to the extent that the amount realized upon such conversion exceeds the cost of such other property.

Accordingly, based on these facts, to the extent that the taxpayer expended the condemnation proceeds in restoring the plantsite so that it could be used in the same manner as it was used prior to the condemnation, he has acquired property similar or related in service or use to the property converted for purposes of section 1033(a) (3) (A) of the Code. Whether all of the expenditures made by the taxpayer were necessary to restore the plantsite to its original usefulness is a question of fact to be determined upon examination of his income tax return for the year in which the transaction occurred.

In addition, the garage erected on land already owned qualifies under section 1033(a) (3) (A) of the Code as property similar or related in service or use to the garage that was condemned.

REVENUE RULING 67–255

1967-2 Cum.Bull. 270.

Advice has been requested whether the investment of condemnation proceeds, under the circumstances set forth below, will qualify as "like kind" replacement of involuntarily converted property for purposes of section 1033(g)** of the Internal Revenue Code of 1954.

After 1957 land which the taxpayer held for investment was condemned. In the same year, the taxpayer expended the proceeds of

---

* See comments at page 914, supra, on redesignation of parts of I.R.C. § 1033. Ed.

** See comments at page 914, supra, on redesignation of I.R.C. § 1033(g) as § 1033(f). Ed.

the condemnation in the construction of an office building to be held for investment purposes on another site which he already owned.

The taxpayer also owned two separate tracts of unimproved rural land, one of which was condemned in a year after 1957. Immediately thereafter, the taxpayer invested the proceeds of the condemnation in the installation of storm drains, water systems, and roads on the remaining tract of rural land.

Section 1033(a) (3) (A) of the Code provides, in effect, that if property is compulsorily or involuntarily converted into money and the taxpayer, during the period specified, purchases other property similar or related in service or use to the property so converted, at the election of the taxpayer the gain shall be recognized only to the extent that the amount realized upon such conversion exceeds the cost of such other property.

Section 1033(g) of the Code provides, in part, that if real property (not including stock in trade or other property held primarily for sale) held for productive use in trade or business or for investment is (as the result of its seizure, requisition, or condemnation, or threat or imminence thereof) compulsorily or involuntarily converted after December 31, 1957, property of a like kind to be held either for productive use in trade or business or for investment shall be treated as property similar or related in service or use to the property so converted.

Section 1.1033(g)–1 of the Income Tax Regulations provides, in part, that, for purposes of applying section 1033 of the Code to the disposition of real property held for productive use in trade or business or for investment, the principles of section 1.1031(a)–1 of the regulations are to be considered in determining whether the replacement property is of a like kind.

Section 1.1031(a)–1 of the regulations provides, in part, that the words "like kind" have reference to the nature or character of the property and not to its grade or quality. The section further states:

(b) * * * One kind or class of property may not, * * * be exchanged for property of a different kind or class. The fact that any real estate involved is improved or unimproved is not material, for that fact relates only to the grade or quality of the property and not to its kind or class. * * *

(c) No gain or loss is recognized if * * * (2) a taxpayer who is not a dealer in real estate exchanges city real estate for a ranch or farm, or exchanges a leasehold of a fee with 30 years or more to run for real estate, or exchanges improved real estate for unimproved real estate * * *.

The effect of section 1033(g) of the Code is to extend the nonrecognition-of-gains benefits of section 1033(a) of the Code to a taxpayer who acquires property of a like kind to real property converted, but not necessarily similar or related in service or use to it.

In considering the "like kind" test, although the term "real estate" is often used to embrace land and improvements thereon, land and improvements are by nature not alike merely because one term is used to describe both. Land is not of the same nature or character as a building, or a storm drain, or a water system, or a road.

Applying the foregoing to the facts in the instant case, the building constructed on land already owned does not qualify as replacement property under section 1033(g) of the Code as being of a like kind to the land involuntarily converted. Nor do the storm drains, water systems and roads constructed on land already owned qualify as replacement property under section 1033(g) as being of a like kind to the land involuntarily converted. However, see Revenue Ruling 67–254, page 269, this Bulletin, for a situation where improvements constructed on land already owned qualify as replacement property under section 1033(a) (3) (A) of the Code.

Accordingly, the investment of the proceeds from an involuntary conversion of land held for investment purposes, in the construction of an office building to be held for investment purposes upon land already owned by the taxpayer, does not qualify as a "like kind" replacement of the converted property within the meaning of section 1033(g) of the Code.

Also, the investment of the proceeds from an involuntary conversion of unimproved rural land in the installation of storm drains, water systems and roads on other unimproved rural land already owned by the taxpayer, does not qualify as a "like kind" replacement of the converted property within the meaning of section 1033(g) of the Code.

Revenue Ruling 55–749, C.B. 1955–2, 295; I.T. 4093, C.B. 1952–2, 130; and Commissioner v. Kate J. Crichton, 122 F.2d 181 (1941), affirming 42 B.T.A. 490 (1940), acquiescence, C.B. 1952–1, 2, are distinguishable because they do not involve land improvements. These rulings and the case hold that mineral interests and water rights are interests in real property and as such are of the same nature or character as fee interests in land.

REVENUE RULING 71–41

1971–4 Int.Rev.Bull. 16.

Advice has been requested whether the investment of condemnation proceeds, under the circumstances set forth below, qualifies for the nonrecognition of gain provisions of section 1033 of the Internal Revenue Code of 1954.

The taxpayer, an individual, owned a warehouse which he rented to third parties. The warehouse and the land upon which it was located were condemned by the State and a gain was realized by the taxpayer on the condemnation. The condemnation proceeds were used by the taxpayer to erect a gas station on other land already owned by the taxpayer. The taxpayer rented the gas station to an oil company.

Section 1033(a) of the Code provides, in part, that if property is, as a result of condemnation, compulsorily or involuntarily converted into money and the taxpayer, during the period specified, purchases other property *similar or related in service or use* to the property so converted, at the election of the taxpayer the gain shall be recognized only to the extent that the amount realized upon such conversion exceeds the cost of the replacement property.

Section 1033(g) * of the Code provides, in part, as follows:

(1) Special rule—For purposes of subsection (a), if real property * * * held for productive use in trade or business or for investment is * * * compulsorily or involuntarily converted, property of a *like kind* to be held either for productive use in a trade or business or for investment *shall be treated* as property similar or related in service or use to the property so converted.

The taxpayer in the instant case did not qualify for the special rule under section 1033(g) of the Code as the replacement property (gas station) and the property converted (land and warehouse) were not properties of a "like kind." The specific question is whether the taxpayer can qualify for treatment under section 1033(a) even though he fails to qualify under section 1033(g) of the Code.

Revenue Ruling 64–237, C.B. 1964–2, 319, in applying section 1033(a) of the Code, states that in considering whether replacement property acquired by an investor for the purpose of leasing is similar in service or use to the converted property, attention will be directed primarily to the similarity in the relationship of the service or uses which the original and replacement properties have to the taxpayer-owner. In applying this test a determination will be made whether the properties are of a similar service to the taxpayer, the nature of the business risks connected with the properties, and what such properties demand of the taxpayer in the way of management, services, and relations to his tenants.

With respect to the property converted by the State, the taxpayer in the instant case was an investor for the production of rental income. As to the property acquired as replacement, the taxpayer is also an investor for the production of rental income. The mere fact that the taxpayer did not qualify under section 1033(g) of the Code does not preclude the taxpayer from the nonrecognition of gain provisions of section 1033 of the Code if the taxpayer is able to demonstrate that

---

* See comments at page 914, supra, on
redesignation of I.R.C. § 1033(g) as
§ 1033(f). Ed.

the replacement property is actually similar or related in service or use to the property converted within the meaning of section 1033(a) of the Code.

Accordingly, under the facts of the instant case, it is held that the gas station is property similar or related in service or use within the meaning of section 1033(a) of the Code. The taxpayer at his election will recognize gain upon the involuntarily converted property only to the extent that the amount realized upon such conversion exceeds the cost of the replacement property, provided, the actual replacement took place within the period of time prescribed by section 1033(a) (3) (B) of the Code.

REVENUE RULING 76–319

1976–34 Int.Rev.Bull. 9.

Advice has been requested whether, under the circumstances described below, property qualifies as replacement property for purposes of section 1033 of the Internal Revenue Code of 1954.

The taxpayer, a domestic corporation, was engaged in the operation of a recreational bowling center prior to the center's complete destruction by fire on June 30, 1974. The bowling center had consisted of bowling alleys, together with a lounge area and a bar. The center was fully insured against loss by fire. As a result of such insurance coverage the taxpayer received insurance proceeds in compensation for the destruction of the bowling center in an amount that exceeded the taxpayer's basis in the property. On its Federal income tax return for 1974, the taxpayer elected to defer recognition of the gain under the provisions of section 1033 of the Code.

Within the period specified in section 1033(a) (3) (B) of the Code, the taxpayer invested the insurance proceeds in a new recreational billiard center. In addition to billiard tables, this center includes a lounge area, and a bar.

Section 1033(a) of the Code provides, in part, that if property (as a result of its destruction in whole or in part) is involuntarily converted into money, the gain shall be recognized except as provided in section 1033(a) (3) (A).* Section 1033(a) (3) (A) provides, in part, that if the taxpayer during the period specified purchases other property similar or related in service or use to the property so converted, at the election of the taxpayer the gain shall be recognized only to the extent that the amount realized on the conversion exceeds the cost of such other property.

---

* See comments at page 914, supra, on redesignation of parts of I.R.C. § 1033. Ed.

The specific question is whether the recreational billiard center (replacement property) is "similar or related in service or use" to the recreational bowling center (involuntarily converted property) within the meaning of section 1033(a) of the Code.

Rev.Rul. 64–237, 1964–2 C.B. 319, states that, with respect to an owner-user, property is not considered similar or related in service or use to the converted property unless the physical characteristics and end uses of the converted and replacement properties are closely similar.

In the instant case, the involuntarily converted property was a bowling center that consisted of bowling alleys together with a lounge area and a bar. The replacement property consists of a billiards center that included billiard tables, a lounge area, and a bar. The physical characteristics of the replacement property are not closely similar to those of the converted property since bowling alleys and bowling equipment are not closely similar to billiard tables and billiard equipment.

Accordingly, in the instant case, the billiard center is not similar or related in service or use to the bowling center within the meaning of section 1033(a) (3) (A) of the Code. Therefore the billiard center does not qualify as replacement property for purposes of section 1033.

PROBLEMS

1. T was in the laundry and dry cleaning business. In 1976 a fire completely destroyed the automatic dry cleaning equipment in his plant. Several years earlier the equipment in his plant had cost him $40,000 and, since its acquisition, T had properly claimed straight-line depreciation on the equipment in the amount of $16,000. After the fire and within 1976, T received $28,000 as insurance covering the loss.

   (a) If the dry cleaning end of the business has been unprofitable and T invests the $28,000 in securities, rather than replacing the equipment, what will be the tax consequences?

   (b) If the capacity of the old equipment was in excess of T's needs and T replaces the old with smaller new equipment at a cost of $26,000

      (1) What will be the immediate tax consequences to T?

      (2) What will be T's basis for the purpose of claiming depreciation on the new equipment?

      (3) What would be the tax consequences to T if he made a quick change of plans and sold the newly acquired equipment for $26,000 before any depreciation became allowable with respect to it?

2. Would the court have reached the same result in *Harry G. Masser* if a single piece of business property had been damaged and,

even though the property could still have been used in the business, the owner of the property "in the exercise of good business judgment" decided, nevertheless, to sell it, and used the sale and insurance proceeds to purchase a piece of replacement property? See C. G. Willis, Inc., 41 T.C. 468 (1964), aff'd per curiam, 342 F.2d 996 (3rd. Cir. 1965).

3. The *Clifton Investment* case reflects a common problem regarding the scope of the term "similar or related in service or use." But suppose in *Clifton Investment*, the taxpayer had bought a hotel rather than stock in a hotel corporation. Would the result in the case be different?

4. Rev.Rul. 70–399, 1970–2 C.B. 164, deals with the repurchase of a new hotel with the insurance proceeds received when an old hotel was destroyed by fire. Despite the intrinsic identity of the properties, the case is placed outside the protective covering of § 1033. The owner had leased the old hotel to others to operate but undertook to operate the new hotel himself. Thus the new property was not similar or related in service or use. Why would § 1033(f) be of no help here?

5. The two questions above are concerned with some of the differences in the definition of "like kind" under §§ 1031 and 1033(f) and "similar or related in service or use" under § 1033(a). In enacting § 1033(g) [now § 1033(f)] the Senate Finance Committee Report stated:

"Both in the case of property involuntarily converted and in the case of the exchange of property held for productive use in trade or business or for investment, gain is not recognized because of the continuity of the investment. Your committee sees no reason why substantially similar rules should not be followed in determining what constitutes a continuity of investment in these two types of situations where there is a condemnation of real property. Moreover, it appears particularly unfortunate that present law requires a closer identity of the destroyed and converted property where the exchange is beyond the control of the taxpayer than that which is applied in the case of the voluntary exchange of business property.

"As a result your committee has added a new subsection to the involuntary conversion (sec. 1033) provision of present law. In this new subsection it has added the 'like kind' test of the voluntary exchange of business property rule of present law as an alternative in the case of involuntary conversions for the rule requiring the substitution of property 'similar or related in service or use.' The 'like kind' rule in this case applies, however, only in the case of real property, does not include inventory or property held primarily for sale, and is limited to seizures, requisitions, condemnations, or the threat of imminence thereof. Nor does it apply in the case of the purchase of stock in acquiring control of a corporation. * * *" Sen.Fin.Comm.Rep. No. 1893, 85th Cong., 2d Sess. (1958), 1958–3 C.B. 922, 993–4.

Is the restriction of § 1033(f) to condemnations of real property too narrow? Should the two tests of §§ 1031 and 1033 be made alternatives under both sections?

D. SALE OF A PRINCIPAL RESIDENCE *

Internal Revenue Code: Sections 121(a) through (c), (d)(7); 1034(a) through (e), (j); 1223(7).
Regulations: Sections 1.121–2(a); 1.1034–1(a), (b), (c)(3) and (4).

EXCERPT FROM HOUSE REPORT NO. 586

82d Cong., 1st Sess. (1951).
1951–2 C.B. 357, 377–378.

Section 303 of this bill amends the present provisions relating to a gain on the sale of a taxpayer's principal residence so as to eliminate a hardship under existing law which provides that when a personal residence is sold at a gain the difference between its adjusted basis and the sale price is taxed as a capital gain. The hardship is accentuated when the transactions are necessitated by such facts as an increase in the size of the family or a change in the place of the taxpayer's employment. In these situations the transaction partakes of the nature of an involuntary conversion. Cases of this type are particularly numerous in periods of rapid change such as mobilization or reconversion. For this reason the need for remedial action at the present time is urgent.

Section 303 of this bill provides that when the sale of the taxpayer's principal residence is followed within a period of 1 year by the purchase of a substitute, or when the substitute is purchased within a year prior to the sale of the taxpayer's principal residence, gain shall be recognized only to the extent that the selling price of the old residence exceeds the cost of the new one. Thus, if a dwelling purchased in 1940 for $10,000 is sold in 1951 for $15,000, there would ordinarily be a taxable gain of $5,000 under existing law. Under this bill no portion of the gain would be taxable provided a substitute "principal residence" is purchased by the taxpayer within the stated period of time for a price of $15,000 or more. If the replacement cost is less than $15,000, say $14,000, the amount taxable as gain will be $1,000.

This special treatment is not limited to the "involuntary conversion" type of case, where the taxpayer is forced to sell his home be-

---

* See Margolis, "Tax-Free Sales and Exchanges of Residences," 17 U.S.C. Tax Inst. 483 (1965).

cause the place of his employment is changed. While the need for relief is especially clear in such cases, an attempt to confine the provision to them would increase the task of administration very much.

The adjusted basis of the new residence will be reduced by the amount of gain not recognized upon the sale of the old residence. Thus, if the replacement is purchased for $19,000, the old residence cost $10,000 and was sold for $15,000, the adjusted basis of the new residence will be $19,000 minus $5,000 or $14,000. This is equal to the cost of the old residence plus the additional funds invested at the time the new residence is purchased. If the second residence had been purchased for $14,000, so that $1,000 of gain on the sale of the old residence would be recognized, its basis would be $14,000 minus $4,000, or $10,000.

For the purpose of qualifying a gain as a long-term capital gain the holding period of the residence acquired as a replacement in a set of transactions which qualify under the terms of this section of the bill will be the combined period of ownership of the successive principal residences of the taxpayer.

* * *

The taxpayer is not required to have actually been occupying his old residence on the date of its sale. Relief will be available even though the taxpayer moved into his new residence and rented the old one temporarily before its sale. Similarly, he may obtain relief even though he rents out his new residence temporarily before occupying it.

The special treatment provided under this section of the bill can be availed of only with respect to one sale or exchange per year, except when the taxpayer's new residence is involuntarily converted. . . .

Section 303 of this bill applies to cases where one residence is exchanged for another, where a replacement residence is constructed by the taxpayer rather than purchased, and where the replacement is a residence which had to be reconstructed in order to permit its occupancy by the taxpayer. However, in cases where the replacement is built or reconstructed, only so much of the cost is counted as an offset against the selling price of his old residence as is properly chargeable against capital account within a period beginning 1 year prior to date of the sale of the old residence and ending 1 year after such date. [The ending periods have been extended to 18 months and 2 years. § 1034(a) and (c) (5) Ed.]

The ownership of stock in a cooperative apartment corporation will be treated as the equivalent of ownership of a residence, provided the purchaser or seller of such stock uses the apartment which it entitles him to occupy as his principal residence.

Regulations will be issued under which the taxpayer and his spouse acting singly or jointly may obtain the benefits of section 303 even though the spouse who sold the old residence was not the same as the one who purchased the new one, or the rights of the spouses in the new residence are not distributed in the same manner as their rights in the old residence. These regulations will apply only if the spouses consent to their application and both old and new residence are used by the taxpayer and his spouse as their principal residence.

Where the taxpayer's residence is part of a property also used for business purposes, as in the case of an apartment over a store building or a home on a farm, and the entire property is sold, the provisions of section 303 will apply only to that part of the property used as a residence, including the environs and outbuildings relating to the dwelling but not to those relating to the business operations.

These provisions apply to a trailer or houseboat if it is actually used as the taxpayer's principal residence.

In order to protect the Government in cases where there is an unreported taxable gain on the sale of the taxpayer's residence, either because he did not carry out his intention to buy a new residence, or because some of the technical requirements were not met, the period for the assessment of a deficiency is extended to 3 years after the taxpayer has notified the Commissioner either that he has purchased a new residence, or that he has not acquired or does not intend to acquire a new residence within the prescribed period of time.

NOTE

The Tax Reduction Act of 1975 increased the replacement period with respect to a principal residence sold after December 31, 1974.[1] In the case of a purchased residence the new period begins eighteen months prior to the sale of the old residence and ends eighteen months thereafter.[2] § 1034(a). If the new residence is constructed the enlarged period is extended to two years following the date the former principal residence is sold, if construction begins within eighteen months.[3] § 1034(c)(5).

The statute expressly requires that both the former residence and the new residence qualify as the taxpayer's principal residence. Thus if a taxpayer resides with his family in a New York City apartment during the week, using a country house only on weekends, the sale of the old, followed by the purchase of another country house will not meet the test of the statute. This is so because the apartment

----

1. P.L. 94–12, § 207(a), 1975–1 C.B. 545, 549.

2. The statutory period cannot be extended. See e. g., Rev.Rul. 75–438, 1975–1 C.B. 334; Rev.Rul. 74–411, 1974–2 C.B. 270.

3. If the taxpayer enters into a contract to purchase a new residence which is under construction by the seller, his acquisition is considered to be by *purchase*. Accordingly the two year construction rule does not apply. Rev.Rul. 57–234, 1957–1 C.B. 263; Rev. Rul. 76–216, 1976–1 C.B. 310. As in the case of a purchased residence, the statutory time period for constructing and using the new residence as a principal residence cannot be enlarged or extended.

is considered the principal residence.[4]   In other circumstances, if both the former residence and new residence otherwise qualify as the principal residence, the House Report and Regulations expressly sanction temporary rental of either dwelling.[5]   Therefore, if at the time the owner moves out, the former dwelling qualifies as the principal residence, it remains qualified even though it is temporarily rented.   In Robert G. Clapham,[6] the taxpayer rented his former residence for three years prior to selling it.   The Tax Court, holding for the taxpayer, concluded that the former residence qualified as the principal residence.   "* * * [The] dominant motive was to sell the property at the earliest possible date rather than to hold the property for the realization of rental income.   Under the facts and circumstances here present, the lease was therefore for a temporary period contemplated by the legislative history and the regulations, * * *."[7]   The question whether a residence is the principal residence is a fact issue.   If, in contrast to the facts in Clapham,[8] the taxpayer converts a residence to income-producing property, making every effort to rent with little or no attempt to sell, the dwelling will no longer qualify as the principal residence at the time it is eventually sold.   In these circumstances, § 1034 will not apply.   This was the result in Richard T. Houlette.[9]   In that case, the taxpayer moved out of his then principal residence.   The dwelling was leased on five separate occasions for over six years.   Two of the leases were for two year periods and sales efforts were minimal.

Quantitatively, a principal residence can include surrounding vast acreage, so long as it is not used for profit.[10]

Although the current statute extends the requisite time periods, the new residence must be *used* as the taxpayer's principal residence within the time period allotted by the statute.   Consider how the taxpayer would have fared in the *Sheahan* case, following this note, if the current statute had been in effect.

UNITED STATES v. SHEAHAN

United States Court of Appeals, Fifth Circuit, 1963.
323 F.2d 383.

WISDOM, CIRCUIT JUDGE.   This is an appeal by the United States from a judgment of the district court granting the taxpayers' claim for a refund based on Section 1034 of the Internal Revenue Code of

---

4. William C. Stolk, 40 T.C. 345 (1963), aff'd. per curiam 326 F.2d 760 (2d Cir. 1964).

5. House Report No. 586, 82d Cong., 1st Sess. (1951), p. 929, supra; Reg. § 1.1034–1(c)(3).

6. 63 T.C. 505 (1975).

7. Id. at 512.

8. Note 6, supra.

9. 48 T.C. 350 (1967).

10. See e. g., Clayburn M. Bennett v. U. S., 61–2 U.S.T.C. ¶ 9697 (D.C.No. Ga.1961).

1954. This section allows a taxpayer, under certain conditions, to make a tax free sale of his "principal residence", if within a year he buys and "uses" another principal residence. The question for decision is whether the evidence is sufficient to sustain the jury's verdict that the taxpayers "used" their newly purchased property as their "principal residence" within one year from the date of the sale of their old residence.

The case was tried to the court and a jury. After the jury returned its verdict in favor of the taxpayers, the Government moved for a judgment notwithstanding the verdict and, in the alternative for a new trial. The district court denied the motions and granted judgment in favor of the taxpayers. We reverse.

[After quoting I.R.C. § 1034(a), the opinion continues:] [1]

As the Treasury Regulations, Sec. 1.1034–1(c) (3), properly state: "Whether or not property is used by the taxpayer as his residence, and whether or not property is used by the taxpayer as his principal residence (in the case of a taxpayer using more than one property as a residence), depends upon all the facts and circumstances in each case, including the good faith of the taxpayer." The essential facts here are virtually undisputed.

On May 8, 1957, the taxpayers, Dr. and Mrs. Edwin L. Sheahan, sold their home in St. Louis County, Missouri, for $270,000 in anticipation of Dr. Sheahan's imminent reitrement from his post as a civilian physician for the Department of the Army. The Sheahans planned to buy a home in Atlanta, Georgia, and live with their daughter and her family. The Army, however, notified Dr. Sheahan that he would be retained in his position for a year. These post-retirement appointments are technically for a year but in practice frequently terminate when a suitable replacement is found. The Sheahans therefore continued in search of a new principal residence in Atlanta in order to move there promptly following Dr. Sheahan's release by the Army. During this time they resided with a second daughter in Godfrey, Illinois. Mrs. Sheahan made several trips to Atlanta in search of a suitable new home, and on March 31, 1958, the taxpayers entered into a contract to purchase a partially completed house at 1265 Swims Valley Drive, Atlanta.

The new house was to be completed and the agreement closed on May 1, 1958, but bad weather caused several delays, and the final contract of sale was not signed until May 8, 1958, precisely one year after the sale of the taxpayers' St. Louis home. At that time Dr. Sheahan had not seen the house. Mrs. Sheahan, who had spent two weeks in Atlanta in March or April after the taxpayers had definitely decided to purchase the house at 1265 Swims Valley Drive, had never actually lived there.

1. [Reg. § 1.1034–1(c) (3) is omitted. Ed.]

The Sheahan's daughter, Mrs. D. T. Lauderdale, and her husband were planning to move into the new house with her parents. Mrs. Lauderdale had done work around the house and supervised some of the construction before May 8. She testified:

"I spent a good bit of time there, checking on the construction, the builders, they didn't seem to feel they had much responsibility for supervising and I found that I had to, so I spent a good many days there, supervising and I would go over the workmen who were supposed to be there, and they wouldn't be there—I would say I spent about four—three to four days a week over there; not all the time, but a good part of the day from—all through April and May, and particularly there in—at the end."

During this period Mrs. Lauderdale did some painting around the house, planted shrubbery, and put up a mailbox with both her husband's and her father's names on it. She also moved in boxes of clothing and other articles belonging to her parents which had been stored in Atlanta after they sold their home in Missouri. She frequently would take a lunch with her and eat in the house.

No one actually slept in the house, however, until May 10, the date when the moving van brought the large pieces of furniture. The Lauderdale family moved in at that time. Mrs. Sheahan did not spend any time in the house until that summer, and although Dr. Sheahan spent two weeks there in June, he did not move in permanently until April 1959. There was no question, however, but that as early as March, 1958, the Sheahans intended to make the new house in Atlanta their principal place of residence and to live there with their daughter and her family.

The taxpayers argue that *intent* to use the new house as the taxpayers' principal residence, coupled with a subsequent use of the house as the principal residence, satisfy the statute. It is true that the good faith of the taxpayer is a circumstance to be weighed, and it may be the decisive factor in a close case in determining whether one of two houses is the *principal* residence, or whether the house is a *residence*, but there must be supporting facts to show that the taxpayer *used* the new property as his principal residence.

In a tax statute, as in any other statute, and whether the statutory purpose is remedial or punitive, the words of the statute must be given their ordinary meaning and they must be construed in harmony with the statute as an organic whole. Lewyt Corporation v. Commissioner, 1955, 349 U.S. 237, 75 S.Ct. 736, 99 L.Ed. 1029. See also Old Colony R. Company v. Commissioner, 1932, 284 U.S. 552, 52 S.Ct. 211, 76 L.Ed. 484; Helvering v. San Joaquin Fruit & Investment Co., 1936, 297 U.S. 496, 56 S.Ct. 569, 80 L.Ed. 824; Helvering v. William Flaccus Oak Leather Co., 1941, 313 U.S. 247, 61 S.Ct. 878, 85 L.Ed. 1310.

In William C. Stolk, 40 T.C. 345, (1963) the Tax Court discussed the meaning of "use", "principal", and "residence" as these terms are employed in Section 1034:

"The ordinary meaning of 'use', 'principal', and 'residence' are clear and well understood, but if dictionary definitions are helpful in recalling the common meanings (see Webster's Unabridged Third New International Dictionary), use (the verb) means a 'putting to service of a thing'; principal means 'chief or main'; and residence means 'the place where one actually lives or has his home.' The context in which 'used' occurs, referring to the 'old residence', connects 'used' with the taxpayers' 'principal residence', thereby making it clear that the property which is sold shall be utilized as the principal residence."

Both the wording and the legislative history of Section 1034 indicate that there must be some actual use, or physical occupancy of the new house in order to satisfy the requirements of the provision. Thus, under the terms of the statute the new property must be "purchased *and used* by the taxpayer as his principal residence" within one year of the sale of the old residence. The absence of any words such as "intended", "treated", or "regarded" and the choice of the word "used" is some evidence that in framing Section 1034 Congress focused on the physical or objective aspects of occupancy rather than on the subjective aspects. See E. C. Schroeder Co. v. Clifton, 10 Cir., 1946, 153 F.2d 385, 390; cert. den'd, 328 U.S. 858, 66 S.Ct. 1351, 90 L.Ed. 1629; reh. den'd, 329 U.S. 821, 67 S.Ct. 33, 91 L.Ed. 699. A further indication that "use" means "occupancy" is given in the Senate hearings on an amendment allowing the taxpayer an additional six months in which to use a house which he has begun constructing within a year of the sale of the old one.[2] The Senate Report states:

"However, under the House bill, where a replacement residence is constructed by the taxpayer, he must occupy the new residence within one year after sale of his old residence. This is the same rule which both your committee's bill and the House bill apply in the case of the purchase of a new residence. However, in the case of new construction *the requirement of occupancy within one year* appears to your committee not to be realistic, particularly during the present period of material and labor shortages." S.Rep.No.781, 82d Cong., 1st Sess. p. 35; 1951–2 Cum.Bull. 458, 583. (Emphasis added.)

In other words, the taxpayer must "occupy" the new house; he must move in and live in the house before the lapse of twelve months after

---

2. [After quoting I.R.C. § 1034(c) (5), this note continues.]

The taxpayers do not claim to be entitled to the 18 month provisions of section 1034(c) (5), because they concede that it is undisputed that the new residence at 1265 Swims Valley Drive, Atlanta, was habitable prior to May 8, 1958, the date on which the final contract of sale was signed.

the sale of the old one. This sort of occupancy—actual or physical occupancy—can be accomplished only when the house is completed.[3]

As far as we find, the particular problem here involved—whether a new house, eventually used as a principal residence, was so used within the statutory period—has been litigated only once before. In John F. Bayley, 35 T.C. 288 (1960) the taxpayer was building a new home, and when it became clear that it would not be finished by October 15, 1955, the date the statutory period expired, he wrote the District Director of Internal Revenue requesting an extension. He was informed that this would be impossible; therefore, on October 14 he moved some of his furniture into an upstairs room which had just been walled off. The taxpayer continued to live elsewhere for two more months before he moved into the new house with the rest of his furniture. Although recognizing the good faith of the taxpayer and his unquestioned intent to use the new house as his principal residence, the Tax Court, as a matter of law, disallowed the nonrecognition of gain on the sale of his old residence, stating:

"The facts of the instant case do not, in our opinion, establish that the petitioners *physically occupied or lived in the new residence on or before* October 15, 1955, the date when the statutory 18-month period expired. Indeed the rather extensive state of incompletion of the new residence—no water or sewerage connections, no appliances in the kitchen, and lights and flooring only in minimal quantities—effectively prevented petitioners from living in the new residence until long after October 15, 1955. Petitioner John Bayley conceded on cross-examination that *they did not sleep in the new residence* until December 28, 1955. Actually, from October 15 to November 15, petitioners continued to live in the house which they had been renting; and from November 15 until December 28, they made their home with various friends. In such circumstances, we feel impelled to hold that within the specified 18-month period, the new residence was not used by the petitioners as their principal residence, within the meaning of the statute. * * * "We fully recognize the equity of the petitioners' position on this issue, for they undoubtedly intended and diligently attempted to meet the statutory requirements for nonrecognition of the gain from the sale of their own residence. But Congress, for reasons satisfactory to it, has established a fixed eighteen-month period within which such requirements must be met; and we feel impelled to conclude that petitioners did not meet these requirements within that fixed period." (Emphasis added.) 35 T.C. at p. 296, 297.

3. See also the report of the House Ways & Means Committee, accompanying the bills that became the Internal Revenue Code of 1954 (H.Rep. No. 1337, 83d Cong., 2d Sess., pp. 79, A268–269 (3 U.S.C. Cong. & Adm. News (1954) 4017) and the report of Senate Finance Committee on the same bills (S.Rep. No. 1622, 83d Cong., 2d Sess., pp. 109, 427 (3 U.S.C. Cong. & Adm.News (1954) 4621).

Ralph L. Trisko, 29 T.C. 515 (1957) does not compel a different conclusion. There the issue was whether the taxpayer's old house retained its status as his principal place of residence while it was rented during his absence from the country. When such rental takes place it is necessary to examine all the facts and circumstances, "including the *bona fides* of the taxpayer" to determine whether this use was intended "in contradistinction to property used in trade or business", that is, as a residence. The Tax Court found only that the rental was a use "in contradistinction", limiting its decision strictly to the facts before it. That case is not authority for the proposition that intent without physical occupancy is sufficient to make a newly acquired house one's principal place of residence.

The taxpayers, however, urge that even if intent by itself is not enough, there was nonetheless sufficient use of the new house by Mrs. Lauderdale on their behalf to bring them within the terms of the statute. They point to the fact that the Sheahans and Lauderdales planned to live in the house at Atlanta as one family group and that they subsequently did so. Thus Mrs. Lauderdale was "using" the house on behalf of the entire family unit when she supervised the builders, ate lunches there, planted shrubbery, put up a mailbox with the Sheahan's name on it, and moved in boxes of the Sheahan's belongings.

There are two difficulties with this argument. First, the Sheahans and Lauderdales did not in fact constitute a single family unit until April 1959, when Dr. Sheahan moved permanently to Atlanta. The taxpayers were not in the position of, for example, a student who, although living temporarily at a college or university, maintains his place of residence with his family. The Sheahans and Lauderdales had functioned as two autonomous family groups, maintaining separate residences before the move to Atlanta, and it is difficult to see how Mrs. Lauderdale's activities can be attributed to the Sheahans, who at that time had been living with another daughter in Godfrey, Illinois, for almost a year.

In Biltmore Homes, Inc. v. Commissioner, 4 Cir., 1961, 288 F.2d 336, a similar argument was made. There the taxpayer had lived with his parents until his marriage in September 1949. His parents continued living in the old residence, which the taxpayer sold to his mother in 1951. Two days before this sale, the taxpayer and his wife moved from a rented house into a new one which they had recently purchased at a price in excess of that which the taxpayer's mother had paid for the old home. The taxpayer sought to avoid recognition of gain on the old home by contending that his parents' home was his principal place of residence until he and his wife moved into their new house. The Fourth Circuit rejected this argument, pointing out that after the taxpayer married and moved out of his parents' home, the house which he and his wife rented was his principal place of residence. In William H. Evans, 21 T.C.M. 339 (1962) the taxpayer had owned and maintained a residence in Neenah, Wisconsin, he and his mother residing there until 1952, when he moved to Milwaukee, ninety miles distant, to practice law. In Milwaukee he lived in his sister's home. In 1956 he sold the old house and bought a new one in which the mother lived until 1960. The taxpayer purchased several appliances for the new house, made repairs from 1956 to the date of trial, and paid the taxes and insurance. The court pointed out that the taxpayer had never stayed at the new Neenah house except on some weekends and ruled that this was no evidence at all that that house had ever been used as his principal residence within the meaning of Section 1034.

Second, even if Mrs. Lauderdale's activities other than putting up the mailbox and moving in boxes of the taxpayers' belongings could enure to the Sheahans' benefit, this token "use" of the house before May 8 was insufficient to satisfy the statutory requirements of the statute. Thus, in John F. Bayley, 35 T.C. 288 (1960), the Tax Court held that the taxpayer's activities in moving furniture into one room of a partially completed house did not constitute the required use. It stated:

"We believe that the 'use' of the new residence, as contemplated by Congress in the enactment of section 1034, is physical occupancy, i. e., that the owners must live therein. * * * The facts of the instant case do not, in our opinion, establish that the petitioners physically occupied or lived in the new residence on or before October 15, 1955, the date when the statutory eighteen month period expired. Indeed, the rather extensive state of incompletion of the new residence—no water or sewerage connections, no appliances in the kitchen, and lights and flooring only in minimal quantities—effectively prevented petitioners from living in the new residence until long after October 15, 1955."

In William C. Stolk, 40 T.C. 345, (1963) the Tax Court had before it both the question whether the old property was used as the taxpayer's principal residence and also the question whether the new property was used as the principal residence. The Court held that

"With respect to each property, petitioner's *use* thereof is determinative. His *use* must be equated with the statutory requirement of 'principal residence.' * * * Petitioner's occupancy and use of the Eden Farm residence during weekends and holidays did not constitute using that residence as his principal residence within a period of one year after the sale of the Chappaqua property. * * * In order to meet the prescribed requirement, the taxpayer must prove that the new property was his *principal* residence. It is not enough to establish that he occupied and used the new property as a residence. It is true that petitioner moved his chief household furnishings into the main dwelling house at Eden Farm within three months after it was purchased; that the main dwelling there was in condition to be lived in; and that petitioner and his wife lived there during weekends and holidays in 1955 and 1956, within the one-year post-sale period. But such use and occupancy was not sufficient to constitute Eden Farm as petitioner's principal residence during the one-year period involved."

On May 8, 1958, the day which terminated the statutory period of one year following the sale of the old residence, the Atlanta house was an empty shell, barren of furniture and unusable as a residence, principal or otherwise. On March 8, 1958, almost all of the taxpayers' clothes, furniture, and personal belongings were either in storage or being used by them in Godfrey, Illinois. At no time during the statutory period had Dr. Sheahan ever seen the house in Atlanta which he was allegedly using as his principal residence. And Mrs. Sheahan had done no more than inspect it. It is true that there is no mechanical test for determining a taxpayer's principal place of residence and that it depends upon all the facts and circumstances of the particular situation. There must, however, be some approach to actual occupancy; the taxpayer must, in effect, "move in." Nothing of the sort occurred here.

We hold that the trial judge erred in not directing a verdict and in not granting the appellant's motion for judgment notwithstanding the verdict. The Judgment of the lower court is Reversed with directions that the judgment be entered in favor of the United States.

EXCERPT FROM SENATE FINANCE COMMITTEE REPORT NO. 830

88th Congress, 2d Session (1964).
1964-1 (Part 2) C.B. 505, 555-557.

Exclusion for gain on the sale of a residence by an individual age 65 or over (sec. 206 of the bill, sec. 121 of the code)

(a) *Present law.*—Under present law (sec. 1034) where an individual sells his old residence and, within a year [now 18 months. Ed.] of that sale, purchases a new residence (or within 18 months [now 2 years. Ed.] thereafter builds a new residence), the gain on the sale of the old residence is not recognized to the extent that it, plus the cost or other basis of the old residence, is invested in the new residence. This postponement of the taxation of the gain is available only where the new residence is purchased or built within the time specified.

(b) *General reasons for the provisions.*—While present law generally provides adequately for the younger individual who is for one reason or another changing residences, it does not do so for the elderly person whose family has grown and who no longer has need for the family homestead. Such an individual may desire to purchase a less expensive home or move to an apartment or to a rental property at another location. He may also require some or all of the funds obtained from the sale of the old residence to meet his and his wife's living expenses. Nevertheless, under present law, such an individual must tie up all of his investment from the old residence in a new residence, if he is to avoid taxation on any of the gain which may be involved.

Your committee agrees with the House that this is an undesirable burden on our elderly taxpayers.

(c) General explanation.—For the reasons given above, the bill provides an exclusion from gross income for a limited amount of gain received from the sale or exchange of a personal residence in the case of taxpayers who have reached age 65 before the sale or exchange occurs. To be eligible for this treatment, they must have owned and used the property involved as their principal residence for 5 out of the last 8 years before the sale or exchange.

(c) (i) Limitations.—In this provision the primary concern is with the average and smaller homestead selling for $20,000 or less. For that reason, the application of this section is limited so that a full exclusion is provided only for the gain attributable to the first $20,000 [Increased in 1976, as noted below. Ed.] of the sales price.[1] Where the sale price of the residence does not exceed $20,000, the entire gain is excluded from income for tax purposes. Where the sale price exceeds $20,000, a proportion of the gain is excluded. The proportion excluded is in the ratio of $20,000 to the actual sale price; for example, if a residence is sold for $60,000 and the gain is $10,000, then the portion of this $10,000 gain which will not be taxable is determined as follows:

Actual sale price $60,000
Ratio of $20,000 to sale price
($20,000/$60,000) .... ⅓
Proportion of $10,000 gain to be excluded from taxable income (⅓ of $10,000) $3,333.33
Remaining gain subject to tax $6,666.67

To prevent taxpayers over age 65 from reusing this section and obtaining numerous exclusions for gains on personal residences, the bill provides that this exclusion is available to a taxpayer and his spouse only once in their lifetimes.

(c) (ii) Other rules.—Since a taxpayer and his spouse may claim the exemption under this provision only once in their lifetimes, the bill provides that the exclusion is elective and may be made or revoked at any time before the expiration of the period for making a claim for credit or refund of tax, generally about 3 years after the year of the sale or exchange. It also was necessary to provide a number of other

1. Actually the determination is made on the basis of adjusted sales price which as provided elsewhere in the code is the gross sales price less any so-called fix-up expenses incurred in selling the property. In this regard, see sec. 1034(b) (1).

special rules for the application of this provision.   [Those special rules are found in § 121(d).   Ed.]

NOTE

For taxable years beginning after December 31, 1976, the adjusted sales price exclusion in § 121(b) (1) is increased from $20,000 to $35,000.   The increase, effected by T.R.A.1976, is an obvious effort to mitigate the rigors of inflation.

PROBLEMS

1.   In 1977 for $70,000 (the "adjusted sales price") Homeowner sold property which he had used as his principal residence for 20 years.   His adjusted basis for the residence was $40,000.   In the same year he acquired and occupied a new condominium which cost him $54,000 and which he used as his principal residence.

(a) If Homeowner is 55 years of age,

    (1) What are the tax consequences of the sale?

    (2) What is his basis for the new residence?

    (3) What is his holding period for the new residence four months after its acquisition?

(b) If Homeowner is 70 years old at the time of the sale,

    (1) To what extent may he avoid tax on the gain realized on the sale?

    (2) If he seeks maximum nonrecognition of his gain, what will be his basis for the new residence?

    (3) And what will be his holding period for the new residence two months after its acquisition?

(c) Same as (b), above, except that Homeowner does not sell his residence.   He dies in 1986, and in that year, three months after his death, his executor sells the residence for $70,000, its then fair market value.

(d) What result to Homeowner in (a), above, in the current and succeeding four years if Buyer pays him $14,000 cash in the current year and Buyer gives him a note under which Buyer agrees to pay him $14,000 in each of the succeeding four years, paying 8% interest on the unpaid balance, and Homeowner elects to report his gain under § 453?   See Rev.Rul. 75, 1953–1 C.B. 83.

2.   Several years ago, Resident paid $60,000 for his residence and the six acres of land which surrounded it.   In the current year he spends $5000 repairing the home to make it more saleable and two months later he sells it for $100,000.   After real estate commissions he receives $95,000.   Resident moves into a motel and three months later he purchases a lot for $20,000 and begins construction

of a new home. Twenty-four months after the original sale, even though construction is not completed Resident and his family move into the new residence when construction costs on it total $50,000. Construction is completed six months later at a total cost of $75,000.

(a) What is Resident's recognized gain on the sale of the old residence? See Kern v. Granquist, 291 F.2d 29 (9th Cir. 1961).

(b) What is Resident's basis for the new residence?

E.   OTHER NONRECOGNITION PROVISIONS

Internal Revenue Code: See Sections 1038; 1039; 1040.

Congress applies the nonrecognition concept to several transactions that fall outside the scope of this book and to some others which, while within, are accorded only brief mention here. For example, a transfer of property to a new corporation in exchange for its shares is a transaction in which gain or loss is clearly realized; and so is a transfer of property to a partnership in exchange for a partnership interest. Nevertheless, such corporate and partnership transactions are usually accorded tax neutrality by way of a nonrecognition provision.[1] Some partnership distributions are similarly treated,[2] as are some distributions in liquidation by corporations.[3] Gain or loss goes unrecognized upon a corporation's transfer of its own shares whether for money or other property, even if the shares are treasury stock.[4] A shareholder's exchange of stock for like stock in the same corporation may be of no immediate tax significance whether he has a realized gain or loss on the exchange.[5] And numerous corporate reorganizations that involve potentially taxable exchanges of stock and other property escape immediate tax consequences to the corporation or the shareholders involved.[6] As in the sections studied, the usual price for nonrecognition is some type of carryover or substitute basis, although the basis rule is of course a compensating advantage where loss is not recognized.

Outside the area of business organizations, the Code provides for nonrecognition of gain or loss upon some exchanges of life insurance,

---

1. As regards corporations, see I.R.C. (26 U.S.C.A.) §§ 351, 358, 362; and as regards partnerships, see I.R.C. (26 U.S.C.A.) §§ 721, 722, 723.

2. I.R.C. (26 U.S.C.A.) §§ 731, 732.

3. I.R.C. (26 U.S.C.A.) §§ 332, 333, 334.

4. I.R.C. (26 U.S.C.A.) § 1032.

5. I.R.C. (26 U.S.C.A.) § 1036; but see § 1031(d).

6. I.R.C. (26 U.S.C.A.) §§ 358, 362(b), 368, 1032.

endowment or annuity contracts for similar contracts [7] and upon the exchange of some United States obligations for other such obligations.[8] It may be a comforting thought that there is sufficient similarity in the nonrecognition provisions so that an understanding of one or several is a great help grasping the significance of another.

The Tax Reform Act of 1969 added § 1039 to the Code to permit nonrecognition of gain on the sale of certain federally assisted low income housing projects. Section 1039 requires that the sale be to the tenants or occupants of the property or to a cooperative type organization made up of the tenants or occupants,[9] and it requires a similar reinvestment by the vendor within a limited period of time.[10] The mechanics of § 1039 are substantially the same as those of § 1033 in that the section is elective and requires a recognition of gain to the extent that the proceeds are not reinvested in another qualified housing project.[11] The basis for the new property is fixed at its cost, less the gain not recognized on the sale of the old property.[12]

It will be recalled that, if an installment sale of property under § 453 is followed by a default and reacquisition of the same property, the vendor's tax liability may be accelerated by the disposition rules of § 453(d). Nevertheless, he is, in a sense, merely restored to the same position he was in prior to the sale. A nonrecognition provision now may provide some relief from the acceleration of tax liability otherwise arising out of a disposition of § 453 obligations. In 1964 Congress enacted § 1038,[13] providing for nonrecognition (or only partial recognition) of gain in certain repossessions, which sometimes would be within the disposition rules of § 453(d).[14] Section 1038 applies only to sales of real property, and only if the obligation was secured by the real property and the vendor reacquires the same property in partial or full satisfaction of the purchaser's indebtedness.[15] Under § 1038, the general effect is to treat amounts previously received on the sale (such as initial and subsequent cash payments) as income, except to the extent that the receipts have previously been reported as income, for example, under § 453(a).[16] But amounts so treated cannot exceed the gain realized on the original sale, reduced by gain previous-

---

7. I.R.C. (26 U.S.C.A.) § 1035.

8. I.R.C. (26 U.S.C.A.) § 1037.

9. I.R.C. (26 U.S.C.A.) § 1039(b) (2).

10. I.R.C. (26 U.S.C.A.) § 1039(b) (3).

11. I.R.C. (26 U.S.C.A.) § 1039(a).

12. I.R.C. (26 U.S.C.A.) § 1039(d).

13. P.L. 88–570, 78 Stat. 854 (1964).
See Hauser, "Effect of Repossessions under Section 1038," 25 N.Y.U.Inst. on Fed.Tax. 47 (1967); Willis, "Repossession of Real Property—Application of Section 1038," 18 U.S.C. Tax Inst. 601 (1966).

14. I.R.C. (26 U.S.C.A.) § 1038 is not limited to § 453 installment sales and may apply to other deferred payment sales of real property, e. g., where initial payments exceed 30% of the selling price or where § 453 is not elected. Sen.Fin.Comm.Rep.No.1361, 88th Cong., 2d Sess. (1964), 1964–2 C.B. 831. See Handler, "Tax Consequences of Mortgage Foreclosures and Transfers of Real Property to the Mortgagee," 31 Tax L.Rev. 193, 215 (1976).

15. I.R.C. (26 U.S.C.A.) § 1038(a).

16. I.R.C. (26 U.S.C.A.) § 1038(b) (1).

ly reported.[17] What this provision seeks to do is to isolate out the amount that the reacquiring vendor has withdrawn from his original investment and to tax him on that amount (but not in excess of the amount of his original gain), to the extent that such withdrawals have previously escaped tax.

If the vendor's property has been returned to him, does he acquire it with the same basis as it had before he sold it? Clearly that would be inappropriate if in the sale and reacquisition he has withdrawn some of his initial investment without being taxed on the entire withdrawal. Section 1038(c), in keeping with other nonrecognition provisions, lays down a special basis rule which takes account of all facets of the sale and reacquisition. The basis for the reacquired property is determined with reference to the vendor's basis for the obligations relinquished in the reacquisition.[18] This will be seen to represent the vendor's basis for the property sold, reduced by prior receipts that went untaxed (for example under § 453(a)) which are in effect a return of capital. To this is added (1) the amount on which the vendor is taxed under § 1038(b),[19] because *taxed* gain should obviously not again be taxed when the reacquired property is sold, and (2) the amount of any payment the vendor made in connection with the reacquisition,[20] because this represents an actual additional cost of or investment in the property.

These remarks are not intended as a comprehensive analysis of § 1038, which can present some complications not discussed. Nevertheless, they touch the main points, and the principles discussed above may be seen at work in the following basic illustration.

Assume T sold a piece of real estate with a basis to him of $60,000 for $100,000. $20,000 was paid in cash in the year of sale and the balance of the price was reflected in a note for $80,000, on which $20,000 was payable in each of the succeeding four years with interest on the unpaid balance (We now dismiss the interest, assuming it to be paid and taxed as due). The $80,000 note was secured by a mortgage on the property. Before any principal payments were made on the note and when the property had appreciated in value to $110,000 the buyer defaulted. T agreed to accept a reconveyance of the property in full satisfaction of the note and to pay the buyer an additional

---

17. I.R.C. (26 U.S.C.A.) § 1038(b) (2). Any further investment by the reacquiring vendor also reduces the income reportable under this provision.

18. Cf. § 453(d) (2).

19. I.R.C. (26 U.S.C.A.) § 1038(c) (1).

20. I.R.C. (26 U.S.C.A.) § 1038(c) (2).

$30,000.[21] If there were no § 1038, T would have had to report $32,000 of income on the disposition, computed as follows:

Portion of fair market value of property received for obligations on reacquisition ($30,000 was received for cash)	$80,000
Less basis for § 453 obligations (§ 453(d) (2))	48,000
Income reportable	$32,000

This is the same amount as would have been reported if the purchaser had paid the obligations in full.[22]

T's basis for the reacquired property would be $110,000. As this is a fully taxable transaction T reacquires the property as if by purchase for a consideration equal to its fair market value at the time of acquisition.[23]

However, under § 1038(b) (1), T's taxable gain is only $2,000, computed as follows:

Money and fair market value of property (other than obligations) received prior to the reacquisition	$20,000
Less prior taxed gain (§ 453(a) gain on the $20,000 was 40,000/100,000 x $20,000 = $8,000)	8,000
Gain taxed (Before the § 1038(b) (2) limitation)	$12,000

On these facts, however, § 1038(b) (2) limits the gain upon which T is taxed on the reacquisition to $2,000, computed as follows:

Excess of sales price over adjusted basis		$40,000
Reduced by:		
Gain taxed before reacquisition	$ 8,000	
Money paid by T upon reacquisition [24]	30,000	
		38,000
Gain taxed on reacquisition		$ 2,000

---

21. It is assumed here that T is paying full value to reacquire the property ($80,000 of purchaser's obligations, plus $30,000 cash equals $110,000). Realistically, the purchaser might accept less, because a forced sale, the alternative to the voluntary arrangement, probably would yield less than the fair market value of the property. See Reg. § 1.1038–1(h), Example (1); and Cf., Reg. § 20.2031–1(b), differentiating "fair market value" and "forced sale price."

22. Reg. § 1.453–5(b) (2).

23. Reg. § 1.453–5(b) (6). As all of T's gain in the property ($40,000)

has been taxed and T has invested another $10,000, the result is the same as if he had originally sold the property for $100,000 cash and has then added $10,000 to purchase new property at a cost of $110,000. (Note that he has taken out $20,000 and put in $30,000 more for a net $10,000 increase in his investment.)

24. This part of the limitation is not especially easy to understand. But notice that, if T had paid upon reacquisition only the same amount as he had withdrawn prior thereto ($20,000), the § 1038(b) (2) limitation would merely equal the amount taxable under § 1038(b) (1) ($40,000 less

Thus under § 1038 T reports only $2,000, instead of the $32,000 otherwise reportable. The cost of this relief is a lower basis for the reacquired property, computed under § 1038(c) as follows:

Basis for the obligations (§ 453(d) (2))	$48,000
Plus gain taxed on the reacquisition (§ 1038(b))ʲ	2,000
Plus amount paid by the vendor in connection with the reacquisition of the property (§ 1038(b) (2) (B))	30,000
Basis	$80,000

A review of the entire transaction and its tax consequences to T will demonstrate the propriety of his new $80,000 basis for the property, which now has a fair market value of $110,000 and a potential $30,000 gain to T upon its sale. At the time of the sale, T had property in which he had a potential $40,000 gain (F.M.V. $100,000 less basis $60,000). He withdrew $20,000 of his original investment of $60,000 but he was taxed on $10,000 of the amount withdrawn ($8,000 at time of sale plus $2,000 upon reacquisition). This should effect a net reduction of $10,000 in his original investment (and basis) because only the $10,000 tax free withdrawal was in the nature of a return of his capital. At this point his basis would have been $50,000 (original $60,000 less $10,000 return of capital). But he has also added $30,000 to his investment ($10,000 of which took account of the post-sale appreciation). Thus his basis becomes $80,000, and T remains potentially taxable on $30,000, the amount of his gain on the original sale which, so far, has gone untaxed.

$8,000, less $20,000 equals $12,000). To the extent that he reinvests more than he has withdrawn, the amount taxed is reduced, because he has increased his net investment, rather than having made a net cash bail-out.

PART EIGHT: CONVERTING TAXABLE INCOME INTO TAX LIABILITY

CHAPTER 27.   COMPUTATIONS

A.   CLASSIFICATION OF TAXPAYERS *

Internal Revenue Code: Sections 1; 2; 3; 6013(a) and (d).   See Sections 11; 73; 142(a); 143(b); 144(a).

Individuals do not all pay federal income tax in accordance with the same tax rates.   There are now *four* separate progressive rate tables, and the particular table applicable to an individual depends upon his classification.   The four classifications are as follows:

1.   Married Individuals Filing Joint Returns [1]

2.   Heads of Household [2]

3.   Unmarried Individuals (not falling within the first two classifications as surviving spouse or head of household.) [3]

4.   Married Individuals Filing Separate Returns. [4]

As indicated, a different rate table applies to each classification.   This is where we are.   Certainly the situation is puzzling enough to invite the question: How did we get here?

For many years all individuals were taxed under a single set of tax rates.   In 1930, however, the Supreme Court held that in community property states earnings and other income of either spouse were taxable one half to each spouse. [5]   Under the then single progressive tax rate table this splitting of income between community property state spouses gave such married persons a major tax advantage over

---

* See Bittker, "Effective Tax Rates: Fact or Fancy?"   122 U.Penn.L.R. 780 (1974) and Bittker, "Federal Income Taxation and the Family," 27 Stan. L.R. 1389 (1975).

1.   I.R.C. (26 U.S.C.A.) § 1(a).   One who qualifies as a "surviving spouse", I.R.C. (26 U.S.C.A.) § 2(a), is also placed in this classification.

2.   I.R.C. (26 U.S.C.A.) § 1(b); the term is defined in I.R.C. (26 U.S.C.A.) § 2 (b).

3.   I.R.C. (26 U.S.C.A.) § 1(c).

4.   I.R.C. (26 U.S.C.A.) § 1(d).   The rates in this table also apply to estates and trusts.

5.   Poe v. Seaborn, 282 U.S. 101, 51 S. Ct. 58 (1930).   While post-marital earnings are split, either spouse may have non-community property, the earnings from which are his or hers, separately.

married persons in common law states. The nature of the advantage should be clear. Not to be outdone, a movement began in the common law states to adopt the community property system.[6] But, as there have always been many more common law states than community property states, it is not surprising that broad relief from the inequality eventually came from Congress. In 1948, the 1939 Code was amended so as to allow a married couple to split their aggregate taxable income for purposes of rate determination; their tax liability then became twice the tax but determined at a (lower) rate on half the income.[7] When the Bill reached the Senate, the Finance Committee Report stated: [8]

"This section amends * * * the Code, relating to surtax on individuals, by adding a new subsection * * * which provides for computation of tax under the plan for the so-called income splitting between husband and wife. This subsection applies only if a joint return for the taxable year involved is made. * * * Under the provisions * * * the combined normal tax and surtax * * * in the case of the husband and wife making the joint return shall be twice the combined normal tax and surtax that would be determined if the net income and the applicable credits * * * were reduced by one-half.

"It is contemplated that under this provision the gross income and adjusted gross income of husband and wife on the joint return will be computed by the same method as under existing law (that is, in an aggregate amount), and that the deductions allowed and the net income will likewise be computed on an aggregate basis. Deductions limited to a percentage of the adjusted gross income, such as the deduction for charitable contributions * * * will be allowed with reference to such aggregate adjusted gross income. Similarly, in the case of a joint return, losses of husband and wife from sales or exchanges of capital assets are combined and such combined losses are allowed * * * only to the extent of the combined gains of the spouses from such sales or exchanges, plus the net income or $1,000 whichever is smaller. The 'net income' referred to * * * is the net income computed before reduction by one-half for the purposes of income splitting and is such net income computed without regard to gains and losses from sales or exchanges of capital assets. Although there are two taxpayers on a joint return, there is only one net income."

The early concept is identifiable in present I.R.C. (26 U.S.C.A.) § 1(a). As was true initially, the special rates are available only if

---

6. Sen. Fin. Comm. Rep. No. 1013, 80th Cong. 2d Sess. (1948), 1948–1 C.B. 301–303. There were also advantages to the community property states under the Estate and Gift Tax provisions which were eliminated by the Rev.Act of 1948. See I.R.C. (26 U.S.C.A.) §§ 2056, 2513, 2523.

7. I.R.C. (1939) §§ 12(d) and 51(b).

8. Sen. Fin. Comm. Rep. No. 1013, supra at 1948–1 C.B. 326.

a joint return is filed. Use of the joint return by married persons is elective and is allowed only if the requirements of § 6013(a) are satisfied. A consequence of filing a joint return is joint and several liability, not only for the tax reported, but also for deficiencies and interest and possibly civil penalties.[9] In almost all circumstances the income-splitting advantage of a joint return will result in less tax liability for the spouses than filing separate returns.[10] But the important thing here is the origin of the split-income device.

In 1954, the "surviving spouse" was fitted into the married joint return classification and remains there.[11] Surviving spouses, as defined in § 2(a), are widows or widowers who for the two years following the year of their spouse's death do not remarry but do maintain certain dependents in their home. If the § 2(a) requirements are met they are allowed to use the § 1(a) rates which, as indicated, are the same income-splitting rates available to married couples filing joint returns.

In 1951, Congress created another set of rates applicable to another category of taxpayers known as "heads of households". The reason for according this new class of taxpayers preferential rates was stated in the House Report:[12]

"It is believed that taxpayers, not having spouses but nevertheless required to maintain a household for the benefit of other individuals, are in a somewhat similar position to married couples who, because they may share their income, are treated under present law substantially as if they were two single individuals each with half of the total income of the couple. The income of a head of household who must maintain a home for a child, for example, is likely to be shared with the child to the extent necessary to maintain the home, and raise and educate the child. This, it is believed, justifies the extension of some of the benefits of income splitting. The hardship appears particularly severe in the case of the individual with children to raise who, upon the death of his spouse, finds himself in the position not only of being denied the spouse's aid in raising the children, but under present law also may find his tax load heavier.

"However, it was not deemed appropriate to give a head of household the full benefits of income splitting because it appears unlikely that there is as much sharing of income in these cases as between spouses. In the case of savings, for example, it appears unlikely that

---

9. I.R.C. (26 U.S.C.A.) § 6013(d)(3); see, however, the innocent spouse rules of §§ 6013(e) and 6653(b).

10. At both the lower and upper income levels this may not be so. At the lower level, whether split or not income may be taxed only at the lowest rate. At the upper level, if each spouse has sufficient income to reach the maximum rate, a shift by way of the elective splitting provision may still leave the maximum rate applicable to the same amount of income.

11. I.R.C. (26 U.S.C.A.) § 1(a) (2).

12. House Rep. No. 586, 82d Cong. 1st Sess. (1951), 1951-2 C.B. 364.

this income will be shared by a widow or widower with his child to the same extent as in the case of spouses. As a result only one-half of the benefits of income splitting are granted to heads of households."

Under the current provisions of the Code "heads of households" are defined in § 2(b) much in line with the comments just quoted. But head of household status is not limited to widows or widowers. It can also apply, for example, to a divorced or legally separated person who maintains as *his* home a household in which unmarried descendants reside.[13] In 1954, the provision was expanded so as to include a taxpayer who maintains *a* household for others, including parents, if they enjoy dependency status under I.R.C. § 151.[14] In 1969, the head of household status was again enlarged so as to permit a person who is actually married to obtain the benefit of that classification, if he would otherwise qualify for head of household status, where the taxpayer and his spouse are physically separated even though not divorced or legally separated.[15] The rates under § 1(b), applicable to such taxpayers, effecting a smaller amnesty, fall between the rates for single persons and the rates for married couples filing joint returns.

And now we have come full circle. In the past, individuals not within the special classes described above and married persons filing separately shared the distinction of paying taxes in accordance with a third schedule of graduated rates, the highest of the three. But in 1969, Congress determined this third schedule was too burdensome for the *unmarried individual* who was not a surviving spouse or a head of household. There emerged a revised third classification and schedule now found in I.R.C. (26 U.S.C.A.) § 1(c), less preferential than the first two, but preferential nevertheless. The Staff of the Joint Committee on Internal Revenue Taxation explains the development as follows:[16]

"Under prior law, the tax rates imposed on single persons were quite heavy relative to those imposed on married couples at the same income level; at some income levels a single person's tax was as much as 42.1 percent higher than the tax paid on a joint return with the same amount of taxable income. The Congress believed that some difference between the rate of tax paid by single persons and joint returns was appropriate to reflect the additional living expenses of married taxpayers but that the prior law differential of as much as 42 percent (the result of income splitting) could not be justified on this basis.

13. I.R.C. (26 U.S.C.A.) § 2(b)(1)(A), (2)(B) and (C), and (c), inconsequentially changed by § 1901(a)(1) of the Tax Reform Act of 1976.

14. I.R.C. (26 U.S.C.A.) § 2(b)(1)(A)(ii) and (B).

15. I.R.C. (26 U.S.C.A.) §§ 2(c) and 143 (b).

16. General Explanation of the Tax Reform Act of 1969, Staff of the Joint Comm. on Int. Rev. Tax, pp. 222–223 (1970).

"The Act provides a new lower rate schedule for single persons effective in 1971. * * * This rate schedule is designed to provide tax liabilities for single persons which are 17 to 20 percent above those for married couples for taxable incomes of between $14,000 and $100,000, with the maximum differential of 20 percent being reached for an income level of $24,000 as shown in table 5 below. (Under prior law, the difference was as great as 42 percent at $24,000 and $28,000.) As income falls below $14,000 where income splitting is less beneficial, the excess of single persons' taxes over those of married couples gradually decreases. This is also true above $100,000 where the benefits of income splitting become less significant.

* * *

"The prior law rate schedule for single persons will continue to be used for married couples filing separate returns and for estates and trusts. The prior law single person rate schedule was retained for married persons filing separate returns because if each spouse were permitted to use the new tax rate schedule for single persons, many (especially those in community property states) could arrange their affairs and income in such a way that their combined tax would be less than that on a joint return.

"With the new rate schedule for single persons, married couples filing a joint return will pay more tax than two single persons with the same total income. This is a necessary result of changing the income splitting relationship between single and joint returns. Moreover, it is justified on the grounds that although a married couple has greater living expenses than a single person and hence should pay less tax, the couple's living expenses are likely to be less than those of two single persons and therefore the couple's tax should be higher than that of two single persons."

As the above quoted remarks indicate, the tag-ender in the rate parade is now the married taxpayer who files separately. A higher rate schedule (§ 1(d)) applies to him. Has Congress thus imposed a tax on virtue? If A and B have equal incomes, or if both have more than nominal incomes, they may be better off living in sin and filing separate returns than marrying. For instance if A has income of $30,000 and B has income of $10,000 and they merely live together and file separately, their total tax liability is $11,480.[17] If they enter the bonds of holy matrimony and file a joint return, their total tax liability increases to $12,140.[18] If they then decide not to adopt the joint return along with the double bed, their combined tax liability climbs to $13,340.[19] This can be a problem for separated but not divorced taxpayers who in many instances do not file jointly and must

---

17. I.R.C. (26 U.S.C.A.) § 1(c) rates. It is unlikely that year-end divorce followed by new year remarriage will be accorded any tax significance. See Rev.Rul. 76–255, 1976–2 C.B. ——, also cited in Chapter 18, supra, at page 508.

18. I.R.C. (26 U.S.C.A.) § 1(a) rates.

19. I.R.C. (26 U.S.C.A.) § 1(d) rates.

use the rates applicable to married taxpayers filing separately. But in some cases the spouse with whom the children reside can now file as head of household even though legally married.[20] Review the above Joint Committee Staff's comments to determine whether the policies underlying the rate variances are justified. Would it be fairer to simply allow married persons to use the lesser of the § 1(a) or 1(c) rates?

In order to provide low-income taxpayers a simplified method of computing their taxes, both the 1939 Code and the 1954 Code have provided tax tables for automatic tax determination without arithmetic computation. The tables are in regulations promulgated under § 3. These tables do not reflect a further different set of individual rates. Instead, they are designed to yield an instant tax figure, determined under the relevant § 1 rates.[21] Entering the table for his proper rate classification, until recently the taxpayer found his tax by reference to his adjusted gross income and total number of exemptions. The tax indicated was computed with the standard deduction.[22] The tables were available through 1969 only to taxpayers with less than $5000 of adjusted gross income but, for years after 1969, they were available to taxpayers with up to $10,000 of adjusted gross income. In two more jumps the critical figure has reached $20,000 for 1976 and after, and *taxable* income, figured with the standard deduction or with itemized deductions is now the measuring device. Use of the tables is no longer optional but is required of taxpayers with $20,000 of taxable income or less.[23]

PROBLEMS

1. Taxpayer is a calendar year taxpayer. In each of the following subparts you are to compute his tax liability before credits at the lowest rates, assuming he has $50,000 of taxable income in 1977.

    (a) Taxpayer is unmarried and has no special status.

    (b) On December 31, 1977 he marries Wife, a calendar year taxpayer who has no income for the year, and they file a joint return.

---

20. I.R.C. (26 U.S.C.A.) §§ 2(c) and 143 (b). See text at note 12, supra.

21. Some rounding off of tax liability occurs because of the bracket approach in the tables.

22. See I.R.C. (26 U.S.C.A.) § 144(a).

23. I.R.C. (26 U.S.C.A.) § 3(a), as amended in 1976.

Under § 51, applicable from 1968 to 1970, Congress imposed a tax surcharge, measured by tax liability computed under the normal rates. The surcharge, which in general ranged from 2½% to 10% per year of the tax conventionally computed, had the effect of increasing one's overall tax rate for the period it was in effect. This was sensibly repealed as a "deadwood" provision by § 1901(a)(7) of the Tax Reform Act of 1976.

(c) Taxpayer was married and two minor children supported by him lived with him and Wife. Wife, who had no income in the year, dies on January 15, 1977.

(d) Same as (c), above, except that Wife died on December 31, 1976.

(e) Same as (c), above, except that Wife died on December 31, 1973.

(f) Same as (e), above, except that Taxpayer remarried on December 31, 1977 and he and his new wife file separate returns for 1977.

(g) Same as (a), above, except that Taxpayer has $14,950 of taxable income. Might Taxpayer have a slight preference for avoiding the § 3 tables, if he could?

2. Husband and Wife, both under 65 and with good eyesight, have two dependent children. In 1977 they file a joint return. They have no § 62 deductions. With what taxable income figure will they enter the § 3 tables if:

(a) They have $15,000 of gross income and $2200 in itemized deductions.

(b) Same as (a), above, except that they have $2500 in itemized deductions.

(c) They have $10,000 of gross income and $2200 in itemized deductions.

(d) Same as (c), above, except that they have $2000 in itemized deductions.

(e) They have $20,000 of gross income and $3000 in itemized deductions.

(f) Same as (e), above, except that they have $2600 in itemized deductions.

B. MINIMUM TAX*

Internal Revenue Code: See Sections 56 through 58.

The Minimum Tax for Tax Preferences entered the Code by way of the Tax Reform Act of 1969. It was sponsored by the fact that some taxpayers were taking advantage, not improperly, of various relief provisions to avoid tax entirely or largely, even though they had

* See Caplin, "Minimum Tax for Tax Preferences and Related Reforms Affecting High Income Individuals," 4 Ind.Legal Forum 71 (1970) and Bersch and King, "Minimum Tax For Tax Preferences," 23 U.S.C. T.I. 111 (1971).

many thousand or even hundreds of thousands of dollars of gross income. Even though it was a fairly modest attack on the problem Congress almost immediately moved to soften the blow. In 1971 subsection 56(c) was added retroactively affording some relief from the new tax. As the ensuing quotations indicate a part of the measure of exemption from the tax has been the amount of the taxpayer's regular income tax plus another stated sum. Congress decided in 1971 to permit a taxpayer to carry over unused exemption to later years. Now sterner thoughts have prevailed. Changes in 1976 reduce the exemption, eliminate the carryover of the unused exemption, increase the tax rate, and add new items of tax preference subject to the special tax. The general nature of the tax and the substance of the recent toughening amendments will be seen from the two excerpts that follow.

EXCERPT FROM THE GENERAL EXPLANATION OF THE TAX REFORM ACT OF 1969

Staff of the Joint Committee on Internal Revenue Taxation, pp. 104–107 (1970).

G. MINIMUM TAX

(Sec. 301 of the Act and secs. 56, 57, and 58 of the code)

Prior law.—Under prior law, many individuals and corporations did not pay tax on a substantial part of their economic income as a result of the receipt of various kinds of tax-favored income or special deductions.

Both individuals and corporations, for example, paid the equivalent of the regular income tax on only part of their long-term capital gains. Individuals with large interest payments on funds borrowed to carry growth stock used the interest deduction to reduce other unrelated taxable income. They could offset practically all their income in this manner and, as a result, paid little or no tax. Similarly, individuals and corporations escaped tax on a large part of their economic income as a result of receiving accelerated depreciation on real property and percentage depletion in excess of cost depletion. Financial institutions also paid lower taxes than other corporations to the extent that their deductions for bad debt reserves exceeded the deductions that would be allowed on the basis of actual loss experience.

General reason for change.—The prior treatment imposed no limit on the amount of income which an individual or corporation could exclude from tax as the result of various tax preferences. As a result, there were large variations in the tax burdens placed on individuals or corporations with similar economic incomes, depending upon the size of their preference income. In general, those individual or corporate taxpayers who received the bulk of their income from personal services or manufacturing were taxed at relatively higher tax rates than others. On the other hand, individuals or corporations which received the bulk of their income from such sources as capital gains or were in a position to benefit from net lease arrangements, from accelerated depreciation on real estate, from percentage depletion, or from other tax-preferred activities tended to pay relatively low rates of tax. In fact, many individuals with high incomes who could benefit from these provisions paid lower effective rates of tax than many individuals with modest incomes. In extreme cases, individuals enjoyed large economic incomes without paying any tax at all. This was true for example in the case of 154 returns in 1966 with adjusted gross incomes of $200,000 a year (apart from those with income exclusions which do not show on the returns filed). Similarly, a number of large corporations paid either no tax at all or taxes which represented very low effective rates.

Explanation of provision.—The Act provides a minimum tax on specified tax preference income received by individuals and corporations in order to make sure that all taxpayers are required to pay significant amounts of tax on their economic income. The minimum tax amounts to 10 percent of the sum of an individual's or corporation's (or estate's or trust's) tax preference income (i. e., income which would be taxed but which is not because of a tax preference) to the extent it exceeds $30,000 plus the regular income tax (reduced by any foreign tax credit, retirement income credit or investment credit). If a taxpayer has a net operating loss that results in loss carryovers to future years, the minimum tax on an amount of preference income equal in size to the carryovers is deferred until the year when the carryovers are used.

The items of tax preference included in the base of the 10 percent tax are as follows:

(a) Excess investment interest.—This is the excess of investment interest over net investment income. Investment income consists of gross income from interest, dividends, rents and royalties, net short-term capital gain from property held for investment purposes, and amounts treated as ordinary income under the recapture rules (secs. 1245 and 1250) but only to the extent that such income and gain are not derived from the conduct of a trade or business. Investment expenses for this purpose include State and local property taxes, bad debts, straight line depreciation, the dividends received deduction, amortizable bond premium, cost depletion, and certain other deductions attributable to the production of income to the extent these expenses are directly attributable to the production of such investment income. Investment interest expense, as distinguished from other interest expense, is interest on indebtedness incurred or continued to purchase or carry property held for investment purposes. Interest with respect to property which is subject to a net lease entered into after October 9, 1969, is treated as a tax preference under this provision.

Excess investment interest is regarded as a preference only for individuals, estates, trusts, subchapter S corporations, and personal holding companies, and only until 1972 when the interest limitation deduction provision becomes applicable. [Excess investment interest is no longer an item of tax preference. But see I.R.C. § 163(d) and footnote 13 at page 469, supra. Ed.]

(b) Accelerated depreciation on personal property subject to a net lease.—This is the accelerated depreciation in excess of the straight-line depreciation. Net leases for this purpose involve those situations where the lessor is either guaranteed a specific return or is guaranteed in whole or in part against the loss of income. Net leases also include those situations where the trade or business expense deductions are less than 15 percent of the rental income produced by the property.

The preference relating to accelerated depreciation on personal property subject to a net lease applies only in the case of individuals, estates, trusts, subchapter S corporations, and personal holding companies.

(c) Accelerated depreciation on real property.—This is the excess of the rapid depreciation allowed over straight line depreciation.

(d) Amortization of rehabilitation expenditures.—This is the excess of the amortization deduction over straight line depreciation.

(e) Amortization of certified pollution control facilities.—This is the excess of the amortization deduction over accelerated depreciation.

(f) Amortization of railroad rolling stock.—This is the excess of the amortization deduction over accelerated depreciation.

(g) Tax benefits from stock options.—In the case of qualified stock options or restricted stock options, this is the excess of the fair market value of the stock at the time of exercise of the option over the option price of the stock.

(h) Bad debt deductions of financial institutions.—In the case of a bank, savings and loan association, mutual saving bank or other financial institution, this is the amount by which the bad debt reserve deduction exceeds the amount which would be allowable to the bank or other institution had it maintained its bad debt reserve on the basis of its own actual bad debt loss experience or in the case of a new institution, industry experience.

(i) Depletion.—This is the excess of the depletion deduction allowance taken for the year over the adjusted basis of the property (reduced for depletion taken in prior years.)

(j) Capital gains.—In the case of individuals, one-half of the net long-term capital gain, to the extent it exceeds the net short-term capital loss. In the case of corporations, the tax preference is the excess of the net long-term capital gain over the net short-term capital loss, multiplied by a ratio in which the denominator is the regular corporate rate (48 percent) and the numerator is the regular corporate rate, minus the rate applicable to capital gains in the case of corporations (28 percent in 1970 and 30 percent thereafter). In other words, the corporate capital gains are included among the tax preferences in the ratio of the difference between their special tax rate and the general corporate tax rate to the general corporate tax rate.

Stock options and capital gains (items (g) and (j) above) which are derived from sources outside the United States, are subject to the minimum tax only if the foreign country taxes them at a preferential rate or does not tax them at all. The remaining items of tax preference, as set forth above, include preferences attributable to income derived from sources outside the United States only to the extent that these items result in foreign losses which reduce taxable income derived from sources within the United States. The amount of tax preferences so included is not to exceed the amount of such foreign losses. The foreign tax credit is not allowed against the 10-percent minimum tax.

Special rules are provided in order to cover the following situations:

(a) In the case of estates or trusts, the items of tax preference are attributed to the estate or trust and the beneficiaries in the same ratio as the income allocable to each. The $30,000 exemption generally available is reduced insofar as the trust or estate is concerned in the proportion in which its income is allocated, to its beneficiaries.

(b) In the case of members of a controlled group of corporations, the $30,000 exemption is apportioned equally among the members of the group unless they agree to share the exemption in some other way.

(c) In the case of subchapter S corporations (where the income is taxed to the shareholders), items of tax preference are apportioned among the shareholders in the manner consistent with the manner in which a net operating loss is apportioned among the shareholders. However, where capital gains are taxed to both the subchapter S corporation and the shareholder (under section 1378 of the code), the capital gains tax preference is subject to the minimum tax at both the corporate and individual levels. In such a case, the amount treated as capital gain by the shareholder is reduced by the tax imposed under section 1378 (as under present law) and by the 10 percent minimum tax imposed at the corporate level.

(d) Regulated investment companies are not subject to the minimum tax to the extent they pass through to shareholders amounts attributable to tax preferences. However, their shareholders are subject to minimum tax on capital gains tax preferences passed through to them. In addition, the shareholders are deemed for purposes of the minimum tax to have received the other tax preferences of the regulated investment company in proportion to the amounts that are distributed to them by the regulated investment company.

(e) The tax preferences of a common trust fund are treated as tax preferences of the participants of the fund and are apportioned pro rata among such participants.

(f) In the case of a husband and wife filing separate returns, the exemption is $15,000 for each spouse.

Effective date.—This provision applies with respect to taxable years ending after December 31, 1969, but in applying the minimum tax to fiscal years beginning in 1969 and ending in 1970, the tax will be imposed on a pro-rata basis.

Revenue effect.—The minimum tax is estimated to increase revenue $590 million in calendar year 1970, $600 million in 1972 and $635 million in the long run.

EXCERPT FROM SUMMARY OF THE
CONFERENCE AGREEMENT
ON H.R. 10612
(THE TAX REFORM ACT OF 1976)

Prepared by the House Committee on Ways and Means on September 14, 1976

sec. 301.   [of the 1976 Act] Minimum tax

Under present law, the minimum tax equals 10 percent of the sum of an individual's or corporation's tax preferences, reduced by a $30,000 exemption plus the taxpayer's regular income taxes (after credits). Regular income taxes that are not used to offset tax preferences in the current year may be carried forward and used to offset tax preferences for up to 7 years. The tax preference items included in the base of the minimum tax are:

(1) Accelerated depreciation on real property in excess of straight-line depreciation;

(2) Accelerated depreciation on personal property subject to a net lease in excess of straight-line depreciation;

(3) Amortization of certified pollution control facilities (the excess of 60-month amortization over regular depreciation);

(4) Amortization of railroad rolling stock (the excess of 60-month amortization over regular depreciation);

(5) Qualified or restricted stock options (the excess of fair market value at the time of exercise over the option price);

(6) Excess bad debt reserves of financial institutions;

(7) Percentage depletion in excess of the adjusted basis of the property;

(8) Capital gains (for individuals, the excluded one-half of net long-term capital gains; for corporations, 18/48 of capital gains); and

(9) Amortization of on-the-job training and child care facilities (the excess of 60-month amortization over regular depreciation).

A. *Minimum tax on individuals*

The conference agreement increases the rate of the minimum tax on individuals from 10 percent to 15 percent. An exemption is provided equal to the greater of $10,000 or one-half of regular income taxes. The carryover of regular taxes that are not used to offset tax preferences in the current year is eliminated. New tax preference items are added for: (1) itemized deductions (other than medical and casualty loss deductions) in excess of 60 percent of adjusted gross income; (2) intangible drilling costs for oil and gas wells in excess of the amount of deduction which would be deductible if intangible drilling costs were capitalized and amortized over 10 years; and (3) accelerated depreciation and amortization on all personal property subject to a lease (including the acceleration that results from the use of the 20-percent variance in useful lives authorized under the ADR rules).

The new preference for intangible drilling expenses applies to those expenses in excess of the amount which could have been deducted had the intangibles been capitalized and either (1) deducted over the life of the well as cost depletion, or (2) deducted ratably over ten years; the taxpayer may choose whichever of these two methods of capitalization is most favorable. This preference does not apply to taxpayers who elect to capitalize their intangible drilling costs. Nor does it apply to nonproductive wells. For this purpose, nonproductive wells are those which are plugged and abandoned without having produced oil and gas in commercial quantities for any substantial period of time.

These revisions of the minimum tax on individuals apply to taxable years beginning after December 31, 1975. The amount of any tax carryover from a taxable year beginning before January 1, 1976, will not be allowed as a tax carryover for any taxable year beginning after December 31, 1975.

B. *Minimum tax on corporations*

The conference agreement increases the rate of the minimum tax on corporations from 10 percent to 15 percent. An exemption is provided equal to the greater of $10,000 or the full amount of regular income taxes. The carryover of regular taxes that are not used to offset tax preferences in the current year is eliminated. The conference agreement does not add any new items of tax preference for corporations. The conference agreement provides special rules for timber income of corporations, including both gains from the cutting of timber and long-term capital gains from the sale of timber. These rules have the effect of exempting timber income from the increase in the minimum tax for corporations. These provisions apply in general for taxable years beginning in 1976. However, for 1976, only one-half of the increase in the minimum tax applies. In addition, commercial banks and financial institutions with excess bad debt reserves are exempt from the increase in the minimum tax for 1976 and 1977.

PROBLEM

Without regard to the minimum tax, Wealthy's tax liability for the year 1977 computed under section 1(c) is $24,000 and he has $2000 of investment credit. He is single and has no dependents. In computing his tax for the year his deductions include: a § 1202 (½ of his net capital gain) deduction of $70,000; and $30,000 of accelerated depreciation on real estate (which would have resulted in only a $20,000 deduction if he used the straight line method). Compute Wealthy's § 56 minimum tax for tax preferences for the year.

C. MAXIMUM TAX ON PERSONAL SERVICE INCOME*

Internal Revenue Code: See Section 1348.

The Puritan Ethic probably does not dictate that we judge major league pitchers on the basis of their *earned* run average, the meaning of ERA in the sports pages. However, the Ethic may have something to do with the way Congress views taxpayers. Seemingly income acquired the hard way is nicer than that achieved through soft investments, entitled to friendlier treatment than unearned income. The current favorable rule, dating only from 1969, in a loosely stated way puts a 50% lid on the rates applicable to what is now called "personal service income." "Now" is 1976 and it is nice to record here that, in addition to making some modest changes of substance in I.R.C. § 1348, the Tax Reform Act of 1976 translated the general rule on the treatment of PSI into essentially intelligible English. If you enjoy horror stories take a look at § 1348(a) before the 1976 change.

The 50% limitation is achieved by a formula that determines the taxpayer's entire tax for the year. Three steps are involved:

First, a tentative tax figure is determined by applying the graduated rates to taxable income up to the point where a rate in excess of 50% would become applicable. For a single person entitled to no special treatment this tentative figure will be $13,290 on taxable income of $38,000 under 1977 § 1(c) rates.

----

* See Asimow, "Section 1348: The Death of Mickey Mouse?" 58 Calif.L. Rev. 801 (1970) and Asimow, "The Maximum Tax on Earned Income: The First Five Years," 27 U.S.C. T.I. 191 (1975).

Second, add to the figure first determined 50% of the amount by which the taxpayer's personal service taxable income exceeds the amount taxed in the first step. This saws off personal service income at the 50% rate. If our taxpayer in the first paragraph had PSI taxable income of $48,000, we would add here $5000 (one half the excess of $48,000 over $38,000) for a tentative total tax of $18,290.

Third, add the amount of § 1 tax on *all* taxable income which exceeds a § 1 tax on PSI taxable income only. If our hypothetical taxpayer had *no* income other than his $48,000 PSI taxable income the addition here would be zero. The tax base for a tax on all taxable income, $48,000, is the same as the tax base for a tax on PSI taxable income, $48,000, and the net amount in paragraph (3) is zero. Well, all right! No part of his PSI taxable income has been taxed at a rate in excess of 50%.

If he does have other income, his combined taxable income might be, let's say, $60,000. The tax on that under § 1(c) is $26,390 (applying rates of 55%, 60% and 62% to the top increment, above $38,000). But now we would subtract the tax under 1(c) on PSI taxable income, $48,000, to get the paragraph (3) addition. This is $18,990. The addition is therefore $7400. Looking back it will be seen that he had $12,000 of taxable income that was not PSI ($60,000–$48,000). His tax on the PSI taxable income was not permitted to exceed a 50% rate, which applied to the top increment under paragraph (2). The $12,000 is taxed at the rates that exceed taxable income of $48,000 in table 1(c) (60% of $2000, or $1200, plus 62% of $10,000, or $6200, equals $7400) to get the paragraph (3) element of his tax. His total tax with the § 1348 limitations is $25,690 ($13,290 plus $5000 plus $7400 = $25,690) as opposed to $26,390, if there were no § 1348 limitation. The device preserves the customary high rates for unfavored income while still protecting PSI itself from the top brackets.

Outside of the improvement in rhetoric mentioned at the beginning of this note, the 1976 changes in I.R.C. § 1348 were not very great. Here is what was said of them in a "Summary of the Conference Agreement on H.R. 10612," prepared by the House Committee on Ways and Means on September 14, 1976:

Sec. 302. Maximum tax

Under present law, the maximum marginal tax rate on earned income is limited to 50 percent. Earned income includes wages, salaries, professional fees or compensation for personal services (including royalty payments to authors and inventors). For individuals engaged in a trade or business where both personal services and capital are material income-producing factors, a reasonable amount (not to exceed 30 percent) of his share of the net profits from the business is treated as earned income. However, deferred compensation, lump-sum distributions from pension plans and distributions from employee annuity plans do not qualify for the maximum tax. In addition, the amount of earned income eligible for the 50-percent maximum tax is reduced by the current year's tax preferences (or, if greater, one-fifth of the tax preferences for the past five years) in excess of $30,000. Taxpayers cannot use the maximum tax if they use income averaging.

The conference agreement eliminates the $30,000 exemption to the preference offset and the 5-year averaging provision. The new tax preferences are added to the preference offset. The maximum tax is extended to pension and annuity income. In addition, the conference agreement redefines "earned income" as "personal service income." These provisions apply to taxable years beginning after December 31, 1976.

PROBLEM

During 1977 Professional, a single taxpayer, earns $75,000, net, in commissions after subtracting $5000 of § 62 business expenses attributable to earning the commissions. He also has $25,000 of income from bank interest. Professional has an additional $20,000 of other deductions and exemptions. Assuming Professional has no items of tax preference, compute his tax liability for the current year taking § 1348 into consideration.

D. CREDITS AGAINST TAX*

Internal Revenue Code: See Sections 31; 37 and 38; 40 through 43; 44A; 6315.

The amount that must be paid by the taxpayer when he files his income tax return may be less than his tax liability for the year. The required payment is often reduced by credits against tax. The statute now uses the term "credit" to refer to items that directly reduce the amount of tax which must be paid. A credit is more advantageous than a deduction because it reduces tax dollar-for-dollar, whereas a deduction reduces tax liability only by way of its impact on taxable income. TRA (1976) reflects some movement away from deductions toward credits, possibly because of a policy decision that credits are fairer. Deductions effect greater tax savings as the taxpayer's income increases; in contrast, credits have the same saving for all taxpayers who otherwise would pay tax, regardless of their tax brackets. The principal credit provisions are cited above, but some of the sections cited are augmented elsewhere, such as §§ 46 through 48 relating to the investment credit provided by § 38.

* See Weidenbaum, "Shifting from Income Tax Deductions to Credits," 51 Taxes 462 (1973).

Withholding and Estimated Tax Payments

The most widely applicable credit provision is § 31, which provides a credit for tax withheld by employers.[1] This credit simply recognizes that tax withheld is in the nature of a prepayment.[2] An actual prepayment occurs when a taxpayer himself makes payments of estimated income tax.[3] These actual and constructive prepayments are treated the same on Form 1040.

The withholding and estimated tax requirements originated in the Current Tax Payment Act of 1943. An initial effect was an acceleration of revenue collections in a time of need during World War II. Their continuing function is to facilitate collection. One wonders whether the current broadly based income tax with its high rates could be administered if all payments were to be made by the taxpayer only at the end of the year.

I.R.C. (26 U.S.C.A.) § 3402(a) requires an employer to act as a tax collector and withhold from an employee an amount of tax generally based upon the employee's wages, exemptions, and tax classification. The Code contains tables [4] to guide employers in determining the amount to withhold, and the employer is personally liable for such amounts as tax imposed on him.[5] The tax applies only if there is an employment relationship,[6] and is imposed on "wages" [7] which are broadly defined.[8] Under statutory changes made in 1969, an employer has alternative methods of determining the amount of tax to be withheld [9] and, if an employee certifies he had no tax liability for the prior year and expects to have none in the current year, he is exempt from withholding.[10]

A second part of the Current Tax Payment Act of 1943 provided for the declaration and payment of estimated tax by non-wage earners or wage earners with outside income.[11] Such prepayments are required on a quarterly basis, for most calendar year taxpayers, on April 15, June 15, September 15, and January 15.[12] There are penalties for failure to file a declaration of estimated tax or to pay the liability.[13]

1. I.R.C. (26 U.S.C.A.) § 3402.

2. See I.R.C. (26 U.S.C.A.) § 6401(b).

3. See I.R.C. (26 U.S.C.A.) §§ 6015 and 6153.

4. I.R.C. (26 U.S.C.A.) § 3402.

5. I.R.C. (26 U.S.C.A.) § 3403.

6. See Reg. § 31.3401(c)–1.

7. I.R.C. (26 U.S.C.A.) § 3402.

8. See I.R.C. (26 U.S.C.A.) § 3401(a) and (f).

9. E. g., I.R.C. (26 U.S.C.A.) § 3401(c) (6).

10. I.R.C. (26 U.S.C.A.) § 3402(n); see also § 3402(m), reducing amounts to be withheld in some circumstances.

11. See I.R.C. (26 U.S.C.A.) § 6015.

12. I.R.C. (26 U.S.C.A.) § 6153.

13. I.R.C. (26 U.S.C.A.) § 6654.

Excessive amounts withheld for social security taxes are treated as if they were withheld as income tax and thus qualify as a credit.[14] This often occurs when an individual changes jobs during the year and withholding by two or more employers exceeds in the aggregate amounts required to be withheld.

The foregoing credit provisions simply take account of what are, at least in effect, prepayments of income tax liability. But there are other credit provisions that do not rest on the notion of any amount having been paid to the government.

Credit for the Elderly

Under 1976 amendments [15] the I.R.C. § 37 "Retirement Income Credit" became the "Credit for the Elderly," with substantial changes. When this matter first attracted congressional attention, the Senate Finance Committee made these comments on the provision in the pending Bill: [16]

> Under existing law, benefits payable under the social security program and certain other retirement programs of the Federal Government are exempt from income tax. No similar exemption is accorded to persons receiving retirement pensions under other publicly administered programs, such as teachers, as well as persons who receive industrial pensions or provide independently for their old age. In order to adjust this differential tax treatment, the House bill grants an individual who is 65 years of age or over a credit against his tax liability equivalent to the tax, at the first bracket rate, on the amount of his retirement income up to $1,200. Retirement income is defined to include pensions and annuities, interest, rents, and dividends. Since some types of retirement pensions are already excluded from gross income, an adjustment is made to avoid duplication. The amount of retirement income up to $1,200 which an individual receives is to be reduced, for purposes of computing the credit, by any social security, railroad retirement, military retirement pension, or other retirement pension which is excluded from gross income. Military disability pensions or workmen's compensation payments, however, do not serve to reduce retirement income.

> Since the benefit of the credit is intended for retired individuals, the bill employs substantially the same test of retirement as that adopted for social-security purposes. An individual would be permitted to earn up to $900 a year as an employee or in self-employment without affecting the amount of the retirement credit. However, earnings in excess of

---

14. I.R.C. (26 U.S.C.A.) § 31(b).

15. See TRA (1976) § 503(a).

16. S.Rep.No.1622, 83rd Cong., 2d Sess. 8 (1954).

$900 reduce, dollar for dollar, the amount of retirement income on which the credit is based. If an individual's earnings equal $2,100, he would receive no tax credit for any retirement income. This provision has been modified by your committee as described below.

The bill also adopts a work-qualifying test similar to one used for social-security purposes to determine whether an income recipient above the age of 65, who is not deriving earned income, is a person who was actually engaged in gainful employment prior to age 65. Thus, to qualify for the credit an individual must have derived earnings of at least $600 a year in each of any 10 years prior to the taxable year. A widow whose spouse would have qualified under this requirement is herself qualified. Where a husband and wife meet this requirement, each can qualify for the retirement credit.

The original provision has been amended many times. Here is a summary of the credit provision in its newest form, as stated by the House Committee on Ways and Means on September 14, 1976:

Sec. 503.   [of TRA 1976]   Revision of retirement income credit

The conference agreement restructures and converts the present retirement income credit to a tax credit for the elderly. The credit for the elderly liberalizes the present retirement income credit in several respects. First, the credit is extended for the first time to earned income and, thus, is available to individuals age 65 or over regardless of whether they receive retirement income or earned income. The reduction in the credit under present law for one-half of the earnings in excess of $1,200 and under $1,700 for all earnings over $1,700 is eliminated. In addition, the present eligibility requirement that an individual must have annual earnings of $600 for 10 years is removed.

Second, the maximum amount of income with respect to which the 15-percent credit may be claimed is increased to $2,500 for a single person age 65 or over and for a married couple filing jointly if only one spouse is age 65 or over and to $3,750 for a married couple filing jointly if both spouses are age 65 or over. These maximum amounts are reduced, as under present law, by social security and railroad retirement benefits and other exempt pension income. In addition, an income phaseout is provided to limit the benefits of the credit to low- and middle-income elderly individuals. The maximum amount on which the credit is based is reduced by $1 for each $2 of adjusted gross income (AGI) in excess of $7,500 for a single person and $10,000 for a married couple filing a joint return. Thus, the credit would no longer be available for a single person when his adjusted gross income reaches $12,500. In the case of married couples, the credit would be available up to an income level of $15,000 if only one spouse is age 65 or over and up to $17,500 if both spouses are age 65 or over. As under present law, the credit for the elderly is nonrefundable (may not exceed the tax for the year).

In the case of individuals under age 65 who receive public retirement pensions, the present retirement income credit is generally retained. However, the maximum amount upon which the credit is based is increased to $2,500 for single persons and $3,750 for married couples filing a joint return. Because the earnings cutback of present law is continued, the adjusted gross income phaseout does not apply. The present eligibility requirement of annual earnings of $600 for 10 years is eliminated. In the case of married couples where one spouse is age 65 or over and therefore eligible for the new elderly credit and the other spouse is under age 65 with public retirement income, the couple must elect for the taxable year whether to use the present retirement income credit or the new credit for the elderly.

This provision applies to taxable years beginning after December 31, 1975.

The Investment Credit

The provision designed to stimulate the economy through the allowance of a credit against tax for capital formation expenditures has been an off-and-on thing for the past decade or so. Now (1976) it is on again for a while, until 1981, and in general at a hearty 10% rate. Detailed rules for allowance and sometimes "recapture"[17] of the I.R.C. section 38 credit are not discussed here.[18]

The Work Incentive Credit

One of the major policy objectives of the Revenue Act of 1971 was to provide expanded "job opportunities for all Americans." In addition to the promulgation of section 188, relating to the amortization of on-the-job training and child care facilities, Congress also provided a tax credit for expenses of work incentive programs, by adding sections 40, 50A and 50B to the Code. The program that had been created in 1967 was ineffectual in placing welfare recipients in jobs.

---

17. Cf. I.R.C. (26 U.S.C.A.) § 1245 considered in Chapter 21.

18. See I.R.C. (26 U.S.C.A.) §§ 46, 47, and 48, as amended by TRA (1976). See page 804, supra.

Commenting on the use of a tax credit to increase the effectiveness of the program, the Joint Committee on Internal Revenue Taxation observed:[19]

* * *

Employment in the private sector represents our major hope for leading present welfare recipients to economic independence. As an incentive for employers in the private sector to hire individuals placed in on-the-job training or employment through the Work Incentive Program, the Act provides a tax credit equal to 20 percent of the wages and salaries paid to these employees during their first 12 months of employment.

Somewhat altered since its inception, the "WIN" credit is still alive and well and somewhat enlarged. These summary comments were made on the provision by the House Ways and Means Committee after agreement of the two Houses of Congress on the 1976 Tax Reform Act:

Under present law, the work incentive (WIN) credit, equal to 20 percent of the wages paid during the first 12 months of employment to qualified AFDC recipients, is available to employers engaged in a trade or business who hire such employees. Qualified participants are certified by the local WIN agency. The credit is not available in the case of an employee who ceases to work for the original employer for an additional 12 months unless the employee voluntarily quits, becomes disabled, or is fired for misconduct. The amount of the credit available in any year is limited to the first $25,000 of tax plus one-half of tax liability in excess of $25,000.

The conference agreement makes the WIN credit available from the date of hiring if employment is not terminated without cause before the end of 6 months. An additional exemption is added to the recapture rules so that there is no recapture of the credit if the employee was laid off due to lack of business. In addition, the limit on the credit is doubled from $25,000 to $50,000 plus one-half of the excess over $50,-000.

Contributions to Candidates

Under I.R.C. section 41, a taxpayer may claim a credit, limited however to $25 ($50 on a joint return), for one half his contributions to candidates for public office.[20] The federal government is pretty

---

19. "General Explanation of the Revenue Act of 1971," Staff of the Joint Committee on Internal Revenue Taxation, pp. 125–127 (1972).

20. Use of the § 41 credit precludes use of the alternative § 218 deduction. See § 218(c) and page 536, supra.

well into the business of financing political campaigns, taking account also of the millions of dollars that taxpayers may designate on their Form 1040's for use in the presidential elections. Even if a laudable motive is discernible, one wonders.

General Tax Credit

A temporary 1975 device to stimulate consumer spending, I.R.C. § 42, initially allowing each taxpayer a credit of $30 multiplied by the number of his I.R.C. § 151(b) and (e) exemptions, was expanded in 1976 and extended through 1977. The credit for Personal Exemptions, as it was first called, has become the General Tax Credit with the critical figure increased to $35. An alternative is now provided allowing the credit to be 2% of taxable income, up to $9000, or a maximum credit under the alternative (There is none under the $35 computation.) of $180. All these figures are halved for married taxpayers filing separately.[21] Not really the type of provision to become a permanent part of the Code, what would determine its further extension?

Earned Income Credit

This is a wage-earner provision with which one might compare I.R.C. § 1348 which puts a maximum 50% rate ceiling on earned income, helping only the "big guy." The credit provided under § 43 is 10% of "earned income"[22] up to $4000, a maximum credit of $400. But a new congressional fad, the phaseout,[23] may eliminate the credit. Just as the credit increases by 10% of each dollar of earned income up to $4000, it is reduced a like amount by each dollar of adjusted gross income over $4000. Thus when adjusted gross is $8000 or more the credit is zip. This "temporary" credit is also scheduled to run through 1977.

Credit for Dependent Care Expenses

For some time I.R.C. § 214 has provided a limited *deduction* for expenses incurred in the care of a dependent (initially only a child), which enabled the taxpayer to work. The Tax Reform Act of 1976 converted this provision to a *credit* under new § 44A and made numerous significant changes.[24] Basically, the credit is "20 percent of the employment related expenses."[25] The credit can never exceed $800 for a taxable year ($400 if there is only one qualifying dependent)[26] and, as is the case of its predecessor deduction, it is the subject of many detailed rules.

---

21. See TRA (1976) § 401.

22. I.R.C. (26 U.S.C.A.) § 43(c)(2).

23. See, for example, I.R.C. (26 U.S.C.A.) § 37(c)(1), as amended in 1976.

24. See TRA (1976) § 504(a) adding new I.R.C. § 44A and repealing § 214.

25. See I.R.C. § 44A(c)(2) for the definition of such expenses.

26. I.R.C. § 44A(d).

Credit for Foreign Taxes

Income taxes imposed by foreign countries may be deducted by one who has paid such taxes, under § 164(a) (3). However, the taxpayer has an alternative of claiming such foreign taxes as a credit.[27] Obviously the deduction and credit cannot both be claimed.[28] Generally, the credit provision will be more advantageous. Why?

Obsolete Credit Provisions

For many years, interest income from certain United States Government obligations was accorded special treatment. The provision allowed individuals a credit of 3% of the amount of interest received on such obligations.[29] However, the credit applied only in the case of obligations issued prior to a critical date in 1941. As no such obligations are now outstanding the "deadwood" provisions of the Tax Reform Act of 1976 sawed off this provision.[30]

For a time a credit was allowed with respect to dividends received from domestic corporations. As a part of measures directed at the "double" tax on corporate income, this provision came into the law [31] at the same time as the limited dividend exclusion.[32] This credit provision was repealed in 1964, and now only the dividend exclusion remains.

A provision of very brief duration allowed taxpayers a credit equal to 5% of the purchase price or construction cost of a new residence, but the credit could not exceed $2000.[33] The provision has little current interest as it was applicable only if construction of the residence was begun before a critical date in March, 1975.

27. I.R.C. (26 U.S.C.A.) §§ 33 and 901 (a).

28. I.R.C. (26 U.S.C.A.) § 275(a)(4).

29. I.R.C. (26 U.S.C.A.) § 35(a); see also § 242 according corporate taxpayers a similar benefit by way of a deduction on determining taxable income for normal tax purposes. Section 242 followed § 35 into limbo in 1976. TRA (1976) § 1901(a)(33).

30. TRA (1976) § 1901(a)(2).

31. I.R.C. (26 U.S.C.A.) § 34.

32. See I.R.C. (26 U.S.C.A.) § 116.

33. I.R.C. (26 U.S.C.A.) § 44.

PART NINE: FEDERAL TAX PROCEDURE

CHAPTER 28. INTRODUCTION

No attempt is made in this book to present a full analysis of procedures involved in the determination and enforcement of federal income tax liability. Many procedural principles are introduced in earlier chapters where the emphasis, however, is on substantive tax law. Here the effort is to present procedural fundamentals in one place for more systematic consideration. The broad questions to consider are: (1) When and how can the taxpayer recover tax that was improperly paid (i. e., successfully assert a right to a refund)? (2) When and how can the government exact additional tax that should have been paid (i. e., successfully assert a deficiency)? (3) What means are available to the taxpayer to resist deficiency assertions? (4) What are the chances of criminal prosecution for tax fraud? Answers to these questions involve all three branches of government. Congress provides the statutory framework. The administration of the law is assigned primarily to the Internal Revenue Service, a branch of the Treasury Department; but the Justice Department enters the picture in some civil and criminal cases. The courts perform their usual role of deciding controversies.

A. CIVIL LIABILITY FOR TAX

Tax liability is determined initially by the taxpayer. Under our system of self-assessment, a potentially taxable individual is required to file an income tax return annually [1] and, upon filing, to pay any amount of tax shown on the return to be due.[2] Taxes so reported are automatically assessed. "Assessment" takes place when the assessment officer in the District Director's office or a Service Center signs the summary record of assessment.[3]

1. I.R.C. (26 U.S.C.A.) §§ 6012(a), 6072 (a). Interestingly, the well-known "Form 1040" came into existence with the inception of the modern income tax in 1913.

2. I.R.C. (26 U.S.C.A.) § 6151(a). Similar rules apply to taxpayers other than individuals, such as corporations, trusts and estates, and to other taxes, such as estate and gift taxes.

Of course large amounts of tax are collected by way of withholding by taxpayers' employers and by quarterly advance payments by taxpayers pursuant to their declarations of estimated tax, as noted at page 963, supra.

3. Reg. § 301.6203–1.

Billions of dollars pour into the Treasury by way of this quasi-voluntary method of tax determination and payment by the taxpayer himself. Yet, the burden placed on the taxpayer is very great. Even just a little experience with the intricacies of substantive tax law should suggest that, quite apart from negligence or any intentional wrong-doing, many mistakes will be made by the taxpayer.

Human error may be at its worst with regard to the simple arithmetic required in the preparation of a return. The statute permits this kind of error to be corrected summarily. If upon examination of a return it is found that tax liability is understated because of a mathematical error appearing on the return, the amount of the tax with the error corrected can be forthwith assessed and the taxpayer billed for the underpayment.[4] Sometimes, on the other hand, a taxpayer is agreeably surprised to receive an automatic refund when the Service discovers he has made an arithmetical error to his disadvantage. If either the government or the taxpayer subsequently asserts that other types of errors appear on the return both administrative and judicial procedures, later discussed, are available to test the validity of such assertions and to enforce the appropriate adjustments.

Controversy over Tax Liability. It taxes credulity to think that a system of voluntary tax payment would work if the government invariably simply accepted the taxpayer's own appraisal of his liability, even after correcting arithmetical errors. This is not the plan. The initial steps in tax payment and collection should be thought of in terms of the following dialogue between the taxpayer and the government:

Taxpayer (the return): "This is what I propose to pay, and why. Check enclosed."

Government (no actual response, but this unstated message): "We've checked your arithmetic, which is O.K. and, since we're pretty busy, we'll call it square."

But at a later date there may be additional *alternative* responses by the government, if the taxpayer's return is selected for audit. How will it be so selected? We do not know.[5] It is the government's policy, perhaps analogous to that behind the unmarked patrol car, to keep taxpayers in the dark in this respect. The *in terrorem* effect is doubtless a boost to taxpayer integrity. Generally, it is more profitable for the government to audit returns reporting large amounts of income, because errors found there may produce much larger amounts of revenue. However, sufficient numbers of very small returns are

---

4. I.R.C. (26 U.S.C.A.) § 6213(b)(1); Reg. § 301.6213–1(b)(1). The same instant assessment authority exists with respect to an underpayment arising out of an overstatement of income tax withheld or estimated income tax paid. I.R.C. § 6201(a)(3).

5. Some circumstances in which an audit is virtually certain are identified in Chommie, Federal Income Taxation, 884–885 (1973); Garbis and Frome, Procedures in Federal Tax Controversies, 1.2–1.4 (1968).

subjected to scrutiny (particularly as to certain items, such as dependency deductions) so that each taxpayer must wonder whether he is next.   Computers now play a role in the selection of returns for audit, for example, by turning up discrepancies between the amount of dividends reported on the return and the amount reported by the paying corporation as paid to the particular taxpayer,[6] but problems seem to persist in matching available data.

Silence is golden, after the filing of a return.   If there is any response, it will be to identify some disagreement with the taxpayer's assertions (although it is possible the reply will indicate the taxpayer overpaid his tax).

Tax audits take several forms.   A return may be reviewed by officials in an audit division of a regional Service Center and questions raised by way of correspondence.[7]   This may be the source of the tax counterpart of the old familiar draft board "Greetings!" which may come by phone or by letter.   In turn, the case may be referred to a District Director's office [8] where it is likely the taxpayer may be asked to appear for an interview,[9] and possibly to bring records.   In such an interview (really at any time) the taxpayer may take the offensive and claim he has overpaid.[10]   Finally, there is a chance of a field audit where the taxpayer and his records may get a going over on his premises.[11]

Taxpayers do not generally enjoy being called onto the carpet any more than schoolboys enjoy a command appearance in the principal's office.   But they have little choice.   Congress has armed tax officials with extensive authority to inquire into matters affecting tax liability and, with judicial assistance, to compel the cooperation of taxpayers and others who may have relevant information.[12]   As in some other situations, inevitability suggests a somewhat quiescent and cooperative attitude; and the attitude of an agent is quite likely to reflect that of the taxpayer.

One possible consequence of an audit is a "no change" letter [13] indicating that, after consideration, no adjustments are required.   The

6. I.R.C. (26 U.S.C.A.) § 6042; and see Cohen, "Automation and Tax Administration," 28 Ohio St.L.J. 69 (1967); Meek, "A.D.P.'s Tax Administration Revolution: Its Advantages, Effects, and Problems," 24 J.Tax. 304 (1966); Caplin, "Automatic Data Processing of Federal Tax Returns," 7 The Practical Lawyer 43 (1961).

7. Reg. § 601.105(b)(2).

8. There are sixty-seven District Directors scattered over the United States. See I.R.C. § 7621; 768 CCH, page 67,-010.

9. Reg. § 601.105(b)(2)(ii).

10. Ibid.

11. Reg. § 601.105(b)(3).

12. See generally, I.R.C. (26 U.S.C.A.) §§ 7602–7604; and see Caplin, "How to Handle a Federal Income Tax Audit," 28 Wash. and Lee L.Rev. 331 (1971).   Under a very recent Supreme Court opinion, the business records even of an individual may be seized subject to a search warrant without offending his privilege against self-incrimination.   Andresen v. Maryland, 427 U.S. 463 (1976).

13. Reg. § 601.105(d).

alternative (disregarding a possible conclusion that there has been an overpayment) is a statement or letter indicating required adjustments and the amount of additional tax to be paid. The taxpayer may very well disagree. If so, still within the District Director's office, the taxpayer may request a conference with the conference staff. Such a conference is an informal proceeding in which the effort is to reach agreement on issues not settled initially with the agent. The taxpayer is not required to take this step; this and some other administrative procedures are not a part of required exhaustion of administrative remedies prior to suit. Indeed, exhaustion of all discretionary administrative procedures might sometimes seem more likely to result in the exhaustion of the taxpayer. But, in fairness, it must be said that the objective is the avoidance of litigation, even more costly for both the taxpayer and the government. Indeed:[14]

> District conferees are authorized to consider and accept settlement proposals by taxpayers, subject to approval of Chief, Conference Staff, Section Chief (Conference Staff), or Chief, Technical Branch (except in Manhattan District) as appropriate, in field and office audit cases when the total amount of proposed additional tax, proposed overassessment, or claimed refund does not exceed $2,500 for any year. This authority includes the right to settle issues on a basis favorable to the taxpayer even though contrary to nonacquiescence in court decisions, revenue rulings, or interpretations of the Service as set forth in ruling letters issued to, or technical advice memorandums concerning, the taxpayer whose case is being considered by the district conferee.

This limited settlement authority was not conferred on district conferees until 1974.

The sequel to a district office conference in an "unagreed" case is a "thirty-day letter," which explains to the taxpayer his further rights to review.[15] By it the taxpayer is informed that within a stated period, usually thirty days, he may take the next possible administrative step by requesting a conference in the Appellate Division.[16] At this stage the taxpayer leaves the District Director's office, if not geographically at least organizationally. The Appellate Division operates directly under the Office of the Regional Commissioner, of which there are seven in the United States,[17] not under any District Director. In most circumstances the Appellate Division's jurisdiction can be invoked only by way of a formal written protest.[18] At the Ap-

---

14. Reg. § 601.105(c)(5).

15. Reg. § 601.105(d). The terms of this letter are not prescribed by statute; indeed, it may emerge as a fifteen-day letter. It is not to be confused with the statutory notice of deficiency, commonly referred to as the "ninety-day letter."

16. The taxpayer does not always have the right to an Appellate Division conference. See Reg. § 601.106(b). This is explained in the thirty-day letter.

17. See 768 CCH, page 67,010.

18. Reg. § 601.106(a)(1).

pellate Division level the taxpayer may hope to find the most experienced Service officials who, in any event, enjoy the greatest latitude and discretion in attempting to reach a settlement on controversial issues.

The three levels of negotiation described (examining officer, district conferee, Appellate Division) probably act pretty effectively, overall, as a series of increasingly finer sieves designed to strain out by agreement as many issues as possible and thus to settle disagreements which otherwise might ripen into litigation. But there will probably always be room for improvement.[19]

Running the described administrative gauntlet might usually be a futile thing if the contested tax liability turned on an issue of law which, for example, was the subject of a Revenue Ruling adverse to the position of the taxpayer. But he need not run it. He has a right to refuse to enter into administrative negotiations or to break them off at any stage and to seek judicial intervention. Before litigation is discussed, however, a brief look should be taken at administrative procedure where the shoe is on the other foot; the taxpayer asserts a right to a refund.

Refund Controversies. Although a draftee never had any such reciprocal opportunity, a taxpayer can sometimes properly send his "Greetings!" to the government. One way in which this possibility arises is for the taxpayer to make a mistake on his return to his own disadvantage and then to discover it later, maybe talking to you at a cocktail party. His next question will be: What can I do about it? In general what he can do, if his action is timely, is to file a refund claim; and if his claim is not allowed, he can then sue for a refund. Chapter 29 gives you some guidance in refund matters.

A refund suit may also arise in another way. As indicated above, the taxpayer can elect utter inactivity in response to deficiency assertions, although he will then have to pay the asserted tax. But this does not necessarily foreclose the recovery of the very tax that he decided initially not to contest. If he has not cut off this possibility,[20] he may still take administrative and judicial steps to contest the liability through a refund claim and suit.

In either case the procedure starts with a claim. In income tax cases the classic form of claim, Form 843, is no longer to be used. Instead, a claim is made by an individual on Form 1040X or on an amended Form 1040.[21] The claim is generally filed in the Service Center serving the Internal Revenue district in which the tax was paid.[22] When filed it commences administrative procedures, includ-

---

19. See Wright, Needed Changes in Internal Revenue Service Conflict Resolution Procedures (1970); Cohen, "Appellate Procedures in Tax Administration," 21 U.S.C.Tax.Inst. 1 (1969).

20. See Finality in Tax Controversies, Chapter 30, infra.

21. See Reg. §§ 601.105(e); 301.6402–3.

22. Reg. § 301.6402–2(a)(2).

ing optional review procedures, which parallel those available in the case of deficiency controversies.[23]　After rejection (or after waiting a stated period of time) the taxpayer may be able to give up on administrative relief and seek judicial intervention by way of a refund suit.

Until 1924 when the Board of Tax Appeals (now the United States Tax Court) was created,[24] the word invariably was pay first—litigate later.　The need for a steady flow of revenue is so great that the taxpayer was restricted to the "refund route" if he wished to contest federal tax liability in the courts.　But now for half a century he has been accorded an alternative.　He stands at the crossroads when he receives a statutory notice of deficiency; he must then decide upon the form and forum for his suit to contest liability.

Tax Litigation.　In general, except in the case of waiver [25] and jeopardy assessment,[26] assessment or collection of an income tax deficiency is barred until a statutory notice of deficiency, the "ninety-day letter," has been sent to the taxpayer.[27]　Moreover, the required terms of this notice give the taxpayer ninety days within which to file a petition in the Tax Court for a "redetermination" of the asserted deficiency; [28] assessment and collection continue to be barred for that period and, if the taxpayer files a petition, until the decision of the Tax Court becomes final.[29]　Limitation periods that otherwise run against the assessment or collection of tax are suspended for the ninety day period or, if a Tax Court petition is filed, for the litigation period and for an additional 60 days after that period.[30]

In the light of all this, efforts to get the taxpayer to agree to the asserted deficiency during the administrative deficiency steps described above are presented in terms of a request that he execute Form 870, which is an authorized waiver of his statutory right to receive a ninety-day letter prior to assessment.[31]

It should be noted here that the government's first determination there may be a deficiency may occur close to the time when assessment would be barred by a statute of limitations.　As indicated above,

---

23.　Reg. § 601.105(e)(2).

24.　Revenue Act of 1924, § 900, 43 Stat. 253 at 336 (1924).

25.　See I.R.C. (26 U.S.C.A.) § 6213(d).

26.　See I.R.C. (26 U.S.C.A.) §§ 6213(a) and 6861.

27.　I.R.C. (26 U.S.C.A.) § 6213(a). See, generally, Worthy, "The Tax Litigation Structure," 5 Ga.L.Rev. 248 (1971); Ferguson, "Jurisdictional Problems in Federal Tax Controversies," 48 Iowa L.Rev. 312 (1963).

28.　Ibid.　The 90-day period is extended to 150 days, if the notice is mailed to a person abroad.

29.　Ibid.

30.　I.R.C. (26 U.S.C.A.) § 6503(a).

31.　I.R.C. (26 U.S.C.A.) § 6213(d).　The execution of a Form 870AD at the Appellate Division level may have further consequences. See Finality in Tax Controversies, Chapter 30, infra at page 1014.

the government's position *could* then be protected by the issuance of the ninety-day letter tolling the statute, but this would tend to foreclose customary negotiations toward an agreed settlement. In such circumstances the taxpayer will be asked to execute a Form 872, which is an authorized extension of the limitation period.[32] As a practical matter a request to sign this extension presents the taxpayer with a Hobson's choice. Refusal to sign will simply bring on the statutory deficiency notice.

Suppose now a taxpayer has received the statutory notice of deficiency giving him ninety days in which to file a petition in the Tax Court. If he files such a petition, he relinquishes all other administrative and judicial remedies otherwise available, except his right to appeal the Tax Court's decision.[33] What he relinquishes specifically is the alternative of permitting the tax to be assessed, paying it, filing a claim for refund and then a suit in either the District Court or the Court of Claims. Thus, receipt of the ninety-day letter places the taxpayer at the cross-roads, if he is determined to litigate.

A suit for refund cannot be filed in the Tax Court whose jurisdiction is in general limited to the redetermination of deficiencies in income, estate and gift taxes.[34] However, if the Tax Court's jurisdiction is properly invoked in response to a deficiency notice the Court can, in addition to finding that there is no deficiency, determine that there has been an overpayment to be refunded to the taxpayer.[35] On the other hand, neither the District Court nor the Court of Claims is given jurisdiction to redetermine deficiencies; tax litigation commenced in those courts rests on the taxpayer's suit for a refund. But of course a refund suit also is a comprehensive determination of income tax liability for the year in question and, where a counterclaim is possible,[36] may result in a deficiency determination.

The losing party in a deficiency proceeding in the Tax Court or in a refund suit in the District Court can appeal the decision (as of right) to the Court of Appeals, with the further possibility of review on certiorari to the Supreme Court.[37] Certiorari to the Supreme Court is the only possibility for review of a decision of the Court of Claims.

---

32. I.R.C. (26 U.S.C.A.) § 6501(c)(4).

33. I.R.C. (26 U.S.C.A.) § 6512(a); and see Emma R. Dorl, 57 T.C. 720 (1972), aff'd, per curiam, 507 F.2d 406 (2d Cir. 1974).

34. See Rules of Practice and Procedure, United States Tax Court, Rule 13. Jurisdiction (1974). It is often questioned whether the Tax Court's jurisdiction should not be extended to refund suits. See Griswold, Federal Taxation, page 91, note 1. (Foundation Press 1966). In 1969 Senator Tydings proposed a bill which would have given the Tax Court exclusive jurisdiction over tax refund suits as well as deficiency suits. S. 1974, 91st Cong. 1st Sess. (1969).

35. I.R.C. (26 U.S.C.A.) § 6512(b). But as regards enforcement of a Tax Court determination of overpayment, see Thelma Rosenberg, 29 TCM 888 (1970).

36. E. g., I.R.C. (26 U.S.C.A.) § 7422(e).

37. See I.R.C. (26 U.S.C.A.) § 7482.

The procedures outlined here are charted in Treasury Publication 612 (November 1968) set out below, which is still up to date except for reference to newly created Service Centers.

INCOME TAX APPEAL PROCEDURE
INTERNAL REVENUE SERVICE

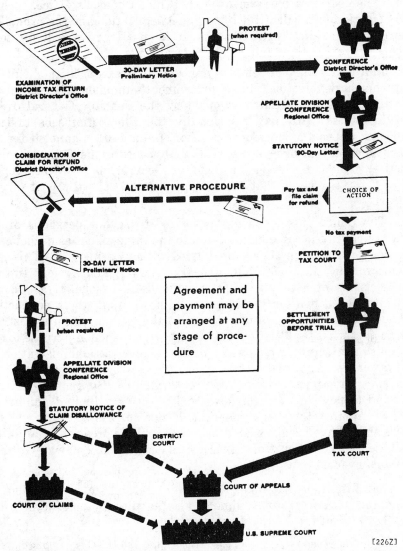

If a taxpayer decides to litigate a tax controversy, he discovers that the government is represented by counsel who are not a part of the Internal Revenue Service organization. Tax Court cases are tried by attorneys in the office of the Chief Counsel *for* the Internal Revenue Service, which is a unit in the Legal Division of the Treasury Department not under the Commissioner of Internal Revenue. Much of the work of the Chief Counsel's office is conducted in the offices of seven Regional Counsel and in the offices of Assistant Regional Counsel located in the district offices. In general, with respect to cases docketed in the Tax Court, settlement authority is either delegated to Regional Counsel or shared by Regional Counsel and the Appellate Division.[38] A great many so-called "session" cases are settled by Regional Counsel just before the Tax Court trial.

Other services performed by the Chief Counsel's office, such as participation in the drafting of proposed legislation and the promulgation of rulings and regulations, make it an attractive spot for some young lawyers with an interest in federal taxes.

If a Tax Court decision is appealed, there is a further shift in governmental personnel. The government's decision whether to appeal a Tax Court decision is made by the Solicitor General of the United States with participation by the Chief Counsel's office.[39] Whoever appeals a Tax Court decision, the appeal is handled for the government by attorneys in the Tax Division of the Department of Justice. And, of course, the Solicitor General also has the responsibility for tax cases that reach the Supreme Court by writ of certiorari.

The Court of Appeals is authorized to review decisions of the Tax Court "in the same manner and to the same extent as decisions of the district courts in civil actions tried without a jury." [40] This procedure for judicial review only appears to be tidy and logical. In fact, the decisions of the Tax Court, a centralized national tribunal, fan out into eleven non-unified appellate bodies. As a result, conflicting interpretations of the statute emerge in the various circuits, destroying in part what the Tax Court believes to be a principal purpose for its establishment, an effort toward uniform national administration of the tax laws. The further review of tax cases by the Supreme Court can only sometimes correct this problem, as the Supreme Court can respond to petitions for certiorari only in a very limited number of cases. Against this background, it is not surprising that over the years there have been repeated proposals for the creation of an intermediate appellate Court of Tax Appeals designed to do away with the present inverted pyramid.[41]

Tax litigation that takes the form of refund suits in the district courts and the Court of Claims is also handled by attorneys in the Tax Division of the Justice Department.

---

38. Reg. § 601.106(a) (2). See, generally, Cohen, "The Chief Counsel's Office," 42 Taxes 191 (1964).

39. See Garbis and Frome, Procedures in Federal Tax Cases, 917 (1968); Walters, "The Role of the Department of Justice in Tax Litigation," 23 S. Car.L.Rev. 193 (1971).

40. I.R.C. (26 U.S.C.A.) § 7482(a).

41. See Del Cotto, "The Need for a Court of Tax Appeals: An Argument and a Study," 12 Buffalo L.Rev. 5 (1962); Griswold, "The Need for a Court of Tax Appeals," 57 Harv.L. Rev. 1153 (1944); Surrey, "Some Suggested Topics in the Field of Tax Ad-

Procedures Generally Unavailable. The injunction and the declaratory judgment might appear to be especially promising remedies in tax controversies. Indeed, the injunction has played something of a role in the history of tax litigation. In an early case, before the ratification of the Sixteenth Amendment, a shareholder successfully enjoined his corporation from paying an income tax that he claimed was unconstitutional.[42] While the use of the injunction in tax cases is not now completely outlawed,[43] its utility is very limited.[44]

It is not difficult to think of circumstances in which a taxpayer might wish to get a declaratory judgment of his tax liability. However, the federal Declaratory Judgments Act [45] provides for such judgments in cases of actual controversy, *except* "with respect to federal taxes." Thus, the remedy is foreclosed.[46] Whether it may be possible to get a declaratory judgment as to rights and obligations that underlie liability for a federal tax is not entirely clear.[47]

On the other hand, there are circumstances in which a taxpayer can obtain a declaratory *ruling*. This has reference to an administrative determination of tax liability, perhaps before a return is filed or before a transaction is undertaken. Numerous Revenue Rulings appear in earlier chapters of this book. Their significance is further explored under the heading "Finality in Tax Controversies" in Chapter 30, infra at page 1014.

Collection of Taxes. As a general rule, valid assessment of tax is a prerequisite to the government's right to collect the tax.[48] It is the act of assessment that establishes the taxpayer's debt to the government. An analogy might be a board of directors' declaration of a dividend, which creates a corporate debt to the shareholder. The statute expressly authorizes the Secretary of the Treasury and of-

ministration," 25 Wash.U.L.Rev. 399, 414–423 (1940).

42. Pollock v. Farmer's Loan & Trust Co., 157 U.S. 429, 15 S.Ct. 673 (1895).

43. E. g., I.R.C. (26 U.S.C.A.) § 6213(a), last sentence, is a statutory exception to § 7421(a).

44. Compare Enochs v. Williams Packing and Navigation Co., Inc., 370 U.S. 1 (1962), with Miller v. Standard Nut Margarine Co., 284 U.S. 498 (1932), and Comm'r v. Shapiro, 424 U.S. 614 (1976).

45. 28 U.S.C.A. § 2201 as amended by § 405 of the Revenue Act of 1935.

46. See, e. g., Sweeney v. U. S., 152 Ct.Cl. 516, 285 F.2d 444 (1961).

47. See King v. U. S., 182 Ct.Cl. 631, 390 F.2d 894 (1968), granting such a judgment; rev'd, 395 U.S. 1, 89 S.Ct. 1501 (1966), on the basis of the limited jurisdiction of the Court of Claims, not unavailability of the remedy.

48. See I.R.C. (26 U.S.C.A.) § 6502. There is some authority supporting collection by suit without assessment. Cf. U. S. v. Ayer, 12 F.2d 194 (1st Cir. 1926), sustaining a suit to collect estate tax without assessment. However, with respect to deficiencies there are parallel obstacles to both assessment and collection, see I.R.C. (26 U.S.C.A.) § 6213(a), and, when the tax can be assessed, it will be.

ficials designated by him to collect assessed federal taxes [49] with substantial latitude as to method of collection.[50]

After proper assessment, the government has six years (or longer by agreement with the taxpayer) within which to collect the tax.[51] This limitation period for *collection* should not be confused with limitation periods within which *assessment* must be made, discussed in Chapter 30.

As might be expected, methods afforded the government for the collection of tax go beyond those available to private creditors. A conventional suit for collection may be brought [52] which, if successful, converts the taxpayer to a judgment debtor. But, additionally, the government may resort to the extraordinary remedies of levy and distraint.[53] This is to say that without judicial intervention the taxpayer's property may be seized and sold to satisfy the tax obligation.[54] Finally, an unpaid federal tax becomes a lien on the taxpayer's property [55] which, when perfected,[56] may be enforced to collect the tax.

A taxpayer cannot thwart the tax gatherer by giving away all his property to avoid payment, or even by dying. Of course, if a tax lien has attached to one's property, it will follow the property into the hands of the donee.[57] Otherwise the liability of the transferee depends upon state law. The Internal Revenue Code invokes state law by permitting enforcement of a taxpayer's tax liability against his transferee, to the extent of the transferee's liability "at law or in equity." [58] Liability "at law" may arise, for example, when a continuing corporation assumes the tax liability of a merging corporation.[59] A transferee's liability "in equity" is likely to be less clear cut, raising as it does conventional problems of creditors' rights.[60] In either event, subject to variation as to such matters as limitation periods [61] and burden of proof,[62] a transferee who is liable for another's tax is placed pretty much in the shoes of the principal taxpayer as regards assessment, payment, and collection of the tax.[63]

49. I.R.C. (26 U.S.C.A.) § 6301. See Thrower, "Current Collection Problems and Procedures," 24 Tax Lawyer 217 (1971).

50. I.R.C. (26 U.S.C.A.) § 6302; see Reg. § 601.104(c).

51. I.R.C. (26 U.S.C.A.) § 6502(a).

52. 28 U.S.C.A. § 1396.

53. I.R.C. (26 U.S.C.A.) § 6331; and see note 50, supra.

54. See, e. g., Martinon v. Fitzgerald, 418 F.2d 1336 (2d Cir. 1969).

55. I.R.C. (26 U.S.C.A.) § 6321.

56. See I.R.C. (26 U.S.C.A.) § 6323(f); Reg. § 601.104(c).

57. E. g., U. S. v. Bess, 357 U.S. 51, 78 S.Ct. 1054 (1958). See Plumb, "Federal Liens and Priorities," 77 Yale L. J. 228, 605, 1104 (1967 and 1968).

58. I.R.C. (26 U.S.C.A.) § 6901.

59. E. g., Turnbull, Inc., Transferee, 22 TCM 1750 (1963); a supplemental opinion at 42 T.C. 582 (1964) was aff'd, 373 F.2d 91 (5th Cir. 1967), cert. den. 389 U.S. 842, 88 S.Ct. 72 (1967).

60. See Comm'r v. Stern, 357 U.S. 39, 78 S.Ct. 1047 (1958), and cases there cited.

61. I.R.C. (26 U.S.C.A.) § 6901(c).

62. I.R.C. (26 U.S.C.A.) § 6902(a).

63. I.R.C. (26 U.S.C.A.) § 6901(a).

This note is intended to be only a general description of civil procedures involved in Federal Income Tax cases. The following books deal in a more comprehensive fashion with these matters: When You Go to the Tax Court (Commerce Clearing House, frequently revised); Wright, Needed Changes in Internal Revenue Service Conflict Resolution Procedures (American Bar Foundation 1970); Chommie, The Internal Revenue Service (Praeger 1970); Garbis and Frome, Procedures in Federal Tax Controversies (Ronald Press 1968); Federal Tax Procedure for General Practitioners, California Continuing Education of the Bar (1968); 9 Mertens, Law of Federal Income Taxation (Rev. 1971; 1976 Supp.); 10 Mertens, Law of Federal Income Taxation (1970; 1976 Supp.); Goodrich and Redman, Procedures Before the Internal Revenue Service (A.L.I. and A.B.A. 1957); Casey, Federal Tax Practice (Callaghan 1955).

B. THE PROFILE OF A TAX FRAUD CASE

This Part B of this chapter is based on a paper prepared by George D. Crowley of the Illinois Bar for presentation in 1973 at the Southern Federal Tax Institute and later published in the Journal of Taxation.[1] Mr. Crowley and the Journal have agreed to adaptation and updating by the authors of this book to serve the purposes of this chapter.

GENERAL DESCRIPTION OF PROCEDURES

The hierarchy of enforcement personnel in the Internal Revenue Service is essentially as follows:

Director, Intelligence Division, National Office
Assistant Regional Commissioner (Intelligence)
Chief, Intelligence Division, District Director's Office
Special Agents (including certain other "technical positions.")[2]

Special Agents of the IRS operate out of the Intelligence Division of the district office. When a tax fraud investigation is approved by the Intelligence Division,[3] a Revenue Agent is assigned by Audit Division for a joint investigation,[4] but he is specifically under

---

1. Crowley, "The Role of the Practitioner When His Client Faces a Criminal Tax Fraud Investigation," 40 J.Tax. 18 (1974). Mr. Crowley is coauthor of the recently published book, Crowley and Manning, Criminal Tax Fraud—Representing the Taxpayer before Trial (PLI 1976).

2. Internal Revenue Manual ¶ 9111 (1976).

3. Among other things, informer's tips, discoveries by revenue agents, and suspicion of classes of taxpayers may indicate the need to investigate.

4. See Randall, "The Tax Man Cometh Back—with a Friend," 5 U. of Toledo L.Rev. 44 (1973).

the control of the Special Agent and, until the criminal aspects of the case are terminated, no civil negotiation concerning the amount of the tax will be allowed.

It is important that a taxpayer's representative recognize a tax fraud investigation is being conducted at the earliest possible time. There is no absolute answer to this problem and some experienced practitioners, in the end, look to their own visceral reactions as to the method by which an audit is being conducted. The most usual time of acquiring knowledge of a tax fraud investigation is when a Special Agent introduces himself into the case and seeks an interview with the taxpayer. This interview is usually preceded by *Miranda* [5]-type warnings [6] and is sought for the purpose of obtaining an initial statement from the taxpayer, which is almost invariably damaging. Among various other indications that a taxpayer may be suspected of fraud is the service of an administrative summons upon the taxpayer's accountant before any other contact by a Special Agent.

When the Special Agent has completed his investigation, if he recommends prosecution, he will do so in a detailed report. This report is similar to the Revenue Agent's Report and contains all necessary facts to support the recommendation. The report is reviewed by the Special Agent's Group Chief.

As a matter of policy, the Service usually provides the taxpayer or his representative a "district intelligence conference" with the Special Agent and his Group Chief before the report is approved,[7] but no "right" to this conference exists.[8] Regulation § 601.107(b) (2) provides that at the conference the IRS conferee will inform the taxpayer's representative of the alleged fraudulent features of the case by a general oral statement and the IRS will disclose the criminal adjustments and methods used by the IRS. The taxpayer will, however, not be furnished a copy of the Special Agent's Report. Useful information may be obtained at this conference which, however, is viewed by the Service chiefly as a vehicle to button up loose ends in its case and to obtain further information. The amount of information obtained by taxpayer's representative will vary with the particular IRS conferee.

The Special Agent's Report, if approved by the Intelligence Division, is forwarded to the Regional Counsel's office in the region where the Intelligence Division is located and the taxpayer is so notified, unless of course the case is in the hands of the United States

---

5. Miranda v. Arizona, 384 U.S. 436 (1966).

6. See Handbook for Special Agents § 242.13: Duty to Inform Individual of his Constitutional Rights.

7. See Reg. § 601.107(b)(2).

8. U. S. v. Goldstein, (unreported) 73–1 USTC ¶ 9163 (E.D.N.Y.1972), rev'd on other grounds 479 F.2d 1061 (2d Cir. 1973), cert. den. 414 U.S. 873 (1973). This case does not reflect the current regulation.

Attorney.[9] Another conference is afforded to the taxpayer or his representative at this level; notice of conference is given in letter form by the Regional Counsel's office. Regional Counsel's analysis of the file is basically limited to a determination (1) that the taxpayer is in fact guilty of tax evasion and (2) that there is a reasonable probability of securing a conviction.

If the Regional Counsel approves the Special Agent's report, the report with the recommendation by Regional Counsel for criminal prosecution is forwarded to the Department of Justice, Tax Division, Criminal Section. Again, it is the policy of Justice to offer the taxpayer or his attorney one conference. The standards for review at Justice are quite similar to those of the Regional Counsel, although the Justice attorneys are more concerned with local prosecution problems and the geographic structure of income tax prosecutions.[10]

If the Department of Justice recommends prosecution, the case is forwarded to the appropriate United States Attorney's office, usually with instructions to secure an indictment. While conferences do take place at the United States Attorney's office prior to indictment, they are not routinely granted. The United States Attorney's office usually has no authority to stop criminal cases in advance of indictment, but will on occasion return the matter to the IRS or Justice for further investigation, or present it to a Grand Jury for examination of unreliable witnesses.

THE EXAMINATION OF WITNESSES AND RECORDS

Section 7602 authorizes the IRS to examine any books, papers, or records, to summon the person liable for the tax or any person having possession or custody or care of relevant books and records to produce them and give relevant testimony, and to take any such testimony under oath of the person summoned as may be relevant or material to the inquiry. This power may be exercised to ascertain the correctness of any return and to determine any tax liability, or to collect any tax due. I.R.C. § 6020 also authorizes the IRS to make a return if the taxpayer has filed none. Under Code Section 7608(b), "a criminal investigator of the Intelligence Division" is authorized to execute and serve search warrants and to serve subpoenas and summonses. The taxpayer may not enjoin the Commissioner from issuing the summons.[11]

The administrative summons is not self-executing and the IRS Agent or hearing examiner has no power of enforcement if the person summoned refuses, or is enjoined from, compliance. The IRS must apply to a district court for enforcement by filing an *ex parte* petition.

---

9. Reg. § 601.107(c).

10. For a more detailed discussion of the difference between the two reviews, see Balter, Tax Fraud and Evasion, ¶'s 3.04(b) and 3.05, (4th Ed. 1976).

11. Reisman v. Caplin, 375 U.S. 440 (1964).

The district court will enter an order directing the person summoned to show cause why the summons should not be enforced and cause the order and the petition to be served. The "show cause" proceeding is a civil and adversary proceeding to which the Federal Rules of Civil Procedure apply.[12] Both the person summoned and anyone affected by a potential disclosure (having a proprietary interest in records sought) may appear or intervene before the district court.[13] The constitutional and other grounds for objection to enforcement of a summons are asserted in the enforcement proceeding and the district court will then either grant or deny enforcement.[14]

If the district court enters an order enforcing the summons, an appeal may be taken to the Court of Appeals. If the district court refuses to stay its order enforcing the summons pending appeal, the taxpayer or person summoned may appeal to the Court of Appeals for a stay of execution of the district court's order. Good faith objections may be raised in the judicial proceedings, whereas contumacious refusal to appear and object to an administrative summons may, upon conviction, subject the person summoned to a $1,000 fine or one year in prison or both.[15]

RESISTING A SUMMONS

A court will not enforce a summons issued for an improper purpose, such as harassment of the taxpayer,[16] pressure to settle a collateral dispute, or any other purpose reflecting on the good faith of a particular investigation,[17] nor one where the leads to the records in question were obtained in an unlawful search and seizure.[18]

The purposes for which a summons may be properly issued do not include the prosecution of tax crimes, but often civil investigation leads to suspicion of fraud. In Donaldson v. U. S.[19] the Court held that a summons under Section 7602 may be issued, if it is issued in good faith, prior to a recommendation for criminal prosecution. A recommendation for criminal prosecution made after issuance of the summons but before enforcement is sought does not invalidate the summons.[20] In United States v. Billingsley,[21] the court held that

---

12. U. S. v. Powell, 379 U.S. 48 (1964).

13. Reisman v. Caplin, supra note 11.

14. Nonconstitutional objections are discussed in Crowley and Manning, supra note 1, at ¶ 8.5.

15. I.R.C. § 7210.

16. Section 7605(b) requires that a taxpayer be subject to only one examination for any taxable year unless he or she is notified in writing by the Service that a further inspection is necessary.

17. U. S. v. Powell, supra note 12.

18. U. S. v. Bank of Commerce, 405 F. 2d 931 (3rd Cir. 1969), but see McGarry's Inc. v. Rose, 344 F.2d 416 (1st Cir. 1965), enforcing a summons where the records were known to the government prior to and independently of an illegal search.

19. 400 U.S. 517 (1971).

20. U. S. v. Cromer, 483 F.2d 99 (9th Cir. 1973).

21. 469 F.2d 1208 (10th Cir. 1972).

the critical recommendation occurs when the Service forwards the case to the Department of Justice. On the other hand, in United States v. Oaks,[22] the court acted on the assumption that a recommendation may have occurred when the Special Agent discussed the case with an Assistant U.S. Attorney and not when a written prosecution report was filed.

Despite the opinions focusing on recommendation dates, it is clear that a recommendation for prosecution is not the only test for proving that a summons was issued for an improper purpose. The question whether a summons is issued in good faith may be raised entirely separately from whether a recommendation for prosecution has been made.[23] Thus, if it can be shown that a firm decision to recommend prosecution has been made, even without any formal recommendation, or if the taxpayer's civil liability has already been determined, presumably the summons has been issued for an improper purpose and is not authorized by § 7602.[24]

If the person summoned intends to comply and the taxpayer has a protectible interest in the records or testimony sought, he may apply to the Federal courts for an injunction enjoining compliance by the person summoned. The result will usually be a petition for enforcement by the IRS and intervention by the taxpayer in that proceeding. If the person summoned refuses to comply, possibly at the suggestion of the taxpayer, the taxpayer may intervene in a subsequent enforcement proceeding if he has a proprietary interest in the records or testimony sought.[25]

It appears from *Donaldson* that the same test will be applied to determine a taxpayer's rights to injunctive relief and to intervention. But they also appear to be very narrow rights; e. g., in order to assert a valid 5th Amendment claim the taxpayer must be the owner or possessor of the records sought,[26] or there must be a privileged relationship (attorney-client) with the possessor of the records or the one whose testimony is sought.[27]

GENERALLY ADDITIONAL TAX MUST BE DUE

Proof of a tax deficiency is ordinarily an essential element in proving tax fraud. The practice has developed of obtaining indictments for filing false returns under Section 7206(1), which does not

22.   360 F.Supp. 855 (C.D.Cal.1973), rev'd on other grounds, 508 F.2d 1403 (9th Cir. 1974).

23.   U. S. v. Lafko, 520 F.2d 622 (3rd Cir. 1975); cf. U. S. v. Wright Motor Co., Inc., 536 F.2d 1090 (5th Cir. 1976).

24.   U. S. v. Wall Corp., 475 F.2d 893 (D.C.Cir. 1972).

25.   U. S. v. Donaldson, supra note 19.

26.   See Couch v. U. S., 409 U.S. 322, 333 (1973).

27.   See Fisher v. U. S.. 425 U.S. 391, 403–405, 96 S.Ct. 1569, 1577 (1976).

require proof of a deficiency. But in other instances, though case law is clear that the demonstration of a mere understatement of taxable income does not prove tax fraud, it is also clear from experience that if the Government can prove sizable understatements of taxable income for a number of years, they are a long way toward proving tax fraud to a judge or jury.

It is important to realize that several options are available to the IRS to prove a deficiency, especially in the early stages of an investigation. Answers to seemingly innocent questions such as "Did you have any cash on hand (i. e., cash other than in bank account) at the beginning of 1975?" or "What bank accounts did you maintain throughout 1974?" can lead to successful prosecution in criminal and civil tax fraud cases. It is therefore essential that a taxpayer's representative be familiar with the methods of proving a deficiency in order to determine the direction of investigation and the problem areas involved.

The IRS is not limited to proving a tax deficiency through the taxpayer's own books and records; the Commissioner is empowered to use less direct methods of proving income. In advance courses students study methods that involve an increase in net worth, a review of bank deposits, an analysis of cash expenditures and available funds, and other indirect methods, such as the "normal markup," "unit of sales" or "unit of profit" methods.[28] For example, in Agnellino v. Comm'r [29] the IRS was permitted to reconstruct taxpayer's income from a motel and restaurant operation by analyzing the number of bed sheets that were rented from a laundry supply company.

Most tax fraud cases that are stopped before indictment are stopped in the early stages of the Intelligence Division's investigation. By and large, this is not because the evidence indicates the taxpayer is innocent but because there is not enough evidence to prove him guilty. The first step any tax advisor should take is to stop the flow of information and evidence to the Special Agent.

MEETING THE SPECIAL AGENT

Virtually every successful tax fraud prosecution contains statements made by the taxpayer to the Special Agent. These statements are almost invariably damaging. If the statements are true, they often amount to a confession or provide damaging elements of the prosecution's case. If the statements are untrue, the Government may go to great efforts to prove they were untrue so as to offer such false exculpatory statements as evidence of *willfulness*, often an es-

28. See Balter, supra note 10, c. 10 ¶ 10.04 (10).

29. 20 TCM 100 (1961), aff'd. in part, 302 F.2d 797 (3rd Cir. 1962).

sential element of the crime charged,[30] i. e., the taxpayer would not have lied if he had not had the guilty knowledge. Moreover, a taxpayer's false statements may themselves constitute an offense punishable under I.R.C. § 7207.

Under no circumstances should the taxpayer be permitted to give a statement to the Special Agent except possibly in voluntary disclosure cases, discussed below. If the taxpayer has previously given a statement to a Special Agent, it is essential to learn what was said. In all but the most routine audits, communications with the Service should be through the taxpayer's representative. It is best that the taxpayer not even be present at any meeting or conferences.

Special Agents are instructed to tell a taxpayer, upon their initial visit, of their function as criminal investigators, and to advise the taxpayer that anything he says may be used against him, that he does not have to incriminate himself by answering questions or producing any documents, and that he may have the assistance of an attorney.[31]

At least two courts have held that this administrative requirement of modified *Miranda* warnings, even if self-imposed and not required by the Constitution itself, is binding on the Service.[32] Recently in Beckwith v. United States [33] the Supreme Court held that a special agent who is investigating suspected criminal tax fraud need not give full *Miranda* warnings unless the taxpayer is taken into custody or the interview is inherently coercive. However, the Special Agent in *Beckwith* had given the warnings mentioned above, required by the Special Agent's manual, so the question remains open (not decided by the Supreme Court) whether the taxpayer has a right to the administrative *Miranda*-type warnings.

CONSTITUTIONAL PROTECTION

The Fifth Amendment privilege against self-incrimination applies to an individual's oral testimony and to documentary communications; this includes the personal and business tax records of an individual.[34] The Fifth Amendment privilege does not apply, however, to corporate records, or those of a partnership.[35] The cus-

---

30. E. g., I.R.C. (26 U.S.C.A.) §§ 7201–7203.

31. Handbook for Special Agents § 242.13, Duty to Inform Individual of his Constitutional Rights. This policy with modification dates back to October 3, 1967 when the IRS issued News Release No. 897.

32. U. S. v. Heffner, 420 F.2d 809 (4th Cir. 1969); U. S. v. Leahey, 434 F.2d 7 (1st Cir. 1970).

33. 425 U.S. 341, 96 S.Ct. 1612 (1976).

34. Bellis v. U. S., 417 U.S. 85 (1974).

35. Ibid.

todian of corporate records is required to turn them over, upon appropriate summons, even if they incriminate him, but not to testify regarding missing records if his testimony might incriminate him.[36] There is no requirement that unrequested corporate records be volunteered to the Service, nor should irrelevant documents be furnished in response to a summons.

An individual taxpayer's books and records have long been legally subject to seizure under the Fourth Amendment if "instrumentalities of a crime," [37] and in Warden v. Hayden,[38] the Supreme Court sustained the seizure of "mere evidence" of a crime, against an assertion of privilege. Now the Supreme Court has held that an individual's Fifth Amendment privilege against self-incrimination does not protect his business records from seizure pursuant to a valid search warrant.[39] There would appear to be little ground left for challenging a search warrant for a taxpayer's books and records.

Unauthorized inspection of records by an IRS Agent constitutes a violation of the Fourth Amendment and the material inspected may be suppressed.[40] However, if a taxpayer fails to make a timely assertion of his rights he may be held to have waived them.[41]

The Special Agent in a fraud investigation will very quickly contact the accountant and attempt to obtain a detailed statement of taxpayer's record keeping practices, method of preparing return and handling of specific transactions. While a taxpayer has no way to silence the accountant, at least two things should be done immediately. First, obtain all of the taxpayer's personal books, records and documents in the accountant's possession (including workpapers) over which the taxpayer can assert an ownership interest. Second, advise the accountant that he is under no obligation to cooperate with the Special Agent and if the Special Agent wants his testimony, he should be required to issue a formal summons to compel the accountant's appearance and testimony. The accountant summoned has ten days to respond to the summons in which time any legal theory or argument to prohibit the testimony may be developed by the taxpayer's attorney.

In Couch v. United States [42] the Supreme Court held that personal books and records of a taxpayer, which had been turned over to

---

36. See Curcio v. U. S., 354 U.S. 118 (1957).

37. U. S. v. Stern, 225 F.Supp. 187 (S. D.N.Y., 1964).

38. 387 U.S. 294 (1967).

39. Andresen v. Maryland, 427 U.S. 463, 96 Sup.Ct. 2737 (1976).

40. U. S. v. Young, 215 F.Supp. 202 (E. D.Mich.1963); Application of Leo-

nardo, 208 F.Supp. 124 (N.D.Cal., 1962).

41. Rife v. Comm'r, 356 F.2d 883 (5th Cir. 1966), taxpayer waived right by failure to timely object to second inspection of his books; accord Moloney v. U. S., 521 F.2d 491 (6th Cir. 1975), cert. den. 423 U.S. 1017 (1975).

42. Supra note 26.

an independent accountant and maintained in the accountant's office for a considerable period of time, must be produced upon a proper summons to the accountant issued by the Special Agent and that the taxpayer did not have constructive possession of the documents. The solution to the Couch situation may be not to leave the records with the accountant, but to require the accountant to work on those records in the taxpayer's place of business.

As a result of the recent decisions in *Fisher*[43] and *Andresen*[44] the following tests must be met in order for a taxpayer to be able constitutionally to protect his books and records. In the case of a subpoena for production of the records, the taxpayer will have a valid Fifth Amendment privilege if he or she has possession of the records.[45]

If the records are in the hands of a 3rd party there must be a privileged relationship (attorney-client) between the parties in order to prevent enforcement of the summons. These tests are to be applied to the facts as they exist at the date of the issuance of the summons, rather than at the time of a subsequent transfer. If a search warrant is used, the taxpayer will not have a Fifth Amendment privilege to prevent seizure of the records and he or she can contest the validity of the search warrant only on the grounds that it violates his Fourth Amendment privilege.[46]

For any accounting work done during an investigation, the accountant should be retained as an agent of the attorney and not the taxpayer. The work should be performed in the attorney's office. All workpapers and memoranda prepared by the accountant should never leave the possession of the attorney. In U. S. v. Brown[47] the Seventh Circuit held that a Special Agent could require a major accounting firm to produce in response to a summons: (1) a memorandum prepared by taxpayer's attorney that was retained in the accounting firm's file and (2) a memorandum prepared by an accountant summarizing the accounting advice given by the accountant at a meeting with taxpayer and his attorney. Because a search warrant is more difficult to obtain than a subpoena, no information of any kind should be retained by the accountant in a tax fraud investigation; if he desires to maintain memoranda, they should be given to the taxpayer and kept in a file in the taxpayer's or his attorney's office where the accountant may consult them.

43. Supra note 27.

44. Supra note 39.

45. While *Couch* left open the possibility that "temporary and insignificant" relinquishment of possession would not defeat the privilege, under the circumstances it would be unwise to rely on such a nebulous exception to this rule.

46. Andresen v. Maryland, supra note 39.

47. 478 F.2d 1038 (7th Cir. 1973).

COOPERATION BY THE TAXPAYER

Any doubts about cooperation with the Special Agent should be resolved against cooperation. The fact that a taxpayer has fully cooperated with the IRS is of minor importance to the IRS in determining whether to recommend prosecution.[48] As previously indicated, the overwhelming number of fraud cases that are won without trial are stopped because there is insufficient evidence to prove guilt, not because there is sufficient evidence to prove innocence.

If a practitioner has decided to cooperate and during the course of the investigation he discovers that the advantages sought are no longer present, he should stop cooperating. Cooperation should be constantly assessed; nothing should be turned over to the Agent unless it has been reviewed and approved by counsel. Cooperation is in order of course to the extent of providing documents or information that the investigator can obtain elsewhere. Otherwise, the taxpayer's attorney should courteously but firmly refuse to turn over information not otherwise available to the Agent until the material has been fully reviewed and specific advantages of cooperation determined.

From 1946 to 1952 the Internal Revenue Service had a formal policy regarding voluntary disclosure. In brief, the policy provided that if prior to audit a taxpayer voluntarily disclosed to a responsible official of the Internal Revenue Service either that he had willfully failed to file his return or had filed a false return, the criminal phase of the case would be forgiven. Voluntary disclosures appear to be effective now only in failure to file cases, if then, and the disclosure must be made in advance of an audit or other IRS contact. Voluntary disclosures in regard to fraudulent returns are, quite frankly, a guess and a gamble; this is a determination that should be made only by an attorney who is experienced in the tax fraud area.

ADMINISTRATIVE REVIEW: IRS

There will usually be an opportunity for conferences with the Group Chief of the investigating Special Agent (the "district intelligence conference") and with the Assistant Regional Commissioner (Intelligence). This later regional conference takes place after the Special Agent has completed his investigation, written his report, and has had the report reviewed and approved by his Group Chief. Therefore, there is little possibility of reversing any decision to recommend prosecution in this conference. Most cases that are stopped in the Intelligence Division are stopped in the investigative, not the review stage.

---

48. See Balter, supra note 10, c. 6.

The conference is viewed by the Service as an opportunity to fill in remaining gaps in their proof of the case. For that reason, it is important that the taxpayer not attend this conference except under the most unusual of circumstances. The conference should be viewed by taxpayer's representative as an opportunity to acquire further information about the case, particularly any information as to how the Government plans to prove "willfulness" or scienter.

The conference with the Assistant Regional Commissioner (Intelligence) is usually waived, as it does not serve an information-gathering purpose.

ADMINISTRATIVE REVIEW: LEGAL

The taxpayer will be provided a conference at the office of Regional Counsel and at the Department of Justice, Tax Division, Criminal Section, prior to the referral to the local United States Attorney's office with directions to secure an indictment. A limited number of cases are stopped at both of these levels, so it is important to know what standards of evaluation are employed by the reviewers and what the substance of a typical conference is.

Regional Counsel. When the case is forwarded to Regional Counsel by the district director, it is assigned to the Assistant Regional Counsel, Enforcement. He then assigns it to one of his assistants. Shortly after he receives the Special Agent's report, he will receive from the Audit Division of the district director's office the original tax returns and the cooperating Revenue Agent's Report. The possession of the original returns prevents any civil tax action from taking place unless it is cleared with Regional Counsel.

It is the function of the Regional Counsel to provide legal advice to the Intelligence Division. He is expected to evaluate evidentiary or other legal problems and to solve them. If they are unsolvable or problematical in important respects, he may return the matter to Intelligence for further investigation or he can decline to recommend prosecution. Although the questions presented to Regional Counsel are (1) whether the taxpayer is in fact guilty of tax evasion and (2) whether his conviction is a reasonable probability, in actual practice the only real question seems to be the probability of conviction.

Conference in the office of the Regional Counsel is not considered a discovery proceeding. The assistant Regional Counsel will usually disclose the theory of the case, e. g., specific item, net worth, bank deposits, etc., and the proposed civil liabilities. Under these circumstances defense counsel should be very careful in the areas he discusses to avoid substantial discovery by the Government. A memorandum should be prepared outlining the history of the case and the points the defense wishes to raise. These arguments are best addressed to legal problems involved in the case or the sufficiency or admissibility of the proofs either generally or specifically.

Normally, officials in the office of Regional Counsel will begin by disclosing the items discussed above, and then sit back and await comments. They do not take the position that the criminal case must be substantiated and defended to taxpayer's representative; the conference is for the purpose of permitting the taxpayer to offer argument and evidence on his behalf. Arguments regarding the taxpayer's health or his excellent reputation, addressed as they usually are in mitigation of the offense, will have no effect upon them. The arguments must convince them that real difficulties exist in prosecution. Thus, if there was misconduct on the part of the investigating Agents that would result in the suppression of evidence, or if impeachment evidence is available against a principal Government witness, or if important parts of the Service's proof of willfulness can be explained away by other circumstances, such arguments should be pressed forcefully with detailed factual recitals and legal arguments. Once a legitimate issue is before them, a frank discussion of its merits is usually forthcoming.

A decision not to prosecute made by Regional Counsel can be protested by the District Director of Intelligence. If the Assistant Regional Commissioner for Intelligence concurs in the protest, the case is forwarded to Washington where it is determined either by the Director, Enforcement Division, in the Commissioner's office, or by the Director, Enforcement Division in the Chief Counsel's Office. The judgment of the latter division is final and unappealable.

Department of Justice. The taxpayer may request a conference at Justice. The Justice Department does not uniformly solicit such a conference but will grant one upon request. The conference is usually held in Washington, D.C. The Justice Department's attorney may make the following recommendations on the case: (1) Prosecute; (2) Forward to U.S. Attorney with instructions for a grand jury investigation of recalcitrant witnesses; (3) Forward to U.S. Attorney with instructions that he exercise discretionary judgment in light of local factors that may have serious jury impact; (4) Return case to IRS for further specific investigation or (5) No prosecution.

Most cases referred to Justice are recommended for prosecution. The Standards for prosecution are the same as in the Regional Counsel's office. However, as attorneys in the Criminal Section of the Tax Division are often called upon to try cases that they recommend be prosecuted, presumably they are more sensitive to jury factors than Regional Counsel. The Chief Counsel's Office may appeal a no prosecution decision by the Justice Department. The Justice Department makes the final decision after reviewing the protest.

TO TRIAL

When the investigation has been completed and, even after administrative review, there is a recommendation of criminal prosecution, the case is forwarded to the appropriate United States Attorney's office, usually with instructions to secure an indictment. The case is then in a trial status and for best results for the taxpayer should long have been in the hands of an experienced criminal trial lawyer. If it is only by this time that tax counsel realizes the matter no longer comes within his specialized understanding of law and legal process but should be under the control of a different expert, he is much too late. Tax counsel should at least be in close cooperation with a tax fraud expert long before the trial begins.

CHAPTER 29. REFUND PROCEDURES

Internal Revenue Code:
§ 6402 Authority to make credits or refunds
§ 6511 Limitations on credit or refund
      (a) Period of limitation of filing claim
      (b) Limitation on allowance of credits and refunds
      (c) Special rules . . . extension of time by agreement
      (d)(1) Special rules applicable to income taxes
§ 6512 (a) Limitations in case of petition to Tax Court
§ 6513 Time return deemed filed and tax considered paid
      (a) Early return or advance payment of tax
      (b) Prepaid income tax
§ 6532 (a) Periods of limitation on suits
§ 6611 (a) Interest on overpayments
§ 6621 Determination of rate of interest
§ 7422 Civil actions for refund
      (a) No suit prior to filing claim for refund
      (b) Protest or duress
      (e) Stay of proceedings
      (f) Limitations on right of action for refund
§ 7502 (a) Timely mailing . . . timely filing and paying

Federal tax procedure is discussed broadly in the introductory note in Chapter 28. In this chapter somewhat more detailed consideration is given to the matter of refunds; Chapter 30 looks at deficiencies. Significant statutory provisions that bear on refunds are listed above; they should be read and then examined closely in connection with the problems following this note. Other provisions cited in the footnotes may be viewed as time permits. It is anticipated that the principal learning activity in this area (as in Chapter 30) will come from a thoughtful examination of important provisions in the statute. It is acknowledged elsewhere, however, that just reading the statute in cold blood is pretty tough going; the problems afford some relief.

In any event, if one riffles through the Code pages of Subtitle F—Procedure and Administration—(beginning with § 6001), some idea of the scope of the procedural rules may be gathered. It seems hardly necessary, therefore, to point out that we have singled out what *may* be some of the most important provisions from which an overview of federal tax procedure may be gained; the treatment is far from comprehensive.

It is axiomatic to say that if a taxpayer seeks a tax refund he must have paid the tax that he seeks to have refunded. However, what constitutes payment is not always so clear. Payments made by an individual in connection with his declaration of estimated tax [1] may give rise to a right to a refund, as such payments are treated as payments on account of the tax for the year.[2] Similarly, even though there is no direct payment by the taxpayer, excessive withholding from a taxpayer's salary or wages [3] is treated as an overpayment for these purposes.[4] Of course in these circumstances the refund due is generally claimed on the return filed for the year, or applied against estimated tax for the following year.[5]

In the course of an audit a taxpayer may make a payment against the amount of a prospective deficiency to stop the running of interest. The Code permits the assessment of any amount paid as tax.[6] Generally, if the amount of the deficiency can be ascertained, the amount paid will be assessed.[7] But if the amount is not assessed the payment may be treated as a cash bond to assure future payment and, as such, it cannot be the subject of a claim for refund.[8]

The taxpayer's procedural choices when a deficiency is asserted will be recalled (to contest in the Tax Court or to pay and follow the refund route). For a time, taxpayers preferring to litigate in the District Court or Court of Claims, rather than the Tax Court, but also wishing not to pay the entire asserted deficiency prior to litigation, undertook to pay a part of the deficiency and then to file a refund claim and suit for that part. A favorable decision would of course in effect be an adjudication that there was no deficiency. The Commissioner challenged the device, and in Flora v. United States the Supreme Court, in agreement with the Commissioner, stated the "full payment" rule, which requires that the entire amount of an asserted deficiency be paid before a refund suit may be maintained.[9] If the taxpayer chooses to pay less than the deficiency asserted, his remedy is a deficiency proceeding in the Tax Court.

1. I.R.C. (26 U.S.C.A.) §§ 6015, 6153.

2. I.R.C. (26 U.S.C.A.) § 6315.

3. I.R.C. (26 U.S.C.A.) § 3402.

4. I.R.C. (26 U.S.C.A.) § 6401(b). On the content of refund claims, see Adams, "The Imperfect Claim for Refund," 22 The Tax Lawyer 309 (1969); Note, "What Should a Refund Claim Contain to Be Effective," 4 Taxation for Accountants 18 (1969).

5. See Reg. § 301.6402–3.

6. I.R.C. (26 U.S.C.A.) § 6213(b) (3).

7. Rev.Proc. 64–13, 1964–1 (Pt. 1) C.B. 674.

8. Ibid. Such amounts will be returned upon request, and they cannot be the subject of a refund claim that would support a suit for refund to determine tax liability. See Farnsworth & Chambers Co., Inc. v. Phinney, 279 F.2d 538 (5th Cir. 1960).

9. 357 U.S. 63, 78 S.Ct. 1079 (1958); on rehearing 362 U.S. 145, 80 S.Ct. 630 (1960). Consider the plight of the taxpayer who lets the 90-day period expire and then cannot fully pay because, whether seized or voluntarily liquidated for payment, his assets are insufficient. See Ferguson, "Jurisdictional Problems in Federal Tax Controversies," 48 Iowa L.Rev. 312, 335 (1963): Nevertheless, this is the current rule. See, e. g., Nogle v. U. S., unreported, 33 AFTR 2d 74–1314 (S.D. Ohio 1974).

In *Flora*, the Supreme Court viewed resort to the refund suit by way of partial payment as destructive of "the harmony of our carefully structured twentieth century system of tax litigation." [10] The Court need hardly have worried. If only part of an asserted deficiency is paid, a deficiency notice can be issued. If the taxpayer does not then petition the Tax Court, the deficiency can be assessed and, if assessed, the tax must be paid, unless of course the taxpayer has no assets. On the other hand, if the taxpayer files a Tax Court petition in response to the deficiency notice, he gives up his refund suit, and the Tax Court takes jurisdiction of the entire controversy. [11]

The allowance of a refund claim does not assure the taxpayer of a receipt of cash. The Code expressly permits the government to credit any overpayment against any internal revenue tax liability of the taxpayer who otherwise would be entitled to a refund. [12] The statute does not seem to permit an overpayment to be credited against a taxpayer's possible tax liability for another year where that liability is contested and the tax has not yet been assessed. However, there is some authority that in such circumstances payment of the refund may be delayed until the question of liability for the other year has been finally determined. [13]

The Code sections cited at the beginning of this Chapter indicate administrative authority to refund overpayments of an individual's income tax. [14] They also suggest, at least by inference, that if one is unsuccessful in his administrative claim for refund, he may properly think in terms of judicial intervention. [15] In either event, a prerequisite to suit is an administrative refund claim [16] and either (1) a six months period of patience, or (2) prior adverse action on the claim. [17]

The requirement of an administrative claim prior to suit is a facet of the doctrine of exhaustion of administrative remedies. If the Internal Revenue Service is going to be principally responsible for administering the tax laws, it should be given a good chance to sort out difficulties before the courts are cluttered up with more controversies. This is "old hat" to any casual student of administrative law; still in

---

10. 362 U.S. 145, 176, 80 S.Ct. 630, 646 (1960).

11. I.R.C. (26 U.S.C.A.) §§ 6512(a), 7422 (e); see Lore, "Supreme Court in Flora Decision Reveals Weakness in Rule Established," 12 J.Tax. 371 (1960).

12. I.R.C. (26 U.S.C.A.) § 6402(a); Reg. § 301.6402–3(a)(6). As a matter of fact, any claim the United States may have against the taxpayer may be set off against the amount otherwise to be refunded. See Garbis and Frome, Procedures in Federal Tax Controversies, 16.16 (1968).

13. See U. S. ex rel. Cole v. Helvering, 73 F.2d 852 (D.C.Cir. 1934).

14. I.R.C. § 6402.

15. I.R.C. § 7422. Suit in the district court against the United States is authorized by U.S.C. Title 28, § 1346. An alternative is a suit against the United States in the Court of Claims, which is authorized by U.S.C. Title 28, § 1491.

16. I.R.C. § 7422(a).

17. I.R.C. § 6532(a)(1).

the tax refund setting (and probably others, too) question can arise whether the claim filed properly supports the suit subsequently brought. The Hornbook-type message here is that the statutory prerequisite to suit is satisfied only if the claim filed gives notice of the nature of the suit which is subsequently brought.[18] The classic failure to meet this requirement was an administrative claim based on a special provision for relief from the World War I Excess Profits Tax, followed by a suit in which the taxpayer asserted as the only ground for a refund a *substantively good* claim for a deduction on account of obsolescence of patents. Failure to assert the valid patent ground in the earlier refund claim nullified the suit.[19]

Taxpayers sometimes fare better where a comprehensive claim is subsequently held to encompass a ground later more specifically asserted in court.[20] Nevertheless, a refund claim should in a sense be viewed as if it were a pleading. Failure to assert grounds on which the taxpayer may later wish to rely in a suit may by procedural error squander a valuable right.

The same precaution must be exercised where a refund claim once filed is sought to be amended. If the amendment in effect involves the assertion of a new ground for recovery a new claim must be filed rather than a mere amendment to the original claim, and of course the new claim must also be filed within the period set by the statute of limitations.[21]

Another fundamental principle in the area of tax refunds is that a taxpayer is entitled to an income tax refund only if he has in fact overpaid his tax for the year.[22] The proposition may seem obvious but actually defeats what might otherwise be an interesting ploy. Toward the end of the period within which a tax deficiency may be asserted, which usually corresponds to the period within which a refund claim may be filed, the taxpayer might assert a refund claim with respect to an item that he had treated erroneously to his disadvantage on the return for the year. For example, the taxpayer might have failed to claim depreciation in the amount of $1000. Assume if you will that on the same return he innocently but erroneously deducted prepaid interest in the amount of $2000. If the commissioner fails to assert a timely deficiency but the taxpayer nips in at the eleventh hour with a timely refund claim, may he isolate the depreciation item and get a refund for tax that would have been saved if the depreciation deduction had been claimed? The answer is no, as he has not

---

18. U. S. v. Felt and Tarrant Mfg. Co., 283 U.S. 269 (1931); see also Susskind v. U. S., 1976–1 U.S.T.C. ¶ 9200 (E.D.N.Y.1976), holding "taxpayers may not change or raise new fact issues or shift to a new legal theory in the District Court."

19. Ibid.

20. See Ford v. U. S., 402 F.2d 791 (6th Cir. 1968), and cases there cited.

21. See I.R.C. § 6511(a).

22. Lewis v. Reynolds, 284 U.S. 281 (1932).

overpaid his tax for the year, even though it is now too late for the Commissioner to assert a deficiency with respect to the improperly claimed interest deduction.

This is a hard and fast rule not to be confused with the equitable defense of recoupment sometimes asserted by the government in a refund suit. The statute of limitations may not stand in the way of the government's assertion of a right to recoupment if the taxpayer has given a different tax treatment to the same transaction in different years. This is an equitable doctrine not always applied mechanically[23] which is to some extent codified now in the statutory provisions concerning "Mitigation of Effect of Limitations * * *," [24] about which a word must be said.

The statutory mitigation rules are highly complex and, while very important and a suitable subject for a graduate course in tax procedure, they cannot be given detailed consideration in an elementary tax course.[25] It may be well to know, however, that the provisions are two-edged and are as likely to work seriously to the taxpayer's disadvantage as they are to benefit him. By way of example, consider the following situation.

T is an accrual method calendar year lawyer. In 1972 he completed a job for a client and billed him $5,000, which the client paid in 1973. T erroneously included the $5,000 in his return for 1973, not reporting it for 1972, as he should have. In January, 1977 he files a timely claim for refund for 1973 on the ground his income for that year was overstated by $5,000. The Commissioner accepts T's position, which is of course inconsistent with his (T's) initial erroneous exclusion of the item for 1972. See § 1311(b). If limitation periods now foreclose the assertion of a deficiency for 1972 (Are they likely to?), can T get his refund for 1973 and never pay tax on the fee? Not by a long shot. Allowance of T's claim for refund is a "determination" within the meaning of § 1311(a), which in these circumstances has the general effect of reopening the year 1972. The year is reopened only briefly, however, affording the Commissioner only one year in which to take corrective action. Moreover, the year is reopened only for correction of the item in question. Thus, on our facts, there could be a redetermination of tax for 1972 taking account of the $5,000 fee. See § 1314. Nevertheless, if T's income for 1972 was subject to higher rates than for 1973, instead of securing a refund T may wind up paying addition tax. It will be noted that on the facts considered the additional tax could not have been collected by unilateral action of the Commissioner. The possibility arises only because T's refund claim, asserting a position inconsistent with his prior

23. See Dysart v. U. S., 340 F.2d 624 (Ct.Cls.1965).

24. I.R.C. § 1311 et seq.

25. An excellent basic analysis appears in Maguire, Surrey, and Traynor, "Section 820 of the Revenue Act of 1938," 48 Yale L.J. 719 (1939).

treatment of the item, resulted in a determination that activates the Code provisions mitigating the statute of limitations. See § 1312(1).

More dramatic illustrations might be given. But the message here is that §§ 1311–1315 are *must* reading prior to embarking on any of the tax procedures discussed.

PROBLEMS

In each of the questions set out below determine what you believe to be the correct answer, indicate the statutory basis for your answer, and to the extent possible and appropriate, determine the reason Congress has adopted the statutory provision that is applied.

1.   Differentiate a refund claim from a refund suit and state the procedural prerequisites for a suit for refund.

2.   Tex Player, a calendar year taxpayer, learns that he has overpaid his tax for the year 1975 in the amount of $500. What is the latest date on which he may file a claim for refund if:

   (a) He filed his 1975 return on April 1, 1976?

   (b) Player's 1975 return was filed late on May 1, 1976?

   (c) Player's 1975 return was timely filed, but the overpayment arose out of an erroneous deficiency assertion by a revenue agent, disallowing a $500 deductible casualty loss, which Player responded to with immediate payment on June 1, 1977?

   (d) Same as (c), above, except that the $500 loss was not a casualty loss but was incurred when XYZ stock for which Player had a $500 basis became worthless during 1975?

3.   With regard to problem 2(b), above, is Player's refund claim timely if, while not received by the Service until May 15, 1979, the claim is postmarked May 1, 1979?

4.   Refunder filed her claim for refund on March 1, 1977.

   (a) If the Service takes no action on her claim, when may she file suit?

   (b) If her claim is denied on March 1, 1978, when must she file a suit for refund in order for the suit to be timely?

   (c) How would your answer to (b), above, be affected by Refunder's waiver of notice of disallowance made at the time she filed the claim?

   (d) Can you think of a circumstance in which the taxpayer would benefit by the waiver permitted in § 6532(a) (3)?

5.   In a suit for refund can the government successfully assert as a defense that the taxpayer paid the amount of tax voluntarily and not under duress or in response to any claim by the government?

6.   If a taxpayer is successful in his refund suit will he recover anything other than the actual amount of overpaid tax?

CHAPTER 30.   DEFICIENCY PROCEDURES

Internal Revenue Code:
§ 6013(e)   Spouse relieved of liability in certain cases
§ 6211(a)   Definition of a deficiency
§ 6212   Notice of deficiency
            (a) In general
            (b)(1) Address for notice of deficiency
            (c)(1) Further deficiency letters restricted
§ 6213   Restrictions applicable to deficiencies; petition to Tax Court.
            (a) Time for filing petition and restriction on assessment
            (b) Exceptions to restrictions on assessment
                (1) Mathematical errors
                (3) Assessment of amount paid
            (c) Failure to file Tax Court petition
            (d) Waiver of restrictions on assessment
§ 6214   (a) Determinations by the Tax Court
§ 6501   Limitations on assessment and collection
            (a) General rule
            (b) Time return filed
                (1) Early return
            (c) Exceptions
                (1) False return
                (2) Willful attempt to evade tax
                (3) No return
                (4) Extension by agreement
            (e)(1)(A) Substantial omission of (income) items
§ 6503   (a)(1) Suspension of running of period of limitation
§ 6601   (a) Interest on underpayment
§ 6621   Determination of rate of interest
§ 6651   (a) Failure to file tax return or to pay tax
§ 6653   Failure to pay tax
            (a) Negligence
            (b) Fraud
§ 6861   Jeopardy assessments
            (a) Authority for making
            (b) Deficiency letters
§ 7121   Closing agreements
§ 7122   Compromises
§ 7421   (a) Prohibition of suits to restrain assessment or collection
§ 7422   Civil actions for refund
            (a) No suit prior to filing claim for refund
            (b) Protest or duress
            (e) Stay of proceedings
§ 7482   Courts of review

The broad outline of tax procedures presented in Chapter 28 encompasses in part the government's assertion of deficiencies. If a formal deficiency notice is issued it is prepared in the form of a determination by the Commissioner of Internal Revenue, the principal officer of the Internal Revenue Service. If the taxpayer files a Tax Court petition in response to a deficiency notice, the Commissioner is the respondent in the Tax Court proceeding and is of course the opposing party in any review of the Tax Court's decision. The early practice, now abandoned, of using the name of the Commissioner in the style of the case explains the prominence in tax litigation of "Helvering." Guy T. Helvering was the Commissioner for a substantial period; and of course uninformed students get less credit than they may think for citing the *Helvering* case on examinations.

In this chapter an attempt is made to afford the student a better grasp of rights and obligations in the deficiency area. The Code sections listed above should be read and then studied in connection with the problems at the end of this chapter. As in Chapter 29, the captions of the various Code provisions cited are set out. It is expected that this will be helpful in working the problems and perhaps at the time of review, especially here where a fairly large number of provisions are examined. The precaution offered in Chapter 28 again applies. The fairly large number of deficiency problems considered really only scratches the surface; perhaps a good overview may be obtained, but the presentation does not come close to being comprehensive.

ADDITIONS TO TAX

Although the Code must be the principal source for learning about deficiency procedures, some comments are presented in text form below either for purposes of emphasis or because they involve matters not easily or even possibly derived from a study of the statute alone.

It should be noticed at the outset that, if the taxpayer loses a deficiency controversy, either by suit or by settlement, he may be required to pay more than the bare amount of the asserted deficiency. For one thing, interest runs against him from the date the amount should have been paid.[1] Additionally, he may be subject to penalties. For example, failure to file a return or failure to pay the tax shown on a return when due, unless occasioned by some reasonable cause, invites penalties at a rate of 5% or 0.5% of the amount of the tax per month respectively but, in either case, not more than 25%.[2] Deficiencies that are the result of taxpayer negligence or his intention-

---

1. I.R.C. (26 U.S.C.A.) § 6601(a). But recall I.R.C. § 163, providing a deduction for interest paid. The rate of interest payable on a deficiency is the same as that receivable on a refund, at present 7%, but determined with reference to the prime rate periodically under I.R.C. § 6621.

2. I.R.C. (26 U.S.C.A.) § 6651.

al disregard of rules and regulations are subject to a penalty in the amount of 5% of the deficiency.[3] If a deficiency is due to fraud, the penalty is 50% of the amount of the deficiency.[4] These are civil, not criminal, sanctions,[5] and in each instance the penalty is simply "added to the tax" and therefore collected *as tax*. But the possibility of criminal sanctions exists as well, as indicted in Chapter 28, and of course criminal penalties are imposed only upon conviction.

Proof of fraud for purposes of sustaining the Commissioner's imposition of the civil fraud penalty may require something less than the proof beyond a reasonable doubt required for conviction for a crime.[6] In Shirley E. Kub [7] the Tax Court sustained the 50% penalty, saying:[8] "Mrs. Kub's consistent omission of [similar income items received in three consecutive years] from her returns, her attempts to conceal the payments, and the fact that she had no reason to believe that they were not taxable income constitute clear and convincing evidence of fraud for all three years." Obviously, perhaps, acquittal of a fraud charge in a criminal proceeding does not foreclose the imposition of the civil fraud penalty.[9]

For purposes of measuring the fraud penalty an individual's income tax return is never considered just a teensy weensy bit fraudulent. The penalty is 50 percent of *the underpayment* if "any part" of the underpayment is due to fraud.[10]

THE INNOCENT SPOUSE

It will be recalled that, if a joint income tax return is filed by husband and wife, both are generally jointly and severally liable for the tax.[11] In the past this sometimes created such an unjust situation that some judges suggested Congress change the law.[12] For example, a widow who had filed a joint return with her deceased husband might suddenly be confronted with a large deficiency including the 50% fraud penalty, arising out of her husband's transgressions that were wholly unknown to her. In 1971, limited relief

3. I.R.C. (26 U.S.C.A.) § 6653(a).

4. I.R.C. (26 U.S.C.A.) § 6653(b). In the case of the income tax this penalty supplants, is not in addition to, that imposed by § 6653(a).

5. Helvering v. Mitchell, 303 U.S. 391 (1938).

6. See Helvering v. Mitchell, supra note 5.

7. 33 TCM 1282 (1974).

8. Id. at 1296. But compare Wiseley v. Comm'r, 185 F.2d 263 (6th Cir., 1950), with Owens v. U. S., 197 F.2d 450 (8th Cir., 1952).

9. Helvering v. Mitchell, supra note 5.

10. Cf. Romm v. Comm'r, 255 F.2d 698 (4th Cir. 1957), cert. den. 358 U.S. 833 (1958), reaching this result under less compelling language of prior law. The case may also be of interest as an example of a successful assertion of fraud circumventing the presumptive three-year statute of limitations. See I.R.C. § 6501(c)(1) and (2).

11. I.R.C. (26 U.S.C.A.) § 6013(d)(3).

12. E. g., Louise M. Scudder, 48 T.C. 36, 41 (1967).

was provided for such situations.[13] The relief provision, I.R.C. § 6013(e), is retroactive to all years affected by the Internal Revenue Code of 1954.[14]

The innocent spouse rule raises the questions whether the one claiming benefit of the rule (1) knew or had reason to know that significant income of the other spouse [15] was omitted from the return, and (2) could equitably be held liable for the tax attributable to the omitted income. If not, the amnesty extends to that tax *and* interest and penalties arising out of the omission. How can the requisite innocence be shown? At least one court thinks the statutory provision invites judicial definition of "minima of reasonable prudence for individual taxpayers or classes of taxpayers," [16] but that the "courts should not limit the relief afforded by § 6013(e) to the case where assessment of the tax would be patently harsh and oppressive but should instead consider the individual situation of each taxpayer who arguably comes within the statute's coverage." [17]

Curiously, Congress elected to treat a fraudulent *deduction* differently from a fraudulent *omission* from gross income. The second sentence of I.R.C. § 6653(b) relieves an *innocent* spouse of liability for the 50 percent fraud penalty in any event.[18] However, fraud of the other spouse may open a year otherwise closed by the statute of limitations and leave an innocent spouse liable for the tax and interest and penalties (other than for fraud), unless the fraud is an income omission which invokes the broader relief of § 6013(e).[19]

THE TAX COURT IN THE JUDICIAL HIERARCHY

The Golsen Doctrine. The Tax Court is briefly introduced in Chapter 2, page 32, supra. By now its substantial role in the development of tax law is probably clear from the large number of Tax Court cases set out or cited earlier in this book. In this chapter the Tax Court is of course front and center, as it is the only tribunal in which the taxpayer may challenge the Commissioner's determination

13. I.R.C. (26 U.S.C.A.) § 6013(e), as added by § 1, P.L. 91–679 (1971).

14. Wissing v. Comm'r, 441 F.2d 533 (6th Cir. 1971); but see U. S. v. Maxwell, 330 F.Supp. 1253, 1257 (N.D. Tex.1971), aff'd, 459 F.2d 22 (5th Cir. 1972), holding that the new provision "does not open a year which has been closed by the statute of limitations, res judicata, or otherwise."

15. See Allen v. Comm'r, 514 F.2d 908 (5th Cir. 1975), dealing with the 25 percent-of-gross-income test and the special rule of I.R.C. § 6013(e)(2) on income from community property.

16. Sanders v. U. S., 509 F.2d 162, note 5 (5th Cir. 1975).

17. Id. at note 6.

18. Under I.R.C. § 6653(b) the question whether a spouse must pay the 50 percent penalty depends only upon whether "some part of the underpayment is due to the fraud of such spouse." In Robert Asmar, 35 TCM 930 (1976), an innocent spouse flunked the rigorous tests of § 6013(e) but nevertheless escaped the 50% fraud penalty under § 6653(b).

19. See S.Rep. 91–1537, 2d Sess. 91st Cong. (1970), 1971–1 C.B. 606, 608.

of an income tax deficiency without first paying the tax. The routine role of the Court will emerge from an examination of the Code provisions cited at the beginning of this chapter. A word is in order here, however, regarding its relationship to the United States Court of Appeals.

The losing party in a Tax Court case may appeal (as of right) to the United States Court of Appeals.[20] The manner and scope of review are the same as in the review of civil, nonjury cases in the district court.[21] Further review is only by way of certiorari to the Supreme Court.[22]

In point of fact of course the Court of Appeals is several courts inasmuch as the ten numbered circuits and the Court of Appeals for the District of Columbia operate independently from each other. Upon review Tax Court decisions fan out in all directions, and some have made reference to this arrangement as an inverted pyramid. Perhaps a mirrored pyramid is closer as things come back together at the Supreme Court; but of course relatively few cases go that far.

Usually, if an individual taxpayer seeks review of a Tax Court decision he or she must appeal to the Court of Appeals for the circuit in which his or her residence is located.[23] For example, a Florida taxpayer would appeal to the 5th Circuit and a New Yorker to the 2nd.[24] Against this background, the question is: If the Court of Appeals to which an appeal may be taken has decided an issue that arises in a Tax Court case, must the Tax Court conform to that decision? For a very long time the Tax Court's stance was one of independence:[25]

* * *

One of the difficult problems which confronted the Tax Court, soon after it was created in 1926 [sic] as the Board of Tax Appeals, was what to do when an issue came before it again after a Court of Appeals had reversed its prior decision on that point. Clearly, it must thoroughly reconsider the problem in the light of the reasoning of the reversing appellate court and, if convinced thereby, the obvious procedure is to follow the higher court. But if still of the opinion that its original result was right, a court of national jurisdiction to avoid confusion should follow its own honest beliefs until the Supreme Court decides the point. The Tax Court early concluded that it should decide all cases as it thought right.

* * *

20. I.R.C. (26 U.S.C.A.) § 7482(a).

21. Ibid.

22. Ibid.

23. I.R.C. (26 U.S.C.A.) § 7482(b).

24. By stipulation the taxpayer and the Commissioner may agree upon review in a different circuit. Ibid.

25. Arthur L. Lawrence, 27 T.C. 713, 716 and 718 (1957).

The Tax Court feels that it is adequately supported in this belief not only by the creating legislation and legislative history but by other circumstances as well. The Tax Court never knows, when it decides a case, where any subsequent appeal from that decision may go, or whether there will be an appeal. It usually, but not always, knows where the return of a taxpayer was filed, and therefore, the circuit to which an appeal could go, but the law permits the parties in all cases to appeal by mutual agreement to any Court of Appeals. Sec. 7482(b) (2), I.R.C.1954. Furthermore, it frequently happens that a decision of the Tax Court is appealable to two or even more Courts of Appeals. * * *

Although the Tax Court had some examples of its single decisions being appealable to two or more circuits, its comment seems almost prophetic as to the difficulty that could be encountered in a departure from its independent position. In 1970, it adopted the opposite, earlier rejected view in deciding Jack E. Golsen,[26] and since then has decided cases in accordance with decisions in the circuits to which appeal probably would be taken. Now two cases,[27] appearing back to back in the report of memorandum decisions, have reached opposite results on an identical issue under the *Golsen* principle. Deciding *Puckett*, the Court said:[28]

* * *

It having been stipulated that Finance was not a personal holding company within the definition of section 542 during its taxable years ended October 31, 1962 and 1963, we hold that its election under section 1372(a) was not terminated by reason of its receipt of interest, under section 1372 (e) (5), House v. Commissioner [72–1 USTC ¶ 9163], 453 F.2d 982 (C.A. 5 1972), reversing a Memorandum Opinion of this Court [Dec. 30,130(M)].

We hasten to add that this decision does not reflect the thinking of this Court on the issue resolved hereby. * * Most recently in *Kenneth W. Doehring* [Dec. 32,762(M)], T.C.Memo.1974–234 a case arising out of the instant facts, we held that Finance's election under section 1372(a) for the years in issue had terminated under section 1372(e) (5).

However, as an appeal from the case at bar would be made to the Fifth Circuit, we consider the precedent established by that circuit in *House* to be controlling, * * *

26. 54 T.C. 742 (1970), aff'd 445 F.2d 895 (10th Cir. 1971), cert. den. 404 U. S. 940 (1971). See also the brief comment in Chapter 1, supra at page 19.

27. Kenneth W. Doehring and Paul E. Puckett, 33 TCM 1035 and 1038 respectively (1974).

28. Id. at 1040.

Some of us "die-hards" still light up when the *Golsen* button is punched.

If the *Golsen* answer to a difficult situation seems only to point up a dilemma, how about a United States Court of Tax Appeals? For early and more recent commentary see, respectively, Griswold, "The Need for a Court of Tax Appeals," 57 Harv.L.Rev. 1153 (1944) and Del Cotto, "The Need for a Court of Tax Appeals: An Argument and a Study," 12 Buffalo L.Rev. 5 (1962).[29]

Concurrent Refund and Deficiency Suits. Perhaps I.R.C. (26 U.S.C.A.) § 7422(e), which is cited at the beginning of this chapter, needs no explanation. Even so, here is a word. Having studied Chapter 29, you are generally acquainted with how and when a taxpayer may have properly filed suit for a refund of income tax in the district court or the Court of Claims. When you are well into this chapter and the Code sections cited here you will know, too, that after a refund suit is commenced the Commissioner *may* still be able to issue a notice of deficiency. You will also know that the receipt of that notice opens up to the taxpayer another trial forum, the Tax Court. Suppose that, having commenced the refund suit, the taxpayer now *also* files a petition for a redetermination of the deficiency? At one time, this created the strange picture of two judicial machines engaged in a race to decision, because a decision in one court would render the matter decided *res judicata* in the other.

Section 7422(e) now presents a more orderly picture when the possibility arises of overlapping refund and deficiency suits. With this much background, little more need be said. The statutory answer is to stay the refund suit for the time within which the taxpayer may file the Tax Court petition, leaving with the taxpayer the customary choice of forum. However, the stay is extended a further 60 days so that, if the taxpayer disdains the Tax Court, the Commissioner may file a counterclaim in the refund suit.

Has Congress only half-assayed the problem? Suppose the taxpayer has filed a timely and otherwise proper Tax Court petition but then, deciding he has really overpaid his tax, he begins to think in terms of a refund claim and suit. Can the race to judgment now blocked by I.R.C. § 7422(e) in other circumstances proceed without impediment here? The answer, which is negative, lies somewhat buried in the verbiage of I.R.C. § 6512(a); the timely filing of a Tax Court petition bars the refund suit with only three limited exceptions in the separately numbered paragraphs of § 6512(a).

29. Consider Arthur L. Lawrence, supra note 25, footnote 2: "The United States Customs Court and the Court of Claims are other national courts operating on the trial court level, but they do not have similar problems since the appeals in each case go to [the Court of Customs and Patent Appeals and the Supreme Court, respectively] an appellate court which also has a nationwide jurisdiction."

Invoking Tax Court Jurisdiction. The statute clearly makes the issuance of a notice of deficiency [30] a prerequisite to a Tax Court suit. It is within ninety days of the mailing of such notice that the taxpayer must file a petition with the Tax Court for a redetermination of the deficiency.[31]

Section 6861 authorizes jeopardy assessments in cases where the usual cumbersome procedures might threaten to impede collection of the tax. In these cases the tax *may* be assessed and collected before issuance of a deficiency notice. It is congressional policy, however, not to foreclose resort to the Tax Court as one of three trial forums in these cases. Accordingly, I.R.C. § 6861(b) requires the issuance of the statutory deficiency notice within 60 days after the mailing of the jeopardy assessment, assuring the taxpayer of his ticket to the Tax Court.

A companion provision to the jeopardy assessment section, section 6851, authorizes the Commissioner to close a taxpayer's year, if he finds the taxpayer designs to take action that may render ineffectual procedures for tax collection, and to make immediate demand for payment. Until recently, it has not been clear whether in these cases the taxpayer is assured of an opportunity to litigate liability in the Tax Court if he chooses to do so. In Laing v. United States [32] the Supreme Court terminated the uncertainty. It held that closing and demand for payment under section 6851 creates a deficiency and, further, that in such circumstances the taxpayer has the right to a formal deficiency notice as provided in section 6861(b) for jeopardy assessments. The consequences are twofold: (1) If the notice of deficiency is not issued the taxpayer *may* enjoin enforcement; he is within an expressed exception to the § 7421(a) proscription of injunctions found in § 6213(a), last sentence. This was the holding in *Laing*. (2) Demand for payment under § 6851(a) is not itself a deficiency notice, so that a taxpayer who petitioned the Tax Court on the basis of such demand had misconceived his remedy; he should have sought to enjoin collection, as held in Musso, Sr. v. Comm'r.[33]

Two further comments might be made regarding access to the Tax Court. Filing a petition within the specified ninety days may be accomplished by a timely *mailing* of the petition.[34] But this is only so if the petition is properly addressed, and the rule was held inapplicable when a petition was addressed to the Court at a New York address where it had office space, rather than to Washington,

30. See I.R.C. (26 U.S.C.A.) § 6212.

31. I.R.C. (26 U.S.C.A.) § 6213. A longer period is provided if the notice is mailed to a taxpayer outside the United States.

32. 423 U.S. 161, 96 Sup.Ct. 473, 493 (1976).

33. 531 F.2d 772 (5th Cir. 1976).

34. I.R.C. (26 U.S.C.A.) § 7502.

D.C.[35]   Whether the mailing is timely may depend upon the "postmark" on the petition.[36]   In a case in which the uncertainty was the date of mailing of the notice of deficiency, which *starts* the running of the 90-day period for timely filing, the Court held that certain so-called "line dates" put on a deficiency notice in a Florida post office were not "postmarks" on which the taxpayer could rely to determine the date of mailing; proof of earlier mailing was accepted to render the taxpayer's petition untimely.[37]   Apparently this same question could arise regarding the time of taxpayer's mailing of his petition.   The case cited offers some learning on the question: What is a postmark?

SMALL TAX CASES

In 1968 the Tax Court announced a new procedure for the handling of small tax cases.   The purpose was to afford taxpayers an opportunity for a speedy adjudication of controversies with the Treasury Department where the taxpayer may not be able to afford or the case does not warrant the expenditures that normally attend a trial.   There are many instances in the law in which it is just too expensive for a person to take the judicial steps needed to enforce his rights.[38]   After the Tax Court made an initial effort to help the small taxpayer, the Tax Reform Act of 1969, by the addition of new Code § 7463, codified, elaborated, and made some changes in the procedure at first administratively adopted.   In general, a "small" tax case within this section is an estate or gift or income tax case in which the amount placed in dispute does not exceed $1500, and the Tax Court is authorized to conduct such cases in accordance with simplified rules of procedure.   The new section can be invoked at the taxpayer's election with the concurrence of the court.   Decisions under it are not subject to appeal and do not serve as precedents. Early comments on the new procedure appear in an article by William M. Drennen, then Chief Judge of the Tax Court, entitled "Procedural Changes Affecting United States Tax Court," 4 Indiana Legal Forum 53, 58–67 (1970).[39]

---

35.   Abbott Hoffman, 63 T.C. 638 (1975). The opinion calls attention to the standard 90-day letter form which gives Box 70, Washingon, D.C. 20044 as the address. But a CCH blurb on this case gives 400 Second Street, N. W., Washington, D.C. 20217. Are both correct?

36.   Separate provisions apply to registered and certified mail. See I.R.C. (26 U.S.C.A.) § 7502(c).   And see Fred Sylvan, 65 T.C. 548 (1975).

37.   Duane M. Traxler, 63 T.C. 534 (1975).

38.   Cf. Nora Payne Hill, 13 T.C. 291 (1949), where taxpayer later went to the Court of Appeals and was reversed and remanded to the Tax Court, in which the deficiency involved was $57.52. She won?

39.   See also Drennen, "The Tax Court's New Look: A View of the New Powers and Small Tax Procedure," 34 J.Tax 82 (1971). Drennen, "New Rules of Practice and Procedure of the Tax Court: How are they Working?" 27 U.Fla.L.Rev. 897, 913 (1975).

It seems likely the Tax Court will tend to support the taxpayer's desire to use the small case procedure over objections by the Commissioner.[40]

A good general understanding of the procedure in Small Tax Cases can be gleaned from Tax Court Rules 170–179 [41] which are set out below, together with Tax Court Form 2, the form to be used to file a petition in a Small Tax Case, copies of which can be obtained from the Clerk of the Court.

TITLE XVII.   SMALL TAX CASES

RULE 170.   GENERAL

The Rules of this Title XVII, referred to herein as the "Small Tax Case Rules," set forth the special provisions which are to be applied to small tax cases as defined in Rule 171. See Code Section 7463 (Appendix II, p. 112). Except as otherwise provided in these Small Tax Case Rules, the other rules of practice of the Court are applicable to such cases.

RULE 171.   SMALL TAX CASE DEFINED

The term "small tax case" means a case in which:

(a) Neither the amount of the deficiency, nor the amount of any claimed overpayment, placed in dispute (including any additions to tax, additional amounts, and penalties) exceeds—

(1) $1,500 for any one taxable year in the case of income or gift taxes, or

(2) $1,500 in the case of estate taxes;

(b) The petitioner has made a request in accordance with Rule 172 to have the proceedings conducted under Code Section 7463; and

(c) The Court has not entered an order in accordance with Rule 172(d) or Rule 173, discontinuing the proceedings in the case under Code Section 7463.

RULE 172.   ELECTION OF SMALL TAX CASE PROCEDURE

With respect to classification of a case as a small tax case under Code Section 7463, the following shall apply:

(a) A petitioner who wishes to have the proceedings in his case conducted under Code Section 7463 may so request at the time he files his petition. See Rule 175.

(b) If the Commissioner opposes the petitioner's request to have the proceedings conducted under Code Section 7463, he shall at the time he files his answer submit an accompanying motion in which he shall set forth the reasons for his opposition.

---

40. See John Dressler, 56 T.C. 210 (1971).

41. As amended through September 2, 1975.

(c) A petitioner may, at any time after the petition is filed and before trial, request that the proceedings be conducted under Code Section 7463. Upon the filing of such request, the Commissioner will be given due time in which to indicate whether he is opposed to it, and he shall state his reasons therefor in the event of such opposition.

(d) If such request is made in accordance with the provisions of this Rule 172, the case will be docketed as a small tax case. The Court, on its own motion or on the motion of a party to the case, may, at any time before the trial commences, enter an order directing that the small tax case designation shall be removed and that the proceedings shall not be conducted under the Small Tax Case Rules. If no such order is entered, the petitioner will be considered to have exercised his option and the Court shall be deemed to have concurred therein, in accordance with Code Section 7463, at the commencement of the trial.

RULE 173. DISCONTINUANCE OF PROCEEDINGS

After the commencement of a trial of a small tax case, but before the decision in the case becomes final, the Court may order that the proceedings be discontinued under Code Section 7463, and that the case be tried under the rules of practice other than the Small Tax Case Rules, but such order will be issued only if (1) there are reasonable grounds for believing that the amount of the deficiency, or the claimed over-payment, in dispute will exceed $1,500 and (2) the Court finds that justice requires the discontinuance of the proceedings under Code Section 7463, taking into consideration the convenience and expenses for both parties that would result from the order.

RULE 174. REPRESENTATION

A petitioner in a small tax case may appear for himself without representation or may be represented by any person admitted to practice before the Court. As to representation, see Rule 24.

RULE 175. PLEADINGS

(a) **Petition:** (1) *Form and Content:* The petition in a small tax case shall be substantially in accordance with Form 2 shown in Appendix I, p. 100, or shall, in the alternative, comply with the requirements of Rule 34(b), and contain additionally (A) the office of the Internal Revenue Service which issued the deficiency notice, (B) the taxpayer identification number (e. g., social security number) of each petitioner, and (C) a request that the proceedings be conducted under Code Section 7463.

(2) *Filing Fee:* The fee for filing a petition shall be $10, payable at the time of filing. The Court may waive payment of the fee if the petitioner establishes to the satisfaction of the Court that he is unable to make such payment.

(3) *Verification Not Required:* The petition need not be verified, unless the Court directs otherwise.

(b) **Answer:** The provisions of Rule 36 shall apply to answers filed by the Commissioner in small tax cases.

(c) Reply: A reply to the answer shall not be filed unless the Court, on its own motion or upon motion of the Commissioner, shall otherwise direct. Any reply shall conform to the requirements of Rule 37(b). In the absence of a requirement of a reply, the provisions of the second sentence of Rule 37(c) shall not apply and the affirmative allegations of the answer will be deemed denied.

RULE 176. PRELIMINARY HEARINGS

If, in a small tax case, it becomes necessary to hold a hearing on a motion or other preliminary matter, the parties may submit their views in writing and may, but shall not ordinarily be required to, appear personally at such hearing. However, if the Court deems it advisable for the petitioner or his counsel to appear personally, the Court will so notify the petitioner or his counsel and will make every effort to schedule such a hearing at a place convenient to them.

RULE 177. TRIAL

(a) Place of Trial: At the time of filing the petition, the petitioner may, in accordance with Form 4 in Appendix I, p. 102, or by other separate writing, request the place where he would prefer the trial to be held. If the petitioner has not filed such a request, the respondent, at the time he files his answer, shall file a request showing the place of trial preferred by him. The Court will make every effort to designate the place of trial at the location most convenient to that requested where suitable facilities are available.

(b) Conduct of Trial and Evidence: Trials of small tax cases will be conducted as informally as possible consistent with orderly procedure, and any evidence deemed by the Court to have probative value shall be admissible.

(c) Briefs: Neither briefs nor oral arguments will be required in small tax cases, but the Court on its own motion or upon request of either party may permit the filing of briefs or memorandum briefs.

RULE 178. TRANSCRIPTS OF PROCEEDINGS

The hearing in, or trial of, a small tax case shall be stenographically reported or otherwise recorded but a transcript thereof need not be made unless the Court otherwise directs.

RULE 179. NUMBER OF COPIES OF PAPERS

Only an original and two conformed copies of *any* paper need be filed in a small tax case. An additional copy shall be filed for each additional docketed case which has been, or is requested to be, consolidated.

FORM 2

PETITION (Small Tax Case)
(Available—Ask for Form 2)

(See Rules 170 through 179)

UNITED STATES TAX COURT

....

Petitioner(s)

v.   Docket No.

COMMISSONER OF INTERNAL REVENUE,

Respondent

PETITION

1. Petitioner(s) request(s) the Court to redetermine the tax deficiency(ies) for the year(s) ...., as set forth in the notice of deficiency dated ...., A COPY OF WHICH IS ATTACHED. The notice was issued by the Office of the Internal Revenue Service at

....
City and State

2. Petitioner(s) taxpayer identification (e.g. social security) number(s) is(are) ....

3. Petitioner(s) make(s) the following claims as to his tax liability:

Year	Amount of Deficiency Disputed	Amount of Addition to Tax, if any, Disputed	Amount of Overpayment Claimed
....	....	....	....
....	....	....	....

4. Set forth those adjustments, i.e. changes, in the notice of deficiency with which you disagree and why you disagree.

....
....
....
....
....

Petitioner(s) request(s) that the proceedings in this case be conducted as a "small tax case" under section 7463 of the Internal Revenue Code of 1954, as amended, and Rule 172 of the Rules of Practice of the United

States Tax Court.* [See pages 76 and 77 of the enclosed booklet.] A decision in a "small tax case" is final and cannot be appealed by either party.

. . . .
          Signature of Petitioner (Husband)   Present Address

. . . .
          Signature of Petitioner (Wife)   Present Address
               (If joint return was filed)

. . . .
          Signature and address of counsel, if retained by petitioner(s)

  * If you do not want to make this request, you should place an "X" in the following box. ☐

BURDEN OF PROOF

In deficiency cases the government is really the moving party, seeking to get money from the taxpayer. Nevertheless, from the standpoint of evidentiary requirements the position of the parties seems to be reversed. The Tax Court Rules provide in general:[42]

> The burden of proof shall be upon the petitioner, except as otherwise provided by statute or determined by the Court; and except that, in respect of any new matter, increases in deficiency, and affirmative defenses, pleaded in his answer, it shall be upon the respondent. As to affirmative defenses, see Rule 39.[43]

There are other situations in which by statute the burden of proof is on the Commissioner. For instance, I.R.C. (26 U.S.C.A.) § 6902(a) provides:

> In proceedings before the Tax Court the burden of proof shall be upon the Secretary or his delegate to show that a petitioner is liable as a transferee of property of a taxpayer, but not to show that the taxpayer was liable for the tax.[44]

And § 7454(a) states:

> In any [Tax Court] proceeding involving the issue whether the petitioner has been guilty of fraud with intent to evade tax, the burden of proof with respect to such issue shall be upon the Secretary or his delegate.[45]

---

42. Rules of Practice and Procedure, United States Tax Court, Rule 142(a), as amended through September 2, 1975.

43. Rule 39 states: "A party shall set forth in his pleading any matter constituting an avoidance or affirmative defense, including res judicata, collateral estoppel, estoppel, waiver, du-

ress, fraud, and the statute of limitations. A mere denial in a responsive pleading will not be sufficient to raise any such issue."

44. See T.C. Rule 142(d).

45. See T.C. Rule 142(b).

The Commissioner also has the burden of proving a major omission from gross income to make applicable the extended statute of limitations for asserting a deficiency.[46]

The shift of the burden on new matters to the Commissioner provided by Rule 142(a) may be cold comfort to the taxpayer. Sometimes in the preparation for a Tax Court trial the Commissioner will turn up new issues on which he can easily meet the burden. The case of Joseph B. Ferguson [47] began with a petition regarding an asserted $1200 deficiency but ended with the Commissioner's successful assertion of several hundred thousand dollars of tax liability.

Does the taxpayer have an easier row to hoe if he contests asserted liability by way of a suit for refund? Under Lewis v. Reynolds [48] a taxpayer must prove that he overpaid his tax. Forbes v. Hassett [49] emphasizes that in a refund suit the taxpayer must prove, not only that the Commissioner was wrong, but also the essential facts upon which a correct determination of liability can be made. Thus, it is sometimes said that the taxpayer has a double burden in refund suits. In the Tax Court, according to the Supreme Court in Helvering v. Taylor,[50] the taxpayer must show that the Commissioner's determination of a deficiency is wrong, but he is not required to show the correct amount of the tax.

Of course in any Tax Court case the taxpayer may present evidence sufficient to establish a prima facie case. If he does, the presumption of correctness that usually or initially attaches to the deficiency notice vanishes, shifting the burden to the Commissioner. If he cannot present evidence to the contrary, the Commissioner cannot win simply by virtue of the lost presumption.[51]

FINALITY IN TAX CONTROVERSIES

One may agree wholeheartedly with Mr. Justice Jackson's analysis of the terminal role of the Supreme Court: "We are not final because we are infallible; but we are infallible only because we are final." [52] But, if there is any question why, there is at least no ques-

---

46. See I.R.C. (26 U.S.C.A.) § 6501(e) and, e. g., C. A. Reis, 1 T.C. 9 (1942). See also I.R.C. (26 U.S.C.A.) § 534 and T.C. Rule 142(e), accumulated earnings tax, and § 7454(b), and T.C. Rule 142(c), foundation managers, for other situations in which the burden of proof is borne by the Commissioner.

47. 47 T.C. 11 (1966).

48. 284 U.S. 281 (1932).

49. 124 F.2d 925 (1st Cir. 1942).

50. 293 U.S. 507 (1935).

51. Paul J. Byrum, 58 T.C. 731 (1972), allowing a contested deduction for stock becoming worthless in 1967. See also Efrain T. Suarez, 61 T.C. 841 (1974), reaching a similar result where the petitioner's deficiency notice lost its presumption of correctness because it was found to rest on evidence obtained in an illegal search and seizure.

52. Jackson, J., concurring in Brown v. Allen, 344 U.S. 443, 540, 73 S.Ct. 397, 427 (1953).

tion whether the Supreme Court is the end of the line. On the other hand, some potential tax controversies come to rest by way of specific statutory provisions, or by administrative action, or by decisions of lower federal courts. This note explores some of these aspects of finality in tax matters.

Statutory Finality. Some principles of finality operate to preclude controversy, rather than to settle a developed controversy. This is often the result of statutes of limitation such as are identified in these chapters on procedure. The presumptive three-year limitation periods on refund claims and deficiency assertions [53] give rise to the phenomenon of the "closed" year. Of course the year may turn out only to be zippered if, for example, there are subsequent assertions of fraud [54] or major omissions of gross income.[55] And, as has been indicated, even a year that is seemingly nailed shut at times is subject to a partial reopening.[56]

In some instances outside the limitation periods the statute forecloses the development of an otherwise possibly controversial issue. For example, if a taxpayer and the government have agreed upon the useful life of a depreciable asset, the agreed life is generally not subject to subsequent challenge.[57]

Administrative Finality. The Code expressly authorizes administrative officials to enter into binding agreements with taxpayers with regard to their liability for taxes.[58] In general such agreements, called "closing agreements," are "final and conclusive." [59]

Many years ago a closing agreement could be executed for the government only by one of the top officials in the Treasury Department.[60] The 1954 Code confers such authority on "the Secretary or his delegate." Subject to various restrictions regarding the nature of the agreement, the authority has been delegated pretty well down the line to the point where District Directors may execute some closing agreements.[61] The Treasury says that most closing agreements

---

53. I.R.C. (26 U.S.C.A.) §§ 6511(a) and 6501(a).

54. I.R.C. (26 U.S.C.A.) § 6501(c) (1 and 2).

55. I.R.C. (26 U.S.C.A.) § 6501(e).

56. I.R.C. (26 U.S.C.A.) § 1311; and see Chapter 29 at page 998.

57. I.R.C. (26 U.S.C.A.) § 167(d); and cf. § 2035(b), last clause, foreclosing the contemplation-of-death issue for estate tax purposes in some circumstances, and § 2504(c), sometimes foreclosing a valuation issue for gift tax purposes.

58. I.R.C. (26 U.S.C.A.) § 7121.

59. Ibid. They may be upset upon a showing of fraud or malfeasance or of misrepresentation of a material fact but, otherwise, must be accorded full effect by taxpayers, the administrators, and the judiciary. I.R.C. (26 U.S.C.A.) § 7121(b) (1) and (2).

60. See I.R.C. (1939) § 3760, requiring participation by the Secretary of the Treasury or the Under Secretary or an Assistant Secretary.

61. See, e. g., Commissioner's Delegation Order No. 97 (Rev. 10), 36 F.R. 13161 (1971).

are now signed by Chiefs and Associate Chiefs of Regional Appellate Division offices.[62]

Closing agreements are of two kinds. The agreement may, for example, fix the income tax liability of a taxpayer for a particular taxable year.[63] On the other hand, the agreement may relate only to one or two questions, such as the fair market value of property received as compensation for services.[64] The latter type of agreement may be useful in situations in which statutes of limitation will afford the taxpayer no all-time assurance on a particular point. For example, whether property was received as compensation and the value of such property might determine the taxpayer's basis for the property which, upon its sale many years later, would determine his gain or loss.[65]

Closely akin to the government's closing agreement authority is its authority to compromise tax controversies.[66] The Treasury views its authority to compromise as limited to two situations: (1) doubt as to liability or (2) doubt as to collectibility, or both.[67] As in the case of a closing agreement, a valid compromise must conform to strict statutory and administrative requirements.[68] In line with the jurisdictional shift from Treasury to Justice which may take place in the course of a tax controversy,[69] the statute provides for action by the "Attorney General or his delegate" in the compromise of a controversy that has been referred to the Department of Justice for prosecution or defense.[70]

Over the years there has been substantial question whether an agreement that did not comply with the rules for the execution of a closing or compromise agreement was binding on either the taxpayer or the government.[71] While there is authority for strict compliance

62. Rev.Proc. 68–16, 1968–1 C.B. 770.

63. Such agreements are executed on Form 866, entitled "Agreement as to Final Determination of Tax Liability."

64. Such agreements are executed on Form 906, entitled "Closing Agreement as to Final Determination Covering Specific Matters."

65. Cf. U. S. v. Frazell, 335 F.2d 487 (5th Cir. 1964).

66. I.R.C. (26 U.S.C.A.) § 7122.

67. Rev.Proc. 64–44, § 8, 1964–2 C.B. 974, 978.

68. Jurisdictional and procedural requirements for compromise settle-

ments are set out in Rev.Proc. 64–44, supra note 67, as amended by Rev. Proc. 66–53, 1966–2 C.B. 1266. The compromise authority of District Directors was expanded by Commissioner's Delegation Order No. 11 (Rev. 6), 36 F.R. 9571 (1971).

69. See Chapter 28, Introduction, supra at page 970.

70. I.R.C. (26 U.S.C.A.) § 7122.

71. See Emmanuel, "The Effect of Waivers in Federal Income Tax Cases," 3 U.Fla.L.Rev. 176, 179 (1950). Congressional and administrative steps such as extensive sub-delegation, which tend to facilitate the execution of de jure closing or compromising agreements, may work toward a reduction of such controversies.

with such rules,[72] there are also cases in which flawed agreements have been accorded finality on estoppel principles.[73]

Form 870, even Form 870AD,[74] by means of which a taxpayer agrees to the assessment of tax without receipt of a statutory deficiency notice, expressly acknowledges that it is not a closing agreement under I.R.C. § 7121. However, Form 870AD does have language of finality which is observed by the government. Uncertainty as to the binding effect on the taxpayer of such language clearly suggests that one who wishes only to relinquish his right to go to the Tax Court, and to maintain his right to litigate in the District Court or the Court of Claims should amend any proffered Form 870AD expressly to preserve his right to file claim and suit for refund.[75]

What is the status of the taxpayer who has requested and received an administrative ruling on a question of federal income tax liability? The best answers to this question can be found in an article by Mitchell Rogovan written when he was Chief Counsel for the Internal Revenue Service.[76] In very brief summary, there is no statutory obstacle to the Service's reneging on a ruling if the matter has not been handled so as to conform with the requirements for a closing or compromise agreement.[77] However, it is only in "rare or unusual circumstances" that the Treasury will apply retroactively its revocation of a ruling so as to upset the expectations of the one to whom the ruling was issued.[78] For this reason, taxpayers feel they can rely on rulings issued to them and, even though procedures have been streamlined, rather rarely seek closing agreements. On the other hand, a "determination letter" is a kind of ruling that is issued by the District Director, which is limited to the tax aspects of transactions that have been completed. Inasmuch as the letter relates only to past transactions and action is not taken by a taxpayer in reliance on such a letter, revocation is automatically retroactive, unless the Commissioner specifically exercises his authority to apply the change only prospectively.[79] As a general rule, oral communication by Service personnel and various Service publications, such as the popular "Your

72. E. g., Botany Worsted Mills v. U. S., 278 U.S. 282, 49 S.Ct. 129 (1929).

73. E. g., Backus v. U. S., 59 F.2d 242 (Ct.Cls.1932), cert. den., 288 U.S. 610, 53 S.Ct. 402 (1933).

74. See Reg. § 601.106(d)(2).

75. In a recent case in which the taxpayer expressly agreed to file no refund claim, a compromise effected by way of a Form 870AD was held to estop him from filing a later claim, even though the Form 870AD did not meet the requirements of a closing or compromise agreement. **Stair** v. U. S., 516 F.2d 560 (2d Cir. 1975).

See also Garbis and Frome, Procedures in Federal Tax Controversies, 1.27 (Ronald Press 1968).

76. Rogovin, "Four R's: Regulations, Rulings, Reliance and Retroactivity," 43 Taxes 756, 763 et seq. (1965).

77. Cf. Dixon v. U. S., 381 U.S. 68, 85 S.Ct. 1301 (1965).

78. Rev.Proc. 67-1, 1967-1 C.B. 544, 553; and see Rogovin, supra note 76, at 769.

79. See I.R.C. (26 U.S.C.A.) § 7805(b).

Federal Income Tax," have no more final effect on the determination of tax liability than the opinion of private tax counsel.[80]

Judicial Finality. The familiar doctrine of res judicata is of course fully applicable to tax controversies.[81] If a taxpayer has won a judgment in a district court in a refund suit, imagine what his reaction would be if told that the Commissioner is now asserting additional income tax liability for the same year and that he must again go to court to preserve his victory. But he need not, of course, because his liability for that year is res judicita.[82] The judgment is controlling not only with respect to the issues litigated but to all issues that could have been raised which bear on the determination of liability for the year.[83] Neither the form of the litigation (refund suit or deficiency proceeding) nor the forum in which the case is tried (Tax Court, District Court, or Court of Claims) makes any difference. While the doctrine is dependent upon a prior adjudication of a controversy between the same parties or their privies, the same-parties requirement is satisfied by the proposition that the contest is between the taxpayer and the government, whether the official party to the proceeding is the United States itself or the Commissioner of Internal Revenue.[84] Moreover, while the Tax Reform Act of 1969 has cured any doubt,[85] even when the Tax Court was an administrative agency [86] an adjudication by the Tax Court, or its predecessor the Board of Tax Appeals, invoked the doctrine.[87]

The related doctrine of collateral estoppel or estoppel by judgment is especially likely to be of importance in tax cases. The landmark opinion outlining the scope of the doctrine of collateral estoppel is that in Commissioner v. Sunnen.[88] A single controversial circumstance may have a bearing on income tax liability for several years. If a judgment fixes liability for one of the years, the broad doctrine of res judicata forecloses only the reopening of that liability. But the related doctrine of collateral estoppel forecloses the relitigation of issues that were in fact raised and decided in the earlier litigation, even when they arise in a new cause of action, such as a dispute as to liability for a later year.[89]

---

80. Rogovin, supra note 76 at 774; and see Kragen, "The Private Ruling: An Anomaly of Our Internal Revenue System," 45 Taxes 331 (1967).

81. Tait v. Western Maryland Ry. Co., 289 U.S. 620, 53 S.Ct. 706 (1933).

82. Even this firm doctrine is subject to exception under the mitigation rules of I.R.C. (26 U.S.C.A.) § 1311 et seq.

83. Cf. Cromwell v. County of Sac., 94 U.S. 351, 352 (1876).

84. Ibid; and see I.R.C. (26 U.S.C.A.) § 7422(c).

85. I.R.C. (26 U.S.C.A.) § 7441.

86. See I.R.C. (26 U.S.C.A.) § 7441, prior to its amendment in 1969.

87. Tait v. Western Maryland Ry. Co., supra note 29; and see I.R.C. (26 U.S.C.A.) § 7481.

88. 333 U.S. 591, 68 S.Ct. 715 (1948); and see Goldstein, "Res Judicata and Collateral Estoppel," 54 A.B.A.J. 1131 (1968).

89. See IB Moore, Federal Practice, 16–17 (1965).

A simple example of the estoppel concept may be helpful. Assume that T is the income beneficiary of a trust. He assigns half his interest gratuitously to his son. The Commissioner asserts that T remains taxable on all the trust income under the fruit-tree doctrine.[90] T successfully contests his liability for tax on half the 1972 trust income in a Tax Court case which is not appealed. Now comes the Commissioner with the same assertion for the year 1973. Res judicata does not protect T, because the cause of action is not the same, i. e., his 1973 tax liability obviously was not decided in the case that involved the 1972 year. But T may be protected by collateral estoppel. Both doctrines reflect a policy that matters judicially determined should not be open for subsequent consideration; and collateral estoppel extends the notion of res judicata to cover a specific issue that has been decided.

However, there are limits to the doctrine. As the Supreme Court has said: [91]

> It must be confined to situations where the matter raised in the second suit is identical in all respects with that decided in the first proceeding and where the controlling facts and applicable legal rules remain unchanged.

The *Sunnen* case itself involved a fruit-tree controversy. But the *Clifford-Horst* line of cases [92] intervened between the first and second controversies. On this ground the Court held in *Sunnen* that the "legal atmosphere" had so changed as to render the doctrine of collateral estoppel inapplicable.

Collateral estoppel may of course work against the taxpayer. For example, a conviction in a criminal case for tax fraud under § 7201 forecloses argument by the taxpayer that he is not liable for the civil fraud penalty under § 6653(b).[93]

PROBLEMS

1. T is a calendar year taxpayer. When can the Commissioner make a timely assertion of an income tax deficiency against T for the year 1975, without resort to special limitation periods, if T filed his return for 1975 on:

    (a) April 1, 1976?

    (b) May 1, 1976?

    (c) If T filed no return for 1975?

90. See Chapter 13, supra at page 275.

91. Comm'r v. Sunnen, supra note 88 at 599–600.

92. Chapters 13 and 14, supra.

93. See Nathaniel M. Stone, 56 T.C. 213 (1971), and cases there cited. On the other hand, an acquittal of the taxpayer in a preceding criminal case does not foreclose assertion of the civil fraud penalty. Helvering v. Mitchell, 303 U.S. 391, 58 S.Ct. 630 (1938).

2. On essentially the same facts as those in problem 1, and assuming that T filed a return on April 1, 1976; what different result would you reach if:

(a) The deficiency asserted rests on an alleged omission of a $20,000 fee for T's services which, if reported, would have increased the gross income reported on the return to $60,000? or

(b) The deficiency asserted rests on an alleged omission from gross income, whatever the amount, done by T with the deliberate attempt to evade tax? (May T be in more than mere financial difficulty? See and broadly differentiate I.R.C. (26 U.S.C.A.) §§ 7201 and 7206(1).)

(c) With regard to the foregoing problems (a) and (b), and making both assumptions ($20,000 *fraudulent omission*), appraise the possible liability of Mrs. T, if she and T filed a joint return, as permitted by I.R.C. (26 U.S.C.A.) § 6013.

3. The Commissioner sent Deficient a ninety day letter dated March 28, 1974. The "letter" was mailed at the post office by the Service on March 29, 1974 and the Service received certified mail notice dated March 29, which also bore the postmark date of March 29, 1974.

(a) Is Deficient's petition timely if it is properly mailed and postmarked on June 27, 1974 and arrives at the Tax Court on July 1, 1974?

(b) What result in (a), above, if the petition is properly mailed on June 29, 1974, but the post office stamps that date on it but fails to postmark it and it arrives at the Tax Court on July 1, 1974? See Duane M. Traxler, 63 T.C. 534 (1975).

(c) Is Deficient's petition timely in (a), above, if it was mailed and postmarked June 27, 1974, but was improperly addressed to the I.R.S. who forwarded it to the Tax Court and it arrived at the Tax Court on July 5, 1974? See Abbott Hoffman, 63 T.C. 638 (1975).

(d) Assume in (a), above, Deficient lived in Town X when the return for the year in question was filed and reported Town X as his address on his return and six months later he moved to Town Y and all subsequent returns show Town Y as his address. If the Commissioner sends the ninety day letter to Town X on the dates above but it is not forwarded to Deficient until April 15, 1974, will Deficient's petition be timely if it is filed by July 10, 1974? See § 6212 (b) (1) and Culver M. Budlong, 58 T.C. 850 (1972).

(e) If in any case above Deficient's petition is not timely and there is no Tax Court jurisdiction has Deficient completely lost his "day in court"?

4. If under § 6501(c) (4) T is asked to execute a Form 872, extending the time for assessment of a deficiency, what practical consideration will affect his response?

5. If under § 6213(d) T executes a simple Form 870, waiving restrictions on assessment of tax, to what extent has he capitulated, i. e., relinquished further opportunities to contest his liability?

6. If the Commissioner makes a jeopardy assessment prior to the issuance of a statutory notice of deficiency, will T lose his right to litigate the question of liability in the Tax Court?

7. Several judicial alternatives are open to taxpayers in tax litigation situations. In the following situations which procedure would the taxpayer be likely to use?

(a) The taxpayer has a factual issue as to which he feels a jury would be favorably disposed.

(b) The taxpayer has no money with which to pay an asserted deficiency.

(c) The taxpayer wishes to stop the running of interest but at the same time litigate the issues. (Consider this carefully).

(d) The litigation involves a very difficult tax law issue.

(e) The litigation involves a legal issue on which there is a split of authority among the circuits. The court of appeals in the circuit in which the taxpayer resides has decided the issue in the government's favor.

Are there further factors that a taxpayer might take into consideration in determining his judicial remedy and forum? See Garbis and Frome, Procedures in Federal Tax Controversies, pp. 2.6–2.13 (Ronald Press, 1968).

*

INDEX

References are to Pages

ACCIDENT INSURANCE
Benefits as gross income, 209

ACCOUNTANTS
Involvement in tax fraud case, 988

ACCOUNTING
See, also, Accrual Methods of Accounting; Cash Method of Accounting; Depreciation
Methods, 538
   Approval for change, 539
   Code provisions, 538
   Defined, 538
   Multiple accounts, 539
   Percentage of completion, 539
Timing principles, 537

ACCRUAL METHOD OF ACCOUNTING
See, also, Accounting; Cash Method of Accounting
Generally, 538
Amount realized for gains, 872
Deduction items,
   Interest on deferred payments, 584
   Reserve funds to cover future costs, 584–596
Income items,
   Advance rent payments, 569
   Deferred income, 572–580
   Embezzled funds, 564
   Inventories, 580
   Judgments, 561
   Prepayment for services, 572
   Profits earned during receivership, 561
   Receipt of earnings, 561
   Total sales, 559
   Unlawful gains, 567
Reserve accounting, 587
Right to receive income, 559–561

ACQUIESCENCES
Generally, 30

ADJUSTED GROSS INCOME
Concept in relation to deductions, 504–506

ADMINISTRATIVE PROCESS
Acquiescences, 30
Regulations, 29
Revenue rulings, 30

ADMISSION TO THE BAR
Amortization of costs, 736

ADVERTISING
Deductible business expense, 409

AGRICULTURE
Deduction of horticulture costs, 418

ALIMONY
Deductibility of payments, 219
   With standard deductions, 221
Ex parte divorce decree, 247
Historically, 219
Indirect benefits, 241
Nondeductible, 219, 248
   Alimony trusts, 249
   Lump sum, 221, 249
   Pre-existing trusts, 251
Periodic payments, 221–241, 248
Premium on life insurance, 241
Rent-free residence, 241
Support payments, 229

AMOUNT REALIZED
See, also, Basis
Closed transactions, 855–885
Community property transfer, 165
Deferred payment sales of personal property, 874
Deferred reporting of gain, 847–854
Defined, 141, 159, 168, 862, 864
Fair market value of real estate contract, 862
Historical background, 862
Installment payments of purchase price,
   Defined, 877
   Interest, 880
   Personal property, 874
   Real property, 874–885
Marital property, transfer of taxable event, 159
Measurement of, 159
Open transactions, 847–854
Trust, transfers to, 178

ANNUITIES
After divorce, gross income, 221
Annual exclusion, 192
Assignment of income, 296
Defined, 190
Gross income, 190–197
Income averaging, 629
Refund features, 193
Variable annuity defined, 191

APPEALS
See Deficiency Procedure; Procedure

APPELLATE COURTS
Jurisdiction, 33

APPORTIONMENT
Defined, 15
Sixteenth amendment, 16

ASSESSMENTS
   See, also, Deficiency Procedures
Agreement for deficiency, 1017
Jeopardy, 1007
Prerequisite to collection of tax, 979

ASSIGNMENT OF INCOME
Acceleration of income, 294
Annuity contract, 296
Anticipatory assignment, 265, 274, 284,
   289
Anticipatory distinguished from sale of
   interest in trust, 674
Anticipatory for value, 292
Bonds, 291
Cattle, 288
Commissions and fees, 270
   Exceptions, 272
Consideration, 295
Contracts for income-splitting, effect of,
   264
Corporations, 265, 300, 331–341
Crop shares as income assets, 290
Dividends, 291–296
   Closely held corporation, 291
Economic gain test, 276
Effect of, 263
Endowment life insurance, 296
Executors and fiduciaries, 270
Fruit-tree doctrine, 265, 279, 288, 291,
   295
Gift, 265–272
Income for services, 263
Interest, 275, 291
Partnerships, 300, 332–331
   Taxation of,
      Family, 322–331
Property, income from, 275, 284, 309–316

ASSIGNMENT OF INCOME—Cont'd
Realization of income, 267, 275, 289,
   293, 296
Rent, 291
State law, effect of, 281
Statutory commissions, 270
Trust income, 279
Trustees, 271
Trusts, 301, 304–317
Unrealized appreciation in value, 289
Waiver, 267, 270

ATHLETIC AWARDS
Gross income, 128

AUDITS
Types of, 972

AUTOMOBILES
Prize or award as gross income, 125–132

AVERAGING OF INCOME
Annuities, 629
Bonuses, 626
Bunched income, 628
Capital gains included, 616
Constructive receipt of income, 620–631
Deferred compensation plans, 620–631
Divorced taxpayer, 617
Employee trusts, 625, 628
Profit-sharing plans, 628
Qualified pension plans, 628
Retirement plans, 630
Self-employment plans, 630
Statutory provisions, 620–631
   133% rule, 613
Stock option plans, 630

AWARDS
See Prizes and Awards

BAD DEBTS
Business bad debts, 816
Corporate loans, guarantee of, 818
Deductions for political parties, 419
Elements of, 808–813
Forgiveness, 814
Loans by shareholder-employees, 817
Nonbusiness, 813
Worthless, 815

BASIS
   See, also, Amount Realized
Adjusted basis, 141
Amount realized in depreciable property,
   168
Carry-over, 154–159
Cost, 142

BASIS—Cont'd
Depreciation related to, 732
Fair market value, 143
Gift, 146–153
Inherited property, 154–159
    Community property, 155, 165
New rule, 156
Transferred, 154
Trust property, 178
Trusts, sale of interest in, 673–679
Zero basis rule, 678

BEQUESTS, DEVICES, OR INHERIT-ANCES
Basis of property received, 154–159
Gross income, exclusions, 89

BILLS
Legislative process, 26

BONDS
Assignment of income from, 275, 291
Holding period, 714–718
Intergovernmental taxation of interest on, 258
Loss incurred in posting bond, 684

BONUSES
Income averaging, 626

BUSINESS
Recovery for injury to, gross income, 215
Regulatory effect of taxation, 1
Travel as gross income, 125

BUSINESS DEDUCTIONS
See Deductions; Trade or Business

BUSINESS EXPENSES
See Deductions; Trade or Business

CAPITAL
Expenses, see Deductions; Trade or Business
Returns of, defined, 141

CAPITAL ASSETS
Characterization, 665–669
Defined, 660
Holding period, 713–718
Inventions, 699
Securities, 668
Special treatment, 665–669

CAPITAL GAINS AND LOSSES
Averaging income, 616
Capital assets,
    Characterization, 665–669
    Defined, 635–640
        Corn products, 680–688

CAPITAL GAINS AND LOSSES—C't'd
Capital assets—Cont'd
    Securities, 668
    Special treatment, 665–669
    Tests to determine ordinary or capital gain or loss, 635, 667–669.
Capital gains,
    Historical treatment, 637
    How to tax, 636
Capital losses, limitations on deductibility, 638
Characterization of, 635
    Term interest, 678
Claim of right earnings, computation of tax, 707
Computation of tax,
    Alternate method, 642–648
        Corporations, 648
    Basic method, 640–642
        Corporations, 648
    Minimum tax for tax preferences, 648
Corn products doctrine, 680–688
Corporations, computation of loss, 658
Defined, 640
Futures transactions, 680–688
Hedging transaction, 680
Holding period, defined, 713–718
Income property,
    Consideration for cancellation of lease, 670
    Release, treatment of funds paid, 673
    Trusts, sale of interest in, 673–679
Judgments settled as gain, 694
Losses,
    Bonds posted as security, 684
    Capital asset, 707
    Carryovers, 653
    Characterized, 650
    Claim of right earnings, 707
    Deductible, 651
    Limitations on long-term, 651
    Procedure, 650
    Property held for sale, corn products, 684
    Short-term, 651
Measurement of term interest, 673–679
Minimum tax for tax preferences, 648
Prior transactions, effect upon characterization, 703
Property held for sale to customers,
    Defined, 660
    Primarily defined, 664

CAPITAL GAINS AND LOSSES—C't'd
Sale or exchange of property,
Correlation with prior transactions, 703–713
Debt-financed property, 701
Defined, 694
Dower rights discharged by divorced husband, 698
Holding period, 713–718
Bonds, 714–718
Real property, 717
Stocks, 715–718
Inventions, 699
Judgment settlement, 694
Losses, defined, 703–713
Patents, franchises, trademarks, and trade names, 700
Trust residence, 689
Trust, sale of interest in, 673–679

CARRYOVERS
Capital losses, computation of tax, 653
Corporations, computation of losses, 658
Net operating losses, computation of tax, 631–634

CASH METHOD OF ACCOUNTING
See, also, Accounting; Accrual Method of Accounting
Generally, 538
Amount realized for gain, 847–854
Constructive payments,
Checks, 551
Defined, 552
Insurance premiums, 555
Interest, 557
Salaries, 551–555
Constructive receipts, 547, 551–555
Credit cards, 551
Disbursements, 551–558
Prizes and awards, 547
Receipts as income,
Checks, 541
After banking hours, 542
Notes, 544

CASUALTY LOSSES
Deductibility of, 475–486
Defined, 478
Depreciation in property value, 478
Federal disaster relief, effect of, 490
Measurement of, 488–493
Sale or exchange of depreciable property, uninsured, 762
Termite infestation, 476
Timing of, 487

CATTLE
Taxable income, assignment of, 288

CHARITABLE CONTRIBUTIONS
Admission to fund raising events, amount of deduction, 827
Appreciated property, 833
Business expense, distinguished, 823
Corporations, 835
Defined, 823
Donation to educational organization, 826
Donative intent, 823
Easements, 843
Fifty per cent deduction, 831
Prior law, 831
Fund-raising activities, amount of deduction, 827
Gifts, defined, 826
Return of gift, computation of tax, 608
State, 843
Voluntary, 826

CHARITIES
Rental income from debt-financed property, computation of tax, 701

CHECKS
Deductible when honored, 551
Income received by cash basis taxpayer, 541–542

CHILD SUPPORT
Dependency exemptions for divorced parents, 499

CIVIL LIABILITY
Assessment of taxes, 970

CLAIM OF RIGHT
Restoration of income, computation of tax, 707

CLIFFORD TRUST
Irrevocable, assignment of property, 309–316

COLLATERAL ESTOPPEL
See Estoppel

COLLEGES AND UNIVERSITIES
Educational expense, deductibility of, 396–404

COMMISSIONS AND FEES
Assignment of income, 270
Exceptions, 272

COMMITTEE REPORTS
Legislative process, 27

COMMODITY FUTURES
Tax treatment, 684

COMMON LAW
Federal taxation, 204

COMMUNITY PROPERTY
Amount realized in divorce, 165
Basis at death of spouse, 155

COMPENSATION FOR INJURIES OR SICKNESS
Accident and health insurance benefits, 209
Computation of damages for gross income, 208
Disability pension benefits, 210
Employee benefits paid for by employer,
Disability exclusion, 214
Gross income, 211
Sick pay, 213
Spouse or dependents, 213
Gross income, defined, 205
Medical malpractice recoveries, 207
Tort recoveries, 206
Workmen's Compensation, 206
Wrongful death, 208

CONDEMNATION
Involuntary conversions, gains or losses, 916, 921–926

CONFERENCES
Tax procedure, 973
Appeals, 973

CONGRESSIONAL RECORD
Debates, 28

CONSTITUTIONAL PROVISIONS
Due process, 20
Fifth Amendment, 20
"From whatever source derived", 16
Income, 16
Power to tax, 14
Self-incrimination, 20
Sixteenth Amendment, 16
Uniformity among states, 18

CONSTRUCTIVE PAYMENTS
See Cash Method of Accounting

CONSTRUCTIVE RECEIPTS
See Cash Method of Accounting

CONTRACTS
Assignment of income, 264

CORN PRODUCTS DOCTRINE
Losses, 680–688

CORPORATIONS
Assignment of income, 265
Anticipatory, 331
Apportionment between persons and organizations, 333
Dividends from closely held corporations, 291
Future dividends, 331
Two businesses jointly controlled, 337
Charitable contributions, 835
Computation of gains, 648
Computation of losses, 658
Contribution to capital as discharge of debt, 201
Gains and losses on stock exchanges, 942
Guarantee of loan loss as bad debt, 818
Income, 300, 331–341
Interest on indebtedness incurred for acquisitions, deductibility, 419
Loans by shareholder-employer, loss as bad debt, 817
Sale or exchange of depreciable property, ownership of 80% of stock, 779
Sale or exchange of property between individuals and close corporation, 889–893
Taxation of assigned income, 333–341
Valid purpose vs. tax-saving activity, 333

COURT OF CLAIMS
Jurisdiction, 33

COURTS OF APPEAL
Jurisdiction, 33
Deficiency procedures, 1004

CREDITS
See, also, Tax Rates
Candidates for public office contributions, 967
Credit cards, constructive payments, 551
Dependent care expenses, 968
Earned income credit, 968
Elderly, 964
Foreign taxes, 969
General tax credit, 968
Investment credit, 966
Obsolete credit, 969
Withholding payments, 963
Estimated tax payments, 963
Retirement income credit, 964
Social Security excessive tax, 964
Work incentive credit, 966

CRIMINAL LIABILITY
See, also, Fraud; Procedure
Generally, 970
Deficiencies, 1002

CROPS
Taxable income, 290

DAMAGES
See, also, Compensation for Injuries
or Sickness
Gross income, 45, 204
Compensatory, 216
Exemplary, 45
Injuries or sickness, compensation,
205–215
Liquidated, 217
Medical malpractice recoveries, 207
Personal injuries, defined, 215
Punitive, 45, 216
Recovery for injury to business or
property, 215
Severance damages, 216
Wrongful death, 208
Torts resulting in bodily injury or sick-
ness, 206

DEATH
Taxation of income upon death of taxpayer, 317–321

DEBATES
Congressional Record, 28

DEBT–FINANCED PROPERTY
Sale or exchange, 701
Tax exempt organizations subject to tax
on rental income, 701

DEBTS
See, also, Bad Debts
Amount realized on trust transfer, 178
Discharge of as gross income, 199
Adjustment of purchase price, 201
Contribution to capital, 201
Forgiveness of student loans, 202
Gifts, 200
Insolvency, 201
Statutory exception, 202

DECLARATORY JUDGMENTS
Remedy foreclosed, 979

DEDUCTIONS
Adjusted gross income concept, 504–506
Avoidance or evasion of income tax, 419

DEDUCTIONS—Cont'd
Bad debt, 808–823
Business bad debts, 816
Corporate loans, guarantee, 818
Elements of, 808–813
Forgiveness, 814
Loans by shareholder-employees, 817
Nonbusiness, 813
Worthless, 815
Business expenses, 343–347
Advertising, 409
Capital expenditure distinguished,
348–355
"Carrying on", 356–362
Elections, 361
Employee, 359
Other employment, 361
Pre-employed, 359
Self-employed, 356
Unemployed, 360
Charitable contribution, distinguished,
823
Dues, 410
Education, 396–404
Entertainment, 405
Home defined, 369–380
Institute, 402
Meals and lodging, 369–380
Medical expenses distinguished, 523
Ordinary and necessary, 344
Defined, 348
"Pursuit of" defined, 358
Rental payments, 383–396
Lease distinguished, 383
Repairs to building, 348–355
Restored income, 598–607
Salaries, reasonable, 363
Summer school, 397
Transfer and leaseback agreements,
386
Travel, 369–380
Trust agreements, 392
Uniforms, 409
Casualty losses, 475–486
Defined, 478
Depreciation in property value, 478
Federal disaster relief, effect of, 490
Measurement of, 488–493
Termite infestation, 476
Timing, 487
Characterization of, 342, 808
Charitable contributions, 823–844
Defined, 504–506
Depreciation, 721–807
Educational expenses, 396–404

DEDUCTIONS—Cont'd
Entertainment, 405
Fines and penalties, 425
Fraud, losses by, 481
Hobby losses, 415, 435
Home, defined for travel expenses,
  369–380
Illegal activities, 420
  Legal expenses, 424
Illegal or improper business expense, 484
Interest, 465–472
  Deferred payments, accounting meth-
    od, 584
  Unpaid, 418
Itemized, 507–509
Kickbacks, 424
Legal expenses, 432
  Antenuptial contract, 445
  Illegal activities, 424
  Ordinary and necessary, 435
Lobbying expenses, 419, 423
Losses, business, 410
  Artificial, 413
Low income allowance, 509
Meals and lodging, 369–380
Medical expenses,
  Air conditioning, 511
  Business expenses distinguished, 523
  Miscellaneous costs, 520
  Rental payments, 513
  Transportation, food and lodging
    costs, 517–521
Moving expenses, 525–534
Nonbusiness expenses,
  "Carrying on a business", 428
  Ordinary and necessary, 428
Personal exemptions, 496
  Dependency exemptions, 496–502
    Defined 497
    Support, 497
  Divorced parents, 502
Political contributions, 536
Production or collection of income, 432
  Legal expenses, 432
  Ordinary and necessary expenses, 432
Profit-making, nonbusiness expenses,
  428–453
  Legal expenses, 432–439
  Ordinary and necessary, 432–439
  Property held for the production of
    income, 432
  Residence held for sale, 458
  Solicitory proxy votes, 439
Public policy against, 481
Reasonable repair rule, 355

DEDUCTIONS—Cont'd
Rental of vacation home expenses, 417
Reserve funds to cover future costs,
  584–596
Restrictions,
  Artificial losses, 413
  Avoidance or evasion of income tax,
    419
  Bad debts of political parties, 419
  Business use of home, 420
  Fines and penalties, 425
  Horticultural development costs, 418
  Illegal activities, 420
    Legal expenses, 424
  Interest on indebtedness incurred for
    corporation acquisitions, 419
  Lobbying expenses, 419, 423
  Unpaid expenses and interest, 418
Sixteenth Amendment, 342
Standard, 507–509
Stock and securities, securing proxy
  vote, 439
Taxes, 472
Theft by fraud, 481
Theft losses, 479
  Measurement of, 490
  Timing, 487
Travel expenses, 369–380
  Medical reasons, 517–521
Unpaid expenses, 418
Vacation homes, rental, expenses, 417

DEFERRED INCOME
Accrual method of accounting, 572–580

DEFICIENCY PROCEDURES
  See, also, Procedure
Agreement for assessment of tax, 1017
Appeal from, 1004
Burden of proof, 1013
Closing agreements, 1015
Closing taxpayer's year, 1007
Criminal sanction, 1002
Demand for payment, 1007
Evidence, 1011
Finality in tax controversies, 1014
  Administrative, 1015
  Judicial, 1018
  Statutory, 1015
Fraud, 1002
Innocent spouse, 1002
Interest, 1001
Jurisdiction of Tax Court, 1006
Limitations, 1015
Notice of deficiency, 1007
Penalties, 1002

DEFICIENCY PROCEDURES—Cont'd
Petition filing, 1007
  Mailing, 1007
Refund, 1006
Ruling, effect of, 1017
Small tax cases, 1008
  Form for petition, 1012
Tax fraud case, 975

DEPENDENTS
Defined, 497
Expenses as credit against tax, 968

DEPRECIATION
Admission to the bar costs, 736
Allowed or allowable, 733
Amount realized in sale of property, 168
Basis, relationship to, 732
Casualty loss in value of property, 478
Cost less salvage value, 726, 750
Cost of asset, 726
Declining balance method, 729, 751
  150% method, 759
  Realty, 759
Deductibility of expenses, nonbusiness
  activity, 455
Defined, 721
Ecological advances stimulated, 734
Education, deductibility of costs, 736
Full-economic-life concept, 748
Methods of computation, 727
Natural resources, cost depletion, 734
Personalty, 758
Prerequisites for deduction, 722
Realty, 759
  Residential housing, 760
    60 month rule, 760
Sale or exchange of depreciable per-
  sonal property,
  Characterization of gain, 779
  Property defined, 789
  Recapture provisions, 786
  Recomputed leases, 787
Sale or exchange of depreciable prop-
  erty,
  Business, 773
  Casualty losses, 762
  Ordinary loss on trade or business
    property, 763
  Ownership of 80% of corporate stock,
    779
  Property held for sale in trade or busi-
    ness, 763, 769

DEPRECIATION—Cont'd
Sale or exchange of depreciable real
  property,
  Accounting methods, 797
  Investment credit property, 798
  Recapture provisions, 797
Sale or exchange of personal property,
  Conversion of business auto to per-
    sonal use, 794
  Player's sport franchise, 791
  Selling price in excess of basis, 793
Sale or exchange of property,
  Business and personal uses by part-
    nership, 752
  Emergency facilities, 802
  Farm property, 802
  Oil or gas property, 804
Salvage value, 748
Sixty-month amortization of capital ex-
  penditures, 734
Sociological improvements benefits, 734
Straight-line method, 727, 751
  60 month rule for rental housing, 760
Sum of the years-digit method, 729, 760
Useful life concept, 722, 747

DETERMINATION LETTER
Final effect upon taxpayer, 1017

DEVISES
See Bequests, Devises, or Inheritances,

DIRECT TAXES
Classification of income, 15
Defined, 14

DISABILITY
Annual exclusion from gross income,
  213
Benefits as gross income, 210

DISCHARGE OF INDEBTEDNESS
Adjustment of purchase price, 201
Contribution to capital, 201
Forgiveness of student loans, 202
Gifts, 200
Insolvency, 201
Payment of debt for less than amount
  owed, 199
Statutory exceptions, 202
Waiver of loan repayment for medical
  student, 139

DISCLOSURES
Voluntary in tax fraud cases, 990

DISTRAINT
Governmental remedy to collect tax, 980

DISTRICT COURTS
Jurisdiction, 33

DIVIDENDS
Assignment of income, 291–296
  Closely-held corporation, 291
Up to $100 excluded from gross income,
  254

DIVORCE
Alimony, 219
Alimony payments, indirect benefits, 241
Alimony trusts, 249
Averaging of income, 617
Community property settlement, amount
  realized, 165
Dependency exemptions for support of
  children, 499
Ex parte decree, 247
Legal expenses, deductibility, 445
Lump sum payments, 249
Periodic and installment payments dis-
  tinguished, 232
Periodic payments, 221–241
Pre-existing trusts, 251
Premiums on life insurance, 241
Property settlement, 221
  Amount realized defined, 159
Property transferred to discharge mari-
  tal obligation, 241
Property transferred to discharge wife's
  dower rights, 221, 698
Rent-free residence, 241
Sham, 508

DOWER
Property transferred to discharge wife's
  right, 698

DUE PROCESS
Generally, 20

DUES
Deductible business expense, 410

EARNED INCOME
Credit against tax, 968

EASEMENTS
Charitable contribution of, 843

ECOLOGY
Depreciation for benefits, 734

EDUCATION
  See, also, Charitable Contributions
Amortization of costs, 736
Deduction for expenses, 396–404
  Institute, 402
  Summer school, 396

ELDERLY
Credits against tax, 964

ELECTIONS
Business expenses, deductibility, 361

EMBEZZLEMENT
Gross income, 50, 564

EMERGENCY FACILITIES
Sale or exchange of depreciable property, 802

EMPLOYERS AND EMPLOYEES
  See, also, Deductions; Trade or Busi-
    ness
Compensation for sickness or injuries,
  Disability exclusion, 214
  Employee benefits paid for by em-
    ployer, 210
    Spouse or dependents, 213
  Sick pay, 213
Employee death benefits, 86
Employer's gift vs. compensation, 77
Fringe benefits as gifts, 110
Intent of gift vs. salary, 78

ENTERTAINMENT
Expenses deductible, 405

ESTIMATED TAX PAYMENTS
Credit against tax, 962

ESTOPPEL
Final effect upon liability of taxpayer,
  1019

EXCLUSIONS
Bequeathed property, 65, 89
  Income from, 65
Bequests, devices, or inheritances, 89
  Compensation for services, 94
Dividends up to $100, p. 64
Fair rental value, 117
  Minister's housing benefits, 122
$5000 limit on payment to widow, 85
Fringe benefits, 99–114
Gifts, 66
Gross income, 64
Honoraria upon retirement, 79
Payments to widow by spouse's em-
  ployer, 81

EXEMPLARY DAMAGES
See Damages

EXEMPTIONS
See Deductions

References are to Pages

EXPENSES
See, also, Deductions
Deductibility of unpaid, 418
Ordinary or capital legal expenses, 435

EXTORTION
Gross income, 50

FAIR MARKET VALUE
Amount realized on divorce transfer, 159
Amount realized on sale of depreciable property, 168
Carryover basis in inherited property, 156
Cost basis, 143
Inherited property, 154

FARMS
Sale or exchange of depreciable property, 802

FEDERAL DISASTER RELIEF
Casualty losses deductions, effect upon, 490

FINES AND PENALTIES
Deductions, 425

FIRE
Involuntary conversion, gains and losses, 926

FOREIGN TAXES
Credit against tax, 969

FOREIGN TRUSTS
Taxation upon assignment of income, 315

FRANCHISES
Sale or exchange of capital asset, 700

FRAUD
Deficiency procedures, 1002
Exemplary damages as gross income, 45
Losses, deductibility of, 481
Procedure in tax fraud case, 981–993

"FRESH START"
Rule as to carryover basis defined, 157

FRINGE BENEFITS
Gifts, 99–114
Group term life insurance, 110
Insurance commissions, 111
Proposed regulations, 99
Split-dollar insurance, 111

GAINS AND LOSSES
See, also, Capital Gains and Losses; Losses
Adjusted basis, open transactions, 847–854
Amount realized, 159, 168
Accrual method, 872
Cash method, 847–854
Closed transactions, 855–885
Timing of, 855–885
Community property transfer, 165
Defined, 862, 864
Fair market value of real estate contract, 862
Historical background, 862
Open transaction, 847–854
Timing, 847–854
Trust, transfers, 178
Carryover basis, 156
Casualty losses on sale or exchange of depreciable property, 762
Closed transactions, 855–885
Contracts for sale of realty with deferred payments, 857
Deferred payment sales of personal property, 874
Deferred reporting of gain,
Closed transactions, 857
Open transactions, 847–854
Gifts, 146–153
Installment payments of purchase price, 862
Defined, 877
Interest, 880
Personal property, 874
Real property, 874–885
Installment sales, disposition defined, 883
Nonrecognition provisions,
Annuity contract exchanges, 943
Corporate exchanges, 942
Defined, 895
Effect of, 896
Endowment contract exchanges, 943
Exchanges of like kind, 897–913
Criteria, 897
Defined, 897–905
Sale or leaseback, 905
Three-cornered transaction, 911
Installment sale of property, 943
Involuntary conversions, 914–927
Condemnation, 916
Proceeds used on remaining property, 921
Proceeds used to improve other property, 922

GAINS AND LOSSES—Cont'd
Nonrecognition provisions—Cont'd
Involuntary conversions—Cont'd
Fire proceeds, 926
Functional or end use test, 917
Similar or related in service or use, defined, 920
Life insurance exchanges, 942
Low income housing projects, 943
Miscellaneous transactions, 942
Partnership exchanges, 942
Sale and reacquisition of property, 943
Sale of principal residence, 929–946
Age 65 or older, 939
Involuntary conversion, 929–931
Replacement period, 931–932
Use of property as, 932
Open transactions,
Closed distinguished, 871
Defined, 850
Property transferred at death, 847
Uncertainties and contingencies existing, 853
Sale or exchange of depreciable property,
Emergency facilities, 802
Farm property, 802
Oil or gas property, 804
Sale or exchange of depreciable real property, 797
Accounting methods, 797
Investment credit property, 798
Recapture provisions, 797
Sale or exchange of personal property,
Characterization of gain, 779
Conversion of business auto to personal use, 794
Player's sport franchise, 791
Property defined, 789
Recapture provisions, 786
Recomputed basis, 787
Selling price in excess of basis, 793

GIFTS
See, also, Assignment of Income; Charitable Contributions
Appreciated property, 833
Assignment of income, 265–272
Basis, 146–153
Cost basis, 154–159
Defined, 826
Discharge of indebtedness, 200
Dominant reason, 81

GIFTS—Cont'd
Excluded from gross income, 66
Employee death benefits, 86
Employer's gift vs. compensation, 77
Honorarium to retired pastor, 79
Intent to give vs. salary, 79
Payments received by widow from spouse's employer, 81
$5000 limit on payment to widows, 85
Fringe benefits,
Group life insurance, 110
Insurance commissions, 111
Proposed regulations, 99
Split dollar insurance, 111
Honorarium upon resignation, 79
Return of, computation of tax, 608
Scholarships and fellowships, 133
Test, determinative of, 66

GRANTOR TRUSTS
Taxation upon assignment of income, 314

GROSS INCOME
See, also, Assignment of Income; Gains and Losses; Income
Adjusted, 504–506
Alimony payments, 219
Annuity payments, 190–197, 221
Annual exclusion, 192
Defined, 190
Refund features, 193
Variable annuity defined, 191
Benefit of grantor, 136
Bequests, devises, or inheritances, 89–97
Compensation for services, 94
Bunched income, 628
Checks received by cash basis taxpayer, 541
After banking hours, 542
Compensation for injuries or sickness 204–215
Employee benefits paid for by employer, 211
Disability exclusion, 214
Sick pay, 213
Spouse or dependents, 213
Damages, 45, 204
Exemplary, 45
Deferred income, 572–580
Defined, 36, 64
Derived from any source, 47
Discharge of indebtedness, 199
Adjustment of purchase price, 201
Contribution to capital, 201
Forgiveness of student loans, 202

GROSS INCOME—Cont'd
Discharge of indebtedness—Cont'd
  Gifts, 200
  Insolvency, 201
  Statutory exceptions, 202
Embezzlement proceeds, 50, 564
Employee death benefits, 86
Exclusions, 65, 253–261
  Bequeathed property, 65
    Income from, 65
  Dividends up to $100, pp. 65, 254
  Employee death benefits, 86
  $5000 limit on payments to widows, 85
  Improvements by lessee, 253
  Income earned abroad, 255
  Military compensation, limited, 254
Extortion proceeds, 50
Fair rental value, 117
  Minister's housing benefits, 122
Federal taxation of state income, 260
Financial benefit received, 37
Foreign, 255
Fringe benefits,
  Group term life insurance, 110
  Insurance commissions, 111
  Proposed regulations, 99
  Split dollar insurance, 111
Gifts defined by courts, 66
Honorarium upon retirement, 79
Illegal activities, 50
Interest free loans, 57
Intergovernmental immunity, 256
Inventories, 580
Judgments, 561
Life insurance proceeds, 188
Loans, 49
  Waiver of repayment, 139
Meals and lodging, 116
Pension payments to minister, 79
Periodic payments, 221–241
Personal injuries, defined, 215
Premium on life insurance as alimony, 241
Prepayment for services, 572
Prizes and awards, 124, 547
  Athletic awards, 128
  Business trip, 125
Profits earned during receivership, 561
Promissory notes received by cash basis taxpayer, 544
Property acquired by gift, bequest, devise or descent, 147
Property not received, 53
Property settlements, 221
Public utilities receipts by states exempt from federal tax, 260

GROSS INCOME—Cont'd
Recoveries for injuries to business or property, 215
Rent, advanced payments, 569
Rent-free residence as alimony, 241
Rental value of building occupied by owner as income, 53
Right to receive income, 559–561
Sales, 559
Scholarships and fellowships, 133
  Compensation for services, 136
  Defined, 135
  Medical interns and residents, stipends, 138
  Research and teaching assistants, stipends, 137
State income taxed by federal government, 260
Support payments, 229
Tax payments as income, 43
Treasure trove, 36
Unlawful gains, 567
Widows, payment received from spouse's employer, 81

HEAD OF HOUSEHOLD
Tax rates, 949

HEALTH INSURANCE
Benefits as gross income, 209

HEARINGS
Legislative process, 26

HEDGING TRANSACTIONS
Tax treatment, 680

HISTORY
Generally, 6

HOBBIES
Expenses, 435
Restriction on deductions of losses, 413

HOLDING PERIOD
Bonds, 714–718
Capital asset, 713–718
Real property, 717
Stocks and securities, 715–718
Trade dates, 714–718

HOME
Defined for travel expenses, 369–380

HONORARIA
Gross income exclusions, 79

HORTICULTURE
Deduction of costs, 418

HOSPITALS
Assignment of income to, 272

HOUSING
See, also, Low Income Housing
Depreciation, 760

HUSBAND AND WIFE
Innocent spouse—deficiency procedures, 1002
Losses on sale or exchange of property to each other, 886–893
Tax rates, 947–953
Filing separately, 951

ILLEGAL ACTIVITIES
Deduction for expenses, 420, 484
Legal expenses, 424
Gains as gross income, 567
Gross income, 50
Kickbacks, deductions, 424

ILLNESS
See Compensation for Injuries or Sickness

IMMUNITY
Intergovernmental tax activities, 256

INCOME
See, also, Assignment of Income; Averaging of Income; Gross Income
Corporations, 300, 331–341
Defined, 36, 147
Ordinary, 796
Partnerships, 300, 322–331
Taxation of upon death, 317–321
Trusts, 304–317

INCOME IN RESPECT OF DECEDENTS
Characterization of, 320
Deductions for expenses, 320
Historical background, 317
Income tax deduction for estate tax, 317
Taxation of, 319

INCOME PRODUCING PROPERTY
See Property Held for the Production of Income

INCOME–SPLITTING
Effect of, 263
Tax rates, 948

INCOME TAXATION
Generally, 1–6
Avoidance or evasion expenses, deductibility, 419

INCOME TAXATION—Cont'd
Constitutionality, 14
Legislative process, 25
Practitioners' tools, 25
Publications, 25
Study of, 1–6

INDICTMENTS
Tax fraud cases, 983

INDIRECT TAXES
Classification of income, 15
Defined, 14

INHERITANCES
See Bequests, Devises, or Inheritances

INJUNCTIONS
Use of prohibited, 979

INJURIES
See Compensation for Injuries or Sickness; Personal Injuries

INNOCENT SPOUSE RULE
Tax consequences, 1002

INSOLVENCY
Discharge of indebtedness, gross income, 201

INSTALLMENT PAYMENTS
Periodic payments, distinguished, 232

INSTALLMENT SALES
See Gains and Losses

INSTITUTES
Educational expense, deductibility of, 402

INSURANCE
Fringe benefit as gift,
Group term life insurance, 110
Insurance commission, 111
Split dollar insurance, 111
Premiums, constructive payments, 555

INTEREST
Assignment of income, 275, 291
Constructive payments, 557
Deductibility of, 465–472
Unpaid, 418
Deduction for interest on deferred payments, accounting method, 584
Deficiency procedures, 1001
Defined, 465–472
Indebtedness incurred by corporation for acquisitions, deductions, 419
Installment payments of purchase price, 880

INTEREST—Cont'd
Intergovernmental taxation of bonds, 258
Loan processing fee, deductibility, 465
Loans free of interest as gross income, 57

INTERGOVERNMENTAL IMMUNITY
Federal-State tax activities, 256

INTERNAL REVENUE CODE
Development of, 8
Study of, 3
Tax laws codified, 25

INTERNAL REVENUE LAWS
Historical background, 7

INTERPRETATION OF TAX LAWS
Judicial process, 31

INVENTORIES
Gross income and accounting methods, 580

INVESTMENTS
Credit against tax, 966
Sale or exchange of depreciable real property, 804

INVOLUNTARY CONVERSIONS
See Deductions; Gains and Losses

JEOPARDY ASSESSMENTS
Effect of, 1007

JUDGMENTS
Settlement as gain, 694

JUDICIAL PROCESS
Interpretation of tax laws, 31

JUSTICE DEPARTMENT
Function of in tax fraud, 992

KICKBACKS
Deduction for illegal activities, 424

LAW SCHOOLS
Assignment of income to, 272

LEASE PURCHASE AGREEMENTS
Rent as deductible, business expenses, 386

LEASES
Cancellation resulting in loss, 670
Improvements by lessee excluded from gross income, 253
Release of, treatment of funds paid, 673
Rental payments distinguished, 383–396

LEGAL AID
Assignment of income to, 274

LEGAL EXPENSES
Antenuptial contract, 445
Deductions, 424, 432–439, 445–453

LEGISLATIVE PROCESS
Bills, 26
Committee reports, 27
Debates, 28
Hearings, 27
Internal Revenue Code, 25
Policy, 5
Prior laws, 28
Reasoning behind tax legislation, 5
Treaties, 28

LEVY
Government remedy to collect tax, 980

LIEN
Unpaid taxes, 980

LIFE INSURANCE
Assignment of income, 296
Gains and losses or exchange of policies, 942
Premiums paid, gross income, 241
Proceeds as income, 188
Wrongful death recoveries, gross income, 208

LOANS
Gross income, 49
Interest-free as gross income, 57
Processing fee, deductible as interest, 465
Waiver of obligation to repay as gross income, 139

LOBBYING
Expenses, deductible, 419

LODGING
See Meals and Lodging

LOOPHOLE
Defined, 2

LOSSES
See, also, Capital Gains and Losses; Gains and Losses
Business, deductibility of, 410
Artificial, 413
Carryovers and carrybacks, 631–634
Casualty, deductible, 475–486
Close corporations and individuals, 889
Family members, between, 886–893
Holding period for capital loss, 713–718

LOSSES—Cont'd
Net operating losses, computation of tax, 631–634
Related taxpayers, 886–893
Sale or exchange of depreciable property,
Ordinary loss on trade or business property, 763
Uninsured, 762

LOW INCOME ALLOWANCE
Standard deductions, 509
Tax rate, 952

LOW INCOME HOUSING
Depreciation, 760
Gains and losses on exchange, 943

MAXIMUM TAX
Earned income, 960

MEALS AND LODGING
Condition of employment test, 119
Convenience of employer test, 118
Deduction as business expense, 369–380
Gross income, 116
Medical deductions, 517–521
Minister's housing benefits, 122

MEDICAL EXPENSES
Deductibility, 511–524
Gross income, 205

MEDICAL INTERNS AND RESIDENTS
Stipends vs. scholarships as gross income, 138
Waiver of loan repayment as gross income, 139

MEDICAL MALPRACTICE
Gross income, recoveries from, 207

MILITARY BENEFITS
Excluded from gross income, 254

MINIMUM TAX
Expanded tax of capital gains to high income taxpayers, 648
Tax preferences, 953–960
Corporations, 959
Individuals, 959

MINISTERS
Fair rental value of housing, 122
Honorarium to retired pastor, gross income, 79

MORTGAGES
Amount realized in depreciable property subject to, 168

MOVING EXPENSES
Deductions, 525–534
Outside U. S., 530

NATURAL RESOURCES
Depreciation of cost depletion, 734

NINETY–DAY LETTER
Statutory notice of deficiency, 975

"NO CHANGE" LETTER
Tax procedure, 972

NONRECOGNITION
See Gains and Losses

OIL AND GAS
Cost depletion, 734
Percentage depletion, relation to tax, 707
Sale or exchange of depreciable property, 804

ORDINARY INCOME
Defined, 796

OVERPAYMENT
Refund of tax paid, 598–607

PARTNERSHIPS
Gains and losses on exchanges, 942
Income, 300, 322–331
Taxation of assigned income, 322–331
Family, 322–331

PATENTS
Sale or exchange of capital asset, 700

PENSION PLANS
See, also, Bonds
Income averaging, 628
Payments to minister, 79

PERIODIC PAYMENTS
See, also, Alimony; Divorce; Separation Agreements
Installment payments, distinguished, 232

PERSONAL EXEMPTIONS
See Deductions

PERSONAL INJURIES
Gross income, defined, 215

PERSONAL PROPERTY
Deferred payment sales, gain on, 874
Depreciation, 758

PHYSICIANS AND SURGEONS
See Medical Interns and Residents

POLICE
Assignment of income, 274

POLITICAL CONTRIBUTIONS
Bad debt deductions,
Credit against tax for, 967
Deductions, 536

POWER TO TAX
Constitutional provisions, 14

PRIOR LAWS
Legislative process, 28

PRIZES AND AWARDS
Athletic awards, gross income, 128
Business trip, 125
Gross income, 124, 547

PROCEDURE
   See, also, Deficiency Procedures; Refund of Tax
Administrative appeals, 973
Appeals, 976, 978
Assessment of tax, 979
Attorneys for government, 978
Audits, 972
Collection of taxes, 979
Conference, 973
   Appeal, 973
Controversy, development of, 972
Declaratory judgments, 979
Declaratory rulings, 979
Distraint, 980
Errors on return, 971
Examining officer, 972
Formal written protest, 973
Jurisdiction of the courts, 976
Levy, 980
Liability of transferee, 980
Liens, 980
Litigation, 975
Ninety-day letter, 975
"No change" letter, 972
Notice of deficiency, 975
Petition, 976
Refund controversies, 974
Self-assessment of tax, 971
Small tax cases 1009
   Claim settlements, 973
   Form for petition, 1012

PROCEDURE—Cont'd
Tax fraud,
   Accountant's involvement, 988
   Administrative review, 990
      Legal, 991
   Conference, 982
   Constitutional protection, 987
   Cooperation with IRS, 990
   Deficiency, proof of, 985
   Department of Justice, 992
   Ex parte petition, 983
   Indictment, 983
   Interview, 982
   Investigation, 981
   Meeting with special agent, 986
   Records, examination of, 983
   Regional counsel, 991
   Search warrants, 983
      Prevent seizure of records, 989
   Self-incrimination, 987
   Special agent's report, 982
   Subpoenas, 983
   Summonses, 983, 989
      Accountant, 988
      Appeals, 984
      Privileged relationship, 989
      Resistance of, 984
   Trial, 992
   Voluntary disclosures, 990
   Witnesses, examination of, 983
Thirty-day letter, 973

PROFIT–SHARING PLANS
Averaging of income, 628

PROGRESSIVE TAX
Defined, 262

PROMISSORY NOTES
Receipts as income, 544

PROPERTY
   See, also, Sale or Exchange
Appreciated, charitable contribution of, 833
Assignment of income from, 275, 284
Depreciation,
   Casualty loss, 478
   Deductibility of expenses, 455
Held for sale to customer,
   Defined, 660
   Primarily defined, 664
Income, 670–679
Recovery for injury to as gross income, 215
Repairs as deductible business expense, 348–355
Reasonable repair rule, 355

PROPERTY HELD FOR THE PRODUCTION OF INCOME
Depreciation expenses, 455
Distinguished from residential property, 458
Maintenance expenses, deductibility of, 458

PROPERTY SETTLEMENTS
Amount realized,
Defined, 159
Divorce, 165

PUBLIC OFFICIALS
Deductibility of election expenses, 361

PUBLIC POLICY
Deductions for fraud, 481
Deductions for illegal activities, 420
Legal expenses, 424

PUBLIC UTILITIES
States' receipts exempt from federal tax, 260

PUNITIVE DAMAGES
See Damages

RATE OF TAX
See Tax Rates

REAL PROPERTY
Charitable contribution of easement, 843
Depreciation, 759
Casualty loss, 478
Deductibility of expenses, 455
Gains and losses on exchanges, 943
Held for sale to customer,
Defined, 660
Primarily defined, 664
Holding period, 717
Installment payments of purchase price, 874–885
Computation of gain realized, 862
Maintenance expenses of property held for sale, 458
Sale of principal residence, gains or losses, 929–946

RECEIVERSHIP
Profits earned as gross income, 561

RECOGNITION
See Gains and Losses

RECORDS
Examination of, 983

RECOUPMENT
Refund suit, 998

REFUND OF TAX
Controversies, 974
Deficiency procedures, 1006
Procedures,
Administrative claim prior to suit, 996
Claim, 996
Credit versus cash payment, 996
Filing claim, 997
Overpayment, 996
Payment of tax, 998
Full payment rule, 994
Recoupment by government, 998
Statutory requisite, 996
Restoration of income previously taxed, 598–607
Reimbursements, 606
Suit for, 1006

REGIONAL COUNSEL
Function of in the tax fraud case, 991

REGULATIONS
Generally, 29
Draft of, 978

REMEDIES
See Procedure

RENT
Advance payments as gross income, 569
Assignment of income, 291
Fair rental value,
Income, 117
Minister's housing benefits, 122
Income producing property, deductibility of expenses, 458
Payments as deductible business expense, 383–396
Lease distinguished, 383
Transfer and leaseback agreements, 386
Trust agreements, 392
Rent-free residence, gross income, 241
Rental value of building occupied by owner as income, 53

REPAIRS, BUILDING
Business expense,
Deductibility of, 348–355
Reasonable repair rule, 355

RES JUDICATA
Final effect upon liability of taxpayer, 1019

RESEARCH ASSISTANTS
Stipends vs. scholarships as gross income, 137

RESERVE ACCOUNTING
See Accrual Method of Accounting

RESIDENCE
See Real Property

RESTORATION OF INCOME
Refund of tax paid, 598–607
Reimbursements, tax paid, 598–607

RETIREMENT
Income averaging plans, 630

RETIREMENT INCOME
Credit against tax, 964

RETURNS
See, also, Deficiency Procedures
Failure to file, 1001
Filing required, 970
Human errors corrected, 971
Individual taxpayers, 947–953

REVENUE ACT OF 1971
General effect, 13

REVENUE ADJUSTMENT ACT OF 1975
General effect, 13

RULINGS
Generally, 30
Declaratory, 979
Draft of, 978
Final effect upon taxpayer, 1017

SALARIES
Constructive payments, cash method of accounting, 552–555
Deductible as business expense, 363
Deferred compensation plans, income averaging, 620–631

SALE AND LEASEBACK
Nonrecognition provisions, 905–913

SALE OR EXCHANGE
Amount realized as taxable, 166
Basis of property acquired by gift, 146–153
Depreciable property,
Amount realized, 168
Business, 773
Casualty losses, 762
Emergency facilities, 802
Farm property, 802
Oil or gas property, 804
Ownership of 80% of corporate stocks, 779

SALE OR EXCHANGE—Cont'd
Property held for sale in trade or business, 763, 769
Property in trade or business, 763
Uninsured, 763
Depreciable real property, 797
Accounting methods, 797
Investment credit property, 798
Recapture provisions, 797
Disposition of property,
Close corporation, 886–893
Family members, 886–893
Related taxpayers, 886–893
Trust res, 689
Nonrecognition provisions, 897–913
Personal property,
Characterization of gain, 779
Conversion of business auto to personal use, 794
Player's sport franchise, 791
Property defined, 789
Recapture provisions, 786
Recomputed basis, 787
Selling price in excess of basis, 793

SCHOLARSHIPS AND FELLOW-SHIPS
Benefit of grantor, 136
Candidate for a degree, 135
Compensation for services, 136
Defined, 135
Expenses incidental to the grant, 134
Grantor a governmental organization, 135
Grantor an exempt organization, 135
Gross income, 133
Medical interns and residents, stipends, 138
Payments for teaching, research, or other services, 135
Research and teaching assistants, stipends, 137

SEARCH WARRANTS
Tax fraud cases, 989
Prevention of record seizure, 989

SELF–EMPLOYMENT
Income averaging plans, 630

SELF–INCRIMINATION
Constitutional provisions, effect upon tax litigation, 20
Tax fraud case, 987

SELF–INSURANCE
Sale or exchange of depreciable property, casualty losses, 762

SEPARATION AGREEMENTS
Payments,
Gross income, 231
Periodic, 231
Periodic and installment payments distinguished, 232

SEVERANCE DAMAGES
Gross income, 216

SICK PAY
See, also, Compensation for Injuries or Sickness
Gross income, 213

SINGLE PERSONS
Tax rates, 950

SMALL TAX CLAIMS
Limited settlement agreements, 973
Procedures, 1008
Form for petition, 1012

SOCIAL SECURITY
Benefits excluded from gross income, 253
Excessive payments credit against tax, 964

STANDARD DEDUCTION
See Deductions

STATE GOVERNMENTS
Charitable contribution to, 843

STATUTE OF LIMITATIONS
See Limitations

STOCK AND SECURITIES
Capital assets, treatment as, 668
Deduction for soliciting proxy votes, 439
Holding period, 714–718
Income averaging through stock options, 630

STUDENTS
See, also, Scholarships and Fellowships
Forgiveness of loans, gross income, 202
Stipends vs. scholarships as gross income, 138
Waiver of loan repayment as gross income, 139

STUDY
Taxation, 1

SUBPOENAS
Tax fraud cases, 983

SUMMONS
Privileged relationship, 989
Tax fraud cases, 983
Accountant, 988
Appeal, 984
Resistance of, 984

SUPPORT
Dependency exemptions, 497
Divorced parents, 502
Gross income, 229
Periodic payments, gross income, 236

SUPREME COURT OF THE UNITED STATES
Jurisdiction, 34

SURVIVING SPOUSE
Tax rates, 949

TAX BENEFIT DOCTRINE
Return of charitable gift, 608

TAX COURT
Appeal from, 1004
Deficiency procedures, 1004
Jurisdiction, 32, 1004
Invoking, 1006
Stare decisis, 19

TAX PRACTITIONERS
Government counsel, 978
Practice of law defined, 4
Tools of the profession, 25

TAX RATES
Generally, 262
Automatic determination, 952
Classification, 947
Credits against tax, 962–969
Candidates for public office, contributions, 967
Dependent care expenses, 968
Earned income credit, 968
Elderly, 964
Estimated tax payments, 963
Foreign taxes, 969
General tax credit, 968
Investment credit, 966
Obsolete credit, 969
Retirement income credit, 964
Social Security excessive tax, 964
Withholding payments, 963
Work incentive credit, 966
Head of household, 949
Individuals, 947
Historical background, 947–953
Joint returns, special rates, 947–953

TAX RATES—Cont'd
Low-income taxpayers, 952
Married taxpayer filing separately, 951
Maximum tax on earned income, 960
Minimum tax for tax preferences, 953–960
  Corporations, 959
  Individuals, 959
Single persons, 950
Surviving spouse, 949

TAX REDUCTION ACT OF 1975
General effect, 13

TAX REFORM ACT
Revision of, 12

TAX RETURNS
See Returns

TAXABLE INCOME
Defined, 36
Realization of, 267, 275, 289

TAXABLE YEAR
Closing by Commissioner, 1007
Timing principles, 537–596

TAXES
Deductibility, 472
Direct and indirect, 14
Intergovernmental immunity, 256
Major tax periodicals, 35
Payment of, as income, 43
Progressive defined, 262
Public utilities receipts to states exempt from federal tax, 260
State income taxed by federal government, 260
Tax expenditures budget as a federal subsidy, 472

TEACHERS
Stipends vs. scholarships as gross income, 137

TERMITES
Infestation as deductible casualty loss, 476

THEFT
Loss as a deduction, 479
  Fraud, 481
  Measurement of, 490
  Timing of, 487

THIRTY–DAY LETTER
Tax procedure, 973

TIMING
See Holding Period

TORTS
Damages for bodily injury or sickness, 206

TRADE NAMES
Sale or exchange of capital asset, 700

TRADE OR BUSINESS
Expenses, 342–344
  Advertising, 409
  Capital expenditures distinguished, 348–355
  "Carrying on", 356–362
    Elections, 361
    Employee, 359
    Other employment, 361
    Pre-employed, 359
    Self-employed, 356
    Unemployed, 360
  Dues, 410
  Education, 396–404
    Institute, 402
    Summer school, 396
  Entertainment, 405
  Meals and lodging, 369–380
  Nonbusiness, 428
  Ordinary and necessary, 344
    Defined, 348
  Rental payments, 383–396
    Lease distinguished, 383
    Transfer and leaseback agreements, 386
    Trust agreements, 392
  Repairs to building, 348–355
    Reasonable repair rule, 355
  Salaries, reasonable, 363
  Uniforms, 409
Interest on indebtedness incurred for corporate acquisitions, 419
Kickbacks, 424
Losses, 410, 475
  Artificial, 413
Ordinary and necessary expense, nonbusiness, 428
"Pursuit of" defined, 358
Vacation homes, expenses, 417

TRADEMARKS
Sale or exchange of capital asset, 700

TRANSACTION ENTERED INTO FOR PROFIT
Defined, 432

TRAVEL
Business trip, gross income, 125
Deductibility as business expense, 369–380
Medical reasons, 517–521

TREATIES
Legislative process, 28

TRIAL
Procedure in tax fraud case, 992

TRUSTS
Alimony trusts, 249
Amount realized in transfer to, 178
Assignment of income, 279, 304–317
  By trustees, 271
  Irrevocable, 309–316
  Revocable, 304
  Short-term, 305–316
  Taxation of, 301–317
Assignment of property,
  Irrevocable, 309–316
Clifford, 309–316
Foreign, 315
Grantor trusts, 314
Income, 301
Income averaging of employee trusts, 625, 628
Pre-existing, 251
Rent as deductible business expense, 392
Sale of income interest in, effect upon capital gains and losses, 673–679
Sale or exchange of trust res, 689

UNIFORMITY
Federal taxing power, 18

UNIFORMS
Deductible business expense, 409

UNIVERSITIES
See Colleges and Universities

UNLAWFUL ACTIVITIES
Gains as gross income, 567

VACATION HOMES
Rental, expenses deductible, 417

VARIABLE ANNUITIES
See Annuities

VETERANS
Benefits excluded from gross income, 253
Limited military benefits excluded from gross income, 254

WAIVER
Gross income, effect on, 267, 270

WASH SALES
Capital assets, 680
Tax consequences, 890–894

WIDOWS AND WIDOWERS
$5000 limit on payments to deceased employee's widow, 85
Payments received from spouse's employer as income, 81
Tax rates, 949

WITHHOLDING TAX PAYMENTS
Credit against tax, 962

WITNESSES
Examination of, 983

WORK INCENTIVE PROGRAMS
Credit against tax, 966

WORKMEN'S COMPENSATION
Gross income, 206

WRONGFUL DEATH
Recoveries, gross income, 208

END OF VOLUME